A Waka Anthology

VOLUME ONE: The Gem-Glistening Cup

A Waka Anthology

VOLUME ONE: The Gem-Glistening Cup

Translated,
with a Commentary and Notes,
by Edwin A. Cranston

Stanford University Press
Stanford, California

Stanford University Press
Stanford, California

© 1993 by the Board of Trustees of the Leland Stanford Junior University
Printed in the United States of America
Published with the assistance of the Japan Foundation
CIP data appear at the end of the book

FOR PHILIP

Cithara crinitus Iopas
personat aurata, docuit quem maximus Atlas.

VIRGIL, Aeneid, 1, 740–41

Preface

This book grew out of a suggestion made to me in the spring of 1974 by Professor Earl Miner of Princeton University. It is the first of an intended four volumes that when completed will carry the story of *waka*, the classical tradition of Japanese poetry, down to the beginning of the sixteenth century. Each of the three volumes to follow will be devoted to one of the periods of the tradition as defined in *Japanese Court Poetry*, the landmark study published in 1961 by the late Robert H. Brower and Professor Miner. This first volume combines two of the Brower-Miner periods, those dealt with in *Japanese Court Poetry* under the titles of "Primitive Song and Poetry, ca. 550–686," and "The Early Literary Period, 686–784." Volume Two will be devoted to the Early Classical Period (784–1100), Volume Three to the Mid-Classical Period (1100–1241), and Volume Four to the Late Classical Period (1241–1502). The terminal date for the Late Classical Period derives from Miner's *Introduction to Japanese Court Poetry* (1968) and represents an extension beyond the original Brower-Miner terminal date of 1350 in order to accommodate the inclusion of important poets of the fifteenth century, among them Sōgi, who died in 1502.

From early on there was an understanding with Stanford University Press that *Japanese Court Poetry* would be followed by an anthology. Eventually, through the good offices of Professor Miner, and with the generous consent of Professor Brower, the happy responsibility of compiling such an anthology devolved upon me. That I have been slow in discharging this responsibility is only too clear. I had been translating waka in one connection or another for a number of years when the publisher offered me a contract for the anthology in the spring of 1976 (two years after the original suggestion by Professor Miner), but the number and variety of poems I had at hand was by no means sufficient to make a book of appropriate balance and amplitude. And it was only in 1978 that I found myself able to begin in earnest. Since then, for over a decade, interwoven with teaching, administrative duties, and other writing projects, through sojourns in Japan and Australia, vacations, and three academic leaves, work on The Book has been a constant preoccupation. The early years were devoted to translating broadly from the period to be covered, full-time during several months in Japan in 1978–79, and for two glorious months in Canberra in the Australian winter of 1985, and otherwise as time allowed, even if only a daily poem before breakfast.

I reached Kyōto in September 1985 accompanied by three fat folders full of poems, but no Book. During the next eleven months the poems told me what kind of book they wanted for themselves, and it became clear that I had embarked on a multivolume project. I left Kyōto in August 1986 with the commentary completed (except for a few later additions), and with the notes begun, for what now appears as Volume One. Thereafter it was a matter of finishing the notes, typing a manuscript of daunting proportions, adding indexes, and seeing the book through the editorial process, chores that to my regret have stretched out over six more years.

Funds from the Reischauer Institute at Harvard University and from the Japan Foundation enabled me to take leave to work on this book in 1978–79 and 1985–86. I thank those organizations for their generosity; without their support in obtaining usable blocks of time the book would not exist. They are by no means responsible for statements made therein, however, or for anything else about it. I would also like to thank several colleagues here and abroad for commenting on aspects of this project, for their guidance, and for their support of my work on waka. My debt to Earl Miner has already been mentioned. Beyond that, my interest in waka was first kindled by the work he shared with Robert H. Brower. Professor Brower, Professor Howard S. Hibbett, and Professor J. R. Hightower, the latter two my colleagues at Harvard, were particularly supportive in their comments on my translations early in my career. Professor Hightower and Professor Donald H. Shively, formerly a colleague at Harvard, obliged me with comments on format. Professor Stephen Owen of Harvard readily responded to questions on matters Chinese. Professor Edward W. Wagner of Harvard provided guidance on Korean romanization. Special thanks go to Professor Christopher Drake of Atomi Gakuen Women's University, who gave a close and very helpful reading to a section of translation from *Nihonshoki*. My first studies in *Man'yōshū* profited from the teaching of Professor Satake Akihiro, then of Kyōto University and now of Seijō University; Professor Kojima Noriyuki of Ōsaka City University; and Professor Kinoshita Masatoshi of Kansai University. I have also benefited from discussions of waka with Professor Nakanishi Susumu of Tsukuba University and Professor Hirano Yukiko of Ochanomizu Women's University, and from very helpful consultation with Professor Komatsu Tomi of Atomi Gakuen Junior College. I would also like to thank Professor Hino Tatsuo of Kyōto University for his administrative and personal support on the occasions of my sojourns in Kyōto. None of these individuals is in the least responsible for any blunders or solecisms that may mar the ensuing pages.

Over the years my students and other dear friends, who will forgive me for not thanking them by name, have given me a deeply appreciated support and have displayed an ever-hopeful belief in the eventual triumph of the author/translator over his tendencies toward an infinite if loving delay. I hope the result will be pleasing in their eyes and useful to them in various ways. One of my students, Stephen Forrest, helped me by devoting a summer to work on the General Index. I wish to express my particular gratitude to him and to the Reischauer Institute for making it possible for him to do so. The dedicatee of this book will know that nothing would have happened but for him and his example. There were also others who knew me and my work but are no longer here to see an anthology too long in the making. To them I offer a special hail and farewell. My wife Fumiko has as always given without stint to a writer whose most consistent product has been a studious frown. She will know the burden and satisfaction of such work. In addition, I would like to remember my first editor, J. G. Bell, whose wit and wisdom, and awesome patience, deserve monographic treatment. His successor, Helen Tartar, deftly and gently guided this project to its first stage of completion. Barbara Mnookin, my copy editor, gave the manuscript a thorough combing-out, and Peter J. Kahn ably saw it through the production process. A generous subsidy from the Japan Foundation helped defray the expense of publication.

Since several of my translations included in this anthology have previously appeared in various journals, I am happy to express my thanks for permission to publish them again to the editors of *Monumenta Nipponica*, *The Journal of the American Oriental Society*, *The Journal of Japanese Studies*, *The Journal of the Association of Teachers of Japanese*, and *The Harvard Journal of Asiatic Studies*. I also thank the following publishers and individuals for permission to quote the work of other translators: Oxford University Press for the quotation from James Robert Hightower, tr., *The Poetry of T'ao Ch'ien* (1970), on p. 831; New Directions for the translation by Kenneth Rexroth, *One Hundred Poems From the Japanese* (1964), on p. 835; E. Bruce Brooks for his translation from his article "A Yakamochi Sampler," *The East-West Review*, III, 1 (Winter, 1966–67), on p. 835; Columbia University Press for the quotation from Burton Watson, tr., *Records of the Grand Historian*, on p. 830; and the University of Minnesota Press for the selection from Richard B. Mather, tr., Liu I-ch'ing, *Shih-shuo Hsin-yü: A New Account of Tales of the World* (1976), on pp. 853–54.

The color photograph of an object from the Shōsōin used in the jacket illustration was provided courtesy of the Office of the Shōsōin Treasurehouse. I am greatly obliged to the former Director, Dr. Abe Hiromu, for making it available, and to the Reischauer Institute for a grant in support of the jacket design. The cobalt-blue goblet with a chased silver stem is 11.2 cm in height, is of handblown alkaline lime glass, and was probably made in T'ang China (the base has a dragon design), though the shape and material are ultimately of Roman origin. This object, preserved in excellent condition in the Shōsōin collection, symbolizes both the cosmopolitan richness of eighth-century Nara culture and the Japanese love of exotic beauty that, cross-fertilizing the rootstock of the native prosody and mystique, informed the poetry of the period.

E.A.C.

Contents

Poem Exchanges and Poem Groups of Multiple Composition 483

The Buddha's Footstone Poems *765*

A Note on Numbering and Source Abbreviations

Two numbering systems are used in this book. The first, appearing on the left-hand side of the page, is simple: a consecutive series from 1 to 1,578 referring to the selections as they are arranged herein. These numbers are also used for cross-reference within the volume.

The second system, of bracketed numbers on the right-hand side, refers the reader to sources. This system has several peculiarities. The numbering of poems drawn from *Man'yōshū* and the various imperial anthologies (*chokusenshū*) takes into account both the traditional numbering in *Kokka Taikan* and the numbering in the new *Shimpen Kokka Taikan*. The first number in all cases is that in *Shimpen*; if the earlier number is different, it appears after a slash. Items left unnumbered in the old system (these include all Man'yō *kanshi* and many variant *waka*) are represented in the present anthology by both the new number and an "a" added to the next previous traditional number (e.g., "MYS VII: 3995/3972a"). This innovation, for which I express my gratitude to the anonymous reader who commented on this book in manuscript for Stanford University Press, should facilitate reference to NKBT, NKBZ, and other commentaries based on the *Kokka Taikan* numeration.

Conversion tables between the consecutive numeration on the left and the source numbers on the right appear as Appendix Tables following the Bibliography.

The following abbreviations are used for the collections treated in the volume:

F	*Fudoki*	KKS	*Kokinshū*
GSS	*Gosenshū*	MYS	*Man'yōshū*
K	*Kojiki*	NS	*Nihonshoki*
KFS	*Kaifūsō*	SIS	*Shūishū*
KHS	*Kakinomoto no*	SKKS	*Shinkokinshū*
	Hitomaro Shū	SN	*Shoku Nihongi*
KKRJ	*Kokinrokujō*		

Introduction

For a poetic anthology, the present volume has a great deal of prose. Some of this consists of translations of prose settings and other information from the original sources, namely the ancient chronicles *Kojiki, Nihonshoki,* and *Shoku Nihongi;* the *fudoki,* a set of eighth-century local gazetteers; *Man'yō-shū,* the great eighth-century compendium of early Japanese poetry; and the *Bussokuseki* poems engraved on a stone tablet at Yakushiji in Nara. It seemed vital to include translations of prose settings where available, because the poems often form part of a literary whole with their attendant prose, such integration being a characteristic feature of early Japanese literature. Thus this anthology, like *Man'yōshū* itself, is open to the full range of literary activity of its period, rather than being single-mindedly "poetic."

The rest, and the great bulk, is my own commentary. The commentary, arranged so as to introduce the poems, and signaled by the device ✳ to demarcate it from the other prose found throughout, attempts to provide historical, biographical, and literary information adequate for an appreciation of the translations. (Additional information, with citation of sources, is provided in the notes at the back of the book, which are keyed to the poem numbers, and in a few cases, chapter titles or subheads.) Aspects of poetic creativity such as theme, genre, structure, and rhetorical devices are discussed where appropriate. Concrete discussions of wording, structure, and the technical use of language refer to the original poems, which are presented in romanization parallel to the translations. Since the commentaries are a special feature of this anthology, I very much hope they will prove helpful rather than the reverse. The ideal of a clean, unencumbered text is esthetically attractive, but I have had occasion to observe how much more clearly and meaningfully a poem can speak with a little help. Short poems in particular benefit from an inhibition of the tendency to swallow them in one unreflecting gulp, as was wisely pointed out to me by my first editor, J. G. Bell.

The commentary also attempts to be fair and sympathetic. It has no theoretical axe to grind. Readers whose basic interest is theory will find slim pickings here. A certain residual tendency toward the old-fashionedly pedantic undoubtedly still crops up here and there in the notes and elsewhere, a bequest of the "scholarly" pressures of graduate schools on both ends of the continent, and of positions on both ends of the teaching log. But my interest has long since shifted—or reverted—to poetry as the voice of people singing out something on their minds. The intersection of feeling and language is where poetry occurs, and where I would prefer to be. The people who utter the poems in this book are real to me, whether I know their biographies or not. Their loves and hates (and admiration of mountains and trees) are not other than my own. And so I have not hesitated to bring myself to this book, a fact that is only partially disguised by its attempt to preserve the decencies of professional decorum.

The main subject matter of this book is *waka*, a term I understand in the sense in which it is used in Brower and Miner's *Japanese Court Poetry*, as encompassing the poetic forms practiced by the early court—namely, the *tanka*, or "short poem"; the *chōka*, or "long poem"; the *katauta*, or "half-poem"; the *sedōka*, or "head-repeated poem"; and the *bussokusekika*, or "Buddha's Footstone poem"—and by extension the earlier, less formally defined verse out of which these forms emerged. I do not use it as a synonym for tanka, a sense in which it is sometimes used elsewhere. The poems appearing in sources outside *Man'yōshū* are sometimes referred to as *kodai kayō*, "ancient song." The song/poem distinction is referred to again later in this book. Here it is sufficient to note that the "songs" of the early chronicles are sometimes formally tanka, though more often a sort of proto-tanka or proto-chōka, and that *Man'yōshū* contains examples of *kodai kayō* along with its more "literary" content. Waka is also to be distinguished from the later linked verse, or *renga*, and from its offshoot, the *haiku*. Finally, the various folk genres such as *saibara*, *kagurauta*, *fūzokuuta*, and *azumaasobiuta*, collected by the Heian court but some of them dating from the period covered by this volume, have been excluded, though valid arguments no doubt could be put forward for including them.

Japanese prosody is based on syllable count, the classically defined forms being made up of arrangements of alternating five- and seven-syllable units. The tanka pattern is 5–7–5–7–7, while the katauta conforms to 5–7–7, the sedōka to 5–7–7–5–7–7, and the bussokusekika to 5–7–5–7–7–7. The chōka alternates fives and sevens to any length, and usually concludes with a 7–7 couplet, after which there may come one or more envoys in tanka form. Hypometric and hypermetric lines are not uncommon; according to certain theories, the latter can be regularized by appeal to rules of synaloepha wherein two vowels elide into one.[1] The rhythms of chōka are complex, involving use of long prosodic periods intersected by parallel structures. Those of tanka are exemplified by the 5–7 rhythm, or *goshichi-chō*, leading to a reading of 5–7/5–7/7. This can be contrasted with the *shichigo-chō*, or 7–5, rhythm that increasingly dominated post-Man'yō poetry, in which the tanka scans 5/7–5/7–7, or 5–7–5/7–7. The shift of the caesura facilitated the eventual development of linked verse, a form that derived from splitting a tanka into 5–7–5 and 7–7. These are only general tendencies and cannot be applied automatically to all the poems in a given form in a given period.

The syllabic units of Japanese prosody are known as *ku*, a term traditionally translated into English as "line." I too call them lines and treat them as such, though this practice has recently been called into question, at least as it applies to tanka. The tanka is usually printed as one vertical line in Japanese books, and, it has been argued, is thought of as a one-line poem.[2] In handwriting it may occupy one or more lines, mainly as a matter of calligraphic esthetics. There is ample evidence, however, that the Japanese have always—or at least since the first statements on the subject in the eighth century—thought of the ku as meaningfully distinct units, to which different formal criteria might apply. The question of lineation would make a fascinating study, one that unfortunately cannot be undertaken here. A place to start would be in the manuscript traditions of the major literary civilizations, and the question to be posed would be, "What is a line?" Do calligraphic arrangements that involve writing continuously in the physically or esthetically available space, whether horizontally or vertically, mean there are no "lines"? What about cases like the Chinese, where line ends are indicated unmistakably by rhymes, even when the calligraphy just flows on and on? And what about chōka, which also just flow on and on? Printing books of poetry that way is very economical—vastly more poems can be gotten onto the page. Someone once likened the standard reference work for waka, *Kokka Taikan*, to the New York phone directory. To me the tanka is in a very meaningful sense a five-line poem, and I have not hesitated to continue using the five-line arrangement I first learned as orthodox for both romanized text and translation from the work of Donald Keene and Brower and Miner.[3] It is partially a matter of habit and personal preference. The advantages of tension and interplay between visually separated lines are something I would be loath to abandon. At the same time I do not deny the possible advantages of other arrangements, even translations in a single line. Anything that works justifies itself, ipso facto.

Another matter having to do with presentation of Japanese text needs to be mentioned here. The language of modern Japan is not phonologically the same as that of the poems in this book. For instance, there were eight vowels in Old Japanese against only five today. Consonant values also have shifted, most notably in the attrition of *F* to *h* to intervocalic *w*, or its total disappearance in some environments. Old initial *w* has disappeared before *o*. Thus the Old Japanese particle *Fa* is now *wa*, and Old *wo* is *o*. The Old verb *omoFu* ("to think," "to long") has become *omou*. The language of the seventh and eighth centuries thus must have sounded quite different from modern standard Japanese. It has been argued with considerable cogency, and not a little scholarly choler, that it should be employed in romanizing Old Japanese texts. On the face of it, the matter would seem to be self-evident. There are two principal reasons why I have nevertheless stuck with what is basically a modern Japanese romanization. One is that I do not know how to pronounce Old Japanese, especially the ï, ë, and ö that have dropped out of the language.[4] But the determinative factor in my decision was an even more practical one. This book is the first of four intended volumes that will carry Japanese poetry forward over several centuries during which the language, like all languages, was in a continuous state of change. It seemed impossible even to decide how many romanization schemes would be required, to say nothing of carrying through the research necessary to put them in place. The easiest way out would be to print the original unromanized script, but there appear to be practical objections to that solution too. In the event, I have presented one sample of Old Japanese at the end of the book, using for the purpose the readings determined for the Buddha's Footstone Poems by a leading advocate of scientifically sound romanization. Otherwise, I have distinguished between Princes Oke and Woke by using the Old Japanese romanization for the younger brother. The rest is mainly what would be expected in modern Japanese, with some adjustments for words no longer in the current lexicon, such as *mononofu* ("man at arms") instead of *mononou*.

Despite its husk of commentary and its tissues of text, this is basically a book of translations, and a few words need to be devoted to the perennially controversial subject of rendering one language into another. Distinct ideals have guided the translation of the prose and the poetry. For the former I have adhered to the best I can recall from graduate school training: make it exact. This determination undoubtedly owes something to the fact that the prose translated herein is all in Chinese. I have never learned any other way to translate Chinese, and such awesome mentors as the late Peter Boodberg still block out any other horizon. Whether I have succeeded in "making it exact" is of course an entirely different question. For the poetry, which with few exceptions is in Japanese, I have listened to other voices. These voices are basically the echoes of poems read and written, echoes that tell me a poem has an inner life that is more than the sum total of its words and cadences, a vital essence that must metamorphose into a new language in translation.

An analogy might be drawn between a book of poem translations and an art catalogue. By writing about illustrated art works, the author of the catalogue makes it possible for the reader/viewer to "see" them for the first time. The instructed eye discerns much that remains latent, obscure to the casual or merely curious glance. It learns to make its way through the now obscure classical references of Renaissance art, receives instruction in Buddhist or Christian iconography, observes the differing perspectives of Chinese and Japanese ink painting, of Giotto and Gauguin and the *Genji* scrolls, sees the light in Poussin and Monet, is disciplined into following line and mass and rhythm so as to make something of Picasso, is made privy to private as well as public mythologies, to the compulsions of Munch and van Gogh, as well as to the shared vocabulary of schools and grand traditions.

A poetic anthology might aim to let the reader "see" the poems in analogous ways. But the analogy goes only so far and then breaks down, or at least becomes suspect. Insofar as the present volume, or any such book, is an anthology of poetry in translation, and the translations correspond to the reproductions in the art catalogue, one must admit a difference. The aim of the art reproduction may be taken to be exact fidelity, and with modern color photography something close to that may be achievable. At least in the case of a two-dimensional work, a painting, one may have the illusion of exact congruity—a picture of a picture, to be sure, a substitute, but with the colors corresponding, the lines all in place, and very like. But a poem paints with words, and the words of one language are not those of another. One cannot "photograph" a poem, even with the latest technology; the "reproduction" that is translation is another matter altogether. Imagine a universe where light breaks up not into one prism, but many, and suppose the resulting colors are mixed in palettes of infinite and mutually obscure complexity, and that the mauves and greens, the shades of red and orange, the blacks and purples of a Gauguin have to be "translated" into some foreign and nameless colors to make them visible. Add the shift to altered laws of modeling and perspective, also necessary to make the painting comprehensible, and one can see that the resulting catalogue would seem very strange indeed.

With the best of intentions, the translator of a poem creates something not less strange, not less other. What are the best of intentions? To care about how a poem goes, what it is as well as what it says; to want it to live again in a new language, to be a living organism even if every cell is altered into an exotic because essentially alien protoplasm. Perhaps therefore the best metaphor is that of the seed that drops on strange soil and grows into a plant adapted to its new conditions. The botanical metaphor blends easily into the traditional Japanese discourse on poetics and suggests an adjustment of Ki no Tsurayuki's famous dictum, "The songs of Yamato have their seed in the human heart and burgeon forth into the myriad leaves of words," to the needs of translation. Certainly the notion of natural growth, of a process not totally under rational control, is seductive to a translator who has worked long at his craft. He descends into the poem and lets something happen. He serves as a medium for the new growth.

Yet in the end this line of metaphorical thinking too misses the mark. The translator is not merely passive. The word "craft" already suggests that he thinks about what he does. He has his ideas of what makes a poem "go," and he gropes about for the life in the original, he listens to it quietly and lets

it keep whispering yes or no to his attempts to make something new. Therefore the translator works under a constant tension—or better, perhaps, a
variable one. The "something new," the "something" that he tries to let
happen, works itself into existence between compulsion and restraint. The
original poem pulls in one direction, stubbornly remaining itself, the starting point and final reference of the whole process. The original is the translator's good angel and the keeper of his bad conscience. But the translation,
for the translator, is the creative part, the goal of the enterprise, the child
waiting to be born. It pulls him in another direction, the direction of its own
life and integrity. Nothing is more persuasive than something that works,
and if a line somehow works, it is hard to abandon it. What will seem to
work will depend on the translator's ear, on what he has come to like and
admire—or even merely to recognize—in versification in the course of a
lifetime. Different translators hear different voices—hence the odium that
sometimes attaches to the rival version. And whether he succeeds or fails,
what he produces has a dubious ontological status.

I would prefer to leave ontology to the philosophers and assert the right
of a poem to exist. Two poems, lined up side by side and looking sus-
piciously over their shoulders at each other. On the left the Japanese, trans-
literated into Roman letters and arranged on the page in the pattern of its
prosody, the alternating long and short lines that are its pulse beat. On the
right an English verse in an equal number of lines, one whose rhythm is
similarly based on expansion and contraction. Though some may feel that
in a book of translations the original is a *dasoku*, as out of place as a leg on a
snake, I have not found that to be the case. Quite the contrary, in fact. The
double track is mutually enhancing; the convenience of being allowed to
read back and forth between the two versions gives a pleasure to be derived
from neither alone. Even with my rudimentary German I experienced this
added enjoyment when reading, for instance, Lucia Getsi's haunting book of
translations from the Austrian poet Georg Trakl.[5] I am aware that writers on
such subjects often remark the uselessness of elements in a book that will
mean nothing to the nonspecialist, and that specialists "can look up for
themselves." For the reasons already stated, I do not believe that that argument applies to the present case. A poem is not a bit of information to be
looked up, or, in this book, a linguistic or philological text to be "checked."
The present volume is obviously intended for students of Japanese literature, but equally for all people who like poetry. Present educational trends
encourage me to hope that increasing numbers of bilingual readers will be
drawn to the double option it represents in years to come.

A valid and interesting way to compile an anthology such as this would
be to call on the talents of a number of translators, assigning different poems
or poets to each. In the event, I chose to do everything myself, even though
there is not a poem in this volume that has not been rendered into English at

least once and sometimes several times before.⁶ One might expect therefore a certain consistency of manner and translation technique to prevail, and to a large extent it has. Yet there are differences. The oldest translations in this book go back over twenty years, and the most recent were done only a month or so before I submitted the manuscript. In the interim my practice shifted from an ampler to a more astringent style, as might be gleaned from an inspection of the handling of the epithetical formulas known as *makura-kotoba* ("pillow words") in, say, MYS II:135 (no. 325) and K 2–5. I am rather glad that I translated most of Hitomaro early on, for I find the full and flowing style with which I was at home at the time suitable to his work. The expansions and displacements, the relative clauses and appositives of

Tsuno sahau	In the Sea of Iwami,
Iwami no umi no	*Where swarming vines crawl on the rocks,*
Koto saeku	Under the Cape of Kara,
Kara no saki naru	*A name for far lands strange of speech,*
Ikuri ni so	On the sunken reefs
Fukamiru ouru	Grows the sea pine in the deep waters,

that create a slow, oceanic rhythm for Hitomaro's vision of an otherworld of unspoiled love give way to the adjectival arrangements of Suserihime's tauter enticements:

Awayuki no	*This soft-snow*
Wakayaru mune o	Bosom quick with youth,
Takuzuno no	*These rope-white arms*
Shiroki tadamuki	In your bare embrace
Sodataki	Take in your hands,
Tadaki managari	Lie close and interlaced.

Preferences among a variety of styles, expansive or terse, esthetics of fleshly contour or of bone structure, will depend on taste and judgment of appropriateness. The reader must ultimately decide which, if any, are acceptable. One particular translation technique used several times in this book needs special comment, however. In addition to the one-line epithet illustrated above, early Japanese poetry makes extensive use of a longer pre-posited structure known as the *jo*, or "preface." The jo is typically a natural image or image cluster preceding the "main statement" of the poem. It is particularly common in love poetry, where it performs a valuable imagistic function. Jo may be of two types. In one there is no logical connection between the imagistic opening and what comes after it. The connection is solely based on wordplay. This type is called the *mushin*, or "meaningless," jo. In the other, called *ushin* ("meaningful"), the prefatory image is logically metaphorical or at least resonates closely with the emotional point of the poem.

Ushin juncture may be simply by juxtaposition, the implied comparison illustrated in K 43:

Iza kodomo	Well, now, boys,
Nobiru tsumi ni	Picking wild garlic,
Hiru tsumi ni	Picking garlic
Wa ga yuku michi no	I went, and there by the path
Kaguwashi	Found a fragrant
Hanatachibana wa	Orange tree all in flower:
Hotsue wa	The upper branches
Tori igarashi	Birds had stripped with their perching,
Shizue wa	The lower branches
Hito torigarashi	People had stripped with their plucking,
Mitsuguri no	But the three-chestnut
Nakatsue no	Middle branches
Hotsumori	Swelled with budding fruit:
Akaraotome o	Redly glowing the maiden—
Iza sasaba	Come, entice her away,
Yorashi na	All will be well!

But the "meaningful" preface may also be joined to the main statement by the suture of wordplay. Whether the jo is ushin or mushin, such juncture will be performed either by repetition of homophones, or by syntactic doubling. MYS IV : 539/536 is an example of the former:

Ou no umi no	Along the Sea of Ou
Shiohi no *kata* no	At low tide the beach lies *bare*:
Kataomoi ni	*Barely* enduring
Omoi ya yukamu	This one-sided love, shall I
Michi no nagate o	Go yearning my long way?

Kata ("beach") is echoed in *kataomoi* ("one-sided love"); the two *kata* are homophones but not homonyms. This type of jo is mushin, though it can readily enough be seen that the opening image subliminally provides the setting for the lover's complaint. The translation here imitates the poem's rhetoric with a pairing of its own (closer to being homonyms, to be sure), rather than translating the juncture words *in situ*. As often, the structural technique of the poem has seemed essential to its proper existence.

The second type of juncture, doubling or zeugma, is referred to in Japanese as *kakekotoba*, or "pivot word." Kakekotoba can exist independently of the jo structure and typically do so in later court poetry, but such instances are rare in this volume. Instead, the doubling usually occurs as the last word, phrase, or line of the jo, functioning simultaneously as the first word, phrase, or line of the "main statement." The following examples will illustrate (all except the first can be considered ushin):

MYS X: 1833/1829

Azusayumi	Taut catalpa bows
Haru yama chikaku	*Spring* mountains close at hand
Ie oreba	You've built your house,
Tsugite kikuramu	And you must live with cries of warblers
Uguisu no koe	Continually about your ears.

MYS II: 114

Aki no ta no	On the autumn fields
Homuki no yoreru	The spears of grain are bending
Kotoyori ni	*In one direction*
Kimi ni yorinana	Toward my lord I'll softly bend,
Kochitakari to mo	Let words sting as they may.

(This example combines zeugma with phonetic repetition.)

MYS XIX: 4242/4218

Shibi tsuku to	To spear the tuna
Ama no tomoseru	Seafolk light their fishing flares
Izaribi no	*Blazing openly*
Ho ni ka idasamu	Shall I let my secret flame
Wa ga shitamoi o	Flash forth for all to see?

MYS XVII: 4028/4002

Katakai no	In Katakai
Kawa no se kiyoku	River the shallows are clear,
Yuku mizu no	The water flows
Tayuru koto naku	*Never ceasing* I shall come
Arigayoimimu	Again and yet again to gaze.

Such translations as the above try to emulate the condensed syntax of their originals. Sometimes a colon alerts the reader:

MYS XI: 2657/2649

Ashihiki no	In the footsore hills
Yamada moru oji	The old man who guards the mountain field
Oku kahi no	Keeps mosquito flares:
Shitakogare nomi	*Always burning with a secret flame*
A ga koioraku	Is the smoldering of my love.

But often there is no warning (any more than in the Japanese original):

MYS X:1912/1908

Haru sareba	After spring has come
Mikusa no ue ni	The remaining rime of frost
Oku shimo no	On water grasses
Ketsutsu mo are wa	*Fading steadily away,*
Koiwataru kamo	Yet I go on in this longing.

I have not always succeeded in incorporating zeugma into the translations of poems where it exists in the original, or indeed cared to make the attempt. Instead, the doubling may dissolve into a simile or some other type of comparative construction:[7]

SKKS XI:993

Isonokami	*As* the early rice
Furu no wasada no	At Furu in Isonokami
Ho ni wa idezu	*Shows yet no grain,*
Kokoro no uchi ni	Shall I too keep hidden
Koi ya wataramu	The love within my heart?

MYS XI:2680/2672

Kono yama no	Close above the peak
Mine ni chikashi to	Of this mountain range I saw
A ga mitsuru	The rising moon—
Tsuki no *sora naru*	Whose track is far across a sky
Koi mo suru kamo	*No more empty* than my love.

The italicization supplied in these examples is absent when the same and similar poems appear later in the book. However, there are a few cases in which I have supplied it in the translation to mark an unusual pillow-word construction or short jo at the beginning of a poem:

MYS I:44

Wagimoko o	*To my own young love*
Izami no yama o	Farewell Mountain's loftiness
Takami ka mo	May be the reason
Yamato no mienu	Why Yamato lies unseen—
Kuni tōmi ka mo	Or is it that the land is far away?

MYS IX:1699/1695

Imo ga kado	*To my sweetheart's gates*
Iri Izumigawa no	*And forth*: Wellspring River:

Tokoname ni	Midst the water-moss
Miyuki nokoreri	Traces of snow still linger—
Imada fuyu ka mo	Is it then winter yet?

Experimental translations like these make up only a small portion of the total number, but represent a direction that I am increasingly drawn to explore.

This book has taken a long time to write. If it turns out to be useful in the study of Japanese poetry, I shall be pleased, but I shall be far more deeply rewarded if it provides even a fraction of the pleasure I have had to myself during years when its poems were my most constant companions.

A Waka Anthology

Songs from the Chronicles and 'Fudoki'

The earliest Japanese books contain a wealth of poetry. *Kojiki* (*Record of Ancient Matters*) was completed in 712, and *Nihonshoki* (*Chronicles of Japan*) in 720. Both books provide accounts of the origins of Japan based on the mythology of its people, legitimize the claim to hegemony asserted by the dominant clan, and detail the events of the reigns of a succession of divine rulers. *Nihonshoki*, the first of a series of *Six National Histories* (*Rikkokushi*), was intended as a comprehensive and authoritative version of events down through the reign of Empress Jitō. It leaves off in 697, a mere generation before the time of its completion. *Kojiki*, a much shorter book, seems by contrast a rather tentative experiment in historiography. Its anecdotal account breaks off in the year 487 with the death of Emperor Kenzō; genealogical records continue through the reign of Empress Suiko, terminating in 628. Both books are the outcome of historiographical initiatives of the seventh century, and represent attempts to provide an official version of the mythology and of the genealogical claims extending from it. *Nihonshoki* often includes several variant versions of a given myth, suggesting the plurality of traditions that must have prevailed among the different clans. *Kojiki* is selective, its version of events no doubt designed to demonstrate the true descent of the imperial clan from the highest deity.

Kojiki, which is in every sense experimental, being Japan's first book and written in an unstable amalgam of Chinese and Japanese, seems particularly close to oral sources of myth, folktale, hero tale, and anecdote. From these sources the earliest scribes strung together the vividly earthy and richly literary accounts that characterize the book far more than its uncertain grasp of history. According to the preface to *Kojiki*, these documents and the genealogies that are the book's other main component were "learned" by a person named Hieda no Are and written down by the author of the preface, Ō no Yasumaro (d. 723). A striking feature of the many stories making up *Kojiki* is the abundance of poetry. The poems are songs uttered by the men, women, and deities whose deeds are the storyteller's matter. *Kojiki* has 113 of these songs.

Nihonshoki has 131 songs, a much smaller concentration considering that it is ten times the length of *Kojiki*, with thirty *maki* ("scrolls") as against three. Its compilation proceeded in a sporadic fashion over a period of nearly forty years, beginning with a review of genealogical and historical documents ordered by Emperor Temmu (d. 686) in 681. The original committee of twelve Princes and nobles included Princes Kawashima (657–91) and Osakabe (d. 705), sons of Emperors Tenji (d. 672) and Temmu, respectively. (For Kakinomoto no Hitomaro's lament on the death of Prince Kawashima, see nos. 336–37.) The final compilation took place under the sponsorship of Empress Gemmei (r. 707–15), and the finished product was presented in 720 in the reign of her daughter Genshō (r. 715–24). Prince Toneri (d. 735), another son of Temmu, saw the book through to completion as chief compiler during the last stage before submission. (For poems by Prince Toneri, see nos. 387 and 879.)

Nihonshoki drew on a wider variety of documentation than *Kojiki* and is a much more detailed and polished work, written in classical Chinese except for its song texts. The ancient anecdotal accounts from which most of the songs probably came clearly existed in variant versions, for in the considerable overlap of songs between *Kojiki* and *Nihonshoki* it is exceptional to find textual identity. In addition, a number of songs that appear in one context in *Kojiki* are assigned to a different story in *Nihonshoki*. Somewhat over half the songs in *Nihonshoki* do not appear in *Kojiki* at all or are given in significantly different versions. On the other hand, the songs telling of the loves of the deity Eight Thousand Spears, a cycle that occurs early in *Kojiki*, are entirely absent from *Nihonshoki*, perhaps part of a deliberate downplaying of the cultic importance of Izumo, where this god reigned. Most of the songs associated with the tragic hero Yamato Takeru no Mikoto are also missing, replaced in some instances by speeches in high-flown Chinese rhetoric. As the chronicle reaches the seventh century with its tangled political strife, there begins to appear a type of song used as satirical counterpoint to the narrative, the so-called *wazauta*, purportedly popular or children's songs of a premonitory character.

Another twenty-three songs are included in the present anthology from a third source, the *fudoki*, or "records of wind and earth." These local gazetteers are a group of documents compiled at imperial command beginning in 713. In that year Empress Gemmei ordered each province to catalogue its products and report on the fertility of its soils. At the same time, provincial authorities were to make orthographic changes, selecting "good characters" for the names of the various administrative units from province down to township. This concern for the auspicious use of language is characteristic of the period and no doubt owes something to both the native belief in word magic and Chinese ideas of propriety. It was accompanied by an antiquarian interest in collecting local legends, the same interest that on a grander scale resulted in the national histories. The fudoki compilers were directed to investigate "the origins of the names of mountains, rivers, plains, and fields, as well as to record old tales and unusual matters passed down by the elderly."

Unfortunately, only five fudoki have survived, and of these only one, that of Izumo, is complete. The other four are those of Hitachi, Harima, Bungo, and Hizen. In addition, a number of other fragments have been preserved, thanks to being quoted in various works. Not surprisingly, some of the origin stories and "old tales and unusual matters" in the fudoki incorporate songs, just as is the case with similar material in the histories. Less predictably, the distribution of songs is uneven—*Izumo Fudoki*, for instance, contains none, whereas there are ten from Hitachi. The richness of Izumo song is attested by *Kojiki*, and so it can hardly have been a lack of anything to collect that accounts for its absence from the fudoki of that province. *Bungo Fudoki* also contains no songs. All but four of the twenty-three songs preserved from Hitachi, Harima, Hizen, Tango, and Ise are in tanka form or a close approximation thereof; and like tanka in the chronicles, they do not represent the most archaic type of versification, though they may have been traditional by the time of compilation in the eighth century. Most of them are love songs, and several no doubt originated in the context of the *utagaki*, or songfest (see nos. 201–8 and 214–15). The prose texts are in Chinese, often polished for literary effect.

The history of the eighth century is told in the second of the *Six National Histories*, *Shoku Nihongi* (*Chronicles of Japan Continued*), which covers the years 697–791. This work, compiled in several stages by a number of different scholars, was submitted to Emperor Kammu (r. 781–806) in 797, shortly after the move away from Nara to the new capital at Heian-kyō. Recording the annals of a fully literate court, it leaves behind the rich mixture of myth, legend, folktale, and song that gives the earlier chronicles and the fudoki their interest as literature. From the handful of songs preserved in its pages, mostly tanka composed on public occasions, one could hardly guess that Nara was one of the great ages of Japanese poetry. With *Shoku Nihongi* and *Man'yōshū*, history and literature have been segregated. The songs of *Shoku Nihongi* are included in the present anthology to show the later stages of a tradition that did not end abruptly with *Nihonshoki*, as much as for their intrinsic interest. In addition to congratulatory tanka, they include a famous ancient war song and a wazauta.

The present anthology begins with a complete translation of the *Kojiki* songs, followed by nonduplicative selections from *Nihonshoki*, the twenty-three fudoki songs, and the eight songs included in *Shoku Nihongi*. The texts used are those in Tsuchihashi Yutaka and Konishi Jin'ichi, eds., *Kodai Kayōshū*, the relevant portions of which are translated in full, including the prose passages introducing and following the songs. For the chronicles, the texts in Kurano Kenji, ed., *Kojiki*, and Sakamoto Tarō et al., eds., *Nihonshoki*, have also been consulted, and, occasionally, preferred. Reference to Donald L. Philippi, tr., *Kojiki*, and W. G. Aston, tr., *Nihongi*, has greatly facilitated work with this material. My numbering of the *Kojiki* and *Nihon-*

shoki songs diverges from Tsuchihashi's in the following instances. The chant of Prince Woke, given herein as K 105 (no. 105), is unnumbered by Tsuchihashi. So is the ritual "blessing on the house" uttered by the same Prince in *Nihonshoki*, here presented as NS 83 (no. 153). The songs I number NS 85 and 86 (nos. 155–56) are also unnumbered by Tsuchihashi. The criterion in all cases seems to be orthographic. The unnumbered songs are written in largely semantic rather than phonetic uses of Chinese characters. As a result of these discrepancies in numbering, *Kodai Kayōshū* lists 112 *Kojiki* songs instead of 113, and 128 rather than 131 *Nihonshoki* songs.

Similar discrepancies obtain in the case of the fudoki songs. The song I number F 2 (no. 201) is not numbered by Tsuchihashi, who omits F 12 and F 13 (nos. 211–12) altogether. The orthography of these songs is semantic rather than phonetic. Thus *Kodai Kayōshū* lists only twenty rather than twenty-three fudoki songs. In addition, I have rearranged the order slightly, grouping together the songs from each province, rather than separating off those taken from the fragmentary sources for Harima and Hizen. Finally, I have rounded off the narratives, given in more abbreviated form by Tsuchihashi, by consulting Akimoto Kichirō, ed., *Fudoki*. This has affected F 8–9 (nos. 207–8), 11 (no. 210), 15–20 (nos. 214–19), and 22 (no. 221). F 12–13 (nos. 211–12) have been supplied in their entirety from Akimoto.

For the most part, the chronicles and fudoki present their songs in the conventional context of impromptu composition and utterance—the songs are indeed sung. The present anthology follows Japanese custom in referring to them as "songs" (*kayō*) rather than "poems" (*waka*), though the distinction is forced in the cases of "songs" that are the same in technique and style as *Man'yōshū* "poems." The basic term is *uta* in either case, and uta means "song," pointing to the oral origins of the art of poetry. The pervasive social role of song, and later of written verse, implied by the most ancient Japanese writings is obvious. The urge to interweave poetry and prose is persistent in Japanese literature, and in this respect the chronicles and fudoki are merely the earliest products of a literary dynamic that resulted in the chief works of the classical tradition. In these earliest books the dynamic clearly operated in such a way as to incorporate songs that were already being sung in different contexts, as well as ones perhaps composed by the compilers to fit the narrative.

'Kojiki' Songs

✳ The first song in *Kojiki* is a bridegroom's celebration of his wedding and his new house. In the *Kojiki* narrative it is sung by the deity Susanoo no Mikoto after his marriage to Kushinadahime in Izumo. Izumo, written with characters meaning "emerging clouds," was the center of a cult devoted to Susanoo and his descendants. The verse is formally a perfect tanka in its 5–7–5–7–7 structure and thus not archaic in its present form. The use of repetition with a strongly rhythmical beat is a sign of an early oral provenance, however. *Ya*, "eight," seems to have been a lucky number, often used to refer to large quantities. In its juxtaposition of a rising, eruptive force with an image of enclosed circularity, the song is appropriate to its nuptial context, and gives Japanese poetry a start on its most ancient subject—the relations between men and women.

1   [K 1]

When this great god first built Suga Palace, clouds rose from that place. And so he composed a song. That song:

Yakumo tatsu	In eight-cloud-rising
Izumo yaegaki	Izumo an eightfold fence
Tsumagomi ni	To enclose my wife
Yaegaki tsukuru	An eightfold fence I build,
Sono yaegaki o	And, oh, that eightfold fence!

✳ Songs 2–5 are a set of four chōka recounting the amorous adventures of Susanoo's descendant, a deity known variously as Yachihoko ("Eight Thousand Spears") and Ōkuninushi ("Great Land Master"). He is the chief deity of the Izumo cult, worshiped at the Grand Shrine of Izumo as a god of marriage, and a cycle of *Kojiki* myth is devoted to telling his story. This cycle is omitted from *Nihonshoki*, but the *Kojiki* account makes it clear that Izumo was the stronghold of the earth deities, who ceded the land to the descendants of the sun goddess in return for guarantees of eternal worship. Replete with phraseology suggesting mime, these songs belong to a tradition of oral presentation specified in their embedded formulas as that of the *amahasezu-*

kai, "the seafolk couriers," an occupational group, or "corporation" (*be*), identified with the seafolk (*ama*) of Ise. Nos. 2–3 form one pair exchanged between the hero and the wise maiden, and nos. 4–5 a second pair, an exchange between the hero and his equally wise wife. The opening lines of no. 2 are a narrative introduction; the remainder of the entire set is cast in direct declaration. See no. 167 for a song closely analogous to nos. 2 and 3.

2 [K 2]

The deity Eight Thousand Spears, going to woo Nunakawahime in the land of Koshi, went, and arriving at the home of Nunakawahime, sang:

Yachihoko no	Eight Thousand Spears,
Kami no mikoto wa	That great, noble god,
Yashimakuni	In the Eight Islands
Tsuma makikanete	Unable to bed a wife,
5 Tōdōshi	Hearing that afar
Koshi no kuni ni	In the far land of Koshi
Sakashime o	Was a wise maiden,
Ari to kikashite	That in a distant province
Kuwashime o	Dwelt a fair maiden,
10 Ari to kikoshite	When he had heard of her
Sayobai ni	Started a-wooing,
Aritatashi	Set off on his way;
Yobai ni	Went off wooing
Arikayowase	Back and forth to her house.
15 Tachi ga o mo	The cord of his sword
Imada tokazute	He had not paused to loosen,
Osui o mo	His hooded mantle
Imada tokaneba	He had not yet undone:
Otome no	By the wooden door
20 Nasu ya itato o	Here where the maiden sleeps
Osoburai	I stand,
Wa ga tatasereba	Pushing and shaking;
Hikozurai	I stand,
Wa ga tatasereba	Pulling and wrenching.
25 Aoyama ni	Now in the green hills
Nue wa nakinu	The thrush is singing;
Sanotsutori	Bird of the moors,
Kigishi wa toyomu	The pheasant is booming;
Niwatsutori	Bird of the barnyard,
30 Kake wa naku	The cock is crowing—
Uretaku mo	Oh, these hateful birds,
Naku naru tori ka	How maddeningly they cry!

Kono tori mo	These birds—
Uchiyamekosene	Someone come and make them stop!
Ishitafu ya	The bottom-swimmers,
Amahasezukai	The seafolk couriers,
Koto no	Have told the story:
Katarigoto mo	The words of the story
Ko o ba	Are these words.

3 [K 3]

Thereupon Nunakawahime, not yet opening the door, sang from within:

Yachihoko no	Eight Thousand Spears,
Kami no mikoto	You great, noble god,
Nuekusa no	I am tender grass,
Me ni shi areba	A yielding maiden,
5 Wa ga kokoro	And my heart
Urasu no tori zo	Is a bird on the sandspits—
Ima koso wa	Still now
Wadori ni arame	A bird of its own,
Nochi wa	But later
10 Nadori ni aramu o	A bird that is yours:
Inochi wa	I pray you then,
Na shisetamai so	Do not lay waste your life.
Ishitafu ya	The bottom-swimmers,
Amahasezukai	The seafolk couriers,
Koto no	Have told the story:
Katarigoto mo	The words of the story
Ko o ba	Are these words.
Aoyama ni	When in the green hills
Hi ga kakuraba	The sun has hidden,
Nubatama no	With the gem-black night
Yo wa idenamu	I would have you come to me:
5 Asahi no	Like the morning sun,
Emisakaekite	Smiling in splendor, come,
Takuzuno no	And these rope-white arms
Shiroki tadamuki	In your bare embrace,
Awayuki no	This soft-snow
10 Wakayaru mune o	Bosom quick with youth
Sodataki	Take in your hands,
Tadaki managari	Lie close and interlaced;
Matamade	Pillowed in these arms,
Tamade sashimaki	These arms precious as jade,

9

15	Momonaga ni	Stretch out your thighs
	I wa nasamu o	In the comfort of your sleep.
	Aya ni	Not so wildly
	Na koikikoshi	Speak words of yearning,
	Yachihoko no	Eight Thousand Spears,
20	Kami no mikoto	You great, noble god.
	Koto no	We have told the story:
	Katarigoto mo	The words of the story
	Ko o ba	Are these words.

And so, they did not meet that night; they met the night of the following day.

4   [K 4]

Again, this god's first consort Suserihime no Mikoto was very jealous of his other wives. Then the god her husband grew tired and decided to go up from Izumo to Yamato. Dressed and about to leave, he stood with one hand on his horse's saddle and one foot in the stirrup, and sang:

	Nubatama no	Jet-berry black
	Kuroki mikeshi o	Is the raiment that I take
	Matsubusa ni	To adorn myself
	Toriyosoi	In my full array;
5	Okitsutori	Bird of the offing
	Muna miru toki	Peering down at its breast,
	Hatatagi mo	Flapping its wings:
	Kore wa fusawazu	These clothes do not become me—
	Hetsunami	I cast them away,
10	So ni nukiute	Waves that draw down the shore.
	Sonidori no	Kingfisher green
	Aoki mikeshi o	Is the raiment that I take
	Matsubusa ni	To adorn myself
	Toriyosoi	In my full array;
15	Okitsutori	Bird of the offing
	Muna miru toki	Peering down at its breast,
	Hatatagi mo	Flapping its wings:
	Ko mo fusawazu	These too do not become me—
	Hetsunami	I cast them away,
20	So ni nukiute	Waves that draw down the shore.
	Yamagata ni	Indigo
	Makishi	Sown in mountain fields:
	Atate tsuki	Pounded
	Someki ga	Dye-plant
25	Shiru ni	Juice-stained

Shimekoromo o	Is the garment that I take
Matsubusa ni	To adorn myself
Toriyosoi	In my full array;
Okitsutori	Bird of the offing
30 Muna miru toki	Peering down at its breast,
Hatatagi mo	Flapping its wings:
Ko shi yoroshi	This will do quite well.
Itoko ya no	My young darling,
Imo no mikoto	Dear and honored lady,
35 Muratori no	When like flocking birds
Wa ga mureinaba	I go flocking with my men,
Hiketori no	When like a following bird
Wa ga hikeinaba	I go following off with them,
Nakaji to wa	Even though you say
40 Na wa iu to mo	You are not going to cry,
Yamato no	On the mountainside
Hitomoto susuki	A single stalk of plumegrass
Unakabushi	Bending its head,
Na ga nakasamaku	You will cry, and your crying
45 Asaame no	Morning rain
Kiri ni tatamu zo	Will rise into a mist,
Wakakusa no	Young grass
Tsuma no mikoto	Tender and noble wife.
Koto no	We have told the story:
Katarigoto mo	The words of the story
Ko o ba	Are these words.

5   [K 5]

Thereupon his consort took the great winecup and came and offered it to him, singing:

Yachihoko no	Eight Thousand Spears,
Kami no mikoto ya	O great, noble god,
A ga Ōkuninushi	My Great Master of the Land,
Na koso wa	You are the one
5 O ni imaseba	Who because you are a man,
Uchimiru	On each and every
Shima no sakizaki	Island cape you ride around,
Kakimiru	Not missing a single
Iso no saki ochizu	Stony cape you climb around,
10 Wakakusa no	Must have wives
Tsuma motaserame	Like the young grass.
A wa mo yo	But as for me,
Me ni shi areba	Because I am a woman,

	Na o kite	Other than you
15	O wa nashi	I have no man,
	Na o kite	Other than you
	Tsuma wa nashi	I have no husband.
	Ayakaki no	Under the fluffiness
	Fuhaya ga shita ni	Of patterned curtains,
20	Mushibusuma	Under the softness
	Nikoya ga shita ni	Of flossy coverlets,
	Takubusuma	Under the rustling
	Sayagu ga shita ni	Of bark-cloth coverlets
	Awayuki no	This soft-snow
25	Wakayaru mune o	Bosom quick with youth,
	Takuzuno no	These rope-white arms
	Shiroki tadamuki	In your bare embrace
	Sodataki	Take in your hands,
	Tadaki managari	Lie close and interlaced;
30	Matamade	Pillowed in these arms,
	Tamade sashimaki	These arms precious as jade,
	Momonaga ni	Stretch out your thighs
	I o shi nase	And rest yourself in sleep.
	Toyomiki	Partake, my lord,
35	Tatematsurase	Of the bountiful fine wine!

Thus singing, they were bound together by the winecup, and with arms around each other's necks, they have remained enshrined to this day. This is a recitation about the gods.

✳ In song 6 Ajishiki Takahikone, a son of Ōkuninushi (Yachihoko), is offended when mistaken for the dead deity Ame no Wakahiko, whose funeral he is attending. He cuts down the funeral house with his sword and flies away. The incident is part of the narrative of the contest between the deities of heaven and earth for the mastery of the land. Ame no Wakahiko, an emissary from heaven, married an earthling deity and disloyally slew the pheasant sent to remind him of his duty. He was killed by the same arrow, hurled back at him from heaven. The analogy of the flashing gems suggests that Ajishiki Takahikone was a god of lightning. His sister Takahime, who sings the song, is the widow of Ame no Wakahiko. The song is labled *hinaburi*, or "rustic measure," probably because it was one of a group with no. 114, which contains the word *hinatsume*, "rustic maid."

6 [K 6]

Then when the god Ajishiki Takahikone, flushed with rage, flew away, his younger full sister Takahime no Mikoto, thinking to reveal his name, sang:

Ame naru ya	In heaven dwelling,
Ototanabata no	The young maiden of the loom
Unagaseru	Wears around her neck
Tama no misumaru	A fair circlet of fine gems.
5 Misumaru ni	On that fair circlet
Anatama wa ya	The pierced gems, how they flash!
Mitani	Across three valleys
Futawatarasu	Twice over gleaming,
Ajishiki	Ajishiki
10 Takahikone no kami so	Takahikone the god is he!

This song is a rustic measure.

✻ Songs 7 and 8 belong to the story of Ho-ori no Mikoto, who married Toyotamahime, the daughter of the sea god. When she came to the land to give birth to their child, she instructed her husband not to look at her during the parturition, for she would revert to her original form. Ho-ori, curious, peeped into the birthing hut and was horrified to see her turn into a *wani*, a creature variously interpreted as "crocodile" and "shark." Realizing she had been spied upon, Toyotamahime left behind her child and husband and returned to the sea. Toyotamahime's song is related by its imagery to the tale in which it is found, but Ho-ori's reply seems to refer to a casual amour of the type associated with utagaki, the country song matches that were arenas of sexual pairing between young men and women. This tale is another version of the myth found in nos. 579-80.

7   [K 7]

While she was resentful of the turn of mind that had led him to spy on her, she was unable to silence her yearning for him, and charging her younger sister Tamayorihime with the task of bringing up his child, had her present a song. That song:

Akadama wa	Red jewels gleam
O sae hikaredo	Even to the very string,
Shiratama no	But the white jewel
Kimi ga yosoi shi	Of your fashion, lord,
Tōtoku arikeri	Noble was it to me!

8   [K 8]

Then her husband answered with this song:

Okitsutori	I shall not forget
Kamo doku shima ni	The young love I took to sleep
Wa ga ineshi	Where wild ducks roost,

Imo wa wasureji Birds of the offing, in the isles—
Yo no kotogoto ni Not a day of my life.

✳ Nos. 9–14 are battle or triumph songs from the campaigns of Kamu-Yamato Iwarebiko no Mikoto (Jimmu, the so-called "First Emperor"), a descendant of the sun goddess to whom *Kojiki* myth ascribes the establishment of the Yamato state. The "he" in the introductory prose passages to all these songs refers to this hero. They were preserved in the repertory of the Kumebe, a hereditary military corporation in the service of the ruling house. No. 9 follows an account of the destruction of the "elder Ukashi," a chieftain opposed to Jimmu who was forced to die in his own trap. It is no doubt a song of independent origin inserted here because of the reference to a trap. It seems to be a jocular feasting song.

9   [K 9]

Afterwards he took the viands presented by the younger Ukashi and gave them all to his troops. Then he composed a song:

Uda no	In the high hold
Takaki ni	Of Uda
Shigiwana haru	I set a trap for snipe,
Wa ga matsu ya	And, oh, I waited.
5 Shigi wa sayarazu	Snipe was not the thing I snared,
Isukuwashi	A fearsome fine
Kujira sayaru	Whale was what I snared.
Konami ga	If the old wife
Na kowasaba	Asks for some vittles,
10 Tachisoba no	Hack her off a hunk
Mi no nakeku o	Lean and with as little flesh
Koki shi hiene	As there's fruit on a spindle tree.
Uwanari ga	If the new wife
Na kowasaba	Asks for some vittles,
15 Ichisakaki	Slice her thick slices,
Mi no ōkeku o	Fat and many as the berries
Kokida hiene	Of the *ichisakaki* bush.
Ee	*Ee*
Shiya ko shiya	The crazy, crazy fools!
20 Ko wa inogou so	This is taunting them.
Aa	*Aa*
Shiya ko shiya	The crazy, crazy fools!
Ko wa azawarau so	This is laughing them to scorn.

✳ Songs 10–14 are remarkable for their ferocity. It has been pointed out that the last five lines of no. 10 are an early example of the *hanka*, or envoy, a prominent feature of *Man'yōshū* poetry. The series 11–13, having to do with the destruction of Jimmu's blood enemy Tomibiko, is dominated by metaphor. The metaphors in nos. 11 and 12 are unitary (i.e., allegorical), whereas no. 13 preserves the distinction between vehicle and tenor. No. 14 provides a contrast to the thumping repetitions and boastful declarations of the preceding set with its admission of weakness (even if only "momentary"). The song is affecting, and the narrative has perhaps been adjusted to provide for its inclusion.

10   [K 10]

When he proceeded from that spot and arrived at the great pit-dwelling of Osaka, eighty braves of the Tsuchigumo, men with tails, were waiting growling in the pit-dwelling. Then by command of the son of the heavenly deity, a feast was given to the eighty braves. He provided eighty servers for the eighty braves, each one armed with a sword, and instructed the servers, "When you hear the song, cut them down at once." The song that was to signal their attack on the Tsuchigumo was this:

Ōsaka no	At Osaka
Ōmuroya ni	In the great pit-dwelling
Hito sawa ni	There are many men
Kiiriori	Who have gone inside to wait.
5 Hito sawa ni	There may be many men
Iriori to mo	Who are waiting there inside,
Mitsumitsushi	But we proud, mighty ones,
Kume no ko ga	We sons of the Kume,
Kubutsutsu i	With our knob-mallet,
10 Ishitsutsu i mochi	With our stone-mallet swords in hand
Uchite shi yamamu	Shall smite them and be done.
Mitsumitsushi	You proud, mighty ones,
Kume no kora ga	You sons of the Kume,
Kubutsutsu i	With your knob-mallet,
15 Ishitsutsu i mochi	With your stone-mallet swords in hand—
Ima utaba yorashi	Now is the time to strike!

Thus singing, they drew their swords and slew the braves at once.

11   [K 11]

Afterwards, when he set about to smite Tomibiko, he sang:

Mitsumitsushi	We proud, mighty ones,
Kume no kora ga	We sons of the Kume, have

Awafu ni wa	In our millet field
Kamira hitomoto	A single stalk of stinking leek:
Sone ga moto	That leek-stalk,
Soneme tsunagite	We shall take it root and bud,
Uchite shi yamamu	Smite it and be done.

12 [K 12]

Again he sang:

Mitsumitsushi	We proud, mighty ones,
Kume no kora ga	We sons of the Kume,
Kakimoto ni	Have by our fence
Ueshi hajikami	A planted pepper tree:
Kuchi hibiku	How it stung my mouth
Ware wa wasureji	I shall not forget:
Uchite shi yamamu	I shall smite it and be done.

13 [K 13]

Again he sang:

Kamukaze no	Over the rocks
Ise no umi no	In the Sea of Ise
Ohishi ni	Of the divine wind
Haimotohorofu	Round and round they crawl,
Shitadami no	The periwinkles:
Ihaimotohori	Thus crawling around the foe
Uchite shi yamamu	We shall smite them and be done.

14 [K 14]

Again when he attacked the elder Shiki and the younger Shiki, his forces were momentarily tired. And so he sang:

Tata namete	Shields aligned to shoot:
Inasa no yama no	On Inasa Mountain
Ko no ma yo mo	From between the trees
Iyukimamorai	We watched their movements,
Tatakaeba	We fought them;
Ware wa ya enu	Now we lie famished.
Shimatsutori	Island-bird
Ukai ga tomo	Cormorant fishers,
Ima suke ni kone	Come soon to our rescue!

❈ The wedding of Jimmu and Isukeyorihime is told in songs 15–19. Jimmu's commander Ōkume no Mikoto serves as go-between and wins Isukeyorihime's consent with the exchange given in nos. 17–18. He answers her katauta with one of his own, replying to her riddle with appropriate form and phraseology. (For another example of rewarded dexterity in versification, see nos. 25–26.) Song 19, a tanka, is a love poem of a type found plentifully in *Man'yōshū* and seems but loosely tied to the *Kojiki* narrative.

15   [K 15]

Hereupon seven maidens were strolling in the field of Takasaji, and Isukeyorihime was among them. Ōkume no Mikoto saw this Isukeyorihime and reported to the Emperor in a song:

Yamato no	Of the seven maidens
Takasajino o	Walking there in the field
Nana yuku	Of Takasaji
Otomedomo	In Yamato,
Tare o shi makamu	Which will you choose to wed?

16   [K 16]

At this time Isukeyorihime was standing in front of the other maidens. The Emperor beheld the maidens, and knowing in his mind that Isukeyorihime was the one standing in front of all the others, he replied in a song:

Katsugatsu mo	If I have to choose,
Iyasakidateru	The one standing there in front—
E o shi makamu	The eldest one I'll wed.

17   [K 17]

Hereupon when Ōkume no Mikoto spoke the Emperor's command to Isukeyorihime, she looked at Ōkume no Mikoto's tattooed eyes and thought them strange.

Ame tsutsu	Rain swallow, wagtail,
Chidori mashitoto	Plover, and meadow bunting:
Nado sakeru tome	Why the sharp, wide-open eyes?

18   [K 18]

When she had sung this, Ōkume no Mikoto sang in reply:

Otome ni	To find a maiden
Tada ni awamu to	Who will meet me face to face
Wa ga sakeru tome	Are my sharp, wide-open eyes.

Thereupon the maiden declared that she would serve the Emperor.

19   [K 19]

Now the house of this Isukeyorihime was on the banks of the Sai River. The

Emperor went to Isukeyorihime's place and slept with her all night. (The reason why this river was called the Sai was that there were many wild lilies growing near the river. Hence they named the river after the wild lilies. The original name of the wild lily was *sai*.) Afterward when this Isukeyorihime came to the palace, the Emperor composed a song:

Ashihara no	In a little house
Shikeshiki oya ni	Hidden deep in the reedbeds
Sugatatami	We spread mats of sedge—
Iyasaya shikite	What a rustling sound they made!—
Wa ga futari neshi	We two, and lay to sleep.

✳ Songs 20–21 are two tanka in the genre of wazauta, veiled predictions of momentous events, and were probably composed to fit the narrative. Tagishimimi no Mikoto, a kind of Japanese Mordred, was the son of Jimmu by his first wife, Ahirahime. In the *Kojiki* narrative the sons of Isukeyorihime, forewarned, kill him.

20 [K 20]

Now after the Emperor died, [his son] the elder half-brother Tagishimimi no Mikoto took [his stepmother] Empress-Consort Isukeyorihime to wife and plotted to do away with his three younger brothers [her sons]. But their mother Isukeyorihime was sorely grieved at this and warned the princes by means of a song. The song went:

Saigawa yo	From Sai River
Kumo tachiwatari	Clouds rise and spread across the sky;
Unebiyama	Unebi Mountain
Konoha sayaginu	Rustles with the leaves of trees:
Kaze fukamu to su	A wind is about to blow.

21 [K 21]

Again she sang:

Unebiyama	Unebi Mountain
Hiru wa kumo toi	In the daytime streams with clouds,
Yū sareba	And when evening falls,
Kaze fukamu to so	Because of the wind about to blow,
Konoha sayageru	Rustles with the leaves of trees.

✳ No. 22 is another premonitory song, this time uttered by a god in human guise. Ōbiko no Mikoto was the uncle of Emperor Sujin, the tenth in the official line of Emperors, who may have lived in the third century. Mimaki

Iribiko was Sujin's name, and the oracle predicts the rebellion (successfully crushed) of Sujin's half-brother Prince Takehaniyasu.

22   [K 22]

Now when Ōbiko no Mikoto was on his way to the land of Koshi, a young girl wearing a waist-skirt stood on the pass of Hera in Yamashiro and sang:

Mimaki Iribiko wa ya	Mimaki Iribiko, alas!
Mimaki Iribiko wa ya	Mimaki Iribiko, alas!
Ono ga o o	That your life
Nusumi shi-semu to	They plot to steal and put to death,
5 Shiritsuto yo	From the rear door
Iyukitagai	Going around and back,
Maetsuto yo	From the front door
Iyukitagai	Going around and back,
Ukagawaku	Watching for their chance,
10 Shirani to	You do not know,
Mimaki Iribiko wa ya	Mimaki Iribiko, alas!

At this, Ōbiko no Mikoto, thinking it strange, turned back his horse and asked the young girl, "What is this that you have said?" The young girl replied, "I have said nothing. I only sang a song." And she abruptly vanished without his seeing where she went.

❋ Songs 23–37 belong to the story of Yamato Takeru no Mikoto, the Brave of Yamato, a hero tale of tragic dimensions. Yamato Takeru was the son of Emperor Keikō, a ruler who may have lived during the fourth century A.D. His headstrong and violent disposition led his father to send him on a series of one-man expeditions to subdue unconquered regions, culminating in a lonely death far from home. The central figure of these legends is brutal and wily toward his enemies, simple and loyal in obedience to authority, boastful, melancholy, and attractive to women. No. 23 is set on the return journey from the west, after Yamato Takeru has slain the braves of the Kumaso in Kyūshū. *Yatsume sasu* is a pillow word for Izumo taken in the sense of "emerging seaweed" (*mo*), rather than "emerging clouds" as in no. 1.

23   [K 23]

Next he entered the land of Izumo. Desiring to kill Izumo Takeru, he formed bonds of friendship with him as soon as he arrived. He made a false sword to wear out of red oak, and they bathed together in the Hi River. Yamato Takeru no Mikoto came up from the river first, and put on the sword that Izumo Takeru had taken off and said, "Let's exchange swords." And so, Izumo Takeru came up from the river after him and put on Yamato

Takeru no Mikoto's false sword. Then Yamato Takeru no Mikoto challenged him, saying, "Come on, let's cross swords!" And so, when each drew his sword, Izumo Takeru could not draw the false sword. Yamato Takeru no Mikoto at once drew his sword and struck and killed Izumo Takeru. Then he composed a song and sang:

Yatsume sasu	In eight-bud-bursting
Izumo Takeru ga	Seaweed-surging Izumo
Hakeru tachi	The Brave wore a sword
Tsuzura sawa maki	All wrapped around with many vines—
Sami nashi ni aware	But without a blade, alas!

And so, having swept aside and pacified [his foes], he went and reported.

❋ The rest of the songs of the Yamato Takeru story come from the hero's expedition to subdue Azuma, the Eastland. The self-sacrificing consort Oto-Tachibanahime is introduced and disposed of in the episode centering on no. 24. In her song she refers to an earlier episode in which Yamato Takeru had been trapped in a fire set by one of his enemies, the local ruler of Sagamu.

24   [K 24]

When he went in from there and was crossing a place where the sea flowed in a swift current, the god of the crossing raised waves and spun the boat around so that it was unable to proceed. Thereupon his consort, whose name was Oto-Tachibanahime no Mikoto, spoke and said, "I shall take the place of the Prince and go into the sea. Let the Prince fulfill his charge of government and return to make his report." And when she was about to go into the sea, they spread eight thicknesses of sedge mats, eight thicknesses of skin mats, and eight thicknesses of silk mats on the waves, and she went down and sat upon them. At this the rough waves calmed of themselves, and the boat was able to proceed. And so his consort sang:

Sane sashi	You who asked of me
Sagamu no ono ni	As you stood amid the flames
Moyuru hi no	Of the burning fire
Honaka ni tachite	On the moor of Sagamu
Toishi kimi wa mo	Of the thrusting peaks—you, lord.

Now, after seven days his consort's comb washed ashore. And they took her comb and made a grave and placed it in the mound.

❋ Songs 25–26 are another example of riddle and answer in paired katauta form. The Kuni no Miyatsuko was in later historical times a court-appointed local ruler. Azuma was the entire Eastland, of imprecise geographical extent, and the account presumably does not reflect a historical reality.

25   [K 25]
Next, from that province he crossed over into Kai, and while he stayed at Sakaori Shrine, he sang:

Niibari	How many nights
Tsukuba o sugite	Have I slept since passing
Iku yo ka netsuru	Niibari and Tsukuba?

26   [K 26]
Thereupon the old man who kindled the fire continued the song, singing:

Kaka nabete	Counting them all up,
Yo ni wa kokonoyo	Nights nine nights
Hi ni wa tōka o	And days ten days.

He praised the old man for this and made him Kuni no Miyatsuko of Azuma.

❋ The chōka exchange of nos. 27-28 is notable for its imagery, structure, and amorous wit. On his way east, Yamato Takeru had pledged to marry Miyazuhime, the ancestress of the Kuni no Miyatsuko of Owari, and now he returns to carry out his promise. The discovery of the menstrual ("monthly") blood leads to punning on the moon and the passage of time. As in many exchanges, the woman adroitly turns the tables on her male interlocutor. The preparation-conclusion technique of no. 27 uses the striking image of the swan's neck in visual analogy to the woman's arm in a manner characteristic of the early poetry. Miyazuhime's reply is introduced by a four-line formula also found in various versions in *Man'yōshū*. The sword Grasscutter (Kusanagi) figures earlier in *Kojiki*, having been discovered in the body of a slain dragon-monster by the god Susanoo no Mikoto. Yamato Takeru used it to mow the grass when trapped on the burning moor of Sagamu. Here he deliberately leaves it behind, determined to conquer the deity of Mount Ibuki with his bare hands. This act of hubris leads to his downfall: he is subsequently punished for speaking disrespectfully to the deity. The magic force of words (presumably correctly employed) is implied in the expression *kotomukete*, translated "quelled with speech" in the prose introduction to no. 27.

27   [K 27]
From that province he crossed over into Shinano Province, where he quelled with speech the god of Shinano Slope; then he returned to the province of Owari. There he entered the house of Miyazuhime, to whom he had made

his vow some time before. While he was being served his meal, Miyazuhime waited on him, offering him the great winecup. It happened that the skirt of Miyazuhime's robe was stained with menstrual blood. When he beheld the menstrual blood, he composed a song:

Hisakata no	Over the sun-bright
Ama no Kaguyama	Heavenly mount of Kagu
Tokama ni	Sharply, raucously
Sawataru kubi	Passes a flying swan:
5 Hiwaboso ni	Supple and slender,
Tawayagaina o	That lissome arm of yours—
Makamu to wa	I was ready
Are wa suredo	To take it for my pillow,
Sanemu to wa	I was eager
10 Are wa omoedo	To lie by your side;
Na ga keseru	But on the skirt
Osui no suso ni	Of the robe you are wearing
Tsuki tachinikeri	I see the moon has risen.

28   [K 28]

Then Miyazuhime sang in reply to his song:

Takahikaru	Divine Child
Hi no miko	Of the High-Shining Sun,
Yasumishishi	Mighty lord
Wa ga ōkimi	Ruling the land in peace:
5 Aratama no	Like a bright, rough gem
Toshi ga kifureba	The new year comes and passes,
Aratama no	Like a bright, rough gem
Tsuki wa kiheyuku	Each month too comes and goes;
Ube na ube na	Well, oh well, may it be
10 Kimi machigata ni	In the hard waiting for you, lord,
Wa ga keseru	That on the skirt
Osui no suso ni	Of the robe I am wearing
Tsuki tatanamu yo	The moon should have risen!

And so they were united, and he went off to conquer the god of Mount Ibuki, leaving his sword Grasscutter with Miyazuhime.

❊ Dazed by a violent, supernaturally induced hailstorm on Mount Ibuki, Yamato Takeru wanders back toward Yamato, reaching Cape Otsu in Ise Province in song 29. There he finds another sword (not Grasscutter) that he had left at the foot of a pine. Probably an Ise folk song, 29 praises the pine, employing the refrain *ase o*, "my brother." In context the song suggests Yamato Takeru's confusion, melancholy, and loneliness.

29   [K 29]

When he arrived at the lone pine of Cape Otsu, he found that the blade he
had worn, and which he had forgotten when he partook of his meal, had not
disappeared but was still there. And so he composed a song:

	Owari ni	Opposite Owari,
	Tada ni mukaeru	Facing straight across the sea
	Otsu no saki naru	On the headland of Otsu
	Hitotsu matsu	A lone pine:
5	Ase o	*My brother!*
	Hitotsu matsu	Lone pine,
	Hito ni ariseba	If you were a man,
	Tachi hakemashi o	I would gird you with my sword,
	Kinu kisemashi o	I would dress you in my clothes.
10	Hitotsu matsu	Lone pine:
	Ase o	*My brother!*

❋ Still heading for home, Yamato Takeru reaches the plain of Nobo near
Suzuka in Ise. No. 30 is a land-praising song integrated into the narrative to
express the hero's homesickness. The mountains of Yamato are a favorite
subject in *Man'yōshū*. No. 31 is directed to the young men and women who
meet at the annual revels (utagaki), urging them to enjoy their youth. In
context the valedictory quality is obvious. The effectively arranged sequence
provides a katauta as a kind of envoy in no. 32. Yamato Takeru's death song
finds him again thinking of his sword Grasscutter, left with Miyazuhime.

30   [K 30]

From there he proceeded until he arrived at the plain of Nobo, where he
sang in yearning for his homeland:

Yamato wa	Yamato
Kuni no mahoroba	Is the crest of the land—
Tatanazuku	In the close-folded
Aokaki	Green-fence
Yamagomoreru	Mountains it is hidden:
Yamato shi uruwashi	Yamato, the beautiful.

31   [K 31]

Again he sang:

Inochi no	Those in whom
Matakemu hito wa	Life is at the full—
Tatamikomo	Let them take
Heguri no yama no	From woven-mat Mount Heguri

Kumakashi ga ha o	Broad leaves of the bear-oak
Uzu ni sase	To thrust in their hair:
Sono ko	You young ones!

This is a song of yearning for the homeland.

32 [K 32]

Again he sang:

Hashike yashi	Yonder from the way
Wagie no kata yo	Where lies my well-loved home
Kumoi tachiku mo	How the clouds now rise and come!

This is a *katauta*.

33 [K 33]

Then his illness worsened rapidly. He composed a song:

Otome no	By the maiden's
Tokonobe ni	Bedside
Wa ga okishi	I left it,
Tsuruki no tachi	The sword I wore—
Sono tachi wa ya	Oh, that sword!

He finished singing, and then he died. They despatched an express rider to the court.

❋ Previously unmentioned consorts and children are introduced as mourners in song 34. Their behavior has been interpreted as an amorous analogy to the vinelike embraces of lovers, reused in a different context as an image of grief. Nevertheless, these paroxysms are described in similar terms from the death of Izanami early in *Kojiki* through the laments of Hitomaro. In no. 34 the fourth line can be taken either as modifying or as end-stopped: creepers of wild yam that crawl, or humans crawl—[like] creepers of wild yam.

34 [K 34]

Thereupon his consorts who lived in Yamato, and all his children, came down and made him a tomb. Crawling around in the muddy paddies, they cried and sang:

Nazuki no	In the sticky fields
Ta no inagara ni	In among the stalks of rice,
Inagara ni	Among the rice stalks,
Haimotohorofu	We crawl around and around
Tokorozura	Creepers of wild yam.

❋ Songs 35 and 37 are based on an effective use of irony, in the first case contrasting earth-bound humans with the freely soaring spirit of the metamorphosed Prince, and in the second bemoaning the inaccessibility of the dead as the spirit recedes into far waters in spite of the implied promise of its name, "plover of the beach." No. 36 employs analogy, continuing the complaint of no. 35, which again has been interpreted, like no. 34, as originally referring to hard going along the path of love.

35   [K 35]

Thereupon he changed into an eight-span white plover, soared into the sky, and flew off toward the beach. And his consorts and his children followed him, weeping and weeping, forgetting their pain though they cut and tore their feet on the stubble of the small bamboo. [Their] song at this time:

Asajinohara	Plain of the dwarf bamboo—
Koshi nazumu	Our legs grow heavy.
Sora wa yukazu	We do not go through the sky,
Ashi yo yuku na	We go upon our feet.

36   [K 36]

Again, a song from when they went into the sea water and waded along:

Umiga yukeba	When we go through the sea
Koshi nazumu	Our legs grow heavy.
Ōkawara no	In the great riverbed
Uegusa	Planted grasses:
Umiga wa	In the sea
Isayou	We waver.

37   [K 37]

A song from when the plover flew again and perched on a rock offshore:

Hama tsu chidori	The plover of the beach
Hama yo wa yukazu	Does not go along the beach
Isozutau	But the rocks offshore.

These four songs were all sung at his funeral. Thus even unto today they sing these songs at an Emperor's funeral.

❋ A fourth- or fifth-century succession struggle forms the background for song 38. Prince Oshikuma and his general, Isahi no Sukune, are the defeated rebels, and Furukuma the victorious general supporting Prince Homudawake (Oshikuma's half brother) and his mother, Empress Jingū. The rebel army has just been slaughtered on the shore of the Sea of Ōmi (Lake Biwa).

38   [K 38]

Thereupon this Prince Oshikuma, together with Isahi no Sukune, being pursued and hard-pressed, got into a boat and launched forth on the sea, singing:

Iza agi	Come, my friend,
Furukuma ga	Instead of bearing
Itate owazu wa	Sore wounds at Furukuma's hand,
Niodori no	Like grebes
Ōmi no umi ni	Let us plunge in the waters
Kazuki sena wa	Of the Sea of Ōmi!

So saying, they went into the sea and died together.

❊ Nos. 39–40 are songs offering and accepting ceremonial *sake*, a beverage made from fermented rice and conventionally referred to in English as rice wine, but perhaps more properly called rice beer. In a song of offering, the singer typically vouches for the quality of the *sake* by disclaiming credit for the fine brew and attributing its success to a deity, in this case the creator god Sukuna Hikona no Mikoto, who in the Izumo cycle of myth helped form the land and then crossed over to Tokoyo, the Elysian realm conceived as across or at the bottom of the sea. "Rock-standing" refers to the stone idols that represented this deity. The acceptance song speaks of the liquor as being brewed to the accompaniment of music, song, and dance. The two songs are made part of the narrative of Prince Homuda-wake, who returns to his mother Okinagatarashihime (Empress Jingū) from purification after the rebellion of Prince Oshikuma. Since the Prince is still a child, the elder statesman Takeshi Uchi no Sukune replies on his behalf. The "waiting *sake*" presumably was intended to extend a magical protection to the person for whom it was prepared.

39   [K 39]

Then when he returned, his parent Okinagatarashihime no Mikoto brewed and offered waiting *sake*. Thus, his parent's song:

	Kono miki wa	This fine liquor
	Wa ga miki narazu	Is not my fine liquor.
	Kushi no kami	The potion-master
	Tokoyo ni imasu	Who dwells in Everworld,
5	Iwa tatasu	The rock-standing
	Sukuna mikami no	Deity Sukuna,
	Kamuhoki	With godly blessing,
	Hokikuruoshi	Blessing in frenzy,

Toyohoki	With abundant blessing,
10 Hokimotooshi	Blessing around and around,
Matsurikoshi	Came and offered
Miki zo	This fine liquor:
Asazu ose	Drink unsparingly,
Sa sa	*Sa! Sa!*

So singing, she offered the ceremonial liquor.

40   [K 40]

Thereupon Takeshi Uchi no Sukune no Mikoto replied on behalf of the Prince:

Kono miki o	He who brewed
Kamikemu hito wa	This fine liquor—was it because
Sono tsuzumi	He took his drum
Usu ni tatete	And standing it up like a mortar,
5 Utaitsutsu	Singing while he brewed
Kamikere ka mo	Did the brewing of the beer,
Maitsutsu	Dancing while he brewed
Kamikere ka mo	Did the brewing of the beer,
Kono miki no	That this fine liquor,
10 Miki no	Fine liquor,
Aya ni utadanoshi	Makes me feel so extra good?
Sa sa	*Sa! Sa!*

These are drinking songs.

❋ No. 41 is a land-praising song attributed to Emperor Ōjin (the now-grown Prince Homuda-wake). It was on this trip to Chikatsu Ōmi (the province around Lake Biwa) that the Emperor met Yagawaehime (see the next song). For a similar land-praising poem, see no. 238. The divinity and bounty of the land are favorite themes of the early singers.

41   [K 41]

Once when the Emperor crossed over to the province of Chikatsu Ōmi, he stood on Uji Fields and looked off toward Kazuno. He sang:

Chiba no	Leafy Kazuno,
Kazuno o mireba	Vinefields of the thousand leaves:
Momochidaru	Looking, I can see
Yaniwa mo miyu	Hundreds, thousands of houses—
Kuni no ho mo miyu	And I can see the summits of the land.

❋ No. 42 is a nuptial-banquet song introduced by reference to what may have been an item on the menu. It is humorous, implying the conviviality of the occasion, and like nos. 2–5 may have been mimed in recitation. The sudden switch in persona at line 13 is particularly effective. The native metaphors and the description of the woman's makeup procedures add considerably to the song's interest and charm. Lines 24–29 exemplify what might be dubbed the Goldilocks pattern of choosing the "just right" alternative among three items, a pattern that was one of the basic structural elements of early Japanese prosody. (See no. 4 for a more extended use of this feature.) The song is here made part of the narrative of the marriage of Emperor Ōjin and Yagawaehime, one of his numerous consorts. The "he" in the prose introduction refers to Yagawaehime's father, Wani no Hifure no Omi. For another performance song with a crab as speaker, see no. 1556.

42   [K 42]

When he presented the viands, he had his daughter Yagawaehime take the great winecup and present it. Then the Emperor, taking the great winecup, composed this song:

	Kono kani ya	This crab here,
	Izuku no kani	Where do you come from, crab?
	Momozutau	Many a day away—
	Tsunuga no kani	I'm a crab from Tsunuga.
5	Yokosarau	Scuttling sideways,
	Izuku ni itaru	Where are you bound?
	Ichijishima	Ichijishima,
	Mishima ni toki	Mishima I reached,
	Niodori no	Like a grebe
10	Kazuki ikizuki	Diving and gasping,
	Shinadayuu	Dragging up the slope
	Sasanamiji o	Of the Sasanami road—
	Sukusuku to	Where *I* sped along,
	Wa ga imaseba ya	Free and easy in my stride;
15	Kohata no	And on the road
	Michi ni	At Kohata,
	Awashishi otome	Ah, the maiden that I met!
	Ushirode wa	From behind
	Odatero kamo	She was a trim little shield,
20	Hanami wa	And the rows of her teeth
	Shii hishi nasu	Were fashioned like acorns, caltrops.
	Ichihii no	At Ichihii

28

Wanisa no ni o	The earth of Wani Hill—
Hatsuni wa	The first earth
25 Hada akarakemi	Having a reddish surface,
Shihani wa	The bottom earth
Niguroki yue	Being a muddy black,
Mitsuguri no	The three-chestnut
Sono nakatsuni o	Middle earth she chose,
30 Kabutsuku	And put it over
Mahi ni wa atezu	No fierce, head-searing fire,
Mayogaki	Eyebrow-painting,
Ko ni kakitare	Thickly drawing down the lines:
Awashishi omina	Ah, the woman that I met!
35 Ka moga to	To have her thus,
Wa ga mishi kora	The sweet girl I saw—
Kaku moga to	To have her so,
A ga mishi ko ni	The girl I saw—whom now
Utatake dani	In mounting pleasure
40 Mukaioru kamo	I sit facing, with whom now
Isoioru kamo	I company side by side!

Thus, when the Emperor had joined with her, she gave birth to a child, Uji no Waki-iratsuko.

❊ In songs 43–46 Emperor Ōjin bestows Kaminagahime ("Lady Long Hair"), a beauty he had selected for himself, on his importunate son Prince Ōsazaki (the future Emperor Nintoku). No. 43 recounts the finding of the maiden, using the same "Goldilocks pattern" as in no. 42. The song is devoted almost entirely to its introduction, or jo, an elaborately detailed consideration of the proper analogy for the "redly glowing maiden" who finally appears in line 14. The pillow word *mitsuguri no* ("three-chestnut") employed in this and the previous song as an epithet for "middle" refers to the three segments in a chestnut.

43   [K 43]

Then the Ō-Omi Takeshi Uchi no Sukune begged the Emperor's command, and the Emperor gave Kaminagahime to his son. The manner in which he gave her was this: on a day of feasting the Emperor had Kaminagahime take the great oak-leaf winecup, which he thus offered to the Crown Prince. Thereupon he composed a song:

Iza kodomo	Well now, boys,
Nobiru tsumi ni	Picking wild garlic,

Hiru tsumi ni	Picking garlic
Wa ga yuku michi no	I went, and there by the path
5 Kaguwashi	Found a fragrant
Hanatachibana wa	Orange tree all in flower:
Hotsue wa	The upper branches
Tori igarashi	Birds had stripped with their perching,
Shizue wa	The lower branches
10 Hito torigarashi	People had stripped with their plucking,
Mitsuguri no	But the three-chestnut
Nakatsue no	Middle branches
Hotsumori	Swelled with budding fruit:
Akaraotome o	Redly glowing the maiden—
15 Iza sasaba	Come, entice her away,
Yorashi na	All will be well!

❋ Song 44 is an expression of regret couched in metaphors of a suggestively sexual nature. Watershield (*nunawa*) is a plant whose stems stretch across the surface of the water; an edible, it is reeled in for harvest.

44   [K 44]

Again he sang:

Mizu tamaru	Where water collects
Yosami no ike no	In the pond of Yosami
Iguiuchi ga	The dikestake-pounding,
Sashikeru shirani	The tamping was done—I didn't know;
Nunawa kuri	The watershield-reeling,
Haekeku shirani	Stretching away—I didn't know.
Wa ga kokoro shi zo	Oh, this heart of mine,
Iya oko ni shite	What a fool it has been:
Ima zo kuyashiki	Now, too late, I regret.

Thus singing, he bestowed her on him.

❋ The paired tanka nos. 45 and 46 are Prince Ōsazaki's exclamations of triumph and delight. Love-in-fulfillment was later largely excluded from the courtly and increasingly melancholy love poetry tradition. *Michi no shiri* ("the end of the road") refers to the remote province of Hyūga in Kyūshū, where Kaminagahime was born. It serves as an epithet for Kohada, her village.

45   [K 45]

After having had the maiden bestowed on him, the Prince sang:

Michi no shiri	Of the nether road
Kohada otome o	Kohada maiden—oh,
Kami no goto	Like unto thunder
Kikoeshikado mo	Was the fame resounding—
Aimakura maku	Yet now we pillow together!

46   [K 46]

Again he sang:

Michi no shiri	How the nether road
Kohada otome wa	Kohada maiden lay
Arasowazu	Without argument
Neshiku o shi zo mo	And slept with me—her meekness
Uruwashimi omou	I remember with delight!

❋ *Kojiki* mentions the Kuzu as an autochthonous people who submitted to Emperor Jimmu in his pacification of the land. They lived in a remote area of the Yoshino mountains and came regularly to court to present their local products, and their songs and dances, on into the Heian period. *Kojiki* preserves two of their songs as nos. 47–48. No. 47, in praise of Ōsazaki's sword, suggests their fealty to this Prince (who later became Emperor Nintoku, though not designated as successor by his father, Emperor Ōjin). While the song has some interpretational obscurities, it is obviously an expression of awe at the Prince's potency. *Sue fuyu*, "swinging at the tip," introduces *fuyuki*, "winter wood," but the usual preparation-conclusion pattern is reversed, with the natural analogue following rather than preceding the object to which it is compared.

47   [K 47]

And the Kuzu of Yoshino, seeing the sword Ōsazaki no Mikoto was wearing, sang:

	Homuta no	Child of the sun
	Hi no miko	From Homuta,
	Ōsazaki	Ōsazaki,
	Ōsazaki	Ōsazaki,
5	Hakaseru tachi	The sword you wear
	Moto tsuruki	Strung from the hilt,
	Sue fuyu	Swinging at the tip:
	Fuyuki no	Swaying underbrush

Sukara ga shitaki no	In the bare-stemmed winter wood—
10 Saya saya	*Saya! Saya!*

❊ No. 48 is another song to accompany the formal presentation of cere-monial liquor. *Maro ga chi,* "our father," may be a refrain like *ase o,* "my brother," in no. 29.

48 [K 48]

And they made a long mortar in the white-oak groves of Yoshino and brewed ceremonial liquor in the long mortar; and when they presented the ceremonial liquor, they beat upon their mouths like drums, showed their skill in the dance, and sang:

Kashi no fu ni	In the white-oak grove
Yokusu o tsukuri	We fashioned a long mortar;
Yokusu ni	In the long mortar
Kamishi ōmiki	We brewed the fine great liquor:
Umara ni	See how good it is—
Kikoshimochiose	Come, partake, down it with joy,
Maro ga chi	Our father.

This song has always been chanted, down to the present, whenever the Kuzu make the great food offering.

❊ Song 49 is positioned in such a way as to serve as an acceptance song to go with no. 48 but belongs to a different anecdote. Here too the liquor is offered by an outlander, the continental immigrant and expert brewer Susu-kori. The results for Emperor Ōjin are both predictable and amusing. Tra-ditional Japanese tolerance for drunkenness, even in the great, is here sug-gested, along with an attitude of awe toward the powers of drink.

49 [K 49]

Then Susukori brewed the ceremonial liquor and presented it. The Em-peror, intoxicated by the ceremonial liquor, sang this song:

Susukori ga	On Susukori's
Kamishi miki ni	Brew of fine strong liquor
Ware einikeri	I have gone and gotten drunk!
Kotonagushi	On this weal-potion,
Egushi ni	This laugh-potion,
Ware einikeri	I have gone and gotten drunk!

Singing thus, he went out and struck a large stone on the Ōsaka road with his stick, whereupon the stone ran out of his way. Hence the proverb, "Even hard stones get out of the drunkard's way."

✳ Songs 50–51 have to do with the attempted coup d'état of Prince Ōyamamori, a son of Emperor Ōjin who turned against the heir-designate, his half brother Uji no Waki-iratsuko, after their father's death. Warned in time, Prince Waki-iratsuko concocted an elaborate ruse in which he disguised himself as a boatman and threw Ōyamamori into the Uji River. Waki-iratsuko's bowmen forced Ōyamamori to drown in the river, but they did not actually shoot him, which must be the significance of the scruples expressed in no. 51. Both songs appear to have an origin independent of the narrative, but the significance of "lord" and "sister" is not clear. In this context they seemingly refer to revulsion against shedding familial blood, a sentiment rather unusual in *Kojiki*. No. 50 seems to express a boatman's desire for a comrade. Whatever the context, the thrust of no. 51 is deeper; the tree-root-branch metaphor is worked out effectively to express a conflict between murderous and compassionate thoughts.

50   [K 50]

When they reached the middle of the river on their way across, he tipped the boat and threw him [Ōyamamori] into the water. He quickly surfaced and was swept down on the current. As he floated along, he sang:

Chihayaburu	A nimble man,
Uji no watari ni	Quick in handling the pole
Sao tori ni	In the crossing
Hayakemu hito shi	Of raging Uji—let him
Wa ga moko ni komu	Come and be my comrade.

Then the troops that lay hidden beside the river rose up at once on both sides, and fitting arrows to their bows, made sure he was swept away. He sank at length when he reached Kawara Point.

51   [K 51]

Then they took up his body, at which time the younger Prince his brother sang:

Chihayahito	At Uji Crossing,
Uji no watari ni	Uji of the raging clans,
Watarize ni	At the crossing shallows
Tateru	There stood
5 Azusayumi mayumi	A catalpa bow, a true-bow tree:
Ikiramu to	I would cut it down,

Kokoro wa moedo	So I had it in my heart;
Itoramu to	I would take it off,
Kokoro wa moedo	So I had it in my heart;
10 Motohe wa	But at the root
Kimi o omoide	I remembered my lord,
Suehe wa	And at the branch
Imo o omoide	I remembered my sister.
Iranakeku	With a sharp pang
15 Soko ni omoide	I remembered him there,
Kanashikeku	With a deep twinge
Koko ni omoide	I remembered her here;
Ikirazu so kuru	I left it uncut and came on,
Azusayumi mayumi	The catalpa bow, the true-bow tree.

❋ Despite his designation as heir by his father, Emperor Ōjin, and his victory over Ōyamamori, Prince Waki-iratsuko was determined to cede the throne to his other half brother, Prince Ōsazaki. Each deferred to the other until the dispute ended abruptly with the untimely demise of Waki-iratsuko. Ōsazaki succeeded as Emperor Nintoku, and the next several songs have to do with his reign. Anecdotes about Nintoku focus on his benevolence and his amorous proclivities, but it is only the latter that have attracted a corpus of song. Songs 52–56 belong to the story of Nintoku and the provincial beauty Kurohime. In this as in other affairs of Nintoku, the jealousy of the Empress, Iwanohime, is the crucial factor in events. No. 52 has the Emperor gazing from his tower in Naniwa (modern Ōsaka), at Kurohime's boat leaving for Kibi down the Inland Sea. The phrase *kurozaya no masazuko* is obscure; "blacksheath the good-luck maiden" is one construction.

52   [K 52]

Thereupon, hearing that the daughter of the chieftain of the seafolk of Kibi—her name was Kurohime—was fair of face, he summoned her and took her into his service. But she fled back to her province in dread of the Empress. The Emperor looked out from his lofty hall at Kurohime's boat leaving port, and sang:

Okie ni wa	Out in the offing
Obune tsuraraku	Little boats go one by one:
Kurozaya no	My young love,
Masazuko wagimo	Blacksheath the good-luck maiden,
Kuni e kudarasu	Is heading away for home.

The Empress was enraged when she heard this song and sent someone after her to Ōura, from where she forced Kurohime to continue her journey on foot.

※ No. 53 seems to be a land-viewing song with no original connection to the narrative. The islands named in the song are not clearly identifiable in terms of Japan's modern topography.

53   [K 53]

Thereupon the Emperor, yearning for Kurohime, deceived the Empress and said he was going to see Awaji Island. He set out and landed on Awaji. Gazing far off into the distance, he sang:

Oshiteru ya	When from the cape
Naniwa no saki yo	Of far-shining Naniwa
Idetachite	I set forth,
Wa ga kuni mireba	Going out to view the land,
Awashima	Awa Island,
Onogoroshima	Onogoro Island, .
Ajimasa no	And the betel-tree
Shima mo miyu	Island stood in view.
Saketsushima miyu	Sake Island stood in view.

※ Songs 54–56 form an interesting study in early tanka. No. 54 is a straight-forward reveling in bucolic pleasures, which in context partakes of the pastoralism prevalent in early poetry. No. 55 employs the technique of analogy and seems to have been a lyric of widespread provenance, since a version is also found in the local gazetteer of Tango province (no. 217). No. 56 also uses an analogical structure, as well as the pattern in which line 5 repeats line 2. Repetitions in general are considered characteristic of early song (see nos. 1, 65, 80, and 111). This brief affair of Kurohime forms a poem-tale that is one of the gems of *Kojiki*, and for the final song the legend-weavers selected a touching expression of the helpless jealousy of the "other woman."

54   [K 54]

He followed on from that island and proceeded to the land of Kibi. There Kurohime had him take up residence in the upland fields, where she brought him food. Once she was picking mustard greens to make broth. When the Emperor came to where the maiden was picking the greens, he sang:

Yamagata ni	Picking mustard greens
Makeru aona mo	Planted in the upland fields—

Kibihito to   How pleasant it is,
Tomo ni shi tsumeba   When you pick them by the side
Tanoshiku mo aru ka   Of one from the land of Kibi!

55   [K 55]

A song presented by Kurohime when the Emperor went up [to Yamato]:

Yamatohe ni   Though the west wind blows
Nishi fukiagete   Toward the land of Yamato,
Kumobanare   And the clouds draw back—
Sokiori to mo   Though you draw away from me,
Ware wasureme ya   When shall I ever forget you?

56   [K 56]

Again she sang:

Yamatohe ni   Off to Yamato
Yuku wa ta ga tsuma   He goes—whose husband is he?
Komorizu no   Like a hidden stream
Shita yo haetsutsu   Flowing away underground
Yuku wa ta ga tsuma   He goes—whose husband is he?

✳ Emperor Nintoku's desire for his half sister Yata no Waki-iratsume and the jealousy of his consort Empress Iwanohime are the context for songs 57–65. Taking advantage of the absence of the Empress on a voyage to Kumano, the Emperor moved Princess Yata into the palace. On her return the Empress was informed of the state of affairs and refused to disembark at Naniwa, going on up the river into Yamashiro. No. 57, given as her utterance, is a song of praise for the ruler. On the surface the song is inappropriate to the emotional situation; it may have been included merely for its geographical references. On the other hand, it is not impossible to read into this paean subtler strains of feeling, such as a woman's resentment against male sexual vainglory or a wife's continuing devotion to her husband. The narrative context continually exerts pressure on the potential meanings of a poem. The final exclamation is introduced by a two-stage jo, a process that raises the recipient of the analogical splendor to an even loftier eminence. The camellia was credited with various magical powers.

57   [K 57]

Thereupon, instead of going into the palace, the Empress had her boat pulled on up the canal; following the river, she went up into Yamashiro. At this time she sang:

Tsuginefu ya	Passing by the peaks
Yamashirogawa o	Up Yamashiro River,
Kawanobori	Up the river
Wa ga noboreba	I have made my way, and now
5 Kawa no he ni	By the riverside
Oidateru	Standing, growing,
Sashibu o	A rosebay, O
Sashibu no ki	A rosebay tree!
Shi ga shita ni	Underneath that tree
10 Oidateru	Standing, growing,
Habiro	Broad-leaved,
Yutsu matsubaki	The sacred camellia:
Shi ga hana no	Like its blossoms
Teriimashi	Shining in splendor,
15 Shi ga ha no	Like its leaves
Hiroriimasu wa	Spreading broad in splendor,
Ōkimiro kamo	You, O mighty lord!

✳ The roundabout course followed by the Empress would have taken her north around the Kazuraki Range, south over Nara Mountain into Yamato, and west to Kazuraki Takamiya, the homeland of the powerful Kazuraki clan to which she belonged. It is not clear why or when she turned back from Yamato to Tsutsuki District in Yamashiro. Nurinomi was an immigrant from Paekche who raised silkworms. The pillow words for Nara and Yamato refer to a locally produced blue pigment and to the shape of the mountains. Song 58 belongs to the longing-for-home genre, exemplified elsewhere in *Kojiki* (e.g., nos. 30, 32, 76, 90).

58   [K 58]

Thereupon she went around from Yamashiro and arrived at the entrance to Nara Mountain, where she sang:

Tsuginefu ya	Passing by the peaks
Yamashirogawa o	Up Yamashiro River,
Miyanobori	Up toward Miya
Wa ga noboreba	I have made my way, and now
5 Aoni yoshi	I pass by
Nara o sugi	Blue-earth Nara,
Odate	I pass by
Yamato o sugi	Little-shield Yamato.
Wa ga	The country
10 Migahoshi kuni wa	I am hungering to see

| Kazuraki Takamiya | Is Kazuraki Takamiya, |
| Wagie no atari | The land around my home. |

Thus singing, she turned back and lodged for a while in the house of a Korean of Tsutsuki named Nurinomi.

✳ No. 59 is a tanka chiefly notable for the sense of urgency created by repetition.

59   [K 59]

The Emperor, hearing that the Empress had gone up through Yamashiro, sent an attendant named Toriyama after her with this song:

Yamashiro ni	Go, Toriyama,
Ishike Toriyama	Catch up in Yamashiro,
Ishike ishike	Catch up, catch up,
A ga hashizuma ni	Catch up with my beloved wife
Ishikiawamu kamo	And meet her there for me!

✳ Two more singing telegrams follow. The first is a textbook example of the roundabout method employed in many early Japanese songs. Like some later chōka, it starts at a high point of divine reference, here to the grove into which a god descends, and ends with the human message. Ōiko ga hara ("Ōiko Plain [hara]") suggests "big wild boar's belly" (ōiko ga hara), and this in turn introduces the pillow word kimo mukau ("entrails [or liver]-facing"), an epithet for kokoro, "heart." The seat of the emotions having been reached, the final plaintive question can be asked. This special use of language is probably an essential part of the earliest Japanese sense of rhetorically heightened speech, and of song as distinct from ordinary discourse.

60   [K 60]

Again, he sent Wani no Omi Kuchiko after [Toriyama] and sang:

Mimoro no	By the sacred grove
Sono takaki naru	Up there in the high hold
Ōiko ga hara	In the moor of the big wild boar,
Ōiko ga	In the belly
Hara ni aru	Of the big wild boar,
Kimo mukau	Facing the liver,
Kokoro o dani ka	The heart: oh, do you never
Aiomowazu aramu	Think of me a little in your heart?

❋ No. 61 reads like a rustic love song and plausibly was incorporated into the narrative because of the pillow word *tsuginefu*, "of the linked peaks," also used with Yamashiro in nos. 57–58. The analogical technique is similar to that of no. 60, but the chief interest is in the barely submerged sexual imagery and the inelegant but vivid likening of a woman's arm to the giant white radish, or daikon. The digging up of the cylindrical white root is imputed to the woman and suggests that because she has aroused the male member, she is responsible for subsequent events. "Root" in a double metaphorical sense thus serves as a pivot for the verse, functioning in both the jo and the main statement.

61   [K 61]

Again he sang:

> Tsuginefu   Passing by the peaks,
> Yamashirome no   The Yamashiro mountain girl
>   Kokuwa mochi   Picked up her mattock,
> Uchishi ōne   Gave a dig to the big white root:
>   Nejiro no   Root-white too
> Shirotadamuki   Were those paired arms on which
> Makazukeba koso   If I had never laid my head
> Shirazu to mo iwame You could say that you don't know me.

❋ Song 62 seems a purely functional piece of verse arranged in tanka form and unlikely to have had an existence independent of the narrative.

62   [K 62]

Now, it rained hard just when Kuchiko no Omi was uttering this song. At this, he made no attempt to get out of the rain, but went and prostrated himself before the front door of the hall. The Empress turned around and went to the back door. He went and prostrated himself at the back door of the hall, and she turned around and went to the front door. Now, while he was crawling back and forth and kneeling in the yard, the water standing in the yard wet him to the waist. The Omi was wearing blue-dyed garments with a red sash, and when the water touched the red sash, the blue all turned red. At this time the younger sister of Kuchiko no Omi, Kuchihime, was in service to the Empress. Kuchihime sang:

> Yamashiro no   Who humbly reports
> Tsutsuki no miya ni   To the palace of Tsutsuki
>   Mono mōsu   In Yamashiro—
> A ga se no kimi wa   The lord my elder brother—
> Namitagumashi mo   Is at the brink of tears.

At this, the Empress inquired the reason. She replied, "My elder brother is Kuchiko no Omi."

✳ Song 63 brings the Emperor himself onto the scene, repeating the opening lines of no. 61. This time the swing line (line 5) is *sawasawa ni*, doubly translated as "slick-slippery" and "stormy," the two senses in which it functions with the jo and the main statement. The Emperor depicts himself and his entourage as a kind of Birnam Wood come to an amorous Dunsinane. And the smooth-skinned daikon *is* slick-slippery. The song climaxes the series with a joint expression of contrition and sexual enticement. The editorial comment following indicates that the songs were performed at court. "Quiet songs," or *shizuuta* (e.g., nos. 92–95), are typically tanka in form and are thought to have been intoned in a stately manner, with a drawing out of the voice line; the "responses" (*utaikaeshi*), by contrast, were usually short chōka and sung in a lively and informal fashion.

63   [K 63]

And so the Emperor stood and sang at the door of the hall where the Empress was:

Tsuginefu	Passing by the peaks,
Yamashirome no	The Yamashiro mountain girl
Kokuwa mochi	Picked up her mattock,
Uchishi ōne	Gave a dig to the big white root:
Sawasawa ni	Slick-slippery
Na ga iese koso	Stormy were your words to me,
Uchiwatasu	So give a look—
Yagahae nasu	Like a great thicket we've come,
Kiirimaikure	Entering in to pay you court.

These six songs sung by the Emperor and Empress are responses to quiet songs.

✳ The songs exchanged between Emperor Nintoku and Princess Yata as nos. 64–65 probably had a prior existence as utagaki wooing songs. The woman replies to the man's amorous solicitude, saying that she has a "great lord," her true love, for whom she is content to wait. The overt recognition of metaphor in the man's song is of interest and is repeated in no. 86. The indirection of analogy serves in these songs as a foil to be brushed aside in the rush of straight talk. The union of Nintoku and his half sister Princess Yata remained childless, apparently the motivation for the establishment of a *minashiro* in her name. A minashiro consisted of a village or other social unit belonging to and named after a member of the imperial family. No. 65 is a sedōka.

64   [K 64]

The Emperor, yearning for Yata no Waki-iratsume, sent her a song. That song:

Yata no	At Yata
Hitomotosuge wa	Shall the single stalk of sedge,
Ko motazu	Having no sprout,
Tachi ka arenamu	Stand and wither desolate?
Atara sugahara	What a waste for the sedge field!
Koto o koso	When it comes to words
Sugahara to iwame	I may talk about sedge fields—
Atara sugashime	What a waste, my fresh young maid!

65   [K 65]

Whereupon Yata no Waki-iratsume replied with this song:

Yata no	At Yata
Hitomotosuge wa	Bides the single stalk of sedge,
Hitori ori to mo	Even though it stays alone;
Ōkimi shi	If but her great lord
Yoshi to kikosaba	Tells her that he thinks it well,
Hitori ori to mo	Even though she stays alone.

Thereupon he established the Yatabe as a namesake group [*minashiro*] for Yata no Waki-iratsume.

✻ The sequence 66–70 tells a story of lust, rebellion, and blood. Emperor Nintoku, whose name was Ōsazaki ("Great Wren"), was rejected by his half sister Princess Medori ("Ladybird") in favor of another half brother, Hayabusawake ("Falcon"). The first three songs in the sequence play on these names. Princess Medori was the full sister of Princess Yata, and so her remark in the preface to song 66 is a sharp one, edged with jealousy and disdain. No. 69 is a revision of an utagaki song found in both *Hizen Fudoki* (no. 215) and *Man'yōshū* (no. 886), and no. 70 is clearly of similar provenance. The *Kojiki* context gives to both songs an ironic quality having to do with doom and early death. "Ladder-standing" renders *hashitate no*, a pillow word for *kurahashi*, "storehouse ladder." The image is of the steep, almost vertical, steps leading up to the raised Japanese storehouse.

66 [K 66]

Again, the Emperor, using his younger brother Prince Hayabusawake as a go-between, courted his younger half sister Princess Medori. But Princess Medori said to Prince Hayabusawake, "Because of the Empress's violent opposition, he has not even been able to keep Yata no Waki-iratsume. Therefore I will not serve him. I intend to become your wife, my lord." And they wed forthwith. Consequently, Prince Hayabusawake did not return to make his report. Thereupon the Emperor betook himself personally to the place where Princess Medori was, and sat upon the doorsill of her hall. Princess Medori was seated at her loom, weaving. The Emperor composed a song:

Medori no	Ladybird,
Wa ga ōkimi no	Medori my Princess,
Orosu hata	For whom to wear
Ta ga tanero ka mo	Is the cloth you are weaving?

67 [K 67]

Princess Medori sang in reply:

Takayuku ya	High-flying, oh!
Hayabusawake no	The falcon Prince for whom I make
Osui ga ne	This hooded mantle.

Thus the Emperor, having learned how things stood, went back to the palace.

68 [K 68]

When her husband Prince Hayabusawake arrived, his wife Princess Medori sang:

Hibari wa	The lark
Ame ni kakeru	Soars in the sky,
Takayuku ya	High-flying, oh!
Hayabusawake	Falcon Prince, I pray you,
Sazaki torasane	Seize the wren!

69 [K 69]

When the Emperor heard this song, he immediately raised troops and set about to kill [the guilty pair]. And so Prince Hayabusawake and Princess Medori fled together and climbed Mount Kurahashi. Thereupon Prince Hayabusawake sang:

Hashitate no	Up ladder-standing
Kurahashiyama o	Storehouse-ladder Mountain
Sagashimi to	The climb is steep:

| Iwa kakikanete | She can't clamber over the boulders, |
| Wa ga te torasu mo | She clings to my hand instead. |

70   [K 70]

Again he sang:

Hashitate no	Ladder-standing
Kurahashiyama wa	Storehouse-ladder Mountain
Sagashikedo	Is steep, and yet
Imo to noboreba	When I climb it with my love,
Sagashiku mo arazu	It isn't steep at all!

And so they fled from there, and when they reached Soni in Uda the Emperor's forces caught up with them and put them to death.

❋ The next three songs have to do with an auspicious event, an anomaly of nature of the sort considered significant in the traditional societies of East Asia. Wild geese wintered in Japan and nested far to the north in the unknown lands of northern Asia or North America. Hence the rarity of finding an egg. Emperor Nintoku consults his oldest living authority, his senior adviser, Takeshi Uchi no Sukune, born nine reigns before and very influential in the time of his grandparents Emperor Chūai and Empress Jingū. The formal dignity of address in nos. 71 and 72 stands in somewhat amusing counterpoint to the brevity and specificity of the question and answer. "Gem-cutting" is one rendering for the obscure pillow word *tamakiwaru* as it applies to the place-name Uchi, said to have been the ancient seat of a gem workers' corporation in Yamato. The epithet "sky-seen" (*sora mitsu*) for Yamato is traditionally related to a myth in *Nihonshoki* to the effect that the deity Nigihayahi no Mikoto looked down on Yamato from the "heavenly rock-boat" as the gods were making an early survey of their future earthly realm. The cithern (koto) is frequently mentioned in connection with soothsaying. No. 73, a *katauta* ("half-song"), interprets the omen.

71   [K 71]

Again, once the Emperor went to Hime Island for feasting. On that island a wild goose had laid an egg. Hence he summoned Takeshi Uchi no Sukune no Mikoto and inquired with a song about the goose having laid the egg. The song:

Tamakiwaru	My elder brother
Uchi no aso	Of gem-cutting Uchi,
Na koso wa	You of all others
Yo no nagahito	Are the longman of the age.

Sora mitsu	Have you heard
Yamato no kuni ni	Of a wild goose laying its egg
Kari komu to kiku ya	In the land of sky-seen Yamato?

72 [K 72]

Hereupon Takeshi Uchi no Sukune spoke with a song:

	Takahikaru	Divine Child
	Hi no miko	Of the high-shining sun,
	Ube shi koso	It is but proper
	Toitamae	You deign to ask me,
5	Ma koso ni	You do well indeed
	Toitamae	To deign to ask me:
	Are koso wa	I of all others
	Yo no nagahito	Am the longman of the age.
	Sora mitsu	I have never heard
10	Yamato no kuni ni	Of a wild goose coming here
	Kari komu to	To lay its egg
	Imada kikazu	In the land of sky-seen Yamato.

73 [K 73]

When he had spoken thus, a cithern was given into his hands, and he sang:

Na ga miko ya	You, my prince!
Tsui ni shiramu to	That you will reign to the end
Kari wa komu rashi	A wild goose lays its egg, it seems.

This is a half-song that is a song of blessing.

❈ Perhaps suggested by the final song in the preceding series, no. 74 is also about a koto. It is a self-contained anecdote and has no overt connection with Emperor Nintoku, the announcement of whose demise immediately follows. No speaker is assigned for the lyrics. Actually, the placement of the anecdote in the *Kojiki* narrative can legitimately be regarded as artistic, in that the life story of the fleet ship built from the giant tree will echo that of the great and tempestuous monarch. The progress from tree to ship to cithern is at once a diminution in scale and a refining toward an essence that finally is music. It would be absurd to push the analogy in detail—Nintoku, for instance, was not cremated, but buried in a huge tumulus. Still, the juxtaposition of ship and monarch can hardly be meaningless. (On this point, see no. 213.) Context always creates meaning. The point of the story is that royal essence may metamorphose but will not pass away. The song itself is structured on a two-part introduction-conclusion pattern. The pattern here is paratactic: the playing of the koto and the swaying of the seaweed. The two are related through the nautical origin of the timbers and the sound-motion analogy in *sayasaya*, a word that could also be rendered "clearly-clearly."

74   [K 74]

In this reign there was a tall tree west of —— River. The tree's shadow cast by the morning sun reached Awaji Island, and when struck by the evening sun, crossed over Takayasu Mountain. Now, they cut down this tree and fashioned a ship from it, and that ship was very swift. They gave the ship the name Karano. Every morning and evening they used this ship to transport drinking water drawn from the springs on Awaji Island to present to the Emperor. After the ship was wrecked, they burned it for salt and fashioned a cithern from the unburnt timbers. The sound of the cithern resounded over seven leagues. Hence this song:

	Karano o	Karano, oh,
	Shio ni yaki	They burned it for salt.
	Shi ga amari	Of its leftovers
	Koto ni tsukuri	They fashioned a cithern
5	Kakihiku ya	For to pluck and play:
	Yura no to no	In Yura Strait
	Tonaka no ikuri ni	In mid-strait on sunken rocks
	Furetatsu	Stand swaying-touching
	Nazu no ki no	Oozy stalks
10	Sayasaya	Softly-softly.

This is a response to a quiet song.

❋ Three innocuous songs, nos. 75–77, are embedded in a bloody account of the succession struggle that followed Nintoku's death. Nintoku's son Richū succeeded and took up residence in Naniwa, his father's capital. While he was there, his younger brother tried to assassinate him, but ultimately himself came to a violent end. Richū's rescue is attributed to Achi, a Chinese who arrived in Japan in his grandfather Ōjin's reign. (The Aya, of which Achi was the ancestor, were silk weavers, and Atae was one of the then-current clan titles.) Nos. 75 and 76 may be about love rather than fratricidal struggle. The first suggests a pair of young lovers sleeping together on the moor, and the second a view from afar of the beloved's home. The *kagiroi*, or "shimmering air," of no. 76 would be "burning" only in a metaphorical sense, perhaps as a vision at sunrise as the husband leaves the woman's house. In its *Kojiki* setting, however, the burning is real, and *kagiroi no* the metaphor. No. 77 responds to a situation reminiscent of that in no. 22.

75   [K 75]

Back when he [Emperor Richū] was staying at Naniwa Palace, one time when he was feasting at the great rice-tasting, he became intoxicated with the ceremonial liquor, and fell asleep. Thereupon his younger brother, Suminoe the Second Prince, thinking to take the Emperor's life, set fire to the great hall. At this, the progenitor of the Aya no Atae, Achi no Atae, smuggled him out, put him on horseback, and got him away to Yamato. Now, when he reached Tajihi moor he woke up and said, "Where am I?" Achi no Atae said, "Suminoe the Second Prince set fire to the great hall. So I took you here—we are escaping to Yamato." At this, the Emperor sang:

Tajihino ni	Had I only known
Nemu to shiriseba	I would sleep on Tajihi moor
Tatsugomo mo	I'd have brought for sure
Mochite komashi o	Matting for a windbreak stand—
Nemu to shiriseba	Had I known I was to sleep here.

76   [K 76]

Arriving at Hanifu Slope, he looked back at the Naniwa Palace far away, and the flames were still burning. Thus the Emperor sang again:

Hanifuzaka	Hanifu Slope:
Wa ga tachimireba	When I stop and take a look,
Kagiroi no	Shimmering air
Moyuru iemura	Burning cluster of houses
Tsuma ga ie no atari	Around about my wife's house.

77   [K 77]

Now, when he arrived at the entrance into the Ōsaka mountain, a woman confronted him. The woman said, "Armed men are blocking this mountain in great numbers. You should make your way around and cross over by the Tagima road." And so the Emperor sang:

Ōsaka ni	At Ōsaka
Au ya otome o	I met her, the maiden,
Michi toeba	And I asked the way;
Tada ni wa norazu	She didn't tell me, "straight over,"
Tagimachi o noru	She told me, "by Tagima Road."

And so he went up and resided at Isonokami Shrine.

❊ The songs dealing with the incest of Prince and Princess Karu, nos. 78–90, constitute the longest sequence in *Kojiki* relating to one event. The romantic and tragic qualities of the story must have inspired the fabricators of the narrative to pull in as many songs as they could. The hapless siblings were the children of Emperor Ingyō, whose traditional reign dates are A.D. 412–53.

The opening song, no. 78, is a chōka based on the preparation-conclusion analogical technique. The image in line 4 leads to the main statement commencing in line 5, and the repeated *shita . . . shita . . . shita* ("down . . . down . . . down") emphasizes the overwhelming secrecy of the whole operation now so successfully concluded. Furthermore, the rural setting of the jo, with its description of hydraulic agriculture, strongly creates the mood for "country matters," along with a kind of rough sexual diagram wherein the furtive goings and weepings take place. Such was no doubt the intent of the song as an independent piece. In the *Kojiki* context the last two lines take on an affecting irony. "Foot-dragging" renders *ashihiki no*, a pillow word for *yama*, "mountain." The editorial note after the song indicates a method of singing with the voice rising in the last line.

78   [K 78]

After the Emperor's decease, it was determined that Prince Kinashi no Karu would rule in the succession of the sun lineage. But while he had not yet mounted the throne he committed folly with his younger sister by the same mother, Karu no Ōiratsume. He sang:

	Ashihiki no	I made a paddy
	Yamada o tsukuri	In the foot-dragging mountain;
	Yamadakami	The mountain was high,
	Shitabi o washise	So I ran a pipe beneath:
5	Shitadoi ni	Undercover I wooed,
	Wa ga tou imo o	I went wooing my young love;
	Shitanaki ni	Undercover I wept,
	Wa ga naku tsuma o	I went weeping for my wife,
	Kozo koso wa	But tonight at last,
10	Yasuku hada fure	Content, I touch her skin.

This is a *shirageuta*.

❋ The appeal of some early love songs, such as nos. 79–80, a pair in tanka form, is in their forthright declaration of desire. Here the common natural analogies are fully adequate to express a headlong and nonchalant male hubris. The middle line of the first song functions syntactically with both the analogical ground (i.e., the jo) and the derived statement. The middle line of no. 80 is a "pillow-word-type jo" (see the note to no. 56), or adverbial *makurakotoba*. The term *ageuta* refers to a high-pitched manner of delivery. It seems likely that the comment refers to both songs.

79 [K 79]

Again he sang:

Sasaba ni	Hail comes pelting down
Utsu ya arare no	On the leaves of bamboo grass
Tashidashi ni	With might and main
Inetemu nochi wa	Once I've taken her to bed,
Hito wa kayu to mo	Let her go where she wants.

80 [K 80]

Uruwashi to	That beauty so fine,
Sane shi saneteba	If I can bed her, just bed her,
Karikomo no	Like sickled rushes
Midareba midare	Let the tangle tangle then,
Sane shi saneteba	If I can bed her, just bed her.

This is an *ageuta* that is a rustic measure.

❉ The sudden turn of events in nos. 81–82 brings out songs of a different sort. No. 81 is artless enough and seems fully integrated into the narrative. As far as the story is concerned, the point of the waiting in the last line could be to let Ōmae-Omae no Sukune weigh the situation. A "metal gate" was one bound with metal fittings. Prince Anaho's arrows no doubt had iron points; Prince Karu's were obsolescent. The behavior of Ōmae-Omae no Sukune, hardly appropriate to the dignity of the leading officer of court, suggests a comic mime of submission used to relax tension. The content of no. 82 reinforces the idea of a mime, with the dancer bending over to touch his garter string (*ayui*, a cord to tie up trousers below the knee). In context the following interpretation is plausible: "Housemen, villagers, beware! The men of court are in a frenzy over the dishonor incurred by one of their number. Do nothing to enrage them further." The song is called a "courtly measure" (*miyahitoburi*) from its opening word.

81 [K 81]

Because of this all the people of the realm from the hundred officials on down turned away from Crown Prince Karu and gave their allegiance to Prince Anaho. And so the Crown Prince took fright and fled to the house of the Ō-Omi, Ōmae-Omae no Sukune, where he fashioned weapons in preparation for battle. (The arrows that he made at that time had bronze tips and so were called *karuya* ["light arrows"].) Prince Anaho also fashioned weapons. (The arrows the Prince fashioned were our present arrows. They are called Anaho arrows.) Then Prince Anaho raised troops and surrounded the house of Ōmae-Ōmae no Sukune. When he arrived at the gate, it was pouring freezing rain. And so he sang:

Ōmae	Come on,
Omae Sukune ga	Let's get under Ōmae
Kanatokage	Omae Sukune's
Kaku yorikone	Metal gate—let's stand here
Ame tachiyamemu	And wait till the rain has stopped.

82   [K 82]

Thereupon Ōmae-Ōmae no Sukune came dancing and prancing out, raising his arms and slapping his knees, singing:

Miyahito no	The little bell
Ayui no kosuzu	On the garter of a man of court
Ochiniki to	Has fallen off—
Miyahito toyomu	Men of court resound in thunder:
Satobito mo yume	Men of home, beware!

This song is a courtly measure.

❋ Songs 83 and 84 seem designed for another context—one in which a young man dallies with the "maidens of Karu." In no. 83 the girl weeps ashamedly when he has his way with her or when he parts with her; no. 84 is a wooing song. These songs have joined the narrative here no doubt because of the place-name Karu. *Amadamu* ("sky-flying") serves as a pillow word because of the resemblance of Karu to *kari*, "wild goose." The first song could also be rendered, "If I cry sorely . . ." in the *Kojiki* context, making it refer to Prince rather than Princess Karu.

83   [K 83]

Thus singing, he came out and said, "My Prince, son of the Heavenly Sovereign, do not attack the Prince your elder brother. If you attack him, people will certainly laugh. Your servant will seize him and deliver him to you." And so he relaxed his battle formation and withdrew. Then Ōmae-Ōmae no Sukune seized Prince Karu, led him out, and delivered him over. The Prince, on being seized, sang:

Amadamu	Sky-flying
Karu no otome	Karu maiden—
Itanakaba	If she cries sorely

Hito shirinubemi	People will be sure to know.
Hasa no yama no	Like doves on the mountain
Hato no	Of Hasa,
Shitanaki ni naku	She cries with a soft crying.

84   [K 84]

Again he sang:

Amadamu	Sky-flying
Karu otome	Karu maiden,
Shitada ni mo	Softly-softly so
Yorinete tōre	Come to me and sleep and go,
Karu otomedomo	You Karu maidens.

❋ Song 85 continues the avian imagery. Birds are often treated as messengers from far away or the beyond in East Asian writings. The term *"amada* measure" for songs 83–85 is said to derive from the epithet with which the first two of them begin.

85   [K 85]

And so they exiled Prince Karu to the hot springs of Iyo. Again, as he was about to be sent into exile, he sang:

Ama tobu	Birds that fly
Tori mo tsukai so	Through the sky are messengers:
Tazu ga ne no	When you hear
Kikoemu toki wa	The cry of a crane, remember,
Wa ga na towasane	And call out my name!

These three songs are *amada* measures.

❋ The use of figurative language (here, metonymy) as a foil for straight speech in song 86 has been encountered before in no. 64. The notation "lowered part" (*kataoroshi*) indicates rendition at a lowered pitch.

86   [K 86]

Again he sang:

Ōkimi o	If you cast your lord
Shima ni haburaba	Into exile in the islands,
Funa amari	He will come again
Igaerikomu zo	Like a boat drawn back toward home:

Wa ga tatami yume	Beware of my sleeping mat!
Koto o koso	When it comes to words
Tatami to iwame	I may talk of sleeping mats—
Wa ga tsuma wa yume	Beware how you touch my wife!

This song is the lowered part of a rustic measure.

✻ Song 87 belongs to the aubade genre, in which the woman attempts to detain her lover by claiming it is still too dark for him to leave. In this early example the imagery is earthy and sharp—for a perhaps barefoot lover! The world evoked is that of the fishing villages and harmonizes with the idea of the island exile. "Sotōshi" was another name for Princess Karu, an encomium for a beauty that "shone through [*tōshi*] her clothing [*so*]."

87   [K 87]

Then Princess Sotōshi presented a song. That song:

Natsukusa no	On Ahine Beach
Ahine no hama no	Where the summer grasses grow
Kakigai ni	Do not go walking,
Ashi fumasu na	Stepping on the oyster shells—
Akashite tōre	Wait till dawn to find your way.

✻ The compilers of *Man'yōshū* were aware of song 88 in its *Kojiki* context, but also as a poem they attributed to Empress Iwanohime, the consort of Emperor Nintoku (no. 231). The image of meeting is of paired leaves.

88   [K 88]

Then afterward, unable to bear her longing, the Princess followed him, at which time she sang:

Kimi ga yuki	Long now are the days
Kenagaku narinu	Since my lord has gone away;
Yamatazu no	As elder leaves meet,
Mukae o yukamu	So shall I go and meet him,
Matsu ni wa mataji	And not wait an endless wait.

What is here called *yamatazu* [elder] is our present *miyatsukogi*.

✻ Song 89 is based on a double analogy—to the banner-flying mountains as emblems of proud and steadfast love, and to bows as familiar, loved objects that can be handled and held close. Each analogy is subdivided into two parts based on size or type to create a quadripartite pattern. All this is for the sake of the parallelism through which the song exists, and which is further emphasized in the internal repetitions of lines 11 and 13. The song shows the basic structural elements of *Man'yōshū* chōka already in place.

89   [K 89]

When she caught up with him he was waiting for her, yearning, and he sang:

	Komoriku no	There on the mountains
	Hatsuse no yama no	Of Hatsuse the hidden land
	Ōo ni wa	On the great summits
	Hata haridate	They put out banners,
5	Saoo ni wa	On the small summits
	Hata haridate	They put out banners.
	Ōo ni shi	Like a great summit
	Naka sadameru	This bond of steadfast love,
	Omoizuma aware	Wife of my longing, alas!
10	Tsukuyumi no	Spindlewood bow
	Koyaru koyari mo	Lying at rest, at rest,
	Azusayumi	Catalpa bow
	Tateri tateri mo	Standing upright, upright,
	Nochi mo torimimu	Afterward I'll take, I'll see:
15	Omoizuma aware	Wife of my longing, alas!

✳ The last song of the series, no. 90, appears also among the anonymous chōka in *Man'yōshū* (see no. 1463). In *Kojiki* it makes a pair with no. 89, both apparently stemming from Hatsuse, the "long valley" known by the epithet *komoriku no*, "the hidden land." In their references to banners, bows, poles, mirrors, and gems, both seem to reflect some ancient Shintō ceremony, perhaps obsequies for a loved one. No. 90 is a textbook example of how preposited imagery is reused metaphorically in a pattern that finds its apotheosis in Kakinomoto no Hitomaro's MYS II: 135 (no. 325). *Yomiuta* are understood to be songs of praise; nos. 89–90 do not fit this description, and so it has been suggested that they were sung to yomiuta tunes or that their imagery associated them with the category.

90   [K 90]

Again he sang:

Komoriku no	There on the river
Hatsuse no kawa no	Of Hatsuse the hidden land

Kamitsuse ni	In the upper shallows
Ikui o uchi	They pound sacred poles,
5 Shimotsuse ni	In the lower shallows
Makui o uchi	They pound splendid poles.
Ikui ni wa	On the sacred poles
Kagami o kake	They hang bright mirrors,
Makui ni wa	On the splendid poles
10 Matama o kake	They hang splendid jewels.
Matama nasu	Like a splendid jewel
A ga mou imo	The dear girl for whom I long,
Kagami nasu	Like a bright mirror
A ga mou tsuma	The dear wife for whom I long:
15 Ari to	If they say
Iwaba koso yo	That she is there, then
Ie ni mo yukame	Shall I go to my home,
Kuni o mo shinowame	Shall I yearn for my country.

Thus singing, they died together by their own hands. These two songs are *yomiuta*.

✳ The Emperor in the setting for song 91 and the next several songs is Yūryaku, whose traditional reign dates are A.D. 456–79. As Nintoku is portrayed as benevolent and amorous, Yūryaku figures as amorous and bloody. His murders draw no songs, though his unstable personality is the occasion for some of the most memorable. He was a problematical entity to the early chroniclers, but as usual his amours provided the greatest opportunity for adding the lyric element that was so intimate a part of their craft. *Kojiki* is a bedroom history of the dynasty. In the setting of no. 91 the Emperor proceeds west over the mountains from Yamato into Kawachi, thus with his "back to the [rising] sun." The song provides the pleasure of a journey through a landscape whose natural features come in pairs, on the trail of an adequate analogy, deeper and deeper into a luxuriant vegetation evocative of the forces of libido, life, and growth. In this Eden stands a tree, surrounded by bamboo, and a man and woman who soon will be as closely interleaved. The song is a small triumph of the roundabout archaic method, where getting there is half the fun. As a love song it is also a vision of the world. Heguri Mountain is called "woven-mat" because its first syllable means "layer." "Thick as thieves" suggested itself as a free translation of *tashi ni*, "firmly."

91   [K 91]

First when the Great Consort was in Kusaka, the Emperor proceeded by the Kusaka direct route over into Kawachi. . . . Thereupon Princess Wakakusakabe spoke to the Emperor: "It is most awesome for Your Majesty to have come with your back to the sun. Rather it is for me to go straight over and wait upon you." At this he returned to the palace, pausing at the top of the slope to sing:

Kusakabe no	Kusakabe
Kochi no yama to	Hither mountain,
Tatamikomo	Woven-mat
Heguri no yama no	Heguri Mountain,
5 Kochigochi no	Hither and yonder
Yama no kai ni	Mountains: in the gorge between
Tachizakayuru	Standing, flourishing,
Habirokumakashi	A broad-leaved bear-oak:
Moto ni wa	At the foot
10 Ikumidake oi	Interlaced the bamboo grow,
Suehe ni wa	Off beyond the tip
Tashimidake oi	Dense the bamboo thickets grow:
Ikumidake	Interlaced bamboo
Ikumi wa nezu	Interlaced we have not lain,
15 Tashimidake	Dense bamboo thickets
Tashi ni wa inezu	Thick as thieves we have not lain—
Nochi mo kuminemu	Yet; but later we'll lie interlaced:
Sono omoizuma aware	That wife of my longing, alas!

And he sent a messenger back with this song.

❋ The strange tale of Yūryaku and the woman Akaiko told in songs 92–95 begs the question of why she ages and he does not, or how the events could be accommodated in a twenty-three-year reign. One may speculate that the story was included to illustrate the capricious nature of this monarch. The four songs, all in tanka form and based on the preparation-conclusion technique with repetitions in the third line, make a nicely balanced set. The first and third make cultic references, while the second and fourth are expressions of a common human regret. The vision of Akaiko as the priestess of an oak-tree cult (even shorn of Druidic overtones) might be enough to frighten a suitor away; but her reply speaks tellingly of the price paid for overlong devotion to a god. And Yūryaku, like other members of his line, was a god.

92   [K 92]

Once when the Emperor was touring his realm he arrived at the river Miwa. A young girl was washing clothes beside the river. Her face was very fair.

The Emperor asked the girl, "Whose child are you?" She replied, "My name is Akaiko of the Hikitabe." Then he said to her, "Do not marry. I shall summon you presently," and returned to the palace. Akaiko respected the Emperor's command and waited; eighty years went by. She thought to herself, "Many years have passed while I have waited for the imperial command. Now I am lean and shriveled, and have no hope. But unless I reveal the feelings of these years of waiting, I shall be unable to bear my stifled resentment." And she went to court with a great array of offerings to present. But the Emperor had long forgotten what he had once commanded and asked Akaiko, "Who are you, old woman? Why have you come here?" Akaiko replied, "Once in a certain year, in a certain month, I received the command of the Emperor and have waited until today for the great summons. Eighty years have gone by. Now my face is old, and I have no hope. But I have come to tell you of my devotion." At this, the Emperor was greatly surprised. "I had long forgotten all about that matter. Yet you have waited faithfully for my summons, letting your youth go by for nought. It is most pitiable." In his heart he wished to wed her but hesitated because of her extreme age. Unable to go through with the marriage, he presented her a song:

Mimoro no	In the sacred grove
Itsukashi ga moto	The trunk of the holy oak,
Kashi ga moto	The white oak trunk:
Yuyushiki kamo	Dread is the power, beware!
Kashihara otome	The maiden of Oak Tree Plain.

93   [K 93]

Again he sang:

Hiketa no	In Hiketa fields
Wakakurusubara	The grove of young chestnut trees:
Wakakuhe ni	Young she would have been,
Inetemashi mono	If only I had lain with her—
Oinikeru kamo	But now she has grown old.

94   [K 94]

The tears Akaiko shed at this went right through her red-dyed sleeves and soaked them. She sang in reply:

Mimoro ni	Round the sacred grove
Tsuku ya tamakaki	They've put up a worship fence;
Tsukiamashi	Too long she's worshiped—
Tare ni ka mo yoramu	On whom now can she rely,
Kami no miyahito	The shrine maid of the god?

95   [K 95]

Again she sang:

> Kusakae no   Kusaka inlet,
> Irie no hachisu   In the inlet lotuses,
> Hanabachisu   Lotuses in bloom:
> Mi no sakaribito   In full flower of their youth,
> Tomoshikiro kamo   How enviable those maidens!

The Emperor bestowed many gifts upon the old woman and sent her back.
These four songs are quiet songs.

❈ Song 96 continues the theme of god and shrine maiden and was probably
originally intended to accompany a shrine maiden's sacred dance. Tokoyo is
here evoked as a paradise of endless youth (see nos. 579–80).

96   [K 96]

Once when the Emperor went to Yoshino Palace there was a maiden beside
the Yoshino River, and her figure was lovely. And so he wed this maiden
and returned to the palace. Later when he visited Yoshino again, he stopped
at the place where he had met the maiden, set up a great royal camp chair,
seated himself on it, and had the young lady dance while he played the cithern. And since the lady danced well, he composed a song. That song:

> Agurai no   To the hand of a god
> Kami no mite mochi   Seated upon a camp chair
> Hiku koto ni   Playing the cithern
> Mai suru omina   She dances, this woman—oh, that
> Tokoyo ni mokamo   This were the eternal land!

❈ Song 97 is a dramatization of an origin tale for one of the traditional
names of Japan. The song seems to have three speakers—someone who announces the abundance of game, someone who challenges him, and a narrator. The *Nihonshoki* version (no. 145) adds a fourth speaker, the Emperor
himself. There are obviously rich possibilities for gesture and mime in both
versions. "Eshino" is an alternative pronunciation of "Yoshino."

97   [K 97]

Then once there was an excursion to the fields of Akizu, and while the royal
hunt was in progress and the Emperor was seated on his camp chair, a
horsefly bit his forearm. A dragonfly came and ate the horsefly and flew
away. . . . At this, the Emperor composed a song. That song:

Mieshino no	In fair Eshino
Omuro ga take ni	On the heights of Omuro
Shishi fusu to	Game lies crouched:
Tare so	Who speaks
5 Ōmae ni mōsu	In the great forecourt?
Yasumishishi	Our great lord
Wa ga ōkimi no	Who rules the land in all tranquility,
Shishi matsu to	Waiting for the game,
Agura ni imashi	Sits on his camp chair.
10 Shirotae no	White barken cloth
Sode kisonau	Are the sleeves that apparel
Takomura ni	His arm's swelling flesh
Amu kakitsuki	Where a horsefly creeps and clings:
Sono amu o	That horsefly, oh,
15 Akizu hayagui	A dragonfly gobbles it down.
Kaku no goto	Thus it came about
Na ni owamu to	That to have this as a name
Sora mitsu	Men began to call
Yamato no kuni o	The land of Sky-Seen Yamato
20 Akizushima tou	Akizushima—Dragonfly Island.

And so it was from this time that these fields began to be called the fields of Akizu.

❋ The *Nihonshoki* version of Yūryaku and the wild boar (no. 146) has an attendant rather than the Emperor himself climb the tree and sing the song given here as no. 98. It is hard to avoid the conclusion that the *Kojiki* narrator is determined to make a fool as well as a knave out of this ruler. The song is a lively and comic one, well suited to some form of enactment. A "humming arrow" had a hollow bulb-shaped head with holes that made a humming or whistling sound in flight.

98   [K 98]

Again, one time the Emperor climbed to the top of Mount Kazuraki. Then a large wild boar appeared. At once the Emperor set about to shoot the boar with a humming arrow. The boar came at him snorting with rage. Terrified by its snorts, the Emperor climbed to the top of an alder tree. Then he sang:

Yasumishishi	Our great lord
Wa ga ōkimi no	Who ruled the land in all tranquility
Asobashishi	Went off a-hunting
Shishi no	For wild boar:

Yamishishi no	Of that wounded boar's
Utaki kashikomi	Snorting I was all a-dread,
Wa ga nigenoborishi	I ran away and clambered up,
Ario no	Up a crag,
Hari no ki no eda	Up an alder tree, onto a branch!

❋ Song 99 uses hyperbole to convey the intensity of blunt male greed. For another memorable early example of hyperbole, see no. 936.

99   [K 99]

Again, when the Emperor went to Kasuga to woo Odohime, the daughter of Wani no Satsuki no Omi, the maiden met him on the road. When she saw him coming, she ran away and hid in the hills. And so he composed a song. That song:

Otome no	Give me mattocks,
Ikakuru oka o	Five hundred iron mattocks—
Kanasuki mo	I'll fix that hill
Iochi mogamo	Where the maiden is a-hiding—
Sukibanuru mono	I'll spade it and fling it aside!

And so they call that hill Kanasuki ("Iron Mattock") Hill.

❋ The body of song attributed to the reign of Yūryaku culminates in a burst of auspicious and adulatory verse celebrating the feasting of the court. Three of these songs, nos. 100–102, are drawn from the repertory of the *amakataribe*, the "seafolk reciters," presumably identical with the "seafolk couriers" of nos. 2–5. Each ends with the formula *koto no katarigoto mo ko o ba*, "The story, the words of the story are these words." The *Kojiki* context points up for one last time Yūryaku's violent and capricious nature, but also emphasizes the suasive powers of song. Since Yūryaku's palace was in Hatsuse and not Makimuku as in no. 100, it seems probable that the sequence originally celebrated some other monarch. As a palace-praising song, no. 100 deserves to be read with MYS I: 50 and MYS I: 52 (nos. 1245 and 1246), as well as with a blessing for a new house such as no. 153. As in the formal and majestic public chōka of Kakinomoto no Hitomaro, the song occupies the high ground at the beginning, with its reference to the sun, divine emblem and entity of sacred rule, and balances this opening with an awed and encomiastic reference to the Emperor as "Child of the Sun" at the end, a pattern adumbrative of Hitomaro's MYS II: 199 (no. 341). The forty-six lines and ladderlike structure of no. 100 make it an effective time-gaining ploy in the *Kojiki* narrative, but more importantly illustrate the heightened suspense inherent in the preparation-conclusion technique as the long-delayed climax is approached by peeling away layer after layer. The danger with this method is that the climax will turn out to be an anticlimax, but here the final references are to the creation myth and the divine sun lineage themselves. The gurgling of the wine, *kōro kōro*, echoes the primordial stirring of the brine with the Heavenly Jeweled Spear by the creator deities Izanagi and Izanami at the beginning of *Kojiki*, thus superimposing the sexual symbolism of that passage on the already suggestive conjunction of the great tree and the "moist, gem-glistening cup." The structure of no. 100 combines features of nos. 43 and 57, but in contrast to the "Goldilocks pattern" of no. 43, it uses the tripartite classification of branches as a vertical progression. "Threefold Mie" renders the literal sense of the place-name, brought to the surface by the pillow word *arikinu no*, "of the mothlike silk."

100   [K 100]

Again, when the Emperor sat banqueting under a hundred-branched zelkova tree at Hatsuse, a palace woman from Mie in the province of Ise offered him the great royal winecup. Just then a leaf fell from the hundred-branched zelkova tree and floated in the winecup. The palace woman, unaware that a leaf was floating in the winecup, persisted in offering the royal wine. The Emperor, seeing the leaf floating in the cup, struck down the palace woman, held his sword to her throat, and was about to put her to death. But she said to the Emperor, "Do not kill me—I have something to say." And she sang:

	Makimuku no	In Makimuku
	Hishiro no miya wa	Hishiro the palace stands,
	Asahi no	A morning-sun
	Hideru miya	Sun-blazing palace,
5	Yūhi no	An evening-sun
	Higakeru miya	Sun-glinting palace,
	Take no ne no	A bamboo-root
	Nedaru miya	Firm-rooted palace,
	Ko no ne no	A tree-root
10	Nebau miya	Root-spreading palace,
	Yaoni yoshi	Yes, an eight-hundred
	Ikizuki no miya	Earthload mallet-pounded palace:
	Maki saku	Fine-timber-splendid
	Hi no mikado	Cypress the fair gates:
15	Niinaeya ni	At the Hall of New Tasting
	Oidateru	Standing, growing,
	Momodaru	A hundredfold-ample
	Tsuki ga e wa	*Tsuki* tree whose branches,
	Hotsue wa	Whose topmost branches
20	Ame o oeri	Overspread the heavens,

Nakatsue wa	Whose midmost branches
Azuma o oeri	Overspread the eastern land,
Shizue wa	Whose bottom branches
Hina o oeri	Overspread the countryside;
25 Hotsue no	From the topmost branch
E no uraba wa	The last leaf on the branch tip
Nakatsue ni	To the midmost branch
Ochifurabae	Drops down and touches;
Nakatsue no	From the midmost branch
30 E no uraba wa	The last leaf on the branch tip
Shimotsue ni	To the bottommost branch
Ochifurabae	Drops down and touches;
Shizue no	From the bottom branch
E no uraba wa	The last leaf on the branch tip
35 Arikinu no	Like floating oil
Mie no ko ga	Into the moist, gem-glistening cup
Sasageru	Raised in offering
Mizutamauki ni	By the girl of threefold Mie
Ukishi abura	Of the mothlike silk
40 Ochinazusai	Drops down, swirling heavily,
Mina kōro	The liquid gurgling,
Kōro ni	Gurgling,
Ko shi mo	Even thus—
Aya ni kashikoshi	Awed, I tremble with dread:
45 Takahikaru	High-Shining
Hi no miko	Child of the Sun.
Koto no	The story,
Katarigoto mo	The words of the story
Ko o ba	Are these words.

And so, when she had presented this song, he forgave her offense.

❋ Song 101 is closely parallel to no. 57 in its employment of the camellia as the image of lordly splendor. Here the Great Consort commands the palace woman to present the wine again.

101   [K 101]

Thereupon the Great Consort sang. Her song:

Yamato no	In Yamato
Kono takechi ni	In this high gathering place,
Kodakaru	On the hillocked
Ichi no tsukasa	High assembly grounds,

5 Niinaeya ni	At the Hall of New Tasting
Oidateru	Standing, growing,
Habiro	Broad-leaved,
Yutsu matsubaki	The sacred camellia:
So ga ha no	The leaves of it
10 Hiroriimashi	Spreading in lordliness,
Sono hana no	Its blossoms
Teriimasu	Beaming in lordliness:
Takahikaru	To the high-shining
Hi no miko ni	Child of the Sun
15 Toyomiki	Raise in offering
Tatematsurase	The abundant royal wine.
Koto no	The story,
Katarigoto mo	The words of the story
Ko o ba	Are these words.

❋ The bird images in song 102 are reminiscent of those in other songs of the ama reciters, especially those in no. 4. The "scarves" of the quail are said to be the white speckles on their breasts. The trailing formal garments of the courtiers are likened to the tails of wagtails.

102   [K 102]

Thereupon the Emperor sang:

Momoshiki no	Men of the palace,
Ōmiyahito wa	Great fortress of the hundred stones,
Uzuratori	Like quail-fowl
Hire torikakete	Hang scarves about their necks,
5 Manabashira	Like wagtails
O yukikae	Cross tails as they go,
Niwasuzume	Like yard sparrows
Uzusumariite	Squat in circles on the ground.
Kyō mo ka mo	Today too for sure
10 Saka mizukurashi	They will be well steeped in drink:
Takahikaru	Men of the palace
Hi no miyahito	Of the high-shining sun.
Koto no	The story,
Katarigoto mo	The words of the story
15 Ko o ba	Are these words.

These three songs are songs recited by the seafolk. And so, at this banquet the Emperor praised the palace woman from Mie and gave her many gifts.

✳ In song 103 the pillow-word construction *mina sosoku* ("water-streaming") is a mock epithet for *omi* ("courtier") through either *umi* ("sea") or *uo* ("fish"). The image is related in a more relevant way to the "spouted flagon," however, and harmonizes with the "outpouring" of bounty intended as the effect of this celebration of the life-enhancing power of the royal wine. Kasuga no Odohime is the reluctant maiden of no. 99.

103   [K 103]

On this day of feasting, Kasuga no Odohime also offered the royal wine, at which time the Emperor sang:

Minasosoku	Water-streaming
Omi no otome	Courtier maiden
Hodari torasu mo	Who hold the spouted flagon,
Hodari tori	Holding the spouted flagon,
Kataku torase	Hold it firmly!
Shitagataku	Hold it firmly with all your heart,
Yagataku torase	Hold it ever more firmly,
Hodari torasu ko	You girl who hold the spouted flagon!

This is a winecup song.

✳ Odohime ends the series with a love song. Songs of this type present the speaker as wishing to substitute for something close to the beloved. For other examples, see nos. 742, 873, 1060, and 1153. The refrain *ase o* ("my brother") appears also in no. 29. Though the exclamation is supposedly directed to the musicians rather than the sense of the song, it fits the sense in both instances.

104   [K 104]

At this Odohime presented a song. That song:

Yasumishishi	Our great lord
Wa ga ōkimi no	Who rules the realm in all tranquility
Asato ni wa	In the morning
Iyoridatashi	Sits up leaning close,
5 Yūto ni wa	In the evening
Iyoridatasu	Sits up leaning close
Wakizuki ga	On his armrest:
Shita no	Would that I
Ita ni moga	Were the plank beneath—
10 Ase o	*My brother!*

This is a quiet song.

❊ The chant of Prince Woke given here as no. 105 is not written in syllable-by-syllable phonetic script, as the other songs are, and thus seems not to have been regarded as the same kind of material. Nevertheless, its imagery and rhetoric are similar to those of many other long songs and differentiate it sharply from prose. The brothers in the story are Princes Oke and Woke, who have been living in disguise in the house of Shijimu as grooms and cowherds since their cousin Emperor Yūryaku murdered their father some years earlier. The younger brother, now that Yūryaku is dead, reveals their identities in this scene from one of the most dramatic stories in the chronicles. Both brothers later succeeded to the throne, Prince Woke as Emperor Kenzō (r. 485–87) and Prince Oke as Emperor Ninken (r. 488–98). The song begins with complimentary references to the elder brother, not now a mere servant but a *mononofu*, or "man at arms," whose sword is associated with the official and auspicious color red. The reference to the red banner on the cord is somewhat obscure, but MYS II:199 (no. 341) uses an image of armies marching under red banners, likened to the renewing flames on the fields in spring. The banner becomes huge enough to hide a whole mountain, where the bamboo bows in obeisance. The eight strings of the cithern also lie in even rows, ready to accompany the mantic phrases vouchsafed to a god-king. Izahowake is Emperor Richū (Yūryaku's uncle), and Ichinobe Oshiha the murdered father of the two Princes. For another chant by Prince Woke, see no. 153; see also nos. 154–56 and 211–12.

105   [K 105]

When Yamabe no Muraji Odate was appointed Governor of the province of Harima, he arrived at the new residence of a commoner of the province, Shijimu by name, and gave a feast. When the feast was in full swing and the liquor was flowing freely, each guest danced in order of precedence. Now, there were two boys to tend the fire, seated by the hearth. When these boys were urged to dance, one of them said, "You, elder brother, dance first." But the elder brother said, "You, younger brother, dance first." They thus deferred to each other, and the people there assembled laughed at the way they kept on deferring. Finally, the elder brother danced first, and when he was finished, the younger brother, before dancing in his turn, chanted:

	Mononofu no	The man at arms
	Wa ga seko ga	My brother wears
	Torihakeru	Girt about him
	Tachi no tagami ni	A sword whose hilt
5	Ni kakitsuke	I rub with ocher,
	Sono o ni wa	On whose cord
	Akahata o tate	I raise a red banner:
	Akahata o	When I look at it,
	Tatete mireba	The red banner I have raised,

10	Ikakuru	It hides
	Yama no	The bamboo
	Mio no take o	On the mountain peaks:
	Kakikari	Hacking, cutting,
	Sue oshinaburu nasu	Laying over end to end—
15	Yatsuo no	Or like an eight-stringed
	Koto o	Cithern
	Shirabetaru goto	Plucked and played in tune,
	Ame no shita	Held reign
	Osametamaishi	Over all beneath the sky
20	Izahowake no	Izahowake
	Sumera mikoto no miko	The noble Sovereign, whose child
	Ichinobe no	Ichinobe
	Oshiha no miko no	Oshiha the Prince:
	Yatsuko	This slave,
25	Misue zo	His scion.

❋ The sequence 106–11 presents the utagaki, or songfest, as the venue for male rivalry rather than male-female flirtation. *Shibi*, the name of Prince Woke's rival, means "tuna"; hence the wordplay in no. 111, where Woke implies that in his frenzy Shibi is only injuring himself. It has been suggested that the songs belong in a different order, but the progression from katauta to tanka to bussokusekika (whose extra line lets Shibi enlarge on his rage) back to tanka is an effective one. So is the interlocking pattern of fence and fish imagery in nos. 108–11 as Shibi continues to taunt Woke on his tumbledown house and its combustible fence, while Woke shifts his ground to ridiculing Shibi's name. Power as well as love was involved in this rivalry. According to the *Kojiki* account, the brothers surrounded Shibi's house the next day and killed him. For a different version of the events involving Shibi, see nos. 158–66.

106 [K 106]

Now, when they were about to rule the realm, the progenitor of the Omi of Heguri, Shibi by name, stood up at a songfest and took the hand of the fair maid whom Woke no Mikoto was going to wed. This maiden was the daughter of the Obito of Uda, and her name was Ōuo ("Great Fish"). And so Woke no Mikoto also stood up at the songfest. Thereupon Shibi no Omi sang:

Ōmiya no	At the great palace
Oto tsu hatade	Yonder eaveline's corners
Sumi katabukeri	Are slumping to the ground.

107   [K 107]

Thus he sang, and when he demanded an ending to his song, Woke no Mikoto sang:

Ōtakumi	It is all because
Ojinami koso	Of a clumsy carpenter
Sumi katabukeri	That the corners are slumping.

108   [K 108]

And so Shibi no Omi sang again:

Ōkimi no	Your heart
Kokoro o yurumi	Is slack, my lord;
Omi no ko no	You are not such
Yae no shibakaki	As will ever stand within
Iritatazu ari	The Omi boy's eightfold brushwood fence.

109   [K 109]

Thereupon the Prince sang again:

Shiose no	Where the riptide
Naori o mireba	Wrinkles into folded waves
Asobikuru	I look and see
Shibi ga hatade ni	Sporting toward me a tuna—
Tsuma tateri miyu	And my wife stands on its fin!

110   [K 110]

And so Shibi no Omi, more and more enraged, sang:

Ōkimi no	My great lord
Miko no shibakaki	My Prince's brushwood fence,
Yafujimari	With eight-knot-fastening
Shimarimotōshi	You may fasten it round about—
Kiremu shibakaki	It will cut, that brushwood fence,
Yakemu shibakaki	It will burn, that brushwood fence.

111   [K 111]

Thereupon the Prince sang again:

Ōuo yoshi	Oh, the Great Fish
Shibi tsuku ama yo	Tuna-spearing fisherman—
Shi ga areba	If she gets away,
Urakōshikemu	How you'll hanker after her,
Shibi tsuku Shibi	Tuna-spearing Tunaman!

Thus singing, they contended until dawn and then withdrew and went their separate ways.

✳ The anecdotal account of *Kojiki* ends with Emperor Kenzō, and the last two songs are sung by that monarch about an old woman he rewarded for helping him find the bones of his murdered father. The "three-stalk" (*sakikusa*) is sometimes identified with the *yamayuri*, or gold-banded lily. Karafukuro was the man who suggested the hunting expedition at Kayano in Ōmi on which Yūryaku shot Prince Ichinobe and buried his cut-up remains in a shallow grave. No. 112 is based on the preparatory image of bell-laden horses wending their way over the plains, an image that introduces *nute*, "bell," in the main statement. The old woman's movements are made to seem as frequent and deliberate as the approach of the horses. No. 113 balances this movement with a journey away beyond the hills.

112   [K 112]

When this Emperor was searching for the remains of his father, Prince Ichinobe, an old peasant woman from Ōmi Province came forth and said, "I know exactly where the Prince's bones are buried. You can identify them by his teeth." (He had teeth that were jammed together like a three-stalk.) And so he got the people together, dug the ground, and searched for the bones. When he found the bones, he made a tomb on the mountain east of Kayano, and he had the sons of Karafukuro guard it. Afterwards he had the bones brought up to the capital. And so he returned to the palace and summoned the old woman. He praised her for having kept her eye on the place so as not to forget and thus having known it, and bestowed on her the name Grandam Okime ("Steady Eye"). Thus he summoned her to the palace and bestowed on her his bounty with a broad and generous hand. And he built a house for the old woman to live in near the palace and summoned her every day without fail. And he hung a bell on the door of the great hall, and whenever he desired to summon the old woman, he would pull the clapper and ring the bell. And he composed a song. That song:

Asajihara	Plains of the shallow reeds,
Odani o sugite	Little valleys they go by
Momozutau	For a hundred leagues
Nute yuraku mo	With a tinkling of the bell
Okime ku rashi mo	Okime seems to be coming!

113   [K 113]

Hereupon the old woman Okime said, "I have become very old and would like to return to my home province." The Emperor let her go as she requested, and as he watched her leave, sang:

Okime mo ya	Okime, oh,
Ōmi no Okime	Okime from Ōmi,
Asu yori wa	From tomorrow
Miyamagakurite	You'll be hidden behind the hills,
Miezu ka mo aramu	Perhaps never more to be seen.

'Nihonshoki' Songs

Nihonshoki, unlike *Kojiki*, follows the Chinese system of recording dates. This system employs the dual cycles of the Ten Stems and Twelve Branches, which, used in conjunction with each other, can designate any point in a sixty-unit cycle. As it applies to the days of the month, this arrangement was used in preference to numbering the days from the beginning of each month. The cumbersome formulas appearing in the prefatory material to song 118, and recurrently from that point on, are typical. The Ten Stems are each named after one of the Five Elements, namely, Wood, Fire, Earth, Metal, and Water, divided respectively into Senior and Junior. The Twelve Branches are named after the Twelve Beasts of the oriental zodiac: the Rat, Ox, Tiger, Hare, Dragon, Serpent, Horse, Sheep, Monkey, Cock, Dog, and Swine. The formula in its full form designates the year (of an Emperor's reign), the month (both year and month by simple numeration), the season, the cyclical signs of the first day of the month, and the cyclical signs of the day of whatever event is being recorded. By counting from the first to the second set of cyclical signs, anyone familiar with the system can determine the day of the month. Thus a day Wood-Junior/Hare of a month beginning Metal-Senior/Rat would be the sixteenth of the month.

❋ The third song in *Nihonshoki* is woven into the incident in *Kojiki* about the god Ajisuki (Ajishiki in *Kojiki*) Takahikone and his rage at being mistaken for the dead Ame no Wakahiko (no. 6). In the *Nihonshoki* account this song follows a shorter version of no. 6. Typically, *Nihonshoki* draws on more than one source as the singer of the songs—either "one among those gathered for the wake" or Ajisuki Takahikone's younger sister, here identified as Shitateruhime. No. 114 is no doubt folk in origin, perhaps a wooing song or a work song to accompany fishing. It is applied to the story of Ajisuki Takahikone through a pun on *mero* ("meshes") in line 7. The word also means "eyes," and *mero yoshi* therefore "give a look." In its contextual use the song is calling the listener's attention to the true identity of Ajisuki Takahikone. *Iwatarasu seto* ("fords the shallows of a stream") also echoes *mitani futawatarasu* ("across three valleys twice over gleaming") in K 6/NS 2. Despite these fortuitous resemblances, the use of this folk song illustrates the extremes to which the chronicles go in forcing alien material into their narratives. The editorial note following the song refers to both NS 2 and NS 3.

114   [NS 3]

Again, she composed a song that went:

Amasakaru	Under other skies
Hinatsume no	In a rustic land a maid
Iwatarasu seto	Fords the narrows of a stream,
Ishikawa katafuchi	A pebble brook, deep below the bank.
Katafuchi ni	Over the deep pool
Ami hariwatashi	I throw out my fishnet:
Mero yoshi ni	Come, little meshes,
Yoshiyorikone	This way, this way, this way come!
Ishikawa katafuchi	Pebble brook, deep below the bank.

These two songs are now called rustic measures.

❋ The next song is inserted into the account of the birth of twins fathered by the grandson of the sun goddess, who had descended to earth to establish the true lineage of divine rulers. He married an earthling, Toyoatatsuhime, who became pregnant in a single night. In order to dispel the Imperial Grandchild's doubts, she swore an oath (*ukehi*) that if the children were legitimate, they would be unharmed by fire, and then set fire to her own parturition hut. The song and the account of the wife's subsequent resentment are not included in the *Kojiki* version of the myth. Although representing a later level of prosodic development than no. 114, this poem like many other early tanka belongs to the world of song matches and folk life in its origins. (See nos. 19, 45–46, 54–56, 69–70, 79–80, 87, and 108–11 for comparable examples.) The burden of the song's complaint seems to be addressed by a would-be lover to an uncooperative ama girl in some seaside village. Plovers, conventionally enjoying a close sexual bonding, serve like the wave-washed seaweed as the contrary example from nature in this negative analogy.

115   [NS 4]

Thus when the Imperial Grandchild took unto him Toyoatatsuhime, she conceived in a single night. The Imperial Grandchild had doubts. . . . At length she bore Hosusori no Mikoto and next gave birth to Ho-ori no Mikoto. His other name was Hikohohodemi no Mikoto. The mother's oath had been put to the test, and now the Imperial Grandchild knew that these were truly his seed. Because of this, Toyoatatsuhime resented the Imperial

Grandchild and would not keep company with him. The Imperial Grandchild grieved and composed a song:

Okitsumo wa	Weed of the offing
He ni wa yoredo mo	Comes a-floating in to shore,
Sanedoko mo	But she won't even
Atawanu kamo yo	Let me come to bed—oh, no,
Hama tsu chidori yo	You plovers of the beach, O!

✳ No. 116 is a song of triumph inserted into the narrative after the account
of Emperor Jimmu's victory over the eighty braves (no. 10). The prose text
contains a phrase adapted from a passage in *Han Shu*, the history of the Former Han Dynasty. "Eaters" (*chiao lei*; i.e., those who are alive to eat and
drink) is a kenning for the populace, here employed with stylistic nicety to
the slaughtered banqueters. The song, on the other hand, is a primordial
chortle of satisfaction, a guffaw of derision at the enemy's defeat, perhaps
the most artless and unsophisticated of the ancient songs. *Ago yo* ("my
boys") is a *hayashikotoba*, a refrain addressed to the audience, but also to the
participants in the action that is the song's context. The Kumebe were the
troops of the Kume, an ancient warrior clan, and this is one of their traditional songs.

116   [NS 10]

When our troops heard the song they all drew their mallet-headed swords
and killed the enemy at once. There was not an enemy left from all those
eaters. The imperial forces were overjoyed and turned their faces to the
heavens and laughed. Thus they sang:

Ima wa yo	Now at last!
Ima wa yo	Now at last!
Aa shiya o	Those fools, oh,
Ima dani mo	Would they even *now*,
Ago yo	My boys,
Ima dani mo	Would they even *now*,
Ago yo	My boys?

It is because of this that the Kumebe nowadays give a great laugh after
singing.

✳ No. 117, another Kumebe song omitted from *Kojiki*, follows immediately after the above. It shows more shaping in the direction of the tanka
form.

117 [NS 11]

Again they sang:

Emishi o	A barbarian,
Hitari	Just one,
Momo na hito	Is worth a hundred men,
Hito wa iedo mo	So the saying goes, and yet
Tamukai mo sezu	They didn't even stand and fight.

These are all songs they sang after receiving the covert instructions. They did not presume to sing of their own accord.

* An event in the reign of Emperor Sujin, a Yamato ruler of the third century A.D., forms the background for songs 118–20. In a time of pestilence a dream came to the Emperor from the deity Ōmononushi, commanding that his descendant Ōtataneko be appointed to worship him. This was done, and the pestilence ceased. To this legend is traced the origin of the Ōmiwa Shrine on Mount Miwa northeast of Asuka. The songs have to do with the worship of Ōmononushi through the offering of sacral wine (*miwa*, a homophone of the name of the shrine; also called *miki*, "fine liquor") and with the ensuing banquet. Ikuhi, the brewer of the liquor, sings the song of offering, using the same opening formula as in no. 39. Ōmononushi ("Great Thing Master") is either identical with or a manifestation of Ōkuninushi ("Great Land Master"), the god of Izumo (also known as Yachihoko no Kami, "the deity Eight Thousand Spears"; see nos. 2–5). In Izumo mythology Ōkuninushi, rather than the primordial pair Izanagi and Izanami, created the land, and the worship of Ōmononushi in the Yamato heartland at Mount Miwa must represent a cultic compromise between Yamato and Izumo. In completing his creation of the land, Ōkuninushi was aided first by a "small" deity, Sukuna Mikami (the brewer claimed for the wine in no. 39) and later by Ōmononushi. The act of worship was apparently conducted at night, and in the order of a *kagura* service, the formal songs and dances were followed by feasting and revelry. The farewell songs are the two tanka 119 and 120, sung as morning approaches. In these songs, both having the ancient structure employing duplicate second and fifth lines, *umasake* ("fine wine") serves as a pillow word for the name of the shrine through its homophone *miwa* ("offertory wine").

118 [NS 15]

On the day Wood-Junior/Hare of the fourth month, whose first day was Metal-Senior/Rat, in the summer of the eighth year, he made Ikuhi, a man of Takahashi village, Provider of the Wine at Ōmiwa. . . . On the day Wood-Junior/Hare of the twelfth month, whose first day was Fire-Senior/Monkey, in winter, the Emperor caused Ōtataneko to worship the great deity of Ōmiwa. On this day Ikuhi personally raised high the ceremonial liquor and offered it to the Emperor. Thus he sang:

Kono miki wa	This fine liquor
Wa ga miki narazu	Is not my fine liquor,
Yamato nasu	It is a liquor
Ōmononushi no	Brewed by Ōmononushi
Kamishi miki	Who made Yamato—
Ikuhisa	For long ages!
Ikuhisa	For long ages!

When he had sung thus they banqueted at the shrine.

119   [NS 16]

Then when the banquet had ended, the nobles sang:

Umasake	Fine wine
Miwa no tono no	Miwa, from its hall,
Asato ni mo	From its morning door
Idete yukana	We would go when we depart—
Miwa no tonoto o	From the door of Miwa's hall.

120   [NS 17]

Thereupon the Emperor sang:

Umasake	Fine wine
Miwa no tono no	Miwa, from its hall,
Asato ni mo	From its morning door
Oshibirakane	Push out and open wide—
Miwa no tonoto o	From the door of Miwa's hall.

He then opened the gates of the shrine and proceeded out.

✳ Also from the reign of Emperor Sujin are the following two versions of a premonitory song that corresponds to no. 22 but is different enough to be included here. The dispatch of the commanders is part of Sujin's campaign to complete the subjugation of the land begun by Emperor Jimmu.

121   [NS 18]

On the day Wood-Senior/Horse of the ninth month, whose first day was Fire-Senior/Dog, he dispatched Ōbiko no Mikoto to the Northern Land [Circuit], Takenunakawa-wake to the Eastern Sea [Circuit], Kibitsuhiko to the Western Circuit, and Taniha no Chinushi to Taniha. And he gave as his command: "If there be any who refuse instruction, raise troops and smite them." He had already given them their insignia and appointed them commanders. When Ōbiko no Mikoto arrived at Wani Slope on the day Water-Senior/Rat, there was a young girl who sang:

Mimaki Iribiko wa ya	Mimaki Iribiko, alas,
Ono ga o o	Unaware of how
Shisemu to	They spy on your
Nusumaku shirani	Life, ready to slay you,
Himenasobi su mo	You dally with your ladies!

Another version goes:

Ōki to yori	From the great door
Ukakaite	Peering in,
Korosamu to	They are ready
Suraku o shirani	To kill you—you do not know,
Himenasobi su mo	You dally with your ladies!

Ōbiko no Mikoto thought this strange and questioned the girl. "What is this you have said?" She said, "I have said nothing. I was just singing." And she sang the same song again and suddenly vanished.

❋ The account of the reign of Emperor Sujin in *Nihonshoki* contains another story about the god Ōmononushi, one that is omitted from *Kojiki*. The heroine of this story, Yamato Todohimomosohime no Mikoto, also called Yamato Todohime no Mikoto, was Sujin's aunt. She was the medium through whom Ōmononushi initially made his displeasure known to the Emperor at the time of the pestilence, and she also interpreted the ominous songs sung to Ōbiko no Mikoto. Eventually Ōmononushi took her as his wife. The following passage tells the outcome. It is one of three *shinkon setsuwa*, or "tales of marriage with a deity," in the chronicles that involve Ōmononushi. In two of them his original form is that of a snake, and in the third he transforms himself into a red-painted arrow, which strikes a maiden's genitals, impregnating her. The curious manner of Todohime's death begins to fit a pattern of sexual symbolism linking arrows, chopsticks, snakes (with fangs), and the phallus. In Japanese cultic belief snakes are also manifestations of lightning, and in this connection the way in which Ōmononushi returns to his shrine is suggestive. The site of Todohime's grave is near the foot of Mount Miwa, the location of the Ōmiwa Shrine, but the stones to build it were brought across the valley from the mountain range that separates the Yamato plain from the littoral of the Inland Sea. The significance of its two-shift manner of construction may lie in the circumstance of marriage between a mortal and a god. The song reads like what the context purports it to be—a song to accompany the building of the chamber of a tumulus, the major use for stonework in early times.

122   [NS 19]

After this, Yamato Todohimomosohime no Mikoto became the wife of the god Ōmononushi. But this deity came only at night and was never seen by day. Yamato Todohime no Mikoto said to her husband, "Since you never appear by day, I am unable to see your face clearly. I wish that you would stay for a little while. Tomorrow morning I would like to gaze upon your lovely features." The great deity replied, "It is most reasonable. Tomorrow morning I shall go into your comb box. I only request that you not be astonished at my form." Yamato Todohime no Mikoto was secretly puzzled in her heart. She waited for the dawn and looked into her comb box, where she found a lovely little snake. Since it was as big as her undersash, she was astonished and screamed. Then the great deity was ashamed and assumed human form, saying to his wife, "You did not control yourself and have shown me shame. In return I shall show you shame." And he climbed Mount Mimoro, treading the sky. Yamato Todohime no Mikoto looked up after him with regret and collapsed onto the floor. . . . In doing so she stabbed herself in the vagina with a chopstick and died. She was laid to rest at Ōchi. Thus the people of that time called her grave "The Grave of the Chopstick." This grave was built by day by men and by night by gods. In bringing stones from Ōsaka Mountain to build it, the people lined up from the mountain to the grave and passed stones from hand to hand. People of that time sang:

Ōsaka ni	All the stone-clusters
Tsuginoboreru	That climb the hill of Ōsaka
Ishimura o	One behind another—
Tagoshi ni kosaba	If we pass them hand to hand,
Koshikatemu kamo	We can bring them down.

❊ The text accompanying no. 123 contains a version of the giant tree legend found elsewhere in connection with no. 74, and in some of the fudoki, as well as in a *fu* by the Chinese poet Chi Shu-yeh (A.D. 223–62). What was probably originally a ceremonial song describing a procession of courtiers has been adapted to the context, *mike* being taken in the sense given in the etymological explanation instead of as "royal tray," a reference to the Emperor's breakfast being carried to him along the palace galleries. *Asashimo* ("morning frost") is a mock epithet for *mike* through *ke* ("melt"). The Emperor in this passage is Keikō, the father of Yamato Takeru no Mikoto (see commentary to no. 23), who in the *Nihonshoki* version conducts his own campaign in Kyūshū before sending his son there.

123   [NS 24]

In autumn, in the seventh month, whose first day was Metal-Junior/Hare, on the day Wood-Senior/Horse, he arrived in Mike in the back province of Tsukushi and took up residence in the temporary palace of Takada. At the time there was a fallen tree whose length was nine hundred seventy spans. The hundred bureaus went back and forth walking along the tree. Someone of the time sang:

Asashimo no	Morning frost
Mike no saobashi	Hoary is the tree-trunk bridge,
Maetsukimi	And all the lordlings
Iwatarasu mo	How they walk across it, oh,
Mike no saobashi	Hoary is the tree-trunk bridge.

Hereupon the Emperor inquired, "What kind of tree is this?" There was an old man who said, "This tree is an oak. Before it fell it used to hide Kishima Mountain when struck by the morning sun and overshadow Mount Aso when struck by the evening sun." The Emperor said, "This tree is a sacred tree. Therefore let this country be named Mike [Divine Tree]."

❋ *Nihonshoki* contains a few songs assigned to the rebellion of Prince Oshikuma (no. 38) that do not appear in *Kojiki*. The following war song is one of them. The Empress is Emperor Chūai's widow Jingū, recently returned from her conquest of Korea. Takeshi Uchi no Sukune is the statesman who served four rulers, Chūai, Jingū, Ōjin, and Nintoku (see nos. 39–40, 43, and 71–72). The Wani, descended from a Paekche scholar of that name who came to the court of Ōjin, were a powerful clan in Yamato that bore the high clan title Omi. Kuma no Kori was the ancestor of the Kazuno clan, who had the low-ranking clan title Obito. This may be the significance of the class distinction in lines 7–10 of the song. "Our brother of gem-cutting Uchi" (*tamakiwaru Uchi no aso*) is Takeshi Uchi no Sukune. The obscure pillow word *tamakiwaru* is interpreted here as "gem-cutting," supposedly a reference to a craft practiced in Uchi, a village in Yamato. A belly full of stones would suggest invulnerability to arrows.

124   [NS 28]

In the third month, whose first day was Fire-Senior/Monkey, on the day Metal-Senior/Rat, the Empress commanded Takeshi Uchi no Sukune and Takefurukuma, the ancestor of the Wani no Omi, to lead a force of several myriad and attack Prince Oshikuma. At this, Takeshi Uchi no Sukune and the other set out from Yamashiro with the pick of their troops. Arriving at Uji, they assembled north of the river. When Prince Oshikuma came out of his encampment ready to fight, there was a man named Kuma no Kori who stood at the point of his vanguard. . . . Thinking to urge on the host, he sang in a loud voice:

Ochikata	Over yonder
Arara matsubara	To the sparse pine barrens,
Matsubara ni	To the pine barrens,
Watariyukite	Let's get over and across—
5 Tsukuyumi ni	Fit your bulb-arrows
Mariya o tague	To your stout zelkova bows!
Umahito wa	You highborn
Umahitodochi ya	With your highborn fellows,
Itoko wa mo	And you my comrades,
10 Itokodochi	Comrades together,
Iza awana ware wa	Come, let's join the battle, we!
Tamakiwaru	Even our brother
Uchi no aso ga	Of gem-cutting Uchi,
Haranuchi wa	Is his belly
15 Isago are ya	Chock-full of stones?
Iza awana ware wa	Come, let's join the battle, we!

❋ After the suicide of Prince Oshikuma and Isahi (Isachi in *Nihonshoki*) no Sukune (see no. 38), Takeshi Uchi no Sukune searches for their bodies. The following two songs, whose original significance may be in reference to cormorant fishing, appear in the *Nihonshoki* account. The Freshwater Sea (Ōmi no Umi) is Lake Biwa. Its waters debouch at Seta and form the Seta River (later in its course called the Uji), flowing past Tanakami and Uji to join the Yodo River and eventually pour into Ōsaka Bay. The context changes the "birds" into metaphors, giving them an ironic significance, since unlike real water birds, these hunted fowl could not survive their plunge.

125   [NS 30]

Then Takeshi Uchi no Sukune sang:

Ōmi no mi	The birds that dived
Seta no watari ni	Into the Freshwater Sea
Kazuku tori	At Seta Crossing
Me ni shi mieneba	Are nowhere to be seen—
Ikidōroshi mo	How tormenting this grim doubt!

Thereupon he searched for their bodies but could not find them.

126 [NS 31]

Several days later they came to light in Uji River. Takeshi Uchi no Sukune
again sang:

Ōmi no mi	The birds that dived
Seta no watari ni	Into the Freshwater Sea
Kazuku tori	At Seta Crossing—
Tanakami sugite	After they passed Tanakami
Uji ni toraetsu	I caught them at Uji.

✳ According to *Nihonshoki*, Emperor Ōjin (the son of Empress Jingū and
half brother of Prince Oshikuma) had a consort from the province of Kibi
named Ehime. One day she and the Emperor were looking out over the Inland Sea from his tower at Naniwa, when she sighed. On inquiring the reason, the Emperor found that she was yearning to see her parents, and he
permitted her to go home and visit them. Song 127 is set in this context.
Awaji and Azuki are two islands between Naniwa and Kibi. Since they are
too distant and far apart to be seen together except in the mind's eye, lines 2
and 4 may mean that each can be seen lined up with another island. In any
case, the idea of being side by side is introduced through the jo technique as
a correspondence to the human situation of Emperor and consort. The anecdote of Ehime's homesickness parallels the story of Emperor Nintoku
(Ōjin's son) and Kurohime in *Kojiki* (see nos. 52–56). Kurohime also was
from Kibi, and Nintoku watched her boat leave Naniwa from his tower,
sang a song about islands, and followed her (as Ōjin does Ehime in *Nihonshoki*). The difference between the two stories is that Kurohime goes
unwillingly, driven out by the jealousy of Nintoku's principal consort,
Iwanohime. *Nihonshoki* omits Kurohime from its account of Nintoku's
reign. It may be noted, however, that the somewhat obscure verb in the seventh line of no. 127 seems to hint at a context where the woman's departure
is involuntary.

127 [NS 40]

In summer, in the fourth month, Ehime set sail from Ōtsu. The Emperor
stayed in his tower and watched Ehime's boat, singing:

Awajishima	Awaji Island—
Iya futanarabi	See the two isles side by side;
Azukishima	Azuki Island—
Iya futanarabi	See the two isles side by side:
Yoroshiki shimashima	Fine they are, these islands.
Ta ka	Who

Tasarearachishi	Took her away from me,
Kibi naru imo o	My young love from Kibi?
Aimitsuru mono	We were meeting face to face.

✳ Among the several anecdotes growing out of the jealousy of Iwanohime, the following appears only in *Nihonshoki*. Nintoku's bestowal of Kugahime on Hayamachi was in vain: she rejected the sexual overtures of her new husband, then fell ill and died. One of several explanations for the obscure pillow-word construction *minasokofu omi* is that *minasokofu* ("water-bottom-swimming"—see the narrative formulas in no. 2 and elsewhere) is a mock epithet impinging on *o* in *omi* ("courtier") in the sense of "fish" (*uo*). Or it may be a mistake for *minasosoku* (see no. 103). *Mikashio* is also an obscure pillow word, variously interpreted as "three-day tide" and "awesome tide," and probably is a mock epithet for *hari* ("brim full") in the name Harima. These question-and-answer songs are thus linked by decorative language having to do with water. The pillow-word construction *iwa kudasu* also refers to rocks rolled down or crushed by a current. Hayamachi's failure as a husband stands in ironic contrast to these vigorous images.

128   [NS 44]

In the sixteenth year, in autumn, in the seventh month, whose first day was Earth-Senior/Tiger, the Emperor pointed out the court lady Kuwata no Kugahime to his personal attendants and said, "We have desired to bestow Our favor on this woman, but many years have gone by without Our being able to wed her because of Our distress at the Empress's jealousy. How can We let her youth go by in vain?" Then he sang:

Minasokofu	The bottom-swimming
Omi no otome o	Courtier maiden—
Tare yashinawamu	Who will take her in his care?

129   [NS 45]

Hayamachi, the ancestor of the Kuni no Miyatsuko of Harima, hereupon came forward and sang:

Mikashio	Riptide
Harima Hayamachi	Harima Hayamachi—
Iwa kudasu	Rock-crushing
Kashikoku to mo	Awesome it may be,
Are yashinawamu	But he shall take her in his care.

That day he gave Kugahime to Hayamachi.

✳ The quarrel of Emperor Nintoku and Empress Iwanohime over Nintoku's desire for his half sister Princess Yata (see nos. 57–65) is the most highly developed chapter in the bedroom biography of this monarch otherwise famed for the Confucian virtue of benevolence. *Nihonshoki* provides several songs not found in *Kojiki*, of which the following five are arranged as a marital debate on polygamy. Since ancient Emperors did in fact have many consorts, the redoubtable Iwanohime's uncompromising stance emerges all the more forcefully as a statement of the monogamous ideal. But her methods of suasion are different from those employed so effectively by Suserihime (no. 5). For an unsympathetic male viewpoint, see no. 9.

In his opening salvo, Nintoku swears an oath (*kotodate*) that he has no intention of replacing his wife, only of supplementing her. The kotodate (or *kotoage*) was a serious matter, one that called the attention of the gods to a statement of intent. Nintoku, it may be noted, claims no divinity for himself, merely that he is highborn (*umahito*), and one may assume that the songs had their origin outside the imperial context. Predictably, the wife is not impressed by the double-bowstring theory of marriage, and Iwanohime answers appropriately (song 131) by tossing back related images at her opponent, in the style of amorous debate honed in the song matches. The songs seem to express a basic social insight by setting at odds the woman's desire for acquisition in the innocent area of clothing and the man's in the more dubious realm of sex. In his rejoinder (no. 132) the Emperor rings more changes on the verb *narabu* ("line up"), this time employing the technique of the jo. Since Nintoku reigned at Naniwa, the locus mentioned in the jo is associatively related to the argument. The last two lines could also be interpreted, "To be doubled up with me must be why that child exists," but this seems less satisfactory. The Emperor's line of argument is the same as that of Prince Atsumichi to his consort in the Heian "poetic diary" *Izumi Shikibu Nikki*—the new lady will be a help, not a threat.

The Empress's next retort (no. 133) reverts to the term *futae* ("double-layered") in no. 131 and develops a related image, that of silkworms in their cocoons. Why the cocoon should be considered "double-layered" is not clear; it has been suggested that the reference is to silkworms that spin cocoons twice (i.e., go through two generations) in a season. The application of the jo to the human situation must envisage the happy husband enjoying the warmth of two bedmates at once. Nintoku's final remark (no. 134), rather bad-tempered, is to the effect that things would be better for his wife if she went two-and-two with a companion. *Asazuma*, "morning wife," suggests a housewife busy about her morning chores, needing all the extra help she can get. It is at the same time the name of a village at the foot of the Kazuraki Mountains, the birthplace of Iwanohime, who belonged to the Kazuraki clan. The song has also been interpreted as referring to the lonely Princess Yata climbing the hills without a companion.

130   [NS 46]

In the first month of spring, in the twenty-second year of his reign, the Emperor spoke to the Empress, saying, "I intend to bring Princess Yata into the palace as my consort." But the Empress would not allow it. And so the Emperor sang a song pleading with the Empress that went:

Umahito no	Oath of a noble,
Tatsuru kotodate	Hear the words now lifted high:
Usayuzuru	For an extra string
Taeba tsugamu ni	To string my bow in case of need
Narabete mogamo	I'd lay her in beside you.

131   [NS 47]

The Empress sang in reply, saying:

Koromo koso	To have your wardrobe
Futae mo yoki	Double layered would be fine,
Sayodoko o	No doubt of that—
Narabemu kimi wa	But you frighten me, my lord,
Kashikokiro kamo	Who would line up beds at night!

132   [NS 48]

The Emperor sang again, saying:

Oshiteru	Out on the cape
Naniwa no saki ni	Of far-shining Naniwa
Narabihama	The double dunes:
Narabemu to koso	To be doubled up with you
Sono ko wa arikeme	Must be why that child was born.

133   [NS 49]

The Empress sang in reply, saying:

Natsumushi no	Summer crawlers,
Himushi no koromo	Silkworms that make double clothes:
Futae kite	Wearing two layers,
Kakumiyadari wa	Sleeping snug and bundled up—
Ani yoku mo arazu	Oh, no, that can't be right!

134   [NS 50]

The Emperor sang again, saying:

Asazuma no	Puffing her way,
Hika no osaka o	Sniffling up the Hika slope
Katanaki ni	At Asazuma—

| Michi yuku mono mo | Of a morning a wife'd be |
| Taguite zo yoki | Better off with company. |

The Empress was silent and did not reply again, for she had no intention of ever giving in.

✳ The following song is also omitted from the *Kojiki* account of the affair of Princess Yata. *Mitsunagashiwa* leaves have been interpreted as trifurcated (*mitsu no*) oak (*kashiwa*) leaves. They were used as drinking vessels at ceremonial court banquets in ancient times. With its altered repetitions, the tanka makes an effective work song. It is conjectured that boats in the service of the court were distinguished by having bells attached to them.

135   [NS 51]

In the thirtieth year, autumn, in the ninth month, whose first day was Wood-Junior/Hare, on the day Wood-Junior/Ox, the Empress journeyed to the land of Ki, arrived at Cape Kumano, and started back with the *mitsunagashiwa* leaves she had obtained there. . . . Hereupon the Emperor, spying an opportunity in the absence of the Empress, wed Princess Yata and brought her into the palace. The Empress meanwhile arrived at Naniwa Crossing. Hearing that the Emperor had married Princess Yata, she felt deeply wronged. She threw the *mitsunagashiwa* leaves she had picked into the sea and refused to go ashore. And so the people of that time named the sea on which she had scattered the leaves Leaf Crossing. Meanwhile the Emperor, not knowing that the Empress was angry and had refused to come ashore, had gone personally to the great port to await her boat. He sang, saying:

Naniwahito	Men of Naniwa,
Suzufune torase	Give a tug to the bell-boat,
Koshi nazumi	Wade through the water,
Sono fune torase	Take that boat and tug it in,
Ōmifune tore	Tug in the royal boat.

✳ After sending messengers in vain (see nos. 59–62), Nintoku follows Iwanohime up Yodo River, singing a song found only in *Nihonshoki*. According to the interpretation adopted here, the mulberry branch stands for Nintoku himself, swept by the current of his passions into every river bend, oscillating between Princess Yata and the Empress. Therefore the Empress will hear of the branch "not indifferently" (*ohoroka ni kikosanu*). "Vine-swarming" (*tsuno sahau*) is a mock epithet for the Empress's name through *iwa* ("rock"). (See no. 325 for another instance of this pillow word.) *Uraguwa* ("leafy mulberry") may be intended to echo *uragoi* ("heart-longing"). The original significance of the song is not clear, but the "Mulberry Branch Legend" (nos. 886–88) is worth thinking about in this regard.

136   [NS 56]

In the eleventh month, whose first day was Wood-Senior/Tiger, on the day Metal-Senior/Monkey, the Emperor launched on the river and betook himself to Yamashiro. Just then a mulberry branch floated by. The Emperor saw the mulberry branch and sang:

Tsuno sahau	Vine-swarming
Iwanohime ga	Rock Princess Iwanohime
Ohoroka ni	Not indifferently
Kikosanu	Will hear of you,
Uraguwa no ki	Leafy mulberry tree:
Yorumashijiki	You shouldn't go near them,
Kawa no kumaguma	All those bending river bends,
Yorohoiyuku kamo	But you round them every one,
Uraguwa no ki	Leafy mulberry tree.

✻ For the story of Princess Medori and Prince Hayabusawake, see nos. 66–70. Song 137 reads like a conflation of nos. 66 and 67. The ominous effect of having the Emperor overhear the weaving women sing this song enhances the narrative, showing an advance over the simple question-and-answer of the *Kojiki* version.

137   [NS 59]

In the fortieth year, in spring, in the second month, desiring to bring Princess Medori into the palace as his consort, he made Prince Hayabusawake his go-between. But Prince Hayabusawake secretly wooed her himself and for a long time gave no report on the success of his mission. Thereupon the Emperor, not knowing she had a husband, went personally to the hall of Princess Medori. At that time the Princess's weaving women sang:

Hisakata no	On a metal loom,
Amekanabata	Loom of heaven high and far,
Medori ga	Ladybird weaving,
Oru kanabata	Weaving on a metal loom
Hayabusawake no	For a falcon prince
Osui ga ne	A hooded mantle.

✻ Song 138 corresponds to no. 68 but has been rationalized to fit the story by eliminating the lark and having the falcon "mount the sky" (*ame ni nobori*). "Over the sacred grove" (*itsuki ga ue*) hints at the falcon's imperial ambitions. Here again the song is sung not by one of the principals in the drama, but by the chorus. The *Nihonshoki* compilers have clearly fashioned a superior narrative from the materials available on this particular story. These allegorical songs have much in common with the premonitory *wazauta*, usually called "children's songs," found later in *Nihonshoki* (nos. 178–82, 193, 195–99).

138 [NS 60]

At this, the Emperor realized that Prince Hayabusawake had secretly wed her and was incensed. . . . Prince Hayabusawake was lying with his head on the Princess's lap when suddenly he said, "Which is swifter, the wren or the falcon?" She said, "The falcon is swifter." Then the Prince said, "Then I'll be first." The Emperor, hearing these words, was yet more deeply incensed. At that time the Prince's housemen sang:

Hayabusa wa	Let the falcon,
Ame ni nobori	Mounting the sky,
Tobikakeri	Flying, soaring,
Itsuki ga ue no	Over the sacred grove
Sazaki torasane	Seize the wren!

❋ The flight of Prince Hayabusawake and Princess Medori leads to the same dénouement as in the *Kojiki* account. According to *Nihonshoki*, the fugitive couple were heading toward Ise to take refuge in the shrine of the sun goddess. Homuchibe no Ofuna and Saeki no Aganoko were the commanders sent to overtake and kill them. No. 139 corresponds most closely to no. 70, and like it and no. 69, probably originates in the context of country love (see also no. 886). *Yasumushiro* ("easy mat") is particularly suggestive of sexual encounter.

139 [NS 61]

Ofuna and his ally pursued them to Uda, where they beset them on Soni Mountain. At that time they hid in the grass and barely managed to escape, fleeing swiftly over the mountain. Thereupon the Prince sang, saying:

Hashitate no	Ladder-standing
Sagashiki yama mo	Steep is the mountain, yet
Wagimoko to	When the two of us,
Futari koyureba	My young love and I, cross over,
Yasumushiro kamo	What an easy mat it is!

At this, Ofuna and his ally, realizing they had escaped, speedily pursued them to the moor of Komoshiro in Ise, where they overtook and killed them.

84

✳ The exchange in songs 140–41 comes from an amorous adventure of Emperor Ingyō (fifth century) not mentioned in *Kojiki*. Like Nintoku, Ingyō came into conflict with his consort over the question of bringing other women into the palace. In this case the other woman is Lady Sotōri, the Empress's sister. (Her name, also read Sotōshi, refers to her beauty that shone "through her clothing." This is another name for Ingyō's daughter Princess Karu in *Kojiki*; see no. 87.) Because of his wife's opposition, the Emperor kept Lady Sotōri in a separate residence at Fujiwara near Asuka, and for the same reason found it difficult to visit her. In Lady Sotōri's song (no. 140) the kenning *sasagane* ("little bamboo crab") is used as an epithet for its synonym *kumo* ("spider"). Chinese as well as Japanese folklore found happy omens in the activity of spiders, which was thought especially to predict the arrival of a guest. This love song is no doubt of independent origin and quite likely inspired the anecdote about Emperor Ingyō and Lady Sotōri. It also inspired the reply, *sasagane* suggesting *sasaragata* ("fine-patterned"), *sasa* in both instances basically meaning "small" or "fine." (*Sasa* as a kind of bamboo refers to dwarf varieties.) *Sasaragata* in turn leads to *nishiki* ("brocade"), *himo* ("sash"), and so forth, and the song composes itself. Lady Sotōri's song also appears in *Kokinshū* as KKS XX: 1110.

140   [NS 65]

In the eighth year, spring, the second month, he [the Emperor] went to Fujiwara and secretly observed the demeanor of Lady Sotōri. That evening Lady Sotōri was alone, yearning for the Emperor. Unaware that the Emperor had come, she composed a song, saying:

Wa ga seko ga	Tonight is the night
Kubeki yoi nari	My young love will come to me:
Sasagane no	Little bamboo crab
Kumo no okonai	Spider's antics make it clear,
Koyoi shirushi mo	Oh, very clear tonight!

141   [NS 66]

The Emperor was moved on hearing this song, and composed a song of his own:

Sasaragata	Fine-patterned
Nishiki no himo o	Sashes of brocade undone,
Tokisakete	Lying at our ease,
Amata wa nezu ni	Many times we have not slept—
Tada hitoyo nomi	Only for a single night.

✳ Emperor Ingyō's next-morning song (no. 142) exemplifies the tendency, recurrent in waka, to work a verb or adjective through its various inflections in a display of technical virtuosity. The Heian poetess Izumi Shikibu was particularly adept at this, and Emperor Temmu's poem MYS I: 27 (no. 264) also provides a well-known example. In no. 142 the verb is *mezu* ("to love," "to adore"). In this instance the playfulness of the technique, which calls attention to itself and tends to become the most prominent feature of a poem, harmonizes well enough with the mixture of exhilaration and ruefulness. It is of interest to note that this is the only song in the chronicles to employ the image of cherry blossoms, eventually to become the prime emblem of Japanese beauty. In this, its earliest usage, the cherry serves as a metaphor for a radiant feminine loveliness.

142   [NS 67]

The next morning the Emperor, seeing the cherry blossoms beside the well, sang:

Hanaguwashi	Fine in your flowers,
Sakura no mede	Cherry tree so loveable—
Koto medeba	Like that to love you
Hayaku wa medezu	But not to have loved you soon enough,
Wa ga mezuru kora	Sweet child I love so well!

When the Empress heard this, she took it very ill.

❋ Because of continued hostility from her elder sister, Lady Sotōri begged Emperor Ingyō to let her live farther away, and the Emperor established a residence for her across the mountains at Chinu in Kawachi on the Inland Sea. His subsequent visits to the area to "go hunting" raised objections from his consort, who requested that he decrease their frequency. At the time of song 143 he has not been to Chinu for over a year. The song follows the reverse of the preparation-conclusion pattern, giving the image-complex (what would otherwise be the jo) at the end, after its significance has been stated. It should be kept in mind that in comparing the Emperor to seaweed, the lady is not demeaning him. The inability to predict when it will be washed ashore is the point of the analogy, but seaweed itself is an image of value and beauty in early poetry (see, e.g., nos. 321 and 325). The anecdote concludes with an etymological origin legend of the sort frequently found in the chronicles and fudoki. For an exploitation of this particular etymology, see no. 464.

143   [NS 68]

In the eleventh year, in spring, in the third month, on the day Fire-Senior/Horse of the month beginning Water-Junior/Hare, the Emperor went to the palace at Chinu. Lady Sotōri sang:

Tokoshie ni	Is it forever
Kimi mo ae ya mo	You will meet with me, my lord?
Isanatori	On the whale-hunting
Umi no hamamo no	Seaside washes glistening weed
Yoru tokidoki o	Only now and then ashore.

Then the Emperor said to Lady Sotōri, "You are to let no one else hear this song. If the Empress were to hear it, she would take it very ill." Thus the people of that time called shore-weed *nanorisomo*, "tell-not weed."

❋ The events that form the setting for song 144 occurred as a result of the assassination of Emperor Ankō, an incident that took place in 456, according to traditional Japanese chronology. Ankō, a son of Emperor Ingyō, was the Prince Anaho who succeeded to the throne when his brother Crown Prince Karu was exiled for incest with his sister (nos. 78–90). (In the *Nihonshoki* account, Princess Karu is exiled rather than her brother, and the guilty pair do not commit lovers' suicide. Prince Karu kills himself later as the result of another sex scandal that resembles the *Kojiki* narrative of the incest affair.) Ankō was murdered in the third year of his reign by a child, Prince Mayowa, whose father, Prince Ōkusaka, he had unjustly put to death because of a slander. In a scene worthy of Shakespeare, the child overhears the Emperor confess to his (Mayowa's) mother, whom he has married and made his Empress, his fears that the boy will take revenge when he learns the circumstances of his father's death. Mayowa waits until the Emperor falls into a drunken sleep on his consort's knees, and then stabs him to death. Ankō's younger brother, Prince Ōhatsuse (later Emperor Yūryaku), promptly takes advantage of the situation to put himself on the throne. He feigns suspicion that his other brothers were involved in an assassination plot and destroys them. Prince Sakai no Kurohiko was one of them, and *Nihonshoki* relates his fate and that of Prince Mayowa. Tsubura, as Ō-Omi ("Great Omi"), the highest officer at court, was a member of the Kazuraki family of Iwanohime, Emperor Nintoku's consort (see nos. 57–63 and 130–34). The powerful Kazuraki clan supported a rival claimant to the throne, Prince Ichinobe Oshiha (the father of Princes Oke and Woke; nos. 105 and 153–56), whom Yūryaku later murdered. This political factor may explain why Princes Kurohiko and Mayowa sought protection from Tsubura. Tsubura's claim that he had not seen a Prince take refuge in the house of a subject seems oblivious to the recent events involving Prince Karu and Ōmae-Omae no Sukune (see nos. 81–84). The "man of old" to whose dictum Tsubura appeals is Confucius in a passage from the *Analects*. The song of Tsubura's wife can be read in an ironic sense as pointing out how some men will insist on the niceties even when they go to their death, and the *Nihonshoki* setting anticipates this interpretation. But the similarity of song and situation to no. 82 is too intriguing to be passed over in silence. Perhaps a comic mimed song of submission has here been revised to give it tragic stature suitable for integration into an anecdote of exemplary loyalty. (Tsubura, unlike Ōmae-Omae no Sukune, does not betray his guest.)

144   [NS 74]

Imperial Prince Sakai no Kurohiko, in fear at being held in deep suspicion, secretly spoke with Prince Mayowa. Finally they found an opportunity to slip away together and fled to the house of Tsubura no Ō-Omi. The Emperor sent a messenger to ask for them, whereupon the Ō-Omi replied by the messenger: "I have heard of a subject fleeing to the palace of a Prince, but I have never before seen a Prince take refuge in the dwelling of a subject. Imperial Prince Sakai no Kurohiko and Prince Mayowa have now given a deep trust to your servant's integrity and have come to your servant's home. How can I deliver them over to you?" Because of this the Emperor raised still more troops and surrounded the Ō-Omi's house. The Ō-Omi went out into his courtyard and called for his garters. The Ō-Omi's wife brought the garters; in sorrow and affliction she sang:

Omi no ko wa	Child of the Omi,
Tae no hakama o	He dons his trousers—seven layers
Nanae oshi	Of barken cloth—
Niwa ni tatashite	And stands in the courtyard
Ayoi nadasu mo	Smoothing his garters, O!

Having finished putting on his gear, the Ō-Omi proceeded to the gate of the Emperor's camp, fell to his knees, and raised his hands in supplication, declaring, "Your servant, though he be slain, will not heed your command. A man of old has said, 'It is hard to take by force the will of a common man.' This fits the case of your servant exactly. I beg on bended knee to make recompense by presenting to the great King my daughter Karahime and my seven houses in Kazuraki." But the Emperor would not allow it; he set fire to the house and burned it down. Thus the Ō-Omi, Imperial Prince Kurohiko, and Prince Mayowa were burned to death together.

✳ No. 145 is a version of no. 97, but with enough differences to be worth including here. A fourth speaker has been added in the person of the Emperor himself, a change that allows some unabashed self-glorification. The problematical character of Yūryaku has been mentioned (commentary to no. 91). The several incidents having to do with hunting in the chronicles of his reign usually portray him as committing some act of violence (as in his murder of Prince Ichinobe Oshiha, which took place on a hunting expedition) or reveal him to be a coward, a hero, or the equal of a god. The bloody annals of dynastic struggle following the death of Nintoku are rich in material for dramatic handling, of which the unstable but larger-than-life figure of Yūryaku provides the most massive cluster.

145   [NS 75]

In autumn, in the eighth month, whose first day was Metal-Junior/Hare, on the day Earth-Senior/Swine, the Emperor went out on the fields of Kawakami. He gave the order for his forester to start the game for the chase, and while he was waiting to get in his shot, a horsefly suddenly flew up and bit his forearm. At this, a dragonfly immediately flew up, ate the horsefly, and flew off. The Emperor was impressed by the dragonfly's spirit and ordered his courtiers, "Compose a song praising the dragonfly on our behalf." But none of them was able to do so. And so the Emperor recited extempore:

Yamato no	In Yamato
Omura no take ni	On the heights of Omura
Shishi fusu to	Game lies crouched:
Tare ka kono koto	Who makes report of this
5 Ōmae ni mōsu	In the great forecourt?
Ōkimi wa	The great lord,
Soko o kikashite	Having heard that news,
Tamamaki no	Stands by on a camp chair
Agora ni tatashi	All festooned with strings of gems,
10 Shitsumaki no	Stands by on a camp chair
Agora ni tatashi	Covered with homespun cloth.
Shishi matsu to	As I sit here
Wa ga imaseba	Waiting for the game,
Sai matsu to	As I stand by
15 Wa ga tataseba	Waiting for wild boar,
Takubura ni	On my arm's swelling flesh
Amu kakitsuki	A horsefly lights and clings:
Sono amu o	That horsefly, oh,
Akizu haya kui	A dragonfly gobbles it down:
20 Hau mushi mo	Even creeping insects
Ōkimi ni matsurau	Do obeisance to the great lord.
Na ga kata wa	Your namesake
Okamu	I shall leave:
Akizushima Yamato	Dragonfly Island Yamato.

Thus this place was named Akizuno ("Dragonfly Fields") in praise of the dragonfly.

❇ The story of Emperor Yūryaku and the wild boar (no. 98) is reworked in song 146 and its attached anecdote. In place of the comic version in which Yūryaku himself climbs a tree to escape, the *Nihonshoki* historians have produced a heroic and didactic tale, making the Emperor slay the charging boar while his attendant climbs the tree. Afterwards the Empress mollifies his anger, and the Emperor returns from the hunt having shown himself not only brave but virtuous. This is one of a number of anecdotes in *Nihonshoki* in which Yūryaku's rage is deflected by words or music. The double image resulting from working with both native and Chinese materials is particularly clear here. The song, which is metrically and otherwise one of the most primitive in the chronicles, is layered about with phraseology taken directly from Chinese sources. Part of the Emperor's speech to his attendant is from *Han Shu*, and the dialogue between the Emperor and Empress is largely adapted from *Chuang-tzu*. The "five emotions" are joy, anger, love, pleasure, and resentment. The *Nihonshoki* version of the song ends with the "*My brother*" refrain of no. 29.

146   [NS 76]

In the fifth year, in spring, in the second month, the Emperor held a hunt on Mount Kazuraki. A weird bird suddenly appeared. It was the size of a crane and had a long tail that trailed on the ground. It cried, "Beware! Beware!" Immediately a raging boar that they had been chasing burst out of the grass and charged them. The hunters climbed trees in great fear. The Emperor proclaimed to his attendant, "Even a wild beast will stop when it meets a man. Fend it off with arrows and then stab it." But the attendant was cowardly and climbed up a tree, losing his color and no longer master of his five emotions. The enraged boar came straight on and was about to gore the Emperor. The Emperor stopped it with a shot from his bow; he raised his foot and trampled it to death. With this the hunt came to an end. The Emperor was going to cut down his attendant, but the attendant, faced with his own execution, composed a song, saying:

Yasumishishi	Our great lord
Wa ga ōkimi no	Who rules the realm in all tranquility
Asobashishi	Went off a-hunting
Shishi no	For wild boar:
5 Utaki kashikomi	Of its snorting I was all a-dread,
Wa ga	I ran,
Nigenoborishi	I clambered up
Ario no	A crag,
Ue no	An alder,
10 Hari ga eda	Out a branch—
Ase o	*My brother!*

The Empress heard this and took pity [on the man]; her feelings aroused,

90

she stayed [the Emperor's hand]. He declared, "The Empress does not side with the Emperor, but takes thought for the attendant." She replied, "The people are all saying that Your Majesty takes his ease in the fields and his pleasure in the beasts. This is hardly proper. If Your Majesty now because of a raging boar slays his attendant, Your Majesty will be no different from a wolf." The Emperor thereupon mounted his carriage with the Empress and returned home. [The hunting party] cried, "Long Live the Emperor!" He exclaimed, "What joy! The others have bagged birds and beasts, but We have brought home good words from Our hunting."

✳ Song 147, also attributed to Emperor Yūryaku, is a land-praising song of the sort associated with early monarchs (no. 238) or heroes (no. 30), or just appearing as anonymous songs (no. 1486). This one is particularly simple and direct, being almost entirely exclamatory rather than descriptive, but out of such beginnings developed both the nature elements in formal excursion and capital-founding poems such as those of Hitomaro (nos. 293–96) and Tanabe no Sakimaro (nos. 677–85), and the paeans to Mount Fuji by Yamabe no Akahito (nos. 537–38) and Takahashi no Mushimaro (nos. 569–71).

147   [NS 77]
In the sixth year, spring, in the second month, whose first day was Water-Senior/Rat, on the day Wood-Junior/Hare, the Emperor made an excursion to the fields of Hatsuse. Gazing at the form of the mountains and the fields, he experienced an upsurge of emotion, and sang this song:

	Komoriku no	Hidden
	Hatsuse no yama wa	Hatsuse Mountain—
	Idetachi no	Going forth,
	Yoroshiki yama	How good is the mountain;
5	Washiride no	Running forth,
	Yoroshiki yama no	How good is the mountain:
	Komoriku no	Hidden
	Hatsuse no yama wa	Hatsuse Mountain—
	Aya ni uraguwashi	Ah, how beautiful it is!
10	Aya ni uraguwashi	Ah, how beautiful it is!

And they named the fields the Fields of Michi.

✳ Another anecdote illustrating Emperor Yūryaku's paranoid and vengeful nature introduces song 148. Tales of artisans of marvelous skill abound in Chinese sources and were also popular in early Japan. In this story the carpenter Mita is building a several-storied tower, no doubt a continental innovation, though it is not clear just how it differed from the towers mentioned in the settings to nos. 52 and 127. That the palace woman is from Ise rather than some other province may point toward the genesis of the anecdote as an explanation of the song, which specifies Ise as the source of the sacred, life-endowed branches. The Mononobe mentioned here are guards, jailers, and executioners under the supervision of the Mononobe clan. The Hada (or Hata) were a prominent clan of Korean origin, specialists in textile manufacture. Also illustrative of the assuasive powers of music, this story is one of several in early Japanese literature that allude to the strange and often supernatural potency attributed to the koto, an instrument anciently used in shamanistic séances (see nos. 74, 96, and 163). The song has been compared to early folk songs of the type known as *saibara* in its expanded repetition of the three-syllable phrase *Ise no. Iofuru kakite* is grammatically implausible; the translation follows an interpretation according to which green-leaved branches were hung in new houses to impart their life force for felicitously long periods of time, here "five-hundred [years]."

148   [NS 78]

In winter, in the tenth month, on the day Water-Senior/Horse of the month beginning Water-Junior/Cock, the Emperor commanded the carpenter Tsuge no Mita . . . and for the first time erected a chambered tower. Mita mounted the tower and ran along the four sides as quickly as if he were flying. At that moment a palace woman from Ise looked up at the top of the tower. In her astonishment at how fast he moved, she fell in the courtyard and spilled the tray she was offering to the Emperor. . . . The Emperor immediately suspected Mita of lewd behavior with the palace woman and turned him over to the Mononobe for punishment. It so happened that Sake no Kimi of the Hada was in attendance. Desiring to awake understanding in the Emperor through the voice of the koto, he placed a koto horizontally and plucked it, saying:

	Kamukaze no	From Ise
	Ise no	Of the divine wind,
	Ise no no no	From the fields of Ise
	Sakae o	Flourishing branches
5	Iofuru kakite	For a five-hundred he hung them,
	Shi ga tsukuru made ni	And as long as they should last
	Ōkimi ni	To his great lord
	Kataku	Firmly
	Tsukaematsuramu to	He vowed obedient service,
10	Wa ga inochi mo	Saying for that end
	Nagaku moga to	How he wished for a long life—
	Iishi takumi wa ya	Oh, the carpenter, alas!
	Atara takumi wa ya	The poor carpenter, alas!

Thereupon the Emperor, brought to understanding through the voice of the koto, pardoned his offense.

✻ The story attached to song 149 gives the opposite case to that of the carpenter Mita. Hatane no Mikoto is guilty of the offense of which Mita was innocent but is able to pay his way out of trouble. His rashly impudent song involves him in further fines but not the death penalty. Hatane no Mikoto, to be sure, had properties to forfeit in lieu of his life. Through his great-great-grandfather Sahohiko he was descended from Emperor Kaika, whose reign was probably in the third century A.D. The Ōmuraji, an official second in prestige to the Ō-Omi, was chief of all the clans having the clan title Muraji. The eight horses and eight swords continue the archaic Japanese attachment to the number eight. Eka was a market town in Kawachi Province. Outdoor markets were known by the kinds of trees planted to shade them. Perhaps Hatane was obliged to sell off his possessions and reimburse the injured party (the Emperor). The implication is that the hamlet of Nagano belonged to Hatane and was given to the Ōmuraji Mononobe no Me as a reward. It is quite possible to imagine the song as the genesis of the story. It intrigues the reader's interest by comparing the value of eight fine horses with that of a woman, and asks for an anecdote to explain the juxtaposition. The setting could as easily have been folk as imperial. Stories of punishment, often involving women, clustered around Emperor Yūryaku, whom the historians evidently wished to portray as unbalanced, and the song could have come to their attention as promising material. The "historians" who joined the song to the story, however, need not have been those of the last generation before the submission of the finished text of *Nihonshoki*.

149   [NS 79]

In the thirteenth year, spring, in the third month, Hatane no Mikoto, the great-great-grandson of Sahohiko, secretly debauched the palace woman Koshimako from Yamanobe. The Emperor heard of it and turned Hatane over to the Ōmuraji Mononobe no Me to be dealt with. Hatane no Mikoto cleansed himself of his offense with [a gift of] eight horses and eight swords. And then he sang, saying:

Yamanobe no	For the sake of
Koshimako yue ni	Koshimako of Yamanobe,
Hito nerau	Eight horses
Uma no yatsugi wa	Such as a man aims to own
Oshikeku mo nashi	Are nothing to begrudge.

The Ōmuraji Me heard this and reported it to the Emperor, who had Hatane lay out all his valuables on the ground at the foot of an orange tree in

Eka market. In the end he bestowed the hamlet of Nagano in Eka on the Ōmuraji Mononobe no Me.

※ A final tale of the cracked-despot variety, showing Yūryaku as not only suspicious but malicious, recounts the trick he played on the carpenter Inabe no Mane. It also illustrates his usual receptiveness to remonstrance in metrical form. The anecdote, made vivid by the use of dialogue and well-integrated songs, is told with economy and wit. The first song (no. 150) is a sedōka, the second a tanka. Both display the ancient oral structure in which one of the long lines is repeated in a refrain-like pattern. A carpenter's ink-string was dipped in ink and stretched tight against a timber to leave a straight line. The metonymy harmonizes with the overall sophistication of this story as compared to that of Tsuge no Mita, with its longer, more openly emotional and less metrically defined song. Concrete particularity is given to the narrative by having it focus on a series of physical objects—adze, stone, loincloths, ink-string, and saddle—that activate the drama by themselves.

150   [NS 80]

In the ninth month the carpenter Inabe no Mane, using a stone for a cutting block, trimmed timbers with an adze, and though he trimmed all day, he never missed and damaged the blade. The Emperor came by and wondered at this, asking, "Don't you ever miss and hit the stone?" Mane replied, "I never miss." And so the Emperor summoned his palace women and had them undress and wrestle in an open place, wearing only loincloths. At this, Mane stopped and looked up for a moment as he went on trimming, and without his realizing it, his hand slipped and he damaged his blade. The Emperor consequently rebuked him, saying, "Where does he come from, this slave who does not fear Us, who with dishonest mind lightly gives false replies?" And he turned him over to the Mononobe to be executed in the fields. At this, one of his fellow carpenters, grieving in regret over Mane, composed a song, saying:

Atarashiki	How sad a loss—
Inabe no takumi	Inabe the carpenter,
Kakeshi suminawa	The ink-string he stretched;
Shi ga nakeba	If he is no more,
Tare ka kakemu yo	Who is going to stretch it?
Atara suminawa	A loss, that ink-string!

151   [NS 81]

When the Emperor heard this song, his feelings changed and he was swept with remorse. Sighing sorely, he said, "We have nearly lost a man." And so he mounted a pardon-bearing messenger on a black colt from Kai and sent him galloping to the execution ground. There the messenger stopped the execution, pardoned the prisoner, and released him from his bonds. And the Emperor composed a song:

Nubatama no	Black as a berry,
Kai no kurokoma	The black colt from Kai—
Kura kiseba	Had we saddled him,
Inochi shinamashi	Someone's life would have been lost,
Kai no kurokoma	The black colt from Kai.

❋ *Nihonshoki* concludes its account of Yūryaku's reign with an anecdote of military valor. In the official chronology the year corresponds to 479, and the abruptly introduced reference to an expedition against Silla at this time is historically suspect, though by no means unique in that regard in the total context of Korean matters as narrated in the Japanese chronicles. Kibi (nos. 52–56) was an area on the north shore of the Inland Sea corresponding to the modern prefectures of Okayama and eastern Hiroshima. Oshiro, who belonged to the Kibi no Omi clan of that region, was leading a company of Emishi, the "barbarian" prior inhabitants of the land, who had largely been pushed into northern Honshū by this time. Pacified Emishi and other non-Japanese ethnic groups, such as the Hayato of Kyūshū, were forced to serve in military units that formed a kind of Praetorian Guard for the imperial house. Saba Harbor is thought to have been near Onomichi in Hiroshima Prefecture. Oshiro's plucking of his bowstring is an act of ritual magic to frighten away evil spirits. (The plucked string of the bow seems to be analogous to the plucking of the koto in shamanistic practice; the sound also invites spirit possession.) The act of singing has a correspondingly powerful effect here. *Ko* ("that boy") is an affectionate diminutive. The song was probably one sung in Kibi about the exploits of a local hero, a young man whose mother was no longer living. In the *Nihonshoki* account, Oshiro pursues the remaining Emishi all the way across Honshū to the Japan Sea, a distance of over a hundred miles.

152   [NS 82]

The general in charge of the expedition against Silla, Kibi no Omi Oshiro, reached the province of Kibi on his way and passed by his home. Later the five hundred Emishi he was leading heard of the Emperor's demise and said to each other, "The Emperor who ruled over our country has passed away. We should not lose this opportunity." And they gathered together in large numbers and attacked and ravaged the neighboring districts. At this, Oshiro came from his home and met the Emishi at Saba Harbor. He did battle with them, but as he shot, the Emishi kept leaping and crouching, skillfully avoiding his arrows and getting away. He simply was unable to hit any of them. So Oshiro plucked on his empty bowstring, after which he shot and killed on the seashore two companies of the leapers and crouchers. He had already used up two quivers of arrows, and so he called to the boatmen and asked for more arrows. But the boatmen were afraid and took themselves off. Oshiro therefore stood his bow on end and grasping the nock, sang:

Michi ni au ya	He faces them down on the road,
Oshiro no ko	That boy Oshiro—
Amo ni koso	To his mother
Kikoezu arame	His fame may never be known,
Kuni ni wa kikoetena	But let it be known to his land!

He finished singing, personally cut down several men, and pursued the remainder into Taniha Province, to the port of Urakake, where he attacked and slew them all.

❋ Songs 153–56 belong to the story of the brothers Oke and Woke (for background on them, see nos. 105 and 211–12). The setting of no. 153 is the same as that for no. 105, and the chant has the same orthographical peculiarity, being written for the most part in semantic rather than phonetic script. But instead of being the point where Prince Woke reveals his identity as the son of the murdered Prince Ichinobe no Oshiha, a moment postponed to nos. 155–56, it is a formula of blessing (*niimurohogi*) on the new house whose construction has been the occasion for the banquet. As a highly wrought use of language, it shows a stage of versification that is clearly earlier than the regularities of the developed chōka form, parallel in a way to proto-chōka such as nos. 57 and 58, and already containing a number of lines five syllables in length, but not tending in the direction of a regular alternation of long and short.

The chant is divided into three parts. The blessing proper, down through line 26, has a structure of its own, being composed of six matching units (except that the first is longer by two lines) ending with the copula *nari* and identifying each part of the house with an aspect of the owner's well-being. Each ritual utterance was no doubt intended to secure the blessing named. The second and third parts of the incantation, lines 27–35 and 36–46, are addressed respectively to the young and the old in the audience and celebrate the virtues of wine and dance. This order—from formal to informal, from the sacred to the profane—is that of the kagura service and of social occasions generally. Parts two and three of the chant abandon the formal structure of part one, being essentially early, not yet regularized chōka. The performer in part three, wearing antlers on his head (and perhaps masked), is apparently a deer dancer. It is thought that such performances were originally to protect the fields from being spoiled by the deer. (For related songs, see nos. 1555–56.) Eka market (see no. 149) has the epithet "sweet-wine" (*umazake*) presumably because such wine was sold there; but, the dancer says, his dance is not for sale. It is fortunate that the *Nihonshoki* compilers considered this authentic early ritual appropriate to the context of their narrative, for to that conjunction we owe its preservation. Prince Woke, who pronounces the blessing, is anachronistically referred to as "the Emperor" because the account comes from the chapter devoted to his reign as Emperor Kenzō.

153   [NS 83]

Hereupon Odate played upon the koto and commanded the torchbearers to get up and dance. At this the elder and younger brother deferred to each other, and for a long time neither got up. Odate spoke sharply, "Why all this delay? Hurry up and get up and dance!" Prince Oke got up and danced first, and when he had finished, the Emperor got up next, straightened his clothing, and pronounced a blessing on the house:

Tsukitatsuru	The rooting vine-ropes
Wakamurotsunane	Of the young dwelling we raise up,
Tsukitatsuru	The pillars
Hashira wa	We raise up
5 Kono iegimi no	Are the coming to rest of the heart
Mikokoro no shizumari nari	Of the master of this house.
Toriaguru	The inner beams
Utsubari wa	That we lift into place
Kono iegimi no	Are the flourishing of the heart
10 Mikokoro no hayashi nari	Of the master of this house.
Toriokeru	The rafters
Haeki wa	That we fit in place
Kono iegimi no	Are the ordering of the heart
Mikokoro no totonoi nari	Of the master of this house.
15 Toriokeru	The sheathing
Etsuri wa	That we fit in place
Kono iegimi no	Is the calming of the heart
Mikokoro no tairagi nari	Of the master of this house.
Toriyueru	The rope-vines
20 Tsunakazura wa	That we tie in place
Kono iegimi no	Are the firming of the life
Miinochi no katame nari	Of the master of this house.
Torifukeru	The thatching
Kaya wa	That we lay in place
25 Kono iegimi no	Is the overflowing of the wealth
Mitomi no amari nari	Of the master of this house.

	Izumo wa	Izumo
	Niibari	Is a new clearing;
	Niibari no	From the new clearing
30	Totsukaine no ho o	Rice ears ten hands long
	Asarake ni	In shallow vessels
	Kameru ōmiki	Brewing the fine great liquor:
	Umara ni o	See how good it is—
	Yarauru gane	Come, it's for you to drink,
35	A ga kodomo	My boys!
	Ashihiki no	When I dance,
	Kono katayama no	Raising on high
	Saoshika no tsuno	The antlers of a stag
	Sasagete	Of this lone
40	A ga maeba	Leg-cramping mountain,
	Umazake	In sweet-wine
	Eka no ichi ni	Eka market
	Atae mochite wa kawazu	You won't buy it for a price.
	Tanasoko o yarara ni	May it please you to applaud,
45	Uchiagetamawane	Strike your palms clap-clap,
	A ga tokoyotachi	My eternal ones!

❋ The next song (no. 154), also placed on the lips of Prince Woke, is in tanka form and is therefore prosodically a strong contrast to the words of blessing, which it immediately follows. A similar song appears in *Eiga Monogatari*, an eleventh-century historical tale, in relation to the prosperity of Fujiwara no Michinaga (966–1027). The metaphors are particularly apt for Princes Oke and Woke, who have bent to the vicissitudes they have endured like the willow's supple fronds but remained firm-rooted. The song thus hints at the revelation of the boys' identities about to be made, while at the same time it can be taken as bestowing further blessings on the house. The sense in which *inamushiro* ("the rice-straw mat") serves as a pillow word for *kawa* ("river") is obscure. "Singing in time" may mean in time to the koto played by Odate.

154   [NS 84]

When the blessing was finished, he sang in time:

Inamushiro	The rice-straw mat
Kawasoiyanagi	River-lining willow fronds
Mizu yukeba	As the water goes
Nabiki okitachi	Trail and lift and rise,
Sono ne wa usezu	But the roots are never lost.

❈ Again the creators of the *Nihonshoki* account show a superior sense of dramatic structure in their handling of the revelation of Prince Woke's identity, disclosing it in suspenseful stages, rather than all at once as in *Kojiki*. The last two songs (nos. 155 and 156) are the official *nanori*, or "announcement of the name," and like the house blessing and the corresponding song in *Kojiki* (no. 105), they were recorded in semantic rather than phonetic orthography. Prince Woke's dance is specified, and then defined in a learned interlinear note. Both songs employ a variety of the preparation-conclusion technique, first speaking of the land or a famous landmark, and then of the person. Yamato really is both the land and its ruler, a familiar Shakespearean usage. In *Harima Fudoki*, which has closely parallel songs (see nos. 211–12), Prince Woke's father Ichinobe Oshiha is given the title Emperor, though according to the official *Nihonshoki* account he never reigned. Elsewhere (e.g., no. 30), Yamato is praised for the green mountains that surround it; here its aspect as open land is sung. Woke is the "younger brother" (*otohi*) of the land and of Prince Oke, whom as in no. 105 he wishes to honor as the heir to the throne. In no. 156 the Princes' murdered father is mentioned by name, and the genealogy of the "slave" is made clear. Furu is the site (now in Tenri City) of the ancient Isonokami Shrine, as well as of the palace of Emperor Richū, Prince Oshiha's father. Ichinobe, where the song claims Oshiha ruled, is nearby. The reference to cutting the base and tip of the sacred shrine cedar of Isonokami is supposedly intended to indicate the awesome power of the sovereign, before whom all the land bends, as in no. 236.

155   [NS 85]

Odate said, "Well done! Pray let me hear more." And so the Emperor performed a *tatsutsumai*. (*Tatsutsumai*: Formerly this kind of dance was called a "standing forth dance"; "standing forth [*tachiide*]" they pronounced *tatsutsu*. It is a dance performed in standing and crouching postures.) And he gravely announced:

Yamato wa	Yamato
Sosochihara	Is a rustling reed plain,
Asajihara no	A shallow reed plain
Otohi	Whose younger brother,
Yatsukorama	This slave, am I.

156   [NS 86]

Odate wondered deeply at this, and he had him recite again, whereupon the Emperor gravely announced:

Isonokami	The godly cedar
Furu no kamusugi	Of Furu of Isonokami—
Moto kiri	His who cut its base,

	Sue oshiharai	His who swept away its tip,
5	Ichinobe no	His who from the palace
	Miya ni	Of Ichinobe
	Ame no shita shirashishi	Ruled the land beneath the sky,
	Ame yorozu kuni yorozu	Sky-myriad, land-myriad,
	Oshiha no Mikoto no	Oshiha the Noble—
10	Mianasue	His scion,
	Yatsukorama	This slave, am I.

Odate was greatly amazed and left his seat. Sorely moved, he bowed twice and offered all his wealth; at the head of his attendants he prostrated himself reverently.

✳ No. 157 is an avowedly "anonymous" popular song in the category of political satire, and thus is related to the genre known as wazauta (see nos. 178–82, 193, and 195–99). The difference lies in the lack of ominous intent and allegorical expression. Emperor Shiraga (posthumous title Seinei) was the son of Yūryaku. He had no heirs and passed the kingdom on to his cousins Princes Oke and Woke. Prince Oke, the elder brother, was designated successor but yielded the throne to his younger brother, Woke (here "the Emperor"), despite the latter's reluctance. Woke reigned first as Emperor Kenzō, and Oke followed as Emperor Ninken. The interregnum under their sister, Princess Iitoyoao, ended with her death within a year of that of Emperor Shiraga.

157 [NS 87]

In the fifth year, spring, first month, Emperor Shiraga passed away. In this month the Prince Imperial (Prince Oke) and the Emperor ceded the throne to each other, and for some time neither would occupy it. Because of this, the Emperor's elder sister, Princess Iitoyoao, took charge of government at Tsunosashi Palace in Oshinumi and called herself Her Highness Iitoyoao of Oshinumi. A songster of the time composed a song, saying:

Yamatohe ni	Up Yamato way
Migahoshi mono wa	What a person wants to see
Oshinumi no	Is this high stronghold
Kono takaki naru	At Oshinumi—
Tsunosashi no miya	The palace of Tsunosashi.

✳ The rivalry between prince Woke and Shibi no Omi (nos. 106–11) is completely reworked in *Nihonshoki* and placed several years later, at the end of the reign of Emperor Ninken. Here too it assumes the form of a poem-tale (nos. 158–66), one even longer than the account in *Kojiki*, and includes an exchange of songs between rivals at an utagaki. Only one of the participants (Shibi) and one of the songs remain the same. Now it is Ninken's son, about to become Emperor Buretsu (official death date 506), who quarrels with Shibi over a young woman (Kagehime, not "Great Fish"). *Nihonshoki* makes clear the political context of the rivalry. Shibi's father, the Ō-Omi Heguri no Matori, has become increasingly arrogant and is about to usurp the throne. The Kagehime affair is the fuse that sets off the Crown Prince's anger, and he proceeds to destroy both father and son before commencing a reign the chroniclers denounce for its wanton cruelty. The interest of the poem-tale itself, however, is focused on the battle of songs and Kagehime's grief for her slain lover. The first song (no. 158) duplicates no. 109, and again the point is the play on Shibi's name. Shibi's retort (no. 159) is a taunt that corresponds to the last three lines of no. 108. Here the *shibakaki* ("brushwood fence") has become a more impressive *karakaki* ("Chinese fence"), but in either case its eight folds surround the prized woman (see no. 1). No. 159 is a katauta, but does not match another song in the same form as in nos. 106–7. The Prince's next song (no. 160) preserves what was no doubt the decorum of the songfest by merely threatening subsequent violence; it can also be read as an assertion of sexual primacy. Shibi's second reply (no. 161) returns to the image of the fence—here a braided or interwoven one—and denies that the Prince, whatever his prowess with a sword, will be able to win and keep a wife. But the Prince has the last word in no. 162, likening his power to that of an earthquake.

158   [NS 90]

Now, the Crown Prince desired to wed Kagehime, the daughter of the Ōmuraji Mononobe no Arakabi, and sent a go-between to Kagehime's house to pledge his troth. Kagehime already had an illicit relationship with Shibi, the son of the Ō-Omi Matori, but she was afraid to reject the Prince's proposal. Her reply was, "Your handmaid, may it please you, wishes to attend on you at the crossroads of Tsuba Market." The Prince, therefore, desiring to go to the appointed place, sent a bodyguard to the house of the Heguri Ō-Omi to present his order for an official horse. The Ō-Omi treated the matter as a joke and gave a facetious reply, saying, "For whom else do I keep the official horses? It shall be as Your Highness wishes." But time went by without his sending a horse. The Prince nursed his anger, but was patient and did not show it on his face. Finally he went to the appointed place and stood among the throng at the songfest. Taking Kagehime's sleeve, he eased her aside and quietly began his wooing. Then all of a sudden Shibi no Omi came up and pushed himself between the Prince and Kagehime. At this, the Prince dropped Kagehime's sleeve and turned to stand face to face with Shibi. And he sang, saying:

Shiose no	Where the riptide
Naori o mireba	Wrinkles into folded waves
Asobikuru	I look and see
Shibi ga hatade ni	Sporting toward me a tuna—
Tsuma tateri miyu	And my wife stands on its fin!

159 [NS 91]

Shibi sang in reply:

Omi no ko no	The Omi boy
Yae ya karakaki	With his eightfold Chinese fence—
Yuruse to ya miko	Prince, can you make him let you in?

160 [NS 92]

The Prince sang:

Ōtachi o	A greatsword
Tarehakitachite	Hangs girded as I stand—
Nukazu to mo	I may not draw it
Sue hatashite mo	Now, but at the end we'll meet
Awamu to zo omou	When I put the tip in play.

161 [NS 93]

Shibi no Omi sang in reply:

Ōkimi no	The great lord
Yae no kumikaki	May want to build a braided fence
Kakamedo mo	Eight folds around,
Na o amashijimi	But you don't know the interweave—
Kakanu kumikaki	You'll build no braided fence.

162 [NS 94]

The Prince sang:

Omi no ko no	The Omi boy's
Yafu no shibakaki	Eight-mesh brushwood fence—
Shitatoyomi	When the ground rumbles
Nai ga yorikoba	And the earth begins to quake,
Yaremu shibakaki	It will tear, that brushwood fence.

❋ The following exchange takes place after the parties have gone home from the songfest. The Prince's song (no. 163) is particularly interesting for its jo (rendered in italics) introducing *kage* ("shadow") in the name Ka-gehime. The "shadow" that comes to a koto (cithern) would be the spirit of a god, or perhaps of a human (see no. 1275). The jo may here be merely decorative, but it provides at least a suggestion that the Prince is playing the koto as a magical means of luring Kagehime (see also nos. 74, 96, 148, and 152–53). For the sentiment of the main statement, see no. 7. The last three lines are based on a repetition of *tama* ("gem," with a subsidiary meaning of "soul"), relating to the shamanistic séance in the jo. Shibi's reply (on behalf of Kagehime) is also introduced by a jo, one that culminates in *musubitare* ("tied and hanging down"), which in turn leads to *tare* ("whom") in the main statement. Again the juncture is purely phonetic, but a vision of the Prince wearing a homespun sash emerges nevertheless.

163 [NS 95]

The Prince sent a song to Kagehime, saying:

Kotogami ni	*To the cithern comes,*
Kiiru Kagehime	*Stays the shadow*: Lady Kage,
Tama naraba	If you were a gem,
A ga horu tama no	The gem that I desire you'd be—
Awabishiratama	A white abalone pearl.

164 [NS 96]

Shibi no Omi replied for Kagehime with a song that went:

Ōkimi no	The homespun fabric
Miobi no shitsuhata	Of the sash the great lord ties
Musubitare	Hangs with trailing end:
Tare ya shi hito mo	In the end, no matter whom,
Aiomowanaku ni	I cannot love some other.

❈ Song 165 is placed in the context of the Crown Prince's revenge. The passage immediately follows the preceding exchange of songs between the Prince and Shibi. Ōtomo no Kanamura, who was instrumental in putting Buretsu on the throne, subsequently served as Ōmuraji under five Em-perors. The song is usually understood as an ancient lament describing the route followed by a funeral procession. It has also been suggested, however, that like nos. 1555–56, it was originally a beggar song, with the places named interchangeable with others, depending on the beggar's itinerary. The rice and water thus become either funeral offerings or alms, according to the interpretation. The route in any case is north from Furu in modern Tenri City to Nara Mountain, north of Nara. Contextually, the song refers neither to a funeral procession (for Kagehime's disposal of her lover's body, see no. 166) nor to begging, but is a *michiyuki*, or travel poem, of grief about a survivor searching for the dead, and thus, mutatis mutandis, a functional equivalent of similar passages in the laments of Hitomaro. Its most prominent structural feature is the list of places, each with a pillow word to introduce it. Furu is associated with Isunokami (a variant of Isonokami), the site of an ancient shrine. *Komomakura* ("rush pillow") is juxtaposed with Takahashi through *taka* ("high"), because such a pillow (wood wrapped in rush matting) was higher than other pillows. *Mono sawa ni* ("things in great abundance") modifies *ō* ("many") in Ōyake. *Haruhi* ("spring sun") applies to *kasu* (from *kasumi*, "spring mist") in Kasuga. *Tsumagomoru* ("wifesecluding"; see no. 325, line 27) is obscure in its relevance to Osaho, but possibly introduces *o* (= *wo*, "man"). The placement of this song in the mouth of the person whose actions it purports to describe suggests the possibility of some form of enactment.

165   [NS 97]

The Prince, now realizing that Shibi had made Kagehime his own, awoke to the full pattern of disrespect he had endured from father and son. Red with fury, he set off to the residence of the Muraji Ōtomo no Kanamura that very night, assembled fighting men, and laid plans. The Muraji Ōtomo led some thousand troops to block the road and killed Shibi no Omi at Nara Mountain. (One text says that Shibi was staying in Kagehime's house and was killed that night.) At this time Kagehime, following after, arrived at the place of the killing and saw that they had killed him. She was amazed and frightened, not knowing where to turn; her eyes filled with tears of grief. Finally she composed a song, saying:

Isunokami	Passing Furu
Furu o sugite	Of Isunokami,
Komomakura	Passing Takahashi
Takahashi sugi	High like a rush pillow,
5 Mono sawa ni	Passing Ōyake
Ōyake sugi	Of things in great abundance,
Haruhi	Passing Kasuga
Kasuga o sugi	Of the misty spring sun,
Tsumagomoru	Passing Osaho
10 Osaho o sugi	The wedded enclosure,
Tamake ni wa	In a gemlike dish
Ii sae mori	Even heaping rice,
Tamamoi ni	In a gemlike bowl
Mizu sae mori	Even brimming water,
15 Nakisohochiyuku mo	Weeping, soaked with tears, she goes—
Kagehime aware	Poor Kagehime, alas!

❋ No. 166, the last song in the tale of Kagehime, is a seven-line chōka, the shortest possible length for a poem in that form. The setting and the song both have the unsparing cruelty of old ballads. Each short line is a pillow-word construction, a feature that contributes to the ballad-like quality. *Minasosoku* ("water-streaming") applies to the meaning of *shibi* ("tuna"), but also resonates with *mizuku* ("dripping") in the previous line. "Hides" (*gomori*), the euphemism for burial, provides an ironic metaphor—Shibi, even in death, is a hunted beast hiding from his pursuers. On the metaphorical level the "young swine" (*inoko*) can be taken as the pursuers, but the savagery of the song comes through best in a literal interpretation.

166   [NS 98]

Then Kagehime, when she had gathered him up and buried him, and it was finished, and she was about to start home, choking with grief, said, "Woe is me! Today I have lost my beloved husband." And again, pouring out tears of sorrow, with heavy heart, she sang:

Aoni yoshi	In blue-earth
Nara no hasama ni	Nara in a narrow cleft
Shishijimono	Like a wild beast
Mizuku hegomori	In a dripping trench he hides,
Minasosoku	Water-streaming
Shibi no wakugo o	Shibi the young lord—
Asarizu na inoko	Do not root him up, young swine.

❋ The successor of Buretsu was Emperor Keitai (r. 507–31). For some reason the marriage of Keitai's son Magari no Ohine (later Emperor Ankan, r. 531–35) attracted an unusual exchange of songs. Perhaps the tradition that Prince Magari wed his cousin Princess Kasuga without a go-between made him a romantic figure. The passage concerning his nuptials is inserted quite abruptly in the midst of accounts of Japan's Korean involvements and stands out as an encapsulated love story told almost entirely in song. The chroniclers were moved to introduce it with a few sentences in literarily heightened prose, using terms culled from Chinese sources. "Pure talk" (*ch'ing t'an*) ordinarily refers to the high-flown philosophical discussions of Taoist eremites, but here to the pillow talk of lovers. "A pattern of flowing lines took shape in words" draws from the *Analects* and *Wen-hsüan*. This Chinese elegance is juxtaposed with an early Japanese wooing song, a chōka strikingly similar to no. 2. Whether song 167 was also in the repertory of the *ama* singers is not specified, but clearly such songs circulated in various versions. *Man'yōshū* has another as MYS XIII: 3324/3310 (no. 1475).

One difference between nos. 2 and 167 is that the latter does not have a

clear split between third-person narration and first-person declamation. The
first ten lines of no. 167 are ambiguous in this regard; the translation has
opted for a unitary speaker and present-tense presentation. Another difference is that no. 167 compresses nos. 2 and 3 into one narrative, taking the
man into the woman's bedroom and letting him actually experience the delights proffered by Nunakawahime in her song of reply. The loss of tension
between would-be lovers separated only by a door (which here opens with
one push) is literarily regrettable, and the crying birds at the end—obviously
a traditional element—interrupt pleasure rather than impatience. Still, the
Nihonshoki version offers a privileged glimpse of bedroom technique and is
interesting precisely for its embodiment of variations on a formulaic pattern. The link between the song and the historical personages of Prince
Magari and Princess Kasuga is probably the mention of Kasuga in the fourth
line. An alternate interpretation of *tsumadori shite* ("I take a wife") in lines 14
and 16 is "I take her by the edge," *tsuma* being a homophone for "wife" and
"edge." It is not clear whether the edge applies to the coverlet (at the head
and the foot of the bed) or the woman's garment. With either interpretation
a great deal of maneuvering, perhaps a struggle, is envisioned. The possibilities are rich for mime. The sexual encounter proceeds in stages from bois-
terous attack, through tentative and then enthusiastic embraces, to complete
joining. The pillow word *shishikushiro* ("game flesh on a spit") in line 23
technically introduces *uma* ("sweet"/"delicious") in *umai* ("sweet sleep"),
but the phallic sense of the image is inescapable. Seldom can an aubade have
been cast in such lusty terms.

167   [NS 99]

In the ninth month Prince Magari no Ohine personally invited Princess Kasuga to be his bride. Then in the moonlit night they held pure talk, unaware
of dawnlight in the sky. Suddenly a pattern of flowing lines took shape in
words, and a song came to the Prince's lips:

	Yashimakuni	In the Eight Islands
	Tsuma makikanete	Unable to bed a wife,
	Haruhi no	Hearing that there is
	Kasuga no kuni ni	In the land of Kasuga
5	Kuwashime o	(Misty with spring sun)
	Ari to kikite	A fair maiden dwelling,
	Yoroshime o	Hearing that there dwells
	Ari to kikite	A comely maiden in that land,
	Maki saku	Pushing her plank door—
10	Hi no itato o	Cypress split from splendid trees—
	Oshihiraki	I open it wide
	Ware irimashi	And make my entrance to her:

	Ato tori	And I take a wife,
	Tsumadori shite	Taking her from the foot;
15	Makura tori	And I take a wife,
	Tsumadori shite	Taking her by the pillow;
	Imo ga te o	And I have my love
	Ware ni makashime	Let me pillow on her arm,
	Wa ga te o ba	And I give my love
20	Imo ni makashime	My arm and have her pillow there:
	Masakizura	Two glorious vines,
	Tadaki azahari	We lie embraced and intertwined;
	Shishikushiro	Game flesh on a spit,
	Umai neshi to ni	We are sleeping sweetly when
25	Niwatsutori	The bird of the yard,
	Kake wa naku nari	The cock is heard crowing;
	Notsutori	The bird of the moors,
	Kigishi wa toyomu	The pheasant begins to boom.
	Hashikeku mo	Before I can say
30	Imada iwazute	How dear you are to me,
	Akenikeri wagimo	The dawn has come, my love.

❋ Princess Kasuga's reply (no. 168) ostensibly expresses sadness at parting in the morning but has clearly been forced into this role with considerable violence. The references to the grief of both nature (the fish) and the people, and to ceremonies in a sacred grove suggest the song may be a lament for an Emperor. It has been pointed out that Emperor Buretsu had the element "Hatsuse" in his name, and that Emperor Keitai had that of "Iware," both places mentioned in the song. Structurally, the song is an extreme and fascinating example of the preparation-conclusion technique, and prosodically, it preserves a feature of old chōka in the 5–3–8 syllabic pattern of lines 3–5 and 16–18. The river, the bamboo, the cithern, and the flute—everything leading up to the sacred grove (*mimoro*) in line 11—are components of an extended jo presenting the lookout platform for the performance of an act of *kunimi* ("land-viewing") as part of a ritual of mourning. The deliberately roundabout route followed is, like that in no. 60 leading to a lady's heart through a moor and the belly of a big wild boar, an expression of the early Japanese delight in the delaying tactics of preparation itself, tactics that create an enjoyable sense of anticipation and arrival. But in no. 168 the elements of the jo are also particularly relevant to the theme of the song—Hatsuse as the probable burial site, the bamboo in the river as a death-countering sign of life, and the cithern and flute as sacred instruments.

Tsuno sahau ("vine-swarming"), the pillow-word construction in line 14, is a mock epithet for Iware through *iwa* ("rock"), and provides an imagistic counterpart to the "interlaced bamboo" (*ikumidake*) in line 5. Iware, an ancient pond constructed by Emperor Richū in the fifth century, no longer exists; it is thought to have been northeast of Mount Kagu, which may therefore be serving as the kunimi platform here, as in no. 238. The mention of the fish sighing in line 18 is the first indication that this is a song of sorrow. The image is striking enough in itself, but it soon becomes apparent that everything to this point is meant to serve as preparation and parallel for the statement of the song's last two lines—the true "main statement"— which are themselves introduced by another elaborate jo. This jo, lines 19–23, uses the same juncture—*tare* ("hang") / *tare* ("who")—as in no. 164. It presents the image of an Emperor, again presumably germane to the original significance of the song. The entire song is thus built of two major sections, lines 1–18 and 19–25, each incorporating its own internal jo. The two main sections have parallel conclusions but different speakers. The first betrays through its self-applied honorific *miseba* ("when We look") that an imperial personage is the subject of the verb. The second section, by contrast, is couched in the language of adulation, using the encomiastic formula *yasumishishi wa ga ōkimi* ("our great lord who rules in tranquility"). It has been suggested that this complex lament found its way into a love story because its opening made it seem like a reply to the old anonymous chōka MYS XIII:3324/3310 (no. 1475), a wooing song for which the present no. 167 was (putatively) later substituted. A proposal more flattering to the literary sensitivity of the *Nihonshoki* compilers could point out the associational relevance of no. 168 to no. 169.

168   [NS 100]

His consort sang in reply:

Komoriku no	Down the river
Hatsuse no kawa yu	Of Hatsuse the hidden land
Nagarekuru	Comes floating
Take no	A bamboo,
5 Ikumidake yodake	Interlaced bamboo, young bamboo:
Motohe o ba	From the trunk
Koto ni tsukuri	They fashion a cithern,
Suehe o ba	From the tip
Fue ni tsukuri	They fashion a flute:
10 Fukinasu	Where they blow the flutes
Mimoro ga ue ni	Up atop the sacred grove
Noboritachi	We climb,
Wa ga miseba	We stand and look:
Tsuno sahau	In the vine-swarming
15 Iware no ike no	Rock pond of Iware
Minashitafu	Even the fish

Uo mo	That pass beneath the water
Ue ni dete nageku	Come to the surface and sigh.
Yasumishishi	Our great lord
20 Wa ga ōkimi no	Who rules the land in all tranquility
Obaseru	Wears around his waist
Sasara no miobi no	A sash of subtle pattern, tied
Musubitare	To hang with trailing end:
Tare ya shi hito mo	In the end they all come forth,
25 Ue ni dete nageku	The people, openly sighing.

❈ The following two songs (nos. 169–70) appear in the *Nihonshoki* entry for the twenty-fourth year of Emperor Keitai's reign, corresponding to 530. At this time matters were going very poorly for Japan in its relations with the kingdoms of the Korean peninsula. The rising power of Silla (J. Shiragi) in the southeast was nibbling away at the Japanese-dominated confederation of Kaya (J. Mimana) on the south coast; two years later in fact it conquered Pon Kaya, one of Mimana's petty states. The *Nihonshoki* account of events is detailed and anecdotal, if confusing and probably unreliable. According to this account, a Japanese force under Kena no Omi had been dispatched to Kaya the previous year charged with restoring Silla's previous depredations and coping with the generally deteriorating situation. Kena no Omi, however, proved so haughty and inept that he alienated the local authorities and brought Silla and Paekche, Silla's traditional enemy in the southwest quadrant of the peninsula, into alliance against him. (It may be noted that Silla and Paekche were in fact allies at this time in their struggle with the northern kingdom of Koguryŏ.) Tsuki no Kishi was another Japanese envoy, a person of Paekche ancestry. Kena no Omi's previous attempt to prevent his returning to Japan with his unfavorable report had precipitated the crisis with Silla and Paekche. As is indicated in an interlinear note in *Nihonshoki*, nothing is known about Mezurako, the envoy who summoned Kena no Omi home. The unexpected death of Kena no Omi at Tsushima shifts the focus of the narrative to the sorrow of his wife, who greets the funeral barge coming up the Yodo River from Hirakata near Naniwa to Ōmi, Kena's home province. The song seems specific to the narrative, though of unknown composition. Perhaps Kena was remembered as a local hero in Ōmi. The use of irony in the song is quite affecting—the flutes, as in no. 168, are playing a dirge.

169   [NS 101]

In winter, in the tenth month, Tsuki no Kishi arrived from Mimana. He reported, "Kena no Omi has a character haughty and perverse, and he does not study statecraft. In the end he has not brought harmony and understanding, but has vexed Kara into riot. Unbridled in his arrogance, he follows his own inclinations; he tolerates calamities instead of preventing them." And so Mezurako was dispatched to summon him back. (The identity of Mezurako is obscure.) This year Kena no Omi, having been summoned, reached Tsushima, contracted an illness, and died. Sending him to burial, they went by the river up into Ōmi. His wife sang:

Hirakata yu	From Hirakata
Fue fukinoboru	He comes up, blowing a flute;
Ōmi no ya	Oh, the young lad
Kena no wakugo i	Kena, he of Ōmi,
Fue fukinoboru	Comes up, blowing a flute.

❋ The song presented to Mezurako on his arrival by the Japanese residents of Mimana expresses the colonists' distrust of the new Governor sent out by the home country. It is a sedōka with duplicate third and sixth lines, a feature probably stemming from exchanges of katauta (see nos. 17–18 and 106–07) and indicative of the ballad-like nature of the form (see nos. 150 and 369–71). "Kara" here probably refers to Korea as a whole. The Iki Islands are off northern Kyūshū, on the way to Tsushima and the south coast of Korea.

170   [NS 102]

When Mezurako first arrived in Mimana, the people from the home country who were there sent him a song, saying:

Karakuni o	Of the land of Kara
Ika ni fu koto so	What did he come to tell us?
Mezurako kitaru	Mezurako has arrived.
Mukasakuru	From Iki Crossing
Iki no watari o	Far beyond the sea from us
Mezurako kitaru	Mezurako has arrived.

❋ The final debacle for Mimana came in 562, when Silla wiped out the remainder of the Kaya Confederation and defeated an expeditionary force sent from Japan to retrieve its overseas territories. The *Nihonshoki* account culminates in the following vignette. The Japanese vice-commander has surrendered and disgraced himself by buying his life at the expense of his wife's honor. Tsuki no Kishi Ikina (of the same family but not the same person as the Tsuki no Kishi of no. 169) displays the opposite extreme of obstinate courage. Ironically, the Tsuki no Kishi—"Kishi" was a clan rank derived from a Korean title—were of Korean extraction. The vivid anecdote of Ikina's defiance, with its extremely physical gut-level conflict, is made the pedestal for the lonely and symbolic gesture of Ikina's wife Ōbako. The incorporation of the two songs into the account is evidence of the continued vitality of the ancient song-centered narrative traditions in the increasingly factual later phases of Japan's first great historiographical project. Both songs contain an honorific (*furasu* for *furu*, "to wave") that indicates they are equally a singer's description of Ōbako's action. The waving of a woman's scarf (*hire*) is a sign of farewell.

171 [NS 103]

Tsuki no Kishi Ikina, who was taken prisoner at the same time, was a man of valiant and fiery character, and never submitted till the end. The Silla commander drew his sword and made as if to cut him down. He compelled Ikina to take off his trousers and then ordered him to point his buttocks toward Japan and shout in a loud voice, "Japanese generals, bite my ass!" But Ikina shouted, "King of Silla, eat my ass!" He kept shouting the same thing even though they tortured him, and so he was killed. His son Ojiko also died, holding his father in his arms. Ikina was always like this—no one could rob him of what he meant to say. Consequently, he alone was mourned by the other commanders. His wife Ōbako was captured with him. Grieving, she sang:

Karakuni no	Standing atop
Ki no e ni tachite	The fortress of Kara,
Ōbako wa	Ōbako
Hire furasu mo	Waves her scarf
Yamato e mukite	Toward Yamato.

172 [NS 104]

Someone said in response:

Karakuni no	Standing atop
Ki no e ni tatashi	The fortress of Kara,
Ōbako wa	Ōbako
Hire furasu miyu	Is seen waving her scarf
Naniwa e mukite	Toward Naniwa.

✳ The next songs in *Nihonshoki* come from the reign of Empress Suiko (554–628). Suiko (r. 593–628), a daughter of Emperor Kimmei (r. 539–71) and granddaughter of Emperor Keitai, was Japan's first reigning Empress in fully historic times. In the following exchange, from the year 612, she and her chief Minister, the Ō-Omi Soga no Umako (d. 626), trade compliments at an imperial banquet. Three generations of the Soga clan, starting with Umako, dominated the court from 587, the year in which they successfully championed the newly introduced Buddhist religion on the field of battle, until their violent overthrow in a coup d'état in 645. For analogues to the songs accompanying the presentation and acceptance of the wine, see nos. 39–40, 48–49, 100–103, and 118–19. It is clear that the early exuberance (if not the wine) has been watered down. The formalities of no. 173 are similar on a small scale to those of the anonymous palace-praising chōka MYS 1:52 (no. 1246). The "heavenly eightyfold shade" (*ama no yasokage*) of line 4 and the "fair sky" (*misora*) of line 6 are metaphors for the lofty palace roof, as are the corresponding terms in lines 38 and 40 of no. 1246. (For an address from the throne bestowing wine on an official, see nos. 698–99.) The repetition of lines 9–10 in lines 11–12 is thought to stem from a scribal error. From the Empress's reply one may assume that horses from Himuka (a province in southern Kyūshū) and swords from Wu (the region in south China occupied by the ancient kingdom of Wu) were highly regarded in seventh-century Japan. "Wu" (J. Kure) may stand for China as a whole.

173   [NS 105]

In the twentieth year, in spring, in the first month, on the day Fire-Junior/Swine of the month beginning Metal-Junior/Serpent, the Empress set out *sake* and feasted her lords. On that day the Ō-Omi offered the cup of long life and sang:

	Yasumishishi	Where our great lord reigns,
	Wa ga ōkimi no	Ruling the realm in all tranquility,
	Kakurimasu	Here as I gaze
	Ama no yasokage	At the heavenly eightyfold shade
5	Idetatasu	In which she shelters,
	Misora o mireba	At the fair sky beneath which she stands,
	Yorozuyo ni	For ten thousand ages
	Kaku shi mogamo	I would have it be as now,
	Chiyo ni mo	For a thousand ages
10	Kaku shi mogamo	I would have it be as now,
	Chiyo ni mo	For a thousand ages
	Kaku shi mogamo	I would have it be as now;
	Kashikomite	And in fearful awe
	Tsukaematsuramu	I shall serve with reverence,
15	Orogamite	Bending to the earth
	Tsukaematsuramu	I shall serve with reverence,
	Utazukimatsuru	I shall offer up my song.

174   [NS 106]

The Empress said in reply:

Masoga yo	O true Soga!
Soga no kora wa	The sons of the Soga,
Uma naraba	Were they horses,

Himuka no koma	Would be steeds from Himuka;
5 Tachi naraba	Were they swords,
Kure no masahi	Would be true blades of Wu.
Ube shi kamo	So it seems most fit,
Soga no kora o	Surely, that the Sovereign
Okimi no	Keep in her service
10 Tsukawasu rashiki	The sons of the Soga!

✵ Song 175 belongs to a pious anecdote about Empress Suiko's nephew, the famous scholar-statesman Shōtoku Taishi (574–621), for whom, and the *Man'yōshū* version of the incident, see no. 237. *Nihon Ryōiki*, an early-ninth-century collection of Buddhist miracle tales, also has a version of the story. In the *Man'yōshū* poem the traveler is already dead, and the lament belongs to the fallen-traveler genre associated particularly with Hitomaro. The *Nihonshoki* song too can be understood in this sense, and the emphasis on the man's starvation is adumbrative of a chōka by Tanabe no Sakimaro (no. 692). The *Nihonshoki* prose account, which is intended to evoke Prince Shōtoku's compassionate nature, incorporates an old lament into an exemplary legend of generosity to the needy rather than identification with the fate of the fallen. The story goes on to add still other elements. The starving man dies, is buried by the Prince, and then vanishes from the tomb, leaving behind the Prince's garment. This resurrection tale is meant to document the legitimacy of Shōtoku's reputation as a holy man, establishing the fact that his virtue has been tested by a Buddhist divinity and found true.

175   [NS 107]

On the day Metal-Senior/Horse, the first of the twelfth month, the Crown Prince made an excursion to Kataoka. At that time there was a starving man lying by the roadside. The Prince asked his name, but the man said nothing. The Prince looked down at him and gave him food and drink. Then he took off his garment and covered the starving man with it, saying, "Rest well!" And he sang, saying:

Shinateru	On slope-shining
Kataokayama ni	Kataoka Mountain,
Ii ni ete	Starved for rice,
Koyaseru	He lies fallen—
5 Sono tahito aware	Alas, that poor traveler!
Oya nashi ni	Without a parent
Nare narikeme ya	Were you born into the world?
Sasu take no	Have you no master
Kimi wa ya naki	Flourishing as young bamboo?
10 Ii ni ete	Starved for rice,

Koyaseru	He lies fallen—
Sono tahito aware	Alas, that poor traveler!

❋ A succession dispute followed the death of Empress Suiko in 628. Soga no Emishi (d. 645), chief Minister (Ō-Omi) and son of Umako, placed Prince Tamura on the throne as Emperor Jomei (r. 629–41), intimidating the other ministers into disregarding the claims of Prince Yamashiro no Ōe (d. 643), the son of Prince Shōtoku. Yamashiro no Ōe's most stalwart supporter, Sakaibe no Omi, came into conflict with Emishi and was put to death. Song 176 is the first of several of political significance, comments or satires on current events, usually employing metaphor or allegory, said to have been popular among the people, or labeled "children's songs." They are generically referred to as wazauta, or "songs of hidden meaning" (see nos. 20–22, 137–38, and 157). The allegory in no. 176 is between the alleged sparseness of the trees on (actually lushly forested) Mount Unebi and the lack of support from the self-effacing Prince Yamashiro no Ōe that had placed Sakaibe no Omi and his family in an impossible position.

176   [NS 108]

The Ō-Omi, intending to kill Sakaibe no Omi, raised troops and dispatched them. Sakaibe no Omi, hearing that a force was arriving, took his second son, Aya, and went out to the gate, where he sat on a camp chair and waited. Then the force arrived, and Kume no Mononobe no Ikuhi was ordered to strangle Sakaibe no Omi. Father and son died together and were buried in the same spot. However, the elder brother, Ketsu, had fled and hidden in a tile-roofed nunnery building. While there he debauched one or two nuns. One of the nuns, jealous, had his whereabouts revealed. The temple was surrounded and an attempt made to capture him, whereupon he left and went to Mount Unebi. And so they searched the mountain, and Ketsu had nowhere left to run. He stabbed himself in the neck and died on the mountain. At that time people sang a song, saying:

Unebiyama	On Mount Unebi
Kotachi usukedo	The stand of trees is thin,
Tanomi ka mo	Yet—did he trust it?—
Ketsu no wakugo no	The young lord Ketsu, so it seems,
Komoraserikemu	Used it for his hiding place.

The year of the following entry is 642. Emishi shows his imperial ambitions by performing the eight-column dance, forbidden to be staged by anyone other than the Emperor, and composes a song in which he hints at his intent. The eight-column dance was actually an ancient Chinese ceremony, and the whole passage is an allusion to the *Analects*, probably to be taken in a metaphorical sense. The song is the same kind of veiled expression found in the wazauta, but placed in the mouth of the main actor rather than the chorus of spectators. Oshi was a place on the Soga River near the Soga clan's ancestral holdings at Kazuraki Takamiya; see no. 58. (The Kazuraki and Soga clans were both descended from Takeshi Uchi no Sukune; see nos. 40, 43, 71–72, and 124–26.)

177   [NS 109]

This year the Soga Ō-Omi Emishi erected an ancestral shrine at Kazuraki Takamiya and performed the eight-column dance. He composed a song, saying:

Yamato no	Intent on the crossing
Oshi no hirose o	Of the wide shallows of Oshi
Wataramu to	In Yamato,
Ayoi tazukuri	I tie up my garter strings
Koshizukurau mo	And gird my loins to make ready.

✳ Song 178, presented as a wazauta, is inserted into the account of the destruction of Prince Yamashiro no Ōe and his family by Soga no Emishi's son Iruka. Emperor Jomei died in 641 and was succeeded by his widow, who reigned as Empress Kōgyoku until 645. Iruka, the third generation of Soga king-makers, wished to secure the next succession for one of Jomei's sons, the subservient Prince Furuhito no Ōe, again passing over Prince Shōtoku's son Yamashiro no Ōe (one of the "Princes of the Upper Palace," as Shō-toku's children were called), although both had Soga mothers. The infamous incident related below occurred in 643. Iruka's rashness in attacking the family of the revered Prince Shōtoku brought the reproof of Iruka's father, Emishi, and led to the downfall of the Soga two years later. Despite the success of Yamashiro no Ōe's clever stratagem to mislead his enemies, he and his followers returned from hiding after several days; he then committed suicide with his family to avoid a civil war. The living quarters at Ikaruga burned by Kose no Tokoda stood on the site of the present eastern precinct of Hōryūji, the famous temple founded by Shōtoku Taishi. The temple, which was adjacent to the west, was itself burned in 670 (see no. 195); today's western precinct is a rebuilding farther to the west. The ranks Lesser Virtue (*shōtoku*) and Greater Benevolence (*dainin*) were second and third in a rank structure instituted in 603.

The song has been explained plausibly as originating in an utagaki, with the little monkey being a young woman who offers a goateed old man some rice in lieu of her sexual favors. The monkey may in fact be plural—a bevy of young women taunting the old man, a scene reminiscent of the one described in the prose introduction to nos. 1528–39, the encounter of the old bamboo-cutter and the nine maidens. The detailed explanation offered by *Nihonshoki* is modeled on similar passages in Chinese historical texts. If an utagaki song was indeed adapted to political satire (whether by "children" or chroniclers), the fact that Prince Yamashiro and his party were starving on Mount Ikoma no doubt has relevance to the offer of the rice.

178   [NS 110]

On the day Earth-Senior/Horse Soga no Omi Iruka plotted by himself to set aside the Princes of the Upper Palace and make Furuhito no Ōe Emperor. At this time there was a children's song that went:

Iwa no e ni	Up on top of a rock
Kosaru kome yaku	A little monkey's parching rice—
Kome dani mo	Come on, old fellow,
Tagete tōrase	At least have some rice and go,
Kamashishi no oji	You old mountain goat, you.

In the eleventh month, whose first day was Fire-Senior/Rat, Soga no Omi Iruka sent Kose no Tokoda no Omi of Lesser Virtue Rank and Haji no Saba no Muraji of Greater Benevolence Rank to carry out a surprise attack on Prince Yamashiro no Ōe and the others at Ikaruga. . . . Thereupon the slave Mitari and several dozen retainers went out and fended them off. Haji no Saba no Muraji was struck by an arrow and died. The troops drew back in fear. They said to each other, "The expression 'One man against a thousand'—does that apply to Mitari?" Yamashiro no Ōe then took the bones of a horse and threw them into his bedchamber. Finally, spotting an opportune moment, he led his consort and family and fled into hiding on Mount Ikoma. . . . The party led by Kose no Tokoda no Omi burned the palace at Ikaruga, and finding bones in the ashes, mistakenly thought that the Prince was dead, and so raised the siege and withdrew. . . . People of that time explained the application of the aforementioned song as follows: "'On top of a rock' refers to the Upper Palace. 'A little monkey' refers to Hayashi no Omi [Iruka]. . . . By 'parching rice' is meant burning the Upper Palace. And in 'Come on, old fellow, at least have some rice and go, you old mountain goat,' there is a reference to Prince Yamashiro's hair being streaked with white like that of a mountain goat. It also corresponds to his abandoning the palace and hiding in the depths of the mountain."

❋ In the rapid buildup of omens pointing toward the overthrow of the Soga in 645, the following song (no. 179) is retrospective, a report submitted in 644 of an incident some years earlier that was now deemed significant in the light of the events at Ikaruga the previous year. This time the allegory has the monkey as Prince Yamashiro no Ōe, and the interloper with the cracked hands as Iruka ("Soga no Kuratsukuri"). This wazauta, instead of being labeled a "children's song" or described as a song popular among the people, is attributed to one of the actors in the anecdote. The "ominous" nature of such songs (when "properly" interpreted) is heightened by their mysterious appearance in the mouths of monkeys, children, or other divinely innocent folk. Like no. 178, no. 179 probably comes out of an utagaki, where a young woman expresses her preference for her "dear lad" over the rough-handed swain who is accosting her.

179   [NS 111]

On the day Wood-Junior/Serpent there was report from Upper Shiki District to the effect that there had been a man who had seen a monkey having a noonday nap on Mount Miwa. He had stealthily seized it by the elbow without injuring its body. The monkey, its eyes still closed, had sung:

Mukatsuo ni	On yonder hilltop
Tateru sera ga	Standing there's a dear lad,
Nikode koso	One whose tender hand
Wa ga te o torame	Well may take this hand of mine;
Ta ga sakide	But this hand so cracked,
Sakide so mo ya	This cracked hand, oh, whose is this?
Wa ga te torasu mo ya	Does it take my hand, oh?

The man had been startled and frightened off by the monkey's song; he had let go and left. This incident was an omen that after the passage of several years the Princes of the Upper Palace would be besieged by Soga no Kuratsukuri at Mount Ikoma.

❋ The account leading up to the assassination of Soga no Iruka on the twelfth of the sixth month of 645 continues with three more wazauta, given in an entry a year earlier, in the sixth month of 644, almost immediately after the report of no. 179. The shamans (or mediums; kamunagi) cluster around the Soga leader, sacred wands in hand, presumably to pour their favorable omens into his ear. This passage duplicates one of the previous year, where the Ō-Omi is Emishi. Presumably the reference here is to Iruka, on whom the narrative concentrates at this point as the ultimate villain. Iruka, however, was not properly the Ō-Omi, though his father had begun to treat him as having the rank. The location of the bridge is not clear. Perhaps it was one across the Asuka River near the Soga estate of Shima no Shō. "A change in customs" is an allusion to Wen-hsüan and implies "for the better."

Songs 180–82, deprived of their ominous interpretations, can be seen as referring to country matters at a songfest. In the first, lovers hide in the tall grass, trying to escape the notice of the other revelers, who can be heard in the distance. The second is by a lover who has been discovered. The cackling of the pheasants is likened to the merciless glee of the onlookers. In the last song a foolish maiden regrets what she has lost, stating her case without recourse to metaphor. Songs such as these seem to be *about* an utagaki, rather than the direct addresses actually used at one. The political interpretation to which they are subjected in *Nihonshoki* comes in an entry a year later, after the events that they supposedly predicted. The interpretation of no. 180 makes the only reference to the erection of a palace by Prince Naka no Ōe, Empress Kōgyoku's son, beside the residence of his enemy Iruka. Naka no Ōe's confederate, Nakatomi no Kamako, is the later Fujiwara no Kamatari, the founder of the Fujiwara clan. According to the *Nihonshoki* account, Naka no Ōe and Kamako laid their plans while walking to and from their lessons with a teacher of Confucian studies. The man appointed by heaven in the interpretation of no. 181 is Naka no Ōe (later Emperor Tenji). Saeki no Komaro and Wakainukai no Amita were the members of Naka no Ōe's faction who delivered the death blows to Iruka in the presence of the Empress.

180   [NS 112]

This month the female and male shamans from throughout the country broke off sprigs of leaves, hung them with streamers of fine barken fiber, waited for the moment when the Ō-Omi crossed the bridge, and vied with each other in uttering the subtle oracles of the gods. There were a great many of these shamans, and it was impossible to distinguish what they were saying. The old people said, "This foretells a change in customs." At that time there were three songs. The first went:

Harobaro ni	Faint and far away
Koto so kikoyuru	Is heard the rustle of voices
Shima no yabuhara	In the thicketed plain of Shima.

181   [NS 113]

The second went:

Ochikata no	Off in the distance
Asano no kigishi	Pheasants in the shallow grass
Toyomosazu	Make the moors resound;
Ware wa neshikado	As for me, I lay softly—
Hito so toyomosu	It's others who make a noise.

182   [NS 114]

The third went:

Obayashi ni	I don't know his face,
Ware o hikirete	Neither do I know his home,

Seshi hito no	The man who took me,
Omote mo shirazu	Led me to the little grove,
Ie mo shirazu mo	And did it to me there.

Thereupon someone explained the first song, saying, "This song's saying, 'Faint and far away is heard the rustle of voices in the thicketed plain of Shima,' is a prediction that a palace would be erected beside the house of Shima no Ō-Omi, and that Naka no Ōe would secretly plan an act of Great Righteousness with Nakatomi no Kamako no Muraji, plotting to kill Iruka." He explained the second song, saying, "This song's saying, 'Off in the distance pheasants in the shallow grass make the moor resound; as for me, I lay softly—it's others who make a noise,' is a prediction that the Princes of the Upper Palace, mild in nature and completely innocent of any crime, would be slain by Iruka, and that though not taking revenge themselves, would have punishment inflicted on their behalf by a man appointed by heaven." He explained the third song, saying, "This song's saying, 'I don't know his face, neither do I know his home, the man who took me, led me to the little grove, and did it to me there,' is a prediction that Iruka no Omi would suddenly be put to death in the palace by Saeki no Muraji Komaro and Wakainukai no Muraji Amita."

✳ Another sign of the times occurring in the year before the downfall of the Soga was the appearance of a strange religion among the people. A person named Ōfube no Ōshi from the Fuji River district in eastern Japan propagated the worship of an enormous caterpillar that fed on orange trees, claiming (perhaps because of its connection with the *tachibana*; see p. 464) that it was the "god of Everworld [Tokoyo]." The cult swept the country with the aid of unscrupulous shamans, and people wasted their wealth on offerings. Hata no Kawakatsu, the head of a prominent kikajin (immigrant) clan with properties at Kazuno in the present city of Kyōto, was a fervent Buddhist, a fact that provides a plausible motivation for his suppression of the new cult. (Kawakatsu was the founder of the temple at Uzumasa in Kyōto known as Kōryūji or Uzumasadera.) The clan title Uzumasa (here Utsumasa) was granted to the Hata in the fifteenth year of the reign of Emperor Yūryaku. (*Hata*, "loom," refers to the clan's occupational specialty of weaving; *uzumasa* supposedly means "piled up higher," referring to piles of woven fabrics.) The title *miyatsuko* indicates that Kawakatsu was in charge of corporations of workers. The song seems to be firmly wedded to the anecdote and may be a genuine popular response to the event. Both song and event make a clearly ominous parallel to the murder of Iruka, the false prophet who was leading the people astray, and whom the shamans are depicted as eager to serve. Prodigies were occurring on all sides—ponds stank and turned strange colors, signs appeared in the sky, voices of monkeys were heard humming, and there were shrieks and cries for which no source could be found. In this context one may wonder if the tale of the caterpillar god also was not invented or elaborated for what were perceived as the proper ends of historiography.

183   [NS 115]

Hereupon Hata no Miyatsuko Kawakatsu of Kazuno, thinking it evil that the people were led astray, struck down Ōfube no Ōshi, and the shamans were afraid and stopped promoting this worship. The people of the time therefore composed a song, saying:

Utsumasa wa	"It's a god, a god!"
Kami to mo kami to	So came its fame resounding,
Kikoekuru	But Utsumasa
Tokoyo no kami o	Has struck down and punished it,
Uchikitamasu mo	That god of Everworld!

❋ One member of the Soga clan, Kurayamada Ishikawa no Maro, was Prince Naka no Ōe's ally in the coup d'état of 645. On the advice of Nakatomi no Kamako, Naka no Ōe had formed a marriage alliance with Ishikawa no Maro, who subsequently played a key role in the plot and was rewarded by being made Minister of the Right. In 649 Maro's half brother Musashi slandered him to Naka no Ōe, who was now Crown Prince, claiming that Maro was about to turn against Naka no Ōe. As a result of the Prince's credulity in this matter, Maro ended by committing suicide along with his family, and his body afterwards was subjected to mutilation. Naka no Ōe repented his rashness when an examination of Maro's personal effects established his innocence. Maro's daughter Miyatsukohime, the consort of Naka no Ōe and probably the same person as Ochi no Iratsume, Maro's elder daughter and mother of the future Empress Jitō, is reported to have died of grief. Nothing is known of Kawara no Maro, whose songs expressed the Prince's sorrow. The Kawara were a kikajin clan from Kawachi Province, and as a *fuhito*, or Scribe, Kawara no Maro was no doubt an educated man.

The first song (no. 184) allegedly shows an acquaintance with the ancient Chinese poetic anthology *Shih Ching* in its image of paired water birds. The analogy is positive—birds and lovers are alike in being well paired—but then is undercut in the last line by the bad outcome that spoils fair beginnings. This pattern too is found in *Shih Ching*, as is negative analogy, the type represented by no. 185. Because of the different syntactic structure of the two languages, the Chinese analogies, whether negative or positive, take the form of a disjunct "symbolic equation," whereas the Japanese usually employ some form of hypotaxis, here a concessive construction (*sakedo mo*—"although they bloom"). No. 115, an earlier example of negative analogy between nature and man, also uses a concessive link. The Man'yō poet Hitomaro, however, realizes a version of the disjunct pattern in the jo to his lament for Princess Asuka (see no. 338). But even in that case there is a mediating line, *nani shi ka mo* ("why, then?"), almost identical to the third line in no. 185. The anecdote also provides interesting evidence of the singing of tanka to koto accompaniment.

184   [NS 116]

The Crown Prince, hearing that Miyatsukohime had passed away, was sorely afflicted and wept in grief, in great extremity. At this, Kawara no Fuhito Maro of Nonaka presented songs. The songs went:

Yamagawa ni	On a mountain stream
Oshi futatsu ite	Once a duck and drake were paired,
Tagui yoku	Well paired were they,
Tagueru imo o	Even as my love and I—
Tare ka inikemu	Who has taken her away?

(The first)

185   [NS 117]

Motogoto ni	From every trunk of tree
Hana wa sakedo mo	Flower out the blossoms now—
Nani to ka mo	How then can it be
Utsukushi imo ga	That my young and precious love
Mata sakidekonu	Does not come to bloom again?

(The second)

In a sudden access of grief the Prince heaved a heavy sigh. "How fine! How sad!" he said in praise. And he provided him with a koto and had him sing them. Afterward he bestowed on him four rolls of silk, twenty pieces of cloth, and two bundles of floss.

❋ After the assassination of Soga no Iruka in 645, Empress Kōgyoku (the mother of Prince Naka no Ōe) abdicated in favor of her younger brother Kōtoku (r. 645–54). Kōtoku moved the capital to Naniwa, at the head of the Inland Sea, where Emperor Nintoku had reigned some two and a half centuries earlier. However, the real power rested with Naka no Ōe, who ruled first through Kōtoku and then through his mother, who returned to the throne on Kōtoku's death in 654. As related in the following account, the Prince simply made off with the court, including Kōtoku's consort Empress Hashihito, when his uncle crossed him by refusing to move the capital back to Asuka in 653. The "Imperial Grandmother" was Kōtoku's mother, Princess Kibi (also the mother of Empress Kōgyoku, and grandmother of Prince Naka no Ōe). Empress Hashihito, Kōtoku's consort, was Naka no Ōe's younger sister. The song captures the doting, suspicious, and possessive love of an older man for a much younger woman. Emperor Kōtoku was fifty-seven at this time, and Empress Hashihito in her early twenties. While there is no way of demonstrating that the song was not composed by Kōtoku himself, it reads very much like a popular ditty about the misfortune of a powerless old monarch. The allegorical mode links it to the wazauta and other satirical songs in this section of *Nihonshoki*.

186   [NS 118]

This year the Crown Prince submitted a request, saying, "May it please you, I desire that the court remove to the Yamato capital." The Emperor refused, and so the Crown Prince, escorting Her Highness the Imperial Grandmother and Empress Hashihito, and taking also his brothers the younger imperial Princes, went to live in a temporary palace at Kawara in Asuka. At this time the high court nobles, the officers of court, and the hundred officials all went along in the transfer. Because of this the Emperor was resentful and wanted to abandon his throne. He had a palace built at Yamazaki and sent a song to Empress Hashihito, saying:

Kanaki tsuke	I kept my pony
A ga kau koma wa	Standing stanchioned in a stall,
Hikide sezu	Never led her out—
A ga kau koma o	How can someone have seen her,
Hito mitsuramu ka	The pony I kept so well?

❋ After the death of Emperor Kōtoku in 654, his sister returned to the throne as Empress Saimei, reigning until her own death in 661. Several brief laments attributed to her are among the most affecting songs in the chronicles. In 658 the young Prince Takeru, a son of Prince Naka no Ōe and therefore grandson of Saimei, died. (Takeru's mother was probably the same Miyatsukohime, the daughter of Soga no Kurayamada Ishikawa no Maro, who had died of grief after her father's suicide; see note to nos. 184–85. Since Prince Takeru must have been born in 651, assuming his age is stated correctly in the account introducing nos. 187–89, it is apparent that Miyatsukohime lived on for at least two years after the tragic events of 649.) Prince Takeru was a mute, a fact that no doubt contributed to the Empress's feelings of pity and attachment. "After ten thousand years and a thousand autumns" is a formula for the future decease of a reigning sovereign. The

Imaki region where the young Prince's temporary tomb was made lies to the southwest of Asuka along the Hinokuma, Soga, and Yoshino rivers. For the significance of the cloud in the first song, see nos. 363 and 1484. The cloud, which seems originally to have stood for the spirit of the dead, blended readily into images of smoke from a funeral pyre on the introduction of cremation at the end of the seventh century (see nos. 354 and 1315-16). The opening two lines of no. 188 are identical to those of no. 1553, an old anonymous poem. In both cases the wounded deer is worked into a jo that culminates in the image of the soft grass on the riverbank where the deer goes to die, leaving a trail of blood. In Saimei's song the grass and the deer function together as a complex vehicle in a metaphor of early death. Song 189 is also based on a jo, one in which the Asuka River serves as the objective counterpart for the flood of grief sweeping over the Empress.

187   [NS 119]

In the fifth month the imperial grandchild Prince Takeru died at the age of eight years. They built a temporary tomb above Imaki Valley and laid him to rest. The Empress had always treasured the imperial grandchild for his docility, and she could not endure her sorrow, afflicting herself with lamentation to an extreme. "After ten thousand years and a thousand autumns he is to be buried together with Us in Our tumulus," she commanded her ministers. Thereupon she composed songs, saying:

Imaki naru	If there were a cloud
Omure ga ue ni	Standing there above the hill
Kumo dani mo	Of Imaki,
Shiruku shi tataba	Plain to see—if only . . .
Nani ka nagekamu	Would I need to grieve?

(The first)

188   [NS 120]

Iyu shishi o	Not that he was young,
Tsunagu kawahe no	I do not say he was so young
Wakakusa no	As the new grass
Wakaku ariki to	Along the river where they track
A ga mowanaku ni	The arrow-wounded deer.

(The second)

189   [NS 121]

| Asukagawa | Asuka River, |
| Minagiraitsutsu | Water brimming bank to bank, |

Yuku mizu no	Flows along the plain—
Aida mo naku mo	Ceaselessly as I am swept
Omōyuru kamo	By the flood of this longing.

(The third)

The Empress sang these songs from time to time and wept bitterly.

❋ Prince Takeru died in the fifth month of 658, and in the tenth month of that year Empress Saimei made an excursion to the hot baths of Ki. According to *Nihonshoki*, her grandson was still on her mind, and the following three additional laments are recorded as having burst from her lips on this occasion. Songs 190 and 191 are tanka; no. 192, which functions as a kind of envoy to the series, is a katauta. The two tanka incorporate a contrast between bright (*omoshiroki*, lit., "face-white") and dark (*kure*). *Omoshiroki* may mean no more than "pleasant," but the reference to Imaki is puzzling. Imaki ("New Fort"), the site of Prince Takeru's temporary burial, was far from the Okamoto Palace where Saimei reigned and, presumably, cared for the motherless young child. It may therefore be the white face of her grandson that the Empress imagines still shining "in Imaki" (*Imaki no uchi*). By contrast, the same region is cast in shadow as she turns away in no. 191 to follow the path of the sea. The sea "goes down" (*unakudari*), perhaps to an underworld, the world of the Yellow Springs (of Ki?), to which she voyages in search of the boy's soul. Speculative as such an interpretation may be, the mingled head-rhyme and repetitions of no. 191 have a hypnotic effect that beckons into some nether realm. The last glow is extinguished, and there is left only the dark rush of waves. It is of particular interest that the text specifies how these orally composed songs were recorded. The Hata, like the Kawara (see nos. 184–85), were of continental extraction.

190   [NS 122]

In winter, in the tenth month, whose first day was Metal-Senior/Dog, on the day Wood-Senior/Rat, there was an imperial excursion to the hot springs of Ki. The Empress remembered the imperial grandson Prince Takeru and wept sadly in her grief. And she cried out, saying:

Yama koete	I may cross mountains,
Umi wataru to mo	I may go across the sea,
Omoshiroki	But there is nowhere
Imaki no uchi wa	A forgetting of that face
Wasurayumashiji	White in its new fortress walls.

(The first)

191   [NS 123]

Minato no	From the harbor
Ushio no kudari	Where the rush of tide goes down,
Unakudari	Where the sea goes down,
Ushiro mo kure ni	Shall I go, leaving what is behind
Okite ka yukamu	In the darkness at my back?

(The second)

192   [NS 124]

Utsukushiki	Shall I go,
A ga wakaki ko o	Leaving him I held so dear,
Okite ka yukamu	My young child, behind?

(The third)

She issued an order to Ōkura no Miyatsuko Maro of the Hata, saying, "Pass down these songs; let them never be forgotten in the world."

✴ In 660, the sixth year of the reign of Empress Saimei, T'ang China entered into an alliance with Silla to destroy Paekche, the Korean state traditionally friendliest to Japan. Paekche crumbled under the combined attack, and King Ŭija was taken to captivity in China. Despite the apparent victory of the invasion forces, however, a resistance movement sprang up and achieved some initial success, only to be crushed in 663. The resistance leaders appealed to Japan for assistance and received a favorable hearing from the Empress. An expeditionary force was organized, and Prince P'ung, a member of the Paekche royal family resident as a hostage at the Japanese court, was returned and proclaimed King.

The following account mentions two evil omens that attended the ill-fated Japanese attempt at intervention and includes a highly obscure, perhaps deliberately scrambled, wazauta text. The translation is based on Tsuchihashi Yutaka's reconstruction. The political meaning to be derived from this version is that enemy soldiers are laying waste to Paekche, and that the Japanese response has been ineffectual. The "broad-backed hunchback" (hirakutsuma) is thought to refer to Tsu no Omi Kutsuma ("the Hunchback"), a Japanese envoy who returned from Paekche in 657. A similar agricultural metaphor to the wild geese ravaging the rice fields is used in the Paekche appeal to Japan, where the Silla allies of T'ang are referred to as "cutworm bandits." "Reversed stern and bow" in the prose narrative presumably means that the new ship was tied to the dock bow-in and was found to have turned 180 degrees during the night. Omino is thought to have been in Ise Province, a long haul from Suruga. Ōsaka Pass is in the high country between Shinano and Mino provinces. *Nihonshoki* reports another huge swarm of flies over Shinano in the summer of 627, the year before Empress Suiko died.

193   [NS 125]

This year it was desired to attack Silla on behalf of Paekche, and a command was issued to the province of Suruga to build a ship. After it was finished they hauled it to Omino, where without cause it reversed stern and bow during the night. People knew we would finally be defeated. Shinano Province reported a swarm of flies heading west over Ōsaka Pass. It was ten spans around and towered into the blue sky. Some knew this was a baneful omen of the defeat of the relief army. There was a children's song that went:

	Hirakutsuma no	In a paddy tilled
	Tsukureru	By a broad-backed hunchback
	Onoeda o	Up on the hilltop
	Karigari no kurau	Flocks of geese devour the rice.
5	Mikari no	The royal hunting
	Tawami to	Has been too timid:
	Onoeda o	In the hill paddy
	Karigari no kurau	Flocks of geese devour the rice.
	Mikoto	The royal command
10	Yowami to	Has been too weak:
	Onoeda o	In the hill paddy
	Karigari no kurau	Flocks of geese devour the rice.

❋ Empress Saimei moved the court to Kyūshū in 661, where she and her son Prince Naka no Ōe oversaw preparations for launching a Japanese expeditionary force to go to the aid of Paekche. (No. 255 recounts an incident along the way.) But the Empress suddenly died in the seventh month, and Naka no Ōe took time out from his military preparations to escort her body back to Asuka for temporary burial. The song attributed to the Prince could easily be read as a love poem from a woman to a man, but the use of *kimi* ("you"/"my lord") is here to be understood as an honorific directed toward the Empress's status. Still, *ō* ("great") is normally prefixed to *kimi* when used to refer to a sovereign. The idiom *me o hori* ("desire for your eyes"), meaning "desire to meet," is particularly powerful in its ironic resonance when referring to someone whose eyes have been closed in death. Naka no Ōe's attempt to rescue Paekche failed, and the remnant of the Japanese fleet returned in defeat in 663.

194   [NS 126]

In winter, in the tenth month, whose first day was Water-Junior/Swine, on the day Earth-Junior/Serpent, the Empress's cortege put to sea on its way

home. Hereupon the Crown Prince, anchoring in the same place, grieved
and yearned for the Empress. And he cried out:

Kimi ga me no	Out of my yearning
Kōshiki kara ni	For your eyes, My Lady,
Hatete ite	I have anchored here,
Kaku ya koimu mo	And that I should yearn so, too,
Kimi ga me o hori	Is from desire for your eyes.

❋ The following entry is from 670. In that year Hōryūji, the temple
founded by Prince Shōtoku, burned down, apparently the victim of an elec-
trical storm. The wazauta that the compilers apply to this event does actually sound like a children's game song, as they make it out to be, though it
has been described as an invitation sung to induce participation in an utagaki. *Nihonshoki* does not provide a gloss, but the compilers must have intended the lyrics to be understood as urging people to flee the burning
buildings. In a few instances, such as this, the wazauta is presented as a comment on an event, rather than as a foretelling of it.

195 [NS 127]

In summer, in the fourth month, whose first day was Water-Junior/Hare,
past midnight on the day Water-Senior/Monkey, there was a conflagration
at Hōryūji. Not one building was left. Heavy rain fell and thunder shook. In
the fifth month there was a children's song that went:

Uchihashi no	Please come out, girl,
Tsume no asobi ni	To the foot of the plank bridge
Idemase ko	Come to the games,
Tamade no ie no	Yaeko the mistress
5 Yaeko no toji	Of the house in Tamade.
Idemashi no	You won't be sorry
Kui wa araji zo	Afterwards for coming out,
Idemase ko	Please come out, girl,
Tamade no ie no	Yaeko the mistress
10 Yaeko no toji	Of the house in Tamade.

❋ In 671 there was a mass conferral of court rank on refugees from the
fallen state of Paekche who were of high status or had specialized training.
These men and their families became Japanese subjects, joining the significant component of the population that had crossed over from the continent
and settled in Japan ever since the fourth century A.D. The ranks bestowed in
671 were part of a system inaugurated by Emperor Tenji in 663. Greater
Brocade Lower was the ninth level from the top, Lesser Brocade Lower the

twelfth, Greater Mountain Lower the fifteenth, Lesser Mountain Upper the sixteenth, and Lesser Mountain Lower the eighteenth. The Department of Laws (Nori no Tsukasa) and Department of Letters (Fumi no Tsukasa) were part of the so-called Ōmi Administrative Code (*Ōmi Ryō*) established by Emperor Tenji in 671. Paekche also had a complex rank structure, of which Yŏ Chasin (one of the resistance leaders) and Sat'aek Somyŏng (a scholar) were in the highest category of "Minister" (*chwap'yŏng*). Most of the others were *talsol*, the second rank. It will be seen that the ranks bestowed on them in Japan were much lower in the corresponding scale.

The wazauta can be understood as satirizing either the fact that the Paekche officials were given Japanese ranks despite their foreign origin or the conferring of rank on so many all at once. *Kojiki* and *Nihonshoki* both report the importation of the tachibana, the ancient Japanese orange, in the reign of Emperor Suinin (third century A.D.?) from "the Land of Everworld," or Tokoyo no Kuni, by Tajimamori, a legendary person of Korean descent. This story undoubtedly points to an actual continental origin for the tachibana, as well as to a special mystique surrounding it. Thus the metaphor in song 196 is appropriate in its foreign associations. Stringing the oranges was done as part of the festivities of the fifth day of the fifth month, all of which aimed to tap the vigor of special flowers, fruits, and medicinal herbs.

196   [NS 128]

In this month the rank of Greater Brocade Lower was conferred on the ministers Yŏ Chasin and Sat'aek Somyŏng (assistants in the Office of Laws). Lesser Brocade Lower was conferred on Koesil Chipsa (head of the Department of Letters). Greater Mountain Lower was conferred on the *talsol* Kongna Jinsu (trained in military tactics), Mokso Kwija (trained in military tactics), Ok Yebongnyu (trained in military tactics), Tappon Ch'unch'o (trained in military tactics), [garbled] (adept in medicine), and Koesil Chipsin (adept in medicine). Lesser Mountain Upper was assigned to the *talsol* Tŏkchŏngsang (adept in medicine), Kiltaesang (adept in medicine), Hŏsolmo (learned in the Five Classics), and Kakpongmo (trained in Yin-Yang). Lesser Mountain Lower was assigned to the remaining *talsol* and others, over fifty individuals. There was a children's song that went:

Tachibana no	Oranges ripen
Ono ga edaeda	Each one on its separate branch,
Nareredo mo	But when the season
Tama ni nuku toki	Comes for stringing them as beads,
Oyaji o ni nuku	They are all strung on one string.

❋ The last songs in *Nihonshoki* are three wazauta presented in the entry on the death of Emperor Tenji, which occurred on the third of the twelfth month of the year corresponding to 671 (=January 7, 672). Tenji's younger brother, Prince Ōama, had recently resigned the succession and retired to Yoshino as a Buddhist monk, correctly reading the Emperor's desire to pass the throne to his son, Prince Ōtomo. There seems to have been bad blood between the brothers over Princess Nukata, who became, willingly or not, the Emperor's concubine after having been loved by Prince Ōama (see commentary to nos. 860–61). Ōama struck back six months after Tenji's death, crushing the forces of Prince Ōtomo (Emperor Kōbun) in a whirlwind campaign known as the Jinshin War, and took the throne as Emperor Temmu (r. 672–86).

The political interpretation intended for the songs is somewhat obscure. No. 197 may be taken to refer to Prince Ōama's difficult situation while in retirement at Yoshino (here "Eshino"), no. 198 to the speed of his military preparations, and no. 199 to the desirability of either direct negotiations or direct action. On another level, no. 197 has been taken as the utterance of the suffering peasants, who contrast their toilsome existence with the free lives of the fish. A grimmer interpretation is also possible. As in the other two songs, the voice may be that of a young woman. Like the speaker of no. 182, she has been taken by a man against her will. Raped, she is left to drown in the river. Unlike the trout, she cannot breathe in the water. As in the Matsura River sequence in *Man'yōshū* (see nos. 1049–59), the free-swimming trout, darting around a woman's body, are sexually suggestive. No. 198 probably describes the ardor of a young Prince on his first night with his bashful bride, a young woman of one of the noble clans. Finally, the red colt in no. 199, which is based on the preparation-conclusion technique of metaphor and application, stands for the diffident suitor, on whom the female speaker urges a more direct approach. This song appears as an anonymous poem in *Man'yōshū* (MYS XII: 3083/3069).

197 [NS 129]

In the twelfth month, whose first day was Water-Junior/Swine, on the day Wood-Junior/Ox, the Emperor passed away at the Ōmi Palace. On Water-Junior/Cock he was given temporary burial at the new palace. At the time there were children's songs that went:

Mieshino no	In fair Eshino
Eshino no ayu	The trout of Eshino—
Ayu koso wa	Oh, yes, the trout,
Shimahe mo eki	They are well by the island.
E kurushie	Ah, the pain of it!
Nagi no moto	Down in the water-leeks,
Seri no moto	Down in the cresses,
Are wa kurushie	Ah, the pain that I am in!

(The first)

198

Omi no ko no   Child of the Omi,
Yae no himo toku   I undo my eightfold sash,
Hitoe dani   But not one fold
Imada tokaneba   Have I yet undone when he,
Miko no himo toku   The Prince, has taken his off.

(The second)

199

Akagoma no   Here the red-roan colt
Iyukihabakaru   Shies away from plunging in—
Makuzuhara   Fields of arrowroot;
Nani no tsutekoto   Why these roundabout reports?
Tada ni shi ekemu   Face to face would be better!

(The third)

'Fudoki' Songs

The first ten songs are from Hitachi. It is thought that the fudoki of this province may have been the compilation of Governor Ishikawa no Naniwamaro, who served there from 714 to 718, and Assistant Governor Kasuga no Oyu, a learned former Buddhist monk. It is to be noted that the poet Takahashi no Mushimaro (see commentary to nos. 569–71) served in Hitachi under the next Governor, Fujiwara no Umakai (694–737). Mushimaro's interest in folklore is well known, but internal evidence suggests that this fudoki had probably been written by the fifth month of 718, before Umakai's arrival in the province. Hitachi is in eastern Japan, in the area of present-day Ibaragi Prefecture. Its most famous landmark was Mount Tsukuha (nos. 201–3; see also nos. 585–88). Tsukuha (now pronounced "Tsukuba") was renowned as a locus of utagaki, and the interest of the compilers in these revels, which seem to have been widespread in the province, is evident in what follows.

The first song (no. 200) apparently had wide distribution, for *Man'yōshū* has a variant version (no. 1542). Mount Hatsuse was in Yamato, not in Hitachi, and it seems likely that the content of the song led either the compilers or an earlier storyteller to join these lines to the legend of the female brigand Yukime. The district whose headquarters are referred to is Niiharu. Yukime (her name can also be read as Abura Okime, "Old Woman Oil") was probably the leader of a band of aborigines (see no. 10 and note). The *mori* ("grove") suggests that she had become a *kami*, and that the "stone chamber" (*iwaya*) was thought to be her grave. The song is a love song addressed by a man to his fearful sweetheart. If "stone fort" (*iwaki*) also refers to a stone burial chamber, the song becomes an appeal for the ultimate refuge of suicide. The somber metonymy of "fort" and "hide" (*komoru*; "take refuge") makes this a highly effective reading. But *iwaki* could also refer to a hilltop fort ringed with stones, and the invitation may be to lovers' flight and a wandering life in the mountains, hiding out in ancient strongholds. A third possibility would be that the lovers are to hide in broken and abandoned tombs.

200   [F 1 : Hitachi]

Fifty leagues east of the district is the village of Kasama. The road by which it is reached is over Mount Ashiho. The old people tell that once there was a mountain brigand there. Her name was Yukime no Mikoto. [Her] stone chamber still exists in the grove. There is a folk song that goes:

Kochitakeba	If their words should hurt,
Obatsuseyama no	Come with me to the stone fort
Iwaki ni mo	On Mount Hatsuse;
Ite komoranamu	Let us hide together there—
Na koi so wagimo	Do not pine, my love.

✳ Song 201 is an ancient chant of blessing translated into four-character Chinese phrases. The translation back into Japanese is conjectural (I have adopted Tsuchihashi Yutaka's), and the English translation is based on the meaning of the Chinese. The identity of the "ancestor deity" is left vague by both the storyteller and the commentators. The gods of Fuji and Tsukuha are the deified mountains themselves. They are imagined to observe (or break) the same taboo on letting outsiders into the house during the first tasting of the early rice that humans observed (or broke) in making the offerings (see no. 1499). Takahashi no Mushimaro describes the "sports and pleasures" of the songfest on Mount Tsukuha in nos. 587–88.

201   [F 2 : Hitachi]

The old people tell that once the ancestor deity made a round of visits to the various gods. He arrived at Mount Fuji in Suruga Province just at nightfall and asked for lodging for the night. But the god of Mount Fuji answered, saying, "It is the first tasting of the early grain, and the house is taboo. This one day I cannot admit you." At this the ancestor deity wept with vexation and cursed him, saying, "How is it that you do not give lodging to your parent? As long as you live, on the mountain where you dwell snow and frost shall fall winter and summer, cold shall pile upon cold, the people shall not climb up, and there shall be none to make offerings of food and drink." Then he climbed Mount Tsukuha and again asked for lodging. This time the god of Tsukuha replied, saying, "Tonight is the tasting of the new grain, but how could I dare refuse your request?" And he prepared food and drink and waited on him respectfully. Thereupon the ancestor deity sang, saying:

Hashiki kamo	Oh, well beloved,
Wa ga ko	My progeny,
Takaki kamo	Oh, lofty
Kamumiya	Shrine of gods!
5 Ame tsuchi no muta	Even with heaven and earth,
Hi tsuki no muta	Together with sun and moon,
Tamikusa tsudoikotohoki	The people shall gather to celebrate

Oshimono yutaka ni	With food and drink abundant,
Yoyo ni tayuru koto naku	Age after age never failing,
10 Hi ni ke ni iyasakaemu	Day after day more flourishing:
Chiyo yorozuyo ni	For a thousand autumns and ten thousand years
Tanoshibi kiwamaraji	Their sports and pleasures never spent.

It is because of this that snow is forever falling on Mount Fuji, making it impossible to climb, whereas on Mount Tsukuha the gathering in throngs, the songs and the dancing, the drinking and feasting, have never ceased to this very day.

❋ The prose setting for songs 202–3 is remarkably similar to that for no. 215, from Hizen. Both describe a mountaintop utagaki, but the songs selected by the Hitachi compilers are distinctive in being the utterances of a jilted lover. Their wry recognition that there are disappointments even in the permissive atmosphere of the annual revels suggests the existence of subgenres of the utagaki song, as well as a sense of humor on the part of the compilers. The mountaintop setting, with its appropriately designated "male" and "female" peaks, and the "supplies of food and drink" lead one to expect a more blissful result than is obtained either by the male speaker of the songs or by the daughter in the popular saying who comes home without a pledge. The two songs are structurally matched—proto-tanka with short second lines. They are presented not as part of a story but as typical songs that people sing. This typicality is to be expected as an aspect of a written account of oral performances set down at some considerable remove from the events. Only the folklorist with his note pad and tape recorder could have preserved the particularity of what one may reasonably suppose went on (poetically) at the ancient songfests. Oral composition must have resulted in songs that were repeated afterward and eventually reached the ear of someone able to write them down and motivated to do so. Mushimaro (nos. 587–88) claims to have been a participant, but he wrote his own poem rather than recording what he heard. It is also probable that original composition was not the sole mode of lyric behavior at the songfest, but that the already existing genre of utagaki songs was more or less freely drawn upon, the songs being altered as needed in the singing.

202   [F 3 : Hitachi]

Now, Mount Tsukuha soars above the clouds. At the summit the west peak is precipitous; it is called the male god and is not to be climbed. The east peak, on the other hand, is surrounded by crags on all four sides, and the ascent and descent are steep. To its side is a spring that never runs dry, summer or winter. When the blossoms open in spring, and when the leaves turn in fall, men and women from the provinces east of the slope come trooping up hand in hand, with supplies of food and drink. They arrive on horseback and on foot, climbing up and looking out from the top. There they frolic merrily and take their ease. [Two of] their songs go:

Tsukuhane ni	She would lie with me
Awamu to	Up on Tsukuha,
Iishi ko wa	She said, that girl—
Ta ga koto kikeba ka	Whose talk has she listened to,
Mine awazukemu	To have left me, lying so?

203   [F 4 : Hitachi]

Tsukuhane ni	Up on Tsukuha
Iorite	Sheltering
Tsuma nashi ni	Without a wife—
Wa ga nemu yoro wa	Here I lie alone tonight,
Haya mo akenu ka mo	And why won't the dawning come?

The songs they sing are many—too many to include all of them here. There is a popular saying that goes, "A daughter who comes home from the wooing on Mount Tsukuha without a pledge-gift is no daughter of mine."

✳ The next two songs are also given a descriptive rather than a narrative setting. This prose piece is one of the more ornate examples of Chinese balanced phraseology in the fudoki, and the lushly elegant spell it weaves is broken by the earthy Japanese voices of the songs. The entire composition nicely juxtaposes the pleasures of the shore with those of the mountains in the previous set (which however it does not follow immediately in the original text), and the two tanka would work easily enough as utagaki songs. One is optimistically amorous, the other modestly plaintive. Each is based on the preparation-conclusion technique, and no. 204 has internal repetition as well, matching its ground image of waves to provide a rhythmic momentum that seems sure to sweep the speaker into the arms of his girl. This sympathetic word-magic is set off against the plea for sympathy in no. 205, where the basic image is the aural one of the moaning wind. The use of *imo* ("sister"/"lover") and *tsuma* ("wife") in the same song is unusual and instructive. *Imo* implies desire, *tsuma* possession. These two songs are finely achieved poems. The locus of the description is Takahama ("High Dunes"), a village along the north shore of Kasumigaura, a huge brackish lake communicating with the sea in present Ibaragi Prefecture. Takahama was near the provincial seat of Hitachi, for which its beaches seem to have provided a resort. "Ninefold luminary" translates *chiu yang*, a term for the sun based on early Chinese myth.

204 [F 5 : Hitachi]

Now, in this land, in the happy time of fragrant and lush growth, and in the cool season of flurry and fall, ordering carriages they set forth, boarding boats they wander at their ease. In spring the blossoms by the bay take on a thousand hues; in autumn the leaves along the shore turn a hundred shades of color. Warblers are heard singing in the fields; cranes are seen wheeling over the drying strand. Village youths and fisher girls converge along the beaches; merchants and farmers pole their little boats back and forth. It goes without saying that on hot mornings in the three [months of] summer, and on evenings parched by the ninefold luminary, they whistle to their friends and lead their servants out to sit lined up on the curving beach, where they look far out across the sea. As the breath of the waves comes fanning over them, they who shun the heat shake off their oppressive cares; as the shadow of the hills gradually lengthens, they who pursue the cool let their joyful spirits expand. There is a song they sing that goes:

Takahama ni	Let the waves roll in
Kiyosuru nami no	To the dunes along the shore,
Okitsunami	Waves from the offing—
Yosu to mo yoraji	But it's not with them I'll be rolling
Kora ni shi yoraba	When I roll in the arms of my girl!

205 [F 6 : Hitachi]

There is also one that goes:

Takahama no	Under the high dunes
Shitakaze sayaku	Moans the wind along the shore—
Imo o koi	I yearn for a girl,
Tsuma to iwaba ya	Someone I could call my wife,
Shikotome shitsu mo	Be she ever so homely or poor.

✳ The Urabe clan served the Kashima Shrine in Hitachi as sacerdotalists. Their drinking song belongs to the same genre as no. 49.

206 [F 7 : Hitachi]

Again, every year on the tenth of the fourth month they have a festival where they pour the wine. Members of the Urabe clan, men and women, gather and make merry singing and dancing day upon day and night after night. They have a song that goes:

Arasaka no	Partake, you said,
Kami no misake o	Of the new and potent wine
Tage to	Of the god—
Iikeba ka mo yo	Oh, that must be the reason
Wa ga einikemu	I have gotten so drunk.

❋ The next two songs are given an elaborate narrative setting. The songs themselves have various obscurities but clearly belong to the utagaki context. The youth's song envisions the maiden dancing with the pine branch in hand, sacred streamers fluttering from it. The fact that the pair are called the god-youth and the god-maiden suggests that they are in the service of a shrine, and that the young woman is a kagura dancer. In the metaphor she is likened to a little island on which the pine tree grows. Her reply gives the impression of lines of youths and maidens facing each other, and picks up the image of the island to apply to all the other women, among whom she is hidden. (For other utagaki songs using images of wave and tide, see nos. 109 and 158.) The setting of the story is the seacoast south from Kashima to Namisaki in Ibaragi Prefecture, Samuta and Aze being places anciently under the local chieftains of Naka and Unakami. The legend of the two pines is told in another example of polished parallel prose. "Jade dew" is an obviously metaphorical decorative term. "Metal wind" is so called because autumn corresponds to metal in the Chinese five-agent system. Both the dew and the wind set the season at autumn. "Shearing" translates *chō* (Ch. *cheng*; Karlgren *t̂eng*, Morohashi 2), here used to represent the sound of wind in the trees. "Cinnamon moon" is from the Chinese legend of a cassia or cinnamon tree growing in the moon. "Wave-Hidden Pine" renders *namimatsu*, in which *nami* is a *kakekotoba* for "wave" and "see-not." "Pine Shavings" is a free rendering of *kotsumatsu*, "shavings pine," a derogatory term. Both names suggest the trees are still ashamed. The open acceptance of sexual encounter in utagaki songs contrasts with the sensitivity on this score that underlies this legend.

207 [F 8 : Hitachi]

To the south is the pine grove of Unai. Long ago there were a young boy and girl. (They are commonly referred to as the god-youth and the god-maiden.) The boy was called the Youth of Samuta of Naka, and the girl was named the Maiden of Aze of Unakami. Both were handsome in form and feature, the radiant blossoms of their villages. They heard of each other's fame and conceived the same desire; their reserve vanished. Months went by, days piled up; they would meet by chance at songfest gatherings. (These are commonly called *utagaki* or *kagai*.) Once the youth sang:

Iyazeru no	Ever more boldly
Aze no komatsu ni	Flourishing before my gaze,
Yū shidete	Strands of barken cloth
Wa o furimiyu mo	Trail from the small pine of Aze:
Azekoshima wa mo	Oh, Aze the little isle!

208 [F 9 : Hitachi]

The maiden sang in reply:

Ushio wa	He said he would stand
Tatamu to iedo	Steadfast in the line of tide,
Nase no ko ga	But that lad of mine
Yasoshimagakuri	Spots me amid eighty isles
Wa o mi sabashiri	Hidden, and comes a-running.

At this point they wanted to talk but were afraid people would know. And so they left the festival grounds and hid under the pines. Hand in hand and knee aligned with knee, they poured out their hearts and confessed their passion. Once they had released the accumulated humors of their old longing, they broke into repeated smiles at their new happiness. It was the time of jade dew on the twigs, the season of metal wind shearing through trees. Off to the west, where the lambent, glistening cinnamon moon shone down, lay the sandbar destination of the raucous cranes; off to the east, where the ruffling, gusting autumn breeze sang cool in the pines, stood the coppiced hill crossed by the wild geese. The mountain was still and lone, the rock spring old; night moaned sere, and the smoky frost was new. The nearby mountain drew their gaze to the color of yellow leaves scattering in the woods; the distant sea let them hear only the voice of blue waves thundering on the rocks. To be together in this place tonight: pleasure beyond all pleasure. They were utterly lost in the sweetness of their colloquy and completely forgot that night would soon be over. Suddenly cocks were crowing, dogs were barking—dawn was in the sky, and the day was bright. Caught by surprise, the young couple did not know what to do. Finally, ashamed to be discovered, they changed into pine trees. The youth they called the Wave-Hidden Pine, and the maiden Pine Shavings. These names were given long ago and have never been altered to the present day.

❋ The text of song 209 is somewhat obscure. The reading and translation given below follow Akimoto. The story to which the song is attached belongs to the worldwide category of metamorphic myth in which birds change into women ("white bird," *hakuchō*, means "swan" in Japanese; see also no. 221). Legends explaining the origin of place-names were of specific interest to the compilers of fudoki. The district referred to was Kashima. Emperor Ikume, better known by his Chinese style of Suinin, should probably be placed in the third century A.D. The song seems to be based on two things: observation of the nest-building of water birds and a play on *tsutsumi* ("embankment") and *tsutsumu* ("enfold").

209   [F 10 : Hitachi]

Thirty leagues north of the district is the village of Shirotori. According to what the old people say, in the time of the Emperor Ikume there were white birds that flew down from the sky and changed into maidens. They would fly back up in the evening and down again in the morning. They picked up stones to make a pond and tried to build a bank, but piled up days and months in vain, for no sooner had they built it than it would crumble. They were unable to build it [in the end]. The maidens [sang]:

Shirotori no	White birds'
Ha ga tsutsumi o	Wings the embankment
Tsutsumu to mo	Embosom, but
Arafu mashiroki	Blotched or pure white,
Ha koe	Wings break.

So singing, they all flew up into the sky and did not come down again. It is because of this that the place is called Shirotori ("White Bird") Village.

✳ The next four songs are from Harima, a province at the eastern end of the Inland Sea corresponding to the southern half of present Hyōgo Prefecture. *Harima Fudoki* is heavily anecdotal, emphasizing stories about Emperor Ōjin and several of the deities that appear in the national mythology recorded in the chronicles. It was probably compiled in 715 or 716. One candidate for compiler is Sazanami no Kafuchi, a kikajin from Paekche who served as Senior Clerk in the province starting in 712.

Ome Moor in the origin anecdote attached to no. 210 was east of Kakogawa, a city west of Akashi on the Inland Sea. Homuda is the name of the sovereign known in dynastic lists as Ōjin Tennō. There are two origin explanations in this story—one for the place-name Ome, and another for the name Sasa. The song, an early chōka, happens to contain both words, no doubt the reason for its inclusion. The original significance of the song is lost, but a metaphorical interpretation is plausible, the beautiful dwarf bamboo perhaps standing for a young woman, and the hail and frost for the forces, social or natural, opposed to her and her lover. The repetitions are typical of early song. (For other mentions of hail, see nos. 215, 461, and 886; for "surveying the four directions," no. 1246.)

210   [F 11 : Harima]

The reason that . . . Omeno is named Omeno is this: When Emperor
Homuda lodged on these fields during a tour of his realm, he surveyed the
four directions and asked, "What is that out there? The sea? A river?" His
attendants replied, "That is mist." Then he said, "The larger shapes are
visible, but there is no detail [ome]." For this reason the place was called
Omeno ["Ome Moor"]. Thereupon his attendants sank a well, and it was
called the Well of Sasa ["Dwarf Bamboo"]. Because of this moor he composed a song:

Utsukushiki	On the lovely leaves
Ome no sasaba ni	Of the dwarf bamboo of Ome
Arare furi	Let the hail come down,
Shimo furu to mo	Let the frost come down, but you,
Na kare so ne	Pray do not wither,
Ome no sasaba	Dwarf bamboo leaves of Ome.

❊ The account in which songs 211–12 are included retells the story of
Princes Oke and Woke (nos. 105, 153–56), who lived in hiding in Harima
after the murder of their father by his cousin Emperor Yūryaku. (The father, here referred to as Emperor Ichibe [or Ichinobe], has not been included
in the official list of sovereigns. Oke and Woke are also called Emperors,
which is what they eventually became.) It is not clear just what the "stone
chamber" in which the Princes and their attendant hid was; see no. 200. The
two chants are recorded primarily in semantic orthography, with only the
epithet *tarachishi* in no. 211 and the suffix -*rama* in no. 212 being written in
phonograms. No. 211 corresponds roughly to the finale of no. 153, where
the dancer addresses his audience on the subject of his dance. The blessing
on the new house, which makes up the main part of no. 153, has been omitted. *Tarachishi* is a mock epithet for Kibi, the name of a province down the
coast from Harima (see no. 54), through *kibi*, "millet." The meaning of the
epithet is either "fulfilling" or "drooping," in either case conveying the image of a rich abundance. The "true metal" is iron, as indicated in the original
orthography. The song is a typical example of preparation-conclusion, with
the first four lines constituting the jo. *Tautsu* ("to till," lit., "to strike a
field") is taken up in *ta ute* ("strike hands"), that is, beat time for the dance.
    No. 212 combines elements of nos. 155–56, as well as no. 105. Again,
the song is based on the preparation-conclusion technique fundamental to
much ancient verse. Here there are three stages of introduction: Ōmi introduces Yamato, Yamato the father, and the father the son. The province of
Ōmi was famous for its great lake (Lake Biwa) and is used to balance the
mention of mountain-ringed Yamato. *Aogaki* ("green-fence"), a traditional

encomium for Yamato (see no. 30), is introduced as a predicate and then reused as an epithet. Such elaborate step-by-step preparation has the effect of crowning the "slave" with all the glories of his land and ancestry. The Princes' mother is Haehime in *Nihonshoki*. The name Tashiraga does not appear in that work, but the then-reigning Emperor, Yūryaku's son Seinei, has the name Shiraga ("Whitehair"). The woman who welcomed the Princes in the *Kojiki* account is their aunt, Princess Iitoyo, who assumed the reins of government after the death of Emperor Shiraga in *Nihonshoki* (no. 157).

211   [F 12 : Harima]

Emperors Oke and Woke were residing in this land because when their father, His Highness the Emperor Ichibe, was killed on Kudawata Moor in the province of Ōmi, they fled there, taking Kusakabe no Muraji Omi with them, and hid in a stone chamber in this village. Afterward Omi, knowing the seriousness of his offense, cut his horse's reins and set it free, and took all his gear, saddles and whatnot, and burned them. Then he hanged himself. Then the two boys hid here and there, wandering east and west, finally being employed in the house of Itomi, the village chief of Shijimi. They were ordered to tend the fire at a party for Itomi's new house and made to sing songs. Hereupon elder and younger brother deferred to each other, until finally the younger stood up and chanted. The words went:

Tarachishi	Drooping millet
Kibi no magane no	Kibi true metal
Saguwa mochi	Mattock in hand,
Tautsu nasu	Tilling the paddy:
Ta ute kora	Clap hands, boys—
Are wa mai semu	I'm going to dance.

212   [F 13 : Harima]

Again he chanted. The words went:

Ōmi wa	Ōmi
Mizu tamaru kuni	Is a land of standing water,
Yamato wa	Yamato
Aogaki	A green fence:
Aogaki no	In green-fence
Yamato ni mashishi	Yamato reigned
Ichibe no sumera mikoto ga	His Sovereign Highness Ichibe,
Mianasue	Whose scion,
Yatsukorama	This slave, am I.

Then everyone came running out in fear and trembling. At this, Yamabe no Muraji Otate, who had been sent to look after Yamato interests in Harima

Province, having listened and observed, spoke: "On account of these boys their mother, Her Highness Tashiraga, does not eat by day and does not sleep at night; she hovers between life and death, weeping and yearning." And thus it was that he went up and reported matters as above. Then she wept in joy and sorrow and sent Otate back to summon them. And they looked at each other, talked to each other, and felt mutual attachment. Afterward [the Princes] went back and built palaces in this land and dwelt there. Thus there are the palaces of Takano, Ono, Kawamura, and Ikeno. Furthermore, the place where they built the imperial granary [*miyake*] is called the village of Miyake, and the place where they built their storehouse [*kura*] is called Mikurao.

❋ Song 213 is reminiscent of no. 74, also about a giant tree made into a boat. As there, it is Emperor Nintoku (who reigned at Naniwa) with whom the anecdote is associated. (For other references to the giant tree legend, see no. 123 and note.) "Let it go at that" could also be rendered "stopped using the boat." The imperial storehouse at Suminoe was the landmark toward which the boat headed on its daily trips to the well at Akashi. The song shows the satirical side of the prevailing interest in names.

213   [F 14 : Harima]

The well of Komate at the Akashi post station: In the time of the Emperor of Takatsu Palace at Naniwa a camphor tree grew by the well. In the morning sun it shaded the island of Awaji, and in the evening sun it shaded Yamato Isle. When they cut down that camphor tree to make a boat, the boat was so swift it seemed to fly—in one oar-stroke it crossed seven waves. And so they named it Swift Bird. Morning and evening they boarded this boat and drew water from this well for the imperial table. Once when it was not in time for the Emperor's meal, someone composed a song and let it go at that. The song went:

Suminoe no	Only if you fly
Ōkura mukite	When you head for the storehouse
Tobaba koso	At Suminoe
Hayatori to iwame	Shall we call you a swift bird—
Nani ka hayatori	What's a swift bird about you?

❋ There are two songs in the portions of *Hizen Fudoki* that have come down to us. The province of Hizen corresponds to the prefectures of Saga and Nagasaki in northwestern Kyūshū. Its fudoki probably was compiled at Dazaifu, like those of the other Kyūshū provinces, but the compiler's name has not been preserved. The surviving work shows interest in the origins of place-names and the Kyūshū campaigns of such national figures as Emperor Keikō, Yamato Takeru, Empress Jingū, and Emperor Sujin.

No. 214 is an utagaki song set in a context that combines a legend of parting with a myth of metamorphic marriage. This combination of disparate elements provides suggestive evidence of the malleable nature of folk song and story. According to *Nihonshoki*, Ōtomo no Sadehiko was twice sent on expeditions to Korea, in 537 and again in 562. The story attached to no. 214, also told as MYS V: 875–79/871–75, belongs to the earlier of these expeditions, one in which Sadehiko successfully carried out a mission to support Mimana against Silla (see no. 169). In the legendary versions preserved in *Hizen Fudoki* and *Man'yōshū*, Sadehiko paused in Kyūshū and married a local beauty, called Otohihime in the former and Matsura no Sayohime in the latter. The *Man'yōshū* account and poems concentrate on the one image of her waving of her scarf (*hire*) to her lover as he departs, at once a gesture of farewell and an act of sympathetic magic designed to ensure his return. The fudoki story incorporates an additional detail, in which the lady drops a mirror that Sadehiko gave her on the day of parting and loses it in a river crossing, thenceforth known as Mirror Crossing. This symbolic loss of the chance to see her man again forecasts her own drowning in the part of the tale translated here. The motif of the scarf-waving is somehow reminiscent of the "Ten Songs of the Seafolk of Shika" (nos. 648–57), in which the doomed boatman Arao waves his sleeve from the sea. It also brings to mind the figure of Ōbako, the wife of Tsuki no Kishi Ikina, waving her scarf from atop the fortress of Kara (nos. 171–72), a detail that *Nihonshoki* includes in its account of the events of 562, the year of Sadehiko's second expedition to Korea. The stormy seas separating Japan and Korea are haunted by these images.

Onto this story of parting is grafted a version of the snake deity myth found elsewhere in early sources (see no. 122, commentary, and note). In its use of the stratagem of the thread it resembles one of the *Kojiki* stories, but the woman's death (rather than pregnancy) as a result of her encounter with the man-snake relates it to the setting of no. 122. This snake seems to be a water monster, one that entices, destroys, and perhaps devours its victims, depending on how literally "bones" is to be taken. This myth makes a sinister mirror-reversal of the water-goddess story in which the female offers eternal life to the mortal male (see nos. 216–20 and 579–80). The third element, the song, in which a man speaks of sleeping with an *otohime*, a "younger [sister] lady," for a single night, belongs to the world of the songfest revels, and says essentially the same thing as no. 79. The fortuitous resemblance of *otohime* to "Otohihime," the name of Sadehiko's bride, may have been suggestive to the *bricoleur* who joined the heterogenous parts of this poem-tale. The ductility of song is illustrated by how easily *kudasamu*

("I'll send her down") takes on a grim significance in its new context. Scarf-Waving Peak is east of Karatsu City in present Saga Prefecture. It commands a view of Matsura Bay; nearby is the village of Kagami ("Mirror").

214   [F 15 : Hizen]

Scarf-Waving Peak. (East of the district. The place of the signal fires is named Scarf-Waving Peak.) When Ōtomo no Sadehiko no Muraji left in his ship to cross over to Mimana, the lady Otohi climbed up to this place and waved her scarf to bring him back. Thus it was named Scarf-Waving Peak. Now, after five days had passed since the parting of the lady Otohi and Sadehiko no Muraji, there was a man who came every night and slept with the woman, leaving early at the break of dawn. His form and figure resembled those of Sadehiko. The woman thought this strange and was unable to keep silent. She secretly attached a thread to the skirt of the man's clothing and followed it up the peak to the edge of the marsh, where she found a sleeping serpent. Its body was that of a human and was sunk on the bottom of the marsh, while its head was that of a snake and was resting on the bank. Suddenly it turned into a man and sang:

Shinohara no	Once I've taken her,
Otohime no ko o	Slept with her a single night—
Sahitoyu mo	That little lady,
Inetemu shida ya	The girl from the bamboo brakes—
Ie ni kudasamu	I'll send her down to her home.

At this, the lady Otohi's maid ran and informed her family, who got up a crowd [of villagers] and climbed up to see. Both the snake and the lady Otohi had vanished. Then they looked down at the bottom of the marsh, and there, all alone, was the corpse of a human being. Each said to the other that these were the bones of the maiden Otohi, and so they built a tomb on the south side of the peak and laid them to rest. This tomb can still be seen.

❋ The similarity in the prose settings of songs 215 and 202–3 has already been pointed out (see also nos. 587–88). There seems to have been a basic descriptive pattern for mountaintop utagaki. (These mountaintop settings are also reminiscent of the preface to no. 1528.) The song is a version of nos. 69 and 886. All of these climax in the amorous gesture of the last line. The epithet *arare furu* ("where the hail comes down") may relate to an onomatopoeic quality in the names Kishima or Kishimi. Mount Kishima is southeast of the city of Takeo in the southern part of present Saga Prefecture.

215   [F 16 : Hizen]

Kishima District. Two leagues south of the district is a solitary mountain. It has three peaks in a line from southwest to northeast. Its name is Kishima. The southwest peak is called Hikogami ["Male God"], the one in the middle is called Himegami ["Female God"], and the one to the northeast is called Mikogami ["Child God"]. (Another name is Ikusagami ["the God of Armies"]; when it moves, troops rise.) Every year the young men and women from the villages, carrying wine and cithern, climb up hand in hand and gaze out over the valley. They play music, drink, sing, and dance, and when the songs are over they go home. The words of [one of their] songs go:

Arare furu	Where the hail comes down
Kishima ga take o	On the heights of Kishima
Sagashimi to	The climb is steep:
Kusa torikanete	I lose my grip on the grasses,
Imo ga te o toru	I grasp the hand of my girl.

This is a Kishima measure.

❋ *Tango Fudoki* exists only in three anecdotal fragments, of which the two containing songs are included here. Tango Province, corresponding to the northern part of Kyōto Prefecture, lay along the Sea of Japan. The longest fragment is the story of Urashima, the young fisherman who achieved immortal marriage in a realm beyond time, but fell victim to homesickness and alienated his luck by returning to his native village and breaking the taboo against opening a forbidden box. The story was retold by Takahashi no Mushimaro in chōka form (nos. 579–80). Mushimaro locates the tale at Suminoe on the Inland Sea. In both versions the hero spends three years of blissful marriage in a land across the sea, only to discover on his return home that time in the mortal world runs by a different clock. In both he opens the box, allowing the escape of an effluvium that could be his luck or his soul. It flies off to Tokoyo, Everworld, leaving him bereft—of life itself in the Man'yō poem, where he abruptly ages and dies. The fudoki account ends more ambiguously. The "fragrant shape" that returns to Tokoyo could be the goddess's spirit that has gone with the hero to keep him safe, but now forsakes him. The narrative stops short of stating that Urashima ages and dies, though that is the classic formulation of the legend as it is generally known in Japan.

In the fudoki version the sea goddess first appears in the form of a tortoise; the corresponding stories in the chronicles (see commentary to nos. 579–80) have her become a *wani* (a crocodile or shark). These metamorphic forms suggest that her palace is at the bottom, rather than merely across, the sea, and in *Kojiki* the palace is said to be made of fish scales and has direct communication with the finny tribe. The fudoki account, however, has a Chinese overlay, in that Tokoyo is specifically identified with P'eng-lai (J. Hōrai), the mythical Taoist island of the immortals. As the abode of the Pleiades and the Hyades, its associations are as much celestial as pelagic. The motif of magic sleep preserves its mystery and is also suggestive of the swift passage of time. A paradise myth of human desire fulfilled, the narrative gives metaphorical expression to the spell of sexual encounter, the time-out-of-time that is the heart of the story.

The myth is made into a legend and given local habitation in the village of Tsutsukawa on the northeast coast of the Yosa Peninsula. The hero is identified with Shimako, the ancestor of a local clan, but an unreconciled separate tradition states that Shimako was the same as Urashima no ko ("the lad Urashima") from Mizunoe on the northwest side of the peninsula. It is apparent that there was already an independent written account of the Urashima legend by Iyobe no Umakai (d. ca. 702), who served as Governor of Tamba Province before 713, the year in which Tango Province (including the Yosa Peninsula) was administratively separated from it, and that this account must have been the source of the conflation of the two traditions. Umakai was a learned official who has a Chinese poem preserved in *Kaifūsō*, and it is likely that his version had something to do with the highly literary style of the fudoki narrative. When homesickness overcomes him, Shimako quotes lines from the *Analects* and the *Classic of Rites*. The tale (like the version in *Nihonshoki*) is placed in the reign of Emperor Yūryaku.

The literary shaping of the legend is continued in the five tanka that are appended to it. They consist of an exchange between the hero and the goddess, followed by the comments of a later person. This structure is identical to that of nos. 1049–59, the elegant Chinese-inspired poem-tale attributed to Ōtomo no Tabito. Four of the songs are related to the story by references to Tokoyo or Urashima and the forbidden box, and were either traditional to the Tango version of the legend or composed to go with this redaction of it. Song 217, however, is a version of no. 55, a song of parting obviously familiar to the tale-makers of both fudoki and *Kojiki*. It is integrated into the present sequence through the image of clouds, present in both no. 216 and the prose narrative. (Clouds are the goddess's chariot, as well as the "fragrant shape" that escapes from the box.) No. 216 belongs to the old tanka structure in which the last line repeats the second, with the modification that the repetition here is altered to an echo that gives back parallel structures and similar sounds, but different meaning. In no. 217 the clouds are part of the jo, which culminates in the syntactic double *sokiori* ("draw back").

Shimako's second song (no. 218) is particularly haunting. *Asato*, the first opening of the door in the morning, should signal a lover's departure, but here instead it provides an outlook over the vast intervening space from which clouds have drawn back, and where only the sea stretches with its endless sound of waves. The word takes on a metaphorical sense of "the door of morning"—a going out into a glistering, naked world of dawn, emptiness, and emotion from which one cannot hide. The wave-beaten beach is that of Tokoyo, now audible across the world but forever unattainable. The "person of a later time" whose contributions complete this journey of lost love speaks first in his own voice, and then in Urashima's. In its "if only he hadn't . . . there might have been" stance, no. 219 is reminiscent of no. 888, also a stranger's comment about a metamorphic marriage. No. 220 is a reprise, like an envoy after a chōka. It brings in the clouds again, drifting as in the first song in the direction of Tokoyo.

216   [F 17 : Tango]

Yosa District, Hioki Township. In this township is the village of Tsutsukawa.

The people hereabout say that the ancestor of the Kusakabe no Obito was called Tsutsukawa no Shimako. From birth he was endowed with an outstanding loveliness of face and figure, an unexampled elegance. This was the well-known lad Urashima of Mizunoe. This does not conflict with what was written by the former Governor Iyobe no Umakai no Muraji. Thus we give a rough account of the essentials of the story.

In the reign of the Emperor who ruled the realm from the Asakura Palace at Hatsuse, Shimako boarded his little boat alone and drifted out on the ocean to hook fish. Three days and nights had gone by without his catching a single fish, when he caught a five-colored tortoise. Thinking it curious and odd, he placed it in the boat. No sooner had he gone to sleep than it turned into a woman. Her appearance was beautiful beyond all compare.

Shimako asked, "Who are you, who have come so suddenly, here far from human habitation on the unpeopled plains of the sea?"

The maiden smiled and replied, "A man of elegance was drifting alone on the blue sea. I was unable to surmount my desire to speak with him close at hand and came on the windy clouds."

Shimako asked again, saying, "Those windy clouds—whence have they come?"

The maiden replied, "I am from the dwellings of the immortals in heaven. I beg you, do not be suspicious of me, but let us be companions in the sweetness of talk."

Then Shimako knew she was a goddess; his mind was filled with caution, dread, and doubt.

The maiden spoke to him, saying, "Your lowly handmaiden's devotion will end with heaven and earth, will last as long as the sun and moon. But what of you, my lord—before going further I must know at once whether or not you agree."

Shimako replied, "There is nothing more to be said. How should I be indifferent?"

The maiden said, "Please ply the oar and let us be on our way to Mount Hōrai." Shimako followed her instructions, and the maiden caused sleep to descend upon his eyes. Before he knew it, they had arrived at a large island in the sea. The ground was as if spread with jewels. Towered gates cast dark shadows, lofty halls gleamed cool as jade. Eyes had never seen, nor ears heard of such a place. He and she strolled hand in hand up to the gate of a grand mansion.

"Wait here a moment, my lord," the maiden said, and opened the gate and went in. Then seven children came and said to each other, "This is Kamehime's husband." Again, eight children came and said to each other, "This is Kamehime's husband." By this he learned that the maiden's name was Kamehime ["Tortoise Princess"]. Then the maiden came out, and when Shimako told her about the children, said, "The seven children are the Pleiades. The eight children are the Hyades. Do not think them strange." And she went ahead of him and escorted him inside.

The maiden's father and mother came out to welcome him, bowed, and settled him on a seat. They explained the difference between the human and immortal realms and talked of the joy of a chance meeting between man and deity. Meanwhile, they pressed on him a hundred delicacies, and the brothers and sisters plied him with wine, lifting high their cups in an exchange of toasts, as bright-faced young girls from neighboring villages mingled merrily among them. Songs of the immortals rang on the air; dances of the deities wound in and out; their joyous carouse surpassed mortals' a myriadfold. What with one thing and another, they were unaware the sun had set, but at twilight the gathered immortals gradually withdrew, until only the maiden was left. Shoulder to shoulder, sleeve touching sleeve, they followed the rule of husband and wife.

Three years had gone by since Shimako had left behind his old home and journeyed to the city of the immortals. Suddenly there arose within him a yearning for his native earth; alone, he longed for his parents. He was always bemoaning his sadness, and his sighs increased from day to day. The maiden asked him, "When I look upon your face these days, my husband, it is different from usual. Pray let me hear your wish."

Shimako responded, "The ancients have said, 'The small man yearns for his native earth, the dying fox rests its head upon its own hill.' Your servant thought these words were empty talk; now he knows their truth."

The maiden asked, "Do you want to go home, my lord?"

Shimako answered, "Of late I left my old, familiar homeland and came far away to the realms of the immortals. My homesickness past enduring, I have broken down and confessed my worthless feelings. What I yearn to do is go back to my native country for a little while and pay my respects to my parents."

The maiden wiped her tears, sighed, and said, "My intent is iron and stone, and I looked forward to ten thousand years together. How can you be so concerned about your village as to abandon me for even a moment?" And she walked with him to and fro, hand in hand, talking and lamenting. Finally she waved her sleeves and they departed, arriving at the forking of the ways. Then the maiden's parents and all her family saw him off, overwhelmed with grief at parting. The maiden took a jewel box and handed it to Shimako, saying, "If in the end you do not abandon your lowly handmaid and have regard to visit me again, hold tight to this box, but be sure never to open it and look inside."

At last they parted, and he boarded his boat. Then she caused sleep to descend upon his eyes. In no time he arrived at the hamlet of Tsutsukawa in his native land. Then he gazed up at the village. Everything and everyone had changed and shifted; there was nothing by which he could orient himself.

Thereupon he asked a villager, "Where is the family of the lad Urashima of Mizunoe?"

The villager replied, "Where are you from, that you ask about someone of the distant past? I have heard that the elders have passed down from of old how in a previous age there was a lad Urashima of Mizunoe who went out alone on the blue sea and never came back. Now over three hundred years has gone by—why all of a sudden are you asking about him?"

Bewildered, Shimako wandered about the village for ten days without meeting anyone he knew. Then he caressed the jewel box and thought lovingly of the goddess. Shimako forgot the terms of the previous day's agreement and suddenly opened the box. Before he could look inside, a fragrant shape trailed out on the windy clouds, flying up into the blue sky. Shimako had broken his vow, and he knew it would be hard to meet again. He turned his head, his footsteps faltering; he choked on his tears, wandering to and fro. Then he wiped his tears and sang:

Tokoyohe ni	Clouds rise, cross over
Kumo tachiwataru	To the way of Everworld;
Mizunoe no	Carrying the words
Urashima no ko ga	Of the lad Urashima
Koto mochiwataru	Of Mizunoe, they cross.

217   [F 18 : Tango]

The goddess sent a fragrant sound flying afar, singing:

Yamatohe ni	Though the wind may blow
Kaze fukiagete	Toward the land of Yamato,
Kumobanare	And the clouds draw back—
Sokiori to mo yo	Though you draw away from me,
Wa o wasurasu na	Do not forget me, lord.

218   [F 19 : Tango]

Still unable to overcome his longing, Shimako sang:

> Kora ni koi   Yearning for my girl,
> Asato o hiraki   I open the morning door,
>   Wa ga oreba   And here I am:
> Tokoyo no hama no   From the shores of Everworld
> Nami no to kikoyu   Comes the sound of breaking waves.

219   [F 20 : Tango]

A person of a later time followed and added songs that went:

> Mizunoe no   Had the jewel box
> Urashima no ko ga   Of the lad Urashima
>   Tamakushige   Of Mizunoe
> Akezu ariseba   Gone unopened, yet again
> Mata mo awamashi o   Might they have had a meeting.

220   [F 21 : Tango]

> Tokoyohe ni   Clouds rise, cross over
> Kumo tachiwataru   To the way of Everworld;
>   Tamakushige   Ever so little
> Hatsuka ni akeshi   I opened the jewel box,
> Ware zo kanashiki   And how sad I am for that!

❋ The story in which no. 221 is set belongs to the worldwide myth of the sky woman (see also no. 209). Like her counterpart the sea woman, she brings blessings to mortals—love, wealth, and hints of immortality. Instead of luring a man away to a magic realm in the sea, she comes, like a bird, as a visitant and then disappears. She may actually be a bird—a graceful swan, or a crane that weaves cloth from its feathers. Or her plumage may be a magic robe, as here and in the Nō play *Hagoromo*. *Hagoromo*, in which a fisherman takes the garment of a sky woman and returns it in exchange for a dance, is based on the same legendary version of the story as the fudoki narrative. The moon maiden Kaguyahime in *Taketori Monogatari*, who brings wealth to her foster parents, also comes out of the same cluster of myth. In the present narrative the wealth comes from a medicinal *sake* brewed by the sky woman, suggestive of the *ochimizu*, or waters of restored youth, said to exist on the moon (see nos. 892 and 1453). The passage in brackets is thought to be a later addition to the original form of the story. The places whose names are explained in the narrative are in the vicinity of Mineyama in northern Kyōto Prefecture. "Muddy bottoms" (*hijikata*) presumably referred to well-watered, fertile fields. Toyoukanome ("Female of

Abundant Provisions"), the identity the sky woman assumes on reaching Nagu ("Tranquil"), was a food deity also mentioned in *Kojiki*. This "capture" of the sky woman as earth goddess probably represents a conflation with another myth. The tanka she sings in her moment of despair expresses a last longing for the lost homeland of the sky, now concealed forever beyond the mist. Like a decaying *apsaras*, the Buddhist angel whose image also lies behind these myths, she has molted beyond redemption and can fly no more. (It should be noted that in the original version of the fudoki story, the cruel foster parents do not return her clothes.) The first two lines of the song are formulaic, but whether the song had an existence independent of the narrative is not clear.

221   [F 22 : Tango]

Tango Province, Tamba District. Northwest of the district headquarters is the township of Hiji. There is a wellspring on the summit of Mount Hiji in this township. It is named Manai ["True Well"]. It has now become a marsh.

Eight sky women came down to bathe in this spring. At this time there was an old couple; they were called the Old Man of Wanasa and the Old Woman of Wanasa. These old people came to the wellspring and stealthily took the clothing of one of the sky women and hid it. Directly, all the maidens who had their clothes flew up into the sky; only the one without clothes remained behind, staying hidden in the water, alone and ashamed.

Hereupon the old man said to the sky woman, "We have no child. Heavenly maiden, please be our child."

[The sky woman replied, "I alone have stayed behind among humans. What can I do but obey you? Please give me back my clothes."

The old man said, "Heavenly maiden, why do you have a deceitful heart?"

The sky woman said, "The decisions of the people of heaven are based on trust. Why is your mind so full of suspicion that you refuse to give me back my clothes?"

The old man replied, "Many doubts and lack of trust are the way of the world. And so, with such a mind I have refused."

Finally he let her have her clothes], and she accompanied them to their home, where they lived together for over ten years. There the sky woman used her skill to brew *sake*. To drink one cup was enough to dispel the ten thousand ills. Cartloads of treasure were sent as the price of a single cup. In time the house overflowed with abundance, and the muddy bottoms [*hiji-kata*] prospered. Hence the township was called Hijikata. Ever since, down to the present day, it has been called the township of Hiji.

Later the old man and his wife spoke to the sky woman, saying, "You are not our child. You have temporarily lived with us, that is all. Now be off with you."

At this the sky woman looked up at heaven and wept in grief, looked down at the earth and moaned in sorrow. She spoke to the old couple, saying, "It was not my idea to come here. It was your wish. Now suddenly you are sick of me and want me to leave. How can you be so cruel?"

The old man glared at her more angrily than before and demanded that she go. The sky woman wept. When she had gone a little beyond the gate, she spoke to the villagers, saying, "For a long time I have been sunken among humankind, and now I cannot return to the sky. Yet I have no kindred here, and I don't know how I can manage to stay. Alas, what am I to do?" Wiping her tears, she looked up at the heavens and sang:

Ama no hara	When I lift my head
Furisakemireba	And gaze across the plains of heaven,
Kasumi tachi	A mist has risen:
Ieji madoite	The way home is lost—perplexed,
Yukue shirazu mo	I don't know where to go.

At last she went away. Arriving at the village of Arashio, she told the villagers, "When I think of what that old man and woman are really like, my heart is a raging tide [*arashio*]." Thus they call the place the village of Arashio in the township of Hiji. Again, she arrived in Nakiki Village in Taniwa Township and leaned against a zelkova tree and wept. Thus they called the place Nakiki ("Weeping Tree") Village. Once more, arriving in the village of Nagu, in Funaki Township, Takano District, she told the villagers, "Here my heart has become tranquil [*nagushiku narinu*]." (*Nagushi* is the old word for "tranquil.") And she stayed on in this village. She is the goddess known as Toyoukanome no Mikoto residing in the Nagu Shrine in Takano District.

❊ Only one of the twelve surviving fragments of *Ise Fudoki* contains a song. The Matokata celebrated in this song was an indentation along the shore of Ise Bay that eventually lost its opening to the sea and became a pond, as stated in the old interlinear note in parentheses. Song 222 is nearly identical to no. 476, attributed to "the Maiden Toneri," a court lady of the late seventh century. It has been argued that her version is the earlier, and that no. 222 is a popularization of it as a song, here ascribed to an early monarch (Emperor Keikō, according to a note attached to the textual fragment). The fudoki version of the fourth line, *iru ya Matokata*, has the formulaic quality of ancient oral verse, in contrast to the grammatically logical *iru Matokata wa* of no. 476. It should be remembered, however, that the reworking of oral materials into written form was one of the chief literary activities of the time. The question of priority is not easily decided. Both versions are based on traditional interest in wordplay; for a discussion, see the commentary on no. 476.

Matokata Bay. This bay is shaped like a target [*mato*]. Thus they made that its name. (Now its traces have vanished and it has become a shorelong pond.) Once the Emperor went down to the shore and sang:

Masurao no	Where the stalwart men
Satsuya tabasami	Take their hunting arrows up,
Mukaitachi	Aim as they stand, and shoot:
Iru ya Matokata	Target Bay, how fair it is,
Hama no sayakesa	How bracing clear its beach!

'Shoku Nihongi' Songs

Song 223 is a typical felicitous New Year's song, one that also exists in a sung version as a *saibara*. The Emperor is Shōmu (701–58; r. 724–49), and the banquet he gives for his nobles in the Daianden, the formal audience hall, occurred on the sixteenth of the first month of 742. The Gosechi dances got their name ("Five-Interval") either from a passage in *Tso Chuan* that mentions the five intervals of ancient Chinese pentatonic music or from a legend that Emperor Temmu was visited by a heavenly maiden who danced to his cithern, waving her sleeves five times. The Gosechi dances became one of the annual rituals of the court, being performed by young girls as part of the First Tasting ceremonies in the eleventh month. "Gosechi field dances" are thought to be the same as simply "Gosechi dances." The Tōka ["Treading Dance"], imported from China, was performed, as here, with congratulatory intent on the fifteenth and sixteenth of the first month. The capital was at Kuni in Yamashiro at this time, rather than at Nara. See pp. 382–83 for a discussion of the political situation.

223   [SN 1]

On the day Water-Senior/Dog [of Tempyō 14 (742).1] the Emperor went to the Daian Hall and feasted his nobles. When the wine was flowing freely, the Gosechi field dances were performed, and when they were over, youths and maidens were made to dance the Tōka. Furthermore, a banquet was held for the rank-holders of the realm and the Scribes of the various bureaus, at which men of the Sixth Rank and under played citherns and sang:

Aratashiki	On this beginning
Toshi no hajime ni	Of the New Year let us thus
Kaku shi koso	In all reverence
Tsukaematsurame	Vow to offer our service
Yorozu yo made ni	For a myriad ages to come!

❊ The next three songs, one of which is by Emperor Shōmu himself, are from the following year (743). Again, the imperial palace is the new one just built in Kuni (see nos. 677–85). The Crown Princess is Shōmu's daughter, the future Empress Kōken (r. 749–58, and again, as Empress Shōtoku,

764–70). The Grand Retired Empress (Daijō Tennō) is Genshō (680–748; r. 715–24), Shōmu's aunt and predecessor on the throne. A longer version of no. 224 appears as a New Year's song in *Kinkafu*. "The Imperial Grand-child" (*mima no mikoto*) is a title for the Emperor, referring to his descent from Ninigi no Mikoto, the grandchild of the sun goddess Amaterasu. For other wine-presenting songs, see nos. 5, 39, 48, 100–101, 118, and 173. See also nos. 698–99, in which Emperor Shōmu bestows rather than partakes of the wine. The use of wine (i.e., *sake*) to solemnize ritual and symbolize the wish for long and auspicious life is honored in Japan today, most notably in the Shintō wedding ceremony.

224   [SN 2]

On the day Water-Junior/Hare [of Tempyō 15 (743). 5] he feasted the nobles in the imperial palace. The Crown Princess personally danced the Gosechi. Minister of the Right Tachibana no Sukune Moroe reported to the Grand Retired Empress in obedience to imperial command. . . . Thus, [the Emperor] composed a song, which went:

Sora mitsu	The sky-seen
Yamato no kuni wa	Land of Yamato
Kamikara shi	Is from its godhead
Tōtoku aru rashi	Clearly fraught with majesty—
Kono mai mireba	When I see this dance!

225   [SN 3]

Again, there was a song that went:

Ama tsu kami	Of heaven's deity
Mima no mikoto no	The imperial grandchild
Torimochite	Here holds court;
Kono toyomiki o	Here he solemnly partakes
Ikatatematsuru	Of this fine, abundant wine.

226   [SN 4]

Again, there was a song that went:

Yasumishishi	Our great lord
Wa go ōkimi wa	Who rules the realm in all tranquility
Tairakeku	Shall long abide
Nagaku imashite	In the level ways of peace:
Toyomiki matsuru	He partakes of the abundant wine.

❋ *Shoku Nihongi* is notable for its collection of sixty-two *semmyō*, or imperial proclamations. These are written in highly formal Japanese prose recorded in a mixture of semantogram and phonogram orthography—that is, with Chinese characters meant to be read in some cases for their meaning and in others for their sound. With some divagations in the direction of Chinese word order, the texts follow Japanese syntax and are meant to be read as Japanese. The characters that are used phonetically in their Sino-Japanese readings are written small and represent particles and inflections. This style, known as *semmyōtai*, is one of the earliest forms of written Japanese prose. The semmyō were proclaimed aloud by public officials and are characterized by a grandiloquent oratorical quality. Semmyō 13, on the discovery of gold in Michinoku Province, has embedded in it an ancient war song of the Ōtomo and Saeki clans, given here as no. 227. The gold was to be used to gild the Great Buddha of Tōdaiji, thus bringing to completion an awesome undertaking of obsessive importance to Emperor Shōmu. It was on this occasion, in the immediately preceding Semmyō 12, that Shōmu proclaimed himself "the slave of the Three Treasures": of the Buddha, the Dharma (the Doctrine), and the Saṅgha (the Community). His abdication was announced later in the same year (749) in Semmyō 14. Semmyō 13 deals not only with the discovery of the gold itself, but with Shōmu's anxiety over the future in the light of the bitter rivalry between the Fujiwara and forces supporting his chief minister, Tachibana no Moroe. The reference to the Ōtomo and Saeki is in the context of an appeal to their loyalty. The whole semmyō, song included, was reworked into a chōka by Ōtomo no Yakamochi (no. 814, the commentary to which may be consulted for the political situation at the time, as well as for an assessment of the famous "oath of the Ōtomo").

227   [SN 5]

In the summer [of Tempyō-Shōhō 1 (749)], in the fourth month, on the first day, Wood-Senior/Horse, the Emperor proceeded to Tōdaiji, went to the hall in front of the statue of Vairocana Buddha, and faced north toward the statue. The Empress and Crown Princess attended with him. The nobles, the hundred bureaus, and the commoners were divided into ranks and drawn up at the rear of the hall. . . . Minister of Central Affairs Isonokami no Asomi Otomaro of Junior Third Rank announced:
 . . . "Further, as you Ōtomo and Saeki no Sukune have always said, you are the men who guard the Emperor's court without a backward glance, men, We hear, whose forefathers handed down these words:

Umi yukaba	If we go on the sea,
Mizuku kabane	Our dead are sodden in water;
Yama yukaba	If we go on the mountains,
Kusamusu kabane	Our dead are grown over with grass.
Ōkimi no	We shall die
He ni koso shiname	By the side of our lord,
Nodo ni wa shinaji	We shall not die in peace."

❋ The large number of participants in Empress Shōtoku's utagaki in the spring of 770 indicates that what had originally been a folk festival (see nos. 587–88), the venue for sexual pairing and rivalry (see nos. 106–11 and 158–64), had become a grand court entertainment by the late eighth century. This courtly utagaki is thought to have come under the influence of the imported Tōka. The men and women who took part in the dance on this occasion were all from clans of continental origin, settled in the Kawachi region where this particular celebration took place while the Empress was on excursion to her detached palace at Yugi (the *nishi no miyako*, or "western royal city," of no. 228). The Yamatomai was another courtly dance of folk origins. The phrase *yorozu yo* ("a myriad ages" or "a myriad lifespans") occurring in both no. 223 and no. 228 marks them as Tōka songs, which always concluded with some form of this felicitous expression. It is worth noting that nos. 228–29 postdate the poems in *Man'yōshū* and show the continuing use of waka on formal occasions after its first great age had passed.

228   [SN 6]

On the day Metal-Junior/Hare [of Hōki 1 (770). 3], two hundred thirty men and women of the six clans of Fujii, Fune, Tsu, Fumi, Takefu, and Kura took part in an *utagaki*. They were all dressed in blue-printed garments of narrow cloth with trailing crimson sashes. The men and women lined up opposite each other in separate rows and advanced slowly in a dignified manner. They sang:

Otomera ni	Men with the maidens
Otoko tachisoi	Now stand up and join in dance,
Fuminarasu	Treading the earth smooth:
Nishi no miyako wa	The western royal city,
Yorozu yo no miya	Palace of a myriad ages.

229   [SN 7]

[One of] the songs at this *utagaki* went:

Fuchi mo se mo	In pool and shallow
Kiyoku sayakeshi	Clear and purling flows the stream:
Hakatagawa	Hakata River,
Chitose o machite	Waiting for a thousand years,
Sumeru kawa kamo	River that will still run pure.

At every turn and bend in song they raised their sleeves to mark the time. The remaining four songs were all old poems, and we have not gone to the trouble of including them here. The palace attendants (*udoneri*) and female officials (*nyoju*) of Fifth Rank and above were ordered to join the rows of *utagaki* dancers. When the songs were over, officials from Kawachi no

Daibu Fujiwara no Asomi Odamaro of Junior Fourth Rank Upper on down performed the Yamatomai. The members of the six clans who took part in the *utagaki* were rewarded with two thousand *tan* of trade cloth and five hundred *ton* of silk floss.

✻ The Emperor referred to in the setting for song 230 is Kōnin (r. 770–81), a grandson of Emperor Tenji who was brought forward as successor when Empress Shōtoku died without issue. The reference to Shōhō is to the Tempyō-Shōhō era (749–57) and to the series of succession disputes that followed the abdication of Emperor Shōmu in 749. Attempted coups d'état had occurred in 757 and 764, and the priest Dōkyō (d. 772), the Empress's favorite, is thought to have had designs on the throne. Though her death in 770 led to Dōkyō's fall, plots and counterplots continued to the end of the Nara period and beyond. In referring to Prince Shirakabe (Kōnin's personal name) as "Emperor" before his accession (during his time as a "latent dragon"), the following account is anachronistic. The wazauta is a folk ballad quite similar to examples preserved in collections from the Heian period. Line 8 has probably been altered to fit the interpretive context into which the song has found its way, *shiratama* ("white gem") being replaced by *shirakabe* ("white wall"). Not only is Shirakabe Emperor Kōnin's personal or taboo name (*imina*), but the characters for *kabe* (Morohashi 5516) and *tama* (Morohashi 21269) differ by only two strokes. The Kazuraki and Toyora temples were in the Asuka area. Sakurai ("Cherry-Tree Well") provides the first syllable of Princess Inoue's name ("Above the Well"). *Oshitodo* and *toshitodo* are hayashikotoba, meaningless ballad refrains.

230   [SN 8]
The Emperor was clement, sincere, and open-minded. Ever since Shōhō there had been no successor to the imperial throne; people were cast into doubt, and many had incurred blame and been brought to ruin. When the Emperor thought of what calamities might lie ahead, he sometimes indulged himself in drink, thus covering his tracks. Time and again he found excuses for evading harm. Also, once before, in the time of the latent dragon, there had been a children's song that went:

	Kazuraki no	In front of the temple
	Tera no mae naru ya	Of Kazuraki—that's where it is,
	Toyora no tera no	West of the temple of Toyora—
	Nishi naru ya	That's where it is:
5	Oshitodo	*Oshitodo*
	Toshitodo	*Toshitodo*
	Sakurai ni	Cherry-Tree Well,
	Shirakabe shizuku ya	With a white wall sunk at the bottom,

	Yoki tama shizuku ya	With a fair gem sunk at the bottom:
10	Oshitodo	*Oshitodo*
	Toshitodo	*Toshitodo*
	Shikashiteba	If that's how it is,
	Kuni so sakayuru ya	The country will flourish for sure,
	Wagiera so sakayuru ya	Our house will flourish for sure:
15	Oshitodo	*Oshitodo*
	Toshitodo	*Toshitodo.*

At that time Imperial Princess Inoue was the Prince's consort. Knowledgeable people made out the meaning thus: "'Well' is the Princess's name; 'White Wall' is the Emperor's taboo name. This must have been an omen of the Emperor's ascending the throne."

Selections from 'Man'yōshū'

Man'yōshū is the earliest surviving anthology of Japanese poetry, the repository of most of what the Japanese themselves would have considered their own literature up to the middle of the eighth century. *Kojiki* and *Nihonshoki* are rich in what we now recognize as literary elements, but to their compilers and first readers, the first two chronicles were simply the true story of their world, race, and nation. The verse in particular is always given a narrative context, and even when that context is clearly specious, the songs can be traced back to a social matrix in which they were not individual creations, but served the purposes of ritual, entertainment, or the perpetuation of myth. They are literature, but folk literature. With *Man'yōshū* the situation changes. The mere decision to compile an anthology is a literary act in itself, and the compilers, men of the eighth century, were educated in Chinese and well aware that literacy, the sine qua non of civilization, implied the existence of literature, and specifically of poetry. And poetry, while still in some sense song and a special use of language, as it had always been, was also the product of individual craft, was in fact an art that could win personal fame, as well as the hand of a girl or rescue in a tight situation. In its content *Man'yōshū* draws on both traditions, the old and the new. There is some overlap with songs in the chronicles, in addition to other poems of a folkish character. A middle ground is occupied by the perfection of chōka and tanka form and the establishment of a generalized voice that is both native and literarily self-confident. And the last generations of Man'yō poets bring individual styles and their own varied voices in poems sometimes overtly Chinese in theme or manner.

The title *Man'yōshū* probably means "Collection for Ten Thousand Generations," though the more common reading of the second character yields the meaning, "Collection of Ten Thousand Leaves." As far as is known, the collection has always had this title, but there is no prefatory material to explain its choice or anything about the motivation or procedure of its compilation. Internal evidence points to Ōtomo no Yakamochi (718–85) as the chief or final compiler and indicates that he drew on existing collections and anthologies, none now extant, as well as writing a great many poems himself. The provenance of some poems is carefully noted, and the hand of the editor is everywhere evident, but still the source of most of the poems, including the vast numbers of anonymous ones, is simply unknown. *Man'yōshū* consists of twenty books or scrolls, a standard number for later court anthologies, and roughly 4,500 poems. The exact number will depend on which variants are counted. The recently revised *Shimpen Kokka Taikan* lists 4,540.

The poems in *Man'yōshū* are arranged according to a variety of schemes—chronological, modal, topical, and geographical—sometimes intermingled, without an overall unified pattern. One book differs from another in its typical content. This variety helps make *Man'yōshū* an endlessly fascinating treasure trove for exploration, but baffles easy generalization. In re-anthologizing poems from *Man'yōshū*, the present work is following in the footsteps of its predecessor, which is itself an anthology of anthologies. The selections are divided into three groups: poems by named authors (given chronologically so far as possible, for dates are often unknown); poetic exchanges and poem groups of multiple authorship; and anonymous poems. The exchanges and poem groups are arranged in chronological order, and the anonymous poems in the order in which they appear in *Man'yōshū*. The editions most frequently consulted have been two four-volume sets entitled *Man'yōshū* in the Iwanami *Nihon Koten Bungaku Taikei* and Shōgakukan *Nihon Koten Bungaku Zenshū*. The translations include the prose material preceding and following the poems.

Poems by Named Poets

Empress Iwanohime (4th or 5th century?)

Ostensibly the earliest poems in *Man'yōshū* are a set of four tanka attributed to the consort of Emperor Nintoku, famous for her jealousy in the chronicles (see nos. 52–70 and 128–36). Attributions earlier than the middle of the seventh century are to be regarded with skepticism, but this admirable set provides a convenient place to begin. They are poems of a woman's yearning for her husband, a basic theme throughout the classical literature, and are arranged into an interesting progression expressing hesitation, despair, determination, and wistfulness. By virtue of the art of arrangement, the compilers are able to investigate the ebb and flow of conflicting emotions. The first poem has a variant in no. 88, a version that appears again as MYS II:90. *Ruijū Karin* ("Classified Forest of Poetry") is referred to several times in *Man'yōshū*. It is no longer extant, but provides further evidence of the anthologizing activities of the eighth century. Its compiler, Yamanoue no Okura, was a leading Man'yō poet and an unusually well-educated man. It goes without saying that his "classifications" were Chinese. The four poems ascribed to Iwanohime begin Book II of *Man'yōshū*, the first part of which is devoted to poems in the category *sōmon*—essentially poems of longing for a loved one. The set can hardly date from before the seventh century, for it shows not only a complete sense of the tanka form, but an understanding that yearning is the basic mode of love in poetry. It can be usefully contrasted with the songs attributed to Nintoku and Iwanohime in *Kojiki*.

231–34   [MYS II:85–88]

Four poems of Empress Iwanohime yearning for the Emperor

(231)   [85]

Kimi ga yuki	My lord's journey
Kenagaku narinu	Has lengthened into many days:
Yama tazune	Shall I go to him,
Mukae ka yukamu	Go and meet him in the hills,
Machi ni ka matamu	Or wait and go on waiting?

The preceding poem is contained in the *Ruijū Karin* of Yamanoue no Okura no Omi.

(232)   [86]

Kaku bakari	Rather than this—
Koitsutsu arazu wa	This constant yearning of love—
Takayama no	Better had it been
Iwane shi makite	To pillow on the mountain crags
Shinamashi mono o	And die, my head among the stones.

(233)   [87]

Aritsutsu mo	Here shall I abide
Kimi o ba matamu	And wait the coming of my lord,
Uchinabiku	Until the streaming
Wa ga kurokami ni	Banner of my long black hair
Shimo no oku made ni	Is stiff and white with frost.

(234)   [88]

Aki no ta no	On the autumn fields,
Ho no he ni kirau	Over ripening spears of grain,
Asakasumi	Drifts the morning mist:
Izuhe no kata ni	Whither will it ever vanish,
Wa ga koi yamamu	My love, and be no more?

Younger Sister of the Naniwa Emperor

It has been suggested that the compilers intended Nintoku by "the Naniwa Emperor," and Princess Yata (see nos. 64–65) by "the younger sister." The other sovereign who reigned at Naniwa was Emperor Kōtoku. Book IV, like Book II, begins with a group of chronologically arranged sōmon poems.

235   [MYS IV : 487/484]

A poem presented by the younger sister of the Naniwa Emperor to her elder brother in Yamato

Hitohi koso	For a single day
Hito mo machiyoki	The waiting would go well enough,
Nagaki ke o	But if there is nothing
Kaku nomi mataba	But this constant daylong wait
Arikatsumashiji	I shall not bear it to the end.

Emperor Yūryaku (r. 456–79)

The opening poem of *Man'yōshū* is attributed to Emperor Yūryaku, whom the chronicles show as often having met and married pretty maids in the countryside (see nos. 92–96). It envisages a similar situation, in which the ruler asks for the name of the girl, and thus for her yielding—like his realm at large. The irregular line length suggests that the poem is indeed early, and it could easily have cropped up as a song in *Kojiki* or *Nihonshoki*. Of the two dominant chōka techniques, preparation-conclusion and parallelism, it employs only the latter, adding to the feeling of simplicity it imparts. Its pride of place in *Man'yōshū* probably has less to do with its amorous subject than with the proud statement of imperial rule in lines 9–14. Book 1 is made up of poems on public themes.

236   [MYS I: I]

A poem composed by the Emperor

	Ko mo yo	With a basket,
	Miko mochi	A pretty basket,
	Fukushi mo yo	And a trowel,
	Mibukushi mochi	A pretty trowel in hand,
5	Kono oka ni	Here on this hillside
	Na tsumasu ko	Gathering herbs: young one,
	Ie kikana	I would hear your home—
	Na norasane	Come, tell me your name!
	Sora mitsu	In the sky-seen
10	Yamato no kuni wa	Land of Yamato
	Oshinabete	Over the bending earth
	Ware koso ore	It is I who reign,
	Shikinabete	Over the yielding realm
	Ware koso imase	It is I who rule:
15	Ware koso ba	I, you may be sure,
	Norame	Shall tell you
	Ie o mo na o mo	My home and my name.

Prince Shōtoku (574–621)

Shōtoku Taishi, nephew of Empress Suiko, was the leading statesman of the early seventh century. An influential patron of Buddhism, he was also active in fostering Confucian learning and close cultural ties with China. He was revered in his own day and afterward as a man of lofty ideals and personal sanctity, and as such attracted a number of legends. The setting for no. 237 belongs to one of these. For a longer version, see no. 175. In its Man'yō version Prince Shōtoku's poem belongs to the genre of laments for dead travelers. These poems persistently emphasize the common humanity of the stranger. The most notable example of the genre is MYS II:220–22, by Hitomaro (nos. 358–60). The tanka ascribed to Shōtoku (here Shōtoko) begins a section of *banka*, or laments, in Book III.

237 [MYS III:418/415]

A poem composed in sorrow when on an excursion to the Well of Takahara Prince Shōtoku of the Upper Palace saw a dead man on Mount Tatsuta

Ie naraba	He who if at home
Imo ga te makamu	Would be pillowed on the arm
Kusamakura	Of his own dear love,
Tabi ni koyaseru	On a journey, grass for pillow,
Kono tabito aware	Here lies sprawled, poor traveler!

Emperor Jomei (593–641)

No. 238 is a land-praising poem, a type already seen in nos. 30, 41, and elsewhere. There was a legend that Mount Kagu near Asuka in Yamato had descended from heaven—hence "Heavenly Mount Kagu." For the *Kojiki* account of the origin of the name "Dragonfly Island," see no. 97. The feeling for the divinity and beauty of the land is one of the most attractive aspects of Man'yō poetry.

238 [MYS I:2]

A poem composed by the Emperor when he ascended Mount Kagu and viewed the land

Yamato ni wa	In Yamato
Murayama areto	There are crowds of mountains,
Toriyorou	But our rampart
Ame no Kaguyama	Is Heavenly Mount Kagu:
5 Noboritachi	When I climb it
Kunimi o sureba	And look out across the land,
Kunihara wa	Over the land-plain
Keburi tachitatsu	Smoke rises and rises;
Unahara wa	Over the sea-plain
10 Kamame tachitatsu	Seagulls rise and rise.
Umashi kuni so	A fair land it is,
Akizushima	Dragonfly Island,
Yamato no kuni wa	The land of Yamato.

❋ Emperor Jomei was known as the Okamoto Sovereign from his palace at Okamoto at the foot of Mount Kagu. No. 239 is one of the earliest references to the autumn mating calls of the deer, a frequent topic in later poetry. The same poem is attributed to Emperor Yūryaku in MYS IX: 1668/1664.

239   [MYS VIII: 1515/1511]

An imperial composition of the Okamoto Sovereign

Yū sareba	The deer that cry
Ogura no yama ni	On Ogura when evening falls
Naku shika wa	Have not cried out
Koyoi wa nakazu	Upon the mountain slopes tonight—
Inenikerashi mo	It must be they have gone to sleep.

Prince Konikishi (active reign of Jomei)

The sole known work of this poet, nos. 240–41, is a remarkable approach to the mature Man'yō style of Kakinomoto no Hitomaro. In fact many of the lines have close echoes in Hitomaro, as a comparison with nos. 325 and 338 will show. The multiple use of pillow words in lines 5, 7, 9, 11, and 21 is also characteristic of Hitomaro's style. But in a poem by Hitomaro the imperial or divine reference (here in lines 9–13) would probably have come at the beginning. This chōka is also the first to be provided with a hanka, an envoy in tanka form. All in all, it is an important poem, both for its quality and for its placement in the first half of the seventh century. As the footnote indicates, the identity of the author—his name has traditionally been read "Ikusa"—is unknown. It has been suggested that he was a scion of the royal house of Paekche settled in Japan.

240–41   [MYS I: 5–6]

A poem composed by Prince Konikishi on seeing the mountains during an imperial progress to Aya District in Sanuki Province

	Kasumi tachi	Mist rose up
	Nagaki haruhi no	Over the long spring day;
	Kurenikeru	Darkness came down,
	Wazuki mo shirazu	But I knew not when it was:
5	Murakimo no	For my heart was sore
	Kokoro o itami	Amid the vitals in my breast,
	Nuekotori	And the cries within me
	Uranakeoreba	Were the cries of a young thrush.
	Tamadasuki	As a jeweled sash
10	Kake no yoroshiku	Girds in splendor, now I speak
	Tōtsu kami	With words that bless
	Wa ga ōkimi no	Of the distant god, our lord:
	Idemashi no	Hither did he travel

	Yama kosu kaze no	To these mountains—where the wind
15	Hitori oru	Comes down the crest
	Wa ga koromode ni	To catch my solitary sleeves
	Asa yoi ni	Morning and evening,
	Kaerainureba	Blowing them back toward home.
	Masurao to	And even I
20	Omoeru ware mo	Who thought myself a valiant man,
	Kusamakura	Since now I pillow
	Tabi ni shi areba	On the grass of a far journey,
	Omoiyaru	Find I do not know
	Tazuki o shirani	The way to clear this longing.
25	Ami no ura no	Out on Ami Bay
	Amaotomera ga	Maidens of the fisherfolk
	Yaku shio no	Burn fires for salt:
	Omoi so yakuru	Fires of longing blaze within,
	Wa ga shitagokoro	Burning my inmost heart.

Envoy

Yamagoshi no	Not a night goes by,
Kaze o tokijimi	What with the unseasonable wind
Nuru yo ochizu	Across the mountains,
Ie naru imo o	That I do not lie and yearn
Kakete shinoitsu	For the wife I left at home.

In examining the above against *Nihonshoki*, we find no record of a progress to Sanuki Province. And Prince Konikishi is not identifiable. However, the *Ruijū Karin* of court noble Yamanoue no Okura states: "The *Chronicles* state: 'The Emperor made a progress to the hot springs of Iyo in winter, the twelfth month of the eleventh year, Earth-Junior/Swine [639], on the Water-Senior/Horse day of the month beginning Earth-Junior/Serpent. . . .' Another work states: 'At this time there were two trees in front of the palace. Large flocks of grosbeaks and hawfinches gathered on the trees. The Emperor ordered a great quantity of rice ears put out to feed the birds. At this a poem was composed. . . .'" Probably the Emperor proceeded from this place [to Sanuki].

Empress Saimei (594–661)

Empress Saimei was the widow of Emperor Jomei, and the following poem may refer to her longing for her dead husband. But Saimei reigned twice, once as Kōgyoku from 642 to 645, and again as Saimei from 655 to 661. (For more on this ruler, see pp. 122–27, 168–74.) Her husband's death was not a recent matter by the time of her second reign, which is the one that took place at the Okamoto Palace. As the *Man'yōshū* compiler points out, the expression "Okamoto Sovereign" is itself ambiguous, since Jomei had also been known by that title. The use of *kimi* ("lord" or "you") suggests that the speaker is a woman in any case. It has been suggested that all ascriptions are unreliable because the poem belongs to folk song. The second *hanka* (characteristically the envoys are referred to as tanka in the prose headnote) plays on two place-names, Ōmiji ("Meeting Road") and Isayagawa ("Uncertain River") in a way that is more subtle than "the moor/belly of the big wild boar" in no. 60. The use of two hanka is also characteristic of the fully developed chōka form. Often, as here, one recapitulates part of the parent poem, while the other extends it by introducing a new thought or image. The poem employs irony in presenting the superabundance of humanity as flocks of teal, and the first hanka nicely transforms the analogical image to a real one, waterfowl whose cries increase the speaker's desolation. Tonally and technically, the poem has the excellence of the best Man'yō verse.

242-44   [MYS IV:488-90/485-87]

A poem by the Okamoto Sovereign; with *tanka*

Kamiyo yori	From the age of the gods,
Aretsugikureba	Born in generations down the years,
Hito sawa ni	Now men are swarming,
Kuni ni wa michite	Filling all the lands of earth,
5 Ajimura no	Going to and fro
Kayoi wa yukedo	Like great flocks of gabbling teal;
Wa ga kouru	But none among them
Kimi ni shi araneba	Is the lord for whom I long.
Hiru wa	By day,
10 Hi no kururu made	And all day long till dusk at eve;
Yoru wa	By night,
Yo no akuru kiwami	And all night long till edge of dawn
Omoitsutsu	I have been yearning,
I mo negateni to	Unable to get to sleep.
15 Akashitsuraku mo	This waiting up till daybreak—
Nagaki kono yo o	The long night I've worn away!

Envoys

Yama no ha ni	Along the mountains
Ajimura sawaki	Go the gabbling flocks of teal—
Yuku naredo	I can hear their cries;
Ware wa sabushie	But I am still and lonely,
Kimi ni shi araneba	For they are not you, my lord.
Ōmiji no	Uncertain River
Toko no yama naru	Winding in its riverbed

Isayagawa   By Toko Mountain:
Ke no korogoro wa   Along Meeting Road the days
Koitsutsu mo aramu   Go by, and I, and endless longing.

On now considering the above, the Palace at Okamoto in Takechi and the Later Okamoto Palace were two different palaces, belonging to different Sovereigns. It is not certain who is meant by saying simply, "the Okamoto Sovereign."

Nakatsu Sumera Mikoto

The identity of Nakatsu Sumera Mikoto ("the Middle Sovereign") is uncertain. The title may refer to Empress Kōgyoku-Saimei herself, but more probably applies to her daughter Princess Hashihito (d. 665). Princess Hashihito married her mother's brother, who reigned as Emperor Kōtoku from 645 to 654. The power behind the throne during these years was Prince Naka no Ōe (626–672), who engineered a coup d'état in 645 and introduced the so-called Taika Reforms. Naka no Ōe ruled through a series of his relatives before formally taking the throne as Emperor Tenji in 668. The first of these was Kōtoku, who reigned at Naniwa. Because of a hostility that developed between the two, Naka no Ōe took his sister Hashihito away from her husband and kept her and their mother, whom he reinstalled as Empress Saimei after Kōtoku's death, at his own headquarters in Asuka. (For Kōtoku's song lamenting the loss of his consort, see no. 186.) During the period from Saimei's death in 661 to her own in 665, Hashihito may have been regarded as the de facto sovereign, thus earning the title Nakatsu Sumera Mikoto. The Emperor referred to in nos. 245–46 is Jomei, at whose death in 641 Princess Hashihito would have been a very young girl, since she was younger than Naka no Ōe. It seems likely that the messenger in the headnote, Hashihito no Muraji Oyu, had some connection with Princess Hashihito's personal name, such as through a female relative who could have been her wet nurse. In view of the princess's no doubt tender years, it has been suggested that Oyu was the real author of the poem. The poem is one of several celebrations of royal hunting in *Man'yōshū*. The morning-evening parallelism is a standard chōka technique for giving a sense of the totality of a scene or experience. The hanka typically concentrates on only one of these bipolar nodes. The *kanahazu*, or "metal bownock," was a device attached to the end of a bow to give an impressive sound. For "gem-cutting Uchi," see the commentary to no. 71.

245–46   [MYS I: 3–4]

A poem that Nakatsu Sumera Mikoto had Hashihito no Muraji Oyu present to the Emperor when he went hunting on the fields of Uchi

Yasumishishi	Our great lord
Wa ga ōkimi no	Who rules the land in all tranquility
Ashita ni wa	Takes in the morning
Torinadetamai	His bow and strokes it with his hand,
5 Yūhe ni wa	Comes in the evening
Iyoritatashishi	And stands beside his mighty bow:
Mitorashi no	The catalpa bow
Azusa no yumi no	Held within his kingly grip—
Kanahazu no	Far comes the clangor
10 Oto su nari	Of metal bownocks.
Asagari ni	To the morning hunt
Ima tatasu rashi	He must now be setting forth,
Yūgari ni	To the evening hunt
Ima tatasu rashi	He must now be setting forth.
15 Mitorashi no	The catalpa bow
Azusa no yumi no	Held within his kingly grip—
Kanahazu no	Far comes the clangor
Oto su nari	Of metal bownocks.

Envoy

Tamakiwaru	Across the vast fields
Uchi no ōno ni	Of gem-cutting Uchi
Uma namete	He lines his steeds,
Asa fumasuramu	He paces them forth in the morning
Sono kusafukano	On those deep fields of grass.

❊ The three tanka grouped as nos. 247–49 seem to be more than mere travel poems. They are entered under the reign of Empress Saimei by the *Man'yōshū* compilers, and the "Sovereign" of the editorial note refers to that monarch. There are three *Nihonshoki* references to visits to the hot springs at Ki during Saimei's reign, and the first two references are quite sinister, involving as they do the alleged plot of Saimei's nephew Prince Arima, son of her brother Emperor Kōtoku. According to the *Nihonshoki* account, Arima's political ambitions were successfully played upon by the minister Soga no Akae, and he was led into discussions of a coup d'état. It seems more than likely that the whole affair was set up by Naka no Ōe; for more details, see nos. 854–59 and note. Prince Arima was executed for treason after questioning by Naka no Ōe at the hot springs of Ki, where the Empress and her son were taking the waters, in 658. As he was being escorted under guard to his interrogation, he tied pine branches at Iwashiro (see no. 854), a gesture of hope that proved futile. Tying branches or grasses together was current magic practice to bring good luck. *Nihonshoki* records that Empress Saimei visited the Ki hot springs again in 659, a few months after her nephew's execution. These events lie in the background of nos. 247–49, poems that imply a woman (the speaker) traveling in the company of a man. Perhaps the pair are Saimei and her son Naka no Ōe, or perhaps Princess Hashihito (Nakatsu Sumera Mikoto) is the author, speaking for and accompanying her mother and brother. The issues are unclear, but the excursion may well have been an uneasy one. It should be pointed out that *seko*, translated "my love" in the second poem, literally means "my brother." For other poems composed by Empress Saimei at this time, see nos. 190–92.

247–49 [MYS I: 10–12]

Poems composed by Nakatsu Sumera Mikoto when she went to the hot springs of Ki

(247) [10]

Kimi ga yo mo	Come, let us tie them,
Wa ga yo mo shiru ya	The grasses on the hillside
Iwashiro no	Of Iwashiro—
Oka no kusane o	This place that has dominion
Iza musubitena	Over your life and mine.

(248) [11]

Wa ga seko wa	If there are no reeds
Kariio tsukurasu	Wherewith my love can fashion
Kaya naku wa	Our hut for the night,
Komatsu ga moto no	Let him cut instead the grass
Kusa o karasane	That grows beneath the pine.

(249) [12]

Wa ga horishi	You have shown me
Noshima wa misetsu	Noshima that I desired,
Soko fukaki	But we have not gathered
Agone no ura no	Pearls from the bay of Agone
Tama so hiriwanu	Whose bottom lies so deep.

In checking the above against the *Ruijū Karin* of the court noble Yamanoue no Okura, we find that the latter states: "These are poems of the Sovereign."

Emperor Tenji (626–72)

Three small eminences abutting the northern end of the Asuka basin, heartland of Yamato rule during most of the seventh century and earlier, are known as the Three Mountains of Yamato. Poems 250−52 recount a legend about how two of the mountains, Kagu (see no. 238) and Miminashi, quarreled over the third, Unebi. Prince Naka no Ōe (the future Emperor Tenji, r. 668−72) uses the story as an allegory of how he and his younger brother Prince Ōama competed for the favors of Princess Nukata (see the commentary to nos. 860−61). Since Naka no Ōe took her away from his brother, there seems more than a little complacency in his treatment of the story. The first hanka is based on a myth recorded in *Harima Fudoki*; an allegorical interpretation would imply that there was a peacemaker in the dispute. The second hanka, as the Man'yō compilers observe, seems to have no connection with the parent poem. But an allegorical interpretation is plausible here too. Sun and moon will stand for Sovereign and Prince, that is, for Empress Saimei (d. 661) and Prince Naka no Ōe himself. It may not be irrelevant that the compilers note that the Prince was next in line. All of this self-congratulation would help explain the bitter enmity between Ōama and Naka no Ōe, which lay behind the Jinshin War of 672. Viewed as a nature poem, no. 252 is the finest achievement in the poetry of its time. This superb tanka hardly seems of a piece with the rest of the set on stylistic grounds as much as for its subject.

250−52   [MYS I: 13−15]

A poem on the Three Mountains by Naka no Ōe (the Sovereign who ruled the realm from the Ōmi Palace)

	Kaguyama wa	Kagu Mountain
	Unebi o oshi to	Was in love with Unebi,
	Miminashi to	And with Miminashi
	Aiarasoiki	Quarreled over her.
5	Kamiyo yori	From the age of the gods
	Kaku ni aru rashi	Things have been this way, it seems.
	Inishie mo	Since in ancient times
	Shika ni are koso	Such already was the way,
	Utsusemi mo	We mortals too,
10	Tsuma o	It seems,
	Arasou rashiki	Quarrel over our wives.

Envoys

Kaguyama to	When Kagu Mountain
Miminashiyama to	Met Miminashi Mountain
Aishi toki	Face to face, there was
Tachite mi ni koshi	A god who rose and came to see—
Inamikunihara	Here to Inamikuni Plain.

| Watatsumi no | Over the great deep |
| Toyohatakumo ni | Stretch the royal banner-clouds |

> Irihi sashi   Bright in the setting sun:
> Koyoi no tsukuyo If only the moon tonight
> Sayakekari koso   Rides cool and clear in the sky!

The above poem on consideration does not seem like an envoy. However, an old text includes it as an envoy. Hence we still include it in this order. Further, the *Chronicles* state that the Emperor [Tenji] was elevated to Crown Prince in the previous fourth year of the sovereign Ame-Toyo-Takara-Ikashi-Hitarashihime [Kōgyoku], Wood-Junior/Serpent [645].

❋ Some tradition or document outside *Man'yōshū* caused the compilers of *Gosenshū* in the middle of the tenth century to ascribe the following poem to Emperor Tenji. It is undoubtedly an old poem from the viewpoint of the tenth century, and has become firmly associated with Tenji in the public mind because of its selection by Fujiwara Teika (1162–1241) for the familiar thirteenth-century mini-anthology *Hyakunin Isshu*. The speaker of the poem is guarding the autumn fields from encroachment by deer and other animals. "Dew" may imply "tears" (of loneliness) as well, and the poem was no doubt admired for its evocation of the mood of autumn sadness. (On Tenji and temporary huts, see nos. 248, 254).

253   [GSS VI: 302; *Hyakunin Isshu* 1]

> Aki no ta no   In the autumn fields
> Kario no io no   This flimsy shelter for the harvest watch
> Toma o arami   Is thatched so roughly
> Wa ga koromode wa That throughout the lonely night
> Tsuyu ni nuretsutsu My sleeves are wet with dew.

Princess Nukata (b. ca. 638–active until 690's)

Princess Nukata has been referred to above as a bone of contention between the brothers Ōama and Naka no Ōe. She was a better poet than either, in fact is the first person in Japanese literary history to leave a reputation primarily as a poet. Her surviving production is very slight—a dozen poems, some of which are in dispute, and one of which is still partially undeciphered. But the evidence indicates that she was admired for her skill, and that she composed poems on request.

  No. 254 is another poem about royalty in a hut. The diligent compilers of *Man'yōshū* lay out the results of their researches on authorship and date. If the lines were composed in 648, Princess Nukata would probably have been too young to have been their author. An "imperial" poem of that date could have been by Emperor Kōtoku or his sister Empress Kōgyoku-

Saimei. If assigned to 659, Nukata becomes more likely, or the composition could be by then-regnant Empress Saimei herself. Out of all this uncertainty emerges another reference to Saimei's excursion to Ki in 659, soon after the execution of Prince Arima. No. 248, perhaps composed on that occasion, also contains a reference to the building of temporary lodgings. Uji, however, would be a more likely resting place on the way from Asuka to Hira on Lake Biwa than to the Ki Peninsula.

Poems like no. 254, written by royalty about thatching huts, smack of the nascent pastoralism soon to become a dominant mode of appreciating nature and the lives of simpler people among the Nara aristocracy. But it must be remembered that Japanese royalty lived in unpretentious thatched buildings until the seventh century. And song 54 portrays Emperor Nintoku's delight in his rustic accommodations during his affair with Kurohime in Kibi.

254   [MYS I:7]
A poem by Princess Nukata [not certain]

Aki no no no	In the autumn fields
Mikusa karifuki	We cut grasses for the thatch,
Yadorerishi	And we lodged the night:
Uji no miyako no	How my thoughts go back again
Kariio shi omōyu	To our palace-hut at Uji!

On examining the above against the *Ruijū Karin* of court noble Yamanoue no Okura, we find that the latter states: "One work states that this is an imperial poem from the excursion to the Hira Palace in the year Earth-Senior/Monkey [648]." However, the *Chronicles* state: "In spring, first month, fifth year [659], on the day Metal-Junior/Serpent of the month beginning Earth-Junior/Hare, the Empress [Saimei] arrived from the hot springs of Ki. In the third month, which began on Earth-Senior/Tiger, the Empress made a progress to the Yoshino Palace and held a banquet. On the Metal-Senior/Dragon day, the Empress made a progress to Hira Bay in Ōmi."

❋ It has been suggested that Princess Nukata composed the following poem at the command of Empress Saimei, whom she apparently accompanied on the voyage of 661. The voyage was a military expedition, a last-ditch attempt to rescue the allied state of Paekche, which was overwhelmed and annihilated by its neighbor Silla two years later, in 663. The expedition proved fatal to Saimei as well (see song 194), for she died suddenly in Kyūshū without being able to emulate the deeds of her remote predecessor Empress Jingū, to whom the chronicles credit the subjugation of the Korean peninsula in the fourth century. Iyo was on the north coast of Shikoku, on the way to Kyūshū. *Ruijū Karin* considered the poem an expression of nostalgia on the part of the Empress as she remembered an earlier stop at Nikitatsu with her husband, Emperor Jomei, twenty-four years before. It seems rather to express eagerness to be away. Scholars have calculated the date and moment of high tide as 2:00 A.M. on the twenty-third of the first month by the lunar calendar. The poem does convey a sense of immediacy and awed anticipation.

255   [MYS 1:8]

A poem by Princess Nukata

Nikitatsu ni	At Nikitatsu
Funanori semu to	We have waited for the moon
Tsuki mateba	Before boarding our boat;
Shio mo kanainu	Now the tide is in at last—
Ima wa kogiidena	Come, let's get to rowing!

On examining the above against the *Ruijū Karin* of court noble Yamanoue no Okura, we find that the latter states: "In the ninth year, Fire-Junior/ Cock [637], of the reign of the Sovereign who ruled the realm from the Okamoto Palace at Asuka beginning in the year Earth-Junior/Ox [629], on the Water-Senior/Horse day of the twelfth month, beginning Earth-Junior/ Serpent, the Emperor and Empress [Jomei and Saimei] made an excursion to the springs of Iyo. In the seventh year, Metal-Junior/Cock [661], of the reign of the Sovereign who ruled the realm from the Later Okamoto Palace, in spring on the Water-Senior/Tiger day of the first month, beginning Fire-Junior/Cock, the imperial barge set off for the west, beginning a sea voyage. On Metal-Senior/ Dog the barge anchored at the temporary palace of Iwayu at Nikitatsu in Iyo. The Empress, seeing things that remained from bygone days, was swept by a feeling of nostalgia. Therefore she composed a poem to express her sorrow." Consequently, this poem is a composition of the Empress. However, there are four other poems that are by Princess Nukata.

❋ Princess Nukata's best-known poem is her defense of autumn against the rival claims of spring, the opening shot in an age-old debate. The topic and occasion are purely literary, and Chinese in inspiration, evidence of the sophistication of the court briefly reigned over by Emperor Tenji on the shores of Lake Biwa during the last years of his life (667–72). The formal beauty of the poem has been greatly admired, and indeed its balanced phraseology shows how readily adaptable the chōka form was to the parallel structures, as well as the topical concerns, of Chinese poetry. The poem is static but perfect in its classical repose. With this polished artifact, chōka comes of age as a literary art fully distinct from its origins in song.

256   [MYS I:16]

When the Emperor [Tenji] commanded the Palace Minister, Fujiwara no Asomi [Kamatari], to match the radiance of the myriad blossoms of the spring mountains against the colors of the thousand leaves of the autumn mountains, Princess Nukata decided the question with this poem:

Fuyugomori	When spring comes forth
Haru sarikureba	That lay in hiding all the winter through,
Nakazarishi	The birds that did not sing
Tori mo kinakinu	Come back and sing to us once more;
5 Sakazarishi	The flowers that did not bloom
Hana mo sakeredo	Have blossomed everywhere again.
Yama o shigemi	Yet so rife the hills
Irite mo torazu	We cannot make our way to pick,
Kusabukami	And so deep the grass
10 Torite mo mizu	We cannot pluck the flowers to see.
Akiyama no	But when on autumn hills
Konoha o mite wa	We gaze upon the leaves of trees,
Momichi o ba	It is the yellow ones
Torite so shinofu	We pluck and marvel for sheer joy,
15 Aoki o ba	And the ones still green,
Okite so nageku	Sighing, leave upon the boughs—
Soko shi urameshi	Those are the ones I hate to lose.
Akiyama so are wa	For me, it is the autumn hills.

❋ Nos. 257–58 belong to the longing-for-home genre, one that is familiar from examples in the chronicles. As the capital was moved again and again during the course of the seventh and eighth centuries, and as courtiers and soldiers were dispatched to distant frontiers, this came to be a recurrent theme in the poetry, echoing in small a similar phenomenon in China. Emperor Tenji's unprecedented decision to move the capital away from both the coast at Naniwa and transmontane Asuka all the way inland to the shores of Lake Biwa may have had to do with his alarm over the reverses suffered in Japan's attempt to stem the tide of events in Korea, where Silla unified the peninsula in 668, and backed by a resurgent, unified China, was perceived as a threat. The experiment was short-lived, and the brief flourishing of the court at Sasanami from 667 to 672 remained to haunt the memories of the Japanese with an image of transient glory. The speaker in nos. 257–58 is clearly reluctant to leave the old capital, and thus the attribution to Tenji, favored by *Ruijū Karin*, seems unlikely. The route out of Yamato goes north past Mount Miwa (homophonous with *miwa*, "offertory wine") and over Nara Mountain (see song 58), which did not yet look down on the imperial city later built nearby. Mount Miwa was the site of an ancient Shintō cult, and thus a particularly sacred spot. The poem is a clinging to the land, and the attribution of volitional force to the clouds is an effective way to displace resentment onto an "enemy" to the poet's happiness. The poem contrasts with no. 256 in its sense of movement, the reluctance of which is conveyed by the use of verbal and syntactic repetitions. This technique is used by Hitomaro in no. 321.

257–58   [MYS 1:17–18]

A poem composed by Princess Nukata when she went down to Ōmi Province

Umasake	O sweet-wine
Miwa no yama	Miwa Mountain!
Aoni yoshi	Until blue-earth
Nara no yama no	Nara Mountain's mountain crest
5 Yama no ma ni	Should come between
Ikakuru made	And you be hidden in behind,
Michi no kuma	Until road-bendings
Itsumoru made ni	Should pile back upon themselves,
Tsubara ni mo	To the very end
10 Mitsutsu yukamu o	I would have kept you in my sight,
Shibashiba mo	Again and yet again
Misakemu yama o	I would have looked afar at you:
Kokoro naku	O my mountain,
Kumo no	What right
15 Kakusaubeshi ya	Have heartless clouds to cover you?

Envoy

Miwayama o	Do you dare to hide
Shika mo kakusu ka	Miwa Mountain in this way?
Kumo dani mo	At least you, O clouds,
Kokoro arana mo	Should have greater heart than that:
Kakusaubeshi ya	What right have you to cover it?

Concerning the above two poems, it is stated in the *Ruijū Karin* of court noble Yamanoue no Okura: "These are poems by the Emperor, in which he gazes on Mount Miwa at the time he transferred the capital to Ōmi Province." It is stated in *Nihonshoki*: "The capital was transferred to Ōmi in the sixth year, Fire-Senior/Tiger [667], spring, third month, on the Earth-Junior/Hare day of the month beginning Metal-Junior/Cock."

❋ Princess Nukata speaks in her private capacity as a woman in love in poem 259. This fine tanka evokes the sudden hope caused by the stirring of the window blind and blends a seasonal sadness with human longing in its effective last line. Several Chinese analogues have been cited for this verse, but its "sincerity" need not be regarded as impugned by such "influence." The poem is completely successful in its own terms, linguistic, affective, and formal. Other poems having to do with Princess Nukata's complicated love life are found in the section on exchanges.

259   [MYS IV: 491/488]
A poem composed by Princess Nukata in longing for the Ōmi Sovereign

Kimi matsu to	While I wait for you,
A ga koioreba	My lord, lost in this longing,
Wa ga yado no	Suddenly there comes
Sudare ugokashi	A stirring of my window blind:
Aki no kaze fuku	The autumn wind is blowing.

Princess Inohe

Princess Inohe is unknown except for this one reference. Her poem is attached to the 257–58 series on leaving for Ōmi Province as a "harmonizing poem"; hence the compilers' footnote. It has been suggested that the poem was composed in the persona of Princess Nukata. It is in any case a love poem with rather intricate references to a story in *Kojiki* about the marriage of the god of Mount Miwa to a mortal. He only came at night, and in order to discover his identity his bride sewed a thread to his garment with a needle (*hari*). In the morning she found that the thread led into a shrine on Mount Miwa. The *hari* of *sanohari* in the poem's middle line means "alder," whose dye "pierces" cloth like a needle—the image of "eye-piercing" love in the last line. For other versions of this *shinkon setsuwa*, see pp. 74–75, 142–43.

260   [MYS I: 19]

Hesokata no	As the alder tree
Hayashi no saki no	On the edge of the woodland
Sanohari no	Of Hesokata
Kinu ni tsuku nasu	Stains cloth like a piercing needle—
Me ni tsuku wagase	So you pierce my love-stained eyes.

In considering the above poem, it does not resemble a harmonizing poem. However, an old text gives it in this order. And so we enter it here nevertheless.

The Great Consort Yamato (fl. 668–71)

The Great Consort (Ōkisaki) Yamato was the daughter of Prince Furuhito no Ōe and became Empress-Consort to Tenji in 668. Her four surviving poems all have to do with her husband's final illness and his death in 672. Laments speak of the spirit of the dead as flying through the air, as here in no. 261; sometimes in the form of a bird, as with the spirit of Yamato Takeru in nos. 35–37 or Hitomaro's wife in no. 348. The contrast with the earth-bound survivors is usually drawn. In no. 261 the Emperor's spirit seems to be hesitating, which may be the significance of the reference in the headnote to the Emperor as gravely ill but not yet dead. However, Kohata is probably meant to refer to the Emperor's burial place. The pillow word *aohata no*, "green-bannered" (with forests), is used effectively with this place-name to create a euphonious sound repetition. No. 262 refers to the custom of presenting a jeweled chaplet at the place of a deceased Emperor's temporary enshrinement. This chaplet was called *kage* or *mikage*, a word that also means "after-image," and the poem exploits both meanings.

261   [MYS II:148]

A poem that according to one text was presented by the Great Consort when, the Ōmi Sovereign having become ill, his illness suddenly worsened

Aohata no	Over green-bannered
Kohata no ue o	Forest-bannered Kohata
Kayou to wa	I can see him pass,
Me ni wa miredo mo	Turn and pass, still wavering;
Tada ni awanu kamo	But we two shall not meet again.

262   [MYS II:149]

A poem composed by the Great Consort Yamato after the demise of the Emperor

Hito wa yoshi	Well for the others—
Omoiyamu to mo	Let them end all their longing;
Tamakazura	His jeweled chaplet
Kage ni mietsutsu	Shining image still appears,
Wasuraenu kamo	And there is no forgetting for me.

Emperor Temmu (d. 686)

Emperor Temmu was that same Prince Ōama who quarreled with his brother Naka no Ōe (Emperor Tenji) over Princess Nukata. After Tenji's death in 672, he overthrew Tenji's son Kōbun and seized the throne in the Jinshin War. His reign (672–86) marked an apogee of imperial power, and the image of the god-emperor in Hitomaro is thought to reflect his majesty. Though not a notable poet, he has left a few compositions preserved in *Man'yōshū*. No. 263 may be his adaptation of an almost identical anonymous poem (MYS I:26) as he remembers his retreat into the Yoshino Mountains before the outbreak of the Jinshin War. No. 264 is a rather ponderous tongue-twister on the name Yoshino ("Goodfield"). For another poem by Temmu, see no. 868.

263   [MYS I:25]

A poem of the Emperor's composition

	Miyoshino no	In fair Yoshino
	Mimiga no mine ni	On the peak of Mimiga
	Toki naku so	Without a season
	Yuki wa furikeru	Snow falls, as I well recall,
5	Ma naku so	Without interval
	Ame wa furikeru	Rain falls, as I well recall.
	Sono yuki no	As that snow comes down
	Toki naki ga goto	Without a special season,
	Sono ame no	As that rain comes down
10	Ma naki ga gotoku	Without interval for rest,
	Kuma mo ochizu	Missing not a turn,
	Omoitsutsu zo koshi	I have pondered on the past
	Sono yamamichi o	All along that mountain trail.

264   [MYS I:27]

A poem by the Emperor at the time of his progress to the palace at Yoshino [in 679]

Yoki hito no	Goodly men of old
Yoshi to yoku mite	Took a good look at its goodness
Yoshi to iishi	And pronounced it good:
Yoshino yoku miyo	You too, good fellows, be good enough
Yoki hito yoku mi	To see Goodfield's goodliness!

The *Chronicles* state that there was an excursion to the palace at Yoshino in the eighth year, Earth-Junior/Hare, on the Wood-Senior/Monkey day of the fifth month, whose first day was Metal-Senior/Dragon.

Princess Ki (d. before 696?)

Princess Ki was a daughter of Emperor Temmu. Her one surviving poem is no. 265. It is impossible to say whom she is thinking of as she compares herself enviously to the wild ducks, but she herself was the recipient of four love poems from Prince Yuge (nos. 279–82). One of these implies the existence of a rival.

265   [MYS III: 393/390]

A poem by Princess Ki

Karu no ike no	When even they,
Urami yukimiru	The wild ducks by the bending shore
Kamo sura ni	Of the pond at Karu,
Tamamo no ue ni	Do not sleep alone at night
Hitori nenaku ni	On the gemlike waterweed . . .

Mistress Fufuki (active ca. 676)

As stated by the compilers, not much is known about this person. Her wish in no. 266 could also be taken as on behalf of Princess Tōchi (the daughter of Prince Ōama and Princess Nukata), in whose service she apparently was. The poem sees a divine force in the boulders that keeps them free of grass—an appealing analogue for the smoothness of a young girl's body.

266   [MYS I: 22]

A poem composed by Mistress Fufuki on seeing the crags on the long mountain flanks of Hata when Princess Tōchi made a pilgrimage to Ise Shrine

Kawa no e no	The thrusting, clustered
Yutsuiwamura ni	Boulders on the riverbank
Kusa musazu	Bear no trace of grass:
Tsune ni mogamo na	Forever young, I too would be
Tokootome nite	A maiden till the end of time.

We as yet have no detailed information about Mistress Fufuki. However, the *Chronicles* state: "In the fourth year of the Emperor [Temmu; i.e., 676], Wood-Junior/Swine, in spring, on the Fire-Junior/Swine day of the second month, whose first day was Wood-Junior/Swine, Princess Tōchi and Princess Ahe set off on a pilgrimage to Ise Shrine."

❋ Nos. 267–68 read like an exchange between a man and a woman, but both poems are attributed to Mistress Fufuki. It seems likely that the first poem was composed by a male admirer, and that the compilers were nodding at this point. It is based on the belief that desire conveys a phantasmal image to its object in a dream. The image of the bridge is germane to this notion, though technically used to introduce the idea of continuousness in *tsugi* ("day and night" in the translation). In the second poem the botanical identity of *itsumo* ("always-plant"), apparently some kind of waterweed, is obscure. The word is used to introduce *itsu mo itsu mo* ("always, always") in the main statement.

267–68   [MYS IV:493–94/490–91]

Two poems by Mistress Fufuki

(267)   [493/490]

> Mano no ura no   Over the still pools
> Yodo no tsugihashi   Of Mano Bay they built a bridge,
> Kokoro yu mo   Planking it by day
> Omoe ya imo ga   And night with all her heart she yearns,
> Ime ni shi miyuru   My love, and comes in dreams.

(268)   [494/491]

> Kawa no e no   Come to me always
> Itsumo no hana no   Like the flower of the always-plant
> Itsu mo itsu mo   Down by the river:
> Kimase wa ga seko   Always, always come, my love—
> Tokijikeme ya mo   You'll never be out of season!

Prince Ōtsu (663–86)

Prince Ōtsu was by all accounts the most talented of Emperor Temmu's numerous sons, but he fell afoul of the ambitions of Temmu's widow, the Empress Jitō (r. 686–97), who was determined to secure the succession for her own son, Prince Kusakabe. Like Prince Arima before him, he was seduced into a plot and thus gotten out of the way, dying by mandatory suicide less than a month after Temmu's death. He is said to have been manly, eloquent, and popular at court, and according to *Nihonshoki*, the practice of composing poetry in Chinese began with him. *Kaifūsō* comments that he had the character of a libertine, a recklessness that can be seen in no. 269. The *Man'yōshū* compilers disclaim knowledge of his affair with Ishikawa no Iratsume but include an exchange between the lovers (see nos. 872–73). This lady had rejected the advances of Prince Ōtsu's half brother Prince Kusakabe, a fact that likely did Ōtsu no good with the Jitō-Kusakabe faction. Ōtsu boasts that he slept with Lady Ishikawa despite the divination conducted by the Yin-Yang Master Tsumori no Tōru. The poem plays on Tsumori's name ("harbor guard") and introduces the image of a ship, along with double meanings for *ura* ("bay"/"divination") and *noramu* ("board"/ "be revealed"). It shows Ōtsu's skill with the intricacies of a poetic style much prized in later ages. No. 270, by contrast, with its use of the pillow word *momozutau* ("on the way to a hundred") as a mock epithet for Iware through the syllable *i* ("fifty"), is in an older, more traditional style. It is the Prince's death poem (he also left one in Chinese) and strikes a note of sober wistfulness. The focus on a last scene of nature makes an effective final gesture, and there is irony in the sense that the mallards cry, but it is he who will fly up into the clouds.

269   [MYS II : 109]

A poem composed by Prince Ōtsu when Tsumori no Muraji Tōru revealed by divination that he had secretly trysted with Ishikawa no Iratsume (the details of this matter are not known)

Ōbune no	We lay together,
Tsumori ga ura ni	Knowing well the harbor guard
Noramu to wa	Would snare our ship,
Masashi ni shirite	Mooring us with magic words,
Wa ga futari neshi	Exposed on the open shore.

270   [MYS III : 419/416]

A poem composed by Prince Ōtsu when, having been condemned to death, he wept on the bank of Iware Pond

Momozutau	On Iware Pond
Iware no ike ni	(*Fifty of a hundredfold*)
Naku kamo o	The mallards cry;
Kyō nomi mite ya	Shall I see them only today
Kumogakurinamu	And vanish into the clouds?

Prince Kusakabe (662–89)

This favorite son of Empress Jitō was known by the unique title of Hinamishi no Mikoto—"His Highness Peer of the Sun." He was made Crown Prince in 681 but died in 689 without succeeding to the throne. Poem 271 is his contribution to the triangle alluded to in no. 269. The plaintive note of this poem is in obvious contrast to Prince Ōtsu's bravado.

271   [MYS II : 110]

A poem sent by Prince Hinamishi no Mikoto to Ishikawa no Iratsume (the lady's name was Ōnako)

Ōnako o	How could I forget
Ochikatanobe ni	Ōnako for the space
Karu kaya no	Of one hand's breadth
Tsuka no aida mo	Of the *kaya* reeds they cut
Ware wasureme ya	In yonder distant fields?

Princess Ōku (661–701)

Princess Ōku was the full sister of Prince Ōtsu. In 673, the second year of her father Temmu's reign, she became the Consecrated Princess, or shrine virgin of Ise. This position of high priestess at the shrine of the sun goddess was traditionally held by an unmarried female relative of the reigning monarch. Princess Ōku held it for thirteen years, returning to the capital in 686 after Temmu's death. Her poems show her to have been very close to her brother, whose secret visit to Ise in 686 no doubt was in connection with the events that ended his life. It was clearly his farewell visit. The reference to autumn in no. 273 places the parting between Emperor Temmu's death on the ninth of the ninth month and the end of the month. Prince Ōtsu died on the third day of the tenth month, the first month of winter. Ōku's six poems are impressive evidence of her love, and of her mastery of pathos and irony. For more on "Ise of the Divine Wind," see no. 341.

272–73   [MYS II: 105–6]

Two poems by Princess Ōku, composed when Prince Ōtsu, having secretly gone down to the shrine at Ise, departed again for the capital

(272)   [105]

> Wa ga seko o   Night had worn away,
> Yamato e yaru to   My brother, when I sent you off
>   Sayo fukete   On the road to Yamato;
> Akatokitsuyu ni   Dawn began to streak the sky,
> Wa ga tachinureshi   And I stood there drenched with dew.

(273)   [106]

> Futari yukedo   Though two were to go,
> Yukisugigataki   The going over would be hard:
>   Akiyama o   The autumn mountains—
> Ika ni ka kimi ga   How are you managing, my lord,
> Hitori koyuramu   To cross them all alone?

274–75   [MYS II: 163–64]

Two poems composed by Princess Ōku when she came up from the Consecrated Shrine at Ise to the capital after the death of Prince Ōtsu

(274)   [163]

> Kamukaze no   In the land they call
> Ise no kuni ni mo   Ise of the Divine Wind
>   Aramashi o   I might have stayed;

Nani shi ka kikemu	For what purpose did I come,
Kimi mo aranaku ni	When I knew you were not here?

(275)   [164]

Mimaku hori	When I knew my lord
A ga suru kimi mo	Whom I desired to look upon
Aranaku ni	Was no longer here,
Nani shi ka kikemu	For what end did I come back—
Uma tsukaruru ni	Merely to tire my horse?

276–77   [MYS II: 165–66]

Two poems composed in sadness and grief by Princess Ōku when the body
of Prince Ōtsu was transferred to Mount Futagami in the Kazuraki Range
for burial

(276)   [165]

Utsusomi no	I, who belong
Hito naru ware ya	To the mortal race of man—
Asu yori wa	From tomorrow
Futagamiyama o	Shall I look on Futagami,
Irose to a ga mimu	A mountain, as my brother?

(277)   [166]

Iso no ue ni	Though with my own hand
Ouru ashibi o	I could pluck andromeda
Taoramedo	On the stony shore,
Misubeki kimi ga	No one says my lord is here
Ari to iwanaku ni	That I might show him flowers.

On reflection, the above does not seem like a poem on transferral for burial.
Perhaps the Princess composed this poem on the way back to the capital
from Ise Shrine, when she saw a flower by the wayside and was choked with
grief.

Prince Kawashima (657–91)

Prince Kawashima was a son of Emperor Tenji noted primarily for his appointment in 681 to the committee that prepared the historiographical materials ultimately resulting in *Nihonshoki*. No. 278 may be another reference to
the fate of Prince Arima (see nos. 247–48 and 854–59). "Offerings" (*tamu-
kekusa*) would refer to cloth strips tied to the trees as oblations for safety on
a journey.

278   [MYS I:34]

A poem composed by Prince Kawashima when the Empress [Jitō] made a progress to the province of Ki (or by Yamanoue no Omi Okura, according to another source)

Shiranami no	Where the white waves splash
Hamamatsu ga e no	Across the branches of the pines
Tamukekusa	Along the sandy shore,
Ikuyo made ni ka	How many ages have they passed,
Toshi no henuramu	These offerings on the boughs?

Nihongi states: "In the fourth year of Akamitori [689], Metal-Senior/Tiger, in autumn, ninth month, the Empress made a progress to the province of Ki."

Prince Yuge (d. 699)

Prince Yuge was a son of Emperor Temmu. *Man'yōshū* shows him in love with his half sister Princess Ki (no. 265), a type of romantic relationship not unusual at the time, when half-siblings were brought up in different households. The sequence 279–82 is structured in a way that is intriguingly parallel to the four poems attributed to Empress Iwanohime (nos. 231–34). An expression of impatience is followed by the topos better-to-have-died, then a poem announcing a decision, and finally a realization that the yearning will go on. The second and fourth poems are particularly close to their counterparts in structure and technique. The use of the rapids of Yoshino River to provide the image of headlong love, recurrent in later poetry, apparently finds its source in no. 279. The reference to "gemweed" (i.e., glistening, gemlike seaweed) in no. 281 is probably metaphorical. In context, the metaphor no doubt refers to Princess Ki (though her connection with Asaka Bay is not clear), but otherwise the poem could be read as expressing the desire for a more casual harvest among the shore girls of Suminoe. No. 282, the final poem in the series (like no. 234), is based on a jo. The swing line *tayutai ni* ("constantly tossing") ties its two halves together. No. 283 uses the already established convention that the cuckoo's call intensifies longing. No. 284 also employs the topos better-to-have-died. It is identical to the anonymous poem MYS X:2258/2254, a fact that can be interpreted in two ways—that Prince Yuge was quoting an old poem, or that the compilers of Book X reused the Prince's poem to illustrate their category of Autumn Love, discarding the author's name in the process.

279–82   [MYS II:119–22]

Four poems in which Prince Yuge yearns for Princess Ki

(279)   [119]

    Yoshinogawa   What I want to know
  Yuku se no hayami   Is, cannot you and I get on
    Shimashiku mo   A bit more quickly,
  Yodomu koto naku   Without this standing still in pools,
  Arikosenu ka mo   But rush like the rapids of Yoshino?

(280)   [120]

    Wagimoko ni   Rather than yearning
  Koitsutsu arazu wa   For my young love as I do,
    Akihagi no   Better had I been
  Sakite chirinuru   An autumn clover blossom
  Hana ni aramashi o   Fallen after flowering!

(281)   [121]

    Yū sareba   When evening falls,
  Shio michikinamu   The salt tide will come flooding in,
    Suminoe no   And that is when
  Asaka no ura ni   I would go down to Suminoe
  Tamamo karitena   To gather gemweed in Asaka Bay.

(282)   [122]

    Ōbune no   Stopped in the roadstead,
  Hatsuru tomari no   A great ship rides at anchor
    Tayutai ni   Constantly tossing
  Monoomoiyasenu   With the burden of my love,
  Hito no ko yue ni   I waste for another's girl.

283   [MYS VIII: 1471/1467]

A poem by Prince Yuge

    Hototogisu   Were there a land
  Nakaru kuni ni mo   Where the cuckoo never comes,
    Yukiteshi ka   There would I go,
  Sono naku koe o   For every time I hear its cry
  Kikeba kurushi mo   My heart is wrung with pain.

284   [MYS VIII: 1612/1608]

A poem by Prince Yuge

    Akihagi no   Better had it been,
  Ue ni okitaru   Like the white dew on the leaves

Shiratsuyu no	Of autumn clover,
Ke ka mo shinamashi	To have dried into the air,
Koitsutsu arazu wa	Rather than live in this yearning.

Empress Jitō (645–702)

Empress Jitō was the daughter of Emperor Tenji and the full sister of Princess Ōta, the mother of Prince Ōtsu and Princess Ōku. She and her sister both became consorts of Emperor Temmu, and one may assume an intense rivalry between them. It was Jitō, the younger sister, who became Empress-Consort and then reigning Empress (686–97). She was politically adept and determined to protect the claims of her own son, Prince Kusakabe, against the brilliance of her nephew and stepson Prince Ōtsu. Since Kusakabe predeceased his mother, she passed on the throne to his son, her grandchild Prince Karu, who reigned as Emperor Mommu from Jitō's abdication in 697 until his death in 707.

No. 285 is Jitō's famous celebration of the onset of summer as evidenced in the bleaching garments laid out against the green of Mount Kagu. "Barken cloth" (*tae*) was made from the fibers of the paper-mulberry tree and figures often as a pillow word for *koromo*, "garment." On "Heavenly Mount Kagu," see no. 238. Mount Kagu was immediately to the east of Jitō's palace at Fujiwara (see nos. 467 and 1245).

285   [MYS I:28]

A poem of the Empress

Haru sugite	Spring must be over,
Natsu kitaru rashi	Summer seems to have arrived:
Shirotae no	White barken-cloth
Koromo hoshitari	Garments are laid out to dry
Ame no Kaguyama	On Heavenly Mount Kagu.

✳ No. 286, the first of Jitō's two tanka mourning her husband, shows great power in its use of irony, though the last line is based on a problematical reading. If the impossible is possible, then death and grief can be endured—this conclusion gains its effect by being forced out of bitter analogy. In the second poem the cloud stands for the deceased (as in the "Suma" chapter of *The Tale of Genji*). The star and moon may be the Empress and her grandson Prince Karu, or vice versa. The moon seems to be associated with Princes, as in nos. 252, 302, and 338.

286–87 [MYS II:160–61]

Two poems that, according to a certain document, were composed by the Grand Retired Sovereign [Jitō] at the demise of the Emperor [Temmu]

(286) [160]

Moyuru hi mo	Even a burning flame
Torite tsutsumite	Do they not say one can take,
Fukuro ni wa	Hold it in one's hand,
Iru to iwazu ya	Bundle it to stuff a bag?
Omo shiranaku mo	But I am not so clever.

(287) [161]

Kitayama ni	On the northern hills
Tanabiku kumo no	Now there trails a band of cloud,
Aokumo no	A blue cloud drifting,
Hoshi sakariyuku	Drawing away from the star,
Tsuki o sakarite	Drawing away from the moon.

Kakinomoto no Hitomaro (active 689–700)

Japanese poetry reached its first full maturity at the end of the seventh century in the work of Kakinomoto no Hitomaro, the earliest poet of any consequence who was not a member of the imperial clan. Just who and what Hitomaro was are questions of the greatest interest, but the answers must be sought in the recorded body of his poetry in *Man'yōshū*, which yields very little in the way of biographical detail. Although he did not belong to a politically prominent or powerful clan, his clan title Asomi, second in the ranking of eight such titles reorganized by Emperor Temmu, indicates remote collateral connections to the reigning house. From his public poetry, largely composed for presentation to or in honor of personages of princely or imperial rank, we can draw the conclusion that he served as at least a semiofficial spokesman for the court, a role that may in its fullest sense have been unique to him, although later poets followed his example in composing paeans and laments for the Emperors and Princes of their day. His known career, datable from four poems commemorating the deaths of members of the imperial family, spans only eleven years, and these largely coincide with the power of Empress Jitō, who assumed the throne after the death of her son Prince Kusakabe in 689 (having ruled informally from the death of her husband Temmu in 686) and continued to rule for a few years through her grandson Emperor Mommu after her abdication in 697. Jitō closely identified herself with her late husband's policies and personal fame, and it has been argued that Hitomaro's role at court was to immortalize in verse the heroic qualities of his era, bringing to new prominence the ancient claim of the blood royal to an actual and living divinity. From his private poetry we learn something of Hitomaro the man—that he traveled extensively in central and western Japan, including to the remote seacoast of Iwami; that he loved a woman in Iwami from whom he parted, and another in Karu near the capital who died, leaving him with a child; and that he had a wife who survived him. Beyond these few facts—facts if the poems from which they are drawn speak a literal truth—all is speculation. The man, if he is to be found, is in the poetry.

The poems connected with the name of Hitomaro fall into three categories. His most secure oeuvre, those poems stated in *Man'yōshū* to have been composed by him, consists of eighteen chōka and sixty-four tanka (thirty-six of which are envoys). There is also a very large body of poems—as many as 370, depending on the interpretation of editorial notes in the text—that are labeled as drawn from "Kakinomoto no Asomi Hitomaro Kashū." This "Hitomaro Collection," as it appears in *Man'yōshū*, consists largely of tanka, but also includes sedōka and chōka. It has been disputed on stylistic and other grounds as not belonging to Hitomaro's work, but also defended. And then there is a scattering of attributions to Hitomaro in later anthologies. The present anthology contains selections from all three categories.

Particularly famous for his poems on parting in life and in death, Hitomaro is the poet of a compassionate sorrow expressed in a heightened style with mythic references and a rich use of formulaic language. His roots in the Japanese past seem deep and nourishing, but he also speaks for a common humanity beyond the bounds of his specific culture. A formal sensuousness runs through his chōka, in a speech at once supple and elevated. It was Hitomaro who realized the full potential of the chōka, orchestrating its pre-posited and parallel structures to provide his prosody with a tensile strength never equaled by any other poet. The voice in these long poems becomes the voice of Everyman, even when it speaks of a personal grief. The independent tanka sometimes let us overhear a quieter speaking voice, a hint of a more quotidian personality, lyric rather than bardic. But this voice in turn blends into the "folk" voice pervasive in the "Hitomaro Collection," and the question of where to draw the lines delineating the "real" Hitomaro constantly recurs. That Hitomaro's accomplishment attracted to him a pre-eminent fame is clear from the references made to his greatness by later poets like Ōtomo no Yakamochi and Ki no Tsurayuki (ca. 868–ca. 945). *Man'yōshū* contains evidence that Hitomaro literally "became a legend in his own time," for we find the final references to him in Book 11 taking on the character of a poem-tale. After a series of poems to comfort the souls of drowning victims and other dead wayfarers, Hitomaro himself lies dying in the wild. His dying verse is followed by one by his wife, and another by a later poet imagining his feelings. Already a tradition is forming in which the individual Hitomaro becomes one with the images in his poetry. He had served the court by enabling it to express and understand grief and glory; now he himself attracts the attentions of others who speak in his name. Ultimately Hitomaro is one with the living gods he worshiped—and yet the final image of him is of the lone mortal dying on the shores of the boundless and unknown sea.

The poems selected below—which include nearly all of Hitomaro's chōka—are arranged in an order following the Man'yō categories of zōka, sōmon, and banka, that is, poems on miscellaneous themes, love poems, and laments. Next come selections from the "Hitomaro Collection," and finally several poems attributed to Hitomaro in later anthologies.

The first poem by Hitomaro in *Man'yōshū*, the chōka-hanka set MYS 1:29–31 (no. 288–90), was composed during the reign of Empress Jitō and takes as its subject the fallen capital at Ōtsu, where Emperor Tenji and his son had held court briefly (667–72) on the shores of Lake Biwa, known as the "Sea of Ōmi." It differs from Hitomaro's other zōka in being a poem of grief—not for a dead Prince, but for a vanished time and its glory. As a public poet Hitomaro did not hesitate to celebrate glory, but as a man he stands puzzled by its passing, which like that of life itself is treated as a sad mystery. By the "monarch [who] reigned at Kashihara" Hitomaro refers to the legendary First Emperor, Jimmu. All his descendants are spoken of as gods, including Emperor Tenji, who transferred the palace to Ōtsu at Sasanami on the lake. The puzzlement expressed concerning his reasons for doing so is echoed in other Hitomaro poems that try to plumb the reason for death. The common ground is awe at the unfathomable, and awe pervades the high poetry of Hitomaro. (For another view of the trip to Ōmi, see nos. 257–58 by Princess Nukata.) Unebi is called "the Jewel-sash Mount" from its first syllable, related to *unaji*, "nape of the neck." The pillow word *tamadasuki* ("jewel-sash") provides an auspicious image with which to begin. The poem is one syntactic unit from this opening image to the final exclamation. A total of seven pillow words add to the richly formal prosody. The two envoys personify features of the land to bring out the ironic contrast between their permanence and the now vanished court. Irony is another of Hitomaro's ways of handling sorrow.

288–90   [MYS 1:29–31]

A poem composed by Kakinomoto no Asomi Hitomaro on passing the ruined capital of Ōmi

Tamadasuki	From that hallowed age
Unebi no yama no	When the monarch Suzerain of the Sun
Kashihara no	Reigned at Kashihara
Hijiri no miyo yu	By Unebi, called the Jewel-sash Mount,

5 Aremashishi	Each and every god
Kami no kotogoto	Made manifest in the world of men,
Tsuga no ki no	One by one in evergreen
Iyatsugitsugi ni	Succession like a line of hemlock trees,
Ame no shita	Ruled under heaven
10 Shirashimeshishi o	All this realm with uncontested sway:
Sora ni mitsu	Yet from sky-seen
Yamato o okite	Yamato did one depart—
Aoni yoshi	Whatever may have been
Narayama o koe	The secret of his sage intent—
15 Ikasama ni	And passed across
Omōshimese ka	The slopes of blue-earth Nara Mountain
Amazakaru	To a land, remote
Hina ni wa aredo	Beyond the distant heaven,
Iwabashiru	The land of Ōmi
20 Ōmi no kuni no	Where water dashes on the rocks,
Sasanami no	To the palace of Ōtsu
Ōtsu no miya ni	In Sasanami of the gently lapping waves;
Ame no shita	And there, as it is said,
Shirashimeshikemu	He ruled this realm beneath the sky:
25 Sumeroki no	That sovereign god,
Kami no mikoto no	August ancestral deity—
Ōmiya wa	His great palace stood
Koko to kikedo mo	Upon this spot, as I have heard;
Ōtono wa	Its mighty halls
30 Koko to iedo mo	Rose here, so all men say;
Harukusa no	Where now spring grasses
Shigeku oitaru	Choke the earth in their rife growth,
Kasumi tachi	And mists rise up
Haruhi no kireru	To hide the dazzling springtime sun;
35 Momoshiki no	Now I view this site
Ōmiyadokoro	Where once the mighty palace stood,
Mireba kanashi mo	And it is sad to see.

Envoys

Sasanami no	Still Cape Kara stands
Shiga no Karasaki	In Shiga of the gently lapping waves,
Sakiku aredo	Changeless from of old;
Ōmiyahito no	But it will wait in vain to see
Fune machikanetsu	The courtiers' boats row back.

Sasanami no	Broad the waters stand
Shiga no ōwada	By Shiga of the gently lapping waves:
Yodomu to mo	The lake is still;

Mukashi no hito ni   But how can it ever meet again
Mata mo awame ya mo   The men of long ago?

❋ An independent tanka composed at an unknown time, but perhaps on
the same journey, serves in a sense as yet another envoy to the poem on
fallen Ōmi. One of Hitomaro's best-loved verses, it shows his mastery of
the short form. Linguistic change has augmented the loveliness of vowel
harmonies (e.g., *afumi nö umi* → *ōmi no umi*) to give the poem an even softer
beauty today than in the language Hitomaro knew, and the wavelike rhythm
remains, together weaving a spell as powerful as anything he achieved in the
greater compass of chōka. Each word is as valuable for its sound as its sense,
and the personification here is more intense and immediate to the speaker of
the poem. Sound, sight, motion, mood—all enhance each other and weigh
on the poet's "helpless heart." No translation could begin to do justice to
what may be the most perfect poem in the language. It was echoed decades
later by Ōtomo no Yakamochi (no. 831), who, however, lacked the grand
theme that deepens the feeling of Hitomaro's meditation on the desolate
lakeshore. Perhaps only a medieval poet like Saigyō (1118–90) could later
match this mood.

291   [MYS III:268/266]

A poem by Kakinomoto no Asomi Hitomaro

    Ōmi no umi   Out on Ōmi Sea
    Yūnami chidori   Plovers on the evening waves,
      Na ga nakeba   When I hear your cries,
    Kokoro mo shino ni   Into my now helpless heart
    Inishie omōyu   Come thoughts of long ago.

❋ On the banks of Uji River on the way back from Ōmi to Yamato,
Hitomaro paused and noticed the waves splashing against the weirs. In his
poem on this scene it is the waves that are helpless, "hesitating." A metaphorical reading reveals nature not as the ironic contrast or the source of
affecting tonal harmony, but as the image of man's fate. Uji River would be
used again for this purpose in *The Tale of Genji*. *Yaso* ("eighty") decorates
the homophonous sense of *uji* as "clan"—the "eighty clans" of warriors
(*mononofu*).

292   [MYS III:266/264]

A poem composed by Kakinomoto no Asomi Hitomaro on reaching Uji
River, coming up from the province of Ōmi

Mononofu no	In Uji River
Yasoujigawa no	(Uji of the eighty warrior clans)
Ajiroki ni	Along the weir-stakes
Isayou nami no	Pile the hesitating waves,
Yukue shirazu mo	Not knowing where they go.

✳ Hitomaro's most notable paeans to the glory of a living ruler are two chōka he composed in honor of a visit by Empress Jitō to the imperial family's pleasure dome at Yoshino. Jitō often visited this spot, no doubt associated in her mind with her late husband Temmu's flight to take refuge in Yoshino before the Jinshin War. Yoshino River runs at the foot of the fastness of the Yoshino Mountains, marking the southern boundary of the Asuka area where the court was traditionally situated. Pleasure trips to the palace at Yoshino are recorded as early as the reign of Yūryaku (see, e.g., no. 96). Hitomaro treats the Empress's visit as a form of land-viewing (see no. 238), this time from atop her palace. The poems are clearly complementary, the first showing the delight of the courtiers, and the second the obeisance of the deified land itself. The opening formulas and the closing line of the second chōka remind us that the Empress too is a divinity. But the emphasis is on creating a vision of clear, unspoiled beauty, an earthly paradise for the Empress to reign over, reflecting her godliness in its own. River valleys and sparkling seacoasts abound in *Man'yōshū*, evidence at once of the high regard in which the native religion held cleanliness, and of a discovery by newly cultivated men and women of the existence of natural beauty as an esthetic quality. Princess Nukata's esthetic vision in no. 256 is here wedded to the native ethos of divine rule. But both esthetic and ethos have achieved a self-conscious definition because of an awareness of continental civilization and governance. This awareness differentiates both Nukata and Hitomaro from their more "primitive" antecedents, the makers of ancient song.

293–96   [MYS I: 36–39]

Poems composed by Kakinomoto no Asomi Hitomaro when the Sovereign went on an excursion to the palace at Yoshino

(293–94)   [36–37]

	Yasumishishi	Where our Sovereign reigns,
	Wa ga ōkimi no	Ruling the earth in all tranquility,
	Kikoshiosu	Under the heaven
	Ame no shita ni	Of this realm she holds in sway,
5	Kuni wa shi mo	Many are the lands,
	Sawa ni aredo mo	But of their multitude,
	Yamakawa no	Seeing the clear pools

	Kiyoki kafuchi to	That form along this mountain stream,
	Mikokoro o	She gave her heart
10	Yoshino no kuni no	To the fair land of Yoshino,
	Hana chirafu	And where blossoms fall
	Akizu no nobe ni	Forever on the fields of Akizu
	Miyabashira	She planted firm
	Futoshikimaseba	The mighty pillars of her palace halls.
15	Momoshiki no	Now the courtiers,
	Ōmiyahito wa	Men of the palace of the hundred stones,
	Fune namete	Line up their boats
	Asakawa watari	To row across the morning stream,
	Funagioi	Vie in their boats
20	Yūkawa wataru	To race upon the evening stream:
	Kono kawa no	And like the stream
	Tayuru koto naku	This place shall last forever,
	Kono yama no	Like these mountains
	Iyatakashirasu	Ever loftier shall rise
25	Minasosoku	Beside the plunging waters
	Taki no miyako wa	Of the torrent her august abode:
	Miredo akanu kamo	Long though I gaze, my eyes will never tire.

Envoy

Miredo akanu	Long though I gaze,
Yoshino no kawa no	Never shall I tire of Yoshino,
Tokoname no	Within whose stream
Tayuru koto naku	The water-moss grows smooth forever,
Mata kaerimimu	As I shall come to view these sights anew.

(295–96)   [38–39]

	Yasumishishi	Our great Sovereign
	Wa ga ōkimi	Who rules the land in all tranquility,
	Kamunagara	She who is a god
	Kamusabi sesu to	In action godlike has ordained
5	Yoshinogawa	That by Yoshino,
	Tagitsu kafuchi ni	Where seething waters deepen into pools,
	Takadono o	Lofty halls shall rise,
	Takashirimashite	Lifting high above the stream;
	Noboritachi	And when she climbs aloft
10	Kunimi o seseba	That she may gaze upon her land,
	Tatanaharu	Fold upon fold
	Aokakiyama	The mountains standing in green walls
	Yamatsumi no	Present as tribute
	Matsuru mitsuki to	Offered by the mountain gods

15	Haruhe ni wa	In springtime
	Hana kazashimochi	Blossoms worn upon the brow,
	Aki tateba	And when autumn comes
	Momichi kazaseri	Deck themselves in yellow leaves.
	Yukisou	Gods of the river too,
20	Kawa no kami mo	That flows along the mountain foot,
	Ōmike ni	In order to provide
	Tsukaematsuru to	The Sovereign's table with good fare,
	Kami tsu se ni	At the upper shallows
	Ukawa o tachi	Start the cormorants downstream,
25	Shimo tsu se ni	And at the lower shallows
	Sade sashiwatasu	Spread their nets from bank to bank.
	Yama kawa mo	Mountain and river
	Yorite tsukauru	Join thus in fealty to serve
	Kami no miyo kamo	The god who rules this glorious age.

Envoy

Yama kawa mo	Whom mountain and river
Yorite tsukauru	Join thus in fealty to serve,
Kamunagara	She who is a god
Tagitsu kafuchi ni	Now sets her boat upon the stream
Funade sesu kamo	Where seething waters deepen into pools.

Concerning the above, *Nihongi* states: "In the third year [689], Earth-Junior/Ox, in the first month, the Sovereign proceeded to the Yoshino Palace. In the eighth month she proceeded to the Yoshino Palace. In the fourth year [690], Metal-Senior/Tiger, in the second month, she proceeded to the Yoshino Palace. In the fifth month she proceeded to the Yoshino Palace. In the fifth year [691], Metal-Junior/Hare, in the first month, she proceeded to the Yoshino Palace. In the fourth month she proceeded to the Yoshino Palace." It is not known precisely in which month the author composed these poems while in the Empress's train.

✳ The formula *kami ni shi maseba* ("is a very god indeed") used by Hitomaro in no. 297 and its variant dates back to poems in honor of Emperor Temmu composed in 672, the year of his victory in the Jinshin War (see nos. 998–99). The "great Sovereign" in this case is Empress Jitō, or in the variant, Prince Osakabe, a son of Emperor Temmu by a different mother. Ikazuchiyama ("Thunder Hill") is a small prominence on the right bank of the Asuka River south of Jitō's palace site at Fujiwara. Hitomaro must have felt the name provided an opportunity too good to miss; the mountain is not much, but the poems work effectively as witty eulogies, the wit giving a buoyancy to the eulogy. They may be contrasted with the laborious changes rung on "Yoshino" by Temmu in no. 264.

297 [MYS III:235]

A poem composed by Kakinomoto no Asomi Hitomaro when the Sovereign went to Thunder Hill

Ōkimi wa	Our great Sovereign
Kami ni shi maseba	Is a very god indeed:
Amakumo no	See how high amidst
Ikazuchi no ue ni	The clouds of heaven she now dwells
Iori seru kamo	Encamped upon the thunder!

298 [MYS III:236/235a]

Concerning the above, it is stated in a certain text that this was presented to Prince Osakabe. There the poem reads:

Ōkimi wa	Because our great lord
Kami ni shi maseba	Is a very god indeed,
Kumogakuru	He builds his palace
Ikazuchiyama ni	Hidden in the covering clouds
Miya shikiimasu	High on Thunder Mountain!

❋ Prince Niitabe (d. 735) was still another of Temmu's numerous progeny. No. 299–300, in praise of the Prince's palace, uses the additional formula *takaterasu hi no miko* ("the Divine Child of the High-Shining Sun") to go with *yasumishishi wa ga ōkimi* ("our great lord who rules the land in all tranquility"). Usage makes it clear that these encomiastic expressions could be applied to other members of the blood royal in addition to the reigning monarch. This, the shortest of Hitomaro's *chōka*, seems to have been occasioned by a snowstorm, and the poet seizes on the steady streaming of the snow as the image of his own fidelity. The envoy is an exclamation of delight, as Hitomaro casts himself in a role much like that of the courtiers sporting on the river under the pleased gaze of their Empress in no. 293. Snow is usually auspicious in *Man'yōshū*—see nos. 868–69, 1169, and 853 (the last poem in the collection).

299–300 [MYS III:263–64/261–62]

A poem presented to Prince Niitabe by Kakinomoto no Asomi Hitomaro; with *tanka*

	Yasumishishi	Our great lord
	Wa ga ōkimi	Who rules the land in all tranquility,
	Takaterasu	The Divine Child
	Hi no miko	Of the High-Shining Sun,
5	Shikiimasu	Laid out these mighty halls
	Ōtono no ue ni	Wherein now he dwells, and whither

Hisakata no	From the far reaches
Amazutaikuru	Of the sky comes streaming snow:
Yukijimono	Steady as the snow,
10 Yukikayoitsutsu	I shall keep upon this path
Iya tokoyo made	Ever more until eternal years.

Envoy

Yatsuriyama	On Mount Yatsuri
Kodachi mo miezu	The forest cannot be seen
Furimagau	Through the mazy drift;
Yuki no sawakeru	How joyous is a morning
Ashita tanoshi mo	When the sky is alive with snow!

❀ The royal hunt is another of the eulogistic topics of Man'yō poetry; no. 245–46, by Nakatsu Sumera Mikoto, has already provided an example. In no. 301–2, his specimen of the genre, Hitomaro adulates the hunter at closer range, bringing the hunting party onto the fields and comparing them to the deer and quail that "kneel down" before the princely presence. This image recurs in no. 341. It is clear that Hitomaro developed a word-store on which he drew in different contexts. The recurrence of such phraseology contributes to the formulaic or bardic quality of his verse. In contrast to the carefully paced exploitation of these elements in the chōka—parallels following the deifying introduction—the first envoy leaps out as a daring and inventive conceit. The images of the sun and its reflection-symbol, the mirror in lines 19–22, have prepared the way for the emergence of another circularity in the heavens—the full moon, often associated with Princes. The envoy is a gesture of kinetic release, in which the Prince throws his net into the sky and snares the moon (now it is night after a day's hunting), which becomes a kind of halo, his silken umbrella, itself a sign of a noble presence. The second hanka, supplied from a different source, reasserts the formula *kami ni shi maseba*, and with it another superhuman feat, the factitious creation of a "sea"—actually a pond—on the mountain. Prince Naga (d. 715), the object of all this adoration, was a son of Emperor Temmu, and full brother of Prince Yuge.

301–2   [MYS III: 240–41/239–40]

A poem composed by Kakinomoto no Asomi Hitomaro when Prince Naga went hunting at the pond of Kariji; with *tanka*

Yasumishishi	Our great lord
Wa ga ōkimi	Who rules the land in all tranquility,
Takahikaru	Our Divine Child
Wa ga hi no miko no	Of the High-Shining Sun,
5 Uma namete	Now lines up his steeds,

	Mikari tataseru	Here begins the royal hunt:
	Wakakomo o	On Kariji fields
	Kariji no ono ni	(Kari of the young rush harvest)
	Shishi koso ba	Surely they are deer
10	Ihaiorogame	That kneel down to worship him,
	Uzura koso	Surely they are quail
	Ihaimotōre	That creep about in circles:
	Shishijimono	Though we are not deer
	Ihaiorogami	We kneel down and worship him,
15	Uzura nasu	We too like quail
	Ihaimotōri	Creep in circles through the grass.
	Kashikomi to	Awed as we are,
	Tsukaematsurite	We render reverent service;
	Hisakata no	As to the sun-bright
20	Ame miru gotoku	Heaven we look up to him,
	Masokagami	A cloudless mirror
	Aogite miredo	On whom we gaze aloft:
	Harukusa no	The new spring grass
	Iyamezurashiki	Is not more marvelous than he,
25	Wa ga ōkimi kamo	The great lord of our delight!

Envoy

Hisakata no	High in the heavens
Ama yuku tsuki o	Where the moon goes sailing by
Ami ni sashi	He has thrown his net:
Wa ga ōkimi wa	Our great lord has caught the moon
Kinugasa ni seri	For his silken parasol!

303   [MYS III : 242/241]

An envoy in a certain text

Ōkimi wa	Our great lord
Kami ni shi maseba	Is a very god indeed:
Maki no tatsu	Where the timber stands
Arayamanaka ni	In the bristling mountain's midst
Umi o nasu kamo	He has made a sea!

❊ Hitomaro the traveler exists in two modes—as the poetic recorder of royal excursions and as a private and often lonely figure bound on journeys whose reasons are not stated. Eight tanka in Book III belong to the latter type. Where Hitomaro was going we do not know, but the points of reference are all at the eastern end of the Inland Sea. The set may have been assembled from more than one journey. These too are *zōka*, "miscellaneous poems," of which travel is one frequent subcategory. The first of the eight contains six characters for which adequate readings have not been agreed upon and is excluded from the translation. Noshima and Kehi are on Awaji Island; the other places named are along the south shore of Honshū. The traveler seems to be bound away from his home in Yamato in nos. 304–8, but in no. 309 he is coming home and sees the mountains of Yamato (*shima,* "isle," referring to a coast seen from the sea) from Akashi Strait. In the last poem the direction is ambiguous. The custom of lovers tying each other's sashes on parting is reflected in no. 305. Two poems, nos. 306 and 308, contain pillow words augmenting the meanings of place-names—*fuji,* the rough-fibered wisteria, and *akashi,* "bright." A series like this, with its glimpses of scenery along the way and its *ryojō,* "mood of travel," looks forward to the extensive travel literature that developed in Heian and later times.

304–10   [MYS III: 251–57/250–56]
[Seven of] eight poems of travel by Kakinomoto no Asomi Hitomaro

(304)   [251/250]
   Tamamo karu   Passing Minume
  Minume o sugite   Where they cut the gemlike weed,
   Natsukusa no   Our boat has come
 Noshima no saki ni   Close by the Point of Noshima,
 Fune chikazukinu   Thick-grown with summer grass.

(305)   [252/251]
    Awaji no   In the shore breeze
Noshima no saki no   Off the Point of Noshima
  Hamakaze ni   On Awaji
 Imo ga musubishi   My sash blows back toward home—
 Himo fukikaesu   The sash my young love tied.

(306)   [253/252]
   Aratae no   On Fujie Bay
 Fujie no ura ni   (Fujie of the rough bark-cloth)
  Suzuki tsuru   Will they look at me
Ama to ka miramu   As a fisherman out for sea bass,
 Tabiyuku ware o   I who am bound away?

(307)   [254/253]
  Inabino mo   As I was thinking
Yukisugigateni   How the moor of Inabi

Omoereba   Was hard to pass by,
Kokoro koishiki   Into view came Kako Island,
Kako no shima miyu.   Dear to my yearning heart.

(308)   [255/254]

Tomoshibi no   He who at sunset
Akashi ōto ni   Enters wide Akashi Strait
Iramu hi ya   (Akashi the torch-bright)—
Kogiwakarenamu   Will he yet row on, away,
Ie no atari mizu   And see his home no more?

(309)   [256/255]

Amazakaru   From beyond far skies
Hina no nagachi yu   Over the long rustic ways
Koikureba   We came in yearning;
Akashi no to yori   Now from the Straits of Akashi
Yamatoshima miyu   Yamato Isle stands in view.

(310)   [257/256]

Kehi no umi no   The sea off Kehi
Niwa yoku arashi   Seems to be good fishing ground,
Karikomo no   For like chopped rushes
Midarete izu miyu   Scattering out they come in view,
Ama no tsuribune   The shorefolk in their boats.

✳ Three tanka recorded in Book 1 show that Hitomaro did not always accompany the court on its excursions. Each poem in this elegant set is cast in the speculative mode, as the poet imagines the activities of the court ladies on the shore. Here we encounter a pastoral vision of aristocrats at play, if "pastoral" may be taken to refer to a well-bred indulgence in or romanticization of pursuits that are work to commoners. The lives of the ama, or shorefolk, were romanticized in this way, and no. 312 has court ladies amusing themselves by gathering seaweed, a daily task to women who lived in seaside villages. In the flanking poems, nos. 311 and 313, the ladies ride in boats. This balanced structure is cut across by a progressive one, as the naughty tide that wets the ladies' skirts in the first poem becomes positively dangerous in the last, and by a clever associational linking between *tamamo* meaning "gemlike skirts" and its homophone meaning "gemlike seaweed" in the first and second poems. The poems create a sea-bright atmosphere of sand, wind, waves, glistening seaweed, and glittering skirts—a visual mélange of distinctly pictorial quality, divorced from the melancholy and mythic resonances usually associated with Hitomaro. *Kushiro tsuku* ("brace-leted") in no. 312 is a mock epithet for Tafushi through *ta* ("arm"). The image is not wasted in this context of gaily dressed young women.

311–13   [MYS I: 40–42]

Poems composed by Kakinomoto no Asomi Hitomaro, who remained in the capital when the court went on an excursion to the province of Ise

(311)   [40]

Ami no ura ni	Out on Ami Bay
Funanori suramu	Where boats must now be launching,
Otomera ga	As the maidens board,
Tamamo no suso ni	Up around their gemlike skirts
Shio mitsuramu ka	Will the salt-sea tide brim full?

(312)   [41]

Kushiro tsuku	On the braceleted
Tafushi no saki ni	Arm of land Cape Tafushi
Kyō mo ka mo	Are the ladies of court
Ōmiyahito no	Again today out gathering
Tamamo karuramu	The gemlike wrack of the sea?

(313)   [42]

Shiosai ni	In the brawling tides
Irago no shimahe	Near the Isle of Irago
Kogu fune ni	The boats row out:
Imo noruramu ka	Might my darling be on board—
Araki shimami o	Around the island's rugged shore?

❋ Both groups of travel poems above contain references to a woman special to Hitomaro. There is no way of knowing the identity of the lady on the boat or the woman who tied his sash. She is simply *imo*, the "little sister," the beloved female. Hitomaro as love poet emerges further in two groups of tanka in Book IV under the rubric *sōmon*, the basic Man'yō term for love poems. Nos. 314–17 are a four-poem series balanced a-b-b'-a', with b' and a' apparently answering b and a. Whether Hitomaro is talking to himself or whether the set is a collapsed exchange remains uncertain. The *hamayū* is a lush seaside plant with white blossoms and abundant leaves, and hence serves to introduce *momoe*, "hundredfold," in the first poem, a word that is re-peated in the last. One may assume that Hitomaro saw the hamayū growing along the coast of Kumano at the southern end of the Kii Peninsula, for it is not a standard image—he is the only poet to refer to this flower in *Man'yō-shū*. The second tanka curiously foreshadows a poem in the "Yūgao" chapter of *The Tale of Genji*.

314–17   [MYS IV: 499–502/496–99]

Four poems by Kakinomoto no Asomi Hitomaro

(314)   [499/496]

    Mikumano no   In fair Kumano
    Ura no hamayū   At the seaside *hamayū*
      Momoe nasu   Grows in abundance:
    Kokoro wa moedo   A hundredfold my heart longs,
    Tada ni awanu kamo   But we meet no more.

(315)   [500/497]

    Inishie ni   They who must have lived
    Arikemu hito no   In the long ago, did they,
      Wa ga goto ka   I wonder,
    Imo ni koitsutsu   Yearning for their loves as I,
    Inekatezukemu   Go sleepless all the night?

(316)   [501/498]

    Ima nomi no   It is not a thing
    Waza ni wa arazu   That began a moment since:
      Inishie no   In the long ago
    Hito so masarite   Men longed yet more sorely—
    Ne ni sae nakishi   They wept aloud for love.

(317)   [502/499]

    Momoe ni mo   Over and over,
    Kishikanu ka mo to   Even to a hundred times,
      Omoe ka mo   Won't you come to me?
    Kimi ga tsukai no   Wondering, I never weary
    Miredo akazaramu   Of seeing your messenger.

❊ The three poems in 318–20 are arranged in a sequence suggesting an old passion with an unhappy ending or interruption. The first poem is built on a double jo, in which the (shrine?) maiden's waving (*furu*) sleeve leads to Mount Furu ("old"), the site of the hoary Isonokami Shrine, which in turn introduces *hisashiki* ("ancient"). Does Hitomaro hint that he was in love with a shrine maiden? The second poem is based on a simpler jo, and the last has none at all, but contains the obscure word *saisai*, translated as "ceaseless rustling." The first and last of the series have extremely close variants among the anonymous poems of other books of *Man'yōshū* (see no. 419; also MYS XIV:3500/3481, which is not included in the present anthology), a fact that raises again the question of the boundaries of Hitomaro's oeuvre.

318-20   [MYS IV: 504-6/ 501-3]
Three poems by Kakinomoto no Asomi Hitomaro

(318)   [504/ 501]

    Otomera ga   Sleeves of a maiden
Sode Furuyama no   Waving Mountain's sacred fence:
    Mizukaki no   From an ancient past
Hisashiki toki yu   Have I kept this love enshrined
Omoiki ware wa   In the longing of my heart.

(319)   [505/ 502]

    Natsuno yuku   Across summer fields
Oshika no tsuno no   Go new-antlered deer whose tines,
    Tsuka no ma mo   One handbreadth long,
Imo ga kokoro o   Are yet longer than the space
Wasurete omoe ya   I could forget the heart of her I love.

(320)   [506/ 503]

    Tamakinu no   Midst all the turmoil—
Saisai shizumi   The ceaseless rustling of her silken skirts—
    Ie no imo ni   I stood in silence;
Mono iwazu kite   My heart sank; without a word
Omoikanetsu mo   I took my grief and left.

❋ In addition to his laments for the dead, to be taken up below, Hitomaro composed two great poems on parting from a loved one in this life. These poems of parting, nos. 320-24 and 325-27, contain his sweetest prosody and most sensuous imagery. As with the Yoshino poems, they form a complementary pair. In them he leaves behind a wife in Iwami on the remote and rugged coast of the Japan Sea and travels up to the capital in Yamato. His connection with Iwami is not known; perhaps he was a provincial official there. Out of Iwami he creates a realm apart, a wild place by the sea, difficult of access, almost foreign. And there he places the woman he loves, from whom the mountains and the unwanted speed of his own horse cut him off. There is here a yearning for the unspoiled, the other, the Tahiti of the heart, where the desired woman is gentle and lithe like seaweed, yielding and sensuously fulfilling. The heartbreak of leaving such a world-beyond-the-mountains is what the poems are about.

Poem 321–24 opens with a defense of the coast and continues through a series of glistening and kinetic images to the woman who lies cradled in them, and from whom in the end the speaker tears himself away, only to look back in vain, and in his helpless rage, bid the intervening mountains to bend down. The second chōka is also structured in this way—with a natural setting that provides the metaphors for the beloved, followed by the parting, the journey away, and the final direct outpouring of emotion. This is the fundamental preparation-conclusion technique of chōka raised to its highest level, interspersed and strengthened with repeated parallels, which here convey the rocking rhythm of waves. Both poems are notable for their skillful use of seaweed imagery to link the untrammeled beauty of the coast to that of the woman, but no. 325–27 goes beyond no. 321–24 in creating an imagistic harmony with related vine images for the land. It is structurally the more complex of the two, with a higher incidence of pillow words and with an internal jo in lines 27–31. In the first chōka the mountains are anonymous barriers, but in the second they are given names rich in meaning, and a celestial imagery of sun and moon is introduced. Man is reduced in proportion, and in the end can only weep, rather than issue a command. The envoys in both cases revert to the waving sleeves and falling leaves through whose flickering curtain the lovers share their last glimpse. Thus the poems begin and end with complementary images—the clinging seaweed and the barrier mountain woods with their coruscating leaves. Each chōka also has an envoy that employs an ironic contrast—between the upheaval of windblown nature and the silent concentration of love, and between the man's reluctance and the vigorous speed of his horse. The abrupt command at the end of no. 321 is softened to a gentler, more resigned negative imperative at the end of all, in no. 327.

321–24, 325–27   [MYS II:131–34, 135–37]

Two poems of Kakinomoto no Asomi Hitomaro when he parted from his wife, coming up to the capital from the province of Iwami; with *tanka*

(321–24)   [131–34]

	Iwami no umi	The Sea of Iwami,
	Tsuno no urami o	The curving coast of Tsuno:
	Ura nashi to	Here is no harbor—
	Hito koso mirame	That is what the stranger sees;
5	Kata nashi to	Here no shorelong mere—
	Hito koso mirame	That is what the stranger sees.

Yoshieyashi	So be it, even so,
Ura wa naku to mo	Though we have no harbor on this coast;
Yoshieyashi	So be it, even so,
10 Kata wa naku to mo	Though we have no sheltered, shorelong mere:
Isanatori	All along this reach
Umibe o sashite	Of the wild, whale-hunting sea,
Nikitazu no	Bearing down on the rocks
Ariso no ue ni	That bristle there on Nikitazu's strand,
15 Kaao naru	Glistening green gems
Tamamo okitsumo	Of seaweed, seaweed from the offing,
Asaha furu	Come driven by the wind
Kaze koso yoseme	That leaps like wings of morning,
Yūha furu	Come carried by the waves
20 Nami koso kiyose	That leap like wings of evening;
Nami no muta	And like the jeweled weed
Ka yori kaku yoru	That slips and floats in the waves,
Tamamo nasu	Riding in their embrace,
Yorineshi imo o	Was she in soft and yielding sleep
25 Tsuyu shimo no	Whom I have left behind,
Okite shi kureba	Helpless as a trace of dew or frost,
Kono michi no	And come upon this road.
Yasokumagoto ni	At the fourscore bendings of the way
Yorozu tabi	Ten thousand times
30 Kaerimi suredo	I turn and look again,
Iyatō ni	But every time
Sato wa sakarinu	Our village is yet further sunk away,
Iyataka ni	And every mountain
Yama mo koekinu	Taller than the one I crossed before.
35 Natsukusa no	Like summer grasses
Omoishinaete	She must droop, sorrowing in her heart,
Shinofuramu	Yearning for her love,
Imo ga kado mimu	The dear girl whose gates I long to see:
Nabike kono yama	O mountains, I command you to bow down!

Two Envoys

Iwami no ya	Far in Iwami,
Takatsunoyama no	From between the trees that grow
Ko no ma yori	On lofty Mount Tsuno,
Wa ga furu sode o	Did my dear one see, I wonder,
Imo mitsuramu ka	The sleeve I waved her in farewell?

Sasa no ha wa	Though whole mountainsides
Miyama mo saya ni	May rustle with the thrashing
Midaru to mo	Of the bamboo-grass,

Ware wa imo omou	Silently I yearn for her,
Wakarekinureba	The dear girl I left behind.

The envoy in a certain text reads:

Iwami naru	There in Iwami,
Takatsunoyama no	Even through the trees that grow
Ko no ma yu mo	On lofty Mount Tsuno,
Wa ga sode furu o	Can my dear one have seen me
Imo mikemu ka mo	As I waved my sleeve in farewell?

(325–27)   [135–37]

Tsuno sahau	In the Sea of Iwami,
Iwami no umi no	Where swarming vines crawl on the rocks,
Koto saeku	Under the Cape of Kara,
Kara no saki naru	A name for far lands strange of speech,
5 Ikuri ni so	On the sunken reefs
Fukamiru ouru	Grows the sea pine in the deep waters,
Ariso ni so	On the stony strand
Tamamo wa ouru	Grows the lovely, gemlike seaweed:
Tamamo nasu	Yielding as gemweed
10 Nabikineshi ko o	Was my young girl when she lay with me,
Fukamiru no	She for whom my love
Fukamete moedo	Is deep as the deeply growing sea pine;
Saneshi yo wa	But those nights were few
Ikuda mo arazu	When we lay thus in our drifting sleep.
15 Hau tsuta no	Now we have parted
Wakare shi kureba	As the crawling ivy vines do branch and part,
Kimo mukau	And I have come away,
Kokoro o itami	Grieving this heart seated amidst
Omoitsutsu	The vitals in my breast,
20 Kaerimi suredo	Turning in longing to look back again.
Ōfune no	But from Mount Watari—
Watari no yama no	*Watari*, crossing, as of a great ship—
Momichiba no	Amidst the wild scattering
Chiri no magai ni	Of the ever-falling yellow leaves
25 Imo ga sode	I could barely see
Saya ni mo miezu	The sleeves of my beloved waving in farewell.
Tsumagomoru	And when—as through the clouds
Yakami no yama no	Over Mount Yakami, a name that tells
Kumoma yori	Of men alone with their wives,
30 Watarau tsuki no	The wandering moon appears and vanishes—
Oshikedo mo	Bitter though my regret,
Kakuroikureba	Those waving sleeves flickered away and were
	hid,

206

Ama tsutau	The heaven-coursing sun
Irihi sashinure	Sank low and shone level with my eyes.
35 Masurao to	Then I, who thought myself
Omoeru ware mo	A valiant man, even I then found
Shikitae no	The sleeves of this robe
Koromo no sode wa	That I spread for my sleep at night
Tōrite nurenu	Were all wet through with tears.

Two Envoys

Aogoma no	Far beyond the clouds,
Agaki o hayami	So swift have been the hoofbeats
Kumoi ni so	Of my blue-gray steed,
Imo ga atari o	Lies now the homeland of my love
Sugite kinikeru	That I have left and come away.

Akiyama ni	O yellow leaves,
Otsuru momichiba	Falling on the autumn hills,
Shimashiku wa	Just for a moment
Na chirimagai so	Do not scatter so wildly—
Imo ga atari mimu	I would see the homeland of my love.

❋ Poem 328–30 is the first of the four banka, or laments, that date the career of Hitomaro. It was composed in 689 for Hinamishi no Miko, "Prince Peer-of-the-Sun," the honorific title by which Empress Jitō's favorite son Kusakabe was known. Kusakabe was the heir to the throne, and his sudden death at the age of twenty-seven was no doubt a great shock to the court. For Hitomaro it provided the opportunity—perhaps the obligation—to set forth that shock and grief in the framework of the sacred imperial myth, elevating and thus sublimating the loss, yet bringing it back to a stunned humanity. Hitomaro's laments rank among the great elegies of the world. Each adjusted in tone to suit its subject, they all begin with a formal introduction; touch the fact of death as a mystery, a perverse and incomprehensible rejection of the goodness of life; and describe the grief of the mourners. Some banka end with a defiant reassertion of the immortality of fame, and some—including this one—do not.

No. 328 is notable for its exceptionally long introduction, extending through line 36, over half the length of the entire chōka. These lines give a telescoped version of the creation and land-bestowal myths and deal not with the defunct Prince, but with his father, Emperor Temmu, who in this vision is coeval with and identical to the Imperial Grandchild of the sun goddess Amaterasu, who first descended to earth to establish rule over the land. Only after Temmu has reascended to heaven at his death does the poet turn to the ostensible object of his lament. These opening lines are cast in highly liturgical language. In their shiritori, or "tail-catching," repetitions—different from the a-b-a'-b' pattern of balanced parallelism—they hark back to songs in *Kojiki* (see nos. 3, 5, and 39). But they also resemble the rhetoric of the *norito*, ancient Shintō prayers of undetermined but probably early date preserved in *Engishiki* (927). Lines 1–24 are particularly close to a passage in "The Great Exorcism of the Last Day of the Sixth Month" (*Minazuki no Tsugomori no Ōharae*). It seems plausible that Hitomaro could have adapted this or some similar ritual text for his lament. Poem 814 shows an even closer adaptation of a semmyō (imperial edict) by Yakamochi. Hitomaro shifts his subject at line 37. The balance of the poem expresses in imagery recurrent in banka how splendid a ruler the Prince would have been "had he been put on," the trust and adoration of his subjects, and the loss of direction they suffer at his death. Death takes the form of a mysterious decision to build a new palace—the funeral hall. The phraseology echoes that in eulogy, but for the ends of a somber irony. The courtiers wait outside the Prince's gates in vain. Members of the royal family were given temporary enshrinement, for periods of several months after their deaths, before burial in sarcophagi beneath the giant tumuli of the time. Rites were conducted, and banka composed, during this period before final burial.

The two envoys make no compromise with grief: the Prince's palace will fall, and the moon—his symbol—has been blotted out. The parallel of the second envoy to no. 252, by Emperor Tenji, is one of mirror-reversal. Temmu's palace at Kiyomi, and Asuka where it was located, had the epithet *tobu tori no* ("of the flying bird"), supposedly because of the presentation of a rare and auspicious red pheasant in the fifteenth year of his reign. The annotation after the envoys refers to Prince Takechi, who became Prime Minister after Prince Kusakabe's death, and himself died and was memorialized by Hitomaro in 696 (see no. 341–44).

328–30   [MYS II: 167–69]

A poem composed by Kakinomoto no Asomi Hitomaro at the time of the temporary enshrinement of His Highness Prince Peer-of-the-Sun; with *tanka*

	Ame tsuchi no	At the beginning
	Hajime no toki	Of the heaven and the earth
	Hisakata no	In the riverbed
	Ama no kawara ni	Of the shining realm of heaven
5	Yaoyorozu	Eight hundred myriad,
	Chiyorozu kami no	A thousand myriad of gods
	Kamutsudoi	In godly assembly
	Tsudoiimashite	Assembled together,
	Kamuhakari	With godly counsel
10	Hakarishi toki ni	Took counsel together:

	Amaterasu
	Hirume no mikoto
	Ame o ba
	Shirashimesu to
15	Ashihara no
	Mizuho no kuni o
	Ame tsuchi no
	Yoriai no kiwami
	Shirashimesu
20	Kami no mikoto to
	Amakumo no
	Yaekakiwakete
	Kamukudashi
	Imasematsurishi
25	Takaterasu
	Hi no miko wa
	Tobu tori no
	Kiyomi no miya ni
	Kamunagara
30	Futoshikimashite
	Sumeroki no
	Shikimasu kuni to
	Ama no hara
	Iwato o hiraki
35	Kamuagari
	Agariimashinu
	Wa go ōkimi
	Miko no mikoto no
	Ame no shita
40	Shirashimeshiseba
	Haruhana no
	Tōtokaramu to
	Mochizuki no
	Tatawashikemu to
45	Ame no shita
	Yomo no hito no
	Ōbune no
	Omoitanomite
	Ama tsu mizu
50	Aogite matsu ni
	Ikasama ni
	Omōshimese ka
	Tsure mo naki

The heaven-illumining
August Goddess of the Sun
    Over heaven
Should be the one to rule,
    And the Plain-of-Reeds
Country of the Sweet Rice-Ears,
    To where heaven and earth
Merge together at their bound
    Should for the august
God who would rule over it
    Have him who brushed aside
The eightfold clouds of heaven,
    Him who was sent down
In godly descent to earth:
    Divine Child
Of the High-Shining Sun,
    At his palace,
Kiyomi of the Flying Bird,
    In all his godhead
He established firm his reign;
    But he knew the land
Was one for Sovereigns to reign in,
    And swinging open
The rock door of heaven's plain,
    In godly ascent
He has ascended and is gone.
    If our great lord,
His Highness our most noble Prince,
    Had come to rule
This realm of all beneath the heaven,
    He would have been
As flourishing as flowers in spring,
    He would have been
As all-fulfilling as the round full moon,
    So under heaven
The people of the four directions thought,
    As in a great ship
Placing their trust in him,
    As for water from heaven
Gazing upward, waiting:
    What was the nature
Of the thought he pondered?
    Where he had no bond,

	Mayumi no oka ni	On the hill of Mayumi,
55	Miyabashira	He planted firm
	Futoshikiimashi	The pillars of his palace halls,
	Miaraka o	He raised on high
	Takashirimashite	The lofty halls of his divine abode.
	Asagoto ni	Morn after morn
60	Mikoto towasanu	Has passed without command,
	Hi tsuki no	Days and months pile up,
	Maneku narinuru	Many, without a word:
	Soko yue ni	All because of this
	Miko no miyahito	The courtiers of the Prince now wait,
65	Yukue shirazu mo	Not knowing where to go.

Two Envoys

Hisakata no	As if we looked
Ame miru gotoku	To the shining realm of heaven,
Aogimishi	So we once gazed up
Miko no mikado no	At our lord our Prince's gates,
Aremaku oshi mo	Whose ruin will be bitter with regret.

Akane sasu	Although, madder-red,
Hi wa teraseredo	The sun illuminates the day,
Nubatama no	Through the jet-black night
Yo wataru tsuki no	The moon no longer sails the sky;
Kakuraku oshi mo	Its dark eclipse is bitter with regret.

One text treats these as envoys of a poem composed at the time of the temporary enshrinement of His Highness the Later Imperial Prince.

❋ Poem 331–35 is classified as a *zōka*, not a *banka*, but it belongs here, after the lament for Hinamishi. Prince Karu (later Emperor Mommu; r. 697–707) was the son of Hinamishi, and it is he who goes to lodge on the fields of Aki, probably his father's hunting grounds. He too may have gone for the hunting, but this poem records no ordinary sporting trip, nor is it a eulogy like no. 301–3 in honor of Prince Naga. This journey is rather—at least as Hitomaro presents it to us—a voyage into the deep past, and the hunting is for the spirit of the dead. A somber atmosphere broods over the poem, twilight and night and dawn on the winter-withered moor. Here is enacted a strange drama of time and memory, involving a circularity that seems about to bring the ghost and all his steeds on stage, but ends with the uncertain irony that the rising of the sun, whose peer the dead Prince was, may dispel the magic moment. The way to that magic moment leads through the formulaic encomium with which the *chōka* opens, and takes the young Prince Karu (perhaps eleven years old at the time) through a superhuman course over the mountains and down to the plain of Aki. The chōka ends with the encampment amid the snow, the dry miscanthus and bamboo, and grass for pillow, at the twilight hour. Then the memories come, and the chōka ends.

The chōka is here only the introduction to the total poetic structure. The four tanka that follow are the heart of the poem. They are spoken by a voice that emerges from among and yet exists apart from the Prince's train—they are the view of an eye that sweeps all horizons. Meditative, descriptive, observant, they probe the minds of the travelers and call forth the monochrome power and meaning of the place. The place is the katami of the dead Prince, the remembrancer, the keepsake, that which evokes the vanished one. And so we know that Hinamishi too had come here to hunt. The third tanka, one of the best-known and loved poems in *Man'yōshū*, arrives at the moment: the first flickers of sunrise and the full moon sinking simultaneously in the west. Between them the great emptiness, played over by a pale, ghostly light, ready for the beginning of the hunt—or for an event that could be the last entrance of the agonist in a Nō play. The power of the scene beggars mere symbolism: dawn and the moon exist to make palpable the cold beauty of the world, rather than for political allegory. In this poem Hitomaro goes beyond whatever may have been required of him as a court poet, and touches the quick of poetry itself.

331-35   [MYS I:45-49]

A poem composed by Kakinomoto no Asomi Hitomaro when Prince Karu lodged on the fields of Aki

	Yasumishishi	Our mighty lord
	Wa ga ōkimi	Who rules the land in all tranquility,
	Takaterasu	The Divine Child
	Hi no miko	Of the High-Shining Sun,
5	Kamunagara	He who is a god
	Kamusabi sesu to	In action godlike now departs
	Futoshikasu	The firm-established
	Miyako o okite	City of the sacred rule,
	Komoriku no	And up mountain slopes
10	Hatsuse no yama wa	By hill-secluded Hatsuse,
	Maki tatsu	On rough mountain tracks
	Araki yamaji o	Where the bristling timber stands,
	Iwagane	Brushing to the earth
	Saeki oshinabe	The rooted rocks and tangled trees,
15	Sakadori no	Like a soaring bird
	Asa koemashite	In the morning clears the crest;

Tamakagiru	And when evening comes
Yū sarikureba	That gleams as softly as a glinting gem,
Miyuki furu	On the snowy plain,
20 Aki no ōno ni	The vast fields of Aki,
Hatasusuki	He spreads the ground
Shino o oshinabe	With bannergrass and small bamboo,
Kusamakura	And grass for pillow
Tabiyadori sesu	Takes a traveler's shelter there,
25 Inishie omoite	Thinking of the days gone by.

Tanka

Aki no no ni	The travelers who take
Yadoru tabibito	Shelter on the fields of Aki—
Uchinabiki	Do they lie at ease,
I mo nurame ya mo	Are they able to find sleep,
Inishie omou ni	When they think of days gone by?

Makusa karu	This place is desolate,
Arano ni wa aredo	A moorland where men cut wild grass,
Momichiba no	But to these fields
Suginishi kimi ga	We come in memory of him,
Katami to so koshi	Our lord who passed like the yellow leaf.

Himugashi no	Eastward on the fields
No ni kagiroi no	A flickering of flame begins
Tatsu miete	To rise against the dark,
Kaerimi sureba	And looking back the sunken moon
Tsuki katabukinu	Is seen to rest upon the land.

Hinamishi no	Peer of the Sun,
Miko no mikoto no	His Highness our most noble Prince
Uma namete	Would line up his steeds
Mikari tatashishi	And start upon the royal hunt
Toki wa kimukau	At this very hour that now has come.

No. 336–37 laments the death of Prince Kawashima in 691. (For a poem by this Prince, see no. 278.) Princess Hatsusebe (d. 741), a daughter of Emperor Temmu, was his consort. Her brother, Prince Osakabe (d. 705), was one of Prince Kawashima's colleagues on the committee of scholars that prepared the historical materials eventually resulting in *Nihonshoki*. For this banka Hitomaro chose to concentrate on the grief of the bereaved wife, and in order to do so compellingly, he made it physical. The aching loss of the young woman robbed of her husband is introduced by water-plant images

in the formal opening. The duality of the image suggests the two young lovers lying together. Later the husband's masculinity is likened to a sword. This tender and protective husband has vanished, leaving the Princess to sleep alone. Her reaction goes beyond the stunned immobility of the courtiers in no. 328. Like a mad Ophelia she wanders about in the dew, searching for what she can never find—the warm and living sharer of her love. Searching for the dead may be an expression of the dementia of grief, rather than a solemn, reflective rite as in Prince Karu's encampment on the fields of Aki.

336–37   [MYS II : 194–95]

A poem presented by Kakinomoto no Asomi Hitomaro to Princess Hatsusebe and Prince Osakabe; with *tanka*

Tobu tori no	In the River of Asuka,
Asuka no kawa no	Asuka of the flying bird,
Kami tsu se ni	The gemweed growing
Ouru tamamo wa	Along the upper shallows,
5 Shimo tsu se ni	Swaying and touching,
Nagarefurabau	Trails with the current toward the shallows
	below:
Tamamo nasu	Like the gemweed, too,
Ka yori kaku yori	Bending to his love and he to yours,
Nabikaishi	Softly interlaced
10 Tsuma no mikoto no	You lay with him who was
Tatanazuku	Your princely husband,
Nikihada sura o	But now must sleep alone
Tsurugitachi	Without one touch
Mi ni soeneneba	Of his fine and tender skin
15 Nubatama no	That used to cling to you
Yodoko mo aruramu	Close as a warrior's long, straight sword,
Soko yue ni	So that in the night,
Nagusamekanete	The night dark as beads of jet,
Kedashiku mo	Your bed must be desolate;
20 Au ya to omoite	And for this reason, inconsolable,
Tamadare no	Have you perhaps now gone,
Ochi no ōno no	Hoping by some chance to meet him there,
Asatsuyu ni	To the fields of Ochi,
Tamamo wa hizuchi	Spattering your skirts with mud
25 Yūgiri ni	In the morning dew,
Koromo wa nurete	Wetting your garments through
Kusamakura	In the evening mist,
Tabine ka mo suru	Sleeping on the grasses of the plain,
Awanu kimi yue	All for the lord whom you will never meet?

Envoy

Shikitae no	He with whom you slept,
Sode kaeshi kimi	Sleeve on sleeve of barken cloth,
Tamadare no	Has passed away
Ochino sugiyuku	Far beyond the fields of Ochi:
Mata mo awame ya mo	How will you meet your lord again?

Concerning the above, it is stated in a certain text that this is a poem presented to Princess Hatsusebe at the time Prince Kawashima was interred on the fields of Ochi. *Nihongi* states that Kawashima, a Prince of Jōdaisan Rank, died in the fifth year of Akamitori, Metal-Junior/Hare [691], in autumn, on the Fire-Junior/Ox day of the ninth month, whose first day was Earth-Junior/Serpent.

❋ In the year 700 Hitomaro went back to the water plants trailing in Asuka River for the opening of another and much longer banka. It was occasioned by the death of Princess Asuka, a daughter of Emperor Tenji and consort of the same Prince Osakabe who was one of the recipients of no. 336–37. This is the last of Hitomaro's datable poems. Quite likely it was the Princess's name that led him to take up and further develop the formal introduction he had composed nine years earlier. The addition of a bridge at each shallows expands the structure, but the more important change is that the renewing life-cycle of the waterweed becomes an ironic contrast with human fate. At the same time, the sinuous image of grasses in water continues to provide the analogical lead-in to the vision of a happy sexual love, now withered and gone. This time it is the woman who has "deserted" her mate, and the man whose desolation is treated in a series of metaphors for heartbreak and distracted grief.

The use of the extended analogical series—here all are closer to Western metaphor, unlike the overt similes of lines 18 and 20—had been developed by Hitomaro four years earlier in his lament for Prince Takechi (no. 341–44). The poet asks three questions: line 26, why? line 62, is it because of this? line 64, what can I do? Why did the Princess choose to die? Is it this terrible and baffling rejection of life that desolates even me, a bystander? How then can I hope to comfort the bereaved husband with my verse? This lament plays back and forth between images of sweet and glorious life, and the denial of that life. First the foreboding note that waterweed withers but grows again; then the sinuous image of love, and the turning away from it in lines 23–26. But the poem reverts to the happy past, letting it flower again in images of conjugal bliss. Then comes the final and abrupt turning away in line 45, as the pleasure palace becomes an "eternal shrine"—the site for lying-in-state.

After his five figures of grief, building to the titanic image of the wave-battered ship, the poet confesses his helplessness. His song has been in vain. But finally he turns about in defiance of death. He seizes a katami, a "keepsake," in the Princess's very name. That name will keep the dead lady's fame alive "for ten thousand ages." What's Hecuba to him? He exclaims *Hashiki yashi* ("O well beloved") and makes his brave gesture. The Asuka River still flows across the plain. But the two envoys retreat from the perfervid insistence on an immortality sanctioned in the land itself. A river is a river—it flows on. Even so, if you block it, the water will stand still. But not human life. And "Asuka," alas, embeds the word *asu*, "tomorrow." Yes, at least tomorrow. The wise ironist in Hitomaro cuts across the excesses of the maker of the paean and the dirge.

338–40   [MYS II: 196–98]

A poem composed by Kakinomoto no Asomi Hitomaro on the occasion of the temporary enshrinement of Princess Asuka at Kinoe; with *tanka*

Tobu tori no	On the River of Asuka,
Asuka no kawa no	Asuka of the flying bird,
Kami tsu se ni	At the upper shallows
Iwahashi watashi	They have built a bridge of stones,
5 Shimo tsu se ni	At the lower shallows
Uchihashi watasu	They have built a spanning bridge.
Iwahashi ni	The gemweed growing,
Oinabikeru	Trailing in the current
Tamamo mo zo	At the bridge of stones,
10 Tayureba ouru	May break, but it will grow again.
Uchihashi ni	The riverweed that grows,
Oiōreru	Softly bending in the current
Kawamo mo zo	At the spanning bridge,
Karureba hayuru	Withers, but it sprouts again.
15 Nani shi ka mo	How then can it be
Wa go ōkimi no	That though she stood by his side
Tataseba	Lithe as the gemweed,
Tamamo no mokoro	And though they lay together
Koyaseba	In the stream of love
20 Kawamo no gotoku	Like strands of riverweed,
Nabikaishi	Our great Princess now
Yoroshiki kimi ga	Forgets the morning palace,
Asamiya o	Shuns and turns her back
Wasuretamau ya	Upon the evening palace
25 Yūmiya o	Of him who was
Somukitamau ya	Her pleasant and most noble lord?

Utsusomi to	In the time when men
Omoishi toki	Still thought her a person of this world
Harube wa	She would come in spring,
30 Hana orikazashi	Breaking sprays of blossom for her brow,
Aki tateba	Or on autumn days
Momichiba kazashi	Deck herself with maple leaves,
Shikitae no	Joining her sleeves,
Sode tazusawari	Her covering sleeves to his,
35 Kagami nasu	The lord on whom
Miredo mo akazu	She looked in ever greater adoration,
Mochitsuki no	Never wearying,
Iyamezurashimi	As on a bright, refulgent mirror
Omōshishi	Or the round full moon;
40 Kimi to tokidoki	Thus hand in hand they would set forth,
Idemashite	Often and again,
Asobitamaishi	To pass their days in pleasure and delight
Mike mukau	At this well-ordered
Kinoe no miya o	Fair Palace of Kinoe:
45 Tokomiya to	The same that now
Sadametamaite	She gives the name of her eternal shrine,
Aji sahau	Ending all words
Megoto mo taenu	And hiding from the eyes of men.
Shikare ka mo	Is it for this
50 Aya ni kanashimi	That when I see him struck with grief,
Nuetori no	A night thrush crying
Katakoitsuma	In unanswered yearning for its mate,
Asatori no	A morning bird
Kayowasu kimi ga	Forever flitting from its nest,
55 Natsukusa no	Like summer grasses
Omoishinaete	Wilted and drooping for love,
Yūtsutsu no	Like the evening star
Ka yuki kaku yuki	Tracing a path of hither and return,
Ōbune no	Or a mighty ship
60 Tayutau mireba	Shuddering in the waves—that when I see
Nagusamuru	Him thus who was her lord,
Kokoro mo aranu	My own heart grows desolate?
Soko yue ni	What know I then
Semu sube shire ya	Of remedy for his more grievous pain?
65 Oto nomi mo	Only your renown,
Na nomi mo taezu	Your name only would I keep alive—
Ame tsuchi no	Farther and longer,
Iyatōnagaku	Even from the ends of heaven and earth
Shinoiyukamu	Shall I remember it:

70	Mina ni kakaseru	And the river, the Asuka that bears
	Asukagawa	The high name you bore,
	Yorozu yo made ni	Until ten thousand ages have gone by—
	Hashiki yashi	O well beloved
	Wa go ōkimi no	Princess!—this stream shall serve
75	Katami ka koko o	For your remembrance in the world of men.

Two Envoys

Asukagawa	Asuka River—
Shigarami watashi	If one were to fence the stream,
Sekamaseba	Blocking it with weirs,
Nagaruru mizu mo	Surely the rushing water
Nodo ni ka aramashi	Would lie calm within its banks.

Asukagawa	Asuka River—
Asu dani mimu to	At least once more—"Tomorrow"—
Omoe ya mo	Would I gaze upon you,
Wa go ōkimi no	Princess: my yearning such
Mina wasure senu	That I do not forget your honored name.

✳ No. 341–44 is a poem of superlatives. It is the longest poem in *Man'yōshū*, a chōka of unexampled scale followed by three envoys. Composed in 696 on the death of Prince Takechi (b. 654), the eldest son of Temmu and a hero of the Jinshin War, it is the most highly wrought in the elevation of its rhetoric of all Hitomaro's poems. The full mystique of imperial rule is evoked, beginning with the four-line opening formula, an almost epic statement of the dread nature of the theme to be taken up. Awe pervades the poem, which is unique in *Man'yōshū* in describing a battle. This heroic event is rendered in a series of Homeric similes that show Hitomaro stretching his versification to achieve new effects. In a passage as long as an average chōka, the introduction deals—as in no. 328—with the late Emperor Temmu, who once built a palace (the symbolic assertion of majesty in *Man'yōshū*), but who now "hides within the stone" of his mighty burial mound. The succeeding lines tell how he raised troops for the Jinshin War of 672 and then turned them over to his son. In the victors' account the vanquished are rebels, to be subdued and brought to obedience. The climax of the first part of the poem is the description of the battle with its panoply of war—drums, horns, banners, bows, and arrows. There is nothing quite like these lines in the literature; even *The Tale of the Heike* does not offer their compact poetic structure. The war songs of the chronicles liken the victorious troops to crawling periwinkles, and the enemy to a stinking leek to be eradicated (see songs 11 and 13). Hitomaro's idea of heroic imagery is different—tigers, flames, and whirlwinds are his similes. This heroism allows no room for the melancholy of soldiers who are starving (no. 14) or who know they will die (no. 227, the old Ōtomo song quoted in no. 814, Yakamochi's chōka on the discovery of gold in Michinoku). The enemy are likened to flying birds, but birds will come to rest at dark. The sun goddess, in a reenactment of a passage in the chronicles, hides herself and deprives the world of light. And, suddenly, the battle is over. This divine intervention in the climactic battle of the Jinshin War is Hitomaro's invention; *Nihonshoki's* detailed account fails to mention it. But "divine wind" (*kamukaze* or *kamikaze*) was already a pillow word for Ise, the site of the shrine of Amaterasu at Watarai, in song 13.

The second half of the poem, beginning in line 87, takes up the Prince's governance—he was made Daijōdaijin, or Prime Minister, in 692—his death, and the grief of his housemen. Lines 89 and 90 probably refer to Emperor Temmu, with a switch in subject to Prince Takechi in line 91. Again, the expectations of a Prince's glory are curtailed by his untimely death, by a palace that becomes a "godly shrine." (Compare the imagery of the grief of the Prince's men to no. 301, Hitomaro's eulogy of Prince Naga. Song 34 might also be reread for its description of the grief of Yamato Takeru's wives and children.) Hitomaro's poem likens the servitors to animals and birds; they are bereft of their human reason and whimper unintelligibly. When the funeral procession wends its way across the plain of Kudara, this theme is continued in the pillow word *koto saeku*, "of unintelligible speech" (rendered as "broken-tongued"), referring technically to Kudara as the Japanese name for the Korean kingdom of Paekche, but for the purposes of the poem reminding the listener that the mourners are still stunned and cannot speak. Hitomaro speaks for them and for the court in the last thirteen lines where, as in the elegy for Princess Asuka, he finds a katami—this time the Prince's palace near Mount Kagu. Hitomaro knows well enough that palaces fall, but once again he makes wish serve as faith, and rounds off the chōka by reiterating the awesomeness of his theme.

The envoys are particularly fine. These too, like the envoys appended to the lament for Princess Asuka, withdraw to a quieter ground, where irony can come into play in place of defiant assertion. These meditative endings are characteristic of Hitomaro and essential to the total structure of a chōka-hanka set. The second envoy reiterates the dazed condition of the Prince's courtiers; it is flanked by verses giving a vision of the Prince now reigning in heaven, a glorious consummation that does little to comfort those left behind. Princess Hinokuma, mentioned in the footnote, is thought to have been Prince Takechi's daughter. The shrine of Nakisawa ("Weeping Fen") still stands at the foot of Mount Kagu. Its deity, the goddess Nakisawame, "Weeping-Fen Woman," was born from Izanagi's tears for his dead spouse Izanami in *Kojiki*. The shrine guarded a spring whose waters were believed to restore life. Hence Princess Hinokuma's resentment. Wazami has the mock epithet *Komatsurugi* ("Korean sword"), a pillow word related to the syllable *wa* ("ring"), from the ringed pommel of such a sword. Azuma ("the Eastland") is called "cock-crowing" (*tori ga naku*), probably from the association of dawn with the east. Kinoe is called "of the hempen skirt" (*asamo yoshi*) because of the hemp fields of the province of Ki, the first syllable of "Kinoe." *Nihongi* is another name for *Nihonshoki*.

341-44   [MYS II: 199-202]

A poem composed by Kakinomoto no Asomi Hitomaro on the occasion of the temporary enshrinement of His Highness Prince Takechi at Kinoe; with *tanka*

Kakemaku mo	I would call it to mind—
Yuyushiki kamo	Yet I shrink from the dread power;
Iwamaku mo	I would speak of it aloud—
Aya ni kashikoki	But my words are lost in awe:
5 Asuka no	He who deigned to choose,
Makami no hara ni	Awesome in his majesty,
Hisakata no	At Asuka
Ama tsu mikado o	In the plain of Makami
Kashikoku mo	The site to build
10 Sadametamaite	His heaven-gated palace halls,
Kamusabu to	The same who now,
Iwagakurimasu	Godlike, hides within the stone,
Yasumishishi	Our great Sovereign
Wa go ōkimi no	Who ruled the land in all tranquility,
15 Kikoshimesu	Once in a province
Sotomo no kuni no	Northward in the realm he held in sway
Maki tatsu	Crossed the timbered slopes
Fuwayama koete	Of Fuwa Mountain, and came down
Komatsurugi	In heaven-descent
20 Wazami ga hara no	To his palace in the fields
Karimiya ni	Of Wazami,
Amoriimashite	Plain of the Korean sword.
Ame no shita	That he might bring rule
Osametamai	To his lands beneath the heaven,
25 Osu kuni o	That he might bring peace
Sadametamau to	To this country of his reign,
Tori ga naku	From cock-crowing
Azuma no kuni no	Azuma, the Eastern Land,
Miikusa o	He summoned a host
30 Meshitamaite	Of warriors to defend his throne.
Chihayaburu	"Pacify the men
Hito o yawase to	Who rage in savage fury,

	Matsurowanu	Subdue the provinces
	Kuni o osame to	That rise in disobedience!"
35	Miko nagara	He charged his son,
	Maketamaeba	And sent him eager to fulfill the task.
	Ōmimi ni	The Prince then took
	Tachi toriobashi	His sword and bound it to his waist,
	Ōmite ni	He gripped his bow
40	Yumi torimotashi	And held it in his mighty hand,
	Miikusa o	And the great war-host
	Adomoitamai	Led forward with a battle cry:
	Totonouru	The crash of drums
	Tsuzumi no oto wa	Signaling the soldiers to draw up
45	Ikazuchi no	Resounded till it seemed
	Oto to kiku made	The sound of thunder fell upon men's ears;
	Fukinaseru	The bray of horns
	Kuda no oto mo	Blown in blasts upon the air
	Ata mitaru	Was like the snarling
50	Tora ka hoyuru to	Of a tiger when it spots its foe,
	Morohito no	And the enemy
	Obiyuru made ni	In all his multitude was seized with fear;
	Sasagetaru	Banners borne aloft
	Hata no nabiki wa	Whipped in the wind; their fluttering
55	Fuyugomori	Was like the fires
	Haru sarikureba	That burn on every field
	Nogoto ni	When winter's done
	Tsukite aru hi no	And spring has come again,
	Kaze no muta	And the flames go
60	Nabiku ga gotoku	Flickering before the wind;
	Torimoteru	The clamor of the bownocks
	Yuhazu no sawaki	Of the bows the warriors held
	Miyuki furu	Was terrible to hear:
	Fuyu no hayashi ni	Men thought the sound was like
65	Tsumuji ka mo	A whirlwind twisting,
	Imakiwataru to	Tearing through a winter forest
	Omou made	In the falling snow,
	Kiki no kashikoku	So dreadful was the noise;
	Hikihanatsu	We drew, we shot,
70	Ya no shigekeku	Our arrows flew as thick
	Ōyuki no	As a blinding blizzard
	Midarete kitare	Pelting down upon the foe:
	Matsurowazu	They, still unsubdued,
	Tachimukaishi mo	Stood and fought our army face to face:
75	Tsuyu shimo no	"If like dew or frost

Kenaba kenubeku	We perish, then let us perish!"
Yuku tori no	And like flying birds
Arasou hashi ni	They went eagerly into the fray.
Watarai no	Then from Watarai,
80 Itsuki no miya yu	From the pure and holy shrine,
Kamukaze ni	A divine wind rose
Ifukimatowashi	And blew confusion on the enemy;
Amakumo o	With clouds of heaven
Hi no me mo misezu	It covered over all the earth,
85 Tokoyami ni	Hiding the eye of the sun,
Ōitamaite	Obscuring the world in utter dark.
Sadameteshi	With peace thus brought
Mizuho no kuni o	To the land of sweet rice spears,
Kamunagara	The Sovereign, a god,
90 Futoshikimashite	Established there a mighty reign,
Yasumishishi	And our great lord
Wa go ōkimi no	Who ruled the land in all tranquility
Ame no shita	Spoke words of government
Mōshitamaeba	To his realm beneath the sky.
95 Yorozu yo ni	Thus would it be
Shika shi mo aramu to	Until ten thousand ages passed,
Yūhana no	So all did say,
Sakayuru toki ni	But when the white flower of his glory
Wa go ōkimi	Bloomed at its fairest,
100 Miko no mikado o	Our great lord our Prince's gates
Kamumiya ni	Became a godly shrine
Yosoimatsurite	And to that end were reverently adorned.
Tsukawashishi	Then the servitors
Mikado no hito mo	Who waited on him in his princely court
105 Shirotae no	Put on rough garments
Asagoromo kite	All of hemp, white as barken cloth,
Haniyasu no	And in the fields
Mikado no hara ni	Before his gates at Haniyasu
Akane sasu	While yet the sun
110 Hi no kotogoto	Shone madder-red to light the day,
Shishijimono	As if they had been deer
Ihaifushitsutsu	Fell down and crawled upon the ground,
Nubatama no	And when swart evening came,
Yūbe ni nareba	Dark as the berry of the leopard flower,
115 Ōtono o	Bent back their necks
Furisakemitsutsu	To gaze aloft at the great hall,
Uzura nasu	And crept like quail
Ihaimotōri	In aimless circles through the grass.

Samoraedo   Serve him though they would,
120 Samoraieneba   There was no way to serve him now,
Harutori no   And so they went forlorn,
Samayoinureba   Whimpering soft as birds are wont in
                                          spring.

Nageki mo   Though their laments
Imada suginu ni   Had not yet passed away,
125 Omoi mo   And while their grief
Imada tsukineba   Had yet to run its course,
Koto saeku   Across the plain
Kudara no hara yu   Of broken-tongued Kudara
Kamuhaburi   They went to burial,
130 Haburiimashite   They went to make the burial of a god;
Asamo yoshi   And to his palace,
Kinoe no miya o   Kinoe called of the hempen skirt,
Tokomiya to   With lofty worship
Takaku matsurite   Gave the name of his eternal shrine,
135 Kamunagara   Wherein at last
Shizumarimashinu   In all his godhead he has gone to rest.
Shikaredo mo   Yet though it be thus,
Wa go ōkimi no   Shall I believe the palace that our great lord
                                          built

Yorozu yo to   By Kagu Mountain,
140 Omōshimeshite   Secure in his sublime intent
Tsukurashishi   That it should stand
Kaguyama no miya   Ten thousand generations on the earth,
Yorozu yo ni   Shall pass away
Sugimu to omoe ya   Although a myriad ages should go by?
145 Ame no goto   As if to heaven
Furisakemitsutsu   I shall lift my head and gaze at it,
Tamatasuki   In yearning close
Kakete shinowamu   As a jewel-sash to the heart,
Kashikokaredo mo   Though I may tremble, lost in sacred awe.

Two Tanka

Hisakata no   For the lord who reigns
Ame shirashinuru   Suzerain of the shining land
Kimi yue ni   Of heaven on high
Hi tsuki mo shirazu   With us a timeless longing still abides,
Koiwataru kamo   Dark to the passage of the sun and moon.

Haniyasu no   Pent within banks,
Ike no tsutsumi no   Waters of the hidden marsh
Komorinu no   Of Haniyasu Pond:

| Yukue o shirani | With no direction for them now, |
| Toneri wa matou | The courtiers wander dazed. |

An envoy in a certain work

Nakisawa no	In the sacred grove
Mori ni miwa sue	Of Weeping Fen we set the jars
Inoredo mo	Of offertory wine,
Wa go ōkimi wa	And pray aloud, but our great lord
Takahi shirashinu	Reigns now as suzerain of the lofty sun.

Concerning the above poem, *Ruijū Karin* states that it is a poem expressing Princess Hinokuma's resentment at Nakisawa Shrine. Turning our attention to *Nihongi*, we observe that it says that His Highness the Later Imperial Prince died in the tenth year, Fire-Senior/Monkey [696], in autumn, on the Metal-Senior/Dog day of the seventh month, which began on the Metal-Junior/Ox day.

❋ Hitomaro three times composed chōka in pairs: his celebrations of the Empress at Yoshino (nos. 293–94 and 295–96), his poems on parting from his wife in Iwami (nos. 321–24 and 325–27), and two outpourings of grief on the death of another woman who was his wife (nos. 345–47 and 348–50). The last lived in Karu, a village in the Asuka area near the imperial capital of the time, and has traditionally been thought of as distinct from the wife in Iwami. As presented in the first chōka, no. 345, the relationship was a secret one, in which the husband visited the wife. (Duolocal marriage among the upper classes remained standard through the Heian period.) The second chōka, no. 348, reveals that she left Hitomaro with a child. These are Hitomaro's personal banka. The death they lament was no affair of state; there was no temporary enshrinement, no grief-stricken court. The grief is intense, though—personal and inconsolable. Even the child, the katami, provides no hope. The poems are outcries of unrelieved sorrow.

As in the laments for Prince Kawashima and Princess Asuka, which are based on a conjugal vision of love, the poet is at pains in the first part of each chōka to establish the value of what has been lost—a sweet and secret intimacy (like a rock-walled pool), a delight in sharing. The seaweed image is used once more to convey a clinging and tactile tenderness. The verse is in Hitomaro's laden style, abounding in metaphor, heavy with treasure. It is interesting to see that in these poems Hitomaro does not question the *reason* for death; he drops the convention that death is an act of will. His wife's passing is treated as a natural event like a sunset, or the moon hiding in the clouds, or the flight of a bird. But this harmony is shattered by the husband's violent and human reaction. The frantic, irrational "searching for the dead"—in the market of Karu, the mountain of Hagai—was never more compellingly rendered. The geographical issues in the second poem are obscure, but this very obscurity contributes to the sense of a random desperation. "She has lost her way"; people tell him she is here, there; he has left her in still another place. These are the evasions and conventions of grief. The event is shaped into poems, which mystify in telling a truth close to the heart of the ultimate mystery. From a variant of no. 348, it appears that the dead wife was cremated. Cremation was new and begins to make an appearance in poetry from about this time. In the poems translated here, however, the images are ancient ones. The soul turns into a bird and flies away. The wife is somewhere in the mountains, perhaps a reference to the custom of abandoning dead bodies in remote locations, not according them burial. The husband comes down out of such a mountain in the last envoy, himself "not as one alive."

As in nos. 83 and 84, no. 345 opens with an epithet for the place Karu, here *ama tobu ya*, "sky-flying." This nicely balances the passage near the end, where birds are singing—meaninglessly—on Mount Unebi. The figure of the messenger, the bearer of sad news, is used again in chōka by Yakamochi (see no. 839, lines 51–54). It is said that messengers carried staffs of *azusa* (catalpa) wood. The catalpa bow, twanging in the distance, becomes a figure for rumor. But the catalpa bow was also the shaman's instrument (like the koto), a means of summoning spirits from the world beyond. This particular messenger was probably the lovers' letter-carrier, which is why the sight of him reminds the poet of "days with her" in no. 347. For "Jewel-sash Mount," see the commentary to no. 288. "Jewel-spear road" renders *tamahoko no michi*. This pillow word probably refers to the phallic stones set up as roadside deities in ancient times. *Tama* might also be translated "soul." The white scarves in the second chōka are reminiscent of the white mourning garments in no. 341, and of the giant white plover that Yamato Takeru turned into at his death (nos. 35–37). Children up to the age of three by the Japanese count (roughly two by the Western) were referred to as *midoriko*, "greenlings." *Ōtori no* ("of the great bird") is a mock epithet for Hagai, from the first syllable, *ha* ("wing"). The locations of Hagai and Hikide are unknown.

345–47, 348–50   [MYS II:207–9, 210–12]

Two poems composed by Kakinomoto no Asomi Hitomaro, sorely grieving with tears of blood, after his wife died; with *tanka*

(345–47)   [207–9]

Ama tobu ya	On the Karu Road,
Karu no michi wa	Karu of the wing-filled sky,
Wagimoko ga	Was the village
Sato ni shi areba	Where she lived, my own dear wife,

5	Nemokoro ni
	Mimaku hoshikedo
	Yamazu yukaba
	Hitome o ōmi
	Maneku yukaba
10	Hito shirinubemi
	Sanekazura
	Ato mo awamu to
	Ōbune no
	Omoitanomite
15	Tamakagiru
	Iwakakifuchi no
	Komori nomi
	Koitsutsu aru ni
	Wataru hi no
20	Kureyuku ga goto
	Teru tsuki no
	Kumogakuru goto
	Okitsumo no
	Nabikishi imo wa
25	Momichiba no
	Sugite iniki to
	Tamazusa no
	Tsukai no ieba
	Azusayumi
30	Oto ni kikite
	Iwamu sube
	Semu sube shirani
	Oto nomi o
	Kikite arieneba
35	Wa ga kouru
	Chie no hitoe mo
	Nagusamuru
	Kokoro mo ari ya to
	Wagimoko ga
40	Yamazu idemishi
	Karu no ichi ni
	Wa ga tachikikeba
	Tamatasuki
	Unebi no yama ni
45	Naku tori no
	Koe mo kikoezu

And to look at her
Was all I wanted in my heart:
　But had I always gone,
There were many eyes of men;
　Had I gone frequently
Others surely would have known.
　So, like branching vines,
After parting we would meet again,
　I thought, as confident
As one who rides in a great ship,
　And though ever yearning,
Kept our love secret, deep and still
　As a pool walled round with rock,
Gleaming softly like a glinting gem.
　But as the coursing sun
Goes down the sky to darkness,
　Or the radiant moon
Is lost to view within the clouds,
　So she who lay with me
As yielding as the seaweed to the wave
　Passed and was gone,
As leaves of autumn pass and are no more:
　It was a messenger,
Azusa-wood staff in hand, who brought the
　　　　　news.

His words buzzed in my ears
Like a distant sound of *azusa*-wood bows:
　Wordless, helpless,
Ignorant of all device,
　I could not bear to stand
Listening to the mere bruit of it,
　And so, imagining
Even the thousandth portion
　Of my longing
Might somehow be assuaged,
　I went where she
Had always gone to look about,
　To the market of Karu,
And there I lingered listening.
　On the hilltop
Of Unebi, called the Jewel-sash Mount,
　The birds were singing,
But I could not hear the voice I knew;

Tamahoko no	Nor were there any
Michi yuku hito mo	Passing on the jewel-spear road,
Hitori dani	Not even one,
50 Nite shi yukaneba	Resembling her, of those that traveled there:
Sube o nami	In my helplessness
Imo ga na yobite	Crying my beloved's name,
Sode so furitsuru	I waved my useless sleeves.

Two Tanka

Akiyama no	On the autumn hills
Momichi o shigemi	The trees are dense with yellow leaves—
Matoinuru	She has lost her way,
Imo o motomemu	And I must go and search for her,
Yamaji shirazu mo	But do not know the mountain path.

Momichiba no	Now that yellow leaves
Chiriyuku nahe ni	Are scattering from the boughs,
Tamazusa no	I see the messenger
Tsukai o mireba	With his *azusa*-wood staff,
Aishi hi omōyu	And days with her return to mind.

(348–50) [210–12]

Utsusemi to	In the days when still
Omoishi toki ni	I thought her a person of this world,
Torimochite	Together she and I
Wa ga futari mishi	Would go to where the elm trees stood
5 Hashiride no	On the embankment,
Tsutsumi ni tateru	Down below the last low hills,
Tsuki no ki no	And pluck the leaves
Kochigochi no e no	To hold and gaze on in our hands:
Haru no ha no	Those rife spring leaves
10 Shigeki ga gotoku	Grew not more thickly on their boughs
Omoerishi	Than the love I held
Imo ni wa aredo	For her, my own dear wife;
Tanomerishi	Than the trust I had
Kora ni wa aredo	In her, child of my heart.
15 Yo no naka o	But she could not turn
Somuki shi eneba	Her back upon what life must bring:
Kagiroi no	Where the shimmering air
Moyuru arano ni	Burns on the wild moorland
Shirotae no	She hid in heavenly scarves,
20 Amahiregakuri	Trailing white as barken cloth;
Torijimono	As if she were a bird
Asa tachiimashite	She flew up in the morning,
Irihi nasu	And like the setting sun

226

	Kakurinishikaba	Vanished to be seen no more.
25	Wagimoko ga	When the little child,
	Katami ni okeru	The greenling keepsake
	Midoriko no	That my darling left,
	Koinaku goto ni	Begs and cries for what it wants,
	Toriatauru	Since there is nothing
30	Mono shi nakereba	That I know to give to it,
	Otokojimono	For all I am a man
	Wakihasamimochi	I hold it clasped beneath my arm.
	Wagimoko to	Where my love and I
	Futari wa ga neshi	Once slept together, in that room,
35	Makurazuku	That pillowed chamber
	Tsumaya no uchi ni	For the nuptial rites, there now
	Hiru wa mo	By day my heart
	Urasabikurashi	Grows cold and dark with grief,
	Yoru wa mo	By night my breath
40	Ikizukiakashi	Is drawn in pain till dawn.
	Nagekedo mo	Lament though I may,
	Semu sube shirani	I know not what to do;
	Kouredo mo	Yearn though I may,
	Au yoshi o nami	We have no way to meet.
45	Ōtori no	Thus when they told me
	Hagai no yama ni	She whom I longed for now abode
	Wa ga kouru	In the great-bird-wing
	Imo wa imasu to	Mountain of Hagai, I came,
	Hito no ieba	Trampling the stones,
50	Iwane sakumite	Kicking aside the rooted rocks,
	Nazumikoshi	Struggling to this spot—
	Yokeku mo so naki	For nothing, it has done no good:
	Utsusemi to	For she whom once
	Omoishi imo ga	I thought a person of this world
55	Tamakagiru	Can no more be seen,
	Honoka ni dani mo	Be it as faintly as the flame
	Mienaku omoeba	That flickers in a glinting gem.

Two Tanka

Kozo miteshi	Though the autumn moon
Aki no tsukuyo wa	On which last fall we gazed together
Teraseredo	Shines again tonight,
Aimishi imo wa	She with whom I watched it then
Iya toshi sakaru	Recedes beyond the gathering years.

Fusumaji o	By Fusuma Road
Hikide no yama ni	In the mountains of Hikide
Imo o okite	I left my love;

Yamaji o yukeba	And I walk the mountain trail,
Ikeri to mo nashi	But not as one alive.

❋ *Uneme* were women from the provinces selected for their beauty and presented to the court to serve as ladies-in-waiting in the palace. In no. 351–53 Hitomaro composed a lament for such a woman. The facts about her are confused. The headnote states that she came from Tsu in Kibi, on the Inland Sea. The two envoys, however, call her the girl from Tsu (or Ōtsu) in Shiga on Lake Biwa. It has even been suggested that she was a legend at court, and that Hitomaro never met her. Uneme were not free to marry, and yet this young woman is said to have left a grieving husband. One interpretation of the first envoy is that she drowned herself, perhaps because her forbidden relationship had been discovered. What is certain in all this is that Hitomaro created a uniquely tender elegy for a lady dying young. Gone is all the high-flown rhetoric of his other banka. The prosody is tentative. Series of truncated lines carry the comparisons to dew and mist, and the unusual 7-7-7 ending of the chōka drifts off, syntactically unfinished. If, as is supposed, the lady was a suicide, the questioning of motive in lines 5 and 6 is no mere convention. Hitomaro places himself in the same position vis-à-vis the actors in his drama as in no. 338, the lament for Princess Asuka. Now he knows regret, but his regret must ever be less than the desolation of the bereaved. Still, it is what he leaves us at the end—the realization only too late of the waste that is indifference.

351–53   [MYS II:217–19]

A poem composed by Kakinomoto no Asomi Hitomaro at the death of a palace woman from Tsu in Kibi; with *tanka*

	Akiyama no	Autumn mountain
	Shitaeru imo	Russet glowing maiden,
	Nayotake no	Slender bamboo
	Tōyoru kora wa	Softly bending, tender child:
5	Ikasama ni	What were her thoughts,
	Omoiore ka	That now it comes to this?
	Takunawa no	Long life was there,
	Nagaki inochi o	A rope of tough bark fiber.
	Tsuyu koso ba	And yet they say
10	Ashita ni okite	It is only dew that gathers
	Yūbe wa	In the dawn
	Kiyu to ie	To dry at dusk;
	Kiri koso ba	And yet they say
	Yūbe ni tachite	It is only mist that rises
15	Ashita ni wa	With the dusk
	Usu to ie	To fade at dawn.

Azusayumi	Even I who hear of this
Oto kiku ware mo	No more than echoes of the twanging bow,
Obo ni mishi	Regret I looked at her
20 Koto kuyashiki o	With the vague glance of one who passes by.
Shikitae no	How much the more must he
Tamakura makite	Who as on finest barken cloth
Tsurugitachi	Pillowed on her arm,
Mi ni soenekemu	Who like a long, straight guardian sword
25 Wakakusa no	Lay close by her side,
Sono tsuma no ko wa	Her husband fresh as the new grass,
Sabushimi ka	Lie in such longing
Omoite nuramu	As comes in loneliness,
Kuyashimi ka	Lost in a yearning
30 Omoikouramu	Bitter with deep regret.
Toki narazu	That this young girl
Suginishi kora ga	Who passed before her time
Asatsuyu no goto	Should, like the morning dew . . .
Yūgiri no goto	Should, like the evening mist . . .

Two Tanka

Sasanami no	The girl from Tsu
Shigatsu no kora ga	In Shiga of the gently lapping waves—
Makariji no	I too am lonely
Kawase no michi o	To see the path she took away,
Mireba sabushi mo	Down by the river shallows.

Sora kazou	Vacantly musing,
Ōtsu no ko ga	To the girl from Ōtsu
Aishi hi ni	On the day she met me
Obo ni mishikaba	I gave but a distant, passing glance—
Ima zo kuyashiki	And now I know the meaning of regret.

❋ The earliest officially recorded cremation in Japan was that of the monk Dōshō in 700. The following poems by Hitomaro perhaps date from about that time. Cremation and Buddhist funeral rites spelled the end of the ancient tumulus burial and its attendant rituals. In this respect as in others, Hitomaro stands at a turning point in time. His public banka glorified the mystique of the archaic burial cult just as it was about to be replaced. But he found a way to incorporate the new custom into his poetry as well. The cloud previously used as the manifestation of the departing spirit (see no. 287) now becomes the smoke cloud from the crematory fire, a familiar image in later literature. The result can be a conceit not dissimilar to the "elegant confusion" of snow and plum blossoms soon to become popular. No. 355-56 may be another commemoration of a suicide. The legends of women who drowned themselves for love found elsewhere in *Man'yōshū* (see nos. 572–73, 574–76, and 837–38) prepared the way for Murasaki Shikibu in her creation of the character Ukifune in *The Tale of Genji*. In no. 356 Hitomaro presents the drowned maiden as an esthetic image. Her long, swirling tresses are at the same time an ironic counterpart to his sensuous water plants.

354   [MYS III: 431/428]

A poem composed by Kakinomoto no Asomi Hitomaro when a maiden of the Hijikata was cremated at Mount Hatsuse:

Komoriku no	In between the hills
Hatsuse no yama no	Of Hatsuse the hidden land
Yama no ma ni	The cloud that hovers
Isayou kumo wa	Hesitant upon the air—
Imo ni ka mo aramu	Might it be the dear one, even she?

355–56   [MYS III: 432–33/429–30]

Two poems composed by Kakinomoto no Asomi Hitomaro when a drowned maiden of Izumo was cremated at Yoshino

(355)   [432/429]

Yama no ma yu	The girl from Izumo,
Izumo no kora wa	Where clouds emerge from the mountains,
Kiri nare ya	Is she a wraith of mist?
Yoshino no yama no	In the mountains of Yoshino
Mine ni tanabiku	The peaks are drifted over.

(356)   [433/430]

Yakumo sasu	The girl from Izumo,
Izumo no kora ga	Land of ever-streaming clouds,
Kurokami wa	Her long black tresses
Yoshino no kawa no	Eddy in the current far
Oki ni nazusau	From Yoshino River's shore.

✳ Victims of starvation or accident also drew Hitomaro's attention. The stranger fallen by the wayside must have been a not uncommon sight, what with the natural hazards of travel and the system of conscript labor that brought men from the provinces to work on public projects. (For a glorifying view of such labor, see no. 1245.) Facilities for travelers must have been few and far between. Hitomaro's tanka below is closely analogous to the poem attributed to Shōtoku Taishi (no. 237). Both assume that the dead man was someone's husband, thereby creating the same kind of pathos found in Hitomaro's laments for Prince Kawashima, Princess Asuka, and his own wife. In no. 357 Hitomaro goes on to inject irony, speaking to the dead man as "in traveler's lodgings," and reproaching him for neglecting his home. This oblique approach perversely creates a stronger effect than the direct exclamation of pity, *aware*, in Prince Shōtoku's poem. We are reminded that the best Man'yō poetry is crafted, if not crafty—not a simple outgushing of the sincere *masurao* ("stalwart") heart. Another irony is that this particular body was discovered on Mount Kagu (one of the "Three Mountains of Yamato"), hardly an arrow's shot from the imperial palace at Fujiwara. There was official concern about such deaths among conscript laborers, and an edict was issued ordering assistance for travelers and burial of the unfortunates who never reached home. In any case, it would have been far from Hitomaro to find in such a misfortune a prediction of "the ruin of the state." The state was divine and coterminous with heaven; but even the "very gods" who were its numinous embodiments, to say nothing of lesser folk, were subject to that greater mystery, death (see also no. 692).

357   [MYS III:429/426]

A poem composed in sadness by Kakinomoto no Asomi Hitomaro on seeing a dead body on Mount Kagu

Kusamakura	Grass for your pillow,
Tabi no yadori ni	Here in traveler's lodgings,
Ta ga tsuma ka	Whose husband are you,
Kuni wasuretaru	Forgetting your own country,
Ie matamaku ni	Though they wait for you at home?

❉ Another encounter between Hitomaro and a stranger who could speak no more, but whom he addresses as a still kindred being, took place on the shore of Samine, a small island off the northeast coast of Shikoku in the Inland Sea. He tells the tale in no. 358–60, the most universal of his poems. In a carefully worked-out structure, he opens with a formal exordium on the divinity of the land, referring to a myth in *Kojiki* to the effect that the island now known as Shikoku ("Four Provinces") is one body with four faces, each a separate god. To one of these divine land-faces, Sanuki, he has come on a voyage. But that face suddenly becomes an angry one as a tempest nearly wrecks the travelers' boat. Taking shelter on the island of Samine, they discover the body of a voyager who has been unluckier than they. The moment has the immediacy of cinematography: "When we looked (*mireba*). . . , you (*kimi*). . . ." The body is "you," and it lies on a rough bed with sand as a pillow. Thus Hitomaro retrieves the dead man as fully human, except that he cannot speak. He is one of us, a brother, a fellow traveler. We might well be lying in his place. As a man, he must have a wife, and as always Hitomaro's thought runs to the bereaved marital partner. She would come if only she knew (but her husband cannot speak, and no one can go to tell her). And what would she do if she came? The first envoy tells: she would pick herbs, prepare a meal for her famished husband. Ah, but the season for herbs is past. At this moment Hitomaro the compassionate ironist quietly reveals once and for all the breadth of his grasp of the human condition. The last envoy turns again to the dead man, speaking to him, but saying nothing, only describing how he lies pillowed on the sea-encircled shore. Man travels across a world of innate divinity, and finds his rest where he must or where the gods will, beneath the sky of his journey.

358–60   [MYS II: 220–22]

A poem composed by Kakinomoto no Asomi Hitomaro on seeing a dead man among the stones of Samine Island in Sanuki; with *tanka*

Tamamo yoshi	Splendid with gemweed,
Sanuki no kuni wa	Yes, rich is the land of Sanuki,
Kunikara ka	A land of good stock—
Miredo mo akanu	Is it for this I gaze but do not weary?
5 Kamukara ka	A land of godhead—
Kokoda tōtoki	Is it for this it bides deep in awe?
Ame tsuchi	Together with heaven,
Hi tsuki to tomo ni	With earth, long as the sun and moon,
Tariyukamu	It will endure and prosper,
10 Kami no miomo to	This land whose face, the legend has come down,
Tsugite kuru	Is the visage of a god.
Naka no minato yu	Having come this far, once more
Fune ukete	We launched our ship
Wa ga kogikureba	And rowed from Naka harbor out to sea:
15 Toki tsu kaze	Then the tidewind blew
Kumoi ni fuku ni	Down from the Dwelling of Clouds;
Oki mireba	When I looked far out
Toinami tachi	Great surging waves towered up,
He mireba	And looking to the beach,
20 Shiranami sawaku	I saw the white waves seething on the shore.
Isanatori	In dread of the wild,
Umi o kashikomi	Whale-hunting sea, we struggled
Yuku fune no	With the oars of our
Kaji hikiorite	Hurtling ship until they bent with strain.
25 Ochikochi no	Everywhere about
Shima wa ōkedo	Were islands, but of their multitude
Nakuwashi	In the end it was

Samine no shima no	The sweet-named isle of Samine
Arisomo ni	Upon whose rocky strand
30 Iorite mireba	We built our shelter and then looked about:
Nami no to no	There on the beach
Shigeki hamabe o	Loud with the ceaseless, pounding surf,
Shikitae no	Sprawled with the sand
Makura ni nashite	For your pillow of fine barken cloth,
35 Aradoko ni	On that rough bed
Korofusu kimi ga	You had laid yourself; and if I knew
Ie shiraba	Where to find your home,
Yukite mo tsugemu	I would go to bear this word;
Tsuma shiraba	Or if your wife but knew,
40 Ki mo towamashi o	Surely she would come to seek you out;
Tamahoko no	But all unknowing
Michi dani shirazu	Even of the jewel-spear road to take,
Oboboshiku	Timidly anxious,
Machi ka kouramu	Even now she must be waiting, yearning,
45 Hashiki tsumara wa	The dear wife that you loved so well.

Two Envoys

Tsuma mo araba	If your wife were here
Tsumite tagemashi	She would pick herbs for you to eat,
Sami no yama	The starworts that grow
No no e no uhagi	In the upland fields of Sami—
Suginikerazu ya	But is their time not long gone by?
Okitsunami	And you who lie asleep
Kiyoru ariso o	Where the long waves wash ashore,
Shikitae no	Taking this rough strand
Makura to makite	For a pillow of fine barken cloth
Naseru kimi kamo	Where you may gently rest your head . . .

✳ The last of the *Man'yōshū* poems directly attributed to Hitomaro in the present anthology is a deathbed verse. But the "bed" is the rough one of stones where fallen travelers lie. Now Hitomaro has become a voice from his own poetry. Now *he* is the man on Mount Kagu or Samine Island, and he speaks in a voice that their mute lips might have uttered, wondering about his wife as he lies dying. The headnote takes him back to remote Iwami; the "beloved wife" must therefore be the woman he left beside the sea. Or so the poem would make us believe. More likely, some unknown poet was moved to provide an appropriate ending for a life story that was already lost. Still, one does not know. Perhaps the final utterance was murmured to a luckier traveler who happened by along the jewel-spear road.

233

361   [MYS II:223]

A poem composed by Kakinomoto no Asomi Hitomaro sorrowing over himself as he lay at the point of death in Iwami Province

Kamoyama no	On Kamo Mountain
Iwane shi makeru	Embedded among boulders
Ware o ka mo	Here I rest my head—
Shirani to imo ga	Unknowing, my beloved wife
Machitsutsu aramu	Must even now be waiting.

A Maiden of the Yosami (poems from early 8th century)

A wife of Hitomaro and author of three tanka in *Man'yōshū*, the Maiden of the Yosami (Yosami no Otome) is usually thought to be the woman Hitomaro loved in Iwami. Other theories place her in Settsu or Kawachi. The compilers of *Man'yōshū* evidently thought of her as Hitomaro's wife in Iwami, since they placed her poems in that geographical context. The following two come immediately after the one in which Hitomaro lies dying on Kamo Mountain. Now he lies in Pebble River (Ishikawa). Is it basically the same place, or has his wife been misinformed, or has his body been taken to the riverbed for cremation? Mention of the clouds in the second poem would tend to support this last hypothesis. Geographical research misses the main point about these poems—they are an *utamonogatari*, a poem-tale, arranged to give the words of a dying man and the perplexed and lonely feelings of his wife. We are no longer in the oeuvre, but in the legend, of Hitomaro.

362–63   [MYS II:224–25]

Two poems composed by his wife, a maiden of the Yosami, when Kakinomoto no Asomi Hitomaro died

(362)   [224]

Kyō kyō to	You for whom I wait
Wa ga matsu kimi wa	Day after day, do they not
Ishikawa no	Say you lie mingled
Kai ni majirite	With the shells, my love,
Ari to iwazu ya mo	In the bed of Pebble River?

(363)   [225]

Tada no ai wa	To meet face to face—
Aikatsumashiji	We shall not meet so any more;
Ishikawa ni	Rise up, O clouds,

Kumo tachiwatare   Stand along Pebble River—
Mitsutsu shinowamu   I would gaze and remember.

Tajihi no Mahito (early 8th century?)

Nothing is known of this poet other than that he left three tanka in *Man'yō-shū*; even his personal name has not been recorded. (Tajihi is his clan name, and Mahito his clan title, the highest in Temmu's reorganized list of eight.) But the headnote to no. 364 makes plain that he or someone like him could be the missing link that would explain Hitomaro's "deathbed" poem (or even his wife's responses) for those not inclined to accept them at face value. It seems plausible that a story circulated that Hitomaro had died as a lonely traveler, and that Tajihi and perhaps others were inspired to imagine his feelings. In such ways do legends grow. Tajihi's poem asks the question that would occur to anyone thinking over the practicalities of the matter. It is nevertheless a fitting last tribute to the mortal gifted to sing of living gods and other humans who flourish briefly before passing beyond the wild fields alone.

364   [MYS II:226]

A poem in reply by Tajihi no Mahito [personal name missing], in imitation of the sentiments of Kakinomoto no Asomi Hitomaro

 Aranami ni   Who will bear the word
Yorikuru tama o   That I am here, am pillowed
 Makura ni oki   Amid the gems of sea
Ware koko ni ari to   Washed by wild waters in to rest
Tare ka tsugenamu   Along the wave-wet shore?

Poems from the "Hitomaro Collection"

There are approximately 360 poems scattered through Books II, III, VII, and IX–XIV of *Man'yōshū* that are noted by the compilers as being from *Kakinomoto no Asomi Hitomaro Kashū*. This "Hitomaro Collection" is one of four in *Man'yōshū* that carry the names of individual poets. Unlike the others, it has long been controversial because of its varied content. There are poems showing familiarity with Chinese versification; poems belonging to the so-called *min'yō*, or "folk song," category of rustic scenes and the traditional means of makurakotoba and jo; poems that are variants of others in the basic body of work stated to have been composed by Hitomaro; poems that are by women, or in which the speaker is a woman; poems in the sedōka form, not found elsewhere in Hitomaro's work; and poems attributed directly to other poets. Detailed study has demonstrated that most of these poems are more closely similar in orthographic usage and vocabulary to the accepted Hitomaro corpus than to a control group of anonymous poems. Other scholars have argued that some are by Hitomaro and others not. The present anthology regards the issue as unresolved and treats the "Hitomaro Collection" as a category separate from both Hitomaro's accepted oeuvre and the anonymous poems at the end of this volume.

Book VII begins with a tanka from the "Hitomaro Collection," one of a group of otherwise anonymous poems "on things" (*eibutsu*), under the general rubric of zōka. The "things" are the natural features and phenomena that were the basic categories of traditional Chinese encyclopedic works. No. 365, in the subcategory "On the Sky," is immediately noticeable for its use of metaphor. Sky, clouds, moon, and stars are made into sea, waves, boat, and forest in a dazzling set of correspondences. The poem is successful as a brilliant imagistic display, but the display calls attention to itself, leaving the impression of a technical paradigm. The surreal boat-in-the-forest image lends a haunting irrationality to an otherwise too perfect scheme. In its use of noun-based metaphor this poem is an anomaly. Traditional Japanese analogical structures tend to work through the verb or adjective, rather than by noun equivalences, or to be based on wordplay or syntactic doublings. The use of direct similes with some form of *goto* ("like") or a similar word was developed by Hitomaro, but these usages are without exception adverbial. When a noun was used in a double sense, the submerged half was left submerged. Metaphors of the x = y variety usually have as tenor a person. The quadripartite metaphorical constellation of no. 365 is an adaptation into Japanese of Chinese norms; the image of the moon-boat can be found in a contemporary kanshi by Emperor Mommu (the Prince Karu of no. 331–35), whose opening couplet may be translated "The moon-boat moves by the misty strand; / The cassia oar drifts past the hazy shore." Is Hitomaro likely to have experimented with a Japanese counterpart of such poems? The bard of the great chōka does not speak in the voice of the urbane Sinologue, but he did create the striking metaphor of no. 302, in which Prince Naga turns the moon into a silken parasol. A variant of no. 365 appears as SIS VIII:488, attributed to Hitomaro.

"On the Sky"

365 [MYS VII: 1072/1068]

Ame no umi ni	In the sea of sky
Kumo no nami tachi	The waves of cloud rise up,
Tsuki no fune	And the moon-boat
Hoshi no hayashi ni	Is seen rowing out of sight
Kogikakuru miyu	Into the forest of the stars.

❋ No. 367 should be compared to no. 306, one of Hitomaro's set of eight poems on travel. Such resemblances of course raise the question of the sources not only of the "Hitomaro Collection," but of the main body of Hitomaro's work: did Hitomaro have an editor, or was he a collector himself? The two poems on Makimuku River make a nice contrast of description and reflection. Ruminations on the evanescence of human life are often taken as shadowings from the penumbra of Buddhist thought. Hitomaro lived during the great Hakuhō age of temple building and sculpture, but his poetry is loyal to an earlier ethos, and his realization of life's brevity must have come from observation and his role as a writer of laments.

"On Rivers"

366   [MYS VII: 1105/1101]

   Nubatama no   When the night comes on,
   Yoru sarikureba   Black as leopard-flower berries,
   Makimuku no   Makimuku
   Kawato takashi mo   River crashes loud—perhaps
   Arashi ka mo toki   A storm is lashing the peak.

"Composed on a Journey"

367   [MYS VII: 1191/1187]

   Abiki suru   Will they look at me
   Ama to ka miramu   As a fisherman, a puller of nets,
   Aku no ura no   I who have come
   Kiyoki ariso o   Only that I too might gaze
   Mi ni koshi ware o   On the clean stone strand of Aku?

"Inspired by a Place"

368   [MYS VII: 1273/1269]

   Makimuku no   We are like foam
   Yamabe toyomite   On rushing water roaring
   Yuku mizu no   Through mountain gorges
   Minawa no gotoshi   Under Makimuku—we
   Yo no hito ware wa   Who are people of this world.

❋ Nos. 369–71 are a set of sedōka with line 6 partially or completely repeating line 3, a feature of ancient song (see nos. 65 and 150). Although placed in the zōka category in Book VII, the three poems are love songs. For Mount Kurahashi in connection with another love story, see nos. 69–70 and commentary. The mountain no doubt was the site of utagaki revels, and these poems seem to refer to such a context. The "white cloud" is the young woman whose sudden appearance attracts the man (or vice versa?). In the second poem the male speaker remembers the adventures of his youth. And in the third we learn that he did not marry the girl ("still sedge"), though he "cut" (harvested) her.

"Sedōka"

369 [MYS VII: 1286/1282]

Hashitate no	White cloud
Kurahashiyama ni	Rising over the mountain,
Tateru shirakumo	Kurahashi the ladder-steep,
Mimaku hori	White cloud
A ga suru nahe ni	Rising at the very instant
Tateru shirakumo	I was gazing with desire.

370 [MYS VII: 1287/1283]

Hashitate no	Across the river,
Kurahashigawa no	Kurahashi the ladder-steep,
Iwa no hashi wa mo	Once on a bridge of stepping stones
Ozakari ni	When I was a young man
Wa ga watariteshi	I went over and across—
Iwa no hashi wa mo	On a bridge of stepping stones.

371 [MYS VII: 1288/1284]

Hashitate no	Down by the river,
Kurahashigawa no	Kurahashi the ladder-steep,
Kawa no shizusuge	Still sedge down by the river
Wa ga karite	I went down and cut,
Kasa ni mo amanu	But I wove no hat for me to wear
Kawa no shizusuge	From the still sedge down by the river.

❋ No. 372 is another sedōka with particularly lovely imagery bringing together sunrise and the moon, expressing the thoughts of a man who does not have a wife about one who does. The slender new moon at twilight would remind a man away on a journey of the hour at which he and his wife would ordinarily meet. For the man without a wife it would be a reminder that he is even more deprived. The mention of sunrise in the pillow word *asazukuhi* subliminally enriches the poem with an allusion to the time of lovers' parting. The new moon is shaped like a bow that shoots afar the arrows of desire.

372   [MYS VII: 1298/1294)

   Asazukuhi   Over the mountains
  Mukai no yama ni   That face the point of sunrise
  Tsuki tateri miyu   The new moon now stands in view:
    Tōzuma o   He who has afar
  Moteramu hito shi   A dear wife for whom he longs
  Mitsutsu shinowamu   Must look on it with yearning.

✻ No. 373 is a tanka belonging to the category of *hiyuka*, the so-called
"metaphorical poems," in which a thought is "related to something" (*kibutsu*) that serves as its vehicle. Poems in this category are usually love poems.
The "pearl" is clearly the object of an amorous quest; the flocks of teal may
also be metaphorical, standing for the inquisitive world. The conceits are
kept dark, however, so that such a poem can be read solely for its surface
meaning.

"Related to Gems"

373   [MYS VII: 1303/1299]

   Ajimura no   That mid flocks of teal
  Tōyoru umi ni   Bobbing lightly on the sea
   Fune ukete   I float my boat
  Shiratama toru to   And go out to gather pearls—
  Hito ni shirayu na   Let nobody know of this!

✻ Many of the poems from the "Hitomaro Collection" in Book IX were
composed at various named places during travel and contain a reference to a
person left at home. Nos. 374–76 are all based on wordplay in their opening
lines. A jeweled comb box (a woman's treasure) "opens" (*ake*) as day dawns
(*ake*) to lovers' regret. Heron Slope Mountain is "white" like a scarf (another feminine article) and the white azaleas growing there. The third of this
set takes the lover directly into (*iri*) his sweetheart's gates in order to introduce Izumi ("come forth") River. In the snow on the water-moss the traveler sees that it is "still winter," not yet the season of renewal.

374   [MYS IX: 1697/1693]

[One of] two poems composed in the province of Ki

   Tamakushige   A jeweled comb box
  Akemaku oshiki   Opening the dawnlight once
   Aratayo o   Ended precious nights—

Koromode karete   And are my sleeves now torn away
Hitori ka mo nemu   From hers as I sleep alone?

375   [MYS IX: 1698/1694]
Composed at Sagisaka

Takuhire no   *Barken-cloth scarf*
Sagisakayama no   White Heron Slope Mountain:
Shiratsutsuji   White azaleas,
Ware ni niowane   Tinge me too with your color—
Imo ni shimesamu   I'd show it to her I love.

376   [MYS IX: 1699/1695]
Composed at Izumi River

Imo ga kado   *To my sweetheart's gates*
Iri Izumigawa no   *And forth:* Wellspring River:
Tokoname ni   Midst the water-moss
Miyuki nokoreri   Traces of snow still linger—
Imada fuyu ka mo   Is it then winter yet?

❋ "Three poems composed at Naki River" use the conceit that the "folks at
home" have sent the spring rain to discourage their traveler from going farther and bring him back to the comfort of dry clothes. Such light and rueful
humor may be found here and there throughout *Man'yōshū* but is not typical of Hitomaro. Why Naki River has the epithet *koromode no* ("garment
sleeve") is not known, but the term does relate well to the image of wet
clothes.

377–79   [MYS IX: 1700–1702/1696–98]
Three poems composed at Naki River
(377)   [1700/1696]

Koromode no   That by garment-sleeve
Naki no kawahe o   Naki River on the bank
Harusame ni   In the rains of spring
Ware tachinuru to   I am standing getting wet—
Ie omouramu ka   Do they imagine it at home?

(378)   [1701/1697]

Iebito no   Now I know for sure:
Tsukai ni arashi   It must be the messenger

Harusame no	Of the folks at home,
Yokuredo ware o	This spring rain, when I consider
Nurasaku omoeba	How it wets me though I dodge it.

(379)   [1702/1698]

Aburihosu	Have I anyone
Hito mo are ya mo	To dry my clothes at the fire?
Iebito no	Yet the folks at home
Harusame sura o	Use of all things the spring rain
Matsukai ni suru	As their messenger to me.

✴ Nos. 380 and 381 are vivid evocations of the wildlife that once abounded at the confluence of the Uji, Yodo, and Izumi rivers south of the present city of Kyōto. A large marshy lake called Ogura (or Ōkura) Pond existed there in ancient times, no doubt providing excellent feeding grounds for waterfowl. These poems make a pleasing contrast with the schematic use of hunting images in formal chōka.

380–81   [MYS IX: 1703–4/1699–1700]

Two poems composed on Uji River

(380)   [1703/1699]

Ōkura no	Thunder in the air
Irie toyomu nari	Over the inlets of Ōkura:
Imehito no	It must be the wild geese
Fushimi ga tai ni	Crossing to Fushimi's paddy fields,
Kari wataru rashi	Where in blinds the hunters lie in wait.

(381)   [1704/1700]

Akikaze ni	On the autumn wind
Yamabuki no se no	Over the roaring in the rapids
Naru nae ni	Of Yamabuki
Amakumo kakeru	They come winging through the clouds—
Kari ni aeru kamo	I have met wild geese descending from the sky!

✴ One may wonder why the following three private poems, one with a love reference, were presented to Prince Yuge (whose own poems are nos. 279–84). The first, no. 382, is also included as an anonymous poem in *Kokinshū* (KKS IV: 192). The feeling in these poems of what would later be called *aware* comes not only from the cold, distant cries of the geese, but also from the motion in each: of the moon, the geese, time. Only the listener remains still, to register the emotions called forth by the passing scene.

382–84   [MYS IX: 1705–7/1701–3]

Three poems presented to Prince Yuge

(382)   [1705/1701]

    Sayonaka to   Night must have deepened
  Yo wa fukenu rashi   Even to the midnight hour:
     Kari ga ne no   A wild goose crying
    Kikoyuru sora o   Heard in flight across the sky,
    Tsuki wataru miyu   The moon in crossing seen.

(383)   [1706/1702]

    Imo ga atari   About her house the air
  Shigeki kari ga ne   Was filled with crying of wild geese;
     Yūgiri ni   Now in the evening mist
    Kinakite suginu   They come and call and pass,
    Subenaki made ni   Until I am helpless.

(384)   [1707/1703]

    Kumogakuri   When the wild geese cry,
  Kari naku toki wa   Hidden high amid the clouds,
     Akiyama no   I wait with single heart
  Momichi katamatsu   For the colors on the autumn hills,
    Toki wa suguredo   Though the season passes by.

❋ Prince Toneri (d. 735), the recipient of nos. 385 and 386 and author of no. 387, was a son of Emperor Temmu. He was the compiler-in-chief of the final version of *Nihonshoki*. The two tanka presented to him seem to have no connection. The first employs the conceit that the mountain mist agitates the waves, perhaps by blocking the stream with its "denseness." Mount Tamu has the pillow word *fusa taori* ("breaking a cluster") because *tamu* also means "to droop." The second poem seems to be a love allegory, one hinting at a plot like that of Hikaru Genji and the girl Murasaki in *The Tale of Genji*. (See also nos. 1159–61 in the section on exchanges.) Prince Toneri's poem may be in response to no. 385, since it is also about mist in the mountains. *Koromode no* ("of the garment sleeves") is a mock epithet for Takaya through *ta* ("arm").

385-86   [MYS IX: 1708-9/1704-5]

Two poems presented to Prince Toneri

(385)   [1708/1704]

   Fusa taori   *Breaking a cluster*
   Tamu no yamagiri   Drooping Tamu Mountain mist—
     Shigemi ka mo   How dense it is!
   Hosokawa no se ni   Whence in Hosokawa's stream
   Nami no sawakeru   The waves splash loud in the shallows?

(386)   [1709/1705]

   Fuyugomori   For winter-dormant
   Haruhe o koite   Springtime I was yearning when
     Ueshi ki no   I planted this tree:
   Mi ni naru toki o   Now I'm half mad with waiting
   Katamatsu ware zo   For the fruit to ripen out.

387   [MYS IX: 1710/1706]

A poem by Prince Toneri

   Nubatama no   In the glistening
   Yogiri wa tachinu   Bead-black night the mists have risen
     Koromode no   Till they drift in bands
   Takaya no ue ni   On the heights of Takaya,
   Tanabiku made ni   Mountain of the garment sleeve.

❋ Nos. 388 and 389 are connected in the sense that each contrasts spring
and fall. Each also involves a playful use of language. *Haru wa hari* ("spring
springs," i.e., "expands," "burgeons") in the first is balanced by *harukusa
o uma kui* ("spring grasses horses eat") to introduce Kuiyama ("Mount
Kui"). The "messenger goose" alludes to the story of Su Wu (ca. 140 B.C. –
60 B.C.), a Chinese general captured by the Hsiung-nu who sent a message
home tied to the leg of a wild goose (see no. 85). Here it brings the message
of autumn's arrival.

388   [MYS IX: 1711/1707]

A poem composed at Sagisaka

   Yamashiro no   In Yamashiro
   Kuse no Sagisaka   Heron Hill at Kuse
     Kamiyo yori   From the Age of Gods

| Haru wa haritsutsu | Has still burgeoned in the spring |
| Aki wa chirikeri | And shed its leaves in fall. |

389 [MYS IX: 1712/1708]

A poem composed beside Izumi River

Harukusa o	Over Mount Kui
Uma Kuiyama yu	Where in spring the horses graze,
Koeku naru	The sound comes closer:
Kari no tsukai wa	The lone messenger goose of autumn
Yadori sugu nari	Passes my lodging in the night.

❊ Praise of mountains and rivers resounds throughout *Man'yōshū*, as in the following seven tanka from the "Hitomaro Collection." The emphasis on the freshness of snow, water, and verdure is typical. The places named are all in the Asuka-Yoshino area. Mutsuta River is another name for a stretch of Yoshino River. The identities of Gannin, Kinu, Shimatari, and Maro are unknown. These private excursions (or so they seem without amplifying context) show a freer working of the delight in nature than could be afforded by such panegyrics as Hitomaro's celebrations of the imperial visit to Yoshino, nos. 293–96. Notice that Maro's poem repeats the last line of the first chōka of that pair. It has been suggested that "Maro" is short for "Hitomaro."

390 [MYS IX: 1713/1709]

A poem presented to Prince Yuge

Mike mukau	Does the rime of snow
Minabuchiyama no	Fallen on the bristling crags
Iwao ni wa	Of Minabuchi
Furishi hadare ka	Remain unmelted, still coating
Kienokoritaru	That mountain of noble abundance?

391–93 [MYS IX: 1724–26/1720–22]

Three poems by Gannin

(391) [1724/1720]

Uma namete	Horses all lined up,
Uchimure koeki	The crowd of us came over,
Ima mitsuru	Down to Yoshino:
Yoshino no kawa o	When shall we come back again
Itsu kaerimimu	To view the river as today?

(392)   [1725/1721]

 Kurushiku mo   It grieves me that the day
 Kureyuku hi kamo At length grows dark despite my wish
  Yoshinogawa   To gaze yet more
 Kiyoki kawara o   On Yoshino's clean river beach,
 Miredo akanaku ni For I am never weary of the sight.

(393)   [1726/1722]

 Yoshinogawa   Yoshino River
 Kawanami takami River waves run high, but why
  Taki no ura o   Go back without seeing
 Mizu ka narinamu The cove by the waterfall?
 Koishikemaku ni   We'll regret it if we do!

394   [MYS IX: 1727/1723]

A poem by Kinu

 Kawazu naku   Riverfrog crying
 Mutsuta no kawa no Mutsuta River bounded
  Kawayagi no   With river willows—
 Nemokoro miredo Rooted to the spot I gaze
 Akanu kawa kamo But never tire of the river.

395   [MYS IX: 1728/1724]

A poem by Shimatari

 Mimaku hori   Eager for the sight,
 Koshiku mo shiruku Lucky that I came to see—
  Yoshinogawa   Yoshino River
 Oto no sayakesa   Has a freshness in its sound;
 Miru ni tomoshiku I gaze and am rapt in wonder.

396   [MYS IX: 1729/1725]

A poem by Maro

 Inishie no   Long though I may gaze
 Sakashiki hito no On the river beach of Yoshino
  Asobikemu   Where wise men of old
 Yoshino no kawara Took pleasure, so the story goes,
 Miredo akanu kamo I can never weary of the sight.

❋ A spring and three autumn poems from the seasonally arranged zōka of
Book x follow. The conventional sign of spring in the first poem (no. 397)

is the *kasumi*, "haze" or "spring mist," distinguished from *kiri*, "autumn mist." This auspicious poem opens Book X. A tradition that was introduced from T'ang China at about this time (i.e., the late seventh century), was the Tanabata myth of the two lover stars, the Weaving Maid (Tanabata, identified with Vega) and the Herdsman (Hikoboshi, the star Altair), who were separated by the River of Heaven (the Milky Way) and could meet only once a year, on the seventh night of the seventh month. The story became very popular in Japan, both as a festival myth and a topic in poetry, and a large number of Man'yō poems were written on the theme. (See note to "Hitomaro Collection.") In no. 398 the Herdsman Star is ready for his annual dash across the Milky Way. The place of his crossing, Yasu no Watari, comes from Yasu no Kawara, the meeting place of the Shintō gods in the chronicles. The other two fall poems are about autumn leaves. "Wife-secluding" (*tsumagomoru*) is a mock epithet for Yano ("Arrowfields") through *ya* ("house").

397   [MYS X: 1816/1812]

> Hisakata no   On sun-radiant
> Ama no Kaguyama   Heavenly Mount Kagu's slopes
> Kono yūhe   In the evening light
> Kasumi tanabiku   Bands of haze are drifting—
> Haru tatsu rashi mo   Spring must be here at last!

"Tanabata"

398   [MYS X: 2004/2000]

> Ama no kawa   Tell my beloved
> Yasu no watari ni   That I wait, my boat in the water
> Fune ukete   At Yasu Crossing,
> Akitachi matsu to   Ready the moment autumn comes
> Imo ni tsuge koso   To launch upon the River in the Sky.

"On Fall Foliage"

399   [MYS X: 2182/2178]

> Tsumagomoru   In wife-secluding
> Yano no kamiyama   Arrowfields the sacred mount
> Tsuyu shimo ni   From the dew and frost
> Nioisometari   Has begun to glow with color:
> Chiramaku oshi mo   How I'll regret the scattering!

400   [MYS X: 2183/2179]

> Asatsuyu ni   On autumn mountains
> Nioisometaru   Now beginning to grow bright

Akiyama ni   From the morning dew,
Shigure na furi so   Drizzly rain, do not rain down,
Ariwataru gane   That the colors may last long.

❋ Book XI opens with a series of twelve sedōka from the "Hitomaro Collection," of which eight are given here. Nos. 401 and 402, 403 and 404, and 406 and 407 form pairs. The whole set has a "folk" quality (i.e., evokes the lives and customs of villagers). Whether they or any other "folkish" poems are actually folk songs in the sense of a common body of song constantly altering from singer to singer is another matter. If ascription to Hitomaro is not to be credited, their authorship remains unknown. The first two, based on an identical analogical technique, are seduction songs at the building of a new house, in which a young woman invites a young man, with honorific language (hence "my lord"), to come in. It seems likely that the songs were part of a nuptial ceremony at which a house was erected for the new couple. The grass-walled house creates a village ambience, intriguingly romantic to courtiers. In no. 402 a shrine maiden is performing a sacred dance to "level" (*narasu*) the earth, clicking (*narasu*) her *magatama* beads as she does so. (For another house-raising ceremony, see no. 153.)

"Sedōka"

401   [MYS XI:2355/2351]

Niimuro no   Come hither, my lord,
Kabekusa kari ni   Cut the grasses for the walls
Imashitamawane   Of the newly finished house.
   Kusa no goto   Here is a maiden,
Yoriau otome wa   Yielding as the grasses yield,
Kimi ga manimani   Yours to do with as you wish.

402   [MYS XI:2356/2352]

Niimuro o   How she clicks her gems,
Fumishizumu ko shi   The girl stamping down the ground
Tadama narasu mo   Of the newly finished house!
   Tama no goto   Tell him to come in,
Teritaru kimi o   The young lord who shines as fair
Uchi ni to mōse   As the gleaming of the gems!

❋ The second sedōka pair is about a different kind of marriage. The man has stolen the woman without the permission of her parents, and now is anxious lest she be discovered. According to another interpretation, it is the wife's beauty that shines "through heaven and earth." But the moon imag-

ery of no. 403 suggests that no. 404 too is dominated by the shafts of the
"bow-moon."

403 [MYS XI:2357/2353]

Hatsuse no	In Hatsuse
Yuzuki ga shita ni	At the foot of Bow-Moon Hill
Kakushitaru tsuma	Is the wife I have hidden.
Akane sashi	Madder-root-shining,
Tereru tsukuyo ni	Beaming is the moonlit night:
Hito mitemu ka mo	Someone may have seen her there.

404 [MYS XI:2358/2354]

Masurao no	Whom the stalwart one,
Omoimidarete	Wildly anxious in his love,
Kakushitaru tsuma	Hid so carefully—that wife,
Ame tsuchi ni	Though through heaven and earth
Tōriteru to mo	The bright moon should shoot its beams,
Arawareme ya mo	Would she let herself be seen?

❋ The effect of the fifth poem in the series, not paired with any other, is
quite delicious. Lulled by the dance rhythm of sedōka, the reader hums
along, only to find the words *haya mo shinanu ka* ("won't she hurry up and
die!"). The effect of such devilish innocence can be stunning, as in some of
the poems of A. E. Housman, but here it is no doubt facetious. The compiler must have inserted the poem at this point for his private satisfaction.

405 [MYS XI:2359/2355]

Uruwashi to	She whom so lovely
A ga omou imo wa	I have thought, that darling girl,
Haya mo shinanu ka	Won't she hurry up and die?
Ikeri to mo	Even if she lives,
Wa ni yorubeshi to	That she will ever come to me
Hito no iwanaku ni	Is what no one ever says.

❋ The pair 406–7 expresses a woman's reluctance to part with her lover in
the morning. Focused on details of clothing, the poems convey a quiet intimacy, and in the case of the first, a coy feminine wit as well.

406 [MYS XI:2360/2356]

Komanishiki	Look! One of your cords
Himo no katahe zo	Brocaded in the Korean style

Toko ni ochinikeru	Has fallen off on the bed!
Asu no yo shi	If you promise me
Kinamu to iwaba	You'll come back again tonight,
Toriokite matamu	I'll keep it for you and wait.

407 [MYS XI:2361/2357]

Asatode no	The dewy meadows
Kimi ga ayuhi o	That will wet your trouser strings
Nurasu tsuyuhara	As you leave the morning door:
Hayaku oki	Let me rise early
Idetsutsu ware mo	And go out along with you,
Mosuso nurasana	Wetting my skirts as I go.

✳ No. 408, the last of the sedōka series, seems closely related to a saibara called "Yamashiro." Replete with repetitions and "rhythm words" (haya-shikotoba) indicating that it was actually sung, "Yamashiro" is based on a poetic text in a 5-7-5-7-5-7-7 pattern, a miniature chōka, and may already have been subjected to revision at court. No. 408 may have come from simi-lar rustic origins and been shaped into a sedōka. In their original form, at least, such folk songs would have been the common property of the people who sang them for entertainment or to accompany work, and not lyrics as-signable to an individual.

408 [MYS XI:2366/2362]

Yamashiro no	That young fellow
Kuse no wakugo ga	From Kuse in Yamashiro—
Hoshi to iu ware	I'm the one he says he wants;
Ausawa ni	He says he wants me,
Ware o hoshi to iu	Brash as can be, that fellow
Yamashiro no Kuse	From Kuse in Yamashiro.

✳ One of the major categories of Book XI is "Expressing Thoughts Di-rectly" (tada ni omoi o noburu). Poems of this type are straight-out declara-tions of emotion, usually of desire, and contrast with the poems in the category "Expressing Thoughts by Reference to Things" (mono ni yosete omoi o noburu), which introduce a name or image, sometimes for analogical use and sometimes not. In individual cases the distinction between the two categories may be difficult to discern. The following ten tanka from the "Hitomaro Collection" illustrate "Expressing Thoughts Directly." Several of the poems are not gender-specific, the sentiments being plausible for either sex. The translations usually make clear the cases where a man or woman can be assumed as the speaker; no. 411, where this may not be so,

can be assumed to be the utterance of the man (compare nos. 418 and 992).
Variants of nos. 411, 417, and 418 appear in *Shūishū*, the third imperial anthology of waka, with attribution to Hitomaro.

"Expressing Thoughts Directly"

409 [MYS XI:2372/2368]

Tarachine no
Haha ga te hanare
Kaku bakari
Sube naki koto wa
Imada senaku ni

Not since the day
I left the hands of my mother
Of the drooping breasts
Have I ever until now
Been as helpless as this.

410 [MYS XI:2373/2369]

Hito no nuru
Umai wa nezute
Hashiki yashi
Kimi ga me sura o
Hori shi nagekau

Not as others lie
In sweet slumber do I sleep;
Oh, the sighs I heave,
My own lover, craving you,
Even your very eyes!

411 [MYS XI:2374/2370]

Koishinaba
Koi mo shine to ya
Tamahoko no
Michiyukibito no
Koto mo tsugenaku

"If you die of love,
Then die of love!" Is that
What you would tell me?
No traveler on the jewel-spear road
Has brought me word of you.

412 [MYS XI:2375/2371]

Kokoro ni wa
Chie ni omoedo
Hito ni iwanu
A ga koizuma o
Mimu yoshi mogamo

Though I long for her
In my heart a thousand fold,
None do I tell
Of the wife of my yearning—
And, oh, that I could see her now!

413 [MYS XI:2376/2372]

Kaku bakari
Koimu mono so to
Shiramaseba
Tōku mibeku mo
Arikeru mono o

If I had known
How desire will hold a man
In such a yearning,
Even I would have been wise
And looked at her far off.

414 [MYS XI:2377/2373]

Itsu wa shi mo
Koinu toki to wa

Be it when it may,
I have never a moment

Aranedo mo
Yū katamakete
Koi wa sube nashi

Free from this longing,
But when evening comes upon me
I am helpless in my love.

415   [MYS XI:2378/2374]

Kaku nomi shi
Koi ya wataramu
Tamakiwaru
Inochi mo shirazu
Toshi wa henitsutsu

Is there nothing else,
Only this constant yearning?
Tell me, to what end,
Life wherein the spirit dwells,
As the years go slipping by?

416   [MYS XI:2381/2377]

Nani semu ni
Inochi tsugikemu
Wagimoko ni
Koizaru saki ni
Shinamashi mono o

Why did I do it—
Go on clinging to my life?
I wish I had died
Before I started this longing
For the love of a young girl.

417   [MYS XI:2394/2390]

Koi suru ni
Shini suru mono ni
Aramaseba
Wa ga mi wa chitabi
Shinikaeramashi

If to burn with love
Were the same thing as to die,
Long before now
I would have died a thousand times,
A thousand times over.

418   [MYS XI:2405/2401]

Koishinaba
Koi mo shine to ya
Wagimoko ga
Wagie no kado o
Sugite yukuramu

"If you die of love,
Then die of love!" Is that
What she would tell me—
My girl who passes by my gate
And never stops to see me?

❋ The following eleven poems from the category "Expressing Thoughts by Reference to Things" are arranged by the status of the "thing"—gods, heaven, moon, mountains, and the sea. Several poems referring to rivers come between mountains and the sea, but are not included here. Five of the poems (nos. 419, 421, and 427–29) employ their category-image in an analogical fashion through a jo or pillow-word formation. The others incorporate it in a variety of ways in formulations that are rhetorically unitary. The first poem (no. 419) is a variant of no. 318, a love poem ascribed directly to Hitomaro. The translation is recast to make the maiden the wavee rather than the waver of the sleeves, which here again introduce Mount Furu ("wave"), and through it the image of the sacred paling as the standard for ancientness (*furu* also means "old"). The same place, the site of the venerable Isonokami Shrine, is mentioned in the third poem (no. 421), which substitutes the sacred cedar for the fence in its jo. The speaker of the fourth poem is less awestruck than impatient when contemplating the gods. He wishes to strike a bargain, to arrange a quid pro quo with an appropriate deity. No. 423 uses the trope naming-the-impossible, a condition (as when "all the seas gang dry") under which, and only under which, the end of love could come about. A different version of no. 424 is quoted by Ōtomo no Ikenushi in a letter to his cousin Yakamochi in the year 749. Yakamochi replies in a poem of his own using the same idea (see nos. 1215 and 1218). Theirs can hardly have been the last variations on the theme.

"Expressing Thoughts by Reference to Things"

419 [MYS XI : 2419/2415]

Otomera o	Maiden, farewell:
Sode Furuyama no	Long ago the waving sleeves;
Mizukaki no	At Furu Mountain
Hisashiki toki yu	The sacred palings sink through time
Omoikeri are wa	No more ancient than my love.

420 [MYS XI : 2420/2416]

Chihayaburu	This life that the gods
Kami no motaseru	Swiftly raging in power
Inochi o ba	Hold in their hands—
Ta ga tame ni ka mo	For whom, then, can you tell me,
Nagaku hori semu	Shall I wish it to be long?

421 [MYS XI : 2421/2417]

Isonokami	At Isonokami
Furu no kamusugi	Over ancient Furu towers
Kamusaburu	A godly cedar:
Koi o mo are wa	Hoary with age, I fall at last
Sara ni suru kamo	In the toils of an old man's love.

422 [MYS XI : 2422/2418]

Ika naramu	Tell me the name—
Na ni ou kami ni	To what god of great renown
Tamuke seba	Shall I make offerings,
A ga omou imo o	That if only in a dream
Ime ni dani mimu	I may see the one I love?

423 [MYS XI:2423/2419]

Ame tsuchi to
Iu na no taete
Araba koso
Imashi to are to
Au koto yamame

If indeed the names
Of heaven and earth should perish
And be heard no more,
Then would you and I, my love,
Tryst not again forever.

424 [MYS XI:2424/2420]

Tsuki mireba
Kuni wa onaji so
Yama henari
Utsukushi imo wa
Henaritaru kamo

Looking at the moon,
We are dwellers in one land—
Oh, but the mountains,
They are barriers between,
Barring my love from me.

425 [MYS XI:2425/2421]

Kuru michi wa
Ishi fumu yama wa
Naku mogamo
A ga matsu kimi ga
Uma tsumazuku ni

On the road he comes
I would have no mountains
With stones to be stepped on,
To be stumbled over by the horse
Of the man for whom I wait.

426 [MYS XI:2426/2422]

Iwane fumu
Kasanaru yama wa
Aranedo mo
Awanu hi manemi
Koiwataru kamo

Between us no mountains
Where we tread the rooted rocks,
Range upon range,
But a multitude of days
Crossed only by my yearning.

427 [MYS XI:2441/2437]

Okitsumo o
Kakusau nami no
Ioenami
Chie shikushiku ni
Koiwataru kamo

Weed of the offing,
Whelmed and hidden by the waves,
Five-hundred-fold waves:
A thousand fold, incessantly,
My love rolls on across the years.

428 [MYS XI:2444/2440]

Ōmi no umi
Oki kogu fune ni
Ikari oroshi
Shinobite kimi ga
Koto matsu ware zo

On the sea of Ōmi
The boat that rows in the offing
Lets down its anchor:
Sheltering from the eyes of men,
I wait for word from you.

429   [MYS XI:2487/2483]

Shikitae no	The beaten-cloth sleeves
Koromode karete	We spread often for our bedding
Tamamo nasu	Now are far apart,
Nabiki ka nuramu	And she must drift like gemweed
Wa o machigate ni	Through the hard waiting of her sleep.

❉ The last selection from the "Hitomaro Collection" is a chōka from Book XIII. "Folk" in its ambience and innocent naïveté, it is composed of two parts and is actually an exchange between a young man and his sweetheart. It is preceded by an anonymous variant in which the two parts of the exchange are numbered separately, and to which envoys have been added. It is curious that the version in the "Hitomaro Collection" is the more primitive. Hitomaro is not known to have composed any chōka without envoys. For the other version, see no. 1471–74.

430   [MYS XIII:3323/3309]

A poem from the Kakinomoto no Asomi Hitomaro Collection

	Mono omowazu	Nothing on my mind,
	Michi yuku yuku mo	Just trudging trudging down the road,
	Aoyama o	Suddenly I reared back
	Furisakemireba	And gazed at the green mountain:
5	Tsutsujihana	Azalea blossom
	Nioeotome	Pinkly glowing maiden,
	Sakurabana	Cherry blossom
	Sakaeotome	Youthful flowering maiden,
	Nare o zo mo	People say of you
10	Ware ni yosu to iu	You are getting close to me,
	Ware o zo mo	People say of me
	Nare ni yosu to iu	I am getting close to you;
	Na wa ika ni omou	What do *you* think, tell me, oh.

	Omoe koso	Oh, I think of *you*,
15	Toshi no yatose o	And so I've waited through the years—
	Kirikami no	Passing my childhood
	Yochiko o sugi	When I kept my hair cut short,
	Tachibana no	Passing the topmost
	Hotsue o suguri	Branches of the orange tree—
20	Kono kawa no	Long and secretly
	Shita ni mo nagaku	As these hidden river depths
	Na ga kokoro mate	Such a signal from your heart.

Poems Attributed to Hitomaro in Later Collections

Over 250 poems are attributed to Hitomaro in the various imperial anthologies, beginning with *Kokinshū* in the tenth century and ending with *Shinzokukokinshū* in the fifteenth. One hundred three poems supposedly by Hitomaro are contained in the third imperial anthology, *Shūishū*, alone, and an unofficial anthology of the tenth century, *Kokinrokujō*, has 123. Some time in the late tenth century, perhaps between the compilation of these two anthologies, there also came into existence a so-called *Kakinomoto no Hitomaro Shū*, various versions of which are still extant. All this activity relating to Hitomaro's poems, and culminating in the extraordinary representation in *Shūishū* at the end of the tenth century, is evidence of the new interest in Man'yō poetry and poets then current, two centuries after the last poem in *Man'yōshū* itself. Exegesis of the *Man'yōshū* text, difficult to decipher by then because of orthographic, phonetic, and grammatical changes in the language, began with the appointment of a committee of scholars in 951. Despite the labors of these and later erudites, however, ability to read *Man'yōshū* remained very uncertain until the linguistic and philological work of the monk Sengaku (1203–after 1272).

The poems attributed to Hitomaro in the imperial anthologies, *Kokinrokujō* and *Kakinomoto no Hitomaro Shū*, a shared corpus, have very little connection with the oeuvre of Hitomaro as seen in *Man'yōshū*. This is not to say that they have nothing in common with Man'yō poetry, however. A great many are in fact duplications of poems in *Man'yōshū*, either verbatim or in variant versions. But the vast majority of these duplications are of poems listed as anonymous or attributed to other poets. In other cases the source is simply not known. It seems clear that an extensive extra-canonical tradition had grown up around the name of Hitomaro by Heian times. A scattering of samples of this material, drawn from three of the imperial anthologies, is given below.

The first three examples are taken from *Kokinshū*, the first of the imperial anthologies, whose preface (which speaks of Hitomaro as *uta no hijiri*, "the sage of poetry") is dated 905. As in the case of all attributions to Hitomaro in *Kokinshū*, the poems are entered as "anonymous" and followed by the statement, "According to a certain person this is a poem by Kakinomoto no Hitomaro." Later anthologies abandon this cautious approach and ascribe their poems directly to Hitomaro. No. 431 is based on the conceit known as "elegant confusion," an alleged inability to distinguish between conventionally similar sense impressions, as here (and typically) falling snow and (white) plum blossoms. This "oblique" attitude toward nature stems from Japanese readings in the Chinese poetry of the late Six Dynasties as imported in such early-sixth-century anthologies as *Wen-hsüan* and *Yü-t'ai Hsin-yung*. Formative later of one strand of Heian taste in poetry, it was already being emulated in waka by the early eighth century. A secure date is provided by a poem composed in 730 by Ōtomo no Tabito (665–731) at a plum-blossom party he hosted (see no. 1018). *Man'yōshū* provides no evidence to link Hitomaro to the beginnings of this new trend, however. No. 431 does repeat in its first two lines phraseology from two Man'yō poems of indefinite date, one (MYS X:2348/2344) anonymous and the other (MYS VIII:1430/1426; no. 567) by Yamabe no Akahito, an important early-eighth-century poet.

It is of interest that the compilers of *Kokinshū*—or at least "a certain person"—thought of Hitomaro in terms of a style much admired and practiced in their own day. The poem appears again in *Shūishū* (SIS I:12), attributed directly to Hitomaro. Neither of the other two *Kokinshū* poems is to be found in *Man'yōshū*, though the first (no. 432) is strongly Man'yō in feeling. The use of nature in no. 433 is typical of the blending with human concerns found in the *Kokinshū* style, a more intricate alternative to the traditional preparation-conclusion analogical technique.

431   [KKS VI:334]

Ume no hana	The pale plum blossoms
Sore to mo miezu	Do not appear as what they are
Hisakata no	When throughout the sky
Amagiru yuki no	A mist of falling snowflakes
Nabete furereba	Drifts down over everything.

According to a certain person this is a poem by Kakinomoto no Hitomaro.

432   [KKS IX:409]

Honobono to	Faintly with the dawn
Akashi no ura no	That glimmers on Akashi Bay,
Asagiri ni	In the morning mist
Shimagakureyuku	A boat goes hidden by the isle—
Fune o shi zo omou	And my thoughts go after it.

According to a certain person this is a poem by Kakinomoto no Hitomaro.

433   [KKS XIII:621]

Awanu yo no	If like falling snow
Furu shirayuki to	White nights of no meeting
Tsumorinaba	Deepen into drifts,
Ware sae tomo ni	I too shall dwindle and vanish
Kenubeki mono o	In the shrinking that will come.

According to a certain person this is a poem by Kakinomoto no Hitomaro.

❋ No. 434 smacks of the Man'yō world with its pillow-word *chihayaburu* ("the furious"), but its use of "reasoning" (the reason for *x* is *y*) and its exploitation of the fire (*hi*) image latent in *omohi* (= *omoi*, "longing") point to a ninth-century or later date. At any rate the poem is not in *Man'yōshū*. Mount Fuji has had periods of volcanic activity within recorded history and figures as a flaming mountain in Man'yō as well as later poetry (see no. 569–71). Here the mountain is regarded as a god.

434 [SIS X : 597]

Chihayaburu	The furious gods
Kami mo omoi no	Also know the flames of love:
Areba koso	Must it not be so,
Toshi hete Fuji no	That across the endless years
Yama mo moyurame	The mountain Fuji burns?

❋ No. 435 is not in *Man'yōshū* either, but the atmosphere of a country market in Yamato Province might be thought appropriate to the more rustic ranges of Man'yō poetry. This market was held once every twelve days, on the Day of the Dragon, whose Japanese name, *tatsu*, puns with "spreading rumor." The bustling fair, a fine place to meet one's lover, or to find one, must have proved disappointing; a too obvious quest has damaged the speaker's reputation.

435 [SIS XII : 700]

Naki na nomi	At the Dragon Fair
Tatsu no ichi to wa	I bartered away my own fair name
Sawagedo mo	For empty rumor,
Isa mada hito o	Though amid the trafficking
Uru yoshi mo nashi	Some did cry, "True love for sale!"

❋ The remaining seven poems, attributed to Hitomaro in later collections, are all in *Man'yōshū* in identical or variant form, and all are entered as anonymous except for the last, a variant that is attributed to a totally obscure poet named Nukike no Obito. Four of the seven are based on a jo, with the shift to the main statement in the third or fourth line. The other three (nos. 438–40) are rhetorically unitary. No. 436 achieves its effect not only by the preparation-conclusion technique, but by repetition, a time-honored element in Japanese versification that here provides a verbal equivalent of the length of the trailing tail.

436   [SIS XIII : 778]

    Ashihiki no   The foot-dragging
Yamadori no o no   Mountain bird has such a tail,
    Shidario no   Such a trailing tail:
Naganagashi yo o   Such a long, long night 'twill be
Hitori ka mo nemu   When I must sleep alone.

437   [SKKS IV : 346]

    Saoshika no   Into the plumegrass
Iruno no susuki   Go the stags of Iruno,
    Hatsuobana   To the first tail-flowers—
Itsu shi ka imo ga   When shall I too lie at ease
Tamakura ni semu   On the pillow of my young love's arm?

438   [SKKS V : 459]

    Saoshika no   On the hills below
Tsumadou yama no   The mountain where the stag cries out
    Okabe naru   In longing for his mate
Wasada wa karaji   I shall not cut the early rice
Shimo wa oku to mo   Though frost should settle on the fields.

439   [SKKS VI : 582]

    Shigure no ame   The cold, drizzly rain
Manaku shi fureba   Falls so ceaselessly one sees
    Maki no ha mo   The very needles
Arasoikanete   Of the evergreens give way
Irozukinikeri   And tinge with a new color.

440   [SKKS VI : 657]

    Yata no no ni   Out on Yata moor
Asaji irozuku   The shallow reeds are coloring:
    Arachiyama   Up Mount Arachi
Mine no awayuki   The light snow on the summit—
Samuku aru rashi   You can tell it must be cold.

441   [SKKS XI : 992]

    Ashihiki no   In the footsore hills
Yamada moru io ni   The hut that guards the mountain field
    Oku kabi no   Keeps mosquito flares
Shitakogaretsutsu   Burning low and burning long,
Wa ga kouraku wa   The smoldering of my love.

442   [SKKS XI:993]
   Isonokami   As the early rice
  Furu no wasada no   At Furu in Isonokami
    Ho ni wa idezu   Shows yet no grain,
  Kokoro no uchi ni   Shall I too keep hidden
  Koi ya wataramu   The love within my heart?

Kawahe no Miyahito (poems from 711)

Except for six poems in *Man'yōshū*, this poet is totally obscure. "Miyahito"
may simply mean "courtier," and "Kawahe" refer to the palace at which he
served. His two poems here, among the last in the banka section of Book II,
continue the genre of laments for victims of drowning. The first poem (no.
443) offers comfort to the soul through immortality in verse (though ironically without the promised name). "Until mosses grow" (*koke musu made
ni*) is a traditional metaphor for an unfathomable venerability, and plays off
against *komatsu* ("young pine") and *hime* ("young lady"). No. 444 is unusual in hinting at the physical ravages of death, and the image of the moss
suddenly comes to suggest a seaweed-shrouded corpse.

443-44   [MYS II:228-29]
Two poems composed by Kawahe no Miyahito, grieving and sighing when
he saw the body of a young woman on the pine-grown shore of Hime
Island, in the fourth year of Wadō [711], year-station Metal-Junior/Swine

(443)   [228]
    Imo ga na wa   The young maiden's name
  Chiyo ni nagaremu   Will flow down a thousand years,
    Himeshima no   Until mosses grow
  Komatsu ga ure ni   All the way to the treetops
  Koke musu made ni   Of the pines on Hime Isle.

(444)   [229]
    Naniwagata   On Naniwa strand
  Shiohi na ari so ne   Let there be no drying of the tide,
   Shizuminishi   For the sunken shape
  Imo ga sugata o   Of the young maid lying there
  Mimaku kurushi mo   Would be hard to look upon.

Takechi no Kurohito (active during Jitō–Mommu reigns, 686–707)

Like Hitomaro and other court poets, Kurohito accompanied the Sovereign
on royal excursions; he seems also to have traveled extensively in a private

capacity. His surviving works, eighteen tanka drawn from his travels, are admired for their descriptions of nature. The Takechi had the clan title Muraji, seventh in the list of eight promulgated by Emperor Temmu, though previously one of the two most prestigious. Kurohito's poems from official excursions do not memorialize the visits themselves, but are private glimpses of scenes along the way. No. 445 is typical. The image of the boat rowing away in the distance seems to have haunted Japanese poets (see nos. 432 and 611), and the *tananashi obune* ("deckless small boat") must have served as a particularly compelling symbol of the fragility of human life. The sense of life as a journey into the unknown pervades the land with its many mountains, and the sea with its infinity of islands behind which the traveler disappears.

445 [MYS I: 58]

A poem from the excursion of the Retired Sovereign [Jitō] to Mikawa Province, in the second year [of Taihō, 702], Water-Senior/Tiger

Izuku ni ka	Where along the shore
Funahate suramu	Will it find a mooring for the night,
Are no saki	The tiny open boat
Kogitamiyukishi	That rowed away around the coast
Tananashi obune	Of the headland of Are?

The above poem is by Takechi no Muraji Kurohito.

❋ No. 446 plays on the name of a bird, *yobukodori* ("calling bird"—perhaps the cuckoo). The mountains of Kisa were directly above and south of the riverside site of the Yoshino pleasure palace at Miyataki. Thus the bird (like the poet?) expresses its yearning for the homeland of the court as it skims over the mountain and north across the river and the Yamato plain.

446 [MYS I: 70]

A poem composed by Takechi no Muraji Kurohito when the Retired Sovereign made an excursion to the Yoshino Palace

Yamato ni wa	Has it come crying
Nakite ka kuramu	All the way to Yamato?
Yobukodori	A calling bird
Kisa no nakayama	Went a-calling as it crossed
Yobi so koyu naru	Over the mountains of Kisa.

❋ The mood of travel in a set of eight poems by Kurohito is more finely attuned to sadness than in the comparable series by Hitomaro (nos. 304–

10). Kurohito is skilled in evoking tones of shaded gray in which scene and feeling fuse, employing a limpid style interwoven with place names but free of wordplay or other rhetorical device. The *yobukodori* poem proves that he does in fact indulge in wordplay, and in the following series too there is one poem (no. 453) based on a heavy use of that principle. The eight poems were no doubt assembled from various travels, and the location of the places named is sometimes obscure. The first five poems (nos. 447–51) are about sea or lake voyages, and the last three have the traveler on land. One explanation of the red-stained boat is that the color was intended to ward off evil spirits. Again, the lone boat in the distance draws the gaze of the viewer, and again, in the third poem, there is a little undecked boat rowing away behind an island. The sense of motion in the middle or far distance unifies the first three tanka; in the fourth the motion is that of the traveler's boat, but the cranes continue to add their raucous cries as in the second. The fifth poem (no. 451) speaks of anchoring—at Hira on Lake Biwa ("Ōmi Sea"). The sixth poem is also about stopping for the night, but on land, along the west shore of the lake. The mood is broken by the determined wit of the seventh poem, which counts one (my love and I), three ("Three Rivers"— Mikawa), two ("Twin Views"—Futami) (or three-two-one in the variant), and is hardly reestablished in the eighth.

447–55   [MYS III: 272–80/270–77]

Eight travel poems by Takechi no Muraji Kurohito

(447)   [272/270]

    Tabi ni shite   Away on a journey,
Monokoishiki ni   The time is lonesome, somehow sad;
    Yamamoto no   Under the mountain
Ake no sohobune   A boat stained red with cinnabar
Oki ni kogu miyu   Rows in view in the offing.

(448)   [273/271]

    Sakurada e   Toward Sakurada
Tazu nakiwataru   Cranes cross over, crying;
    Ayuchigata   On Ayuchi strand
Shio hinikerashi   The tide must now be dried away:
Tazu nakiwataru   Cranes cross over, crying.

(449)   [274/272]

    Shihatsuyama   Shihatsu Mountain—
Uchikoemireba   Over I cross and look down:
    Kasanui no   By Kasanui,

Shima kogikakuru | Rowing away behind the isle,
Tananashi obune | A tiny open boat.

(450) [275/273]

Iso no saki | As we round the cape,
Kogitamiyukeba | Rowing past the rocky shore,
Ōmi no umi | Along Ōmi Sea
Yaso no minato ni | In all its eighty inlets
Tazu sawa ni naku | The teeming cranes are crying.

([Authorship] obscure)

(451) [276/274]

Wa ga fune wa | Let's have our boat
Hira no minato ni | Row to anchor in the inlet
Kogihatemu | At Hira;
Oki e na sakari | Don't go out to the offing—
Sayo fukenikeri | The night is far advanced.

(452) [277/275]

Izuku ni ka | Where shall we stop
Wa ga yadori semu | To find lodging for the night
Takashima no | When on the wide fields
Katsuno no hara ni | Of Katsu at Takashima
Kono hi kurenaba | This day has drawn to dusk?

(453) [278/276]

Imo mo are mo | That my love and I
Hitotsu nare ka mo | Are One Flesh must be the reason
Mikawa naru | Why at the road-fork
Futami no michi yu | Of Twin Views in Three Rivers
Wakarekanetsuru | We cannot separate.

(454) [279/276a]

Another text says:

Mikawa no | If we separate
Futami no michi yu | At the road-fork of Twin Views
Wakarenaba | In Three Rivers,
Wa ga se mo are mo | I'm afraid my man and I
Hitori ka mo ikamu | Must go on One by One.

(455)   [280/277]

Haya kite mo	Had I come quickly
Mitemashi mono o	I'd have been in time to see,
Yamashiro no	But they've shed their leaves,
Taka no tsukimura	The elm groves on the mountainside
Chirinikeru kamo	At Taka in Yamashiro.

❋ The peculiar effect of no. 456 depends on a knowledge of the events at Sasanami, depends indeed for its plenitude on a reading of Hitomaro's series on the fallen capital (nos. 288–90). It is as if Hitomaro had insisted on taking Kurohito along to see the site/sight, so that he could share the feeling of unbounded sorrow he experienced there. The later (younger?) poet is less eager to have his heart riven. In a poem such as this the existence of a poetic tradition begins to take on shape and force. The primary emotional field associated with a place can now be assumed; the place has entered the vocabulary of the art, or in Japanese parlance has become a "song-pillow" (*utamakura*) on which the poet can share the dreams of generations past.

456   [MYS III: 308/305]
A poem by Takechi no Muraji Kurohito on the old capital in Ōmi

Kaku yue ni	It would be like this,
Miji to iu mono o	I knew, I told you I'd no desire
Sasanami no	To see the old palace
Furuki miyako o	At Sasanami of the lapping waves—
Misetsutsu motona	But you'd show it, you gave me no peace.

According to a certain book the above poem is by Shōben. Just who this Shōben was is not clear.

Takechi no Furuhito (late 7th century?)

Nothing is known of this poet other than the following two poems. His very existence is in doubt: the name Furuhito ("man of old") may be nothing more than a scribal confusion based on the first two characters ("old-man") of no. 457. In short, a copyist may have written "Furuhito" instead of "Kurohito." If so, the confusion already existed at the time of the compilation of *Man'yōshū*, as the headnote indicates. No. 457 is in the mode of Hitomaro, and if by Kurohito, shows him reacting in a more orthodox manner to the ruined capital. But no. 458, with its indictment of the god of the land for having hardened his heart, is powerfully original.

457–58   [MYS I:32–33]

Poems composed by Takechi no Furuhito in grief over the former capital at Ōmi (another source states that the poems are by Takechi no Muraji Kurohito)

(457)   [32]

Inishie no	Is it that I too
Hito ni ware are ya	Am a man of long ago?
Sasanami no	At Sasanami
Furuki miyako o	I gazed at the old capital,
Mireba kanashiki	And it was sad to see.

(458)   [33]

Sasanami no	Ruin rusts the heart
Kuni tsu mikami no	Of the deity that guards the land
Urasabite	At Sasanami:
Aretaru miyako	The capital lies desolate,
Mireba kanashi mo	And, oh, it is sad to see.

Wife of Tagima no Mahito Maro (poem from Jitō's reign, 686–97)

The existence of Tagima no Maro and his wife is known because of this one poem, which through some fluke was recorded twice in Man'yōshū. The headnote in the other instance (MYS IV:514/511) states that the poem was composed while the husband was away in the entourage of the Empress on an excursion to Ise Province. It is clear therefore that he was an officer at court; his clan title, Mahito, was the highest in Temmu's list of eight. The anxiety of the wife for a husband away on a journey, treated from many angles in Man'yō poetry, is again the theme here. Oki tsu mo no ("of the offshore seaweed") is a mock epithet for Nabari through its homophone meaning "to hide."

459   [MYS I:43]

A poem composed by the wife of Tagima no Mahito Maro

Wa ga seko wa	Where is he passing,
Izuku yukuramu	My husband, as he goes along?
Oki tsu mo no	Today is he crossing
Nabari no yama o	The mountains of Nabari
Kyō ka koyuramu	Of the hidden offshore weed?

Prince Naga (d. 715)

This is the same Prince Naga who was the royal huntsman and object of Hitomaro's panegyric in no. 301–3. The three tanka given here show him as a poet in the amorous mode. In the first he reverses the situation in the poem by Tagima no Maro's wife (no. 459)—this time it is the male lover who remains behind, and the woman who lodges on Mount Nabari. The first two lines are a jo, again to introduce the name Nabari through the verb *nabari*, but this time with a special sense relevant to the poem as a whole. The devising of this sort of meaningful introduction (the so-called *ushin no jo*) is one of the fine points of waka versification. The last two lines of the translation are the ostensible content of the poem, but they exist in a useful contrast with the bedroom scene implied in the jo. No. 461 is thought to refer to one of the Prince's light loves, perhaps one of the harbor prostitutes at Suminoe on the Inland Sea. Whoever his playmate may have been, the poem concerns itself mainly with a play on the place-name Arare ("Hailstone"). In no. 462 the Prince is thinking of home, whither he bids the wind to blow, and where the pine and camellia await his return. It is impossible to say whom these auspicious plants represent, but the focus on the "young love" (*wagimoko*) in the first line suggests they may be intended as aspects of this one woman.

460   [MYS 1:60]

A poem by Prince Naga

> Yoi ni aite   When we met at eve
> Ashita omo nami   In the morning she would hide
> Nabari ni ka   Her face, her color
> Kenagaki imo ga   Mounting high on Mount Nabari
> Iori serikemu   Has she lodged, my long-departed love?

461   [MYS 1:65]

A poem by Prince Naga

> Arare utsu   A rare sight they are,
> Arare matsubara   The hail-lashed pines of Hailstone Beach,
> Suminoe no   And I could watch
> Otohi otome to   Forever by Otohi's side—
> Miredo akanu kamo   By this maiden of Suminoe.

462   [MYS 1:73]

A poem by Prince Naga

> Wagimoko o   To see my young love:
> Hayami hamakaze   Swift wind along the sandy shore,

Yamato naru	Do not fail to blow
Ware matsu tsubaki	Where the camellia waits for me,
Fukazaru na yume	And the pine, in Yamato.

The Maiden of Suminoe (poem from Mommu's reign, 697–707)

Perhaps this is the same Otohi who figures as Prince Naga's companion in no. 461. The poem is one of a group composed during a visit by the abdicated Empress Jitō to Naniwa. It is a poem of parting, and the red for the garments, as for the boat in no. 447, may have been intended as a charm to ward off misfortune.

463   [MYS I:69]

Kusamakura	Had I known you, lord,
Tabi yuku kimi to	A traveler, one who takes
Shiramaseba	Grass for his pillow,
Kishi no hanifu ni	With the red clay of the bank
Niowasamashi o	I would have stained your garments.

The above poem was presented to Prince Naga by a maiden of Suminoe (her family has not been identified).

Tajihi no Kasamaro (active late 7th century)

Kasamaro is remembered for this one chōka-hanka set and one other poem, all that the Man'yōshū compilers preserved of him. This exiguous evidence reveals him to be an accomplished chōka poet, and one may assume much has been lost. No. 464 shows good control of the techniques of parallelism and preposited analogy, with a fine sense of pacing and narrative form. The poem combines sadness on leaving home with appreciation of the land, two of the basic concerns of Man'yō poetry. It is composed of two long sentences, the first ending at line 12. The fine and powerful flow carries the prosody past the numerous place-names to the resonance of *ie no shima* (line 41—"Isle of Home") with its sudden memories and the pun in line 45 on *nanoriso*, a kind of seaweed whose name can be glossed as "do not tell," which in turn leads to the final anguished question. The envoy extends the thought raised at the end of the chōka, creating a specific scene to make the traveler's regret at being far from home compelling.

464–65   [MYS IV:512–13/509–10]

A poem composed by Tajihi no Mahito Kasamaro when he went down to the province of Tsukushi; with *tanka*

266

Tawayame no	Lying in port at Mitsu,
Kushige ni noreru	Whose beach-encircled waters sparkle
Kagami nasu	Like the bright mirror
Mitsu no hamabe ni	That a tender maiden places
5 Sanitsurau	On her chest of combs,
Himo tokisakezu	I spent the nights in yearning
Wagimoko ni	For my own dear love,
Koitsutsu oreba	Never loosening my red-tinged garment cords;
Akekure no	But as from cranes
10 Asagirigakuri	That cry hidden in the morning mist
Naku tazu no	When dawn begins to break,
Ne nomi shi nakayu	Cries of longing came pouring from my lips.
Wa ga kouru	Thinking to assuage
Chie no hitoe mo	Even the thousandth part of my yearning,
15 Nagusamoru	To ease my heart
Kokoro mo ari ya to	I stood and gazed toward home,
Ie no atari	But all that reach of land
Wa ga tachimireba	Lay hidden under the white clouds
Aohata no	Floating in bands upon
20 Kazurakiyama ni	The peaks of Kazuraki, the mountain
Tanabikeru	Bannered green with trees.
Shirakumogakuru	Passing Awaji, which lies
Amasagaru	Full opposite those lands,
Hina no kunibe ni	Those rustic lands, remote as where
25 Tada mukau	The heavens bend down to earth,
Awaji o sugi	Which were our journey's end, we rowed along,
Awashima o	Still looking back
Sogai ni mitsutsu	At the Isle of Awa dropping far astern.
Asanagi ni	In the morning calm
30 Kako no koe yobi	The sailors' voices came across the deep,
Yūnagi ni	And in the evening calm
Kaji no to shitsutsu	We traveled to the creaking of the oars.
Nami no e no	On and on we went,
Iyukisagukumi	Forcing our path across the endless waves,
35 Iwa no ma o	Threading our way between
Iyukimotōri	The rocks that closed on every side,
Inabitsuma	Past Inabi Head
Urami o sugite	And the curving coast that lies beyond,
Torijimono	Boats bobbing on the sea
40 Nazusaiyukeba	Like a scattered flock of water birds.
Ie no shima	And at the Isle of Home
Ariso no ue ni	The wild and stony beach was strewn
Uchinabiki	With a wrack of kelp

Shiji ni oitaru	That grows so rife about these shores,
45 Nanoriso ga	The plant men call "Tell-Not":
Nado ka mo imo ni	In truth, why did I come away,
Norazu kinikemu	Not telling my dear one all my heart?

Envoy

Shirotae no	In each other's arms,
Sode tokikaete	Loosening each the other's sleeves,
Kaerikomu	We should have lain
Tsukihi o yomite	To count the days till I might come again,
Yukite komashi o	Before I made a journey such as this.

Princess Yoza (d. 706)

Practically nothing is known of this Princess except for her one poem and the year of her death. The poem shows her continuing the dialogue of the parted man and woman, expressing anxiety over the well-being of her spouse away on a journey—while presumably hoping that he is indeed sleeping alone. *Tsuma* puns "whirlwind" (*tsumujikaze*) with "husband" (*tsuma*).

466 [MYS I: 59]

A poem by Princess Yoza

Nagarauru	The wind sweeps over,
Tsuma fuku kaze no	Swirling, blowing where he lies—
Samuki yo ni	In the cold night,
Wa ga se no kimi wa	Will the husband of my heart
Hitori ka nuramu	Be sleeping all alone?

Prince Shiki (d. 715)

Prince Shiki was a son of Emperor Tenji and the father of Emperor Kōnin (r. 770–81), during whose reign he was posthumously raised to the rank of Emperor. The shift from the Asuka to the Fujiwara Palace referred to in the headnote to no. 467 took place in 694, eight years after the death of Emperor Temmu, who had ruled at the Kiyomihara Palace in Asuka. His widow Jitō built a new palace farther north at Fujiwara. The Asuka area is compact, and the two palaces are only a morning's stroll apart, but the transfer to the one meant the abandonment of the other as the capital—a psychological distance that the Prince captures in a memorable image. No. 468 is a more intense expression of homesickness. Naniwa, famed for its reedbeds along the shore, was across the mountains from Yamato, the inland kingdom that held tiny Asuka in its midst. Evening is always the hour for longing; mallards return to their nests, and the poet's thoughts to home.

467 [MYS I: 51]

A poem composed by Prince Shiki after the move from the Asuka Palace to the Fujiwara Palace

Uneme no	Winds of Asuka
Sode fukikaesu	Blowing back the waving sleeves
Asukakaze	Of palace women—
Miyako o tōmi	Now the capital is far,
Itazura ni fuku	And you blow in vain.

468 [MYS I: 64]

A poem composed by Prince Shiki when he visited the Naniwa Palace in the third year of Kyōun [706], Fire-Senior/Horse

Ashihe yuku	In among the reeds
Kamo no hagai ni	Go the mallards through the frost
Shimo furite	Falling on their wings:
Samuki yūhe wa	Cold twilight, the still hour
Yamato shi omōyu	Of longing for Yamato.

Okisome no Azumato (active during Mommu's reign, 697–707)

This poet is known also for a banka he composed on the death of Prince Yuge in 699. No. 469 shows him balanced between indolent pleasure in his outing at the beach and the yearning for home that is axiomatic in this poetry.

469 [MYS I: 66]

A poem of the time the Retired Sovereign [Jitō] made an excursion to the Naniwa Palace

Ōtomo no	Though I lie at ease
Takashi no hama no	Here at Ōtomo on the sands
Matsu ga ne o	Of Takashi Beach,
Makurakinuredo	Pillowed on the roots of a pine,
Ie shi shinohayu	Still there comes a longing for my home.

The above poem is by Okisome no Azumato.

Kasuga no Oyu (active late 7th–early 8th centuries)

Kasuga no Oyu was at one time a Buddhist monk with the name Benki, but was secularized by official order in 701 and given the clan title Kurabito. In addition to his seven waka in *Man'yōshū*, one Chinese poem is preserved in *Kaifūsō*. The identity of the Mino no Muraji referred to in the headnote to no. 470, which was unknown to the compilers of *Man'yōshū*, was discovered in 1872 from a grave marker in Ikoma, Nara Prefecture. The missing personal name is Okamaro, a member of the official embassy to T'ang in 702. Okamaro (662–728) returned safely and went on to a career in the Nara bureacracy. The Straits of Tsushima lie between Japan and Korea, a bit to the north of the usual course for China. It was customary for sea voyagers to make offerings to the deities of the sea to secure a safe journey, here in the form of *nusa*, sacred white strips of cloth. In an emergency more valuable objects might be sacrificed, such as a bronze mirror. For a reference to (voluntary) human sacrifice, see no. 24.

470   [MYS I:62]

A poem composed by Kasuga no Kurabito Oyu when Mino no Muraji (personal name missing) departed for T'ang

Arine yoshi	Where the sharp peaks rise
Tsushima no watari	In the Straits of Tsushima,
Watanaka ni	In the midmost deep
Nusa torimukete	Scatter offerings to the god,
Haya kaerikone	And hasten your return!

❋ Kasuga no Oyu's two poems in Book III bespeak two contrasting aspects of travel—its arduousness and its unexpected opportunities for pleasure. Iware is called "of the crawling vines" (*tsuno sahau*) from the element *iwa* ("rock").

471   [MYS III:285/282]

A poem by Kasuga no Kurabito Oyu

Tsuno sahau	Not even yet past
Iware mo sugizu	Iware of the crawling vines,
Hatsuseyama	When shall I manage
Itsu ka mo koemu	To cross Hatsuse Mountain?—
Yo wa fukenitsutsu	And the night is getting late!

472   [MYS III:287/284]

A poem by Kasuga no Kurabito Oyu

Yakizuhe ni	I was on my way,
Wa ga yukishikaba	Going down past Yakizu,

Suruga naru	Taking the Ahe road
Ahe no ichiji ni	To the marketplace in Suruga—
Aishi kora wa mo	And, oh, the girl I met!

Isonokami no Maro (640–717)

Isonokami no Maro was a prominent statesman of the early eighth century, rising to Minister of the Left in 708. No. 473 is his only preserved poem. As the footnote makes clear, there was opposition to this particular excursion of the much-traveled Empress Jitō, and in this regard Maro's verse has a peculiar resonance. Yamato, the seat of government and its responsibilities, is out of sight, and the entourage is safely on its way to Ise, with the then minor court official dutifully following along. The opening line is a pillow-word construction serving to introduce iza ("farewell") in the name Izami. Whether Maro intended it in a personally meaningful sense is hard to say, but it does add a whole human dimension to the poem. The Counselor Takechimaro who admonished the Empress in vain lived from 657 to 706 and was a veteran of the Jinshin War. During her excursion, according to Nihonshoki, the Empress made a great show of exempting the local people from taxation and rewarding her porters, as well as granting a general amnesty. Whether Takechimaro felt foolish or exonerated is not recorded. "Broad Fourth Pure Rank" (Jōkōshii) was a rank reserved for Princes in the system then in effect.

473 [MYS I: 44]

A poem composed by Minister Isonokami on accompanying the imperial palanquin

Wagimoko o	*To my own young love*
Izami no yama o	Farewell Mountain's loftiness
Takami ka mo	May be the reason
Yamato no mienu	Why Yamato lies unseen—
Kuni tōmi ka mo	Or is it that the land is far away?

Concerning the above, Nihonshoki states: "In the sixth year of Akamitori [692], in spring, third month, on the Earth-Senior/Dragon day, the month having begun on Fire-Senior/Tiger, Prince Hirose of the Broad Fourth Pure Rank and others were appointed keepers of the palace [during the Sovereign's absence]. Thereupon Middle Counselor Miwa no Asomi Takechimaro removed his headdress and proffered it to the throne, repeating his admonishment: 'The movement of the imperial entourage before the conclusion of agricultural activity is improper.' On the Metal-Junior/Sheep day the Empress disregarded this admonishment and set off on her progress to

Ise. On the Metal-Senior/Horse day of the fifth month, which began with Wood-Junior/Ox, she proceeded to the temporary palace at Ago."

Empress Gemmei (661–721)

Empress Gemmei was a daughter of emperor Tenji and half sister of Empress Jitō (their mothers were also sisters; see note to nos. 184–85). She married Prince Kusakabe (Jitō's son, her nephew) and was the mother of Prince Karu (Emperor Mommu) and a daughter who became Empress Genshō (r. 715–24). On Mommu's death in 707 she succeeded her son and reigned until 715, when she abdicated in favor of her daughter. Her years on the throne saw the move to the new capital at Nara in 710, the completion of *Kojiki* (712), the first Japanese coinage, and developments in law and administration. As far as can be told from her meager representation in *Man'yōshū*, she lacked the poetic flair of her elder sister Jitō (see especially nos. 286–87). In no. 474 she takes advantage of passing by a mountain in Ki Province named Senoyama (or Se no Yama, "Husband Mountain") to compose a tanka implying her longing for her late husband Prince Kusakabe (d. 689; see no. 328–30). Ahe was her name as a Princess. No. 475 is reminiscent of Nakatsu Sumera Mikoto's no. 245. The sound of bows—here the string slapping against the *tomo*, a leather guard worn on the left wrist—makes the hearer imagine a scene of armed men. The sound comes from afar (*oto su nari*), and an action is assumed (*rashi mo*). Why the great ministers of court should be standing under arms has not been adequately explained. One of them would be Minister of the Left Isonokami no Maro, author of no. 473, above.

474   [MYS I:35]

A poem composed by Princess Ahe when crossing over Senoyama

Kore ya kono	Is this then the spot
Yamato ni shite wa	For which I yearned in Yamato,
A ga kouru	The famous mountain
Kiji ni ari to iu	Said to lie along the road to Ki,
Na ni ou Senoyama	Senoyama, Husband Peak?

475   [MYS I:76]

A poem by the Empress in the first year of Wadō [708], Earth-Senior/Monkey

Masurao no	There comes the sounding
Tomo no oto su nari	Of the wrist-guards of the stalwart men:
Mononofu no	Officers of court,

| Ōmaetsukimi | The great ministers must stand, |
| Tate tatsu rashi mo | Their shields lined up in view. |

The Maiden Toneri (active late 7th–early 8th centuries)

The *toneri* were the personal attendants of the royal family, the servitors who appear in Hitomaro's laments stunned at the loss of their lord. Whether Toneri no Otome was so called because she was the daughter of such a person is not known. She was clearly a lady-in-waiting at successive courts, from Jitō to Gemmei, but nothing else is known about her. In no. 476 she is presumably in attendance on the former Empress Jitō on one of her many excursions. Everything in her poem down through *iru* ("shoot") in the fourth line is a jo to introduce *mato* ("target") in Matokata. It has been suggested that *sayakeshi* ("bracing clear") refers also to the sound of the arrow hitting the target. In a poem so dominated by its jo, and where the juncture is through wordplay, the thrill of finding the "target" word provides an esthetic experience based on a kind of suspense (as in no. 60, which gets to the "heart" of the matter by a roundabout intestine route). But this is only half the truth. In a sense the word *mato* in Matokata has generated the jo, and through it the poem. But by tonal and imagistic resonance the jo then infuses the main statement with an atmosphere—sharp, clear, masculine—that defines the sense of the predication: clear, bracing, like an arrow hitting a target. Such effects were available in the repertory of rhetoric for poets—and for ancient anonymous singers—able to use them. For the relation of this poem to the *Ise Fudoki* song F 23, see the commentary to no. 222.

476   [MYS 1:61]

A poem composed by the Maiden Toneri, accompanying the imperial palanquin

Masurao no	Where the stalwart men
Satsuya tabasami	Take their hunting arrows up,
Tachimukai	Stand and aim and shoot,
Iru Matokata wa	Target Lake lies fair in view:
Miru ni sayakeshi	How bracing clear the sight!

Hashihito no Ōura (active early 8th century)

Nothing is known of this poet other than his four poems in *Man'yōshū*. The first (no. 477) is a very striking poem indeed. The effect is achieved partly by substituting the metaphor for the object, and in this regard the "moon-boat" poem from the "Hitomaro Collection" (no. 365) serves as a useful contrast. There is also the sense of vastness and wonder created by the opening two lines, which are used seven times in *Man'yōshū*. The brilliant, sharp image is set in a field of boundless space, and the tension is increased by the use of the verb *harite* ("drawn," "stretched"). The last line implies that such a crescent moon meant good luck on the journey. Its effect as a literal light-giver would be brief, for the new moon sets early. The second poem—despite the headnote—is about the waning moon that shows its crescent before dawn in the eastern sky. The poet blames its paleness on the height of the mountain over which it has had to rise, and perhaps also on the "darkness" lurking in the word *kura* ("dark") in Kurahashi.

477–78 [MYS III: 292–93/289–90]

Two poems by Hashihito no Sukune Ōura on the new moon

(477) [292/289]

Ama no hara	When I gaze aloft
Furisakemireba	Far across the plains of heaven
Shiramayumi	I see hanging there
Harite kaketari	A drawn bow of purest white:
Yomichi wa yokemu	The night journey should go well.

(478) [293/290]

Kurahashi no	Perhaps the loftiness
Yama o takami ka	Of Kurahashi's somber peak
Yogomori ni	Is what makes the moon
Idekuru tsuki no	That lurked hidden all the night
Hikari tomoshiki	Rise with such feeble rays.

❋ There is some doubt whether the author of nos. 479–80 is the same man who wrote the two poems above, since the personal name was omitted by the compilers of *Man'yōshū*. Both poems on river foam are based on a form of elegant confusion, and the second is as well a conceit alluding to the Tanabata story (see no. 398).

479–80 [MYS IX: 1689–90/1685–86]

Two poems composed by Hashihito no Sukune on the banks of the Izumi River

(479) [1689/1685]

Kawa no se no	Where the rapids churn
Tagichi o mireba	I gaze upon the river foam—
Tama ka mo	Are these pearls

Chirimidaretaru	That scatter wildly as they fall,
Kawa no tsune ka mo	Or but the river's wonted face?

(480) [1690/1686]

Hikohoshi no	Surely these are pearls
Kazashi no tama shi	Cascading from the hairpin
Tsumagoi ni	Of the Herdsman Star,
Midarenikerashi	Wild with longing for his wife,
Kono kawa no se ni	Into these river rapids.

Princess Tajima (d. 708)

Princess Tajima was a daughter of Emperor Temmu, and thus a half sister of Prince Hozumi and Prince Takechi, the other principals in the triangle revealed below. For whatever reason, her preference ultimately was not for the hero of the Jinshin War. Prince Takechi's surviving poems do not mention her, but her other brother/lover composed a tanka on her grave (no. 484). Nos. 481 and 482 are reminiscent of two poems in the set of four attributed to Empress Iwanohime (nos. 231–34). Like no. 234, no. 481 incorporates an image of the ripe autumn fields into an expression of the burden of love, with similar syntactic overlap at the point of juncture. And no. 482 is based on the same opening structure and rhetoric as no. 232. But instead of concluding that it would be better to die than stay behind, Princess Tajima asks for signs along the road—perhaps branches tied together, as was done in vain by Prince Arima (see no. 854 and commentary to nos. 247–49). It has been suggested that Prince Hozumi was banished to Shiga, perhaps to become a monk at Sūfukuji, because of his liaison with Princess Tajima. In her third poem (no. 483) the Princess stands on the brink of her own small Rubicon, the stream that the speaker of no. 370 crossed on stepping stones "when he was a young man." For the Princess there may be no stepping stones. She takes her life and her skirts in her hands at the morning hour of parting; the stream is a complex symbol of her resolution, her risking all for love, and of her desire to flee the stinging words of the world.

481 [MYS II:114]

A poem composed by Princess Tajima in longing for Prince Hozumi, at the time she was living in the palace of Prince Takechi

Aki no ta no	On the autumn fields
Homuki no yoreru	The spears of grain are bending
Kotoyori ni	In one direction
Kimi ni yorinana	Toward my lord I'll softly bend,
Kochitakari to mo	Let words sting as they may.

482 [MYS II:115]

A poem composed by Princess Tajima when Prince Hozumi was sent by imperial command to the mountain temple of Shiga in Ōmi

Okureite	Rather than be thus,
Koitsutsu arazu wa	Left behind in my yearning,
Oishikamu	I shall follow you:
Michi no kumami ni	My love, tie a sign for me
Shime yue wagase	At every bend of the road!

483 [MYS II:116]

A poem composed by Princess Tajima when she was living in the palace of Prince Takechi, and it had been revealed that she had trysted secretly with Prince Hozumi

Hitogoto o	Rumors are rife,
Shigemi kochitami	Gossip is a stinging swarm:
Ono ga yo ni	The time has come
Imada wataranu	For me to cross the morning stream
Asakawa wataru	That I have never crossed before.

Prince Hozumi (d. 715)

Prince Hozumi was a son of Emperor Temmu and younger half brother of Prince Takechi. After the death of Princess Tajima, he married Lady Ōtomo of Sakanoue, the aunt of Yakamochi. Whatever trouble came to him because of his liaison with Princess Tajima, it did not permanently affect his political career, since he became Prime Minister in 705, well before her death. The events reflected in her poems occurred before Prince Takechi's death in 696, so that Prince Hozumi is looking back over a past of considerable depth in no. 484, probably composed in 708. The beginnings of a secret love between him and the Princess and his gazing at her grave years later are all that remains of this love story. It is thought that she left Takechi to join him, and so it seems probable that they lived together in marriage until her death. The personification of nature in this poem typically takes the form of direct address and a displacement of human feeling onto a feature of the land. The hill of Ikai at Yonabari near Hatsuse was the site of Princess Tajima's grave.

484 [MYS II:203]

A poem composed by Prince Hozumi after the demise of Princess Tajima, when, grieving and in tears, he gazed far off at her tomb on a snowy winter day

Furu yuki wa	O you falling snow,
Awa ni na furi so	Do not snow so heavily,
Yonabari no	Lest Yonabari
Ikai no oka no	And the hill of Ikai
Samukaramaku ni	Should come to feel the cold.

❋ Nos. 485–86 show Prince Hozumi as a native poet employing the "reasoning" style that was to remain popular into the Heian period. The cries of the wild geese (returning to winter in Japan) tell him that Mount Kasuga must be decked out in its autumn colors; the scattering of the reed blossoms suggests that the bush clover must be in bloom. Nature poetry in this mode provides two scenes for the price of one: one observed, the other deduced. The direct personal engagement in the last line of no. 485 goes beyond this elegant intellectual balance.

485–86   [MYS VIII: 1517–18/1513–14]

Two poems by Prince Hozumi

(485)   [1517/1513]

Kesa no asake	At daybreak this morning
Kari ga ne kikitsu	I heard the crying of wild geese:
Kasugayama	Kasuga Mountain
Momichin·kerashi	Must have turned to golden flame;
Wa ga kokoro itashi	My heart aches at the thought.

(486)   [1518/1514]

Akihagi wa	Autumn bush clover
Sakubeku aru rashi	Must by now have come to bloom,
Wa ga yado no	For the blossoms
Asaji ga hana no	Of the reeds around my house
Chiriyuku mireba	I see scattered on the ground.

❋ Perhaps the best-known poem by Prince Hozumi is the following tanka with its rueful recognition of the power of love, the slave that masters its master, the genie out of the bottle. The poem has a spring in it, thrusting upward and outward through its spiral of modifying clauses to its pointed participial -te, the assertive, nonfinal form of the verb. There is no ending—either to the poem or to the impudent, erectile force it mimics. No wonder its author, who had some experience in these matters, enjoyed reciting it when the mood was upon him.

487   [MYS XVI: 3838/3816]

A poem by Prince Hozumi

Ie ni arishi	In the house I had
Hitsu ni kagi sashi	A chest, wherein I thrust him,
Osameteshi	Locked him with a key,
Koi no yatsuko no	The slave called love—now
Tsukamikakarite	Clawing, clutching at my throat!

Prince Hozumi was fond of reciting the above poem at banquets when the drinking was in full swing, always to great applause.

Naga no Okimaro (active late 7th–early 8th centuries)

Nothing is known of the life of Naga no Okimaro other than that he was a courtier and wit of Emperor Mommu's reign. Imiki, his clan title, was number four in Emperor Temmu's list, bestowed on clans of provincial and foreign ancestry. The excursion referred to in the headnote to no. 488 is the same one that drew forth poems by Takechi no Kurohito, Prince Naga, Princess Yoza, and the Maiden Toneri (nos. 445, 460, 466, and 476). Like Princess Yoza and Prince Naga, Okimaro apparently stayed home, since he asks the poem's unknown recipient to come back with visible proof of the journey. A black dye was extracted from the fruit and bark of the alder, but it is not clear what color stain would result from brushing through the leaves.

488   [MYS I: 57]

A poem of the time of the Retired Sovereign [Jitō's] excursion to Mikawa Province in the second year [of Daihō, 702], Water-Senior/Tiger

Hikumano ni	Go into the fields
Niou harihara	Bright with leaves at Hikuma,
Irimidare	Brush through the alder,
Koromo niowase	Bring your garments back all stained
Tabi no shirushi ni	As a sign of your journey.

The above poem is by Naga no Imiki Okimaro.

❋ No. 489 may have been composed on an excursion of former Empress Jitō or Emperor Mommu to Naniwa. In any case it has a seaside setting.

489   [MYS III: 239/238]

A poem composed by Naga no Imiki Okimaro in response to imperial command

Ōmiya no	Here in the palace,
Uchi made kikoyu	Even here there comes the sound:
Abiki su to	Shouts of the seafolk
Ago totonouru	Keeping the netmen in rhythm
Ama no yobikoe	As they pull the nets ashore.

❋ Okimaro's poem about being caught in the rain at Sano served as inspiration for a famous allusive variation by Fujiwara Teika (1162–1241), in which the rain is changed to snow and the vivid immediacy of what was no doubt an actual experience is transmuted into an imagined scene of lonely, monochrome beauty.

490   [MYS III:267/265]

A poem by Naga no Imiki Okimaro

Kurushiku mo	Look at it come down—
Furikuru ame ka	What a miserable rain!
Miwa no saki	And it's not as if
Sano no watari ni	There were houses hereabout
Ie mo aranaku ni	At Sano ford in Miwa.

❋ The next eight poems (nos. 491–98) are evidence of the playful use of poetry that stemmed no doubt from the inveterate Japanese fondness for wordplay, a fondness that would lead in due course to the parlor-game aspect of linked verse, the more freewheeling and earthy ranges of *haikai*, and the "mad poems" (*kyōka*) of the eighteenth century. Happily, *Man'yōshū* preserves examples of an early-eighth-century game in which courtiers challenged each other to combine a variety of disparate objects in one poem, as speedily and cleverly as they could. Naga no Okimaro was evidently very good at this game. The anecdote appended to no. 491 suggests the context out of which such compositions sprang. The "third watch" would be about four o'clock in the morning. Okimaro's response involves some double entendres, in which *tsu* ("inlet") is embedded in *hitsu* ("box") and the place-name Ichihitsu, and in which *komu* ("will come") rhymes with *kon*, the sound of the fox's bark. In no. 492 "chaps" translates *mukabaki*, leg protectors of deerskin, bearskin or horsehide worn when traveling or riding on horseback.

491–98   [MYS XVI:3846–53/3824–31]

Eight poems by Naga no Imiki Okimaro

(491)   [3846/3824]

    Sashinabe ni   Get the kettle, boys,
  Yu wakase kodomo   Boil some water—we'll be ready
    Ichihitsu no   For the barking fox:
  Hihashi yori komu   When he comes by Boxwood Cove
  Kitsu ni amusamu   We'll douse him on the cypress bridge.

Concerning the above poem, it is related that once several people got together for a drinking party. At the third watch of night there was heard the bark of a fox. Everyone challenged Okimaro, saying, "Make up a poem right away about these vessels and utensils, the voice of the fox, and a bridge over a stream." He immediately composed this poem in response.

(492)   [3847/3825]

A poem about chaps, greens, a dining mat, and the beams of a house

    Sukomo shiki   Spread the dining mat,
  Aona nimochiko   Boil the greens and bring them on—
    Utsuhari ni   The lord is waiting,
  Mukabaki kakete   Resting with chaps off and dangling
  Yasumu kono kimi   Where he hung them from the beam.

❋ The next two poems are different from the others in that their topics are singular. No. 493 is an *eibutsuka*, a poem written about some "thing," which may be simply descriptive of the "thing" or may use it as a metaphor for something else. Okimaro's poem loses its savor without a metaphorical reading: a beautiful stranger and a homely wife. No. 494 plays with the name for markings on backgammon dice, and with a juggling of numbers that gives it a busyness comparable to the verses on multiple topics.

(493)   [3848/3826]

A poem about lotus leaves

    Hachisuha wa   Lotus leaves—
  Kaku koso aru mono   So this is the way they look!
    Okimaro ga   What Okimaro
  Ie ni aru mono wa   Has at home turns out to be
  Umo no ha ni arashi   Nothing but leaves of taro!

(494)   [3849/3827]

A poem about backgammon dice

    Hito futa no   One eye, two eyes—no,
  Me nomi ni arazu   That's not all the eyes there are:

Itsutsu mutsu	Five eyes, six eyes,
Mitsu yotsu sae ari	Even three or four you'll find—
Suguroku no sae	Oddly, on backgammon dice!

✳ Nos. 495–96 form a pair with their negative imperatives and culinary contrasts. A whiff of the scatological serves as a reminder of the esthetic breadth for which *Man'yōshū* is famous, and of how far back the roots of the haikai spirit probe. A sexually explicit graffito found in a Nara temple makes the same point. In the midst of their ambitious strivings for high civilization, the people of the time would pause to give a wink to the natural man. This is not to overlook the fact that no. 495 is highly abusive to a member of the lower classes. The derogatory term used for the carp combines with the river bend to get across the essentials of the required word "privy" (*kawaya*). No. 496 was perhaps less of a challenge, since all the terms are comestibles.

(495)   [3850/3828]

A poem about incense, a pagoda, a privy, excrement, crucian carp, and a slave

Kori nureru	Don't come near the pagoda—
Tō ni na yori so	It's been rubbed with fragrant oil—
Kawakuma no	You filthy slave girl,
Kusobuna hameru	Mouth reeking of the shit-carp caught
Itaki meyatsuko	In the stinking river bend!

(496)   [3851/3829]

A poem about vinegar, salted bean paste, garlic, sea bream, and water leek

Hishio su ni	Don't show a fellow
Hiru tsukikatete	Who's begging for a nice sea bream
Tai negau	All fixed with bean paste,
Ware ni na mise so	With vinegar and pounded garlic,
Nagi no atsumono	Such a thing as water-leek soup!

✳ The *tamabahaki* ("gem-whisk") in no. 497 may refer to a deciduous shrub now called *kōyabōki* rather than to the "broom laced through with gems" used by the Empress for the ceremonial sweeping of the silkworm platforms in spring, an example of which is preserved among the many precious eighth-century objects in the Shōsōin collection in Nara. But the whimsicality of Okimaro's poem is enhanced by supposing that he imagines using the implement of a Chinese ritual to sweep his garden. Ōtomo no

Yakamochi's awed reaction to handling one of these brooms is recorded in no. 851.

(497)   [3852/3830]

A poem about a gem-whisk, a sickle, a juniper, and a jujube

Tamabahaki	Sickle, go and cut,
Kariko kamamaro	Cut a broom laced through with gems,
Muro no ki to	That I may sweep the ground
Natsume ga moto to	All around my juniper
Kakihakamu tame	And the trunk of the jujube tree.

✳ The facetious question in the last of Okimaro's eight poems relates a heron with a stick in its beak to the figure of Kongō Rikishi, the Thunderbolt Strongman, a Buddhist guardian deity seen in pairs at temple gates, and also in the contemporary masked dance performance known as Gigaku. In the Rikishimai, or Strongman Dance, Kongō Rikishi, armed with a halberd, cut off the phallus of a lustful barbarian named Konron who was in pursuit of the Woman of Wu. Gigaku, then recently introduced from Paekche, is unfortunately not among the traditional performing arts that have survived in Japan to modern times. It is known only from descriptions, depictions, and the large collection of masks and other accouterments in the Shōsōin. Okimaro's poem is thus precious evidence of its familiarity to a courtier at the beginning of the eighth century. The image of Kongō Rikishi whirling his halberd seems to have come readily to mind. The location of Ikegami is not known.

(498)   [3853/3831]

A poem about a white heron flying with a stick in its beak

Ikegami no	What is it doing—
Rikishimai ka mo	The Strongman Dance they hold
Shirasagi no	At Ikegami?—
Hoko kuimochite	This white heron flying away
Tobiwataruramu	With a halberd in its beak!

Mikata no Sami (active late 7th–early 8th centuries)

Whether or not this poet was a śrāmaṇera, or Buddhist novice—the meaning of the derived Japanese word sami—is uncertain. It has been suggested that Sami was merely his name. For evidence of his having married, see nos. 881–83. No. 499 appears in a series of poems by parted lovers. The celebration of snow (no. 500–501), apparently composed to please Fujiwara no

Fusasaki (681–737), the founder of the "Northern" branch of the Fujiwara clan, reached Ōtomo no Yakamochi in the year 750 in Etchū Province, where he was serving as Governor. Yakamochi, the author of the compiler's note, seems to have been well informed on the transmission of the poem. Kasa no Kogimi may have been a name familiar to Yakamochi, but nothing else is known of him now. Kume no Hirotsune, however, was Yakamochi's subordinate, and Yakamochi undoubtedly heard the poem directly from him. This kind of evidence of the oral transmission of poetry is very suggestive in regard to later attributions to Man'yō poets (or even attributions within *Man'yōshū*, for that matter), especially when, as here, a textual variant leads to the alternate interpretation that someone merely recited, rather than composed, the poem.

499   [MYS IV : 511 / 508]
A poem by Mikata no Sami

Koromode no	From this evening
Wakaru koyoi yu	Of the parting of our sleeves,
Imo mo ware mo	My love and I,
Itaku koimu na	Ah, how sorely we shall yearn—
Au yoshi o nami	For we have no way to meet.

500–501   [MYS XIX : 4251–52 / 4227–28]

	Ōtono no	All around the hall
	Kono motōri no	My lord's grounds lie buried deep:
	Yuki na fumi so ne	Don't go walking on his snow!
	Shibashiba mo	It's not every day
5	Furazaru yuki so	You will see a snow like this.
	Yama nomi ni	Only the mountains
	Furishi yuki so	Ever have such snow as this.
	Yume yoru na	Don't you dare come near,
	Hito ya	You people!
10	Na fumi so ne	Don't go walking
	Yuki wa	On the snow!

Envoy

Aritsutsu mo	Just the way it is
Meshitamawamu so	He'll be pleased to gaze at it;
Ōtono no	All around the hall
Kono motōri no	My lord's grounds lie buried deep:
Yuki na fumi so ne	Don't go walking on his snow!

The two poems above are ones that Mikata no Sami composed and recited on receiving the words of the posthumous Minister of the Left, the Northern Lord of the Fujiwara. The person who heard the poems and passed them on was Kasa no Asomi Kogimi; later Kume no Asomi Hirotsuna, the Secretary of Etchū Province, again recited them and passed them on.

Tori no Senryō (active early 8th century)

Tori no Senryō (his personal name means something like "ordinance") was presumably a learned man, for he became tutor to the Crown Prince (future Emperor Shōmu) and left Chinese poems in *Kaifūsō* as well as Chinese prose compositions in a later anthology. No. 502 shows him bemused at Yoshino, echoing "white waves" (*shiranami*) in "not know" (*shiranedo mo*). What past he is thinking of is not clear, but the Yoshino Palace had been the object of over twenty visits by Empress Jitō, and her relation to the place had been immortalized by Hitomaro (no. 293–96). There are also stories in *Kojiki* about Emperor Yūryaku's visits there (see nos. 96 and 97). In no. 503 the cuckoo sings from deep within a sacred grove, invisible in the permanent shade. Both poems capture a sense of mystery, contrasting light (white) and dark (shadow). The cuckoo's cry was an aching sound, both sought and shunned for its burden of remembrance. Iwase is "of the men of court" (*mononofu no*) because its first syllable is a homophone of the word meaning "fifty," suggesting the large number of court officials.

502   [MYS III: 316/313]

A poem by Tori no Senryō

Miyoshino no	In fair Yoshino
Taki no shiranami	The white waves of the torrent fall:
Shiranedo mo	What fell here once
Katari shi tsugeba	I cannot say, and yet I muse
Inishie omōyu	On tales men tell of long ago.

503   [MYS VIII: 1474/1470]

A poem by Tori no Senryō

Mononofu no	Cuckoo in the wood,
Iwase no mori no	The deep grove of Iwase
Hototogisu	Of the men of court,
Ima mo nakanu ka	Won't you sing out this moment
Yama no tokage ni	From the hill's eternal shade?

Prince Mutobe (d. 729)

Prince Mutobe's genealogy is unknown. He was apparently in the train of Retired Empress Jitō on one of her excursions to Naniwa, where the following poem was composed. It belongs to the thoughts-of-home genre and as usual focuses on the wife left behind. Since royal excursions were of frequent occurrence, the pangs of separation expressed on these occasions were a literary convention. A literary convention may coincide with genuine feelings, and the literary tradition may provide forms and modes for expressing such feelings. Or a poem may owe its existence more or less to the demands of the convention. Prince Mutobe, walking on the beach at Naniwa, picks up a single shell—one-half of a bivalve, a "forgetting shell"—and remembering, uses the occasion to declare he will never forget. Or: wishing to assert his fidelity, he makes up an imagistic jo to go with the expression of it, being at the time some miles from the beach.

504   [MYS 1:68]

A poem of the time the Retired Sovereign [Jitō] made an excursion to the Naniwa Palace

Ōtomo no	Here on the beach
Mitsu no hama naru	At Mitsu of Ōtomo,
Wasuregai	A forgetting shell:
Ie naru imo o	How can I forget the lass
Wasurete omoe ya	I left behind at home?

The above poem is by Prince Mutobe.

Prince Nagaya (676–729)

A son of Prince Takechi, Prince Nagaya revived something of his father's power, rising to a dominant position at court in the 720's as Minister of the Left. This reassertion of princely primacy brought him into conflict with the ambitions of the Fujiwara, who turned the tables on him in 729 with charges of treason that led to his compulsory suicide. Prince Nagaya was at the center of a circle of devotees of Chinese poetry, and left three kanshi in Kaifūsō. No. 505 probably was composed in 701. The cold endured by the lonely traveler is the theme here. The Prince was not alone of course, but in the company of the Emperor and other courtiers. But travel away from home is cold and lonely by convention, no matter what the actual circumstances. By making it so, the poets brought out the essence—what later ages would call the hon'i—of the experience.

505   [MYS 1:75]

A poem of the time the late Sovereign [Mommu] went on excursion to Yoshino Palace

| Ujimayama | On Mount Ujima |
| Asakaze samushi | The wind is cold in the morning: |

Tabi ni shite	Off on a journey,
Koromo kasubeki	Here I am without my love
Imo mo aranaku ni	To lend me her warm robe.

The above poem is by Prince Nagaya.

Prince Aki (active 720's–40's)

Prince Aki was the grandson of Prince Shiki (nos. 467–68). The event for which he is chiefly known in *Man'yōshū*, his illicit marriage with a palace woman (uneme) from Inaba, probably took place about 724. The Prince also had another wife, Lady Ki (nos. 509–11 and 1154–55). His no. 506 (it also appears in a variant version as SIS III:141) is about the onset of autumn, adopting what became a well-established convention, that the wind starts to get cool as soon as the boundary between the sixth and seventh months is crossed. Actually, in terms of the calendar now in use, this would have been somewhere in August, a month of almost unrelieved heat and sultriness in most of Japan. Autumn *should* be cool, spring *should* be warm. Japanese poets remained loyal for centuries to the fiction that their calendar actually corresponded to the observed seasonal changes in temperature, weather, and the cycle of growth. In this, as in the convention that travel must be lonely, they were formulating what they conceived as a poetic truth, a hon'i.

506   [MYS VIII: 1559/1555]

A poem by Prince Aki

Aki tachite	Since autumn began
Ikuka mo araneba	Hardly a day or two has passed,
Kono nenuru	And yet I wake
Asake no kaze wa	To find the wind upon my sleeves
Tamoto samushi mo	Blows coldly in the dawn.

✳ The compiler of Book IV explains in his footnote the circumstances that gave rise to no. 507–8. The Prince's affliction is evident without this note; the poem is clearly a cry from the heart. The yearning to be free of earthly constraints, the feeling of helplessness, the desire to be safe and whole in love, all ring true. "Even as I see her now" (*ima mo miru goto*) must mean "in my mind's eye" or "in the image that comes in dreams." For she "is no longer here"; she has been sent back in disgrace to Inaba. The palace woman from Tsu (no. 351–53) comes to mind. What penalty Prince Aki suffered beyond the deprivation of his love is not known, but the guilty man was subject to exile in such cases. The story of Nakatomi no Yakamori and Sano no Otogami (nos. 935–97) is the best-known example in *Man'yōshū* of punishment for an improper marriage, though Otogami was not an uneme. (The reader may also recall that Genji withdrew from court to Suma after his affair with Oborozukiyo was discovered.) The Prince may claim his beloved as *tōzuma*, his "distant wife," but time is telling against them, as the envoy makes poignantly clear. The passing of the year mocks the best and most defiant intentions.

507–8   [MYS IV : 537–38/534–35]

A poem by Prince Aki; with *tanka*

Tōzuma no	Since my distant wife
Koko ni araneba	Is no longer here with me,
Tamahoko no	And the jewel-spear road
Michi o tatōmi	Is a far road to travel,
5 Omou sora	My empty longing
Yasukenaku ni	Is no easy thing to bear,
Nageku sora	My empty sighing
Yasukaranu mono o	Never lets me rest in peace.
Misora yuku	Could I be a cloud
10 Kumo ni mogamo	Drifting in the boundless sky,
Takatobu	Could I be a bird
Tori ni mogamo	Flying high into the clouds,
Asu yukite	I'd go tomorrow
Imo ni kotodoi	To call on my beloved.
15 Wa ga tame ni	Let her for my sake
Imo mo koto naku	Be safe from every ill;
Imo ga tame	Let me for her sake
Ware mo koto naku	Be safe from every ill:
Ima mo miru goto	Even as I see her now
20 Taguite mogamo	Let me have her by my side.

Envoy

Shikitae no	Her spread barken-cloth
Tamakura makazu	Pillowing arm unpillowed
Aida okite	In an empty space
Toshi so henikeru	I have let a year go by:
Awanaku omoeba	A whole year of no meeting.

Concerning the above, Prince Aki took a palace woman from Yakami in Inaba as his wife. Just when his passion was most intense and his tender love for her at its height, he was charged with the crime of lèse-majesté and she was obliged to return to her home province. Thereupon the Prince, afflicted and distressed, composed this poem, inadequate though it was.

Lady Ki (active 720's–40's)

Lady Ki (Prince Aki's other wife; see preceding commentary) has left three exceptionally intense and bitter poems of parting (nos. 509–11). Here the *Man'yōshū* compiler fails us, providing no context. Perhaps the label "poems of resentment" and the note that the Lady was the Prince's wife are enough. No. 509 again uses crossing a stream as a metaphor for a woman's resolution (see no. 483). The Lady may have been referring to separation/divorce, an attempt to win back her husband, or simply to enduring whatever situation she was in. Apparently she finds returning as tedious as go o'er, and the reference to "women of the world" is telling in a poem laden with jealousy. She uses the name of the river as a way to exclaim, "Oh, my husband!" (*ana se*), and the exclamation surely is one of reproach and dismay. The helplessness implied in no. 509 is made explicit in nos. 510 and 511 in complementary images: a rope slipping away, a day approaching. Whatever that day brought, Lady Ki survived it, and as an older woman, she attracted the amorous attention of the young Ōtomo no Yakamochi in the 740's. For some of the poems they exchanged, see nos. 1154–56.

509–11   [MYS IV : 646–48/643–45]

Three poems of resentment by Lady Ki (the daughter of the court noble Kahito, her name was Oshika. She was the wife of Prince Aki)

(509)   [646/643]

Yo no naka no	If I were a woman
Omina ni shi araba	Such as are women in this world,
Wa ga wataru	Would I have trouble
Anase no kawa o	Crossing the stream of Anase,
Watarikaneme ya	Husband, that I now must cross?

(510)   [647/644]

Ima wa wa wa	Now I have fallen
Wabi so shinikeru	To the depths of my despair,
Iki no o ni	For I have let you go,
Omoishi kimi o	Loosening, slipping from my hands,
Yurusaku omoeba	You who were the rope of my life.

(511)   [648/645]

Shirotae no	The day when white
Sode wakarubeki	Sleeves of barken cloth must part
Hi o chikami	Is near at hand;
Kokoro ni musehi	I am strangled in my heart,
Ne nomi shi nakayu	Cries pour from my throat.

Kurumamochi no Chitose (active 720's–30's)

Chitose was one of a number of court poets of the early Nara period who carried on the tradition of commemorating visits made to outlying palaces and spas in the royal entourage. An official visit to Yoshino in 723 would have been in the company of Empress Genshō. Now that the capital was at Nara, visits to Yoshino by reigning monarchs were less frequent. Poem 512–15 celebrates the land and bemoans Chitose's separation from someone (his wife?) left behind, but omits any reference to the monarch, thus altering the formula established by Hitomaro in his Yoshino poems. In Chitose's formulation the imperial progress has become a version of "travel" (tabi), and the traveler is all alone, a concept found in other early-eighth-century poets such as Prince Mutobe and Prince Nagaya (nos. 504–5). Here the chōka concentrates on the strange (aya, also meaning "twill") fascination of Yoshino, evoked at the outset by the paired pillow-word constructions. As usual, parallel couplets fill out the middle part of the poem, and then the poet reveals his personal deprivation (himo tokanu tabi, "a journey with cords never untied") and regrets (oshi mo) that he cannot show the scene to that special person who did the tying of the cords. The first envoy brings together awe at nature and yearning for home, and thus provides an instructive contrast with Hitomaro's envoy MYS I: 37 (no. 294), which yearns for return visits to Yoshino. The referent of kimi in the second envoy is not clear. "Friend" or "you" might be better than "lord." In any case it does not refer to the Sovereign (ōkimi). Madder root (akane) was the source of a red dye, and thus a pillow word for hi ("day"/"sun"). Mist rising from sighs became a well-established poetic conceit. The point of the footnote is that Chitose's poem is one of a series on imperial progresses.

512–15   [MYS VI:918–21/913–16]

A poem composed by Kurumamochi no Asomi Chitose; with tanka

	Umakori	Cleverly fashioned
	Aya ni tomoshiku	Fine twill, strange the troubling desire;
	Naru kami no	Thunder far off,
	Oto nomi kikishi	A renown of which I had heard:
5	Miyoshino no	Now at last here I stand
	Maki tatsu yama yu	On the forested mountains of Yoshino
	Mioroseba	And look down at the stream.
	Kawa no se goto ni	Wherever the water is shallow,
	Akekureba	When dawn lights the sky
10	Asagiri tachi	The mists of the morning arise,
	Yū sareba	And when evening comes
	Kawazu naku nabe	The frogs start their singing.
	Himo tokanu	But this is a journey
	Tabi ni shi areba	When the cords of my garments

15 Wa nomi shite   Are never untied,
  Kiyoki kawara o   And deep is the ache that I feel as I gaze
  Miraku shi oshi mo   All alone on the clean river beach.

Envoy
  Tagi no e no   The mountain Mifune
 Mifune no yama wa   That stands where the cataract plummets
  Kashikokedo   Is fearsome with awe,
 Omoiwasururu   But still there is one whom I never
 Toki mo hi mo nashi   Forget, not an hour or a day.

The envoys in a certain text read:
  Chidori naku   Where the sanderlings cry
 Miyoshinogawa no   By fair Yoshino's river
  Kawato nasu   The sound of the river
 Yamu toki nashi ni   Continues forever, as ever
 Omōyuru kimi   My thoughts that go out to my lord.

  Akane sasu   Though the madder-root
 Hi narabenaku ni   Days have not gone beyond number,
  Wa ga koi wa   Already the love
 Yoshino no kawa no   In my heart has arisen and stands
 Kiri ni tachitsutsu   As a mist over Yoshino River.

Concerning the above [two envoys], the date is not precisely known. However, they are entered here because of the type of poem to which they belong. It is stated in a certain text that they were composed on the occasion of an imperial excursion to Yoshino in the fifth month of Yōrō 7 [723].

Kasa no Kanamura (active 715–33)

More extensively preserved than Kurumamochi no Chitose, but with hardly more known about his personal life, Kasa no Kanamura was like him a court poet (i.e., a member of the imperial entourage) during the first decades of the Nara capital. His debt to Hitomaro is even more apparent, but his lament for Prince Shiki is cast in an entirely different mold. This poem, which concludes the banka section in Book II, is based on a dramatic dialogue in which the speaker of the poem discovers the meaning of a funeral procession from a passerby. The concept of dialogue in a chōka harks back to such ancient songs as no. 42, but in the context of banka it is highly original and completely breaks the pattern established by Hitomaro. Because of this fact, and because of its source in *Kasa no Asomi Kanamura no Kashū*, the "Kanamura Collection," and a date eight years earlier than the earliest dated poem of Kanamura not designated as taken from this collection, some doubt might be entertained about whether no. 516–20 is from the same hand as other poems attributed to Kanamura. But unlike the "Hitomaro Collection," the "Kanamura Collection" is usually accepted as the work of the poet whose name it bears, and there is no valid reason for depriving Kanamura of the credit for originality.

The chōka opens with an extended jo similar to the one in the Maiden Toneri's no. 476. Introducing Takamato ("High Target") Mountain, it provides vivid images of men armed with bows and arrows—images that resonate with the sudden fires in line 7. Here there is a searching for meaning, an urgent need to know, responded to in stages by the tears and broken speech of the mourner. Finally the truth comes out: a Prince—as in Hitomaro, a living god—is dead. And the fire image is reintroduced at the end in a brilliant alternative to Hitomaro's searching-for-the-dead, and with an irony worthy of him. The prosody is rapid and impatient, pausing for only one parallelistic passage, in lines 21–24. The imagistic conclusion, still in the mourner's quoted speech, avoids Hitomaro's usual personal comment. The four envoys provide this element of the total structure. They are reflective, reverting to the original speaker or assuming a third, neutral voice, the voice of one who thinks about the meaning of the passing of time. As such they balance the urgency of the chōka and provide a component very much in the mode established by Hitomaro. The date given in the headnote for Prince Shiki's death is one year earlier than the date in *Shoku Nihongi*, the official history of the Nara period.

516–20 [MYS II:230–34]

A poem from the time of the demise of Prince Shiki in autumn, the ninth month of the first year of Reiki [715], Wood-Junior/Hare in the order of the years; with *tanka*

Azusayumi	Their catalpa bows
Te ni torimochite	They have taken in their hands;
Masurao no	Now the stalwart men
Satsuya tabasami	Take their hunting arrows up,
5 Tachimukau	Stand and draw an aim:
Takamatoyama ni	On High Target Mountain
Haruno yaku	Those blazing fires—
Nobi to miru made	When they burn the fields in spring
Moyuru hi o	We see such fires,
10 Ika ni to toeba	But these—? I turned to ask,
Tamahoko no	And he wept,
Michi kuru hito no	The man who came along
Naku namida	The jewel-spear road,
Kosame ni furite	His tears came spilling down,
15 Shirotae no	A rain that muddied
Koromo hizuchite	The white barken cloth he wore.

Tachitomari	He stopped,
Ware ni kataraku	And this is what he said to me:
Nani shi ka mo	What're you doing,
20 Motona toburau	Pestering people with questions?
Kikeba	I hear you,
Ne nomi shi nakayu	And all I can do is cry;
Katareba	I start to tell you,
Kokoro so itaki	But my heart is choked with pain.
25 Sumeroki no	Our sovereign lord,
Kami no miko no	Our Prince who was a god,
Idemashi no	Has gone forth:
Tabi no hikari so	Torches of his escort shining
Kokoda teritaru	Throng all the ways with light.

Two Tanka

Takamato no	In the wild moorland
Nobe no akihagi	Of Takamato this autumn
Itazura ni	Will the bush clover
Saki ka chiruramu	Bloom and fall in vain,
Miru hito nashi ni	No one there to see?
Mikasayama	Is the road that winds
Nobe yuku michi wa	Along the foot of Mikasa
Kokidaku mo	Over the wild moors
Shiji ni aretaru ka	Already so rank with grass?
Hisa ni aranaku ni	For the time is not long gone.

The above poem appears in the collection of Kasa no Asomi Kanamura.

The [envoy] poems in a certain text read:

Takamato no	Bush clover blooming
Nobe no akihagi	On the moors of Takamato,
Na chiri so ne	Do not scatter yet—
Kimi ga katami ni	I would look at you awhile
Mitsutsu shinowamu	As a remembrance of my lord.
Mikasayama	See the road that winds
Nobe yu yuku michi	Along the foot of Mikasa
Kokidaku mo	Over the wild moors—
Arenikeru kamo	Utterly abandoned in the grass!
Hisa ni aranaku ni	Though the time is not long gone.

❋ The sequence 521–24 finds Kanamura on a journey. His path takes him over Mount Shiotsu at the northern end of Lake Biwa and down to Tsunoga (modern Tsuruga) on the Japan Sea. The two tanka composed at the top of the pass refer to folk beliefs. A traveler wishing to pray for success in arms or safety on a journey would shoot an arrow into the trunk of a cedar standing at a fork in the path as an offering to the god dwelling in the tree. Kanamura, proud of his shot and calling himself a *masurao*, "a stalwart man," hopes that later travelers will take note of his feat. The euphoria of the first tanka is set against the sudden reminder in the second that he is away from home, where the thoughts of those who long for him cause his horse to stumble. Thus the pair achieves a balance: a palpable hit, and a near miss.

521–22   [MYS III : 367–68/364–65]

Two poems composed by Kasa no Asomi Kanamura at Mount Shiotsu

(521)   [367/364]

> Masurao no   Here a stalwart man,
> Yuzue furiokoshi   Raising his bow-tip with a flourish,
> Itsuru ya o   Has shot an arrow:
> Nochi mimu hito wa   Let him who sees it afterward
> Kataritsugu gane   Tell others what he saw!

(522)   [368/365]

> Shiotsuyama   Up the mountain slopes,
> Uchikoeyukeba   Through the pass of Shiotsu
> Wa ga noreru   My horse carried me,
> Uma so tsumazuku   When suddenly it stumbled:
> Ie kou rashi mo   At home they must be missing me!

❊ In nos. 523–24 Kanamura takes a ship from Tsunoga on a voyage of unspecified destination. Though he says in line 15 that he is alone, the vessel is called an *ōbune* ("large boat"), and it seems likely that there are boatmen doing the rowing, probably in a boat with several sets of oars. Perhaps he is the only traveler; the traveler is existentially alone in any case. The poem is about longing for home, and the wild breath of sea only makes the speaker think of inland Yamato. Even the ama girls—voyagers, including Kanamura, found them attractive—cannot distract him. He is Hitomaro's friend from Samine—Everyman bound away, yearning for his home. Luck let him live to write his own poem. One speculation about the epithet "the Stalwart" (*masurao no*) for Tayui Bay is that *tayui* (the word is not recorded as a common noun) may have been the name of some article of warrior's wear, such as a gauntlet.

523-24 [MYS III : 369-70/366-67]

A poem composed by Kasa no Asomi Kanamura when he boarded ship at the port of Tsunoga; with *tanka*

Koshi no umi no	By the Koshi Sea,
Tsunoga no hama yu	On the beach at Tsunoga,
Ōbune ni	We thrust down the oars
Makaji nukioroshi	In the oarlocks of our ship,
5 Isanatori	And to the whale-hunting
Umiji ni idete	Path of the wild sea we went,
Aekitsutsu	Gasping for breath
Wa ga kogiyukeba	As we rowed along our way.
Masurao no	At Tayui Bay
10 Tayui ga ura ni	(Called the Stalwart for its name)
Amaotome	Smoke rose from the fires
Shio yaku keburi	That the shore girls burn for salt;
Kusamakura	But this was a journey
Tabi ni shi areba	Where one's pillow must be grass,
15 Hitori shite	And I was alone—
Miru shirushi nami	To watch would gain me nothing.
Watatsumi no	Close as the jewel-sash
Te ni makashitaru	That the god of ocean deeps
Tamadasuki	Binds across his arms
20 Kakete shinoitsu	There was bound about my heart
Yamatoshimane o	A yearning for Yamato Isle.

Envoy

Koshi no umi no	How my heart is drawn
Tayui ga ura no	By the Bay of Tayui
Tabi ni shite	On Koshi Sea—
Mireba tomoshimi	As I travel past the shore
Yamato shinoitsu	I yearn for Yamato.

❊ Like Hitomaro, Kanamura composed two chōka-hanka sets on imperial visits to Yoshino. They provide instructive comparisons and contrasts with the earlier pair. Cast in a public mode, they avoid reference to personal loneliness of the sort found in Kurumamochi no Chitose (no. 512-15) and Kanamura's own travel poems. They also at many points echo or use verbatim lines from Hitomaro. More important, they preserve his vision of eternity, of a virgin and numinous land that will draw the speaker back again and again. But the emphasis has shifted away from the monarch, whose superior divinity dominates Hitomaro's gods of mountain and stream. The Sovereigns whom Kanamura served in song—Empress Genshō in the year 723 and Emperor Shōmu (or again Genshō as Retired Empress) in 725—were served less lavishly in these poems. The Sovereign is the assumed subject of the verb *shirasamu* ("will rule") in no. 525, line 8, but otherwise is invisible, a sacred majesty implied perhaps by the unblemished beauty of the land, but left unmentioned. The jo that introduces the one incorporation of the imperial person into the amalgam of divinity draws its images from the very place being praised. The "men of the palace" (*ōmiyahito*) appear in the second chōka, but they wander through purlieus where nature seems the all-in-all. In his final envoy Kanamura expresses the wish for a life changeless as stone. But his poems point to a change affecting the concept of divine rule as the hero-image of Temmu fades away. Shōmu would eventually declare himself "the slave of the Three Treasures" in a capital whose most overpowering presence was a colossal Buddha. The image of the pristine land remains in the white "flowers" of *yū* cloth, the same image that served as the emblem of Prince Takechi's short-lived glory in no. 341.

525–30   [MYS VI:912–17/907–12]

A poem composed by Kasa no Asomi Kanamura at the time of an imperial excursion to the detached palace at Yoshino, in summer, in the fifth month of Yōrō 7 [723], Water-Junior/Swine; with *tanka*

Tagi no e no	As on this mountain,
Mifune no yama ni	Mifune where the torrent plunges,
Mizue sashi	Branched in tender green,
Shiji ni oitaru	Luxuriant and flourishing
5 Toga no ki no	The hemlock grow
Iyatsutsugi ni	Trunk upon trunk, so year after year
Yorozuyo ni	Until ten thousand ages
Kaku shi shirasamu	She will rule this land as now,
Miyoshino no	Will reign at Akizu,
10 Akizu no miya wa	Her palace in fair Yoshino.
Kamukara ka	Perhaps from its godhead
Tōtoku aruramu	Comes its awesome majesty,
Kunikara ka	Perhaps from its landstock
Migahoshikaramu	It is most sweet to look upon.
15 Yama kawa o	Mountain and river
Kiyomi sayakemi	Are so clear, so limpid pure,
Ube shi kamiyo yu	All men can see the reason why
Sadamekerashi mo	This site was chosen from the Age of Gods.

Two Envoys

Toshinoha ni	Year after year
Kaku mo miteshika	Would I gaze upon this sight:
Miyoshino no	At fair Yoshino

Kiyoki kafuchi no	The clear pools in the torrent
Tagitsu shiranami	Where the white waves plunge and boil.

Yama takami	The mountain is high,
Shirayūhana ni	The plunging torrent foams,
Ochitagitsu	A white barken cloth
Tagi no kafuchi wa	Flower on the river pool:
Miredo akanu kamo	Long though I gaze, my eyes will never tire.

The envoys in a certain text read:

Kamukara ka	Perhaps for their godhead
Migahoshikaramu	They are most sweet to look upon,
Miyoshino no	The deep river pools
Tagi no kafuchi wa	In the torrent of fair Yoshino:
Miredo akanu kamo	Long though I gaze, my eyes will never tire.

Miyoshino no	In fair Yoshino
Akizu no kawa no	Akizu River still shall flow
Yorozuyo ni	Ten thousand ages hence:
Tayuru koto naku	As ceaselessly shall I return
Mata kaerimimu	To view these sights anew.

Hatsuseme no	The barken-cloth flowers
Tsukuru yūhana	Fashioned by the girls of Hatsuse—
Miyoshino no	Have they not come to bloom
Tagi no minawa ni	In the foam beneath the torrent
Sakinikerazu ya	That plunges at fair Yoshino?

531–33 [MYS VI : 925–27/920–22]

A poem composed by Kasa no Asomi Kanamura at the time of an imperial excursion to the detached palace at Yoshino, in summer, in the fifth month of Jinki 2 [725], Wood-Junior/Ox; with *tanka*

Ashihiki no	Whole foot-wearying
Miyama mo saya ni	Mountains rustle with the force
Ochitagitsu	Of the boiling plunge
Yoshino no kawa no	When Yoshino River falls;
5 Kawa no se no	I see the clearness
Kiyoki o mireba	Where the river rapids form,
Kamibe ni wa	Hear the plovers
Chidori shibanaki	Crying ceaselessly above,
Shimobe ni wa	The songfrogs calling
10 Kawazu tsuma yobu	To their mates below this spot;
Momoshiki no	Men of the palace
Ōmiyahito mo	Built of a hundred stones

	And timbers wander
Ochikochi ni	
Shiji ni shi areba	Through these grounds in multitudes.
15 Miru goto ni	Each time I behold
Aya ni tomoshimi	These scenes a strange longing comes:
Tamakazura	As the tangling vine
Tayuru koto naku	Twists on without an ending,
Yorozuyo ni	For ten thousand years
20 Kaku shi mogamo to	May it all endure as now,
Ame tsuchi no	I pray to the gods
Kami o so inoru	Of the heaven and the earth—
Kashikokaredo mo	Though I tremble, lost in awe.

Two Envoys

Yorozuyo ni	Though ten thousand years
Mi to mo akame ya	Should pass, how should I weary
Miyoshino no	Of fair Yoshino,
Tagitsu kafuchi no	Of gazing at the palace
Ōmiyadokoro	By the deep and seething pools?

Minahito no	Would that all men's lives,
Inochi mo ware mo	My own as well, were changeless
Miyoshino no	As eternal stone
Taki no tokiwa no	Standing against the raging
Tsune naranu ka mo	Torrent of fair Yoshino!

✻ In no. 534–36 Kanamura returns to the ama girls past whose rustic charms he rowed disconsolately in no. 523. This time he is on the Inland Sea, stopped with the imperial train on the shores of Harima Province, opposite the island of Awaji. The valor of his manly (*masurao*) heart is called into question by the helpless hankering he feels, lacking a boat (he says) for crossing to the imagined enticements of the far shore. He likens himself to a *tawayame* "a weak-armed girl"—he who had shot a stalwart's arrow once—because of his inability to take direct, masculine action. The power of the romantic, pastoral ideal that was lodged in the minds of courtiers by this time is evident in this poem. It takes precedence for once even over the conventional (or real) longing for home. But nature remains as a solace, and in the last envoy the poet contents himself with walking on the beach and watching the splashing waves.

534-36   [MYS VI:940-42/935-37]

A poem composed by Kasa no Asomi Kanamura at the time of an imperial excursion to Inami District in Harima Province, on the fifteenth day of the ninth month of the third year [of Jinki, 726], Fire-Senior/Tiger; with *tanka*

Nakizumi no	From where we stay
Funase yu miyuru	Here in the roads of Nakizumi,
Awajishima	Over in Awaji
Matsuho no ura ni	The Bay of Matsuho lies in view:
5 Asanagi ni	There, as I have heard,
Tamamo karitsutsu	When the sea lies still in the morning calm
Yūnagi ni	The shore girls come
Moshio yakitsutsu	To take their harvest of the gemlike weed,
Amaotome	And in the evening calm
10 Ari to wa kikedo	They light their fires to burn the weed for salt.
Mi ni yukamu	But since I have no means
Yoshi no nakereba	Whereby I too might go to see the sight,
Masurao no	I linger here, bereft
Kokoro wa nashi ni	Of the valor of my manly heart,
15 Tawayame no	Drooping in my thoughts
Omoitawamite	Like a tender, peaking maiden,
Tamotōri	Timidly wandering,
Ware wa so kouru	So longing-stricken am I now,
Fune kaji o nami	I who have no boat, no oar.

Two Envoys

Tamamo karu	Oh, for a boat, an oar!
Amaotomedomo	That I might go and see those girls,
Mi ni yukamu	The dwellers of the shore,
Fune kaji mogamo	Taking their harvest of the gemlike weed—
Nami takaku to mo	What matter though the waves be high?

Yukimeguri	By the circling bay
Mi to mo akame ya	Let me ramble, gazing, never
Nakizumi no	Tiring of white waves,
Funase no hama ni	Wave on wave across the sand
Shikiru shiranami	Of the roadstead of Nakizumi.

Yamabe no Akahito (active 724–36)

Yamabe (or Yamanobe) no Akahito is a very famous poet about whom even less is known than about Hitomaro. Like Chitose and Kanamura, with whose poems his often appear in the same series, he accompanied the court on its peregrinations and composed poems in honor of the Emperor's visits to various places. It is apparent from his poems, of which fewer than fifty survive, that he traveled in eastern Japan as well as in the Inland Sea area. It is thought that the Yamabe were descended from Kumebe no Odate, the man who discovered the Princes Oke and Woke in hiding during the reign of Emperor Seinei (nos. 105, 153–56). According to *Nihonshoki*, Odate was granted the clan name and title Yamabe no Muraji by Emperor Kenzō in gratitude. The clan title was later changed from Muraji to Sukune under Emperor Temmu.

Akahito and Hitomaro were later linked by Ki no Tsurayuki in his *Kokinshū* preface as two poets of such equal ability as to make it impossible to choose between them, and they have tended to be thought of as the twin stars of *Man'yōshū* ever since. Akahito was actually a lesser poet, but one justly admired for the depiction of nature in some of his poetry, and for his mastery of the tanka. His work begins with an undated poem on Mount Fuji, a landmark that now first makes its appearance in Japanese poetry. (But see the folktale treatment in no. 201.) The majestic peak was far outside the geographical range of most Man'yō poets, and Japanese poetry cannot be said to have grown up in its shadow. The encomia for the mountains of Yamato speak of them as green walls surrounding the heartland, and there was usually an emotional identification with them as the hills of home. Many of them are indeed noble mountains; others, such as Mount Kagu and "Thunder Hill," are only small prominences (see nos. 238 and 297–98). None could prepare the viewer for the sweeping grandeur of Japan's highest mountain, snowcapped and then still a live volcano. Akahito shows it for its own sake. The mountain is an icon in the religion of the sacred land: it has both beauty and mystery—godhead. The chōka falls into three parts—the introduction of the subject, the development of the theme of power and wonder, and the personal statement. The effect is dazzling, but a comparison with Takahashi no Mushimaro's very similar poem (no. 569) will demonstrate what is evident from a reading of Akahito's other chōka as well. Akahito tends to be brief and not to exploit the full potential of the chōka form. His is not the highly wrought and laden style of Hitomaro. No. 537–38 is entirely lacking in pillow words and is shy of delving too deeply into the mystery of the mountain, or of employing the exclamatory particle *kamo*. Akahito's masterstroke is reserved for the envoy. This brilliantly pictorial tanka is one of the most admired of Japanese poems, and the best evidence of Akahito's special genius. A comparison with the envoys to Mushimaro's no. 569 will show the difference between a poet using words to tell and one using them to show. The anecdotal, a trip in a boat out of Tago Bay, has achieved the permanence of vision—not "vision" in the mystical sense, but the crystallization of a visual entity registered in all its sharpness by the observing eye.

537–38   [MYS III : 320–21 / 317–18]

A poem on a distant view of Mount Fuji by Yamabe no Sukune Akahito; with *tanka*

Ame tsuchi no   From the division
Wakareshi toki yu   Of the heaven and the earth,

Kamusabite	Instinct with godhead,
Takaku tōtoki	Lofty and noble has there stood,
5 Suruga naru	Rising in Suruga,
Fuji no takane o	The towering cone of Fuji:
Ama no hara	When I gaze afar
Furisakemireba	Across the distant plains of heaven
Wataru hi no	The wandering sun
10 Kage mo kakurai	With all its beams is blotted out,
Teru tsuki no	The shining moon
Hikari mo miezu	And all its light is lost to view;
Shirakumo mo	The white clouds fear
Iyukihabakari	To drift across the mountain face,
15 Tokijiku so	And in all seasons
Yuki wa furikeru	Snow still falls upon the peak:
Kataritsugi	I shall tell the tale,
Iitsugiyukamu	I shall talk for all my days
Fuji no takane wa	About Fuji's towering cone.

Envoy

Tago no ura yu	When from Tago shore
Uchiidete mireba	We rowed far out and turned to look,
Mashiro ni so	Pure white it was,
Fuji no takane ni	The towering cone of Fuji
Yuki wa furikeru	Gleaming under fallen snow!

❋ For the background of poem 539–40, see no. 255. Here Akahito stands where Empress Saimei stood in 661, and Saimei and her husband Emperor Jomei before that, in 639. The date of Akahito's visit to Iyo is not known, but nearly a century must have gone by since the time Saimei looked back on with such nostalgia. Akahito is groping into a deep past, much more remote than was ruined Ōmi to Hitomaro, and claims he does not know the date, probably referring to Saimei's ill-fated expedition to Tsukushi and to Princess Nukata's poem. Akahito here employs the elevated style of Hitomaro to good effect, achieving a grave and mournful beauty worthy of his public theme. He also refers to an account preserved in *Iyo Fudoki*, the eighth-century local gazetteer of Iyo Province, to the effect that Emperor Jomei fed rice to the birds perched in the fir trees at Iyo.

539–40 [MYS III : 325–26/322–23]

A poem composed by Yamabe no Sukune Akahito on arriving at the hot springs of Iyo; with *tanka*

Sumeroki no	Where our august line
Kami no mikoto no	Of sovereign ancestral gods

Shikiimasu	Rules in majesty,
Kuni no kotogoto	Everywhere throughout this land
5 Yu wa shi mo	Are many springs,
Sawa ni aredo mo	But of their multitude,
Shima yama no	Knowing it a land
Yoroshiki kuni to	Blessed in mountain and in isle,
Kogoshi kamo	On the lofty peak
10 Iyo no takane no	Of Iyo of the beetling crags,
Izaniwa no	On Izaniwa Hill
Oka ni tatashite	Our monarch deigned to stand,
Uta omoi	Devising poems,
Koto omōshishi	Meditating on their words:
15 Miyu no ue no	As I view the grove
Komura o mireba	Nearby the waters of that honored spring,
Omi no ki mo	I can see the firs
Oitsuginikeri	Still flourishing in their generations,
Naku tori no	While singing birds
20 Koe mo kawarazu	Cry out in strains unaltered.
Tōki yo ni	Until far ages
Kamusabiyukamu	It will endure in godhead,
Idemashidokoro	This site of the imperial tour.

Envoy

Momoshiki no	No one now can say
Ōmiyahito no	When they came to board their boats
Nikitatsu ni	At Nikitatsu,
Funanori shikemu	The men of that mighty court—
Toshi no shiranaku	Even the year is lost.

❋ Akahito's longing for the past is further explored in no. 541–42, a poem about his return to Asuka, long since abandoned as the capital, to climb Kamuoka, the "God Hill" identified with that "Thunder Hill" on which Hitomaro had placed his divine Sovereign in no. 297. One can only speculate about his reason for climbing Kamuoka, but it seems clear that he shared with Hitomaro a need to brood upon the past (and indeed, by now the fallen capital constituted a topos in Japanese poetry). For a man of Nara, Asuka represented the past, as Ōmi had for Hitomaro. The chōka begins with a jo in which the hill appears as a sacred site, a *mimoro* or *kamunabi*, both of which mean a place where a god descends to inhabit the wood. The hill in the opening lines provides in its vegetation the emblems of seriation and endlessness that lead into the primary level of discourse, and at the same time is the hill that has been climbed, serving—as Iwami did for Hitomaro— as both setting and metaphor. Akahito's paratactic view from the top elevates the hills of Asuka and broadens its stream to more majestic proportions than a prosaic inspection would allow, for the end of creating a vision of a lost kingdom left to the paired guardians of its natural beauty. This vision, charged with remembrances, causes the poet to "weep aloud," as Hitomaro had grieved at Ōmi. But here there is no mention of the vanished glories of the palace, of the many palaces of the generations at Asuka. It is as if the great empty anadem of the land contained in itself both the power of the past and the eternality of an ever-youthful godhead. The poet explains his tears in the envoy, finding in the land a counter-image for his own still longing.

541–42   [MYS III: 327–28/324–25]

A poem composed by Yamabe no Sukune Akahito on climbing Kamuoka; with *tanka*

	Mimoro no	As on this mountain
	Kamunabiyama ni	Where the god descends into the sacred grove,
	Ioe sashi	Five-hundred-branched,
	Shiji ni oitaru	Luxuriant and flourishing
5	Tsuga no ki no	The hemlock grow,
	Iyatsugitsugi ni	Trunk upon trunk, again and yet again,
	Tamakazura	Like the tangling vine
	Tayuru koto naku	For endlessness, unfailingly
	Aritsutsu mo	While yet I live
10	Yamazu kayowamu	Shall I return to Asuka,
	Asuka no	Forever to
	Furuki miyako wa	This capital of olden times:
	Yama takami	Here the hills are high,
	Kawa tōshiroshi	The river broad across the plain.
15	Haru no hi wa	On the days of spring
	Yama shi migahoshi	How fair the mountains are to see!
	Aki no yo wa	On the nights of fall
	Kawa shi sayakeshi	How clear the river is to hear!
	Asakumo ni	In the morning clouds
20	Tazu wa midare	Cranes go swirling in mad flight,
	Yūgiri ni	In the evening mist
	Kawazu wa sawaku	Songfrogs clamor noisily.
	Miru goto ni	Each time I look
	Ne nomi shi nakayu	I can only weep aloud
25	Inishie omoeba	As I think upon the past.

Envoy

Asukagawa	For this longing
Kawayodo sarazu	Will not vanish from my heart
Tatsu kiri no	Like the rising mist

| Omoisugubeki | That hovers on the river pools, |
| Koi ni aranaku ni | The quiet pools of Asuka. |

❊ As they did with Hitomaro and Takechi no Kurohito, the compilers of *Man'yōshū* included a set of tanka on travel by Akahito. Most of the places that can be identified in Akahito's set of six are near the eastern end of the Inland Sea. Poems 543–44, with their images of small boats in the offing, are reminiscent of Kurohito; no. 545 expresses the "yearning for Yamato" that is a staple of the whole tradition, going back to the songs of *Kojiki*. No. 546 places the poet on the seashore and develops the thought of home to include his wife. The *tamamo* ("gemlike seaweed") would be a practical, edible gift. The wife is the speaker in no. 547, worrying at home about her traveling husband. In this context no. 548, the last poem, comes as an ironic twist. The speaker, far from thinking of his wife at home, is wooing an ama girl—and with a bold proposition at that. But this tanka is very much in the mode of the so-called "folk song" (*min'yō*), and the speaker would normally be assumed to be a village youth. With the intrusion of a third voice the concept of a sequence breaks down.

543–548   [MYS III : 360–65/357–62]

Six poems by Yamabe no Sukune Akahito

(543)   [360/357]

Nawa no ura yu	Out from Nawa Bay
Sogai ni miyuru	Beyond these waters can be seen
Oki tsu shima	An island in the offing:
Kogimiru fune wa	The boats that row around its shore
Tsuri shi su rashi mo	Seem angling there for fish.

(544)   [361/358]

Muko no ura o	Around Muko Bay,
Kogimiru obune	See, there rows a little boat
Awashima o	Looking out beyond
Sogai ni mitsutsu	At the Island of Awa—
Tomoshiki obune	How you draw me, little boat!

(545)   [362/359]

Ahe no shima	Out on Ahe Isle
U no sumu iso ni	Cormorants nest on the stony strand,
Yosuru nami	And the waves roll in:
Ma naku kono koro	Without respite these past days,
Yamato shi omōyu	My yearning for Yamato.

(546) [363/360]

> Shio hinaba
> Tamamo karitsume
>   Ie no imo ga
> Hamazuto kowaba
> Nani o shimesamu

> When the tide is out,
> Cut a store of the gemlike weed:
>   If my wife at home
> Should beg some trophy of the beach,
> What else shall I have to show?

(547) [364/361]

>   Akikaze no
> Samuki asake o
>   Sanu no oka
> Koyuramu kimi ni
> Kinu kasamashi o

>   You who cross the hill
> Of Sanu at cold daybreak
>   In the autumn wind,
> Would that I had lent you
> Garments to keep you warm.

(548) [365/362]

>   Misago iru
> Isomi ni ouru
>   Nanoriso no
> Na wa norashite yo
> Oya wa shiru to mo

>   In the rock-lined waters
> Of this bay, haunt of the osprey,
>   Grows the "naming weed":
> Tell your name to me, lass—
> Who cares if your parents know?

❋ No. 549–50 is a love poem in the guise of a visit to a famous place. Here Akahito goes up into Kasuga Fields near Nara, but instead of developing a theme of loyalty to the land and its history as in the poem about climbing Kamuoka, he uses the images provided by the setting to serve as analogues of his desire "for a girl I cannot meet." Thus what looks like a public poem at the outset turns out to be a private one, as the last line makes specifically clear. The marshaled order of the images—first in the preparation, then re-used in the conclusion—presses on to an unexpected dénouement. The case is somewhat different from Hitomaro's use of special places—Iwami or Karu—as settings for his private poems. Kasuga and Mount Mikasa are associated with the imperial capital—are "public" places—Kasuga the site of the Fujiwara-founded Kasuga Shrine, and Mikasa here adorned with the epithet *takakura no* ("like a royal throne"). The expectations created are palpably public in nature. Neither is this a poem of longing for home on an official tour. The poet is seemingly alone on the fields of Kasuga, and the woman of whom he thinks is not the "wife at home" of the travel poems, but *awanu ko*, the girl he longs for but has not won. The *kaho* bird has not been identified; it may be the cuckoo.

549–50   [MYS III : 375–76/372–73]

A poem composed by Yamabe no Sukune Akahito on climbing to Kasuga Fields; with *tanka*

Haruhi o	On Kasuga Mountain
Kasuga no yama no	(Hazy as a day in spring),
Takakura no	On Mikasa Peak
Mikasa no yama ni	(Lofty as a royal throne),
5 Asa sarazu	Morning without fail
Kumoi tanabiki	Clouds lie drifting in long bands,
Kahotori no	And the *kaho* bird
Ma naku shibanaku	Cries constantly, never ceasing.
Kumoi nasu	Like the bands of cloud
10 Kokoro isayoi	My heart hovers hesitant,
Sono tori no	Like the calling bird
Katakoi nomi ni	I long with a one-sided love.
Hiru wa mo	In the light of day,
Hi no kotogoto	And all day long from dawn to dusk,
15 Yoru wa mo	In the dark of night,
Yo no kotogoto	And all night long from dusk to dawn,
Tachite ite	Rising, sitting,
Omoi so wa ga suru	Restless ever do I yearn
Awanu ko yue ni	For a girl I cannot meet.

Envoy

Takakura no	On Mikasa Peak
Mikasa no yama ni	(Lofty as a royal throne)
Naku tori no	The calling bird
Yameba tsugaruru	Ceases only to begin again—
Koi mo suru kamo	Endlessly as my yearning.

✳ Fujiwara no Fuhito, Minister of the Right and head of government, died in 720. He was the son of Kamatari (614–69), the original Fujiwara and architect of the Taika Reforms that set Japan on its new course of adopting Chinese institutions in the mid-seventh century. Fuhito was himself the father of sons and daughters who dominated the court in their day. He was posthumously awarded the title of Prime Minister (*daijōdaijin*). No. 551 suggests that Akahito may have had a patron–client relationship with him or some member of his family. The poem is a miniature variation on the theme of the fallen capital. Probably written in the 730's, it provides more evidence of the pull of the past on Akahito.

551 [MYS III : 381/378]

A poem composed by Yamabe no Sukune Akahito on the landscape garden
of the late Prime Minister Fujiwara

Inishie no	The old embankment,
Furuki tsutsumi wa	Relic of a vanished past:
Toshi fukami	The deepening years
Ike no nagisa ni	Along the margin of the pond
Mikusa oinikeri	Lie buried in the tangled reeds.

❋ No. 552 is an entirely different kind of poem. It is personal, allegorical,
open to interpretation. Saying one thing, it means another; unless, that is,
Akahito is simply making horticultural notes, which is unlikely. He is more
probably practicing the allegorical mode (hiyuka) than that of eibutsu, "the
poem about things."

552 [MYS III : 387/384]

A poem by Yamabe no Sukune Akahito

Wa ga yado ni	Cockscomb I planted,
Karaai makiōshi	I grew it here before my house;
Karenuredo	Now it has withered,
Korizute mata mo	But I have not learned despair:
Makamu to so omou	I intend to plant again.

❋ A number of poets of the Nara period, Akahito among them, were interested in local legends (an official concern of the fudoki) and recorded
them in verse. One group of legends had to do with the marriage-rejecting
maiden who commits suicide, usually by drowning, rather than choose between or among suitors, a plot that later received its classic formulation in
the story of Ukifune in *The Tale of Genji*. The exemplars of this character
type in *Man'yōshū* lack the psychological detail provided by the mind of
Murasaki Shikibu; indeed, in the naïveté of their conception lies their romantic charm. Akahito's contribution to this theme concerns the Maiden of
Mama, a village in the region of Katsushika on the shore of what is now
known as Tōkyō Bay. As usual, Akahito's narrative interest is slight; a
longer poem by Mushimaro (no. 572–73) reveals that the Maiden, a true
rustic beauty, attracted such a rush of male attention that she chose "to lie
down in her barrow beside the harbor loud with waves." Akahito merely
mentions passing her grave—now lost in the passage of time—and presents

himself as one in whom the legend has lodged, and who will transmit it. The opening lines need not be read to mean that the Maiden of Mama was successfully courted in the manner described; they are probably intended as a jo to introduce *tsumadoi shikemu* ("they wooed her, so the story goes"). The word *tegona* (or *tego*), etymologically "babe in arms," was eastern dialect for "maiden." Akahito uses it almost as a personal name, and it is so rendered in the translation.

553-55   [MYS III : 434–36/431–33]

A poem by Yamabe no Sukune Akahito on passing the grave of the Maiden of Mama in Katsushika; with *tanka*. (In the speech of the easterners she is called Kazushika no Mama no Tego.)

Inishie ni	In times now gone
Arikemu hito no	Lovers in this place, the story goes,
Shitsuhata no	Used to loosen each
Obi tokikaete	The other's homespun sash;
5 Fuseya tate	They built their bowers—
Tsumadoi shikemu	It was the wooing of a wife.
Katsushika no	And of Tegona,
Mama no tegona ga	The maid of Mama in Katsushika:
Okutsuki o	Her barrow, I have heard,
10 Koko to wa kikedo	Once stood upon this spot; but now—
Maki no ha ya	The dense-boughed timber
Shigeritaruramu	Has grown too wild, perhaps,
Matsu ga ne ya	Or the pine roots
Tōku hisashiki	Long: too long a time ago.
15 Koto nomi mo	But as for me,
Na nomi mo ware wa	Her story and her name, if only these,
Wasurayumashiji	Will surely never be forgot.

Envoys

Ware mo mitsu	I too have seen it,
Hito ni mo tsugemu	I shall tell of it abroad:
Katsushika no	The barrow-site
Mama no tegona ga	Of the Maiden Tegona
Okutsukitokoro	Of Mama in Katsushika.
Katsushika no	She who men say
Mama no irie ni	Gathered the gemweed floating here
Uchinabiku	Along this inlet
Tamamo karikemu	At Mama in Katsushika—
Tegona shi omōyu	The Maiden Tegona comes now to my thought.

✳ One of Akahito's finest poems in the public mode is no. 556–58, a celebration of a visit by Emperor Shōmu to the seashore near Wakanoura on the Ki Peninsula. The typically short chōka balances the imperial with the natural dignity in a view from the detached palace toward a windswept, wavewashed offshore island. The picture of vigorous, cleansing natural forces at work is completed by the presence of the shore-dwellers going about their daily task of gathering seaweed. Everything in view is elemental, a harmony of man and nature placed pictorially or cinematically at the end of a vista. At the opposite end are the courtiers, who exist to observe, and to record in poetry. The first envoy takes the courtiers abruptly across to the rocks on the island coast. In a close-up, they look down at the seaweed about to be swallowed by the tide. A romantic longing overcomes them, not for the seaweed so much as for the simple life of gatherers that they can enjoy only for a day. In the second envoy the tide pours in, the seastrand vanishes, the cranes fly off—and the courtiers too must leave the wild scene that has so entranced them. Akahito has used the excursion poem here for subtler purposes than the straightforward vision of peace, joy, and reverence that Hitomaro created at Yoshino. In Akahito's more shaded conception the courtiers do not merely sport on the waters under the pleased gaze of their divine Sovereign. They know discontent and longing for a romantically conceived "other"—a safe regret, to be sure, but one that suggests their relative modernity. None of this would be apparent without the two envoys, which alter the whole perspective of the poem. The footnote contradicts the precise dating of the headnote, implying that the compiler(s) supplied the latter to a source document lacking dates.

556–58   [MYS VI: 922–24/917–19]

A poem composed by Yamabe no Sukune Akahito at the time of an imperial excursion to the province of Ki, on the fifth day of the tenth month, winter, of Jinki 1 [724], Wood-Senior/Rat; with *tanka*

Yasumishishi	Where our great lord reigns,
Wa go ōkimi no	Ruling the land in all tranquility,
Tokomiya to	From this eternal palace
Tsukaematsureru	Where we wait upon his will
5 Sahikano yu	Here in Sahika Fields,
Sogai ni miyuru	Beyond these precincts can be seen
Oki tsu shima	An island in the offing.
Kiyoki nagisa ni	Along the clean-swept margin of its waves
Kaze fukeba	When the wind blows fresh
10 Shiranami sawaki	White billows storm across the beach,
Shio fureba	And when the tide is out
Tamamo karitsutsu	The seafolk bend and cut the gemlike weed.

Kamiyo yori	From the Age of Gods
Shika so tōtoki	Awesome and noble has it stood,
15 Tamatsushimayama	The sea-mount Tamatsushima.

Two Envoys

Oki tsu shima	When the tide comes in
Ariso no tamamo	And the gemlike weeds on the rocks
Shiohi michite	Of this island coast
Kakuroiyukaba	Hide themselves slowly in the waves,
Omōemu ka mo	Will our thoughts go after them?

Wakanoura ni	When the tide pours in
Shio michikureba	Across the flats of Waka Bay
Kata o nami	The seastrand vanishes,
Ashibe o sashite	And the cranes with raucous cries
Tazu nakiwataru	Fly off to shelter in the reeds.

No date was given for the above. However, the text mentions accompanying the imperial palanquin to Tamatsushima. Hence we enter the poem here, based on our investigation of the date of the imperial excursion.

❋ Akahito's public poems usually lack dates, a fact referred to more than once by the compilers. Two chōka-hanka sets (nos. 559–61 and 562–63) composed at Yoshino are grouped together under one headnote. The first chōka is highly derivative from Hitomaro's Yoshino poems and is hardly a very impressive performance. Akahito seems to be rushing through it in order to reach the envoys, which are among his best. Fully independent tanka with little relation to the parent poem, they form a matched pair with their descriptions of birdsong by day and by night. Each concentrates on creating a mood by sound and rhythm—the bright sounds of day and the cool, quiet ones of night. These are nature poems pure and simple, making no reference to the conventional awesomeness of the occasion.

The other poem set is on the royal hunting and deserves comparison with Nakatsu Sumera Mikoto's no. 245–46 and Hitomaro's no. 301–2. Akahito is clearly doing something quite different from those poets. Though all three use paratactic structures, the paired parallel couplets that are basic to the developed chōka form, Akahito employs them to create a visual pattern, a kind of diorama of the hunt, with trackers and bowmen stationed here and there, animals and birds appearing at designated times. This visual effect is underscored by the hanka, in which the huntsmen advance in formation across the hills, and which ends with the distancing verb *miyu* ("are seen"). In contrast, Hitomaro's poem is not really about hunting at all, but the adoration of a Prince, and its striking visual effect in the envoy is a brilliant flight of fancy. Except in the envoy, which is close to the ending Akahito has given his chōka, the poem by Nakatsu Sumera Mikoto is cast in the speculative mode and achieves its hypnotic effect through auditory rather than visual means, and through the ritual repetition of a whole section of the poem.

559–63   [MYS VI:928–32/923–27]

Two poems composed by Yamabe no Sukune Akahito; with *tanka*

(559–61)   [928–30/923–25]

Yasumishishi	Our great Sovereign
Wa go ōkimi no	Who rules the land in all tranquility
Takashirasu	By high decree
Yoshino no miya wa	Has raised at Yoshino a palace
5 Tatanazuku	Nestled among walls
Aokakigomori	Of green around it fold on fold,
Kawanami no	Where clear pools form
Kiyoki kafuchi so	Along the winding river course:
Harube wa	In springtime
10 Hana sakiōri	Blossoms load the bending boughs,
Aki sareba	And when autumn comes
Kiri tachiwataru	Mists rise and spread across the hills.
Sono yama no	As those mountains
Iya masumasu ni	March ever onward range on range,
15 Kono kawa no	As this river
Tayuru koto naku	Flows forever without end,
Momoshiki no	So the courtiers,
Ōmiyahito wa	Men of the Palace of the Hundred Stones,
Tsune ni kayowamu	Will always make their journeys to this place.

Two Envoys

Miyoshino no	In fair Yoshino,
Kisayama no ma no	In the vale that lies between
Konure ni wa	The mountains of Kisa,
Kokoda mo sawaku	From every treetop rise the voices
Tori no koe kamo	Of the gaily singing birds.
Nubatama no	As the night grows deep
Yo no fukeyukeba	In darkness black as beads of jet,
Hisaki ouru	Where the red oak grow
Kiyoki kawara ni	Along the clean-swept river beach
Chidori shibanaku	The plovers keep endlessly crying.

(562-63)   [931-32/926-27]

Yasumishishi	Our great Sovereign
Wa go ōkimi wa	Who rules the land in all tranquility,
Miyoshino no	In fair Yoshino
Akizu no ono no	On the plain of Akizu
5 No no e ni wa	Stations trackers
Tomi sueokite	In the fields to follow game,
Miyama ni wa	Spreads across the hills
Ime tatewatashi	The shelters where his bowmen watch.
Asakari ni	In the morning hunt
10 Shishi fumiokoshi	The animals are driven from their lairs,
Yūkari ni	And in the evening hunt
Tori fumitate	The birds are startled into flight.
Uma namete	Lining up his steeds,
Mikari so tatasu	He leads forth the royal hunt
15 Haru no shigeno ni	Across the verdant fields of spring.

Envoy

Ashihiki no	All across the fields,
Yama ni mo no ni mo	High upon the footsore hills,
Mikaribito	The huntsmen can be seen
Satsuya tabasami	Excitedly advancing
Sawakitari miyu	With their game bows in their hands.

The order of the above is not precisely known. However, it seems expedient to give them in this order.

❋ Akahito's visual patterns are nowhere more vividly illustrated than in a tanka he composed at Naniwa in 734. Again the occasion is a royal hunt. This time there is a bipartite division between the men and the women—the masurao who go off to the hunt and the court ladies who remain behind. The energy of the former is set off against the elegant grace of the latter, so that the short poem is informed by two contrasting movements, one rapid and departing, the other leisurely and occupying the center of attention. The ladies are dressed in scarlet skirts, which sweep across the clean sand of the beach in this most painterly poem. This part of the scene is reminiscent of Hitomaro's tanka set 311-13.

564   [MYS VI: 1006/1001]

[One of] six poems composed [by various poets] on the occasion of an imperial excursion to the Naniwa Palace in spring, in the third month [of 734]:

Masurao wa	The stalwart warriors
Mikari ni tatashi	Set off on the royal hunt,
Otomera wa	While courtly maidens
Akamo susobiku	Trail the scarlet of their skirts
Kiyoki hamabi o	Along a clean, white-sanded shore.

The above poem was composed by Yamabe no Sukune Akahito.

✳ Four spring tanka by Akahito in Book VIII form a sequence arranged in the reverse of the seasonal order, with violets blooming in the first poem, cherry blossoms in the second, plum blossoms amid the snow in the third, and snow falling onto the first herbs in the last. It has been suggested that the first poem is allegorical, with the violets referring to a young woman, and an allegorical interpretation could be pressed in the second poem as well. More likely, these are simply poems about a love for flowers, a topic that becomes established about this time in Japanese poetry. The third is an early example of "elegant confusion," approximately contemporary with Ōtomo no Tabito's dated snow/plum poem of 730 (no. 1018). The plum blooms early enough to meet the snowflakes of February (early spring by the old Japanese calendar). The fourth poem probably refers to the custom of picking spring herbs for medicinal purposes on the first Day of the Rat of the new year. "Marking the fields" meant setting aside a special area against intrusion by outsiders. Again, snow often spoiled the occasion, inspiring many poems like this. These elegant and much-admired poems by Akahito look forward in tone and topic to the seasonal verse of the Heian period.

565–68   [MYS VIII: 1428–31/1424–27]

Four poems by Yamabe no Sukune Akahito

(565)   [1428/1424]

Haru no no ni	To the fields of spring
Sumire tsumi ni to	To pick violets I came—
Koshi ware so	I who in fondness
No o natsukashimi	For those fields could not depart,
Hitoyo nenikeru	But stayed and slept the night.

(566)   [1429/1425]

Ashihiki no	If the wild cherry
Yamasakurabana	Flowered every day as now
Hi narabete	Far in the trailing hills,
Kaku sakitaraba	How would I ever come to know
Ito koime ya mo	The sharpness of this longing?

(567)   [1430/1426]

Wa ga seko ni   To you, dear friend,
Misemu to omoishi   I was set to show the blossoms
      Ume no hana   Of my flowering plum—
Sore to mo miezu   But they are nowhere to be seen,
Yuki no furereba   Now that snowflakes fill the air.

(568)   [1431/1427]

Asu yori wa   Starting tomorrow,
Wakana tsumamu to   I was off to pick young herbs,
   Shimeshi no ni   And I marked my fields;
Kinō mo kyō mo   But yesterday and now today
Yuki wa furitsutsu   Those fields have filled with falling snow.

Takahashi no Mushimaro (active 720's–30's)

Takahashi no Mushimaro has left a distinctive body of work from which it is apparent that, like Akahito, he traveled in eastern Japan, was interested in local legends, and wrote poems about mountains. Practically nothing is known of either his personal or his public life, but no. 581–82 makes it seem likely that he was at some point a subordinate of Fujiwara no Umakai (694–737), a son of Fuhito. His familiarity with Mount Tsukuha suggests that he served in the administration of Hitachi Province. Mushimaro and Akahito were contemporaries and twice wrote chōka on the same subject, poems that are strikingly similar and yet instructively different. The connection between these two poets, if there was one, is not clear. What is clear is that Mushimaro, perhaps more than any other poet in *Man'yōshū*, had those narrative interests and talents that are so notably lacking in Akahito. He tells, rather than shows, and has the storyteller's love of stringing out words. As far as can be ascertained from his surviving poems, Mushimaro was not a court poet in the sense of Hitomaro, Akahito, and others. There is no record of his accompanying an imperial excursion, and he has not left any panegyrics on the monarchy. His connections seem to have been noble rather than royal; his poems show him in the company of lords instead of sovereigns. Thus he and Akahito may have moved in different circles and never met. But it is well-nigh impossible to believe that they were not aware of each other, or that their poems on Mount Fuji have no connection.

No. 569–71 appears immediately following "On a Distant View of Mount Fuji," in the middle of a series of poems by Akahito. Despite the compiler's note, which is sometimes taken to refer only to the second envoy, its authorship has long been controversial. I follow the Japanese scholars who accept it as Mushimaro's work. The plenitude and exuberance of the style suit Mushimaro, whose other work is known for these qualities. Mushimaro must have seen Mount Fuji when he traveled in the east, and his delight in mountains is attested by several poems on Mount Tsukuha in Hitachi Province. Mushimaro's version of the Fuji poem differs from Akahito's in being about twice the length, and in using that length to build up to an overpowering climax, replete with the use of exclamation, parallel couplets, two parallel quatrains, and four syntactic units ending in *kamo*. All of this creates an effect quite at variance with Akahito's spare exposition. Both poems treat the mountain as spectacularly awesome and outside the normal range of experience, a vortex of power where the workings of nature are disordered. But Mushimaro, who is not aiming for primarily visual effects, deepens the sense of mystery and exploits paradox more fully. He begins with an obscure pillow word, *namayomi no* (here rendered "grim-shadowed"), and builds step by step a setting for the mountain, which wells up from the earth, driven by its own inner force. It disturbs not only the clouds but the birds. Instead of the bright images of the sun and moon in Akahito, here a paradox reigns in fire and snow locked in eternal combat. The mountain is a "living god" (*imasu kami*). The poem reaches a first climax in line 20, then begins again in what may be a structural flaw, but one that allows the poet to elaborate on those natural features, lakes and rivers, that help make the mountain a national treasure. (The "Sea of Barnacles," a literal rendering of *se no umi*, was a lake that was split into two by an eruption in 864.) This ultimate land-praising poem is comparable in its successful evocation of a dread theme to Hitomaro's handling of the death of Prince Takechi in no. 341. Again in sharp contrast to Akahito, Mushimaro continues to narrate even in the first envoy, deploying a further paradox. The second envoy is a reprise, relating back to the parent poem in a way often used by Hitomaro.

569–71   [MYS III : 322–24/319–21]

A poem composed on Mount Fuji; with *tanka*

Namayomi no	From the borderland
Kai no kuni	Where grim-shadowed Kai
Uchiyosuru	Lies by the flank
Suruga no kuni to	Of wave-worn Suruga,
5 Kochigochi no	From the scattered lands,
Kuni no minaka yu	Rising from the midst of them,
Idetateru	Swells and soars aloft
Fuji no takane wa	The towering cone of Fuji:
Amakumo mo	Clouds of the sky
10 Iyukihabakari	Fear to drift across its face,
Tobu tori mo	Birds of the air

Tobi mo noborazu	Cannot rise upon the wing;
Moyuru hi o	Burning fire
Yuki mochikechi	It quenches in smothering snow,
15 Furu yuki o	And falling snow
Hi mochikechitsutsu	Forever devours in fire:
Ii mo ezu	I cannot speak,
Nazuke mo shirazu	I cannot find a name to give
Kusushiku mo	For the dark riddle
20 Imasu kami kamo	Of this awesome living god.
Se no umi to	The Sea of Barnacles,
Nazukete aru mo	Such the name it has been given,
Sono yama no	Is a sea embosomed
Tsutsumeru umi so	In the mountain's wide embrace;
25 Fujikawa to	The Fuji River,
Hito no wataru mo	Known to men who cross its stream,
Sono yama no	Is a fresh torrent
Mizu no tagichi so	Rushing from the mountain slopes.
Hi no moto no	Here in Yamato,
30 Yamato no kuni no	Land of the rising of the sun,
Shizume to mo	Guardian of its peace,
Imasu kami kamo	Abides this living god forever;
Takara to mo	Treasure of the realm,
Nareru yama kamo	Stands this peerless mountain peak:
35 Suruga naru	Rising in Suruga,
Fuji no takane wa	The towering cone of Fuji
Miredo akanu kamo	Will never tire my steadfast gaze.

Envoys

Fuji no ne ni	'Tis said the snow that piles
Furioku yuki wa	All year long on Fuji's cone
Minazuki no	Melts when the moon is full
Mochi ni kenureba	In the middle of the month of June,
Sono yo furikeri	But falls again that very night.

Fuji no ne o	Lofty and dreadful
Takami kashikomi	Is the cone of Fuji—
Amakumo mo	Clouds of the sky,
Iyukihabakari	Fearing to drift across its face,
Tanabiku mono o	Trail hesitant upon the air.

The above poem appears in the poems of Takahashi no Muraji Mushimaro. We include it here because of its similarity [to Akahito's poem on Mount Fuji].

✳ Mushimaro's interest in local legend inspired his most characteristic poetry. The long narrative poem never became established as a Japanese form,
but Mushimaro clearly felt an urge to push the chōka in that direction. No.
572–73 is his counterpart to Akahito's poem on the Maiden of Mama in Katsushika. Over twice as long, it concentrates on what Akahito neglects,
namely, the story. Akahito seems to assume that the story is known (though
he might not have been interested in telling it anyway); he says "he too" has
seen the gravesite—but that all sign of the grave itself has disappeared. He
seems to be commenting on an earlier poem, and there is an attractive plausibility to the supposition that he had read (or heard) Mushimaro. In Mushimaro's poem we can see the storyteller warming to his subject, delighted to
be able to create an appealing innocent, dressing her, contrasting her favorably with a rich girl. He adopts the convention used by Hitomaro in writing
about death and other mysteries: "What was the reason?" The implied reason is that the maiden is too tender-hearted to endure the spectacle of men in
rivalry. She chooses to remove herself as the cause of conflict. (The fierce-
ness of the conflict is the focus of the story of the Maiden Unai, told by both
Mushimaro in no. 574–76 and Ōtomo no Yakamochi, no. 837–38.) The
remorselessness and admirable economy of a ballad take the heroine to her
grave without the pages of agonizing that a prose narrative makes possible
for Ukifune in *The Tale of Genji*. Mushimaro has found the chōka well
suited to his purposes in its flexible but never excessive length.

572–73   [MYS IX : 1811–12/1807–8]

A poem about the Maiden of Mama in Katsushika; with *tanka*

Tori ga naku	In cock-crowing
Azuma no kuni ni	Azuma the Eastern Land
Inishie ni	From the long ago
Arikeru koto to	There comes a story that still now,
5 Ima made ni	Even to this day,
Taezu iikeru	They have never ceased to tell:
Katsushika no	Of the Maid Tegona
Mama no tegona ga	Of Mama in Katsushika,
Asaginu ni	Who put blue collars
10 Aokubi tsuke	On her simple flaxen frocks,
Hitasao o	And wove skirts to wear
Mo ni wa orikite	Out of fibers of plain hemp,
Kami dani mo	Who never dressed her hair
Kaki wa kezurazu	Or even drew a comb through it,
15 Kutsu o dani	And who went about
Hakazu yukedo mo	With no sandals for her feet.
Nishiki aya no	(Yet what pampered child

Naka ni tsutsumeru	Wrapped around in figured silks,
Iwaiko mo	Bundled in brocades,
20 Imo ni shikame ya	Could ever compare with this sweet girl?)
Mochizuki no	The round full moon
Tareru omowa ni	Was not more perfect than her face,
Hana no goto	And when like a flower
Emite tatereba	She stood smiling at her door,
25 Natsumushi no	Like summer insects
Hi ni iru ga goto	Entering into the flame,
Minatoiri ni	Or a crowd of boats
Fune kogu gotoku	Rowing into the harbor,
Yukikagure	They came to claim her,
30 Hito no iu toki	The men with their talk. And then—
Ikubaku mo	What was the reason,
Ikeraji mono o	When though she lived she would not
Nani su to ka	Live forever?—
Mi o tanashirite	Brooding deeply on herself,
35 Nami no oto no	The dear one lay down
Sawaku minato no	Where now she lies in her barrow
Okutsuki ni	By the harbor
Imo ga koyaseru	Busy with the sound of waves.
Tōki yo ni	It happened long ago
40 Arikeru koto o	In a distant age, this thing,
Kinō shi mo	But it is as if
Mikemu ga goto mo	I had seen it yesterday,
Omōyuru kamo	When the thoughts come over me.

Envoy

Katsushika no	When I see the well
Mama no i mireba	Of Mama in Katsushika,
Tachinarashi	Whither she wore a path
Mizu kumashikemu	Going to draw water, so men say,
Tegona shi omōyu	The Maiden Tegona comes to my thought.

❊ In the story of the Maiden Unai a young girl is torn between two particular suitors, not simply overwhelmed, as the Maiden Tegona is, by men who come like boats to a harbor, who make a hedge about the house. (The first metaphor in the tale of Tegona—moths flying into a lamp flame—suits the legend of Unai better, since both of her principal wooers destroy themselves with her.) Unai is thought to have been a village in the Ashinoya (now Ashiya) district west of Naniwa, but Mushimaro uses it as the maiden's name as well. One rival comes from the same village, and the other from

Chinu, the seacoast south and east of Naniwa. Thus the scene of this tale is set in western rather than eastern Japan, indicating Mushimaro's connection with both areas.

It has been suggested that Mushimaro drew his story from a legend about a group of tumuli visible to travelers going past Ashinoya, but that he also was familiar with a poem in the sixth-century Chinese anthology *Yü-t'ai Hsin-yung* about a forcibly separated husband and wife who committed suicide and were buried together. Whatever his inspiration, the poet-storyteller is obviously eager to make his tale an exciting one, and he uses a fluid style with seven pillow words and a number of other strongly imagistic lines. Unai presumably would have put up her hair at the age of fifteen or sixteen, having worn it loose until then. It is interesting to note Mushimaro's penchant for creating contrasting heroines. Tegona went barefoot and never combed her hair, yet was more winsome than the *iwaiko* ("pampered child") in her silks and brocades. Unai is precisely that iwaiko, kept secluded and beautifully groomed. And unlike Tegona, she incurs the guilt of an unconfessed passion, as well as the deaths of men. The pillow word *utsuyū no* ("of the hollow *yū*") is obscure. *Yū* was a bleached white fiber made from paper-mulberry bark and was normally used for sacramental purposes in Shintō worship. Artificial flowers were also made of it (see no. 341, line 97). How it applies as an epithet to *komorite* ("staying in seclusion") has not been adequately explained. Line 17 may mean that the two youths burned each other's houses (or the honeymoon huts they were building for Unai?); another school of thought, followed here, is that *yaki* ("burn") introduces *susu* ("soot") in *susushikioi* ("came at each other"). As often, Mushimaro involves his narrative stance closely with the story by the use of the diminutive endearment *wagimoko* ("my young darling," lit., "my little sister").

Line 37's *shishikushiro* ("gameflesh on a spit"; see no. 167) is a pillow word for *yomi*. Yomi is the land of the dead, but homophonous with *yomi*, "good flavor." The epithet is a strong one in the mouth of a young woman, especially when rendered into English, but so is the decision to wait in hell. Kan'ami's Nō play *Motomezuka*, based on the Unai legend, has the maiden tormented by fiends in hell after her death. The foreboding pillow word in this poem seems to foreshadow that terrible vision, in which the grave mound is the very image of hell. To be sure, Kan'ami's hell is Buddhist, and a place of punishment, whereas Unai's may have been only the indigenous land of darkness (*yomi/yami*). Still, the usage is intriguing. The fact that Unai appeared in a dream to the Youth of Chinu and not to his rival could mean either of two things in the beliefs of the time—that she loved him, or that his love for her was stronger than the Youth of Unai's. The final envoy favors the first interpretation. Compare the Youth of Unai's reaction with lines 60–63 of Yamanoue no Okura's poem on the death of his son, no. 629–31. Mushimaro is at his best when he recasts the three suicides into metaphors of flight and pursuit, a device that enables him to convey in terms rich with irony the ineluctable blindness of passion. In particular, the spectacle of the youth of Unai on the warpath to the underworld is so striking a parable as to make a Buddhist hell not inappropriate. Mushimaro's treatment of the legend already has the seeds of fire that Kan'ami fanned into dark flame.

574-76 [MYS IX: 1813-15/1809-11]

A poem on seeing the grave of the Maiden Unai; with *tanka*

Ashinoya no	In Ashinoya
Unai otome no	Lived the Maiden of Unai:
Yatoseko no	From a child of eight,
Kataoi no toki yu	A half-grown girl, until
5 Obanari ni	She tied her hair
Kami taku made ni	To hang short on either side,
Narabioru	She was never seen
Ie ni mo miezu	In the houses on the street,
Utsuyū no	But stayed secluded
10 Komorite oreba	As in a hollow of bleached cloth:
Miteshika to	They fought for air,
Ibusemu toki no	The men who would see her;
Kakiho nasu	They formed a fence,
Hito no tou toki	The men who came to call.
15 Chinu otoko	Then the Youth of Chinu
Unai otoko no	And the Youth of Unai
Fuseya yaki	Came at each other,
Susushikioi	Black as the soot from torched hovels,
Aiyobai	Fierce in their wooing,
20 Shikeru toki ni wa	Rivals for one woman's love.
Yakitachi no	Twisting the hilts
Takami oshineri	Of their swords of tempered steel,
Shiramayumi	Strapping on their backs
Yuki torioite	Their quivers and their whitewood bows,
25 Mizu ni iri	They faced each other,
Hi ni mo iramu to	Ready to plunge into water,
Tachimukai	Ready to plunge in flame.
Kioishi toki ni	In the midst of their contending,
Wagimoko ga	My young darling went
30 Haha ni kataraku	And to her mother she said this:
Shitsutamaki	"A homespun bracelet,
Iyashiki wa ga yue	I am lowly, yet for me
Masurao no	The stalwart men
Arasou mireba	Fall into strife; when I see it,

35 Ikeri to mo	I know I could never wed,
Aubeku are ya	Even if I were to live."
Shishikushiro	Gameflesh on a spit,
Yomi ni matamu to	In the dark land I'll wait, she whispered,
Komorinu no	Keeping this intent
40 Shitahaeokite	As deep as water in a hidden marsh.
Uchinageki	She sighed,
Imo ga inureba	The darling girl, and went her way.
Chinu otoko	The Youth of Chinu
Sono yo ime ni mi	Saw her that night in a dream,
45 Toritsutsuki	Clung to her,
Oiyukikereba	Followed her where she went;
Okuretaru	And, now left behind,
Unai otoko i	He, the Youth of Unai,
Ame aogi	Gazed up to heaven,
50 Sakebi orabi	Shouted, shrieked at the sky,
Tsuchi o fumi	Stamped on the ground,
Kikamitakebite	Gnashed his teeth in defiance,
Mokoroo ni	And swore he'd not
Makete wa araji to	Be bested by no more a man than he.
55 Kakehaki no	He slung on his sword,
Odachi torihaki	Belting it tight at his hip,
Tokorozura	And went to find them,
Tomeyukikereba	Following like a creeper of wild yam.
Ugaradochi	And so the kinfolk
60 Iyukitsudoi	Came together to decide:
Nagaki yo ni	That for long ages
Shirushi ni semu to	They might stand as monuments,
Tōki yo ni	That in distant years
Kataritsugamu to	The tale might still be told,
65 Otomehaka	They raised a tomb
Naka ni tsukurioki	For the maiden in the middle,
Otokohaka	And tombs for the youths
Konomo kanomo ni	One on either side of her.
Tsukuriokeru	When I heard of it,
70 Yueyoshi kikite	All the story of these graves,
Shiranedo mo	Though I knew nothing
Niimo no goto mo	Of those times, I wept aloud,
Ne nakitsuru kamo	As in mourning for the newly dead.

Envoys

Ashinoya no	When on my travels
Unai otome no	I pass by the barrow site
Okutsuki o	At Ashinoya,

320

Yukiku to mireba	The grave of the Maiden Unai,
Ne nomi shi nakayu	I can only weep aloud.

Haka no ue no	Over one grave
Ko no e nabikeri	Trailed the branches of a tree:
Kikishi goto	Just as I had heard,
Chinu otoko ni shi	It was to the Youth of Chinu
Yorinikerashi mo	That she inclined in her heart.

The above five poems [i.e., nos. 572–76] appear in the collection of Takahashi no Muraji Mushimaro.

❋ No. 577–78 is a sympathetic, warmly related tale of the making of a village wanton. Unlike most of the legends about lovers, it does not end in the death of one or all. Tamana is not the romantic suicide that touched the tragic fancy of storytellers and poets, but a wild girl darting off with her lovers into the night, a local beauty unable to resist the passion aroused by her own ample charms. She is the contrasting case to the Tegona of no. 572–73. Both stand smiling (innocently?), with as magnetic and disturbing an effect as Mount Fuji on the denizens of the air, but instead of going to lie in her grave, Tamana goes out to lie with men. This is a tale told by a poet, not by a corporation of singers as in the ancient songs of the chronicles, and the poet's judgment can be adjusted in any way he sees fit. Mushimaro says of Tegona's decision for suicide, *mi o tanashirite* ("brooding deeply on herself"—knowing herself utterly), and of Tamana's wantonness, *mi wa tanashirazu* ("with no thought for what she did"—utterly oblivious of herself). Some irony, or even the seeds of a psychology, may lurk in these matched phrases, but Mushimaro is intent on telling his stories and presses the matter no further. It is not known why Awa has the epithet *shinagadori* ("long-breath bird," i.e., the diving grebe), but Sue doubles for *sue* ("end"—of the catalpa bow). Sue village was on the eastern shore of what is now Tōkyō Bay.

577–78   [MYS IX : 1742–43 / 1738–39]

A poem about the Maiden Tamana of Sue in Kamitsufusa; with *tanka*

Shinagadori	By the long-breath bird
Awa ni tsugitaru	Land of Awa lies the last
Azusayumi	Of the villages,
Sue no Tamana wa	Sue the tip of the catalpa bow:
5 Munewake no	There dwelt Tamana,
Hiroki wagimo	My sweet girl with swelling breasts,
Koshiboso no	Slender at the waist,
Sugaru otome no	The wasp-maiden of Sue.
Sono kao no	Shapely she was and smooth,

10 Kirakirashiki ni All her person soft with sheen,
   Hana no goto   And when like a flower
   Emite tatereba She stood smiling at her door,
   Tamahoko no   Men who were bound away,
   Michiyukibito wa Traveling down the jewel-spear road,
15   Ono ga yuku   Gave up their journeys
   Michi wa yukazute And went no more along the way,
   Yobanaku ni   But reached her gate
   Kado ni itarinu And stopped, though she had not called.
   Sashinarabu   Neighbors in houses
20 Tonari no kimi wa Standing lined along the lane,
   Arakajime   Heads of households,
   Onozuma karete Separated from their wives
   Kowanaku ni   And without her asking
   Kagi sae matsuru Offered up their very keys.
25   Hito mina no   Everyone was mad
   Kaku matoereba For her, wandering thus lost,
   Uchishinai   And so she yielded,
   Yorite so imo wa That fair one, and went with them
   Tawarete arikeru In the wild ways of desire.

Envoy

   Kanato ni shi   Someone had come,
   Hito no kitateba Was standing by the metal gate:
   Yonaka ni mo   In the dead of night
   Mi wa tanashirazu With no thought for what she did
   Idete so aikeru She went and kept her tryst.

❋ Mushimaro's longest poem, and the masterpiece of narrative art in *Man'yōshū*, is his version of the Urashima legend, no. 579–80. Urashima no ko, or Urashima Tarō, is a fisherman who meets and marries the daughter of the sea god, but foolishly rejects immortality in her palace in order to return to his village. There he opens a forbidden box she has given him, turns old, and dies. The Mushimaro version is associated with the Settsu area west of Naniwa on the Inland Sea, but the story is also known on the Japan Sea coast. For the *Tango Fudoki* version, see nos. 216–20. A brief account of the legend, placed in Tamba Province, also appears in *Nihonshoki* as an entry for the twenty-second year of the reign of Emperor Yūryaku.

The Urashima story is made up of three widely distributed myths: the visit to another world and marriage with a woman of that place; the story of the forbidden box; and the sudden discovery of the passage of time by a hero whose life has been unnaturally prolonged. The first of these stories is particularly important in Japan, where it has been incorporated into the central national myth. Nos. 7–8 and NS 5–6 are songs set in the latter stages of an account that takes an ancestor of the First Emperor down to the bottom of the sea, where he marries Toyotamahime, the sea god's daughter. In that story too the hero breaks a taboo when he spies on his wife in childbirth. In revenge she denies him access to the realms of the undersea. This undersea kingdom is a version of Tokoyo, "Everworld," the eternal land sometimes thought of as across the sea. Tokoyo became fused in the Japanese imagination with the Chinese Taoist paradise of P'eng-lai (J. Hōrai), envisioned as an island in the eastern sea. The image of a separate realm and the woman who lives there seems to haunt Hitomaro's Iwami poems as well (nos. 321–27).

Mushimaro devotes particular care to the opening of no. 579–80. He creates a setting for his narrative and establishes a relaxed mood for story-telling in the first eight lines of the chōka, a narratological equivalent of the formal imagistic introductions of the ancient preparation-conclusion struc-ture. The long narrative songs in the chronicles (e.g., nos. 2–5) may come to mind in this regard, but there the narrator's acknowledgment comes in at the end in the appended formulas. And such songs seem likely to have been mimed, which is to say, are dramatic as much as narrative. Mushimaro as narrator comes in at the beginning of the tale of Urashima, gathers his lis-teners around him, and begins to spin his story. The story is developed skill-fully in two movements, in and out—in to the subtle and delicate hall (*tae naru tono*) in the center of the poem, and out again to the world. The para-digm is certainly a sexual one, with the pride of ignorant youth at the begin-ning and the helplessness of old age at the end. Even the motions of fishing are parodied in the paroxysms of death, and together they frame the soft entrance, "hand in hand," into the palace of love. The eternal woman, eter-nally young, remains behind at the crux of the story in that other realm where man's desires are fulfilled, but where, since it is a dream world, he can never stay. In the tale of Urashima, the hero *could* have stayed, which is why the poet abuses him in the envoy. The *tama* of the *tamakushige*, or "jeweled comb chest," also means "soul," and it is Urashima's soul, kept safe in the chest, that flies away as a cloud to the lost land of heart's desire, leaving him to die on the beach.

579–80   [MYS IX : 1744–45 / 1740–41]

A poem composed on the subject of the youth Urashima of Mizunoe; with *tanka*

	Haru no hi no	On a day in spring
	Kasumeru toki ni	When the air was soft with haze
	Suminoe no	I traveled down
	Kishi ni ideite	To Suminoe shore, and as I watched
5	Tsuribune no	The fishing boats
	Tōrau mireba	Bob gently on the sea,

Inishie no	There came to mind
Koto so omōyuru	A tale of long ago.
Mizunoe no	Young Urashima
10 Urashima no ko ga	Of Mizunoe fished for bonito,
Katsuo tsuri	Fished for golden bream,
Tai tsurihokori	And proud he was of his fine catch.
Nanuka made	On the seventh day
Ie ni mo kozute	He still had not come home;
15 Unasaka o	He rowed beyond
Sugite kogiyuku ni	The slope of sea, rowed on
Watatsumi no	Until he met by chance
Kami no otome ni	The daughter of the mighty deep.
Tamasaka ni	They spoke enticing words
20 Ikogimukai	Each to the other, challenge and reply,
Aiatorai	And when the thing
Koto narishikaba	That they desired had come about,
Kakimusubi	Fast bound in troth
Tokoyo ni itari	They reached the realm of Everworld.
25 Watatsumi no	There in the palace
Kami no miya no	Of the god of the great deep
Uchi no e no	They made their way
Tae naru tono ni	Together, hand in hand,
Tazusawari	Into the chamber
30 Futari iriite	Of the inmost mystery.
Oi mo sezu	They might have lived
Shini mo sezu shite	Forever in those wondrous halls,
Nagaki yo ni	Never growing old
Arikeru mono o	Or dying, through long ages,
35 Yo no naka no	But this fool
Orokahito no	Of all the foolish world,
Wagimoko ni	He went to his love,
Tsugete kataraku	And this is what he said to her:
Shimashiku wa	"Let me go home,
40 Ie ni kaerite	Just for a little while,
Chichi haha ni	To tell Father and Mother
Koto mo katarai	All that's happened to me—
Asu no goto	I'll come back to you
Ware wa kinamu to	In a day or two, I swear,"
45 Iikereba	He said, and she,
Imo ga ieraku	His lady love, spoke thus:
Tokoyohe ni	"If you would come again
Mata kaerikite	To this realm of Everworld
Ima no goto	And meet me
50 Awamu to naraba	Just as now, heed well:

324

	Kono kushige	Take this comb chest,
	Hiraku na yume to	But never open it—beware!"
	Sokoraku ni	Over and over
	Katameshi koto o	She pressed her warnings on him.
55	Suminoe ni	But when he reached
	Kaerikitarite	The shores of Suminoe
	Ie miredo	And looked for his house,
	Ie mo mikanete	There was no house for him to find;
	Sato miredo	When he sought his village,
60	Sato mo mikanete	There was no village anywhere.
	Ayashi to	"How strange!" he thought,
	Soko ni omowaku	And wondered thereupon,
	Ie yu idete	"In the three years
	Mitose no hoto ni	Since the day I left my home
65	Kaki mo naku	How could the house
	Ie useme ya to	Have vanished, the fence be gone?
	Kono hako o	Maybe if I take
	Hirakite miteba	This box and open it
	Moto no goto	There'll be a house here
70	Ie wa aramu to	Just the way there was before."
	Tamakushige	Then he opened it,
	Sukoshi hiraku ni	The jeweled comb chest, only a little—
	Shirakumo no	And a white cloud
	Hako yori idete	Flew out and drifted off
75	Tokoyohe ni	In a trailing vapor
	Tanabikininureba	Toward the realm of Everworld:
	Tachihashiri	Wildly he ran,
	Sakebi sode furi	Shouted, waved his sleeves,
	Koimarobi	Rolled upon the ground;
80	Ashizuri shitsutsu	He stamped his feet in frenzy;
	Tachimachi ni	Suddenly
	Kokoro keusenu	His heart grew faint, he fell.
	Wakakarishi	Wrinkles spread across
	Hada mo shiwaminu	The skin that had been smooth and young,
85	Kurokarishi	Whiteness fell upon
	Kami mo shirakenu	The locks that had been gleaming black.
	Yunayuna wa	Moment by moment
	Iki sae taete	His breath ebbed away, was gone;
	Ato tsui ni	At last it was over,
90	Inochi shinikeru	Life died within him:
	Mizunoe no	Young Urashima,
	Urashima no ko ga	The fisherman of Mizunoe,
	Iedokoro miyu	Here is seen the site of his abode.

Envoy

Tokoyohe ni	You should have stayed there
Sumubeki mono o	In the realm of Everworld—
Tsurugitachi	Rusty-bladed sword,
Na ga kokoro kara	Dullard were you on the day
Oso ya kono kimi	You willed otherwise, you fool!

✴ Regional Commanders (*setsudoshi*) in charge of military preparedness were first appointed for the several "circuits" (*dō*) in 732. Fujiwara no Umakai, apparently the patron of Mushimaro, was given the Saikaidō, or Western Sea Circuit, consisting of Kyūshū and its outlying islands. Umakai had previously served in the north and had some experience as a military commander against the unpacified inhabitants of that remote region. His appointment to the new post in Kyūshū is commemorated in a four-line Chinese poem in *Kaifūsō* in which he bemoans his posting and the drudgery of commanding provincial troops. Mushimaro also wrote a poem on the subject, no. 581–82, in which he lavishes on the scion of the Fujiwara some of the hero worship accorded to imperial princes by other poets. Here it is a nobleman who makes the superhuman progress through the mountains (see Hitomaro's no. 331). Matters stop short of actual warfare, and the whole *chōka* is framed with autumn leaves and spring flowers rather than the exclamations of awe found in Hitomaro's battle piece, no. 341. Mushimaro employs the traditional formula (also known from norito, the ancient Shintō ritual prayers) about the wandering toad (*taniguku no sawataru kiwami*) in an effective contrast to the desired return of his lord "swiftly as a flying bird" (*tobu tori no hayaku*). He offers the traveler the enticements of home to bring him back from distant exile. The envoy is of particular interest for its reference to *kotoage*, "lifting up words," in a magical spell. Kotoage could achieve the results specified in the words through the efficacy of the *kotodama*, or "word soul," but the practice was hedged with peril. Inappropriately performed kotoage could unleash forces that would rebound on the person uttering the words (this is what killed Yamato Takeru; see commentary to nos. 27–28). Fortunately Umakai's military prowess was such, in Mushimaro's estimation, that he did not need to have recourse to magic. This is the only poem attributed to Mushimaro in the headnote; the others are all from the "Collection" or noted afterward as "from the poems of Takahashi no Muraji Mushimaro."

581–82   [MYS VI : 976–77/971–72]

A poem composed by Takahashi no Muraji Mushimaro when Lord Fujiwara no Umakai was dispatched as Regional Commander of the Western

Sea Circuit in the fourth year [of Tempyō, 732], Water-Senior/Monkey;
with *tanka*

Shirakumo no	Where the white clouds rise
Tatsuta no yama no	On Tatsuta the mountain slopes
Tsuyu shimo ni	Now with dew and frost
Irozuku toki ni	Brighten in their autumn hues
5 Uchikoete	As you, my lord,
Tabi yuku kimi wa	Cross over on your journey.
Ioeyama	Five hundred mountains
Iyukisakumi	You shall spurn, brushing trees aside,
Ata mamoru	To reach Tsukushi,
10 Tsukushi ni itari	Our defense against the foe.
Yama no soki	There you will divide
No no soki miyo to	The company of your command
Tomonobe o	To guard the ramparts
Akachitsukawashi	Of the mountains and the moors,
15 Yamabiko no	Observing how the land
Kotaemu kiwami	Is formed in all its vast extent,
Taniguku no	Far as the boundary
Sawataru kiwami	From which the mountain sprite replies,
Kunikata o	Far as the boundary
20 Meshitamaite	Reached by the wandering valley toad.
Fuyugomori	But when spring returns
Haru sariyukaba	That lay hidden all the winter long,
Tobu tori no	Come back, my lord,
Hayaku kimasane	Swiftly as a flying bird:
25 Tatsutaji no	When the roadsides
Okabe no michi ni	Over the hills to Tatsuta
Nitsutsuji no	Glow with the colors
Niowamu toki no	Of azaleas all in red,
Sakurabana	And cherry blossoms
30 Sakinamu toki ni	Burst into first flowering,
Yamatazu no	As elder leaves meet,
Mukaemaidemu	So shall I go out to meet you,
Kimi ga kimasaba	My lord, when you come back again.

Envoy

Chiyorozu no	Though you faced a foe
Ikusa nari to mo	A thousand myriads in strength,
Kotoage sezu	You are such a man
Torite kinubeki	As without lifting up of words
Onoko to so omou	Could bring them captive back.

On examining the records of official appointments, it appears that Regional Commanders were appointed for the Tōzan, San'in, and Saikai [Circuits] on the seventeenth of the eighth month [of 732].

❋ The occasion for the following poem is not known, but Fujiwara no Umakai served as officer in charge of the construction of a palace at Naniwa in the 720's and went there for the observation of its completion in the third month of 732. The poems composed by Mushimaro, who apparently was part of the entourage, are really about the cherry blossoms seen along the way and place Mushimaro among the first Japanese poets to take up the theme of their perishability. (In this regard no. 566, by Akahito, is also of interest.) Generally the plum seems to have been the more fashionable tree to admire in the eighth century, but neither the plum nor the cherry was of much interest to poets before that time.

583–84   [MYS IX : 1751–52 / 1747–48]

[One of] two poems composed in spring, in the third month, when the lords and great officers of court went down to Naniwa; with *tanka*

	Shirakumo no	Where white clouds rise
	Tatsuta no yama no	Above soaring Tatsuta
	Taki no ue no	And the mountain torrent
	Ogura no mine ni	Plummets down Ogura's peak,
5	Sakiōru	Blossoming cherries
	Sakura no hana wa	Burgeon in great swirls of bloom;
	Yama takami	But the mountain is high
	Kaze shi yamaneba	And the wind is never still,
	Harusame no	And the spring rain
10	Tsugite shi fureba	Goes on falling day by day,
	Hotsue wa	So that by now the petals
	Chirisuginikeri	Have scattered from the upper branches.
	Shizue ni	O blossoms remaining
	Nokoreru hana wa	On the branches down below,
15	Shimashiku wa	For a little while
	Chiri na midare so	Do not scatter so wildly,
	Kusamakura	Until my lords return
	Tabi yuku kimi ga	From the journey where they go,
	Kaerikuru made	Grass for their pillow.

Envoy

	Wa ga yuki wa	This journey of mine
	Nanuka wa sugiji	Will not last beyond seven days:

Tatsutahiko	God of Tatsuta,
Yume kono hana o	I charge you, do not let the wind
Kaze ni na chirashi	Scatter these blossoms to the ground.

✳ Mushimaro composed four poems about Mount Tsukuha in Hitachi Province, northeast of the present city of Tōkyō. He seems to have climbed the mountain repeatedly, and with a keen sense of exhilaration and joy. In no. 585–86 he finds an almost Wordsworthian sense of comfort and consolation in nature. Here nature is not an awesome deity, or a landmark of home, or a barrier, or a picture, but a place to go to be alone and let the cares of life drop away. There is something here of the land-viewing, land-praising tradition, but Mushimaro is no Emperor, and what he finds on Tsukuha is universal, not culture-bound. The wind, waves, grass, and cries of birds, in the midst of solitude, work their magic, and the poet is restored to himself. So much so that in the envoy he reaches out to another human presence, the tiny figure of a peasant girl reaping far away. To him she may be a cousin of Tegona or Tamana (nos. 572–73, 577–78); as with them, he refers to her intimately as *imo* ("little sister"), the ubiquitous endearment of ancient Japan.

585–86   [MYS IX : 1761–62 / 1757–58]

A poem on climbing Mount Tsukuha; with *tanka*

	Kusamakura	Grass for my pillow,
	Tabi no uree o	Travel-worn and sad, I thought
	Nagusamoru	Here perhaps might be
	Koto mo ari ya to	Some solace for these sorrows,
5	Tsukuhane ni	And up Tsukuha's
	Noborite mireba	Famed peak I climbed and gazed about:
	Obana chiru	Where plumegrass scattered
	Shizuku no tai ni	On the fields of Shizuku
	Karigane mo	Wild geese had come,
10	Samuku kinakinu	Their voices coldly crying;
	Niibari no	At Niibari
	Toba no ōmi mo	Out on the lake of Toba
	Akikaze ni	White waves had risen,
	Shiranami tachinu	Brisk before the autumn wind.
15	Tsukuhane no	As I gazed upon
	Yokeku o mireba	The good things of fair Tsukuha
	Nagaki ke ni	The long day's burden
	Omoitsumikoshi	Carried heaped within my heart
	Uree wa yaminu	Of sorrow lightened and was gone.

Envoy

Tsukuhane no	Let me break a branch
Susomi no tai ni	Of yellow leaves—I'll send it
Akita karu	To the girl down there
Imogari yaramu	Harvesting the autumn fields
Momichi taorana	Along the skirts of Tsukuha.

❋ No. 587–88 presents a very different kind of experience on Mount Tsukuha. The mountain served other needs besides those of the melancholy traveler; at certain times of the year it was the site of sexual license rather than solitary contemplation, and Mushimaro shows himself apt for this kind of consolation as well. The "song-matches" (kagai), also known as utagaki (see nos. 106–11, 158–62, 201–8, and 214–15), were orgiastic affairs, probably originally intended to ensure fertility in the fields, which included not only sexual frolics but much singing and dancing, and especially the use of song as challenge and reply, either between men and women or male rivals. Mushimaro's record of his (wholehearted) participation in these rites reveals that he had a wife (if we are to assume the "factuality" of the poem), and that she accompanied him to the revels. Needless to say, all of this is of considerable interest from the viewpoint of the customs of the time.

The chōka has a sprightly rhythm based partly on shiritori ("tail-catching") repetition and overflows with a sense of exultation and release, from its opening image to its final admonition. It is easy to see the eager progress of the throngs of youths and maidens up the mountain (this contrasts with another of Mushimaro's poems on Mount Tsukuha, MYS IX : 1757–58/1753–54, in which he records sweating his way up, clutching the roots of trees), and the promiscuous joys that await them are suggested in words such as *majirawamu* ("shall be keeping company") and *kagau* ("match songs"), which have secondary sexual meanings. The "haven" (*tsu*) of lines 3–4 presumably refers to a watered glen, a *locus amoenus* less sedate than the hallowed banks of the Yoshino. According to another interpretation, the last two lines are exchanged between Mushimaro's wife and himself, she saying, "Do not pity me," and he replying, "Don't blame me." Mount Tsukuha has twin peaks, one male, one female. Appropriately, the envoy climaxes the riotous proceedings by having clouds of rain (a classical Chinese allusion to a female sex partner) swirl around Male God Peak and drench the ecstatic poet, who is only too willing to be drenched. Indeed, why go home?

587–88   [MYS IX : 1763–64/1759–60]

A poem composed on the day he climbed Mount Tsukuha and took part in the song-matches; with *tanka*

Washi no sumu	To where eagles dwell
Tsukuha no yama no	On the Mountain of Tsukuha,
Mohakitsu no	Up to the haven,
Sono tsu no ue ni	The haven of Mohaki,
5 Adomoite	Urging each other
Otome otoko no	With shouts, the youths and the maidens,
Yukitsudoi	Thronging together,
Kagau kagai ni	Go to match songs in the song-match.
Hitozuma ni	Since with others' wives
10 Wa mo majirawamu	I shall be keeping company,
Wa ga tsuma ni	So with my own wife
Hito mo kototoe	Let others banter as they will.
Kono yama o	The gods that keep
Uchihaku kami no	This mountain from of old
15 Mukashi yori	Have never interposed
Isamenu waza zo	Their ban against these usages.
Kyō nomi wa	This one day alone,
Megushi mo na mi so	Sweetling, do not look at me,
Koto mo togamu na	Do not question what I do.

Envoy

Hikokami ni	Over Male God Peak
Kumo tachinobori	Clouds boil up, hang in the air,
Shigure furi	Rain comes scudding down;
Nuretōru to mo	But though I end up sopping wet,
Ware kaerame ya	Will I go home for that?

Ōtomo no Tabito (665–731)

Ōtomo no Tabito came of an ancient clan distinguished for military service to the imperial house. He rose to Major Counselor of Junior Second Rank after serving as Governor-General of Dazaifu, the military procuracy in northern Kyūshū, from 728 to 730. There he fostered the composition of poetry among his subordinates and was the host of a famous plum-blossom party whose poetic harvest is presented in the section on poem groups of multiple composition (nos. 1011–42). Tabito may have been of the same generation as Hitomaro, but he lived on into the new age of Nara and became one of its most highly Sinicized poets. The plum-blossom party itself is one evidence of his determination to emulate Chinese-style elegance. The Matsura River sequence (nos. 1049–59) is another. A third bit of chinoiserie is his set of thirteen tanka in praise of wine, nos. 592–604 below. Tabito's family was clearly a cultured one, devoted both to Chinese learning and the practice and preservation of waka. Probably they had a large collection of the work of contemporary and earlier Japanese poets, as well as a Chinese library. The numerous Ōtomo who figure in the pages of *Man'yōshū* no doubt looked up to Tabito as the most learned and politically successful of their number. He was also the clan head. Tabito's son Yakamochi was a far greater poet, and the master anthologizer whom we have to thank for *Man'yōshū* itself, but in his day the Ōtomo clan was in rapid decline, and his career was marked by vicissitudes. Yakamochi's copious poetic production is from his early and middle years, and the last twenty-six years of his life are a blank as far as poetry is concerned. The converse is true of Tabito—what we have are the poems of the end of his career.

For at least the first thirty-five years of his life, Tabito was a contemporary of Hitomaro, but there is little in his extant work to show that he belonged to the same world. Tabito's only surviving chōka, no. 589, illustrates the point. Perhaps no more than a preliminary draft (it was never submitted, although composed on imperial command), it is a feeble effort to produce something in the tradition of Hitomaro's Yoshino poems. Its eleven derivative lines not only fail to praise the Sovereign, but are devoid of both the traditional preposited structures of jo and pillow word and any but the most generalized imagery. The brook of Kisa, mentioned in the envoy, flows down out of the Yoshino Mountains from the south and joins the Yoshino River at Miyataki, the site of the detached palace. The poem may have been composed in 724.

589–90   [MYS III: 318–19/315–16]

A poem composed on imperial command by Middle Counselor Lord Ōtomo in the last month of spring on the occasion of an excursion to the detached palace at Yoshino; with *tanka* (a poem not yet presented to the throne)

Miyoshino no	In fair Yoshino
Yoshino no miya wa	There Yoshino the palace stands—
Yamakara shi	Clearly its majesty
Tōtoku arashi	Comes from the grandeur of the hills,
5 Kawakara shi	Clearly its purity
Sayakeku arashi	Comes from the freshness of the stream.
Ame tsuchi to	Together with heaven,
Nagaku hisashiku	With earth, long and enduring,
Yorozuyo ni	For ten thousand ages
10 Kawarazu aramu	It will still remain unchanged,
Idemashi no miya	This palace of the imperial tour.

Envoy

Mukashi mishi	When I look today
Kisa no ogawa o	Upon the rivulet of Kisa

Ima mireba	Where I oft have gazed,
Iyoyo sayakeku	Its waters sparkle yet more pure
Narinikeru kamo	Than when I saw it long ago.

✻ The following tanka dates from Tabito's years as Governor-General of Dazaifu (728–30). He has produced a much better poem on Yoshino from the distance of his post in Kyūshū, when not under the pressure of an imperial command and obliged to write in a form (the chōka) for which he probably had little talent. His poem introduces interesting and outlandish people and images for comparison with the beloved Yoshino. The Hayahito were the aboriginal inhabitants of southern Kyūshū and were still causing the Yamato court some trouble as late as the eighth century. Pacified, they served as guards in the capital. The -keri ending of the poem tells that the poet has verified his (homesick) preferences for Yamato on viewing the vaunted local splendors. There is also an implied statement of the superiority of the central power over the fractious periphery.

591   [MYS VI:965/960]

A poem composed by Governor-General Lord Ōtomo, thinking from afar of the detached palace at Yoshino

Hayahito no	In the sea passage
Seto no iwao mo	In the country of the Haya folk
Ayu hashiru	Are great bristling rocks,
Yoshino no tagi ni	But the sight cannot compare
Nao shikazukeri	To the trout-darting torrent of Yoshino.

✻ It has been suggested that Tabito's thirteen tanka on the joys of drink (nos. 592–604), another product of his years at Dazaifu, were a response to his sorrow over the recent death of his wife. The refrain of "drunken tears" lends plausibility to this hypothesis. The many learned references in the poems make the sequence quite a different matter from the songs in the chronicles celebrating the manufacture and imbibing of the Japanese national drink (see nos. 39–40, 48–49, and 118). Making *sake* was a process steeped in ritual, performed with dance and invocations of the gods; drinking it produced a state of triumphant intoxication expressed in the exclamation *ware einikeri* ("I have gone and gotten drunk!"). Tabito's toper is a more erudite reprobate, and his pleasures are those of the *naki jōgo*, the crying drunk.

The sequence is artistically arranged, structured around theme, elaboration, and refrain. Poem one (no. 592) announces the theme: wine is best. (The translation renders the rice brew as "wine" throughout.) And *nigoreru sake* ("cloudy wine"), the unrefined beverage, is specified. That clue is developed in the next two poems (nos. 593–94). In China refined wine was called Sage (*sheng*) and cloudy wine Worthy (*hsien*): and so the speaker is himself a worthy. These terms were drinkers' argot at a time of prohibition in the Wei Dynasty (A.D. 220–64). The second poem is thus ironic—there was no "great sage" (*ōki hijiri*). But the term sounds good, even to a mere worthy. There *were* Seven Wise Men (*nana no sakashiki*), the famous Seven Sages of the Bamboo Grove, a group of bibulous, world-rejecting scholars in the Western Chin Dynasty (A.D. 265–317). The reference in poem three (no. 594) establishes Tabito's drinker as a man who enjoys dabbling in the escapist philosophy of a degenerate Taoism. The refrain *einaki suru* ("weeping drunken tears"), which occurs three times in the series, appears for the first time in poem four (no. 595); the continued reference to wisdom links the poem to its predecessor.

The fifth poem (no. 596) restates the theme and begins a new subsequence. Poems six and seven (nos. 597–98) provide the concrete image groped for in the abstract thematic enunciation. The Omaresque image of the winepot is based on another Chinese anecdote, about a drinker of the Wu Dynasty (A.D. 222–80) who wished to turn to clay in the earth and be reshaped into a wine vessel. Poem seven (no. 598) echoes poem four (no. 595) in its contempt for pretentiousness. Perhaps Tabito had some particular teetotaler in mind with his reference to a face like a monkey's. He continues the elaboration of the theme with a matched pair on treasures, no doubt examples of the *shirushi naki mono* ("things of no virtue") mentioned in the first poem. "Treasures beyond price" (*atai naki takara*), a Buddhist term, is a phrase echoed in a poem by Tabito's friend Yamanoue no Okura (no. 628), where the "superior treasure" (*masareru takara*)—superior to silver, gold, or jewels—is not wine, but a child. "Gems that shine at night" (*yoru hikaru tama*) are mentioned in early Chinese sources, one of which says they come from the Southern Seas and are the eyes of whales. Here such a marvel is contrasted unfavorably with "letting your heart fly free" (*kokoro o yaru*), at the same time that its mention establishes a night scene of drinking by some softly glowing light (the moon?). The refreshment of the cool night and the emotional release are picked up by the tenth poem (no. 601), where *suzushiki* means both "cool" and "refreshing," and where the refrain *einaki suru* appears for the second time. Poems eleven and twelve (nos. 602–3) give the theme its last twist. They are pure carpe diem philosophy; both advocate hedonism, and no. 602 takes a swipe at the Buddhist doctrine of metempsychosis as well. The final poem restates the theme, refers back to poems four (no. 595) and seven (no. 598), and brings in the refrain one last time.

592–604 [MYS III: 341–53/338–50]

Thirteen poems in praise of *sake* by Lord Ōtomo, Governor-General of Dazaifu

(592)   [341/338]

    Shirushi naki   Things of no value—
Mono omowazu wa   Better not waste your thoughts on them;
    Hitotsuki no   But to take a cup
Nigoreru sake o   Brimming with the cloudy wine . . .
Nomubeku aru rashi   Yes, and drain it to the lees!

(593)   [342/339]

    Sake no na o   He named it Sage—
Hijiri to ōseshi   This was the name he gave to wine,
    Inishie no   That ancient wise man,
Ōki hijiri no   That great sage of long ago—
Koto no yoroshisa   And how fine the word he chose!

(594)   [343/340]

    Inishie no   In the bygone days
Nana no sakashiki   Seven wise men did there live,
    Hitotachi mo   Seven sagely men
Hori seshi mono wa   With but one desire, 'tis said,
Sake ni shi aru rashi   One thing they wanted—that was wine!

(595)   [344/341]

    Sakashimi to   Better than prating
Mono iu yori wa   With false display of wisdom,
    Sake nomite   Or so I've been told,
Einaki suru shi   Is to take wine, and to drink,
Masaritaru rashi   And to weep with drunken tears.

(596)   [345/342]

    Iwamu sube   Wine is so precious—
Semu sube shirazu   From the things that I've heard tell—
    Kiwamarite   That I hardly know
Tōtoki mono wa   What to say or what to do
Sake ni shi aru rashi   To make you see its excellence.

(597)   [346/343]

    Nakanaka ni   Not this middling life,
Hito to arazu wa   Neither sober nor yet drunk,
    Sakatsuho ni   That we humans live:
Nariniteshi kamo   I'll be a winepot, and I'll soak,
Sake ni shiminamu   I'll soak all day in wine!

(598)   [347/344]

    Ana miniku   What an ugly sight!
  Sakashira o su to   Look well and tell me, has he not,
    Sake nomanu   This wise know-it-all,
  Hito o yoku miba   This prig who never touches wine,
  Saru ni ka mo niru   A face just like a monkey?

(599)   [348/345]

    Atai naki   Treasures beyond price—
  Takara to iu to mo   Yes, talk of them all you want;
    Hitotsuki no   What I say is this:
  Nigoreru sake ni   How could they be better than
  Ani masame ya mo   One cup of cloudy wine?

(600)   [349/346]

    Yoru hikaru   Gems that shine at night—
  Tama to iu to mo   Talk of such things all you want,
    Sake nomite   Could they be as rare
  Kokoro o yaru ni   As the joy of drinking wine
  Ani shikame ya mo   And letting your heart fly free?

(601)   [350/347]

    Yo no naka no   In this world of ours
  Asobi no michi ni   Along the path of pleasure
    Suzushiki wa   There's one thing, they say,
  Einaki suru ni   Sure to make you feel refreshed—
  Arubekaru rashi   It's weeping drunken tears.

(602)   [351/348]

    Kono yo ni shi   In this life at least
  Tanoshiku araba   Let me just enjoy myself,
    Komu yo ni wa   And in lives to come
  Mushi ni tori ni mo   I'll be perfectly content
  Ware wa narinamu   To be a bug, a bird.

(603)   [352/349]

    Ikeru hito   Every living man
  Tsui ni mo shinuru   Is a creature that at last
    Mono ni areba   Must come to die—
  Kono yo naru ma wa   So while I'm here in this world
  Tanoshiku o arana   I'd like to have some fun.

(604)   [353/350]

Moda orite	Not your sullen pride,
Sakashira suru wa	Nor your air of wise disdain
Sake nomite	Will ever equal
Einaki suru ni	Solace found in drinking wine
Nao shikazukeri	And weeping drunken tears.

Ōtomo no Yotsuna (active 730's–40's)

Yotsuna was Tabito's subordinate at Dazaifu in 730, but it is not clear how they were related within the Ōtomo clan. Tabito's departure for the capital in early 731 was the occasion of no. 605. The Ashiki post station, where official mounts would have been available, was four kilometers from Dazaifu, a convenient place for farewell parties. The farewell poem was a much-practiced Chinese genre, now adapted to waka, as the Japanese too began to experience the comings and goings of a Chinese-style bureaucracy. One can assume that the wine flowed, and perhaps the drunken tears.

605   [MYS IV: 574/571]

When the Governor-General of Dazaifu, Lord Ōtomo, was appointed Major Counselor and was about to leave for the capital, his officials held a farewell banquet for him at the Ashiki post station in Chikuzen Province. [One of] four poems composed on that occasion:

Tsukuyo yoshi	Tonight the moon is fair,
Kawato sayakeshi	The tinkle of the stream is clear:
Iza koko ni	Let us pause awhile,
Yuku mo yukanu mo	Those who go and those who stay,
Asobite yukamu	To seek pleasure ere we part.

The above poem is by Assistant of the Bureau of Coastal Guards Ōtomo no Yotsuna.

❋ The designation "banquet poem" (*enseki no uta*) indicates that a poem was recited at a banquet, not that it necessarily was composed on the occasion or by the person who recited it. No. 606 presupposes a pair of correspondents, probably lovers, and it is not clear what brought it forth at the party. One is reminded that Prince Hozumi liked to recite his poem about the slave called love (no. 487) on similar occasions. No doubt it was best to be prepared.

606   [MYS IV:632/629]

A banquet poem by Ōtomo no Yotsuna

Nani su to ka	What are you doing,
Tsukai no kitsuru	Sending me a messenger?
Kimi o koso	It is you yourself
Ka ni mo kaku ni mo	All these fidgets are about—
Machikateni sure	This insufferable waiting!

Koshima (poems from 731)

Koshima was a courtesan of Ōtomo no Tabito's acquaintance in Kyūshū, and it is thought that the traveler in the headnote to no. 607 was Tabito himself. Elsewhere in *Man'yōshū* she exchanges farewell poems with him on his departure for the capital (see nos. 1073–76). That Koshima and Tabito were attached to each other is evident from those poems; from this one, we can feel the young woman's fine sense of propriety and relinquishment.

607   [MYS III:384/381]

A poem sent to a traveler by a young woman of Tsukushi (her name was Koshima)

Ie omou to	Longing for your home,
Kokoro susumu na	Do not spur that eager heart;
Kazamamori	Watch the wind well,
Yoku shite imase	Go with a grave and weather eye:
Arashi sono michi	They are wild, those paths of sea.

Manzei (active 704–31)

"Manzei" was the Buddhist name taken by Kasa no Maro, a highly successful official of the Nara provincial bureaucracy when he became a sami, or Buddhist novice, to pray for the health of the dying former Empress Gemmei in 721. In his lay career he had won commendation for opening a highway through the mountains of Kiso, and in 723 he was appointed Intendant for the Construction of Kanzeonji, a large Buddhist temple near Dazaifu in Kyūshū. There he met Ōtomo no Tabito in 728 and became part of his poetic circle. In addition to the four tanka below, he composed a poem at Tabito's plum-blossom party in 730 (no. 1017) and exchanged poems with Tabito after Tabito's return to the capital (nos. 1077–80).

No. 608, dating from Manzei's time in Kyūshū, as perhaps all his extant poems do, may be nothing more than an interesting reference to a local product, the leavings from silkworm cocoons that were used to make warm padded clothing. But though the compilers of *Man'yōshū* (the chief of whom—Yakamochi—was an Ōtomo and probably knew Manzei as a boy) list this poem in the *zō*, or "miscellaneous," section of Book III, it reads very much as if it belonged to the allegorical mode (hiyuka) or to the metaphorical range of "expressing thoughts by reference to things" (*kibutsu chinshi*). Nos. 609 and 610, also by Manzei and also "referring to things," are in fact labeled hiyuka. These two are supposed to be disguised confessions of a love interest but are no more plausibly so than no. 608. The presence of young women like Koshima around Dazaifu suggests that what Manzei fantasized wearing next to his person might have been very soft and warm indeed. "Unruly spirits" translates *shiranuhi*, a somewhat obscure pillow word for Tsukushi (i.e., Kyūshū). The construction is probably *shiranu hi tsuku* ("unruly spirits possess"), introducing "Tsukushi" through its first two syllables. The sense of the epithet is not inappropriate to a lust-plagued *śrāmaṇera*.

608   [MYS III: 339/336]

A poem by Sami Manzei on the subject of silk floss (Intendant for the Construction of Kannonji in Tsukushi; lay name Kasa no Asomi Maro)

Shiranuhi	Floss from Tsukushi
Tsukushi no wata wa	Of the unruly spirits—
Mi ni tsukete	I have never yet
Imada wa kinedo	Worn it next to my body,
Atatakeku miyu	But how warm it looks to be!

❋ No. 608 is entered with a group of poems from Tabito's poetic circle at Dazaifu, including his own series on drinking *sake*. Nos. 609 and 610 are in the hiyuka section, grouped with other poems having nothing to do with Kyūshū. The fortuitous element of local reference in no. 608 may have determined the arrangement, ignoring in the process the poetically more significant question of mode. The surface meaning of no. 609 has to do with cutting down a tree set aside for boat-building. Someone has cut and removed the tree without the owner's permission. The dark conceit is that parties unknown have made off with the speaker's woman. It is not hard to see this far through the skin of the allegory. But what about "erecting the crown"? The reverent Shintō custom was to cut off the top of the felled tree and insert it into the stump as an offering to the god of the mountain. The disappointed woodsman/lover arrives on the scene and finds that his property has been removed but that a sign has been left—a sign whose proud erectness tells him that the tree-poacher has acted with exquisite deliberation, following all the sacred rites, asserting ownership by sticking a luxuriant stake into the newly opened wood. Ashigara Mountain in the

Hakone area was known for good ship timber, but this carpenter will never build his boat. The moon too is a boat, as no. 365 in the "Hitomaro Collection" diagrammatically demonstrates; in no. 610 it hesitates to launch on the sea of sky. It is late, past the middle of the lunar month, but the poet still waits. The moon is a woman, and she will come over the mountain at last, though the beached boat-builder can only gaze at her from afar.

609   [MYS III: 394/391]

A poem by Sami Manzei, Intendant for the Construction of Kanzeonji in Tsukushi

Tobusa tate	Erecting the crown,
Ashigarayama ni	On Ashigara Mountain
Funagi kiri	They cut my boat-tree,
Ki ni kiri yukitsu	They cut it down and took it off—
Atara funagi o	Oh, that precious boat-tree!

610   [MYS III: 396/393]

A poem by Manzei Sami

Miezu to mo	Though still unseen,
Tare koizarame	Who does not yearn for it?
Yama no ha ni	On the mountain crest
Isayou tsuki o	Soon the hesitant moon will rise,
Yoso ni miteshika	And, oh, for a distant glance!

❋ Manzei's finest poem is another one about a boat. Positioned after Tabito's sequence on wine, it expresses the emptiness of the world, the *yo no naka* to which Tabito's toper would cling for a few more rounds, in the telling image of a boat that rows away, its wake vanishing. The lonely, far-glimpsed boat of travel poems such as Kurohito's nos. 447 and 449 here receives an overtly symbolic treatment. The act of comparison is also overt: the poet opens the poem by asking for a true analogy and ends by stating it. The structure is thus simple, with no concealed rhetorical devices or conceits. This mode of speaking directly to the listener is responsible for the poem's effect, along with the image of the boat itself, with all the pull of its mystery. The parable is a Buddhist one, and a rebuke to Tabito's levity. It is the only Buddhist poem we have by the novice Manzei.

611   [MYS III: 354/351]

A poem by Sami Manzei

| Yo no naka o | To what |
| Nani ni tatoemu | Shall I compare the world? |

Asabiraki   It is like the wake
Kogiinishi fune no   Vanishing behind a boat
Ato naki gotoshi   That has rowed away at dawn.

Ōtomo no Momoyo (active 730's–40's)

Ōtomo no Momoyo was another clansman of Tabito's who was a subordinate during his tenure at Dazaifu. Seven of his tanka have been preserved in *Man'yōshū*. As Senior Secretary (*daiken*) at Dazaifu, Momoyo may have been close to Tabito; in any case, his poem at the famous plum-blossom party of 730 immediately follows and responds to Tabito's (nos. 1018–19). No. 612 is a quite different plum-blossom poem. Situated between Manzei's two allegories (nos. 609–10), it too says one thing and means another. The white plum blossom in the bead-black night, like Manzei's white silk floss, is a metaphor for a desired woman not possessed. Apparently she was out of reach, and so the poet "forgets" his desire. The sharpness of the disappointment is conveyed by the specificity of *sono yo* ("that night").

612   [MYS III : 395/392]

A plum poem by Senior Secretary of Dazaifu Ōtomo no Sukune Momoyo

Nubatama no   Black as a berry,
Sono yo no ume o   That night of the white plum flower;
Tawasurete   Yet I came away
Orazu kinikeri   Without breaking off a branch,
Omoishi mono o   Forgetting those blossoms of desire.

❋ The location of the following "four love poems" in Book IV suggests that they were composed during Momoyo's time at Dazaifu. Momoyo went on to occupy other official posts elsewhere into the late 740's, and so it may be proper to give an elastic interpretation to the "waves of old age" (*oinami*) in no. 613. Perhaps Momoyo indeed was, or felt himself to be, an old man, like Tabito and Okura (and Manzei?). Whether or not he was, the stance is literarily productive: the frustrated love of an old man for a younger woman lends a peculiar intensity to the meaning of *koi*. *Koi* is yearning for what one does not have, and for an old man time is running out, as stated in the second poem. He seems to be counting his days (*ikeru hi*), knowing each one will not return. The last two poems refer to beliefs of the time and shift to a lighter mood of wry self-amusement. The sacred grove of Mikasa was near Dazaifu in northern Kyūshū; its deity is invoked to witness the sincerity of the poet's love. The lady is apparently not impressed, however, since the poet is still waiting in the last poem. Scratching the eyebrows is not mentioned just as a nervous mannerism; itching eyebrows were supposed to be a sign that one was about to meet one's lover (see nos. 722 and 1409). The image of the old man is here given the twist of caricature, fooled as he is even by his own body.

613–16   [MYS IV : 562–65 / 559–62]

Four love poems by Senior Secretary of Dazaifu Ōtomo no Sukune Momoyo

(613)   [562 / 559]

    Koto mo naku
Ikikoshi mono o
    Oinami ni
Kakaru koi ni mo
Are wa aeru kamo

    Without misfortune
I have lived my life till now—
    Only as the waves
Of old age come over me
To meet such love as this.

(614)   [563 / 560]

    Koishinamu
Nochi wa nani semu
    Ikeru hi no
Tame koso imo o
Mimaku hori sure

    What good will it do
After I have yearned to death?
    It is for the days
When I still have life in me
That I would meet my love.

(615)   [564 / 561]

    Omowanu o
Omou to iwaba
    Ōno naru
Mikasa no mori no
Kami shi shirasamu

    If I do not love,
For all I say I love you,
    The god in the grove
Of Mikasa in Ōno
Will know that I have lied.

(616)   [565 / 562]

    Itoma naku
Hito no mayone o
    Itazura ni
Kakashimetsutsu mo
Awanu imo kamo

    You keep a body
Busy scratching his eyebrows,
    But all for nothing—
Here I am, in a frenzy,
But still you never meet me.

Yo no Myōgun (poems from 731)

Yo no Myōgun belonged to the royal lineage of the defunct Korean state of Paekche, which had been defeated and absorbed by its rival Silla in 663. Japan had been an ally of Paekche in the wars leading to the unification of the Korean peninsula under Silla, and the refugees from the fallen state added to the already significant Korean-derived population in Japan. Despite his royal blood, Yo no Myōgun was no more than a government orderly (*shijin*), assigned to Ōtomo no Tabito as one of Tabito's perquisites of rank and office. He was deeply devoted to Tabito and composed a series of laments in tanka form at the time of his death. No. 617 below, however, is another in the series of hiyuka in Book III, following Manzei's poem on the hesitating moon (no. 610). In Myōgun's poem it is a pine (a "little pine"—*komatsu*) that serves as metaphor for the woman. The poet has "roped off" (*shime yuite*) his pine to show ownership and seems confident of better luck than Manzei had in no. 609.

617   [MYS III : 397/394]

A poem by Yo no Myōgun

Shime yuite	That little pine
Wa ga sadameteshi	On the beach at Suminoe,
Suminoe no	The one I chose
Hama no komatsu wa	And tied with a rope around—
Nochi mo wa ga matsu	It will always be my pine.

Ahe no Hironiwa (659–732)

Ahe no Hironiwa, the son of Minister of the Right Ahe no Miushi (d. 703), followed a career of court and provincial service that took him to the position of Middle Counselor in 727. In addition to four tanka in *Man'yōshū*, he left two Chinese poems in *Kaifūsō*. No. 618 presents him as pleased enough with his current situation to wish for a long life to enjoy it. Without a context it is impossible to know which of the various contentments and pleasures that life affords *kaku shitsutsu* ("doing this") refers to. It has been suggested that the occasion might have been a drinking party, but it is equally possible that the preference is simply for life over the alternative. "Soulbound" renders the obscure pillow word *tamakiwaru*, an epithet for *inochi* ("life"), interpreting *tama* as "soul" and *kiwaru* as equivalent to *kiwamaru* ("reaches its limit").

618   [MYS VI : 980/975]

A poem by Middle Counselor Lord Ahe no Hironiwa

Kaku shitsutsu	Best of all would be
Araku o yomi zo	To go on just as I am;
Tamakiwaru	That's why I crave
Mijikaki inochi o	For this soul-bound little life
Nagaku hori suru	A length beyond its limits.

Yamanoue no Okura (660–ca. 733)

Yamanoue no Okura is the most original voice in *Man'yōshū*. This is another way of saying that unlike other major Man'yō poets, he is not a follower of Hitomaro. The ethos of land, love, death, and divine monarchy for which Hitomaro spoke and which he largely formulated seems to have haunted the minds of poets to the end of the Man'yō age and not to have been lost until the poetically obscure period extending from 759 on into the ninth century. It would be misleading to assert that Okura stands entirely outside this tradition, since he is the author of poems glorifying both the mystique of Yamato and the deeds of its rulers. But Okura does not belong to the privileged rout of poets who went to Yoshino or elsewhere with the Sovereign and composed, in however etiolated a fashion, something in the manner of Hitomaro's nos. 293–96. Nor was he, like Mushimaro, in the train of a noble patron. He does not speak his grief for a fallen capital or for a stranger fallen by the wayside. His one chōka on the death of a wife is not for his own, but for his friend Tabito's, a substitute-poem (*daisaku*). Fundamentally, Okura breaks away from the harmonious vision of Hitomaro in his most significant work, substituting a critical and fragmenting social conscience and pessimism for the tragic acceptance of divine mystery in the earlier poet.

Hitomaro's intellectual formation, like the man himself, is obscured by his very universality; half-mythic, he blends into the world of his poems. Okura, a nearly exact contemporary who lived on into the Nara age, is another matter. That he was an educated man, which is to say, well read in Chinese books, is only too apparent from the insistent name-dropping allusions in his kambun writings. Okura's great adventure was not going to Yoshino or far Iwami, or climbing Tsukuha, but making the perilous and momentous passage to T'ang China. When he was selected as a member of the official embassy of 701 he was already in his forties; in order to have been chosen, he must have been known as something of an erudite. Okura's early life is obscure, but recent research has led to the conclusion that his origins were Korean, that he was in fact born in Paekche, Japan's ally on the Korean peninsula, and was brought to Japan in the wave of refugees that came when that state was extinguished by its rival Silla in 663. Okura would have been in his fourth year. His father, a doctor who entered the service of the Japanese court, no doubt provided his son with a thorough Chinese-style education. This education is amply evident in Okura's surviving work, but his putative foreign origins are not. When he speaks of his adopted country he seems to speak as a native son.

When Okura returned from China in 707 his official career at last got under way. He attained Junior Fifth Rank, Lower Grade, in 714 and was given an appointment as Tutor to the Crown Prince (later Emperor Shōmu) in 721. But poetically the most memorable period of his life came at the end.

He was appointed Governor of Chikuzen Province in northern Kyūshū about 728 and became part of Ōtomo no Tabito's circle during Tabito's incumbency at Dazaifu (728–30). Okura is known mostly through his literary production during his Kyūshū years and after his return to Nara, where he died probably in 733. Tabito and Okura seem to have been cronies in the manner of Chinese literati, or later of Ōtomo no Yakamochi and his cousin Ikenushi (see nos. 1174–1221). Both Okura and Tabito are poets of old age, and both delight in displaying their literary sophistication through learned Chinese references. But there is little doubt that Okura was the more creative of the two, as well as the more learned. Partly because of their close literary involvement, there is considerable controversy over the authorship of certain items, but Okura's mastery of the chōka is indisputable, whereas Tabito's is questionable. The most generous count credits Okura with twelve chōka (to Tabito's one), sixty-nine tanka (of which twenty-eight are envoys), two kanshi, and twelve extended pieces of Chinese prose. Okura's activity as a literary man also included the compilation of a waka anthology, *Ruijū Karin* (*Classified Forest of Poetry*). This book unfortunately has not survived, but it is quoted frequently in the compilers' notes in *Man'yōshū*. It is quite plausible that Okura exerted a great influence on his friend's young son Yakamochi (who himself played the Chinese literatus on occasion), an influence to which we may owe the existence of *Man'yōshū* itself.

The following tanka, one of the earliest poems by Okura to have been preserved, is atypical of most of his known work in its youthful vigor and headlong rhythms and in its feeling of hope. It is an irony that the Man'yō poet most devoted to Chinese studies should be introduced by a poem composed in China expressing an urgent desire to go home to Japan. The verse can be compared with another poem allegedly composed in China, that attributed to Ahe no Nakamaro (no. 697). Nakamaro's melancholy and homesickness contrast with Okura's call for action. For Okura, it is the pines in Japan that are "pining" for the return of the embassy. Whether other poems from Okura's forties or earlier would have shown these qualities is a question that cannot now be answered. Okura's clan title Omi, the sixth in Emperor Temmu's reorganized list, implies an ancient lineage stemming ultimately from the Japanese imperial family. The newly arrived immigrants often tried in this way to graft their way onto prestigious family trees. The name Yamanoue ("On the Mountain") may have come from the location of property granted to Okura's father. The Ōtomo district of seacoast at the head of the Inland Sea was the location of Mitsu, the royal port from which the envoys had departed (i.e., the port of Naniwa).

619   [MYS I:63]

A poem composed by Yamanoue no Omi Okura when he was in Great T'ang and thought of his homeland

Iza kodomo	Quick, boys,
Hayaku Yamato e	Let's set out for Yamato!
Ōtomo no	The pines on the shore
Mitsu no hamamatsu	At Mitsu of Ōtomo
Machikoinuramu	Must long for our return.

✳ It was during Okura's lifetime that the Chinese topos of the seventh night meeting of the lover stars Herdsman and Weaving Maid was introduced to Japan (see commentary to no. 398). The myth inspired countless poems over the centuries. Nos. 620–23 are four tanka from a group of twelve poems (one of which is a chōka) that Okura composed on the topic over a period of several years. They show him practicing within a set convention, and very capably, too, even though the romantic story on which he embroiders his variations was hardly in his usual vein. This capability may be taken as evidence of Okura's professionalism, his ability to write from the mind as well as the heart (so put, hardly a distinction he would have understood). But this said, there remains an erotic element in some of the poems that is there by the poet's choice, and that suggests a willingness to respond to his theme with a more than intellectual appreciation of its possibilities.

The first of the twelve poems, no. 620, is an example. This utterance of the Weaving Maid is an explicitly sexual handling of the theme: instead of running down to the edge of the River of Heaven (the Milky Way) to greet her lover, as in no. 622, she seems to be running to her bed. It must be remembered that Okura and other Nara "literati" regarded the elegantly pornographic Chinese poem-tale *Yu-hsien-k'u* (*Journey to the Cave of Immortals*) by their contemporary Chang Wen-ch'eng (ca. 657–730) as a classic to be quoted in their ornate kambun pastiches, though they left nothing remotely approaching its salaciousness. (This book was snapped up and brought back to Japan probably about the time of Okura's visit to China.) The frankly amorous declarations and sensuous images of the early Japanese love tradition were no doubt validated by the example of the more "explicit" though highly metaphorical approach to love making in *Yu-hsien-k'u*.

The command in response to which no. 620 was composed was presumably issued by Emperor Shōmu, who had succeeded to the throne earlier in the year (724). Okura had been tutor to Shōmu as Crown Prince since 721. The other three poems (nos. 621–23) form a sequence. The first and third provide evidence, in the "reasoning" manner learned from Six Dynasties Chinese poetry, of the Herdsman's departure across the Milky Way, the first in the form of a conceit lodged in the perception of the earth-bound observer (spray from the Herdsman's oars makes a mist), and the third as perceived by the Weaving Maid. These frame the middle poem, where the direct statement of action is concentrated. Here too there is an element of the erotic in the "wet skirts."

620–23 [MYS VIII: 1522/1518, 1531–33/1527–29]
[Four of] twelve poems of Yamanoue no Omi Okura on Seventh Night

(620) [1522/1518]

Amanogawa	We gazed at each other
Aimukitachite	Across the River in the Sky,
Wa ga koishi	And I yearned for him,
Kimi kimasu nari	The lord whose coming I can hear—
Himo tokimakena	I'll loosen my sash and make ready.

The above was composed in response to command on the seventh day of the seventh month of Yōrō 8 (724).

(621) [1531/1527]

Hikohoshi no	The Herdsman Star
Tsumamukaebune	Must now be rowing in the boat
Kogizu rashi	That takes him to his wife:
Ama no kawara ni	A mist has risen on the shores
Kiri no tateru wa	Of the River in the Sky.

(622) [1532/1528]

Kasumi tatsu	While I wait my lord
Ama no kawara ni	On the shores of the haze-enshrouded
Kimi matsu to	River in the Sky,
Ikayou hoto ni	My steps keep seeking the water's edge
Mo no suso nurenu	Until my skirts are wet along the hem.

(623) [1533/1529]

Amanogawa	The sound of waves
Ukitsu no namito	Slapping against the dock is borne across
Sawaku nari	The River in the Sky:
Wa ga matsu kimi shi	My long-awaited lord must now
Funade su rashi mo	Have launched his boat upon the stream.

✳ No. 624–25 relates more centrally to the main thrust of Okura's work. The sardonic realist, defender of family values and foe of fools and their pride, is much in evidence. This is the Okura schooled in Confucian ethics and ready to expound them to a world in need of correction. What we have here is in fact Okura's preachiest poem. No doubt Master Spurn-the-World (Baizoku Sensei) is a mere construct, a straw dog to beat in order to make a point. The placement of the poem in Book v shows it to be a product of Okura's term as Governor of Chikuzen, and some have suggested that in it he speaks in the role of moral instructor to the province. It is worth noting that the earthy images and down-to-earth advice that give the poem its pungency are combined with an appeal to the sanction of the divine land and sovereign. Here Okura is creating a Shintō-Confucian amalgam, looking ahead to dual elements in the development of Japanese ethics. He is also creating a new literary form, the highly polished Chinese prose preface followed by one or more poems in Japanese (or sometimes Chinese). The challenge of versatility, of showing brilliance in two languages and in widely differing literary forms, must underlie this development. It later attracted Yakamochi and Ikenushi as well, Okura's main followers in *Man'yōshū*. There was also the precedent of the chronicles and fudoki, with their song texts embedded in prose narrative.

Okura's originality is shown again in the experimental structure of the chōka. No. 624 is a tripartite poem, three times culminating in couplets of long lines. The first part of the poem, through line 9, is a statement of the theme of domestic love and responsibility; the second part, through line 16, introduces the figure of the malfeasant; and the last part gives the grand framework for the practical advice in the envoy. The preface and the poem are well integrated in tone and imagery, despite the linguistic difference. The whole composition amounts to a Confucian attack on Taoist (and Buddhist) pretensions to superiority through noninvolvement or withdrawal, and makes interesting reading in connection with Tabito's series on drinking wine (nos. 592–604), with its sneers at those who "prate with false display of wisdom." This is not to suggest that Tabito was the model for Master Spurn-the-World, or Okura for the abstainer with a face like a monkey, but there is a savor to the conjecture that the two old gentlemen may have been aware of the nice contrast in philosophical positions adopted in their respective poems.

The "Three Bonds" were those between ruler and subject, father and son, and husband and wife; the "Five Teachings," another Confucian term, stipulate that the father should be righteous, the mother compassionate, the elder brother friendly, the younger brother obedient, and the child filial. The reference to "absconding into the hills and marshes" probably refers to peasants who abandoned their fields to seek a freer life on the fringes of cultivation. The first nine lines of the chōka sum up Okura's mature understanding of the human condition. Love is balanced by anxiety and care, but this is *kotowari* ("in accord with nature"). We are trapped in our humanity like birds in birdlime. Not a happy vision, but an honest one. We must accept what we are, for there is no escape. Okura says this in one way or another in poem after poem, and the bird is a favorite image. The bird is the image of freedom from worldly restraints, but "we are not birds" (no. 635). Master Spurn-the-World thinks he is a bird, and his pride "soars above the blue clouds." But he is like the rest of us, trapped in the human dimension. The simile of the cast-off shoe has been traced back through *Wen-hsüan* to *Shih Chi*, a Chinese history dating from the first century B.C. "Heaven" in the last section of the chōka and the envoy resonates with the image of the bird and probably stands more for a Taoist otherworld than for the native realm of the high gods. For the "wandering toad," see no. 581 by Mushimaro.

624–25   [MYS V : 804–805 / 800–801]

A poem to correct a straying heart; with preface

There is a certain person who, knowing that he should respect his parents, yet forgets to care for them; who gives no thought to his wife and children, treating them with less regard than a cast-off shoe. He calls himself Master Spurn-the-World. His pride soars above the blue clouds, but his body remains in the dust. There is no evidence of his being a sage who has attained the Way through practice of austerities; perhaps he is a commoner who has absconded into the hills and marshes. It devolves upon me to point out the Three Bonds and to give further instruction in the Five Teachings. I impart them with a poem, in order to turn him back from his delusion. The poem goes:

	Chichi haha o	Father and mother
	Mireba tōtoshi	Are reverend to look upon.
	Me ko mireba	To look on wife and child
	Megushi utsukushi	Stings the heart, brings anxious love.
5	Yo no naka wa	For life to be thus
	Kaku zo kotowari	Is in accord with nature.
	Mochidori no	Like birds caught in lime
	Kakarahashi mo yo	We are stuck fast with no escape,
	Yukue shiraneba	For we know not where to go.
10	Ukegutsu o	Like a worn-out shoe,
	Nukitsuru gotoku	Gaping holes and cast aside,
	Fuminukite	He casts them away
	Yuku chū hito wa	And turns to go: that man,
	Iwaki yori	Was it from stone or wood
15	Narideshi hito ka	That he came forth into the world?
	Na ga na norasane	Be so good as to speak your name!
	Ame e yukaba	If you go to heaven
	Na ga manimani	All will be as you wish,
	Tsuchi naraba	But if here on earth

20 Ōkimi imasu	Our great lord is in command.
Kono terasu	Here beneath the light
Hi tsuki no shita wa	Of the shining sun and moon,
Amakumo no	Far as the borders
Mukabusu kiwami	Where heaven clouds touch the ground,
25 Taniguku no	Far as the borders
Sawataru kiwami	Reached by the wandering toad,
Kikoshiosu	Our Sovereign's realm
Kuni no mahora zo	Stretches in its majesty.
Ka ni kaku ni	In each and every way
30 Hoshiki manimani	You live by your selfish will.
Shika ni wa araji ka	Is it not as I have said?

Envoy

Hisakata no	Far is the road
Amaji wa tōshi	To the shining land of heaven;
Naonao ni	Now the thing for you
Ie ni kaerite	Is quietly to go back home
Nari o shimasani	And tend the planting of your fields.

❈ If Okura's several references to his children are to be understood biographically rather than merely as explorations of the theme of parental love, one must conclude that he had a young wife or concubine in his old age. The children are always young—crying, fretful, playful, painfully loved. The following tanka is grouped with other poems of the Dazaifu circle and must have been composed when Okura was about seventy. Amusingly enough, it immediately precedes Tabito's sequence on *sake*. In this poem Okura's voice emerges as that of the crotchety old man, a loyal husband and loving father whose vision of domesticity is completely at ease with quotidian reality. One can almost see him heave himself erect and go, leaving his host (Tabito?) to discourse on the virtues of wine. The use of a personal name to refer to oneself is a humble convention. It is impossible to say how many children Okura had; in other poems there seem to be more than one, and here too *ko* ("child") may be plural. This banquet poem of Okura's old age shares the spontaneity of his home-thoughts-from-abroad tanka (no. 619). Both speak of going home to something or someone who is waiting. But in no. 626 the poet "withdraws" (*makaramu*), and the flat-footed insistence of the repeated *ramu* conveys not exuberance, but a weary recognition of responsibilities and routines. The distances have shortened, the scope has narrowed from a homeland to a specific home, and the speed has slowed from *hayaku* ("quickly") to the hobble of an elderly man.

626   [MYS III: 340/337]

A poem by Yamanoue no Okura Omi on leaving a banquet

> Okurara wa   This time Okura
> Ima wa makaramu   Really must excuse himself;
> Ko nakuramu   His child is crying,
> Sore sono haha mo   Yes, and its mother is waiting—
> Wa o matsuramu so   Of that he's pretty sure.

✳ Okura's love for his children is the tenderest side of his character as revealed in his poetry. In no. 627–28 he takes up the theme of parental love in
a Buddhist rather than Confucian framework. Once again he uses the format of a Chinese preface followed by a chōka and envoy. The preface refers
to the son, Rāhula, fathered by Śākyamuni while still in secular life, and
alludes to scriptural passages in which this human tie is made the standard
for the Buddha's love for all humanity. This brief and touching preface is of
particular interest as evidence of Okura's familiarity with the Buddhist as
well as the Confucian canon. But more is involved in his appeal to a Buddhist sanction for family love. Okura's vision of the human condition as
a trap from which we cannot (must not try to) escape, revealed in no.
624–25, conforms with the ironic realization that the sage of all sages could
not free himself from the same snare. The Buddha here is not the Enlightened One, but the father caught—like us—in an ineluctable human
bond. The paradox might be capable of resolution in the infinite regress of
Buddhist dialectic, but Okura has no interest in that. Here is the essence of
his irony: the warmest human relations are filled with the most pain. Pain
can be struck at the root in Buddhist teaching by realizing its source in attachment. But the Buddha himself was the victim of the same attachment.
To try to break free is contrary to nature and doomed to failure: we are condemned to a love that is our burden and the definition of our humanity. The
"golden mouth" of Śākyamuni Tathāgata (Shaka Nyorai, the "Thus Come")
is a reference to both the excellence of his doctrine and the golden color that
was a sign of his Buddhahood. "Green grass of the world" renders *yo no
naka no aohitokusa*. *Aohitokusa* ("green human grass") is a term for the human species found in *Kojiki* and *Nihonshoki*.

The nine-line chōka is a quiet cry, appealing in its imagery and stylistic
simplicity, one of the most accessible expressions of love in the language.
The images of fruit and nuts may have been suggested by a poem of T'ao
Ch'ien (A.D. 365–427), the great Chinese poet of reclusion, with whose
work Okura was undoubtedly familiar. They lend Okura's chōka the savor
of a sorrow that gathers in the mouth, juicy like tears, gritty like sand, sweet
and flavorsome and impossible to forget. The old man is a child, eating mel-

ons, eating chestnuts, swallowing his grief with each bite. The unusual rhyming lines, *uri hameba . . . kuri hameba*, strengthen the childlike effect. Of course he is remembering his children eating these foods they loved. The verbs *omōyu* ("come to mind") and *shinuhayu* ("long") show that the children are not there. There has been a separation of parent and child, though whether in life or death is not made clear. But the children are with the speaker of the poem in his dreams. True to the troublesome nature of children, they keep him from his sleep. The envoy sums up the lesson of the entire composition. It has been pointed out that "silver, gold, and jewels" are meant to contrast with the humble melons and chestnuts of the chōka. They are also among the "Seven Precious Things" (*nanakusa no takara*) of Buddhist scripture Okura mentions in the next poem, and hence round out the composition with another Buddhist reference. Once more, compare this envoy with Tabito's poems on wine, nos. 599 and 600.

627–28   [MYS V: 806–7/802–3]

A poem of longing for his children; with preface

> Shaka Nyorai preached truly with his golden mouth that he had equal compassion for all beings, even as for Rāhula. He also preached that there is no love surpassing that for a child. The greatest sage still had the feeling of love for his child. Who then of the green grass of the world would not love his children?

Uri hameba	When I eat melons
Kodomo omōyu	My children come to my mind;
Kuri hameba	When I eat chestnuts
Mashite shinuhayu	The longing is even worse.
Izuku yori	Where do they come from,
Kitarishi mono so	Flickering before my eyes,
Manakai ni	Making me helpless
Motona kakarite	Incessantly night after night,
Yasui shi nasanu	Not letting me sleep in peace?

Envoy

Shirogane mo	What are they to me,
Kugane mo tama mo	Silver, or gold, or jewels?
Nani semu ni	How could they ever
Masareru takara	Equal the greater treasure
Ko ni shikame ya mo	That is a child?

❋ At the end of Book V, a section heavily dominated by the compositions of Yamanoue no Okura, appears an elegy for a dead child. Consisting of a chōka and two envoys, it is followed by a note indicating that the authorship is unknown, but that the work is included where it is because of its similarity to Okura's style. One opinion holds that the note refers to the entire chōka-hanka set, another that it refers only to the second envoy. The elegy is included here on the assumption that Okura wrote all three parts of it, and that it is his most intense statement of the theme of parental love.

The question of whether the child was Okura's own has been much debated. Okura died in his early seventies, and most of his extant compositions, both prose and poetry, are from the last five years of his life. This material refers again and again to young children. It may justifiably be felt that the elegy poses no more of a problem in this regard than the other references, such as those in nos. 626 and 627–28. Despite the ill health of which he complained, it is not impossible that Okura fathered one or more children in his sixties. On the other hand, Okura shows an obvious interest in treating generalized social topics and is known to have composed daisaku, poems (or prose) in which he speaks for someone else. He did this for Tabito on occasion, and the "Ten Songs of the Seafolk of Shika" (nos. 648–57) are an example of his treatment in semifictionalized fashion of a local event. The name of the dead child in nos. 629–31 is Furuhi. Research has shown this to be an unusual name for a boy, a son of a courtier, in the early Nara period. It has been suggested that Furuhi was the child of local people in Chikuzen, the province Okura governed in northern Kyūshū. The undeniable intensity and immediacy of the poem would be due to Okura thinking back to a similar event earlier in his own life. Such a double-image theory is of course sheer speculation.

The chōka opens with a rhetorical question and comparison echoing the envoy in no. 627–28. This passage takes the place of the formal introductions Hitomaro developed out of the archaic preparation-conclusion structure, but its referent is Buddhist (i.e., foreign rather than native). There are various lists of "Seven Precious Things" in different scriptures. In the *Lotus Sutra* they are gold, silver, lapis lazuli, giant clam shell, agate, pearl, and carnelian. This time the child is made into a treasure similar in kind but by implication more precious, a single white pearl whose radiance is the counterpart on earth of the glowing grain of the morning and evening star mentioned in the next part of the poem. The poem is based on a structure of value destroyed, expectations defeated, and in this it is similar to Hitomaro's laments on nuptial love and death. Okura uses the formula *ōbune no omoitanomu ni* ("confident as they who trust in a great ship," basically the same as Hitomaro's in no. 345, lines 13–14). But Okura, a realist, incorporates more of the homely detail of life. In a unique passage his child speaks directly to its parents, urging them to let him make with them a *sakikusa*, a three-stalked plant. Hitomaro's vision is of lovers lying together, sinuous and yielding like strands of waterweed. Okura alters the metaphor to include the child. It is the difference between two kinds of love, both physical, but one primarily sexual and romantic, and the other domestic and affectionate. With Hitomaro (no. 348) the child is an afterthought, a katami. For Okura, it is the center, the value of all values. The endearing words of the child are what "grow faint and few" when, after line 33, misfortune suddenly strikes. They are replaced by the useless words of the father, whose prayers to the gods are in vain.

The gentle ways of the child and parents contrast with the increasingly frenetic action in the last part of the poem. The child dies quietly, but the father is thrown into paroxysms of grief, as if he were the one undergoing the death agonies, the *shinimonogurui*. Again comparisons and contrasts with Hitomaro come to mind. Hitomaro finds oblique and symbolic ways to speak of death, which is always laden with mystery. Okura, whose father was a doctor, and who was much concerned with his own ill health, describes the progress of the child's disease in spare and telling phrases. But for Okura, as for Hitomaro and other poets and singers of this early period, the soul is something that flies away at the end. The image is of an escaped bird. Then there is nothing left but for the poet to make the final exclamation, *yo no naka no michi*, a bitter realization that "the way of the world" (in which we are ensnared like birds in lime) provides freedom only for the dead. But this resolution too is undercut by the anxious envoys. The soul is no longer a free-flying bird, but a child again, one bound for "the realms below" (*shitahe*). The father will pay for his safe conduct. The indeterminacy of the ancient Japanese concept of the afterlife is further indicated in the second envoy (whose authorship is uncertain). Now the path leads upward into heaven, but still a guide is necessary. There is an irony in the "beseeching prayer," since such petitions have been useless in saving the child's life.

629–31 [MYS v:909–11/904–6]

Three poems of yearning for his son named Furuhi: one *chōka*, two *tanka*

Yo no hito no	As for the treasures,
Tōtobinegau	The precious things of seven kinds,
Nanakusa no	Reverenced and craved
Takara mo ware wa	By all the people of the world,
5 Nani semu ni	What are they to me?
Wa ga naka no	Our treasure was
Umareidetaru	Our son Furuhi, the white lustrous pearl
Shiratama no	Born of our love,
A ga ko Furuhi wa	Who on mornings when at dawn
10 Akaboshi no	The bright star hung
Akuru ashita wa	Upon the brightening sky,
Shikitae no	Would stay with us
Toko no he sarazu	Beneath the covers of our bed,

	Tateredo mo	And whether we stood
15	Oredo mo	Or sat to rest
	Tomo ni tawabure	Frolicked with us all the day.
	Yūtsuzu no	Then when evening
	Yūhe ni nareba	And the evening star drew on,
	Iza neyo to	"Come on, go to bed,"
20	Te o tazusawari	He urged us, pulling us by the hand.
	Chichi haha mo	"Father and Mother,
	Ue wa na sakari	Don't go away from me,
	Sakikusa no	I'll sleep between,
	Naka ni o nemu to	We'll be stalks of splitty-grass."
25	Utsukushiku	Sweet were his ways
	Shi ga kataraeba	As he chattered on to us.
	Itsu shi ka mo	For the day to come
	Hito to nariidete	When he would grow into a man
	Ashikeku mo	And we might see
30	Yokeku mo mimu to	Full-formed his character for good or ill
	Ōbune no	We waited, confident
	Omoitanomu ni	As they who trust to a great ship.
	Omowanu ni	Then suddenly
	Yokoshimakaze no	An ill wind blew athwart our lives,
35	Nifufuka ni	A baneful blast
	Ōikinureba	Overtook us, unprepared.
	Semu sube no	What could I do?
	Tadoki o shirani	Not knowing where to reach for help,
	Shirotae no	I bound my sleeves,
40	Tasuki o kake	My white barken sleeves with cords,
	Masokagami	And in my hands
	Te ni torimochite	Grasping our round cloudless mirror,
	Ama tsu kami	To the gods of heaven
	Aogikoinomi	I raised my voice in beseeching prayer,
45	Kuni tsu kami	And to the gods of earth
	Fushite nukatsuki	I bowed and pressed my brow into the dust.
	Kakarazu mo	"To save him from this fate,
	Kakari mo	Or let him die—
	Kami no manimani to	It lies within the pleasure of the gods."
50	Tachiazari	With distracted steps
	Ware koinomedo	I wandered in beseeching prayer,
	Shimashiku mo	But all in vain—
	Yokeku wa nashi ni	Not for a moment did his body mend,
	Yakuyaku ni	While inexorably
55	Katachi kuzuhori	A cruel devastation ravaged his sweet face.
	Asana asana	Morning by morning

Iu koto yami	His utterances grew faint and few;
Tamakiwaru	At last, his soul flown free,
Inochi taenure	Life ebbed, dwindled, and was gone.
60 Tachiodori	I leaped into the air
Ashisuri sakebi	And stamped upon the ground. I cried aloud.
Fushiaogi	Falling to the earth, I gazed aloft.
Mune uchi nageki	I beat my breast now wracked with sobs.
Te ni moteru	The child I held in my arms,
65 A ga ko tobashitsu	I have let him go like a bird in flight.
Yo no naka no michi	This too is the way of the world.

Envoys

Wakakereba	Young as he is,
Michi yukishiraji	He can hardly know the way:
Mai wa semu	I'll bribe you well,
Shitahe no tsukai	Messenger from the realms below,
Oite tōrase	Carry him safely on your back.

Fuse okite	First my offering,
Are wa koinomu	Now I make beseeching prayer:
Azamukazu	Practice no deceit,
Tada ni iyukite	Take him straight and teach him true
Amaji shirashime	The road that leads to heaven.

The author of the above poem is not known for certain. However, we include it here in view of its stylistic resemblance to the manner of Yamanoue.

✳ Okura's most sweeping comment on the human condition comes in no. 632–33, a poem that culminates a series opening Book v. "A Poem to Correct a Straying Heart" (no. 624–25) and "A Poem of Longing for His Children" (no. 627–28) are in the same series. If the note following no. 633 refers to the entire series, as is thought, we should infer that Okura made his final version of all the poems on the date mentioned, not that he composed several of his major chōka and prefaces in one day. The question of "final versions" of waka is always problematical, however. No. 632 in particular shows ample evidence of variant lines, a common phenomenon in Man'yō chōka. In this instance the translation incorporates them, in brackets, as an enrichment of the poem.

The kambun preface, composed in the usual Six Dynasties style of balanced prose, lays out the theme to be elaborated in the poem: the difficulty of life in this world. The Eight Great Pains enumerated in *Mahāparinirvāna Sūtra* are those of birth, old age, illness, death, being unable to obtain what one seeks, parting from a loved one, meeting someone one hates, and the pains of the Five Skandhas, the physical and mental components of a human being. The two colors of hair are black and white, the mingling of which is a sign of advancing age.

The chōka is schematically structured, with a (re) statement of the theme in lines 1–8, sections on young women (lines 9–19) and their aging (lines 23–35), young men (lines 38–47), young men visiting young women as lovers (lines 50–55), and men in their old age (lines 58–63). The various sections are concluded with generalizing comments, in lines 20–22, 36–37, 48–49, 56–57, and 64–65, and the whole chōka has its summation in lines 66–68. The envoy provides still another statement of the theme, placing the image of a great, unchanging rock, with which the poet seeks to identify himself, amid the flood of time mentioned in lines 3 and 4 of the chōka. Here life is like a stream sweeping all before it; instead of struggling to be free, man fights merely to stand still, but always in vain. The various ages of man are given even more detailed treatment in an anonymous chōka, no. 1528, that reads like a parody of Okura's manner. The old man who speaks that poem stubbornly insists that old men should be treated with respect. Here Okura observes bitterly that they are not. He sighs again and again that this is the way of the world. But the aging Confucian reveals something in this poem about his own preferences: he too would rather be young. Old age is a miserable time, and he makes no suggestion that it is anything but natural that the old are treated with scorn. His evocation of youthful beauty and ardor, culminating in the passage on lovers' trysts that echoes the amorous songs of the chronicles, has preempted the poem, and the stance is very different from the strict moralism of "A Poem to Correct a Straying Heart."

632–33   [MYS V: 808–9/804–5]

A poem lamenting the difficulty of life in this world; with preface

> What gather easily but are hard to disperse are the Eight Great Pains; what are hard to gain and easy to lose are the praise and pleasures of a hundred years. These facts were lamented by men of old, and now it is still the same. And so by writing one poetic composition I dispel the sorrows of the two [colors of] hair. The poem goes:

	Yo no naka no	In the world of man
	Sube naki mono wa	There are things beyond our strength:
	Toshitsuki wa	The years and months
	Nagaruru gotoshi	Flow past in an unending stream,
5	Toritsutsuki	And in their wake,
	Oikuru mono wa	One upon another without rest,
	Momokusa ni	Come flooding ills
	Semeyorikitaru	Of many kinds in grim assault.
	Otomera ga	Little maidens,

10 Otome sabisu to	In the manner of young maids everywhere,
Karatama o	Wind their wrists about
Tamoto ni makashi	With costly gems from foreign lands,
[Shirotae no	[Wave back and forth
Sode furikawashi	Their sleeves of fine white barken cloth,
15 Kurenai no	Trail along the ground
Akamo susobiki]	The hems of their scarlet skirts,]
Yochikora to	And joining hand in hand
Te tazusawarite	With other children of their age,
Asobikemu	Go out to play;
20 Toki no sakari o	But the glory of this blossom time
Todomikane	Cannot be made to stay,
Sugushiyaritsure	And when the years are gone, the time is spent,
Mina no wata	Upon the locks that glistened
Kaguroki kami ni	Black as the gut of the *mina* snail,
25 Itsu no ma ka	In an unknown hour
Shimo no furikemu	A winter of white frost descends;
Kurenai no	And to those faces
[Ni no ho nasu]	That glowed with a fair crimson flush,
Omote no ue ni	[As ruddy as the rice in ear,]
30 Izuku yu ka	No one can say whence,
Shiwa ga kitarishi	The wrinkles of old age have come.
[Tsune narishi	[The accustomed smiles,
Emai mayobiki	The lovely long-drawn eyebrows,
Saku hana no	As with flowers in bloom,
35 Utsuroinikeri	Wither and are gone.
Yo no naka wa	Thus ever
Kaku nomi narashi]	Seems to be the world of man.]
Masurao no	And the brave young men,
Otoko sabisu to	Displaying all their manly valor,
40 Tsurugitachi	Take their long, straight swords
Koshi ni torihaki	And belt them tight about their hips,
Satsuyumi o	Take their hunting bows
Tanigirimochite	And grip them fiercely in their hands,
Akagoma ni	On their red-roan steeds
45 Shitsukura uchioki	Throw saddles of homespun cloth,
Hainorite	Scramble on their mounts,
Asobiarukishi	And sally forth to sport:
Yo no naka ya	But is there aught
Tsune ni arikeru	Of constancy in the world of man?
50 Otomera ga	The youths push open
Sanasu itato o	Wooden doors to where the maidens lie
Oshihiraki	In waiting sleep;

Itadoriyorite	Slowly they grope closer in the dark,
Matamade no	Till jewel-like arms outstretched
55 Tamade sashikae	Meet precious arms in close embrace;
Saneshi yo no	But the nights are few
Ikuda mo araneba	Young lovers sleep in such delight.
Tatsukazue	Soon their hands will clutch
Koshi ni taganete	A cane pressed close to their tottering hips;
60 Ka yukeba	When they come hither
Hito ni itowae	They will be shunned with bitter scorn;
Kaku yukeba	When they go thither
Hito ni nikumae	They will meet with loathing hate.
Oyoshio wa	The aged ones
65 Kaku nomi narashi	Seem ever to be treated thus.
Tamakiwaru	Precious it is,
Inochi oshikedo	Life wherein the spirit dwells,
Semu sube mo nashi	But these are things beyond our strength.

Envoy

Tokiwa nasu	Changeless as stone,
Kaku shi mogamo to	Thus would I be forever,
Omoedo mo	Had I my desire,
Yo no koto nareba	But since this is the world of man
Todomikanetsu mo	There is no way to hold it fast.

Completed on Jinki 5 [728].7.21 in Kama District.—Governor of
Chikuzen Province Yamanoue no Okura

❃ With Okura Japanese poetry begins to develop themes outside its traditional trinity of love, death, and divinity. A poetry of family life and social concern becomes possible. Tabito's experiment with the theme of release through intoxication is trivial when compared with the series of major chōka in which his friend Okura staked out new ground. But even within the century-long tradition of Man'yō poetry, Okura had few followers; when that tradition collapsed in the late eighth century, his accomplishment was doubly lost. There was no personal collection to preserve his name and fame in later times, in however diluted and unreliable a fashion, as there was for Hitomaro, Akahito, and Yakamochi. To the extent that Okura's social themes were dealt with by later poets, they were dealt with in kanshi, poetry in the Chinese language. Okura's Chinese education made him aware that the hardships of the common people were a legitimate poetic theme. He also knew that as a Governor the welfare of the inhabitants of his province was his responsibility. He must also have been familiar with the Chinese tradition of retirement into poverty by a government official, one powerfully enunciated as a poetic stance by T'ao Ch'ien three hundred years earlier. Okura's genius was that he was able to recast such thematic materials into Japanese, and it was out of them that he created his most brilliant and bitter poem.

"A Dialogue on Poverty" (no. 634–35) is two poems in one, with a final comment in the form of an envoy. The first speaker is the Poor Man, represented by the character *bin* in the title *Bingū Mondō*; he is answered by the Destitute Man (*gū*). The translation follows Brower and Miner in inserting the names of the speakers. The Poor Man is probably Okura himself (on his claim of straitened circumstances, see nos. 643 and 644), now retired from his governorship and without adequate resources. Poor, proud, and irascible: one feels that the man in the portrait is Okura to the life. On a cold night he warms himself with drink, but instead of "weeping drunken tears" he sniffles as his nose begins to run. The homely touch is typical of Okura and seems like a parody of his late friend Tabito. Even his attempt at self-importance is defeated by the undeniable cold, but instead of indulging in further self-pity, he turns his thoughts to those who have even less. It is the gesture of the poor scholar toward the destitute farmer.

The last thirteen lines of this part of the poem are taken up with conjecturing the miseries of the lower class. And the conjectures turn out to be quite accurate. But Okura's Destitute Man, the speaker of the second part of the poem, is no ordinary peasant. He is far more eloquent than the Poor Man and devoid of his wry humor. Instead of sodden nights for an opening, we are given a vision of the splendors of heaven and earth that are denied to the highly self-aware, desperate, and angry human being of these lines. Okura has dropped his realism here in favor of creating a mouthpiece for his own outrage. He can be amused at himself but not at the plight of the starving. The detail is grim enough, but charged with poetic power. Hitomaro's favorite image of sexual love, the sinuous, caressing seaweed, is here a simile for rotten shreds of clothing, tattered and oozing clammy moisture, which are all the Destitute Man has to wear—the remains of a sleeveless frock, of which the Poor Man seems to have so many. Starvation is at hand—the family is moaning with hunger. The Poor Man is alone, but the Destitute Man has parents and progeny, is in the midst of the struggle for life. The masterstroke is the image of the spiderweb in the rice pot—it says all. But Okura is not content to let the family simply starve or freeze. He brings on the village boss, in charge of recruiting for corvée labor. This man has a whip and is the representative of authority. These lines are the most subversive in *Man'yōshū*. The strong Chinese tradition of sympathy for the oppressed lies behind them, but they must have caused the former Governor some reflection.

The poem ends with the same line uttered by the father of Furuhi (no. 629–31)—*yo no naka no michi*. With it Okura comes back to his basic stance: we are helpless to alter things. Rage and grief are equally futile. This is

Okura's acceptance—not of a numinous, mysterious whole as in Hitomaro, but of a flawed and bitter reality. Okura was no revolutionary, but he insisted on seeing life straight on. The envoy brings in shame and frustration, to endure as best he can. These final five lines seem to be spoken by a third voice, one that sums up the lessons of the dialogue. A final note indicates that Okura presented this composition to someone. It has been suggested that the recipient was Tajihi no Agatamori (668–737), an official whose career closely paralleled Okura's, and who in 731 and again in 732 received appointments that took him to western Japan in a supervisory capacity. Okura, who had served as Governor in those regions, may have been making a personal report on local conditions.

634–35   [MYS V : 896–97 / 892–93]

A poem: "Dialogue on Poverty"; with *tanka*

(The Poor Man)

	Kaze majie	On sodden nights
	Ame furu yo no	When rain comes gusting on the wind,
	Ame majie	On freezing nights
	Yuki furu yo wa	When snow falls mingled with the rain,
5	Sube mo naku	Shivering helplessly
	Samuku shi areba	In the all-pervading cold,
	Katashio o	I take a lump
	Toritsuzushiroi	Of hardened salt and nibble on it
	Kasuyuzake	While I sip diluted
10	Uchisusuroite	Lees of *sake* from my cup.
	Shiwabukai	Clearing my throat,
	Hana bishibishi ni	Sniffling as my nose begins to run,
	Shika to aranu	Stroking the few hairs
	Hige kakinadete	Of my meager, scraggly beard,
15	Are o okite	I puff myself up:
	Hito wa araji to	"What do people matter anyway,
	Hokoroedo	Aside from me?"
	Samuku shi areba	But still I'm cold, and so I take
	Asabusuma	My hempen quilt
20	Hikikagafuri	And pull it up around my shoulders.
	Nunokataginu	I put on every
	Ari no kotogoto	Sleeveless homespun frock I own,
	Kisoedo mo	Layer upon layer,
	Samuki yo sura o	But the night is cold. And he,
25	Ware yori mo	The man more destitute
	Mazushiki hito no	Than even I, on such a night
	Chichi haha wa	His father and mother

Uekogoyuramu
　Me kodomo wa
30 Niyobinakuramu
　Kono toki wa
Ika ni shitsutsu ka
Na ga yo wa wataru

Must be starving, bodies chill and numb;
　His wife and children
Moaning softly in the dark:
　Yes, you—at times like these
How do you manage to go on,
How do you get through your life?

(The Destitute Man)

Ame tsuchi wa
Hiroshi to iedo
　A ga tame wa
Saku ya narinuru
5　Hi tsuki wa
Akashi to iedo
　A ga tame wa
Teri ya tamawanu
Hito mina ka
10 Are nomi ya saru
Wakuraba ni
Hito to wa aru o
Hitonami ni
Are mo tsukuru o
15　Wata mo naki
Nunokataginu no
　Miru no goto
Wawakesagareru
Kakafu nomi
20 Kata ni uchikake
Fuseio no
Mageio no uchi ni
Hitatsuchi ni
Wara tokishikite
25　Chichi haha wa
Makura no kata ni
　Me kodomo wa
Ato no kata ni
Kakumiite
30 Ureesamayoi
　Kamado ni wa
Hoke fukitatezu
Koshiki ni wa
Kumo no su kakite
35　Ii kashiku
Koto mo wasurete

Although men say
That heaven and earth are vast,
　Have they not dwindled
To a narrow frame for me?
　Although men say
That the sun and moon are bright,
　Have they not refused
To grant their shining unto me?
　Are all men thus,
Or am I alone deprived?
　Though by rare chance
I was born into the world of men,
　And as any man
I toil to make my living on the land,
　Yet must I throw rags
About my shoulders, mere rotten
　Shreds of a sleeveless
Frock, hemp with no padding,
　Dangling like branches
Of sea pine over my bones;
　And in this crazy hut,
This flimsy, tumbling hovel,
　Flat on the ground
I spread my bedding of loose straw.
　By my pillowside
My father and my mother crouch,
　And at my feet
My wife and children; thus am I
　Surrounded by grief
And hungry, piteous cries.
　But on the hearth
No kettle sends up clouds of steam,
　And in our pot
A spider spins its web.
　We have forgotten
The very way of cooking rice;

	Nuedori no	Then where we huddle,
	Nodoyoioru ni	Faintly whimpering like *nue* birds,
	Itonokite	Deliberately,
40	Mijikaki mono o	As the saying goes, to cut
	Hashi kiru to	The end of what
	Ieru ga gotoku	Was short enough before,
	Shimoto toru	There comes the voice
	Satoosa ga koe wa	Of the village chief with his whip,
45	Neyado made	Standing, shouting for me,
	Kitachiyobainu	There outside the place we sleep.
	Kaku bakari	Does it come to this—
	Sube naki mono ka	Is it such a helpless thing,
	Yo no naka no michi	The path of man in this world?
	Yo no naka o	Though we may think
	Ushi to yasashi to	Our lives are mean and frustrate
	Omoedo mo	In this world of men,
	Tobitachikanetsu	We cannot fly into the air,
	Tori ni shi araneba	It being so we are not birds.

Respectfully presented with deep obeisance by Yamanoue no Okura

✳ An official embassy to China was announced in 732 and departed in the fourth month of the following year. The Ambassador was Tajihi no Hironari (d. 739), younger brother of the Agatamori mentioned in the commentary to no. 634–35. About a month before Hironari's departure, Okura presented him with a poem (no. 636–38) wishing him bon voyage and a safe return. No doubt memories of his own embarkation some thirty years earlier made the gesture a particularly meaningful one. This chōka-hanka set shows a very different world from that in the broodings on human life. As in Okura's tanka composed in China (no. 619), the world is that of the Japanese homeland, now not merely represented by a few pine trees, but presented in all its ancient mystique. In its worshipful attitude toward the gods of Japan and the divinity of the land, the chōka almost outdoes Hitomaro, and if nothing else, shows that Okura had more than one string to his bow. It opens with a formal introduction in the Hitomaro manner identifying Yamato as the unique land ruled by the sun deity, and in its evocation of the "word soul" (kotodama; see no. 582) harks back to the most archaic native feelings about the inherent magic of language. The poem itself was undoubtedly intended to be a function of that magic, a charm for a safe voyage, in which auspicious words achieve auspicious results. Here lies the motivation for the plethora of gods and godly services that the poem invokes, and for Okura's adoption of a manner at variance with his usual style. Only by speaking thus can he tap the mystic resources of the divine land to ensure the safety of his friend. It is clear why the poem is devoid of a single Buddhist or Confucian reference: the gods must not be offended by such foreign intrusions.

The introductory fourteen lines are followed by a shift of attention to the Ambassador himself, his selection, and his voyage. Lines 21–24 refer to the fact that Hironari's father Shima had served as Minister of the Right and of the Left under Jitō and Mommu. Hironari's ship will be guided by the gods of the ocean waters, and a humble verb is used for their "service," indicating they are subordinate to the representative of the divine heaven-descended court. From the sky the greater gods look down, one of them the spirit of the land itself. It is a stirring vision, and the "matters" (*koto*) to be concluded in "Grand Cathay" (Morokoshi) are mentioned in one line, and then the magic safety net for the return voyage is woven in its turn. "Ajikaoshi" is obscure, but the headlands of Chika would be on the outer islands off the northern Kyūshū coast. Mitsu of Ōtomo is the same port (Naniwa) to which Okura wished to return in no. 619. On "ink-string" (*suminawa*), see no. 150.

The two envoys place Okura himself in the welcoming position of the pine trees in his poem composed in China. Having finished his blessing in the chōka, the poet turns the focus from the gods to his very human self. Though he may seem like a Shintō god sweeping beneath the pine trees in disguise, the second envoy shows him as an eager, half-dressed mortal running to meet his friend come home. Sadly, he did not live to see the day; he is thought to have died within the year in which he wrote the poem. In the appended cover note Okura humbly refers to himself by name, signs the letter, and gives the addressee in the last line, as is customary. "Records Chamber" (*kishitsu*) is a polite ending, suggesting that the sender is too lowly to address the recipient directly and so entrusts the letter to his secretary.

636–38 [MYS V: 898–900/894–96]

A poem for a good departure and a good return; with two envoys

	Kamiyo yori	From the Age of Gods
	Iitsutekuraku	This has been the saying passed down:
	Sora mitsu	Sky-seen Yamato
	Yamato no kuni wa	Is a land hallowed in power
5	Sumekami no	Wielded in the hand
	Itsukushiki kuni	Of a sovereign deity,
	Kotodama no	A land where the word soul
	Sakiwau kuni to	Works its potency for weal:
	Kataritsugi	This have they told,
10	Iitsugaikeri	Passing down the saying age to age;
	Ima no yo no	And in this present reign
	Hito mo kotogoto	Each and every living man

	Ma no mae ni	Knows the truth of it,
	Mitari shiritari	Sees it here before his eyes.
15	Hito sawa ni	Men in their numbers
	Michite wa aredo mo	Overflow the earth, and yet
	Takahikaru	The Great Imperial
	Hi no ōmikado	Gate of the High-Shining Sun
	Kamunagara	In all its godhead,
20	Mede no sakari ni	In the fullness of its love
	Ame no shita	Chose for this mission
	Mōshitamaishi	The son of a house well schooled
	Ie no ko to	In the governing
	Erahitamaite	Of this realm beneath the sky.
25	Ōmikoto	With the Great Command
	Itadakimochite	Bestowed and safe in your hands
	Morokoshi no	You are now dispatched
	Tōki sakai ni	To the distant boundaries
	Tsukawasare	Of Grand Cathay:
30	Makariimase	When you shall have departed,
	Unahara no	They who keep the waters,
	He ni mo oki ni mo	Both the onshore and the offing,
	Kamuzumari	Of the plains of sea,
	Ushihakiimasu	They who dwell as deities,
35	Moromoro no	All the various,
	Ōmikamitachi	All the numerous great gods
	Funa no he ni	On the prow of your ship
	Michibikimōshi	Will serve to guide you on your way.
	Ame tsuchi no	And the great gods
40	Ōmikamitachi	Of the heaven and the earth,
	Yamato no	The great Land Soul
	Ōkunimitama	Of the land of Yamato,
	Hisakata no	Will gaze afar,
	Ama no misora yu	Beating their wings in heaven,
45	Amakakeri	Soaring through the void
	Miwatashitamai	Of the everlasting sky.
	Koto owari	With matters settled,
	Kaeramu hi ni wa	On the day you start for home
	Mata sara ni	Again they will come,
50	Ōmikamitachi	The great gods, and lay their hands
	Funa no he ni	On the prow of the ship,
	Mite uchikakete	And you will be drawn away
	Suminawa o	Straight as an ink-string
	Haetaru gotoku	Stretching across the sea.
55	Ajikaoshi	From Ajikaoshi,

Chika no saki yori	The headlands of Chika,
Ōtomo no	To the sandy shores
Mitsu no hamabi ni	Of Mitsu of Ōtomo,
Tadahate ni	Direct to its mooring
60 Mifune wa hatemu	Your ship will come home and moor.
Tsutsumi naku	Go without mishap,
Sakiku imashite	Safe in the power of your luck,
Haya kaerimase	And quickly return, my lord.

Envoys

Ōtomo no	I'll sweep the pine grove
Mitsu no matsubara	By the harbor of Mitsu
Kakihakite	Of Ōtomo,
Ware tachimatamu	And then stand and wait for you—
Haya kaerimase	Quickly return, my lord!

Naniwatsu ni	When I hear your ship
Mifune hatenu to	Has tied up at Naniwa,
Kikoekoba	I'll be off at a run
Himo tokisakete	Down to the port to see you in,
Tachibashiri semu	My sash all loose and flying.

On the first of the third month of Tempyō 5 [733] we met at [Oku]ra's
house. I presented the poem on the third.—Yamanoue no Okura
Respectfully submitted, Lord Ambassador to Great T'ang,
Records Chamber

❊ In strong contrast to the nativism of the farewell to Hironari, the follow-ing selection, entirely in Chinese, is a tissue of learned references. It consists of a *chüeh-chü*, a four-line Chinese poem, this one in the seven-character line, prefaced by one of Okura's longer Chinese prose compositions. A fea-ture of *Man'yōshū* is that it includes writings in both Japanese and Chinese. *Shih* is the generic term for the main types of Chinese poetry, one of which is the *chüeh-chü*. In this instance the preface is clearly dominant over the brief four-line poetic form. It follows an even longer prose composition dilating on Okura's various illnesses that is addressed to the same situation: the four elements of earth, water, fire, and wind that combine temporarily into a hu-man being are about to disperse; Okura is facing his death and writing a meditation on it.

The essay opens with a statement of the equivalence of the two doc-trines, Buddhism and Confucianism. This happy syncretism should prove that all is well in the world; the balance of the composition is intended to show that such is not the case. The evidence of mutability is hammered home, and then the hard-won resignation acquired from these lessons is undercut in the last sentence. The knowledge of existence and annihilation is too great a burden to carry. The essay has its own internal commentary explaining some of the references; the whole method of argument is by reference. Chou and K'ung are the Duke of Chou and Confucius. The Duke of Chou, an ancient Chinese statesman at the beginning of the Chou Dynasty (1122 B.C.–255 B.C.), was admired by Confucius as an exemplar of ethical conduct; together, their doctrines stand for Confucianism, as those of the historical and future Buddhas (Śākyamuni and Maitreya) do for Buddhism. The Springs or Yellow Springs are the Chinese abode of the dead, a counterpart of the Japanese netherworld Yomi. The white horse often appears in early Chinese writings as a metaphor for the speed with which life passes. Okura adjusts the metaphor to a race between life (the white horse) and death (the Yellow Springs).

The "sword of faith" refers to an account in *Shih Chi* about Chi Cha of the Kingdom of Wu, who, knowing that the ruler of Hsü desired his sword, returned from a journey to give it to him, only to find that he had died. He left it tied to a pine tree on the grave mound. The "white poplar" is an allusion to a poem in *Wen-hsüan* about a ruinous graveyard. The "platform of long night" is the grave, a reference to a poem in *Wen-hsüan*. Vimalakīrti was a rich Buddhist layman, a contemporary of Śākyamuni. He was in ill health and is depicted as sitting up in bed discoursing with the Buddha's disciples or the Bodhisattva Mañjuśri. He is said to have lived in a ten-foot-square hut. The historical Buddha is supposed to have died, or "passed into nirvāṇa," surrounded by four pairs of *śāl* (teak) trees. The Inner Teaching is Buddhism, so distinguished from Confucianism and other doctrines. Kālarātri and Lakṣmī are Hindu goddesses, of death and birth, respectively, adopted into the Buddhist pantheon.

The chief stylistic feature of the preface is its balanced phraseology. Buddhism and Confucianism are each given two sponsors (Shaku and Ji, Chou and K'ung) and classes of three and five precepts. "A hundred years" goes with "a thousand generations," and so on throughout the essay. The compound sentence is the basic structural unit. The echoing is carried to a nicety with "green pine" balancing "white poplar," and "jade body" corresponding to "golden countenance." In employing this ornate and mannered style, known as *p'ien-wen*, Okura is being faithful to Six Dynasties and early T'ang ideals of elegant prose. The poem reiterates phraseology from the preface in its first two lines, and in the last two applies the generalized lessons of the whole composition to the poet's personal situation. The four lines provide a metrical, rhyming coda to Okura's variations on the theme of mortality.

639   [MYS V: 901 / 896a]

A *shih* sorrowing and sighing over how on the path of this world the ele-

ments combine only to separate, easily dispersed and hard to make stay;
with preface

> If I may venture the observation, the teachings of Shaku and Ji (this re-
> fers to [Śākyamuni of the] Śākya clan and [Maitreya] the Compassionate
> One) have already opened the way of the Three Surrenders (this refers to
> taking refuge in the Buddha, the Dharma, and the Monastic Order) and
> the Five Commandments, thus converting the whole world (this refers
> to, one, not taking life; two, not stealing; three, not committing adul-
> tery; four, not lying; five, not drinking wine); the doctrines of Chou and
> K'ung have stretched the rope of the Three Bonds (these refer to ruler
> and subject, father and son, husband and wife) and the Five Teachings,
> thus saving the country (this refers to the father being righteous, the
> mother compassionate, the elder brother friendly, the younger brother
> obedient, the son filial). Thus we learn that the ways by which we are led
> are two, but the enlightenment obtained is one and the same.

> However, in the world there is no permanent substance, and for this
> reason hills and valleys interchange; for man there is no set span, and
> from this fact comes the difference between long life and early death.
> The hundred years of life pass in an eyeblink, a thousand generations
> vanish into nothing while one stretches out his arm. In the morning one
> lords it as host on the dais, but by evening one is a guest below the
> Springs. No matter how fast the white horse runs, how can it catch up
> with the Yellow Springs? The sword of faith hangs emptily from the
> green pine on the grave mound; the white poplar in the wasteland blows
> aimlessly in the mournful wind. From this we learn that from the start
> the world provides no retreat for retirement; there is only the platform
> of long night in the moorland. The former sages are already gone, and
> the latter worthies have not stayed. If one could escape for a redemption
> fee, who among the ancients would have lacked the price in gold? I have
> yet to hear of a single person who lived to see the end of the age. There-
> fore the Mahāsattva Vimalakīrti was afflicted with illness in his jade
> body in the ten-foot-square hut, and Śākyamuni the Benevolent shaded
> his golden countenance under the twin trees. It is said in the Inner Teach-
> ing, "If you do not desire Kālarātri to come after, do not admit Lakṣmī
> when she arrives first." (Lakṣmī is birth; Kālarātri is death.) Thus we
> learn that where there is birth there must be death. If one does not want
> to die, the best thing is not to be born. However—need one add?—even
> if one has awakened to the unvarying destiny of beginning and end, how
> is he to ponder the Great Rule of existence and annihilation?

> > On our worldly path change comes in an eyeblink;
> > The web of human affairs lasts the stretching of an arm.
> > In emptiness that drifts with floating clouds in the great void,
> > Mind and muscle both spent, I have no resort.

✳ Okura's poem set 640–46, dated in the sixth month of Tempyō 5 [733], may have come close to the end of his life. It is devoted to the question of readiness for death. Old and ill, Okura says he would as soon die. But again his children are brought in—it is they that hold him back. To take them as literary inventions on the grounds that Okura was too old to have fathered them is biologically unprovable and literarily devastating to the integrity of the self-portrait the poet is at pains to create. It is also rather insulting to a man whose creative virility in old age is otherwise unquestionable. Okura, whose self-pity is always accompanied by a bitter smile, talks of himself in the chōka as one of the walking wounded, one whose only treatment is to get salt rubbed into his wounds; or as an old packhorse, overburdened with a top-heavy load of infirmities. Somebody is behind it all—such seems the implication of the object-marker o in yamai o to (line 19): "add on some illness." But this is a mere aggrieved gesture, and there is no pause to ask who could be so cruel. One knows the answer by this time anyway: yo no naka no michi ("the way of the world"). Lines 21–24 closely echo lines 37–40 in no. 348, Hitomaro's second chōka on the death of his wife in Karu. The paired couplets on suffering by day and by night may have been a formula, like the last line, which appears sixteen times in Man'yōshū. Line 30 serves as the logical conclusion of Okura's account of his ills, but his wish to die is immediately subverted by his ties to his children. The children are "like flies in May" (sabae nasu)—constantly in motion, playing, quarreling, disturbing their father's rest, manakai ni motona kakarite (no. 627), "flickering before my eyes, making me helpless." That helplessness, expressed in the last line, ne nomi shi nakayu, is picked up in the first envoy in the recurrent image of the bird, this time one crying in the clouds. The second envoy recapitulates the chōka in small—"these" (kora) suggesting "children" (kora). The third and fourth envoys focus on the poet's poverty, in an echo of his "Dialogue on Poverty." This time the "rich" are brought in to contrast with the poor scholar who cannot afford the warm garments for his children that wealthy families let go to waste. The economic spectrum of rich-poor-destitute is thus completed. Okura chose to end the series with two envoys in which he wishes not for death, but for life. Even in context, the wish does not seem to be for the sake of the children, but the revelation of a will to live—plaintive, but still defiant. The old man, it seems, is not ready yet. The first footnote (showing the poet in the process of manipulating his work) refers to the last envoy, the second to the rest of the composition.

640–46   [MYS V:902–8/897–903]

Seven poems on the multiple illnesses afflicting this aged body, the years of bitter suffering, and thoughts of my children: one chōka, six tanka

   Tamakiwaru   Within the limits
   Uchi no kagiri wa   Of this soul-bound present life

Tairakeku	I would be at peace,
Yasuku mo aramu o	I would rest here at my ease
5 Koto mo naku	Without a bother,
Mo naku mo aramu o	Without a grief to mourn.
Yo no naka no	But the thwarted hopes
Ukeku tsurakeku	And the hardships of this world
Itonokite	Are like pouring
10 Itaki kizu ni wa	Salt into a smarting wound,
Karashio o	Deliberately adding
Sosoku chū ga gotoku	To a hurt the sting of bitter brine;
Masumasu mo	Or like throwing
Omoki umani ni	Yet more baggage on a horse
15 Uwani utsu to	Heavily laden—
Iu koto no goto	Yes, just like things like these
Oi nite aru	Is the way they ordered
Wa ga mi no ue ni	Illness piled atop this frame of mine,
Yamai o to	This body that is old:
20 Kuwaete areba	With these added burdens now
Hiru wa mo	By day my sighs
Nagekaikurashi	Go on and on till dark,
Yoru wa mo	By night my breath
Ikizukiakashi	Is drawn in pain till dawn.
25 Toshi nagaku	Across the long years
Yami shi watareba	I trail my maladies,
Tsuki kasane	And the months pile up
Uree samayoi	Amid grief and querulous complaints.
Kotokoto wa	Take it all in all,
30 Shinana to omoedo	I'd sooner die and be done.
Sabae nasu	But the children,
Sawaku kodomo o	Buzzing about like flies in May—
Utsutete wa	To abandon them
Shini wa shirazu	And die is quite beyond me:
35 Mitsutsu areba	As I look at them
Kokoro wa moenu	Something burns in my heart.
Ka ni kaku ni	Pulled this way and that,
Omoiwazurai	I am vexed for what to do,
Ne nomi shi nakayu	And can only weep aloud.

Envoys

Nagusamuru	With no heart in me
Kokoro wa nashi ni	Touched by any comfort here,
Kumogakuri	I am like a bird
Nakiyuku tori no	Crying somewhere in the clouds,
Ne nomi shi nakayu	For I can only weep aloud.

Sube mo naku	In my helplessness
Kurushiku areba	I cannot endure the pain—
Idehashiri	I would run away,
Inana to omoedo	I would sooner leave than stay—
Kora ni sayarinu	But I am held back by these.

Tomihito no	Children of the rich
Ie no kodomo no	Have more clothes than they can wear—
Kiru mi nami	They must let them rot,
Kutashisutsuramu	Those fine padded garments
Kinuwatara wa mo	Stuffed with warm silk floss.

Aratae no	Even rough-woven
Nunokinu o dani	Clothing of coarse barken cloth
Kisekateni	Is beyond my means—
Kaku ya nagekamu	Must I sigh thus, helpless
Semu sube o nami	To dress them at least in that?

Minawa nasu	I have prayed all day
Moroki inochi mo	That this fragile life of mine,
Takunawa no	Froth on the water,
Chihiro ni moga to	Might be a stout bark-fiber rope
Negaikurashitsu	A thousand fathoms long.

Shitsutamaki	A homespun bracelet,
Kazu ni mo aranu	Not a thing to count for much,
Mi ni wa aredo	That is all I am—
Chitose ni moga to	But the thought has come to me
Omōyuru kamo	To wish for a thousand years.

I composed this [last] poem in the second year of Jinki [725], but include it here because of its resemblance.

Composed in the fifth year of Tempyō [733], in the sixth month, whose first day was Fire-Senior/Monkey, on the third day, Earth-Senior/Dog.

❋ In what is probably his last poem Okura shows himself still unready to die. This time it is ten thousand, not a thousand years he speaks of, and he speaks what may be the truth about his stubborn will to live: the desire for fame. Fame may be many things. Is Okura thinking about his career as an official, of his paltry rank of Junior Fifth Lower? Of his scholarly attainments that have produced no great work? Does he regret the poems he never wrote? We can only be sure that he was conscious of his worth and wished to be remembered. If Hitomaro's dying was absorbed into a legend of lonely wayfarers he himself created, Okura's is a deliberately reported enactment of the role of the old scholar's farewell. Unlike Hitomaro, who merged into the world of mountains and wave-washed seacoasts, Okura consciously used his last years and months to create his most distinct image: his dying is his final creative act, and what is created is an individual man very plainly present, sitting up in bed and reciting poems. Though reported by others, this final scene is consonant with Okura's self-portraits. Okura, despite his low rank, was clearly well known at court, having served as Tutor to the now-reigning Emperor. Fujiwara no Yatsuka (d. 766), a member of what turned out to be the dominant branch of the Fujiwara, was in 733 a young man with a promising career ahead of him, the son of Fusasaki, a high-ranking officer at court. Kawahe no Azumato, who was sent by Yatsuka to inquire after Okura, may have been a steward (*karei*) in Fusasaki's household. In the footnote Okura's clan title Omi is placed after his personal name, an honor ordinarily reserved for dignitaries of the Third Rank and above. It has been suggested that this rearrangement indicates the passage is from the records of someone with deep respect for Okura—such as Ōtomo no Yakamochi.

647   [MYS VI:983/978]

A poem of Yamanoue no Omi Okura's at a time of grave illness

Onoko ya mo	A man—
Munashikarubeki	Is he to be nothing,
Yorozuyo ni	Leave no name
Kataritsugubeki	To be handed down
Na wa tatezu shite	For ten thousand years?

Concerning the above: When Yamanoue no Okura Omi lay gravely ill, Fujiwara no Asomi Yatsuka sent Kawahe no Asomi Azumato to inquire after him. When Okura Omi had finished his reply, he paused and then, wiping his tears, sighed sadly and recited this poem.

❋ Among the poems uncertainly ascribed to Okura are ten tanka in Book XVI. As the footnote explains, they are supposed to have been composed by the widow and children of a drowned fisherman named Arao, but may in fact have been produced by Okura, the Governor of the province in which Arao lived. The tragic story is of the sort to which one feels Okura would have been attracted, a tale about a simple man who paid with his life for an act of generosity to a friend, and who left behind him a wife and children bereft of support. The incident occurred in the Jinki period (724–29), just before Okura arrived in Chikuzen. Tsushima, to which Arao was delivering supplies when he vanished at sea, is an island outpost of Japan midway between Kyūshū and Korea, and it was the responsibility of the various nearby provinces to keep it supplied with foodstuffs. The ten tanka, which the headnote suggests were sung by the local seafolk, form a sequence rich in sorrow, irony, and futile hope—the staples of Okura's major poems. Various schemes for rearranging these compositions have been suggested, but their present order seems quite adequate to achieve a powerful poetic effect. The first four poems (nos. 648–51) form one subsequence, introduced by the bitter statement that Arao went on his fatal voyage of his own will (no doubt against the wishes of his wife). It is a poem of farewell, with Arao last seen waving his sleeve in the offing. No. 649 is about the waiting; spoken by the wife, as the entire sequence seems to be, it shows her preparing the food that is the symbol of home, an enticement that can never bring her husband back from his last wandering. Nos. 650 and 651 sweep more broadly over what Arao left behind—the mountains and the marshfields, now devastated and lonely, emblems therefore of the wife herself.

The sequence begins again with poem five (no. 652), a restatement of Arao's "wisdom" (i.e., his folly). Again he waves his sleeve—this time amid the waves. Is it a gesture of farewell, or is he drowning? In poem six (no. 653) the family again is waiting—has been waiting for years. The next two poems (nos. 654–55) reach out to the coast, as did nos. 650–51—here to the Cape of Yara. The fiction is still maintained that Arao might some day return. His boat is introduced and given a name, providing a link to the boat images in the last two poems. Thus the sequence proceeds in two echoing movements of four poems each; the final two (nos. 656–57) are a tailpiece entirely in the ironic mode. The first imagines sending a gift, as if Arao were sojourning in a place where gifts could reach him. The futility of the idea is displaced onto factitious worry about the security of the package. Arao's wife is the *hashiki tsumara*, "the wife that you loved so well," of Hitomaro's Samine poem (no. 358–60), who would have picked herbs for her shipwrecked husband had the season not been past. *Akara obune* ("boats of reddish hue") may have been so marked to ward off evil, or because they were in government service (see no. 447). The last poem imagines a search expedition, its futility and probable fate.

648–57   [MYS XVI: 3882–91 / 3860–69]
Ten songs of the seafolk of Shika in Chikuzen Province

(648)   [3882 / 3860]

Ōkimi no	Not that he was sent
Tsukawasanaku ni	By order of our mighty lord—
Sakashira ni	In his own wisdom
Yukishi Araora	He went out, our Arao,
Oki ni sode furu	Who waves his sleeve in the offing.

(649)   [3883/3861]

        Araora o   Our Arao—
    Komu ka koji ka to   Maybe tonight's the night he'll come;
        Ii morite   Heaping his dish with rice,
    Kado ni idetachi   I go out to the gate and stand,
    Matedo kimasanu   And wait, but he does not come.

(650)   [3884/3862]

        Shika no yama   The mountains of Shika,
    Itaku na kiri so   Do not cut them so sorely—
        Araora ga   Our Arao
    Yosuka no yama to   Made those mountains his landmark:
    Mitsutsu shinowamu   I would look and remember.

(651)   [3885/3863]

        Araora ga   Since the day
    Yukinishi hi yori   Our Arao departed,
        Shika no ama no   How lonely the marshfields
    Ōura tanu wa   Of the fishers of Shika
    Sabushiku mo aru ka   Beside the open shore.

(652)   [3886/3864]

        Tsukasa koso   The government—sure,
    Sashite mo yarame   It could tell him to go out,
        Sakashira ni   But in his wisdom
    Yukishi Araora   Our Arao went freely;
    Nami ni sode furu   Mid the billows he waves his sleeve.

(653)   [3887/3865]

        Araora wa   Our Arao
    Meko no nari o ba   Never thinks of the livelihood
        Omowazu ro   Of his wife and child—
    Toshi no yatose o   Years we have waited, many years,
    Matedo kimasanu   But he does not come again.

(654)   [3888/3866]

        Okitsutori   Bird of the offing,
    Kamo tou fune no   Wild Duck did he call his boat:
        Kaerikoba   If it should return,
    Yara no sakimori   Guardian of the Cape of Yara,
    Hayaku tsuge koso   Come quickly and bring me word.

(655)   [3889/3867]

Okitsutori	Bird of the offing,
Kamo tou fune wa	Wild Duck did he call his boat:
Yara no saki	That round Cape Yara
Tamite kogiku to	It is rowing home again
Kikoekonu ka mo	Will the tidings never come?

(656)   [3890/3868]

Oki yuku ya	Far in the offing
Akara obune ni	Go the boats of reddish hue—
Tsuto yaraba	If I send a gift
Kedashi hito mite	Someone may see the package
Hirakimimu ka mo	And open and look inside.

(657)   [3891/3869]

Ōfune ni	Though we sent a great boat
Obune hikisoe	With a small boat tied astern
Kazuku to mo	And plunged them down,
Shika no Arao ni	Would they meet Arao of Shika
Kazukiawame ya mo	In their plunge beneath the sea?

Concerning the above, in the Jinki period the Dazaifu issued orders to Tsumaro of the Munakatabe, a commoner of Munakata District in Chikuzen Province, appointing him helmsman of the boat to deliver supplies to Tsushima. Tsumaro went to the fisherman Arao of Shika Village, Kasuya District, and said, "I have a small request. I wonder if you will grant it." Arao replied, "I am from a different district, but have been your shipmate many a long day. I love you like a brother, and even if it led to my death, how could I refuse you?" Tsumaro said, "The government has given me orders appointing me helmsman of the boat to deliver supplies to Tsushima. But I am old and decrepit and not up to making this voyage. And so I've come here to ask a favor. Will you be so kind as to take my place?" Arao agreed and finally went about fulfilling his promise. He launched his boat from Cape Mineraku in the Matsura District of Hizen Province and headed straight across the sea toward Tsushima. Suddenly the sky darkened, and a violent wind came up, mixed with rain. In the end there was no favorable wind, and Arao sank in the sea. Hence it was that his wife and children, yearning for him like calves [for the mother cow], composed these poems. Others say that Yamanoue no Okura Omi, the Governor of Chikuzen, saddened at the grief of the wife and children, composed these poems to express their feelings.

Kamikoso no Oyumaro (poems from 733)

Nothing is known of this poet other than that he composed the following two poems in 733, the year in which Yamanoue no Okura probably died. Kusaka Mountain separates inland Yamato from Naniwa and the sea. The point of both poems is that Oyumaro is looking down at a scene of sunlight reflected off the sea and strand around Naniwa, a panorama of great beauty, one he intends to describe to his wife when he returns home. *Nagori* in no. 658 may refer to little waves on tidal pools rather than the seaweed deposited by the dropping tide. No. 659 suggests how Naniwa got its epithet *oshiteru ya*, here interpreted as "shining waves."

658–59   [MYS VI: 981–82/976–77]

Two poems composed by Kamikoso no Imiki Oyumaro when crossing Kusaka Mountain in the fifth year [of Tempyō, 733], Water-Junior/Cock

(658)   [981/976]

Naniwagata	On Naniwa strand
Shiohi no nagori	Well shall I look at the sea wrack
Yoku mitemu	Left by the dropping tide,
Ie naru imo ga	For my wife at home is waiting
Machitowamu tame	With many a thing to ask.

(659)   [982/977]

Tadakoe no	Surely it was here
Kono michi ni shite	On the path at Tada Pass
Oshiteru ya	That they gave the name
Naniwa no umi to	Shining Waves to Naniwa
Nazukekerashi mo	Afloat in its sunlit sea.

Ono no Oyu (d. 737)

Ono no Oyu served under Ōtomo no Tabito in the Dazaifu administration, eventually rising to be Assistant Governor-General (*daini*). Including the poem below, three tanka of his have been preserved, one of them composed at Tabito's plum-blossom party in 730 (see nos. 1011–42). No. 660 is a memorable evocation of what the new capital at Nara, then about twenty years old, meant to courtiers of the time. The lack of a speculative ending to the final verb suggests that Oyu has the city before his gaze, but the likelihood is that he was writing at his duty post in Kyūshū, and that Nara is an absolute fixed image in his mind. The poem stands at the head of a series on longing for the capital. The placement of the clan title after the personal name is complimentary.

660   [MYS III : 331/328]

A poem of Junior Assistant Governor-General of Dazaifu Ono no Oyu
Asomi

Aoni yoshi	The royal city,
Nara no miyako wa	Nara of the blue-green earth,
Saku hana no	Like blossoming trees
Niou ga gotoku	That shimmer into fragrant bloom,
Ima sakari nari	Is at the height of splendor now.

Ama no Inukai no Okamaro (poem from 734)

This poet survives only through this one poem, in which he claims his life
was worth living because it came when it did. Emperor Shōmu, at whose
command the poem was composed, had been reigning for twelve years, and
the great city of Nara with its many temples and palaces had taken form. No
doubt it is these things to which Okamaro refers. It was indeed a great age
of art, literature, religion, statecraft, and civilization generally, one whose
splendor can be judged faintly from the relics that remain in Nara, and from
Man'yōshū itself. It was also a restless time of bloody intrigues and coups
d'état, but of that these poems say nothing. For Okamaro as for Ono no
Oyu and others, Nara was a flower in full bloom. The foreboding implications of the image go unnoticed.

661   [MYS VI : 1001/996]

A poem in response to imperial command by Ama no Inukai no Sukune
Okamaro in the sixth year [of Tempyō, 734], Wood-Senior/Dog

Mitami ware	I, loyal subject,
Ikeru shirushi ari	Have lived to some avail:
Ame tsuchi no	I have but to think
Sakayuru toki ni	How I have come into a time
Aeraku omoeba	When heaven and earth are in flower.

Ōami no Hitonushi (poem from 730's or 740's?)

Ōami no Hitonushi is another poet preserved through just one poem, one
he sang at a banquet. The date of the banquet is unknown, and it is uncertain
whether he composed the poem or merely recited it. It is grouped with the
hiyuka of Book III. Based on the technique of the jo, it uses the image of
coarsely woven garments to convey a love that is still new and unfamiliar,
not yet worn soft. Suma on the Inland Sea west of Naniwa was known as a
place where the shore-dwellers made salt by burning brine-drenched sea-

weed. Wisteria garments (*fujigoromo*), woven of fibers made from wisteria bark, were very rough. The clan title Kimi was given to regional clans of imperial descent.

662 [MYS III: 416/413]

A poem sung by Ōami no Kimi Hitonushi at a banquet

Suma no ama no	Seafolk of Suma
Shioyakikinu no	Wear for burning salt rough cord
Fujigoromo	Spun of wisteria:
Matō ni shi areba	Woven sparse, our web of days
Imada kinarezu	Not yet fits soft about us.

Prince Yuhara (active 730's)

Prince Yuhara was a son of Prince Shiki (nos. 467–68) and an uncle of Prince Aki (nos. 506–8). Prince Yuhara has left several love poems, some of which are translated in the section on exchanges, but one of his finest efforts is this nature poem, which bears a marked resemblance to his father's tanka on twilight amid the reeds of Naniwa (no. 468). Both poems evoke an atmosphere of loneliness and longing through images of wild ducks, their questing for shelter and their cries. Both employ a setting away from home, at Naniwa or Yoshino, and though structured differently, convey a similar sense of stillness and fading light.

663 [MYS III: 378/375]

A poem composed by Prince Yuhara at Yoshino

Yoshino naru	From the river pools
Natsumi no kawa no	At Natsumi in Yoshino,
Kawayodo ni	From those quiet pools
Kamo so naku naru	Comes the sound of mallards crying
Yamakage ni shite	Beneath the shadow of the hills.

❋ The next two tanka are set at a party at which the Prince tells his host (or honored guest) of his admiration for a young woman whose waving sleeves suggest she is dancing. *Tamakushige* ("jeweled comb chest") in no. 664 is a pillow word for *oku* ("deep inside"—in the Prince's heart). No. 665 is based on a jo in which the white clouds serve as an analogue for the young woman through their power to draw a man's gaze.

664–65 [MYS III: 379–80/376–77]

Two banquet poems by Prince Yuhara

(664)   [379/376)

Akizuha no   Look at her, my lord,
Sode furu imo o   The darling girl waving her sleeves
Tamakushige   Like dragonfly wings;
Oku ni omou o   She is to me as a chest of combs,
Mitamae a ga kimi   A treasure of my deep longing.

(665)   [380/377]

Aoyama no   Marvelous, my lord—
Mine no shirakumo   White clouds on blue mountain peaks,
Asa ni ke ni   Morning and by day
Tsune ni miredo mo   Constantly I gaze at her,
Mezurashi a ga kimi   But she delights me ever.

✳ The second of Prince Yuhara's "two moon poems" (nos. 666–67) is addressed to a friend to whose visit he looks forward. The first is no doubt to be understood in the same context, as a wish for a long night of talk. Both are based on conceits. The "bowman of the crescent moon" (*tsukuyomi otoko*) is asked to prolong the night five hundred times over in the first poem and is depicted as standing on tiptoe waiting for the friend's arrival in the second. This moon deity is first mentioned in the chronicles as the younger brother of the sun goddess.

666–67   [MYS VI:990–91/985–86]

Two moon poems by Prince Yuhara

(666)   [990/985]

Ame ni masu   Heaven-abiding
Tsukuyomi otoko   Bowman of the crescent moon,
Mai wa semu   I'll bribe you well:
Koyoi no nagasa   Let the evening tonight
Ioyo tsugi koso   Be long five hundred nights.

(667)   [991/986]

Hashiki yashi   Ah, my dearest friend,
Machikaki sato no   For you to come from that village
Kimi komu to   Of yours so nearby
Ōnobi ni kamo   The very moon is standing
Tsuki no teritaru   On tiptoe as it shines!

The Maiden Ōyake (poems from 730's?)

Nothing is known of this poet other than that she was a young woman of Buzen Province in northern Kyūshū who left two poems about love and the moon, of which one is translated below. The moon has a special fascination for lovers: it is a large and radiant object that they can gaze at simultaneously from widely separated places (see no. 424 in the "Hitomaro Collection"). The moon comes to seem the witness and guarantor of their love, and the image becomes meaningful in this sense in Ōyake's poem.

668   [MYS VI: 989/984]

A moon poem by a maiden of Buzen Province (the maiden's name was Ōyake, but her family is unknown)

Kumogakuri	Hidden in the clouds,
Yukue o nami to	Where it goes we cannot say,
Wa ga kouru	But I yearn for it—
Tsuki o ya kimi ga	The moon, my love, are you eager
Mimaku hori suru	To gaze on it as I?

The Maiden Ato no Tobira (poem from 730's?)

Nothing is known about this maiden. There is only her one poem to reveal that there was such a person, and that she dreamed of a man she glimpsed once by moonlight. There is something peculiarly haunting about one-poem poets, especially when they write of their passions, fires of which only one spark has somehow been preserved.

669   [MYS IV: 713/710]

A poem by the Maiden Ato no Tobira

Misora yuku	Only one fleeting
Tsuki no hikari ni	Glance by the light of the moon,
Tada hitome	The sky-traveler,
Aimishi hito no	Had that man and I, and yet
Ime ni shi miyuru	Now I see him in my dreams.

Prince Kadobe (d. 745)

Prince Kadobe was the grandson of Prince Naga (nos. 460–62) and great-grandson of Emperor Temmu. In 739 he and his brother were reduced to nonroyal status and given the clan name and title Ōhara no Mahito. (Mahito was the highest of the clan titles on Temmu's revised list of eight.) This was a way of thinning overpopulated royal ranks, and several of the noble houses owed their origins to it. The former Prince served in various governorships and other offices, eventually rising to be Minister of the Treasury. He had a reputation as an elegant and took part in a formal court version of the uta-gaki songfest held at the main gate of the capital in 734. Only five of his poems, all tanka, have been preserved. In the Nara capital trade was regulated in the Chinese fashion, buying and selling being confined to two official marketplaces, an eastern and a western, open from noon till sundown. The bustle of a marketplace was a convenient cover for the meetings of lovers; it is the lack of such meetings, not the trees in the marketplace, that is the subject of no. 670.

670   [MYS III: 313/310]

A poem composed by Prince Kadobe on the subject of the trees planted in the eastern market (he was later granted the clan name Ōhara no Mahito)

Himugashi no	The trees they planted
Ichi no ueki no	In the eastern marketplace
Kodaru made	Now trail to the ground;
Awazu hisashimi	It's a long time since we met—
Ube koinikeri	No wonder I long for you!

❋ In the above poem the sight of the trees with their trailing branches suggests the length of time the lovers have not met; in the following one the sight of the flares at Akashi implies the flaming openness of the poet's love. Both embody types of analogy, but no. 670 is kept on the primary level of discourse, as a factual statement (though perhaps hyperbolic), whereas no. 671 employs the sleight of hand of metaphor through the jo technique with doubling at the juncture in line four.

671   [MYS III: 329/326]

A poem composed by Prince Kadobe when he was in Naniwa and saw the flares of the fishermen

Miwataseba	When I gaze far out
Akashi no ura ni	Across Akashi Bay I see
Tomosu hi no	The lighted flares:
Ho ni so idenuru	Flaming openly, my love
Imo ni kouraku	Burns bright for my darling girl.

❋ The next two poems were composed during Prince Kadobe's tenure as Governor of Izumo, probably before 719. In one he longs for home, and in the other for a woman. Both mention the "Sea of Ou," an indentation of the

Izumo coastline. The plovers there remind him of those for which the Saho River at Nara was famous. *Na ga nakeba* ("when you raise your call") is the same line Hitomaro employed in his poem about the plovers of Ōmi (no. 291). Both poets are reminded of the past. The second poem (no. 673) is based on a jo with repetition: *kata* ("beach") / *kataomoi* ("one-sided love"). The poem may have been given to the young woman before the Prince made a trip to the capital to report, as provincial Governors were required to do. In its outward aspects the situation is perhaps a repetition of the one that produced Hitomaro's poems on leaving his wife in Iwami (nos. 321–27).

672   [MYS III : 374/371]

A poem by Prince Kadobe, Governor of Izumo, in yearning for the capital

Ou no umi	Plovers on the sands
Kawara no chidori	Where the river joins the sea at Ou,
Na ga nakeba	When you raise your call
Wa ga Sahogawa no	Don't you know how the thoughts come back
Omōyuraku ni	Of my own Saho River?

673   [MYS IV : 539/536]

A love poem by Prince Kadobe

Ou no umi no	Along the Sea of Ou
Shiohi no kata no	At low tide the beach lies bare:
Kataomoi ni	Barely enduring
Omoi ya yukamu	This one-sided love, shall I
Michi no nagate o	Go yearning my long way?

Concerning the above: Prince Kadobe took a young woman on his staff as wife during his appointment as Governor of Izumo. But before long he completely stopped visiting her. After several months had gone by, he again started to have tender feelings for her. Thus he wrote this poem and sent it to her.

Tanabe no Sakimaro (active 740's)

Tanabe no Sakimaro was a minor court official who continued in a major way the tradition of public chōka stemming from Hitomaro. The late 730's and early 740's were a time of great uneasiness at the Japanese court. In 737 a smallpox epidemic caused the deaths of the heads of the four Fujiwara houses, Fusasaki (681–737), Maro (695–737), Muchimaro (680–737), and Umakai (694–737). This cumulative disaster to Fujiwara power allowed the advancement of Tachibana no Moroe (684–757), a half brother of Emperor Shōmu's consort, who took Muchimaro's place as Minister of the Right in 738. It was twenty years before the Fujiwara fully reasserted their influence over the throne. In 740 Fujiwara no Hirotsugu, a son of Umakai who was serving as Junior Assistant Governor-General of Dazaifu, raised a revolt in Kyūshū, demanding the expulsion from government of advisers hostile to the Fujiwara. His revolt was quickly put down, and he was executed before the end of the year, but the event alarmed Emperor Shōmu into abandoning the capital at Nara. At the end of 740 he chose a new and presumably more defensible site several miles north, at Kuni in Yamashiro Province, where he held court for the first time in 741. The years 744 and 745 brought further shifts as Shōmu vacillated between staying at Kuni, moving the capital to Naniwa, going farther north to Shigaraki in Ōmi Province (where he had a detached palace and where the colossal icon of Vairocana subsequently known as the Nara Daibutsu was at first planned to be erected), and returning to Nara. The court took up residence in Nara again after a series of earthquakes in 745, and stayed there until 784. The building and abandonment of capitals is Sakimaro's major theme, the subject of several chōka preserved in *Tanabe no Sakimaro Kashū*, a collection of his poems that has been incorporated into *Man'yōshū* at least in part. All the poems translated here are from this "Sakimaro Collection."

Nara as abandoned capital provided a grand subject for poets, and it is surprising that more was not done with it. The following chōka-hanka set by Sakimaro (no. 674-76) is the principal commemoration of the temporary fall of the great city. There are also three anonymous tanka (nos. 1253-55) that deserve to be read along with Sakimaro's poem in conjunction with the evocations of Nara's glory by Ono no Oyu and Ama no Inukai no Okamaro (nos. 660-61). The episode of the 740's was a false alarm, and the Nara capital entered into its full flourishing after Shōmu's return in 745, with the erection of Tōdaiji to house the Great Buddha (on which see no. 814-17) and the continued development of religious art and institutions. Man'yō poetry, however, had only fourteen years left, as far as we can tell from the abruptly truncated form in which it has come down to us. When the court finally moved away from Nara in 784, partly to escape those religious institutions, there was no chōka poet to mourn its departure, or if there was, his works were lost in the shuffle at the end of the age.

Sakimaro is faithful to his model in beginning, as Hitomaro would have done, with an evocation of the majesty and antiquity of the imperial house, complete with opening pillow word, elaborated through the concept of a foreordained succession of divine rulers. (On these elements of public chōka, see nos. 288, 328, and 341). In Sakimaro's superbly anachronistic vision, the capital at Nara has been designated in advance by the "ancestral god" (*sumeroki no kami*, i.e., the First Emperor, Jimmu) and is to last to an archaic equivalent of eternity (eight million years, with an added thousand for good measure). After this introduction come two parallel eight-line passages on spring and fall at the capital, with local names and staple images; they are followed by parallel couplets summing up the attractions of the city and its setting. This celebratory central passage goes back ultimately to Hitomaro's Yoshino River poems (nos. 293–96). The poem begins again in line 37, this time addressing itself to desolation rather than celebration. The formula *mononofu no yasotomo no o* is as deeply resonant of the archaic past as the formula with which the poem opens, but these "great officers of court" who through their clans control the labor of the "eighty allied crafts" are no more prescient than the divine ancestor. Furthermore, when their Sovereign moves, they move too—like flocking birds—and the city is abandoned. The final image is of empty streets. Not only did the courtiers leave, but the two markets were forced to move to Kuni in 741. In the first envoy the empty streets begin to be lost in grass and weeds, an image that harks back to Hitomaro's lament for the fallen capital at Ōmi in no. 288. But though Nara seems something of a ghost town, someone is still there: Sakimaro himself comes out to wander through the desolation in the second envoy.

674–76   [MYS VI: 1051–53 / 1047–49]

A poem composed in sadness over the old homeland of Nara; with *tanka*

	Yasumishishi	Where our great lord reigns,
	Wa ga ōkimi no	Ruling the eight corners of the earth,
	Takashikasu	The land of Yamato,
	Yamato no kuni wa	Held beneath his lofty sway,
5	Sumeroki no	From the hallowed age
	Kami no miyo yori	Of that far ancestral god,
	Shikimaseru	Has been a land
	Kuni ni shi areba	Of sovereign dominion:
	Aremasamu	Therefore that Princes
10	Miko no tsugitsugi	To be born into the world
	Ame no shita	Might in their generations
	Shirashimasamu to	There rule the land beneath the sky
	Yaoyorozu	He foreordained
	Chitose o kanete	For eight hundred myriad
15	Sadamekemu	And a thousand years
	Nara no miyako wa	The royal city of Nara.
	Kagiroi no	When of a springtime,
	Haru ni shi nareba	With the air a shimmering haze
	Kasugayama	On Kasuga Mountain
20	Mikasa no nohe ni	And the high fields of Mikasa,
	Sakurabana	Trees are hung with shade
	Ko no kuregakuri	From the blossoming cherry,
	Kahotori wa	Hidden in the bloom
	Ma naku shibanaku	The *kaho* bird cries, never ceasing.

25 Tsuyu shimo no	And when autumn comes,
Aki sarikureba	Bringing back the frost and dew,
Ikomayama	On Mount Ikoma,
Tobuhi ga oka ni	On the hill of signal fires,
Hagi no e o	Scattering flowers
30 Shigaramichirashi	From the tangling clover stems,
Saoshika wa	Young stags call to their mates,
Tsuma yobitoyomu	Bellowing till the cliffs resound.
Yama mireba	When you view the hills,
Yama mo migahoshi	The hills are fair to look upon;
35 Sato mireba	When you view the town,
Sato mo sumiyoshi	The town is a good place to live.
Mononofu no	The eighty clansmen,
Yasotomo no o no	The great officers of court,
Uchihaete	Thinking of times to come,
40 Omoerishiku wa	Were sure in their minds of this:
Ame tsuchi no	Until heaven and earth
Yoriai no kiwami	Should merge together at their far frontier,
Yorozuyo ni	For ten thousand ages
Sakaeyukamu to	It would go on in glory;
45 Omoerishi	So they thought,
Ōmiya sura o	For it was a mighty palace—yet,
Tanomerishi	The royal city,
Nara no miyako o	Nara where they placed their trust,
Aratayo no	Now that a new age
50 Koto ni shi areba	Comes upon us, they do leave,
Ōkimi no	Meekly following
Hiki no manimani	Whither their great lord will lead:
Haruhana no	As the flowers in spring
Utsuroikawari	Fade and wither, their affections change.
55 Muratori no	Like flocking birds
Asadachiyukeba	They fly up and away in the morning.
Sasu take no	Live as young bamboo,
Ōmiyahito no	The courtiers once thronged
Fuminarashi	Along these streets,
60 Kayoishi michi wa	Treading the earth smooth and flat;
Uma mo ikazu	Now no horses go,
Hito mo yukaneba	And no people walk the ways—
Arenikeru kamo	How desolate they have become!

Two Envoys

Tachikawari	Now that times have changed
Furuki miyako to	And the city has become
Narinureba	The old capital,

Michi no shibakusa	The wild grass of the roadside
Nagaku oinikeri	Grows tall along the streets.
Natsukinishi	How at home we were
Nara no miyako no	In Nara the royal city!
Areyukeba	Its desolation
Idetatsu goto ni	Draws more sighs from me each time
Nageki shi masaru	I go out in the spreading ruin.

❋ Lo and behold, here is Sakimaro with two chōka in praise of the new capital at Kuni. His delight in the new seems at least equal to his sorrow over the old; the delight and the sorrow are two sides of his role as a court poet, one who could express on public occasions the feelings appropriate to the time. In no. 677–79 the echoes of Yoshino are particularly strong. Both the four-line introduction and the many-one technique of lines 5–18 are closely modeled on, or adaptations of, the same formulas in the equivalent passages in no. 293. The seasonal passage that follows reverses the usual order of spring and autumn, but otherwise occupies a similar position to lines 11–26 of no. 295. In Sakimaro's version the pleasance of river and mountain, divinity and eternity, is still radiant with a dawn-of-the-world freshness. One almost believes in the new beginning—that Kuni will last. In fact it was abandoned in less than five years. The vision is of an ideal outside of history, and can ignore the dust and blood of battle and political intrigue. History teaches that the accounts of Kuni to which Shōmu listened as he sought a safer seat of rule included those of Tachibana no Moroe, who had estates in the area and no doubt favored a move away from Nara with its entrenched Fujiwara.

The second chōka (no. 680) again sings the praises of the new capital in terms appropriate to an earthly paradise, terms originally used for a detached palace at an excursion site. Nara's streets have been trodden smooth by the feet of its thronging courtiers, and now only weeds grow along them. The great halls of Kuni rise in the pristine ambience of mountain and stream amid the roar of water and the deep verdure of the forest. Poetically, the move to Kuni is a retreat from urbanity and its problems into the haloed mist of the Japanese past, to a monarchy of woodland and fields and tribal memories. This second chōka is provided with five envoys. They form a garland of place-names surrounding the new capital and allow the poet to embroider his theme. The first two find a warrant in the forms of river and mountain for the eternality of the imperial abode and are thus serious restatements of the theme. The last three are more informal. The third is based on a pun in the pivot word *kase*, meaning both "spindle" and Mount Kase. The fourth envoy continues the reference to this mountain, combining it with a reference to the warblers mentioned in the chōka. The final envoy employs an associational technique in going from warbler to cuckoo, and ends the series with a conceit about the bird crossing only at a river ford. One may be forgiven for feeling that Sakimaro indulged himself in too many envoys here, and that numbers three and five are tonally inappropriate to the artistic effect of the poem as a whole.

677-85   [MYS VI: 1054-62/1050-58]

Two poems in praise of the new capital at Kuni; with *tanka*

(677-79)   [1054-56/1050-52]

Akitsukami	Where our great lord reigns
Wa go ōkimi no	A god incarnate, master
Ame no shita	Of all under heaven,
Yashima no uchi ni	In the eight great islands of the realm
5 Kuni wa shi mo	There are provinces,
Sawa ni aredo mo	Many are they, but of them all—
Sato wa shi mo	There are villages,
Sawa ni aredo mo	Many are they, but of them all,
Yamanami no	Choosing a province
10 Yoroshiki kuni to	Where mountains fall in lovely folds,
Kawanami no	Choosing a village
Tachiau sato to	Where rivers blend their waves in one,
Yamashiro no	In Yamashiro,
Kaseyama no ma ni	In the mountains of Kase
15 Miyabashira	He planted firm
Futoshikimatsuri	The pillars of his palace halls,
Takashirasu	He raised on high
Futagi no miya wa	His lofty halls at Futagi:
Kawa chikami	Close by is the stream,
20 Se no to so kiyoki	Its rapids sounding clean and clear,
Yama chikami	Close by are the hills
Tori ga ne toyomu	That echo with the calls of birds.
Aki sareba	When autumn comes,
Yama mo todoro ni	The young stags bellow for their mates
25 Saoshika wa	Until the slopes resound,
Tsuma yobitoyome	The mountains tremble with the sound of it;
Haru sareba	When spring arrives,
Okabe mo shiji ni	The hillsides are a mass of bloom,
Iwao ni wa	Cascading blossoms
30 Hana sakiōri	In wild profusion from the rocks.
Ana omoshiro	How pleasant
Futagi no hara	Are Futagi's fields,
Ito tōto	How filled with awe

Ōmiyadokoro
35   Ube shi koso
Wa go ōkimi wa
Kimi nagara
Kikashitamaite
Sasu take no
40   Ōmiya koko to
Sadamekerashi mo

The site of these great palace halls!
   Surely it was for this
That our great lord, our Sovereign,
   When in his lordliness
He listened from his throne to men's accounts,
   Fixed upon this place
To found a palace that might stand
Forever flourishing as young bamboo.

Two Envoys

Mika no hara
Futagi no nobe o
   Kiyomi koso
Ōmiyadokoro
Sadamekerashi mo

The meadows of Mika,
The field land of Futagi—
   It must have been
Their purity for which he chose
This region as his palace site.

Yama takaku
Kawa no se kiyoshi
   Momoyo made
Kamushimiyukamu
Ōmiyadokoro

The mountains are high,
The river shallows clean and clear:
   A hundred ages
It will endure in godhead,
The site of these great palace halls!

(680–85)

[1057–62/1053–58]

Wa go ōkimi
Kami no mikoto no
Takashirasu
Futagi no miya wa
5   Momoki moku
Yama wa kodakashi
Ochitagitsu
Se no to mo kiyoshi
Uguisu no
10 Kinaku harube wa
Iwao wa
Yamashita hikari
Nishiki nasu
Hana sakiōri
15 Saoshika no
Tsuma yobu aki wa
Amagirau
Shigure o itami
Sanitsurau
20 Momichi chiritsutsu
Yachitose ni

Where our great lord,
Sovereign and august god,
   Has raised at Futagi
A lofty palace for his rule
   The hundred trees grow thick,
The mountains are high-forested.
   The plunging, seething
Rapids' roar rings clean upon the air.
   In springtime,
When the warbler comes to sing,
   The mountain crags
Are mantled in a crimson glow,
   As blossoms like brocade
Descend in riot from the hills.
   In autumn,
When young stags call to their mates,
   Bitten by the cold
Of chill rains misting all the sky,
   Leaves of ruddy hue
Scatter ceaselessly to earth.
   For a myriad years

388

Aretsugashitsutsu	Ceaselessly our Sovereigns
Ame no shita	In unbroken line
Shirashimesamu to	Shall rule this realm beneath the sky,
25 Momoyo ni mo	And for a hundred ages
Kawarumashijiki	The great halls shall stand unchanged
Ōmiyadokoro	Within these mighty palace grounds.

Five Envoys

Izumigawa	If the water flowing
Yukuse no mizu no	In the rapids of Izumi River
Taeba koso	Were to run no more,
Ōmiyadokoro	Then alone could come decay
Utsuroiyukame	To these mighty palace grounds.

Futagiyama	Futagi Mountain—
Yamanami mireba	Behold the mountain range's sweep:
Momoyo ni mo	For a hundred ages
Kawarumashijiki	The great halls shall stand unchanged
Ōmiyadokoro	Within these mighty palace grounds.

Otomera ga	Maidens spin the flax
Umio kaku tou	And wind the thread on spindles—
Kase no yama	And Spindle Mountain
Toki no yukereba	With the turning of the years
Miyako to narinu	Has become our capital.

Kase no yama	On Kase Mountain,
Kodachi o shigemi	So lush is the growth of trees,
Asa sarazu	Each morning without fail
Kinakitoyomosu	They come, they sing, the slopes resound
Uguisu no koe	To the warbler's joyous call.

Komayama ni	On Koma Mountain
Naku hototogisu	Cries the cuckoo from the wood:
Izumigawa	The river ford
Watari o tōmi	Of Izumi is far from here—
Koko ni kayowazu	And so he never comes across.

❋ Sakimaro was again at hand when it came time to lament the abandonment of Kuni. In poem 686–88 he enlarges on the natural beauties of the site but acknowledges that this capital with its high mountains and clear view is now "a town belonging to the past" (*furinishi sato*). There is no "divine overture" to this poem; perhaps the whole episode seemed too embarrassing a mistake to associate with the throne. *Kaku arikeru ka* ("was it all to come to this?"), he exclaims. Now Kuni is empty and desolate like Nara. But the last look back focuses on the blossoms and the birds, not on the grass in the streets. Thus even desolation is mantled in beauty. "Desolation" (*aruraku*) means absence of human habitation, but as the poet says in the second envoy, "there has been no change in the color of the things in bloom." Tu Fu (712–70) wrote a little over a decade later a line meaning "the country is destroyed; the mountains and rivers remain." The grief of the Chinese poet seems but faintly foreshadowed here. Kuni had no history; hardly built, it slipped back easily into the natural loveliness that surrounded it. There is regret—the topos demanded that—but the sense of a futile gesture hangs over the loss. The ruined capital at Ōmi was equally short-lived, but it fell in a fratricidal war and represented to Hitomaro (no. 288–90) more than "a pleasant place to dwell." It is rather the image of Yoshino that is superimposed on Sakimaro's vision of a fallen capital.

686–88   [MYS VI: 1063–65 / 1059–61]

A poem composed on a day in spring in sorrow and grief over the desolate remains at Mika Fields; with *tanka*

	Mika no hara	At this capital,
	Kuni no miyako wa	Kuni on the fields of Mika,
	Yama takaku	The mountains are high,
	Kawa no se kiyoshi	The river rapids fresh and clear.
5	Sumiyoshi to	Although people say
	Hito wa iedo mo	This is a pleasant place to dwell,
	Ariyoshi to	And although I too
	Ware wa omoedo	Find it pleasant to be here,
	Furinishi	Since it is now
10	Sato ni shi areba	A town belonging to the past,
	Kuni miredo	Though I look at the land,
	Hito mo kayowazu	There are no people going to and fro;
	Sato mireba	When I look at the town,
	Ie mo aretari	The houses all stand desolate.
15	Hashike yashi	Ah, wellaway!
	Kaku arikeru ka	Was it all to come to this?
	Mimoro tsuku	On Kase Mountain
	Kaseyama no ma ni	Where a shrine was fashioned for the god
	Saku hana no	The bursting blossoms
20	Iro mezurashiku	Spread the colors that I long to see,
	Momotori no	The hundred birds
	Koe natsukashiku	Sing with the voices that I yearn to hear:
	Arigahoshi	Bitterly I regret
	Sumiyoki sato no	The desolation of this pleasant town,
25	Aruraku oshi mo	The place where I would spend my days.

Two Envoys

Mika no hara	This capital,
Kuni no miyako wa	Kuni on the fields of Mika,
Arenikeri	Has grown desolate,
Ōmiyahito no	For now the courtiers have left,
Utsuroinureba	Departing for their new abode.

Saku hana no	There has been no change
Iro wa kawarazu	In the colors of the things in bloom;
Momoshiki no	It is they who served
Ōmiyahito zo	In the Palace of the Hundred Stones
Tachikawarikeru	Who have changed to other scenes.

❊ Sakimaro also composed a land-praising poem divorced from imperial ambitions and their projects. Minume Bay was part of the coast of the Inland Sea at a spot now incorporated into the city of Kōbe. Sakimaro's no. 689–91 combines several of the elements of land worship—mythological depth, a universally experienced sense of awe, immaculate cleanliness, and peerless beauty—with a strong pictorial quality reminiscent of Akahito. Like an impressionist seascape, the panorama shimmers with white on blue— sails, breakers, and dazzling white beaches seen across the sunlit water. Wind, waves, seaweed, and boats are all in motion, while the observing eye travels down the coast. The freedom from any emotional involvement other than sheer admiration is important to the effect of the poem. It is very pure, this picture, framed by a mythic past and bequeathed to the future, but itself an absolute and timeless moment. Subjected to a cultic interpretation, such poems can be described as making an icon of the land itself, and the sacred image of the sun-mirror in the first envoy comes to mind in this regard. But their appeal is not limited by such considerations. They are retinal afterimages of moments in the sun. For the deity Eight Thousand Spears (Yachihoko no Kami), here representing the "Age of the Gods," see nos. 2–5.

689–91   [MYS VI: 1069–71 / 1065–67]

A poem composed on passing Minume Bay; with *tanka*

	Yachihoko no	From the glorious age
	Kami no miyo yori	Of the deity Eight Thousand Spears
	Momofune no	The hundred boatman
	Hatsuru tomari to	Of the eight great islands of the realm
5	Yashimaguni	Have fixed by a firm custom
	Momofunahito no	The roadstead for the anchoring
	Sadameteshi	Of their hundred ships
	Minume no ura wa	Here in the waters of Minume Bay.

Asakaze ni	In the morning breeze
10 Uranami sawaki	The brisk waves whip across the bay,
Yūnami ni	And in the evening waves
Tamamo wa kiyoru	The gemlike seaweed washes on the shore.
Shiramanago	Though I turn and look
Kiyoki hamabe wa	Times without number at the fine white sand
15 Yuki kaeri	Of that clean-swept beach,
Miredo mo akazu	My eyes will never weary of the sight.
Ube shi koso	Well has it been said
Miru hitogoto ni	That every man who ever looked
Kataritsugi	Has told the tale,
20 Shinoikerashiki	Has sung his longing for this place:
Momoyo hete	Through a hundred ages
Shinohaeyukamu	Men will sing their praises still
Kiyoki shirahama	For this clean, white-sanded shore.

Two Envoys

Masokagami	Bright as a mirror,
Minume no ura wa	The sparkling Bay of Minume
Momofune no	Is not ringed
Sugite yukubeki	By such a beach as would allow
Hama ni aranaku ni	The hundred ships to pass it by.

Hama kiyoku	With its clean-swept beach,
Ura uruwashimi	The dazzling beauty of its bay,
Kamiyo yori	From the Age of the Gods
Chifune no hatsuru	A thousand ships have anchored here
Ōwada no hama	By Ōwada's peerless shore.

❊ A journey west by sea took Sakimaro past the dazzling beaches of Minume; one east by land brought him to Ashigara Pass near Hakone, and there he found what Hitomaro had found on Samine: the body of a man. For Hitomaro the wild beaches of the Inland Sea were the setting for a drama, not a radiant seascape. For Sakimaro the mountain pass merely happened to be the place where the man lay. Hitomaro in his one poem brings the worlds of nature and man together for a full sense of the cosmic dimensions of human life. Sakimaro in his two poems deals separately with nature and with man. Despite its identical topic, no. 692 is thus a very different poem from Hitomaro's no. 358–60. Hitomaro speaks of the world, and of himself, and then of and to the man. Sakimaro's poem begins where Hitomaro's ends. The man is addressed immediately at the outset of the poem. His home is imagined; his wife and his garments are described. He is very gaunt, and we are told why—his loyal service to the court has worn him out. This is not Everyman, but a conscript laborer or soldier on his way home (see no. 357). The poet does not identify with him, merely praises and pities him. The poet imagines everything, reconstructs what must have happened. The irony is there, in the Hitomaro manner: the dead man must be cold under his thin cloak. But the poet in making his unfortunate traveler vivid and real removes the mystery that is at the heart of Hitomaro's vision. The dead man in Sakimaro's poem is an unfortunate victim of the hazards of travel and a harsh system of taxation through labor. But he is not you or me.

692   [MYS IX: 1804/1800]

A poem composed on seeing a dead man while passing along the slope of Ashigara

	Okakitsu no	She your darling wife
	Asa o hikihoshi	Must have pulled and dried the hemp
	Imonane ga	Within your hedge
	Tsukurikisekemu	And fashioned whitened garments
5	Shirotae no	For your wear,
	Himo o mo tokazu	Whose strings you never loosened,
	Hitoe yuu	But wound about you
	Obi o mie yui	Thrice the sash that should have gone but once,
	Kurushiki ni	And gave yourself
10	Tsukaematsurite	To all the pains of loyal service.
	Ima dani mo	Now at last
	Kuni ni makarite	You left the court for home,
	Chichi haha mo	Eager in your heart
	Tsuma o mo mimu to	To see your father and mother
15	Omoitsutsu	And your wife again,
	Yukikemu kimi wa	Journeying back to your province.
	Tori ga naku	But along this slope,
	Azuma no kuni no	Guarded by the fearsome gods
	Kashikoki ya	Of Azuma, where speech
20	Kami no misaka ni	Of men resembles cries of birds,
	Nikitae no	You must be cold
	Koromo samura ni	Beneath the thin, soft cloak you wear,
	Nubatama no	And your jet locks
	Kami wa midarete	Are tangled and undone.
25	Kuni toedo	I ask your province,
	Kuni o mo norazu	But you do not speak its name;
	Ie toedo	I ask your home,
	Ie o mo iwazu	But you do not tell me where it is.
	Masurao no	You, a valiant man,
30	Yuki no manimani	Still intent on your journey,
	Koko ni koyaseru	Here have laid yourself to rest.

Takahashi no Asomi (poem from 744?)

As the compilers of *Man'yōshū* note, this poet's personal name is unknown. The clan title Asomi differentiates his family from that of Takahashi no Mushimaro, who was a Muraji. The Takahashi no Asomi were hereditary stewards to the Emperor. The following chōka-hanka set, no. 693–95, is this obscure person's only extant poem. Its position in Book III suggests that the year of composition was 744. As a lament for a dead wife the poem bears a striking resemblance to Hitomaro's no. 348–50. In both poems death is spoken of as a fading or flying away into the wild world; in both the wife has left behind a *midoriko*, or "greenling" infant, that the bereaved husband struggles clumsily to care for. And in both the wife is said to have gone into the mountains, which become the final focus of the husband's attention.

Takahashi's poem, like Hitomaro's, is laden with reproach for the mate who has abandoned her husband and child, a reproach that is an altered way of speaking of the demands of love. The opening is intimate, with the pair shown in bed, exchanging vows. These vows are broken through no wish of theirs, but still the wife is spoken of as having gone away. For Yamanoue no Okura this would have been a case of *yo no naka no michi*, and Hitomaro too mentions *yo no naka* ("what life must bring") at this point in his poem. Takahashi does not, leaving the break unmediated. The significance of "the new age" (*aratayo*, line 7) is not clear. Perhaps the phenomenon of a peripatetic capital dealt with by Sakimaro has some bearing on it, or the term may betray an awareness that the Nara age was in fact an adventure in new institutions and rapidly changing ways of life.

The vision the poem holds out (and dashes) of an old couple living on into new days is an effective way of expressing mutual devotion, but the quasi-political facet is one not found in Hitomaro's private poetry. The wild archaic "search for the dead" that is so important in Hitomaro is also tempered here. The speaker of the poem does not struggle frantically through the mountains looking for his love but merely gazes at the mountain from a distance. The mountain is a *yosuka*, a "landmark," as for the wife of the fisherman Arao (no. 650). It is where his love "went in" (*irinishi*)—where her body was taken for burial or whatever disposition was made of it—and the mountain is now identified with her. Princess Ōku's poem (no. 276) on Mount Futagami sixty years earlier had made this identification even more closely. The variant forms *utsusomi/utsusemi* link her poem to the first envoy of Takahashi's lament. The meaning may have shifted, as historically it did, from "actual person" (i.e., human being) to "empty cicada" (*utsu-semi*, the cast-off husk of a cicada), a prime metaphor for the vacuity of life. This *utsu-semi no yo* would then be the final ironic comment on the *aratayo* of line 7. (On *aratayo*, see also line 49 of Sakimaro's chōka about the abandonment of Nara, no. 674.)

693-95

A poem composed by Takahashi no Asomi, grieving for his dead wife; with
tanka

Shirotae no	White barken-cloth
Sode sashikaete	Sleeves thrust out to each other,
Nabikineshi	Nestled we lay:
Wa ga kurokami no	My black hair in your embrace
5 Mashiraka ni	Would turn pure white
Narinamu kiwami	At the border of some distant day
Aratayo ni	And we still be
Tomo ni aramu to	Together side by side in the new age.
Tama no o no	Thread of my soul,
10 Taeji i imo to	Never should I be sundered from you:
Musubiteshi	We bound ourselves—
Koto wa hatasazu	With words not kept to the end;
Omoerishi	We loved each other—
Kokoro wa togezu	With hearts left unfulfilled.
15 Shirotae no	For you have parted
Tamoto o wakare	From these sleeves of barken white,
Nikibinishi	You have gone away
Ie yu mo idete	From the house you made so sweet;
Midoriko no	You have abandoned
20 Naku o mo okite	The crying of our greenling child.
Asakiri no	As in morning mist
Ō ni naritsutsu	You faded to a distant blur,
Yamashiro no	Slowly receding
Sagarakayama no	Into the mountains, the valleys
25 Yama no ma ni	Between the mountains
Yukisuginureba	Of Sagaraka in Yamashiro.
Iwamu sube	What can I say,
Semu sube shirani	What can I do? I know nothing.
Wagimoko to	Into the bower
30 Saneshi tsumaya ni	Where I slept with my young love
Ashita ni wa	Of a morning
Idetachi shinoi	I go to stand remembering,
Yūhe ni wa	Of an evening
Irii nagekai	I enter and sit sighing.
35 Wakibasamu	Crooked beneath my arm
Ko no naku goto ni	Our baby cries, and I try again,
Otokojimono	Man though I am,
Oimi mudakimi	Carrying it on my back or held in front.
Asatori no	Like a morning bird
40 Ne nomi nakitsutsu	I keep crying, weeping aloud,

Kouredo mo	Yearning for her
Shirushi o nami to	Without any sign of help.
Kototowanu	And so I turn,
Mono ni wa aredo	Though it is a speechless thing,
45 Wagimoko ga	To the mountain
Irinishi yama o	Where my young love went in
Yosuka to zo omou	As the landmark of my longing.

Envoys

Utsusemi no	From the empty husk
Yo no koto nareba	Of the world of the living
Yoso ni mishi	Shall I turn now
Yama o ya ima wa	My once incurious gaze
Yosuka to omowamu	To a mountain as the landmark of my love?

Asatori no	Like a morning bird
Ne nomi shi nakamu	I shall cry, weeping aloud:
Wagimoko ni	For with my young love,
Ima mata sara ni	Now that it has come to this,
Au yoshi o nami	There is no way to meet again.

The above three poems were composed on the twentieth of the seventh month by Takahashi no Asomi. Research has not yet revealed his personal name. But he is said to have been a man who served in the Office of the Imperial Table.

Ahe no Mushimaro (d. 752)

Ahe no Mushimaro was a minor court official who left a handful of tanka in *Man'yōshū*. In 740 he was a member of the expeditionary force to put down the rebellion of Fujiwara no Hirotsugu, and was rewarded for his exploits by promotion to a higher court rank. He was the first cousin of Lady Ōtomo of Sakanoue and engaged in what purports to be a mock love exchange with her (nos. 1130–32). Mushimaro's poem on Mount Mikasa and the late-rising moon is closely echoed in a similar observation by Lady Ōtomo (no. 719). Mount Mikasa, one of the hills east of Nara, has the epithet "rain-sheltering" (*amagomori*) from its name, "Royal Umbrella."

696   [MYS VI:985/980]

A moon poem by Ahe no Asomi Mushimaro

Amagomori	Rain-sheltering
Mikasa no yama o	Mount Mikasa is so high—
Takami ka mo	Perhaps that's why the moon

Tsuki no idekonu
Yo wa kutachitsutsu

Has yet to come up over it,
Even while night wastes away.

Ahe no Nakamaro (ca. 700–770)

Ahe no Nakamaro was sent to China in the embassy of 717 as a young student and ended by staying there the rest of his life. He adopted a Chinese name, served the T'ang court, and was known by the Chinese poets of the day. His attempt to return to Japan with a later embassy in 751 was foiled by storms. Nakamaro's only known waka was supposedly composed on the occasion of this attempted departure. It does not appear in *Man'yōshū*, but turns up among the travel poems in *Kokinshū*, and in a variant version in *Tosa Nikki*, the tenth-century fictionalized travel diary of Ki no Tsurayuki. Nakamaro's success in China was applauded from afar in his home country, where he posthumously received the honor of being elevated to Senior Second Rank.

It is possible that the poem and the anecdote connected with it are the embellishments of legend-makers in Japan. Nevertheless, Nakamaro was a man of the Man'yō age, and the poem associated with him belongs here. In it he thinks of home, as Yamanoue no Okura (no. 619) did, in terms of a particular place. Nakamaro's place is the same as that referred to by his kinsman Mushimaro in poem 696. Here the moon is risen, and Nakamaro sees it in his mind's eye over Mount Mikasa. It is a fine poem, for all that its ringing opening lines are a formula that appears seven times in *Man'yōshū*. The third and fourth lines occur three times, twice in conjunction with a moon image. None of this diminishes the quality of the poem in the least, or even of itself casts doubt on Nakamaro's authorship. The number of shared lines in *Man'yōshū* is very high in any case, and clearly there was a tradition of associating the moon with Mount Mikasa. The fact remains that the poem attributed to Nakamaro is more memorable than any of the others. Its strong cadences and vast sweep match each other well, and the final image of the moon floats above an arpeggio based on repetitions of the bright, open vowel *a*. Whoever put the poem together knew how to use the language.

697 [KKS IX : 406]

Composed on seeing the moon in China

Ama no hara
Furisakemireba
Kasuga naru
Mikasa no yama ni
Ideshi tsuki kamo

When I gaze afar
High into the plain of heaven,
    I see the moon—
The same that once in Kasuga
Stood risen on Mikasa Mount.

Concerning this poem the following story is told: Long ago Nakamaro was sent to China with instructions to acquire learning. He spent many years there without being able to return home. Finally another ambassador went from our country, and Nakamaro decided to go back with him. The people of that country held a farewell banquet on the seashore at a place called Ming-chou [Ningpo]. Night came, and the moon rose in all its beauty. Nakamaro composed this poem at the sight.

Emperor Shōmu (701–56)

Emperor Shōmu was the son of Emperor Mommu. When Mommu died in 707, he was succeeded by his mother, who reigned as Empress Gemmei until 715 and moved the capital to Nara. Gemmei abdicated in favor of her daughter, Mommu's sister, whose reign name was Genshō, and who in turn abdicated in 724. This brought Shōmu to the throne, where he remained until his own abdication in 749. The Nara period ended the presumption that a sovereign would reign until his or her death. Of the Emperors and Empresses whose reigns terminated in the eighth century, two died in office, five abdicated, and one was deposed. Vicious rivalries within the imperial house and within and between the noble families characterized the period. In the midst of this, Shōmu's twenty-five years on the throne were a time of artistic and literary florescence such as had never been seen before. Despite its vicissitudes, Nara continued to grow as a great and increasingly Buddhist city. Shōmu and his consort Kōmyōshi, the daughter of a Fujiwara father and a Tachibana mother, were fervent adherents of the faith and lavish imperial patrons. When Shōmu abdicated in favor of his equally devout daughter in 749, he declared himself "the slave of the Three Treasures" (Buddha, Dharma, Sangha) and devoted his remaining years to his great project of creating the largest temple and icon in the world. When he died in 756 his widow donated his personal collection of objets d'art from all over Asia to form the basis of the unbelievably rich and refined holdings of the Shōsōin. It was a cosmopolitan age, and the image of its monarch seems vastly removed from that still moment on the fields of Aki when, Hitomaro tells us, Shōmu's father the young Prince Karu greeted the dawn and a ghostly hunter (see no. 331–35).

Shōmu was the author of ten tanka and one chōka preserved in *Man'yōshū*. The chōka is of the greatest interest as an example of a sovereign speaking to his subjects, employing a style replete with self-applied honorifics. This composition, no. 698–99, immediately follows Takahashi no Mushimaro's poem on the dispatch of Fujiwara no Umakai as Regional Commander of the Western Sea Circuit (no. 581–82) and commemorates the same occasion. The date is therefore 732. Other appointments at this time included Fujiwara no Fusasaki to the Eastern Sea Circuit (Tōkaidō) and Eastern Mountain Circuit (Tōsandō), and Tajihi no Agatamori (see the commentary on no. 634–35, Okura's "Dialogue on Poverty") to the North-of-the-Mountains Circuit (San'indō).

The chronicles preserve numerous examples of early songs on the presentation of wine to the ruler (nos. 39–40, 48–49, 100–101, 103, 118, 173). The reverse situation, where the ruler presents drink to his subjects or shares it with them, is less frequently encountered but may be found in nos. 43, 102, 119–20, and 153, as well as in nos. 1169–73. In none of these is found anything like the rhetoric of Shōmu's no. 698. There are echoes here of no. 236 in the unhesitating assertion of power and rule, but for Shōmu the promised caress is a metaphor of state rather than the goal of an amorous quest. The pomp and dignity of the address associate it with the figure of the god-Sovereign created by Hitomaro, but there is no invocation of the divine myth, and no solar image. The monarch's folded arms suggest an ideal of rule through the unmoving embodiment of the Mandate of Heaven on the ancient Chinese model. At the same time, the chōka's metrical irregularity, with four short lines followed by three long ones, suggests that the poem is an incantation, a vehicle for the word soul (kotodama) intended to bestow blessings on the departing officials. It is an altogether unusual performance and needs to be read in conjunction with the farewell poems by Mushimaro (no. 581–82) and Okura (no. 636–38). The appeal to heroism in the envoy is particularly interesting as a parallel to the envoy in Mushimaro's poem. Okura's many gods appear not at all in Shōmu's chōka; he himself is the guarantor of all. The final note probably refers to the envoy rather than to the entire poem. Former Empress Genshō, Shōmu's aunt, lived on until 748.

698–99   [MYS VI: 978–79/973–74]

A poem composed by the Emperor, bestowing wine on the Regional Commanders; with *tanka*

	Osu kuni no	In the land We rule
	Tō no mikado ni	To Our distant royal gates
	Imashira ga	You now take your way,
	Kaku makarinaba	Departing thus from Our presence:
5	Tairakeku	We shall be at peace,
	Ware wa asobamu	Untroubled in Our leisure;
	Tamudakite	We shall fold Our arms,
	Ware wa imasamu	Seated secure in power.
	Sumera wa ga	We your Sovereign
10	Uzu no mite mochi	With Our peerless royal hand
	Kakinade so	Shall stroke you,
	Negitamau	Bestowing Our reward;
	Uchinade so	Shall caress you,
	Negitamau	Bestowing Our reward:

15 Kaerikomu hi   On the day that you return
    Ainomamu ki so   We shall drink this wine together,
    Kono toyomiki wa   This rich and royal wine.

Envoy

   Masurao no   Roads of stalwart men
  Yuku tou michi so   Are the roads you travel on:
    Ōroka ni   Take them not lightly
  Omoite yuku na   As you go upon your way,
  Masurao no tomo   You band of stalwart men.

The above poem is said by some to be a composition of the Retired Sovereign [Genshō].

Princess Yashiro (known dates 737–58)

Princess Yashiro, whose genealogy is unknown, was a recipient of the favors of Emperor Shōmu. After his death she was reduced in rank because she committed the lèse-majesté of loving someone else. She left one poem in *Man'yōshū*, and another is attributed to her in *Shinkokinshū*. The significance of a stream of water for a woman with a secret love has been explored in connection with nos. 483 by Princess Tajima and 509 by Lady Ki. For Princess Yashiro the river is a river of lustral cleansing (*misogi*). In no. 700 she would flee Nara for Asuka and wash her love away in Asuka River. In no. 701, a version preserved in *Shinkokinshū*, the prayer has altered to one for the affair to continue in secret, and the place of lustration is in the opposite direction. *Nara no ogawa* ("the oak stream") refers to the water from the Kamo River that runs through the Upper Kamo Shrine north of, but antedating, the city of Kyōto. Nara here is not the city of that name.

700   [MYS IV: 629/626]

A poem presented by Princess Yashiro to the Emperor

   Kimi ni yori   Since because of you
  Koto no skigeki o   Talk has grown to a thicket,
    Furusato no   I shall make my way
  Asuka no kawa ni   Back to the old capital
  Misogi shi ni yuku   And cleanse in Asuka River.

701   [SKKS XV: 1376/1375]

   Misogi suru   Over the oak stream
  Nara no ogawa no   Where the cleansing rites are held
    Kawakaze ni   My prayer is wafted

| Inori zo wataru | Far upon the river wind, |
| Shita ni taeji to | That our secret may not die. |

Tachibana no Moroe (684–757)

Tachibana no Moroe was a leading statesman of the Nara period, and the dominant political figure during the latter part of Emperor Shōmu's reign. The son of Prince Mino and Agata Inukai Tachibana no Michiyo, he was half brother of Empress-Consort Kōmyōshi on his mother's side. He was known as Prince Katsuragi until 736, at which time he gave up his royal status and took his mother's clan name of Tachibana. Thanks to the fatalities among the Fujiwara leaders in the smallpox epidemic of 737, he rose rapidly to power, becoming Minister of the Right in 738 and Minister of the Left in 743. In 749 he reached the supreme rank of Senior First, an extremely unusual honor. But his last years were clouded by resurgent Fujiwara influence, wielded by Muchimaro's son Nakamaro (706–64). He resigned from office in the year former Emperor Shōmu died and died himself the following year. The Ōtomo were factionally allied to Moroe, and it has been suggested that he motivated Yakamochi to compile the collection that became known as *Man'yōshū*. Moroe was not himself a poet of much talent. No. 702 is one of several tanka he composed on social occasions, an appropriate response to a visit from former Emperor Shōmu, the ruler whom he had served for many years. Other examples of his work appear in the section on poetic exchanges.

702   [MYS XIX : 4294 / 4270]

[One of] four poems composed at a banquet at the house of Minister of the Left Tachibana no Asomi on the eighth of the eleventh month [of 752]

Mugura hau	Round this mean hovel
Iyashiki yado mo	Overgrown with crawling weeds,
Ōkimi no	Had I only known
Masamu to shiraba	My Sovereign would come to call,
Tama shikamashi o	I would have spread a path of jewels.

The above poem is by Minister of the Left Lord Tachibana.

Ōtomo no Ikenushi (active 730's–50's; living in 757)

Ōtomo no Ikenushi was a minor court and provincial official whose service as provincial Secretary of Etchū in the late 740's coincided with Yakamochi's governorship of that province. He and Yakamochi, with whom his genealogical relationship is not clear, exchanged a copious correspondence in poetry (both Chinese and Japanese) and prose, and most of Ikenushi's work translated in the present anthology will be found in the section on poetic exchanges. After his service in Etchū from 746 until no later than 749, Ikenushi was transferred to the neighboring province of Echizen in the same capacity. He was back in the province of Yamato by 753 and was incarcerated four years later for joining in the attempted coup of Tachibana no Naramaro, the son of Moroe. His subsequent fate is unknown. His bright and loquacious personality emerges strongly in his correspondence with Yakamochi, of whom he seems to have been very fond. The following poem is earlier, composed at a winter banquet in the year 738. The poem is not exceptional, merely an appropriate response to the occasion, but read in retrospect it takes on a somber resonance. Naramaro, the young host of the party (he was then sixteen or seventeen), some twenty years later attempted to move against resurgent Fujiwara power within months of his father's death. He failed and was executed in 757, and many of his Ōtomo allies were dragged down with him.

703   [MYS VIII: 1594/1590]

[One of] eleven poems from a party held by Tachibana no Asomi Naramaro

Kaminazuki	The bright leaves of fall
Shigure ni aeru	That have known the chilly showers
Momichiba no	Of harsh November
Fukaba chirinamu	Will fly before the slightest wind,
Kaze no manimani	Whirling, eddying at its will.

The above poem is by Ōtomo no Sukune Ikenushi.

Tajihi no Kunihito (active 730's–50's; living in 757)

Tajihi no Kunihito is another courtier who was implicated in Tachibana no Naramaro's revolt, resulting in his exile to Izu in eastern Japan. Before that he served in various posts, provincial and metropolitan, following the typical career of a minor official. His relationship to Tajihi no Kasamaro (nos. 464–65) is not known. One of Kunihito's three extant poems is the following chōka-hanka set. (For another, see no. 906.) In this poem Kunihito follows the example of Takahashi no Mushimaro in climbing Mount Tsukuha. Kunihito's ascent is early in the year, with snow still on the ground, but the mountain's magnetism does not allow him to forgo the challenge. (Mushimaro records having climbed the mountain in the heat of summer, as well as in spring and fall.) The *kunimi* ("land-surveying") to be done on Tsukuha is not the imperial rite of no. 238, though this poem like that employs the many/one formula, but as with Mushimaro (no. 585–86) a private exhilaration that comes from "wading to the top" and seeing the world spread out below. The mention of the twin peaks (one male, one female) looks ahead to the rites of spring (no. 587–88).

704–5   [MYS III: 385–86/382–83]

A poem composed by Tajihi no Mahito Kunihito on climbing the peak of Tsukuha; with *tanka*

Tori ga naku	In the cock-crowing
Azuma no kuni ni	Eastern Land of Azuma
Takayama wa	Towering mountains
Sawa ni aredo mo	Fill the earth with their numbers,
5 Futagami no	But the twin-god
Tōtoki yama no	Noble mountain of two crests
Namitachi no	Rising side by side
Migahoshi yama to	Is the mountain all would see:
Kamiyo yori	From the Age of the Gods
10 Hito no iitsugi	Men have spoken of it so—
Kunimi suru	The land-surveying
Tsukuha no yama o	Lookout mountain of Tsukuha.
Fuyugomori	The winter-hidden
Tokijiki toki to	Season still unseasonable,
15 Mizute ikaba	I might pass it by—
Mashite koishimi	To yearn the more for what I had not seen:
Yukige suru	Hence through the snow-melt
Yamamichi sura o	All along this mountain trail
Nazumi zo a ga keru	I have waded till I reached the top.

Envoy

Tsukuhane o	Unable to pass by
Yoso nomi mitsutsu	The peak of Tsukuha with only
Arikanete	An indifferent glance,
Yukige no michi o	Through the snow-melt on the trail
Nazumikeru kamo	I have waded to the top.

Imube no Kuromaro (active 730's; living in 762)

Little is known of this minor court official from a clan of Shintō sacer-dotalists. Kuromaro's ancient clan title of Obito was not on Emperor Temmu's revised list of eight; he was granted Muraji in 759. Among Kuromaro's four tanka in *Man'yōshū*, the following two are of interest as contrasting treatments of autumn imagery. The first is purely seasonal, an evocation of the time of coming cold in the just-harvested rice fields. The hut in the fields (see no. 253) is to guard against the depredations of the geese, and of the deer mentioned in the next poem. This next poem (no.

707) is a love poem, with the autumn imagery incorporated in a jo occupying the first three lines and overlapping with the main statement in the swing line, line 4. "Rough fields" (*arakida*) are paddies newly brought under cultivation. The anecdote about the poem having been composed in a dream adds its own extraneous interest.

706   [MYS VIII: 1560/1556]

A poem by Imube no Obito Kuromaro

Akita karu	We've not yet pulled down
Kario mo imada	The hut that guards the autumn fields
Kobotaneba	In harvest time,
Kari ga ne samushi	But the cries of geese are cold,
Shimo mo okinu gani	And frost is in the air.

707   [MYS XVI: 3870/3848]

A poem composed in a dream

Arakida no	From the rough fields,
Shishida no ine o	The deer fields, I put the rice
Kura ni agete	Up in the storehouse:
Ana hinehineshi	Oh, these dry and bitter hulls
A ga kouraku wa	Of a longing left untouched!

Concerning the above poem: Imube no Obito Kuromaro composed and sent this poem to a friend in a dream. When he woke up, he had his friend recite it, and it came out just as it had been.

Fujiwara no Yatsuka (715–66)

Fujiwara no Yatsuka was the son of Fusasaki, one of the Fujiwara leaders who died in the smallpox epidemic of 737, and was the person who dispatched a messenger to inquire after the dying Okura (see no. 647) in 733. Admired for his probity and lack of self-interest in a politically vicious age, he rose to the position of Major Counselor (*dainagon*), just below the uppermost echelons of power. From his line descended the main political branch of the Fujiwara that dominated the court in the Heian period. Yatsuka as poet is represented by a handful of tanka and a sedōka, none of which show qualities commensurate with his virtues. Poems 708 and 709 are metaphorical references to an unknown budding beauty. The unusual collocation *itsu mo itsu mo* in no. 708 presumably expresses both eagerness and readiness.

708–9   [MYS III: 401–2/398–99]

Two plum poems by Fujiwara no Asomi Yatsuka (Yatsuka: later name Matate, third son of Fusasaki)

(708)   [401/398]

    Imo ga ie no   At my darling's house
    Sakitaru ume no   The plum tree now blossoming
      Itsu mo itsu mo   Ever whenever
    Narinamu toki ni   It shall come into the fruit
    Koto wa sadamemu   The matter will be settled.

(709)   [402/399]

    Imo ga ie ni   At my darling's house
    Sakitaru hana no   The flower now blossoming,
      Ume no hana   Flower of the plum:
    Mi ni shi narinaba   When it comes into the fruit,
    Ka mo kaku mo semu   I'll enjoy it as I please.

Kawahe no Azumato (poem from 730's?; living in 770)

Kawahe no Azumato was the messenger sent by Fujiwara no Yatsuka to inquire after Okura (see no. 647). He has left one tanka in Man'yōshū. Azumato, a client of the family of Fujiwara no Fusasaki, seems to have had a
career as a minor official and was serving as Governor of Iwami in 770. His
poem is an early expression of concern for the cherry blossom, a fully explored theme in later poetry. Shikushiku ("incessantly") has an onomatopoeic quality expressive of splashing rain.

710   [MYS VIII: 1444/1440]

A poem by Kawahe no Asomi Azumato

    Harusame no   Showers of spring rain
    Shikushiku furu ni   Swishing, splashing on the hills—
      Takamato no   On Takamato
    Yama no sakura wa   How will the mountain cherry
    Ika ni ka aruramu   Be faring in all this wet?

Ōtomo no Katami (poems from 730's or 740's; living in 772)

Katami's known career, that of a minor official, is datable to the third
quarter of the eighth century, but the placement of his five tanka suggests
they are love poems of his youth. His relation to the other Ōtomo is not
known. In no. 711 Katami's use of kimi, normally reserved for males, implies that the lady who is the object of his ardor is above him socially. The
poem's intensity is achieved through the force of the emphatic particle so at
the end of each of the two urgent sentences, through the pillow-word image
karikomo no ("of sickled rushes"), and through the constrainedly polite but

bristling negative imperative with its four *k*-consonants in the opening two lines. *Tadaka*, the "direct fragrance," and by extension the self, suggests the compelling and intimate nature of the rage that explodes in these well-chosen words.

711   [MYS IV : 700/697]

[One of] three poems by Ōtomo no Sukune Katami

Wa ga kiki ni	Not in my hearing
Kakete na ii so	Shall you ever speak of her;
Karikomo no	That lady's fragrance
Midarete omou	Is a wildness in my longing
Kimi ga tadaka so	Like tangles of sickled rushes.

Ōtomo no Miyori (d. 774)

Another Ōtomo of obscure genealogical affiliations, Miyori served in Kyūshū during Tabito's incumbency as Governor-General of Dazaifu, and otherwise pursued the usual career of a minor official, serving as Governor of three different provinces. His four *tanka* date from the 730's and possibly 740's. As Katami did in no. 711, Miyori uses *kimi* for a woman in no. 712; it has been suggested that this mark of respect was intended for Princess Kamo (see following section). He refers to himself as *wake*, a familiar or self-demeaning term for young males. "On the double" renders *futahashi-ruramu* ("twice running"), an outcry against the fickleness of a changeable love. In no. 713 Miyori addresses his (different?) lady with a familiar *wagimoko* ("my darling girl"). His reassuring greeting suggests she has been living in Tokoyo, the mythical land of immortality, since last they met.

712   [MYS IV : 555/552]

A poem by Ōtomo no Sukune Miyori

A ga kimi wa	Is my lady then
Wake o ba shine to	Intent on the death of her young swain—
Omoe ka mo	Is that what she wants?
Au yo awanu yo	Nights together, nights apart,
Futahashiruramu	She keeps him on the double.

713   [MYS IV : 653/650]

A poem by Ōtomo no Sukune Miyori, in joy at meeting after separation

Wagimoko wa	My own darling girl
Tokoyo no kuni ni	Must have been living somewhere
Sumikerashi	In the Timeless Land:

| Mukashi mishi yori | She has grown even younger |
| Ochimashinikeri | Than when I saw her last. |

Princess Kamo (poems from 730's)

As stated in the headnote to no. 714, Princess Kamo was the daughter of Prince Nagaya (no. 505). In this poem she has gone down to Naniwa to see off Ōtomo no Miyori on his way to Tsukushi (Kyūshū). The pillow and pivot words in no. 715 suggest they are meeting in the same place (Mitsu of Ōtomo), perhaps after his return. *Mitsu* puns on the word for "I saw"; the Princess promises to keep the tryst secret (all the while revealing it in her poem).

714   [MYS IV: 559/556]

A poem sent to Ōtomo no Sukune Miyori by Princess Kamo (daughter of the late Minister of the Left Prince Nagaya)

Tsukushibune	The Tsukushi boat
Imada mo koneba	Has not even come, and yet
Arakajime	Already
Araburu kimi o	The sadness of seeing you
Miru ga kanashisa	Grow distant in your heart.

715   [MYS IV: 568/565]

A poem by Princess Kamo

Ōtomo no	At Ōtomo
Mitsu to wa iwaji	*Mitsu*—"I saw him!"—never
Akane sashi	Shall I tell it, though
Tereru tsukuyo ni	Under the madder-shining moon
Tada ni aeri to mo	We are meeting face to face.

Lady Ōtomo of Sakanoue (b. ca. 695?—active until 750)

Lady Ōtomo of Sakanoue (Ōtomo no Sakanoue no Iratsume) was the half sister of Tabito and the aunt of Yakamochi. In her youth she married Prince Hozumi (see commentary to no. 484) and after his death in 715 she was courted and won by Fujiwara no Maro, one of the Fujiwara leaders who died in the epidemic of 737. Her relationship with Maro had ended well before the 730's, however, and she had married her half brother Sukunamaro, by whom she had two daughters; the elder became the wife of Yakamochi. After the death of Tabito's wife in 728, Lady Ōtomo went to Dazaifu, where she took on the role of foster-mother to her young nephew. When Tabito himself died three years later, she seems to have been for a time the de facto head of the Ōtomo clan. Clearly a woman of great energy and acumen, she is also the major woman poet of *Man'yōshū*. Her eighty-four extant poems include a number of notable essays in the amorous mode, but these are sometimes accompanied by notes explaining away her apparent passion as familial affection or a literary game. The impression that she was a woman of rich sexual experience is nevertheless hard to avoid, though the nature of that experience and its relevance to her poetry raise puzzling questions. A noticeable intimacy pervades her manner of expression, whether she is addressing her daughter, her son-in-law, or one of her numerous cousins. Aside from her own importance as a poet, it seems inevitable that she must have been a major influence on Yakamochi, and through him on *Man'yōshū* itself. The preservation of so many of her poems was no doubt a return favor. Several of her poems are dated or datable; others are not. The translations below start with the first group and continue with the second. Other poems by Lady Ōtomo appear in the section on poetic exchanges.

In the year 733 Ōtomo no Tabito was dead, and his son and successor as head of the Ōtomo clan, Yakamochi, was only about fifteen years of age. These facts may account for the role in which Lady Ōtomo of Sakanoue portrays herself in no. 716–17, the most unusual of her poems. The poem shows her conducting formal Shintō worship of the clan gods. The Ōtomo lineage stemmed from Ame no Oshihi no Mikoto, a god who participated as armed vanguard in the descent of the original Heavenly Sun Child, the grandson of the sun goddess, to rule the earth. In her ceremony Lady Ōtomo is worshiping this ancestral god and his descendants. She serves as clan priestess, whether or not this was her usual role, and performs the sacred actions of waving the holy *sakaki* branch with its streamers of white fiber (*yū*) made from paper-mulberry bark, setting up the jars of offertory wine, and kneeling in prayer, decked out in strings of bamboo disks. All this is provided with a formal four-line introduction directly addressing the gods. But then in the last three lines, and in the envoy, the rite becomes personal and private, a prayer that she may meet a man—her lover? Rather than judge the lady sacrilegious, however, it is more satisfactory to interpret the first sixteen lines of the poem as an extended metaphor for the intense anxiety of her passion, a metaphor suggested to her by actually having enacted the rite. This seems to be the significance of the prose note that follows the poem. Nevertheless, the result is a striking juxtaposition of high cultic language with the most intimate of personal desires. The identity of the object of the lady's prayerful attentions is not known. Her husband Sukunamaro is thought to have died in the 720's, leaving her a widow and perhaps free to engage in what affairs were to her liking. She would have been in her thirties at this time.

716–17   [MYS III: 382–83/379–80]

A poem in which Lady Ōtomo of Sakanoue worships her gods; with *tanka*

	Hisakata no	From the sun-bright realm,
	Ama no hara yori	The plains of heaven on high,
	Arekitaru	Born into this world,
	Kami no mikoto	You gods mighty of word:
5	Okuyama no	To the sacred branch,
	Sakaki no eda ni	*Sakaki* from the distant hills,
	Shiraka tsuke	I tie white-tresses,
	Yū toritsukete	Take and tie fine barken strands;
	Iwaihe o	Offertory jars
10	Iwaihorisue	I offer set into the earth,
	Takatama o	Disks of fine bamboo
	Shiji ni nukitare	String thick upon a dangling cord,
	Shishijimono	And like a deer
	Hiza orifushite	Fall forward on my bended knees,
15	Tawayame no	Casting about me
	Osuhi torikake	The stole of a tender maiden:
	Kaku dani mo	Even in such ways
	Are wa koinamu	Shall I beg for him I love—
	Kimi ni awaji ka mo	But I fear we shall not meet.

Envoy

	Yūtatami	The bark-fiber mat
	Te ni torimochite	I take and hold in my hands:
	Kaku dani mo	Even in such ways
	Are wa koinamu	Shall I beg for him I love—
	Kimi ni awaji ka mo	But I fear we shall not meet.

The above poem is one to whose composition she gave some small effort in the winter of Tempyō 5 [733], when she worshiped the Ōtomo clan gods in the eleventh month. Hence it is called a poem in which she worships her gods.

❊ Composed in the same year as the preceding poem, as seems likely from its placement in Book VI, is a tanka in which Lady Ōtomo expresses her solicitude for her nephew Yakamochi. She is apparently in residence at the main Ōtomo mansion at Saho north of the capital, and Yakamochi is leaving for another residence, perhaps that at Sakanoue. She refers to him as *wa ga seko*, an endearment usually applied to a husband or lover. Lady Ōtomo is noted for this tendency to define her relationships in amorous terms. Yakamochi, then about fifteen, was her intended son-in-law. The poem well conveys her motherly feelings. The cold winds of Saho suggest that the poem was composed in the same season as the rite of supplication described in no. 716–17.

718   [MYS VI:984/979]

A poem given by Lady Ōtomo of Sakanoue to her nephew Yakamochi on his return from Saho to the western residence

Wa ga seko ga	This young man of mine,
Keru kinu usushi	The garments that he wears are thin—
Sahokaze wa	Winds of Saho,
Itaku na fuki so	Blow not harshly upon him
Ie ni itaru made	Till he arrives at his home.

✳ Three poems on the moon by Lady Ōtomo display a variety of approaches to nature. The first (no. 719) immediately follows a similar poem by Ahe no Mushimaro (no. 696). Since the two were cousins, and very intimate ones at that (see nos. 1130–32 in the section on exchanges), it seems more than likely that the similarity is not accidental, and indeed the poems may have been composed at the same moon-viewing party. The question of precedence may be a red herring, though. Since an earlier tanka by Isonokami no Maro (no. 473) also employs the middle line *takami ka mo* ("is it because it is high?"), it seems plausible that there was an established trope in which the poet inquired what lay behind a high mountain. Lady Ōtomo's working out of the trope is particularly effective because of the triple repetition of *taka* ("high"), an element that appears in the two place-names that are the seed of the poem, making it seem inevitable, if perhaps a little trite.

The second poem (no. 720), by contrast, is a pure appreciation of the visual quality and emotional overtones of a night scene, free from rhetorical device other than the introductory epithet *nubatama no* ("bead-black"). The association of melancholy with a scene, the perception of moods in nature—these are elements in poetic sensibility, elements found also in the poetry of Lady Ōtomo's nephew Yakamochi, pointing to one of the lines of development that Japanese poetry would take. When Hitomaro feels the melancholy in the cries of the plovers on Lake Biwa (no. 291), he is moved by more than the sound and the scene. These are part of the tragic history of the place. When Yakamochi employs similar phraseology in no. 831, he is showing his sensitivity to *mono no aware*, the sadness of things.

The third poem (no. 721) is particularly interesting for its note on the source of inspiration. One may assume that the information came from Lady Ōtomo herself, with whom the anthologist (Yakamochi) had a privileged relationship. The term *sasaraeotoko* seems to be a *hapax legomenon*. From the word to the poem; from the sight to the poem: the distinction is too simple and rigid to describe the creative process, but these three poems do exemplify it. The first and third grow out of a fascination with words, while the second attempts to find words to capture a mood existing inchoate in the mind. A Wordsworthian "interfusion" makes the mood seem to inhere in both observer and observed, a poetically productive ambiguity echoed in the bivalence of Japanese adjectives. *Mireba kanashisa*, "the sadness upon gazing": one is sad because, somehow, the scene itself is sad. These poems too are from the year 733.

719-21   [MYS VI:986-88/981-83]

Three moon poems by Lady Ōtomo of Sakanoue

(719)   [986/981]

    Karitaka no   By the Hunting Heights
Takamatoyama o   The High Target Mountain soars
    Takami ka mo   High into the sky,
Idekuru tsuki no   Whence perhaps the rising moon
Osoku teruramu   Is so late with its shining.

(720)   [987/982]

    Nubatama no   Over the dark sky,
Yogiri no tachite   Bead-black with glistening night,
    Oboboshiku   A mist has risen:
Tereru tsukuyo no   And the sadness of gazing
Mireba kanashisa   At the vaguely shimmering moon.

(721)   [988/983]

    Yama no ha no   From the mountain crest
Sasaraeotoko   Like a fine and handsome youth
    Ama no hara   Across fields of sky
Towataru hikari   He fords the night, and his shining
Miraku shi yoshi mo   Is fair to look upon.

Concerning the above poem, a certain source says that *sasaraeotoko* ["fine and handsome youth"] is another name for the moon. The author was inspired by the word to compose this poem.

* A final moon poem from the year 733, no. 722, is based on the same superstition about scratching the eyebrows as in Ōtomo no Momoyo's no. 616 (see also no. 1408-09), except that here the action brings rather than predicts the result of meeting a lover. The person the Lady met is not known. She plays on the crescent moon, now visible in the evening sky, and the crescent shape of her "three-day-moon" (*mikazuki*) eyebrows, an elegantly fashionable feature of feminine cosmetic adornment. It is of interest to note that this poem is followed by one by Yakamochi on the crescent eyebrows of someone he once glimpsed (his earliest datable poem: no. 756).

722   [MYS VI: 998 / 993]

A new-moon poem by the same Lady Sakanoue

Tsuki tachite	All I did was scratch
Tada mikazuki no	These eyebrows that are crescent moons,
Mayone kaki	And now the moon is out
Kenagaku koishi	I am meeting you, my lord,
Kimi ni aeru kamo	Whom I've longed for these long days.

✻ Lady Ōtomo's longest poem is her lament on the death of Rigan, a Korean nun who lived as a dependent of the Ōtomo family at Saho. According to the poem (no. 723- 24) and the footnote, Rigan seems to have come from Silla during the lifetime of Lady Ōtomo's father Yasumaro (d. 714) and died in 735. The reasons for her coming to Japan and for her protection by the Ōtomo are no longer known. For the former the poem supplies as answer the complacent Japanese attitude toward its Korean neighbor that seems to have been an article of national belief by this time: the virtue of Japan attracts the (benighted) foreigner. Toward the latter, the formula of puzzlement, *ikasama ni omoikeme ka* ("how can she have been thinking?"), a staple of chōka since Hitomaro, is the readily available stance. By 676 Silla ruled a unified Korean peninsula, so that to say the nun came from Silla is merely to say she came from Korea. Japan had absorbed a considerable Korean population over a period of more than three centuries by this time, and when Silla and T'ang destroyed Japan's ally Paekche in the 660's, there had been an influx of refugees. But Rigan's arrival was presumably subsequent to those events, and for reasons that the poem conceals rather than explains. She apparently was under the care of Lady Ōtomo's mother, the "Grand Mistress" (*ōtoji*) of the note.

The chōka-hanka set continues the tradition of Man'yō elegy with its mournful evocation of the mystery of death and its elevated handling of grief. It is a study in traditional formulas. There are nine pillow-word constructions, providing an essential ingredient of the grand chōka manner developed by Hitomaro. The poem reaches back in time and comes down to the present, making possible the building up of a precious entity to be destroyed in the inevitable victory of "the thing called death" (*shinu to iu koto*). Lines 21–24 are crucial to the creation of this entity, the two epithets, *shikitae no* ("like spread barken cloth") and *aratama no* ("like a rough gem"), implying the simple comforts of the nun's life and the inestimable value of each year. Rigan's passing is couched in terms familiar from Hitomaro and other poets (see nos. 348–50 and 693–95): she vanishes into the mountains and the moors, her ghost fading from sight into the natural world. But most interesting is the way "crossing the morning river" (*asakawa watari*), used in no. 483 as a metaphor for a woman's decision for love, is here the final going over into the unknown beyond. The striking enactments of the archaic dementia of grief and "searching for the dead" are reduced to two lines (45–46) in Lady Ōtomo's lament, but the element is preserved as a part of the total structure in this small token. The chōka ends with a conceit in which the poet's tears and sighs are envisaged as gathering and falling as rain. Into these traditional means of the lament is incorporated a situational explanation in lines 31–34, giving the information that Rigan's death occurred while family members were away. The last three lines of the chōka are a reminder of this circumstance: they reveal that the whole poem is addressed to Lady Ōtomo's mother, away taking the waters at Arima. The Major Counselor and Military Commander in the note is Lady Ōtomo's late father Yasumaro.

723–24   [MYS III: 463–64 / 460–61]

A poem composed by Lady Ōtomo of Sakanoue in the seventh year [of Tempyō, 735], Wood-Junior / Swine, in grief at the death of the nun Rigan; with *tanka*

	Takuzuno no	From Shiraki, the land
	Shiraki no kuni yu	Of the white bark-fiber ropes,
	Hitogoto o	Thinking fair the words
	Yoshi to kikashite	She heard men speaking of our land,
5	Toisakuru	She came across
	Ugara haragara	To this country where she had no kin,
	Naki kuni ni	No brothers or sisters
	Watarikimashite	With whom to talk and ease her heart.
	Ōkimi no	Where our great lord rules
10	Shikimasu kuni ni	In all this country subject to his will,
	Uchihi sasu	Villages abound,
	Miyako shimimi ni	And in his capital, flashing in the sun,
	Sato ie wa	Houses crowd together:
	Sawa ni aredo mo	Yet of places in such multitudes—
15	Ikasama ni	Why, we do not know,
	Omoikeme ka mo	But she must have had good reason—
	Tsure mo naki	She came to the hillsides
	Saho no yamahe ni	Of Saho, here where she had no tie:
	Naku ko nasu	Like a crying child

20 Shitaikimashite	She came as yearning for her home.
Shikitae no	Here she built a house,
Ie o mo tsukuri	Soft with the white of barken cloth,
Aratama no	And while the years went by,
Toshi no o nagaku	Like rough gems, fresh from the earth,
25 Sumaitsutsu	She might have dwelt
Imashishi mono o	Until they formed a string of endless time.
Ikeru hito	Yet the truth is still
Shinu to iu koto ni	That those who live cannot escape
Manukarenu	The thing called death:
30 Mono ni shi areba	Hence it came about that while
Tanomerishi	All of the people,
Hito no kotogoto	Each and every one on whom she leaned,
Kusamakura	Had gone away
Tabi naru aida ni	On a journey, grass for pillow,
35 Sahogawa o	She crossed the river
Asakawa watari	Of Saho, the morning river,
Kasugano o	And while looking
Sogai ni mitsutsu	At the fields of Kasuga beyond,
Ashihiki no	Made her way straight
40 Yamabe o sashite	Toward the mountains, weary to men's feet,
Yūyami to	And as in evening darkness
Kakurimashinure	Vanished forever from our sight.
Iwamu sube	Hence it comes that I
Semu sube shirani	Who know not what to say or do
45 Tamotōri	Can only wander
Tada hitori shite	In aimless circles all alone:
Shirotae no	I cannot dry the sleeves
Koromode hosazu	Of my garment of white barken cloth.
Nagekitsutsu	And the tears I shed
50 Wa ga naku namita	With the endless grieving of my sighs—
Arimayama	Have they gathered
Kumoi tanabiki	To float in clouds on Arima,
Ame ni furiki ya	And did they fall as rain?

Envoy

Todomeenu	Since this is a life
Inochi ni shi areba	That cannot be held back,
Shikitae no	She went from her house,
Ie yu wa idete	Soft with the white of barken cloth,
Kumogakuriniki	And vanished in the clouds.

The nun from the country of Silla referred to above was called Rigan. Far off she was moved by the royal virtue and came hither to give her allegiance to our sagely court. Thereupon she took up residence in the house of Major Counselor and Military Commander Lord Ōtomo, where she lived some dozens of years. Then she suddenly sank into her fatal illness in the seventh year of Tempyō, Wood-Junior/Swine [735] and departed forthwith to the realm of the [Yellow] Springs. At this time Grand Mistress Ishikawa no Myōbu had gone to Arima hot springs for a cure [to her own illness] and missed the funeral. Only the Lady [Ōtomo of Sakanoue] had remained behind. She saw to the burial of the coffin and afterward composed this poem and sent it to the hot springs.

✳ The rest of the poems by Lady Ōtomo of Sakanoue presented in this section are undated. Nos. 725–26 seem to refer to one or the other of the Lady's two daughters, known as Ō-otome (the Elder Maiden) and Oto-otome (the Younger Maiden). During the late 730's Lady Ōtomo was occupied with marriage plans for these girls, offspring of her now-deceased husband Sukunamaro. The Elder Maiden married Yakamochi, apparently in the fall of 739. The Younger Maiden was courted by Ōtomo no Surugamaro (see the commentary to nos. 1113–16), with what success is not known. The most plausible referent for *ie naru hito* ("the person at home") in the first tanka is the Elder Maiden, for whom Lady Ōtomo's strong affection is attested in no. 727–28. The "symbolic equation" of no. 725 strongly implies that the gathering dew finds a counterpart in the tears of the person who waits, longing. The allegory of no. 726 hints that matters have begun between Yakamochi and the Elder Maiden. A physical bonding between mother and daughter is strikingly conveyed by the image of the pillow as substitute. The poem communicates in thirty-one syllables the psychological complexity of a mother's pride and loss.

725–26   [MYS IV : 654–55 / 651–52]

Two poems by Lady Ōtomo of Sakanoue

(725)   [654/651]

Hisakata no	Dew of the heavens
Ame no tsuyushimo	That endure forever gathers
Okinikeri	Here upon the earth;
Ie naru hito mo	She who waits for me at home
Machikoinuramu	Must weep in her longing.

(726)   [655/652]

Tamanushi ni	I have entrusted
Tama wa sazukete	The jewel to the jewel-keeper;
Katsugatsu mo	Whether we will or no,

Makura to ware wa	Come, let us sleep together,
Iza futari nemu	Pillow and I, we two.

❋ Lady Ōtomo's feelings about the Elder Maiden are expressed at greater length in a chōka and envoy written when they were apart. The Lady has gone to an Ōtomo estate at Tomi, perhaps in the Asuka area, since it is referred to as the *furusato* ("old homeland"). The Elder Maiden is at home, presumably at Sakanoue near Nara. Troubled by dreams of her daughter (envoy) and by the memory of a sadness in her face at farewell, the Lady finds herself wasting away, unable to endure a month's separation. Her daughter is now grown up, the *toji*, or "mistress of the house," during her absence, and probably already married to Yakamochi. But the mother is a woman who "yearns desperately" (*motona shi koiba*). She reveals much of herself in a poem such as this, in which the paramountcy of parental love seen in Yamanoue no Okura is joined to a need for closeness that is almost erotic. For Okura, too, children come in troubling dreams (see no. 627–28), and both poets use the adverb *motona* ("desperately," "irrationally"). Lady Ōtomo, however, does not stop there, but uses the lovers' image of tangled hair to evoke her daughter's putative distress (actually her own) at the separation. One is reminded of her sigh as she turned to her pillow as a bedmate (no. 726).

727–28   [MYS IV : 726–27 / 723–24]

A poem sent from the Tomi estate by Lady Ōtomo of Sakanoue to her daughter, the Elder Maiden, who had remained at home; with *tanka*

Tokoyo ni to	I was not leaving
Wa ga yukanaku ni	For the Land of Endless Time,
Okanato ni	But I could tell
Monoganashira ni	There was a sadness in her face
5 Omoerishi	By the metal-bound gate,
A ga ko no toji o	She the mistress of the house, my child:
Nubatama no	Through the bead-black night,
Yoru hiru to iwazu	And through the day, 'tis all the same,
Omou ni shi	I long for her,
10 A ga mi wa yasenu	And my body wastes away;
Nageku ni shi	I sigh for her,
Sode sae nurenu	And am wet to the very sleeves.
Kaku bakari	If I am to yearn
Motona shi koiba	With so desperate a need
15 Furusato ni	There is little chance
Kono tsukigoro mo	I shall bear it to the end,
Arikatsumashiji	This month in the old homeland.

Envoy

Asakami no	Morning-hair-tangled,
Omoimidarete	Thoughts distracted with your love,
Kaku bakari	Your yearning for me
Nane ga koure so	Has been so strong, sweet child,
Ime ni miekeru	You have come to me in dreams.

The above poem is in reply to one sent by the Elder Maiden.

✳ The same theme is couched in the form of an analogy in no. 729. Lady Ōtomo is again away from home, writing to her daughter from Taketa, another Ōtomo estate in the "old homeland" (*furusato*), this one northeast of Mount Miminashi. Her clan responsibilities may have obliged her to visit these various properties on a regular basis. Cranes crying in the distant fields provide an auditory image of ceaselessness structured into a *jo* to introduce the statement of longing in the last two lines. The "crying" of the cranes balances the "longing" of the woman on opposite sides of the swing line (line 4), an implied equivalent that is also an agent to call the longing forth, with a gaze across the fields and toward home.

729   [MYS IV : 763 / 760]

[One of] two poems sent by Lady Ōtomo of Sakanoue from the Taketa estate to her daughter the Elder Maiden

Uchiwatasu	Gazing across the fields,
Taketa no hara ni	At Taketa I hear the cranes
Naku tazu no	Ceaselessly crying:
Ma naku toki nashi	Not a space, not a moment
Wa ga kouraku wa	Of pause in my longing.

✳ Two more tanka composed on tour of the Ōtomo properties are found in Book VIII. Nos. 730 and 731 evince an affinity with nature without direct reference to human ties. One is about bush clover (*hagi*), the other about deer. They form a pair because deer and bush clover were traditionally linked. The bush clover blooms in the fall, when the mating deer are bleating in the hills. Deer push their way through the thickets of bush clover, scattering the blooms. Bush clover is even spoken of as the "wife" of the deer. The first poem opens with a pillow-word construction serving as direct object of a place-name interpreted as a verb. This ingenious device calls attention to the content of the epithet, and one wonders if the endearment *imo* is not intended again for the beloved daughter. Misome no Saki ("Lookout Point") has not been identified, but the two place-names in the second poem are in the Hatsuse area, suggesting the location of the Tomi estate. In both poems the hills are laden with longing, and this quality draws the poet to identify with and "envy" the life that goes on there.

730–31   [MYS VIII: 1564–65 / 1560–61]

Two poems composed by Lady Ōtomo of Sakanoue at the Tomi estate

(730)   [1564 / 1560]

> Imo ga me o
> Misome no Saki no
>   Akihagi wa
> Kono tsukigoro wa
> Chirikosu na yume

> *Eyes of my darling*:
> Steady on the Lookout Point
>   May the clover bloom;
> For a while yet this autumn
> Do not let your flowers fall.

(731)   [1565 / 1561]

> Yonabari no
> Ikai no yama ni
>   Fusu shika no
> Tsuma yobu koe o
> Kiku ga tomoshisa

> How I envy them,
> The deer that crouch on Mount Ikai
>   In Yonabari,
> When I hear their voices cry
> In yearning for their mates.

✳ Lady Ōtomo as love poet appears in a number of undated sequences in Book IV. The preponderance of these are or appear to be exchanges, and some of them raise intriguing questions having to do with factuality, fictionality, the Lady's role as poet, and her relations with her male cousins. A few of these sequences are presented and discussed in the section on poetic exchanges. The following seven tanka, nos. 732–38, are assumed for the purposes of this anthology to be addressed to an unknown man, although they are followed by a poem of parting (with whom it is uncertain) by Lady Ōtomo's kinsman Miyori (for whom see nos. 712–13). The seven poems have about them an intensity that seems altogether genuine. The fear of talk (in the first poem with overtones of the powerful Japanese "word soul," kotodama), the sense of urgency and frustration, the dwelling on barriers of time and space, are as vivid here as anywhere in the love tradition.

Lady Ōtomo has been both praised and blamed for her variations on earlier poems, often anonymous, collections of which may have been among the Ōtomo literary holdings. The second poem (no. 733) is clearly such a variation. The source poem is no. 405, a sedōka in the "Hitomaro Collection." There the poet asks if the girl he loves will not please hurry up and die, there being no sign that she will give herself to him. Lady Ōtomo adopts the role of the woman and declares that she *will* die, her man being similarly uncooperative. The placement of the poem in the sequence leads into the third poem (no. 734), in which the lovers are kept apart by people's talk. The striking metaphor of swords in a double sheath seems to be original with Lady Ōtomo. (There actually were double and even triple sheaths.) The fourth and fifth poems deal with the passage of time and the intensification of blocked desire. Dams crumble, the river of desire rushes on, and in the sixth poem (no. 737) the lover is enjoined not to smile with a too-knowing smile. This verse shares its last two lines with an anonymous poem from Book XI (no. 1396). But it is the original part, the image of the white cloud against the blue mountain, that accounts for the poem's peculiar charm. The last poem returns the lovers to the basics of their situation—the frustration and lean pickings of a secret affair.

732–38   [MYS IV : 686–92 / 683–89]

Seven poems by Lady Ōtomo of Sakanoue

(732)   [686/683]

Iu koto no	This is a country
Kashikoki kuni so	Where talk is a fearsome thing;
Kurenai no	Do not let this out
Iro ni na ide so	In the open blush of crimson,
Omoishinu to mo	Not though you die of longing.

(733)   [687/684]

Ima wa a wa	Now I am going
Shinamu yo wagase	To die, O you man of mine,
Ikeri to mo	For though I live
Wa ni yorubeshi to	There is never any word
Iu to iwanaku ni	You will give yourself to me.

(734)   [688/685]

Hitogoto o	Do you hide beyond
Shigemi ya kimi ga	The thickets of people's talk,
Futasaya no	Longing for me,
Ie o hedatete	Keeping to your house, as I to mine,
Koitsutsu masamu	Like swords in a double sheath?

(735)   [689/686]

Kono koro wa	These days a thousand
Chitose ya yuki mo	Years seem to have passed us by—
Suginuru to	Why should it be so—
Ware ya shika omou	Is it only my fancy,
Mimaku hori ka mo	Or this desire to see you?

(736)   [690/687]

    Uruwashi to   My heart beats fast,
A ga omou kokoro   This heart that thinks you so splendid:
    Hayakawa no   A rushing river
Seki ni seku to mo   I may block with all my dams,
Nao ya kuenamu   But the dams will soon crumble.

(737)   [691/688]

    Aoyama o   Do not smile at me
Yokogiru kumo no   Plainly as a plain white cloud
    Ichishiroku   Drifting straight across
Ware to emashite   The face of a blue mountain—
Hito ni shirayu na   People are sure to know.

(738)   [692/689]

    Umi yama mo   There are no mountains
Hedataranaku ni   And no seas to cut us off—
    Nani shi ka mo   How then can it be
Mekoto o dani mo   That even times to meet and talk
Kokoda tomoshiki   Are so desperately few?

✳ A tanka, no. 739, among the spring love poems (*haru no sōmon*) in Book
VIII is a general comment on the pains of those emotions the Lady seems
most to have cultivated. The "lushness of love" (*koi no shigeki*) is meant to
match the new green growth of spring.

739   [MYS VIII: 1454/1450]

A poem by Lady Ōtomo no Sukune of Sakanoue

    Kokoroguki   What a heart burden
Mono ni so arikeru   I have found this thing to be—
    Harukasumi   The lushness of love
Tanabiku toki ni   In the season of spring mists
Koi no shigeki wa   That trail along the hills.

✳ Most of Lady Ōtomo's poetic doings as they have come down to us are
founded on the highly interwoven affairs of the Ōtomo clan with its numerous marriages between cousins and half siblings. The "clannishness" of
these affairs is given a special sense of romantic intimacy and excitement,
combined with an encompassing motherly warmth, in the poetry of this
ambiguous and fascinating woman. Depending on whether we read the sex-

ual passion in her poems as the imprint of actual experiences or as something else—an arch game of poetic badinage, training in amatory *ars poetica* for her kinsmen—she may seem like the queen tree in a garden of ancient incest, or like the chief mother-poet of her tribe. Three of her poems, however, show that she had contacts outside the family on the highest level. The recipient is Emperor Shōmu himself. The first of the three *tanka* (no. 740) was apparently intended to accompany a gift of some rustic local herb or product and is unassuming in its proper humility. The poem is most interesting for its use of the term *miyabi* ("elegance"), a quality of courtier life that also had overtones of romantic dalliance and sexual receptivity. The other two tanka (nos. 741–42) are couched in amorous terms. In the first Lady Ōtomo addresses the water in the palace pond, asking it to reflect her image before the Emperor. In the second she wishes she could be a wild duck living in that pond. Are these political poems, allegories of Ōtomo fidelity to the Sovereign? Yakamochi was to write a whole chōka (no. 814) on that theme. Is the Lady in love with her Emperor? And if so, is the love itself political or personal? Or is the amorous mode simply her basic manner of address? Aided by her anthologist nephew, the Lady has created a mystery, and is smiling somewhere behind it.

740   [MYS IV : 724 / 721]

A poem presented to the Emperor (composed by Lady Ōtomo of Sakanoue at her home in Saho)

Ashihiki no	Off here as we are
Yama ni shi oreba	In the leg-cramping mountains,
Miyabi nami	We lack elegance;
Wa ga suru waza o	Prithee then, do not reproach
Togametamau na	This small gesture of mine.

741–42   [MYS IV : 728–29 / 725–26]

Two poems presented to the Emperor (composed by Lady Ōtomo of Sakanoue at the village of Kasuga)

(741)   [728 / 725]

Niodori no	Water in the pond
Kazuku ikemizu	Where the diving grebes plunge down,
Kokoro araba	If you have a heart
Kimi ni a ga kouru	Show my heart unto My Lord,
Kokoro shimesane	This heart in all its yearning.

(742)   [729 / 726]

Yoso ni ite	Rather than living,
Koitsutsu arazu wa	Yearning, in a distant place,

Kimi ga ie no	Would that I could be
Ike ni sumu to iu	A wild duck of the ducks that dwell,
Kamo ni aramashi o	So they say, in the pond of My Lord.

The Elder Maiden of the Ōtomo of Tamura (active 730's)

The Elder Maiden of the Ōtomo of Tamura (Ōtomo no Tamura no Ō-otome) was the Lady Ōtomo of Sakanoue's stepdaughter, the child of Ōtomo no Sukunamaro by a wife whose identity has been lost, but who lived at Tamura, apparently Sukunamaro's principal residence at Nara. This Elder Maiden was older than Lady Ōtomo's daughter of the same designation, and it is assumed that she was the offspring of a first, or at least an earlier, marriage. Her mother may no longer have been living by the time Lady Ōtomo of Sakanoue married Sukunamaro. The nine extant tanka by the Elder Maiden of Tamura are all addressed to her half sister, expressing the desire to meet. Whether the sisters in fact did not meet often is now impossible to know, but the keen sense of yearning in Tamura's poems is undeniable. This craving to be with other Ōtomo, resulting in expressions of warm affection (and sometimes riskier emotions), seems to have been shared throughout the circle around Lady Ōtomo of Sakanoue, as later between Yakamochi and his cousin Ikenushi.

The first four poems below (nos. 743–46) exude a girlish charm that gives them a special place in the range of early Japanese emotional expression. These innocent verses open a small window on the private lives and feelings of an ancient family, supplementing the larger documentation of sexual passion and parental love. For once it is permissible to translate the endearment *imo* in its proper sense of "sister." Two further tanka, nos. 747–48, datable to the autumn of 739 (the period when it is believed that the marriage of Yakamochi and the Elder Maiden of Sakanoue began), pick up the image of the house in the last poem of the previous set. Instead of the conventional weed patch around the equally conventional humble abode, this time the Elder Maiden of Tamura offers the beauty of bush clover in bloom and flaming autumn leaves. No. 747 is particularly admirable, an imaginative capturing of a magical moment. It may have been suggested by an anonymous tanka, MYS X : 2288 / 2284, in which the poet wishes to see his "sister's" figure, likened to the pliant bending of bush-clover stems.

743–46   [MYS IV : 759–62 / 756–59]

Four poems sent by the Elder Maiden of the Tamura Ōtomo family to her younger sister, the Elder Maiden of Sakanoue

(743)   [759 / 756]

Yoso ni ite	When we are apart,
Koureba kurushi	I yearn for you terribly;

Wagimoko o
Tsugite aimimu
Koto hakari seyo

Let my young sister
Cleverly devise some plan
Whereby we keep on meeting.

(744) [760/757]

Tōku araba
Wabite mo aramu o
    Sato chikaku
Ari to kikitsutsu
Minu ga sube nasa

If you were far away
I would give up in despair,
    But I keep hearing
How your house is close to mine—
And yet I'm helpless to see you!

(745) [761/758]

Shirakumo no
Tanabiku yama no
    Takataka ni
Wa ga mou imo o
Mimu yoshi mogamo

Isn't there some way
For me to see my sister,
    For whom my longing
Reaches up into the sky,
To the cloud-capped mountaintops?

(746) [762/759]

Ika naramu
Toki ni ka imo o
    Mugurafu no
Kitanaki yado ni
Ireimasetemu

When will come a time
For me to have my sister here
    To this patch of weeds,
To this shabby house of mine,
And treat her as my guest?

Concerning the above, both the Elder Maiden of Tamura and the Elder Maiden of Sakanoue were daughters of the Major Controller of the Right, the nobleman Ōtomo no Sukunamaro. Since the nobleman resided in the village of Tamura, [his daughter] was called the Elder Maiden of Tamura. But her younger sister, since her mother lived in the village of Sakanoue, was called the Elder Maiden of Sakanoue. At this time the sisters corresponded by means of poems.

747-48 [MYS VIII: 1626-27/1622-23]

Two poems given by the Elder Maiden of the Ōtomo of Tamura to her younger sister, the Elder Maiden of Sakanoue

(747) [1626/1622]

Wa ga yado no
Aki no hagi saku
    Yūkage ni
Ima mo miteshi ka
Imo ga sugata o

All about my house
The autumn clover is in bloom:
    Oh, that I could see
My sister's figure standing there,
Bathed in the evening light!

(748)   [1628 / 1623]

<table>
<tr><td>Wa ga yado ni</td><td>Every time I see</td></tr>
<tr><td>Momitsu kaerude</td><td>The maples brightening into flame</td></tr>
<tr><td>Miru goto ni</td><td>Here about my house,</td></tr>
<tr><td>Imo o kaketsutsu</td><td>There's not a day I do not yearn</td></tr>
<tr><td>Koinu hi wa nashi</td><td>With all my heart for my sister.</td></tr>
</table>

The Elder Maiden of the Ōtomo of Sakanoue (active 730's–40's)

The Elder Maiden of the Ōtomo of Sakanoue (Ōtomo no Sakanoue no Ō-otome) was the older of two daughters born to Lady Ōtomo of Sakanoue and her third husband, Ōtomo no Sukunamaro. She married her cousin Yakamochi, with whom she exchanged love poems preserved in Books IV and VIII. She also received poems from her mother and from her half sister, the Elder Maiden of the Ōtomo of Tamura, but her replies are not recorded. Thus she exists entirely as a love poet in *Man'yōshū*. For her exchanges with Yakamochi, see nos. 1145–53. The following set of four tanka (nos. 749–52) is also noted as having been sent in reply, but the other half of this particular correspondence is not extant. The content of the poems and their placement suggests that they are from early in the relationship, before it was formalized, supposedly in the fall of 739. The young lovers seem quite desperate, both ardent and hesitant. The circumstances of Ōtomo marriages are known better than most in the period, which is not saying a great deal. It is commonly assumed that Lady Ōtomo smiled upon her nephew Yakamochi as a prospective son-in-law. We have evidence that she was also ardently attached to her daughter (nos. 725–29). But from these four poems (and others) it appears that Yakamochi and his bride-to-be went through the usual excitements and agonies of a secret love affair. Since marriages began with secret visits in any case, this is perhaps not surprising, but the intensity is striking, especially in the first poem. Again the Ōtomo love of love seems to be in evidence, though there is no necessary presumption that the emotions described are not utterly sincere. The first poem (no. 749) reads like the record of an actual dream and has an urgency lacking in the others. Competition in love pangs (no. 750) became traditional and was always implied by the structure of the love exchange as challenge and reply, going back to the early song-matches (utagaki). In the third poem "moongrass" (*tsukikusa*) is a name for the dayflower or spiderwort, whose blue flowers yielded an easily fading dye. As is commonly the case, the woman contrasts her own constancy with the man's supposed lack of seriousness. The image of clouds in poem four may seem a poor choice as an emblem of fidelity, but the hovering quality of clouds is an apt analogue for the uncertainty the woman is forced to endure.

749–52   [MYS IV : 584–87 / 581–84]

Four poems sent in reply to Ōtomo no Sukune Yakamochi by the Elder Maiden of the Ōtomo family of Sakanoue

(749)   [584 / 581]

Ikite araba	If we are alive
Mimaku mo shirazu	We may see each other yet,
Nani shi ka mo	For all we know;
Shinamu yo imo to	Why did you come in my dream,
Ime ni mietsuru	Saying, "Darling, I shall die"?

(750)   [585 / 582]

Masurao mo	Though the stalwart man
Kaku koikeru o	May also suffer from the pangs of love,
Tawayame no	What comparison
Kouru kokoro ni	Could he offer to the heart
Tagui arame ya mo	Of the tender, yearning maiden?

(751)   [586 / 583]

Tsukikusa no	Does he have for me
Utsuroiyasuku	A love as quick to fade
Omoe ka mo	As the moongrass,
A ga omou hito no	That from him for whom I long
Koto mo tsugekonu	There comes no message?

(752)   [587 / 584]

Kasugayama	Clouds of a morning
Asa tatsu kumo no	Rising daily on the slopes
Inu hi naku	Of Mount Kasuga
Mimaku no hoshiki	Hover no more constantly
Kimi ni mo aru kamo	Than my wish to see my love!

Lady Kasa (active 730's)

Of Lady Kasa (Kasa no Iratsume) all that is known is that she wrote twenty-nine love poems to Ōtomo no Yakamochi, to which he gave two in reply. Twenty-four of her poems, with Yakamochi's two replies, appear in the section on poetic exchanges. The three presented here (nos. 753–55) have no recorded response. They are fine and intense poems, and their preservation would suggest that Yakamochi valued them, and the woman from whom they came. Their placement indicates that they date from the 730's, when Yakamochi was in his teens and early twenties. As a young man he received ardent poems from a number of women in addition to his prospective wife and mother-in-law. Such attentions can hardly have been other than beneficial to his self-esteem.

Lady Kasa's tanka set is unified by botanical references. In the first poem the plant is the *murasaki*, a lowly herb (the "common gromwell") that gives its name to the color purple, from a dye extracted from the root. No. 753 is thus an early example of the poetic use of a regnant image whose final enthronement came in *The Tale of Genji* at the beginning of the eleventh century. Lady Kasa's allegory implies that she has fallen in love (dyed her cloth), but that the love has been discovered (the color revealed) before it could be consummated (before she could wear the dress). The location of Tsukuma moor is not known, but some suppose it to have been near Maibara on the shore of Lake Biwa. The reed plain of Mano (no. 754) was farther away, in distant Michinoku in northern Honshū. This utamakura (famous place of poetic reference) here makes its first appearance. The fact that, though distant, it can be summoned to the mind's eye in an *omokage*, or mental image, is meant to contrast with the lover's nonappearance though he lives close by. The third plant is the sedge (*suge*), whose roots strike deep and thus serve as an objective correlative for devotion. No. 755 is based on a jo using this image, and with its verb *musubishi* ("bound"), indicates a progression through time to a love that is now "deep" (i.e., established in physical fact). The deep root is needless to say a potential phallic image. But after all this tour through the wild places, the woman is abandoned, left to ponder forgetting and remembrance.

753–55   [MYS III: 398–400 / 395–97]

Three poems sent to Ōtomo no Sukune Yakamochi by Lady Kasa

(753)   [398 / 395]

    Tsukumano ni   With the purple plant
    Ouru murasaki   Growing on Tsukuma moor
      Kinu ni shime   I stained my cloth—
    Imada kizu shite   But before I could wear the dress
    Iro ni idenikeri   Its color was revealed.

(754)   [399 / 396]

    Michinoku no   The Plain of *Kaya* Reeds
    Mano no kayahara   At Mano in Michinoku—
      Tōkedo mo   Distant though it is,
    Omokage ni shite   And if only as a daydream,
    Miyu to iu mono o   Yet, they say, it can be seen.

(755)   [400 / 397]
Okuyama no   Remote in the mountains
Iwamotosuge o   Sedges grow below the rocks—
   Ne fukamete   Their roots go deep:
Musubishi kokoro   Deep were the bonds that bound our hearts
Wasurekanetsu mo   In a love I can never forget.

Ōtomo no Yakamochi (718?–85)

Ōtomo no Yakamochi is the key literary figure of eighth-century Japan, for it was through his efforts that the corpus of poetry (and prose) known as *Man'yōshū* was brought together in its twenty books and over 4,500 poems. Such a statement can be supported only by internal evidence, for no preface or external source reveals Yakamochi to have been the compiler. And indeed, *Man'yōshū* drew from a variety of sources and probably was worked over at different stages by more than one person. But Yakamochi's 479 waka (432 tanka, 46 chōka, 1 sedōka), plus his compositions in Chinese prose and verse, comprising over a tenth of the anthology, strongly suggest him as the dominant personality behind the work as a whole. No other poet comes close to being as copiously represented.

Yakamochi's writings are concentrated in Books III, IV, VI, and VIII, and dominate the last four books, XVII–XX. This last part of *Man'yōshū* is clearly Yakamochi's personal compilation, one whose dated entries and first-person usages make of it a rough poetic journal. Its content includes poems he received, heard, or collected, as well as his own compositions, thus displaying the anthologist at work. The fact that there is an overlap in time between the earliest section of these chronologically arranged last four books and the numerous youthful poems given elsewhere in the anthology raises interesting questions of editorial policy and control. Are the last four books a draft manuscript that Yakamochi never had time to refine by rearranging the poems under the categories of Books III, IV, VI, and VIII? Or did the chronological substructure running through most of the books of *Man'yōshū* simply surface at the end as the basic format? Did Yakamochi deliberately choose to display his versatility as an anthologist by using his own poems to illustrate different principles? Does a chronological framework betray a loss of interest, or the triumph of the diaristic urge in Japanese letters?

The date of Yakamochi's birth is in dispute; 718 is commonly cited, but 716 and 717 have also been put forward. In its outward course his life must be reckoned less successful and his career more precarious than his father Tabito's. We know little of Tabito's early career, but in lives of very nearly the same length (Tabito died at sixty-seven by the Japanese count, Yakamochi at sixty-eight, if born in 718) the father rose to the rank of Junior

Second, with an appointment as Major Counselor (*dainagon*), whereas the son concluded his career as a Middle Counselor (*chūnagon*) with Junior Third Rank. Dry as such data may seem, they represent vital concerns of the people whose careers they encapsulate. The decline from father to son further reflects a permanent decline in the fortunes of the Ōtomo clan, a matter of the utmost moment to Yakamochi in his position as clan head. When Tabito died in 731, Nara was in its palmy early days; when Yakamochi died in 785 it was being abandoned in despair. The ancient and proud Ōtomo clan was really never in the running for the prizes of power in competition with the upstart Fujiwara in the Nara years. The fight was among the Fujiwara, elements in the imperial house they served and wished to control, and the Tachibana, who emerged briefly in the second quarter of the century. Nevertheless, Tabito may have been enough of a presence that it was felt wisest to remove him from the scene of high politics by sending him to remote Dazaifu in 728 while the Fujiwara engineered the downfall and suicide of Prince Nagaya in 729.

When the four Fujiwara leaders perished in the epidemic of 737, Empress-Consort Kōmyō's half brother, the former Prince Tachibana no Moroe, came to the fore, monopolizing power and holding the Fujiwara in check for a generation. But by the early 750's the influence of this adviser of Emperor Shōmu had been undermined by Nakamaro, the son of Muchimaro, one of the fallen Fujiwara brothers of 737. Moroe died in 757, the year after his imperial patron, and the stage was set for a clash between Nakamaro and Moroe's son Naramaro. The Ōtomo, who had enjoyed a close alliance with Moroe, were inevitably involved when Naramaro made his move later in 757. Naramaro's attempted coup failed, and his party was destroyed. Yakamochi had been watching the developing situation and tried to steer his clan away from dangerous waters. He personally survived the debacle, but Ōtomo prestige had received a damaging blow. Yakamochi's cousin Komaro was put to death, and Ikenushi, Yakamochi's favorite poetic correspondent, suffered imprisonment. Yakamochi himself had his career derailed, being sent to govern the province of Inaba in 758, an assignment that represented a demotion.

In 762 Yakamochi returned to take up an office in the capital, only to join another abortive plot against Nakamaro and be sent to the remotest post in southern Kyūshū as Governor of Satsuma. In the year of Yakamochi's exile, 764, Nakamaro himself rebelled against former Empress Kōken, Shōmu's daughter, who with her favorite, the priest Dōkyō, had usurped power from reigning Emperor Junnin. Nakamaro was defeated and killed. Kōken promptly deposed Junnin and reascended the throne as Empress Shōtoku. After a great scandal involving Dōkyō and his alleged imperial ambitions (as well as his alleged illicit relations with the Empress), Shōtoku died and was replaced by Emperor Kōnin in 770. Yakamochi's career continued in the doldrums under Shōtoku, but a politically favorable climate led to his advancement to Senior Fourth Rank Upper and various prestigious offices during the reign of Kōnin.

By the time Emperor Kammu succeeded the elderly Kōnin in 781, Yakamochi's life and career were reaching their final phase; he received his last promotion, to Junior Third Rank, shortly after Kammu took power. Nevertheless, he was politically disgraced twice more, once in 782 for joining yet another plot against the throne, and again immediately after his death in 785. In the first case he was banished but pardoned after a few months. The following year he was promoted to Middle Counselor, his highest post, and in 784 he was given additional duties of a military nature in northeastern Japan, where he was put in charge of subduing the unruly inhabitants of the region and securing the imperial presence. He was occupied with these duties when he died on the twenty-eighth of the eighth month in 785. About a month later two of his Ōtomo kinsmen, acting on behalf of Emperor Kammu's brother Prince Sawara, assassinated Fujiwara no Tanetsugu. This event occurred at Nagaoka, a site just south of modern Kyōto, where Emperor Kammu was building a new capital to replace Nara. Tanetsugu was in charge of the construction, and Prince Sawara led the party opposed to the move. The affair put a curse on the new capital, leading to its transfer to Heian-kyō (modern Kyōto), but also brought on the final debacle of Ōtomo fortunes. Yakamochi had served in the household of Prince Sawara (who was starved to death on the way to exile) and was regarded with suspicion. The family property was confiscated, and Yakamochi was posthumously stripped of rank, his remains banished to the Oki Islands along with his son. The punitive edicts were revoked in 806 by a court that had been terrorized by the "angry ghosts" of Prince Sawara and his party.

In the midst of all this turmoil of late Nara, the poet disappears, and only Yakamochi the durable official and perhaps increasingly desperate plotter remains. There are no poems after New Year's Day of the year corresponding to 759. The great silence may be no more than a matter of the hazards besetting textual survival. *Man'yōshū* was not the only anthology of the period. Like *Kaifūsō*, it survived; others, mentioned in *Man'yōshū*, did not. If *Man'yōshū* too had disappeared, we would have little idea of the poetic riches of pre-Heian times. It is implausible that late Nara became a poetic desert in 759. And yet there is evidence in *Man'yōshū* itself that the poetic tradition was narrowing down to banquet poems, that Yakamochi had spent himself as a creative force by the time he was forty, and that he was indeed the last practitioner of the grand chōka. Poets do fall silent, and perhaps he was one of these. Yet political turmoil per se may as easily be stimulating as inimical to poetic activity, and when a whole tradition falls silent, the cause must lie deep. The erosion of the mythic underpinnings of the chōka by an increasingly Buddhist and Confucian ethos at court, with a consequent lack of interest and patronage, suggest themselves as factors here. Yakamochi personalized the chōka, using it for everyday incident, rather than (or in addition to) elevated and romantic themes. His skill and devotion to poetry—at least during the first half of his life—enabled him to achieve success in this endeavor, but the effort may have seemed arduous and pointless to less gifted people. In any case, when the waka tradition revived in vigor and official favor about a hundred years after the last Man'yō poem, the chōka was among the casualties of the interim. Tanka, which survived, found no Yakamochi to collect them until in due course they found their Tsurayuki.

Yakamochi the poet is therefore Yakamochi to the age of forty. He is the ultimate in versatility, writing in Chinese (prose and poetry), as well as Japanese, and in a variety of manners on a range of themes that represents the breadth of *Man'yōshū* itself. The major poetic influences on him were no doubt his father Tabito, his aunt and mother-in-law Lady Ōtomo of Sakanoue, his father's friend Yamanoue no Okura, and, through his reading, the oeuvre of Hitomaro. To this list should be added the numerous anonymous "folk" poems no doubt preserved in the Ōtomo library, plus the standard Chinese readings of an educated man of Nara, notably (in a poetic context) *Wen-hsüan, Yü-t'ai Hsin-yung*, and *Yu-hsien-k'u*. Finally, Yakamochi's political patron during the early part of his career, Tachibana no Moroe, is thought to have been instrumental in his development as an anthologist.

Yakamochi accompanied his father to Dazaifu when he was about ten years old, and one may assume was impressed by the poetic atmosphere Tabito was at pains to foster there. His earliest training in poetry, as well as his basic education, no doubt were seen to by the family, and the example of the two old Sinophiles, Tabito and Okura, must have been in his mind when he exchanged Chinese correspondence and both Chinese and Japanese poems with his cousin Ikenushi during his governorship of the province of Etchū in the late 740's. It is interesting to note that both father and son were at their most creative when, isolated from the capital, they duplicated its poetic world in miniature.

Yakamochi's earliest recorded poems are from the 730's, after Tabito's return from Dazaifu and his death in 731. The young Yakamochi is primarily a love poet, working intensively in the amorous style in exchanges with a number of women in addition to the one he married, his cousin the Elder Maiden of Sakanoue. Some of these love poems employ images derived from *Yu-hsien-k'u*, the erotic T'ang novelette brought back from China perhaps by Okura himself. Yakamochi's marriage to the Elder Maiden is thought to have taken place late in 739, after the death of a favorite concubine whom he mourned in a notable series of poems (nos. 1135–42). About a year later Yakamochi followed Emperor Shōmu in his flight from Nara at the time of the rebellion of Fujiwara no Hirotsugu. Yakamochi was a Palace Attendant (*udoneri*) at the time. Several of his poems are addressed to the Elder Maiden at home in Nara. Another of his poetic correspondents during his early years and on into his Etchū period was his mother-in-law (and aunt), Lady Ōtomo of Sakanoue. Her peculiarly amorous quality of address is reciprocated by the young poet, who was in some sense her pro-tégé. The manner is also found in three intriguing poems on parting from a friend (nos. 765–67) and was shared between Yakamochi and Ikenushi in Etchū.

The Etchū appointment came in the fall of 746 and lasted until 751. These were Yakamochi's most productive years as a poet, the period of his best and most plentiful chōka, as well as his exchanges with Ikenushi. The chōka range over public and private matters, excursions, friendship, love in separation, the landscape, legend, and death. They show Yakamochi experimenting and growing, making the long poetic form serve a variety of ends, but present no unified vision such as can be found in Hitomaro. Yakamochi, the last chōka poet, looked back at Hitomaro as a master to be emulated, as can be gleaned from a remark he made in a letter to Ikenushi (see the preface to nos. 1189–92). But everything about him—his sense of history, his self-conscious personalism and anecdotal quality, his experimentalism, his literary poses, and even his melancholy show him to be a different voice for a different age.

When Yakamochi left his mountain fastness and returned to the maelstrom of Nara in 751, his melancholy increased, and three of his late tanka (nos. 843–45) are imbued with an indefinable sadness that blends nature with human perception in a way that was to be much practiced in the future. That future, practically speaking, might have been greatly different but for the prior example of *Man'yōshū*. It is not unreasonable to assume that the model of Okura (whom Yakamochi also admired, according to his letter to Ikenushi) excited Yakamochi to collect poems and arrange them in categories. Okura, it will be remembered, was the compiler of the now lost *Ruijū Karin* (*Classified Forest of Poetry*), a collection whose content someone, most plausibly Yakamochi, drew upon for *Man'yōshū*. The actual impetus to compile a poetic anthology "for ten thousand ages" may have come from Moroe, along with the nucleus of the collection in the form of its first two books.

Yakamochi's earliest datable poem, from 733 according to its placement in Book VI, is a tanka about the eyebrows of a woman he once glimpsed. It immediately follows one by his aunt, Lady Ōtomo of Sakanoue (no. 722), using the same image. The Lady speaks of a rendezvous enjoyed, the boy (Yakamochi was about fifteen at this time) of an image that floats remote and unattained.

756   [MYS VI: 999/994]

A poem by Ōtomo no Sukune Yakamochi on the new moon

| Furisakete | When I gaze aloft, |
| Mikazuki mireba | Seeing there the crescent moon, |

Hitome mishi	I am reminded
Hito no mayobiki	Of the eyebrows of a person
Omōyuru kamo	Whom once I briefly glimpsed.

✳ The tanka set 757–60 is dated to the ninth month of 736 and is placed among the autumn love poems in Book VIII. Although each of the four poems is dominated by its natural images, and only the second contains an overt reference to longing, the sequence is rich in implications of love. "Early rice" (*wasa*) in no. 757 and "grain that is full" (*hotachi*) in no. 758 carry strong suggestions of ripening passion, and the cries of the wild geese echo those of the poet's desire. Everything is held in, "hidden in the clouds" (*kumogakuri*), in the first two poems, and this stifling (*ibusemi*) is made explicit and broken in the third. The poet goes out and lifts his eyes from the fields to the hills, where a new color (a new and open passion) is revealed. In the fourth poem the moon shines down from a rain-washed sky, and the poet asks the clouds not to cover it again. The progression is clear enough, but the object of these metaphorical designs is not known. The sequence is preceded by exchanges between Yakamochi and two young women, but could as well have been intended for the Elder Maiden as for one of them. The arrangement in this portion of Book VIII seems to be based on imagistic association.

757–60   [MYS VIII: 1570–73 / 1566–69]

Four autumn poems by Ōtomo no Yakamochi

(757)   [1570 / 1566]

Hisakata no	From the distant sky
Amama mo okazu	Come the cries of the wild geese
Kumogakuri	Hidden in the clouds,
Naki so yuku naru	Ceaseless even in the rain,
Wasada karigane	Over fields of early rice.

(758)   [1571 / 1567]

Kumogakuri	Hidden in the clouds,
Naku naru kari no	The wild geese are calling—
Yukite imu	I can hear them go,
Akita no hotachi	Soon to flock in autumn fields
Shigeku shi omōyu	Whose grain is full as my longing.

(759)   [1572 / 1568]

Amagomori	Sheltered from the rain,
Kokoro ibusemi	I've stayed in until, heart-stifled,

Idemireba
Kasuga no yama wa
Irozukinikeri

I go forth and look:
Over Kasuga the hills
Are tinged with a new color.

(760) [1573 / 1569]

Ame harete
Kiyoku teritaru
Kono tsukuyo
Mata sara ni shite
Kumo na tanabiki

The rain has lifted,
From a sparkling sky the moon
Shines clear tonight;
Do not cover it again,
Clouds that have trailed away.

The above four poems were composed in Tempyō 8 [736], Fire-Senior / Rat, autumn, ninth month.

❋ Seventh Night, the myth of the lover stars Weaving Maid and Herdsman (see nos. 398 and 620–23), is the topic of another early tanka by Yakamochi. Based on the "reasoning" conceits learned from Six Dynasties Chinese poetry (see clouds, deduce spray), Yakamochi's poem is also faithful to the Chinese version of the myth, in which the Weaving Maid goes to her lover rather than vice versa, as was usually the case in Japanese versions. The poem is from Book XVII, Yakamochi's poetic journal, and therefore the headnote is rendered in the first person. The term *jukkai*, "stating the feelings," is adopted from T'ang usage.

761 [MYS XVII: 3922 / 3900]

A poem on looking up alone at the River of Heaven on the night of the seventh of the seventh month, in the tenth year [of Tempyō, 738], stating a little of my feelings

Tanabata shi
Funanori su rashi
Masokagami
Kiyoki tsukuyo ni
Kumo tachiwataru

'Tis the Weaving Maid—
She must be out in her boat:
Across the clear moon
Like a mirror in the night
Clouds are rising, drifting.

❋ Three undated tanka by Yakamochi, probably from the late 730's, appear in the hiyuka section of Book III. They are dispersed among a group of poems, some by other members of the Ōtomo clan, using similar images. The woman (a jewel, a pink, a sedge) is to be kept safe in the poet's possession. The first two of Yakamochi's poems are specifically addressed to the Elder Maiden, and the third may have been intended for her as well. In objectifying the woman in this way, the poems betray the speaker's insecurity.

The third in particular clearly indicates that the relationship is yet to be consummated. Not enough detail is available about Yakamochi's love life to know whether his apprehensions were plausible or merely conventional. It is particularly puzzling to conceive what boulders would have cramped his style in wooing his cousin. Perhaps Lady Ōtomo's mother love was the problem (though Yakamochi was her "fair-haired boy"), or perhaps cousin Surugamaro was interested in the elder as well as the younger Sakanoue daughter. The use of *koi* ("long") in the second poem is unusual. *Koi* properly refers to yearning for what is not at hand; to say one would yearn for what *is* in one's hands is a striking confession of the illogicality of love.

762   [MYS III: 406/403]

A poem sent by Ōtomo no Sukune Yakamochi to the Elder Maiden of the
. . . Sakanoue family

Asa ni ke ni	At morning, all day,
Mimaku hori suru	A desire is in me
Sono tama o	To see that jewel:
Ika ni seba ka mo	What can I do to make certain
Te yu karezu aramu	That it never leaves my hands?

763   [MYS III: 411/408]

A poem sent by Ōtomo no Sukune Yakamochi to the Elder Maiden of the
same Sakanoue family

Nadeshiko ga	If you were only
Sono hana ni mo ga	One of these flowers, these pinks,
Asanasana	Morning by morning
Te ni torimochite	Taking you into my hands,
Koinu hi nakemu	Not a day I wouldn't long.

764   [MYS III: 417/414]

A poem by Ōtomo no Sukune Yakamochi

Ashihiki no	The leg-cramping
Iwane kogoshimi	Boulders bristle so sharply
Suga no ne o	It would be a task
Hikaba katami to	To pull the sedge up by the root:
Shime nomi so yuu	I'll just fence it off for now.

✻ The following set of three tanka may also be assumed to belong to the 730's, but just when and to whom the poems were written remains a mystery. The recipient was a man, as is indicated by the Chinese term for "companion" in the headnote, but the language of the poems is that of a lover. It is intriguing to suppose that Yakamochi had homosexual as well as heterosexual involvements, and these three poems certainly do nothing to discourage such speculation. In the absence of a literature dealing with the subject, it is impossible to discuss homosexuality in the Nara period, though one may assume it existed. The jealousy and general intensity expressed in these poems seem to strain the conventions of ordinary male friendship. But there are extraordinary friendships, which may exist with or without an overtly sexual bond, and the amorous modes of expression learned from Lady Ōtomo may be of relevance here.

765-67   [MYS IV: 683–85 / 680–82]

Three poems by Ōtomo no Sukune Yakamochi on parting from a companion

(765)   [683/680]

Kedashiku mo	Could it be, my lord,
Hito no nakagoto	You have listened to slander?
Kikase ka mo	I have been waiting
Kokodaku matedo	By now for a long, long time,
Kimi ga kimasanu	But you do not come to me.

(766)   [684/681]

Nakanaka ni	It would be better
Tayu to shi iwaba	If you said you'd break with me:
Kaku bakari	How could I then
Iki no o ni shite	Go on with this yearning for you,
Are koime ya mo	Making you the thread of my life?

(767)   [685/682]

Omouramu	When you are not such
Hito ni aranaku ni	As would ever care for me,
Nemokoro ni	Why do I go on,
Kokoro tsukushite	Pouring out my very heart
Kouru are ka mo	Down to the roots of longing?

❊ The next two poems by Yakamochi in Book IV (which is devoted entirely to love poems) are addressed to an unknown woman, apparently one who served at court. The lover's reproach seems essentially the same whether intended for a man or a woman, one of its modes being the rhetorical question. No. 768's image of obsession "mounted on my heart" (*kokoro ni norite*) is striking, but not original to Yakamochi, occurring twice elsewhere in *Man'yōshū*. It is less common than the *iki no o* ("thread of my life") of no. 766, however, which appears in various constructions sixteen times. Nevertheless, the addresses to the "companion" carry a greater intensity than those to the young woman. The one has a sense of desperation, the other the air of an amorous game.

768–69   [MYS IV : 694–95 / 691–92]

Two poems sent to a young woman by Ōtomo no Sukune Yakamochi

(768)   [694 / 691]

    Momoshiki no   Oh, they are many,
    Ōmiyahito wa   They who dwell in the great court
      Ōkaredo   Of the hundred stones,
    Kokoro ni norite   But one girl obsesses me—
    Omōyuru imo   She rides mounted on my heart.

(769)   [695 / 692]

    Uwahe naki   No skin of kindness
    Imo ni mo aru kamo   Has my young girl for her love—
      Kaku bakari   What else can I think
    Hito no kokoro o   When I see how she spares him
    Tsukusaku omoeba   Nothing of heart's travail?

❋ Yakamochi complains of a cool reception in no. 770, an isolated tanka from the 730's. Again the complaint is couched in the interrogative mode.

770   [MYS IV : 703 / 700]

A poem by Ōtomo no Sukune Yakamochi on arriving at a young woman's gate

    Kaku shite ya   Is this all there is?
    Nao ya makaramu   After all, must I go back,
      Chikakaranu   Having gotten here
    Michi no aida o   After struggling up a road
    Nazumimaikite   Where the distance was not short?

❋ The series "Seven Poems to a Young Woman" (nos. 771–77) preserves the anonymity of the recipient, though the mention of Saho River in the second poem suggests a resident on the Ōtomo property there. Poems sent to the Elder Maiden are usually labeled as such, and so the identity of this *otome* remains obscure. The second poem in any case is modeled closely on nos. 1006 and 1009, two of a set of four poems Lady Ōtomo of Sakanoue exchanged with Fujiwara no Maro around the time Yakamochi was born. Yakamochi's seven poems can be seen as an examination of the theme of isolation in love. The sequence opens with a statement of the theme, contrasting *yoshi* ("means," "chance," "opportunity") with *yoso* ("another place," "a remote place"). The idea of "crossing" in *wataredo* links this poem to the next, a fantasy of crossing Saho River on horseback. But this cry for action is plaintive, like the cries of the plovers, and in no. 773, the next poem, the journey becomes one in the world of dreams, and even this is uncertain. Blocked, the lover loses confidence in having his love reciprocated, and in no. 774 he suggests the dreadful possibility that his is a one-sided passion. Poem 775 rescues him: his love has appeared in a dream, indicating that she thinks of him. But at the same time he is condemned to renewed torture, not being able to go to her. The momentary vision past, the lover falls further into agony in the last two poems, pining away in isolation and sure that his sufferings are ignored.

It has been suggested that poem six (no. 776) incorporates elements of no. 1076, in the section on poetic exchanges, by Yakamochi's father Tabito, as well as of an anonymous tanka, MYS XI: 2589 / 2584, but some form of the locution *masurao to omoeru ware* ("I who thought myself a valiant man") seems to be a Man'yō formula. It appears, for instance, in no. 325 by Hitomaro. For Yakamochi, as an Ōtomo, the ideal of the masurao was particularly important, however. But the main point about such sequential structures as this is that they are a species of literature in which the facts of an affair and the conventions of love poetry interact to create an account of the passion that reaches out from the circumstantial toward the typical. This typicality was to be the grand route of waka in its classical ages.

771–77   [MYS IV: 717–23 / 714–20]
Seven poems sent to a young woman by Ōtomo no Sukune Yakamochi

(771)   [717 / 714]

Kokoro ni wa	Although in my heart
Omoiwataredo	I still go on in my longing,
Yoshi o nami	I have no choice:
Yoso nomi ni shite	In this place where you are not
Nageki so a ga suru	Sighing is the thing I do.

(772)   [718 / 715]

Chidori naku	Where the plovers cry
Saho no kawato no	On the lip of Saho River,
Kiyoki se o	Through the clear shallows

Uma uchiwatashi　　　　　Splashing as I whip my horse,
Itsu ka kayowamu　　　　　When shall I come to you again?

(773)　　　　　　　　　　　　　　　　　　　　　　　　　[719/716]

　　Yoru hiru to　　　　　　Whether night or day,
　Iu waki shiranu　　　　　My love knows no difference—
　　A ga kouru　　　　　　　Did my yearning
　Kokoro wa kedashi　　　　Heart perhaps appear to you
　Ime ni mieki ya　　　　　In a dream of desire?

(774)　　　　　　　　　　　　　　　　　　　　　　　　　[720/717]

　　Tsuremonaku　　　　　　To long for someone
　Aruramu hito o　　　　　　With a one-sided longing,
　　Kataomoi ni　　　　　　　When for all I know
　Ware wa omoeba　　　　　She is quite indifferent—
　Kurushiku mo aru ka　　　Ah, the torment of it!

(775)　　　　　　　　　　　　　　　　　　　　　　　　　[721/718]

　　Omowanu ni　　　　　　Without my thinking,
　Imo ga emai o　　　　　　Suddenly I saw it in a dream,
　　Ime ni mite　　　　　　　My love's smiling face,
　Kokoro no uchi ni　　　　Since when within my heart
　Moetsutsu so oru　　　　　I have been living in flames.

(776)　　　　　　　　　　　　　　　　　　　　　　　　　[722/719]

　　Masurao to　　　　　　　Can it come to this—
　Omoeru ware o　　　　　　That I who thought myself
　　Kaku bakari　　　　　　　A valiant man
　Mitsure ni mitsure　　　　Should peak and pine in my weakness,
　Kataomoi o semu　　　　　Worn out with one-sided love?

(777)　　　　　　　　　　　　　　　　　　　　　　　　　[723/720]

　　Murakimo no　　　　　　Can it be that she
　Kokoro kudakete　　　　　Knows nothing of my yearning,
　　Kaku bakari　　　　　　　How my heart is smashed
　A ga kouraku o　　　　　　Midst the vitals in my breast,
　Shirazu ka aruramu　　　　So unbearable this love?

❋ The following two tanka begin a series of exchanges in Book IV between Yakamochi and the Elder Maiden. The whole series is undated but is supposed by some to belong to the fall of 739, after the death of Yakamochi's concubine. No. 778 is based on the Chinese-derived popular belief that the day lily, known in Japanese poetry as *wasuregusa* ("forgetting grass"), had the power to make people forget their unhappiness. As with Prince Hozumi's helplessness before "the slave called love" (no. 487), measures of a cautionary kind have proven ineffectual: Yakamochi confesses that he has never been able to rid himself of his longing for the Maiden. The second poem expresses the probably universal desire of lovers to be left undisturbed, a desire intensified in the conventional (and no doubt real) atmosphere of prying eyes that is a constant of Japanese love poetry.

778-79   [MYS IV:730-31/727-28]

Two poems sent by Ōtomo no Sukune Yakamochi to the Elder Maiden of the Sakanoue family (after some years of separation they met again and exchanged endearments)

(778)   [730/727]

Wasuregusa	In my undersash
Wa ga shitabimo ni	Grasses of forgetfulness
Tsuketaredo	I tucked away—
Shiko no shikogusa	Oh, that scurvy scurvy-grass,
Koto ni shi arikeri	I see it was so much talk.

(779)   [731/728]

Hito mo naki	Isn't there any
Kuni mo aranu ka	Country where no people are?
Wagimoko to	With my darling girl
Tazusaiyukite	I would go there hand in hand,
Taguite oramu	We would live there side by side.

✳ The sequence "Fifteen Additional Poems Sent to the Elder Maiden of Sakanoue" (nos. 780–94) is so positioned as to form the climax of the section beginning with poems 778–79. They are probably a collection of poems sent at various times rather than an integrated sequence, but their arrangement seems not to be totally haphazard. There is a progression from meeting in dreams to meeting in fact, working against an ironic undertow as the lover discovers that pain does not cease when trysting begins. There are pairs of poems on the physical effects and sensations of yearning (nos. 781–82), and on keepsakes (nos. 785–86). The set ends with two poems on parting at dawn that have the same opening line. Throughout there is a lacing together by references to "seeing"—in dream, in fact, and in *omokage*, the daydream image retained in the mind or hovering as a retinal aftereffect.

Four of the poems—nos. 780, 781, 783, and 794—may have been sug-

gested by passages in *Yu-hsien-k'u*. The excellence of no. 780 has been recognized by several fine translations. The general conclusion is stated first,
with the *-keri* ending warranting it as the poet's realization, and the evidence
follows, building from an assertive *-te* to a concessive *-do* to a conditional
-ba, leaving both the syntax and the awakened dreamer's hand groping at
the end. The dark emptiness at the heart of longing is nowhere better expressed, and although apparently based closely on a *Yu-hsien-k'u* passage,
the poem works in its own language, with its own patterns, to powerful
effect. No. 781 is more perfunctorily related to *Yu-hsien-k'u*; the image of
the sash that goes around three times when it should go only once is also in
Sakimaro's poem on finding a dead man at Ashigara Pass (no. 692). There
seems to be a perhaps not fortuitous association between the bed and the
groping in no. 780 and dressing and tying a sash in no. 781.

In the third poem (no. 782) the gesture of encircling the waist changes to
hanging something around the neck. "Thousand-puller stones" (*chibiki no
ishi*) are boulders it would take a thousand men to pull, and are mentioned in
the *Kojiki* and *Nihonshoki* passages describing how Izanagi the creator god
blocked the mouth of Yomi to save himself from the fury of his dead mate
Izanami. The term probably referred originally to the great boulders used to
build the burial crypts of ancient tombs. The lover expresses his sincerity by
leaving the outcome to the gods, having already invoked them indirectly
through the mention of the stones. The conceit of the open or unbarred
door to let in the dream-lover in the fourth poem (no. 783) was also probably suggested by a passage in *Yu-hsien-k'u*; it is used as well in an anonymous Man'yō poem, MYS XII: 2924/2912. Poem five (no. 784) alters the
dream visit to real "seeing," and is reminiscent of no. 763 in its special dis-
tortion of the ordinary meaning of *koi*.

Poems six and seven (nos. 785–86) exclaim over two gifts Yakamochi
has received from the Elder Maiden. The satisfying intimacy of wearing a
garment from a lover next to one's skin is often referred to in *Man'yōshū*,
along with the (perhaps inconvenient?) custom of not taking it off until the
next rendezvous. Yakamochi's ecstatic reaction to the gift of a sack suggests
that he was not behindhand in grasping sexual symbolism. These two
thank-you poems are the last happy ones. In the next, no. 787, he is contemplating death, deciding it is better to brave the wounds of gossip than
waste away in thwarted passion. The thwarting becomes worse in no. 788,
where he is denied even a meeting in a dream. This implies the lady is not
thinking of him, whence his accusation in the last line. Poem ten (no. 789)
moves the affair to the stage of actual visits, but only to reveal new levels of
pain. The urgency of desire brought on by the renewed intimacy makes the
numbness of despair seem better in retrospect; the ineffectual "grasses of
forgetfulness" (no. 778) have been forgotten. In no. 790 the lover is described as having gone mad with passion, even when meetings are now fre-

quent. He is haunted by the loved one's omokage in no. 791, and at the same time is surrounded by thickets of peering eyes. The use of the "seeing" motif is particularly striking here. No. 792 is a specific statement of the truth that desire feeds on desire, the sort of truth that the waka tradition is keen at pointing out. The last two poems take the lover from his beloved's bed out into a disintegrating night invaded by the gray of dawn, where the last glimpse of the woman's faintly seen face hovers in omokage. Each repetition of this parting tears the lover's heart a little more. The final poem looks back to a passage in *Yu-hsien-k'u*, the penultimate forward to the *yōen* style of Fujiwara Teika.

780–94 [MYS IV : 744–58 / 741–55]

Fifteen additional poems sent to the Elder Maiden of Sakanoue by Ōtomo no Sukune Yakamochi

(780) [744 / 741]

Ime no ai wa   Meeting in a dream
Kurushikarikeri   Is a cruel way to meet:
Odorokite   For you wake,
Kakisaguredo mo   Suddenly groping, but nothing
Te ni mo fureneba   Is there for your hand to touch.

(781) [745 / 742]

Hitoe nomi   The sash you fasten,
Imo ga musubamu   Darling, once around, round me
Obi o sura   Would go three times
Mie musububeku   Before I finally tied the knot,
A ga mi wa narinu   So thin have I become.

(782) [746 / 743]

A ga koi wa   This yearning of mine
Chibiki no ishi o   Hangs as heavy round my neck
Nana bakari   As seven stones,
Kubi ni kakemu mo   Each a thousand-puller weight:
Kami no manimani   Be it as the gods may will.

(783) [747 / 744]

Yū saraba   When evening falls
Yado akemakete   I shall leave my door open
Ware matamu   And wait for one
Ime ni aimi ni   Who said that she would come
Komu to iu hito o   To visit me in a dream.

(784)   [748/745]

    Asa yoi ni   Were I to see her
Mimu toki sae ya   Even every morn and eve,
    Wagimoko ga   Still would I yearn
Mi to mo minu goto   For my darling just as if
Nao koishikemu   I never saw her at all.

(785)   [749/746]

    Ikeru yo ni   Never in my life
Wa wa imada mizu   Have I seen a thing like this—
    Koto taete   Words fail me now,
Kaku omoshiroku   So cunningly is it fashioned,
Nueru fukuro wa   This sack you have sewn for me.

(786)   [750/747]

Wagimoko ga   I wear underneath
Katami no koromo   The keepsake garment that my love
    Shita ni kite   Has given me,
Tada ni au made wa   And shall I ever take it off
Ware nukame ya mo   Till the day we meet again?

(787)   [751/748]

Koishinamu   If I yearn to death
Soko mo onaji so   I shall be no better off—
    Nani semu ni   Why should I worry,
Hitome hitogoto   Making such a thorny thing
Kochitami are semu   Of what people see and say?

(788)   [752/749]

Ime ni dani   I might yet survive
Mieba koso are   If you came to me in dreams,
    Kaku bakari   But even there
Miezu shi aru wa   I can catch no glimpse of you—
Koite shine to ka   Is it, "Yearn till you die!" then?

(789)   [753/750]

Omoitae   All my longings dead,
Wabinishi mono o   I lay languishing in despair;
    Nakanaka ni   What was I thinking,
Nani ka kurushiku   To start meeting you again,
Aimisomekemu   Painfully, in cruel hope?

(790)   [754/751]

    Aimite wa   Since last we met
  Ikuda mo henu o   Not so many days have passed;
    Kokodaku mo   Must I long for you
  Kurui ni kurui   In such helplessness as this—
  Omōyuru ka mo   In madness piled on madness?

(791)   [755/752]

    Kaku bakari   If you come to me
  Omokage nomi ni   Thus constantly in daydreamed
    Omōeba   Shadows of a face,
  Ika ni ka mo semu   What shall I do, I wonder,
  Hitome shigekute   In this jungle of men's eyes?

(792)   [756/753]

    Aimiteba   If we were to meet,
  Shimashiku koi wa   I thought this yearning would lie still
    Nagimu ka to   For a little while,
  Omoedo iyoyo   But instead desire swells
  Koi masarikeri   More enormous than before.

(793)   [757/754]

  Yo no hodoro   In the lees of night
  Wa ga idete kureba   I went out and came away
    Wagimoko ga   From my darling girl:
  Omoerishiku shi   Now the thoughts she brooded on
  Omokage ni miyu   Show in her shadow-face.

(794)   [758/755]

  Yo no hodoro   In the lees of night
  Idetsutsu kuraku   Many are the times I've left
    Tabi maneku   And come away,
  Nareba a ga mune   So many that by now my breast
  Kiriyaku gotoshi   Is as if pierced and burned.

✳ Two tanka dated to the summer of 740 lower the level of intensity as they gracefully play on the floral gifts they accompany, very much in the manner of Heian romance. The second poem without being distinctly allegorical suggests that the poet's love has brightened to autumn colors in the full tide of its summer.

795–96   [MYS VIII: 1631–32 / 1627–28]

Two poems sent to the Elder Maiden of Sakanoue by Ōtomo no Sukune Yakamochi with two things he had plucked—out-of-season wisteria blossoms and autumn leaves

(795)   [1631 / 1627]

> Wa ga yado no   An out-of-season
> Tokijiki fuji no   Wisteria from my garden—
> Mezurashiku   How unusual!
> Ima mo miteshika   How rare my beloved: this instant
> Imo ga emai o   I would gaze upon her smile.

(796)   [1632 / 1628]

> Wa ga yado no   The underleaves
> Hagi no shitaba wa   Of bush clover from my garden
> Akikaze mo   Have turned this bright
> Imada fukaneba   Even though the autumn wind
> Kaku so momiteru   Has not yet begun to blow.

The above two poems went back and forth in Tempyō 12 [740], Metal-Senior / Dragon, summer, sixth month.

❋ Among the earliest of Yakamochi's chōka-hanka sets is no. 797–98, which from its placement should be from the year 740. Addressed to the Elder Maiden, it echoes the complaint of the fifteen-poem sequence, nos. 780–94. In popular lore the mountain pheasant and its mate spend nights on opposite peaks, but for Yakamochi even "a single day or night" (*hitohi hitoyo*) apart is an unbearable deprivation. The complaint is conventional, that is, true, in terms of human feelings, but flies blithely in the face of duo-local, or visiting type, marriage customs and Yakamochi's other amorous interests. A perusal of Hitomaro's poems on parting from his wife in Iwami, especially no. 325, and on the death of his wife in Karu (nos. 345–50) reveals Yakamochi's debt to him. The lovers' embrace that does not last for-ever and the quest for solace in wandering are adapted to a situation of a rather quotidian nature; there is no heartbreak, only impatience. The flowers on the hillsides mock the poet's need to forget "the thing called love" (i.e., yearning: *koi to iu mono*), reminding him of the very flower he cannot (constantly) pluck. Yakamochi thinks of the human being as ephem-eral, an *utsusemi* (line 19). This term, a pillow word for *hito* ("man"), begins to change its sense from "person of the actual world" to "empty locust" (*utsu-semi*) about this time. The brevity of life heightens the despair of thwarted passion. In the envoy Yakamochi skillfully uses the traditional technique of the jo to blend the images of the *kaobana* (lit., "face-flower") and the omokage of the woman who haunts him.

797–98   [MYS VIII : 1633–34 / 1629–30]

A poem to the Elder Maiden of Sakanoue, by Ōtomo no Sukune Ya-kamochi; with *tanka*

Nemokoro ni	When I brood on things
Mono o omoeba	In the deep roots of my mind
Iwamu sube	I am left speechless,
Semu sube mo nashi	And I know not what to do.
5 Imo to are to	She, my love, and I,
Te tazusawarite	Taking each the other's hand,
Ashita ni wa	Oft of a morning
Niwa ni idetachi	Would go out in the garden,
Yūhe ni wa	And when evening came
10 Toko uchiharai	Spread our sleeping mats all smooth.
Shirotae no	Were the nights we lay
Sode sashikaete	With our sleeves of white bark cloth
Saneshi yo ya	In mutual embrace
Tsune ni arikeru	Something that lasted forever?
15 Ashihiki no	In the footsore hills
Yamadori koso ba	The mountain pheasant, so they say,
Omukai ni	Calls to its mate
Tsumadoi su to ie	From a neighboring summit—
Utsusemi no	But I who am a man,
20 Hito naru are ya	The castings of a locust,
Nani su to ka	What am I doing
Hitohi hitoyo mo	Even for a single day or night
Sakariite	To stay apart from her,
Nagekikouramu	Sighing, yearning in vain?
25 Koko omoeba	When I think of it
Mune koso itaki	I hurt right here in my breast.
Soko yue ni	And for this reason,
Kokoro nagu ya to	Thinking that my heart might calm,
Takamato no	I went to the mountain
30 Yama ni mo no no ni mo	And the moor of Takamato,
Uchiyukite	Rambling at my ease
Asobiarukedo	All across the upland fields.
Hana nomi shi	But only flowers
Nioite areba	Shed their glow along those slopes,
35 Miru goto ni	And each time I looked
Mashite shinohayu	The longing grew within me.
Ika ni shite	How can it be done,

Wasururu mono so	This business of forgetting
Koi to iu mono o	The thing that we call love?

Envoy

Takamato no	Flowers of bindweed
Nohe no kaobana	On the Takamato moor
Omokage ni	Linger in my eye
Mietsutsu imo wa	Like the shadow of a face—
Wasurekanetsu mo	Hers that I cannot forget.

❀ A real separation was imposed on Yakamochi and the Elder Maiden by the events of late 740. Fujiwara no Hirotsugu's rebellion in the ninth month led to Emperor Shōmu's abandonment of Nara in the tenth. The Emperor took his court on a great circle eastward through Iga and Ise provinces, north to Mino, and then back west and south along the shore of Lake Biwa, settling at last at Kuni in the hills north of Nara by the fifteenth of the twelfth month. (For poems about Kuni, see nos. 677–88). Yakamochi was in the entourage and wrote poems from various stops along the way. The following is one, composed at Kawaguchi in Ise Province, where the court stayed from the second to the eleventh of the eleventh month. The person on Yakamochi's mind is presumably the Elder Maiden, though he was not without his other interests at the time. It is noticeable that there is less agony here than in the fifteen poems or the chōka-hanka above.

799   [MYS VI: 1033 / 1029]

A poem composed by Palace Attendant Ōtomo no Sukune Yakamochi at the temporary palace at Kawaguchi when the Emperor proceeded to the province of Ise in the tenth month, winter, of the twelfth year [of Tempyō, 740], Metal-Senior/Dragon, because of the raising of a rebel army by Junior Assistant Governor-General of Dazaifu Fujiwara no Asomi Hirotsugu

Kawaguchi no	Since we made our camp
Nohe ni iorite	On the fields of Kawaguchi,
Yo no fureba	Nights have gone by—
Imo ga tamoto shi	How the thoughts steal over me
Omōyuru kamo	Of the sleeves of one I love!

❀ The location of Sasa is unknown, but somewhere along the coast at a place of that name Yakamochi composed the following pair of tanka. The first continues the thought of no. 799, its burden being love in separation, and its vehicle the image of the loved one's arm or sleeve, the pillow for lovers' nights. The second deals with the issue of separation in a different way, less direct but potentially more affecting because of its overtones. In the solitary boat rowing away in the distance, Yakamochi creates an image of loneliness that speaks for him, that says more about his feelings than the open complaint does. The image is obviously not original to Yakamochi, who must be thinking back to Kurohito (see nos. 445, 447, and 449) and other poets. If he fails to capture the mood of those poems—leaving out a detail, speculating too closely about who is in the boat, not emphasizing the boat's fragility or unknown destination—it is nevertheless significant that he understood the effectiveness of using the image for one in his situation. The province of Shima had the pillow word *miketsukuni* ("land of royal provisions") because of its rich tribute in fish and seaweed. Kumano, the southern part of the Kii Peninsula, was known for its fine boat timber.

800–801   [MYS VI: 1036–37/1032–33]

Two poems composed by Ōtomo no Sukune Yakamochi at the temporary palace at Sasa

(800)   [1036/1032]

   Ōkimi no   Ever in the train
Miyuki no manima   Of our great lord on his journey,
  Wagimoko ga   Since last I pillowed
Tamakura makazu   On the pillow of my young love's arm
Tsuki so henikeru   A whole month has gone by.

(801)   [1037/1033]

  Miketsukuni   Over there, riding
Shima no ama narashi   In the small Kumano boat,
  Makumano no   Must be a shoreman
Obune ni norite   Of Shima the royal provider;
Okihe kogu miyu   He rows in view in the offing.

From the twenty-sixth to the twenty-ninth of the eleventh month of 740, the court was encamped at Tagi on the Tado River in Mino Province. There Yakamochi wrote a poem not about his personal feelings, but in the public mode of Hitomaro, Akahito, and other poets who had accompanied official retinues. Only a gesture in tanka form, it suggests that Tagi had long been a place of imperial resort. The poet laureate of Shōmu's reign was Sakimaro, not Yakamochi, but even this tanka touches briefly on the essential point in the litany of palace-praise—*kiyomi*, the "clearness" (or "cleanness") of the land and its waters.

802   [MYS VI: 1039/1035]

A poem composed by Ōtomo no Sukune Yakamochi

Tadokawa no	Perhaps from the clearness
Taki o kiyomi ka	Of the falls of Tado River,
Inishie yu	From an ancient time
Miyatsukaekemu	Palaces have flourished here
Tagi no no no ue ni	Above the moors of Tagi.

❋ The next stop was at Fuwa, where the court rested from the first to the fifth of the twelfth month. Fuwa was the remotest spot reached on the journey and the site of a famous "barrier," or inspection point (as well as of the fateful battle of Sekigahara 860 years later). Yakamochi was 120 kilometers from Nara, a five-day journey, but Fuwa Barrier proved too good an image to pass up. Lovers are always being separated by some barrier or other, and here was one labeled as such. Yakamochi reverts to the pillowing arm as the image of enticement at the far end of the vista.

803   [MYS VI: 1040/1036]

A poem composed by Ōtomo no Sukune Yakamochi at the temporary palace at Fuwa

Seki naku wa	But for the barrier
Kaeri ni dani mo	I would spur across the hills
Uchiyukite	To a brief homecoming;
Imo ga tamakura	Pillowed with my darling's arm
Makite nemashi o	For my pillow I would sleep.

❋ By the fifteenth of the twelfth month the court was in Kuni, where it remained for about three years. Early in the following year, 741, in the season of spring mists, Yakamochi sent the Elder Maiden a poem about time and a barrier, this time the barrier of the mountains themselves.

804   [MYS VIII: 1468/1464]

A poem sent by Ōtomo no Yakamochi to the Elder Maiden of Sakanoue

Harukasumi	Hazy in the spring,
Tanabiku yama no	Mist-drifted mountains rise
Henarereba	To stand between us;
Imo ni awazute	Without meeting my darling
Tsuki so henikeru	I have let the months go by.

The above was sent from the capital at Kuni to his residence in Nara.

❋ The complaints continued to be sent across the hills from Kuni to Nara; the following two are probably also from 741. In the first Yakamochi reproaches his wife, in the second himself. Kuni is less than ten kilometers from Nara as the crow flies, but this was apparently too far for the two to get together either in dream or in fact.

805-6   [MYS IV: 770-771 / 767-68]

Two more poems sent to the Elder Maiden by Ōtomo no Sukune Yakamochi

(805)   [770 / 767]

> Miyakoji o   Is the way so far
> Tōmi ka imo ga   Down the road from Miyako?
>   Kono koro wa   Lately, beloved,
> Ukeite nuredo   Though I pray before I sleep,
> Ime ni miekonu   You do not come to me in dreams.

(806)   [771 / 768]

> Ima shirasu   In this capital,
> Kuni no miyako ni   Kuni, where our lord now reigns,
>   Imo ni awazu   Since I met my love
> Hisashiku narinu   I've spent an everlasting time—
> Yukite haya mina   I must go and see her soon.

❋ In the fall of 746, the year after the capital was moved back to Nara, Yakamochi was appointed Governor of Etchū, a province on the Japan Sea nearly 250 kilometers northeast of the Yamato basin. It was a land of high, snowy mountains and rushing rivers, a remote and wild country area where Yakamochi enjoyed an active outdoor life (he turned thirty in the third year of his appointment) and wrote most of his best and most characteristic poetry. The following chōka-hanka set (no. 807-11) was composed about a year after he had taken up his post. It is on a personal subject, the loss of a favorite hawk, but employs the formal opening that might be expected in a public poem. The prosody is vigorous, with a good command of speed and pacing, parallel structures being strategically placed to slow down the rush of the unfolding exposition. The sudden shift from delight to disgust at line 47 is handled with particularly good effect, and the use of direct quotation (lines 11–12, 21–22, 54, 55–60, and 85–104) constitutes a special feature adding to the vivid freshness of the poem. Yakamochi has clearly found his own unique voice in this composition, which should be compared with the presentations of hunting as a royal rite in such poems as nos. 245–46, 301–3, and 562–63.

The chōka falls into five parts. The first ten lines make up a formal introduction of the land that Yakamochi has gone to govern. ("Koshi" was a general term for the area "across" the mountains, of which Etchū was a part.) It
is a *tō no mikado*, "a distant court," an outpost of imperial power, a term
used elsewhere by Hitomaro and Okura, but most frequently by Yakamochi himself. Lines 7–8 echo Akahito in no. 541, but here apply to the
landscape more plausibly. The second section, lines 11–46, leads into the
description of the hawk through parallel passages on cormorant fishing (for
Yakamochi's delight in which see no. 834–36) and hawking. The "great
black" is a three-year-old female hawk, described in the appended prose
passage as a "blue hawk." The picture of the young aristocrat out in the
fields and hills with his hawk on his wrist is another image of Yakamochi to
be placed alongside the lovesick swain of the early poems and the indisposed
Chinese-style literatus of his correspondence with Ikenushi (nos. 1182–99).

The smile is suddenly stricken from Yakamochi's lips by the news that
old Yamada has lost the great black. This third section (lines 47–62) is particularly good in the Okura-esque touch at the end of the old man clearing
his throat. Section four gives Yakamochi's reaction to the loss—confusion,
yearning, practical measures, and prayer. Unlike Okura, who prayed in vain
for the life of Furuhi, Yakamochi is rewarded: a divine messenger comes to
him in a dream. Her long speech makes up the last section. But, alas, the
poet learns that gods and dreams deceive. The promise that the hawk will be
found within seven days is revealed to have been empty by the first envoy. A
month has gone by, and still no hawk. The second envoy recapitulates the
practical measures, and the good dream, reversing the order of events with
regard to the first envoy, but effectuates another sharp switch in mood to
the third envoy, a scathing denunciation of old Yamada. *Matsugaeri*, a pillow
word for *shii* ("dumb," "numb"), is obscure, but may refer to the molting
of hawks perched in pines, suggesting the image of a bald (and useless) old
man. Yakamochi rewrites the story in Chinese prose at the end. It is interesting to note that he sees the poem as a way to purge himself of his resentment, suggesting perhaps something of the ancient magical force of the
"word soul" in chōka. But his "faith in a happy outcome" seems dubious.
The last envoy has him wondering if now he will lose all pleasure in hunting. Suka no Yama ("Mount Suka") was an actual place, echoing as well the
suka in *sukanaku*, "devoid of pleasure."

807–11   [MYS XVII: 4035–39/4011–15]

A poem composed in joy when, longing for my hawk that had been let
loose and escaped, I saw it in a dream; with *tanka*

Ōkimi no	Of our great lord
Tō no mikado so	We are the distant court,
Miyuki furu	Here in a hinterland
Koshi to na ni oeru	Remote beyond the farthest skies,

5	Amazakaru
	Hina ni shi areba
	Yama takami
	Kawa tōshiroshi
	No o hiromi
10	Kusa koso shigeki
	Ayu hashiru
	Natsu no sakari to
	Shimatsutori
	Ukai ga tomo wa
15	Yuku kawa no
	Kiyoki se goto ni
	Kagari sashi
	Nazusainoboru
	Tsuyu shimo no
20	Aki ni itareba
	No mo sawa ni
	Tori sudakeri to
	Masurao no
	Tomo izanaite
25	Taka wa shi mo
	Amata aredo mo
	Yakatao no
	A ga ōguro ni
	Shiranuri no
30	Suzu toritsukete
	Asagari ni
	Iotsutori tate
	Yūgari ni
	Chitori fumitate
35	Ou goto ni
	Yurusu koto naku
	Tabanare mo
	Ochi mo kayasuki
	Kore o okite
40	Mata wa arigatashi
	Sanaraeru
	Taka wa nakemu to
	Kokoro ni wa
	Omoihokorite
45	Emaitsutsu
	Wataru aida ni
	Taburetaru
	Shiko tsu okina no

Having for its name
Koshi of the falling snow:
    The mountains are high,
The rivers vast across the plain;
    The wild moors are wide,
And grass grows dense in thickets.
    "Here it's high summer,
Trout are running in the streams,"
    Say the island-bird
Cormorant fishers, and go out,
    Shining their flares
In every limpid shallow stretch
    Of flowing water,
Wading up against the buffeting stream.
    When the year draws on
To autumn with its frost and dew,
    "All across the moors
Birds are flocking. Come!"
    I invite my men,
My band of valiant hunters.
    I have many hawks,
But of them all I choose
    My great black
With the arrow-feather tail,
    And attach to her
A silver-plated tinkle bell.
    In the morning hunt
We start five hundred birds,
    In the evening hunt
We flush out a thousand birds,
    In each pursuit
We never lose our prey.
    She handles easily
In release and in return:
    Hard would it be
To find another one like her;
    No one has a hawk,
Surely, so beautifully trained—
    So I thought, my heart
Alive with happy pride,
    Smiling along my way
Across the days of my content.
    And then—that idiot!
That unspeakable old man,

	Koto dani mo	Without a word
50	Ware ni wa tsugezu	Or a by-your-leave to me,
	Tonogumori	Picked a rainy day
	Ame no furu hi o	When all the sky was under clouds,
	Togari su to	Just gave his name
	Na nomi o norite	And said, "I'm going hawking."
55	Mishimano o	"Looking off beyond
	Sogai ni mitsutsu	At the moors of Mishima,
	Futagami no	She flew up and crossed
	Yama tobikoete	Twin-peaked Futagami Mountain,
	Kumogakuri	Winging away,
60	Kakeriiniki to	Disappearing in the clouds,"
	Kaerikite	So on his return
	Shiwaburetsugure	He announced, clearing his throat.
	Oku yoshi no	Since there was no way
	Soko ni nakereba	Ready at hand to call her back,
65	Iu sube no	And as I knew no trick
	Tadoki o shirani	Nor anything to say or do,
	Kokoro ni wa	In my heart at length
	Hi sae moetsutsu	A fire began to burn, a burning
	Omoikoi	Of yearning, longing,
70	Ikizukiamari	And the heaving of endless sighs.
	Kedashiku mo	And yet after all
	Au koto ari ya to	Maybe I really could find her:
	Ashihiki no	Hither and yon
	Otemo konomo ni	Along the foot-dragging slopes
75	Tonami hari	I stretched bird nets,
	Morihe o suete	I placed lookouts on watch.
	Chihayaburu	To the holy shrine
	Kami no yashiro ni	Of the fierce, swift-shaking gods
	Teru kagami	A shining mirror
80	Shitsu ni torisoe	Joined to bolts of native cloth
	Koinomite	I gave, beseeching,
	A ga matsu toki ni	And while I waited after prayer
	Otomera ga	A maiden came
	Ime ni tsuguraku	And announced to me in a dream:
85	Na ga kouru	"That superb hawk
	Sono hotsutaka wa	You miss so sorely, yearning,
	Matsudae no	Flew along the beach
	Hama yukigurashi	Of Matsudae until dark,
	Tsunashi toru	Past Himi Inlet
90	Himinoe sugite	Where men fish for gizzard shad,
	Tako no shima	On over Tako Isle
	Tobitamotōri	Wheeled about in circling flight;

Ashigamo no
Sudaku Furue ni
95   Ototsuhi mo
Kinō mo aritsu
  Chikaku araba
Ima futsuka dami
  Tōku araba
100 Nanuka no ochi wa
  Sugime ya mo
Kinamu wa ga seko
  Nemokoro ni
Na koi so yo to so
105 Ima ni tsugetsuru

Two days ago
And yesterday again she stayed
  Where the mallards flock
Among the reeds of Furue.
  If soon,
In another day or two;
  If late,
The far side of seven days
  Will not have passed:
She'll come back, my brother.
  Do not, I bid you,
So burden yourself with yearning."
Thus she announced in my dream.

Yakatao no
Taka o te ni sue
  Mishimano ni
Karanu hi maneku
Tsuki so henikeru

On my hand a hawk
With an arrow-feather tail, I went
  To Mishima moor;
Now day after day of no hunting—
See, a whole month has gone by!

Futagami no
Otemo konomo ni
  Ami sashite
A ga matsu taka o
Ime ni tsugetsu mo

Hither and yon
Around twin-peaked Futagami
  I set the traps,
And I waited for my hawk—
And then came news in a dream!

Matsugaeri
Shii nite are ka mo
  Sayamada no
Oji ga sono hi ni
Motomeawazukemu

That pine-molting
Doddering baldpate numbskull,
  Old man Yamada,
If he'd had a brain in his head that day,
He'd have found my hawk for sure.

Kokoro ni wa
Yuruu koto naku
  Suka no yama
Sukanaku nomi ya
Koiwatarinamu

Shall I then go on
With this yearning in my heart
  Never lessening,
Bereft of all my pleasure
And the hills that were hills of joy?

Concerning the above: I caught a blue hawk at Furue Village in Imizu District. It was a handsome bird and fierce beyond other hawks. Then its keeper Yamada no Fubito Kimimaro lost all sense of the season for training and ignored the proper time for hunting on the moors. It soared off on its wind-beating wings and disappeared into the clouds; the bait of a rotten mouse was without effect in calling it back. Thereupon I stretched netting in readiness and watched for the unwonted; I made offerings of dedicatory cloth to the gods and relied on the unexpected. Lo and behold, there was a maiden in

a dream. She instructed me, saying, "Gentle magistrate, do not worry your-self, expending your vital force in vain. You will capture that hawk of yours before much longer." A moment later I was wide awake, and there was joy in my heart. Thus I composed a poem to rid myself of resentment, thereby expressing my faith in a happy outcome.
—Governor Ōtomo no Sukune Yakamochi. Composed on the twenty-sixth day of the ninth month [of 747].

❋ The red skirts of young women often caught the eyes of poets (see, for instance, nos. 311, 564, and 1057). In no. 812, a tanka datable to 748, Yakamochi uses the "reasoning" technique to explain the crimson glow re-flected in a river. The artifice of the "oblique" approach to description (the maidens must have been in full view) is quite in accord with the elegant standards of the Six Dynasties style.

812   [MYS XVII: 4045 / 4021]
A poem composed on the banks of the Okami River in Tonami District

> Okamigawa   Okami River
> Kurenai niou   Shimmers with a crimson flush:
> Otomera shi   Young maidens
> Ashitsuki toru to   Must be standing in the shallows
> Se ni tatasu rashi   Picking beadmoss from the rocks.

❋ In the third month of 748 Tanabe no Sakimaro came to visit Yakamochi in Etchū as an emissary from Minister of the Left Tachibana no Moroe. He was entertained by the provincial officials at a series of banquets where the composition of poems was part of the socializing. Poem 813 is from a party that took place on the twenty-sixth of the month. Kume no Hironawa, the host on this occasion, was Yakamochi's subordinate and friend. Fubito, Sakimaro's clan title, originated as a designation of record-keepers (*fumi-hito*). Most of the poems on this occasion were about the cuckoo (*hototo-gisu*), and Hironawa's residence is said to have been a favorable place to hear its song. The cuckoo was associated with night and the moon.

813   [MYS XVIII: 4078 / 4054]
[One of] four poems at a banquet in honor of Tanabe no Fubito Sakimaro, held at the residence of Secretary Kume no Asomi Hironawa

> Hototogisu   Cuckoo, do you
> Ko yo nakiwatare   Fly singing before me—
> Tomoshibi o   This torchlight

Tsukuyo ni nasoe   I shall liken to the moon
Sono kage mo mimu   And watch your shape flit by.

The above is by Ōtomo no Sukune Yakamochi.

❋ In the second month of 749 gold was discovered in the Oda district of Michinoku Province, and on the first of the fourth month Emperor Shōmu went before the recently cast monumental bronze icon of Vairocana Buddha in Nara and proclaimed two edicts. In the first, addressed to the icon, the Emperor declared himself the "slave of the Three Treasures" and expressed his joy and thanks for the propitious discovery of the metal with which to gild and thus complete the statue. In the second, addressed to his officials and people, he detailed at greater length his anxiety about having enough gold for his project and his consequent relief, rewarded his loyal ministers and family, and bestowed blessings and amnesties on his subjects. He revealed his view of Buddhism as the prime means of protecting the nation, at the same time rehearsing his own divine ancestry and invoking the native gods.

These edicts (semmyō) are a unique feature of *Shoku Nihongi*. They stand out from the surrounding kambun text by virtue of being written in Japanese, in a combination of phonetic and semantic orthography not unlike the principles used in many Man'yō poems, but with the characters representing inflections and particles written small for easy identification. And they are prose—a prose of a highly elaborate and formal character whose rhetorical dignity and oratorical splendor are reminiscent of the grand chōka manner of Hitomaro, but structurally and rhythmically distinct. The resemblance is close enough, however, that Yakamochi probably had little difficulty adapting portions of Shōmu's second proclamation into chōka form. The result is no. 814–17, composed in Etchū about a month and a half after the Emperor issued his edicts in Nara. (As a provincial Governor, Yakamochi was no doubt promptly supplied official copies.)

The main reason why Yakamochi was attracted to this experiment is probably to be found in a passage in the second edict directed to the Ōtomo clan, praising (and reminding them of) their tradition of loyalty to the throne. Given the incessant intrigues of the period, the monarch needed to issue such reminders, and Shōmu may well have been particularly worried at this point, for he was about to abdicate in favor of his daughter Kōken (he did so in the seventh month). Kōken was under the influence of Fujiwara no Nakamaro, the enemy of Tachibana no Moroe. And the Ōtomo were allies of Moroe. Shōmu's fears were realized in 757, the year after his death, when Moroe's son Naramaro staged an abortive coup. For his part, Yakamochi probably was more interested in the fate of his clan than in the Great Buddha, which had been under construction while he was away in Etchū. Waka in any case rarely extended its realm to descriptions of Buddhist iconography or architecture. In Yakamochi's chōka the Emperor's cherished project is simply *yoki koto*, "the good work."

The chōka is an interweaving of passages adapted from or suggested by the semmyō with others supplied by Yakamochi. The adulatory introduction in the Hitomaro manner generally reflects a passage early in the second semmyō. Yakamochi greatly expands this section, and leads skillfully from the rich tribute into the main topic—gold (line 25). Lines 20–58 are more or less closely adapted from the text of the proclamation, but with the elements rearranged into a new order of exposition. Individual words like *izanaitamai* ("with high exhortation"; line 22) and *aiuzunai* ("rejoice"; line 38) are incorporated with minor grammatical adjustments. However, in lines 41–44 Yakamochi is at pains to insert a reference not found in his source, to the discovery of gold in Tsushima in 701. Yakamochi's great-uncle Miyuki (d. 701) had been in charge of having the gold refined and presented to court. The first half of the chōka, down through line 62, is completed by a description of the Emperor's beneficence suggested in a vague fashion by the conclusion of the semmyō.

Beginning with line 63, Yakamochi turns from the Emperor to his own clan, the Ōtomo, and writes what is really a second poem. The Ōtomo too have "a remote god-ancestor" (*tōtsu kamuoya*) and are thus coeval with the imperial line itself. According to the *Kojiki* account, this ancestor was Ame no Oshihi no Mikoto, but Yakamochi, who should have known his own clan's lineage, identifies him as Ōkumenushi. This "Great Master of the Kume" does not appear in the chronicles, but both the Ōtomo and the Kume were clans of warriors in the service of the imperial house, and the ancestors of both descended together with the sun goddess's grandchild, according to *Kojiki*. The designation Ōkumenushi suggests that the Kume were subordinate to the Ōtomo. The ancient song in italics, the "oath of the Ōtomo," is also incorporated in the semmyō (see no. 227); Yakamochi has altered the ending, *nodo ni wa shinaji* ("we shall not die in peace"), to *kaerimi wa seji* ("we shall never look back"). The song stands out from the matrix in which it is embedded, no less in the chōka than in the semmyō. Simple, inevitable, and sad, it goes directly to the heart of loyalty—the willingness to die. In its vision of war as perseverance and death (no mention of victory), it is far more moving than the heroics of Hitomaro's battle piece (no. 341), and it makes the rest of Yakamochi's chōka seem to be straining for effect—which of course it is. The song was put to music and sung during the Second World War, telling only too well the fate of Japan's far-flung expeditionary forces.

The rest of the chōka is a reworking and elaboration of the semmyō text. The Saeki clan, mentioned in line 84, was a branch of the Ōtomo. Yakamochi seeks to serve both his clan and his Emperor in this poem, but for all the stirring rhetoric, the times were against him. Nevertheless, despite the straining, it is his most impressive poem in the public mode. The three envoys strike a nice balance, with a refrain-like repetition of the last three lines in the first, references to the (Ōtomo) past in the second, and to the Sovereign's present (and future) in the last. The "inner hold" (*okutsuki*) in the second envoy is the grave; it is not clear exactly what kind of sign is intended, perhaps the stringing of a sacred rope. *Masurao* ("valiant man") in the first envoy represents the Ōtomo ideal that Yakamochi is trying to preserve.

814–17   [MYS XVIII: 4118–21 / 4094–97]

A poem in celebration of the imperial rescript on the discovery of gold in Michinoku Province; with *tanka*

Ashihara no	To the reed-plain
Mizuho no kuni o	Country of the sweet rice spears
Amakudari	In heaven-descent
Shirashimeshikeru	Came to an all-knowing rule
5 Sumeroki no	The ancestral gods,
Kami no mikoto no	Sovereign noble deities
Miyo kasane	Age upon age
Ama no hitsugi to	In the sun-succession of the sky:
Shirashikuru	And in every age
10 Kimi no miyo miyo	Of their wise and lordly rule
Shikimaseru	From well-governed lands
Yomo no kuni ni wa	In all the four directions came,
Yamakawa o	Out of the breadth and depth
Hiromi atsumi to	Of the mountains and the rivers,
15 Tatematsuru	High-held offerings,
Mitsuki takara wa	Tribute, treasures of the land
Kazoeezu	Beyond all counting,
Tsukushi mo kanetsu	Inexhaustible by man.
Shikaredo mo	Yet though it was thus,
20 Wa go ōkimi no	Our great lord was calling
Morohito o	With high exhortation
Izanaitamai	All the people of his realm,
Yoki koto o	He was setting forth
Hajimetamaite	To accomplish the good work:
25 Kugane ka mo	Gold—would there be
Tashikeku aramu to	Amounts sufficient to the task,
Omōshite	He wondered,
Shitanayamasu ni	Afflicting his inmost heart.
Tori ga naku	Then: "In cock-crowing
30 Azuma no kuni no	Azuma the Eastern Land,
Michinoku no	In Michinoku
Oda naru yama ni	In the mountains of Oda

	Kugane ari to	Gold has been found,"
	Mōshitamaere	So it was reported to the throne.
35	Mikokoro o	The august mind
	Akirametamai	Brightened in a flood of cheer:
	Ame tsuchi no	"The gods of heaven
	Kami aiuzunai	And the gods of earth rejoice,
	Sumeroki no	The august spirits
40	Mitama tasukete	Of Our Sovereign Ancestors give aid,
	Tōki yo ni	That which was thus
	Kakarishi koto o	In a distant age once more
	Wa ga miyo ni	In Our very reign
	Arawashite areba	Making manifest to all.
45	Osu kuni wa	This land We feast upon
	Sakaemu mono to	Shall burst like a flower into bloom."
	Kamunagara	So he deigned to think,
	Omōshimeshite	He, the Sovereign, a god.
	Mononofu no	And his men at arms,
50	Yaso tomo no o o	His eighty officers of court
	Matsuroe no	He commands to obey,
	Muke no manimani	Directing them to carry out his will:
	Oihito mo	He succors the aged,
	Omina warawa mo	The women and the children,
55	Shi ga negau	Granting their pleas,
	Kokorodarai ni	Fulfilling the desires of their hearts;
	Nadetamai	He soothes them,
	Osametamaeba	He governs them wisely and well.
	Koko o shi mo	And I wondered,
60	Aya ni tōtomi	Strangely moved to reverence,
	Ureshikeku	Thinking more and more
	Iyoyo omoite	Of my joy at such a reign.
	Ōtomo no	We Ōtomo
	Tōtsu kamuoya no	Spring from a remote god-ancestor,
65	Sono na o ba	And as for his name,
	Ōkumenushi to	Ōkumenushi was
	Oimochite	The proud name he bore;
	Tsukaeshi tsukasa	And the office he performed:
	Umi yukaba	*"If we go on the sea,*
70	*Mitsuku kabane*	*Our dead are sodden in water;*
	Yama yukaba	*If we go on the mountains,*
	Kusamusu kabane	*Our dead are grown over with grass.*
	Ōkimi no	*We shall die*
	He ni koso shiname	*By the side of our lord,*
75	*Kaerimi wa*	*We shall never*
	Seji to kotodate	*Look back."* So they proclaimed,

Masurao no	They who passed down
Kiyoki sono na o	From the ancient time till now
Inishie yo	In our present day
80 Ima no otsutsu ni	That pure name of valiant men,
Nagasaeru	They the fathers
Oya no kodomo so	Of the sons we are:
Ōtomo to	The Ōtomo
Saeki no uji wa	And the Saeki clans
85 Hito no oya no	Are bound in duty
Tatsuru kotodate	Set forth in the words held high,
Hito no ko wa	Words of the fathers
Oya no na tatazu	That the sons may never break,
Ōkimi ni	To serve our great lord
90 Matsurou mono to	In worshipful attendance:
Iitsugeru	They bequeathed to us
Koto no tsukasa so	This testament of office.
Azusayumi	The catalpa bow
Te ni torimochite	We shall take into our hand,
95 Tsurugitachi	And the long, straight sword
Koshi ni torihaki	We shall belt about our hips.
Asamamori	For the morning watch,
Yū no mamori ni	For the watch at evening,
Ōkimi no	For the sentry watch
100 Mikado no mamori	At the gates of our great lord
Ware o okite	There will be no men
Hito wa araji to	Other than we. Ever more clearly,
Iyatate	Lofty with pride,
Omoi shi masaru	This knowledge fills my thoughts:
105 Ōkimi no	To the peal of glory
Mikoto no saki o	Bursting from our great lord's royal word
Kikeba tōtomi	I listen, reverent with awe.

Three Envoys

Masurao no	My thoughts go out
Kokoro omōyu	To the hearts of valiant men;
Ōkimi no	To the peal of glory
Mikoto no saki o	Bursting from our great lord's royal word
Kikeba tōtomi	I listen, reverent with awe.
Ōtomo no	On the inner hold
Tōtsu kamuoya no	Of the remote god-ancestor
Okutsuki wa	Of the Ōtomo
Shiruku shime tate	Clearly set the sacred sign,
Hito no shirubeku	That men may know the spot.

Sumeroki no	Let our Sovereign's reign
Miyo sakaemu to	Open now in glorious flower:
Azuma naru	In the Eastern Land,
Michinokuyama ni	In the mountains of Michinoku,
Kuganehana saku	The golden blossoms bloom.

Composed by Ōtomo no Sukune Yakamochi at the Governor's Residence in Etchū Province on the twelfth day of the fifth month of the first year of Tempyō-Kampō [749].

❋ Immediately following his poem on the discovery of gold in Michinoku, Yakamochi included a poem that is of more interest for its headnote than for itself. The headnote reveals that the Yoshino poem had become such a set genre that examples were being composed in advance to be ready for submission on an appropriate occasion. This poem was composed in Etchū in 749, far from Yoshino and any chance to be included in an imperial excursion. The elements of a Yoshino chōka are nevertheless marshaled for review: the Sovereign, the founding of the palace, the courtiers (in the old formula *mononofu no yaso tomo no o*), the ever-present mountains and river— Hitomaro revisited, but from a great distance. (It will be remembered that Yakamochi's father Tabito had also composed a Yoshino poem that he never submitted; see no. 589–90.) It is not clear for whom the encomia in the first part of the poem are intended. Emperor Yūryaku (no. 96) is recorded to have visited a palace at Yoshino, and in more recent times the place was associated particularly with Empress Jitō. *Na* ("name") in line 18 may be taken to mean family honor or fame. This is the last salute to Yoshino in *Man'yōshū*; with it a tradition dies. When Yoshino reappears in later poetry it is as a famous site for cherry blossoms. The mountains and the river remain, in poetry as in fact, but the palace and the faithful courtiers are gone. Yoshino becomes a place for monks and hermits in search of solitude. Yakamochi can hardly have been conscious of the irony of his final lines.

818–20   [MYS XVIII: 4122–24 / 4098–4100]

A poem composed in advance for the time when the Emperor would make an excursion to the detached palace at Yoshino; with *tanka*

Takamikura	Enthroned on high,
Ama no hitsugi to	Scion of the sun in heaven,
Ame no shita	Lord of all the earth
Shirashimeshikeru	Beneath the circle of the sky,
5 Sumeroki no	Sovereign ruler,
Kami no mikoto no	August god, that mighty one of old
Kashikoku mo	It was who in dread

Hajimetamaite	Majesty began the task,
Tōtoku mo	Who with awesome
10 Sadametamaeru	Purpose founded on this spot
Miyoshino no	The great palace
Kono ōmiya ni	Of fair Yoshino; and now we see
Arigayoi	How in steadfast round
Meshitamau rashi	Our present lord goes forth to view this site.
15 Mononofu no	And the men at arms,
Yaso tomo no o mo	The eighty officers at court,
Ono ga oeru	Bearing each his name,
Ono ga na oite	The name he bears as servitor—
Ōkimi no	At our lord's command
20 Make no manimani	They too shall make their journeys here,
Kono kawa no	And as the river flows
Tayuru koto naku	Forever without running dry,
Kono yama no	As these mountains rise
Iyatsugitsugi ni	Range beyond range, again and yet again,
25 Kaku shi koso	Even as now,
Tsukaematsurame	Shall render reverent service to the throne
Iyatōnaga ni	Beyond the utmost reaches of the years.
Inishie o	He seems to ponder
Omōsu rashi mo	On the days now past and gone:
Wa go ōkimi	Our great lord
Yoshino no miya o	Goes forth in steadfast round to view
Arigayoitsutsu	His palace in fair Yoshino.
Mononofu no	And the men at arms,
Yasoujibito mo	The clansmen of the eighty clans,
Yoshinogawa	Shall gaze on Yoshino
Tayuru koto naku	Forever, as the river flows,
Tsukaetsutsu mimu	While they render service to their lord.

✳ Two days after his poem on the discovery of gold (and one day after the Yoshino poem?), according to his footnote, Yakamochi wrote a poem for his wife. The Elder Maiden had been left behind in Nara but not forgotten. In no. 821–25 Yakamochi wishes to send her pearls, to the round number of five hundred, from the islands adjacent to his realm. The sentiment and prosodic liveliness of this chōka-hanka set make it one of his most appealing poems. Gone is the lover's obsession with his own sufferings that dominates the early love poems; instead, we have the husband's concern and sympathy for his wife. He imagines *her* longing for *him*, alone in her half-empty bed, and not bothering to comb her hair in the morning. This image of the sleep-tangled hair is curiously reminiscent of no. 728, Lady Ōtomo of Sakanoue's poem to her daughter; mother and husband have had the same vision of the woman left behind in her yearning.

Yakamochi's chōka is particularly impressive for the way, beginning with line 7, it sweeps on to the end in one continuous syntactic stream, stringing together all the things he wants his wife to wear with the pearls and arriving at its conclusion still not out of breath. Suzu (in the first line) is at the tip of the Noto Peninsula, to the north of Yakamochi's provincial seat across Toyama Bay. "The ocean god" (*oki tsu mikami*) refers to the shrines of the Seven Islands and Hekura Island, where the seafolk of Noto went to dive for abalone. These islands, north of Noto in the Sea of Japan, are still prime diving grounds. In the ama communities of this area it is the women who do the diving, hence the translation "her" in the final envoy.

The chōka contains a few niceties in the way of *engo* ("related words"). The *awabitama* ("abalone gems," i.e., pearls) resonate with the *nubatama* ("*nuba*-berries") that are the epithet for *yo* ("night")—nacreous white against glistening black. And the husband counts the pearls, whereas the wife counts the days and months. In a way, one serves as a recompense for the other, a *kokoro nagusa* ("consolation for the heart"). The four envoys recapitulate and embroider various points in the main poem, the last corresponding to the opening passage and presenting the superb image of an ama girl offering a double handful of gleaming pearls. Yakamochi does not say whether he ever obtained them, but as a government official he must have been in an advantageous position to do so.

821–25   [MYS XVIII : 4125–29 / 4101–5]

A poem requesting pearls to send to my home in the capital; with *tanka*

	Suzu no ama no	The seafolk of Suzu
	Oki tsu mikami ni	Go out far across the deep
	Iwatarite	To the ocean god
	Kazukitoru to iu	And dive for abalone, so 'tis said,
5	Awabitama	And oh that I could have
	Iochi mogamo	Five hundred of those abalone pearls!
	Hashiki yoshi	To my dearest one,
	Tsuma no mikoto no	My most honored wife, who since
	Koromode no	I parted from her sleeves
10	Wakareshi toki yu	And came away into this place
	Nubatama no	Has lain alone,
	Yodoko katasari	Her bed half-empty in the bead-black night,
	Asanegami	Who does not touch a comb
	Kaki mo kezurazu	To the tangles of her morning hair,
15	Idete koshi	But must be sighing
	Tsukihi yomitsutsu	As she counts the months and days

Nagekuramu	Since I set forth,
Kokoro nagusa ni	As consolation for her heart,
Hototogisu	With admonition that
20 Kinaku satsuki no	She string them as a garland for her hair
Ayamegusa	Together with sweet flag
Hanatachibana ni	That grows in June when cuckoos sing,
Nukimajie	And fragrant blossoms
Kazura ni seyo to	Of the flowering orange,
25 Tsutsumite yaramu	I'd wrap and send them as my gift!

Shiratama o	If I wrap white pearls
Tsutsumite yaraba	And send them to her as a gift,
Ayamegusa	They'll be the very thing
Hanatachibana ni	To string together with sweet flag
Ae mo nuku gane	And blossoms of the flowering orange.

Oki tsu shima	To the isles of the offing
Iyukiwatarite	'Tis said the seafolk go to dive:
Kazuku chū	Oh, that I might have
Awabitama moga	Their take of abalone pearls—
Tsutsumite yaramu	I'd wrap and send them to my wife.

Wagimoko ga	Oh, for white pearls
Kokoro nagusa ni	From the islands of the offing,
Yaramu tame	For me to send
Oki tsu shima naru	As a consolation to the heart
Shiratama mogamo	Of my own sweet darling girl!

Shiratama no	How I would prize her,
Iotsu tsudoi o	The diver who would bring me pearls,
Te ni musubi	Pearls of gleaming white,
Okosemu ama wa	Five hundred gathered together,
Mugashiku mo aru ka	Heaped in her offering hands!

The above was composed by Ōtomo no Sukune Yakamochi on the fourteenth day of the fifth month [of 749].

✳ The *tachibana* tree, an exotic long naturalized in Japan by the Nara period, and mentioned over thirty times in *Man'yōshū*, is dealt with at greatest length by Yakamochi in no. 826–27, written a little over a month after the poem about pearls, in which it also appears. It is not clear just how the ancient tachibana relates to the modern *mikan*, the mandarin orange or tangerine, a highly edible fruit. References in *Man'yōshū* indicate that the tree was admired for its fragrant flowers and evergreen leaves, and that both the fruit and the flowers were strung in garlands. Yakamochi's chōka gives the plant's annual cycle: budding in spring; flowering in the fifth month (corresponding roughly to June), at which time it was associated with the cuckoo (hototogisu); the collection of petals and unripe fruit; the display of tree-ripened fruit in the fall; and the retention of green leaves in winter.

The tachibana's lush beauty in every season, and its glowing green and orange colors, made it a special, almost magical, tree. Yakamochi recounts the myth of its importation from Tokoyo no Kuni, "the Land of Everworld," found in both *Kojiki* and *Nihonshoki*. The concept of Tokoyo, the land of immortality across the sea (or at its bottom in some versions), may have been influenced by the Chinese myth of P'eng-lai (J. Hōrai), the island of the Taoist immortals (see nos. 216–20 and 579–80). Like Tajimamori, sent by Emperor Suinin (third century?) to Tokoyo for the Seasonless Fragrant Tree, one of the characters in the early Heian tale *Taketori Monogatari* is sent to Hōrai for the branch of a magic tree. Tajimamori was of Korean descent, according to the legendary accounts in the Japanese chronicles. *Kojiki* recounts a legend concerning his Korean antecedents in which there figures a red jewel born to a woman impregnated by the rays of the sun. It is tempting to suppose that this jewel might have some significance in connection with the glowing fruit of the tachibana. But the early accounts do not suggest that Tokoyo was identified with Korea. A southern origin for the orange is more likely; in Korea nowadays the mikan grows only on Cheju Island off the southern coast of the peninsula.

826–27   [MYS XVIII: 4135–36/4111–12]

A poem on the *tachibana*; with *tanka*

	Kakemaku mo	I would call it to mind,
	Aya ni kashikoshi	But my thoughts are lost in awe—
	Sumeroki no	In the mighty reign
	Kami no ōmiyo ni	Of a sovereign ancestral god
5	Tajimamori	Tajimamori
	Tokoyo ni watari	Crossed the sea to Everworld,
	Yahoko mochi	And when he returned,
	Maidekoshi toki	Carrying with him the eight spears,
	Tokijiku no	He bestowed on us,
10	Kaku no konomi o	Wondrously, in a later age,
	Kashikoku mo	The bright, glowing fruit
	Nokoshitamaere	Of the Seasonless Fragrant Tree—
	Kuni mo se ni	Whence now our land
	Oitachisakae	Overflows with its bounty:
15	Haru sareba	When spring comes on
	Hikoe moitsutsu	The new twigs burst forth in bud,
	Hototogisu	And in the month of June

Naku satsuki ni wa	When the little cuckoo cries
Hatsuhana o	We break whole branches
20 Eda ni taorite	For their burden of first bloom
Otomera ni	To send as trophies
Tsuto ni mo yarimi	To the maidens of our choice,
Shirotae no	Or strip the petals
Sode ni mo kokire	Into sleeves of white bark cloth,
25 Kaguwashimi	For their fine fragrance
Okite karashimi	Leaving them until they dry;
Ayuru mi wa	The windfallen fruit
Tama ni nukitsutsu	We string like beads, one by one,
Te ni makite	Winding them about
30 Miredo mo akazu	Our arms, never sated with gazing.
Akizukeba	When autumn sets in
Shigure no ame furi	The chill rains fall in sudden showers,
Ashihiki no	And the tips of trees
Yama no konure wa	Along the foot-wearying mountains
35 Kurenai ni	Spread a crimson glow
Nioichiredo mo	As the leaves come scattering down;
Tachibana no	But the fruit of the orange,
Nareru sono mi wa	All now fully formed and ripe,
Hitateri ni	Shines with a brilliance
40 Iya migahoshiku	Ever brighter day by day.
Miyuki furu	And then when we arrive
Fuyu ni itareba	In the snow-falling winter
Shimo okedo mo	Hoarfrost may rime them,
Sono ha mo karezu	Yet the leaves never wither,
45 Tokiwa nasu	In lustrous glory
Iya sakabae ni	Changeless as the mountain crags.
Shikare koso	For this very cause
Kami no miyo yori	Seems it—and most fittingly—
Yoroshinae	From the Age of Gods
50 Kono tachibana o	This *tachibana* has been called
Tokijiku no	The Seasonless Tree
Kaku no konomi to	Of the glowing, fragrant fruit—
Nazukekerashi mo	That name given so long ago.

Envoy

Tachibana wa	I have seen the orange
Hana ni mo mi ni mo	In the flower and the fruit,
Mitsuredo mo	But the desire
Iya tokijiku ni	Still is in me to see it
Nao shi migahoshi	Yet more in every season.

Composed by Ōtomo no Sukune Yakamochi on the twenty-third day of the intercalary fifth month [of 749].

❋ Some of Yakamochi's finest tanka open Book XIX of *Man'yōshū*, dated to the first few days of the third month of 750. The opening pair is a contrasting study in red and white. The first poem in particular is excellently conceived and executed. Lines 1 and 2 paint an overall impression of crimson glow in the garden. Lines 3 and 4 locate its source in peach blossoms casting their colored shade on the ground. And the last line completes the picture with a young woman standing on the garden path, bathed in the warm light. Finally the reader notices that she too is presented, through her youthful beauty, as a source, not merely a recipient, of the glow. An advance of Yakamochi's art in tanka beyond the traditional amorous modes he inherited is well evidenced by this gem of a poem, whose taut construction and suffusion with warm color and femininity make one think of the work of the early-twentieth-century poet Yosano Akiko. The matching verse is about the white blossoms of the damson plum and is an early example of "elegant confusion," the Chinese conceit perhaps introduced to Japanese poetry by Yakamochi's father Tabito (see no. 1018).

828–29   [MYS XIX: 4163–64 / 4139–40]

Two poems composed on gazing at the blossoms of the peach and damson trees in my spring garden, on the evening of the first of the third month of Tempyō-Shōhō 2 [750]

(828)   [4163 / 4139]

> Haru no sono   My whole spring arbor
> Kurenai niou   Radiates a crimson glow:
>   Momo no hana   Blossoms of the peach
> Shitaderu michi ni   Shine down on the garden path
> Idetatsu otome   Where a maiden steps in view.

(829)   [4164 / 4140]

> Wa ga sono no   Is it the blossom
> Sumomo no hana ka   Of the damson in my arbor
>   Niwa ni chiru   Scattered in the yard,
> Hadare no imada   Or a dusting of snowflakes
> Nokoritaru ka mo   That still lingers on the ground?

❋ In no. 830, written at about the same time, Yakamochi again brings together young women and a flower. This poem, however, is built on contrast—between the lively commotion of the women around a well and the quietude of a single bloom in the crannies. It is tempting to interpret the pink sweet-lily metaphorically as a shy maiden, but that would likely be a romantic over-reading. But Yakamochi plays another game here, using the epithet *mononofu no* ("men at arms" or "court officers," according to different interpretations), with its dignified archaic resonance, not for *yasotomo no o* ("heads of eighty crafts") or *yaso ujibito* ("men of eighty clans"), but for *yaso otomera*, "eighty maidens," with a no doubt calculated comic effect.

830   [MYS XIX: 4167 / 4143]

A poem on plucking a pink sweet-lily

Mononofu no	The eighty maidens,
Yaso otomera ga	Busy as the officers at court,
Kumimagau	Bustle about
Terai no ue no	Drawing water from the temple well—
Katakago no hana	Where this pink sweet-lily blooms.

✳ Also belonging to the poems composed early in the third month of 750 are a pair of tanka on the cries of plovers at night. It has been suggested that "the men of old" (*mukashi no hito*) in no. 832 could be an allusion to Akahito's evocation of the plovers of Yoshino in no. 561. This may well be so, for Akahito's justly admired verse would have been known to Yakamochi as an anthologist. But Yakamochi is doing something quite different in these poems. He is not trying to embroider scenes of natural beauty on the tapestry of an imperial progress, but attempting to show himself as a sensitive man. He lets us come very close and see him lying in bed, utterly passive, absorbing the sounds that come to him and reacting to the inchoate sadness they convey. This receptivity, surely we are to understand, qualifies him as a poet. It is a modern, romantic conception, a kind of "negative capability." The poems are lovely in sound and rhythm, especially the first one with its sonorous fourth line and falling cadence at the end. Yakamochi seems to like such rare and mysterious-sounding terms as *yogutachi* ("slack of night") and *yo no hodoro* ("lees of night"; see nos. 793–94). He may have found the former in an anonymous poem, MYS VII: 1128 / 1124, also about listening to plovers on a sleepless night (see also no. 291 by Hitomaro). *Yogutachi* refers to a time past midnight when the night is "declining" or "decaying," whereas *hodoro*, perhaps cognate with *hadare* ("flurrying snowflakes"), is the shimmering away of the blackness of night in the gray of dawn.

831–32   [MYS XIX: 4170–71 / 4146–47]

Two poems on hearing the plovers' cries during the night

(831) [4170/4146]

>   Yogutachi ni   In the slack of night
>   Nezamete oreba   I lie awake, my heart grown
>   Kawase tome   Helpless at the sound
>   Kokoro mo shino ni Of plovers crying in the stream,
>   Naku chidori kamo   Seeking the shallow water.

(832) [4171/4147]

>   Yo kutachite   When the night grows slack
>   Naku kawachidori   And the river plovers cry,
>   Ube shi koso   It comes to me
>   Mukashi no hito mo   How the men of old were moved
>   Shinoikinikere   To sing in helpless longing.

❋ Yakamochi's residence in Etchū was on the east bank of the Imizu River near the modern city of Takaoka. From there he heard the plovers in the river, and at dawn, boatmen singing.

833 [MYS XIX:4174/4150]

A poem on hearing far off the song of the boatmen going up the river

>   Asatoko ni   Faint and far away
>   Kikeba harokeshi   As I listen in my morning bed,
>   Imizugawa   From Imizu River
>   Asakogi shitsutsu   Comes the sound of boatmen singing,
>   Utau funabito   Rowing on the stream at dawn.

❋ No. 834–36, another poem listed for the third month of 750, once more shows Yakamochi as a vigorous outdoorsman engaging in a favorite sport. This time it is cormorant fishing, conducted at night by torchlight. It is spring; the Sakita River is a rushing torrent of snow melt and young trout. By day the mountain slopes are aglow with bloom; even the new year has the pillow word *aratama no* ("like a rough gem"). The shining and glowing continue into the night scene as the torches illuminate the swift current against which Yakamochi and his followers wade, and the bright crimson skirts of his drenched attire. Like the maidens in no. 812, he stains the stream red. The garment is a reminder of his wife, who sent it to him, and to whom he will soon return, but in the exhilaration of the moment he declares his intention to come back to Etchū every year for the sport, as long as the river and the trout shall run. Such formulaic declarations were made in a public context by Hitomaro and his followers at Yoshino. Sakita River is indeed another version of the river valley as *locus amoenus*.

834–36   [MYS XIX: 4180–82/4156–58]

A poem on cormorant fishing; with *tanka*

Aratama no	When the year comes round,
Toshi yukikaeri	The new year precious as a gem from the earth,
Haru sareba	And spring returns once more,
Hana nomi niou	The lower mountain slopes, aglow
5 Ashihiki no	With the flush of bloom,
Yamashita toyomi	Reecho to the thunder of the stream
Ochitagichi	Where Sakita River
Nagaru Sakita no	Plunges in a boiling cataract;
Kawa no se ni	And where the rapids flow
10 Ayuko sabashiru	The waters are alive with darting trout.
Shima tsu tori	So it was one night
Ukai tomonae	I led the trainers of cormorants,
Kagari sashi	Birds of the islands,
Nazusaiyukeba	And torches lit, we labored up the stream.
15 Wagimoko ga	That night even the skirts
Katamigatera to	Of the garment that my darling girl
Kurenai no	Dyed to a bright crimson—
Yashio ni somete	Eight times into the vat it went—
Okosetaru	And sent to me
20 Koromo no suso mo	As a remembrance of her love
Tōrite nurenu	Were wet in every stitch.
Kurenai no	I shall come again
Koromo niowashi	To stain the waters with my crimson garb;
Sakitagawa	As Sakita River
Tayuru koto naku	Flows forever, never shall I fail
Ware kaerimimu	To return and see these sights anew.
Toshinoha ni	As long as the trout
Ayu shi hashiraba	Shall run, year after year,
Sakitagawa	I shall seek once more
U yatsu kazukete	The rapids of Sakita River,
Kawase tazunemu	Eight cormorants diving on my string!

❊ About two months later, on the sixth of the fifth month of 750, Yakamochi relates, he was moved to write a poem on the legend of the maiden of Unai. The result is no. 837–38. Since he was far from the area around Ashiya on the Inland Sea where the events of the story are supposed to have taken place, and where the sight of the grave mounds inspired Takahashi no Mushimaro to his version of the legend (no. 574–76), it is tempting to speculate that Yakamochi was going through Mushimaro's poems, perhaps at work compiling *Man'yōshū* during his spare time in Etchū. In any case he does not attempt to duplicate Mushimaro's dramatic intensity or rival his narrative gift. Yakamochi assumes that the story is known and gives a rapid, condensed account of its main features, a lyrical rendering concentrating on the maiden Unai's (and his own) emotional reactions. All is sad and beautiful and mysterious and lost in the past; there is no shrieking or gnashing of teeth, and Unai vanishes like a fragile flower fallen at its peak. Unai is the entire focus; the rival lovers are mentioned only as the impetus to her self-immolation. Dead, she seems to be buried alone, and the tree trails its branches over her grave, not that of the young Chinu. The theme has altered from obsession to *aware*, and the "sinfulness" of the lovers has been diluted to the vanishing point. Yakamochi introduces the image of a succession of trees growing from the maiden's boxwood comb: the story is an old one, and the poet no longer mourns "as for the newly dead" (*niimo no goto*: no. 574, line 72).

837–38   [MYS XIX: 4235–36 / 4211–12]

A contribution on the theme of the Maiden's grave mound; with *tanka*

	Inishie ni	Long ago, men say,
	Arikeru waza no	An event occurred, a thing
	Kusubashiki	Surpassingly strange:
	Koto to iitsugu	According to the tale,
5	Chinu otoko	The youth of Chinu
	Unai otoko no	And the youth of Unai,
	Utsusemi no	Quarreling together
	Na o arasou to	Over their honor in this world,
	Tamakiwaru	Casting life to the winds,
10	Inochi mo sutete	Even life wherein the spirit dwells,
	Arasoi ni	In fierce rivalry
	Tsumadoi shikeru	Wooed one maiden; and when I heard
	Otomera ga	That maiden's story
	Kikeba kanashisa	I felt deep sadness sink upon my heart.
15	Haruhana no	She whose beauty glowed
	Nioesakaete	With a soft bloom as of flowers in spring,
	Aki no ha no	Who shone as crimson
	Nioi ni tereru	As the colored leaves of autumn,
	Atarashiki	She who stood now
20	Mi no sakari sura	In the heartbreaking prime of loveliness
	Masurao no	Felt such compassion
	Koto itawashimi	For the vows her valiant lovers swore
	Chichi haha ni	That she bade farewell
	Mōshiwakarete	To her father and her mother,

25	Iezakari	Left her home behind,
	Umibe ni idetachi	And turned her footsteps toward the sea.
	Asa yoi ni	Even one moment
	Michikuru shio no	Of her life—a time as short
	Yaenami ni	As a segment
30	Nabiku tamamo no	Of gemweed floating on the eightfold waves
	Fushi no ma mo	When the tide comes in
	Oshiki inochi o	At morn and eve—so brief a span
	Tsuyu shimo no	Was precious, but that life
	Sugimashinikere	Soon had passed away like frost or dew.
35	Okutsuki o	And so they settled
	Koko to sadamete	On this site to make her grave,
	Nochi no yo no	And that later men
	Kikitsugu hito mo	Might hear and tell her story
	Iyatō ni	Age upon age,
40	Shinoi ni seyo to	As a remembrance her people
	Tsugeogushi	Thrust into the earth,
	Shika sashikerashi	It seems, the boxwood comb she wore:
	Oite nabikeri	It grew, and now the branches trail.

	Otomera ga	From the boxwood comb
	Nochi no shirushi to	Placed for the Maiden's emblem
	Tsugeogushi	To posterity,
	Oikawarioite	Tree after tree has grown, it seems,
	Nabikikerashi mo	With branches trailing on her grave.

The above was composed by Ōtomo no Sukune Yakamochi thanks to a sudden inspiration on the sixth day of the fifth month.

❋ On the twenty-seventh of the fifth month of this same year, 750, Yakamochi wrote a lament on the death of a lady. She was his son-in-law's mother, as we learn from his diligently appended note, but beyond that her identity is uncertain. Even the son-in-law's identity is in dispute. At first blush it may seem premature for Yakamochi, now about thirty-two, to have a son-in-law. But Yakamochi's concubine, who died in the fall of 739, left him a baby (see no. 1140). It is thought that this baby was a daughter, and that it is she who was the object of inquiries from Fujiwara no Kuzumaro recorded in an undated series of exchanges with Yakamochi at the end of Book IV (nos. 1162–68). Since the child is referred to as a midoriko in no. 1140, a term applied to children up to three years of age by the Japanese count (or roughly two by the Western), Yakamochi's daughter could have been as much as thirteen years old (Western count) by this time. Based on the evidence in Book IV, Kuzumaro would be the most plausible husband for this young person. However, he was not the second son of the Minister of the Right, as specified in the footnote. Moreover, the man who was the second son of the then Minister of the Right, Fujiwara no Toyonari (704–65), had other marital arrangements, and there is no record of his being an in-law of the Ōtomo. Kuzumaro was the eldest son of Nakamaro, Toyonari's younger brother, the same Nakamaro who was the political foe of Tachibana no Moroe and his Ōtomo allies. Nakamaro himself later became Minister of the Right, and the note may take cognizance of this fact. To complicate further these questions of politics and bedfellows, Kuzumaro too had another wife, and so Yakamochi's daughter may have been his concubine.

Faithful to the formal chōka manner, Yakamochi begins his lament on a high plane of reference, remote from the actual event toward which he works in what is still a version of the ancient preparation-conclusion technique. There is no metaphorical jo, to be sure, but time is immediately established in the prologue as a frame within which human events can be viewed. By taking "the beginning of heaven and earth" (*ame tsuchi no hajime*) as his starting point, Yakamochi gives resonance to his exhortation for stoic masurao acceptance at the end. Man and his griefs are after all a momentary affair, *tsune naku arikeri* ("they have no permanence"; line 34). The imperium is from time eternal, and its servants go on their distant journeys without regard to personal feelings. Yet within this stern frame feelings dominate, and Yakamochi makes it clear that he too is a passional man, unable to check his tears and be a masurao. The lament is intensified by being set against a value structure that overrides it.

Yakamochi the poet of male friendship emerges strongly in his lines of sympathy with the bereaved son-in-law. There is a collegiality, here of grief, that is typical of the man. His mentor Okura is echoed in lines 29–34 and again in the final envoy. But the poem partakes most powerfully of the central tradition of banka going back to Hitomaro in its valorization of the deceased as a precious entity whose loss is inexplicable and unacceptable, and in its exposition of the way the word of death comes by a messenger who surely cannot be believed. (On the twanging of the azusa bow, see nos. 345 and 351.) Even Hitomaro's favorite image of seaweed appears in lines 47–48, transformed into a metaphor for helplessness. The "flowing water" (*yuku mizu*) that takes the lady away is echoed in the "flowing tears" (*nagaruru namida*) of the poet at the end. Both are "impossible to hold in check" (*todomekanetsu*). These elements are set forth with a masterly control of chōka prosody, a rhythmic alternation of long and short periods that builds to a climax in the description of the lady and her passing, with its series of structural parallels beginning in line 39, followed by the more compressed syntax, echoes, and half-rhymes of the last seven lines. The envoys restate, share, and attempt to distance the grief, reasserting at the end the values with which the poem began.

839-41   [MYS XIX: 4238-40 / 4214-16]

A lament; with *tanka*

Ame tsuchi no	From the beginning
Hajime no toki yu	Of the heaven and the earth
Utsusomi no	Among mortal men
Yaso tomo no o wa	The eighty officers of court
5 Ōkimi ni	Have had as the task
Matsurou mono to	Fixed for the offices they hold
Sadamareru	Reverent service
Tsukasa ni shi areba	Rendered to our sovereign lord.
Ōkimi no	Hence I too in fear
10 Mikoto kashikomi	Obeyed our great lord's mandate
Hinasakaru	To govern this land,
Kuni o osamu to	Remote though it lies, beyond
Ashihiki no	The foot-wearying
Yama kawa henari	Mountain ranges and rivers.
15 Kaze kumo ni	Though on wind and cloud
Koto wa kayoedo	Your words and mine may find their way,
Tada ni awazu	The days have piled up
Hi no kasanareba	Since last we saw each other's face.
Omoikoi	So in longing thought
20 Ikizukioru ni	I lay, with many a sigh,
Tamahoko no	When a man came
Michi kuru hito no	Along the jewel-spear road:
Tsutekoto ni	In his message,
Ware ni kataraku	In the words he spoke to me,
25 Hashiki yoshi	Ah, my cherished lord,
Kimi wa kono koro	I find that you now pass your days
Urasabite	In loneliness of heart
Nagekaiimasu	And repetition of a sad lament.
Yo no naka no	The way of the world—
30 Ukeku tsurakeku	How hateful and harsh it is!
Saku hana mo	Flowering petals
Toki ni utsurou	Fade with time and lose their bloom,
Utsusemi mo	And the life of man
Tsune naku arikeri	Passes in mutability.
35 Tarachine no	Your esteemed parent,
Mioya no mikoto	She who bounteously fostered you—
Nani shi ka mo	How can it be?
Toki shi wa aramu o	There would have been a time for this—
Masokagami	Though she held men's gaze
40 Miredo mo akazu	Like a burnished mirror, perfectly,
Tama no o no	In life's bright flower

Oshiki sakari ni	Precious as a string of jewels,
Tatsu kiri no	Now like rising mist
Useyuku gotoku	That thins and vanishes away,
45 Oku tsuyu no	Or like the settled dew
Kenuru ga goto	That dries into the parching air,
Tamamo nasu	Helpless as gemweed
Nabikikoifushi	Lay drifting in the tides of pain,
Yuku mizu no	And like flowing water
50 Todomekanetsu to	There was no way to hold her fast.
Magakoto ya	Are these but wild words,
Hito no iitsuru	Crooked and bent, this man has spoken,
Oyozure o	A deceitful tale
Hito no tsugetsuru	He brings hither as his message?
55 Azusayumi	I who hear this news
Tsuma hiku yoto no	Distantly resounding like the sound
Tōto ni mo	Of *azusa*-wood bows
Kikeba kanashimi	Plucked at night by palace guards,
Niwatazumi	Am saddened, and my tears
60 Nagaruru namida	That flow now in a sudden freshet
Todomekanetsu mo	Are beyond my power to hold in check.

Two Envoys

Tōto ni mo	As a sound far off
Kimi ga nageku to	I hear the news of your lament,
Kikitsureba	And my own grief
Ne nomi shi nakayu	Wells up in tears; I weep aloud,
Aiomou ware wa	I who share your every thought.

Yo no naka no	The way of the world,
Tsune naki koto wa	That nothing ever stays the same,
Shiruramu o	You know it well—
Kokoro tsukusu na	And so do not wear out your heart,
Masurao ni shite	But bear your sorrow like a man.

The above was composed by Ōtomo no Sukune Yakamochi in condolence for the grief of his son-in-law, the second son of the Southern Fujiwara house of the Minister of the Right, at the loss of his loving mother. Fifth month, twenty-seventh day.

❋ From the general evidence of the Etchū years the following tanka on secret love (also from the fifth month of 750) seems to be an exercise in the use of the metaphorical formula of the jo. Biographical readings are customary for Man'yō poets, but here Yakamochi is probably "writing poetry," an activity whose occasions, rituals, and rules eventually make it possible and even necessary to read the most esteemed poetry as true in a typical or essential rather than circumstantial sense. Whether or not Yakamochi had a "secret flame" matters for our understanding of Yakamochi, but not for our evaluation of this thoroughly traditional love poem.

842   [MYS XIX:4242/4218]

A poem on seeing the lights of the fishermen's fires

Shibi tsuku to	To spear the tuna
Ama no tomoseru	Seafolk light their fishing flares
Izaribi no	Blazing openly
Ho ni ka idasamu	Shall I let my secret flame
Wa ga shitamoi o	Flash forth for all to see?

❋ Book XIX of *Man'yōshū* ends, as it begins, with a few of Yakamochi's best tanka. The last three (nos. 843–45) are from the second month of 753, by which time Yakamochi had been back in the capital for nearly two and a half years. Again the poems are meditations on spring as seen from his garden. The mood is subdued and melancholy—*uraganashi*, *kokoroganashi*, adjectives meaning "sad at heart," specify the emotion in poems one and three, while the middle one has *kasokeki*, "faint," in reference to the sound of the wind. The season corresponds to early April by the Western calendar. The time is dusk in the first two poems, daylight in the third, but in all there is a stillness enhanced by a faint cry or the rustling of bamboo. The stillness is really in the heart of the poet, here more finely "interfused" with nature than in any other poems in *Man'yōshū*. *Uraganashi* in no. 843 is meant to apply to what follows as well as what precedes, and to the poet as well.

Each of the verses is a small triumph in the sensitive handling of language, with a use of sound to convey the softness of the mood through subtle and quiet rhythms and vowel harmonies. There is a touch of onomatopoeia in *isasa muratake* ("small bamboo clusters") and *kasokeki*, suggesting the rustling of bamboo leaves, and the final poem exploits the repetitions of internal rhyme and assonance (*uraura . . . tereru . . . haruhi . . . hibari agari*) to create an updraft for the skylark in its flight. The first two poems are based on a unified mood, whereas the last incorporates a contrast. The skylark sings high in the sunlit sky, but the poet remains alone with his thoughts. The sequence shows Yakamochi's continued advance in poetic skill and surely conveys something personal about him as a man of sensibility, but it is too determined a biographical reading that would attempt to find in these gossamer verses a statement of his political discouragement. In his footnote Yakamochi quotes from the ancient Chinese poetic collection *Shih Ching* and shows his awareness of Chinese theory on the function of poetry. The new style evidenced in such tanka as these may owe more than a little to Chinese example, but if so, the lessons have been applied with consummate skill.

843-44   [MYS XIX: 4314-15 / 4290-91]

Two poems composed from heightened feeling on the twenty-third

(843)   [4314 / 4290]

Haru no no ni	Over the spring moors
Kasumi tanabiki	Hovers a hazy, drifting mist
Uraganashi	All too sad at heart
Kono yūkage ni	Somewhere in this shadowed light
Uguisu naku mo	At evening a warbler sings.

(844)   [4315 / 4291]

Wa ga yado no	In the small clusters
Isasa muratake	Of bamboo around my house
Fuku kaze no	A wind is stirring:
Oto no kasokeki	Tonight the faintest rustling comes
Kono yūhe kamo	Across the dusky air.

845   [MYS XIX: 4316 / 4292]

A poem composed on the twenty-fifth

Uraura ni	In the endless calm
Tereru haruhi ni	Of a spring day bright with sun
Hibari agari	A skylark rises;
Kokoroganashi mo	And my heart—how sad it is
Hitori shi omoeba	As I ponder here alone.

The spring days are lengthening, the orioles are in full cry. Without poetry it would be hard indeed to dispel my cares. And so I compose these poems to loosen my knotted feelings. . . .

❋ In 755, in the seventh year of the reign of Shōmu's daughter Empress Kōken, Yakamochi wrote a poem in the public mode with the specification "private" in its title. It belongs to the genre of poems in praise of palaces and their founders, of which the Yoshino poem was the most cultivated subspecies. This time the palace is at Naniwa, a subsidiary capital under Kōken. The chōka-hanka set 846–48 follows the established pattern of historical reference, selection of a site for its unspoiled natural beauty, depiction of the busy activity of the subjects in bringing tribute, and assertion of the poet's desire to return or remain. The theme is thoroughly public; the title must therefore mean that the poem is not a command performance, that Yakamochi was speaking on a private occasion, not as the official voice of an imperial excursion, and that like his father's Yoshino poem (no. 589–90) and his own "composed in advance" (no. 818–20), this composition may never have been presented to the throne.

Be that as it may, the poem is a splendid example of the vigor and skill the mature Yakamochi brought to chōka, and conveys an undiminished sense of conviction in its handling of the time-honored vision of monarch and realm. The fusion of past and present inherent in the superimposed images of divine ancestor and reigning Sovereign (compare nos. 328 and 341), a fusion that is part of the Japanese mystique of legitimate rule, informs and imposes its cohesion on this chōka. In this case the sovereign ancestor is probably the fourth-century Emperor Nintoku, who first ruled at Naniwa, the thought of whom brings on the formula of awe *kakemaku mo aya ni kashikoki* in lines 9–10. The founding of the present palace occurs in lines 25–26 but is reenvisaged as an event in the remote past in the final lines of the chōka. Bracketed by these three points are the two long sections of exposition, lines 11–26 and 27–52. In the first the Empress is drawn to enact her role of founder by the power residing in the divinity of the land; in the second her own divine power, enshrined in her palace, draws mankind to present nature's tribute. This diagrammatic structure is enlivened with color and activity. The vision of mountain and stream in the first part could belong to Yoshino or to Kuni, but the canal (a project of Nintoku's reign) and the broad, heaving sea are purely Naniwa's. Life is everywhere abundant, and spring is at its height. The poet's delight is also part of the formal conventions of praise poetry, conveyed here in the two envoys. The whole performance—and performance it undoubtedly is—gives no hint that the encomiastic tradition and its vehicle the chōka were both on the verge of collapse. The "season of splendor" was almost over for Japan's first poetic flourishing, if not for the court that had sponsored it.

846-48   [MYS XX:4384–86/4360–62]

A poem privately stating my humble feelings; with *tanka*

Sumeroki no	In distant ages
Tōki miyo ni mo	Of our sovereign ancestors,
Oshiteru	In the land
Naniwa no kuni ni	Of sea-bright Naniwa
5　Ame no shita	They already ruled
Shirashimeshiki to	The realm of all beneath the sky,
Ima no yo ni	So it still is said
Taezu iitsutsu	Even to our present day:

	Kakemaku mo	I would call it to mind,
10	Aya ni kashikoki	But my thoughts are lost in awe.
	Kamunagara	Our great lord
	Wa go ōkimi no	In the godhead of her reign
	Uchinabiku	At the beginning
	Haru no hajime wa	Of the laden, bending spring,
15	Yachikusa ni	When the land was aglow
	Hana sakinioi	With blossoms in their thousand kinds,
	Yama mireba	Looked at the mountains,
	Mi no tomoshiku	Eyes famished for such loveliness;
	Kawa mireba	Looked at the river,
20	Mi no sayakeku	Eyes sparkling at such clarity:
	Monogoto ni	She beheld a world
	Sakayuru toki to	Where all things were at their height,
	Meshitamai	A season of splendor,
	Akirametamai	And she gladdened her heart
25	Shikimaseru	And founded here
	Naniwa no miya wa	The palace of fair Naniwa.
	Kikoshiosu	Hither from the lands
	Yomo no kuni yori	Sustaining her attentive rule
	Tatematsuru	From all directions
30	Mitsuki no fune wa	Come boats with tribute offerings.
	Horie yori	Along the canal
	Miobiki shitsutsu	They come plying the channel,
	Asanagi ni	In the morning calm
	Kaji hiki nobori	Rowing up with sculling oars,
35	Yūshio ni	On the evening tide
	Sao sashi kudari	Dropping down with punting poles.
	Ajimura no	Like flocks of teal
	Sawakikioite	People come clamoring, squabbling
	Hama ni idete	Down to the beach
40	Unahara mireba	And look off at the heaving plain:
	Shiranami no	On the white waves
	Yaeoru ga ue ni	Cresting, breaking fold on fold,
	Amaobune	Bob the little boats
	Harara ni ukite	Of the shorefolk, widely scattered.
45	Ōmike ni	To render service
	Tsukaematsuru to	To the table of their lord,
	Ochikochi ni	In every quarter,
	Izaritsurikeri	See! they fish, they dip their lines.
	Sokidaku mo	What a sweep of sea,
50	Ogironaki kamo	The vastness of these waters!
	Kokibaku mo	What abundant life

Yutakeki kamo	In these teeming, boundless deeps!
Koko mireba	One has but to look—
Ube shi kamiyo yu	No wonder from the age of gods
55 Hajimekerashi mo	Began the building of this site.
Sakurabana	The cherry blossoms
Ima sakari nari	Now are out in full splendor;
Naniwa no umi	In the shining palace
Oshiteru miya ni	At sea-bright Naniwa she reigns,
Kikoshimesu nahe	Grave in the flowering time.
Unahara no	As I gaze across
Yutakeki mitsutsu	The plain of heaving, teeming sea,
Ashi ga chiru	There comes the thought:
Naniwa ni toshi wa	Here would I pass my years away
Henubeku omōyu	At Naniwa of the scattering reeds.

The above is by Junior Assistant Minister of Military Affairs Ōtomo no Sukune Yakamochi, thirteenth day, second month [of 755].

✽ By the sixth month of 756 Tachibana no Moroe had fallen from power and former Emperor Shōmu was dead. The faction led by Fujiwara no Nakamaro dominated the court, and one of Yakamochi's kinsmen had recently been stripped of office for criticizing the government. Events were building toward the crisis of 757, the unsuccessful coup of Tachibana no Naramaro. Two poems from a group dated to the seventeenth of the sixth month reveal Yakamochi to be sick in bed, turning his thoughts to religion. These two tanka (nos. 849–50) are that rarity in *Man'yōshū*, poems of Buddhist devotion. The only term used for the faith is *michi*, "the Way," but in conjunction with the implications of ephemerality in *utsusemi* ("mortal man" / "empty locust") and the assumptions of reincarnation in *mata mo awamu* ("to meet it again"), it is enough. Yakamochi's father Tabito had made a hedonist gibe at reincarnation in one of his drinking poems (no. 602), claiming that he would be content to be an insect or a bird in the next life as long as he could have his fill of pleasure in this, but Yakamochi is eager to seek the Way (fighting against the swift passage of time) in this life, so that he will be worthy to be reborn as a human and find it again in the next. The evidence in these poems is hardly enough to prove that Yakamochi was a devout Buddhist, though the city and the age in which he lived had seen the sudden rise of the great temples, and the occupants of the throne were ardent believers. The poets of Nara rarely wrote of this side of their lives; Yakamochi here provides a small exception. In the first poem he movingly identifies the traditional purity of nature with the metaphysics of

the faith. It may not be irrelevant to remember that the next development in
Japanese Buddhism was a flight from the politically enmired urban temples
to the remote purity of mountains and streams.

849–50   [MYS XX: 4492–93 / 4468–69]

Two poems composed when lying ill, in sadness over impermanence, desiring to practice the Way

(849)   [4492 / 4468]

Utsusemi wa	Man counts for nothing,
Kazu naki mi nari	A body empty, ephemeral—
Yama kawa no	Let me gaze on beauty
Sayakeki mitsutsu	In clear mountains and rivers
Michi o tazunena	While I search for the Way.

(850)   [4493 / 4469]

Wataru hi no	Vying with the light
Kage ni kioite	Of the heaven-coursing sun,
Tazunetena	Oh, let me search,
Kiyoki sono michi	That I find it once again—
Mata mo awamu tame	The Way that was so pure.

❋ In 758, one year before the end of *Man'yōshū*, Yakamochi was among the
officials attending a banquet at the imperial palace on the first Day of the Rat
of the new year. His headnote to no. 851 explains the occasion. Following
Chinese custom, the plow and the whisk (for sweeping out the silkworm
platforms; see no. 497) were brought out for display on this day to symbolize the monarchy's solicitude for agriculture. Two of the "jewel brooms"
that Tōdaiji presented on this occasion are still in the Shōsōin. The Palace
Minister was Fujiwara no Nakamaro, who had survived the coup attempt of
the previous year and was about to replace Empress Kōken with the more
subservient Emperor Junnin (r. 758–64). Yakamochi records only his own
poem, for the reason he states. The position he occupied involved supervisory responsibilities in the Treasury—of which he was relieved when later
that year he was "exiled" as Governor of Inaba. The poem is the sort of
felicitous expression expected on formal auspicious occasions. It puns on
tama no o ("thread of jewels," but also "thread of my soul").

851   [MYS XX: 4517 / 4493]

In the second year [758], spring, on the third day of the first month, the
Empress summoned her Chamberlains, Pages, Princes, and Ministers, as-

sembled them at the foot of the enclosure of the eastern pavilion in the palace, provided them with jewel brooms, and held a banquet. The Palace Minister, Fujiwara no Asomi, received the imperial command and declared, "Princes and Lords, pray compose Japanese and Chinese poems as your thoughts direct you, in accordance with your several preferences." Thus they composed both Japanese and Chinese verses in response to this command, giving expression each to his own thoughts. (I have not been able to obtain [these] poems.)

Hatsuharu no	At the first of spring
Hatsune no kyō no	On the first Day of the Rat
Tamabahaki	I take in hand
Te ni toru kara ni	The jewel broom, and all my soul
Yuraku tama no o	Tingles with the tinkling gems.

The above verse was composed by Middle Controller of the Right Ōtomo no Sukune Yakamochi. However, he was unable to submit it because of his responsibilities at the Treasury.

✻ Another poem by Yakamochi from early in 758 is an appreciation of flowers in a garden. Not one of his best efforts in the genre, it is still a graceful reflection of a graceful spring scene. The *ashibi* is the andromeda, a flowering plant with clusters of pendulous white blossoms.

852   [MYS XX:4536/4512]

[One of] three poems composed on viewing a landscape garden

Ikemizu ni	Here along the pond
Kage sae miete	Its reflection blooms again
Sakiniou	Down in the water—
Ashibi no hana o	Come, pluck the shining *ashibi*,
Sode in kokirena	Strip its flowers into your sleeves!

The above poem is by Middle Controller of the Right Ōtomo no Sukune Yakamochi.

✻ In the sixth month of 758 Yakamochi was appointed Governor of Inaba Province on the Sea of Japan in western Honshū. On New Year's Day of the following year he hosted a banquet for his officials. The poem he composed on that occasion is the last we have of him, and of *Man'yōshū*. It fulfills the auspicious needs of the occasion, but if Yakamochi deliberately selected it to end the anthology (and there too a felicitous flourish would be appropriate), it contains contextual ironies. A heavy snow on New Year's Day is said to predict rich crops, but the early harvest of Japanese poetry was over. And snow is an unreliable metaphor for glory.

853   [MYS XX:4540/4516]

A poem composed at a banquet for the provincial and district officials held at the government office of Inaba Province on the first day of the first month of the third year [of Tempyō-Hōji, 759]

Aratashiki	Like the snow that falls
Toshi no hajime no	On this first day of the year
Hatsuharu no	In early spring,
Kyō furu yuki no	From today may our blessings
Iyashike yogoto	Accumulate forevermore!

The above poem was composed by the Governor, Ōtomo no Sukune Yakamochi.

Poem Exchanges and Poem Groups
of Multiple Composition

Many of the poems in *Man'yōshū* are inconvenient to list under a single author because they are part of an exchange or of a group of poems composed
by several people on a set occasion. Sometimes the "occasion" extends over
time as different poets revert to a theme or add further verses to a series.
Material of this nature is presented here, as far as possible in chronological
order, though dates are often unknown. It has seemed expedient to make
two chronological series—a general one, followed by a second devoted to
compositions by or associated with members of the Ōtomo clan, thus preserving the cohesion of that interrelated body of work.

Prince Arima and the Bound Pine

A series of six tanka, nos. 854–59, commemorates an event that clearly impressed the people of subsequent decades as cruel and pathetic. Prince Arima
was a son of Emperor Kōtoku and a nephew of reigning Empress Saimei,
through whom her son Naka no Ōe (future Emperor Tenji) governed. (For
Kōtoku's falling-out with Naka no Ōe, see no. 186.) *Nihonshoki*, in a perhaps slanted account, describes Prince Arima as of crafty character and recounts how he plotted treason with the minister Soga no Akae while the
Empress and her son were away at the hot springs of Ki in the eleventh
month of 658. At the very least Akae seems to have been an agent pro-
vocateur, for he had Prince Arima arrested the next day and sent under
guard to Muro for questioning by Naka no Ōe. Along the way at Iwashiro
on the coast of Ki, Prince Arima tied the branches of a pine as a good luck
charm. The precaution was in vain, however, for when he was asked to give
a reason for his plot, his cryptic answer, "Only Heaven and Akae know; I
do not know," did not please his interrogator, and he was taken back up the
coast to be executed by strangulation at Fujishiro on the eleventh of the
month. He was nineteen by the Japanese count.

   The first two poems (nos. 854–55) are by Prince Arima himself, or attributed to him. The first poem is similar to an *ukehi*, an utterance that
attempts to discover truth or influence events by swearing an oath whose
validity will be demonstrated by one of two alternative outcomes. The

binding of the pine branches is an act of ritual magic, and the poem is
the incantation said over them. The tragic outcome shows the failure of the
spell, and the irony of the manner of the Prince's execution adds the final
mockery. The privations of travel are the theme of the second poem; these
too are ironic, a mentioning of the small in place of the great. The other
poems are by later men, travelers who pass by and remember. Naga no
Okimaro, known for his clever pranks in verse (see nos. 491–98), is one.
No. 856 is clearly ascribed to him, but the compiler seems to have had some
uncertainty about no. 857. The question in no. 856 is a way of touching the
pathos of the event but could also reflect real curiosity. Prince Arima's road
back from Muro went by Iwashiro to its last stop at Fujishiro. The correspondence of nature and man that is the constant play of metaphor underlies
the "symbolic equation" of no. 857, through the technique of the jo. The
vision of Prince Arima's soul hovering over the pine echoes no. 261 on
the death of Emperor Tenji, by the Great Consort Yamato. But there the
speaker claims to see the spirit with more than the mind's eye, whereas here
it is only the pine that knows. This is the earliest poem by Yamanoue no
Okura to have been preserved. In the footnote to no. 858, "pulling a coffin"
translates the literal sense of the genre name banka. The final poem is dated
and attributed to the "Hitomaro Collection." The excursion of 701 was by
Emperor Mommu. It has been suggested that Okimaro and Okura were
also members of the entourage on this occasion. If Hitomaro himself was
the author of no. 859, this opens the interesting possibility that Okimaro,
Okura, and Hitomaro were all together at one time and place. Although a
member of the official embassy to T'ang of 701, Okura would still have
been in Japan, for the embassy's departure was delayed until the following
year. However, the headnote to Okura's poem does not claim that he actually saw the pine.

854–55   [MYS II: 141–42]

Two poems in which Prince Arima, grieving over himself, ties together
pine branches

(854)   [141]

Iwashiro no	I pull the branches
Hamamatsu ga e o	Of the pine of Iwashiro Beach
Hikimusubi	And bind them together;
Masakiku araba	I shall pass this way again
Mata kaerimimu	And see them, if all goes well.

(855)   [142]

| Ie ni areba | When I am at home |
| Ke ni moru ii o | I eat my rice heaped in a dish, |

484

Kusamakura	But since I am away
Tabi ni shi areba	On a journey, grass for pillow,
Shii no ha ni moru	I heap it on leaves of oak.

856–57   [MYS II: 143–44]

Two poems by Naga no Imiki Okimaro, choked with sorrow on seeing the bound pine

(856)   [143]

Iwashiro no	He who bound the boughs
Kishi no matsu ga e	Of this pine tree on the cliff
Musubikemu	At Iwashiro,
Hito wa kaerite	Did he pass this way again
Mata mikemu ka mo	And see them as before?

(857)   [144]

Iwashiro no	At Iwashiro
Nonaka ni tateru	In the middle of the moor
Musubimatsu	Stands a bound pine:
Kokoro mo tokezu	Never loosening, my heart
Inishie omōyu	Is wrapped in thoughts of the past.

858   [MYS II: 145]

A poem written later in concert with the above by Yamanoue no Omi Okura

Tsubasa nasu	Soaring on birdwing,
Arigayoitsutsu	He must ever pass and turn
Miramedo mo	And watch it well;
Hito koso shirane	People cannot know him there,
Matsu wa shiruramu	But the pine tree surely knows.

The poems in the above series were not composed at the time of pulling a coffin, but their sense is equivalent to poems in that genre, and so we include them in the *banka* category.

859   [MYS II: 146]

A poem on seeing the bound pine at the time of an imperial excursion to Ki Province in Daihō 1 [701], Metal-Junior/Ox (this poem appears in *Kakinomoto no Asomi Hitomaro Kashū*)

| Nochi mimu to | Thinking that later |
| Kimi ga musuberu | He would look at them again, |

Iwashiro no	He bound the branch tips
Komatsu ga ure o	Of the pine of Iwashiro—
Mata mikemu ka mo	Did he ever see them more?

Princess Nukata and the Crown Prince

In 668 Naka no Ōe formally assumed the throne as Emperor Tenji, reigning at Ōtsu on the shores of Lake Biwa, where he had moved the court in 667. At some time prior to these events, Princess Nukata, the most talented poet at his court, became one of his lesser consorts. She had previously enjoyed the favor of Tenji's younger brother, Prince Ōama, and it is not clear whether the shift in alliance was voluntary or forced. Nos. 860–61 are an exchange between the former lovers. The "hunting" of the headnote refers to plucking herbs on a *shimeno* ("staked field"), a tract set aside for the imperial pleasure. Kamafu Fields were on the eastern shore of Lake Biwa. The Prince's feelings are clear; those of the Princess are ambiguous, but not indifferent. The exchange is in the mode of challenge and reply stemming from the ancient song matches (utagaki). The challenge is bright with color and busy with activity. The color is doubled: *akane sasu* ("madder-shining") sheds an epithetical splendor over *murasaki* ("purple"). Both *akane* and *murasaki* were sources of dye, both plants relevant to the day's "hunting" and suggestive of imperial favor as well as flaunted love. The line of motion is also doubled in the two *yuki* ("go"), giving an impression of the constant patrolling of the keeper of the grounds. And above all this a sleeve is waving in the air, the wave being a gesture of beckoning, not of farewell. The Prince's reply is couched as a rhetorical question and returns to the giver an image from her poem, true to the utagaki style. *Hitozuma* ("another's wife") appears twelve times in *Man'yōshū*, suggesting the topical importance of illicit desire.

860 [MYS 1:20]

A poem composed by Princess Nukata when the Sovereign went hunting on Kamafu Fields

Akane sasu	The madder-shining
Murasakino yuki	Purple fields he goes around,
Shimeno yuki	The staked fields around:
Nomori wa mizu ya	Won't the guardian of the fields
Kimi ga sode furu	See you wave your sleeve, my lord?

861 [MYS 1:21]

A poem in reply by the Crown Prince (the Sovereign who ruled the realm at the Asuka Palace; posthumously called Emperor Temmu)

Murasaki no	Like the purple-root
Nioeru imo o	Glowing is my comely love:
Nikuku araba	Felt I some fault in her
Hitozuma yue ni	Would I for another's wife
Are koime ya mo	Subject myself to this yearning?

It is stated in the *Chronicles*: The Sovereign hunted on Kamafu Fields on the fifth day of the fifth month, in the summer of the seventh year [of his reign], Fire-Junior/Hare [667]. The Imperial Prince his younger brother, the various Princes, the Palace Minister, and the other Ministers all accompanied him on this occasion.

Laments for Emperor Tenji

Several laments for Emperior Tenji, who died in the twelfth month of the year corresponding to 671 (January 7, 672, by the Western calendar) are recorded in Book II. All are by consorts or other women at his court. The following pair of tanka appear under one headnote. Poem 862, by Princess Nukata, can be interpreted in two ways. The guardian rope might be a magic barrier against evil spirits boarding the royal barge, or it could have a metaphorical sense as a means of preventing the escape of the Emperor's soul. Toneri no Yoshitoshi (or Kine) was a court lady (for another poem by her, see no. 864). Her poem is strongly reminiscent of Hitomaro's no. 289 on the ruined capital at Ōmi. Tenji, the only Emperor to rule on the shores of the great lake (other than his unfortunate son, who is not counted in the official list of rulers), remains identified with it.

862-63 [MYS II: 151-52]

Two poems from the time of the Emperor's temporary enshrinement

(862) [151]

Kakaramu to	Had I known before
Kanete shiriseba	That such as this would come to pass,
Ōmifune	I would have tied
Hateshi tomari ni	A guardian rope across the berth
Shime yuwamashi o	Where the royal barge lies moored.

(Princess Nukata)

(863) [152]

Yasumishishi	For the royal barge
Wa go ōkimi no	Of our great lord who ruled the earth
Ōmifune	In all tranquility,

Machi ka kouramu   Is it waiting, yearning now,
Shiga no Karasaki   Cape Kara in Shiga?

(Toneri no Yoshitoshi)

Toneri no Yoshitoshi and Tanabe no Ichihiko

The following undated exchange between a court official and a court lady probably took place in the 670's or 680's. Toneri no Yoshitoshi is the same lady who presented a lament on the death of Emperor Tenji; Tanabe no Ichihiko is known only from this exchange, and it is not clear to what office he was appointed at Dazaifu. The poems are full of the rue and pain of parting, the side of love that the waka tradition was best at treating over the centuries. Each has a special quality of emotion or imagery that distinguishes it. No. 864, by Yoshitoshi, presses the Japanese psychological lever now known as *amae*, by which one tries to get one's way by adopting a dependent, childlike role. The helpless pleading covers anger and reproach. Ichihiko responds in no. 865 by restoring the sad and sensuous beauty of an adult woman, revealing at the same time that his regret matches hers. The authorship of the final two poems is not specifically labeled, but no. 866 is clearly the man's. Suddenly he too is angry at the too great pain of parting; this is the real requital of the lady's possessive verse. The use of *kimi* ("my lord"/"you") in no. 867 argues that it is by the woman, but everything else about it contradicts that argument. The man goes away to the west and looks back, where the waning crescent moon at dawn hangs in the brightening sky. The poem is structured on the jo, the moon being that of which one never wearies, that which on the other side of the equation is the loved woman left behind the hills. This poem is one of a small number in *Man'yōshū* in which *kimi* is used to refer to a woman.

864–67   [MYS IV : 495–98 / 492–95]

Four poems from the time when Tanabe no Imiki Ichihiko was appointed to Dazai

(864)   [495 / 492]

Koromode ni   Leaving me behind,
Toritodokōri   Worse off than a wailing child
  Naku ko ni mo   Clinging hard as glue
Masareru ware o   To the sleeves of its mother—
Okite ika ni semu   What are you doing to me?

(Toneri no Yoshitoshi)

(865)   [496/493]

    Okite yukaba   How my love will pine
    Imo koimu kamo   If I leave her when I go,
      Shikitae no   Spreading her black hair
    Kurokami shikite   Like a bedspread of fine cloth,
    Nagaki kono yo o   Alone these long autumn nights.

(Tanabe no Imiki Ichihiko)

(866)   [497/494]

    Wagimoko o   Now that this longing
    Aishirashimeshi   Rises to cover me
      Hito o koso   I remember
    Koi no masareba   Bitterly the go-between
    Urameshimi omoe   Who brought us together.

(867)   [498/495]

    Asahikage   Above mountainsides
    Nioeru yama ni   Now glowing in the morning sun
      Teru tsuki no   Hangs the moon at dawn:
    Akazaru kimi o   Beauty of which I cannot weary,
    Yamagoshi ni okite   I have left you behind the hills.

Emperor Temmu and Lady Fujiwara

Of a different sort is a bantering exchange between Emperor Temmu and
Lady Fujiwara, one of his consorts. (Lady Fujiwara was the daughter of Fujiwara no Kamatari, the major statesman of Emperor Tenji's reign and the
founder of the Fujiwara clan.) Temmu seems to have had a penchant for
rapid-fire repetitions, judging from no. 264 and this verse he sent to his consort on a snowy day. Her father's residence at Ōhara ("Great Pastures") was
about a kilometer southeast of his own palace. Her *furinishi sato* ("village
that has gotten old") is paradoxically without a fall (*furi*) of snow, but may
get some later. The plays on *fureri*, *furinishi*, and *furamaku*, and the echoing
of *ōyuki* ("great snow") and *ōhara* are what the poem is about, and show the
Emperor in a playful mood. The lady responds in kind, assuring him that
the snowstorm was caused by the dragon god of her hill, and that he has
hardly seen what real snow is like. The point in jest is not to be overawed by
your opponent.

868   [MYS II: 103]

A poem given by the Emperor to Lady Fujiwara

>   Wa ga sato ni   Here in *my* village
>   Ōyuki fureri   We have had a great snowfall,
>   Ōhara no   But in Great Pastures,
>   Furinishi sato ni   *Your* tumbledown old village,
>   Furamaku wa nochi   Snow will fall later, if at all.

869   [MYS II: 104]

A poem presented later by Lady Fujiwara

>   Wa ga oka no   It was by speaking
>   Okami ni iite   To the dragon of my hill
>   Furashimeshi   I caused this snowfall;
>   Yuki no kudake shi   A few flakes may have scattered,
>   Soko ni chirikemu   No doubt, out there where you are.

Prince Omi's Exile

An image of exile not as demotion to Governor of some distant province, but as a life of deprivation and want is provided by a pair of poems in Book I. The exile, Prince Omi, is otherwise unknown, and his offense is not specified in *Nihonshoki*, though it is conjectured that he opposed the reforms of Emperor Temmu. The *Man'yōshū* context has him exchanging poems with a sympathizer, ruefully admitting that his life is no better than that of the ama, the peasant fisherfolk. As the footnote makes clear, the whole affair is surrounded by uncertainties. He may not even have been exiled to Irago; his poem may be apocryphal, and the image of exile a romantic fiction. But perhaps not. Crossing an Emperor could lead to more serious consequences than exile, as we know from the story of Prince Arima. "Beaten hemp" (*uchiso*) is a pillow word for *omi* ("spun hemp"), which also happens to be the Prince's name. Irago on modern maps is the tip of the Atsumi Peninsula, jutting out to the west toward Ise across the mouth of Ise Bay (see no. 313). It may or may not have referred to an offshore island in ancient times. The "Island of Izu" may be Ōshima off the Izu Peninsula. The Chika Islands are off the northwest coast of Kyūshū.

870   [MYS I: 23]

A poem composed in sorrow when Prince Omi was exiled to Irago Island

>   Uchiso o   Is our Prince Omi
>   Omi no ōkimi   (Omi of the beaten hemp)

Ama nare ya	Some rude shore-fellow,
Irago no shima no	That he now must harvest
Tamamo karimasu	The gemweed round Irago's Isle?

871   [MYS I:24]

A poem in which Prince Omi, having heard this, replies, sorrowing

Utsusemi no	Chary of my life,
Inochi o oshimi	And loath to leave this mortal world,
Nami ni nure	Though wet with waves,
Irago no shima no	I harvest and I dine upon
Tamamo karihamu	The gemweed round Irago's isle.

Concerning the above, on consulting *Nihongi* we find the latter states: "In the fourth year of the Emperor [675], Wood-Junior/Swine, in summer, fourth month, on the Wood-Junior/Hare day of the month beginning Earth-Senior/Dog, Prince Omi of the Third Rank was exiled to Inaba for an offense. One child was exiled to the Island of Izu, and another to the Chika Islands." Perhaps the statement that he was exiled to Irago Island in Ise Province is a mistaken notation by a later person based on the words of the poem.

Prince Ōtsu and Ishikawa no Iratsume

The fate of Prince Arima was reenacted almost thirty years later by Prince Ōtsu, who was forced to commit suicide in 686. For two poems by him and six by his sister Princess Ōku, see nos. 269–70 and 272–77. The love triangle of Prince Ōtsu, Prince Kusakabe, and Ishikawa no Iratsume is also mentioned there. In the following exchange between Prince Ōtsu and Ishikawa no Iratsume, the lover's complaint is mollified in the most intimate way, and in the process his poem is taken apart, reassembled, and sent back in a rearranged pattern—a good example of the style of an effective reply. Duplicate second and fifth lines in tanka, as in no. 872, are an old structural formula (see nos. 56 and 80).

872   [MYS II:107]

A poem sent by Prince Ōtsu to Ishikawa no Iratsume

Ashihiki no	In the dripping
Yama no shizuku ni	Of the foot-dragging mountain
Imo matsu to	I waited for you,
Ware tachinurenu	I got wet from standing there
Yama no shizuku ni	In the dripping of the mountain.

873 [MYS II:108]

A poem presented in reply by Ishikawa no Iratsume

A o matsu to	The dripping
Kimi ga nurekemu	Of the foot-dragging mountain
Ashihiki no	Where you grew wet
Yama no shizuku ni	As you waited there for me
Naramashi mono o	Is what I wish I had been.

Prince Yuge and Princess Nukata

At some point during the reign of Empress Jitō (686–97), Prince Yuge and Princess Nukata exchanged poems. Prince Yuge was a son of Emperor Temmu, and Princess Nukata had enjoyed Temmu's favor when he was still a Prince (see nos. 860–61). Whether there was any further connection between them is not clear. Prince Yuge, who has accompanied Empress Jitō to Yoshino, writes to Princess Nukata at Asuka about a bird that cried as it flew by. She identifies the bird in her reply as the cuckoo, associated with yearning for the past. Perhaps both are thinking of the recently deceased Emperor Temmu. The Prince breaks off a mossy pine branch and sends it, no doubt with a poem (not given, however); the Princess replies. It is all very much a preview of Heian romance. There is evidence at this point of Princess Nukata's poetic activity under three reigns.

874 [MYS II:111]

A poem sent by Prince Yuge to Princess Nukata at the time of an imperial visit to Yoshino Palace

Inishie ni	Could it be a bird
Kouru tori ka mo	That yearns for the days gone by?
Yuzuruha no	Over the royal pool
Mii no ue yori	Of Yuzuruha it flies,
Nakiwatariyuku	Making its cry as it goes.

875 [MYS II:112]

A poem presented by Princess Nukata (sent from the capital in Yamato)

Inishie ni	If there was a bird
Kouramu tori wa	That seemed to yearn for days gone by,
Hototogisu	It was the cuckoo:
Kedashi ya nakishi	I am sure it must have cried
A ga kouru goto	From a longing such as mine.

876   [MYS II: 113]

A poem presented by Princess Nukata when [Prince Yuge] broke off a
mossy pine branch at Yoshino and sent it to her

Miyoshino no	From fair Yoshino
Tamamatsu ga e wa	This bough of the gemlike pine—
Hashiki kamo	How dear to me,
Kimi ga mikoto o	Serving as messenger to bear
Mochite kayowamu	Your gracious words, my lord!

Prince Yuge and Prince Kasuga

In another exchange at Yoshino, Prince Yuge speaks of the brevity of life.
The ever-clouded peak of Mount Mifune by the Yoshino River serves as the
contrary example from nature. Prince Kasuga (d. 699?), otherwise unrepre-
sented in *Man'yōshū*, seeks to draw a positive analogy in his reply.

877   [MYS III: 243 / 242]

A poem of the time when Pringe Yuge went on an excursion to Yoshino

Taki no ue no	For I know well enough
Mifune no yama ni	I shall not be here forever
Iru kumo no	Like the cloud that rests
Tsune ni aramu to	Along the crest of Mifune
Wa ga omowanaku ni	Over the racing water.

878   [MYS III: 244 / 243]

A poem presented in reply by Prince Kasuga

Ōkimi wa	My great lord
Chitose ni masamu	Will surely live a thousand years;
Shirakumo mo	Shall the white clouds
Mifune no yama ni	Along the crest of Mifune
Tayuru hi arame ya	Vanish for a single day?

Prince Toneri and the Maiden Toneri

An amorous exchange between Prince Toneri (for whom, see no. 387) and
the woman known as the Maiden Toneri (no. 476) is preserved in Book II.
Prince Toneri, who died in 735, was the final compiler of *Nihonshoki*, a son
of Emperor Temmu and the father of Emperor Junnin. The Maiden Toneri
was a lady of the court in the reign of Empress Jitō. One may speculate that
the name by which she is known came from her connection with the Prince,

but nothing beyond this one exchange exists to tell what that may have been. The Prince's rueful self-disparagement employs the term *masurao* ("stalwart"). The masurao was not supposed to weep or be weak and womanish (see nos. 325, 534, and 841), but men found it difficult to live up to the ideal. The Maiden's reply is a gentle reminder that a woman may be drawn to the "weak" (i.e., emotional) quality of a man, rather than to his vaunted strength. Both poems, however, have about them a self-amused hyperbole that makes them slightly comic as well as amorous. The lover's sighs have carried such a charge of moisture that not only the woman but her hair is undone.

879   [MYS II: 117]

A poem by Prince Toneri

> Masurao ya   Does a stalwart man
> Katakoi semu to   Hanker for a heartless girl
>   Nagekedo mo   Who loves him not?
> Shiko no masurao   What a shabby stalwart, this—
> Nao koinikeri   He still mopes, sighing, yearning.

880   [MYS II: 118]

A poem presented in reply by the Maiden Toneri

> Nagekitsutsu   It is your yearning
> Masura onoko no   And your sighs, O stalwart man,
>   Koure koso   That have undone me—
> Wa ga yuu kami no   All my hair is hanging loose,
> Hichite nurekere   The plaits are dripping wet.

Mikata no Sami and the Daughter of Sono no Omi Ikuha

For Mikata no Sami, see nos. 499–501. Two poems from the following exchange with his very young wife concentrate on her hair, which she is still wearing loose in the childish fashion. As a participant in a duolocal or visiting type marriage, the bedridden Sami would not be able to see his bride, who is probably still living with her parents. All the wise grownups are telling her the time has come to put up her hair, no doubt in the looped double topknot popular at the time, but she, true to her status as a woman in love, refuses to change what her lover saw. The first two poems (nos. 881–82) are both based on repetitions, giving an engaging impression of the waywardness of the unmanageable tresses and the insistence of the busybodies. The third poem is based on a jo, "the eight crossroads" (*yachimata*) being those of the city and of the husband's perplexity. The image of people (lovers?) strolling along in the shade is undoubtedly intended to contrast with the confined condition of the invalid husband. The streets referred to are those of Empress Jitō's capital at Fujiwara, north of Asuka (and south of the not-yet-founded Nara). Orange trees (tachibana; see the commentary to no. 826–27) were planted in the marketplaces of Nara and presumably also at Fujiwara. The headnote ascribing all three poems to Sami must be in error, unless he is assuming a feminine persona in the second poem.

881–83   [MYS II:123–25]

Three poems composed by Mikata no Sami when he fell ill not long after marrying the daughter of Sono no Omi Ikuha

(881)   [123]

Takeba nure	Tied up they came loose,
Takaneba nagaki	When not tied they were too long;
Imo ga kami	My dear one's tresses
Kono koro minu ni	All this time I have not seen—
Kakiretsuramu ka	Has she combed them into place?

(Mikata no Sami)

(882)   [124]

Hito wa mina	Everybody says
Ima wa nagashi to	My hair is getting long now—
Take to iedo	Bind it up, they say;
Kimi ga mishi kami	But this hair you looked upon,
Midaretari to mo	I'll leave it, though in tangles.

(The young woman)

(883)   [125]

Tachibana no	People stroll along,
Kage fumu michi no	Walking in the orange-tree shade
Yachimata ni	To the eight crossroads:
Mono o so omou	Crossed, sore vexed in grief am I,
Imo ni awazute	Not meeting the girl I love.

(Mikata no Sami)

An Excursion of Emperor Mommu

Emperor Mommu is known to have visited Naniwa in 699 and 706. Two tanka by members of his entourage are recorded in Book 1. The first (no. 884) is a "yearning for Yamato" poem reminiscent of no. 468 by Prince

Shiki, which may have been composed on the same occasion. Nothing further is known of the author, Osakabe no Otomaro. The stated author of the second poem, Fujiwara no Umakai (694–737), a leading political figure of early Nara and founder of the Ceremonial House, one of the four branches of the Fujiwara clan, is well known indeed. But his tender age in 706 (not to mention 699) casts serious doubt on the attribution. One *Man'yōshū* manuscript lists the poem as author unknown. Whoever the author was, he found the attractions of the shore greater than those of the sea. It has been suggested that he is thinking of a courtesan of Naniwa.

884–85   [MYS I: 71–72]

Poems from the time of the late Emperor's visit to the Naniwa Palace

(884)   [71]

Yamato koi	When I cannot sleep
I no neraenu ni	In my yearning for Yamato,
Kokoro naku	Must they cry,
Kono susakimi ni	Heartlessly, these cranes
Tazu nakubeshi ya	On the edge of the sandspit?

The above poem is by Osakabe no Otomaro.

(885)   [72]

Tamamo karu	I shall row no more
Okihe wa kogaji	To the offing for the gemlike weed:
Shikitae no	I cannot forget
Makura no atari	The pillow of spread barken cloth,
Wasurekanetsu mo	And one who lay beside me.

The above poem is by Minister of Ceremonial Fujiwara no Umakai.

The Nymph Mulberry Branch

There is a curious set of three tanka in Book III linked to the legend of Umashine, a fisherman who caught a mulberry branch in his fish trap, only to have it turn into a beautiful young woman whom he then married. As in most folktales about marriages between mortals and immortals, the story apparently ended unhappily, with the nymph deserting her husband because of slanders. The work entitled *Shashiden* (*The Mulberry-Branch Legend*) is no longer extant, and the story is known only in fragments. Other than these in *Man'yōshū* there are several references in kanshi in *Kaifūsō*, and a retelling in chōka form in *Shoku Nihon Kōki*, the fourth of the *Six National Histories* (*Rikkokushi*), a work of the ninth century. The *Man'yōshū* poems really say very little about the legend itself. The first poem is a variant of no. 69 (see also no. 139), and there is another version in *Hizen Fudoki* (no. 215). All these poems are no doubt utagaki songs or elopement songs in their origins, and no. 886 is an accretion that has crept into the legend from an unknown source. The location of Kishimi is uncertain; the word is probably a version of the Kishima in the *Hizen Fudoki* song. *Arare furi* ("where the hail comes down") is an epithet, perhaps from onomatopoeic qualities in *Kishimi/Kishima*. The other two poems are comments on the legend. The first is anonymous; the second is by a poet about whom practically nothing is known, but who from the placement of the series was probably active in the 730's. Both comments seem to imagine how pleasant it would be to meet a complaisant mulberry branch. Ayumaro's poem implies, however, that there was only one, and it has already been caught.

886-88   [MYS III: 388-90/385-87]

Three poems of the nymph Mulberry Branch

(886)   [388/385]

Arare furi	Where the hail comes down
Kishimi ga take o	On the heights of Kishimi
Sagashimi to	The climb is steep:
Kusa torikanawa	I lose my grip on the grasses,
Imo ga te o toru	I grasp the hand of my girl.

Concerning the above poem it is also stated that it is a poem given to the Mulberry-Branch nymph by Umashine, a man of Yoshino. But an inspection of *The Mulberry-Branch Legend* fails to reveal such a poem.

(887)   [389/386]

Kono yūhe	If this evening
Tsumi no saeda no	A branch of wild mulberry
Nagarekoba	Should come floating by,
Yana wa utazute	I've set no traps to catch it in,
Torazu ka mo aramu	And it might get away.

Above, one poem

(888)   [390/387]

Inishie ni	If it had not been
Yana utsu hito no	For the man who long ago
Nakariseba	Set traps in the water,
Koko ni mo aramashi	Here too there might have been
Tsumi no eda wa mo	A branch of wild mulberry.

The above poem is by Wakamiya no Ayumaro.

A Young Woman and Saeki no Sukune Akamaro

Among the liveliest exchanges in *Man'yōshū* are those between Saeki no Akamaro (of whom nothing else is known) and an anonymous young woman. The first three poems (nos. 889–91) constitute a set in the hiyuka poems of Book III. They seem to date to the late 730's from their placement among the poems of the Ōtomo clan. The poems are a dialogue between a young woman and a married man, cast in an allegorical mode. The first is already a reply, but the poem it answers has not survived. It reveals the young woman to be well disposed for country matters, but restrained from sowing the fields by fear of the deity that guards them. The choice of Kasuga for the location of the fields is guided no doubt by the existence of the famous shrine nearby. "Thousand-rock-smashing" (*chihayaburu*) is a pillow word for *kami* ("deity"). "Her" as a reference to this deity opens a hole in the allegory not provided by the sexually nonspecific original, though one of the deities of Kasuga is in fact a goddess. The choice of millet (*awa*) as the grain to be sown also is not fortuitous. The Japanese text offers its own opening into the allegory through the pivot-word device of *awa maka-* ("sow millet") / *awamaku* ("to meet you").

Akamaro's reply regrets that they have never sown their seed, for if they had, it would of course be necessary to go out every night to guard the crop. The woman is simply prudent, not surprisingly when her would-be lover joins her in regarding the power of the "deity" as immovable. The maiden's final comment is the ultimate withering rejoinder and comes close to blowing the allegorical decorum away. The sarcasm and scorn seem to be triggered by the word *urameshi* ("hateful") in Akamaro's poem, a spineless plea for sympathy that puts a biting edge on *masurao* ("stalwart") in the reply. The young woman of the second exchange (nos. 892–93), the same, one would judge from her sharp tongue, again twits Akamaro for being a masurao-manqué, though this time it is his age that is the objection. The *ochimizu*, or "waters of replenished youth," are said to be in the moon (see no. 1453), and so Akamaro has far to go on his search. As a weak but amiable and persistent amorist he is a forerunner of Heichū, the hero of the Heian work *Heichū Monogatari*.

889   [MYS III : 407 / 404]

A poem by a young woman in reply to one sent her by Saeki no Sukune Akamaro

Chihayaburu	Thousand-rock-smashing,
Kami no yashiro shi	A fierce deity abides
Nakariseba	In the godly shrine:
Kasuga no nohe ni	But for her I'd be well pleased
Awa makamashi o	To sow our millet in Kasuga fields.

890 [MYS III: 408 / 405]

Another poem sent by Saeki no Sukune Akamaro

Kasugano ni	Had we sown millet
Awa makeriseba	In the fields of Kasuga,
Shishimachi ni	I'd go every night
Tsugite ikamashi	To stalk deer amid the grain—
Yashiro shi urameshi	Oh, how I hate that shrine!

891 [MYS III: 409 / 406]

A poem in which the young woman replies again

Wa ga matsuru	She is not a god
Kami ni wa arazu	That I worship, rest assured,
Masurao ni	She's a god, rather,
Tsukitaru kami so	That possesses you, my stalwart—
Yoku matsurubeshi	Worship her well, I say.

892 [MYS IV: 630 / 627]

A poem sent by a young woman in reply to Saeki no Sukune Akamaro

Wa ga tamoto	If you wish to rest
Makamu to owowamu	Your head upon this arm of mine,
Masurao wa	O my good stalwart,
Ochimizu motome	Seek first the waters of replenished youth
Shiraka oinitari	For the white hairs growing on your brow.

893 [MYS IV: 631 / 628]

A poem in reply by Saeki no Sukune Akamaro

Shiraka ouru	Without wasting thought
Koto wa omowazu	For the white hairs on my brow,
Ochimizu wa	I'll be off today,
Ka ni mo kaku ni mo	Searching hither, searching yon,
Motomete yukamu	For those waters of replenished youth.

Prince Yuhara and a Young Woman

A more evenly matched series of undated amorous exchanges (nos. 894–905) takes place between Prince Yuhara and a young woman. The Prince's opening poem is reminiscent of two by Yakamochi, perhaps dating from about the same time (the 730's?)—see no. 769 for the opening line and no. 770 for the essence of the complaint. The cassia tree in the moon in the second poem is a Chinese image. The woman's first reply (no. 896) acknowledges the intensity of the Prince's desire through a reference to the prevalent belief about the source of dreams. This poem also implies the existence of a custom of setting out an extra pillow in hopes of a dream (or actual) visit, no doubt an act of sympathetic magic. The fourth poem (no. 897) makes it clear that Prince Yuhara too is a married man, but conveys a very different attitude on the part of the "other woman" from that of Akamaro's correspondent. There are two ways of interpreting this poem—one as translated, and the other by assuming that the wife is the subject of the first two lines. In the latter case the poem becomes a complaint that the wife has all the luck.

At this point in the series it is the Prince who is the more sought-after member of the amorous pair, and he offers consolation in the form of his esteem and his robe (nos. 898–99). The affair is to remain enclosed, intimate, clandestine, like a jewel in a chest wrapped in a costly fabric. The young woman accepts this arrangement in her next reply (no. 900)—she will sleep with the Prince's robe while he is detained elsewhere. The next three poems (nos. 901–3) reverse the situation again. Now it is once more the Prince who is desperate. Time and space are irrational enemies—they seem great when they are small. The final two poems (nos. 904–5) are far and away the most interesting, both for their images and for their psychological probing. The woman accuses the man of substituting compassion for true passion, of lacking the commitment that would make the affair turn out "luckily" (*sakiku*). His "tempered blade" (*yakitachi*) is no longer enough. On his side the man wonders how to extricate himself from the tangle. For that purpose his spindle seems as useless as his sword.

894–95   [MYS IV: 634–35 / 631–32]

Two poems sent to a young woman by Prince Yuhara (the son of Prince Shiki)

(894)   [634 / 631]

> Uwahe naki   Not the merest skin
> Mono kamo hito wa   Of kindness has someone like you,
> Kaku bakari   Sending me back
> Tōki ieji o   After I'd come all that way
> Kaesaku omoeba   On the long road to your home.

(895)   [635 / 632]

> Me ni wa mite   What shall I do
> Te ni wa toraenu   About my dear girl whom I see
> Tsuki no uchi no   But cannot ever touch?
> Katsura no gotoki   She is like the cassia tree
> Imo o ika ni semu   Growing afar in the moon.

896–97   [MYS IV:636–37/633–34]

Two poems sent in reply by the young woman

(896)   [636/633]

Kokodaku ni   Did you long for me
Omoikeme ka mo   With so desperate a love
  Shikitae no   That to the barken-cloth
Makura katasaru   Pillow beside where I lay
Ime ni miekoshi   I saw you come in my dream?

(897)   [637/634]

Ie ni shite   Here in my house
Miredo akanu o   I never tire of seeing you;
  Kusamakura   How I envy her
Tabi ni mo tsuma to   Who can even be your wife
Aru ga tomoshisa   On journeys, grass for pillow.

898–99   [MYS IV:638–39/635–36]

Two more poems sent by Prince Yuhara

(898)   [638/635]

Kusamakura   Though on my journeys,
Tabi ni wa tsuma wa   Grass for pillow, it is true
  Itaredo mo   I take my wife,
Kushige no uchi no   My thoughts are always turning back
Tama koso omōyure   To the jewel in the chest of combs.

(899)   [639/636]

A ga koromo   For remembrance
Katami ni matsuru   I offer you this robe of mine:
  Shikitae no   Always keep it close,
Makura o sakezu   By your pillow of fine barken cloth;
Makite sanemase   Wrap it round you when you sleep.

900   [MYS IV:640/637]

Another poem sent in reply by the young woman

Wa ga seko ga   I shall wear this robe
Katami no koromo   As my true love's remembrance
  Tsumadoi ni   Next to my body;
A ga mi wa sakeji   It shall be yourself come courting,
Koto towazu to mo   Though it speak me not a word.

901   [MYS IV : 641 / 638]

Another poem sent by Prince Yuhara

    Tada hitoyo   Only a single night
    Hedateshi kara ni   Have we been apart, and yet
    Aratama no   The unpolished gem
    Tsuki ka henuru to   Of a whole month has gone by—
    Kokoro matoinu   It seems to my disordered heart.

902   [MYS IV : 642 / 639]

Another poem sent in reply by the young woman

    Wa ga seko ga   So it is because
    Kaku koure koso   My true love so yearns for me,
    Nubatama no   That he comes in dreams
    Ime ni mietsutsu   In the night as black as beads—
    Ineraezukere   And for me there is no sleep.

903   [MYS IV : 643 / 640]

Another poem sent by Prince Yuhara

    Hashike yashi   Ah, woe is me!
    Machikaki sato o   When your village is so close,
    Kumoi ni ya   Must I go yearning
    Koitsutsu oramu   As if it were beyond the clouds,
    Tsuki mo henaku ni   And a month not yet gone by?

904   [MYS IV : 644 / 641]

Another poem sent in reply by the young woman

    Tayu to iwaba   You know I'd be broken
    Wabishimi semu to   If you said our love must end,
    Yakitachi no   And so you stick by me
    Hetsukau koto wa   Like a sword of tempered steel—
    Sakiku ya a ga kimi   And yet, is it well, my lord?

905   [MYS IV : 645 / 642]

A poem by Prince Yuhara

    Wagimoko ni   If I went crazy,
    Koite midareba   All a tangle of heartstrings
    Kurubeki ni   Over my darling,
    Kakete yoramu to   I could wind them straight again
    A ga koisomeshi   On a spindle: so began this love.

Banquet Poems at Toyura Temple

Toyura Temple at the foot of Amagashi Hill in Asuka was Japan's first nunnery, founded on the site of Empress Suiko's palace early in the seventh century. The following three tanka were composed there at a banquet in the cell of one of the nuns some time in the 730's. The headnote does not elaborate on what such a party would have been like, but the poems are about admiring the autumn-flowering bush clover (*hagi*). They are by a man, Tajihi no Kunihito (see no. 704–5), and two novice nuns (*samini*). The "old capital" refers to Asuka. The authors of the poems have a keen awareness of the passing of time and beauty, and a delight in each other's company. The novices are still half in lay life, and perhaps all are worldly friends of the resident nun. The final poem employs an image capable of metaphorical interpretation in the worldliest of senses.

906–8   [MYS VIII: 1561–63 / 1557–59]

Three poems at a banquet in the private quarters of a nun at the Toyura Temple in the old capital

(906)   [1561 / 1557]

Asukagawa	Where Asuka River
Yukimiru oka no	Winds around the foot of the hill
Akihagi wa	The autumn clover
Kyō furu ame ni	In this pelting rain today
Chiri ka suginamu	May shed its blossoms on the slopes.

The above poem is by Tajihi no Mahito Kunihito.

(907)   [1562 / 1558]

Uzura naku	In this fallen village,
Furinishi sato no	Old and filled with cries of quail,
Akihagi o	We've gazed together
Omou hitodochi	One in heart upon the autumn fields
Aimitsuru kamo	Where the tall bush clover blooms.

(908)   [1563 / 1559]

Akihagi wa	The full flowering
Sakarisuguru o	Of the autumn clover bush
Itazura ni	Will soon be past—
Kazashi ni sasazu	And shall we part and never wear
Kaerinamu to ya	Its blossoms upon our brows?

The above two poems are by novice nuns.

From the Embassy to Silla of 736

The first part of Book XV (MYS XV: 3600–3744 / 3578–3722) is made up of a unique collection of travel poems composed by members of an official embassy to Silla that departed from Naniwa about the beginning of the sixth month of 736. Apparently the intention was to be back home by the fall of the year, but there were delays, and it was the ninth month before the boats reached Tsushima. One member of the party died on the outward voyage, and the Ambassador was dead too before the envoys returned to Nara in the first month of 737. The reception in Silla had been chilly, and so all in all the embassy was not a great success. The poems are largely about the sorrows of parting and being away from home, with mention of sights and incidents along the way. There are unfortunately no poems composed in Silla, the state that then ruled the Korean peninsula, and of course no attempts to deal with the political significance of the journey. The following are selections. The collection begins with a number of exchanges between husbands and wives, all anonymous. The first poem (no. 909), by a wife, presents a parent-child image of warm nurturing. Muko Bay, the place mentioned in the jo, is the site of the modern city of Kōbe, just to the west of Naniwa (Ōsaka). The husband, receptive to his wife's feelings, replies in kind. The second exchange employs a frequently encountered conceit about sighs forming mist. The reply provides evidence of the intended return date of the embassy.

Exchanges of the envoys to Silla, sad over parting, and statements of their thoughts when moved by the afflictions of the voyage, with old poems they recited here and there along the way:

909   [MYS XV: 3600 / 3578]

Muko no ura no	Birds along the strand
Irie no sudori	In the inlets of Muko Bay
Hagukumoru	Nestled secure
Kimi o hanarete	I lay warm beneath your wings,
Koi ni shinubeshi	And parted must die of longing.

910   [MYS XV: 3601 / 3579]

Ōbune ni	Were it allowed
Imo noru mono ni	That my dear one board our ship,
Aramaseba	I would nestle her
Hagukumimochite	Warm beneath my wings and go,
Yukamashi mono o	Taking her on our way.

911   [MYS XV: 3602/3580]

    Kimi ga yuku   If on your way
  Umihe no yado ni   Where you lodge along the sea
     Kiri tataba   The mist should rise,
  A ga tachinageku   Please know it is my breath
  Iki to shirimase   Sighed as I stand here waiting.

912   [MYS XV: 3603/3581]

    Aki saraba   When autumn comes
  Aimimu mono o   We shall see each other once again;
    Nani shi ka mo   Why then, my darling,
  Kiri ni tatsubeku   Need you sigh until your sighs
  Nageki shi masamu   Stand risen in a mist?

✳ After running from port to port down the north shore of the Inland Sea, the embassy passed through the straits between the island of Ōshima and the mainland of Suō Province about the middle of the sixth month. Near the modern city of Yanai in Yamaguchi Prefecture, the opposing coasts form a "roaring narrows" (*naruto*) through which the tide rushes with swirling waters. A poem by Tanabe no Akiniwa (otherwise unknown) remarks on the ama girls out gathering seaweed in the rough water.

913   [MYS XV: 3660/3638]

[One of] two poems composed after two nights had passed since going by the tide race of Ōshima

    Kore ya kono   Are these then the girls,
  Na ni ou Naruto no   Daughters of the dwellers of the shore,
    Uzushio ni   Who in the swirling tides
  Tamamo karu tou   That roar past storied Naruto
  Amaotomedomo   Go out in boats to cut the gemlike weed?

The above poem is by Tanabe no Akiniwa.

✳ A little farther down the coast of Suō, near the modern city of Hōfu, the party ran into bad weather and was blown out into Suō Nada and across to northern Kyūshū, where it sheltered near the modern city of Nakatsu. As usual, the men consoled themselves by composing poems in which they thought of home. No. 914 is based on the supposition that the soul travels in a dream to the one it loves, here that of the wife at home to her husband away on his journey. Two other poems composed at this time take the opposite direction, asking for light from fishing flares or the moon, so that the yearning gaze can find its Yamato homeland at the other end of the Inland Sea. In their feeling for Yamato these poems are faithful to modes of expression going back to Hitomaro (see particularly nos. 308–9). The authors of these poems are unknown. No. 916 is carefully identified as a by now rare sedōka.

914–16   [MYS XV : 3669 / 3647, 3670 / 3648, 3673 / 3651]

Suddenly they encountered adverse winds in the waters off Saba and were swept along on swelling waves. After a night they fortunately obtained a favorable wind and arrived at Wakuma Bay in Shimotsumike District, Buzen Province. [The following are three of] eight poems composed in sadness and pain as they recollected their distress.

(914)   [3669 / 3647]

    Wagimoko ga   My young love at home,
    Ika ni omoe ka   How she must be yearning for me,
    Nubatama no   That she should appear
    Hitoyo mo ochizu   So faithfully in dreams by night,
    Ime ni shi miyuru   Coming ever in the glistening dark!

(915)   [3670 / 3648]

    Unahara no   You in the offing
    Okihe ni tomoshi   Lighting flares for the fishing
    Izaru hi wa   On the plains of sea,
    Akashite tomose   Burn your flares even brighter—
    Yamatoshima mimu   I would see Yamato Isle.

(916)   [3673 / 3651]

    Nubatama no   Black as a berry
    Yo wataru tsuki wa   Is the night—the fording moon,
    Haya mo idenu ka mo Won't it hurry up and rise?
    Unahara no   Across plains of sea
    Yasoshima no ue yu   Over the eighty islands
    Imo ga atari mimu   I would see my love's homeland.

(This is a sedōka.)

✱ Arriving at the provincial capital of Chikuzen, near modern Fukuoka, the travel-worn envoys rested part of the seventh month, then gradually moved westward toward their launching point across the Korea Strait. The following anonymous tanka was probably composed on Hakata Bay. It is based on a jo with juncture in the pivot word *kuru* ("haul"/"come").

"Ropeweed" (*nawanori*) is a ropelike seaweed not precisely identified. It was now autumn by the Japanese calendar, the promised season of return.

917   [MYS XV: 3685 / 3663]

[One of] nine poems composed on gazing at the moon by the sea

Watatsumi no	In ocean waters
Oki tsu nawanori	Far off shore they haul ropeweed,
Kuru toki to	Hand over hand,
Imo ga matsuramu	Homecoming soon, she waits for me,
Tsuki wa henitsutsu	But the months go passing by.

❋ About the middle of the seventh month, at a favorable time for moon-viewing, the party stopped for a few days at Kara, an anchorage on the western side of the mouth of Hakata Bay. The following set of six poems (nos. 918–23) was composed there. "This blossom in the sky" in the head-note probably stems from "moon blossom," a phrase found in several Chinese poems. "The Ambassador," the author of the first poem, was Ahe no Tsugimaro, who died in Tsushima on the return voyage, perhaps of small-pox. He employs the traditional formula for those who carry out the impe-rial will under far skies (compare no. 807), thus revealing his sense of mis-sion, but admits in the same breath his human frailty. The next three poems (nos. 919–21) go to the heart of that frailty, the yearning for home and the woman who waits there. The Senior Secretary who wrote the second poem was Mibu no Udamaro, whose career as an official can be traced into the 750's. The other four poems are anonymous. The first of them (no. 920) is based on a contrastive structure common in early tanka and very closely du-plicated in an old anonymous poem in *Kokinshū*. The fantasy in the second (no. 921) must be based on the perception of the moon as a movable object, but flies in the face of its westward course through the night sky. Still, it is a pleasant conceit, this idea of coming as a shining lantern (or as a "flower in the sky"?) to the beloved who, as in Udamaro's no. 919, is no doubt waiting in a dark that is emotional as well as visual. The last two poems turn their attention to the scene at hand, the first being a purely descriptive panorama of light-dazzled water, and the second an evocation of the power of the sea, a foreboding of the crossing soon to be made.

918–23   [MYS XV: 3690–95 / 3668–73]

They arrived at Kara Roadstead in Shima District of the province of Chikuzen and spent three days at anchor. The moon shone down at night with a flowing white brilliance. The sadness of travel overcame them sud-denly at this blossom in the sky, and each gave some small effort to express-ing his emotions, thus fashioning six poems:

(918)   [3690 / 3668]

     Ōkimi no   Of our great lord
  Tō no mikado to   We are the distant court,
     Omoeredo   We know it well—
  Kenagaku shi areba   And yet the number of the days
  Koinikeru kamo   Is long, and we yearn for home.

The above poem is by the Ambassador.

(919)   [3691 / 3669]

     Tabi ni aredo   Though on a journey,
  Yoru wa hi tomoshi   All night by the lighted torch
     Oru ware o   I take my rest,
  Yami ni ya imo ga   While my love must lie alone,
  Koitsutsu aruramu   Yearning in the dark.

The above poem is by the Senior Secretary.

(920)   [3692 / 3670]

     Karatomari   Though there are days
  Noko no uranami   When no waves rise in Kara Roads
     Tatanu hi wa   By Noko's curving shore,
  Aredo mo ie ni   There's not a day I do not long
  Koinu hi wa nashi   With all my heart for home.

(921)   [3693 / 3671]

     Nubatama no   If I were the moon
  Yo wataru tsuki ni   That crosses the bead-black night,
     Aramaseba   I would go to her,
  Ie naru imo ni   My dear love who waits at home,
  Aite komashi o   And come again by dawn.

(922)   [3694 / 3672]

     Hisakata no   The sun-resplendent
  Tsuki wa teritari   Moon is out and shining down;
     Itoma naku   Without rest the flares
  Ama no izari wa   Of the seafolk as they fish
  Tomoshiaeri miyu   Flash back and forth in view.

(923)   [3695 / 3673]

     Kaze fukeba   The winds are blowing,
  Oki tsu shiranami   White waves from the offing rise,
     Kashikomi to   Awesome in power;

Noko no tomari ni	Many are the nights we sleep,
Amata yo so nuru	Fearful, in the roadstead of Noko.

✳ The member of the embassy who died en route to Korea was Yuki no Yakamaro, of whom nothing further is known. His death occurred on the island of Iki (pronounced Yuki in two of the poems), between the northern coast of Kyūshū and Tsushima. The party reached Iki some time during the eighth or ninth month, after further delays. Yakamaro fell victim to a contagion that may have been the early stage of the smallpox epidemic that swept into Japan from the west in the following year, taking the lives of many, including the four leaders of the Fujiwara clan. The following chōka-hanka set is the first of a series of laments for Yakamaro. Its author is unknown. The formal opening again employs the formula for distant service, altering it from ōkimi ("great lord") to sumeroki, the sovereign in his aspect as the ancestor god. The fallen companion is wagase ("our brother"), a term that makes specific the implied kinship in Hitomaro's encounter with the drowned man on Samine Island (no. 358–60). Yakamaro's death on a "rough, upthrusting isle" (araki shimane) reminds us strongly of the sense of man's fate as a lone traveler in Hitomaro's work, though this dead man had his companions to bury him and compose the laments to quiet his soul, if that was indeed their intended function. The speculation about the (supernatural) cause of the death is more specific here than in Hitomaro's laments, and the image of the home folk waiting in ignorance is also further developed. The final address to the dead man as kimi at the end of the chōka is very like no. 360, the second envoy of Hitomaro's Samine poem, with Hitomaro's kindly, ironic naseru ("rest") corresponding to yadori ("lodge"). The first envoy for Yakamaro is particularly fine in the way it turns to the dead man, now so safely lodged, for an answer to one of life's hardest questions. The second envoy implies that Yakamaro had a touch of Okura about him.

924–26   [MYS XV: 3710–12 / 3688–90]

A poem composed when Yuki no Muraji Yakamaro, having arrived at Yuki Island, suddenly encountered pestilence and died; with tanka

Sumeroki no	With us, the distant court
Tō no mikado to	Of our Primordial Sovereign,
Karakuni ni	You too, our brother,
Wataru wagase wa	Were crossing to the land of Kara:
5 Iebito no	Perhaps your people
Iwai matane ka	Did not wait in abstinence,
Tadami ka mo	Perhaps you yourself
Ayamachi shikemu	Carelessly broke some taboo.

	Aki saraba	When autumn came
10	Kaerimasamu to	You would be at home again,
	Tarachine no	You told your mother
	Haha ni mōshite	Of the milk-abundant breasts.
	Toki mo sugi	Time passed,
	Tsuki mo henureba	And the months went by.
15	Kyō ka komu	"He'll come home today,
	Asu ka mo komu to	He'll be home tomorrow for sure,"
	Iebito wa	Your people must hope,
	Machikouramu ni	Waiting for you, longing.
	Tō no kuni	But not yet arrived
20	Imada mo tsukazu	In the distant country,
	Yamato o mo	Far from Yamato,
	Tōku sakarite	Cut off in a remote place
	Iwagane no	Among rooted rocks
	Araki shimane ni	In the rough, upthrusting isles
25	Yadori suru kimi	You have found your lodging.

Two Envoys

Iwatano ni	You who find lodging
Yadori suru kimi	On the moors of Iwata,
Iebito no	What shall I say,
Izura to ware o	What shall I tell your people
Towaba ika ni iwamu	If they ask me where you are?

Yo no naka wa	Shall I yearn for you
Tsune kaku nomi to	Who parted from us at the end,
Wakarenuru	Saying the world is thus
Kimi ni ya motona	And ever has been—shall I go on
A ga koiyukamu	Ceaselessly, senselessly longing?

The above three poems are laments.

❋ The embassy apparently reached Tsushima, the last outpost of Japanese territory before Korea, at some point during the ninth month. It put up in Takashiki Bay on the north coast of the southern island and stayed there long enough for relationships to be formed of the type implied by poems 927–28. There are two theories about Tamatsuki—that she was a harlot, and that she was a pearl diver. The local place name Tamatsuki ("pearl tribute") may have been the source of her cognomen. In any case she is an island girl and knows she will be left behind. Her lover's boat rows by the autumn mountain slopes that plunge into the sea, its red gleam (compare no. 447) blending with the reflections of colored leaves. The seaweed swaying in the wake of the boat is the objective correlative of the waves left in the young woman's heart. If her lover was perchance the Ambassador himself, the anticipated return was a sad one, for he died on the island on the way back to Nara. (For farewells by local courtesans, see nos. 463, 607, and 1073–74.) A sense of weariness and loss of time is conveyed by two other poems—anonymous—from the same set. "The long month" (*nagatsuki*) is the ninth month, the last month of autumn by the old lunar calendar, corresponding roughly to October. These are the last poems of the outward voyage; the collection contains nothing more save a group of five tanka composed when the embassy reached the province of Harima on the way home.

927–30   [MYS XV: 3726–27 / 3704–5, 3738–39 / 3716–17]

[Four of] eighteen poems composed setting forth their feelings when the boat was in port at Takashiki Bay

(927)   [3726 / 3704]

Momichiba no	Where the colored leaves
Chirau yamahe yu	Are scattering on the mountain slopes
Kogu fune no	His boat rows by:
Nioi ni medete	Dazzled by its gleam in the water,
Idete kinikeri	I have come to see it pass.

(928)   [3727 / 3705]

Takashiki no	When my lord rows out
Tamamo nabikashi	And sets the seaweed swaying
Kogidenamu	In Takashiki Bay,
Kimi ga mifune o	How long shall I have to wait
Itsu to ka matamu	To see his boat come back again?

The above two poems are by a maid of Tsushima named Tamatsuki.

(929)   [3738 / 3716]

Amakumo no	While we tossed at sea
Tayutaikureba	Like clouds churning in the sky,
Nagatsuki no	Mountain slopes aflame
Momichi no yama mo	With the leaves of the long month
Utsuroinikeri	Altered to faded hues.

(930)   [3739 / 3717]

Tabi nite mo	Though on a journey,
Mo naku haya ko to	Be safe and come back soon,
Wagimoko ga	My darling said,
Musubishi himo wa	And she tied this sash for me—
Narenikeru kamo	See how worn it has become!

Prince Kadobe and Tachibana no Ayanari

In the first month of 737 a banquet was held at the residence of Prince Kadobe (see nos. 670–73). The following two poems are illustrations of the formal exchange between host and guest. The Prince here employs essentially the same "had I known" formula as Tachibana no Moroe employed fifteen years later at a banquet at his own house (see no. 702). Nothing is known about the author of the reply beyond what is stated in the footnote. His poem is as stiff and lifelessly polite as can be managed in the tanka form and well matches the schematic quality of the verse it answers. These poems are good for explaining grammar. The Tachibana Lesser Lord is Moroe's younger brother Tachibana no Sai.

931–32   [MYS VI: 1018–19 / 1013–14]

Two poems composed at a banquet when the Tachibana Lesser Lord and the great officers of court assembled at the home of Prince Kadobe, President of the Board of Censors, in spring, the first month of the ninth year [of Tempyō, 737], Fire-Junior / Ox

(931)   [1018 / 1013]

Arakajime	Had I known before
Kimi kimasamu to	My lords would come to me this day,
Shiramaseba	In the gateway,
Kado ni mo yado ni mo	In the doorway of my house
Tama shikamashi o	I would have spread a path of jewels

The above poem is by the host, Prince Kadobe (he was later granted the clan name Ōhara no Mahito).

(932)   [1019 / 1014]

Ototsuhi mo	Though we have met you
Kinō mo kyō mo	Two days since, and yesterday,
Mitsuredo mo	And again today,
Asu sae mimaku	Tomorrow still we'll have desire
Hoshiki kimi kamo	To meet my lord once more.

The above poem is by Tachibana no Sukune Ayanari (that is, the son of the Lesser Lord).

Kosobe no Tsushima and Tachibana no Moroe

Another formal exchange between guest and host at a banquet has been preserved from the following year. Of the guest, Kosobe no Tsushima, it is known that he occupied provincial posts in the 730's, and from the exchange he appears to have been a protégé of Tachibana no Moroe, who had become Minister of the Right in the first month of the year. The placement of the clan rank Asomi after rather than before Tsushima's name could be a sign of special favor (see the commentary to no. 647). Tsushima fashions a jo out of a reference to an island in the province of his governance (a political plum from Moroe, perhaps) to lead into *okumaete* ("deep within"). His wish for a thousand years for his patron is bettered by one third in the reply. Tsushima uses the respectful *kimi* ("lord"), and Moroe the intimate *seko* ("brother"). The exchange is successful in its complementary as well as complimentary diction, and conveys a warmer tone than the exchange between Prince Kadobe and Ayanari (nos. 931–32).

933–34   [MYS VI: 1028–29 / 1024–25]

[Two of] four poems from a banquet held at the home of Minister of the Right Tachibana in autumn, the twentieth of the eighth month [of 738]

(933)   [1028 / 1024]

Nagato naru	In Nagato lies
Oki tsu Karishima	Deep in the offing Kari Isle:
Okumaete	Deep within my heart
A ga omou kimi wa	Is the love I bear my lord—
Chitose ni mogamo	May he live a thousand years!

The above poem is by Kosobe no Tsushima no Asomi, Governor of Nagato.

(934)   [1029 / 1025]

Okumaete	You who care for me
Ware o omoeru	Deep within your loyal heart,
Wa ga seko wa	You, my brother—
Chitose iotose	Cannot life go on for you
Arikosenu ka mo	A thousand, five hundred years?

The above poem is the reply of the Minister of the Right.

Sano no Otogami and Nakatomi no Yakamori

The latter part of Book XV consists of sixty-three tanka (MYS XV:3745–3807 / 3723–85, nos. 935–97) exchanged between an exiled husband and his wife. The husband was Yakamori, a minor official of the ancient Shintō sacerdotal Nakatomi clan, who is known to have been still living in the early 760's. Around 738, or at the latest by 740, he married Sano no Otogami, a woman employed in the Treasury Office (*kura no tsukasa*), the court bureau charged with keeping the sacred regalia, imperial vestments, and other important valuables. It is commonly thought that his exile—to Echizen Province—was due to this marriage, perhaps because it was entered into without the parties obtaining permission. Whatever the offense, it was regarded seriously enough for Yakamori to be excluded by name from the amnesty of the sixth month of 740. He was eventually pardoned and returned to the capital. In 764 he became involved in the abortive coup of Fujiwara no Nakamaro and had his name stricken from the list of officials. He held offices in the Department of Shrines (*jingikan*), where he rose to be Senior Assistant Head (*tayū*). The Treasury Office, where Otogami was one of ten low-ranking *nyoju*, or "female servants," was located in the women's quarters of the palace and was staffed entirely by women.

The series opens with a set of four tanka by Otogami. The first word of the first poem is *ashihiki* ("footsore," "foot-dragging," "leg-cramping"), an epithet for *yama* ("mountain"). Thus pain and mountains to be crossed are announced as the themes of this examination of the sorrow of parting. She holds him in her heart (*kokoro ni mochite*), declaring the struggle of wish against reality, a tension that deprives her of rest (*yasukeku mo nashi*). In an intense and brilliant metaphor the second poem seeks to wipe out the road that will take Yakamori into exile, hauling it back by the end like a strip of cloth that the fire of a just heaven will burn away. The deliberate, heavy motion of the imagined pulling of the road works against the dragging, reluctant forward progress of feet over mountain trails. The third poem, by contrast, is all weakness and resignation, hiding from rather than combating reality. Poem four (no. 938) makes clear for the first time what is stated in the footnote—it is the last night before Yakamori's departure. The disjunction between now (*kono koro*) and what comes "after dawn" (*akete ochi*) is clearly drawn. The clinging now is to what remains, and the last line acknowledges helplessness. A kaleidoscope of emotion is compressed into these poems.

935–97   [MYS XV: 3745–3807 / 3723–85]

Poems exchanged between Nakatomi no Asomi Yakamori and the Maiden Sano no Otogami

(935)   [3745 / 3723]

    Ashihiki no   Over the footsore
    Yamaji koemu to   Mountains you must climb the trails,
      Suru kimi o   Soon, O my lord;
    Kokoro ni mochite   I hold you back, clasped in my heart,
    Yasukeku mo nashi   And have not a moment's peace.

(936)   [3746 / 3724]

    Kimi ga yuku   The long road, my lord,
    Michi no nagate o   That you must go, I'll seize it,

Kuritatane	Reel it, roll it,
Yakihorobosamu	Stack it up into a pile—
Ame no hi mogamo	May heaven's fire burn it away!

(937) [3747/3725]

Wa ga seko shi	If indeed, my love,
Kedashi makaraba	It happens you should go away,
Shirotae no	Wave me, I beg you,
Sode o furasane	Your sleeve of white barken cloth,
Mitsutsu shinowamu	That I may gaze and remember.

(938) [3748/3726]

Kono koro wa	For this little while
Koitsutsu mo aramu	Let us hold our tenderness;
Tamakushige	When the gem-bright dawn
Akete ochi yori	Opens the day that is to come,
Sube nakarubeshi	There will be no help for us.

The above four poems were composed by the Maiden on the eve of parting.

❋ Yakamori answers with a four-tanka set composed along the road. Each poem has images of earth or walking. Granted that Yakamori is in official disgrace, the humility of the male lover toward the woman in no. 939 is nevertheless striking in a tradition that does not come out of chivalric adoration of the "fair sex." The next three poems take Yakamori out of Nara and up the mountain trails, where he finds the real reason why the climb is hard. The power of Otogami's love is "holding him in her heart" (no. 935), and he has to fight against it in order to take a step ahead. In no. 942 a moment of crisis comes as he blurts out her name at the shrine on what is probably Arachi Pass, the crossing point between the provinces of Ōmi and Echizen. The gods of mountains and mountain passes were thought to be fierce and dangerous; one spoke to them with care, as Yamato Takeru no Mikoto learned to his sorrow (see commentary to nos. 27-28). Yakamori has guarded his secret from the mountain god, but something makes him call out Otogami's name as he is about to descend into the land of his exile. (For a comparable poem, see no. 1495.)

(939) [3749/3727]

Chirihiji no	Less than dust or mire
Kazu ni mo aranu	Do I count my worth, and yet
Ware yue ni	For such a one
Omoiwaburamu	My beloved is cast down—
Imo ga kanashisa	She the darling of my heart.

(940)   [3750/3728]

    Aoni yoshi   In blue-earth Nara
  Nara no ōchi wa   The great avenues run smooth,
    Yukiyokedo   Fine to walk upon,
  Kono yamamichi wa   But these stony mountain trails
  Yukiashikarikeri   Make hard going for my stumbling feet.

(941)   [3751/3729]

    Uruwashi to   Is it then because
  A ga mou imo o   My thoughts fly constantly to her,
    Omoitsutsu   My handsome darling,
  Yukeba ka motona   That each step I take ahead
  Yukiashikaruramu   Should be so desperately hard?

(942)   [3752/3730]

  Kashikomi to   Dread of the mountain
  Norazu arishi o   Kept me silent as I climbed,
    Mikoshiji no   But at last I stood
  Tamuke ni tachite   On the high pass of Koshi—
  Imo ga na noritsu   And I spoke her name at the shrine.

The above four poems were composed by Nakatomi no Asomi Yakamori as he went up the road.

❈ The longest section of the exchange is the third, fourteen poems by Yakamori composed in exile. Exile is the theme of the first poem (no. 943): if wishes were horses, he would cross the ranges that bar him from his love. This wish-world is the counterpart of that of Otogami with which the sequence begins. Time rather than space is the matter of the second verse (no. 944), a time that oscillates meaninglessly between day and night, completely filled because completely empty. Yakamori makes no pretense at being a masurao. After defining his situation through the twin concepts of space and time, he turns in no. 945 to an immediate and concrete manifestation of love—the katami, or keepsake. The garment is something that can be touched, held on to, a lifeline as it were, and as such corresponds in an opposite sense to the road that Otogami would have rolled up and destroyed. But the road has been taken to its destination, and no. 946 reverts to the hopelessness of barrier mountains and deprivation.

    Poems 947–51 form a distinct subsequence, in which Yakamori's mood turns petulant and argumentative, as if answering doubts about his constancy. In no. 947, and again in no. 950, the common belief that the one who yearns travels in a dream to the one who is yearned for is turned around: it is the yearner who draws the object of desire to appear in his dream. The honorific language in no. 948 (*omōshimesu na*, "pray do not think") is unparalleled from a man to a woman. Since Otogami occupied a not particularly elevated position in the palace, Yakamori's use of honorifics and the description of himself as "less than dust or mire" (no. 939) point toward a personality that found pleasure in self-abnegation. (This is to be distinguished from the kind of jocularity used in no. 712.) But abnormally honorific language can be a sign of suppressed anger as well as of supplication. The next poem (no. 949) lets some of that feeling show, even if in the form of playful mock-anger. It illustrates the truth that *koi* is not "love" in its amplitude, but "yearning," a pain that can only be annihilated by coming together with its object. Poem 951 restates this thesis, with the further lesson that the trouble can be cut at the root by not making that first not-innocent glance. The lesson seems to be in accord with fundamental Buddhist teaching on the source of suffering in desire, though one would hesitate to say these poems have been directly influenced by Buddhism. (For a similar poem, see no. 413 in the "Hitomaro Collection.")

The final five poems of this group (nos. 952–56) form another subsequence. Longing is triumphant and demands hope. It begins with the trope of the extreme condition, one whose very extremity warrants the truth that could be negated by it alone. It is also an appeal to the gods to prove their existence and their power. The same trope is used by Kasa no Iratsume in a poem to Ōtomo no Yakamochi (no. 1105). Nos. 953 and 954 examine two sides of perseverance—confidence in a happy ending and uncertainty about when it will come. The next-to-last poem in this section (no. 955) is a convoluted attempt to define the innocent-sounding word *tabi* ("journey") in terms that reach out toward the English cognates travel/travail. The deprivation that is part of *tabi* is approached through the elaborate construction *sukunaku mo . . . subenakenaku ni* ("not being only slightly lacking in means [of coping]"). The difficulty of this tormented locution is no doubt meant to reflect the inner torment of *tabi* and to contrast with the "easy" (*yasuki*) and superficial syllables that come so quickly to the tongue. Finally, in no. 956, Yakamori declares where he stands: all for love, which means continuing in no. 954's *tokoyami* ("unchanging dark") of yearning.

(943)   [3753/3731]

Omou e ni	If by mere longing
Au mono naraba	Lovers' trysts could be arranged,
Shimashiku mo	Even for a moment
Imo ga me karete	Would I stay in this exile
Are orame ya mo	From the eyes of my darling girl?

(944)   [3754/3732]

| Akane sasu | All the madder-red |
| Hiru wa mono omoi | Daytime I am lost in thought, |

Nubatama no
Yoru wa sugara ni
Ne nomi shi nakayu

And the berry-black
Night is never long enough
For the crying that I do.

(945)   [3755 / 3733]

Wagimoko ga
Katami no koromo
Nakariseba
Nani mono mote ka
Inochi tsugamashi

But for the garment
My young darling gave to me
As a remembrance,
What would I have that I could use
To keep my life together?

(946)   [3756 / 3734]

Tōki yama
Seki mo koekinu
Ima sara ni
Aubeki yoshi no
Naki ga sabushisa

Over far mountains,
Past the barrier I've come;
Never again
Will there be a chance to meet—
And, oh, the loneliness of that!

(947)   [3757 / 3735]

Omowazu mo
Makoto ariemu ya
Sanuru yo no
Ime ni mo imo ga
Miezaranaku ni

Could I in all truth
Live and never think of you?
Even in my sleep
There is not a night, my love,
You do not come in dreams.

(948)   [3758 / 3736]

Tōku areba
Hitohi hitoyo mo
Omowazute
Aruramu mono to
Omōshimesu na

Do not, I pray you,
Think because I'm far away
There might come a time,
A single day, a single night,
When I do not long for you.

(949)   [3759 / 3737]

Hito yori wa
Imo so mo ashiki
Koi mo naku
Aramashi mono o
Omowashimetsutsu

She gives me trouble
Worse than any stranger would—
When I could have lived
Free of the yearning of such love,
She binds me in constant longing.

(950)   [3760 / 3738]

Omoitsutsu
Nureba ka motona
Nubatama no

Is it this longing
In my restless sleep that brings
Through the glistening dark

Hitoyo mo ochizu　　　　The wild flickering of dreams
Ime ni shi miyuru　　　　Wherein I see her night by night?

(951)　　　　　　　　　　　　　　　[3761/3739]

　　Kaku bakari　　　　　　Had I only known
Koimu to kanete　　　From the start how burdensome
　　Shiramaseba　　　　　　Would be this yearning,
Imo o ba mizu so　　　I could well have gone without
Arubeku arikeru　　　That first glance at her I love.

(952)　　　　　　　　　　　　　　　[3762/3740]

　　Ame tsuchi no　　　　　If there are no gods
Kami naki mono ni　　Either in heaven or on earth,
　　Araba koso　　　　　　　Then and then alone
A ga mou imo ni　　　Shall I never meet my love,
Awazu shini seme　　But die in my longing.

(953)　　　　　　　　　　　　　　　[3763/3741]

　　Inochi o shi　　　　　　If my life remains
Mataku shi araba　　Intact—yes, if only that,
　　Arikinu no　　　　　　　Then the days may draw
Arite nochi ni mo　　Long as the silk of the silkworm,
Awazarame ya mo　　But shall we not meet at last?

(954)　　　　　　　　　　　　　　　[3764/3742]

　　Awamu hi o　　　　　　　The day we shall meet
Sono hi to shirazu　　Is a day I do not know;
　　Tokoyami ni　　　　　　In unchanging dark
Izure no hi made　　Until what far day must I
Are koioramu　　　　Go on in this sore yearning?

(955)　　　　　　　　　　　　　　　[3765/3743]

　　Tabi to ieba　　　　　　We speak of journeys,
Koto ni so yasuki　　And the word comes easily;
　　Sukunaku mo　　　　　　But the helplessness
Imo ni koitsutsu　　Of unquenchable yearning
Subenakenaku ni　　Is mine in no small measure.

(956)　　　　　　　　　　　　　　　[3766/3744]

　　Wagimoko ni　　　　　　I shall give myself
Kouru ni are wa　　To yearning for my young love:
　　Tamakiwaru　　　　　　Nothing will matter,

Mijikaki inochi mo   Not this brief life and the soul
Oshikeku mo nashi   Expiring with my final breath.

The above fourteen poems are by Nakatomi no Asomi Yakamori.

✻ The next batch of nine poems (nos. 957–65) is from Otogami. It begins with a reaction to Yakamori's desperate statement in no. 956, harking back to no. 953 as well. She woos her husband back from the brink of despair, and then begins her own complaints in no. 958. These incorporate honorifics down through no. 961. The complaint about unplanted fields in no. 958 is the one suggestion in the entire exchange of the purely practical inconveniences of being an exile's wife. If the fields are to be taken as real rice paddies, and not as a metaphor for general economic support, the first two lines seem to paint a picture of everyone else out planting, with only Otogami's fields left untended. The following poem (no. 959) has her sitting in her house staring at pine needles, no doubt because *matsu* ("pine") also means "to wait," and the next points out what an inferior place Yakamori has chosen to live. These two end with the same couplet, which becomes a kind of refrain. The whole effect of the series 957–60 is to induce a desire to return, whether through guilt feelings or self-interest, and is thus an ironic fiction in view of Yakamori's actual situation. Poem 960 in particular ever so faintly echoes *Chao Hun*, the "Summons to the Soul" attributed to Sung Yü, a Chinese poet of the third century B.C., which attempts to entice back the soul of an ailing ruler (or of the dead poet Ch'ü Yüan, according to the traditional interpretation) from alien and frightful realms away from home. Otogami's next poem (no. 961) is the counterpart of Yakamori's no. 954, and no. 962 is a declaration that chimes with no. 956. In no. 963 she sends him one of her underrobes, apparently in addition to the garment mentioned in no. 945. Perhaps a third garment arrives in no. 965, one sewn especially for Yakamori. *Omoimidarete* ("distracted with longing") is an engo associated with *nueru* ("sew") because *midarete* can refer to snarled thread. But the word also refers back to the penultimate poem in this series (no. 964) with its evocation of a state of raveled emotions.

(957)   [3767/3745]

    Inochi araba   If we have life,
  Au koto mo aramu   There will be a time to meet;
      Wa ga yue ni   Do not for me
    Hada na omoi so   Torment yourself with longing:
    Inochi dani heba   If at least life still endures.

(958)   [3768/3746]

    Hito no uuru   You do not, my lord,
  Ta wa uemasazu   Plant the fields that others plant;

Ima sara ni
Kuniwakare shite
Are wa ika ni semu

How shall I manage,
Now that you have gone away
Into some far-off province?

(959) [3769/3747]

Wa ga yado no
Matsu no ha mitsutsu
Are matamu
Haya kaerimase
Koishinanu to ni

I shall wait for you,
Looking at the needles of the pine
There before my house;
Hasten back to me, my lord,
Ere I die of my yearning.

(960) [3770/3748]

Hitokuni wa
Sumiashi to so iu
Sumuyakeku
Haya kaerimase
Koishinanu to ni

The far provinces
Are ill places to live, they say:
Therefore with all speed
Hasten back to me, my lord,
Ere I die of my yearning.

(961) [3771/3749]

Hitokuni ni
Kimi o imasete
Itsu made ka
A ga koioramu
Toki no shiranaku

To a far province
I have let my lord depart,
Though without knowing
Until when I shall go on
In the toils of this yearning.

(962) [3772/3750]

Ame tsuchi no
Sokohi no ura ni
A ga gotoku
Kimi ni kouramu
Hito wa sane araji

In all the vast reach
To the utmost limits of
The sky and the earth
There is surely no other
Who yearns for her lord as I.

(963) [3773/3751]

Shirotae no
A ga shitagoromo
Ushinawazu
Motere wa ga seko
Tada ni au made ni

This white barken-cloth
Underrobe of mine I send,
Do not lose it, love,
Keep it with you till we meet
One fine day, face to face.

(964) [3774/3752]

Haru no hi no
Uraganashiki ni

In the heart-sorrow
Of this day in spring I stay

Okureite	Left behind at home,
Kimi ni koitsutsu	Lost in yearning for my lord,
Utsushikeme ya mo	Unsure anything is real.

(965)   [3775 / 3753]

Awamu hi no	Till the day we meet
Katami ni seyo to	Keep it for a remembrance—
Tawayame no	Your tender maiden
Omoimidarete	Has stitched you a garment
Nueru koromo so	From the snarled strands of her longing.

The above nine poems are by the Maiden.

❉ Since the text is not specific on this point, we do not know how often poems went back and forth between Otogami and Yakamori, or by what means. The preceding group of nine culminates in references to gifts of clothing; perhaps the entire set accompanied the gifts, or perhaps only the relevant poems. The next group of thirteen (nos. 966–78), from Yakamori, similarly culminates in two poems referring to unspecified presents from him to Otogami. It opens with a poem wishing for a more frequent means of communication. As *Kojiki* has the exiled Prince Karu remark, "the birds are also messengers" (no. 85). Yakamori addresses himself in no. 966 to the cuckoo, a bird associated with love and longing for the past. The cuckoo needs no passport to fly over the barrier at the frontier—its flights have the freedom denied to human travelers, who must carry a *kaso* (gate pass). The kaso was a long wooden strip with the name of the traveler, his destination, the barriers he would pass, and other information written on it. It was obtained from metropolitan or provincial authorities, and failure to possess one meant trouble at the inspection point. Yakamori is the only poet in *Man'yōshū* to use the term, and his poem has been admired for its originality.

The next verse (no. 967) is more conventional, a statement of the human as distinguished from the avian condition. Its opening line duplicates that of no. 941. *Uruwashi* is expressive of a kind of bold and striking beauty and is usually applied to men; Yakamori's description of Otogami in such terms echoes his use of honorifics and the humility of his first poem (no. 939). The last line is the same as the last line of Otogami's first poem (no. 935), and it corresponds as well to the restless motion envisaged for the cuckoo in no. 966. In the next two poems Yakamori again, as in nos. 943–44, examines time and space, and finds a fracture in each. The tension in no. 969 seems an outcome of that in no. 935, and its vision of a heart left at home leads to no. 970, where Yakamori wonders what is really going on there. No doubt he has reasons to be familiar with the favorite sports of the courtiers. This is the only poem that deals head-on with sexual jealousy, but the fantasy is vivid, since the verb *naburi* ("toy") has a quite physical sense. The next three poems (nos. 971–73) show the result of Yakamori's anguish—sleepless nights—and his philosophical conclusion about its cause. Poem 973 does seem to show the influence of Buddhist *inga* ("cause and effect") doctrine, and *tsune no kotowari* ("changeless law of life") is no doubt, as has been suggested, a rendering of some Chinese phrase. The "planted seed" (*sueshi tane*) at once harks back ironically to the unplanted fields complained of in no. 958, and carries an obvious sexual sense.

Travel and separation are again the themes of poems 974–76. No. 974 has the wit and complexity of paronomasia. Ausaka, the pass between Yamashiro and Ōmi provinces, on Yakamori's probable route to Echizen, puns on *au* ("to meet"), and *wagimoko ni au* means "to meet my sweetheart." The poem complains that famous places do not live up to their names. *Wagimoko ni* is here a pillow-word construction, a mere epithet for *au*; if the syntax is followed literally, the thought is illogical, since Yakamori is traveling away from his love. But illogicality is to be expected in the topsy-turvy world of journeys against one's will over mountains that betray their names. Having played with language in this poem, Yakamori reverts to a serious inquiry into its nature in no. 975, picking up again the word that so troubles him, *tabi* (see no. 955), and again being left where he started. He is behind the mountains and rivers (nos. 967 and 976) but home with Otogami in his heart (nos. 969 and 976). The final two poems of this set accompany some gift or gifts from Yakamori to Otogami. Since they can be hidden (no. 977) and are small enough to sew into a sash (no. 978), they may be gems or pearls. Whatever they are, he hopes that the sight of them will remind her of him. The pillow word *masokagami* ("bright mirror") suggests yet another precious possession of a woman, one that is privileged to look at her when she looks at it.

(966)   [3776/3754]

Kaso nashi ni	Cuckoo, you who fly
Seki tobikoyuru	Over all the barriers
Hototogisu	Without a gate pass,
Maneku ako ni mo	You must go to my sweetheart,
Yamazu kayowamu	Many times, constantly.

(967)   [3777/3755]

Uruwashi to	She I think so fine,
A ga mou imo o	My handsome darling, and I her love,
Yama kawa o	Have in between us
Naka ni henarite	Whole mountain ranges and rivers—
Yasukeku mo nashi	And there is no rest for me.

(968)   [3778 / 3756]

    Mukaiite   I could gaze at her
  Hitohi mo ochizu   Face to face, day after day,
    Mishikado mo   And never weary—
  Itowanu imo o   My beloved girl, from whom
  Tsuki wataru made   I cross the widening months.

(969)   [3779 / 3757]

    A ga mi koso   Although my body
  Sekiyama koete   May have crossed the barrier
    Koko ni arame   Mountains to this place,
  Kokoro wa imo ni   My heart remains behind at home,
  Yorinishi mono o   Close to the girl I love.

(970)   [3780 / 3758]

  Sasu dake no   Do they, I wonder,
  Ōmiyahito wa   Those elegant courtiers,
    Ima mo ka mo   Fresh as new bamboo,
  Hitonaburi nomi   Still find their greatest pleasure
  Konomitaruramu   In toying with women?

(971)   [3781 / 3759]

  Tachikaeri   Over and over
  Nakedo mo are wa   I could turn and weep aloud,
    Shirushi nami   And be no better,
  Omoiwaburete   Wherefore the nights are many
  Nuru yo shi so ōki   When I lie listless with longing.

(972)   [3782 / 3760]

  Sanuru yo wa   Many are the nights
  Ōku aredo mo   When I lay me down to sleep;
    Mono mowazu   There are none, though,
  Yasuku nuru yo wa   When I do not think of things—
  Sane naki mono o   No nights of peaceful slumber.

(973)   [3783 / 3761]

  Yo no naka no   It is the working
  Tsune no kotowari   Of some changeless law of life
    Kaku sama ni   That seems finally
  Narikinikerashi   To have brought me to this pass:
  Sueshi tane kara   All from the seed I planted.

(974)   [3784/3762]

    Wagimoko ni   I wept as I went up
    Ausakayama o   The slope of Lovers' Meeting Mount,
      Koete kite   I wept as I came down;
    Nakitsutsu oredo   There was for all the tears I shed
    Au yoshi mo nashi   No meeting to be found.

(975)   [3785/3763]

      Tabi to ieba   We speak of journeys,
    Koto ni so yasuki   And the word comes easily;
      Sube mo naku   But though a journey
    Kurushiki tabi mo   Is cruel beyond bearing,
    Koto ni masame ya mo Is there a better word for it?

(976)   [3786/3764]

     Yama kawa o   We have between us
    Naka ni henarite   Whole mountain ranges and rivers,
      Tōku to mo   We are far apart;
    Kokoro o chikaku   Yet I want you to believe
    Omōse wagimo   Our hearts are close, my love.

(977)   [3787/3765]

    Masokagami   These my offerings
    Kakete shinue to   Use to keep my image clear
      Matsuridasu   As a bright mirror:
    Katami no mono o   They are for remembrance—
    Hito ni shimesu na   Do not show them to another.

(978)   [3788/3766]

    Uruwashi to   If your heart is pleased
    Omoi shi omowaba   By the beauty of these gifts,
      Shitabimo ni   Carry them with you
    Yuitsukemochite   Sewn into your undersash,
    Yamazu shinowase   And always think of me.

The above thirteen poems are by Nakatomi no Asomi Yakamori.

❋ The next set is eight poems by Otogami (nos. 979–86). A gift of jewels from Yakamori is further hinted in the opening poem, since Otogami says that she has received his soul (*tamashii*). *Tamashii* is a synonym for *tama*, and *tama* means both "jewel" and "soul." She receives this gift "morning and evening" (*ashita yūhe ni*)—or whenever she puts on or takes off the under-sash into which the jewels are sewn? But the gift is not enough to save her from the onrush of longing. The next poem (no. 980) further develops the theme of helplessness. The third (no. 981) seems to refer back to no. 938 and the last night together. Does the self-reproach mean that Otogami did not see Yakamori off when he left for exile at dawn? The balance of this section deals with the idea of Yakamori's return or of being with him in exile. In no. 982 she imagines him on the fields of Ajima (near the modern city of Takefu in Fukui Prefecture). Whether Yakamori really "lodged on the fields" cannot be known, but the image of rusticity is useful as a contrast with the palace in no. 983. The generalization of anxiety about Yakamori to include his sympathizers at court prepares the way for the public event of the exiles' return in no. 984. If the reference in no. 984 is to the amnesty of the sixth month of 740, as is commonly supposed, one must assume from the poem that Otogami did not know her husband had been excluded from it. It is the shock of (false) joy that almost kills her; the keen disappointment is only implied. As she says in the next poem, *yoki koto mo nashi* ("there is nothing good"). It is not clear whether she in fact had the option of accompanying her husband into exile. The gift with which she ends this series is her life. *Inochi nokosamu* ("I shall retain my life") suggests a state of mind in which she has contemplated not doing so, and thus the depth of her shock at not finding Yakamori among the returned exiles.

(979)   [3789 / 3767]

    Tamashii wa   Love, it is your soul
    Ashita yūhe ni   Whose gift is always with me,
      Tamauredo   Morning and evening;
    A ga mune itashi   But my breast is torn with pain
    Koi no shigeki ni   Beneath this rush of longing.

(980)   [3790 / 3768]

    Kono koro wa   I have grown helpless:
    Kimi o omou to   When I think of you these days
      Sube mo naki   All that I can do
    Koi nomi shitsutsu   Is yearn, over and over;
    Ne nomi shi so naku   All I can utter are cries.

(981)   [3791 / 3769]

    Nubatama no   In the blackberry
    Yoru mishi kimi o   Night I saw you one last time,
      Akuru ashita   But I let you go
    Awazuma ni shite   Without meeting you at dawn,
    Ima so kuyashiki   And now I have learned regret.

(982)   [3792 / 3770]

    Ajimano ni   You who lodge afar
  Yadoreru kimi ga   On the fields of Ajima,
    Kaerikomu   My lord, I wonder—
  Toki no mukae o   How long shall I have to wait
  Itsu to ka matamu   To greet the hour of your return?

(983)   [3793 / 3771]

    Miyahito no   Throughout the palace
  Yasui mo nezute   Sweet sleep surely never comes
    Kyō kyō to   To those who wait
  Matsuramu mono o   Day by day for your return,
  Mienu kimi kamo   My lord—for they see no sign.

(984)   [3794 / 3772]

    Kaerikeru   The exiles were back,
  Hito kitareri to   The ones who were to return—
    Iishikaba   They had just arrived:
  Hotohoto shiniki   I almost died on the spot,
  Kimi ka to omoite   Thinking they spoke of you.

(985)   [3795 / 3773]

    Kimi ga muta   Now, too late, I wish
  Yukamashi mono o   I had gone along with you—
    Onaji koto   It is all the same,
  Okurete oredo   Though I stay here left behind,
  Yoki koto mo nashi   Nothing is any good.

(986)   [3796 / 3774]

    Wa ga seko ga   Against that far time
  Kaerikimasamu   When my lover will return,
    Toki no tame   I shall let my life
  Inochi nokosamu   Remain set aside for him:
  Wasuretamau na   My lord, do not forget me!

The above eight poems are by the Maiden.

❊ The exchange proper ends with a pair of two-poem sets. The first is by
Yakamori, and its first poem (no. 987) suggests the passage of many years
but could well be a conventional exaggeration. Similarly phrased expressions of faithfulness are found elsewhere in *Man'yōshū* among the anonymous poems of Books XI (2403 / 2399) and XIV (3501 / 3482). Years are called

"unpolished gems" (*aratama*) because of the word's similarity to *aratamaru* ("to begin again"). Yakamori's second poem (no. 988) sounds like a confession of clandestine love, but this sudden vivid memory could equally well refer to the accustomed rendezvous point where he waited for Otogami to come out of the palace after getting off duty. In any case the poem stands out in its remembered joy from the melancholy tone that dominates the series. In her poem 989 Otogami too misses the daily meetings; this poem is an answer to no. 988. The last poem (no. 990) takes the long view and seems intended as a reply to no. 987, as well as an auspicious and prayerful ending to the entire exchange.

(987)   [3797/3775]

Aratama no	Unpolished gems,
Toshi no o nagaku	The string of years is long
Awazaredo	Since last we met,
Keshiki kokoro o	But of an unfaithful heart
A ga mowanaku ni	There is nothing in my thoughts.

(988)   [3798/3776]

Kyō mo ka mo	Today as ever,
Miyako nariseba	If I were in the capital
Mimaku hori	I would be standing,
Nishi no mimaya no	All eagerness to meet you,
To ni tateramashi	Outside the western stables.

The above two poems are by Nakatomi no Asomi Yakamori.

(989)   [3799/3777]

Kinō kyō	Yesterday, today,
Kimi ni awazute	I did not meet you, my lord—
Suru sube no	I have grown helpless,
Tadoki o shirani	I do not know what to do,
Ne nomi shi so naku	Only to weep aloud.

(990)   [3800/3778]

Shirotae no	My white barken-cloth
Wa ga koromode o	Garment sleeves take in your hands,
Torimochite	Hold them to the god:
Iwae wa ga seko	Purify yourself with prayer,
Tada ni au made ni	My love, till we meet again.

The above two poems are by the Maiden.

✳ The final seven poems (991–97) are an addendum by Yakamori, a set of variations on the theme of the cuckoo as love bird. They are not addressed to Otogami, and there is no indication that they were sent to her, but they belong here as part of this story of love and exile. The series begins with a poem on orange blossoms, a flower associated with the cuckoo, so that in a way the bird is present although not mentioned. Yakamori is thinking of his long-unseen house in the capital, and the poem is cast in the speculative mode. In no. 992 he turns directly to the cuckoo, the passportless free flyer of no. 966, here presented in a more traditional guise. (For other poems with the same opening formula, see nos. 411 and 418 in the "Hitomaro Collection." In these other poems it is a woman, not the cuckoo, who is to be the death of the poet.) From no. 992 on, the haunting cry of the cuckoo is revealed as the source of suffering. In nos. 993 and 995 the fact that the poet is away from home is stressed. The cuckoo that would have sung among his orange blossoms at home has sought him out in the village of his exile (nos. 994–95), reminding him of all he has lost. The bird chooses the times when he is sunk in longing to come with its sad cries (994–96). He expostulates with the bird (no. 996) and then begs it for mercy (no. 997). The sequence is nicely structured and builds to a climax, employing a conventional topos to good effect in a lyrical solo flight that provides an aerial perspective on the entire actual/poetic experience as a work of literary art.

(991) [3801/3779]

> Wa ga yado no   All around my house
> Hanatachibana wa   Blossoms of the flowering orange
> Itazura ni   Must be scattering,
> Chiri ka suguramu   Drifting down till the bloom is gone,
> Miru hito nashi ni   Wasted with no one to see.

(992) [3802/3780]

> Koishinaba   If you die for love,
> Koi mo shine to ya   Die then for love—is such
> Hototogisu   Your wish, O cuckoo,
> Mono mou toki ni   Pouring your tumultuous cries
> Kinakitoyomosu   In this hour of my longing?

(993) [3803/3781]

> Tabi ni shite   Far away from home
> Mono mou toki ni   In this hour of my longing,
> Hototogisu   Cuckoo, do not cry
> Motona na naki so   With that strange, wild urgency,
> A ga koi masaru   Lest my yearning should increase.

(994)   [3804 / 3782]

> Amagomori
> Mono mou toki ni
>   Hototogisu
> Wa ga sumu sato ni
> Kinakitoyomosu

> Kept in by rain—
> In this hour of my longing,
>   Cuckoo, you have come
> To the village where I dwell,
> Pouring the tumult of your cries.

(995)   [3805 / 3783]

> Tabi ni shite
> Imo ni koureba
>   Hototogisu
> Wa ga sumu sato ni
> Ko yo nakiwataru

> Far away from home
> I lie yearning for my love;
>   Then the cuckoo comes
> To the village where I dwell,
> And flies past me crying.

(996)   [3806 / 3784]

> Kokoro naki
> Tori ni so arikeru
>   Hototogisu
> Mono mou toki ni
> Nakubeki mono ka

> What a heartless bird
> You reveal yourself to be!
>   O cuckoo, must you
> Choose this hour of my longing
> To pour forth your mournful cries?

(997)   [3807 / 3785]

> Hototogisu
> Aida shimashi oke
>   Na ga nakeba
> A ga mou kokoro
> Ita mo sube nashi

> Cuckoo, leave some space
> In the tumult of your song:
>   When I hear your cry
> This longing within my heart
> Grows impossible to bear.

The above seven poems were composed by Nakatomi no Asomi Yakamori, expressing his feelings through references to flowers and birds.

Poems After the Pacification of Jinshin

Exchanges and poem groups of multiple composition involving the Ōtomo go back at least as far as these two tanka from Book XIX. They were probably composed in 672 or soon afterward, since they refer to the reestablishment of the capital at Asuka after Emperor Temmu's victory in the Jinshin War of that year. ("Jinshin" is the Sino-Japanese reading of "Mizunoe / Saru" ["Water-Senior / Monkey"], the cyclical designation of the year corresponding to 672.) One is by Ōtomo no Miyuki, an uncle of Tabito, and the other is anonymous. Like other members of the Ōtomo clan, Miyuki fought on Temmu's side in the war; for this he was honored after his death in 701 by a posthumous appointment as Minister of the Right. The footnote is by Yakamochi and implies that he had been unaware of his grand-uncle's poem until 752. The two poems are interesting evidence of the hero image of Emperor Temmu that took form after 672, and that was extended to his consort Jitō and his sons. (For Hitomaro's use of the opening formula, see nos. 297 and 303.) The wilderness that was Asuka after Tenji moved the court to Ōmi in 667 is simply and powerfully evoked by the central image in each poem, and the power to transform wilderness to civilization, to found and erect palaces (as in public poetry generally), is presented as that of a god.

998-99   [MYS XIX : 4284-85 / 4260-61]

Two poems after the pacification of the disturbances of the year Jinshin

(998)   [4284 / 4260]

Ōkimi wa	Our great Sovereign
Kami ni shi maseba	Is a very god indeed:
Akagoma no	Where red-roan stallions
Harabau tai o	Once rubbed their bellies in the paddy fields
Miyako to nashitsu	He has made his capital.

The above poem is by Lord Ōtomo, General and posthumous Minister of the Right [Miyuki].

(999)   [4285 / 4261]

Ōkimi wa	Our great Sovereign
Kami ni shi maseba	Is a very god indeed:
Mizutori no	Where waterfowl
Sudaku minuma o	Once flocked gabbling in the marshes
Miyako to nashitsu	He has made his capital.

Author unknown. I heard the above two poems on Tempyō-Shōhō 4 [752].2.2 and include them verbatim.

Ishikawa no Iratsume and Ōtomo no Tanushi

The reputation of Ōtomo no Miyuki's nephew Tanushi (the son of Yasumaro and younger brother of Tabito) was not as a masurao, but as a *miyabio*, or "man of elegance." In his one surviving poem (no. 1001) he defends himself as such, and the following exchange tells why the defense was necessary. The incident occurred during the reign of Empress Jitō (686–97). Ishikawa no Iratsume (Lady Ishikawa), the other party, may or may not be the same woman whose affair with Prince Ōtsu is recorded in nos. 269 and 872–73. She is no doubt to be distinguished from the mother of Lady

Ōtomo of Sakanoue, who is also referred to as Ishikawa no Iratsume in the footnote to no. 1132. Whoever she was, she had initiative, daring, and wit. The account of her escapade provides a peep at the amorous goings-on of aristocratic society, especially as they concern the Ōtomo. Whoever compiled Book II of *Man'yōshū* must have thought the anecdote too choice to leave out. It has been pointed out, however, that this gem owes something to Chinese sources in its manner of narration. One may assume that to the lady in this story a *miyabio* would be quick rather than "slow" (*oso*)—quick to size up a situation and take appropriate action, especially in a case like this, when a woman comes asking for fire in the middle of the night. Tanushi, who no doubt thought himself sophisticated as well as handsome, does seem to have been slow, but tries to recoup his loss of face by pretending that he was on to the lady's game all along, and simply decided to give her a lesson in true elegance by the practical joke of putting fire in her pot and sending her home. The third poem of the set would seem to grow out of the lady's continued interest in and annoyance with Tanushi. She ribs him on his leg trouble, making jokes about her ears and his legs (*ashi*), both of which are likened to reeds (*ashi*). As a woman of saucy wit she rivals Saeki no Akamaro's correspondent (nos. 889–93).

1000   [MYS II: 126]

A poem sent by Ishikawa no Iratsume to Ōtomo no Sukune Tanushi (i.e., the second son of Lord Ōtomo the Saho Major Counselor; his mother was Kose no Asomi)

Miyabio to	A man of elegance—
Ware wa kikeru o	So I had heard my lord to be;
Yado kasazu	Yet he sent me home
Ware o kaeseri	With no lodging for the night:
Oso no miyabio	A bit slow, this elegant!

Ōtomo no Tanushi was familiarly known as Chūrō ["Second Son"]. His appearance was graceful, his elegance superb; no one who saw or heard him failed to heave a sigh. At the time there was a person called Ishikawa no Iratsume. She conceived a desire to live with him and always felt sad because it was hard for her to sleep alone. She wanted to send him a letter but could find no reliable messenger. And so she thought of the expedient of making herself up to look like an old pauper woman. She took an earthen pot, and carrying it, went to where Tanushi was sleeping. Voice quavering and step tottering, she knocked on his door and said, deceiving him, "I am your neighbor to the east, the poor woman, and I've come to get some fire." In the dark Chūrō failed to recognize her beneath her disguise, and since it was all quite unexpected, did not fall in with her stratagem for love-making. He got fire for her as she had requested and sent her off the way she had come.

When it grew light, the lady was embarrassed at having been so shameless as to be her own go-between and resentful that her cherished desire had not been fulfilled. Thus she composed this poem and sent it in mocking jest.

1001 [MYS II:127]

A poem sent in reply by Ōtomo no Sukune Tanushi

Miyabio ni	A man of elegance—
Ware wa arikeri	Yes indeed, that's what I am!
Yado kasazu	I who sent you home
Kaeshishi ware so	With no lodging for the night
Miyabio ni wa aru	Am just what they mean by an elegant!

1002 [MYS II:128]

Another poem sent by the same Ishikawa no Iratsume to Ōtomo no Tanushi Chūrō

Wa ga kikishi	I pricked up my ears
Mimi ni yoku niru	When I heard—like reed tips swaying
Ashi no ure no	Are the reedy legs
Ashi hiku wagase	You drag, they say: just so—
Tsutometabubeshi	Have a care for your health, my brother!

She sent the above poem as an inquiry on hearing that Chūrō was suffering from leg trouble.

Fujiwara no Maro and Lady Ōtomo of Sakanoue

After Lady Ōtomo of Sakanoue's first husband, Prince Hozumi, died in 715, she was courted by Fujiwara no Maro (695–737), one of the four Fujiwara brothers who died in the epidemic of 737. How long they continued seeing each other, whether the relationship was stable enough to be characterized as marriage, and what came of it beyond a handful of love poems are questions that cannot now be answered. It has been conjectured that the following exchange dates from soon after Prince Hozumi's death, perhaps around 717. At this time Maro was in his early twenties, and the lady perhaps a few years younger. It should be noted, however, that Maro did not hold the office specified in the headnote until 721. Whatever his actual age, Maro complains in no. 1003 of an unwanted venerability (*kamusabi*—"godliness") brought on by neglect. The jo that takes up the first three lines of the poem and blends into the main statement in the fourth line assumes that combs age through use. It is not clear whether the irony was perceived by the author. The next poem (no. 1004) seems to be modeled on an early anonymous envoy, no. 1464. The third poem (no. 1005), Maro's best, opens with two lines almost identical to lines 20–21 of no. 5. *Kojiki* had been presented to court in 712, less than ten years earlier, but the extent to which Nara courtiers were familiar with it would be hard to determine. Perhaps the ancient songs of the amahasezukai ("the seafolk couriers") were still to be heard.

Lady Ōtomo too shows herself an impatient lover. Her first poem (no. 1006) is based closely on another anonymous envoy from Book XIII (no. 1478), simply localizing the scene to Saho River. The same can be said for no. 1007, which is based on yet another anonymous envoy (no. 1452), though with more reshaping. Line 4, the swing line between jo and main statement, has been moved up from its final position in the anonymous poem. The wordplay of no. 1008 represents a phenomenon that goes back at least as far as Emperor Temmu's Yoshino tongue-twister (no. 264) and produces notable examples in the poetry of Izumi Shikibu in the early eleventh century. The laying of a plank bridge in no. 1009 is the same action demanded of the Weaving Maid by the Herdsman in an anonymous tanka, MYS X:2060/2056. But the lover stars can meet only once a year. Despite their complaints, one can assume Lady Ōtomo and her young Fujiwara did better than that. The Saho Major Counselor in the footnote was Ōtomo no Yasumaro, also the father of Tabito, Tanushi, and Sukunamaro. No. 1010 presumably belongs to the affair, if not to the exchange, and is appended here as in the *Man'yōshū* text. It is a sedōka, and its sprightly rhythm and "folk" atmosphere transform the lady and her lover into a country girl and boy who will hide together in the underbrush come spring. The image may be no more fictional than that of Maro splashing across Saho River on a black horse at night. Here as elsewhere the tradition has provided two people with things to say about their love.

1003–5   [MYS IV:525–27/522–24]

Three poems sent to Lady Ōtomo by the Fujiwara Master of the Capital Offices (this nobleman's personal name was Maro)

(1003)   [525/522]

Otomera ga   As a shining comb
Tamakushige naru   In a maiden's box of combs
Tamakushi no   Turns to an antique,
Kamusabikemu mo   So must I have grown hoary,
Imo ni awazu areba   Never meeting my love.

(1004)   [526/523]

Yoku wataru   They say there are
Hito wa toshi ni mo   People who have no trouble
Ari to iu o   Getting through a year,

Itsu no ma ni so mo   But as for me, this yearning came
A ga koinikeru   Quicker than I can tell.

(1005)   [527/524]

     Mushibusuma   Under the softness
Nagoya ga shita ni   Of my warm and flossy quilts
     Fuseredo mo   I lie down to sleep,
Imo to shi neneba   But I do not lie with you, love,
Hada shi samushi mo   And my skin is cold.

1006-9   [MYS IV: 528-31/525-28]

Four poems in reply by Lady Ōtomo

(1006)   [528/525]

     Sahogawa no   Why cannot they be
Koishi fumiwatari   All year long, those nights you come
     Nubatama no   On your blackberry steed,
Kuroma no ku yo wa   Splashing across the pebbles
Toshi ni mo aranu ka   Of Saho River?

(1007)   [529/526]

     Chidori naku   Where the plovers cry
Saho no kawase no   In the shallows of Saho River
     Sazarenami   The rippling waves
Yamu toki mo nashi   Never still for a moment,
A ga kouraku wa   This time of my yearning.

(1008)   [530/527]

     Komu to iu mo   Though you say you'll come,
Konu toki aru o   There are times you do not come;
     Koji to iu o   Now you say you won't come—
Komu to wa mataji   I'll not wait for your coming,
Koji to iu mono o   Not when you say you won't come.

(1009)   [531/528]

     Chidori naku   Where the plovers cry
Saho no kawato no   On the lip of Saho River
     Se o hiromi   The shallows are broad—
Uchihashi watasu   I'll lay a plank bridge for you,
Na ga ku to omoeba   For I'm sure that you will come.

Concerning the above, the Lady was the daughter of his lordship the Saho Major Counselor. She first married Hozumi, a Prince of the First Rank, and was the object of his unparalleled devotion. After the Prince died, Fujiwara no Maro, Master [of the Capital Offices], courted the Lady. The Lady had her home in the village of Sakanoue; hence her kinsmen called her the Lady of Sakanoue.

1010   [MYS IV: 532 / 529]

Another poem by Lady Ōtomo of Sakanoue

Sahogawa no	Don't you cut the brush
Kishi no tsukasa no	Growing on the riverbank
Shiba na kari so ne	High above Saho River;
Aritsutsu mo	Leave it as it is,
Haru shi kitaraba	So when springtime comes around
Tachikakuru gane	We'll have a place to hide.

Tabito's Plum-Blossom Party

The most famous of the poetic activities of Ōtomo no Tabito during his stint as Governor-General of Dazaifu is the plum-blossom party he held in the first month of 730, when he and thirty-one guests from as far away as Satsuma and Tsushima gathered in his garden and engaged in elegant amusements such as admiring the blossoming plum trees and newly verdant willows, breaking off sprigs of each to adorn their brows, drinking wine, and composing tanka. The tanka have been preserved in Book V, along with a Chinese preface. The fête was doubtless intended to be the last word in elegance, but it is merely the best recorded of many that took place in the poetry circles of the capital and wherever cultivated gentlemen congregated, as later in Etchū when Tabito's son Yakamochi was Governor there. The poems composed on these occasions were sometimes kanshi, but the requisite expertise in Chinese versification was of course more limited in distribution than the ability to compose in the native tongue, and waka were the order of the day for Tabito's guests.

The waka produced (given here as nos. 1011–42) show abundant Chinese influence in subject, decorum, and technique, and the idea of a poetic garden party itself was a Chinese importation. Readings in the self-indulgent and mannered verse of the late Six Dynasties were generally formative of the nascent Japanese taste for a Chinese style of literary behavior, supplemented by early T'ang writings of similar nature and a selective appreciation of older works. By "literary behavior" is meant both such a gala as Tabito's and the prose and verse that came out of it. Like all such compositions in *Man'yōshū*, the kambun preface to "Thirty-two Plum Poems" is a pastiche of phrases adopted or adapted from Chinese sources, in this case notably the famous "Preface on the Orchid Pavilion Collection" (*Lan-t'ing-*

chi Hsü) by the great Chinese calligrapher Wang Hsi-chih (A.D. 321–79). In its structure and phraseology it also owes much to prefaces by early T'ang poets such as Wang Po (647–75) and Lo Pin-wang (d. 684). Written in the balanced style favored in the Six Dynasties, employing antithesis in constructions of matching four- or six-character phrases, the preface is itself closer to verse than to prose in the ordinary sense, its insistent and recherché metaphors too being a feature of the poetry produced and admired at southern Chinese courts during the sixth century. The metaphors are sometimes condensed enough to need explanation, as in "powder before a mirror," which likens the white of plum blossoms to a woman with a white-powdered face. "After a sachet" is meant to balance "before a mirror," but in doing so changes the sense of the modification from spatial to temporal. "Old geese" are the winter migrants returning north to nest. The world of the preface, it need hardly be said, is more an imaginary pleasure realm than a description of Tabito's garden. Who wrote the preface is a matter of some dispute. Ascription to Tabito himself runs into trouble in the complimentary term *sochi no okina*, translated "the venerable Governor-General." Some suppose the author to be Yamanoue no Okura, who did more than one daisaku ("substitute composition") and was the best Chinese scholar among the guests.

The thirty-two tanka are arranged more or less in order of their authors' social prominence as determined by court rank. The main exception to this rule is that the host, who with Senior Third has by far the highest rank, allows all his guests of the Fourth and Fifth Ranks to precede him. Guests of Sixth Rank and under follow him in a not completely consistent ordering. The above may represent the actual order of recitation at the party; if decorum prevailed over liquid refreshment, one would expect this to be the case. Tabito had his Dazaifu staff out in force, and in addition eight of the eleven provinces of the Western Sea Circuit were represented by one or more official guests. Each poem is followed by the name, and usually the title, of its author. (For further information on the contributors, where available, consult the backnotes.) The poems are much of a piece—smooth, mildly enthusiastic, and above all decorous expressions of the pleasure of being together in spring, along with an occasional twinge of anxiety that spring may not last forever. The principal images are plum blossoms, green willows, warblers, and wine. The tone is celebratory, shadowless as the diffused light of a spring day.

Spring arrives in the first poem (no. 1011) bringing its plum blossoms, which are urged to stay awhile in no. 1012. In both poems, the blossoms are personified. The willow is introduced in the third poem (no. 1013), a light green to contrast with the white of the plums. Plum blossoms are auspicious for their purity of color and fragrance, and for being the first blossoms to come out in the still-cold spring. Willows stand for friendship and unwillingness to part, because the Chinese words for "willow" and "stay" are homophones. Both are thoroughly Chinese images and never appear in ancient Japanese song. An antique elegance is conveyed by the picture of the gentlemen wearing chaplets of willow catkins. Most of the poems, like no. 1013, are addressed to the fellow revelers.

The fourth poem (no. 1014) is by Yamanoue no Okura and strikes the only note of loneliness. It also suggests, like one or two others, that poems may have been composed in advance and brought to the party. The next poem (no. 1015) incorporates love (i.e., longing, or *koi*), into a plum-blossom verse and is thus also atypical. The desire to be a plum blossom hints at a desire for early death, but this is far too solemn for the occasion, and to be the cynosure of admiring eyes may be the substance of the wish. Or to be pure and free from passion. Outright celebration is reasserted in no. 1016, which reverts to the ancient song form of duplicate second and fifth lines. Hedonism and a touch of carpe diem inform no. 1017, which brings back the willow and introduces drink. The headier atmosphere at decadent southern Chinese courts is hinted here. (It may be remarked that a feminine component in Tabito's revels is notable for its absence—there are no lady guests and no singing or dancing girls, or at least none who appear in the poems or preface.)

Tabito's own poem comes next (no. 1018). It is one of four on the occasion employing some form of comparison between snow and plum blossoms—the most common version of "elegant confusion" as it came to be practiced in Japan. Tabito's question, "or is it snow?," whispers across the ages. The first susurrations of the concert can be heard in kanshi, of which *Kaifūsō* preserves a number, including one by Emperor Mommu and one by Tabito himself. (For a contemporary example in waka, see Akahito's no. 567.) Tabito's statement that the plum blossoms are scattering is contradicted in no. 1019, by his kinsman Momoyo. It is a rare moment in the history of waka when a realist scoffs at a prized literary pretense on one of its first appearances. No blossoms are scattering, but it is actually snowing, as you can see if you look over there at the mountain. Through the falling flakes the careful observer might also have detected an Emperor with no clothes. This is the most surprising poem produced at the party, a bit jarring to the bland decorum but clearly acceptable to the genial host. It also provides evidence of actual give-and-take between poets. The day of the party, it may be noted, corresponded to February 8 by the Western calendar. But in the absence of an actual weather report for the day, we cannot be sure that Momoyo's gibe was not equally fictional.

The next poem (no. 1020) works out a compromise—the petals' scattering is regretted in advance—and introduces the warbler, a traditionally associated bird. The tradition, however, lay almost entirely in the future; warblers, like willows and plum blossoms, were something new to waka, an eighth-century phenomenon infused from Chinese poetry. The uguisu, to be sure, was a native Japanese species, not an exotic like the plum and willow. During the Nara period and forever after it became the bird of early spring in the new literary cult of the four seasons. Here it sings in a bamboo grove. Bamboo certainly appears in ancient song, but as an elegant image associated with singing birds it too is Chinese. Plum and willow are brought together in no. 1021, then separated and compared in no. 1022. In no. 1023 the warbler is in the plum tree, where its location can only be judged by its cries. Another exclamation of delight follows in no. 1024.

The only mention of cherry blossoms recorded at the party is in the next poem (no. 1025). The cherry, eventually to become the prime emblem of Japanese beauty, one rich in overtones of *aware* because of its perishability, is a poor second to the plum in *Man'yōshū*. Man'yō poets adopted Chinese preferences in this regard, along with the whole genre of flower-garden poems. Here the attitude is determinedly bright and cheerful—even when we lose the plum blossoms there will still be something to look forward to. The stability of joy and beauty is stressed in no. 1026—a stance as fully determined by the decorum of the occasion as were the predictions of eternality for imperial abodes in the Yoshino poems. *Aware* has no place in these sunny glades. Personification comes in again with no. 1027, addressed to the plum blossoms and expressing what may be anxiety but is more likely an intoxication with the blossoms' beauty. The limits of joy are implied in no. 1028—this day is a special time. But no. 1029 promptly reasserts the ongoing nature of the celebration and again mentions drinking. The opening lines of no. 1016 are picked up in no. 1030; the fullness of bloom is to be matched by a full-throated chorus of birds. Full satisfaction is expressed in nos. 1031 and 1032, and by now the general fullness begins to be stultifying. The warbler is back in no. 1033, which shows a little more invention than the previous two poems and firmly establishes the link between the tree and the bird. The author of no. 1034 backs up the host in claiming to see scattering blossom, though only in the distance. Elegant confusion follows in no. 1035—here with such effect that the onlooker sees not only snow but mist, so heavy is the drift of bloom.

Attention is redirected to amenities closer at hand in no. 1036, which suggests a rather large wine bowl—one that someone has decorated while the guests were gazing off into the distance. The second line functions doubly, predicating the first and modifying the third. The author of no. 1037 combines the blossoming and scattering into one continuous movement, spurred on by the warbler's song. Here as in a few other instances the scene is the poet's own garden, rather than Tabito's. The next poem (no. 1038) is another example of this. A common "pathetic fallacy" has the warbler "cry" (*naku*, the all-purpose verb for bird and animal sounds and human weeping) in anticipation of the coming loss of the plum blossoms. Though it displaces the emotion onto the bird, this poem plumbs what depths of despair are to be found in the series. Thoughts of Nara (and its poetry parties, no doubt) intrude for the first and only time in no. 1039, though consciousness of being far from home was surely strong in many of these men, not least of all the host. Elegant confusion makes its last appearance in no. 1040, which like no. 1015 is exceptional in introducing a love element. The imaginary scene here is neither Tabito's residence nor the poet's, but that of a woman. The woman on the poet's mind balances the warbler with blossoms on its mind in the somewhat more interesting treatment provided by no. 1041. The warbler is eager to have the blossoms bloom, and the poet to have them last. Each is anxious, and the insistent serenity of the "satisfied" poems is dispelled by an inner dynamic. The final poem, however, reasserts the dominant theme. The day has been a grand success, and since it is a spring day, it is by definition long. Length gives scope for an ever-increasing fondness for the blossoms that appropriately occupy the last line. But fondness too implies clinging, and therefore farewell.

The occasion was à la chinoise, and the poems too, in their imagery, in their deliberately limited tonal and emotional range, and in their view of the world as a garden, are faithful to aspects of their Six Dynasties' predecessors. Mediocre as much of the verse is, it embodies traits important in the development of Japanese nature poetry. The poetry of the Heian period did not draw its inspiration mainly from the majestic mountains and sparkling beaches lauded by Akahito and other Man'yō poets. Refinement and adaptation of the Chinese legacy were to create a kind of nature poetry fundamentally at variance with much that is found in *Man'yōshū*. In a sense the poems produced at Tabito's party are very "pure," which may be only another way of pointing out their limitations. They are straightforwardly descriptive or exclamatory, and the only "device" they employ to any effect is "elegant confusion." Artfully "oblique" viewpoints, "reasoning," and other characteristics of sixth-century Chinese court poetry are absent. These qualities were adapted later to waka, and indeed can be found elsewhere in *Man'yōshū* itself. On the other hand, the poems lack the conceptual and rhetorical complexity of traditional Japanese verse. There is only one pillow word (*hisakata no* in no. 1018) in the whole set, and not a single jo. Personification is present, but metaphor is not. The jo is a feature of verse where a human situation is to be worked toward through, explained in terms of, or otherwise compared with an image, usually from nature. That is why it is prevalent in early love poetry, which is about human situations. When a poem is *only* about nature the need for a jo evaporates. When one is nevertheless used, as in KKS 1:9, by Ki no Tsurayuki, it constitutes an adaptation of an old technique to the new needs of natural description, and is part of an effort to increase the structural density of the tanka form. Nothing of the sort happened at Tabito's party.

It is by no means fortuitous that this particular set has survived out of what must have been many poetic products of garden parties in the Nara period. The role of Yakamochi in compiling *Man'yōshū* made it inevitable that he would draw heavily on Ōtomo sources. He himself wrote far better *waka* in the Chinese mode than any produced by his father's guests in 730 (see especially nos. 828–29 and 843–45). The experiments by Akahito in nos. 565–68 are also more appealing, partially because of their greater variety. The virtue of "Thirty-two Plum Poems" as an artifact of literary history is that it shows what could be done by a patron eager to foster versifying even when he had available only the local talent brought within reach by the accident of appointment to a distant outpost. Most of the participants in Tabito's party are totally obscure as poets, but all acquitted themselves adequately, preserving a unified tone and a sense of participation in what was after all an act of civilization, a gesture toward the fraternity of cultivated men. This sense of being an elite with commonly held tastes and abilities was to receive further refinement as Japanese court culture continued to develop.

1011–42   [MYS V : 819–50 / 815–46]

Thirty-two Plum Poems; with preface

On the thirteenth day of the first month of Tempyō 2 [730] people gathered at the residence of the venerable Governor-General and held a party.

It is now the choice month of early spring; the weather is fine, the wind is soft. The plum blossoms open—powder before a mirror; the orchids exhale—fragrance after a sachet. Furthermore, clouds move across dawn peaks; pines are draped with gauze, holding sunshades over their shoulders; evening summits are caught in mist, and birds wander lost in the grove, closed in by silken veils. In the garden new butterflies dance; in the sky old geese return home.

And so, with heaven as a parasol and earth as a mat, seated knee to knee, the guests send the winecup flying. Words are forgotten in the chamber, collars are turned out to the smoky haze. In lightness comes release, in pleasure contentment.

Were it not for the garden of letters, with what could we express our feelings? In Chinese poetry there are sets on the fallen plum blossoms: how is the past then different from the present? Let us take the plums in the arbor as our topic and spend a while making short compositions.

(1011)   [819/815]

    Mutsuki tachi   When spring has arrived
    Haru no kitaraba   With the rising of the New Year month,

Kaku shi koso   Let us spend the day
Ume o okitsutsu   In such pleasures as bring us now
Tanoshiki oeme   To give welcome to the plum.

(Assistant Governor-General Lord Ki)

(1012)   [820/816]

Ume no hana   Blossoms of the plum,
Ima sakeru goto   Will you not, blooming as now,
Chirisugizu   Without scattering,
Wagae no sono ni   Without passing stay with me
Arikosenu ka mo   In the arbor of my home?

(Junior Assistant Governor-General Officer Ono)

(1013)   [821/817]

Ume no hana   Here in this arbor
Sakitaru sono no   All a-flower with the plum,
Aoyagi wa   See the green willow—
Kazura ni subeku   Has it not grown long enough
Narinikerazu ya   To make chaplets for our brows?

(Junior Assistant Governor-General Officer Awata)

(1014)   [822/818]

Haru sareba   The plum by my door
Mazu saku yado no   That when spring arrives blooms first
Ume no hana   Of all my trees—
Hitori mitsutsu ya   Shall I gaze upon its blossoms
Haruhi kurasamu   Alone, this long spring day?

(Governor of Chikuzen Officer Yamanoue)

(1015)   [823/819]

Yo no naka wa   In the world of men
Koi shigeshi e ya   Longing grows in dense thickets;
Kaku shi araba   If things must be thus
Ume no hana ni mo   I would rather have been born
Naramashi mono o   As a flower of the plum.

(Governor of Bungo Officer Ōtomo)

(1016)   [824/820]

Ume no hana   Blossoms of the plum
Ima sakari nari   Now are out in full flower;

Omou dochi   Boon companions all,
Kazashi ni shite na   Let us deck our brows with bloom—
Ima sakari nari   Now is the full of the flower!

(Governor of Chikugo Officer Fujii)

(1017)   [825/821]

Aoyanagi   After green willow
Ume to no hana o   And the flower of the plum
Orikazashi   Have decked our brows,
Nomite no nochi wa   And the drinking all is done—
Chirinu to mo yoshi   *Then* let the blossoms scatter!

(Kasa no Sami)

(1018)   [826/822]

Wa ga sono ni   In my arbor now
Ume no hana chiru   Petals scatter from the plum—
Hisakata no   Or is it snow
Ame yori yuki no   That floats down drifting over us
Nagarekuru ka mo   From the boundless sky?

(The host)

(1019)   [827/823]

Ume no hana   Petals of the plum—
Chiraku wa izuku   Where is it they are scattering?
Shikasuga ni   One thing is certain—
Kono Kinoyama ni   Yonder on Fortress Mountain
Yuki wa furitsutsu   It is snowing even now.

(Senior Secretary Ōtomo no Momoyo)

(1020)   [828/824]

Ume no hana   Petals of the plum
Chiramaku oshimi   Soon must scatter: in regret
Wa ga sono no   In my arbor now
Take no hayashi ni   In the thicket of bamboo
Uguisu naku mo   Oh, how the warbler cries!

(Junior Secretary Ahe no Okishima?)

(1021)   [829/825]

Ume no hana   Here in this arbor
Sakitaru sono no   All a-flower with the plum,

Aoyagi o	Take we green willow—
Kazura ni shitsutsu	Making chaplets for our brows,
Asobikurasana	Let us spend the day in joy!

(Junior Secretary Hanishi no Momomura?)

(1022)   [830 / 826]

Uchinabiku	Between this willow
Haru no yanagi to	Trailing its springtime branches
Wa ga yado no	And the plum tree
Ume no hana to o	Blossoming before my house
Ika ni ka wakamu	How am I to make a choice?

(Senior Clerk Fubito no Ōhara)

(1023)   [831 / 827]

Haru sareba	Now that spring has come
Konuregakurite	We hear the warbler descending
Uguisu so	Hidden by the twigs,
Nakite inu naru	Singing deep inside the leaves,
Ume ga shizue ni	To the plum tree's lowest branch.

(Junior Clerk Yamaguchi no Wakamaro)

(1024)   [832 / 828]

Hitogoto ni	Every one of us
Orikazashitsutsu	Has plucked a branch to deck his hair
Asobedo mo	In these our revels—
Iyamezurashiki	Ah, but how adorable,
Ume no hana kamo	Ever more, these flowering plums!

(Senior Judge Tajihi [Taniwa?] no Maro)

(1025)   [833 / 829]

Ume no hana	When the time has come
Sakite chirinaba	For the plum to flower and fall,
Sakurabana	Will not cherry blossoms
Tsugite sakubeku	Be the next to burst in bloom,
Nari nite arazu ya	Following close behind them?

(Master of Medicine Chō no Fukushi)

(1026)   [834 / 830]

Yorozuyo ni	Though for a myriad
Toshi wa kifu to mo	Ages the years come and go,

544

Ume no hana ·   Blossoms of the plum
Tayuru koto naku   Are sure to go on flowering,
Sakiwatarubeshi   Never ceasing to bloom.

(Assistant Governor of Chikuzen Saeki no Koobito)

(1027)   [835/831]

Haru nareba   Now that spring is here
Ube mo sakitaru   You who blossom well and true,
Ume no hana   Flower of the plum,
Kimi o omou to   When I think of you at night,
Yoi mo nenaku ni   Alas, I cannot sleep.

(Governor of Iki Itamochi no Yasumaro)

(1028)   [836/832]

Ume no hana   Flowers of the plum—
Orite kazaseru   We who break them for our brows,
Morohito wa   All here assembled,
Kyō no aida wa   Today at least for this brief while
Tanoshiku arubeshi   Must rest secure in joy.

(Head Shintō Priest Kōji no Inashiki)

(1029)   [837/833]

Toshinoha ni   If at the outset
Haru no kitaraba   Of each year the spring comes round,
Kaku shi koso   Let us always then
Ume o kazashite   Deck our brows with plum as now,
Tanoshiku nomame   And drink our wine in joy.

(Senior Legal Secretary Ono no Sukunamaro)

(1030)   [838/834]

Ume no hana   Blossoms of the plum
Ima sakari nari   Now are out in full flower:
Momotori no   Spring has come for sure,
Koe no kōshiki   When we yearn for the voices
Haru kitaru rashi   Of the hundred singing birds.

(Junior Legal Secretary Denji no Komahito)

(1031)   [839/835]

Haru saraba   When spring should come
Awamu to moishi   I would be eager to meet them—

Ume no hana | Blossoms of the plum:
Kyō no asobi ni | And now today's festivity
Aimitsuru kamo | Brings us together at last.

(Master of Medicine Kōji no Yoshimichi)

(1032)   [840/836]

Ume no hana | Today is a day
Taorikazashite | We can break off sprigs of plum
Asobedo mo | To deck our hair
Akidaranu hi wa | And never know discontent
Kyō ni shi arikeri | However long our frolic.

(Master of Divination Isobe no Norimaro?)

(1033)   [841/837]

Haru no no ni | The warbler singing
Naku ya uguisu | In the unplowed springtime fields—
Natsukemu to | That it be content
Wa ga he no sono ni | To live close at hand the plum
Ume ga hana saku | Blooms in my arbor now.

(Master of Computation Shiki no Ōmichi)

(1034)   [842/838]

Ume no hana | Where the plum blossoms
Chirimagaitaru | Scatter in their mazy swirls
Okabi ni wa | On yonder hillside
Uguisu naku mo | A warbler is out singing,
Haru katamakete | Spring being now at the ready.

(Clerk of Ōsumi Kaji no Hachimaro)

(1035)   [843/839]

Haru no no ni | Over spring fields
Kiri tachiwatari | Mist rises, spreads across the ground,
Furu yuki to | And snow sifts down—
Hito no miru made | Or so we see it as we watch
Ume no hana saku | Plum blossoms scattering.

(Clerk of Chikuzen Tanabe no Makami)

(1036)   [844/840]

Haru yanagi | Spring willow broken
Kazura ni orishi | For twining into a chaplet,

Ume no hana   Flowers of the plum—
Tare ka ukabeshi   Who has set these things afloat
Sakazuki no he ni   In our brimming bowl of wine?

(Clerk of Iki Murakuni no Ochikata?)

(1037)   [845/841]

Uguisu no   Now that I've heard it,
Oto kiku nahe ni   The sound of the warbler singing,
Ume no hana   Petals of the plum
Wagie no sono ni   In my arbor blossom forth
Sakite chiru miyu   And scatter before my gaze.

(Clerk of Tsushima Takamuko no Oyu?)

(1038)   [846/842]

Wa ga yado no   On the lowest branch
Ume no shizue ni   Of the plum tree at my house,
Asobitsutsu   Flitting to and fro,
Uguisu naku mo   How the warbler cries these days,
Chiramaku oshimi   Regretful of the scattering to come!

(Clerk of Satsuma Kōji no Ama)

(1039)   [847/843]

Ume no hana   When I see the sight
Orikazashitsutsu   Of all this company of men
Morohito no   Taking their pleasure,
Asobu o mireba   Plucking plum blossom for their brows,
Miyako shi zo mou   I think of the royal city.

(Hanishi no Mimichi)

(1040)   [848/844]

Imo ga ie ni   It must be snowing
Yuki ka mo furu to   At the dwelling of my love—
Miru made ni   So almost I think,
Kokoda mo magau   When I see the wild swirling
Ume no hana kamo   Of these blossoms of the plum!

(Ono no Kunikata)

(1041)   [849/845]

Uguisu no   Blossoms of the plum
Machikateni seshi   That the warbler could not wait

Ume ga hana   To have in bloom—
Chirazu ari koso   Let them remain unscattered
Omou ko ga tame   For the young girl I love.

(Secretary of Chikuzen Kadobe no Muraji Isotari)

(1042)   [850/846]

Kasumi tatsu   Through the long spring day,
Nagaki haruhi o   Hazy with its rising mist,
Kazaseredo   We keep our brows
Iyanatsukashiki   Decked with blossoms of the plum,
Ume no hana kamo   But only grow the fonder.

(Ono no Tamori)

✳ The six tanka following the poetic harvest of Tabito's plum-blossom party constitute attachments and are meant to be read with it. The first two (nos. 1043–44) are labeled "supernumerary" (*ingai*); their theme is not the blossoms, but the desire to return to youth and to the capital. Though the author is not given, the Taoist references and the yearning for Nara found both here and elsewhere in Tabito's poetry suggest they are his work. If like a Taoist adept he could fly on a cloud, it would be no matter to reach Nara, but the cloud-flying potion itself would not cure his old age (Tabito was then sixty-four or sixty-five years old); only seeing Miyako, the royal city, could do that. The reference to elixirs and flying indicates familiarity with the Taoist work *Pao-p'u-tzu* (A.D. 317) and the relevant portions of the T'ang encyclopedia *I-wen Lei-chü*.

1043–44   [MYS V:851–52/847–48]

Two supernumerary poems on longing for home

(1043)   [851/847]

Wa ga sakari   My prime has fallen
Itaku kutachinu   Sorely to decay at last:
Kumo ni tobu   Even if I drink
Kusuri hamu to mo   Quintessence of Cloud-Flying
Mata ochime ya mo   Will youth come back again?

(1044)   [852/848]

Kumo ni tobu   It is not drinking
Kusuri hamu yo wa   Quintessence of Cloud-Flying,
Miyako miba   But seeing Miyako

Iyashiki a ga mi   That will cure this villainous old age
Mata ochinubeshi   And give me my youth again.

❋ A further four tanka (nos. 1045–48) follow, "added later in harmony" (*tsuiwa suru*) in accordance with Chinese practice. Again the author is probably Tabito. The treatment of the blossom-snow motif in the first poem does not constitute "elegant confusion" in the full sense, since the two elements are kept distinct in order to set up a conceit in which the blossoms are urged not to take the place of the melting snow. In the second poem *iro o ubaite* ("stealing their color") is based directly on a Chinese expression. The desire for someone with whom to share the beauty here and in the next poem is consonant with the Chinese poetic ethos of friendship. The most interesting of the set is the last, in which the blossoms appear to the poet in a dream and ask to be floated in wine. A fantasy in which a koto speaks in a dream is elaborated in a poetic exchange between Tabito and Fujiwara no Fusasaki (682–737) immediately preceding the plum-blossom poems in Book v. It has been suggested that such fantasies owe something to readings in *Yu-hsien-k'u.*

1045–48   [MYS V : 853–56 / 849–52]
Four poems added later in harmony with the plum poems

(1045)   [853 / 849]
    Nokoritaru   Blossoms of the plum
  Yuki ni majireru   Mingling with the lingering snow,
    Ume no hana   Pray do not hasten
  Hayaku na chiri so   To go scattering to the ground
  Yuki wa kenu to mo   Though the snow should melt away.

(1046)   [854 / 850]
    Yuki no iro o   Stealing their color
  Ubaite sakeru   From the snow, these flowering
    Ume no hana   Blossoms of the plum
  Ima sakari nari   Now are at the height of bloom—
  Mimu hito mogamo   Oh, for someone to see them!

(1047)   [855 / 851]
    Wa ga yado ni   Here around my house
  Sakari ni sakeru   Flowering at the height of bloom,
    Ume no hana   Blossoms of the plum

Chirubeku narinu	Have reached the brink of scattering—
Mimu hito mogamo	Oh, for someone to see them!

(1048) [856/852]

Ume no hana	Blossoms of the plum
Ime ni kataraku	Spoke to me within a dream:
Miyabitaru	"Elegant flowers
Hana to are mou	Do we think ourselves to be—
Sake ni ukabe koso	You should float us in the wine!"

An Excursion to Matsura River

The plum-blossom sequence in Book V is followed by another experiment in combining a Chinese prose preface with Japanese poetry. This experiment (nos. 1049–59) is fictional in nature, taking the form of a little poem-tale inspired in part by two Chinese works, *Yu-hsien-k'u* and *Lo-shen Fu* (*Rhyme-Prose on the Goddess of the Lo*); the latter is by Ts'ao Chih (A.D. 192–232). Both of these works tell of meetings between a mortal man and mysterious or supernatural females, with an exchange of amorous badinage in verse. Ts'ao Chih's fu suggests the riverside setting, but the T'ang novelette is the more heavily drawn upon for phraseology in the preface. Specific phrases are also taken from the *Analects* and a variety of other works. Despite these Chinese borrowings, the specific locale and the fishing motif come out of Japanese legend. According to *Nihonshoki*, Empress Jingū paused at Tamashima to catch fish in the Matsura River on her way to conquer Korea; according to *Kojiki* she did so after her triumphant return. Both accounts say she drew a thread from her clothing, stood on a rock in the river, and angled for trout. Thereafter it was the custom of the local young women to fish in the river in the fourth month. The author of the preface, who may have been either Tabito or Okura, was no doubt drawn to the idea of superimposing a Chinese vision of fantastic encounters and amorous adventure on a setting already beautified by local legend and folkways. Thus the references to the "banks of the Lo" and "gorges of Wu," taken from Chinese fu, are allowed to float free over the geographical specifics of northern Kyūshū. The linguistic medium of the preface and its author's attempt to emulate his sources inevitably spin a dream world in which the maidens are indeed Chinese goddesses. This world dissolves in the poems, and the maidens become Japanese fishing girls on the Matsura River, but equally mysterious, the products of an imagination trying to create nymphs out of peasant lasses of the sort glimpsed by Yakamochi in no. 812. There is a double image here too, the frequently romanticized ama girls being obliged to enact the role of "highborn" (*umahito*) ladies discovered in rustic surroundings, a topos popularized in Japan by *Yu-hsien-k'u*, and formative of basic situations in amatory fiction throughout the Heian period.

The eleven tanka in the set are grouped into two exchanges and an appended comment in a different voice. The man addresses the maidens in the first poem (no. 1049), and the maidens reply in the second. Referring back to their claim in the preface that they are "daughters of fishermen," he says he has seen through to their real nature as *umahito* or well-born. They in turn admit something about themselves, that they lied when they said they had "neither village nor home." The exchange thus repeats in the language of waka the complimentary approach, "Are you perhaps immortals?," the denial, and the telling "all about ourselves" found in the kambun of the preface.

The next six poems (nos. 1051–56) are a dialogue based on the amorous intent of "What is there for us now but to grow old together with you?" and "As you wish, I am yours to command," but with the order reversed, giving to the man, here called "the wanderer," the right of male initiative sanctified in Japan's primal nuptial myth. The three poems of the wanderer form a progression from a focus on the immediate scene (no. 1051), to a hint that he would like to learn the girls' address (no. 1052), to a declaration of what he intends to do when he reaches it (no. 1053). They are closely integrated through the image of the girls standing in the river, occupying the middle line of each. The rhythm is rapid, the auditory and visual quality bright and lively, appropriate to the rushing water and quickening emotion. The erotic image of the wet skirts in no. 1051 leads on to the vision of intimacy in no. 1053. *Tōtsuhito* ("one far off") is a mock epithet for Matsura through *matsu* ("to wait"), conveying the idea of the young woman waiting in her home. The next three poems (nos. 1054–56) are the replies of the maidens, who now seem to be three in number. Each addresses a different poem of the wanderer. The first, by the girl with wet skirts, uses the image of waves (*nami*) to reply to no. 1051 and doubles its repetitions, retaining that of "river" (*gawa/kawa* or *kawa/kawa*), and introducing a play on *nami* ("waves") and *nami* ("ordinary"), the second *nami* being the juncture point at the end of the *jo* that occupies the first three lines. The second reply refers back to no. 1052 with its reference to the girls' home; its darting fish are metaphors for the emotion of the speaker. And in the third reply the desired waiting is promised in emphatic terms through the use of negative analogy.

All these poems and the set as an entity are clearly on a higher level of competence than the products of Tabito's plum-blossom party. Their authorship is in dispute, only the final three (nos. 1057–59) being attributed directly to Tabito. These are cast in the speculative mode by a speaker who regrets not having been on hand to see what "the wanderer" saw. Each relates, however, to the previous sets of three by referring to wet skirts (no. 1057), expressing a desire to travel to where the girls are (no. 1058), and expressing envy (no. 1059). If the entire set is not by one hand, then it is an example of skillful "harmonizing." Since the whole composition is a fiction in any case, there is no reason of a purely literary nature why one author (e.g., Tabito) could not have introduced a second male persona in the last three poems, a stay-at-home old fellow who envies the wanderer his adventures. However, the term of respect translated "venerable" can, as in the headnote to the plum-blossom preface, be argued to indicate that at least the bit of prose in which it appears is by another hand; a hand that may have drafted the entire composition. Okura is again the most likely candidate. An orthographic usage in no. 1050 has been adduced as evidence of his composition—or recording—of at least that poem. One hypothesis attempts to divide the set in three: preface and first two poems by Okura, middle six poems by one or more of Tabito's officials, and final three poems by Tabito himself. This elaborate scheme, however, ignores the evidence of careful artistic integration of the whole composition.

Preface on an Excursion to Matsura River

> Once I happened to go to Matsura District. During my aimless rambling I chanced to pass by the banks of Tamashima Pool, and as I was sauntering along gazing at the water, I came upon some maidens angling for fish. Their flowerlike faces were beyond compare, their shining forms unparagoned. Willow leaves opened in their brows; peach blossoms bloomed upon their cheeks. In lively spirit they soared above the clouds; in elegance they surpassed the world. I asked them, "From what village, from what families do you come? Are you perhaps immortals?" The maidens all smiled and replied, "We girls are daughters of fishermen; we are lowly dwellers in grass huts and have neither village nor home. How can we presume to tell you our names? We are merely those whose nature it is to take pleasure in the water, and whose hearts delight in the mountains. At times we sit on the banks of the Lo in useless envy of the gemlike fish; at others we lie in the gorges of Wu and gaze emptily at the smoky haze. Now that we have chanced to meet a noble traveler, we have been unable to control our feelings and have told all about ourselves. What is there for us now but to grow old together with you?" The lowly official replied, "As you wish, I am yours to command." By this time the sun was going down west of the mountains, and my sable steed was restless to depart. Finally I spoke forth the burden of my heart; thus I presented a poem of my composition:

1049   [MYS V: 857/853]

    Asari suru   Fisher girls, they say,
    Ama no kodomo to   Daughters of the river folk—
    Hito wa iedo   But with one glance

| Miru ni shiraenu | I know them for what they are: |
| Umahito no ko to | Children of a highborn clan. |

1050 [MYS V:858/854]

Their reply poem said:

Tamashima no	Though we have a home
Kono kawakami ni	Upstream from here along this river
Ie wa aredo	Of Tamashima,
Kimi o yasashimi	From bashfulness before our lord
Arawasazu ariki	We did not let him know of it.

1051–53 [MYS V:859–61/855–57]

Three more poems by the wanderer

(1051) [859/855]

Matsuragawa	Where Matsura River
Kawa no se hikari	River shallows flash in the sun,
Ayu tsuru to	Angling for trout
Tataseru imo ga	The darling girl stands in the stream,
Mo no suso nurenu	Her skirts all wet along the hem.

(1052) [860/856]

Matsura naru	Here in Matsura
Tamashimagawa ni	Along Tamashima River
Ayu tsuru to	Angling for trout
Tataseru kora ga	The young girls stand; alas,
Ieji shirazu mo	I know not where to find their home.

(1053) [861/857]

Tōtsuhito	Waiting as for one
Matsura no kawa ni	Far off, this Matsura River:
Wakayu tsuru	Angling for young trout,
Imo ga tamoto o	The darling girl upon whose arm
Ware koso makame	I would be the one to pillow.

1054–56 [MYS V:862–64/858–60]

Three further poems in reply by the maidens

(1054) [862/858]

| Wakayu tsuru | If you are to me |
| Matsura no kawa no | A wave among the river waves |

Kawanami no	Of Matsura River
Nami ni shi mowaba	Where we angle for young trout,
Ware koime ya mo	Why should I so yearn for you?

(1055) [863/859]

Haru sareba	When spring arrives
Wagie no sato no	The little fish go darting
Kawato ni wa	In the river ford
Ayuko sabashiru	Beside the village where we live
Kimi machigate ni	All eager for our lord to come.

(1056) [864/860]

Matsuragawa	On Matsura River
Nanase no yodo wa	Below the seven shallows are still pools:
Yodomu to mo	Let them be still!
Ware wa yodomazu	I shall not still this eager heart,
Kimi o shi matamu	But wait the coming of my lord.

1057–59 [MYS V:865–67/861–63]

Three poems added in reply by a later person (the venerable Governor-General)

(1057) [865/861]

Matsuragawa	In Matsura River
Kawa no se hayami	The river shallows are so swift,
Kurenai no	Do those girls now stand,
Mo no suso nurete	Angling for trout, their scarlet skirts
Ayu ka tsururamu	All wet along the hem?

(1058) [866/862]

Hito mina no	The others all have seen
Miramu Matsura no	Tamashima in Matsura—
Tamashima o	Must I alone
Mizute ya ware wa	Forgo the sight, stay where I am,
Koitsutsu oramu	Merely yearning for the place?

(1059) [867/863]

Matsuragawa	How envious I am
Tamashima no ura ni	Of those who see the darling girls
Wakayu tsuru	Angling for young trout
Imora o miramu	Where the Matsura River
Hito no tomoshisa	Winds past Tamashima!

A Letter and Poetic Response from Yoshida no Yoroshi

Further evidence of the poetic activity of the Ōtomo and their circle is provided in a letter and four poems written by Yoshida no Yoroshi on the tenth day of the seventh month of 730. The addressee of the letter is not stated but is commonly assumed to be Ōtomo no Tabito. The letter and poems (nos. 1060–63) immediately follow the "Thirty-two Plum Poems" and "Excursion to Matsura River" in Book v and are a response to them. It seems clear that Tabito sent these two poetic sequences to Yoroshi in the capital along with a letter dated the sixth of the fourth month, probably immediately after the composition of the "Excursion" preface and poems. Why Tabito wished to share these compositions with Yoroshi, who appears from his own letter to have been an admirer and probably a political client, is anybody's guess. Were they for Yoroshi's private delectation, or was he perhaps expected to circulate them among the dilettanti of the capital? Yoshida no Yoroshi, like Yamanoue no Okura, was of Paekche origins, and like Okura's father, he was a specialist in medicine and hence a learned man. He is thought to have been about sixty years old in 730. His early career was as a Buddhist monk, but he returned to lay life in 700 on imperial command with the aim of fostering the medical art. Late in his career he served as head of the Bureau of Books and Drawings (*zushoryō*) and the Bureau of Medicine (*ten'yakuryō*). He has two Chinese poems in *Kaifūsō*, which lists his years as seventy.

Yoroshi's letter is another flowery example of the four-six balanced style of Six Dynasties Chinese prose. A self-indulgent excursion into the realm of allusion, and at the same time an exercise in the declensions of obsequiousness, it (like the other kambun letters, prefaces, and compositions in *Man'yōshū*) sets forth for inspection an array of the intellectual furnishings of the newly learned Nara mind. More surface dazzle than depth, the style nevertheless conveys a rococo exuberance that is not without its appeal. T'ai Ch'u is a character in an anecdote from the fifth-century Chinese collection *Shih-shuo Hsin-yü* who was said to beam so brightly that it was as if the sun and moon shone in his breast. Similarly, Yüeh Kuang, whose biography appears in the official history of the Chin Dynasty (A.D. 265–420), was described as having a personality cloudless as a clear sky. The "border fortress" is a reference to Dazaifu. How the perfected man and the princely man should behave is recommended in the Taoist classic *Chuang-tzu* and the ancient divinatory text *I Ching*, respectively. Pheasants came without fear to Lu Kung, a benevolent district magistrate of Later Han (A.D. 25–220). K'ung Yü bought a captive turtle and released it in the Chin Dynasty, and was later rewarded for his virtue. Chang and Chao are Chang Ch'ang and Chao Kuang-han, able officials under the Former Han (206 B.C.–A.D. 8). Sung and Ch'iao refer to Ch'ih Sung Tzu and Wang Tzu Ch'iao, legendary Taoist immortals of antiquity. By mentioning the "Sayings on the Apricot

Altar," Yoroshi likens Tabito and his guests to Confucius and his disciples. A discussion on a hill called the "Apricot Altar" is mentioned in *Chuang-tzu*, and similar gatherings for talk are recorded in the *Analects*. "Unhitching the Carriage at Spikenard Marshes" connects the Matsura River sequence to the "Rhyme-Prose on the Goddess of the Lo" by Ts'ao Chih, where the speaker of the fu stops his horses to view the Lo River at a place called Spikenard Marshes. The "node" (*sechi*) of early fall is the point midway between the summer solstice and the autumnal equinox, August 8 by the Gregorian calendar, but corresponding roughly to the Tanabata festival on the seventh of the seventh month in the old Japanese lunar calendar. The celebration of Tanabata at the Nara court included wrestling (*sumai*) exhibitions, and recruitment officers (*kotoritsukai*) were sent to the provinces to find talent for the matches. Now that Tanabata is over, Yoroshi entrusts his letter to the officer taking his charges back to Tsukushi.

Two of Yoroshi's four tanka are "harmonizations" with the two sequences he has received from Tabito. The first (no. 1060) seems to refer particularly to no. 1015, with which it shares two lines. In Yoroshi's poem the yearning (*koi*) is directed toward Tabito and occasioned by regret at not having been at the party. Similarly, in using the pillow-word construction *kimi o matsu* ("waiting for their lord") as the first line of no. 1061, he is echoing *tōtsuhito* ("one far off") in no. 1053, both being mock epithets for the meaning "wait" (*matsu*) in "Matsura." The question in no. 1061 rephrases the question in the preface, "Are you perhaps immortals," but at the same time recognizes the maidens' double identity as ama girls. Yoroshi's last two poems (nos. 1062–63) are addressed to Tabito himself and the desire he expresses in nos. 1043–44 to return to Nara. No. 1063 refers to Tabito's family estate at Saho, whose landscape garden (*shima*; "island") has taken on a primeval look during its owner's absence.

Yoroshi respectfully states:

> With obeisance I have received your letter of the sixth of the fourth month. Falling to my knees, I opened the sealed case; reverently I read your fragrant screed. My spirit opened into serene light as if embracing T'ai Ch'u's moon; my savage mood was banished as though I were unfurling Yüeh Kuang's sky. But when I see that, traveling to a border fortress, you afflict your heart with memories of the past; and that, the arrows of the years never stopping, you shed tears as you recollect your youth—all I can say is, the perfected man is content to go with the way of things, and the princely man does not agonize.
>
> Suppliant, I beg that in the morning you extend the transforming favor of your care to the pheasant; that in the evening you preserve the way of the released tortoise; that you emblazon Chang and Chao for a hundred ages; and that you follow Sung and Ch'iao to a thousand years of age.

With this, I receive intelligence of a fragrant spread in the plum arbor where assembled luminaries spin out their strands of verse; of badinage with immortal damsels by the jade pool of Matsura: these are like the "Sayings on the Apricot Altar"; I almost think they are "Unhitching the Carriage at Spikenard Marshes." Deeply absorbed in reading, I chant aloud; grateful as to a kinsman, I revel in delight.

The sincerity with which Yoroshi yearns for his master exceeds that of a dog or horse; the spirit with which he looks up to his virtue is the same as that of a sunflower for the sun. But the jade-green sea splits the land, and the white clouds separate the heavens. In vain I load on the weight of longing. How can I comfort my weary heartstrings?

Early fall arrives at the node; may the myriad blessings renew themselves this day, I pray. Now I humbly entrust this scrap of paper to the wrestlers' recruitment officer.

Yoroshi humbly states: nothing further.

1060   [MYS V: 868/864]

A composition presented to harmonize with the plum-blossom poems of the various poets

Okureite	Rather than this—
Nagakoi sezu wa	This long yearning when too late—
Misonofu no	Rather had I been
Ume no hana ni mo	A blossom on a plum tree there
Naramashi mono o	In the arbor of my lord.

1061   [MYS V: 869/865]

A composition harmonizing with the poems on the lady immortals of Matsura

Kimi o matsu	*Waiting for their lord,*
Matsura no ura no	Maidens of the river cove
Otomera wa	Of Matsura River—
Tokoyo no kuni no	Maidens of the fisherfolk
Amaotome ka mo	Of the Land of Everworld?

1062–63   [MYS V: 870–71/866–67]

Two further poems indited out of a yet-unexhausted longing for his lord

(1062)   [870/866]

Haroharo ni	Far and far away
Omōyuru kamo	Off beyond a thousand clouds
Shirakumo no	Do my longings fly,
Chie ni hedatsuru	Brooding over a land cut off—
Tsukushi no kuni wa	The land of Tsukushi.

(1063)   [871 / 867]

Kimi ga yuki	My lord's journey
Kenagaku narinu	Has lengthened into many days,
Naraji naru	And the island groves
Shima no kodachi mo	Of his retreat on Nara Road
Kamusabinikeri	Are godly with hoary age.

Tempyō 2 [730], seventh month, tenth day

Ōtomo no Yotsuna and Ōtomo no Tabito

As Tabito's subordinate, Ōtomo no Yotsuna might have been expected to be among the guests at the garden party, but for whatever reason, his name does not appear. (His farewell poem to Tabito on the latter's departure from Dazaifu in early 731 appears as no. 605.) In the following undated exchange (nos. 1064–70), he and Tabito compare notes on their homesickness. This exchange immediately follows the celebration of Nara by Ono no Oyu, who was also on Tabito's staff (no. 660). Oyu proclaimed Nara "now at its height of bloom" (*ima sakari nari*). In poem 1065 Yotsuna describes the "waves of wisteria" (*fujinami*) in the same terms and associates them with a remembered image of Nara. Tabito takes the term *sakari* and applies it to himself (no. 1066), where he finds no flowering. His five tanka are plaintive, pessimistic, and full of nostalgia. These sentiments may be regarded as conventional, but in fact Tabito did fall seriously ill in the summer of 730, and died in the year after his return to the capital. In the light of these facts his poems take on a special poignancy. The formal decorum of the plum-blossom party and the artifice of the Matsura River sequence are laid aside, and the poet here lets us come close to him and his real feelings.

Kisa in no. 1067 is a small stream flowing into the Yoshino River; for another poem giving Tabito's feelings for Yoshino, see no. 591. *Asajihara* ("plain of shallow reeds") in no. 1068 serves as a pillow word for *tsubara tsubara* ("thoroughly, through and through") because of the -*jihara*/*tsubara* (Old Japanese *difara*/*tubara*) sound resemblance, but at the same time raises the image of a desolate plain. This poem is thought to refer not to Nara, but to the older capital at Asuka where Tabito had lived the first half of his life. The reference to Kagu Mountain in no. 1069 shows that Tabito is still thinking of Asuka. The inefficacy of his method of effacing memory was later denounced by his son Yakamochi (see no. 778). The final poem in the set (no. 1070) is again about Yoshino. "The Bend of Dreams" (*ime no wada*) was a pool in the Yoshino River near the pleasure palace at Miyataki. The name seems to be used in a meaningful sense here; Yoshida no Yoroshi also mentions it in a kanshi in *Kaifūsō* (KFS 80).

1064–65   [MYS III: 332–33 / 329–30]

Two poems by Assistant of the Bureau of Coastal Guards Ōtomo no Yotsuna

(1064)   [332 / 329]

Yasumishishi	He who rules in peace,
Wa ga ōkimi no	Our great lord, has many lands
Shikimaseru	Subject to his will,
Kuni no uchi ni wa	But of all his provinces
Miyako shi omōyu	I long most for Miyako.

(1065)   [333 / 330]

Fujinami no	Waves of wisteria,
Hana wa sakari ni	Now at the height of their bloom,
Narinikeri	Flower across the land;
Nara no miyako o	Do you long for it, my lord,
Omōsu ya kimi	The capital at Nara?

1066–70   [MYS III: 334–38 / 331–35]

Five poems by Governor-General Lord Ōtomo

(1066)   [334 / 331]

Wa ga sakari	My own blossoming
Mata ochime ya mo	Youth—can it come back to me?
Hotohoto ni	Unless I am wrong,
Nara no miyako o	The chances are I shall not see
Mizu ka narinamu	The Nara capital again.

(1067)   [335 / 332]

Wa ga inochi mo	Is there no life in me
Tsune ni aranu ka	Such as would last forever—
Mukashi mishi	So that I could go
Kisa no ogawa o	And see the brook of Kisa
Yukite mimu tame	As I saw it long ago?

(1068)   [336 / 333]

Asajihara	Plain of shallow reeds:
Tsubara tsubara ni	End to end they choke my heart,
Mono omoeba	These dark thoughts of home—
Furinishi sato shi	How the memories come back
Omōyuru kamo	Of the place where once we lived!

(1069)   [337/334]

    Wasuregusa   That I may forget
  Wa ga himo ni tsuku   The old home where once I lived
    Kaguyama no   By Kagu Mountain,
  Furinishi sato o   In my undersash I tuck
  Wasuremu ga tame   Grasses of forgetfulness.

(1070)   [338/335]

    Wa ga yuki wa   My tour of duty
  Hisa ni wa araji   Will not last much longer now:
    Ime no wada   May the Bend of Dreams
  Se ni wa narazute   Not have become a shallows,
  Fuchi ni ari koso   But remain the pool I knew.

Seeing Off the Post Riders

The compiler's note appended to the second of the following two poems explains in detail the circumstances of their composition. On Ōtomo no Inagimi, see his exchange with Yakamochi, nos. 1081–82. Tabito's nephew Komaro has left no poems in *Man'yōshū*. As Vice-Ambassador on the official embassy to China of 752, he argued successfully for improvement in the diplomatic courtesies accorded to Japan. He was put to death in 757 for his part in the rebellion of Tachibana no Naramaro. Several of Ōtomo no Momoyo's poems have been given, including his response to Tabito's "elegant confusion" at the plum-blossom party (no. 1019). Yamaguchi no Wakamaro also composed a poem at the party (no. 1023). He is otherwise totally obscure, but his name and poem suggest he came from either Suwa (later Suō) or Nagato Province. Yamaguchi and Iwakuni are still principal cities in modern Yamaguchi Prefecture. The last line of Wakamaro's poem is identical to that of Koshima's farewell to Tabito (no. 607). On fearsome mountain gods, see no. 942. The mention of Yakamochi here is the earliest in *Man'yōshū*. He would have been about twelve years old, and no poem is credited to him on the occasion.

1071–72   [MYS IV: 569–70/ 566–67]

Two poems given to the post riders by Senior Secretary of Dazaifu Ōtomo no Momoyo and another person

(1071)   [569/566]

    Kusamakura   Grass for your pillow,
  Tabi yuku kimi o   You have started your journey:
    Uruwashimi   Such splendid fellows,

Taguite so koshi   We have tagged along with you
Shika no hamahe o   As far as the sands of Shika.

The above poem is by Senior Secretary Ōtomo no Sukune Momoyo.

(1072)   [570/567]

     Suwa ni aru   On the day you cross
Iwakuniyama o   The mountain at Iwakuni
    Koemu hi wa   In Suwa Province,
Tamuke yoku seyo   Make full offerings to the god:
Arashi sono michi   It is wild, that stretch of road.

The above poem is by Junior Clerk Yamaguchi no Imiki Wakamaro.

Previously, in the sixth month, summer, of Tempyō 2 [730], Metal-Senior/Horse, Governor-General Lord Ōtomo suddenly developed a tumor on his leg and lay sick in bed. Thereupon he dispatched a [messenger by] post horse to submit a report, stating that he desired to impart his last injunctions to his half brother Inagimi and his nephew Komaro. An imperial command was issued to Assistant of the Right Armory Ōtomo no Sukune Inagimi and Junior Secretary of the Ministry of Civil Administration Ōtomo no Sukune Komaro. They were provided with post horses and sent off with instructions to care for Lord [Ōtomo] during his illness. As it happened, after several weeks he was fortunately able to make a complete recovery. Thus since the illness was cured, Inagimi and Komaro left Dazaifu for the capital. Senior Secretary Ōtomo no Sukune Momoyo, Junior Clerk Yamaguchi no Imiki Wakamaro, and the Lord's son Yakamochi escorted the post riders, accompanying them as far as Hinamori post station. They drank a little [wine] and lamented their parting, whereupon they composed these poems.

Koshima and Ōtomo no Tabito

When Tabito left Dazaifu in the last month of Tempyō 2 (early 731 by the Western calendar), the courtesan Koshima (no. 607) was among those who saw him off. Farewell poems were exchanged between her and Tabito atop the Mizuki, or Water Fortress, a dike northwest of Dazaifu erected in 664 under Emperor Tenji as a defense work after the destruction of Japan's ally Paekche in 663. A fourteen-meter-high remnant still runs for a kilometer in a northeast-southwest direction. There is some question whether the dike ever held water, as its name implies and as *Nihonshoki* states was its purpose. The fine complexity of feeling in Koshima's poems shows to good advantage against the punning and bathos of Tabito's replies. Her two poems balance scruple and impulse in a way that reinforces both in a dynamic of

tension and release. The final pathos of the farewell is provided by the realization that she will wave her sleeve only when Tabito is out of sight beyond
the clouds. In his replies Tabito plays on the place-name Koshima (modern
Kojima in Okayama Prefecture), which he will pass on his way home, and
on the term Water Fortress. He makes up an epithet, *mizukuki no* ("of the
water-steeped fortress"?) to go with *mizuki*, and then adds the image of his
tears in the standard self-reproach of the masurao-manqué, for a thoroughly
wet farewell.

1073–74 [MYS VI: 970–71 / 965–66]

Two poems composed by a young woman when Governor-General of
Dazaifu Lord Ōtomo went up to the capital in winter, the twelfth month [of
Tempyō 2, early 731]

(1073) [970 / 965]

Oho naraba	Were you a common man,
Kamokamo semu o	Oh, the things that I would do—
Kashikomi to	But I am in awe,
Furitaki sode o	And this sleeve I want to wave
Shinobite aru kamo	I shall be wise and hold still.

(1074) [971 / 966]

Yamatoji wa	The Yamato Road
Kumogakuretari	Is hidden behind clouds,
Shikaredo mo	Yet I wave good-bye—
Wa ga furu sode o	Do not think my fluttering sleeve
Nameshi to mou na	Too discourteous a farewell.

Regarding the above, the Governor-General of Dazaifu, Lord Ōtomo,
having received a concurrent appointment as Major Counselor, set off on
the road to the capital. That day he stopped his horse on top of the Water
Fortress and looked back at the buildings of Dazaifu. There happened to be
a courtesan among the officials who were seeing him off; her familiar name
was Koshima. At this point this young woman, grieving over how easy it
was to part and sighing over how difficult it was to meet, wiped her tears
and sang a song about waving her sleeve.

1075–76 [MYS VI: 972–73 / 967–68]

Two poems in reply by Major Counselor Lord Ōtomo

(1075) [972 / 967]

Yamatoji no	Going through Kibi
Kibi no Koshima o	On the road to Yamato

Sugite ikaba	I'll pass Koshima,
Tsukushi no Koshima	And how the memories will come
Omōemu kamo	Of Koshima in Tsukushi!

(1076)   [973 / 968]

Masurao to	What am I doing,
Omoeru ware ya	I who thought myself a valiant man,
Mizukuki no	Wiping my tears
Mizuki no ue ni	Here on the Water Fortress,
Namita nogowamu	This fortress steeped in water?

Manzei and Ōtomo no Tabito

In 731 the Novice Manzei, one of the guests of the plum-blossom party (no. 1017; see also nos. 608–11), sent Tabito, now back in the capital, two tanka, 1077–78, expressing distress over the loss of his company. Tabito replied in kind (1079–80). In his first poem Manzei speaks of his desolation, using the image of a perfectly burnished mirror (*masokagami*) as a pillow word for "gaze" (*mi*) and as a metaphor for a shining that contrasts with his own darkened and desolate (*sabi*) spirit. The mention of black hair turned white (it would appear that as a novice, Manzei had not shaved his head) follows naturally in the second poem from the idea of looking in a mirror. Tabito's first reply (no. 1079) gives a vivid sense of the feeling of dislocation experienced on returning home from a sojourn overseas. *Shira-* in the third line is a pivot word meaning both "not know" and "white," an early example of what became a common doubling. On the far side of the mountains that block his view in the direction of Tsukushi lies Kusaka Bay, where the Yamato and Yodo rivers debouch through a complex of channel islands into the Inland Sea. The jo upon which Tabito's second reply is based works technically through the phonetic link between *tazu* ("crane") and *tazuta-zushi* ("uncertain"), but at the same time successfully exploits the "direction" (*kata*) of Tsukushi mentioned in the preceding poem.

1077–78   [MYS IV: 575–76 / 572–73]

Two poems sent by Sami Manzei to Lord Ōtomo, Governor-General of Dazaifu, after he went up to the capital

(1077)   [575 / 572]

Masokagami	My lord, by you,
Miakanu kimi ni	The spotless mirror that I never
Okurete ya	Tire to gaze upon,
Ashita yūbe ni	Am I abandoned; morn and eve
Sabitsutsu oramu	I shall rust in solitude.

(1078) [576 / 573]

Nubatama no	Black as a berry,
Kurokami kawari	The locks of a young man's hair
Shirakete mo	May change and whiten,
Itaki koi ni wa	But there still can come a day
Au toki arikeri	He meets sore longing.

1079–80 [MYS IV : 577–78 / 574–75]

Two poems in reply by Major Counselor Lord Ōtomo

(1079) [577 / 574]

Koko ni shite	Now that I am here
Tsukushi ya izuku	I wonder where Tsukushi is;
Shirakumo no	Beyond the mountains
Tanabiku yama no	Drifted with white cloud must be
Kata ni shi aru rashi	The direction where it lies.

(1080) [578 / 575]

Kusakae no	On Kusaka Bay
Irie ni asaru	Down by the inlet the reed cranes
Ashitazu no	Are scratching for food:
Ana tazutazushi	Bobbing, craning, uncertain,
Tomo nashi ni shite	So faltering without my friend.

Ōtomo no Inagimi and Ōtomo no Yakamochi

An undated seasonal exchange between the young Yakamochi and his uncle Inagimi is found among the autumn poems of Book VIII. Inagimi was one of the Ōtomo family members who went to be with Tabito during his illness in the summer of 730. The exchange with Yakamochi probably took place later in the 730's. Inagimi was Tabito's younger half brother and a full brother of Lady Ōtomo of Sakanoue. He served in various provincial and metropolitan positions into the 750's. The poems, although not particularly distinguished individually, strike a nice balance as an exchange, pointing to the paradoxical effects of *shigure*, the sudden cold showers of late fall and early winter that both bring out and quench the autumn colors. Poems on *momichi*, the bright fall foliage that is an annual spectacle in Japan, show a Chinese-inspired esthetic appreciation of nature that begins to appear as early as Princess Nukata's famous poem, no. 256, but that unlike the praise of plum and willow, is tied to the wild native landscape. *Mikasa* has the epithet *ōkimi no* ("of our great lord") because of its meaning, "royal parasol" (see nos. 696–97).

1081   [MYS VIII: 1557 / 1553]

A poem by Senior Lieutenant of the Outer Palace Guards Ōtomo no Sukune Inagimi

Shigure no ame	Cold autumnal rain
Manaku shi fureba	Drizzles down so ceaselessly,
Mikasayama	On Mount Mikasa
Konure amaneku	Everywhere across the hill
Irozukinikeri	The treetops have turned color.

1082   [MYS VIII: 1558 / 1554]

A poem in reply by Ōtomo no Yakamochi

Ōkimi no	On Mount Mikasa
Mikasa no yama no	(Our great lord's Royal Parasol)
Momichiba wa	The autumn leaves
Kyō no shigure ni	Will soon be gone, all scattered
Chiri ka suginamu	In today's chill, drizzling rain.

The Maiden Maso of the Kamunagibe and Ōtomo no Yakamochi

Yakamochi's exchange with the Maiden Maso, like the next one with the Maiden Heki no Nagae, is in the Autumn-Miscellaneous (*aki no zōka*) section of Book VIII, instead of the autumn subdivision of the love poems (*sōmon*), even though they are exchanges with young women. The Kamunagibe were a clan whose function was to produce female shamans, or *kamunagi*. Maso is the author of four poems in *Man'yōshū*, including no. 1083. That her interest in geese had something to do with her interest in Yakamochi is indicated by the final line. Yakamochi hints more indirectly that the lines of the analogy will not soon converge.

1083   [MYS VIII: 1566 / 1562]

A poem on a wild goose by the Maiden Maso of the Kamunagibe

Tare kikitsu	Who has heard the sound?
Ko yu nakiwataru	The voice of a wild goose crying,
Karigane no	Flying overhead,
Tsuma yobu koe no	Calling to its distant mate—
Tomoshiku mo aru o	And I am seized with envy!

1084   [MYS VIII: 1567 / 1563]

A poem in reply by Ōtomo no Yakamochi

Kikitsu ya to	Did I hear the sound?
Imo ga towaseru	You ask me, love—yes,

Kari ga ne wa	A wild goose
Makoto mo tōku	Far away indeed
Kumogakuru nari	Calls faintly in the clouds.

The Maiden Heki no Nagae and Ōtomo no Yakamochi

Heki no Nagae has left only one poem and is otherwise totally obscure. Her feelings for Yakamochi are made the subject of her supposedly "miscellaneous" tanka, based on the analogical technique of the jo. Yakamochi replies a bit more encouragingly than he does to Maso, yet rather in the vein of an absent-minded Genji with a full social calendar. His bush clover (*hagi*) matches her plumegrass (*obana*), though it exists on the primary level of discourse and will provide an occasion rather than an analogy.

1085   [MYS VIII: 1568 / 1564]

A poem by the Maiden Heki no Nagae

Akizukeba	I faint with longing,
Obana ga ue ni	As the dew that gathers
Oku tsuyu no	On the plumegrass
Kenubeku mo a wa	With autumn's onset
Omōyuru kamo	Soon fades away.

1086   [MYS VIII: 1569 / 1565]

A poem in reply by Ōtomo no Yakamochi

Wa ga yado no	The bush-clover clump
Hitomura hagi o	Here by my house—how close I came
Omou ko ni	To letting its blossoms
Misezu hotohoto	Scatter without showing them
Chirashitsuru kamo	To the girl for whom I long!

Lady Kasa and Ōtomo no Yakamochi

Three of Lady Kasa's poems appear as nos. 753–55. The following undated exchange also comes out of Yakamochi's youth in the 730's. Lady Kasa's twenty-four poems (nos. 1087–1110) are an intense and engaging confession of love, and it is hard to believe that they moved Yakamochi to no more than the two despairing replies he records (nos. 1111–12). His side of the affair must have been edited out for reasons no longer apparent. Since we do not know who Lady Kasa was, we do not know what kept the lovers apart. His commitment to the Elder Maiden (and others?) comes to mind, but there is little jealousy in Lady Kasa's poems. Accusations of neglect abound,

566

however, and so perhaps the affair was indeed largely one-sided. The conventions of lovers' agony, already explored in several sequences, here focus on the woman who waits in vain. But the voice in these poems emerges as that of a real woman, and they carry a conviction that is more than merely conventional.

The series begins with the gift of an unspecified keepsake (katami), something that speaks of the past, establishing the fact that this love has its history, at the same time that it looks forward through the coming year—a year of longing. *Aratama* ("rough gem"), a mock epithet for *toshi* ("year") through the homophonous *aratama* ("begin again"), relates to *o* ("thread") in the expression *toshi no o* ("thread of the year") to provide an image of a string of jewels. The second poem (no. 1088) continues the theme of time and waiting. *Shiratori no* ("of the white bird") is a mock epithet for Tobayama ("Mount Toba") through *tob-*, a stem of the verb *tobu* ("to fly"). *Matsu* ("pine") introduces *machitsutsu* ("pining") at the juncture of the jo. *Toba* is also a homophone of a word meaning "forever." From this rhetorical complexity emerges the image of the woman / lone bird / lone pine, a cluster expressive of fidelity unto death. The third poem (no. 1089) takes Lady Kasa to her home in the village of Uchimi (location unknown). It happens that *uchi* means "to pound," and therefore Uchimi is receptive to the mock epithet *koromode o* ("garment sleeves"). Fulling cloth at night, the sound of the fulling paddle resounding in the stillness, is an auditory image of wifely loneliness and fidelity well established in Chinese, and later Japanese, poetry. This poem provides an early example.

1087–1110   [MYS IV: 590–613 / 587–610]

Twenty-four poems sent by Lady Kasa to Ōtomo no Sukune Yakamochi

(1087)   [590 / 587]

    Wa ga katami   Look at this keepsake
  Mitsutsu shinowase   And remember me, my love;
      Aratama no   All the gem-bright year,
  Toshi no o nagaku   Long as its thread of shining days,
  Ware wa omowamu   I too shall think of you.

(1088)   [591 / 588]

    Shiratori no   Where the white bird soars,
  Tobayamamamatsu no   On Mount Toba stands a pine:
    Machitsutsu so   Pining forever,
  A ga koiwataru   I have passed these many months
  Kono tsukigoro o   With a waiting love.

(1089)   [592 / 589]

Koromode o   Where the fullers pound
Uchimi no sato ni   Garment sleeves at Uchimi
  Aru ware o   Is my village home:
Shirani so hito wa   But he does not know me now—
Matedo kozukeru   I wait, he does not come.

❋ The next two poems are about secrecy. *Aratama no* again introduces
"year" in no. 1090, but this time years that have passed. The passage of time
gives no carte blanche for talk in the woman's view, and male carelessness in
this regard is an anxiety. Neglect and possible exposure are the two complementary complaints most often voiced in feminine love poetry throughout
its long history, and they are the basics of this series as well. The symbolism
of the closed box informs the central image in the anxiety dream recorded in
no. 1091. Opening a box would be a clear enough metaphor for disclosure
of secrets in itself, but the element *tama* in *tamakushige* ("jeweled comb
box") is also "soul," no doubt its significance in line 71 of Mushimaro's
chōka on the Urashima legend (no. 579). The escape of something from a
box also lies behind both the Pandora myth in the West and Prince Hozumi's
"love-slave" poem (no. 487). A sexual significance for *kushige* is suggested
by the story attached to no. 122.

(1090)   [593 / 590]

Aratama no   For the gem-bright years
Toshi no henureba   That have passed since first we met,
  Ima shi wa to   Do not think, my love,
Yume yo wa ga seko   "Now, surely"—no, I tell you,
Wa ga na norasu na   Never must you speak my name!

(1091)   [594 / 591]

Wa ga omoi o   Have I let my love
Hito ni shirure ya   Slip out where the world may know?
  Tamakushige   I had a dream
Hirakiaketsu to   Where I saw my box of combs—
Ime ni shi miyuru   And I was opening it!

❋ The theme of the poems reverts to yearning in separation. A crane cries
in no. 1092 in a darkness (*yami*) that is located in the analogical introduction,
but is also a reflection of the speaker's mood. In no. 1093 she stands sighing
under a pine ("pining") tree that grows on the primary level of discourse

(unlike that in no. 1088) but nevertheless is in the poem for its name. The structure and imagery of no. 1094 are those of the Maiden Heki no Nagae's no. 1085. The next poem (no. 1095) is a logical outgrowth of the perception of life as of limited duration—what there is of it will be devoted to memory, though memory increases longing.

(1092)   [595/592]

Yami no yo ni   As one hears the cry
Naku naru tazu no   Of a crane in the darkness
   Yoso nomi ni   Far off at night,
Kikitsutsu ka aramu   Must I hear but rumors of you,
Au to wa nashi ni   With never a chance to meet?

(1093)   [596/593]

Kimi ni koi   Yearning for you,
Ita mo sube nami   I am helpless in my love;
   Narayama no   All I can do
Komatsu ga moto ni   Is stand sighing by the pine
Tachinageku kamo   That grows on Nara Mountain.

(1094)   [597/594]

Wa ga yado no   The white drops of dew
Yūkagekusa no   That glisten in the evening sun
   Shiratsuyu no   There in my garden
Kenu gani motona   Fade no more quickly from the grass
Omōyuru kamo   Than I faint from my desire.

(1095)   [598/595]

Wa ga inochi no   While yet my life
Matakemu kagiri   Remains whole within me
   Wasureme ya   Shall I forget you?
Iya hi ni ke ni wa   Not though my longing should increase
Omoi masu to mo   By day and hour and minute!

❋ The next two poems form a pair—contrasting perceptions of space as it relates to desire. No. 1096 takes the imagination into a vast open space of sand, which yet does not compass the vastness of love. In no. 1097 the world is closed in by thickets of eyes, and the merest step across a bridge of stones cannot be taken. The image of the bridge is reminiscent of the anonymous sedōka no. 370 in the "Hitomaro Collection," and the stream is that of Princess Tajima (no. 483) and Lady Ki (no. 509).

(1096)   [599 / 596]

    Yaoka yuku   On so vast a shore
Hama no manago mo   That one could walk eight hundred days
    A ga koi ni   Would the grains of sand
Ani masaraji ka   Number greater than my love,
Oki tsu shimamori   O guardian of the outer isles?

(1097)   [600 / 597]

    Utsusemi no   In the world of men
Hitome o shigemi   Everywhere the eyes are thick:
    Ishibashi no   Near though you are,
Machikaki kimi ni   A step across a bridge of stones,
Koiwataru kamo   I pass my days in yearning.

❋ Lady Kasa is again at the brink of death in nos. 1098–99. The first poem is divided into an abstract truism and an image that warrants its validity. The image itself is a self-betraying metaphor. A waterless river should be flowing secretly beneath the sands, but Lady Kasa wastes away with an inner meagerness instead. The claim in the second poem that she has but glimpsed Yakamochi vaguely should no doubt be taken as a conventional exaggeration, though the conditions of secret nocturnal visits (again, no. 122!) could make it true enough.

(1098)   [601 / 598]

    Koi ni mo so   From yearning also
Hito wa shini suru   People have been known to die:
    Minasegawa   A waterless river,
Shita yu are yasu   Underneath I waste for you
Tsuki ni hi ni ke ni   By month and day and hour.

(1099)   [602 / 599]

    Asagiri no   For a man I saw
Oho ni aimishi   As vaguely as the morning mist—
    Hito yue ni   Yes, for that one glance
Inochi shinubeku   I am about to lose my life
Koiwataru kamo   With this ceaseless yearning!

❋ Lady Kasa's emotions reach a stormy climax in no. 1100, where her love becomes a raging sea in which her premonitions of death may be fulfilled.

(1100)   [603 / 600]

    Ise no umi no   On the stony strand
    Iso mo todoro ni   The wild waves of Ise Sea
      Yosuru nami   Crash with their thunder:
    Kashikoki hito ni   Awesome is my highborn love,
    Koiwataru kamo   For whom this ceaseless yearning!

✳ The peculiar sense of things being wrong in no. 1101 echoes the sentiment of no. 1097: so near and yet so far. Yakamochi's *omokage*, his remembered image, is the only visitor the lady has (no. 1102), and once more she broods on death (no. 1103). Finally there comes another symbolic dream (no. 1104), the meaning of whose sword image is not hard to fathom. (Recall Hitomaro's use of the sword metaphor in nos. 336 and 351.)

(1101)   [604 / 601]

    Kokoro yu mo   In my heart
    A wa omowazuki   I never dreamed it would be thus:
      Yama kawa mo   With no barrier
    Hedataranaku ni   Of stream or mountain in between
    Kaku koimu to wa   To yearn so hopelessly.

(1102)   [605 / 602]

    Yū sareba   When evening comes
    Monomoimasaru   I sink deeper into longing,
      Mishi hito no   For the one I loved
    Kototou sugata   Hovers then before my eyes
    Omokage ni shite   As he were speaking to me.

(1103)   [606 / 603]

    Omoi ni shi   If by her longing
    Shini suru mono ni   She who longs were doomed to die,
      Aramaseba   Then for this same cause
    Chitabi so ware wa   Long ere this I would have died,
    Shinikaeramashi   And died a thousand times.

(1104)   [607 / 604]

    Tsurugitachi   In a dream I saw
    Mi ni torisou to   How I bound a long, straight sword
      Ime ni mitsu   Tight to my body:
    Nani no saga so mo   What portent lies within this sign?—
    Kimi ni awamu tame   Because I want to meet you!

❋ Nakatomi no Yakamori's challenge to the gods in no. 952 is repeated by Lady Kasa in poem 1105, though the likelihood is that hers is the earlier of the two. The link between them is obscure. To die without ever meeting again is accepted and given a positive sense in no. 1106, where the emptily blowing wind becomes a metaphor for remembrance.

(1105)   [608/605]

    Ame tsuchi no   If there is no truth
  Kami no kotowari   In all the gods of heaven and earth,
     Naku wa koso   Then and then alone
  A ga omou kimi ni   Shall I never meet my love,
  Awazu shini seme   But die in my longing.

(1106)   [609/606]

    Ware mo omou   I shall think of you;
  Hito mo na wasure   You too do not forget me:
     Ōnawa ni   Like the wind that sweeps
  Ura fuku kaze no   Ceaselessly across the bay,
  Yamu toki nakere   Let us never cease our love.

❋ Curfew in Nara was 10:00 P.M., when an official at the Bureau of Divination (ommyōryō) struck four bells. But the lady is alone with her thoughts (no. 1107) and cannot sleep. A *gaki* was a sinner condemned after death to a starving existence as a punishment for greed. Statues of them are said to have been placed as a warning in the large temples of Nara. Graphic representations of gaki depict them as hideously grotesque creatures with swollen bellies and emaciated limbs, living on offal. It is to the backside of such a creature that Lady Kasa imagines herself bowing in no. 1108, in a strong poem whose rue spills over into anger. These two poems, the last apparently that Yakamochi received before the final break, are particularly interesting for their incorporation of elements of culture not usually found in waka. And nothing in the entire series leads one to expect an outburst like that in no. 1108, the literary equivalent of slamming the door after delivering a few choice words. Unfortunately, the lady retreats to her usual meekness in the wake of parting. In no. 1109 it seems that she has gone home to where she grew up, but in no. 1110 she implies that she is not far away. This final poem is somewhat reminiscent of no. 938 by Sano no Otogami.

(1107)   [610/607]

    Minahito o   Though I hear the bell
  Neyo to no kane wa   Whose striking tells the city,
    Utsu naredo   "Sleep, all good people,"

Kimi o shi omoeba	When I think of you, my love,
Inekatenu kamo	There is no sleep for me.

(1108)   [611/608]

Aiomowanu	To long for a man
Hito o omou wa	Who does not long the least for you
Ōtera no	Is like knocking your head
Gaki no shirihe ni	On the floor of a great temple
Nukatsuku gotoshi	To the rump of a hungry ghost!

(1109)   [612/609]

Kokoro yu mo	In my heart
A wa omowazuki	I never dreamed it would be thus:
Mata sara ni	That even now
Wa ga furusato ni	I should come again to this,
Kaerikomu to wa	The place where once I lived.

(1110)   [613/610]

Chikaku areba	Since you are near
Minedo mo aru o	I can live and not see you,
Iyatō ni	But if you go away
Kimi ga imasaba	Into some more distant place
Arikatsumashiji	I shall not bear it to the end.

The last two poems arrived separately after parting.

❋ Yakamochi's replies—the only poems he is recorded to have written to
Lady Kasa—are pained, resigned, and regretful. The first shows him in
the agony of loss, experiencing feelings that are immediate and physical.
But in the second rueful reflection has taken over, and the lover is wise after
the fact.

1111–12   [MYS IV:614–15/611–12]

Two poems in reply by Ōtomo no Sukune Yakamochi

(1111)   [614/611]

Ima sara ni	Never again
Imo ni awame ya to	Shall I meet the girl I love—
Omoe ka mo	Is it this thought
Kokodaku a ga mune	That tightens all my chest
Ibuseku aruramu	Until I cannot breathe?

(1112)   [615/612]

Nakanaka ni	When after all
Moda mo aramashi o	We could just have kept our peace!
Nani su to ka	What were we thinking
Aimisomekemu	When we started out to love?
Togezaramaku ni	For we knew how small the chance.

Ōtomo no Surugamaro and Lady Ōtomo of Sakanoue

Lady Ōtomo of Sakanoue has already appeared in these pages as poet, woman in love, and materfamilias to the Ōtomo clan. Her relationship to Yakamochi as aunt and mother-in-law has also been mentioned. Yakamochi was not the only younger male relation for whom she had warm feelings, however. Her exchanges with Surugamaro, the grandson of her own uncle Miyuki, are of an ardent nature whose implications should be unmistakable, but which the compiler (Yakamochi?) attempts to explain away in a footnote. Surugamaro (d. 776) followed a career that was roughly parallel to Yakamochi's, taking him to several governorships and a military appointment in the north. Like his cousin, he fell afoul of Fujiwara power, being punished and then pardoned for his involvement with Tachibana no Naramaro in 757. He ended his career at Senior Fourth Upper, as compared with Yakamochi's Junior Third. Another significant parallel is that Surugamaro courted the younger sister of Yakamochi's wife (with what success we do not know), thus placing himself in a triangular relationship with mother and daughter that may or may not have been of the same character (whatever that character really was) as that enjoyed by Yakamochi. Certainly in Surugamaro's case Lady Ōtomo's poems cannot be dismissed as expressive of a merely motherly interest. It has been argued that even the Lady's more daring exchanges are part and parcel of the banquet repartee in which she also engaged, and this may indeed be what Yakamochi hoped his readers would believe. The following translations are based on the conviction that there are love poems involved that should be allowed to burn forth and shed their uncertain light on the enigma.

The exchanges between Surugamaro and Lady Ōtomo presented here come from sections of Books III and IV that probably place them in the late 730's. The first four (nos. 1113–16) are followed by the explanatory footnote mentioned above. It is incorrect in describing the Lady and Surugamaro as aunt and nephew; they were first cousins once removed. The Saho Major Counselor was Ōtomo no Yasumaro (d. 714), and the great lord from Takechi was his elder brother Miyuki (no. 998). It is interesting that such notes are often found after poems by Lady Ōtomo (see nos. 716–17, 723–24, 1003–9, and 1131–32). Surugamaro's first poem (no.

1113) casts him in the familiar mold of the "weak stalwart," the man whose tender passions unman him and make him unworthy to be called a masurao. Lady Ōtomo's reply (no. 1114) adopts a corresponding feminine convention—the fear of being involved in an affair that will cause talk. Since she says she has not forgotten him, it is apparent that the affair already exists. The next two poems presuppose this also. They seem a bit intimate for mere social inquiries. One speculation is that Surugamaro is actually addressing Lady Ōtomo's daughter, and that the mother is replying in her stead. Since there are no poems by the younger daughter in *Man'yōshū*, perhaps she did not share the Ōtomo gift of words. Poem 1116 could be read as a mother's reproof to her daughter's suitor for his lack of attention.

1113 [MYS IV : 649 / 646]

A poem by Ōtomo no Sukune Surugamaro

Masurao no	These many sighs
Omoiwabitsutsu	Sighed by a stalwart man
Tabi maneku	In hopeless longing—
Nageku nageki o	Will you never take them
Owanu mono ka mo	For the burden of your heart?

1114 [MYS IV : 650 / 647]

A poem by Lady Ōtomo of Sakanoue

Kokoro ni wa	Though in my heart
Wasururu hi naku	I have longed for you, never
Omoedo mo	Forgetting for a day,
Hito no koto koso	You are a man over whom
Shigeki kimi ni are	Talk grows like a jungle.

1115 [MYS IV : 651 / 648]

A poem by Ōtomo no Sukune Surugamaro

Aimizute	Long days have gone by
Ke nagaku narinu	Since we saw each other last;
Kono koro wa	I worry about you,
Ika ni sakiku ya	How you get on, is everything
Ifukashi wagimo	Well with you, my darling?

1116 [MYS IV : 652 / 649]

A poem by Lady Ōtomo of Sakanoue

Natsukuzu no	When the summer vine
Taenu tsukai no	Endlessly arriving stream
Yodomereba	Of your messages

Koto shi mo aru goto   Grew stagnant, I began
Omoitsuru kamo   Suspecting something was wrong.

The above Lady of Sakanoue was the daughter of his lordship the Saho Major Counselor. Surugamaro was the grandson of our great lord from Takechi. The two nobles were brothers, so that the daughter and the grandson of their respective families were related as aunt and nephew. Because of this, they exchanged poems inquiring after each other's welfare.

✳ Three poems by Surugamaro, MYS IV:656–58/653–55, of which the first two are translated here (the third has an undeciphered line), fairly pale and even apologetic, set off an intense avalanche of six by Lady Ōtomo. Surugamaro's second poem (no. 1118) has an honorific in the last line: he seems very much the timid young man addressing the older woman. This poem could hardly have been intended for the daughter. Lady Ōtomo picks up Surugamaro's suggestion that he might be yearning and throws the word (*kou*) back at him (no. 1119). This is typical of lovers who compete over who is suffering more, but the Lady's last line implies that she has much to be offended about. Her emotional dominance of the exchange is clear throughout. In her second poem (no. 1120), one of her best, she reproaches not her lover but herself, which is another way of stating the intensity of her feelings. The almond (*hanezu*) yielded a dye known to fade quickly. The third poem is in the same vein, addressed to herself, but in the fourth (no. 1122) she turns back to her correspondent. *Shieya* ("fie on them!") is a strong expression of disgust. This is the negative counterpart of the positive appeal in no. 1123: two lovers fighting against a hostile world. The stance has changed from rebuke to reflection to resolution. In no. 1123 Lady Ōtomo uses the familiar *na* ("you"), unusual from a woman to a man, but follows it with the more respectful *kimi* ("my lord" / "you"). The final poem is a thrust into the heart of the matter—how to spend the time-out-of-time that lovers can steal for each other. The focus is on words, through whose magic love (fictive or real) is created.

1117–18   [MYS IV:656–57/653–54]

[Two of] three poems by Ōtomo no Sukune Surugamaro

(1117)   [656/653]

Kokoro ni wa   Though in my heart
Wasurenu mono o   I have never forgotten,
Tamasaka ni   Somehow or other
Minu hi samaneku   Many days without meeting—
Tsuki so henikeru   A whole month has gone by.

(1118)   [657/654]

    Aimite wa   When not a month
  Tsuki mo henaku ni   Has gone by since last we met,
      Kou to iwaba   You will think me
  Osoro to ware o   Too impetuous, I fear,
  Omōsamu ka mo   If I talk now of yearning.

1119-24   [MYS IV:659-64/656-61]

Six poems by Lady Ōtomo of Sakanoue

(1119)   [659/656]

    Are nomi so   It is only I
  Kimi ni wa kouru   Who am yearning for you;
    Wa ga seko ga   When my lover
  Kou to iu koto wa   Talks about how he yearns
  Koto no nagusa so   He gives me soothing words.

(1120)   [660/657]

    Omowaji to   I shall long no more,
  Iiteshi mono o   I said, that thing is finished;
    Hanezuiro no   Oh, but the almond
  Utsuroiyasuki   Gives a color that alters
  A ga kokoro kamo   No more quickly than my heart.

(1121)   [661/658]

    Omoedo mo   Though I long for you,
  Shirushi mo nashi to   My longing gets me nowhere,
    Shiru mono o   I know it well—
  Nani ka kokodaku   Why must it be so endless,
  A ga koiwataru   This voyage of my love?

(1122)   [662/659]

    Arakajime   Before we've begun,
  Hitogoto shigeshi   What a swamp of talk there is!
    Kaku shi araba   If it's like this now,
  Shieya wa ga seko   Fie on them, lover of mine,
  Oki mo ika ni arame   We've heavy going ahead.

(1123)   [663/660]

    Na o to wa o   You and I, they say,
  Hito so saku naru   People are set to pull apart;

Ide a ga kimi	Pray you, my love,
Hito no nakagoto	Do not listen to the words
Kikikosu na yume	That come between us—never!

(1124)   [664/661]

Koikoite	After all our lust,
Aeru toki dani	When the hour has come at last,
Utsukushiki	Pour out your words,
Koto tsukushite yo	All those lovely words of love,
Nagaku to omowaba	If you want this to be long.

❋ There is no way of knowing whether the following three poems (nos. 1125–27) were composed before or after those given above. But it is clear that they refer to a different aspect of the relationship between Surugamaro and Lady Ōtomo. They are to be found among the hiyuka of Book III, and their metaphors are not hard to fathom. The plum branch in no. 1125 is a young woman in whom Surugamaro has preemptive interest, presumably Lady Ōtomo's second daughter, and he seems to have heard rumors that she has formed another connection. In the following exchange at a banquet the mountain must be Surugamaro, about whom Lady Ōtomo apparently has heard similar gossip. Her roping off of the mountain would be on her daughter's behalf. Surugamaro admits the rumor may be true but wants to maintain his bond with Lady Ōtomo's daughter—and Lady Ōtomo herself, perhaps. The arch tone of these poems distinguishes them readily enough from serious love poetry.

1125   [MYS III: 403/400]

A plum poem by Ōtomo no Sukune Surugamaro

Ume no hana	Someone said to me,
Sakite chirinu to	All the plums have blossomed out,
Hito wa iedo	Flowered and fallen;
Wa ga shime yuishi	He could not have meant the branch
Eda narame ya mo	I tied with sacred straw.

1126   [MYS III: 404/401]

A poem sung at a banquet for her kinsfolk by Lady Ōtomo of Sakanoue

Yamamori no	Since I didn't know
Arikeru shirani	The mountain had a guardian,
Sono yama ni	I roped it off,
Shime yuitatete	I bound that mountain all around—
Yui no haji shitsu	A bond that brings me shame!

1127   [MYS III: 405 / 402]

A poem in which Ōtomo no Sukune Surugamaro immediately replied

Yamamori wa	There may be indeed
Kedashi ari to mo	A guardian of the mountain,
Wagimoko ga	But who would dare
Yuikemu shime o	Undo the bond my dear one bound
Hito tokame ya mo	When she roped this hillside round?

※ Two more poems of the same type follow shortly after in Book III. The author of the second is not given but is suspected to be Surugamaro. The matter is the same; only the metaphor has changed. The most plausible reading is that Surugamaro is declaring his intention to bring his suit of Lady Ōtomo's daughter to a successful conclusion. The "very close" (*ito chikaku*) could refer to consanguinity, though that seems to be a rule rather than an exception in Ōtomo marriages.

1128   [MYS III: 413 / 410]

An orange-tree poem by Lady Ōtomo of Sakanoue

Tachibana o	For the orange tree
Yado ni ueōshi	I planted by the house and tended
Tachite ite	I am ill at ease:
Nochi ni kuyu to mo	Though later I have regrets,
Shirushi arame ya mo	What good will it do then?

1129   [MYS III: 414 / 411]

A poem in reply

Wagimoko ga	My dear lady
Yado no tachibana	Planted the orange tree by her house
Ito chikaku	Very close to mine,
Ueteshi yue ni	For which reason I feel sure
Narazu wa yamaji	It cannot but bear fruit.

Ahe no Mushimaro and Lady Ōtomo of Sakanoue

Man'yōshū records yet another provocative exchange, nos. 1130–32, followed by another "explanatory" note, between Lady Ōtomo and one of her blood relations. This time the man is Ahe no Mushimaro, her first cousin (no. 696). It is worth stressing that there was nothing unusual or shocking in amorous exchange between cousins. Lady Ōtomo, after all, married her own half brother Sukunamaro. What needs explanation is why the compiler of Book IV, presumably Yakamochi, felt it necessary to attach the kind of note that follows nos. 1113–16 and nos. 1130–32. If, as is thought, Lady Ōtomo was by this time (late 730's) a widow, she would have been free to pursue what amours she pleased. But the writer of the footnotes keeps insisting that hers was a game of words, and not of love. There is no evidence of a triangular relationship involving one of her own daughters in the case of Mushimaro. The theory that these are banquet poems is lent some support by no. 1130, in which Mushimaro sits facing Lady Ōtomo, too overpowered by her fascination to be able to leave. Lady Ōtomo's two poems, which like her six to Surugamaro are replies merely by juxtaposition, seem better suited to a more private ambience. If these are "playful poems" (*kika*), as the footnote claims, they set a strenuous standard of play. Perhaps Lady Ōtomo was offering her cousins lessons in how to write love poems; if so, the opening of nos. 1124 and 1132 may have been one she thought particularly effective.

1130   [MYS IV: 668 / 665]

A poem by Ahe no Asomi Mushimaro

Mukaiite	I sit facing her,
Miredo mo akanu	But can never gaze my fill
Wagimoko ni	At my dearest one:
Tachihanareikamu	I am utterly bereft
Tazuki shirazu mo	Of the means to rise and leave!

1131–32   [MYS IV: 669–70 / 666–67]

Two poems by Lady Ōtomo of Sakanoue

(1131)   [669 / 666]

Aiminu wa	Since last I saw you
Ikubisasa ni mo	No such endless succession
Aranaku ni	Of long whiles has passed—
Kokodaku are wa	Yet am I thus sore beset
Koitsutsu mo aru ka	By this eternal yearning!

(1132)   [670 / 667]

Koikoite	After all our lust
Aitaru mono o	Here we are, alone at last;
Tsuki shi areba	Since the moon is out,
Yo wa komoruramu	Deeps of night must lie ahead—
Shimashi wa arimate	Stay with me yet awhile!

Concerning the above: The mother of Lady Ōtomo of Sakanoue, Inner Palace Lady Ishikawa, and the mother of Ahe no Asomi Mushimaro, Outer

Palace Lady Azumi, were sisters who lived together and enjoyed the intimacy of kin. Because of this, the Lady [Ōtomo of Sakanoue] and Mushimaro were by no means distant in the way they looked at each other and had long been on the closest terms in their conversation. They put some little effort into composing playful poems and conducting a dialogue.

Ōtomo no Yakamochi and a Young Girl

The significance of feathered chaplets (*hanekazura*) has been lost; one suggestion is that they were a part of the regalia for a coming-of-age ceremony. Whoever the girl was who wore one in the following exchange, she deserves to be remembered for her saucy indifference to Yakamochi's soft, insinuating ways. In a tradition dominated by expressions of desire, it is always refreshing to find someone not in love. But the tradition also teaches that a coy initial reply need not be taken as an outright rejection. Where she "wasn't" (*nakarishi*) presumably means in Yakamochi's dream. (People believed that, spectrally speaking, they actually moved about in dreams.) Yakamochi plays with *ima* ("now"), *imo* ("little sister," i.e., "young maiden"), and *ime* ("dream") in his poem, a challenge to which the reply does not quite rise. This undated exchange is also probably from the late 730's.

1133   [MYS IV:708/705]

A poem sent to a young girl by Ōtomo no Sukune Yakamochi

Hanekazura	In a dream I saw
Ima suru imo o	The young maiden who now wears
Ime ni mite	A feather chaplet,
Kokoro no uchi ni	Since when within my heart
Koiwataru kamo	I drift on seas of longing.

1134   [MYS IV:709/706]

A poem in response by the young girl

Hanekazura	Since she wasn't there,
Ima suru imo wa	The young maiden who now wears
Nakarishi o	A feather chaplet,
Izure no imo so	For what young maiden can it be
Sokoba koitaru	You are so lost in longing?

Ōtomo no Yakamochi and Ōtomo no Fumimochi

A woman of importance in Yakamochi's life who becomes known only on her death is designated with the character for "concubine"—perhaps, it has been suggested, out of consideration for Yakamochi's wife, the Elder Maiden of Sakanoue. Her name is not known. She was probably the mother of Yakamochi's daughter (see the commentaries to nos. 839–41 and 1162–68), and it is thought that only after her death did Yakamochi make his final advances to the Elder Maiden. She died in the sixth month of 739 and was mourned by Yakamochi in a series of laments preserved in Book III. Several are included here, among the poetic exchanges, because of Fumimochi's response to Yakamochi's first poem. Fumimochi (d. 746) was Yakamochi's younger brother and has left eleven other tanka in *Man'yōshū*. (In a lament on his death, MYS XVII: 3979–81 / 3957–59, which occurred during Yakamochi's incumbency as Governor of Etchū, Yakamochi noted that his brother loved flowers and trees.) By referring in his first poem here (no. 1135) to the oncoming long nights and cold winds of autumn, Yakamochi creates a mood harmonious with his grief over his concubine's death and his sense of deprivation. Fumimochi's reply (no. 1136) is sympathetic but undistinguished. One senses a close bond between the brothers. Poem 1137 is particularly affecting in its use of direct quotation and an uncommented floral link with the past. The word for "pinks," *nadeshiko*, suggests "petted child." In no. 1138 Yakamochi reverts to the cold autumn wind. The effect of the poem need not be diminished by calculating that the first of the seventh month (the beginning of autumn) for A.D. 739 corresponds to the ninth of August.

1135   [MYS III: 465 / 462]

A poem by Ōtomo no Sukune Yakamochi composed in mourning for his concubine who died in summer, in the sixth month of the eleventh year [of Tempyō, 739], Earth-Junior / Hare

Ima yori wa	Now is the season
Akikaze samuku	When we feel the autumn wind
Fukinamu o	Begin to blow cold;
Ika ni ka hitori	How if I must sleep alone
Nagaki yo o nemu	Shall I endure the long nights?

1136   [MYS III: 466 / 463]

A poem in which his younger brother Ōtomo no Sukune Fumimochi promptly replied

Nagaki yo o	Through the long nights
Hitori ya nemu to	You'll be sleeping all alone—
Kimi ga ieba	At these words of yours
Suginishi hito no	How the memories come back
Omōyuraku ni	Of her who now is gone.

1137   [MYS III: 467 / 464]

Another poem composed by Yakamochi on seeing the fringed pinks beside the flagstones under the eaves

Aki saraba	*When autumn has come,*
Mitsutsu shinoe to	*Look at these and remember:*
Imo ga ueshi	The pinks she planted
Yado no nadeshiko	By the borders of our house
Sakinikeru kamo	Have at last begun to bloom.

1138   [MYS III: 468 / 465]

A poem composed by Yakamochi after the first of the new month, sighing sadly over the autumn wind

Utsusemi no	That the locust-husk
Yo wa tsune nashi to	World is without permanence
Shiru mono o	I know well enough;
Akikaze samumi	But the autumn wind is cold,
Shinobitsuru kamo	It has made me remember.

✳ A chōka and three envoys (nos. 1139–42) follow. The image of the pinks established in no. 1137 is used effectively as a frame in the first four lines of the chōka and in the final envoy. The flowers by which his concubine wished to be remembered bring no comfort, perhaps only greater sadness. Within the frame are memories, images of connubial happiness (lines 5–10) that fulfill the need of the lament to establish the value of what has been lost. Yakamochi's reflections on the ephemerality of the "locust-husk" (*utsusemi*) world begin here, in lines 11–14, and in poem 1138. The conceptualization of the dead as vanishing into wild nature (lines 15–18) is part of the lament pattern perfected by Hitomaro. Lines 21–22 are those of Takahashi no Mushimaro about Mount Fuji (no. 569, lines 17–18), and the final three lines of the chōka are in no small measure reminiscent of Okura. The first envoy provides the evidence for the child, and like no. 693 by Takahashi no Asomi, blames its mother for abandoning it. Yakamochi's hyperbole in the second envoy recalls, but does not match, Sano no Otogami's in no. 936.

1139–42   [MYS III: 469–72 / 466–69]

Another poem composed by Yakamochi; with *tanka*

Wa ga yado ni	All around my house
Hana so sakitaru	Flowers are gaily blooming;
So o miredo	Yet though I look at them
Kokoro mo yukazu	There is no lifting in my heart.

5   Hashiki yashi
Imo ga ariseba
   Mikamo nasu
Futari narabii
   Taorite mo
10   Misemashi mono o
Utsusemi no
   Kareru mi nareba
Tsuyu shimo no
   Kenuru ga gotoku
15   Ashihiki no
Yamaji o sashite
   Irihi nasu
Kakurinishikaba
   Soko omou ni
20   Mune koso itaki
   Ii mo ezu
Nazuke mo shirazu
   Ato mo naki
Yo no naka nareba
25   Semu sube mo nashi

Ah, my beloved—
If she were here alive today,
   Like ducks in water
We two would be side by side;
   We would pick blossoms
And show them to each other.
   But our locust-husk
Bodies are but borrowed flesh:
   It melts away
And vanishes like dew or frost.
   To the foot-weary
Mountain paths she made her way,
   And like the setting sun
Hid herself behind the hills.
   When I think of this
My breast is fraught with pain,
   But I cannot speak,
I cannot find a name for it.
   Since ours is a world
That will leave no trace behind,
There is nothing I can do.

Envoys

   Toki wa shi mo
Itsu mo aramu o
   Kokoro itaku
Iyuku wagimo ka
Midoriko o okite

When there would be times,
More than enough for such a thing,
   Why did my darling
Bring me this grief by her going,
Leaving our greenling behind?

   Idete yuku
Michi shiramaseba
   Arakajime
Imo o todomemu
Seki mo okamashi o

If I had but known
The road my love would take away,
   Before she could have gone
I would have put a barrier
Across to hold her back.

   Imo ga mishi
Yado ni hana saki
   Toki wa henu
Wa ga naku namita
Imada hinaku ni

Flowers are in bloom
In the garden that she knew,
   And time goes by;
But still there has been no drying
Of the tears I shed for her.

Ōtomo no Yakamochi and Lady Ōtomo of Sakanoue

In the eighth month of 739, about two months after the death of his concubine, Yakamochi paid a visit to his aunt on her Taketa estate near Asuka, on which occasion the following exchange took place. The two tanka are very warm, cast in the ardent language found in Lady Sakanoue's exchanges with both her daughter and her nephew. *Imo* ("little sister" / "dearest") and its accompanying exclamation *hashiki yashi* ("well beloved") are usually lovers' terms. People who dream of each other in waka are usually lovers, too. Still, the terms are general enough that in the absence of more specific signals—sexual symbolism, need for secrecy, fear of gossip, exchange of intimate clothing, and so forth—they may best be taken here to point toward affection rather than eros. The Lady's poem is very skillful as a reply, answering *tamahoko no* with *aratama no*, both epithets containing the word *tama* ("jewel"), supplying *imo* to match *ime* ("dream") at the beginning of the fourth line, and echoing the grammatical structure of Yakamochi's last line in her own. *Aratama no* ("of the rough gem") applies to *tsuki* ("moon" / "month") in the same sense as to *toshi* ("year"), through the homophone *aratama[ru]* ("to begin again").

1143   [MYS VIII: 1623 / 1619]

A poem composed by Ōtomo no Yakamochi on arriving at the Taketa estate of his aunt, Lady Sakanoue

Tamahoko no	Though the jewel-spear road
Michi wa tōkedo	Is a far road, I have come,
Hashiki yashi	O my dearest one,
Imo o aimi ni	Well beloved, to meet you,
Idete so a ga koshi	Setting out along that way.

1144   [MYS VIII: 1624 / 1620]

A poem in reply by Lady Ōtomo of Sakanoue

Aratama no	Till the rough-gem moon
Tsuki tatsu made ni	Stood renewed in the sky
Kimasaneba	You did not come—
Ime ni shi mitsutsu	I have seen you in my dreams,
Omoi so a ga seshi	Longing for you all the while.

The above two poems were composed in Tempyō 11 [739], Earth-Junior / Hare, autumn, eighth month.

The Elder Maiden of Sakanoue and Ōtomo no Yakamochi

It is not unlikely that Yakamochi's visit to his aunt was for the purpose of renewing his intimacy with her daughter. If so, the venture seems to have been a success, judging from the following exchange in the ninth month. The Elder Maiden sends Yakamochi a katami in the form of a wreath of ripened rice, perhaps from the fields of Taketa. The golden, full grains are surely intended to be symbolic of her love, and of a relationship that has reached fruition. Yakamochi's reply is appreciative but not particularly inventive. Another gift arrives, this time a garment. Yakamochi promises to wear it under his clothes, a secret pledge of love. This time his reference to the "cold autumnal wind" could be more than conventional, for the month is October.

1145   [MYS VIII: 1628 / 1624]

A poem by the Elder Maiden of Sakanoue, sending a garland of autumnal rice to Ōtomo no Sukune Yakamochi

Wa ga makeru	From the seed I sowed
Wasada no hotachi	In the fields of early rice
Tsukuritaru	Here are heads of grain
Kazura so mitsutsu	Fashioned in a garland—look,
Shinowase wagase	And remember me, my love.

1146   [MYS VIII: 1629 / 1625]

A poem sent in reply by Ōtomo no Sukune Yakamochi

Wagimoko ga	Out of her harvest
Nari to tsukureru	In the autumn fields of rice
Aki no ta no	My darling fashioned
Wasaho no kazura	From the early grain this garland—
Miredo akanu kamo	I shall look and not weary.

1147   [MYS VIII: 1630 / 1626]

Another poem, in requital of the gift of a garment that she took off and sent to Yakamochi

Akikaze no	Now in the season
Samuki kono koro	Of the cold autumnal wind
Shita ni kimu	I'll wear it under
Imo ga katami to	As a keepsake of my love,
Katsu mo shinowamu	This while as I remember.

These three poems passed back and forth in Tempyō 11 [739], Earth-Junior / Hare, autumn, ninth month.

❋ Since the following exchange (nos. 1148–53) is undated, it is impossible to know whether it came before or after the above. The poems are agitated and speak of rumor and separation, and so one might suspect them of reflecting an earlier stage in the relationship, but given the vagueness of all the fragments of evidence bearing on the question of Yakamochi's marriage, not to mention the proverbially uncertain course of love, one cannot be sure.

Yakamochi's three replies take up the Elder Maiden's poems in reverse order. In the first (no. 1148) she expresses the need for reassurance by actual possession, and in his last (no. 1153) he agrees that it would be better to be so possessed. Yakamochi himself later used a more ingenious version of the same conceit in his farewell to Ikenushi (no. 1210). The idea of carrying one's lover or friend as a string of jewels wrapped around one's arm may have something to do with the *tama / tama* ("jewel" / "soul") homophony. Yakamochi's first poem (no. 1151) is clearly an answer to the Elder Maiden's last (no. 1150); they make a complementary pair on the theme of rumor. The middle pair (nos. 1149 and 1152) are twins bound at the waist: the female rues the fatal night, the male all nights but that.

1148-50   [MYS IV: 732-34 / 729-31]

Three poems by the Elder Maiden of the Ōtomo of Sakanoue to Ōtomo no Sukune Yakamochi

(1148)   [732/729]

  Tama naraba   Were you a string of beads
 Te ni mo makamu o   I would wind you about my arm,
   Utsusemi no   But since you are a man
 Yo no hito nareba   Of the actual, mortal world,
 Te ni makigatashi   You are hard in the winding.

(1149)   [733/730]

  Awamu yo wa   When we could have met
 Itsu mo aramu o   Any time, any night,
   Nani su to ka   Why did we do it—
 Sono yoi aite   Why did we choose that night to meet,
 Koto no shigeki mo   And all this thicket of talk?

(1150)   [734/731]

  Wa ga na wa mo   Let this name of mine
 China no iona ni   Be bandied on five hundred
   Tachinu to mo   Or a thousand tongues;
 Kimi ga na tataba   But if rumor touched your name,
 Oshimi koso nake   I would weep for very rage.

1151-53   [MYS IV: 735-37 / 732-34]

Three further poems in reply by Ōtomo no Sukune Yakamochi

(1151)   [735/732]

  Ima shi wa shi   There is in me now,
 Na no oshikeku mo   Oh, now indeed, no remnant

Ware wa nashi	Of care about my name,
Imo ni yorite wa	Though rumor rise a thousand times
Chitabi tatsu to mo	Because of my young love.

(1152) [736/733]

Utsusemi no	Through the locust-husk
Yo ya mo futayuku	World do we pass twice over?
Nani su to ka	What am I doing,
Imo ni awazute	Sleeping all alone at night,
A ga hitori nemu	Never meeting my young love?

(1153) [737/734]

Wa ga omoi	Than that my longing
Kakute arazu wa	Should be thus, it were better
Tama ni mo ga	To be a bead-string,
Makoto mo imo ga	Truly to be wound around
Te ni makaremu o	The arm of my young love!

Lady Ki and Ōtomo no Yakamochi

On Lady Ki and her husband Prince Aki, see nos. 506–11. The Lady may have been a widow when Yakamochi engaged her attention in the early 740's. Their exchanges, of which one is given here, probably took place at Kuni, Emperor Shōmu's temporary capital during 740–44. The Lady pleads age in her first poem—not that she is too old now, but that her eventual abandonment will be harder to bear. She seems to be proposing a platonic relationship in the second (no. 1155). The term *awao* ("foam thread") may refer to lightly twined cord. Yakamochi anticipates Thomas Moore in his feigned disdain for endearing young charms, while painting a more graphic picture of the "dear ruin." Yakamochi was about twenty-two; Lady Ki's age is unknown.

1154–55 [MYS IV: 765–66/762–63]

Two poems sent by Lady Ki to Ōtomo no Sukune Yakamochi (the lady's name was Oshika)

(1154) [765/762]

Kamusabu to	Not for my hoary years
Ina ni wa arazu	Is it that the answer's "No!"
Hata ya hata	Only, it's only
Kaku shite nochi ni	If we do this, what later
Sabushikemu ka mo	Shall I know of loneliness?

(1155)   [766 / 763]

   Tama no o o   If we were to leave
   Awao ni yorite   The two threads that are our souls
     Musuberaba   Twined as light as foam,
   Arite nochi ni mo   Would they not as time goes by
   Awazarame ya mo   Still come round to a meeting?

1156   [MYS IV : 767 / 764]

A poem in which Ōtomo no Sukune Yakamochi replies

   Momotose ni   At a hundred years
   Oishita idete   Drooling from a doddering tongue
     Yoyomu to mo   And crumpled over . . .
   Are wa itowaji   I'd not shun you even then—
   Koi wa masu to mo   If anything, I'd want you more!

Ōtomo no Yakamochi and Lady Fujiwara

The identity of the Lady Fujiwara (Fujiwara no Iratsume) of poem 1158 is unknown. By 741 Yakamochi's marriage was clearly an established fact to be commented on by sympathetic third parties. Yakamochi's mention of the moon in no. 1157 shows that he is watching it too, in a triangulation repeated in no. 1215. The poems are bound not only by the speculative mode, but by the causation of *tsukuyo yomi* ("because the moon is fine") and *michi tōmi* ("because the road is far").

1157   [MYS IV : 768 / 765]

A poem composed by Ōtomo no Sukune Yakamochi in the Kuni capital, thinking of the Elder Maiden of Sakanoue, who had remained behind at the house in Nara

   Hitoeyama   We are held apart
   Henareru mono o   Only by one range of hills—
     Tsukuyo yomi   Does my love go out
   Kado ni idetachi   To stand waiting by the gate,
   Imo ka matsuramu   Now that the moon is so fine?

1158   [MYS IV : 769 / 766]

A poem composed by Lady Fujiwara on hearing this

   Michi tōmi   Though the road is far,
   Koji to wa shireru   And she knows you will not come,
     Mono kara ni   She must be waiting

Shika so matsuramu	Even so as you have said,
Kimi ga me o hori	Eager for your eyes, my lord.

A Certain Person, a Nun, and Ōtomo no Yakamochi

An unusual exchange ends the section of Book VIII devoted to autumn love poems, and its placement suggests a date sometime while the capital was at Kuni (740–44). The unique feature of the exchange is that the final tanka is divided in two, the first three lines (the *tōku*) composed by a nun, and the last two (the *matsuku*) by Yakamochi. The identical division characterizes linked verse (renga), a major poetic form that flourished from the thirteenth to the nineteenth century, and that began with such playful splittings of tanka as this. No. 1161 thus has the historical distinction of being the "first renga." The whole exchange is cast in the allegorical mode, the planting metaphors of the tanka by "a certain person" being familiar from poems like no. 1128. One line of interpretation is that "a certain person" is a man who has been raising a daughter of the nun born before she entered religion. Now the girl is coming of age, and the man wonders if his trouble will be rewarded. The nun's reply stops at an ambiguous point, and it is Yakamochi's final two lines that supply the answer. Who the nun was and why she turned to Yakamochi to complete her poem remain mysteries. The Korean nun Rigan, a dependent of the Ōtomo family, comes to mind (see nos. 723–24). As a foreigner she might have needed help with her waka, and so recruited the talents of the young Yakamochi. Rigan died in 735, however, too early for the series in which nos. 1159–61 are found, unless the three poems are an out-of-sequence addition tacked on at the end. In any case, since Yakamochi was "challenged" (*atoraerarete*) to complete the poem, there seems more wit than helplessness involved.

1159–60   [MYS VIII: 1637–38 / 1633–34]

Two poems sent to a nun by a certain person

(1159)   [1637 / 1633]

Te mo sumani	Hands never resting,
Ueshi hagi ni ya	I toiled to plant the clover bush—
Kaerite wa	And must my reward
Miredo mo akazu	Be thus to wear my heart away
Kokoro tsukusamu	Gazing with avid eyes?

(1160)   [1638 / 1634]

Koromode ni	In the paddy field
Mishibu tsuku made	Until sleeves were foul with scum

Ueshi ta o	I toiled at planting—
Hikita wa ga hae	And it was I who strung the clapper
Mamoreru kurushi	To guard the crop—a weary task!

1161   [MYS VIII: 1639 / 1635]

A poem in reply, of which the first three lines were written by the nun, and the last two added by Ōtomo no Sukune Yakamochi, who was challenged by her [to complete the verse]

Saogawa no	Damming the waters
Mizu o sekiagete	Of Sao River, he planted
Ueshi ta o	The paddy field

(By the nun)

| Karu wasaii wa | Whose first harvest of young rice |
| Hitori narubeshi | Will be his alone to taste. |

(Added by Yakamochi)

Ōtomo no Yakamochi and Fujiwara no Kuzumaro

On Fujiwara no Kuzumaro's relationship to Yakamochi, see the commentary to nos. 839–41. An undated exchange between the two men (nos. 1162–68) is recorded at the end of Book IV. It is clear enough from context and convention that the subject of the exchange is a young girl in whom Kuzumaro is interested, the plum serving the same metaphorical function as the orange in no. 1128 and the bush clover and rice in the immediately preceding series. If the girl was Yakamochi's daughter, she must have been very young indeed, for the set comes directly after poems from the early 740's, when Yakamochi was barely in his twenties. A proposal intended to get around this difficulty has been made to the effect that the girl may have been the offspring of Yakamochi's concubine from a previous relationship. It seems preferable to admit the limits of our knowledge, rather than compound ambiguity with speculation.

The exchange opens with Yakamochi replying to a poem or poems by Kuzumaro that have not been preserved. His first poem (no. 1162) is an orthodox allegorical treatment of the plum image, an elegantly indirect way of asking Kuzumaro to be patient. The second poem (no. 1163) is more intriguing—why does Yakamochi feel he is in a dream when Kuzumaro sends his repeated messages? Is he honored, or is there something unreal about the situation, given his own age and that of the young girl? No. 1164 reverts to the plum metaphor, joining it to the latent vegetal force of *shigemi* ("lush") to create another puzzle. Why are people talking? Is it a gabble of avid suitors, or does the world suspect Yakamochi of an improper propinquity to the young plum? Yakamochi is still bemused in his second set of poems (nos. 1165–66), and it is clear that the suit being pressed is causing him some worry. The whole exchange is set in spring, no doubt because that is when it took place, but also appropriately to the images of budding and immaturity. Here spring mist and spring wind add to the dreamy atmosphere. In no. 1166 he reassures Kuzumaro that time and the effect of rumor are in his favor. In his first reply (no. 1167) Kuzumaro uses a representative jo of the type often found in love poetry to provide the objective correlative of his emotion. The jo is tied to the main statement through the repeated *ne* ("root") in *nemokoro* ("cordially"), a word whose derivation is *ne-mokoro* ("rootlike"). Kuzumaro's second reply (no. 1168) responds to Yakamochi's first (no. 1162). It seems likely that in both cases "spring rain" (*harusame*) stands for the constant shower of Kuzumaro's attentions. It is not clear whether Kuzumaro's own young plum grows on the ground of primary reference (i.e., is a tree in his garden), or whether it continues the metaphor, in which case we are to understand that he too has a young daughter.

1162–64   [MYS IV : 789–91 / 786–88]

Three poems sent in reply to Fujiwara no Asomi Kuzumaro by Ōtomo no Sukune Yakamochi

(1162)   [789 / 786]

Haru no ame wa	That the rains of spring
Iyashikifuru ni	Come down daily more, and yet
Ume no hana	The blossom of the plum
Imada sakanaku	Has not yet come forth in bloom—
Ito wakami kamo	Perhaps it's still a bit too young?

(1163)   [790 / 787]

Ime no goto	How like a dream
Omōyuru kamo	The feeling comes over me,
Hashiki yashi	My cherished lord,
Kimi ga tsukai no	When I see your many messengers
Maneku kayoeba	Come beating a path to my door!

(1164)   [791 / 788]

Urawakami	Tender little twigs
Hana sakigataki	Hardly set to break in bloom,
Ume o uete	The plum I planted—
Hito no koto shigemi	And yet such a thicket of gossip
Omoi so wa ga suru	That I'm lost for what to do!

1165–66   [MYS IV : 792–93 / 789–90]

Two more poems sent by Yakamochi to Fujiwara no Asomi Kuzumaro

(1165)   [792 / 789]

    Kokoroguku   How my heart fails
    Omōyuru kamo   All this weary, worried time!
      Harukasumi   Days of hazy spring
    Tanabiku toki ni   Stretching on and on in mist—
    Koto no kayoeba   And the messages keep coming.

(1166)   [793 / 790]

    Harukaze no   When like wind in spring
    Oto ni shi denaba   Whispers run across the land
      Arisarite   And the days go by,
    Ima narazu to mo   Even if not now, at last
    Kimi ga manimani   All will be as you desire.

1167–68   [MYS IV : 794–95 / 791–92]

Two poems coming from Fujiwara no Asomi Kuzumaro in reply

(1167)   [794 / 791]

    Okuyama no   In inner mountains
    Iwakage ni ouru   In the shadow of the rocks
      Suga no ne no   Grows the rooted sedge—
    Nemokoro ware mo   Fine, tenacious roots of love
    Aimowazare ya   Sink no less deep in me.

(1168)   [795 / 792]

    Harusame o   Spring rain—oh, indeed
    Matsu to ni shi arashi   That is what it's waiting for;
      Wa ga yado no   The young plum tree
    Wakaki no ume mo   At my own house too has still
    Imada fufumeri   Its bloom held close in bud.

An Impromptu Snow Party

Unlike Ōtomo no Tabito's plum-blossom event of 730, which no doubt was planned well in advance, the celebration of an unusually heavy snowfall in the first month of 746 was a spur-of-the-moment affair, and of the twenty-two poems composed on the occasion, only five were written down. Yakamochi, one of the participants, included them in Book XVIII. His headnote gives an account of what transpired, and in his footnote he lists all those present. For the first time in five years the court was back in Nara for the new year, and so no doubt the snow seemed doubly auspicious (see no. 853). The Minister of the Left, Tachibana no Moroe, then at the height of his power, personally led his entourage of Princes and officials to the residence of former Empress Genshō (680–748; r. 715–24), the sister of Emperor Mommu and aunt of Emperor Shōmu. Fujiwara no Toyonari, the brother of Nakamaro (though not belonging to his faction), was a rising figure at court and would be made Minister of the Right in another three years.

The first poem (no. 1169) is by Moroe, and speaks of his service to the *ōkimi*, the "great lord"—that is, the occupant of the throne, who both then and at the time of his rise to power in 738 was Emperor Shōmu, though no doubt here the term is intended to extend by courtesy to the former Empress. Snow, the designated topic, is skillfully worked into a reference to Moroe's venerable locks. The author of the next poem (no. 1170), Ki no Kiyohito (d. 753), was a scholar who served as tutor to Shōmu when he was Crown Prince. He rose to be *monjō hakase* ("Doctor of Literature") at the official university and also served as a court-appointed historian. In his poem he does not presume to speak of his own services in the wake of the Minister of the Left, but does echo his respectful last line. *Yuki no hikari* ("the shining of snow") is a translation term from Chinese, and probably is intended as a metaphor for the imperial favor.

Ki no Okaji, the author of no. 1171, was a minor official whose known career runs from the 740's into the 760's. In 746 he was Assistant Director of the Board of Censors (*danjōdai no suke*). From his poem we learn that it had been snowing for three days. He is also the most observant of visual detail; unlike the others, he does not address himself to the auspicious significance of the snow. Fujii no Moroai (no. 1172) gives documentation for the belief that snow at New Year augurs a rich harvest. He deliberately uses the noun *toshi* twice in his poem, once in its derived sense of "year," and once in its original meaning of "rice harvest." Moroai was a minor official who at this time held the rank of Outer Junior Fifth Lower. The Outer ranks were inferior to the Inner or regular ones and were assigned to officials of undistinguished families. Yakamochi lists Moroai's poem before his own as a courtesy, though he held the higher regular rank of Junior Fifth Lower. In no. 1173 Yakamochi echoes the auspicious vision of Kiyohito's poem (no. 1170), ending with a terminal formula of praise used twenty times in *Man'yōshū*, starting with MYS 1:36 (no. 293) by Hitomaro.

Information on the participants whose poems were not written down is given in the backnote on this exchange. Hada no Chōgan, the object of Tachibana no Moroe's witticism, was a learned professor of medicine and the Chinese language. He was born in China, though his father was a student member of the Japanese official embassy of 702. In 719 he was made a Hada (the Hada [or Hata] were of Korean ancestry) and given the clan title Imiki, used for clans of foreign descent. He eventually rose to be Chief of the Bureau of Statistics (*kazoe no kami*). The point of Moroe's jest seems to be double—as a "foreigner" Chōgan might be excused for having trouble with waka, but as a doctor he could be expected to possess the rare and expensive musk, a substance obtained from musk deer in Tibet and South China, and no doubt of medicinal as well as aromatic properties.

In the first month of Tempyō 18 [746] much white snow fell, and several inches accumulated on the ground. Hereupon Minister of the Left Lord Tachibana escorted Major Counselor Fujiwara no Toyonari Asomi and several Princes and courtiers to the residence of the Retired Sovereign (the west precinct of the Empress's palace), where they performed the service of sweeping away the snow. At this she issued a command that the Great Ministers, the Imperial Advisers, and the Princes wait upon her in the great hall, and the Ministers and Masters in the narrow hall, where she had them served with wine and feasted them. By imperial order she proclaimed, "You, my Princes and Lords, be so good as to make a few compositions on this snowfall and severally submit your poems."

1169   [MYS XVII: 3944 / 3922]

A poem by Minister of the Left Tachibana no Sukune in response to imperial command

Furu yuki no	Until falling snow
Shirokami made ni	Is no whiter than my hair
Ōkimi ni	In loyal service
Tsukaematsureba	I have waited on my lord,
Tōtoku mo aru ka	And my heart is filled with awe.

1170   [MYS XVII: 3945 / 3923]

A poem by Ki no Asomi Kiyohito in response to imperial command

Ame no shita	All under heaven
Sude ni ōite	Covered over completely
Furu yuki no	By the falling snow—
Hikari o mireba	When I look at the shining
Tōtoku mo aru ka	My heart is filled with awe.

1171   [MYS XVII: 3946 / 3924]

A poem by Ki no Asomi Okaji in response to imperial command

Yama no kai	The mountain chasm
Soko to mo miezu	Cannot be seen where once it was
Ototsuhi mo	Now that this snowfall

| Kinō mo kyō mo | Has gone on from two days ago |
| Yuki no furereba | Through yesterday and today. |

1172   [MYS XVII: 3947 / 3925]

A poem by Fujii no Muraji Moroai in response to imperial command

Aratashiki	At the beginning
Toshi no hajime ni	Of the new year the coming
Toyo no toshi	Of bountiful harvest
Shirusu to narashi	Surely is augured already
Yuki no fureru wa	In the falling of the snow.

1173   [MYS XVII: 3948 / 3926]

A poem by Ōtomo no Sukune Yakamochi in response to imperial command

Ōmiya no	Until a shining
Uchi ni mo to ni mo	Fills the palace and the land
Hikaru made	Beyond its gates,
Furasu shirayuki	To our joy the white snow falls—
Miredo akanu kamo	I gaze but do not weary.

Fujiwara no Toyonari Asomi, Kose no Natemaro Asomi, Ōtomo no Ushi-kai Sukune, Fujiwara no Nakamaro Asomi, Prince Mihara, Prince Chinu, Prince Funa, Prince Ōchi, Prince Oda, Prince Hayashi, Hozumi no Asomi Oyu, Oda no Asomi Morohito, Ono no Asomi Tsunate, Takahashi no Asomi Kunitari, Ō no Asomi Tokotari, Takaoka no Muraji Kafuchi, Hada no Imiki Chōgan, Narahara no Miyatsuko Azumato

[Seventeen of the eighteen Princes and courtiers named above] composed poems in response to command, and submitted them in order. Their poems were not written down at the time and so have been lost. However, in the case of Hada no Imiki Chōgan, Minister of the Left Lord Tachibana made sport of him, saying, "If you are not able to compose a poem, you may make amends by presenting musk." Because of this he kept silent.

Ōtomo no Yakamochi and Ōtomo no Ikenushi I: Poems at a Banquet

In the seventh month of the year of the snow poems (746) Yakamochi was appointed Governor of Etchū and went to take up residence in that province. The following exchange (nos. 1174–81) took place a month later. His partner in the exchange is his kinsman Ikenushi, the provincial Secretary. Apparently the rice was ripening in the fields of Etchū on a date corresponding to August 27 in the Western calendar, and Ikenushi may have been out inspecting the crops during the day. Yakamochi's first poem (no. 1174) immediately reveals the warm and easy affection that existed between the two men. Ikenushi has apparently brought back a bouquet of *ominaeshi* ("maiden flowers"), a yellow-flowering autumn grass growing wild in the fields. Yakamochi quite possibly is also suggesting that Ikenushi has been flirting with the farm girls ("maiden flowers") on his way. Ikenushi answers in kind (no. 1175). He has indeed been wandering among the maiden flowers but has remained true to his friend. "To come the long way round" (*tamotōri-kinu*) means to go to a rendezvous by a circuitous route in order to escape detection (see no. 1297). Thus Ikenushi joins in the Ōtomo love of verbal love-play.

Ikenushi's next two poems (nos. 1176–77) deal with the cold and loneliness of autumn, and the tone is more serious. Ikenushi and Yakamochi have both left their wives behind in the capital. But Ikenushi's no. 1177 shows he has been in the province longer than Yakamochi: the cuckoo, a bird of summer, is now gone from its erstwhile haunts. Yakamochi responds by countering Ikenushi's vanished cuckoo with the newly arriving wild geese that winter in Japan. His no. 1178 is well integrated in mood with what Ikenushi has just provided. It is instructive that such sere, cold poems could be composed at presumably convivial banquets. In his second reply (no. 1179) Yakamochi addresses himself to Ikenushi's no. 1176. The wished-for garment becomes a sash actually tied by his wife. The focus has shifted from deprivation to fidelity. (Interestingly enough, Yakamochi received in the mail twelve ardent love poems from a woman not his wife shortly after arriving in Etchū. He includes them sans reply.) Ikenushi's next response (no. 1180) preserves a solidarity of virtue with his friend. Yakamochi's final poem plays the theme of self-denial out to its maudlin end, hinting a need to reassure himself of his unwavering integrity, and suggesting also that the time has come to clear the cups away.

1174–81   [MYS XVII: 3965–72 / 3943–50]

Poems from the banquet held at the official residence of Governor Ōtomo no Sukune Yakamochi on the night of the seventh of the eighth month [of 746]

(1174)   [3965 / 3943]

Aki no ta no	Through the autumn fields
Homuki migateri	You went to see the nodding grain,
Wa ga seko ga	But all the while
Fusa taorikeru	You were pulling from their stems,
Ominaeshi kamo	Old friend, these maiden flowers!

The above poem is by Governor Ōtomo no Sukune Yakamochi.

(1175)   [3966 / 3944]

    Ominaeshi   Where maiden flowers
Sakitaru nohe o   Blossomed in the meadowland
    Yukimeguri   I went to and fro,
Kimi o omoide   And then remembering my lord,
Tamotōrikinu   I came the long way round.

(1176)   [3967 / 3945]

    Aki no yo wa   These autumn nights
Akatoki samushi   It is cold in the dawning:
    Shirotae no   Oh, how I wish
Imo ga koromode   I could have my darling's robe
Kimu yoshi mogamo   Of white bark cloth to wear!

(1177)   [3968 / 3946]

    Hototogisu   Down from the hillside
Nakite suginishi   Where the cuckoo sang one day
    Okabi naru   As he passed me by,
Akikaze fukinu   Now the autumn wind comes blowing—
Yoshi mo aranaku ni   And no way to bear the cold!

The above three poems are by Secretary Ōtomo no Sukune Ikenushi.

(1178)   [3969 / 3947]

    Kesa no asake   The autumn wind was cold
Akikaze samushi   At break of day this morning;
    Tōtsuhito   Has the time drawn near
Kari ga kinakamu   For wild geese to come crying,
Toki chikami ka mo   Visitors from a far land?

(1179)   [3970 / 3948]

    Amazakaru   In this country place
Hina ni tsuki henu   Far beyond the skies of home
    Shikaredo mo   A month has gone by,
Yuiteshi himo o   But the sash she tied for me
Toki mo akenaku ni   I have not loosened to this day.

The above two poems are by Governor Ōtomo no Sukune Yakamochi.

(1180)   [3971 / 3949]

    Amazakaru   Surely she must know
Hina ni aru ware o   Beyond doubt that we would never
    Utagata mo   Take off our sashes,

Himo tokisakete   Though here we are in the country
Omōsurame ya   Up beyond the skies of home.

The above poem is by Secretary Ōtomo no Sukune Ikenushi.

(1181)   [3972/3950]

   Ie ni shite   Who would ever know
Yuiteshi himo o   How my longing heart is bent
  Tokisakezu   On never loosening
Omou kokoro o   The sash she tied around me
Tare ka shiramu mo   In our house before I left?

The above poem is by Governor Ōtomo no Sukune Yakamochi.

Ōtomo no Yakamochi and Ōtomo no Ikenushi II: Yakamochi's Illness

Yakamochi fell ill in the second month of 747 and during his convalescence exchanged several letters, chōka, tanka, and kanshi with Ikenushi. This correspondence (nos. 1185–99), in which Yakamochi and Ikenushi write back and forth to each other in two languages and four literary forms, documents better than any other passage in *Man'yōshū* the culturally and linguistically complex nature of the Nara literatus and his modes of expression. There is a special fascination in listening to the same voices alter their modes of expression as they shift from the conventions of Six Dynasties prose and poetry to those of the by now highly developed native verse. The correspondence also documents a special friendship. For all the fancy language, the unfeigned delight of the two men in each other is unmistakable. The Chinese literary ethos of friendship gives the means of expression to what Yakamochi and Ikenushi must have felt for each other, and also, as literature will, encourages them to have the feelings so expressed. Again, it is of interest to see how they carry over these feelings into waka. Yakamochi and Ikenushi may be said to have invented a waka of male companionship.

Though the first poem here, the chōka-hanka set 1182–84, is not addressed to Ikenushi, and thus strictly speaking is not part of the exchange, it introduces the subject of Yakamochi's illness and so seems the best place to begin. It may have been intended for Yakamochi's wife and her mother, who were on his mind as he wrote, but more likely, as he implies in his footnote, Yakamochi wrote it for himself and laid it aside. Lines 45–48 of the chōka say that he "cannot" send a message to his wife (who has remained in Nara). This may be another way of saying he has no intention of doing so, that by the time the messenger arrived he would be either dead or well. Or perhaps he wishes to spare his wife the worry.

As in a number of other chōka he wrote in Etchū, Yakamochi begins the poem with a passage on how he came as Governor at imperial command, projecting a heroic image of himself as a faithful official crossing the mountains to a distant realm. This masurao image (line 3) is always on Yakamochi's mind, an acknowledgment even in private poems of his public duty. Here he is able to use it as a contrast to his common mortality (lines 13–14), a conjunction repeated at the end, where he calls himself an *arashio*, a "rough man" (line 56). As he lies in bed he thinks first of his "mother"— really a reference to Lady Ōtomo of Sakanoue—and then of his wife. *Haha* ("mother") is given its usual epithet *tarachine no*, variously understood as "drooping-breasted," "nourishing," or "female pendulous with milk." Both *haha* and *tsuma* ("wife"; line 20) are followed by the respectful *no mikoto*, translated "my honored." His wife folds back her sleeves (*Koromode o / Orikaeshitsutsu*; lines 31–32) as a charm to obtain the dream she desires. The family picture of the two yearning women is completed by reference to Yakamochi's children. Like Okura's (no. 626, 640), his children are fretting and crying. We learn here that he has at least one son and daughter (to be distinguished from the child or children left by his concubine). The poet's reluctance to die in a far country, and his helplessness, are conveyed powerfully at the end. The first envoy is a sigh, blending a perception of the world as empty with an ironic vision of dying amid the scattering blossoms of spring. The second redirects the line of sight from fluttering petals (perhaps visible outside Yakamochi's bedroom) to the *omokage* of a distant, beloved woman.

1182–84 [MYS XVII: 3984–86 / 3962–64]

Suddenly I sank into an inexplicable illness; I was well on my way to the [Yellow] Springs. And so I composed these lyrics to express my sad feelings: one poem with *tanka*

	Ōkimi no	To our great lord's charge
	Make no manimani	Obedient, I came away,
	Masurao no	Rousing in myself
	Kokoro furiokoshi	The heart of a valiant man;
5	Ashihiki no	Over leg-cramping
	Yamasaka koete	Mountain slopes I crossed
	Amazakaru	And came down
	Hina ni kudariki	To a hinterland beneath far skies.
	Iki dani mo	While still I gasp
10	Imada yasumezu	Without rest to catch my breath,
	Toshitsuki mo	And the years and months
	Ikura mo aranu ni	Come yet to nothing at all,
	Utsusemi no	Being but a man
	Yo no hito nareba	Of the actual, mortal world,
15	Uchinabiki	Now I lie stretched out
	Toko ni koifushi	Tossing on a bed of pain,

	Itakeku shi	The hurt in my body
	Hi ni ke ni masaru	Growing worse from day to day.
	Tarachine no	My honored mother,
20	Haha no mikoto no	She who bounteously fostered me,
	Ōbune no	Must now be waiting,
	Yukura yukura ni	Yearning down deep, uneasy
	Shitagoi ni	As a great ship
	Itsu ka mo komu to	Riding, rolling in the waves,
25	Matasuramu	Wondering when I'll come,
	Kokoro sabushiku	Sad at heart and lonely.
	Hashiki yoshi	And—well beloved!—
	Tsuma no mikoto mo	She my honored wife must too
	Akekureba	When the dawn has come
30	Kado ni yoritachi	Go out and stand by the gate,
	Koromode o	Or when evening falls
	Orikaeshitsutsu	Brush smooth our bed for sleep,
	Yū sareba	First and always
	Toko uchiharai	Turning back the sleeves of her robe,
35	Nubatama no	And, spreading out
	Kurokami shikite	Her hair that gleams jetberry-black,
	Itsu shi ka to	Lie down to her sighing,
	Nagekasuramu so	Wondering when, when, how long.
	Imo mo se mo	Sisters and brothers,
40	Wakaki kodomo wa	The little children too
	Ochikochi ni	Will be fretful,
	Sawakinakuramu	Crying on every side.
	Tamahoko no	For the jewel-spear road
	Michi o tadōmi	Stretches far and far away—
45	Matsukai mo	It will do no good
	Yaru yoshi mo nashi	To dispatch a messenger,
	Omōshiki	And I cannot send
	Kototsute yarazu	The words that burden my thoughts,
	Kouru ni shi	So that in yearning
50	Kokoro wa moenu	All my heart is burnt away.
	Tamakiwaru	Greedy of my life,
	Inochi oshikedo	Life wherein the spirit dwells,
	Semu sube no	Yet I know nothing,
	Tadoki o shirani	No remedy I might employ—
55	Kaku shite ya	Must it then be thus
	Arashio sura ni	That even a rough and stalwart man
	Nagekifuseramu	Moans and lies down at last?
	Yo no naka wa	When you count the world
	Kazu naki mono ka	Does it then add up to nothing?
	Haruhana no	For if one must die

Chiri no magai ni	Amid the flickering swirl of bloom
Shinubeki omoeba	When the petals of spring flowers fall . . .

Yama kawa no	Since it is a far way
Sokie o tōmi	Over mountains and rivers,
Hashiki yoshi	Must I lie sighing,
Imo o aimizu	Never seeing my dear one,
Kaku ya nagekamu	The dear woman I love so well?

Concerning the above, I distracted myself by composing these verses when I lay ill and afflicted with grief at the Governor's Residence in the province of Etchū, on the twentieth day of the second month, in the spring of Tempyō 19 [747].

❋ Nine days after composing the above poem Yakamochi wrote to Ikenushi. His letter manages to combine stylistic niceties such as the playful repetition of "spring" (an admired Six Dynasties ornamentation, and not intended for comic effect) with information on his physical condition (one senses his convalescence is progressing well) and a mock humility that characterizes the correspondence on both sides. The disclaimer about dislocating Ikenushi's estimable (lit., "jade") jaw is derived from a Chinese source, and of course the whole flowery and (potentially) bibulous ambience is highly Chinese. The term for "yearning" in "my yearning grows ever deeper" is of a peculiarly romantic intensity. The two tanka (nos. 1185–86) recapitulate the desire for "a good time" in terms of enjoying the spring blossoms with Ikenushi. The spring blossom associated with the warbler is most often the plum, but even in the snow country of Etchū the season must have been too late for those earliest bloomers by a date corresponding to April 13 in the Julian calendar. In his replies Ikenushi mentions cherry blossoms and the *yamabuki*, both of which bloom later than the plum.

1185–86   [MYS XVII: 3987–88 / 3965–66]

Two sad poems sent by Governor Ōtomo no Sukune Yakamochi to Secretary Ōtomo no Sukune Ikenushi

Suddenly I sank into an inexplicable illness and suffered pain for several weeks. I prayed to a hundred gods and have obtained some relief. But my body is still aching and listless, my muscles weakened and soft. Since I am not yet up to calling on you to render my thanks, my yearning grows ever deeper. Just now on spring mornings the spring flowers pour their fragrance through the spring garden, and on spring evenings the spring warblers twitter among the spring groves. This is the season for enjoying cithern and wine cask. I am in the mood for a good time but unable to face the effort of hobbling along with a cane. Lying alone within my curtains, I dash off these trivial verses, which I take the liberty of presenting to you, committing the offense of dislocating your estimable jaw [with laughter]. They go as follows:

(1185)   [3987/3965]

Haru no hana	The spring blossoms
Ima wa sakari ni	Must now be out in splendor,
Niouramu	In all their fragrance:
Orite kazasamu	Oh, if I only had the strength
Tajikara mogamo	To break a sprig for my brow!

(1186)   [3988/3966]

Uguisu no	These spring blossoms
Nakichirasuramu	That the warbler must be scattering
Haru no hana	All the while he sings—
Itsu shi ka kimi to	When shall I go out with you
Taorikazasamu	And break sprigs to adorn our brows?

Second month, twenty-ninth day [747]. Ōtomo no Sukune Yakamochi.

❋ Ikenushi dates his reply a few days later. The parallel prose of his letter is even more ornate than Yakamochi's, embossed with terms, phrases, and images from half a dozen Chinese sources. His metaphors are harmonized with the central theme of spring in a garden. The peach and the butterfly are new arrivals on the Japanese poetic scene. The *ying*, or Chinese oriole, corresponds to the *uguisu*, or Japanese warbler. Orchid and melilotus stand for the worthy and the gentleman (i.e., for Yakamochi and Ikenushi). Wisteria fiber is particularly rough and therefore ill matched with brocade. Overall, Ikenushi's composition reflects the structure of Yakamochi's, and like his combines the exhilaration of writing in a rich and foreign idiom with the bright enthusiasm of friendship. He matches Yakamochi's two tanka with two of his own. Yakamochi's undifferentiated spring blossoms are defined as cherry and wild mountain rose (the yellow-flowering *yamabuki*). The wish in Yakamochi's first poem is responded to by a wish in Ikenushi's first, and the blossom-scattering warbler in the second merely sings in Ikenushi's reply. Nature holds its breath and waits for Yakamochi to recover.

1187–88   [MYS XVII: 3989–90/3967–68]

Unexpectedly I have been honored by your fragrant epistle, a garden of letters soaring above the clouds. In addition you have bestowed on me Japanese poems, a grove of words spread out like brocade. I have murmured them to myself, I have recited them aloud, and have succeeded in relieving the longing in my heart. Spring is a time for enjoyment, and the scenery of late spring is the most moving of all. The red peach blooms brightly, and the merry butterfly flutters around the blossoms; the green willow trails gracefully, and the charming oriole hides in the leaves and sings. How enjoyable it is! To sit close together in open comradeship, so that minds commune and words are forgotten—how pleasant it is, how beautiful it is: how worthy of praise the inner reaches of our hearts! But how could we have foreseen this—that orchid and melilotus would be separated by thickets of grass, and that without recourse to cithern and wine cask we should let the brave season go by in vain, so that nature scorns man? This is my grievance, and I cannot remain silent. I know I shall be joining wisteria [fabric] to brocade, as the vulgar phrase has it. My one aim is to provide you a little amusement.

(1187)   [3989 / 3967]

Yamagai ni	If I could show you
Sakeru sakura o	The cherry trees a-flower
Tada hitome	In the mountain folds,
Kimi ni miseteba	Were it but a single glance,
Nani o ka omowamu	What more could I desire?

(1188)   [3990 / 3968]

Uguisu no	The wild mountain rose
Kinaku yamabuki	Where the warbler comes to sing—
Utagata mo	In all truth I ask,
Kimi ga te furezu	Would it ever drop its bloom
Hana chirame ya mo	Without a touch from your hand?

Third month, second day [747]. Secretary Ōtomo no Sukune Ikenushi.

※ In his next letter, dated the following day, Yakamochi does not attempt to match the density of Ikenushi's style; little of the phraseology has been traced to specific Chinese works. The composition is of particular interest, however, for providing a rare glimpse of a self-aware Nara poet thinking about literature. The insistent self-deprecation is of course dictated by the conventions of the correspondence and must therefore be disregarded. What emerges from the two sentences, "However, when young . . . ," and "In my tender years . . ." is that Yakamochi thought of "the niceties of style," presumably kambun style, in terms of training in "the garden of the arts," either the court university or the poetic circles devoted to Chinese composition, and of "fashioning a poem" (i.e., a waka) as something one learned from a master poet. Yakamochi's masters (taking his disclaimer in the negative) were "Yama and Kaki." "Kaki" is surely Kakinomoto no Hitomaro;

"Yama" may be either Yamabe no Akahito or Yamanoue no Okura. Hitomaro had passed from the scene long before Yakamochi's birth, and so betaking oneself to his gates must mean studying his collected works. Such study, as well as Yakamochi's activities as an anthologist, speaks of a consciously held idea of literature as a cumulative learned tradition based on written documents. The idea is hardly amazing from our point of view, but represents an enormous and crucial change from the concept Hitomaro himself inherited of a poetic art still in the process of emerging from bardic song. Yakamochi quite likely did know Okura as a boy, and could have known Akahito, but it is probable that he here regards whichever one of them he was referring to in the same light as Hitomaro—as a poet whose poems are down on paper and form part of his nation's literature.

This time Yakamochi's letter is followed by a chōka with three envoys, nos. 1189–92. The chōka draws from no. 1182 extensively in its description of his illness, leaving out the part about his wife and "mother," and adding a section on the pleasures of spring. In particular, lines 1–2, 9–12, and 23–32 correspond to 1–2, 15–18, 43–48, and 51–54 of the earlier poem, in most cases identically. This large-scale reworking of a poem written only a fortnight before suggests that Yakamochi had decided to regard it as a first draft, not to be sent out. Fortunately, he later decided to include it in *Man'yōshū*, so that it is possible to observe this practical example of the poet at work, integrating old lines into a new structure. Given the prevalence in *Man'yōshū* of formulaic lines that were the common property of all poets, we must recognize in this a process that on one level or another was going on all the time. The contrast between the author as *masurao* and as sick and suffering man elaborated in no. 1182, then, forms the first half of no. 1189, down to line 36. The second half of the poem sets up another contrast, between all that Yakamochi is missing by being shut in and the pleasure he experiences at Ikenushi's thoughtfulness. The vision of spring adds red-skirted girls to the blossoms and birds already celebrated. As so often, the red skirts are wet, perhaps clinging, in an incipiently erotic image bespeaking a resurgence of life force. The last seven lines turn directly to Ikenushi in a characteristic expression of fondness, speaking for the "solaced heart" (*nagusamuru kokoro*) lacking earlier (lines 35–36). The first two envoys are a direct reply to Ikenushi's nos. 1187–88, reasserting a plaintive note of envy. The third, like a wave of lassitude, carries the poet back to bed and listless moping.

1189–92   [MYS XVII: 3991–94 / 3969–72]

A further poem I sent; with *tanka*

> Your magnanimous virtue has condescended to give thought to this wormwood body; your incalculable favor has extended comfort to this petty mind. I am overwhelmed by your attentions, for which there is no

possible comparison. However, when young I did not frequent the garden of arts, and consequently the products of my flowing brush are naturally deficient in the niceties of style. In my tender years I never betook myself to the gates of Yama or Kaki, so that now when it comes to fashioning a poem I lose my words amidst thickets of grass and trees. And in this connection I am abashed at your reference to joining wisteria to brocade; rather, I have gone on to indite a composition that is tantamount to mixing stones with gems. It is my old habit, vulgar and stupid, of being unable to remain silent. And so I present you a few lines, whereby I shall repay your kindness with a laugh. They go as follows:

Ōkimi no	To our great lord's charge
Make no manimani	Obedient, I came away
Shinazakaru	Over the many-folded
Koshi o osame ni	Mountains to Koshi, the far land
5　Idete koshi	Of my governance;
Masura ware sura	Stalwart was I—and yet
Yo no naka no	The world is such
Tsune shi nakereba	That nothing in it stays for long:
Uchinabiki	Soon I lay stretched out,
10　Toko ni koifushi	Tossing on a bed of pain.
Itakeku no	The hurt in my body
Hi ni ke ni maseba	Grew worse from day to day,
Kanashikeku	And sad memories
Koko ni omoide	Began to rise in my mind,
15　Iranakeku	Sharp, stabbing thorns
Soko ni omoide	In every memory that came.
Nageku sora	My moody sighs
Yasukenaku ni	Trailed off uneasily,
Omou sora	My brooding sorrows
20　Kurushiki mono o	Were hard to bear alone—but now
Ashihiki no	Leg-cramping mountains
Yama kihenarite	Stood as barriers between,
Tamahoko no	And the jewel-spear road
Michi no tōkeba	Stretched far and far away:
25　Matsukai mo	It would do no good
Yaru yoshi mo nami	To dispatch a messenger;
Omōshiki	My burdened thoughts
Koto mo kayowazu	Would never reach their goal.
Tamakiwaru	Greedy of my life,
30　Inochi oshikedo	Life wherein the spirit dwells,
Semu sube no	Yet I knew nothing,
Tadoki o shirani	No remedy I might employ,
Komoriite	And so stayed closed in,

606

	Omoinagekai	Brooding and lost in sighs,
35	Nagusamuru	Without a solace
	Kokoro wa nashi ni	To bring comfort to my heart:
	Haruhana no	The blossoms of spring
	Sakeru sakari ni	Bloom now in all their splendor,
	Omou dochi	But I do not go
40	Taorikazasazu	With friends to pluck them for my brow;
	Haru no no no	On the springtime fields
	Shigemi tobikuku	The warbler plunges in and out
	Uguisu no	Through the lush new growth,
	Koe dani kikazu	But I do not even hear its song.
45	Otomera ga	The unmarried girls,
	Haruna tsumasu to	Going out to pick spring herbs,
	Kurenai no	Walk to and fro
	Akamo no suso no	In skirts of crimson red
	Harusame ni	Whose hems must now
50	Nioihizuchite	Be shining in the wetness
	Kayouramu	Of the soft spring rain.
	Toki no sakari o	All this splendor of the season
	Itazura ni	Has passed me by,
	Sugushiyaritsure	Wasted and thrown away.
55	Shinowaseru	Yet you thought of me,
	Kimi ga kokoro o	And the fineness of your gentle heart
	Uruwashimi	Touched me so deeply
	Kono yo sugara ni	That last night the whole night through
	I mo nezu ni	I could not sleep,
60	Kyō mo shimera ni	And again today I cannot find
	Koitsutsu so oru	Hours enough for my yearning.

Ashihiki no	If with you, my friend,
Yamasakurabana	I could see the cherry blossoms
Hitome dani	In the footsore hills,
Kimi to shi miteba	Were it but a single glance,
Are koime ya mo	Would I still feel this yearning?

Yamabuki no	How I envy you,
Shigemi tobikuku	Listening to the warbler
Uguisu no	Singing as it flies,
Koe o kikuramu	Plunging deep in the lushness
Kimi wa tomoshi mo	Of the yellow mountain rose!

Idetatamu	Staying in at home,
Chikara o nami to	Since I haven't strength enough
Komoriite	To start upon my way,

Kimi ni kouru ni   I lie here yearning for you,
Kokorodo mo nashi   With no heart for anything.

Third month, third day [747].—Ōtomo no Sukune Yakamochi

❊ Following Chinese custom, the officials of the Etchū provincial administration held a winding-water banquet (*kyokusui no en*) on the third of the
third month, even though the Governor was indisposed and could not attend. So much, at least, we are to assume from the following composition
by Ikenushi. The composition consists of a prose preface and a kanshi in
eight lines of seven characters each, one of the standard forms of shih. (For
another example of preface and shih, see no. 639.) In the original the even-
numbered lines of the poem rhyme. The two lines of each couplet are structurally parallel, the second and third couplets being particularly strict in this
regard. The structure of the preface too observes the syntactic and imagistic
rhythms of parallel prose, so that esthetically the whole piece partakes of the
virtues and vices of highly ornate metrical writing.

Lustral ceremonies originally held on the first Day of the Serpent in the
third month lay behind the spring poetry-and-wine party of the double
third; hence the reference in the first sentence of the preface and the second
line of the poem. "The company of orchids" (see Ikenushi's previous letter,
nos. 1187–88) is that of worthies and gentlemen. "Mellowing its light"
refers to a passage in the Taoist classic *Lao-tzu* and suggests the noblesse
oblige of superior beings tempering their brilliance so as to mingle with
ordinary mortals. Yakamochi is of course the "star of virtue" that is missing. To "strike silence" (in order to obtain a sound) and to "mouth phrases"
are metaphors for composition drawn from fu in *Wen-hsüan*, the first from
Wen Fu ("Rhyme-Prose on Literature") by Lu Chi (A.D. 261–303), and the
second from *Shu-tu Fu* ("Rhyme-Prose on the Shu Capital") by Tso Ssu
(d. ca. A.D. 300).

The general phrasing of the first three lines of the poem bears a close
resemblance to a shih by the early T'ang poet Ch'en Tzu-ang (661–702).
"Peach Spring" is the realm lost to time described by T'ao Ch'ien (365–427)
in his "Account of Peach-Blossom Spring" (*T'ao-hua-yüan Chi*). The "boats
of the immortals" are the winecups floating down the stream of the winding-water banquet. The "wing cups" and the "nine bends" in line 6 also
refer to this game, in which each guest was to compose a poem before the
cup reached him. Cassia twigs were steeped in the wine to add their flavor
of cinnamon. "Cloud vessels" were earthenware wine jars decorated with
friezes in a conventionalized cloud-and-thunder motif. The wing cups were
either cups with winglike flanges or elaborate vessels made in the shape of
birds, with wings, head, and tail. The "nine bends" alludes to a passage in

Yu-hsien-k'u. The wholehearted celebration of intoxication in the last two lines gives some idea of the sort of thing Tabito was adapting to waka in his sequence on drinking wine (nos. 592–604).

1193   [MYS XVII: 3995 / 3972a]

A poem on an excursion on the third day of the last month of spring, in the seven-word line; with preface

> On this brilliant occasion of the first Day of the Serpent, the late spring scenery is at its finest. Peach blossoms shed their glow on eyelids, sharing in crimson; willow color contains the moss and vies in greenness. Now we join hands and gaze afar over the banks of the rivers; in quest of wine we go to call at the distant house of a dweller in the fields. Already fully under the influence of cithern and wine cask, the company of orchids has mellowed its light. Alas, there is still one thing to regret to-day—that the stars of virtue are already too few. Unless I strike silence and mouth phrases, how can I relate the manner of our loitering? At once I give the task to my inadequate brush and roughly inscribe four rhymes.

> The smiling days of remaining spring may well be cherished.
> The scenery on the First Serpent is worth an excursion.
> Rows of willows by the river cast bright patterns on our gala dress.
> Peach Spring connects to the sea and carries boats of the immortals.
> We dip cassia from cloud vessels brimming with clear wine.
> Wing cups urge us on, floating past the nine bends.
> Unrestrainedly drunk, our ecstatic hearts forget me and thee.
> Hopelessly soused, there isn't anywhere we don't plop down for a stay.

> Third month, fourth day.—Ōtomo no Sukune Ikenushi

❋ Having widened the discourse to include kanshi in his dispatch of the fourth, Ikenushi goes on the next day to answer Yakamochi's letter and chōka-hanka set of the third. In his kambun he works himself up to new heights of adulation of his friend, using the opportunity to display further his mastery of style and allusion. In the process he assures Yakamochi that he (Yakamochi), not Yama or Kaki, is the greatest poet Japan has produced. All this might smack of sycophancy from a subordinate were it not for the quite different tone of the chōka that follows, where Ikenushi takes Yakamochi to task for self-pity. The cordial warmth of the Japanese establishes an atmosphere of easy, teasing informality that retroactively enables us to see the knowing smile behind the formal ecstasies of the Chinese as well. Ikenushi is a schoolboy exulting in his Horatian imitations and expects

Yakamochi to know it. The expression translated "My offense deserves death" is a set phrase in the humilific language of such documents as memorials to the throne. The terms behind "master spirit" and "stellar phenomenon" are found in writings by the early T'ang poet Wang Po (647–75). The preference of the wise for the water and the benevolent for the mountains was established by a passage in the Confucian *Analects*. P'an Yüeh (d. A.D. 300), like his contemporary Lu Chi, was a fu writer of the Chin Dynasty. In the important Six Dynasties critical work *Shih P'in* by Chung Hung (fl. ca. 483–513), P'an Yüeh's talent is likened to a river, and Lu Chi's to a sea. It was Ts'ao Chih (A.D. 192–232), the author of *Lo Shen Fu*, who, anecdote tells, composed a poem while taking seven steps. The description of literary ornamentation as "carving dragons" goes back to Liu Hsiang (79 B.C.– 8 B.C.), a writer of the Former Han Dynasty.

In his accompanying chōka-hanka set (nos. 1194–96) Ikenushi maintains the formal public stance of Yakamochi's no. 1189 in his opening passage, and like him concludes it with *masurao* (line 7). Yakamochi's stalwart soon found he was only too susceptible to human ills, and the balance of the poem is a complaint. Ikenushi also makes an ironic maneuver at the corresponding point, but the burden of his argument is not that Yakamochi is weak, but that he is strong. In his attempt to reactivate his friend's life-force and dispel his self-pity he uses sarcasm, pointing out (lines 9–12) the absurdity of Yakamochi's pretense that he cannot correspond with Nara. In lines 17–20 Ikenushi echoes Yakamochi's gloomy question in no. 1183—a poem Yakamochi presumably did not send—only to demolish it with the ultimate weapon, an appeal to those instincts most oriented toward life. Painting a fresh, enticing picture of spring, Ikenushi dangles a vision of cherry blossom, birdsong, and red-skirted girls before Yakamochi's famished gaze. But in his two envoys he turns away and admits his own longing and sadness. It is never made clear why he cannot visit Yakamochi.

1194–96   [MYS XVII: 3996–98 / 3973–75]

Yesterday I related my paltry sentiments, and this morning I defile your ears and eyes. Having been honored by your gracious letter, I go on once more to present my rambling thoughts. My offense deserves death. Far from neglecting this vile person, you have frequently bestowed the blessing of your virtuous epistles. Yours is a master spirit, a stellar phenomenon. Your outstanding meters surpass those of other men. Your nature, which being wise loves the water, and being benevolent loves the mountains, contains within it the shining of a lovely jewel; your talent, which like P'an Yüeh's is a river, and like Lu Chi's is a sea, of itself qualifies you for a place in the palace of letters. Your conceptions are extraordinary, your feelings governed in accordance with reason. You finish a composition in seven paces, and the numerous poems fill your paper to overflowing. Skillfully you drive away the heavy distress of the grieved one; capably you dispel the accumulated longings of the lovesick one. Compared with this, the fountain of poetry of Yama and Kaki was as nothing. I have been afforded a brilliant glimpse of a sea of letters where genius carves dragons. Your servant is fully aware of his good fortune. The poem in which he respectfully replies goes as follows:

Ōkimi no	In obedient dread
Mikoto kashikomi	Of the word of our great lord,
Ashihiki no	By foot-wearying
Yama no sawarazu	Mountains and moors unhindered,
5 Amazakaru	Who this hinterland
Hina mo osamuru	Beyond the borne of sky do rule,
Masurao ya	You stalwart man!
Nani ka mono mou	Where is the cause for this brooding?
Aoni yoshi	Do the messengers
10 Naraji kikayou	With their staffs of catalpa
Tamazusa no	No longer come and go
Tsukai taeme ya	Along the blue-earth Nara road?
Komorikoi	Keeping indoors, yearning,
Ikizukiwatari	Heaving sighs as you pass the day,
15 Shitamoi ni	A hidden longing
Nagekau wagase	In all your complaints, my brother:
Inishie yu	From long ago
Iitsugiku rashi	It seems the saying has come down
Yo no naka wa	That the world
20 Kazu naki mono so	Is not worth the counting.
Nagusamuru	Still might we find
Koto mo aramu to	Something here for our solace,
Satobito no	So the villagers
Are ni tsuguraku	Thought when they told me this:
25 Yamabi ni wa	On the mountainside
Sakurabana chiri	Cherry bloom is scattering,
Kahotori no	And where the *kaho* bird
Manaku shibanaku	Sings without pause, incessantly,
Haru no no ni	To the spring moorland
30 Sumire o tsumu to	The unmarried girls have come
Shirotae no	To pick violets,
Sode orikaeshi	Sleeves of white bark cloth turned back,
Kurenai no	And crimson skirts
Akamo susobiki	Trailing behind them on the ground:
35 Otomera wa	I hear they are waiting,
Omoimidarete	Yearning in their inmost hearts
Kimi matsu to	For you to come,

Uragoi su nari	Their breasts a turmoil of longing.
Kokorogushi	You will drown in gloom!
40 Iza mi ni yukana	Come, let's go and see the girls:
Koto wa tanayui	Your word—the matter's settled!

Yamabuki wa	The wild mountain rose
Hi ni hi ni sakinu	Blooms more lushly day by day.
Uruwashi to	Of you whom I think
A ga mou kimi wa	So splendid the memories
Shikushiku omōyu	Come, and wave on wave of longing.

Wa ga seko ni	Nothing can help me,
Koi subenagari	Yearning thus for my brother;
Ashikaki no	I who make my plaints
Hoka ni nagekau	Cut off as by a reed fence,
Are shi kanashi mo	I if anyone am sad.

Third month, fifth day [747]—Ōtomo no Sukune Ikenushi

※ Yakamochi replies in kind to Ikenushi's kambun and kanshi compositions, but his final response in Japanese is brief—two tanka (nos. 1198–99)—and the correspondence terminates. The "jade grasses" presumably refer to Ikenushi's Chinese poem, and the "superlative lines" to his waka. "Difficult to carve" is an allusion to a passage in the *Analects*, as well as a modest demurral from Ikenushi's "carving dragons." The theory of inborn genius enunciated by Yakamochi (following his classic description of writer's block) is in accord with one important strain of Chinese thinking on the nature of composition. Yakamochi's hesitancy about composing Chinese poetry seems to have been justified, for he made far more mistakes than Ikenushi in handling the tonal patterns prescribed for *lü shih*, the "regulated" form of eight-line Chinese verse. The wisdom of the village child is here based on a four-character phrase in *Shih Ching*. In the poem he alludes to one of the "Nineteen Old Poems" in *Wen-hsüan* (line 3), as well as to a passage in a Han work of syncretic erudition, *Huai-nan-tzu*, which also provides the image in line 4. The lustration mentioned in line 6 is that for the first Day of the Serpent. A comparison of the two kanshi, the one by Ikenushi and Yakamochi's reply, shows that they correspond line for line, even to the differently caused but commensurate totteriness in the last line of each. In this juxtaposition lies the wit of the exchange.

1197   [MYS XVII: 3999/3975a]

Last evening's messenger to my great good fortune bestowed upon me your *shih* on a late spring excursion; your second message this morning, of which I am shamefully unworthy, presents me your *uta* inviting me to view the fields. First on looking at your jade grasses my melancholy gradually abated, then on intoning your superlative lines my grief vanished completely. Without this exhilarating panorama who would be able to liberate his feelings? And yet your lowly servant has a nature difficult to carve, a dark spirit impossible to burnish. I take my brush in hand and rot the tip; I face the inkstone and forget it is dry; all day I watch the water flowing, but am unable to compose. Writing is an innate gift, not something to be learned. By searching for characters and choosing rhymes, how should I be able to harmonize with your elegant compositions? Yet when I asked a village child, he said the ancients never lacked a response to whatever was said to them. I have roughed out a clumsy *shih*, by which I respectfully intend to release a burst of laughter. [Now I arrange words and choose rhymes, and put them together with your elegantly composed piece. How can this be different from mixing stones with gems or indulging myself by humming my own tunes? It is like the nonsense sung by a child. I respectfully set it down on a scrap of paper and let it serve as an envoy. It goes:]

A Poem in Seven-Word Lines

The remaining days at the end of spring are lovely with smiling scenery.
The gentle breeze on the First Serpent sweeps lightly in accordance with
    its nature.
The arriving swallow comes with mud in its beak to bring felicitations to
    the house.
The departing goose trails a reed and heads away for the offing.
I hear that you chant poems with your friends and have made a new
    winding watercourse;
That at the drinking for the lustration you urge winecups on each other,
    and float them in the cleanness of the stream.
Although I would like to go in search of your fine banquet,
I know that I am permeated with afflictions, and my legs are tottery.

❋ Yakamochi's final two tanka, with which he apparently bade farewell to the subject of his illness, are in answer to the two envoys (nos. 1195–96) to Ikenushi's chōka. There is no reply to the chōka itself. Perhaps Yakamochi was exhausted by his efforts with the Chinese, for he wrote the kambun, the kanshi, and the waka all on the same day, after receiving Ikenushi's compositions the previous evening and the same morning. The first tanka (no. 1198) is actually a version of an anonymous poem (no. 1368) that has *hagi* in place of *yamabuki*. Perhaps Yakamochi expected Ikenushi to recognize the variation. In his second tanka Yakamochi picks up the image of the reed fence (*ashikaki*) from no. 1196, seeming to change it from an epithetical to a real fence. But the reality is a reality in a dream—a dream caused by Ikenushi's yearning, and revealing him standing outside looking in.

1198–99   [MYS XVII: 4000–4001/3976–77]
Two *tanka*

(1198)   [4000/3976]

Sakeri to mo	So they are in bloom—
Shirazu shi araba	Ah, I could have kept my peace
Moda mo aramu	If I had not known;
Kono yamabuki o	But you go showing them to me,
Misetsutsu motona	These blossoms of the mountain rose.

(1199)   [4001/3977]

Ashikaki no	By the fence of reeds
Hoka ni mo kimi ga	You stood, you came that far,
Yoritatashi	But stopped outside—
Koikere koso ba	And your yearning was so strong
Ime ni miekere	I saw you in my dream.

Composed on the fifth day of the third month [747] by Ōtomo no Sukune Yakamochi as he lay sick in bed.

Ōtomo no Yakamochi and Ōtomo no Ikenushi III: An Outing to Lake Fuse

Yakamochi was well enough by late in the fourth month of 747 to go on an extended excursion up the coast to Lake Fuse, one of the local beauty spots. He and Ikenushi celebrated the outing in an exchange of chōka and hanka, nos. 1200–1203. These in a sense belong to the tradition of land-praising poems, but the land they praise has been shorn of all awesomeness. Nature in these poems is not so much numinous as exhilarating, a wonderful scenic realm in which to enjoy the great outdoors. The poems are equally celebrations of companionship, both poets using the term *omou dochi* ("dear comrades"). Although thoroughly Japanese in setting, technique, and imagery, the two chōka are labeled *fu* by their authors, a continuation of their game of posing as Chinese literati, perhaps. Ikenushi even goes so far as to call his envoy a *chüeh*, a short form of Chinese verse in four lines of five syllables each. The grand and glorious descriptions of a highly fantasized nature in Chinese fu are far beyond the resources of the Japanese lexicon, but clearly Yakamochi and Ikenushi drew the parallel between chōka and fu in their own minds, an interesting point to remember in view of the somewhat prolix and breathless quality of these particular poems.

Yakamochi begins (no. 1200) with the two-line formula for court officials *mononofu no yasotomo no o no*, by which he means himself and his gubernatorial staff. The resounding thunder of the phrase is immediately mellowed into *omou dochi*: all are friends together on the picnic day. The poem develops as a descriptive narrative, taking the party past one sight after another along the shore. The parallel to travel literature suggests itself, but this miniature *kikō* is innocent of any melancholy overtones of *ryojō*, the "mood of travel." Rather, nature is a smiling place in which to shed one's dark, inactive vapors. Active sport—cormorant fishing (for Yakamochi's love of which, see nos. 834–36)—balances sight-seeing from horseback and boat. In strong contrast to Yakamochi's listless bedridden poems, all is energy and motion—horses, waves, cormorants and fishers, boats and rowers, teal. Yakamochi does not call himself a masurao here—he is having too good a time. The ideal of masurao-hood seems to have largely ironic overtones in *Man'yōshū*, and especially so for Yakamochi. Lines 29 and 31 are pillow-word constructions, the former a mock epithet for *futa* ("lid") in Futagamiyama ("Twin-Peak Mountain"), and the latter an adverbial metaphor for *wakare* ("fork"/"part"). The envoy is a rephrasing of the last five lines of the chōka, using the technique of the jo to provide an image from nature for the intended constancy of return.

1200–1201   [MYS XVII: 4015–16/3991–92]

A *fu* on making an excursion to Lake Fuse; with *tanka* (this lake is in Furue Village in Imizu District)

Mononofu no	We men at arms,
Yasotomo no o no	We eighty officers of court,
Omou dochi	Dear comrades all,
Kokoro yaramu to	Wanting to chase our gloom away,
5 Uma namete	Lined up our horses
Uchikuchiburi no	And set out along the rocky coast.
Shiranami no	Where the white waves roll,
Ariso ni yosuru	Splashing far and near along the shore,
Shibutani no	We skirted out
10 Saki tamotōri	Around Cape Shibutani,
Matsudae no	And left behind us
Nagahama sugite	Matsudae and its long sand beach.
Unaigawa	At Unai River
Kiyoki segoto ni	We set cormorants to work
15 Ukawa tachi	In each clear shallows:
Ka yuki kaku yuki	Up and down the stream we went
Mitsuredo mo	To see what sport we'd find;
Soko mo akani to	But being soon dissatisfied,
Fuse no umi ni	Went on to Fuse,
20 Fune ukesuete	And put our boats afloat upon the lake.
Okihe kogi	We rowed far out,
He ni kogimireba	We rowed along the shore and looked:

	Nagisa ni wa	Great flocks of teal
	Ajimura sawaki	Were clamoring at the water's edge,
25	Shimami ni wa	And round the isle
	Konure hana saki	Hung blossoms from the slender twigs of trees.
	Kokobaku mo	Could there be a scene
	Mi no sayakeki ka	In all the world as fair to gaze upon?
	Tamakushige	A jeweled comb chest:
30	Futagamiyama ni	Covering the slopes of Mount Futagami,
	Hau tsuta no	Crawling ivy forks:
	Yuki wa wakarezu	Never let us branch and part,
	Arigayoi	But come and return,
	Iya toshi no ha ni	Ever as the year comes round,
35	Omou dochi	Dear comrades all,
	Kaku shi asobamu	To revel in these sights anew,
	Ima mo miru goto	Even as we see them now.

	Fuse no umi no	Out on Fuse Sea
	Oki tsu shiranami	White waves from the offing roll,
	Arigayoi	Ever washing in:
	Iya toshi no ha ni	Every year without fail
	Mitsutsu shinowamu	We shall come to gaze and wonder.

The above was composed by the Governor, Ōtomo no Sukune Yakamochi. Fourth month, twenty-fourth day [747].

❊ Ikenushi's reply (nos. 1202–3) was written two days later, and he seems to have spread himself to the task. His chōka has an elaborate introduction setting the season and its mood as background for the outing. The opening image, "waves of wisteria" (*fujinami*), sets up a gentle swaying motion consonant with the feelings of lines 9–10 and anticipating the waves of the sea and lake mentioned in line 27 and the envoy. With the wisteria scattered, earliest summer is past, and now the white-blossomed *unohana* (deutzia; here "hareflower") is in bloom, and the summer bird, the *hototogisu* ("cuckoo"), heralds its full flowering. All of this elaborates Yakamochi's line 4, *kokoro yaramu to* ("wanting to chase our gloom away").

In his description of the outing itself, Ikenushi selects out the cormorant fishing, which he replaces with birds searching for food on the tidal flats. His version of the trip is more leisurely than Yakamochi's: he pauses to watch the tide come in and to make a garland of seaweed for some dear girl (simply *imo*; line 31). But once arrived at the lake he is all energy, leading the others in his boat. His account of the boating is slightly more elaborate, but closely parallels Yakamochi's, and he too concludes his chōka with a vow to return. Similarly, his envoy is cast as a recapitulation of this vow, structured in a jo hinging on the pivot word *yo* ("segment," as of seaweed, but mean-ing also "world" / "life"). One senses a certain *hariai*, a competitiveness, in the way Ikenushi matches his friend and slightly outdoes him.

1202-3   [MYS XVII:4017–18/3993–94]

A poem in respectful reply to your *fu* on our excursion to Lake Fuse; with a *chüeh*

	Fujinami wa	The waves of wisteria
	Sakite chiriniki	Had flowered and scattered away.
	Unohana wa	Now the hareflower
	Ima so sakari to	Bloomed in its prime, the cuckoo sang,
5	Ashihiki no	And the song resounded
	Yama ni mo no ni mo	Over the fields and up the slopes
	Hototogisu	Of mountains where men go
	Naki shi toyomeba	With dragging feet; so that my heart,
	Uchinabiku	Charmed to submission,
10	Kokoro mo shino ni	Fell to long and quiet thoughts.
	Soko o shi mo	At last the longing
	Uragoishimi to	In my bosom grew so strong
	Omou dochi	That I joined dear friends,
	Uma uchimurete	And trooping our horses as we went,
15	Tazusawari	Linking hand to hand,
	Idetachi mireba	We set forth together upon the road.
	Imizugawa	First we observed
	Minato no sudori	How on the sand island at the mouth
	Asanagi ni	Of Imizu River
20	Kata ni asari shi	In the morning calm birds searched the strand
		for food,
	Shio miteba	And when the tide came in
	Tsuma yobikawasu	Called to their mates in signal and reply.
	Tomoshiki ni	Gazing in envy,
	Mitsutsu sugiyuki	We went our way, passing on
25	Shibutani no	To Shibutani's
	Ariso no saki ni	Rock-encrusted cape, where
	Oki tsu nami	Waves of the offing
	Yosekuru tamamo	Sweep ashore the gemlike weed;
	Katayori ni	Which with a twist
30	Kazura ni tsukuri	I twined into a garland
	Imo ga tame	To give my sweetheart,
	Te ni makimochite	And carried wrapped about my arm.
	Uraguwashi	Then to the smiling
	Fuse no mizuumi ni	Waters of Lake Fuse, where,

35 Amabune ni	Taking fishing boats,
Makaji kainuki	We thrust the oars into the oarlocks,
Shirotae no	And I waved my white sleeves
Sode furikaeshi	Until they blew backward in the wind
Adomoite	As I shouted aloud
40 Wa ga kogiyukeba	For all to follow me, and rowed out on the lake.
Ofu no saki	At Cape Ofu
Hana chirimagai	Blossoms showered on us in mad swirls,
Nagisa ni wa	While along the water's edge
Ashigamo sawaki	Mallards clamored in among the reeds,
45 Sazarenami	And little wavelets
Tachite mo ite mo	Gently splashed, as standing to the oars
Kogimeguri	Or resting, we circled
Miredo mo akazu	The shore, and never wearied of all we saw.
Aki saraba	When autumn comes,
50 Momichi no toki ni	In the time of crimson leaves,
Haru saraba	And when spring arrives
Hana no sakari ni	And the blossoms flaunt their glory,
Ka mo kaku mo	Whatever the season,
Kimi ga manima to	So be it one that please my lord,
55 Kaku shi koso	Let us thus go forth
Mi mo akirameme	To sights that bring refreshment to our hearts:
Tayuru hi arame ya	Can ever a day come to bring the end of joy?
Shiranami no	Long as I shall live,
Yosekuru tamamo	Oft as the white waves wash ashore
Yo no aida mo	The gemlike weed,
Tsugite mi ni komu	I shall come to see again
Kiyoki hamabi o	The sands of this clean-swept beach.

The above is the composition of Secretary Ōtomo no Sukune Ikenushi. A response of the twenty-sixth of the fourth month [747].

Ōtomo no Yakamochi and Ōtomo no Ikenushi IV: Mount Tachi

The day after Ikenushi's response completed the exchange on Lake Fuse, Yakamochi wrote a "fu" (no. 1204–6) on another prominent feature of his realm, Mount Tachi, a commanding range of peaks in the eastern part of the province. It is thought that Tsurugigatake ("Sword Peak"; elevation 2,998 m) is the individual peak referred to. Ikenushi replied (nos. 1207–9) a day later. These poems restore the numinousness of the land with a vengeance. In their deification of the mountain they are strongly reminiscent of Akahito's and Mushimaro's poems on Mount Fuji (nos. 537–38, 569–71),

whose mysterious snow-in-midsummer appears again as a source of wonder. The many-one pattern at the outset of Yakamochi's chōka (no. 1204),
however, is that of the land-praising poem attributed to Emperor Jomei (no.
238). The handling of the mist image in lines 17–24 perhaps owes something to no. 541–42, Akahito's poem on climbing Kamuoka. "Midmost
Koshi" (line 3) is another way of saying Etchū, the middle of the three provinces into which the land of Koshi was divided for administrative purposes.
Akahito too ends his chōka on Mount Fuji by declaring, "I shall tell the
tale" (*kataritsugi*). The eternal return and telling the tale are also formulaic
endings for poems that praise the land. Ikenushi's reply (again his envoys are
chüeh) follows Yakamochi in evoking the divine majesty of the mountain
and the mystery of its snow. But once again he outdoes his friend in his
expression of wonder (lines 15–20), and develops the mist image into an
extended preparation-conclusion analogy (lines 21–32) that is the heart of
the second half of the chōka. "Telling the tale" is given five lines at the end,
as compared with Yakamochi's eleven. Ikenushi's two envoys are clearly intended to duplicate Yakamochi's as closely as possible, though the second
one replaces Yakamochi's syntactic doubling in the fourth line with the
more disjunct structure of a simile.

1204-6   [MYS XVII: 4024–26 / 4000–4002]

A *fu* on Mount Tachi; with *tanka* (this mountain is in Niikawa District)

	Amazakaru	Beyond far skies,
	Hina ni na kakasu	Famed among rustic lands,
	Koshi no naka	Midmost Koshi has
	Kunuchi kotogoto	Everywhere throughout the province
5	Yama wa shi mo	Abounding mountains—
	Shiji ni aredo mo	They crowd against each other;
	Kawa wa shi mo	Plentiful rivers—
	Sawa ni yukedo mo	Their waters swarm across the earth.
	Sumekami no	Yet of these it is
10	Ushihakiimasu	Where the guardian god holds sway
	Niikawa no	Over New River,
	Sono Tachiyama ni	On Mount Tachi rising there
	Tokonatsu ni	That all summer long
	Yuki furishikite	Snow lies fallen in great sheets.
15	Obaseru	Girdling the mountain
	Katakaigawa no	Katakai River runs,
	Kiyoki se ni	Over whose clear shallows
	Asa yoi goto ni	Morn and evening without fail
	Tatsu kiri no	Rise the vagrant mists:
20	Omoisugime ya	But my longing will not vanish so.

Arigayoi	I shall come again,
Iya toshi no ha ni	Ceaselessly year after year,
Yoso nomi mo	And if but from afar
Furisakemitsutsu	Shall lift my head and gaze.
25 Yorozuyo no	I shall tell the tale,
Kataraigusa to	That for a myriad ages yet to come
Imada minu	Men who have not seen the sight
Hito ni mo tsugemu	May make of it their daily talk.
Oto nomi mo	Though but by report,
30 Na nomi mo kikite	Though they hear its fame alone,
Tomoshiburu gane	They will surely envy us the sight.
Tachiyama ni	The snow that lies
Furiokeru yuki o	Deep-drifted on Mount Tachi
Tokonatsu ni	I could gaze upon
Miredo mo akazu	Through endless summer, never tiring:
Kamukara narashi	Surely a sign the mountain is a god.
Katakai no	In Katakai
Kawa no se kiyoku	River the shallows are clear,
Yuku mizu no	The water flows
Tayuru koto naku	Never ceasing I shall come
Arigayoimimu	Again and yet again to gaze.

Ōtomo no Sukune Yakamochi composed this on the twenty-seventh of the fourth month [747].

1207–9   [MYS XVII: 4027–29 / 4003–5]

A poem replying respectfully to the *fu* on Mount Tachi; with two *chüeh*

Asahi sashi	Where the morning sun
Sogai ni miyuru	Rises dazzling, from the land
Kamunagara	Beyond these precincts
Mina ni obaseru	Can be seen in all its godhead,
5 Shirakumo no	Thrusting aside
Chie o oshiwake	The thousand layers of white cloud,
Ama sosori	Towering into heaven,
Takaki Tachiyama	Lofty Tachi, called the Standing Peak.
Fuyu natsu to	In winter, in summer,
10 Waku koto mo naku	Regardless of the time of year,
Shirotae ni	The snow lies thick
Yuki wa furiokite	In sheets as white as barken cloth.
Inishie yu	From a time long past
Arikinikereba	They have stood where now they stand,
15 Kogoshi kamo	The headlong crags

Iwa no kamusabi	Bristling in their godly power:
Tamakiwaru	How many ages
Ikuyo henikeru	Have gone by of soul-abiding time?
Tachite ite	I stand and gaze, I sit,
20 Miredo mo ayashi	The wonder is forever new.
Minedakami	So lofty is the peak,
Tani o fukami to	The valley deep, the clear pools
Ochitagitsu	Wherein the river
Kiyoki kafuchi ni	Plummets in a raging torrent,
25 Asa sarazu	Morning without fail
Kiri tachiwatari	Are covered with a rising mist,
Yū sareba	And when evening comes
Kumoi tanabiki	Cloud banners float upon the air.
Kumoi nasu	My heart drifts too
30 Kokoro mo shino ni	As softly as a floating cloud,
Tatsu kiri no	But unlike the mist
Omoisugusazu	My longing will not pass away:
Yuku mizu no	Clearly as the sound
Oto mo sayakeku	That the flowing water makes
35 Yorozuyo ni	I shall tell the tale,
Iitsugiyukamu	That men may know ten thousand ages hence,
Kawa shi taezu wa	If the river does not cease its flow.
Tachiyama ni	The snow that lies
Furiokeru yuki no	Deep-drifted on Mount Tachi
Tokonatsu ni	Remains unmelted
Kezute wataru wa	Through endless summer; a sign,
Kamunagara to so	Men say, the mountain is a god.
Ochitagitsu	Plummeting, raging,
Katakaigawa no	Katakai River runs
Taenu goto	A ceaseless torrent:
Ima miru hito mo	So, too, we who view it now
Yamazu kayowamu	Shall ceaselessly return.

In the above, Secretary Ōtomo no Sukune Ikenushi replies.—Fourth month, twenty-eighth day [747].

Ōtomo no Yakamochi and Ōtomo no Ikenushi V: Leaving for the Capital

For some time Yakamochi had been preparing to go up to the capital with the provincial tax register and make his report. His approaching departure was the occasion for an exchange between him and Ikenushi (nos.

1210–14). It was the most Chinese of occasions—the parting of two men, one of whom goes away on the Emperor's business. But it drew forth no kanshi from Yakamochi and Ikenushi, or none that found their way into *Man'yōshū*. Instead, the exchange took the form of chōka-hanka, employing the traditional images and formulas of waka, appealing to native gods and describing native scenes, reaching for the inner truth of friendship through the means available to men writing in their own tongue. None of this would have come out the same had they chosen to write in Chinese, even had they avoided the formalistic superficialities of the late Six Dynasties court style. Whether or not prompted by such considerations, in this instance the two cousins failed to don their Chinese masks despite the apparent appropriateness of the occasion.

Yakamochi's chōka (no. 1210) is composed of four sections: a formal introduction (lines 1–6), an evocation of shared experience (7–30), the parting (31–46), and a final wish (47–53). The introductory lines, which are not otherwise related to the rest of the poem, have been plausibly explained as a metaphor for the clan relationship of Yakamochi (root) and Ikenushi (branch). *Kakikazou* ("counted on the fingers") is a pillow word for *futa* ("two") in Futagami ("Twin Peak"). The second passage of the poem is remarkable for its pictorial sense, the windswept harbor and hurrying boats at evening having the strong visual impact of a seascape by Turner. But more vital to the theme of the poem is the way in which it sums up what Yakamochi and Ikenushi meant to each other. They are not simply taking a walk or admiring nature. Rather, they are experiencing together a special moment, a kind of wordless epiphany that binds them as brothers beyond the merely conventional sense of *wagase* ("my elder brother") in line 8. In this respect the passage is a counterpart to the storm through which Hitomaro discovered the brotherhood of all men on the beach at Samine (no. 358–60). Yakamochi defines elsewhere (MYS XVII: 4041 / 4017) the dialect word *ayu* as meaning "east wind." His use of it may be attributable to his interest in local color. The section on parting (lines 35–46) raises the image of the awesome ancestral sovereign (*sumeroki*) often found at the beginning of chōka. This chōka treats a private grief in the context of public duty, and for once the poet has chosen to put the personal part first. (For the opposite pattern, see Yakamochi's poems on his illness, nos. 1182 and 1189.) "The road of the sacred spears" is another translation of the pillow-word construction *tamahoko no michi*, elsewhere "the jewel-spear road." The whole passage is strongly nativistic in feeling and phraseology. The last seven lines employ lovers' language in a conceit reminiscent of nos. 1148 and 1153, but with the added and delightful fantasy of stringing the cuckoo's note on the same thread with the beloved. The envoy is a reprise of this section.

[MYS XVII: 4030–31 / 4006–7]

As the time to go in to the capital gradually approached, the feeling of sadness became harder to drive away. A poem expressing these thoughts; with a *chüeh*

Kakikazou	On twice-counted
Futagamiyama ni	Double-peaked Mount Futagami
Kamusabite	Stands the godlike tree,
Tateru tsuga no ki	The hemlock, venerable, sublime:
5 Moto mo e mo	Both root and branch
Oyaji tokiwa ni	Spring from the same eternal stock.
Hashiki yoshi	O well-beloved
Wagase no kimi o	Brother, you and I have met
Asa sarazu	These mornings without fail
10 Aite kotodoi	To talk of what the day might bring,
Yū sareba	And when evening came
Te tazusawarite	Then hand in hand have made our way
Imizukawa	Down to the river,
Kiyoki kafuchi ni	To the clear pools of Imizu,
15 Idetachite	And stood on the bank.
Wa ga tachimireba	Oft as we stood and gazed about
Ayu no kaze	The east wind came,
Itaku shi fukeba	The one called *ayu*, sharply blowing,
Minato ni wa	So that the harbor
20 Shiranami takami	Whitened under towering waves;
Tsuma yobu to	Birds on the sandspits
Sudori wa sawaku	Clamored as they called their mates,
Ashi karu to	And the little boats
Ama no obune wa	Used by the shorefolk cutting reeds
25 Irie kogu	Rowed for the rivermouth,
Kaji no oto takashi	Their oarstrokes crashing loudly.
Soko o shi mo	Ah, such scenes as these,
Aya ni tomoshimi	How strangely they have drawn me:
Shinoitsutsu	A constant wonder
30 Asobu sakari o	Fills me, and my rambles fill my days.
Sumeroki no	But ours is a land
Osu kuni nareba	Our Sovereign summons to his will,
Mikoto mochi	Wherefore I must bear
Tachiwakarenaba	His dread command even to this parting.
35 Okuretaru	You who stay behind—
Kimi wa aredo mo	Things may go well enough for you;
Tamahoko no	But I who travel
Michi yuku ware wa	The road of the sacred spears,

Shirakumo no	When beneath white clouds
40 Tanabiku yama o	Adrift upon the mountain peaks
Iwane fumi	I tread the rooted rocks
Koehenarinaba	And cross the ranges, and go down,
Koishikeku	Then will the days begin,
Ke no nagakemu so	The long days of my yearning:
45 Soko moeba	When I think of it
Kokoro shi itashi	My heart is wrung with pain.
Hototogisu	Were you but a bead,
Koe ni aenuku	I would thread you on one string
Tama ni moga	With the cuckoo's song;
50 Te ni makimochite	Winding you around my arm,
Asa yoi ni	Morning and evening
Mitsutsu yukamu o	I would see you as I went:
Okite ikaba oshi	To go without you is bitter.

Wa ga seko wa	As for my brother,
Tama ni mogamo na	I would have him be a bead:
Hototogisu	With the cuckoo's song
Koe ni aenuki	I would thread him on one string,
Te ni makite yukamu	And carry him wrapped round my arm!

The above was sent by Ōtomo no Sukune Yakamochi to Secretary Ōtomo no Sukune Ikenushi.—Fourth month, thirtieth day [747]

❋ Ikenushi's reply (no. 1212–14) maintains the same serious and intimate mood. He speaks briefly of the consolation Yakamochi's society has provided him, and at greater length of his sadness at parting. There is nothing to correspond to the scene of shared experience in Yakamochi's poem; rather, the climax comes in the prayer at the end to the god of Mount Tonami, which Yakamochi will have to cross on his way to Nara. Dread of this god is the reason why Ikenushi does not dare to speak his thoughts (lines 31–32; compare no. 942). The reference to traveler's luck (*masakiku*, line 39) is reminiscent of the conclusion of Okura's chōka on the departure of the ambassador to China (no. 636–38). Ikenushi hopes to have his friend back before fall (which began with the seventh month). The pinks also bloomed in the sixth month of the year Yakamochi's concubine died (see no. 1137). In the first envoy Ikenushi expands his appeal to all the gods of travel; the "sacred spears" (*tamahoko*) were themselves gods of the roadside. In the second envoy he responds to Yakamochi's conceit with one of his own. His kambun preface incorporates hyperbole from *Yu-hsien-k'u*.

1212-14   [MYS XVII: 4032-34 / 4008-10]

When suddenly I was presented with your composition relating your regrets at going in to the capital, I felt the sadness of partings in this life as if my entrails had been cut a myriad times, and my feelings of resentment were hard to deny. A poem in which I present some small indication of my thoughts; with two *chüeh*

	Aoni yoshi	Though blue-earth Nara
	Nara o kihanare	Now had long been left behind
	Amazakaru	For a hinterland
	Hina ni wa aredo	Far beyond the farthest sky,
5	Wa ga seko o	Yet I comforted
	Mitsutsu shi oreba	Myself, for day by day
	Omoiyaru	I had occasion
	Koto mo arishi o	To meet with my dear brother.
	Ōkimi no	But in obedient
10	Mikoto kashikomi	Dread of our great lord's command
	Osu kuni no	You have taken up
	Koto torimochite	This charge in the land he rules;
	Wakakusa no	And when you have tied
	Ayui tazukuri	Thongs like young grass around your legs
15	Muratori no	And started on your way
	Asadachi inaba	Like the bird flocks starting up at dawn,
	Okuretaru	Will I who stay
	Are ya kanashiki	Be of us two the sadder,
	Tabi ni yuku	Or you who go
20	Kimi ka mo koimu	More stricken in your yearning?
	Omou sora	This anxious mood
	Yasuku araneba	Leaves me no peace—I can but sigh,
	Nagekaku o	And the sighs escape
	Todome mo kanete	Beyond my power to stop them.
25	Miwataseba	When I gaze afar,
	Unohanayama no	On the hareflower mountains
	Hototogisu	The cuckoo is crying:
	Ne nomi shi nakayu	Cries come, and nothing else.
	Asagiri no	My heart is troubled,
30	Midaruru kokoro	Torn like the morning mist,
	Koto ni idete	And I dare not speak
	Iwaba yuyushimi	What thoughts arise in me.
	Tonamiyama	Therefore to the god
	Tamuke no kami ni	Of travelers on Tonami Mount
35	Nusa matsuri	I make offerings
	A ga koinomaku	And beseech him in my prayer:

Hashike yashi	That he guard you well,
Kimi ga tadaka o	Dear friend, hovering constantly
Masakiku mo	About you, close upon you,
40 Aritamotōri	So your luck may bear you through;
Tsuki tataba	And when a month has gone,
Toki mo kawasazu	Before the season changes,
Nadeshiko ga	That he bring you back
Hana no sakari ni	When the wild pinks are in flower,
45 Aimishime to so	And let us meet again.

Tamahoko no	All you gods who guard
Michi no kamitachi	The road of the sacred spears,
Mai wa semu	I'll bribe you well:
A ga omou kimi o	Upon the lord for whom I long,
Natsukashimi seyo	Look kindly, I bid you.

Uragoishi	You for whom I yearn
Wagase no kimi wa	With all my heart, my brother,
Nadeshiko ga	I would have you be
Hana ni mogamo na	The flower of the wild fringed pink—
Asana sana mimu	I'd look at you each morning.

The above is the answering poem sent in response by Ōtomo no Sukune Ikenushi.—Fifth month, second day [747]

Ōtomo no Yakamochi and Ōtomo no Ikenushi VI: In Separate Provinces

Ikenushi was transferred to the neighboring province of Echizen at some time subsequent to Yakamochi's departure for Nara in the fifth month of 747. The following correspondence (nos. 1215–21) dates from 749. Fukami Village was on the border with Etchū; east-northeast would be a more accurate statement of the direction in which Ikenushi should have looked. Ikenushi's brief note is in an informal style, while the quotation from Yakamochi's letter is in balanced four-character phrases. Ikenushi's first poem (no. 1215) is a variant of no. 424 from the "Hitomaro Collection." Here Ikenushi is hard up against Mount Tonami, separating Echizen from Etchū. Yakamochi answers from the other side (no. 1218). Now it is Ikenushi (no. 1216) who feels too listless to go out and see the blossoms, and Yakamochi (no. 1219) who sends the invitation to come and view them. Having spoken of the moon and cherry blossoms, Ikenushi comes directly to his feelings in no. 1217. The feelings are those of a neglected lover, and Yakamochi's reply (no. 1220) is couched in even more intense terms. Again the language of love poetry makes its pervasive influence felt in the writings of the Ōtomo. The last poem, by Yakamochi (no. 1221), is a supernumerary meditation on the weather—spring mist (*kasumi*), but still a persistence of snow.

1215-17   [MYS XVIII:4097-99 / 4073-75]

Three poems sent by Ōtomo no Sukune Ikenushi, the Secretary of Echizen Province

On the fourteenth of this month I went to Fukami Village and gazed respectfully toward the north. When shall I ever cease to think constantly of your fragrant virtue? Moreover, since we are neighbors, my yearning for you has suddenly increased. Further, as you said in your recent letter, "Late spring leaves regret; we have not had an occasion to sit knee to knee. The sorrow of partings in this life—how shall we express it?" I face the paper and am overcome with grief; these notes are too disorderly to present.

Third month, fifteenth day [749].—Ōtomo no Sukune Ikenushi

(1215)   [4097 / 4073]

A man of old said:

Tsuki mireba	When you look at the moon,
Onaji kuni nari	This is all the same country;
Yama koso ba	It is the mountains
Kimi ga atari o	That have made the barrier
Hedatetarikere	Between your land and mine.

(1216)   [4098 / 4074]

Inspired by the sight of something

Sakurabana	The cherry blossoms
Ima so sakari to	Now are at their very height,
Hito wa iedo	So people say,
Ware wa sabushi mo	But I am sunk in loneliness,
Kimi to shi araneba	For I am not with you.

(1217)   [4099 / 4075]

A poem about my feelings

Aiomowazu	What is it ails me,
Aruramu kimi o	That I sigh the livelong day
Ayashiku mo	For someone like you
Nagekiwataru ka	Who likely never thinks of me—
Hito no tou made	People are starting to ask.

1218–21   [MYS XVIII : 4100–4103 / 4076–79]

Four poems sent in reply by Ōtomo no Yakamochi, Governor of Etchū
Province

(1218)   [4100 / 4076]

In reply to the saying by the man of old

Ashihiki no	How I wish them gone,
Yama wa naku moga	These foot-wearying mountains:
Tsuki mireba	When we see the moon
Onajiki sato o	We are all in one village,
Kokoro hedatetsu	But *they* have split our hearts.

(1219)   [4101 / 4077]

In reply to the poem inspired by the sight of something, with further reference to the cherry tree at the northwest corner of the residence you had before your transfer

Wa ga seko ga	Inside the old fence
Furuki kakitsu no	Where once you lived, my brother,
Sakurabana	The cherry blossoms
Imada fufumeri	Still are closed within the bud—
Hitome mi ni kone	You'd best come and have a look!

(1220)   [4102 / 4078]

Replying to your poem about your feelings, and at the same time adapting
to the sense of the present a poem left by a man of old

Kou to iu wa	What they call yearning,
E mo nazuketari	Yes, there's a name for that;
Iu sube no	But as for me,
Tazuki mo naki wa	There is no way to speak of it,
A ga mi narikeri	This helpless thing I feel.

(1221)   [4103 / 4079]

A further poem inspired by the sight of something

Mishimano ni	Mist is hovering
Kasumi tanabiki	On the moors of Mishima,
Shikasuga ni	But for all of that,
Kinō mo kyō mo	Yesterday we had some snow,
Yuki wa furitsutsu	And today it snowed again.

Third month, sixteenth day [749].

Songs of the Sakimori

In 664, the year after the collapse of efforts to revive the Korean state of Paekche, Japan took measures to defend itself against possible aggression from T'ang China and its Korean ally, Silla. Among these measures was the garrisoning of conscript soldiers, the so-called *sakimori* or "guardians of the capes," in northern Kyūshū and its outlying islands Tsushima and Iki. The conscripts came mostly from eastern Japan, whose men had the reputation of good soldiers, and served for three years. The force numbered three thousand men, and the tours of duty were staggered, with a new contingent of one thousand assembling at the embarkation point of Naniwa once a year. The system was still in effect a century later, when Ōtomo no Yakamochi was stationed at Naniwa as Junior Assistant Minister of Military Affairs in 755. Yakamochi's duties included overseeing the processing of the sakimori, and he took it upon himself to collect the poems, mostly sad ones, that they composed on setting out for their distant duty. Book XX contains a large collection of these poems. Unlike the poems in the smaller collection in Book XIV (nos. 1520-24), each poem in Book XX is followed by the name of its author. Some few are by Yakamochi himself, harmonizing with the topic, but most are by men otherwise unknown, mostly of low estate. The poems were collected from the men and submitted to Yakamochi by the several recruiting officers who were in charge of transporting the sakimori to Naniwa. Yakamochi excluded what he considered to be inferior poems, and it is not inconceivable that he revised others, or even that he assigned the composition of the poems as extra duty in order to provide material for *Man'yōshū*. But these poems do reinforce the impression of widespread poem-making in the provinces one receives from Book XIV and other collections of anonymous verse. Such making does not necessarily imply literacy, or, as here, that the products of oral composition need be folk songs. What seems to be clear is the widespread use of the tanka form.

Draft-eligible men (ages twenty-one to sixty) were classified into several categories of *yohoro*, a term that denotes "hollow of the knee," suggesting leg power, but that may be translated "able-bodied male." Most of the authors of the sakimori poems given below have family names ending in *-be*, showing their origins in the occupational groups (*be*) under the control of noble clans in ancient Japan. The *be* system itself had been abolished as part of the Taika Reforms in 646, but the names remained a century later. The youth of these sakimori is suggested by the many poems that speak of parting with parents rather than wives and children. Of the selection given here, the first seven poems (nos. 1222-28) are from Tōtōmi Province, the western part of present Shizuoka Prefecture; nos. 1229-31 are from Sagami, farther east, corresponding to Kanagawa Prefecture; nos. 1232-34 are from a group by Yakamochi; and nos. 1235-44 are from Suruga, the province between Tōtōmi and Sagami. The other poems in the series, not translated here, are from Kazusa, Hitachi, Shimotsuke, Shimōsa, Shinano, Kōzuke, and Musashi. The poems, like those in Book XIV, employ eastern dialect—for example, *yuri* for *yori* ("from"), *kae* for *kaya* ("wild grass"), and *imu* for *imo* ("sweetheart") in no. 1222.

Poem 1222 introduces the series with the arrival of the draft notice. The reverent attitude toward authority is the same as that expressed by Yakamochi in such chōka as nos. 1182 and 1189, but the conscript's reaction goes straight to the heart of his deprivation.

Songs of the *sakimori* sent out as replacements to Tsukushi from the provinces in the second month of Tempyō-Shōhō 7 [755], Wood-Junior / Sheep

1222–31   [MYS XX: 4345–54/4321–30]

(1222)   [4345/4321]

Kashikoki ya	The dread command
Mikoto kagafuri	Has descended from on high;
Asu yuri ya	Shall I tomorrow
Kae ga muta nemu	Be sleeping with the wild grass,
Imu nashi ni shite	No sweetheart by my side?

The above poem is by Mononobe no Akimochi of Lower Naga District, an able-bodied male in the service of the District Chief.

❋ The author of no. 1223 is already on his way, but his wife's soul follows him, appearing as a reflection in his drinking water in what may be a variant on the folk belief concerning dreams that is found pervasively in early Japanese poetry (see nos. 728 and 773).

(1223)   [4346/4322]

Wa ga tsuma wa	My wife misses me—
Itaku koi rashi	See, with how sore a yearning:
Nomu mizu ni	In the very water
Kago sae miete	That I drink her face appears;
Yo ni wasurarezu	I can never forget her.

The above poem is by Wakayamatobe no Mimaro of Aratama District, an able-bodied male in the service of the Chief Clerk.

❋ Though the following poem appears similar in concept and mode of expression to no. 185, it makes quite another point. Instead of lamenting the difference between flowers that bloom every year and humans that flower only once, the author of no. 1224 regrets that he cannot carry his mother with him like a blossom (compare no. 1226).

(1224) [4347/4323]

Tokitoki no	Season by season
Hana wa saketo mo	All the flowers come in bloom—
Nani sure so	Why is it, then,
Haha tou hana no	That a flower called "mother"
Sakidekozukemu	Has never come blossoming forth?

The above poem is by Hasebe no Mamaro of Yamana District, a *sakimori*.

❋ The author of the next poem has apparently reached Nie no Ura ("Sacrifice Bay"), somewhere between Toetōmi (Tōtōmi) Province and Naniwa. Shiruha no Iso ("Whitewing Strand") was probably in his home district of Yamana.

(1225) [4348/4324]

Toetōmi	If the stony strand
Shiruha no iso to	Of Whitewing in Toetōmi
Nie no ura to	And Sacrifice Bay
Aite shi araba	Could only find a way to meet,
Koto mo kayuwamu	How the messages would fly!

The above poem is by Hasebe no Kawai of the same district.

❋ The desire expressed in no. 1226 is one of the conventions of parting; for a more elaborate version, see no. 1210, lines 47–52. See also no. 1214 for the wish that the loved one be a flower. These poems seem to ignore the implications of the floral image as an expression of fragility (no. 1487) or seasonal recurrence (no. 185).

(1226) [4349/4325]

Chichi haha mo	Father and Mother—
Hana ni mogamo ya	Could they only be flowers!
Kusamakura	How I would hold them,
Tabi wa yuku to mo	Though on a grasspillow journey,
Sasagote yukamu	High in my hands as I go!

The above poem is by Hasebe no Kuromasa of Saya District.

❊ Poem 1227 is structured on a jo with linkage through repetition. Comparatively few of the sakimori poems in this section use the jo technique; their preference for the mode of direct statement may be a function of their authors' untutored sincerity, or the result of unfamiliarity with poetic composition. In this regard one would be curious to look at the poems eliminated by Yakamochi. The "manor house" (*tono*) could be simple hyperbole or a tongue-in-cheek way of referring to the family's no doubt humble abode. "Hundred-year grasses" (*momoyogusa*) have not been identified; one suggestion is that they are chrysanthemums, a flower associated with longevity.

(1227)   [4350 / 4326]

Chichi haha ga	Father and Mother
Tono no shirihe no	Have behind their manor house
Momoyogusa	Hundred-year grasses:
Momoyo idemase	May they for a hundred years
Wa ga kitaru made	Abide till I come again.

The above poem is by Ikutamabe no Tarikuni of the same district.

❊ Poem 1228 is interesting in various ways. It implies familiarity with pictures (*e*) of some sort and the ability to execute them (given the time), both items that suggest the author possessed a degree of high culture. The Mononobe clan, and its dependent *be* groups, were originally specialists in warfare. The poem is a more practical expression of the symbolic urge found in no. 1226, and makes clear the cultural niche waiting to be filled by the Polaroid camera. It also has a resonance as the realistic counterpart of no. 1223.

(1228)   [4351 / 4327]

Wa ga tsuma mo	Oh, for the leisure
E ni kakitoramu	To take down my wife's features,
Itsuma moga	Captured in a sketch—
Tabi yuku are wa	I who go along my way
Mitsutsu shinowamu	Would look at it and remember.

The above poem is by Mononobe no Komaro of Lower Naga District.

On the sixth of the second month the Recorder of Tōtōmi Province, Sakamoto no Asomi Hitokami, the recruitment officer of the *sakimori*, submitted eighteen poems. However, eleven were eliminated because of their inferiority.

✳ The three poems from Sagami Province were all apparently composed at Naniwa on the eve of embarkation for Tsukushi. The first of them (no. 1229) echoes the opening poem from Tōtōmi in its conception and phraseology, carrying the journey forward to the second major departure point. Parents take the place of the sweetheart of the earlier poem. Nos. 1230 and 1231 are unusual in sounding a positive note. The authors of both look forward with excitement to their great adventure and only regret that no one from home is there to see them off.

(1229)   [4352/4328]

Ōkimi no	Awed by the command
Mikoto kashikomi	Of our great lord, I shall go:
Iso ni furi	Skirting stony strands,
Unohara wataru	I shall cross the plains of sea,
Chichi haha o okite	Leaving Father and Mother.

The above poem is by Hasebe no Miyatsuko Hitomaro, assistant able-bodied male.

(1230)   [4353/4329]

Yaso kuni wa	All the eighty lands
Naniwa ni tsudoi	Have gathered in Naniwa;
Funakazari	Would there were someone
A ga semu hiro o	To watch me on the day I dress
Mimo hito mogamo	Our ship in its finery.

The above poem is by Tajihibe no Kunihito of Lower Ashigara District, able-bodied male, active duty.

(1231)   [4354/4330]

Naniwatsu ni	In Naniwa port
Yosoiyosoite	Ready as ready we can be,
Kyō no hi ya	Now at last today—
Idete makaramu	But must I embark on this journey
Miru haha nashi ni	Without Mother to watch me go?

The above poem is by Maroko no Muraji Ōmaro of Kamakura District, able-bodied male, active duty.

On the seventh of the second month the Governor, Fujiwara no Asomi Sukunamaro, Junior Fifth Rank Lower, the recruitment officer for the *sakimori* of Sagami Province, submitted eight poems. However, five inferior poems were eliminated.

❋ The next three poems are from a group inserted by Yakamochi of his own composition, in which he addresses the sakimori or comments on their themes. *Saki* ("blossom") in no. 1233 also means "split"; either way, it is an image of the foaming sea. The canal in no. 1234 is the famous one at Naniwa dug in the reign of Nintoku in the early fifth century. Boats made by the boatwrights of Izu were famed for their speed.

1232–34   [MYS XX:4358–60/4334–36]

(1232)   [4358/4334]

  Unahara o   Whither you shall go,
  Tōku watarite   Far across the plains of sea,
   Toshi fu to mo   Though the years pass by
  Kora ga musuberu   Never dream of undoing
  Himo toku na yume   The sash your sweetheart tied!

(1233)   [4359/4335]

  Ima kawaru   Now the time has come
  Niisakimori ga   For the changing of the guard:
   Funade suru   New *sakimori*
  Unahara no ue ni   Embark across the plains of sea—
  Nami na saki so ne   Waves, do not blossom there.

(1234)   [4360/4336]

  Sakimori no   The *sakimori*
  Horie kogizuru   Cannot row their Izu boats
   Izutebune   Out from the canal
  Kaji toru ma naku   With an oarstroke more incessant
  Koi wa shigekemu   Than the beat of their longing.

The above were composed by Ōtomo no Sukune Yakamochi on the ninth.

❋ The first three poems from Suruga (nos. 1235–37) are based on the jo technique. No. 1235 employs a swing line (line 2) to join the natural image and the human application, effectively evoking the confusion and hurry of leave-taking in a way somehow reminiscent of no. 320 by Hitomaro. No. 1236 works through incremental repetition to introduce the idea of parting by an image of separation. Its simple final exclamation expresses the heart of the whole series. *Tatamikeme* (dialect for *tatamikomo*, "woven-mat") is a mock epithet for Muraji through *mu*, an allophone of *u*, the first syllable of *umu*, "to spin." No. 1237 again evokes the restlessness of travel through an image of birds of passage. *Iwaite* in the last line refers to a complex of ritual behavior designed to assure the safety of a traveler, involving the utterance of auspicious formulas and the avoidance of taboos. (No. 924 provides a negative instance in lines 5–6.)

1235–44   [MYS XX: 4361–70 / 4337–46]

(1235)   [4361 / 4337]

Mizutori no	Water birds rising:
Tachi no isogi ni	In the rush of our parting
Chichi haha ni	To Father and Mother
Monowazu kinite	I said not a word and came away;
Ima zo kuyashiki	Now I know the meaning of regret.

The above poem is by Utobe no Ushimaro, able-bodied male, active duty.

(1236)   [4362 / 4338]

Tatamikeme	Yonder rocky shore
Muraji ga iso no	Of woven-mat Muraji,
Hanariso no	Island far away;
Haha o hararete	Far away from my mother
Yuku ga kanashisa	Have I gone—oh, the sadness.

The above poem is by Mibube no Michimaro, assistant able-bodied male.

(1237)   [4363 / 4339]

Kuni meguru	Touring the country,
Atori kama keri	Chaffinch, mallard, and lapwing:
Yukimeguri	Till I've done my tour
Kairiku made ni	And come home to you again
Iwaite matane	Prayerfully wait, and well.

The above poem is by Osakabe no Mushimaro.

❋ The "water-immersed pearl" (*mizuku shiratama*) of no. 1238 probably stands for the exotic riches of an imagined Tsukushi; less likely, it could be a metaphor for a Tsukushi bride (would she be welcome in Suruga?). In any case the image is almost certainly part of a kind of mutual deception in which parents and recruit agree to speak of his military service as a pleasure cruise.

(1238)   [4364 / 4340]

Tochi haha e	Father and Mother,
Iwaite matane	Prayerfully wait, and well,
Tsukushi naru	Till I come again

| Mizuku shiratama | With the white pearl of Tsukushi |
| Torite ku made ni | Wet from its watery bed. |

The above poem is by Kawara no Mushimaro.

❋ The following three poems form a set focusing on, respectively, father, mother, and wife and children. The first (no. 1239) is unadorned and moving in its straightforward simplicity. The poem is one exclamatory sentence, regular in its syntax, devoid of figurative language. It shows the possibilities of plain speech. Miori is presumably the home village of the speaker. Tachibana may have been an area in what is now the city of Shimizu. The poem for Mother (no. 1240), by contrast, employs a majestic simile. (For the kind of chant referred to, see no. 153.) The cry of despair with which the third poem (no. 1241) begins may be compared with no. 975 by Nakatomi no Yakamori. On journeys you need expect nothing but the worst—the worst, perhaps, being the aging of the precious woman, mother or wife, left behind.

(1239)   [4365/4341]

Tachibana no	Leaving my father
Miori no sato ni	In the village of Miori
Chichi o okite	In Tachibana,
Michi no nagachi wa	It is more than I can bear
Yukikatenu kamo	To travel the long, long road.

The above poem is by Hasebe no Tarimaro.

(1240)   [4366/4342]

Makebashira	Like the cypress pillar
Homete tsukureru	Of a great hall erected
Tono no goto	To a chant of praise,
Imase hahatoji	Stay, Mother, mistress of the house—
Omogawari sezu	And may your face never change.

The above poem is by Sakatabe no Obitomaro.

(1241)   [4367/4343]

Waro tabi wa	This is a journey,
Tabi to omeodo	Yes, I know it's a journey—
Ii ni shite	But she's at home
Komechi yasuramu	And must be worn thin with the children—
Wa ga mi kanashi mo	My wife, oh, how dear to me!

The above poem is by Tamatsukuribe no Hirome.

❋ The truth that travel is no escape from thoughts is discovered again by the author of no. 1242. This poem sums up the pain in the previous three.

(1242) [4368 / 4344]

Wasuramu te	Wanting to forget,
No yuki yama yuki	Over moor, over mountain
Ware kuredo	I came away;
Wa ga chichi haha wa	But there was no forgetting them,
Wasure senu kamo	My father and mother.

The above poem is by Aki no Osa no Obito Maro.

❋ The "high peak of Suruga" (*Suruga no nera*) toward which the longing of no. 1243 is displaced is probably Mount Fuji, rising on the border of Suruga and Kai provinces (see no. 569).

(1243) [4369 / 4345]

Wagimeko to	How I long for it,
Futari wa ga mishi	The high peak of Suruga
Uchiesuru	Of the rolling waves
Suruga no nera wa	That I and my sweetheart
Kufushiku me aru ka	Used to gaze at together.

The above poem is by Kasugabe no Maro.

❋ The last poem by the sakimori of Suruga is another affectingly simple statement like no. 1239, but this one so designed as to frame in its middle line the farewell blessing of the parents left at home.

(1244) [4370 / 4346]

Chichi haha ga	Father and Mother
Kashira kakinade	Stroked my head and said to me,
Saku are te	"Good luck be with you!"
Iishi ketoba ze	Those words I have never
Wasurekanetsuru	Been able to forget.

The above poem is by Hasebe no Inamaro.

On the seventh of the second month—actually on the ninth—the Governor, Fuse no Asomi Hitonushi, Junior Fifth Rank Lower, the recruitment officer for the *sakimori* of Suruga Province, submitted twenty poems. However, the inferior poems were eliminated.

Anonymous Poems

Almost half of the poems in *Man'yōshū* are anonymous. If they are under-represented in the present anthology, it is not out of any lack of appreciation for their quality and interest. That interest has both intrinsic and literary-historical dimensions. Few of the anonymous poems achieve the power of Hitomaro or Okura, or the fresh vision occasionally attained by Akahito and Yakamochi, but their level of poetic competence, though varied, is generally high, and for vast stretches they maintain an even plane that may indeed be the true voice of *Man'yōshū*. The accomplishments of the known poets can be appreciated retrospectively against this background. In addition, in innumerable cases the anonymous poems break through their conventions to speak in voices of a lively and immediate appeal. Earthy images, forthright declarations, and a communally shared viewpoint bespeak folk origins for many poems. A few are really ancient songs and provide a link with the material drawn from the chronicles. Others show Chinese influence or serve as pieces in the new game of literary categories.

The bulk of the anonymous poetry in *Man'yōshū* is concentrated in eight of its twenty books—Book VII and Books X–XVI. Books VII, X, XI, and XII are collections of tanka arranged according to various modal and topical schemes. The compilers' interest seems to have been in the categories to be illustrated, and it is possible that authors' names were deliberately omitted even when known, thus avoiding biographical distraction. Book XIII is a collection of old anonymous chōka, and Book XIV assembles tanka from the provinces of eastern Japan. These two books are evidence of the interest in the old and geographically remote that was part of Nara literary culture. The poems and songs of these collections were intended to be appreciated for their rustic and archaic qualities, but were nevertheless arranged according to modal and other literary categories. The anonymous content of Book XV—those poems from the 736 embassy to Silla lacking authors' names—presents a different picture and was dealt with earlier. Finally, Book XVI is a grand and glorious grab bag of chōka and tanka, mostly anonymous, some old, and many accompanied by a prose anecdote. It is the true miscellany of *Man'yōshū*. Outside these eight books the basic principle of the compilers was to provide authors' names where available. Since names were not always available, there are also a number of anonymous poems to be found outside the so-called "anonymous books." Their inclusion where they are points toward the variety of editorial principles at work in *Man'yōshū*.

The principles on which *Man'yōshū* was compiled are numerous and overlapping. One of the basic ones, to be observed in individual books and with many divagations as a general thrust in the anthology as a whole, is chronological. But the "anonymous books" are exceptions to this rule. Though the content of the several books may be relatively old or new, chronology is not of paramount concern. Elsewhere in the present anthology Man'yō poems have been largely rearranged precisely for a greater chronological coherence, but in this final section it has seemed wisest to sidestep the pitfalls of attempting a relative dating of disparate and anonymous verse. The sampling presented here, then, has the virtue, if such it is, of following *Man'yōshū* itself.

Books I–VI

The first selections are from Book 1, a formally arranged chronological collection of *zōka*, or "Miscellaneous Poems." This book culminates in some of the public poetry of Hitomaro, and the following two poems (nos. 1245 and 1246–47) are very much in his manner. They even form a pair, a feature characteristic of his surviving chōka. No. 1245, ascribed to the conscript laborers who built Empress Jitō's Fujiwara Palace, has the formulaic quality and the long, swelling rhythms of Hitomaro's prosody. The opening four-line formula is one that Hitomaro may have put together from its paired two-line encomia, elements found separately in, for example, nos. 72 and 97. The high incidence of pillow words (ten) is also typical of his style. The choosing of the palace site (lines 5–12), the tribute rendered by nature (lines 13–24) and man (lines 25–46), and the conclusion (line 47) on the Sovereign's divinity are all elements set forth in Hitomaro's Yoshino poems (nos. 293–96), and the Sovereign (Empress Jitō) is the same monarch he served.

The description of nature's largesse and the devotion of the subjects is if anything livelier than can be found elsewhere in the genre. The use of pivot words (kakekotoba) in lines 34 and 40 is also reminiscent of Hitomaro's use of the technique in lines 9 and 10 of no. 293. Pivot words, as distinguished from entire swing lines, were still an unusual device in Man'yō times. The carefully crafted double jo in lines 31–40 technically goes beyond anything in the attested work of Hitomaro, but bespeaks experience with the kind of extended figures of speech found in lines 27–32 of no. 325 and the Homeric similes of no. 341. This massive parenthesis exists for the purpose of introducing the auspicious omen of the sacred tortoise. It takes off from the point in line 30 where the commoners are toiling in the river, and deposits them on dry land at the end (line 41), still carrying the timbers for the palace. In between are the two pivot constructions, *yoshikoseji* in line 34 and *Izumi no kawa* in line 40, marking the shift from the first jo to the second, and from the second back to the main line of exposition. *Yoshikose* ("let them draw near") pivots into Koseji ("Kose Road"), where the tortoise was discovered, and *izu* ("comes forth") into Izumi, the name of the river whither the people are transporting the timbers. The result is like the spectacular flourish of a gymnast doing an extra two turns in the air. Perhaps only Hitomaro would have been capable of such athletic versification.

Prodigious beasts were regarded as omens in East Asia, and their appearance was recorded in the histories of China, and therefore also in the Japanese chronicles. *Nihonshoki* fails to report a tortoise with auspicious markings having been discovered at the time of the building of the Fujiwara palace, however. The locus classicus for the tortoise with mystic markings on its carapace is a passage in the K'ung An-kuo commentary to *Shu-ching*. The markings were a code to the ninefold Great Plan for the governance of mankind, and so the tortoise became the most sacred of the prodigious animals. *Aratae no* ("rough-fibered") in line 5 is a mock epithet for Fujiwara through *fuji* ("wisteria"). *Koromode no* ("garment-sleeved") in line 17 similarly applies to *ta* ("arm") in Tanakami. *Yasouji* ("eighty clans") in line 22 involves a doubling with the name of the Uji River. Izumi, the name of the river mentioned in line 40, means "Wellspring." The transportation route for the timbers is south along the Uji and Izumi rivers, and then overland past Nara Mountain, and down the Saho and up the Hatsuse rivers. Fujiwara, at the northern end of the Asuka area, was the last stopping point before the court moved to Nara in 710. The foundations of the huge palace with outlying temples Empress Jitō erected there can still be seen. The poem's vision of subjects "eagerly at work" belies the fact that forced labor—corvée—was used for such projects.

1245   [MYS 1: 50]

A poem composed by the laborers on the Fujiwara Palace

Yasumishishi	Our great Sovereign
Wa ga ōkimi	Who rules the land in all tranquility,
Takaterasu	The Divine Child
Hi no miko	Of the High-Shining Sun,
5 Aratae no	Deigning to choose
Fujiwara ga ue ni	Rough-fibered Fujiwara as the seat
Osu kuni o	Whence to hold in sway
Meshitamawamu to	The provinces of this her realm,
Miaraka wa	Thinking to build here
10 Takashirasamu to	The lofty halls of her divine abode,

Kamunagara	She who is a god
Omōsu nahe ni	Conceived this plan: and at her thought
Ame tsuchi mo	The heavens and the earth
Yorite are koso	Drew near to listen and obey.
15 Iwabashiru	Hence in Ōmi,
Ōmi no kuni no	Where water dashes on the rocks,
Koromode no	On the wooded slopes
Tanakamiyama no	Of garment-sleeved Mount Tanakami
Maki saku	Splendid trees were split
20 Hi no tsumade o	And timbers of fine cypress came
Mononofu no	Cascading down Uji—
Yasoujigawa ni	River named of the eighty clans that fill
Tamamo nasu	The hundred offices at court—
Ukabenagasere	Set afloat like gemweed on the stream.
25 So o toru to	To grasp these timbers
Sawaku mitami mo	The milling crowds of commoners,
Ie wasure	Forgetful of their homes,
Mi mo tanashirazu	Oblivious even of life and limb,
Kamojimono	Bob on the surface
30 Mizu ni ukiite	Of the water like a flock of ducks.
Wa ga tsukuru	To the gates we build,
Hi no mikado ni	The lofty Gates of the Sun,
Shiranu kuni	Let unknown lands
Yoshikoseji yori	In obedience draw near: from Kose Road,
35 Wa ga kuni wa	Bearing on its back
Tokoyo ni naramu	Strange markings that proclaim
Aya oeru	Our land the Deathless Land,
Kusushiki kame mo	A sacred tortoise has come forth,
Ayatayo to	Foretelling a new age:
40 Izumi no kawa ni	Wellspring River, Izumi—thither
Mochikoseru	Do the people now
Maki no tsumade o	Carry overland the timbered logs,
Momotarazu	Lashing them together
Ikada ni tsukuri	Into multitudes of rafts
45 Nobosuramu	To take up the stream.
Isowaku mireba	When I see her subjects eagerly at work,
Kamukara narashi	How clear our Sovereign is a god!

Concerning the above, *Nihongi* states: "In the seventh year of Shuchō [693], Water-Junior / Serpent, in autumn, in the eighth month, the Sovereign visited the site of the Fujiwara Palace. In the eighth year [694], Wood-Junior / Horse, in spring, in the first month, she visited the Fujiwara Palace. In winter, in the twelfth month, whose first day was Metal-Senior / Dog, on the day Wood-Junior/Hare, she moved her abode and took up residence in the Fujiwara Palace."

✻ The matching composition (no. 1246–47), whose author is said to be unknown, is a palace-praising poem cast in the form of a geographical diagram. The Fujiwara site is located by the coordinates of the mountains that frame it—the "Three Mountains of Yamato" (see no. 250), Kagu, Unebi, and Miminashi, to the east, west, and north, and the ranges of Yoshino in the far distance to the south. Each mountain is described in terms of its beauty and lushness, as well as its position, in a series of parallel passages that seem to be performing a sacred rite of blessing for the land. In this paradise-like realm rises (without effort by milling crowds of commoners) the palace whose towering roof is itself an image of the mountains surrounding it. (See no. 173 for similar phraseology.) From the distance the Empress looks on, as in no. 295, so that the poem is also a kunimi, a viewing of the land. The water of the palace well, the poem's ostensible subject, is mentioned at the end, an image of coolness and refreshment that juxtaposes this poem with no. 1245's frenetic splashing in the rivers. The poems are clearly intended as a complementary pair contrasting activity and stillness. When the palace has thus been twice blessed, the poet (if he is one and the same) at last turns in the envoy to an expression of a courtier's desire for the company of palace ladies, a charmingly informal grace note after the outpouring of ritual praise.

1246–47   [MYS I: 52–53]

A poem on the well of Fujiwara Palace

Yasumishishi	Our great Sovereign
Wa go ōkimi	Who rules the land in all tranquility,
Takaterasu	The Divine Child
Hi no miko	Of the High-Shining Sun,
5 Aratae no	Deigns to begin
Fujii ga hara ni	The building of her palace gates
Ōmikado	In the well-field
Hajimetamaite	Of Fuji the rough-fibered,
Haniyasu no	Goes and takes her stand
10 Tsutsumi no ue ni	On the bankments of the pond
Aritatashi	Of Haniyasu,
Meshitamaeba	There to gaze upon her realm:
Yamato no	Yamato
Aokaguyama wa	Green Kagu Mountain,
15 Hi no tate no	At the rise-of-sun

Ōki mikado ni	Great eastern palace gate,
Haruyama to	A spring mountain,
Shimisabitateri	Stands luxuriantly dense;
Unebi no	Unebi,
20 Kono mizuyama wa	That lush mountain,
Hi no yoko no	At the set-of-sun
Ōki mikado ni	Great western palace gate,
Mizuyama to	A lush mountain,
Yamasabiimasu	Rises mountain-perfect;
25 Miminashi no	Miminashi,
Aosugayama wa	Green-sedge mountain,
Sotomo no	At the back-face
Ōki mikado ni	Great northern palace gate
Yoroshinahe	In full splendor
30 Kamusabitateri	Stands in godliness;
Naguwashiki	Lovely in their name,
Yoshino no yama wa	The mountains of Yoshino,
Kagetomo no	From the light-face
Ōki mikado yu	Great southern palace gate
35 Kumoi ni so	Lie far off
Tōku arikeru	In the cloudland of the sky.
Takashiru ya	Towering aloft,
Ame no mikage	The heaven-shelter that she built;
Ame shiru ya	Towering to heaven,
40 Hi no mikage no	Her high shelter of the sun:
Mizu koso ba	This shady water
Tsune ni arame	Shall endure throughout all time,
Mii no sumimizu	This fresh water of the palace well.

Tanka

Fujiwara no	How enviable
Ōmiyatsukae	The company of maidens
Aretsuku ya	Born to serve at court
Otome ga tomo wa	In the mighty palace halls
Tomoshikiro kamo	Of royal Fujiwara!

The author of the above poem is unknown.

❋ No. 1248, one of a group of poems composed during travel, is an example of compositions about whose authorship the *Man'yōshū* compilers express uncertainty. If the poem is indeed by Emperor Mommu (Empress Jitō's grandson and successor), it can be regarded as an experiment in the genre of the sorrows of a traveler.

1248   [MYS I:74]

A poem from the time of the late Sovereign [Mommu's] visit to the Yoshino
Palace

Miyoshino no	Evening in the cold
Yama no arashi no	Of fair Yoshino's mountains,
Samukeku ni	Swept by the harsh wind:
Hata ya koyoi mo	Will this be another night
A ga hitori nemu	When I must sleep alone?

It is also claimed that the above poem is a composition of the Sovereign.

✳ The next poem, from Book II, is a variant of no. 233, attributed to Empress Iwanohime. The existence of such variants is evidence of an apparently
large floating repertory of orally transmitted tanka. *Kokashū* ("Collection of
Old Poems") may be either a common or a proper noun.

1249   [MYS II:89]

There is a poem in a certain text that reads as follows:

Iakashite	Waking until dawn,
Kimi o ba matamu	I shall wait my lord's return,
Nubatama no	Though upon my hair,
Wa ga kurokami ni	Black now as lustrous beads of jet,
Shimo wa furu to mo	The white frost softly falls.

The above poem appears in *Kokashū*.

✳ No. 1250 immediately follows the series on Hitomaro's death (nos. 361–
64) and seems to have been intended to be read as part of it. The reference to
"leaving" is to the abandonment of a dead body. For a similar and perhaps
source poem, see no. 350 by Hitomaro.

1250   [MYS II:227]

There is a poem in a certain text that reads as follows:

Amazakaru	Under remote skies
Hina no arano ni	In the wasteland of the countryside
Kimi o okite	I left you, my lord;
Omoitsutsu areba	Now I go on in this longing
Ikeru to mo nashi	Without the strength to live.

The author of the above poem is unknown. However, an old text gives it in
this order.

✸ The chōka-hanka set 1251–52 on travel on the Inland Sea concludes the *zōka* section of Book III. The compiler notes that it was recited by Waka-miya no Ayumaro, the author of the final poem in the "Mulberry Branch" group (no. 888). The implied oral transmission of (in this case anonymous) chōka is of interest as an activity still occurring in the eighth century. The poem is particularly effective in evoking the interfusion of divinity with land and sea that characterizes much of the nature poetry in *Man'yōshū*. Awaji Island lies athwart the head of the Inland Sea and would be clearly visible to travelers going west through Akashi Strait. Iyo, one of the provinces of Shikoku, probably stands for the whole island. The mystery and quiet majesty of no. 1251 are worthy of the powers of any of the best chōka poets, and the vivid sense of dawn at the end is especially satisfying. Minume was on the coast near modern Kōbe; it would be off the starboard beam of a ship heading away from Yamato toward Akashi Strait. The envoy deals with the feeling of departure in its aspect of homesickness, whereas the chōka focuses on eagerness to be on the way.

1251–52   [MYS III: 391–92 / 388–89]

A travel poem; with *tanka*

	Watatsumi wa	Mystic are the ways
	Kusushiki mono ka	Of the god of the great deep:
	Awajishima	He sets Awaji
	Naka ni tateokite	As the midmost of the isles,
5	Shiranami o	He girdles Iyo
	Iyo ni motōshi	With the white of breaking waves;
	Imachizuki	Through Akashi Strait
	Akashi no to yu wa	(Bright Akashi of the waited moon)
	Yū sareba	When evening comes
10	Shio o mitashime	He brings the tide to full,
	Ake sareba	When morning comes
	Shio o kareshimu	He dries the tide away.
	Shiosai no	In dread of the waves
	Nami o kashikomi	That clash in the brawling tides,
15	Awajishima	On Awaji Isle
	Isogakuriite	We lie sheltered on the strand,
	Itsu shi ka mo	Wondering when night
	Kono yo no akemu to	Will brighten into dawn,
	Samorau ni	Biding our time
20	I no nekateneba	In watchful, sleepless waiting;
	Taki no ue no	Till above the falls
	Asano no kigishi	In the fields of shallow grass
	Akenu to shi	The pheasants cry dawn
	Tachisawaku rashi	Has come, in strident clamor:

25 Iza kodomo   Come, boys,
    Aete kogidemu   Let's row out with a will—
    Niwa mo shizukeshi   The broad sea fields are calm.

Envoy

    Shimazutai   Rowing down the coast,
    Minume no saki o   We round the cape of Minume—
    Kogimireba   And then they come,
    Yamato koishiku   The longing for Yamato,
    Tazu sawa ni naku   The cries of the flocking cranes.

The above poem was recited by Wakamiya no Ayumaro, but the author is unknown.

❊ The following three tanka follow poems dated to the first month of 744 and immediately precede Tanabe no Sakimaro's chōka-hanka set on Nara in its abandonment (no. 674–76), whose subject they share. The image of permeation (drawn from dyeing fabric in deep safflower red) in poem 1253 suggests the red-painted pillars of the palace, now taken away to the new capital at Kuni, and hence the colorlessness of the city once the court has gone. In no. 1254 Nara fades like a flower or colored leaf, and the latent botanical image is continued in the opening mock epithet of no. 1255. *Mata* is "forks" with *iwatsuna no* ("rock ivy"), "again" with *mata ochikaeri* ("return to youth again"). The ancient true epithet for Nara, *aoni yoshi*, appears in the third line, harmonizing with the crimson in the first poem, so that Nara assumes throughout the guise of a gorgeously colored but flowerlike and ephemeral Miyako, or royal city.

1253–55   [MYS VI: 1048–50 / 1044–46]

Three poems composed in affliction and regret over the desolate remains of the Nara capital (author uncertain)

(1253)   [1048 / 1044]

    Kurenai ni   Shall a heart that soaked
    Fukaku shiminishi   Deeply, even to crimson,
    Kokoro ka mo   In the royal city
    Nara no miyako ni   Go on living in Nara
    Toshi no henubeku   Through the passing of the years?

(1254)   [1049 / 1045]

    Yo no naka o   Now at last I learn
    Tsune naki mono to   That the world in which we live

Ima so shiru
Nara no miyako no
Utsurou mireba

Is ephemeral—
Now that I see it fade away,
The royal city of Nara.

(1255)   [1050/1046]

Iwatsuna no
Mata ochikaeri
Aoni yoshi
Nara no miyako o
Mata mo mimu ka mo

Ivy on a rock—
Might I turn and cling again
To a long-lost youth,
Once more to see Miyako
In Nara of the blue-green earth?

Book *VII*

Book VII is the first of the "anonymous books." It includes tanka and sedōka from the "Hitomaro Collection," as well as contributions from *Kokashū* ("Collection of Old Poems"), but is basically a collection of anonymous tanka of unknown origin. The content is arranged under three general headings—zōka ("Miscellaneous Poems"), hiyuka ("Allegorical Poems"), and banka ("Laments")—but also includes poems on travel and other topics. Many of the zōka are of the modal type eibutsu, "Poems on Things," while the hiyuka are largely kibutsu, "Poems in Reference to Things." The distinction is one between descriptive and metaphorical expression, but also involves a grouping into nature and love poems. The category hiyuka, itself modal, properly means a poem of completely metaphorical (i.e., allegorical) expression, but not all examples are of this type. These categorical arrangements are thought to have been modeled on the original "Hitomaro Collection" before it was cut up and distributed throughout *Man'yōshū*. The ultimate sources for genre distinctions are Chinese, however, largely late Six Dynasties and early T'ang. *Wen-hsüan* was of particular importance, and the existence of reference works such as the T'ang encyclopedia *I-wen Lei-chü* facilitated topical composition. The use of topics indicates a growing interest in literary theory in the Nara period. The poems themselves probably run from the late seventh to the early eighth century and reflect both court and country.

"On the Moon" is the second of the eibutsu categories of the zōka section. (The first, "On the Sky," is represented by the "moon-boat" poem from the "Hitomaro Collection"; see no. 365. The particular metaphorical nature of that poem is atypical of eibutsu as a whole, indeed, of tanka in general.) The following seven tanka belong to the moon category. All are exemplary of the refined viewpoints of courtiers for whom admiration of the moon is an elegant pastime, and nos. 1260 and 1261 present specifically courtly scenes. The general theme is one of regret for the setting of the moon or for its late rising, interspersed with expressions of pleasure (nos.

1257 and 1261) or loneliness (no. 1260). A banquet ambience is suggested by nos. 1256, 1259, 1261, and 1262. True to the eibutsu mode, the poems generally avoid metaphor and concentrate on description or exclamation. The jo in no. 1257 and the pillow-word construction in no. 1262 are exceptions. It is not in Chinese-influenced appreciations of nature such as these that the traditional Japanese rhetorical devices are usually found. Conceits are another matter (nos. 1259 and 1262). The "hesitating moon" (*isayou tsuki*) in no. 1258 refers to the waning moon, which rises about an hour later each night.

"On the Moon"

1256   [MYS VII: 1073 / 1069]

Tsune wa sane	Never until now
Omowanu mono o	Have I troubled at such thoughts,
Kono tsuki no	But, oh, tonight
Sugikakuramaku	How I regret this moon must sink
Oshiki yoi kamo	And vanish from our sight!

1257   [MYS VII: 1074 / 1070]

Masurao no	Stalwart men brandish
Yuzue furiokoshi	Their hunting bows, shafts upright,
Karitaka no	And from Hunting Hill
Nohe sae kiyoku	Even the distant fields lie clear
Teru tsukuyo kamo	This night of radiant moon.

1258   [MYS VII: 1075 / 1071]

Yama no ha ni	On the mountain crest
Isayou tsuki o	Soon the hesitating moon
Idemu ka to	Surely will come forth—
Machitsutsu oru ni	But while I have waited
Yo so fukenikeru	The night has worn away.

1259   [MYS VII: 1076 / 1072]

Asu no yoi	Night of the moon
Teramu tsukuyo wa	That will shine tomorrow night,
Katayori ni	Let it come over,
Koyoi ni yorite	Let it merge into tonight—
Yo nagakaranamu	For, oh, that this night may be long!

1260   [MYS VII: 1077 / 1073]

Tamadare no	Through beaded curtains
Osu no matōshi	By myself I sit and gaze—

Hitori ite / But she wastes the hour
Miru shirushi naki / Who watches all alone the moon
Yūzukuyo kamo / Grow bright in the evening sky.

1261   [MYS VII: 1080 / 1076]

Momoshiki no / How clear is the moon
Ōmiyahito no / On this night of banqueting
Makariidete / When the courtiers
Asobu koyoi no / Of the palace fortress-strong
Tsuki no sayakesa / Have left to take their pleasure!

1262   [MYS VII: 1081 / 1077]

Nubatama no / That we might hold back
Yo wataru tsuki o / The moon that crosses through the night
Todomemu ni / Of *nuba*-berry black,
Nishi no yamahe ni / Is there no barrier on its path
Seki mo aranu ka mo / Across the western hills?

❊ No. 1263, "On Rain," is an example of the tendency of the compilers to slip love poems into their eibutsu category, whether from inattentiveness or for some other reason. The poem is not about rain, but about the poet's desire to share the experience of his sweetheart. Similarly, no. 1264, "On Mountains," is really more about the speaker's sense of aging than about Mount Kagu as such. The ancient matters may be those referred to in no. 250–52 by Emperor Tenji. Mount Kagu has the epithet *ame no* ("heavenly") because of the legend that it descended from heaven.

"On Rain"

1263   [MYS VII: 1094 / 1090]

Wagimoko ga / Would that even I
Akamo no suso no / Might be wet in this small rain
Hizutsuramu / Wherein today
Kyō no kosame ni / My darling's had her scarlet skirt
Ware sae nurena / All splashed along the hem.

"On Mountains"

1264   [MYS VII: 1100 / 1096]

Inishie no / Though I do not know
Koto wa shiranu o / Those matters of the ancient time,
Ware mite mo / It has been long enough
Hisashiku narinu / Since the day that I first gazed
Ame no Kaguyama / On heaven-sent Kagu Mountain.

✻ Most of the following poems "On Rivers" keep their focus on the natural scene and the delight to be drawn from it, and the compilers seem to have found in Yoshino poems and similar expressions of rapt pleasure in running water proper material for their category. The first (no. 1265) is an exuberant conceit reminiscent of Hitomaro's moon-parasol in no. 302. The conceit is perhaps overburdened, however, since the mountain is at once anthropomorphized to take a sash (the rivulet) and exploited for the meaning of its name (Mikasa = "Royal Parasol") in order to take the pillow-word construction *ōkimi no* ("of our great Sovereign"). In the next six poems (nos. 1266–71) can be heard the voice of the courtier of Nara or Fujiwara as he gazes on local beauty spots celebrated for the clean refreshment of their rushing streams and quiet pools. This courtier's preferences are in accord with the emphasis on purity in his native Shintō religion, but at the same time are informed by an esthetic of nature-observation inspired by Chinese example. Like Yakamochi, he is a culturally composite man. The metaphor in no. 1270, referring to the bleached cloth *yū* made from paper-mulberry bark fibers, was one of the highest emblems of beauty (see no. 341, lines 97–98). A woman's love poem has been included as no. 1272. *Sahinokuma* is a pillow-word duplication, with prefix *sa*, of the name of the river, a repetition that lends the verse an archaic songlike quality. The name Furukawa ("Ancient River") in no. 1270 no doubt suggested the poem.

"On Rivers"

1265   [MYS VII: 1106 / 1102]

    Ōkimi no   How pure the sound
Mikasa no yama no   The narrow valley rivulet
    Obi ni seru   Makes that winds about,
Hosotanigawa no   A sash on our great Sovereign's
Oto no sayakesa   Royal Parasol Mountain!

1266   [MYS VII: 1107 / 1103]

    Imashiku wa   Hardly should I see
Mime ya to omoishi   Before long time had passed, I thought,
    Miyoshino no   The great quiet pool
  Ōkawayodo o   In the river of fair Yoshino—
Kyō mitsuru kamo   That I have seen today!

1267   [MYS VII: 1108 / 1104]

    Uma namete   To line up our steeds
Miyoshinogawa o   And set off to see the river
   Mimaku hori   Of fair Yoshino—
Uchikoekite so   From this desire we've crossed the hills
Taki ni asobitsuru   And taken pleasure by the torrent here.

1268   [MYS VII: 1109/1105]

      Oto ni kiki   I have seen today
  Me ni wa imada minu   The quiet pool of Mutsuta
       Yoshinogawa   In Yoshino River,
  Mutsuta no yodo o   Of whose renown I'd heard before,
  Kyō mitsuru kamo   But never looked on with my eyes.

1269   [MYS VII: 1110/1106]

      Kawazu naku   One last look today
  Kiyoki kawara o   At this clean-swept river beach
    Kyō mite wa   Where the songfrogs cry,
  Itsu ka koekite   And when will I cross the hills again
  Mitsutsu shinowamu   To feast my eyes as now?

1270   [MYS VII: 1111/1107]

      Hatsusegawa   On Hatsuse River
  Shirayūhana ni   A white flower of barken cloth,
    Ochitagitsu   The plunging rapids foam:
  Se o sayakemi to   So sparkling pure their waters,
  Mi ni koshi ware o   Behold me here to see the sight!

1271   [MYS VII: 1112/1108]

      Hatsusegawa   On Hatsuse River
  Nagaruru mio no   The rapids in the current
    Se o hayami   Flow so swiftly
  Ide kosu nami no   There is cleanness in the sound
  Oto no kiyokeku   Of waves across the dam.

1272   [MYS VII: 1113/1109]

      Sahinokuma   Sahinokuma
  Hinokumagawa no   Hinokuma River runs
    Se o hayami   Swift in the shallows—
  Kimi ga te toraba   If I were to take your hand
  Koto yosemu ka mo   Would we be talked about?

1273   [MYS VII: 1115/1111]

      Inishie mo   In former times
  Kaku kikitsutsu ka   Did men with eager joy
    Shinoikemu   Listen as now
  Kono Furukawa no   To the purity of sound
  Kiyoki se no oto o   Of the rapids of Ancient River?

✻ Similarly to no. 1273, the name Aone ("Green Pinnacle") in the following poem "On Moss" was presumably the seed from which its playful conceit grew.

"On Moss"

1274 [MYS VII: 1124 / 1120]

Miyoshino no	Who was it wove,
Aone ga mine no	Without a thread for warp or weft,
Kokemushiro	The coverlet of moss
Tare ka orikemu	That drapes the heights of Aone,
Tatenuki nashi ni	The Greentop Peak of Yoshino?

✻ "On a Japanese Cithern" is the last of the eibutsu poems in Book VII. The topic follows "On an Old Village" and "On a Well," the only other categories of man-made things. The Japanese cithern (*yamatogoto* or *wagon*) had six strings, in contrast to the seven-stringed Chinese cithern. The cithern's "pipe" (*shitabi*) refers to the sounding chamber. For evidence that the cithern was believed able to summon the spirit of a woman, see no. 163. The cithern had been used in shamanistic rites of spirit possession since prehistoric times.

"On a Japanese Cithern"

1275 [MYS VII: 1133 / 1129]

Koto toreba	I take the cithern—
Nageki sakidatsu	Before all else a sigh escapes:
Kedashiku mo	Can it really be
Koto no shitabi ni	That deep down in the cithern's pipe
Tsuma ya komoreru	My wife is lurking?

✻ Poems composed at various places follow the eibutsu category under the zōka division of Book VII. One of these places is Yoshino. Nos. 1276 and 1277 are typical of Yoshino poems in tanka form, praising the pureness and eternality of the site according to conventional formulations: the reason for x is y (no. 1276), and x will last as long as y (no. 1277).

"Composed at Yoshino"

1276 [MYS VII: 1135 / 1131]

Minahito no	When I see today
Kouru Miyoshino	Fair Yoshino all men have loved,

Kyō mireba	The cause is clear:
Ube mo koikeri	None but must have loved this place
Yama kawa kiyomi	For the pureness of its hills and stream.

1277   [MYS VII: 1138/1134]

Yoshinogawa	To Yoshino River
Iwa to kashiwa to	I shall return forever,
Tokiwa nasu	As steadily
Ware wa kayowamu	As the changeless stones and oaks,
Yorozuyo made ni	Until ten thousand ages pass.

❋ The poems composed at various places logically belong with the next category, "Composed on a Journey." The first poem in the following sample (no. 1278) is a hiyuka, although not labeled as such. This example of nature used for love allegory (that the "sea lentil" is a woman is hinted by its name, *nanoriso*, "tell-not weed") is native in imagery, atmosphere, and technique. Its rusticity contrasts with the estheticism of most of the moon poems. The next poem (no. 1279) is intriguingly ambiguous. The seacoast setting and the evocation of wild nature join it to the world of no. 1278, but it reads like a nature poem, the memory a traveler has of his days along the wave-swept coast. It is tempting, however, to take the *tamamo* ("gemweed") as metaphorical, in which case the memories become those of amorous days spent with ama women. The third example (no. 1280) is definitely a love poem, of a very old type involving contrast between nature and man (see no. 115). It is also traditional and native in being introduced by a pillow word, *natsusobiku* ("summer-hemp-stretching"), a mock epithet for the place-name Unakami through *u*, related phonetically to *umu* ("spin"). Unakami is thought to have been in the Eastland, in present Chiba Prefecture. The poem shares its first three lines with MYS XIV: 3362/3348.

"Composed on a Journey"

1278   [MYS VII: 1171/1167]

Asari su to	Once, foraging upon
Iso ni wa ga mishi	The rocks along this coast, I found
Nanoriso o	Where the sea lentil grows;
Izure no shima no	And from what island did he come,
Ama ka karikemu	The fisherman who took it all away?

1279   [MYS VII: 1172/1168]

Kyō mo ka mo	Today once more
Oki tsu tamamo wa	Will the gemweed from the offing
Shiranami no	Be tumbling in wild skeins

| Yaeoru ga ue ni | Where the white waves, fold on fold, |
| Midarete aruramu | Break in sheets of shivering foam? |

1280 [MYS VII:1179/1176]

Natsusobiku	Summer-hemp-stretching
Unakamigata no	Unakami strand is lined
Oki tsu su ni	With offshore sandbars:
Tori wa sudakedo	Seabirds flock and clamor there,
Kimi wa oto mo sezu	But you, my love, are silent.

✳ The remaining examples of the travel category are mostly straightforward descriptions or exclamations. Their generally positive mood shows that the vague sadness found in the travel poems of, say, Takechi no Kurohito (nos. 445–55) is not typical of the genre throughout. Wakasa and Lake Mikata (no. 1281) are on the shores of the Sea of Japan. Inamino (nos. 1282–83; compare no. 251) is along the Inland Sea west of Akashi. *Amazutau* ("heaven-coursing") is a mock epithet for Hikasa through *hi* ("sun"). The viewpoint of no. 1283 reverses the usual yearning for home while on a journey. The next poem (no. 1284) suggests the combined fear and fascination that wild coastlines stirred in early mariners.

1281 [MYS VII:1181/1177]

Wakasa naru	Here in Wakasa
Mikata no umi no	The shore of Lake Mikata
Hama kiyomi	Sparkles so cleanly,
Iyukikaerai	Every time I leave I come again—
Miredo akanu kamo	Long though I gaze, my eyes will never tire.

1282 [MYS VII:1182/1178]

Inamino wa	Past Inamino
Yukisuginu rashi	We must now have made our way,
Amazutau	For the heaven-coursing
Hikasa no ura ni	Sun-shade Bay of Hikasa
Nami tateri miyu	Stands wave-bright in view.

1283 [MYS VII:1183/1179]

Ie ni shite	When I am at home
Are wa koimu na	Surely I shall yearn for this—
Inamino no	Once again to be
Asaji ga ue ni	Underneath the moon that beamed
Terishi tsukuyo o	On the reeds of Inamino.

1284 [MYS VII: 1184/1180]

Ariso kosu   Dreading the wild waves
Nami o kashikomi   That crash across its rocky strand,
Awajishima   Shall we pass it by
Mizu ya suginamu   All unseen though close at hand,
Kokoda chikaki o   The coast of Awaji Isle?

✳ The traditional looking back toward the Yamato homeland is expressed
in no. 1285. The next poem (no. 1286) is unusual in making the perception
of visual correspondence its subject. Tomo was near present Fukuyama City
in Hiroshima Prefecture. No. 1287 is also set at Tomo and incorporates a jo
elaborating the meaning of its name ("handguard"). Here the two-line jo
serves the same rhetorical function as a one-line pillow word of the mock-
epithet variety. A haunting evocation of the loneliness of travel is provided
by no. 1288, atypical of this group. The affective content is left vacant in no.
1289, which like nos. 1282 and 1286 ends in the spontaneous-passive verb
miyu ("is-seen"), the open, receptive eye of Man'yō poetry.

1285 [MYS VII: 1185/1181]

Asagasumi   Tatsuta Mountain,
Yamazu tanabiku   Where the morning mist forever
Tatsutayama   Drifts along the slopes—
Funade shinamu hi   On the day we launch our boat
Are koimu kamo   I shall look back in longing.

1286 [MYS VII: 1186/1182]

Amaobune   All across the bay
Ho ka mo hareru to   Fishing boats had hoisted sail,
Miru made ni   So it looked to me
Tomo no urami ni   When the waves stood up in view
Nami tateri miyu   By Tomo's curving shore.

1287 [MYS VII: 1187/1183]

Masakikute   Let our luck hold good,
Mata kaerimimu   We'll come again and see it,
Masurao no   The Bay of Tomo—
Te ni makimoteru   Tomo the Handguard bound about
Tomo no urami o   The wrist of the stalwart man!

1288 [MYS VII: 1188/1184]

Torijimono   As if I were a bird
Umi ni ukiite   I rest floating on the sea,

Oki tsu nami
Sawaku o kikeba
Amata kanashi mo

And the sound of waves
Splashing about in the offing
Brings many sadnesses.

1289   [MYS VII: 1189/1185]

Asanagi ni
Makaji kogidete
Mitsutsu koshi
Mitsu no matsubara
Namigoshi ni miyu

In the morning calm
Full-oared we rowed away,
Watching as we went
The pine-barrens of Mitsu—
Now in view across the waves.

❋ Poems like no. 1290 over the centuries established the courtier's concept of the hardships of the ama that finds its ultimate expression in the Nō play *Matsukaze*. The next poem (no. 1291) is susceptible to an allegorical interpretation. Ina (no. 1292) was between present Kōbe and Ōsaka. It takes the mock epithet *shinagadori* ("long-breath bird," a name for the grebe, which can stay submerged for extended periods) through *i* ("lead"), because grebes run across the water in pairs, one "leading" the other. The next two poems (nos. 1293–94) are far separate in the *Man'yōshū* text but form a pair in their hortatory address. One implies eagerness for the light of day, the other fear of the dark. The location of Nagoe is unknown; Akashi is on the Inland Sea opposite Awaji Island. The speaker of no. 1295 must be a native of northern Kyūshū, for Mount Yū is near the spa of Beppu on the coast of Ōita Prefecture. The first two lines are a jo impinging on *yū* in the sense of "tie up" (*yuu*). An imagistic parallel between flowing hair (*hanari no kami*) and trailing clouds also operates in the poem. Shika (no. 1296) is also in northern Kyūshū, near Fukuoka on the north coast (see nos. 648–57). The last three poems are in a group noted as taken from *Koshū* ("The Old Collection"). Again the term may be a common noun.

1290   [MYS VII: 1190/1186]

Asari suru
Amaotomera ga
Sode tōri
Nurenishi koromo
Hosedo kawakazu

Foraging by the sea,
Maidens of the fisherfolk
Work in sodden clothes,
Sleeves wet through and will not dry,
Though they hang them in the wind.

1291   [MYS VII: 1192/1188]

Yama koete
Tōtsu no hama no
Iwatsutsuji
Wa ga kuru made ni
Fufumite arimate

Over the mountains
Far away on Tōtsu Beach,
O wild azalea,
Wait until I come again,
Holding your flowers in bud.

1292   [MYS VII: 1193 / 1189]

   Ōki umi ni   Wind of the great sea,
Arashi na fuki so   Stormwind do not blow a storm
   Shinagatori   Till the long-breath-bird
Ina no minato ni   Boat has moored in the harbor
Fune hatsuru made   At Ina of the plunging grebe.

1293   [MYS VII: 1194 / 1190]

   Fune hatete   Let's tie up the boat,
Kashi furitatete   Let's pound in a mooring pole,
   Iori semu   Let's spend the night:
Nagoe no hamahe   The sandy shores of Nagoe
Sugikatenu kamo   Are a sight we can't go by.

1294   [MYS VII: 1233 / 1229]

   Wa ga fune wa   Let's have our boat
Akashi no mito ni   Row to harbor in the port
   Kogihatemu   At Akashi;
Okihe na sakari   Don't go out to the offing—
Sayo fukenikeri   The night is far advanced.

1295   [MYS VII: 1248 / 1244]

   Otomera ga   Young maidens all
Hanari no kami o   Do up their loose and flowing hair:
   Yū no yama   Flow not, O clouds,
Kumo na tanabiki   Across the face of Yū Mountain—
Ie no atari mimu   I would look upon my home.

1296   [MYS VII: 1250 / 1246]

   Shika no ama no   The shorefolk of Shika
Shio yaku keburi   Burn the seaweed to make salt,
   Kaze o itami   But the wind is strong:
Tachi wa noborazu   The smoke does not tower up—
Yama ni tanabiku   It drifts along the hills.

❋ The category "On an Occasion" (*rinji*) is somewhat mysterious; the poems entered under it are mostly in the mode of rustic love. No. 1297 is an example. For a reworking by Ōtomo no Ikenushi, see no. 1175. Here as there the roundabout route is the safe one. *Harukasumi* ("spring mist") is a mock epithet on *i* ("well") through *i* ("linger"). The poem is from *Kokashū*.

"On an Occasion"

1297   [MYS VII: 1260 / 1256]

> Harukasumi   Spring mist hovering:
> I no e yu tada ni   By the well I might have gone
>   Michi wa aredo   Where the road runs straight,
> Kimi ni awamu to   But to tryst with you, my love,
> Tamotōriku mo   I came the long way round.

✳ No. 1298 is the sole example in the category "Arousing Thoughts by Reference to Things" (*kibutsu hasshi*), a rubric that seems essentially the same as the "Expressing Thoughts by Reference to Things" (*kibutsu chinshi*) in Books XI and XII. Kibutsu poems usually employ the "thing" referred to in a love context, but here the "thing"—the moon—is used as a symbol of inconstancy. This poem too is from *Kokashū*.

"Arousing Thoughts by Reference to Things"

1298   [MYS VII: 1274 / 1270]

> Komoriku no   Over the mountains
> Hatsuse no yama ni   Of Hatsuse the hidden land
>   Teru tsuki wa   Stands the shining moon:
> Michikake shikeri   How it waxes and it wanes—
> Hito no tsune naki   The inconstancy of man!

✳ The second major division of Book VII is hiyuka. Hiyuka are properly allegories, poems in which an image is used in a metaphorical sense throughout, without the tenor of the metaphor being spelled out. Not all examples abide by this definition, however. Within the hiyuka section the dominant mode is kibutsu ("Reference to Things"), which results in an encyclopedic array of categories like that of the eibutsu in the zōka section. In this case the "things" are the vehicles of the metaphor. In the first example (no. 1299) the single thread stands for a one-sided love. Its dyeing (a love image) by a maiden is suggestive of the source of the passion.

"In Reference to Thread"

1299   [MYS VII: 1320 / 1316]

> Kafuchime no   The thread dyed by the hand
> Tesome no ito o   Of a maid of Kafuchi
>   Kurikaeshi   Spins around and round—
> Kataito ni aredo   It is but a single thread,
> Taemu to omoe ya   But can I believe it will break?

❊ In the next two poems the pearl is obviously a desired woman. The world of the pearl divers comes to life strongly in no. 1301, where the diver cries out (as was customary) the name of a god of the sea before plunging down. In ancient times there were both male and female divers, though nowadays diving is a woman's occupation. These poems are very close to Japanese folkways, but at the same time evoke memories of the magical undersea realm found by Urashima (no. 579–80).

"In Reference to Gems"

1300 [MYS VII: 1321 / 1317]

Wata no soko	On the ocean floor
Shizuku shiratama	Sunken lies a shining pearl—
Kaze fukite	Though the wind may blow
Umi wa aru to mo	And the sea grow wild with waves,
Torazu wa yamaji	I shall not stop till I have it.

1301 [MYS VII: 1322 / 1318]

Soko kiyomi	On the sunken pearl
Shizukeru tama o	Where the ocean floor lay clear
Mimaku hori	He desired to gaze—
Chitabi so norishi	A thousand times the diver
Kazuki suru ama	Cried out and plunged in the sea.

❊ The first poem in the section relating to grasses plays with fire to good if rueful effect. Its image is situated in a conceit—phrased as a rhetorical question—rather than being worked into a jo, and the range of power available to conceited hyperbole is well exemplified. The speaker's gender is not directly specified, but the translation assumes that the burning of fields—and therefore, in this instance, of hearts—is a male activity.

"In Reference to Grasses"

1302 [MYS VII: 1340 / 1336]

Fuyugomori	Hidden-in-winter
Haru no ōno o	The spring moors are all aflame—
Yaku hito wa	And he who burns them,
Yakitarane ka mo	Can he never burn enough,
Wa ga kokoro yaku	That he now sets fire to my heart?

❊ The following poem, also from the section on grasses, reverses the usual order by placing the natural image (the vehicle of the metaphor, or in Japanese terms what would normally be the jo) second, and the human application (the tenor of the metaphor) first. In giving the tenor it also diverges from the strict definition of hiyuka. *Nunawa* is a kind of water plant (*junsai* or "water-shield"). The poem captures the meaningless though not unpleasant motion of a love affair that is going nowhere.

1303   [MYS VII: 1356 / 1352]

   A ga kokoro   My heart lies afloat
Yuta ni tayuta ni   Riding, slipping in the waves:
   Ukinunawa   Like the *nunawa*
He ni mo oki ni mo   It drifts neither in nor out,
Yorikatsumashiji   But bobs upon the water.

❋ The next example fulfills the requirements of hiyuka by keeping the tenor dark. The reference is presumably to a girl still too young to marry (see nos. 1125–27 and 1159–61).

"In Reference to Rice"

1304   [MYS VII: 1357 / 1353]

   Isonokami   Though the early rice
Furu no wasada o   At Furu of Isonokami
   Hidezu to mo   Is not yet in ear,
Nawa dani hae yo   String at least a rope around—
Moritsutsu oramu   I intend to guard it well.

❋ Since the first three lines in the next poem are taken as a jo, that is, as splitting the poem into vehicle and tenor, this example too seems unsatisfactory as a hiyuka. This type belongs rather to the *kibutsu chinshi* ("Expressing Thoughts by Reference to Things") mode of Books XI and XII.

"In Reference to Thunder"

1305   [MYS VII: 1373 / 1369]

   Amakumo ni   As when clouds fly near
Chikaku hikarite   With their flash and thunder
   Naru kami no   Of the rumbling god,
Mireba kashikomi   There is one I tremble to see—
Mineba kanashi mo   But how sad when I don't see him!

❋ The moon stands for a sweetheart in no. 1306, a thoroughly orthodox hiyuka. But no. 1307, as the compilers note, is not a hiyuka, though it contains an analogy in the first two lines. The note is of interest as evidence that, despite inconsistencies, the compilers were paying attention to their self-imposed task. It also shows that at least some of the time they were working from manuscript collections of individual poets.

"In Reference to the Moon"

1306 [MYS VII: 1378 / 1374]

> Yami no yo wa | A night of darkness
> Kurushiki mono o | Is a cruel thing to bear;
> Itsu shi ka to | When will it come out—
> A ga matsu tsuki mo | Won't the moon I'm waiting for
> Haya mo teranu ka | Please hurry up and shine?

1307 [MYS VII: 1379 / 1375]

> Asashimo no | Life that vanishes
> Keyasuki inochi | Quicker than the morning frost—
> Ta ga tame ni | Is it for another
> Chitose mogamo to | That I wish it a thousand years?
> Wa ga omowanaku ni | No, for no one but you!

The above poem does not belong to the category of metaphorical poems [*hiyuka*]. However, the author of the "night of darkness" poem, because of what he had in his heart, also composed this poem. Thus we enter this poem in the present order.

❋ "In Reference to Rivers" is about lovers kept apart.

"In Reference to Rivers"

1308 [MYS VII: 1384 / 1380]

> Asukagawa | Gemlike waterweed
> Seze ni tamamo wa | Grows in every shallow place
> Oitaredo | Of Asuka River,
> Shigarami areba | But since the stream is fenced with weirs
> Nabikiaenaku ni | The trailing grasses cannot touch.

❋ No. 1309, the first of four poems "In Reference to Waterweed," disqualifies itself as hiyuka by stepping outside the vehicle. The same may be said of the next one. No. 1310, however, is unusually interesting in the significance it attributes to its vehicle. The significance lies in the name *nanoriso* ("tell-not"), *nanoriso* being a seaweed one may imagine to be everywhere about in the world of the ama, reminding the speaker of his or her burden of secret love. All these poems evoke the folk world of the coastal villages, and so it is surprising to find that there may be an adaptation of phraseology from *Yu-hsien-k'u* in the line *yamai to nareri* ("has turned into a sickness"). The other two poems (nos. 1311–12) are true *hiyuka*, keeping the tenor of the metaphor concealed inside its vehicle. The first is very similar to no. 1278, which clearly belongs in this section. Nataka (a place on the coast of the Kii Peninsula) takes the epithet *murasaki no* ("purple") because *nataka* means "renowned," and purple is the noblest of the colors. The speaker of this poem plays a waiting game; that of no. 1312 expresses the view that the rustic setting (or perhaps opposition) is well worth putting up with in view of the prize.

"In Reference to Waterweed"

1309   [MYS VII: 1398 / 1394]

Shio miteba	Is it then because
Irinuru iso no	She is grass upon the reefs
Kusa nare ya	That drown in the tide?
Miraku sukunaku	Few are the times I see her,
Kouraku no ōki	Many the hours of longing.

1310   [MYS VII: 1399 / 1395]

Oki tsu nami	The "tell-not" weed,
Yosuru ariso no	Swept in by the waves of the offing
Nanoriso wa	To these rocky shores,
Kokoro no uchi ni	Has turned into a sickness
Yamai to nareri	In the depths of my heart.

1311   [MYS VII: 1400 / 1396]

Murasaki no	In the Bay of Nataka
Nataka no ura no	(Called the Purple for its lofty name)
Nanoriso no	Floats the sea lentil;
Iso ni nabikamu	And here I sit, alone on the rocks,
Toki matsu ware o	Waiting for it to wash ashore.

1312   [MYS VII: 1401 / 1397]

Ariso kosu	Dreadful are the waves
Nami wa kashikoshi	That break across this rocky strand,
Shikasuga ni	But for all of that
Umi no tamamo no	I think that no one looks askance
Nikuku wa arazu shite	At the gemlike weed of the sea.

❋ The last of the major divisions of Book VII, *banka* ("Laments"), is generic rather than modal. This group of thirteen tanka provides the most extensive evidence in *Man'yōshū* for the practice of cremation, which gradually replaced tomb burial from the beginning of the eighth century. The gathering of the bones is the subject of no. 1313—white fragments likened to shining orange blossoms. In the unexpected simile one can sense the wonder at alteration "into something rich and strange," and the rueful disbelief that this is all that is left of "you." The next poem (no. 1314) and the last (no. 1319) are about the scattering of the ashes. Scattering was practiced instead of interment by those who were not wealthy or powerful. The ashes and bone fragments disappear readily into the long grass, blending like flowers among the wildflowers (no. 1319). The "gemlike bough" (*tamazusa*) is the one traditionally carried by the messenger (no. 347). The cloud of smoke from the crematory fire also figures in the imagery of these poems (nos. 1315–16); it becomes a poetic conceit, one already employed by Hitomaro in no. 354, a poem that is a variant of no. 1316. The convention of disbelief finds its place in these brief laments (no. 1317), in phraseology that should be compared with no. 839, lines 51–54. The dead live in the mountains (nos. 1317–18), in an ironic use of ancient belief that antedates cremation and scattering (see nos. 348, lines 45–48; 693, lines 21–26; and 924, lines 23–25). The dead are said to have downcast faces (no. 1318) as they go off into the autumn hills to hide amid the colored leaves—leaves whose beauty draws them away.

1313   [MYS VII: 1408 / 1404]

> Kagami nasu
> Wa ga mishi kimi o
> Aba no no no
> Hanatachibana no
> Tama ni hiriitsu

> You, on whom I gazed
> As one might on a mirror,
> I have gathered today
> Like gems of flowering orange
> From the fields of Aba moor.

1314   [MYS VII: 1409 / 1405]

> Akizuno o
> Hito no kakureba
> Asa makishi
> Kimi ga omōete
> Nageki wa yamazu

> Akizu moor:
> People have but to say the name,
> And you come to me,
> You that I scattered in the morning—
> And the grief that never ends.

1315   [MYS VII: 1410 / 1406]

> Akizuno ni
> Asa iru kumo no
> Useyukeba
> Kinō mo kyō mo
> Naki hito omōyu

> Akizu moor—
> The cloud that hung in the morning
> Has thinned away:
> Yesterday, today, thoughts come
> Of the one who is no more.

1316   [MYS VII: 1411 / 1407]

> Komoriku no   On the mountainsides
> Hatsuse no yama ni   Of Hatsuse the hidden land
> Kasumi tachi   The haze that rises,
> Tanabiku kumo wa   The cloud that hovers there—
> Imo ni ka mo aramu   Might they be my young love, even she?

1317   [MYS VII: 1412 / 1408]

> Tawakoto ka   Are these mad ravings?
> Oyozurekoto ka   Is it a deceitful tale?
> Komoriku no   In the hidden land,
> Hatsuse no yama ni   The mountains of Hatsuse,
> Iori seri to iu   They say you make your lodging.

1318   [MYS VII: 1413 / 1409]

> Akiyama no   To autumn mountains
> Momichi aware to   The bright foliage drew her;
> Uraburete   With a downcast look
> Irinishi imo wa   She went in, my beloved—
> Matedo kimasazu   I wait, but she does not come.

1319   [MYS VII: 1420 / 1416]

> Tamazusa no   A handful of petals,
> Imo wa hana ka mo   My love of the gemlike bough?
> Ashihiki no   Under the shadow
> Kono yamakage ni   Of this foot-weary mountain
> Makeba usenuru   Scattered and lost in the grass.

Book IX

Book IX is not among the "anonymous books," but it does contain a substantial number of poems of unknown or uncertain authorship. The following are examples. The first two (nos. 1320–21) are from an excursion of Empress Saimei to Ki, perhaps that of 658, the fateful occasion of Prince Arima's execution (nos. 854–59). Another group of poems from that journey, nos. 247–49, attributed to Saimei's daughter Nakatsu Sumera Mikoto (or to Saimei herself), concludes with a poem to which no. 1320 reads almost like a reply. But no. 1320 equally well matches the poem with which it is paired here, the one being the traveler's thought of the girl he left at home, the other her thought of him on his journey.

1320–21   [MYS IX : 1669–70 / 1665–66]

Two poems from the time the Sovereign who ruled the realm from the Okamoto Palace made an excursion to the province of Ki

(1320)   [1669 / 1665]

Imo ga tame	For the girl I love
Ware tama hiriu	I shall gather gleaming gems:
Okihe naru	Bring from the offing
Tama yosemochiko	Gems swirling in to the shore,
Oki tsu shiranami	White waves of the distant sea.

(1321)   [1670 / 1666]

Asagiri ni	Wet with morning mist,
Nurenishi koromo	And none to dry your garments,
Hosazu shite	Do you now go
Hitori ka kimi ga	Alone, my lord, along the path
Yamaji koyuramu	Across the mountain slopes?

The authors of the above two poems are as yet unknown.

✳ Another two tanka (nos. 1322–23) from the anonymous poems in Book IX were composed during one of the numerous imperial excursions to Yoshino in the late seventh or early eighth century. The first makes a playful pun on *yobukodori* ("calling bird"), a species that has not been identified but is thought perhaps to be a name for the *kakkō*, a cuckoo larger than the much-sung *hototogisu*. The bird is flying downstream toward the palace site at Akizu, and the whim of the poet asks for whom its cries are intended. The other poem is an admirable exercise in nature description, one that might stand as an exemplar of the descriptive mode in waka. It is purely objective, following the course of a river from cataract, to rapid, to still pool, ending with the open-eyed verb *miyu* focused on the reflected moon, whose roundness dots the rondure of calm water.

1322–23   [MYS IX : 1717–18 / 1713–14]

Two poems from the time the Sovereign made an excursion to the detached palace at Yoshino

(1322)   [1717 / 1713]

Taki no ue no	Over the torrent
Mifune no yama yu	On the mount of Mifune
Akizuhe ni	Toward Akizu

Kinakiwataru wa   Crossing, crying as it comes—
Tare yobukodori   For whom is it a calling bird?

(1323)   [1718/1714]

   Ochitagichi   Plummeting, seething,
Nagaruru mizu no   As it flows along the water
   Iwa ni fure   Strikes against the rocks
Yodomeru yodo ni   Until it calms in quiet pools
Tsuki no kage miyu   Where the image of the moon is seen.

The author of the above two poems is as yet unknown.

Book x

Book x, the second of the "anonymous books," is a collection of tanka (and two chōka) arranged by the four seasons, an innovation looking forward to the structure of the imperial anthologies in the Heian period and later. Unlike those anthologies, however, Book x of *Man'yōshū* divides each season into zōka and sōmon (miscellaneous and love), thus treating two of the three major categories distinguished in *Kokinshū* and its successors as aspects of the third, season. In this regard Book x follows the organization of Book VIII, but instead of named poets chronologically arranged as the third level of organization, it uses the eibutsu-kibutsu scheme already familiar from Book VII, along with a number of other subcategories, some modal, some formal, and some topical. The content of Book x draws in part on the "Hitomaro Collection" and for the rest seems distributed from the late seventh to the early eighth century. Like the other "anonymous books," Book x contains poems duplicating or similar to those by named poets elsewhere in the anthology. Such anonymous collections may have been used as reference books in poetic typology in the Nara period, both drawing on and feeding into the works of known poets. Even so, the reason for the existence of such large numbers of anonymous poems (539 in Book x alone) has not been adequately explained.

Two eibutsu poems "On Birds" from the Spring-Miscellaneous section of Book x display the delight in birdsong learned from Chinese poetry. The *uguisu* ("warbler") corresponds to the Chinese *ying* ("yellow bird"), an oriole, in its association with blossoms and new verdure, as well as in the character with which its name is written. The first poem (no. 1324) combines the elegant theme with the traditional Japanese pillow-word device, *azusa-yumi* ("catalpa bow") being a mock epithet for *haru* ("spring") through *haru* ("stretch"). The poem is a conversational address to a friend. The second poem also begins with a pillow word, this one a true epithet, *uchinabiku* ("trailing"), referring to the bending grasses and fronds of spring.

"On Birds"

1324 [MYS X: 1833 / 1829]

Azusayumi	Taut catalpa bows
Haruyama chikaku	Spring mountains close at hand
Ie oreba	You've built your house,
Tsugite kikuramu	And you must live with cries of warblers
Uguisu no koe	Continually about your ears.

1325 [MYS X: 1834 / 1830]

Uchinabiku	Now that trailing spring
Haru sarikureba	Has made its round to us again,
Shino no ure ni	Flirting wing and tail
Oha uchifurete	On the slender bamboo branches,
Uguisu naku mo	Oh, how the warblers sing!

❋ The topical categories are sometimes filled in with love poems, as in the following, "On Snow." This is by the woman to the man; for a similar poem by the man to the woman, see no. 1374. *Egu* ("galingale") was an edible marsh plant.

"On Snow"

1326 [MYS X: 1843 / 1839]

Kimi ga tame	When I went to pluck
Yamada no sawa ni	For my love the galingale
Egu tsumu to	In mountain marshes,
Yukige no mizu ni	All the edges of my skirt
Mo no suso nurenu	Grew wet in snow-melt water.

❋ The following poem, "On Rivers," could almost equally well be "On Rain," the category that precedes it. The poem expresses the longing for the homeland (Asuka, the old capital) and the fascination with rushing streams that are part of what might be termed the Yoshino tradition.

"On Rivers"

1327 [MYS X: 1882 / 1878]

Ima yukite	Oh, that I could go
Kiku mono ni moga	And listen now to this one thing,
Asukagawa	The sound the rapids make
Harusame furite	Roaring in the seething torrent
Tagitsu se no to o	While spring rain falls on Asuka.

✳ At the end of the Spring-Miscellaneous section the compilers placed a single hiyuka, one whose allegory relates to spring through the image of a ripening peach. The fuzziness of the peach combines with the significance of the moon in the female sexual cycle (see nos. 27–28) to make the allegory plain enough, except that it is not clear whether the person delighted over first menstruation is intended to be the girl herself or her parents. The peach is a female symbol, perhaps because of a fancied resemblance to a woman's genitalia (Momotarō was born from a peach in Japanese folklore).

"A Metaphorical Poem"

1328   [MYS X: 1893 / 1889]

Wa ga yado no	Under the fuzzy peach
Kemomo no shita ni	In the doorway of my house
Tsukuyo sashi	The moon in shining:
Shitagokoro yoshi	How good I feel, deep in my heart—
Utate kono koro	Lately things have been so strange!

✳ The following kibutsu poems from the Spring-Love section include both those based on a jo and those whose statement is rhetorically unitary. The habits of the shrike seem to be the subject of "In Reference to Birds" (no. 1329) until the last line reveals that lines 3 and 4 refer also to a reclusive lover. The use of *kimi* shows this to be the woman's poem. "In Reference to Flowers" (no. 1330) is by the man. A poem of unitary expression, it presumably mourns the fact that the woman has now moved away, though it could be some other circumstance that keeps the lover from crossing her hedge. The *unohana* (the deutzia, or "hareflower") blossomed in early summer by the old lunar calendar, and so the poem is seasonally puzzling. That the seasonal arrangement of these poems did not receive the careful attention lavished on such aspects of anthologizing in *Kokinshū* and later is further evidenced by the late appearance of the category "In Reference to Frost" (no. 1331). This and the next poem, "In Reference to Mist" (no. 1332), are based on jo, with juncture respectively in the fourth and third lines. "In Reference to Rain" (no. 1333) is a straightforward statement of love's power.

"In Reference to Birds"

1329   [MYS X: 1901 / 1897]

Haru sareba	After spring has come
Mozu no kayaguki	The shrike goes plunging in the reeds
Miezu to mo	And cannot be seen—
Ware wa miyaramu	But I will spy it out, my love,
Kimi ga atari o ba	The place where you have your home.

"In Reference to Flowers"

1330 [MYS X: 1903 / 1899]

  Haru sareba   Once when spring had come
Unohanagutashi   I would ruin the hareflowers
  Wa ga koeshi   Crossing her hedge;
Imo ga kakima wa   Now the gap is overgrown
Arenikeru kamo   That let me in to my love.

"In Reference to Frost"

1331 [MYS X: 1912 / 1908]

  Haru sareba   After spring has come
Mikusa no ue ni   The remaining rime of frost
  Oku shimo no   On water grasses
Ketsutsu mo are wa   Fading steadily away,
Koiwataru kamo   Yet I go on in this longing.

"In Reference to Mist"

1332 [MYS X: 1913 / 1909]

  Harukasumi   The mist in spring
Yama ni tanabiki   Trails along the mountainside
  Ohohoshiku   In a filmy haze
Imo o aimite   Dreamily I gaze at her—
Nochi koimu ka mo   Later to suffer longing?

"In Reference to Rain"

1333 [MYS X: 1919 / 1915]

  Wa ga seko ni   Being helpless
Koite sube nami   In my desire for him,
  Harusame no   I came out,
Furu waki shirazu   Unaware of the spring rain
Idete koshi kamo   That was falling even then.

❇ Wisteria bloomed from late spring to early summer; in the first of the following two poems "On Flowers" from the Summer-Miscellaneous section the "hunters" are out looking for herbs to use in the "fragrance balls" mentioned in the second poem. The fragrance balls (*kusudama*) were one of the decorations displayed during the festival of the fifth of the fifth month. Composed of various fragrant herbs and flowers, they were attached to the clothing and were thought to ward off illness. In the second poem the speaker has been unwilling to wait until the fifth month.

"On Flowers"

1334   [MYS X: 1978 / 1974]

Kasugano no	On Kasuga Fields
Fuji wa chiri nite	The wisteria has scattered—
Nani o ka mo	What will the hunters
Mikari no hito no	Find now in the moorland
Orite kazasamu	To break and adorn their brows?

1335   [MYS X: 1979 / 1975]

Toki narazu	Though out of season,
Tama o so nukeru	We have strung our fragrance balls,
Unohana no	For the fifth month
Satsuki o mataba	When the hareflower comes in bloom
Hisashiku arubemi	Is a long time for waiting.

❋ An exchange (nos. 1336–37) following the last of the eibutsu poems in the Summer section associates the cuckoo (*hototogisu*) with the *unohana*, and both with the rains of the fifth month monsoon season.

"An Exchange"

1336   [MYS X: 1980 / 1976]

Unohana no	Over the hillside
Sakichiru oka yu	Where the hareflower blooms and falls
Hototogisu	A cuckoo flew,
Nakite sawataru	Crying as it crossed the slope—
Kimi wa kikitsu ya	Friend, did you hear its song?

1337   [MYS X: 1981 / 1977]

Kikitsu ya to	Did I hear it?
Kimi ga towaseru	Friend, you kindly inquired:
Hototogisu	That cuckoo flew,
Shinono ni nurete	Crying as it went by here,
Ko yu nakiwataru	All in a flutter of wet.

❋ The other flower most frequently associated with the cuckoo was the orange blossom (*hanatachibana*; see nos. 991–97). The hiyuka with which the Summer-Miscellaneous section concludes is based on this association. The cries of the cuckoo here stand for gossip, and the orange-blossom village for the home of the desired woman.

"A Metaphorical Poem"

1338   [MYS X:1982/1978]

    Tachibana no   Were I to frequent
   Hana chiru sato ni   The village where from the fragrant orange
     Kayoinaba   The blossoms fall,
   Yamahototogisu   Might the mountain cuckoo come
   Toyomosamu ka mo   With all its tumult of cries?

❋ The Summer-Love section is made up entirely of kibutsu poems, of which the following is the first. For a summer poem it has the peculiarity of beginning with *haru*, "spring." A plausible reading is that in spring the wasps hatch out and buzz about on fields where now in summer the cuckoo sings. The cuckoo is a summer bird in poetry, and the compilers have been guided by that fact in placing the poem here. The compressed syntax of the first three lines constitutes a jo introducing *hotohoto* ("almost") in the fourth line by phonetic repetition with *hototogisu*. The main statement of the poem is focused on love, not season, though thanks to the jo one may imagine the lover wandering around in the moorland all through spring and summer.

"In Reference to Birds"

1339   [MYS X:1983/1979]

    Haru sareba   After spring arrives
   Sugaru nasu no no   All alive with whining wasps,
     Hototogisu   The moorland cuckoo:
   Hotohoto imo ni   You who are my own dear girl
   Awazu kinikeri   I almost missed on the way.

❋ The dusk cicada (*higurashi*) cries in the twilight of evening and morning, but the speaker of no. 1340 does not so limit himself. This use of negative analogy is structured into the main statement of the poem, without recourse to the sometimes fortuitous imagistic augmentation provided by the device of the jo. Whether or not to employ the device was a fundamental decision for any poem-maker of the time.

"In Reference to Cicadas"

1340   [MYS X:1986/1982]

    Higurashi wa   The dusk cicada
   Toki to nakedo mo   Cries at its appointed times,
     Koishiku ni   But in my yearning
   Tawayame are wa   I who am a tender maiden
   Sadamarazu naku   Cry in and out of season.

❊ The second line serves as a one-line positive analogy, this too a type of jo structure, in the next poem (no. 1341). The likening of talk to rife vegetation through the adjective *shigeshi* ("thick-grown") is traditional in waka. Here the image of entanglement is completed by the final line. It is a shared equivalent of the self-centered travel-first, pay-later plan of no. 80.

"In Reference to Grasses"

1341   [MYS X: 1987 / 1983]

Hitogoto wa	What though people's talk
Natsuno no kusa no	Grows as thick as the grasses
Shigeku to mo	On the summer moor,
Imo to are to shi	As long as you and I, my love,
Tazusawarineba	Have bedded hand in hand?

❊ As in no. 1299, a single thread signals a one-sided love in poem 1342, which is a kind of hiyuka in which the flowering orange stands for the man's heart. The tachibana is a summer bloom. The *kusudama* referred to in no. 1335 may be the intended image. The fruit of the tachibana was also strung (see nos. 196 and 826–27).

"In Reference to Flowers"

1342   [MYS X: 1991 / 1987]

Katayori ni	With a single twine
Ito o so a ga yoru	I have twined this string of mine,
Wa ga seko ga	Thinking all the while
Hanatachibana o	How to string the flowering orange
Nukamu to moite	Of my very own dear man.

❊ The following poem seems to be by the woman. It is her lover, not she, who must leave at dew-drenched dawn, but she has her own source of moisture to dampen her sleeves. The hyperbolic treatment of tears became a feature of Heian waka but is a comparative rarity in *Man'yōshū*.

"In Reference to Dew"

1343   [MYS X: 1998 / 1994]

Natsukusa no	For all I do not wear
Tsuyuwakegoromo	Garments that have parted dew
Tsukenaku ni	On the summer grass,
Wa ga koromode no	There is no time for the drying
Furu toki mo naki	Of the sleeve-ends of my gown.

✳ The Autumn-Miscellaneous section of Book x contains the category "On Crickets." Crickets are common in post-Man'yō poetry, but there are two differences. *Kōrogi*, the term used here (and in modern Japanese), was replaced by *kirigirisu* (which in modern Japanese means "grasshopper") in Heian poetry. There are no *kirigirisu* in *Man'yōshū*, or *kōrogi* in later classical poetry. The other difference is one of mood, somber in later poetry, but one of quiet enjoyment here. "On Frogs" (no. 1345) is the traditional paean to Yoshino, transposed for a chorus of frogs.

"On Crickets"

1344   [MYS X: 2163 / 2159]

Kagekusa no	In sunlit grasses
Oitaru yado no	Growing here beside my house
Yūkage ni	Lurks evening shadow
Naku kōrogi wa	Where the chirping crickets cry—
Kikedo akanu kamo	And I listen, but do not weary.

"On Frogs"

1345   [MYS X: 2165 / 2161]

Miyoshino no	The songfrogs that cry
Iwamoto sarazu	By every rock in Yoshino—
Naku kawazu	Not for nothing
Ube mo nakikeri	Do they raise their cries of joy,
Kawa o sayakemi	Where the river runs so clear.

✳ Three poems "On Dew" are set in a harvest hut. The first (no. 1346) in particular is close to poem 253, attributed to Emperor Tenji in *Gosenshū*, and suggests its origins in anonymous verse. The other two poems, despite their rustic setting, depend on the "evidence"-based speculative mode learned from Six Dynasties poetry.

"On Dew"

1346   [MYS X: 2178 / 2174]

Akita karu	In the autumn fields
Kario o tsukuri	I build myself at harvest time
Wa ga oreba	A flimsy shelter;
Koromode samuku	Crouching there I feel my sleeves
Tsuyu so okinikeru	Grow cold in the gathering dew.

1347 [MYS X : 2179 / 2175]

   Kono koro no   These last few days
  Akikaze samushi   The autumn wind has turned cold;
    Hagi no hana   The white dew
  Chirasu shiratsuyu   That scatters the bush-clover bloom
  Okinikerashi mo   Must have gathered out there.

1348 [MYS X : 2180 / 2176]

   Akita karu   In the autumn fields
  Io ugoku nari   The harvest hut makes a stirring:
   Shiratsuyu shi   It's the white dew come
  Oku hota nashi to   Seemingly to let me know
  Tsuge ni kinu rashi   The ripe grain where it gathered is gone.

❋ The importance of autumn leaves in Japanese poetry dates from *Man'-yōshū*. Princess Nukata's famous *chōka* comparing spring and autumn (no. 256) is a landmark and speaks for the estheticization of nature that was one result of Chinese influence. But no doubt because Japan is blessed with particularly brilliant fall colors, the topic is much more important in Japanese than in Chinese poetry. The Autumn-Miscellaneous section of Book X contains one of the principal early collections of poems on this topic. "On Mountains," immediately preceding this section, is reminiscent of Princess Nukata's poem and is closely allied with what follows. Its seasonal panorama and the prosodic pacing and buildup to an exclamatory finish make it one of the most successful nature poems in *Man'yōshū*.

"On Mountains"

1349 [MYS X : 2181 / 2177]

   Haru wa moe   In spring they put forth,
  Natsu wa midori ni   In summer are a mass of green,
    Kurenai no   And then in autumn
  Shimiiro ni miyuru   How the mountains look all tinged
  Aki no yama kamo   With a wash of crimson color!

❋ The use of *kurenai* ("crimson") to describe the autumn mountains in no. 1349 casts some doubt on the validity of the suggestion that yellow is the basic color intended by Man'yō poets when they use the term *momichi*. *Momichi* (in Heian times and later, *momiji*) is foliage whose color has changed as a result of fall frosts, regardless of what the changed color may be, and is related to the verbs *momitsu* and *momitasu*, intransitive and transitive for the specific phenomenon of leaves changing color. In *Man'yōshū* orthography *momichi* is regularly written "yellow leaves," whereas in post-Man'yō times "crimson leaves" was more common. It has also been suggested that the Man'yō orthographic preference owes to Chinese example. In the aggregate, the translations of the following examples of *momichi* poems reflect the real lack of color specificity in the term.

The "long month" (*nagatsuki*) was the ninth month—not that it was longer than the others, but it came at the end of autumn, whose nights were conventionally "long." The ninth and tenth were the months for *shigure*, the sudden cold showers of late fall and early winter. The *shigure*, along with the frost and dew, was an agent for bringing about the color shift in leaves. In current terms the time of year may be anywhere from late September to early November in the first poem (no. 1350).

Wild geese returning to winter in Japan are another sign of the season. The syntactic doubling of *samuki* ("cold") in no. 1351 applies both to their cries and to the dawn. *Hagi*, or bush clover (no. 1352), is one of the prime emblems of autumn in *Man'yōshū*.

"On Yellow Leaves"

1350   [MYS X:2184/2180]

> Nagatsuki no   The long month—
> Shigure no ame ni   And the seasonal chill rains
>   Nuretōri   Come drenching down;
> Kasuga no yama wa   Now in Kasuga the hills
> Irozukinikeri   Begin to tinge with color.

1351   [MYS X:2185/2181]

> Kari ga ne no   Cries of wild geese
> Samuki asake no   At daybreak cold
>   Tsuyu narashi   Over Kasuga
> Kasuga no yama o   The morning dewdrops
> Momitasu mono wa   Turning hills to flame.

1352   [MYS X:2186/2182]

> Kono koro no   These days as the dawn
> Akatokitsuyu ni   Reddens over fields of dew
>   Wa ga yado no   Before my dwelling,
> Hagi no shitaba wa   Bright colors have come again
> Irozukinikeri   To the underleaves of clover.

❋ The next two poems abandon the simple descriptive stance of the previous three. The first addresses the leaves, expressing impatience for their appearance. The second, by forbidding their mention, implies even greater attachment. The situation of the speaker may be that of Yakamochi in no. 1198.

1353   [MYS X:2187/2183]

   Karigane wa   The wild geese have come—
Ima wa kinakinu   Now at last I hear their cries;
  Wa ga machishi   Bright leaves of autumn
Momichi haya tsuge   That I long have waited for,
Mateba kurushi mo   Hurry, the waiting's been hard!

1354   [MYS X:2188/2184]

   Akiyama o   Of autumn mountains
Yume hito kaku na   Do not, I forbid you, speak:
  Wasurenishi   I had forgotten
Sono momichiba no   The bright leaves on all the hills,
Omōyuraku ni   But the memory now returns.

✳ The arrangement of "Yellow Leaves" takes a rather uncertain course through autumn. The scattering of leaves starts early, in nos. 1355 and 1357, which bracket a poem in which autumn has just arrived. The vagaries of coloring and scattering during an actual fall may be no less spasmodic, however. Ōsaka Pass (no. 1355) leads over the Kazuraki Range from the Yamato basin to the coast. Futagami (see no. 276) is a mountain near the northern end of the range. The coloring of reeds (nos. 1356 and 1360), grasses (no. 1361), and brush (no. 1360), as well as trees, is important in the Man'yō image of autumn. *Imo ga sode* ("my darling's sleeve") in no. 1357 is a mock epithet for Makiki, the name of a mountain, through *maki* ("pillow on"). Regret is the other side of pleasure.

1355   [MYS X:2189/2185]

   Ōsaka o   As I came over
Wa ga koekureba   Ōsaka mountain pass
  Futagami ni   On Futagami
Momichiba nagaru   Yellow leaves were cascading
Shigure furitsutsu   While the chill rain fell and fell.

1356   [MYS X:2190/2186]

   Aki sareba   Now that autumn's here,
Oku shiratsuyu ni   In the gathering white dew
  Wa ga kado no   The leaftips

Asaji ga uraha	Of the shallow reeds by my gate
Irozukinikeri	Have brightened into color.

1357 [MYS X:2191 / 2187]

Imo ga sode	Now my darling's sleeve
Makiki no yama no	Pillow Mountain in the dew
Asatsuyu ni	At morning glow
Niou momichi no	Yellow leaves whose scattering
Chiramaku oshi mo	Overcomes me with regret.

❋ In the midst of the appreciations of nature come two poems whose primary concern is human. The "unpaired pear" (*tsumanashi no ki*) is a pun on *nashi* ("pear" / "lacking"). To pluck its leaves is to experience the rue of having no *tsuma* ("mate"—either wife or husband), perhaps through loss. So in no. 1358 the speaker turns away from the splendor of the season to his or her personal sorrow. The second poem is particularly affecting. A true *hiyuka*, it has the autumn wind, symbolic of loneliness, turn the leaves of the imaginary tree to the bright colors of fall, a statement of the intensity of a suffering that matches the visible glow of autumn.

1358 [MYS X:2192 / 2188]

Momichiba no	Bright fall foliage
Nioi wa shigeshi	Has a glow that is intense,
Shikaredo mo	But let that be:
Tsumanashi no ki o	I shall pluck to deck myself
Taori kazasamu	Leaves of the unpaired pear.

1359 [MYS X:2193 / 2189]

Tsuyu shimo no	By the autumn wind
Samuki yūhe no	On evenings chilly with the fall
Akikaze ni	Of frost and dew
Momichinikerashi	See how their color has been turned,
Tsumanashi no ki wa	The leaves of the unpaired pear!

❋ The next two poems are about moments of transition. The coloring of the reeds at the gate in no. 1360 is taken to imply a more advanced stage of autumn in the highlands of Yonabari near Hatsuse. Coloring and scattering emerge as complementary "waves" in nature, one advancing while the other recedes. *Namishiba* ("wave-brush") may be a place-name, but it serves as an image in any case. In no. 1361 the cries of the wild geese are taken as a signal, a catalyst, for the color change sweeping over the land.

1360   [MYS X: 2194 / 2190]

    Wa ga kado no   The sparse reeds
    Asaji irozuku   Around my gate are coloring;
      Yonabari no   At Yonabari
    Namishiba no no no   The waves of brush on the moorland
    Momichi chiru rashi   Must be scattering bright leaves.

1361   [MYS X: 2195 / 2191]

    Kari ga ne o   Cries of the wild geese—
    Kikitsuru nahe ni   From the moment I heard them,
      Takamatsu no   On Takamatsu
    No no e no kusa so   The grass on the high moorland
    Irozukinikeru   Began to tinge with new color.

❋ In the next poem coloring comes even to the "true trees," the evergreen *maki*—cypress, cedar, and the like. Such supposedly nondeciduous trees actually drop their needles on a staggered schedule, but the poem converts this normal phenomenon into an unsuccessful struggle against the cold rain. This poem is attributed to Hitomaro in *Shinkokinshū* (see no. 439) and appears three times in two post-Man'yō personal collections of what were thought to be his work.

1362   [MYS X: 2200 / 2196]

    Shigure no ame   The cold, drizzly rain
    Manaku shi fureba   Falls so ceaselessly, one sees
      Maki no ha mo   The very needles
    Arasoikanete   Of the evergreens give way
    Irozukinikeri   And tinge with a new color.

❋ A final example of the colored-leaf poems leaps to the moon in an elaborate Chinese conceit. Because of the Chinese myth of a cassia tree growing in the moon (see the note to no. 365), the golden color of the rising moon in autumn could poetically be attributed to the coloring of its leaves, which in turn would signal the advent of earthly *momichi*. The moon-man (*tsukihito*), who lives at the foot of the tree, is part of the Chinese myth, and the see *x*, deduce *y* paradigm is also in the Chinese mode.

1363   [MYS X: 2206 / 2202]

    Momichi suru   Now the time has come
    Toki ni naru rashi   For our leaves to turn golden—
      Tsukihito no   So much one can judge

| Katsura no eda no | By the coloring of the branch |
| Irozuku mireba | Of the moon-man's cassia. |

❋ Also from Autumn-Miscellaneous, "On the Moon" may be compared with both the above poem and no. 365 from the "Hitomaro Collection." It also should be read in connection with the kanshi by Emperor Mommu previously quoted (p. 236). All four belong to a world of celestial Chinese myth that includes the Tanabata story as well. As in the poem from the "Hitomaro Collection," the creator of "On the Moon" transforms the moon into a boat, one rowed by the moon-man with an oar made from his cassia tree. The poem has only two correspondences rather than the four in no. 365 and is a long way from capturing the mystery of rowing off into a forest.

"On the Moon"

1364   [MYS X: 2227 / 2223]

Ame no umi ni	On the sea of heaven
Tsuki no fune uke	One is seen who sets afloat
Katsurakaji	The moon-boat on the wave
Kakete kogu miyu	And rows with a cassia oar:
Tsukihito otoko	The man the dweller in the moon.

❋ In the Autumn-Love section the following poem, "In Reference to Paddy Fields," brings to mind no. 958 by Sano no Otogami. Rice was presumably not the only harvest with which the singer of no. 1365 was concerned. *Tachibana o* ("orange-tree") makes a pillow-word construction as the object of *mori* ("guard") in the name of the unknown village of Morihe. It has been suggested that orange trees were precious enough to have watchmen posted over them. Perhaps the "watchman" subliminally frightens off the helper from coming to cut the early rice. The poem can also be read as a hiyuka in which field and rice are metaphorical for a young daughter of marriageable age spurned by her suitor.

"In Reference to Paddy Fields"

1365   [MYS X: 2255 / 2251]

Tachibana o	In orange-tree
Morihe no sato no	Watchman's Village the early rice
Kadotawase	In my gateside field
Karu toki suginu	Has passed the time for harvesting—
Koji to su rashi mo	It looks like he won't come this year.

❋ The jo in "In Reference to Grasses" is intended as a negative analogy. The identity of *omoigusa* ("grasses of longing") is somewhat obscure; a flower called *nambangiseru* ("southern barbarian pipe," or broomrape) is one possibility.

"In Reference to Grasses"

1366   [MYS X: 2274 / 2270]

Michinobe no	Down on the roadside
Obana ga shita no	Under the clumps of tail-flower
Omoigusa	Grasses of longing:
Imasara sara ni	Why should I longer grow pensive,
Nani ka omowamu	When the longing is over and done?

❋ The analogy is positive in the next poem. The jo making up the first three lines is joined to the last two not by wordplay, but by the suggestive image of the *hatsuobana* ("the first tail-flowers"), the newly tasseled pampas grass that associates in the speaker's mind with his young sweetheart. The parallel between the stags and the would-be lover completes the symbolic equation.

"In Reference to Blossoms"

1367   [MYS X: 2281 / 2277]

Saoshika no	In plumegrass hollows
Irino no susuki	Entered by the stags of Irino
Hatsuobana	The first tail-flowers—
Itsu shi ka imo ga	When shall I too lie at ease,
Te o makurakamu	Pillowed on my young love's arm?

❋ Another poem "In Reference to Blossoms" is the likely source of Yakamochi's complaint in no. 1198.

1368   [MYS X: 2297 / 2293]

Sakeri to mo	So they are in bloom—
Shirazu shi araba	Ah, I could have kept my peace
Moda mo aramu	If I had not known;
Kono akihagi o	But you go showing them to me,
Misetsutsu motona	These blossoms of autumn clover.

❋ The following three poems "In Reference to Night" state their emotions directly, "reference" being part of the primary statement rather than perched in an imagistic introduction. The first (no. 1369) acknowledges the power of the season and its mood to affect our feelings. Nos. 1370–71 examine "night" more directly. Autumn nights are conventionally long, but the perception of time slips back and forth under the pressure of pleasure and melancholy, so that those who are happily employed find the nights short (how heartless that they should be so), while for one who lies alone they never end.

"In Reference to Night"

1369   [MYS X : 2305 / 2301]

    Yoshieyashi   Let him go, then,
    Koiji to suredo   I'll long no more, I said;
      Akikaze no   Yet when the autumn wind
    Samuku fuku yo wa   Blows cold at night the old thoughts come,
    Kimi o shi so omou   And I am longing for you once again.

1370   [MYS X : 2306 / 2302]

    Aru hito no   There are those who think,
    Ana kokoro na to   Ah, how heartless! as they watch
      Omouramu   The hours slip away
    Aki no nagayo o   On the long nights of autumn—
    Nesamefusu nomi   While I lie sleepless, alone.

1371   [MYS X : 2307 / 2303]

    Aki no yo o   Autumn nights
    Nagashi to iedo   Are long, they say,
      Tsumorinishi   But for pouring out
    Koi o tsukuseba   My stored-up yearning
    Mijikaku arikeri   I found them all too short.

❋ Among the snow poems in the Winter-Miscellaneous section of Book x, no. 1372 was clearly composed in blithe disregard of an anthologist's need to classify it as either a seasonal or a love poem. The impatience of *ima ka ima ka* ("Not yet? Not yet?") matches the unsettled sky and the snow-speckled ground—the inner and outer weather seem the same. A rhetorically split-level treatment of the same scene would place the snow in a metaphorical jo.

"On Snow"

1372   [MYS X : 2327 / 2323]

    Wa ga seko o   I kept going out
    Ima ka ima ka to   To see if he was coming,

Idemireba	That man of mine—
Awayuki fureri	Fluffy snow was coming down,
Niwa mo hodoro ni	The yard was all in speckles.

✳ Plum-blossom poems appear in both the Spring and the Winter section, as they do later in *Kokinshū*. The blossoming of the plum occurs at the dividing line of the seasons by the old lunar calendar. The scattering of plum petals in the moonlight makes a refinedly elegant picture to contrast with the homelier scene in no. 1372.

"On Blossoms"

1373   [MYS X : 2329 / 2325]

Ta ga sono no	From whose arbor
Ume no hana so mo	Come these petals of the plum?
Hisakata no	Under a clear moon
Kiyoki tsukuyo ni	In the everlasting sky
Kokoda chirikuru	Their fluttering throngs the night.

✳ "On Dew," like "On Snow," combines love and nature. By the time of *Kokinshū*, dew was considered an autumn image and is not to be found in the Winter section, though it does occur once in Spring.

"On Dew"

1374   [MYS X : 2334 / 2330]

Imo ga tame	When for my young love
Hotsue no ume o	I reached up to break a twig
Taoru to wa	From the plum's highest branch,
Shizue no tsuyu ni	What a wetting I received
Nurenikeru kamo	From the underbranches' dew!

✳ In the next poem the two places mentioned are far apart. Yata moor is in Yamato not far from Nara (see no. 440), and Mount Arachi is beyond the northern end of Lake Biwa on the way to Echizen, the pass crossed by Nakatomi no Yakamori going into exile (no. 942). No doubt, as has been suggested, the poet is thinking of someone heading for the north country.

"On Yellow Leaves"

1375   [MYS X : 2335 / 2331]

| Yata no no no | Out on Yata moor |
| Asaji irozuku | The shallow bladygrass tinges: |

Arachiyama	On Mount Arachi
Mine no awayuki	Light snow must be falling
Samuku furu rashi	Cold on the highest peak.

❈ Winter-Love is the last section of Book x. "In Reference to Frost" is spoken by a woman who wishes to detain her lover. The *yuzasa*, the "awful" or "taboo" bamboo grass, is so called from its being used as a sacred wand in Shintō ceremonies. Typifying it in this way somehow makes the night seem more dreadful and the woman's bed more inviting.

"In Reference to Frost"

1376 [MYS X:2340/2336]

Hanahada mo	It's terribly late—
Yo fukete na yuki	Don't go now in the dead of night—
Michi no he no	All along the path
Yuzasa no ue ni	On the awful bamboo grass
Shimo no furu yo o	Frost is falling tonight.

❈ In the next poem the *sasa* is ordinary bamboo grass, but the thought structure is of more than ordinary complexity. The first three lines are a jo, with *kenaba ka mo* the swing line. "If," one lover says, "I / we fade away (like melting snow), would I / we forget you / each other then?" Whatever the answer, the implication is that short of death there will be no forgetting, which is why the speaker of the last line says what he / she does. The implied comparison of life to flakes of wet snow lends a compelling immediacy to the question.

"In Reference to Snow"

1377 [MYS X:2341/2337]

Sasa no ha ni	Flakes of wet snow
Hadare furiōi	Cover leaves of bamboo grass:
Kenaba ka mo	Once the melting comes
Wasuremu to ieba	Will the memories fade too?—
Mashite omōyu	You ask, and longing deepens.

❈ The penultimate and final poems in Book x are by a woman longing for her lover. As in no. 1373, the eibutsu poem "On Blossoms," a kibutsu poem "In Reference to Blossoms" combines flowering plums with moonlight, adding only the human element of waiting for a companion, the element that classifies the verse as sōmon instead of zōka. In no. 1379 the woman, not having acquired the wished-for companion, complains of cold nights alone. The order of the two poems is seasonally reversed, with plum blossoms preceding the onset of winter storms.

"In Reference to Blossoms"

1378   [MYS X: 2353 / 2349]

Wa ga yado ni	Here in my garden
Sakitaru ume o	All in flower is the plum,
Tsukuyo yomi	And the moon is fine—
Yoiyoi misemu	Night by night I wait for you,
Kimi o koso mate	You only, to show them.

"In Reference to Night"

1379   [MYS X: 2354 / 2350]

Ashihiki no	Not yet does the wind
Yama no arashi wa	Sweep the foot-wearying mountains
Fukanedo mo	With its stormy blast,
Kimi naki yoi wa	But on nights without you, love,
Kanete samushi mo	I already feel the cold.

Books XI and XII

❊ Books XI and XII are collections of anonymous love poems in the tanka and sedōka forms, drawing in part on the "Hitomaro Collection" and *Kokashū*. (For selections from the "Hitomaro Collection" portions of Book XI, see nos. 401–29.) Both books center on modal categories in their organization. As the only two books to use the terms *seijutsu shinsho* ("Expressing Thoughts Directly") and *kibutsu chinshi* ("Expressing Thoughts by Reference to Things"), they form an obvious pair. *Seijutsu shinsho* (*tada ni omoi o noburu* in the native Japanese reading) poems are those of direct expression, not based on metaphor. *Kibutsu chinshi* (or *mono ni yosete omoi o noburu*) is the same as the kibutsu category of Book X. Such poems in "referring to a thing" tend to use it as a metaphor and to be based on the split-level structure of jo and main statement. That such is not always the case has been amply demonstrated by kibutsu poems already examined. Therefore, since *seijutsu shinsho* poems are not devoid of imagery, even though non-metaphorical, in practice there is considerable overlap between the two categories, another way of saying that modal distinctions were not rigidly adhered to by the compilers. The third stage of modality, the allegorical hiyuka, is also represented in Book XI. The compilers of Book VII, it will be recalled, use kibutsu as a subcategory of hiyuka. Like the other modally arranged anonymous books, Books XI and XII seem to have been used as poetic samplers by the Ōtomo poets in particular.

Book XI begins with a formal rather than a modal category—a collection of seventeen sedōka. Most of them were taken from the "Hitomaro Collection" (nos. 401–8). The following is noted as being from *Kokashū*. Each half of the evenly structured sedōka begins with a pillow-word construction, and together they form a contrastive pair. The flashing light of the sun surrounds the dazzling vision of an unattainable love, which in turn leads to the inward flame of the tangled jewels (*tama* = "jewel" / "soul") that entwine the agonized figure of the would-be lover. Day in the first half is set against night in the second.

"Sedōka"

1380   [MYS XI:2369/2365]

    Uchihi sasu   For another's wife
  Miyaji ni aishi   Met on the highroad leading
  Hitozuma yue ni   To the sun-bright capital,
    Tama no o no   Like a string of jewels
  Omoimidarete   My cord of life is tangled
  Nuru yo shi so ōki   With desire and sleepless nights.

❋ The following two tanka from the "Expressing Thoughts Directly" category might form a pair, though they are not so arranged. The first is by the woman, who complains of gossip based only on her carrying on a private correspondence. The man's poem complains that his sweetheart never sends him word, despite the heavy traffic in the light messages of love that he can see going on all around him.

"Expressing Thoughts Directly"

1381   [MYS XI:2529/2524]

  Wa ga seko ni   If I had met you
  Tada ni awaba koso   Face to face, my love, oh, then,
    Na wa tatame   Then might the rumors fly—
  Koto no kayoi ni   But for messages exchanged,
  Nani ka soko yue   Why for nothing but that?

1382   [MYS XI:2534/2529]

    Iebito wa   Back and forth they go,
  Michi mo shimimi ni   Such an abundance of housemen—
  Kayoedo mo   They clog the roads;

| A ga matsu imo ga | But, oh, from the girl I wait for |
| Tsukai konu kamo | A messenger never comes. |

✳ The homely image in poem 1383, also a "direct" expression despite the almost symbolic importance attached to the sleeping mat, is particularly telling. The implied contrast of two sleepers wearing away the mat quickly hovers just out of sight. This is a woman's poem, and belongs to the genre of expressions of fidelity until some distant and unlikely time.

1383 [MYS XI: 2543 / 2538]

Hitorinu to	Sleeping alone
Komo kuchime ya mo	Hardly wears a mat away,
Ayamushiro	But I'll wait for you
O ni naru made ni	Until this twill-patterned pallet
Kimi o shi matamu	Is a bundle of loose cords.

✳ Another two poems are linked by the shared image of a woman's hair. In no. 1384 the girl is just coming of age (compare nos. 574 and 881–82). In order to appear older she lengthens her hair with grass, though it is not quite clear how this would be done. The sense may be that she ties it up in the adult fashion with the aid of grass. For more on this tangled topic, see nos. 1528 and 1548. The woman who speaks in no. 1385 repeats the vow of the young wife in no. 882.

1384 [MYS XI: 2545 / 2540]

Furiwake no	She whose hair was short,
Kami o mijikami	Hanging loose to either side,
Aokusa o	Who perhaps now binds
Kami ni takuramu	Green grasses to lengthen it—
Imo o shi so omou	How I do long for that girl!

1385 [MYS XI: 2583 / 2578]

Asanegami	Tangled though it be
Ware wa kezuraji	With morning sleep, I shall not
Uruwashiki	Comb this hair you touched,
Kimi ga tamakura	My precious one, when I lay
Fureteshi mono o	All night on your pillowing arm.

✳ The rather plain and unheightened version of a meeting along the road given in no. 1386 may be compared with the dazzling sedōka no. 1380, as

well as with the rollicking chōka given in different versions as nos. 430 and
1471. Its only adornment is the perhaps by this time dead metaphor in the
epithet *tamahoko no* ("jewel-spear"); nevertheless, the poem works very well
because it captures a universally recognizable human experience.

1386   [MYS XI: 2610 / 2605]

> Tamahoko no   Down the jewel-spear road
> Michiyukiburi ni   I was walking on my way,
> Omowanu ni   And I never thought—
> Imo o aimite   But suddenly I met her:
> Kouru koro kamo   And now's the time for yearning!

✳ The next "directly expressed" poem states the case on parting rather than
on meeting. It appears again as an anonymous love poem in *Shinkokinshū*,
SKKS XV: 1359 / 1358.

1387   [MYS XI: 2613 / 2608]

> Imo ga sode   Since the day I parted
> Wakareshi hi yori   From the sleeves of my beloved
> Shirotae no   The white barken cloth
> Koromo katashiki   Of my cloak spread out alone
> Koitsutsu so nuru   Has been the bed of my longing.

✳ Unlike the kibutsu poems in Books VII and X, the entries under "Expressing Thoughts by Reference to Things" are not accompanied by categorical headings specifying the "thing" referred to. In the first of the following sample of *kibutsu chinshi* poems, the object is obviously a mirror.
The image is situated in the first line of a jo that serves to introduce the
swing phrase *asanasana mimu* ("look at morning after morning"). This syntactic doubling does not involve the use of the particle *no*, which typically
results in an analogy translatable into either simile or metaphor. Rather, the
compression shifts the object of seeing from mirror to lover without specifying their logical relationship. In such a rhetorical situation the image can
nevertheless have metaphorical implications, and does so here, standing
for the beauty and perfection of the loved one, not for narcissistic self-
contemplation.

"Expressing Thoughts by Reference to Things"

1388   [MYS XI: 2641 / 2633]

> Masokagami   The gleaming mirror
> Te ni torimochite   I hold grasped within my hands

Asanasana
Mimu toki sae ya
Koi no shigekemu

Morn after morn
Though I should look upon you,
Each time would my longing grow.

❋ The next poem has a touch of magic. Presumably "referring" to a *to-moshibi*, a lamp or torch, it plays with the sounds and meanings of *kage*, a word that can mean either "light" or "shadow," and that appears also as part of the verb *kagayou* ("to flicker"). There is a memory of lamplight on a woman's face, a memory presented in the non-past, over which is imposed the *omokage*, the mental image, literally "the shadow of a face." The distinction between past and present is deliberately blurred but is still crucial. The woman is given the epithet *utsusemi no* ("actual, real") as a reminder of what was, of the experience behind the now-disembodied smile.

1389   [MYS XI: 2650 / 2642]

Tomoshibi no
Kage ni kagayou
Utsusemi no
Imo ga emai shi
Omokage ni miyu

The lamp flame
Played its light across her face,
    And she was real—
My love whose flickering smile
Now hovers in shadowed air.

❋ Fire-related topics continue in the next two poems. In no. 1390 a meta-phorical jo pivots on *shitakogare* ("burn low" / "burn secretly") to provide a rustic backdrop for a love kept hidden and remote. The smudgy mosquito flares relate the poem to the even homelier imagery of no. 1391, also structured on a jo, with double function in the third line. The jo draws into its world the speaker of the poem and his familiar but ever-adorable wife.

1390   [MYS XI: 2657 / 2649]

Ashihiki no
Yamada moru oji
Oku kahi no
Shitakogare nomi
A ga koioraku

In the footsore hills
The old man who guards the mountain field
    Keeps mosquito flares:
Always burning with a secret flame
Is the smoldering of my love.

1391   [MYS XI: 2659 / 2651]

Naniwahito
Ashihi taku ya no
Sushite aredo
Ono ga tsuma koso
Toko mezurashiki

Naniwa folk
Burn reed-fires in their huts:
    Darkened with soot,
Still my own wife is the one
Ever lovable to me.

✳ Judging by adjacent poems, the topical reference of no. 1392 must be a horse. The poem is an intricate piece of joinery, with two jo and reversed syntax. *Imo ga kami age* ("my young love's hair done up") reads like part of the main statement of a love poem, and in a sense it is. But its primary technical function is to introduce *tak-* in *takahano* ("Bamboo Leaf Pasture"; location unknown). *Tak-* is the stem of *taku* ("to tie up"), and *taka* is an allomorph of *take* ("bamboo"). The double jo concludes in the swing line *arabinikerashi* ("seem to have gone wild" / "seem to be hostile"). The last line gives the speaker's reason for supposing that such wild / rough / ruinous conditions prevail in his woman's heart (and, tangentially, in her hair?). The image of the "free-running colts" (*hanaregoma*) suggests she is in rebellion, has slipped her halter, as it were (see no. 186).

1392 [MYS XI: 2660 / 2652]

Imo ga kami	My young love's hair
Agetakahano no	Done up with Bamboo Leaf Pasture's
Hanaregoma	Free-running colts
Arabinikerashi	Gone wild, a ruin now, it seems,
Awanaku omoeba	Considering how we never meet.

✳ *Sora* ("sky" / "empty") is the pivot word that connects the jo to the main statement in the next poem. The image of the moon is metaphorically relevant in that the moon, like the would-be lover, must travel across a vast emptiness.

1393 [MYS XI: 2680 / 2672]

Kono yama no	Close above the peak
Mine ni chikashi to	Of this mountain range I saw
A ga mitsuru	The rising moon—
Tsuki no sora naru	Whose track is far across a sky
Koi mo suru kamo	No more empty than my love.

✳ Although no. 1394 must "refer" to sand or seawater, its images are handled differently from those in the last several poems. They are organized into a preposited three-line unit, but there is no juncture through syntactic doubling—no swing line or pivot word. The comparison is direct and specifically metaphorical. By contrast, no. 1395 is not only based on a jo, but based on one whose juncture is through phonetic repetition (*hisagi* / *hisashiku*), the least logical structure. The "reference" must be to "waves" or "beach," or perhaps to "grasses"—all images located in the jo. As usual, the jo subliminally directs the reader to think of the "matter" of the poem as taking place in the world it depicts.

1394 [MYS XI: 2743 / 2734]

Shio miteba	Sand amid the surf,
Minawa ni ukabu	Floating in the churning water
Manago ni mo	With the advancing tide:
Are wa ikeru ka	Even thus am I living,
Koi wa shinazute	Locked in death-struggle with love!

1395 [MYS XI: 2763 / 2753]

Nami no ma yu	Long are the days
Miyuru koshima no	Since last I met you, long
Hamahisagi	As the sweet beach-bramble
Hisashiku narinu	Growing where the island dunes
Kimi ni awazu shite	Are glimpsed between wave and wave.

✳ In no. 1396 the phonetic linkage of the jo is also semantic, *niko* in both cases meaning "soft." This anonymous poem may be the source of Lady Ōtomo of Sakanoue's no. 737.

1396 [MYS XI: 2772 / 2762]

Ashikaki no	Do not look at me
Naka no nikogusa	Tenderly as tender-grass
Nikoyoka ni	In a fence of reeds—
Ware to emashite	If you smile at me like that
Hito ni shirayu na	People are sure to know.

✳ The next four poems relate to seaweed. The first three are built on jo, with syntactic doubling (nos. 1397–98) or adjectival modification (no. 1399); the fourth confines its jo to one line (line 3). A one-line jo can be considered a pillow-word construction, the adverbial makurakotoba being functionally identical to an adverbial jo. The voice in nos. 1397 and 1399 is the man's, and in no. 1400 the woman's. The second poem (no. 1398) could be by either sex.

1397 [MYS XI: 2788 / 2778]

Minasoko ni	The gemweed growing
Ouru tamamo no	On the floor of the ocean

Oiidezu   Does not reach the top:
Yoshi kono koro wa   Well then, for some time to come
Kakute kayowamu   I'll make my visits under cover too.

1398   [MYS XI: 2789 / 2779]

Unahara no   On the broad sea plains
Oki tsu nawanori   Ropeweed of the offing drifts
Uchinabiki   Where the current goes:
Kokoro mo shino ni   So tenderly my heart drifts on
Omōyuru kamo   In unending thoughts of you.

1399   [MYS XI: 2790 / 2780]

Murasaki no   In the Bay of Nataka
Nataka no ura no   (Called the Purple for its lofty name)
Nabikimo no   The drifting seaweed
Kokoro wa imo ni   Is my heart which now has washed ashore
Yorinishi mono o   On the coastline of my own dear girl.

1400   [MYS XI: 2792 / 2782]

Sanu gani wa   If it is but sleep,
Tare to mo nemedo   Why, I can sleep with anyone;
Oki tsu mo no   But it is you, my love,
Nabikishi kimi ga   Who drifted with me like the seaweed
Koto matsu ware o   Of the offing, for whose word I wait.

❋ The following poem uses parallel images, *iki no o* ("thread of breath") and *tama no o* ("jewel-thread"), which have the additional meanings of "thread of life" and "thread of the soul," respectively. The poem deliberately points to the images as metaphors and examines them. Concealed love is a lifeline but as painful as held-in breath. *Kurushi* ("painful") contains *kuru* ("to reel"), an engo for *o* ("thread"). *Tama no o* is a string of gems, but also the image of the thread that ties the soul to the body. Its "breaking" is a metaphor for disclosure, for "spilling the beans"—but also for the ultimate danger and the ultimate release. The complexity of this poem demonstrates the alternate avenues to be pursued by waka beyond the traditional structure of the jo.

1401   [MYS XI: 2798 / 2788]

Iki no o ni   As the thread of my breath
Omoeba kurushi   This held longing: reeling pain;

Tama no o no	Let the jewel-thread snap,
Taete midarena	The wild scattering begin—
Shiraba shiru to mo	And if the world knows, it knows.

※ By contrast, the next poem fairly glories in the delaying tactics of jo technique. It begins with a pillow-word construction, *ashihiki no* ("leg-cramping"), the ancient epithet for *yama* ("mountain"), and builds up step by step through a series of *no* modifying phrases and repetitions of the *o* sound to the longness of the trailing tail of the bird on the mountain, a length promptly transformed at the juncture point in line 4 into that of the nights the speaker must sleep alone. The long process of arriving at the nights undoubtedly makes them seem longer. This catchy poem was associated with Hitomaro in the post-*Man'yōshū* tradition, appearing under his name in both *Kakinomoto no Hitomaro Shū* and *Shūishū* (SIS XIII:778), the third of the imperial anthologies (see no. 436).

1402   [MYS XI:2813/2802a]

Ashihiki no	In the leg-cramping
Yamadori no o no	Mountains the mountain pheasant's tail,
Shidario no	That trailing tail,
Naganagashi yo o	Is it longer than the long, long nights
Hitori ka mo nemu	When I must sleep alone?

※ Like the above poem, the following series clearly belongs to a set referring to birds. The first three are all based on jo with juncture in the third line. The first employs negative analogy, while the other two are positive. The wife in no. 1403 stifles her sobs so as to avoid calling attention to the cockcrow departure of her husband, with whom her relationship is still secret. The next two poems are in the voice of a woman whose man is away. The jo in no. 1404 is joined to the main statement by repetition, that in no. 1405 by semantic doubling. In both the birds fly high, across mountains and seas, their flight a metaphor of the desired homecoming.

1403   [MYS XI:2814/2803]

Satonaka ni	Off in the village
Naku naru kake no	Hear the crying of the cock—
Yobitatete	Not so does she cry,
Itaku wa nakanu	Out loud, so clamorously,
Komorizuma wa mo	This secret wife of mine.

1404   [MYS XI:2815/2804]

        Takayama ni   The teal are flying
      Takabe sawatari   Over the tall mountains high—
        Takataka ni   Tall, tall if I stand
    A ga matsu kimi o   On tiptoe in my heightened heart
   Machiidemu ka mo   Shall I make you come home to me?

1405   [MYS XI:2816/2805]

       Ise no umi yu   If like the cranes that cry,
    Nakikuru tazu no   Coming over Ise Sea
       Otodoro mo   In distant thunder,
    Kimi ga kikosaba   You but let me hear your voice,
    Are koime ya mo   My love, would I be lonely?

❊ The next two poems form a contrastive pair. The first is in the voice of a man, the second in that of a woman. One complains of separation and sleepless nights, the other of desires still unsatisfied despite a night spent pillowed together. In the man's poem it is night, and the birds are silent; in the woman's dawn, and the birds burst forth in song. The man's poem has a jo in an unusual medial position, introducing only the last line. The woman's poem has no jo at all—the birds are real, not metaphorical, though their abundant energy does serve as a parallel to the speaker's unspent sexual drive and emotional need. There is even a contrast between a relative preponderance of o's in no. 1406 and of a's in no. 1407. In the latter poem *akenubeku* ("about to dawn") and *akanaku ni* ("still unsatisfied") echo each other's sound and comment on each other's meaning.

1406   [MYS XI:2817/2806]

      Wagimoko ni   Out of my longing
    Koure ni ka aramu   For my darling it must be
      Oki ni sumu   Come these nights when sleep
   Kamo no ukine no   Floats with wild ducks in the offing
   Yasukeku mo naki   But brings no peace to me.

1407   [MYS XI:2818/2807]

      Akenubeku   Dawnlight is breaking,
  Chitori shibanaku   A thousand birds burst forth in song—
     Shirotae no   Pillowed on white cloth,
   Kimi ga tamakura   Here I lie within your arms,
   Imada akanaku ni   My love, not yet grown weary.

❋ Each of the main modal sections of Book XI is followed by poetic exchanges. A selection of these is presented here with the anonymous poems, rather than being integrated into the exchanges section, where the identity of at least one of the poets is known. In the first exchange the enumerated phenomena are symptomatic of an oncoming visit from a lover (see no. 616). The footnote refers to MYS XI:2412/2408, an almost identical poem in the "Hitomaro Collection."

"Exchanges"
1408–9   [MYS XI:2819–20/2808–9]
(1408)   [2819/2808]

Mayone kaki	Scratching her eyebrows,
Hana hi himo toke	Sneezing, sash coming undone,
Materi ya mo	Maybe she's waiting—
Itsu ka mo mimu to	When can we get together,
Koikoshi are o	I wondered, yearning, and came.

The above is found previously among the poems of Kakinomoto no Asomi Hitomaro. However, because it is part of an exchange we have included it again here.

(1409)   [2820/2809]

Kyō nareba	Today was the day—
Hana no hanahi shi	No wonder my eyebrows were itchy,
Mayo kayumi	My nose busy sneezing
Omoishi koto wa	Those sneezes: I thought it was strange,
Kimi ni shi arikeri	But it was all because of you!

❋ The next exchange centers on the pillow word *masokagami* ("cloudless mirror"), used as a concrete symbol of meeting "face to face" (*tadame*) and as an epithet for the moon. The man's poem shows vile hesitation, and the woman, hurt and offended, claims that the listening moon—suggested by the round mirror in his poem—has been blotted out by her tears.

1410–11   [MYS XI:2821–22/2810–11]
(1410)   [2821/2810]

Oto nomi o	Shall I yearn for her,
Kikite ya koimu	Merely listening to report?
Masokagami	A cloudless mirror
Tadame ni aite	Meeting face to face might leave
Koimaku mo itaku	A longing just as painful.

(1411)   [2822/2811]

　Kono koto o   To these words of yours
　Kikamu to narashi   It seems to be listening—
　　Masokagami   Now the cloudless mirror
　Tereru tsukuyo mo   Beaming moon itself becomes
　Yami nomi ni mitsu   Mere darkness to my eyes.

❋ Folding back one's sleeves before sleeping was a magical means of meeting in dreams. Sometimes it was the folder of the sleeves who had the dream, sometimes the one for whom they were folded, as in the following exchange.

1412–13   [MYS XI:2823–24/2812–13]

(1412)   [2823/2812]

　Wagimoko ni   In my helplessness
　Koite sube nami   To bear this longing for my girl,
　　Shirotae no   Taking up my sleeves
　Sode kaeshishi wa   Of white bark cloth, I turned them back—
　Ime ni mieki ya   Did you see it in your dreams?

(1413)   [2824/2813]

　Wa ga seko ga   So it was a dream—
　Sode kaesu yo no   My lover folded back his sleeves
　　Ime narashi   Before he slept that night—
　Makoto mo kimi ni   But to me it was as real
　Aitaru gotoshi   As if I'd truly met you.

❋ The next exchange is based on the same assumption—that one dreams because one is loved, not because one loves.

1414–15   [MYS XI:2825–26/2814–15]

(1414)   [2825/2814]

　A ga koi wa   I find no comfort
　Nagusamekanetsu   For these pangs of yearning love;
　　Make nagaku   The years have gone,
　Ime ni miezute   Each with its long count of days,
　Toshi no henureba   And she comes never to my dreams.

(1415)   [2826/2815]

　Make nagaku   Our bonds are broken,
　Ime ni mo miezu   Long the count of precious days

696

Taenu to mo	With no dream of you—
A ga katakoi wa	Yet this one-sided love of mine
Yamu toki mo araji	Seems never to find an end.

✻ Matching structures, message first and metaphor second, bind the following exchange. Both partners speak of their own love—the "waterless river" (*minasegawa*) is a figure for the speaker's submerged passion, questing secretly toward its object.

1416–17   [MYS XI: 2827–28 / 2816–17]

(1416)   [2827 / 2816]

Uraburete	Do not be downcast,
Mono na omoi so	Sunken into brooding thoughts,
Amakumo no	For my love is not
Tayutau kokoro	A plaything of the airy clouds,
Wa ga omowanaku ni	Tossed upon every wind.

(1417)   [2828 / 2817]

Uraburete	I won't be downcast,
Mono wa omowaji	Sunken into brooding thoughts:
Minasegawa	A waterless river,
Arite mo mizu wa	So they say, still moves on—
Yuku to iu mono o	Its water flows underneath.

✻ The tenor of the metaphors in nos. 1418–19 may be gleaned by glancing back at no. 371. *Kakitsuhata* ("ground iris") in no. 1418 is a mock epithet for the place-name Sakinu through *saki* ("bloom"). The man apparently has had his way with the woman, but not married her, and she is now "old hat." The poems are examples of hiyuka.

1418–19   [MYS XI: 2829–30 / 2818–19]

(1418)   [2829 / 2818]

Kakitsuhata	From the ground iris
Sakinu no suge o	Blossoming Marsh I have taken
Kasa ni nui	Sedge and sewn a hat,
Kimu hi o matsu ni	But the years have passed me by
Toshi so henikeru	While I waited the day to wear it.

(1419)   [2830 / 2819]

| Oshiteru | The hat you fashioned |
| Naniwa sugakasa | From sedge of far-shining Naniwa |

<table>
<tr><td>Okifurushi</td><td>Lies around unused,</td></tr>
<tr><td>Nochi wa ta ga kimu</td><td>Getting old—but it's no hat</td></tr>
<tr><td>Kasa naranaku ni</td><td>For someone else to wear.</td></tr>
</table>

❉ In the following exchange both lovers have the moon for companion, one unwillingly, the other forgetting all else in its splendor. The use of *imo* ("sister," "young love") in no. 1420 indicates it is the man's, but usual roles are reversed, with the man waiting and the woman out wandering around. It has been suggested that *imo* is a mistake for *kimi*.

1420–21   [MYS XI: 2831–32 / 2820–21]

(1420)   [2831 / 2820]

<table>
<tr><td>Kaku dani mo</td><td>Even thus</td></tr>
<tr><td>Imo o machinamu</td><td>Shall I wait for my young love,</td></tr>
<tr><td>Sayo fukete</td><td>Far into the night</td></tr>
<tr><td>Idekoshi tsuki no</td><td>At long last the moon came out—</td></tr>
<tr><td>Katabuku made ni</td><td>I shall wait until it sets.</td></tr>
</table>

(1421)   [2832 / 2821]

<table>
<tr><td>Ko no ma yori</td><td>Down between the trees</td></tr>
<tr><td>Utsurou tsuki no</td><td>The shifting moonlight found its path,</td></tr>
<tr><td>Kage o oshimi</td><td>And I have followed,</td></tr>
<tr><td>Tachimotōru ni</td><td>Wandering entranced by the shining</td></tr>
<tr><td>Sayo fukenikeri</td><td>Till the night has worn away.</td></tr>
</table>

❉ The *mizukakeron*, or "water-splashing argument," futile in real life, can result in some of the more stimulating exchanges. In the following the lover accuses his sweetheart of becoming distant toward him, using waves on a beach as a negative analogy for his inability to approach her. *Araburu* suggests both the "roughness" of the sweetheart and the "wild" impatience of the waves. The woman shoves all this back at him with her opening blast— *kaerama* ("on the contrary"), a word that carries the idea of a receding wave. In her view, the waves never do anything but recede. The first poem positions its imagistic *jo* at the beginning, whereas the reply has it in lines 3 and 4. In both poems *takuhire no* ("mulberry-scarf," i.e., a scarf made of cloth from the paper-mulberry) is an epithet for *shira* ("white").

1422–23   [MYS XI: 2833–34 / 2822–23]

(1422)   [2833 / 2822]

<table>
<tr><td>Takuhire no</td><td>Mulberry-scarf</td></tr>
<tr><td>Shirahamanami no</td><td>White beachwaves come surging</td></tr>
</table>

Yori mo aezu	Closer I cannot
Araburu imo ni	Get to my harsh-hearted love,
Koitsutsu so oru	So pass my days in longing.

(1423)   [2834/2823]

Kaerama ni	Turnabout, my love—
Kimi koso ware ni	You're the one who never comes,
Takuhire no	A mulberry-scarf
Shirahamanami no	White beachwave, surging
Yoru toki mo naki	Across the sands to me.

❋ The conceit of scattering gems as a welcome for honored guests is used several times in *Man'yōshū*, and no. 1424 below has a close analogue in no. 702. The reply states the essence of a theme of romantic love that was a favorite with the courtly writers of the Heian period.

1424-25   [MYS XI:2835-36/2824-25]

(1424)   [2835/2824]

Omou hito	If I'd only known
Komu to shiriseba	The man I long for was coming,
Yaemugura	Over the weed patch
Ōeru niwa ni	Of this overgrown garden
Tama shikamashi o	I'd have scattered jewels, but oh.

(1425)   [2836/2825]

Tama shikeru	What are they to me,
Ie mo nani semu	Houses all scattered with jewels?
Yaemugura	Even a hovel
Ōeru oya mo	Buried deep within the weeds,
Imo to oriteba	If only alone with my love!

❋ Book XI ends with a section of hiyuka, here as in Book VII combined with kibutsu topical designations. As there, the "allegorical" treatment of metaphor that preponderantly distinguishes hiyuka is somewhat uncertainly maintained. Kibutsu as a modal category contrasting with eibutsu and sei-jutsu ("direct statement") poems, both of which are nonmetaphorical, tends to be demoted to a subcategory of hiyuka, but when used independently maintains a useful distinction between open and closed metaphor. The failure to exploit critical terminology with sufficient rigor is regrettable, but the terminology, whether of Chinese (eibutsu) or of analogous Japanese (kibutsu) derivation, must have postdated in its application many of the poems it purports to label, and so it is remarkable that it was made to fit the ways of waka as well as it does. No doubt, too, it began to influence the way waka were conceived and written, both on the allegorical (hiyuka) and the descriptive (eibutsu) end of the modal spectrum. The native (despite its Chinese name) technique of the jo remains in the middle, as usually—but not always—the trope that kibutsu in practice implies.

The analogy in no. 1426 is between a love affair and a crimson garment. The staining or dyeing of cloth as a metaphor for love was established by the Nara period, if not earlier (see, e.g., nos. 260 and 753); the stain was also conceived as applying directly to the person (no. 1538). Coloring as a visible sign and therefore a betrayal of love's secrecy is an allied metaphor (see no. 732). Here the two are combined. Since the garment is "deeply dyed" (*fukasome*), the passion must be intense. The crimson garb can also stand for the woman herself, as is seen in no. 1427.

"Analogies"

1426–27 [MYS XI: 2839–40 / 2828–29]

(1426) [2839 / 2828]

Kurenai no	Were I to wear
Fukasome no kinu o	Beneath my clothes a garment
Shita ni kiba	Of deep crimson dye,
Hito no miraku ni	People would look, and when they looked,
Nioiidemu ka mo	Might a tinge come blushing through?

(1427) [2840 / 2829]

Koromo shi mo	When it comes to clothes,
Ōku aranamu	The more the better, I would say;
Torikaete	But you keep changing
Kireba ya kimi ga	And have tried so many on,
Omo wasuretaru	By now you've forgotten my looks.

The above two poems express thoughts metaphorically through reference to clothing.

❋ A bow makes a seductively complex image of sexual dynamics in that it combines resistance with obedience, concentrated effort with release. The bow as a symbolic object of male affection is implied in no. 245, and in such poems as KKS XII: 605 by Ki no Tsurayuki.

1428 [MYS XI: 2841 / 2830]

| Azusayumi | Your catalpa bow— |
| Yuzuka makikae | Round and round you wrap the grip, |

Nakami sashi   Set the sighting true:
Sara ni hiku to mo   Now you've but to draw the string
Kimi ga manimani   And bend me to your will.

The above poem expresses thoughts metaphorically through reference to a bow.

✳ The following poem employs its reference as an explicit comparison rather than a submerged metaphor. The effect of the doubling of *iru* ("rest") is to delay the liberating tide and make the waiting seem longer.

1429   [MYS XI: 2842 / 2831]

Misago iru   Where the ospreys rest,
Su ni iru fune no   Where the boat rests on the sand,
Yūshio o   The stranded boatman
Matsuramu yori wa   Cannot wait the evening tide
Ware koso masare   More impatiently than I.

The above poem expresses thoughts metaphorically through reference to a boat.

✳ A true hiyuka, no. 1430 achieves its effect of disreputable self-satisfaction precisely by making the vehicle carry all the weight of the metaphor. The concealment of the tenor in the allegorical structure is part and counterpart of the successful concealment of the adultery.

1430   [MYS XI: 2843 / 2832]

Yamagawa ni   In the mountain creek
Ue o shi fusete   He laid his funnel trap,
Mori mo aezu   But couldn't guard it—
Toshi no yatose o   It's now been a good eight years
Wa ga nusumaishi   That I've been stealing his fish.

The above poem expresses thoughts metaphorically through reference to fish.

✳ As in no. 1429, the final selection from Book XI sets up a strong contrast between the world of the self and the world of the referent image. The squabbling ducks may suggest a scolding wife, and the stranded boat the difficulties of attaining a rendezvous, but the main function of these images is to exist outside the speaker's situation and serve as marks against which human reactions can be measured. The fish thief is inside the vehicle; the impatient lover and the patient husband are outside, looking toward points of reference that are comparative but not strictly metaphorical.

1431   [MYS XI:2844/2833]

Ashigamo no	Where the flocking reed-ducks
Sudaku ikemizu	Clamor on the surface of the pond
Hafuru to mo	Water overflows
Makemizo no he ni	The spillways—but shall *I*
Ware koeme ya mo	Go spilling in another's ditch?

✳ Book XII follows the same model as Book XI in concentrating on the two modal categories of *seijutsu shinsho* ("Expressing Thoughts Directly") and *kibutsu chinshi* ("Expressing Thoughts by Reference to Things"). It also includes poems of travel and of parting, but lacks the sedōka section of Book XI. Both books are composed completely of love poems, and as such exhibit little Chinese influence compared with the eibutsuka ("Poems on Things") of Books VII and X.

True to the "directness" of its expression, the following poem does not allow itself to be detained by imagery, much less metaphor. It is all regret and remembrance.

"Expressing Thoughts Directly"

1432   [MYS XII:2879/2867]

Kaku bakari	Had I only known
Koimu mono so to	I would yearn for you like this,
Shiramaseba	On that night
Sono yo wa yuta ni	I might well have found the time
Aramashi mono o	To stay awhile at ease.

✳ The next two poems are on dreams. The first is in a style that may be labeled "passionate confusion," in which intense feeling leads one to lose the ability to distinguish dream from reality, self from other, or past from present. Dream remained an important category of love poem on into *Kokinshū* times and beyond, and took on a deep cultural resonance because of the importance in Buddhism of the dialectic noumenon (void; *śūnyatā*) vs. phenomenon (apparent reality; *rūpa*). The second poem reverses the effect of the magical technique mentioned in no. 1412: by turning back his sleeves the lover receives rather than sends a dream.

1433   [MYS XII: 2929 / 2917]

    Utsutsu ni ka   In reality
  Imo ga kimaseru   Did my darling come to me,
     Ime ni ka mo   Or was it all a dream,
  Ware wa matoeru   And I but lost and wandering
  Koi no shigeki ni   In the thickets of longing?

1434   [MY XII: 2949 / 2937]

    Shirotae no   All through the night,
  Sode orikaeshi   Sleeves of white bark cloth turned back,
     Koureba ka   I yearned for her—
  Imo ga sugata no   Was it perhaps because of this
  Ime ni shi miyuru   I saw her figure in a dream?

❉ Each of the following three poems incorporates a jo, which is normal for the *kibutsu chinshi* mode. The first two obviously "refer" to seaweed, although as in Book XI the topic is not specified. The first is by a woman, whereas the gender of the second speaker is left open. *Nawanori* ("rope-weed") contains the phrase *na wa nori* ("tell a name"), and hence introduces *na* ("name"). The juncture through wordplay leaves the jo of no. 1436 in the subliminal position of suggesting a seaside backdrop for the secret lovers, whereas in no. 1435 the relationship between jo and main statement is analogical. The cord of a single strand in no. 1437 is the same metaphor for one-sided love encountered in nos. 1299 and 1342, and the "disorder" (*midaruru toki*) implies the same "scattering" (*midare*) as in no. 1401.

"Expressing Thoughts by Reference to Things"

1435   [MYS XII: 3093 / 3079]

  Watatsumi no   As the gemweed drifts
  Oki tsu tamamo no   In the offing of the mighty deep,
    Nabikinemu   So let us drift in sleep:
  Haya kimase kimi   Come to me quickly, O my love,
  Mataba kurushi mo   For I must suffer if you make me wait.

1436   [MYS XII: 3094 / 3080]

  Watatsumi no   In the mighty deep
  Oki ni oitaru   Far off the shore there grows
    Nawanori no   The ropeweed "Name-Teller":
  Na wa sane noraji   Your name I shall never tell,
  Koi wa shinu to mo   Not though I should die of love.

1437 [MYS XII: 3095 / 3081]

Tama no o o	When a string of jewels
Katao ni yorite	Is twisted from a single strand
O o yowami	It has no strength:
Midaruru toki ni	What can I do but yearn for you
Koizu arame ya mo	When weakness brings disorder?

❋ Another intertwining of seaweed and love is found in no. 1438, from a category of travel poems. The speaker may be imagined to be one of the ama ("shore girls") mentioned in the jo. "Tell-not weed" (*nanoriso*), like *nawanori*, serves to introduce *na* ("name"). As in no. 236 and elsewhere, telling the name implies the establishment of a sexual bond, which is the point of the euphemism and the impatience with the evasive male here.

"Thoughts Inspired on a Journey"

1438 [MYS XII: 3191 / 3177]

Shika no ama no	On the stony beach
Iso ni karihosu	The shore girls of Shika dry
Nanoriso no	Their take of tell-not weed,
Na wa noriteshi o	But now I've told my name to you
Nani ka aigataki	How can you say it's hard to meet?

❋ Only one of the following poems selected from the category "Sorrow at Parting" incorporates a jo. Although not devoid of imagery or incidental metaphor, they are mainly in the mode of "direct statement." The "parting of the sleeves" (*sode no wakare*) in no. 1439 is the parting of lovers, and in fact most of the poems express the feelings of a woman whose man is leaving on a journey. Sleeves are appropriate as a synecdoche of parting because they imply the mutual embrace of lovers in a bed where clothes served as covers, and because they were waved in farewell. Here the "tangle of longing" (*omoimidare*) is the subjective correlative of the intertwining of the sleeves.

"Poems of Sorrow at Parting"

1439 [MYS XII: 3196 / 3182]

Shirotae no	It was bitter,
Sode no wakare wa	The parting of our sleeves
Oshikedo mo	White as barken cloth,
Omoimidarete	But in a tangle of longing
Yurushitsuru kamo	Helplessly I let him go.

❊ In no. 1440 the constant coming undone of the woman's sash must be a sign of her desire for the return of her man, rather than a prediction of it as in no. 1408. The woman's feeling in no. 1441 may be the same as that of Koshima when she said good-bye to Ōtomo no Tabito (see nos. 1073–74). But here the need for secrecy proves paramount, or perhaps the reluctance of a woman to call attention to herself and her love.

1440   [MYS XII: 3197/3183]

  Miyakohe ni   Since you went away
 Kimi wa inishi o   To the capital, my love,
   Tare toke ka   Who can it be
 Wa ga himo no o no That keeps loosening my sash?
 Yuu te tayuki mo   My hands are limp with tying.

1441   [MYS XII: 3198/3184]

  Kusamakura   Grasspillow
 Tabi yuku kimi o   Journey: you go away,
   Hitome ōmi   Men's eyes are many—
 Sode furazu shite   I make no move to wave my sleeve,
 Amata kuyashi mo   And now am thronged with regret.

❊ The next poem is based on a jo in which the mirror (one of white bronze, as suggested by the orthography for *maso*) introduces the idea of avid gazing, whose object then becomes *kimi* ("you"). The implied cherishing of the beloved works to intensify the sense of loss in his departure. The parting could be one in death rather than in life.

1442   [MYS XII: 3199/3185]

  Masokagami   The flawless mirror
 Te ni torimochite   I have taken in my hands,
   Miredo akanu   Gazed on without tiring:
 Kimi ni okurete   You, my love, have left me here
 Ikeri to mo nashi   Abandoned, hardly alive.

❊ The next three poems all have the lover (or friend) crossing mountains on his journey.

1443   [MYS XII: 3200/3186]

  Kumoriyo no   How long shall I wait,
 Tadoki mo shiranu   When will you come home again

Yama koete	Who now cross mountains
Imasu kimi o ba	Dark to my groping as a night
Itsu to ka matamu	Lost under layered clouds?

1444 [MYS XII: 3201 / 3187]

Tatanazuku	When folded ranges
Aokakiyama no	Of the green-fence mountains rise
Henarinaba	In barriers between,
Shibashiba kimi o	Won't I find I can no more
Kototowaji ka mo	Inquire of you constantly?

1445 [MYS XII: 3202 / 3188]

Asakasumi	When you cross the hills
Tanabiku yama o	Covered in drifting mist
Koete inaba	In the morning,
Ware wa koimu na	How I shall long for you,
Awamu hi made ni	Till the day we meet again.

❋ A final two poems on parting conclude this sampling of Book XII. The first shares its first two lines with no. 1429, but unlike that hiyuka does not use the image of the boat on the sandspit for comparative purposes. The ospreys, sandspit, boat, and speaker are all on the same level of discourse, in a poem of "direct statement." The maker of the statement is facing the deprivation of a temporary separation, and thus is in better case than Tamatsuki, the Maid of Tsushima (no. 928). The second poem, however, achieves its effect precisely by the use of metaphor, the *hiyu* of *tamamo* ("gemweed") referring to the glistening enticements to be found in ama villages down Tsukushi way. The first poem might be the voice of one of those ama girls, the second that of the wife at home.

1446 [MYS XII: 3217 / 3203]

Misago iru	Out on the sandspit,
Su ni iru fune no	Resting where the ospreys rest,
Kogidenaba	He left his boat;
Uragoishikemu	I'll be lonely when it rows away,
Nochi wa ainu to mo	Though we lie together after.

1447 [MYS XII: 3220 / 3206]

Tsukushiji no	Can it be my love
Ariso no tamamo	Tarries along Tsukushi Road

Karu to ka mo	To gather gemweed
Kimi ga hisashiku	Growing by the rocky shore?
Matedo kimasanu	However long I wait, he does not come.

Book XIII

Book XIII is a chōka collection; almost all the tanka (and the one sedōka) included in it are envoys. Many of the chōka are metrically irregular, and several employ older alternatives to the 7-7 ending of the classically defined form, in particular the patterns 5-3-7 and 7-7-7. These characteristics, unsophisticated prosody (especially in the handling of repetitions), and a predominance of folk settings, suggest that many of the poems are early, belonging to the world of ancient song found in the chronicles. Several of the chōka lack envoys, another feature typical of early song. However, there are also echoings or prefigurings of Hitomaro, and indications that some of the poems may be as late as the Nara period. Except for one hiyuka, modal categories are not to be found in the labeling of the content of this book. The basic scheme is by genre—zōka, sōmon, and banka—along with a section of exchanges.

An example of a short chōka with the 5-3-7 ending is provided by the following poem (see nos. 49, 83, and 145 for approximations of this pattern, realized precisely in no. 236). This panegyric to a sacred mountain is based on substitution-pattern parallelism (lines 3–6) framed by the repetition of identical (*moru . . . moru, yama . . . yama . . . yama*) and nearly identical (*moro . . . moru*) elements. *Naku ko* ("crying child"), a jo-type preposited phrase embedded in a single line, introduces *moru* ("guard") by serving as its object. This piece of wordplay has led to the suggestion that the poem is an ancient lullaby. *Ashibi* is a plant with pendulous white blossom clusters known as andromeda in English.

"Miscellaneous Poems"

1448   [MYS XIII: 3236/3222]

Mimoro wa	The guarded mountain,
Hito no moru yama	Mountain of the sacred grove—
Motohe ni wa	Along the foot
Ashibi hana saki	*Ashibi* are flowering,
Suehe ni wa	Along the top
Tsubaki hana saku	Camellias are flowering.
Uraguwashi	What a lovely
Yama so	Mountain is
Naku ko moru yama	The mountain guarded like a crying child.

❋ The following chōka employs a narrative version of the preparation-
conclusion pattern (see no. 165) that is similar to a jo in the sense that it
delays the moment of truth for the poem—here the image of the Yoshino
rapids—but different because it is part of the main line of discourse, not an
analogical structure or one tangentially pinned on by wordplay. It would be
easy to shift the passage through line 7 into the jo mode by interpreting
shima ("island") literally, in which case the raft is cruising around an actual
island, whose attractions (line 8) are then applied to the river scene at
Yoshino. But *shima* was also used to refer to a shore seen across water, and is
undoubtedly the winding riverbank here. The log raft also belongs on a
river. The last three lines of the chōka, once arrived at, are repeated verbatim in the envoy—the only envoy in *Man'yōshū* that is a sedōka rather
than a tanka—and then altered to bring in the one element not related
directly to the natural scene. Mention of "the girl I left behind me"
(*tomarinishi imo*) shifts the zōka in the direction of sōmon at the end, and the
balanced structure of the sedōka makes the shift prosodically effective.

1449–50   [MYS XIII: 3246–47 / 3232–33]

Ono torite	Taking an axe,
Nifu no hiyama no	Cutting down the cypress trees
Ki korikite	On Nifu's mountains,
Ikada ni tsukuri	Fashioning from them a raft,
5 Makaji nuki	Attaching oars,
Iso kogimitsutsu	And rowing round the stony strand,
Shimazutai	Coasting the island,
Miredo mo akazu	Never weary of the sight:
Miyoshino no	The white waves
10 Taki mo todoro ni	In the torrent that descends
Otsuru shiranami	In thunder at fair Yoshino.

Envoy

Miyoshino no	The white waves
Taki mo todoro ni	In the torrent that descends
Otsuru shiranami	In thunder at fair Yoshino—
Tomarinishi	The white waves
Imo ni misemaku	That I want to show the girl
Hoshiki shiranami	I left behind me when I came!

❋ No doubt can be entertained about the existence of a jo in the next poem.
There are in fact two of them, one introducing the next, in the chōka, and a
third in the envoy. (For the double-jo technique, see no. 1245.) The image
of spun thread in the first three lines is meant to introduce *naga* ("long") in

the place-name Nagato; in turn, the tidal characteristics of Nagato Bay provide twin analogies for the speaker's yearning for a woman he has been
thinking about as he journeys along (his journey no doubt taking him by
Nagato Bay). The location of Ago is not known, but it was presumably in
the same area of the western reaches of the Inland Sea as Nagato. Once
there, the speaker observes a third set of maidens (in addition to those in the
jo and his sweetheart). His attention is drawn to one of the maidens by a
waving sleeve—note the balance achieved with the textile image in the jo—
and an amorous message flashes to him like the flashing of a white scarf in
the sunlight. The envoy reasserts his yearning—for his original sweetheart,
apparently, rather than for the friendly ama girl. This envoy may have been
the model for no. 1007 by Lady Ōtomo of Sakanoue.

1451-52   [MYS XIII: 3257-58 / 3243-44]

Otomera ga	Maidens spinning hemp
Oke ni taretaru	Catch the spun thread in baskets,
Umio nasu	The long loops of thread:
Nagato no ura ni	Out on long Nagato Bay
5　Asanagi ni	In the morning calm
Michikuru shio no	The tide comes flooding in,
Yūnagi ni	In the evening calm
Yosekuru nami no	The waves come sweeping in:
Sono shio no	Like that tide
10　Iya masumasu ni	Deeper and ever deeper,
Sono nami no	Like those waves
Iya shikushiku ni	Ceaselessly, with mounting force,
Wagimoko ni	I yearn for her,
Koitsutsu kureba	My own true love, as I come.
15　Ago no umi no	On the sea of Ago,
Ariso no ue ni	On the wild and stony shore
Hamana tsumu	Picking the beach herbs,
Amaotomera ga	Daughters of the fisherfolk:
Unagaseru	Draped around their necks,
20　Hire mo teru gani	Scarves—and one now flashing;
Te ni makeru	Wound around their wrists,
Tama mo yurara ni	Gems—and I hear the click:
Shirotae no	White as barken cloth
Sode furu mietsu	A sleeve waves suddenly in view—
25　Aiomou rashi mo	Ah, it seems she fancies me.

Envoy

Ago no umi no	On the sea of Ago,
Ariso no ue no	On the wild and stony shore

Sazarenami	The rippling waves:
A ga kouraku wa	This time of my yearning,
Yamu toki mo nashi	Never still for a moment.

❋ The following poem, which could be by a wife to her husband or a courtier to his lord, is based on the belief that the moon god Tsukuyomi (born from the right eye of the creator god Izanagi, and thus the brother of Amaterasu the sun deity) possessed the magic youth-restoring water *ochimizu*. The moon is an obvious symbol of both aging and rebirth. Assuming that no. 1453–54 is spoken by a woman to an older man, it makes a nice contrast with no. 892. Akamaro was told to find his own *ochimizu*, but this woman is willing to climb to the moon to get it for the man she loves. The envoy takes off from the image of scaling the heavens in its use of the moon and sun as similes. (For more on the myth of the restorative water, see the commentary to nos. 1528–39.)

1453–54   [MYS XIII: 3259–60 / 3245–46]

Amahashi mo	A ladder to heaven—
Nagaku mogamo	And let it be a long one;
Takayama mo	A lofty mountain—
Takaku mogamo	And oh that it be high:
Tsukuyomi no	I would go and get
Moteru ochimizu	The water of replenished youth
Itorikite	Kept by the moon god
Kimi ni matsurite	And offer it to you, my lord,
Ochieteshi kamo	To make you young again.

Envoy

Ame naru ya	You to me, my lord,
Tsuki hi no gotoku	Are as the moon and sun
A ga omoeru	In heaven;
Kimi ga hi ni ke ni	How bitter is my regret
Oyuraku oshi mo	At your aging more each day.

❋ The above two chōka-hanka sets are listed under zōka, but seem to belong better to the category of sōmon. The Love poems officially begin with no. 1455–56. The chōka employs the many-one paradigm to ask why a woman must spend sleepless nights yearning for one man when there are many. The envoy rephrases the question, suggesting that it is in the uniqueness of a passion that its pain resides. Shikishima, near present Sakurai City in Nara Prefecture, was the residence of Emperors Sujin (third century A.D.) and Kimmei (r. 539–71). The name is used as a pillow word for Yamato, or sometimes as a synonym for Japan. Wisteria vines twist like tortured thoughts, and young grass suggests the tenderness of a young lover (compare no. 351).

"Love Poems"

1455–56 [MYS XIII: 3262–63 / 3248–49]

Shikishima no	Though in Yamato,
Yamato no kuni ni	The land called Shikishima,
Hito sawa ni	Men in their numbers
Michite aredo mo	Fill the land to overflowing,
5 Fujinami no	Waves of wisteria
Omoimotōri	Are my encircling longings,
Wakakusa no	Young grasses
Omoitsukinishi	Are the longings that take root
Kimi ga me ni	For your eyes
10 Koi ya akasamu	Must I still keep vigil of desire,
Nagaki kono yo o	Long though this night may be?

Envoy

Shikishima no	If in Yamato,
Yamato no kuni ni	The land called Shikishima,
Hito futari	I thought there were two—
Ari to shi omowaba	Two men—what then, I wonder,
Nani ka nagekamu	Could ever grieve my heart?

Above, two poems.

❋ The following poem takes the form of a kotoage, a "lifting up of words" in appeal to the gods, considered a dangerous procedure (see nos. 582 and 942). The voice is that of a woman. For the legendary source of the epithet *akizushima* ("Dragonfly Island") see nos. 97 and 145. The direct challenge to the gods to prove their power, omniscience, or existence by coming to the aid of a lovelorn heart may be compared to that in no. 952 by Nakatomi no Yakamori, while the ironic use of sun and moon in lines 11–14 recalls the opening words of the Destitute Man in no. 634. The "flawless mirror" (*masokagami*) in line 25 resonates with these celestial images. The two envoys reveal that the man has left on a journey, the implications of the pillow words *ōbune no* ("as on a great ship") and *kusamakura* ("on a grass pillow") being "by sea" and "by land."

1457–59   [MYS XIII : 3264–66 / 3250–52]

	Akizushima	Dragonfly Island
	Yamato no kuni wa	Land of Yamato—
	Kamukara to	A land of godhead
	Kotoage senu kuni	Where men do not lift up words;
5	Shikaredo mo	Yet though it be thus,
	Are wa kotoage su	I shall lift up words for this:
	Ame tsuchi no	Are the deities
	Kami mo hanahada	Of heaven and earth so utterly
	A ga omou	Ignorant of my heart
10	Kokoro shirazu ya	And all its burden of longing?
	Yuku kage no	The moving splendor
	Tsuki mo heyukeba	Of the moon goes by in months,
	Tamakagiru	The gem-glinting light
	Hi mo kasanarite	Of the sun piles up in days
15	Omoe ka mo	Of ceaseless longing,
	Mune yasukaranu	So that my breast is never peaceful;
	Koure ka mo	Of ceaseless yearning,
	Kokoro no itaki	So that my heart is sore.
	Sue tsui ni	In the end at last
20	Kimi ni awazu wa	If I never meet you, love,
	Wa ga inochi no	All my life
	Ikeramu kiwami	For as long as I shall live
	Koitsutsu mo	I shall go on
	Are wa wataramu	In continual yearning.
25	Masokagami	A flawless mirror
	Masame ni kimi o	Bright before me, face to face:
	Aimiteba koso	Only if I meet you thus
	A ga koi yamame	Will my longing find an end.

Envoys

Ōbune no	As on a great ship
Omoitanomeru	I rely on you, my love,
Kimi yue ni	For whom my longing
Tsukusu kokoro wa	Draws the very heart of me—
Oshikeku mo nashi	A spending without regret.

Hisakata no	The everlasting
Miyako o okite	Capital of kings you leave,
Kusamakura	On a grass-pillow
Tabi yuku kimi o	Journey you depart, my love:
Itsu to ka matamu	Till when shall I await you?

❋ A quadripartite structural principle in early chōka, already seen in lines 5–12 of no. 1451–52, is further illustrated in the next poem. The jo provides matching couplets in the pattern a-b-a'-b', which are then applied to the main statement of the poem in a second pair of couplets. (For further examples, see nos. 263 and 1468–69.) Oharida and Ayuji are thought to have been in the Asuka area. The first envoy is a formulaic poem with variants in Book XII (2893 / 2881, 2904 / 2892, 2953 / 2941, 2972 / 2960, not included in the present anthology). The footnote points out a recurrent phenomenon in Book XIII, namely, that the hanka does not always match the chōka. The envoy "from a certain text" employs an opening formula identical to lines found in nos. 318 and 419.

1460–62   [MYS XIII : 3274–76 / 3260–62]

	Oharida no	At Oharida
	Ayuji no mizu o	The water of Ayuji
	Ma naku so	Without resting
	Hito wa kumu to iu	People draw, they say,
5	Tokijiku so	In and out of season
	Hito wa nomu to iu	People drink, they say:
	Kumu hito no	As they who draw it
	Ma naki ga gotoku	Take no interval for rest,
	Nomu hito no	As they who drink it
10	Tokijiki ga goto	Drink it all the year around,
	Wagimoko ni	So for my young girl
	A ga kouraku wa	Does my yearning never find
	Yamu toki mo nashi	A season when it might cease.

Envoy

Omoiyaru	To clear my longing,
Sube no tazuki mo	Of device or skillful way
Ima wa nashi	I now have none—
Kimi ni awazute	Now that the years have passed me by
Toshi no henureba	And I never meet my lord.

On present consideration, it is not logical for this envoy to say *kimi ni awazu* ["not meeting my lord"]; it should say *imo ni awazu* ["not meeting my girl"].

The envoy in a certain text reads:

Mizukaki no	From a time as old
Hisashiki toki yu	As these sacred palings
Koi sureba	I have yearned for you:
A ga obi yuruu	My sash hangs more loosely
Asa yoi goto ni	With every morn and eve.

❋ The death song of Prince Karu in *Kojiki* (no. 90) has found its way into *Man'yōshū* as an anonymous chōka (no. 1463), with only a slight variation in the final lines. This poem of longing for a woman left at home, or perhaps for a lost wife, fits the *Kojiki* context, in which the lovers commit suicide together, only poorly. The elaborate pattern of the jo and the way it joins the main statement of the poem are developments from the schema seen in no. 1460. Neither envoy probably belonged with the chōka originally. The first, which may be the source for no. 1004 by Fujiwara no Maro, contradicts the sentiment of the poem to which it is attached. The other expresses the reluctance of a Buddhist monk to return to secular life.

1463–65   [MYS XIII : 3277–79 / 3263–65]

Komoriku no	There on the river
Hatsuse no kawa no	Of Hatsuse the hidden land
Kami tsu se ni	In the upper shallows
Ikui o uchi	They pound sacred poles,
5 Shimo tsu se ni	In the lower shallows
Makui o uchi	They pound splendid poles.
Ikui ni wa	On the sacred poles
Kagami o kake	They hang bright mirrors,
Makui ni wa	On the splendid poles
10 Matama o kake	They hang splendid jewels.
Matama nasu	Like a splendid jewel
A ga omou imo mo	The dear girl for whom I long,
Kagami nasu	Like a bright mirror
A ga omou imo mo	The dear girl for whom I long:
15 Ari to iwaba koso	If they say that she is there,
Kuni ni mo	Then shall I go
Ie ni mo yukame	To my country, to my home:
Ta ga yue ka yukamu	Else for whose sake should I go?

In checking this against *Kojiki*, we find that this is said to be a poem that Crown Prince Kinashi no Karu composed when he died by his own hand.

Envoy

Toshi wataru	They do say there are
Made ni mo hito wa	Those who are content to wait
Ari to iu o	Till a year goes by,
Itsu no ma ni so mo	But for me the yearning came
A ga koinikeru	Quicker than I can tell.

The envoy in a certain text reads:

Yo no naka o	I who thought the world
Ushi to omoite	Useless, and abandoned it,

714

Iede seshi	Leaving my home,
Are ya nani ni ka	What would I amount to
Kaerite naramu	Even if I did return?

❋ Wolf Plain (Makami no Hara; see also no. 341) is south of Asuka Village, and so the Kamunabi, the "deity-endowed" mountain referred to in the next poem, may be Ikazuchi no Oka ("Thunder Hill"; no. 297). The poem, presumably by a woman whose lover or husband has left unusually early in the evening, is reminiscent of no. 718, in which Lady Ōtomo of Sakanoue expresses similar solicitude for her nephew Yakamochi. Her term for him, *seko* ("young brother") is more specifically an endearment than the *hito* ("person") translated as "lover" here. Atmospherics—sacred groves, clouds, rain, menacing place-names, and pillow words evoking darkness—lend a brooding quality to this nocturne.

1466-67   [MYS XIII: 3282-83/3268-69]

Mimoro no	Over Kamunabi,
Kamunabiyama yu	Mountain of the sacred groves,
Tonogumori	The dark clouds stretch
Ame wa furikinu	And the rain begins to fall,
5 Amagirai	The sky is misted
Kaze sae fukinu	And the wind now starts to blow.
Ōkuchi no	Over the wide fields,
Makami no hara yu	Wolf Plain called of the gaping jaws,
Omoitsutsu	Lost in his yearning
10 Kaerinishi hito	My departing lover went—
Ie ni itariki ya	Is he safe at home by now?

Envoy

Kaerinishi	After he left
Hito o omou to	I lay thinking of him:
Nubatama no	In the blackberry
Sono yo wa ware mo	Night that night I too
I mo nekaneteki	Could find no more of sleep.

❋ The similarity between the next chōka and no. 263 has been remarked. The pattern seems to be an old one in folk song, giving the singer a chance to bring in the weather, the most universal of topics, for analogies to whatever may be the burden of his song. The burden here is love for a woman, presented in its essence, *tadaka*, "the direct fragrance." The jo of the envoy, returning to the setting at the beginning of the chōka, conveys the singularity of the fatal glance.

1468–69 [MYS XIII:3307–8/3293–94]

Miyoshino no	In fair Yoshino
Mikane no take ni	On the peak of Mikane
Ma naku zo	Without interval
Ame wa furu to iu	It rains, so people say,
5 Tokijiku so	Though out of season
Yuki wa furu to iu	It snows, so people say:
Sono ame no	As that rain comes down
Ma naki ga gotoku	Without interval for rest,
Sono yuki no	As that snow comes down
10 Tokijiki ga goto	Even though out of season,
Ma mo ochizu	Not missing a moment
Are wa so kouru	I yearn all my time away
Imo ga tadaka ni	For the bare scent of my love.

Envoy

Miyuki furu	Where the fair snow falls
Yoshino no take ni	On the high peaks of Yoshino
Iru kumo no	Perches a lone cloud:
Yoso ni mishi ko ni	Afar off I saw that girl,
Koiwataru kamo	And know no rest from yearning!

❋ The following vigorous and busy chōka is in the voice of a young *ama* man who has been separated from his sweetheart by village opposition. It has some of the power of Hitomaro prosody, being composed of one long syntactic unit down to the last, reversed-syntax line. The cadence is swift, flowing over the dam set up by the double imagistic parallels and their matching couplets in lines 11–18, and through the weirs of a double jo in lines 21–27. The seaweed images are also reminiscent of Hitomaro (compare nos. 321–27). The junctural structure of vehicle and tenor in lines 11–18, and similar passages in other anonymous chōka (e.g., no. 1463, lines 7–14), give evidence of the continuity of technique that existed between nameless singers and Hitomaro, the perfecter of the chōka form. The double image of baby and bowman in lines 21–27, however, may be overstraining the potentialities of the jo, though it does manage to convey the speaker's frantic state of mind.

1470 [MYS XIII:3316/3302]

Ki no kuni no	Here beside the cove
Muro no e no he ni	Of Muro in the land of Ki
Chitose ni	We thought to live thus
Sawaru koto naku	A thousand years unhindered

5 Yorozuyo ni	In our happiness,
Kaku shi mo aramu to	Ten thousand ages in a love
Ōbune no	Secure as they
Omoitanomite	Who trust themselves to a great ship.
Idetachi no	Along the clean-swept
10 Kiyoki nagisa ni	Margin of the waves at Idetachi
Asanagi ni	In the morning calm
Kiyoru fukamiru	Deep sea pine washing on the shore,
Yūnagi ni	And in the evening calm
Kiyoru nawanori	Ropeweed washing on the shore:
15 Fukamiru no	The girl I held
Fukameshi kora o	Deep as deep sea pine in my heart,
Nawanori no	Did they think that if,
Hikeba tayu to ya	Ropeweed-like, they pulled us we would part?
Satobito no	Those hateful villagers
20 Yuki no tsudoi ni	Clustered in their busy throngs
Naku ko nasu	Have torn us apart,
Yuki torisaguri	As a bowman groping in his quiver—
Azusayumi	Like a crying baby
Yubara furiokoshi	Groping for its mother's breast—
25 Shinogiha o	Brandishes his bow,
Futatsu tabasami	Grasps two tempest-quelling arrows,
Hanachikemu	And sends them tearing forth:
Hito shi kuyashi mo	How I do loathe the people who did this,
Kouraku omoeba	When I think how well I loved that girl!

✳ The "Exchanges" section in Book XIII begins with a pair of folk songs that are slightly longer versions of no. 430, given in the "Hitomaro Collection" section. The two chōka (nos. 1471 and 1473) may be thought of as the original part of the exchange, with the envoys (lacking in the "Hitomaro Collection" version) later additions. The youth couches his poem to the maiden (no. 1471) in nonchalant and teasing terms, but the maiden's reply (no. 1473) reads its message correctly. Together the chōka imply a childhood romance of the type found in the Nō play *Izutsu*. Such songs are of course not those of particular individuals, but part of the common and constantly altered repertory of folksingers. The integration of setting, metaphor, and message is concise and effective in no. 1471. On the amorous activities of mountains, see no. 250-51. The measuring of the girl's height by the orange tree (instead of a well curb, as in *Izutsu*) must be hyperbole. The two envoys are conventional love complaints, and in their intensity are ill sorted with the naïve charm of the chōka.

"Exchanges"

1471–74
(1471–72)

[MYS XIII: 3319–22/3305–8]
[3319–20/3305–6]

Mono omowazu	Nothing on my mind,
Michi yuku yuku mo	Just trudging trudging down the road,
Aoyama o	Suddently I reared back
Furisakemireba	And gazed at the green mountain:
5 Tsutsujihana	Azalea blossom
Nioeotome	Pinkly glowing maiden,
Sakurabana	Cherry blossom
Sakaeotome	Youthful flowering maiden,
Nare o so mo	People say of you
10 Ware ni yosu to iu	You are getting close to me,
Ware o mo so	People say of me
Nare ni yosu to iu	I am getting close to you;
Arayama mo	Even the bare mountain
Hito shi yosureba	Should someone say it's getting close
15 Yosoru to zo iu	Would come close of its own accord:
Na ga kokoro yume	Watch what happens to your heart!

Envoy

Ika ni shite	What should I do
Koiyamu mono zo	To bring these love pangs to an end?
Ame tsuchi no	Though I pray for help
Kami o inoredo	To the gods of heaven and earth,
Are ya omoimasu	My longing only grows the more.

(1473–74)

[3321–22/3307–8]

Shikare koso	So it is indeed
Toshi no yatose o	I have waited through the years—
Kirikami no	Passing my childhood
Yochiko o sugi	When I kept my hair cut short,
Tachibana no	Passing the topmost
Hotsue o sugite	Branches of the orange tree—
Kono kawa no	Long and secretly
Shita ni mo nagaku	As these secret river depths
Na ga kokoro mate	Such a signal from your heart.

Envoy

Ame tsuchi no	I prayed to them all—
Kami o mo are wa	The gods of heaven, the gods of earth—
Inoriteki	This thing called love

Koi to iu mono wa	Has not ceased for a moment
Sane yamazukeri	To torment me as before.

❋ The formulaic quality of early song can be seen very clearly by comparing no. 1475, the first member of the following exchange, with nos. 2 and
167, more highly elaborated versions of a wooing song that always concludes with a maddening chorus of birds at daybreak. These songs are based
on the Japanese custom of the wooer making a nocturnal visit to his intended bride, and achieve their interest by observing his difficulties (nos. 2
and 1475) or his amorous activities (no. 167). Like no. 2, no. 1475 ends with
the hero still outside the door, calling to the woman on the other side. Her
answer (no. 1477) is quite unlike Nunakawahime's, however. There is no
promise of amorous delights to be obtained at the price of a little patience.
Instead, the "secret wife" (*komorizuma*) emphasizes her own problems—
namely, the awkward presence of her mother and father. She addresses her
lover as *sumeroki* ("sovereign"), which may point toward a lost context in
which the song formed part of a tale about an amorous Emperor. The wife's
envoy (no. 1478) is the probable source poem for no. 1006 by Lady Ōtomo
of Sakanoue. Its image of a black horse clattering over the stony riverbed
may imply that the "stepping" in the husband's envoy is also that of his
mount. However, it seems poorly matched with the complaint in the chōka
it follows and may be a later addition.

1475–78	[MYS XIII: 3324–27 / 3310–13]
(1475–76)	[3324–25 / 3310–11]

Komoriku no	When to Hatsuse,
Hatsuse no kuni ni	Hatsuse the hidden land,
Sayobai ni	I come a-calling,
Wa ga kitareba	Creeping in to you by night,
5 Tanagumori	The sky clouds up
Yuki wa furiku	And the snow begins to fall,
Sagumori	It gets all cloudy
Ame wa furiku	And the rain begins to fall;
No tsu tori	The bird of the moor,
10 Kigishi wa toyomu	The pheasant is booming,
Ie tsu tori	The bird of the house,
Kake mo naku	The cock is crowing, too;
Sayo wa ake	Dawn is in the sky,
Kono yo wa akenu	This night has reached the dawn:
15 Irite katsu nemu	I want to go in and sleep now,
Kono to hirakase	Please open this door for me.

Envoy

Komoriku no	Here in Hatsuse
Hatsuse oguni ni	The hidden little country
Tsuma shi areba	I have a wife:
Ishi wa fumedo mo	Though I've had to step on stones,
Nao shi kinikeri	Still I have come to her.

(1477–78)   [3326–27/3312–13]

	Komoriku no	Here in Hatsuse
	Hatsuse oguni ni	The hidden little country
	Yobai sesu	Where by night you come
	A ga sumeroki yo	Creeping in to me, my sovereign,
5	Okutoko ni	In the inner bed
	Haha wa inetari	My mother is sleeping,
	Todoko ni	In the outer bed
	Chichi wa inetari	My father is sleeping;
	Okitataba	If I get up
10	Haha shirinubeshi	Mother is sure to know,
	Idete ikaba	If I go out
	Chichi shirinubeshi	Father is sure to know.
	Nubatama no	The blackberry night
	Yo wa akeyukinu	Has already reached the dawn.
15	Kokodaku mo	Does a secret wife
	Omou goto naranu	Have to put up with all this?
	Komorizuma ka mo	Nothing goes the way I want.

Envoy

Kawa no se no	Why cannot they be
Ishi fumiwatari	Every night, those nights you come
Nubatama no	On your blackberry steed,
Kuroma no ku yo wa	Splashing across the cobbles
Tsune ni aranu ka mo	In the shallows of the river?

❋ A horse is the subject of the next exchange, between a self-sacrificing wife and her equally noble husband. The conjugality of the songs is touching, but the wife's effusion plays more heavily on the listener's heartstrings than the situation would seem to warrant, indeed is probably the most sentimental poem in *Man'yōshū*. Though the husband's reply, limited to one tanka, manages to avoid the banalities of bathetic prolixity, it is pitched to much the same too-melting note. These poems sound less like folk ballads than the condescending creations of well-intentioned popularizers. The "envoy in a certain text" (no. 1481), however, uses the mirror image in an interestingly complex way. "Dragonfly scarves" (*akizuhire*) are ones transparent as a dragonfly's wings.

1479-82   [MYS XIII: 3328-31 / 3314-17]
(1479-81)   [3328-30 / 3314-16]

Tsuginefu	Down the highway
Yamashiroji o	To peak-strung Yamashiro
Hitozuma no	Other husbands go
Uma yori yuku ni	Mounted on their horses' backs,
5 Onozuma shi	But my own husband
Kachi yori yukeba	Trudges down that road on foot.
Miru goto ni	Each time I see him
Ne nomi shi nakayu	Sobs come welling from my throat;
Soko omou ni	When I think of it
10 Kokoro shi itashi	My heart is sore within me.
Tarachine no	Take then the keepsake
Haha ga katami to	Of my mother who fed me
Wa ga moteru	The milk of her breasts,
Masomikagami ni	This flawless-fine mirror she left me,
15 Akizuhire	And my dragonfly scarves—
Oinamemochite	Pack them up and take them away,
Uma kae wagase	Go and buy a horse, my love.

Envoy

Izumigawa	Izumi River—
Watarize fukami	So deep is the crossing place
Wa ga seko ga	I fear my dear one's
Tabiyukigoromo	Travel garments will be wet,
Nurehitamu ka mo	Sopping from fording over.

The envoy in a certain text reads:

Masokagami	A flawless mirror
Moteredo ware wa	Shows me nothing to my good
Shirushi nashi	Though I keep it close—
Kimi ga kachi yori	All I can see is the trudging
Nazumiyuku mireba	Of my weary love afoot.

(1482)   [3331 / 3317]

Uma kawaba	If I buy a horse,
Imo kachi naramu	Still my girl must go afoot;
Yoshieyashi	Let us be content—

| Ishi wa fumu to mo | Though we walk upon the stones, |
| Wa wa futari yukamu | We two shall go together. |

❋ The "Laments" section in Book XIII begins with a major banka in the grand manner associated with Hitomaro and presumably developed by him. Not only is the poem in Hitomaro's style, but it draws extensively from the actual text of no. 341, his lament for Prince Takechi, and other lines come from nos. 325 and 328. Because this lament is set in the time of the Fujiwara capital (694–710), it has been suggested that the Prince for whom it was composed may have been Prince Yuge (d. 699; see nos. 279–84 and 874–78) or Emperor Mommu himself (r. 697–707), who died at the age of twenty-four. Even given the existence of a common body of formulas—pillow words and other recurrent phraseology—the unknown singer's debt to Hitomaro is unmistakable. Both the opening and closing of the poem are closely adapted from the lament for Prince Takechi, as are lines 67–72, describing the funeral procession. Hitomaro was a contemporary of the author, and the poem's wholesale adoption of his lines, along with its imitation of his style, suggests the currency of his work during his own lifetime. The funeral of Prince Kusakabe (no. 328–30) took place in 689, followed by the funerals of Prince Kawashima (no. 336–37), Prince Takechi (no. 341–44), and Princess Asuka (no. 338–40) in 691, 696, and 700. If Hitomaro's laments were recited aloud on these occasions, they must still have been echoing in the ears of whoever composed no. 1483–84.

The chōka opens with the formula for expressing awe and continues through the many-one technique (lines 3–16) to focus on the particular lord of whom the poet sings. As with Prince Kusakabe, his time of full flourishing has not come (lines 17–22), which makes it seem unlikely that the subject could be a reigning sovereign like Mommu. In three parallel passages (lines 23–43) his seasonal activities (summer omitted) are described. Among them is kunimi, the rite of "land-viewing," a monarchical function that suggests the deceased might be Mommu after all. The location of Uetsuki has not been established; it may have been near the present city of Yamatokōriyama, a short distance southwest of Nara. *Matsu* ("pines") in line 26 has the mock epithet *tōtsuhito* ("faraway person") as the object of *matsu* in the sense of "wait."

It is interesting that the other two seasonal activities are private in nature and balance the elegant appreciation of dew-laden bush clover against the masculine sport of hunting with bow and arrow. The conventional summing up of the happy situation before the intrusion of mortality (lines 45–52) is suddenly and effectively reversed by the introduction of the weeping speaker in line 53. Disbelief (lines 54, 63–64) punctuates the evidence of death, presented, as in no. 341, by the image of white-clad courtiers and a palace transformed into a shrine by white funeral decorations. The stunned reaction of the speaker in lines 63–66 occupies the place in the pattern of grief taken up in Hitomaro's laments by extended descriptions of irrational behavior, with analogies to birds and beasts. Mention of Iware (line 70, and again in the envoy) permits use of the mock epithet *tsuno sahau* ("where vines swarm"), applying to the element *iwa* ("rock"), as in the opening of no. 325. The katami at the poem's end turns out to be a pine tree, presumably one of those under which the Prince (or Sovereign) climbed to view the land. The envoy, like several other laments in early Japanese poetry, equates a cloud with the dead (for other examples, see nos. 187, 287, 354, 363, and 1315–16).

1483-84   [MYS XIII: 3338-39/3324-25]

Kakemaku mo	I would call it to mind,
Aya ni kashikoshi	But my thoughts are lost in awe:
Fujiwara no	At Fujiwara,
Miyako shimimi ni	Filling all that royal city
5 Hito wa shi mo	There are throngs of men—
Michite aredo mo	They overflow the streets;
Kimi wa shi mo	There are many lords
Ōku imasedo	Dwelling in princely splendor.
Yukimukau	But to the royal gates
10 Toshi no o nagaku	Of the lord whom I have served
Tsukaekoshi	While years came and went,
Kimi ga mikado o	Long in their unending chain,
Ame no goto	I have lifted my face,
Aogite mitsutsu	Gazing up as to heaven;
15 Kashikokedo	I have given my trust,
Omoitanomite	Humble before their power.
Itsu shi ka mo	For the time to come
Hi tarashimashite	When his days would be fulfilled,
Mochizuki no	Waxing to greatness
20 Tatawashikemu to	Like the brimming circle of the moon,
A ga omou	I waited, expectant
Miko no mikoto wa	Of His Highness our most noble Prince:
Haru sareba	He who in springtime
Uetsuki ga ue no	Over Uetsuki ascended
25 Tōtsuhito	By the roadway
Matsu no shitaji yu	Leading up beneath the pines
Noborashite	(*Pines for the one far off*),
Kunimi asobashi	There to gaze upon his land;
Nagatsuki no	Or who in showery

30 Shigure no aki wa
   Ōtono no
Migiri shimimi ni
   Tsuyu oite
Nabikeru hagi o
35   Tamadasuki
Kakete shinowashi
   Miyuki furu
Fuyu no ashita wa
   Sashiyanagi
40 Nehariazusa o
   Ōmite ni
Torashitamaite
   Asobashishi
Wa ga ōkimi o
45   Keburi tatsu
Haru no hi kurashi
   Masokagami
Miredo akaneba
   Yorozuyo ni
50 Kaku shi mogamo to
   Ōbune no
Tanomeru toki ni
   Naku ware
Me ka mo matoeru
55   Ōtono o
Furisakemireba
   Shirotae ni
Kazarimatsurite
   Uchihi sasu
60 Miya no toneri mo
   Tae no ho no
Asaginu kereba
   Ime ka mo
Utsutsu ka mo to
65   Kumoriyo no
Matoeru aida ni
   Asamo yoshi
Kinoe no michi yu
   Tsuno sahau
70 Iware o mitsutsu
   Kamuhaburi
Haburimatsureba

Long-Month autumn admired
   With a wonder close
As a jewel-sash to the heart
   The bush clover bending
Over flagstone walks beneath
   The eaves of his great hall,
Weighed down with the plenteous dew;
   Or who of a morning
In the snow-falling winter
   Took his well-strung bow,
Catalpa tough as willow root,
   In his mighty hand,
And sallied forth to sport,
   Roaming the open fields:
This was the great lord on whom
   Through the smoke-rising
Days of spring all day till dusk
   I gazed unwearied
As on a flawless mirror,
   Wishing for that time
To go on ten thousand ages,
   Confident as they
Who place their trust in a great ship.
   Then—I was weeping
(Were my eyes wandering lost?),
   I bent back my head
To gaze aloft at the great hall:
   They had adorned it
With the white of barken cloth,
   And the servitors
In the palace bright with sun
   Were dressed in hemp—
Hemp like tassels of the fibrous bark.
   Was it a dream?
Could it be that this was real?
   While in clouded night
I was lost and wandering,
   Down Kinoe Road—
Kinoe called of the hempen skirt—
   Looking toward Iware,
Where swarming vines crawl on the rocks,
   They went to burial,
To reverent burial of a god.

724

	Yuku michi no	But there is for me
	Tazuki o shirani	No way to find the road to take;
75	Omoedo mo	It does no good
	Shirushi o nami	However much I long for him,
	Nagekedo mo	There is no end
	Okuka o nami	To all the sighs I sigh for him.
	Ōmisode	Therefore, though this pine
80	Yukifureshi matsu o	That his princely sleeve brushed by
	Koto towanu	Is but a tree
	Ki ni wa ari to mo	That has not power of speech,
	Aratama no	As the rough gems
	Tatsu tsuki goto ni	Of the months arise and pass,
85	Ama no hara	As if to heaven's plain
	Furisakemitsutsu	Let me lift my head and gaze at it
	Tamadasuki	In yearning close
	Kakete shinowana	As a jewel-sash to the heart,
	Kashikoku ari to mo	Though I may tremble, lost in sacred awe.

Envoy

Tsuno sahau	On Mount Iware,
Iware no yama ni	Where swarming vines crawl on the rocks,
Shirotae ni	Rests a cloud
Kakareru kumo wa	In the white of barken cloth—
Sumera miko ka mo	Could it be our sovereign Prince?

❉ In contrast to the flowing Hitomaro style that employs parallels to vary the cadence, the rocking-horse rhythm of the following lament is dominated by them totally. With its triplet ending and insistent repetitions, the poem belongs to the world of early song. As such it demonstrates the possibilities as well as the limitations of a prosody based on preparation-conclusion and parallelism. The a-b-a'-b' pattern marches forward so mechanically that it brings about exact duplication (a-b-a-b) in lines 11-14. Lines 1-2, 15-16, and 29-30 stand outside the pattern, which is enlarged to a-b-c-d/a'-b'-c'-d' in lines 21-28. The regular alternation within four-line units opens up because of this expansion, but the overall effect does not escape monotony. The other basic structural feature, preparation-conclusion, is handled more artfully. The cormorants in the preparation, a variety of jo, exist meaningfully in the conclusion as well. They provide the trout that the remorseful husband denied to his deceased wife. Not only that, but the verb that expresses their feeding, *kuwashime* ("cause to eat"), introduces by phonetic duplication the adjective *kuwashi* ("fine and slender") by which the wife is characterized. The early and persistent Japanese delight in wordplay functions here to good effect. The image of the woman's death in lines 15–16 is a powerful version of the disappearance motif, usually expressed as flight or a receding into the distance. And the ironic negative analogies of lines 21–28 are appropriate to the loss of a wife, as well as providing complex overtones in *tama*, which means "soul" as well as "gem." Thus the poem combines elements of artistry and naïveté.

1485 [MYS XIII:3344/3330]

Komoriku no
Hatsuse no kawa no
Kami tsu se ni
U o yatsu kazuke
Shimo tsu se ni
U o yatsu kazuke
Kami tsu se no
Ayu o kuwashime
Shimo tsu se no
Ayu o kuwashime
Kuwashi imo ni
Ayu o oshimi
Kuwashi imo ni
Ayu o oshimi
Naguru sa no
Tōzakariite
Omou sora
Yasukenaku ni
Nageku sora
Yasukenaku ni
Kinu koso ba
Sore yarenureba
Tsugitsutsu mo
Mata mo au to ie
Tama koso ba
O no taenureba
Kukuritsutsu
Mata mo au to ie
Mata mo awanu mono wa
Tsuma ni shi arikeri

Along the river
Of Hatsuse the hidden land
In the upper shallows
I keep eight cormorants diving,
In the lower shallows
I keep eight cormorants diving.
From the upper shallows
I give them the little trout to eat,
From the lower shallows
I give them the little trout to eat.
Little the trout I gave
To my fine and slender love,
Little the trout I gave
To my fine and slender love;
Like a hurled arrow
She has fled afar from me.
This brooding emptiness
Is no easy thing to bear,
This sighing emptiness
Is no easy thing to bear.
When you tear your clothes,
Clothes they say can be mended—
You sew them together
And the torn edges meet again;
When you break a string
And the gems go scattering,
Gems can be strung again—
They say snapped ends can be mated:
But the mate that you have lost
You will never meet again.

❋ The next poem, also early in technique, with its simple parallels and 5-3-7 ending, is a lament only if the last three lines are considered a metonymy. Osaka Mountain near Hatsuse is the site of both Emperor Jomei's tumulus and the tomb of his daughter Princess Kagami. Otherwise the poem is a song in praise of mountains, very similar to no. 147, attributed to Emperor Yūryaku. In its "environmentalist" ending, however, the *Man'yōshū* version is reminiscent of no. 650, one of the poems on the death of the sailor Arao.

1486   [MYS XIII: 3345 / 3331]

Komoriku no	Hidden
Hatsuse no yama	Hatsuse Mountain,
Aohata no	Green-bannered
Osaka no yama wa	Osaka Mountain—
5 Hashiride no	In the way they run,
Yoroshiki yama no	How good are these mountains;
Idetachi no	In the way they rise,
Kuwashiki yama zo	How fine are these mountains:
Atarashiki	These precious
10 Yama no	Mountains—
Aremaku oshi mo	How bitter will be their waste.

❋ The last selection from Book XIII is a lament not for an individual, but for mankind in general. It is also an early and explicit expression of the theme of man's ephemerality, a theme implicit in Hitomaro and of great concern to Chinese-influenced poets like Okura and Yakamochi, but not characteristic of ancient song, to which no. 1487 structurally belongs. The straightforward comparison of people to blossoms contrasts with the ancient rhetorical technique of preposited juxtaposition, as well as with the allegorical method extensively employed in *Man'yōshū*. Theme and technique are thus at odds with structure in suggesting formative foreign influence.

1487   [MYS XIII: 3346 / 3332]

Takayama to	The high mountain
Umi to koso ba	And the sea—yes, they:
Yama nagara	Only a mountain,
Kaku mo utsushiku	But the mountain is real;
Umi nagara	Only the sea,
Shika tada narame	But the sea is always there.
Hito wa hanamono so	People are but blossoms,
Utsusemi yohito	People of the mortal world.

Book XIV

Book XIV is the only book of *Man'yōshū* organized on a geographical basis. It is composed of Azumauta, or "Songs of the Eastland," tanka from provinces extending eastward from Tōtōmi and Shinano. Ninety poems of known provenance are followed by 140 whose province of origin was unknown to the compilers. The standard categories of zōka, sōmon, hiyuka, and banka form the main internal organization, with grouping by province (where known) as the second level. Many of the poems employ eastern dialect, and a rustic ambience is prevalent throughout the book. The poems are often thought of as genuine folk songs, but the fact that they are all in tanka form requires a careful definition of the term "folk." As a classical form of comparatively late evolution, the tanka was not the primary vehicle of ancient oral composition, whose origins are to be sought in the archaic proto-chōka, the katauta, and the double katauta or sedōka. But the tanka was unquestionably in widespread use in the seventh and eighth centuries, as its presence in the chronicles and its overwhelming numerical dominance in *Man'yōshū* attest. The problem posed by the status of tanka composition in Book XIV is not essentially different from that encountered in Books XI and XII and other places where courtly authorship is unlikely. It is an unsolved problem, but there is adequate evidence to show that untutored easterners were indeed composing tanka in the middle of the Nara period (witness the songs of the sakimori, nos. 1222–44), whether or not their compositions deserve the label of "folk song."

When the cuckoo sings in the wild fields of the up-country of Shinano ("Shinanu" in eastern dialect), the farmers know the time is ripe for transplanting rice in their paddies—that is one interpretation of the following poem. But the last line refers to the passing of a season rather than to its arrival. It may be merely spring that has passed, since the cuckoo is a summer bird. Or it could be the season for love, or the season of waiting for love. The compilers did not find these resonances in the poem, however, for they placed it among the Miscellaneous rather than the Love verses.

"Songs of the Eastland"

1488   [MYS XIV : 3366 / 3352]

Shinanu naru	In the wild moorland
Suga no arano ni	Of Suga in Shinanu
Hototogisu	Hear the cuckoo cry—
Naku koe kikeba	When you listen to his song
Toki suginikeri	You know the time has gone by.

The above is a poem from Shinanu Province.

✳ Love in the provinces is the subject of the next series. Kihe in Tōtōmi (= Tōtsu Ōmi) is thought to have gotten its name from the skilled (*ki*) workers of a weavers' occupational group (*he*, or *be*) that settled in the area. The poem refers to such local occupations in its *jo*, and in its main statement to the preferred activity they suggest to the speaker.

"Love Poems"

1489   [MYS XIV: 3368 / 3354]

Kihehito no	In the dappled quilts
Madarabusuma ni	Of the Kihe folk they stuff
Wata sawada	Batches of silk floss—
Ininamashi mono	How I wish I'd snuggled in
Imo ga odoko ni	Like that in the bed of my girl!

The above is [one of] two poems from Tōtsu Ōmi Province.

✳ Farther east in Suruga, the way of a vine with a rock suggests an image of dependence to an *ama* girl who can no longer cling to her mother.

1490   [MYS XIV: 3375 / 3359]

Suruga no umi	To the rocky shore
Oshihe ni ouru	Of the sea of Suruga
Hamatsuzura	Clings the beach-creeper:
Imashi o tanomi	Just so have I clung to you
Haha ni tagainu	And gone against my mother.

The above is [one of] five poems from Suruga Province.

✳ On Mount Ashigara in Sagami (Sagamu) Province the snares are no doubt set for birds or animals, but imply the local opposition that the two lovers have cleverly eluded. Whatever game has been caught merely distracts attention from the Saikakuesque pair intent on their immediate concerns.

1491   [MYS XIV: 3377 / 3361]

Ashigara no	On Ashigara
Ote mo konomo ni	Here and on the yonder side
Sasu wana no	They set their snares—
Kanaru ma shizumi	And while the racket quiets down
Koro are himo toku	That girl and I undress.

❋ The next poem is one of direct expression, devoid of metaphor. Kamakura is the place now occupied by the city of that name, and Minanose River is a short creek now called Inase.

1492 [MYS XIV: 3383 / 3366]

Makanashimi	Haunted by her face,
Sane ni wa wa yuku	I set off to sleep with her—
Kamakura no	At Kamakura
Minanosegawa ni	Will the Minanose River
Shio mitsunamu ka	Be flooded at high tide?

❋ "Ashigari" in the next three poems is a variant pronunciation of "Ashigara." The first is based on the technique of repetition, the second on that of comparison. These invitations would fit well into the context of country revels, the utagaki, sometimes held on mountaintops (see no. 587–88).

1493 [MYS XIV: 3386 / 3369]

Ashigari no	Why do you pillow
Mama no kosuge no	On a pillow made of sedge,
Sugamakura	Of the little sedges
Aze ka makasamu	On the bank at Ashigari?
Koro se tamakura	Girl, come pillow on my arm!

1494 [MYS XIV: 3387 / 3370]

Ashigari no	Are you a flower-bride,
Hakone no nero no	A soft maidenhair fern
Nikogusa no	From the upland fields
Hana tsu tsuma nare ya	Of Hakone at Ashigari,
Himo tokazu nemu	That you never sleep with sash undone?

❋ For the possible significance of the next poem, see no. 942; the fearsome deity of Ashigara is also alluded to in no. 692. A passage in *Kojiki* relates how Yamato Takeru no Mikoto killed the deity of Ashigara in its incarnation as a white deer.

1495 [MYS XIV: 3388 / 3371]

Ashigari no	Overcome with awe
Misaka kashikomi	On the Ashigari slope,
Kumoriyo no	I spoke it forth,

A ga shitabae o   The thing that dark as clouded night
Kochidetsuru kamo   I kept secret in my heart.

The above are [five of] twelve poems from Sagamu Province.

✳ From Musashi (Muzashi) come two poems giving local scenes and customs. The first ties its jo into the main statement by phonetic repetition—
sarasu ("bleach") / *sarasara ni* ("so helplessly"). *Sarasara* also is onomatopoeic for "rustling" (of the homespun cloth), so that juncture is by semantic as well as phonetic doubling. As often, the jo gives a glimpse of a possible world in which the poem's main concern can be pictured. The next poem depicts scapulamancy, the burning of the shoulder bone of a deer for oracular purposes. The diviner read the oracle in the cracks caused by the fire. Just how a name would be determined by this means is not clear. Presumably the young woman is trying to conceal her lover's name from her inquisitive parents.

1496   [MYS XIV: 3390 / 3373]

    Tamagawa ni   By Tama River
    Sarasu tezukuri   Rustling homespun out to bleach:
        Sarasara ni   Rustling, trembling,
    Nani so kono ko no   Why, oh why, so helplessly
    Kokoda kanashiki   Do I dote on that darling girl?

1497   [MYS XIV: 3391 / 3374]

    Muzashino ni   On Muzashi moor
    Urahe kata yaki   The diviner burned the bone—
        Masade ni mo   Sure, the truth was there:
    Noranu kimi ga na   Your name that I'd never spoken
    Ura ni denikeri   Came out in the signs.

The above are [two of] nine poems from Muzashi Province.

✳ The following from Kazusa (Kamitsufusa) Province is in the genre of home thoughts from abroad. As in Hitomaro's nos. 321 and 325 and elsewhere, mountains are a barrier between a man and a woman.

1498   [MYS XIV: 3401 / 3383]

    Umaguta no   Hidden by the peaks
    Nero ni kakurii   Of the Umaguta Hills,

Kaku dani mo	Home's so far away—
Kuni no tōkaba	How I'm going to crave the sight
Na ga me hori semu	Of the very eyes of you!

The above is [one of] two poems from Kamitsufusa Province.

❋ The importunings of sexual desire are treated in a pair of poems from separate provinces. In the first, from Shimōsa (Shimotsufusa), a young woman of Kazushika (see nos. 553–55 and 572–73) is willing to commit a sacrilege in order to meet her lover. As an unmarried daughter she alone remains in the house to offer the first fruits to the god at the annual rite of harvest (see no. 201). Other family members are forbidden to come near, creating an opportunity for privacy too good to be missed. *Niodori no* ("grebe-plunging") is a mock epithet for Kazushika through *kazuku* ("dive"). In the second poem, from Hitachi Province, an amorous man is once again waiting to come in to a woman. The situation is reminiscent of the tale of Tamana in no. 577–78, except that Tamana needed no advice from third parties. The advice and the mention of Mount Tsukuha in the jo (see no. 587–88) suggest that this is an utagaki poem, and that what the "young lord" (*kimi*) cannot pass by is not a house, but the place on the mountain where one of the merrymaking maidens is standing.

1499   [MYS XIV:3404/3386]

Niodori no	Grebe-plunging
Kazushika wase o	Kazushika's early harvest
Nie su to mo	I serve to the god,
Sono kanashiki o	But shall I keep my own sweetheart
To ni tateme ya mo	Standing outside the door?

The above is [one of] four poems from Shimotsufusa Province.

1500   [MYS XIV:3406/3388]

Tsukuhane no	Up on Tsukuha
Nero ni kasumii	On the summit trailing mist:
Sugikateni	He can't trail on by,
Ikizuku kimi o	The young lord there sighing—
Inete yarasane	Bring him, bed him, let him go.

The above is [one of] ten poems from Hitachi Province.

❋ A road was opened into the wild mountains of Shinano in 713, a date that gives an approximate time of composition to the following poem, if not to others in the collection. The advice is reminiscent of that in no. 87, but strikes a more practical note. *Kutsu* ("shoes") could refer to a variety of footgear, such as straw sandals.

1501   [MYS XIV: 3417/3399]

Shinanuji wa	The Shinanu Road
Ima no harimichi	Is a road that's just been cut—
Karibane ni	Don't step on the stumps
Ashi fumashimu na	And give your feet a bruising:
Kutsu hake wagase	Wear your shoes, my man.

The above is [one of] four poems from Shinanu Province.

❋ In the method of harvesting hemp referred to in poem 1502, the reapers clasped the stalk (up to two meters in height) and bent backward to pull it down on top of themselves. This image swings around the pivot of line 3 into an expression of unsatisfied desire. Hemp harvesting was women's work, and the speaker of the poem is probably a woman. As a "folk song" it reads like a mockery of female lust.

1502   [MYS XIV: 3422/3404]

Kamitsukeno	In Kamitsukeno,
Aso no masomura	In Aso thickets of the hemp:
Kakimudaki	With arms wrapped round you
Nuredo akanu o	Down I lie—what shall I do?
Ado ka a ga semu	I can never get enough!

The above is [one of] twenty-two poems from Kamitsukeno Province.

❋ The sturdy, rustic simile in the following poem probably refers to the new leaves of the oak, and thus is an image of flourishing youth. The question means "Whom will she marry?"

1503   [MYS XIV: 3443/3424]

Shimotsukeno	She who's like the oaks,
Mikamo no yama no	The young oaks of Mount Mikamo
Konara nosu	In Shimotsukeno,
Maguwashi koro wa	That girl so fine to look at,
Ta ga ke ka motamu	Whose dishes will she hold?

The above is [one of] two poems from Shimotsukeno Province.

❋ Michinoku and Tsukushi were at the northern and southern extremities of Japan, a fact that augments the polarity that is the subject of the next poem. It seems likely the composition reflects an experience of a sakimori.

1504   [MYS XIV: 3446/3427]

Tsukushi naru	For a Tsukushi girl
Niou ko yue ni	Blushing in her loveliness
Michinoku no	I now undo
Katori otome no	The sash that a maiden tied
Yuishi himo toku	At Katori in Michinoku.

The above is [one of] three poems from Michinoku Province.

❋ The hiyuka in Book XIV, as elsewhere in *Man'yōshū*, are love poems. The first is not a complete allegory, but rather in the kibutsu mode of image and application. *Miotsukushi* ("channel stakes") are markers stuck in a bay or river to indicate a navigable channel, and are thus something to be trusted. The poem seems to be a woman's complaint at not having been taken advantage of. The man could have told her the lies she wanted to hear, allowing her to fall in love. As it is, she has had no chance to launch her boat at all. The word *miotsukushi* conceals the phrase *mi o tsukushi* ("exhaust oneself"), something that Heian poets were well aware of. It is not clear whether the author of no. 1505 intended this extra meaning. If so, it could apply to the (nonexistent) efforts of the failed lover.

"Metaphorical Poems"

1505   [MYS XIV: 3448/3429]

Tōtsu Ōmi	In Tōtsu Ōmi
Inasa hosoe no	Up Inasa Creek there stand
Miotsukushi	The channel stakes—
Are o tanomete	You could have made me follow
Asamashi mono o	And left me high and dry.

The above is a poem from Tōtsu Ōmi Province.

❋ The next poem is a true hiyuka, unified on the level of the metaphor. "Rowing back and forth" suggests the actions of a hesitant lover, a man who "has his reasons" for passing in front of a woman's door.

1506   [MYS XIV: 3449/3430]

Shida no ura o	Out on Shida Bay
Asa kogu fune wa	Boats do not row of a morning

Yoshi nashi ni	Without a reason—
Kogurame ka mo yo	Sure, they have their reasons
Yoshi kosarurame	For rowing to and fro.

The above is a poem from Suruga Province.

❋ In no. 1507 a lover compares his plight to the way newly hewn boats are brought down the mountains, held from behind to keep them from turning end over end. An invisible cord seems to be under similar tension as he tries to go home from visiting his girl. The comparison, structured into a jo, should make the poem kibutsu rather than hiyuka.

1507   [MYS XIV: 3450/3431]

Ashigari no	With a taut hawser
Akina no yama ni	Tied astern they inch their boats
Hiko fune no	Down Mount Akina
Shirihikashi mo yo	In Ashigari: a backward drag
Kokoba ko ga ta ni	Holds me, and all for that girl.

The above is [one of] three poems from Sagamu Province.

❋ For alder stain as a love metaphor, see nos. 260 and 1538. The following poem employs the trope in true hiyuka fashion, maintaining but not explaining the allegory. Alder dye, made from the fruit and bark of the tree, was brown or black. It is surprising that these dark colors served as love images no less than the warm and bright *murasaki* ("purple"; no. 753) and *kurenai* ("crimson"; no. 1426). It is probably not so much the color itself as the action of staining that is suggestive of an altered state of feeling. Alder trees were known for rubbing off their color on the garments of passersby (no. 488).

1508   [MYS XIV: 3454/3435]

Ikahoro no	Let the alder field
Soi no harihara	That lies by Ikahoro
Wa ga kinu ni	Stain my garments,
Tsukiyorashi mo yo	For its dye will suit me well—
Hitae to omoeba	I know it comes straight through.

The above is [one of] three poems from Kamitsukeno Province.

❋ The hiyu in no. 1509 is an unstrung bow, and its application is to a man who tries to revive a long-dead love affair.

1509 [MYS XIV: 3456 / 3437]

Michinoku no	A stout spindle bow
Adatara mayumi	From Adatara in Michinoku:
Hajikiokite	Leave it long unstrung
Serashimekinaba	And then try to bend it back—
Tsura hakame ka mo	Are you going to nock that string?

The above is a poem from Michinoku Province.

❊ The rest of the poems in Book XIV are from unknown provinces. They begin with a section of zōka, which as it happens are mostly about amorous matters. The compilers of the Azumauta seem to have found love the most engrossing topic among the inhabitants of eastern Japan. The first poem is a traveler's song. The official courier system of the Nara period maintained a network of stables along the main routes, where mounts were kept in readiness for travelers on official business. Such government horses were distinguished by the bells they wore (see no. 112). *Hayuma umaya* ("swift-horse horsebarn") makes a pretty series of syllables (*Fayuma umaya* in Old Japanese), and there seems to be no doubt about the oral nature of this lilting song. In a song any traveler might sing, it is pointless to inquire what sort of girl the *imo* might be, whether stablekeeper's daughter, local harlot, or fantasy sweetheart.

"Miscellaneous Poems"

1510 [MYS XIV: 3458 / 3439]

Suzu ga ne no	At the jingle-bell
Hayuma umaya no	Swift-horse horsebarn wellhead
Tsutsumii no	Let me have water,
Mizu o tamaena	Have it from the rock-walled well,
Imo ga tadate yo	Have it from my true love's hand.

❊ The sense of the immodest proposal in no. 1511 depends on interpreting *yochi* ("children of like age," "playmates") as a lewd metaphor for the sexual parts of the man and woman; *ko* ("child") in the last line also enters into this rustic argot. Risqué talk is no guarantee of folk origins, but it seems plausible that this version of the fair maid surprised represents a class of ribald songs appropriate to the most unbuttoned stages of communal celebration.

1511 [MYS XIV: 3459 / 3440]

Kono kawa ni	Here in the river
Asana arau ko	Washing your greens in the morning, girl,

Nare mo are mo	You and me—we both
Yochi o so moteru	Have a little playmate—so,
Ide ko tabarani	Come on, give your missy to me.

✻ It has been proposed that the following poem from the sōmon section is a rice-hulling woman's work song. Rice was hulled with a wooden pestle over a meter in length, grasped firmly at the middle and brought down repeatedly on the grains in a wooden mortar.

"Love Songs"

1512   [MYS XIV: 3478 / 3459]

Ine tsukeba	These cracked hands of mine,
Kakaru a ga te o	Hardened from the rice-hulling—
Koyoi mo ka	Tonight once again
Tono no wakugo ga	Will the young lord of the manor
Torite nagekamu	Hold them in his and sigh?

✻ The "evening omen" (*yūke*) was an augury taken by interpreting the words of passersby at a crossroads in the evening.

1513   [MYS XIV: 3488 / 3469]

Yūke ni mo	By evening omen
Koyoi to noraro	It's been said tonight's the night:
Wa ga sena wa	Husband, where are you?
Aze so mo koyoi	I don't see you on the path—
Yoshiro kimasanu	Heavens, why don't you come?

✻ Adultery as a subtheme of the general topic of love is often clued by the term *hitozuma*, "another's wife" (or "husband"), which appears fifteen times in *Man'yōshū*. The following halfhearted complaint hardly speaks from the same passion as nos. 861 and 1380.

1514   [MYS XIV: 3491 / 3472]

Hitozuma to	Why do people say,
Aze ka so o iwamu	"She's somebody else's wife . . ."?
Shikaraba ka	If that's how it is,
Tonari no kinu o	Can't we even borrow
Karite kinawamo	Our neighbor's clothes to wear?

✳ In no. 1515 the poet uses *osagi* (eastern dialect for *usagi*, "rabbit") to introduce *osaosa* ("hardly at all"). The image of the young man as hunter applies to both halves of the poem. A world remote from the capital is strongly evoked.

1515   [MYS XIV : 3550 / 3529]

Toya no no ni	Out on Toya moor
Osagi nerawari	Stalking coneys in the grass:
Osaosa mo	Lying in wait,
Nenae ko yue ni	But not lying yet with her—
Haha ni korohae	And still her mother scolds me!

✳ *Ayaokado* ("it is dangerous—but"), the swing line in no. 1516, balances vehicle and tenor in a stasis of terror and desire in another exploration of the *hitozuma* theme.

1516   [MYS XIV : 3561 / 3539]

Azu no ue ni	The danger of it:
Koma o tsunagite	Tying my horse on the lip
Ayaokado	Of a crumbling ravine—
Hitozuma koro o	Yet she is my breath of life,
Iki ni wa ga suru	That girl the wife of another.

✳ The next poem, structured into an explicit simile, plays off *sero* ("rapids") against *sero* ("sweetheart").

1517   [MYS XIV : 3570 / 3548]

Naru sero ni	Like driftwood
Kotsu no yosu nasu	Down the roaring rapids
Itonokite	They come milling,
Kanashike sero ni	Bobbing around my sweetheart,
Hito sae yosu mo	My special man, those girls.

✳ Another rice-pounding song plays on *ina* and *ine*. The woman complains that she has been left to sleep alone despite her willingness—pounding the rice (*ine*) with a big push (*oshite*) does not mean she's saying *ina* ("No!"). The play of the pestle here is unmistakably sexual in connotation. As in no. 1502 the intent may be to burlesque female desire.

738

1518 [MYS XIV: 3572 / 3550]

Oshite ina to	Forcing out a "No!"
Ine wa tsukanedo	As I hull the rice?—not I!
Nami no ho no	No, but a wave-crest
Itaburashi mo yo	Crashing on the shore was I
Kiso hitori nete	Last night as I lay alone.

✳ When waves break across a reef, the sea grasses growing along the ridge rise with the force of the water and thrash about in wild agitation. The jo in no. 1519 employs this image as the counterpart of the way a woman starts up anxiously and goes to the door to look for her lover when overwhelmed by a wave of emotion. The seaweed *wakame* carries a second meaning of "young woman."

1519 [MYS XIV: 3585 / 3563]

Hitagata no	As the maiden-weed
Iso no wakame no	Growing on the reefs of Hita rises
Tachimidae	In a wild wavering,
Wa o ka matsunamo	Has she waited for me night by night,
Kiso mo koyoi mo	Ever starting, trembling, to her feet?

✳ Book XIV includes five anonymous sakimori poems of the sort collected more copiously in Book XX (nos. 1222–44). Like most of those, they deal with the pain of parting as the conscript soldier leaves his village for Naniwa. All five are in the mode of direct expression that does not use the device of the jo, though the first two, an exchange between a sakimori and his wife or sweetheart, employ metaphorical fantasy according to the pattern "I wish I / you could be . . . ," expressive of intimacy and surrender between friends and lovers. (For other examples, see nos. 104, 873, 1148, 1153, 1210–11, and 1214.)

"Songs of the Sakimori"

1520–21 [MYS XIV: 3589–90 / 3567–68]

(1520) [3589 / 3567]

Okite ikaba	Her face will haunt me
Imo wa makanashi	If I leave her when I go—
Mochite yuku	Would that she could be
Azusa no yumi no	The grip on my catalpa bow
Yuzuka ni mogamo	That I have always with me.

(1521)   [3590/3568]

    Okureite   To be left behind
  Koiba kurushi mo   Yearning will be hard for me—
     Asagari no   Would I could become
  Kimi ga yumi ni mo   The bow you take out hunting
  Naramashi mono o   On the morning hunt, my love.

The above two poems are an exchange.

❋ The next two poems form a pair: dawn departure and evening encampment, a woman weeping and a man remembering. Leaves of reeds and mallards' cries in no. 1523 suggest Naniwa (see no. 468), the assembly point for sakimori heading west to Tsukushi. This moody poem evokes the fine melancholy of the courtly tradition.

1522   [MYS XIV:3591/3569]

    Sakimori ni   When in the dawnlight
  Tachishi asake no   I went out the metal-bound gate
    Kanatode ni   To serve as a soldier
  Tabanare oshimi   My sweet girl was crying—
  Nakishi kora wa mo   She was loath to let me go.

1523   [MYS XIV:3592/3570]

    Ashi no ha ni   When the evening mist
  Yūgiri tachite   Rises over leaves of reeds
    Kamo ga ne no   And the mallards' cries
  Samuki yūhe shi   Echo coldly in the dusk
  Na o ba shinowamu   I shall be longing for you.

❋ The situation is not clear in no. 1524—where has the sakimori left his wife, and why? He seems bewildered as well as anxious. The "dread command" (no. 1222) has necessitated desperate domestic rearrangements; or perhaps the wife has followed her soldier husband and fallen ill along the way.

1524   [MYS XIV:3593/3571]

    Onozuma o   My wife—I left her
  Hito no sato ni oki   In a village of strangers;
    Ohohoshiku   Anxiously
  Mitsutsu so kinuru   Turning to look back, I came:
  Kono michi no aida   All this time on the road.

❋ A brief section of hiyuka follows the sakimori poems. In no. 1525 *yamakazurakage* ("cypress moss") contains the word *kage*, meaning both "shade" and "chaplet," repeated in line 4. These intertwined images (*kazura* also means both "vine" and "chaplet") all stand for a desirable woman, no easy prize to win and not to be left to "wither on the vine."

"Metaphorical Poems"

1525   [MYS XIV : 3595 / 3573]

Ashihiki no	The shady chaplet
Yamakazurakage	Of the cypress moss that grows
Mashiba ni mo	High in the footsore hills
Egataki kage o	Is no easy crown to get—
Oki ya karasamu	How can I let it wither?

❋ The staining metaphor of no. 1508 is used again in no. 1526 to imply sexual intimacy. The dyeing process is probably deliberate rather than accidental. The water-leek has bluish-purple blossoms.

1526   [MYS XIV : 3598 / 3576]

Nawashiro no	As I rub my clothes
Konagi ga hana o	With flowers of the water-leek
Kinu ni suri	From the seedling bed,
Naruru manimani	The color grows more familiar—
Aze ka kanashike	Why is it so dear to me?

❋ Book XIV ends with a single brief lament for a dead wife. The mountain sedge (*yamasuge*) grows with its leaves pointed in different directions.

"A Lament"

1527   [MYS XIV : 3599 / 3577]

Kanashi imo o	That dear one—
Izuchi yukame to	Did I think she'd go away?
Yamasuge no	How I now regret
Sogai ni neshiku	The times when like the mountain sedge
Ima shi kuyashi mo	We slept back turned to back.

Book XVI

Book XVI gives every indication of being the receptacle for a variety of material left over from the compiling of the other books—material both anonymous and by known authors—a miscellany intended to round off the anthology. The last four books, XVII–XX, are in a sense an addendum, Yakamochi's personal compilation, his *shikashū* or "private collection" pasted on at the end. The compiler of Book XVI gave it the title *Yuen aru uta narabi ni zōka*, "Poems with a Story and Miscellaneous Poems." The "Poems with a Story" are accompanied by kambun passages in the form of either headnotes or footnotes explaining how the poems came to be composed. These stories are nuggets of fiction, and like similar prose-verse combinations in the chronicles and fudoki, are forerunners of the Heian genre of utamonogatari, or "poem-tale." Book XVI also contains early folk and minstrel songs, and examples of what would later be called *haikai*, such pranks and ploys as the enumerative poems of Naga no Okimaro. Low imagery and vulgar vocabulary occasionally add to the back-of-the-book flavor.

Among the "Poems with a Story" is one extraordinary composition, nos. 1528–39, which includes a kambun preface, the second-longest chōka in *Man'yōshū*, two envoys, and nine replies in tanka form. The unknown author drew on a fragmentary version of the tale prevalent in early Japan of a meeting between mortal and immortal, a theme that he used for satiric purposes and cosmeticized with references to *Yu-hsien-k'u* and other Chinese works. He added a moralizing element from Chinese didactic fiction and was at pains to display his knowledge of sartorial culture. The result is very strange indeed, baffling because it points in several different directions at once, as well as being fraught with orthographic obscurities.

The Old Bamboo-Cutter who is the principal figure and the speaker of the chōka and envoys recurs in *Taketori Monogatari* (*The Tale of the Bamboo-Cutter*), an early Heian work reputed in the days of Murasaki Shikibu at the beginning of the eleventh century to have been "the ancestor of all tales." In *Taketori Monogatari* the Old Bamboo-Cutter encounters a woman who is young and tiny, an exquisite child he discovers in the bole of a bamboo. She grows with preternatural swiftness to normal human size and lives as a foster daughter with him and his wife before returning to her home on the moon. In nos. 1528–39 the old man encounters not one, but nine women, and in the fragment constituting the "story" matters take a very different course. Instead of bringing the old man wealth, as in *Taketori Monogatari* (see also no. 221), the maidens ridicule him. But they are very beautiful, and the aged hero readily becomes their butt. The parallel between this story and the Matsura River sequence (nos. 1049–59) is instructive. The authors in both cases drew on *Yu-hsien-k'u* and its sexual exoticism in their descriptions of the maidens, who are clearly no ordinary village girls. An exchange of poems follows in both sequences. But at Matsura River the traveler is young, and the women are romantically drawn to him. The Old Bamboo-Cutter, on the other hand, hobbles along instead of arriving on a dashing steed. The women invite him to "blow on their fire" and then laugh in his face. He takes revenge by subjecting them to a thorough account of his past glories, but his poem is a satiric accretion to a story that must originally have developed in a somewhat different way.

The encounter of age and youth, mortal and immortal, is the common element in the two *taketori* stories. This set of juxtapositions is also found in no. 178, presented as a wazauta of political significance, but also interpreted as a song of sexual mockery. The "monkey" on the rock offers rice to the "old goat," and in doing so invites him to come near, as do the maidens who tease the Old Bamboo-Cutter. It seems likely that the *Nihonshoki* song and the *Man'yōshū* poem set are referring to the same story, and that the food—rice or broth—has some special significance. The significance might be suggested by other tales of meetings across the barrier of here and there, young and old. When young Urashima travels to the watery paradise of Tokoyo no Kuni, across or at the bottom of the sea, in nos. 216–20 and 579–80, it is to wed the enticing daughter of the sea god. When he leaves her and returns to the mortal world he turns into an old man and dies. In another version of this myth, recounted in both *Kojiki* and *Nihonshoki* (see nos. 7–8), the hero climbs a cassia tree at the gate of the sea god's palace and is offered water from a well before he meets his bride. The parallel of the water with the rice in no. 178 and the broth in the preface to no. 1528 points toward the hypothesis that these are magic foods or drinks, and that their main property is to restore or preserve youth—perhaps to make a mortal immortal.

There seem to be two versions of the myth—one in which contact with a woman provides a magic and sexual charm that preserves the life of a man as long as the spell is not broken (as with Urashima), and another in which an old man pleads for the spell and is mocked. This inverted version lies behind the exchange between "a young woman" and Saeki no Akamaro, nos. 892–93. Akamaro does not receive the *ochimizu* ("water of replenished youth") from the hand of the woman he desires, but is sent away to search for it on his own. The *ochimizu* is to be found on the moon (see nos. 1453–54), whose waxing and waning make it the symbol of aging and rebirth, and from which Kaguyahime, the heroine of *Taketori Monogatari*, came. The moon is also the home of the cassia tree (see nos. 1363–64), completing the correspondence of the sea palace and moon as realms of immortality. A third realm, that of the mountains, appears in the "story" accompanying no. 1528 (and in no. 178?), but is linked to memories of the sea realm in lines 66–69 of the chōka. That in a lost version of the myth the moon/sea/mountain woman used her charm to provide an old man youth as well as wealth (*Taketori Monogatari*) may be hinted in the replies of the nine maidens in nos. 1528–39. One by one they declare their intention to "submit." The verb is *yoru* ("to come close"), and the implications are sexual: the Old Bamboo-Cutter (bamboo itself is a symbol of lusty youth) is to regain his powers and reign over a harem of life-restoring nymphs.

The faint *pentimento* of some such story is overlaid in the kambun preface by brushstrokes from the gorgeous palette of *Yu-hsien-k'u* in various turns of phrase, and in the chōka by a thick parodic / didactic gouache. The poem, which is offered as an "atonement" for the old man's offense, turns out to be a long essay in vainglory, one whose retrospective self-satisfaction reflects and yet burlesques the vision of the stages of human life in Okura's no. 632–33. In both the good days are those of youthful vigor, and the old are treated with loathing and scorn. But the Old Bamboo-Cutter goes into such endless detail about his former good looks and wardrobe that the poem becomes a travesty of the "dressing of the hero." The comic garrulity of the old man undercuts the seriousness of the theme. His fussing with his hair (lines 16–23), his delight in fine clothes, his narrow waist (lines 66–71), and his admiration of his looks (lines 72–75) suggest that he is describing himself as a woman, but are no doubt meant as expressions of an exaggerated dandyism. He lines up mirrors, and the women line up to woo him. The poem becomes a parody of Takahashi no Mushimaro's narratives of Tegona and Unai (nos. 572–76). It is as if acquaintance with Gentleman Chang, the ladykiller hero of *Yu-hsien-k'u*, had inspired in the author the desire to create a set of fashion plates to illustrate the Life of a Handsome Man. The resulting composite is a portrait totally lacking in moral depth, and the moralizing last ten lines seem strangely out of place. Their didacticism, and that of the two envoys, has only a shallow purchase on the poem. The effect again is comic, as if the old man had suddenly remembered what he wanted to say. The reference is to a Chinese tale of filiality. Yüan Ku, ordered by his father to transport the aged grandfather to the hills and abandon him, complies but brings back the cart. Asked why, he replies that he will need it again when his father's time comes. The father experiences a salutary shock and has Yüan Ku go and bring his grandfather home, where he is thereafter treated with filial devotion.

The structure of the chōka takes the narrator from infancy to adulthood through a series of stages defined in terms of clothing and hair style. A first climax is reached in line 46, where his looks start attracting feminine attention. The socks and shoes given him by one woman take him to another, who gives him a sash. The sash emphasizes his slender figure and brings him a second round of attention—from himself, the birds and clouds, and the men and women of the court (lines 72–97). All this is then contrasted with the disdain of the nine maidens (lines 102–5). The adult raiment worn by the Old Bamboo-Cutter in lines 24–45 is a fanciful combination of rich silks, brocades, and home-made hempen and bark-cloth garments. The catalogue is of interest as a list of fabric-related industries and their products in Nara Japan. Dyeing and weaving had long been practiced by communities of craftsmen of kikajin origin in the area at the head of the Inland Sea. "Far Ono" (Ori Ono or Tōsato Ono) is now part of the cities of Ōsaka and Sakai. Koma (line 32) was the Japanese name for the Korean state of Koguryŏ. The Asuka shoemaker (lines 52–55) does not touch the shoes during the rainy season, presumably because the black is a lacquer, and lacquer does not set well during wet weather. The transition at lines 57–59 is very abrupt, but apparently a second woman is introduced here, and line 58 is directed toward her suitor. It is not clear exactly what a "drawing sash" (*hikiobi*) was, or how it would be worn as a "foreign sash" (*karaobi*). There is a self-applied honorific in line 65. The repeated last line of the chōka suggests oral recitation, but the poem as a whole is definitely a learned and not a folk product. Of known Man'yō poets, Yamanoue no Okura is the most appropriate candidate for author, on the grounds of his learning, his moralizing, and his interest in the course of human life. The garrulous style is also not unlike his. The crotchety Old Bamboo-Cutter could be self-parody.

The replies of the nine maidens are arranged in a series in which the first poem poses a question to which the other eight reply. Chastened, all the women agree to "submit." The impression of a comic chorus line deliberately fostered by the "naïve," repetitious prosody of the first five replies gives way to intimations of something more intense in the last three poems. The change is brought about by the introduction of imagery and the analogical mode. By having the first six maidens present themselves as feather-brained, falling over each other in their eagerness to submit, the author is continuing his basic satirical thrust. He varies the sameness of the replies by appeals to unanimity in nos. 1534 and 1535, and by the self-parodies of nos. 1532 and 1536, whose speakers wordily claim silence or insist on being different from the others, only to show themselves to be the same. The last three replies, however, are not parodistic but serious love poems. They build from the intimations of secret passion in no. 1537 to its threefold expression in no. 1538, and then recede to the gentler statement of no. 1539. Pillow word, paradox, and jo are successively employed in related images to give the subsequence its own unity. In a fine adjustment, the last poem alone ends in reversed syntax instead of the flatfooted final verb. In this shift in tone two-thirds of the way through the series of replies, the author seems to remind himself of the serious dimension of the myth with which he has played as suited his fancy.

1528–30   [MYS XVI: 3813–15 / 3791–93]

Once there was an old man who was called the Old Bamboo-Cutter. On a day in the last month of spring this old man climbed to the top of a hill and looked far out over the surrounding countryside. Suddenly he came upon nine maidens boiling broth. Their hundred charms were beyond compare, their flowerlike faces without peer. With a teasing laugh they called out, "Here, old man, come and blow on our fire!" "Aye, aye," the old man replied, and slowly and deliberately made his way over to where they were seated. After a while the maidens started to giggle and nudge each other. "Who invited this old man?" they asked. Thereupon the Old Bamboo-Cutter humbly said, "When without the slightest inkling I happened to encounter this band of immortals, my mind was thrown into uncontrollable confusion, and I dared to profane your presence. I beg you to let me atone for my mischief with a poem." And he composed the following poem along with its envoys.

	Midoriko no	A little greenling,
	Wakugo ga mi ni wa	Just a little youngling—in those days
	Tarachishi	I was cradled in arms
	Haha ni udakae	By my drooping-breasted mother;
5	Himutsuki no	In leading strings,
	Hau ko ga mi ni wa	Just a little crawling child—in those days
	Yuukataginu	They sewed a sleeveless frock
	Hitsura ni nuiki	Of lined bark cloth for me to wear;
	Kubitsuki no	With my collared jacket
10	Warawa ga mi ni wa	Now I was a bright young lad—in those days
	Yuihata no	A tunic with sleeves,
	Sodetsukegoromo	Made all of tie-dyed cloth—
	Kishi ware o	That was what I wore!
	Nioiyoru	And when I was the age
15	Kora ga yochi ni wa	You blushing girls are now—those days
	Mina no wata	I took my raven locks—
	Kaguroshi kami o	Black as the bowels of a mud-snail—
	Makushi mochi	And with a fine comb
	Koko ni kakitari	Combed them down to here—all loose;
20	Toritsukane	Sometimes I bound them
	Agete mo makimi	In a bun, seeing how they'd look done up,
	Tokimidari	And then again
	Warawa ni nashimi	Let them hang loose like a boy's.
	Sanitsukau	A fine tinge of red
25	Iro natsukashiki	Gave a warm, appealing color
	Murasaki no	To my purple silks
	Ōaya no kinu	With damask patterns woven large;
	Suminoe no	From Suminoe,
	Tōsato Ono no	From the village of Far Ono,
30	Mahari mochi	They take alder dye
	Nioshishi kinu ni	To give their silks a glowing hue;
	Komanishiki	Brocade from Koma
	Himo ni nuitsuke	Was sewn on these silks for cords:
	Sasau kasanau	Garments such as these I wore
35	Namikasaneki	Layer on layer, fold on fold.

	Utsuso yashi	Oh, the beaten-hemp
	Omi no kora	Flax-spinning girls,
	Arikinu no	Webs of mothlike silk
	Takara no kora ga	Treasure-fashioning girls—
40	Uchitae wa	The bark cloth they beat
	Hete oru nuno	And warp and weave in fabrics,
	Hisarashi no	The long sun-bleached
	Asatezukuri o	Homespun hempen swatches,
	Hiremo nasu	Trailing in scarves and trains—
45	Hashiki ni torishiki	I flaunted them in fetching style.
	Ie ni furu	The grainkeeper's girl
	Inaki omina ga	Who busied herself about her house
	Tsumadou to	Set to wooing me,
	Ware ni okoseshi	Sent me presents such as these:
50	Ochikata no	From a far-off land
	Futaaya shitakutsu	Stockings in two different twills,
	Tobu tori no	And from bird-flying
	Asuka otoko ga	Asuka, sewn by a man
	Nagame imi	Who never touched them
55	Nuishi kurokutsu	While the long rains fell, black shoes:
	Sashihakite	I put them right on
	Niwa ni tatazume	And strolled about the garden.
	Makari na tachi to	Off with you! Don't loiter there!
	Sauru otome ga	They hindered the maiden;
60	Honokikite	She'd caught a rumor
	Ware ni okoseshi	And so sent a present too:
	Mihanada no	An indigo silk
	Kinu no obi o	Sash, which like a drawing sash
	Hikiobi nasu	I did them all the honor
65	Karaobi ni torashi	To wear in the manner of a foreign sash;
	Watatsumi no	Tight about my waist—
	Tono no iraka ni	Slender as the digger wasp
	Tobikakeru	Skimming the roof tiles
	Sugaru no gotoki	Of the sea god's palace halls—
70	Koshiboso ni	I wound it round
	Torikazarai	And made myself as handsome as could be.
	Masokagami	Bright, well-polished mirrors
	Torinamekakete	I took and hung up in a row
	Ono ga kao	To admire my face,
75	Kaeraimitsutsu	Turning to look and look again.
	Haru sarite	When spring came on
	Nohe o megureba	And I went about the fields,
	Omoshiromi	Birds of the moorland—
	Ware o omoe ka	Was it that they found my looks

80   Sanotsutori
Kinakikakerau
Aki sarite
Yamahe o yukeba
Natsukashi to
85   Ware o omoe ka
Amakumo mo
Yukitanabikeru
Kaeritachi
Michi o kureba
90   Uchihi sasu
Miyaomina
Sasu take no
Toneri otoko mo
Shinoburai
95   Kaeraimitsutsu
Ta ga ko so to ya
Omowaete aru
Kaku no goto
Serareshi yue ni
100   Inishie
Sazakishi ware ya
Hashiki yashi
Kyō ya mo kora ni
Isa ni to ya
105 Omowaete aru
Kaku no goto
Serareshi yue ni
Inishie no
Sakashiki hito mo
110   Nochi no yo no
Kagami ni semu to
Oihito o
Okurishi kuruma
Mochikaerikoshi
115 Mochikaerikoshi

Two Envoys

Shinaba koso
Aimizu arame
Ikite araba
Shirokami kora ni
Oizarame ya mo

Delightful to behold?—
Came crying, flocking all around.
Then when autumn came
And I went out walking in the hills,
Clouds in the heavens—
Was it that they found my charm
Too irresistible?—
Came and drifted alongside.
Starting off for home,
I would pass along the street,
And then the ladies
Of the sun-bright palace,
The gentlemen of court,
Flourishing as new bamboo,
Would stealthily look round
To watch me as I passed them by,
Guessing at who I was:
I was wondered at, all right.
That was the way
I was treated long ago—
Yes, those good old days,
I was quite the fellow then!
But now—oh me, oh my!
Today I'm treated by you girls
As if you wonder
Whether you should let me get too close!
That was the way
Men were treated long ago,
And that's the reason why
The sagely man of ancient times
To set an example
For all ages yet to come
Took the hand-drawn cart
In which he'd carried the old man off
And brought it home with him again,
And brought it home with him again.

If you die, well then,
Of course you'll never see it;
But if you live on,
White hair is going to grow on you
Young girls one day for sure.

748

Shirokami shi	And if indeed white hair
Kora mo oinaba	Should grow on you young girls one day,
Kaku no goto	How can you be sure
Wakakemu kora ni	You'll not be, as I am now,
Noraekaneme ya	Mocked by girls who'll be young then?

1531-39 [MYS XVI : 3816-24 / 3794-3802]

Nine poems in reply by the maidens

(1531) [3816/3794]

Hashiki yashi	Dear oh dear oh dear,
Okina no uta ni	What shall we nine maidens do—
Ohohoshiki	Silly as we are,
Kokono no kora ya	Shall we let ourselves be swayed
Kamakete oramu	By this old man's song?

(1532) [3817/3795]

Haji o shinobi	Enduring my shame,
Haji o modashite	Bearing my shame in silence,
Koto mo naku	Without resistance,
Mono iwanu saki ni	Before even saying a thing,
Ware wa yorinamu	I am going to submit.

(1533) [3818/3796]

Ina mo o mo	Whether no or yes,
Hoshiki manimani	Anything at all he wants
Yurusubeki	I shall not deny:
Katachi wa miyu ya	Can he see it in my face?
Ware mo yorinamu	I too am going to submit.

(1534) [3819/3797]

Shini mo iki mo	Dying or living,
Oyaji kokoro to	We all swore our hearts would be
Musubiteshi	Bound into one—
Tomo ya tagawamu	How can friends like that fall out?
Ware mo yorinamu	I too am going to submit.

(1535) [3820/3798]

Nani semu ni	What good would it do
Tagai wa oramu	For me to go against the others?
Ina mo o mo	Whether no or yes,
Tomo no naminami	I shall do just as my friends:
Ware mo yorinamu	I too am going to submit.

(1536) [3821/3799]

Ani mo araji	There's no need for all this.
Ono ga mi no kara	Being the kind of girl I am,
Hito no ko no	Unlike the others
Koto mo tsukusaji	I shall not go on wasting words:
Ware mo yorinamu	I too am going to submit.

(1537) [3822/3800]

Hadasusuki	Plumegrass in tassel,
Ho ni wa na ide to	Openly flaunting—not you,
Omoite aru	I said to my heart;
Kokoro wa shirayu	But my feelings now are known.
Ware mo yorinamu	I too am going to submit.

(1538) [3823/3801]

Suminoe no	Though they should stain me
Kishino no hari ni	With the alder of Kishino
Niouredo	In Suminoe,
Niowanu ware ya	I would not be stained—not I!—
Nioite oramu	Who shall now go stained through life.

(1539) [3824/3802]

Haru no no no	The under-grasses
Shitakusa nabiki	Bending in the fields of spring:
Ware mo yori	I too submit;
Nioiyorinamu	I am stained and shall submit,
Tomo no manimani	Even as my friends have done.

❋ The next few poem-tales include several on disappointed wives. It seems likely that the author of the kambun was motivated by the same desire to provide fictional settings for poems that resulted in many of the stories in *Ise Monogatari* two centuries later, the main difference being that the *Man'yōshū* settings are in Chinese. In other words the poems may have existed separately from and prior to the stories. Such reuse of poetic materials was a well-established procedure in the chronicles. The urge to write love stories interweaving prose and poetry, growing out of the pervasive social role of poetry in early Japanese society and finding expression in the classics of Heian courtly literature, drew also on the dazzling example of *Yu-hsien-k'u*, with which the author of the following story was clearly familiar. The two tanka are love poems vague enough in their reference to make it unlikely that they were composed to go with the anecdote.

1540-41   [MYS XVI: 3826-27 / 3804-5]

(1540)   [3826 / 3804]

Once there was a man. He had just celebrated a new marriage. Then before any time at all had gone by he was suddenly dispatched as an express courier to a distant region. His duties kept him bound; there were no days off when he and his wife could meet. The young woman felt heartbroken about this, and in despair fell ill and took to her bed. Years piled up, and at last the man came back and reported on his mission. This done, he went home and looked: the young woman was wasted in the extreme, and her appearance had greatly altered. Words stuck in their throats. Then he heaved a pitiful sigh and wept. Fashioning a poem, he recited it to her. That poem:

Kaku nomi ni	So it had come to this—
Arikeru mono o	All the while I never knew;
Inagawa no	No, but I longed for you
Oki o fukamete	Deeply in my secret depths
Wa ga moerikeru	As the sea off Ina River.

(1541)   [3827 / 3805]

As she lay there, the young woman raised her head from the pillow on hearing her husband's poem, and in response to his voice replied:

Nubatama no	Have you come to me
Kurokami nurete	Through the fluffy, falling snow,
Awayuki no	Wetting the blackness
Furu ni ya kimasu	Of your lovely, gem-black hair
Kokoda koureba	To answer my great longing?

On present consideration, this poem suggests that it was winter and snowing when the husband returned after his years as courier. Perhaps this is why the young woman composed the line about the fluffy snow.

❋ A variant of the next poem crops up as a "provincial song" (*kunibito no uta*) in the province of Hitachi in eastern Japan (see no. 200). In the *Man'yōshū* version the wording of the poem, and the narrative context, reverse the situation. A young woman addresses her fainthearted lover, urging him to be prepared to join her in flight. Whether the flight is to death depends again on the interpretation of *iwaki* ("stone fort"), a term that could either refer to a hilltop stronghold or serve as a kenning for the burial chamber of a grave. The "story" has shifted in position to an editorial note at the end.

1542   [MYS XVI: 3828 / 3806]

   Koto shi araba   If they make trouble,
Obatsuseyama no   And you hide in the stone fort
   Iwaki ni mo   On Mount Hatsuse,
Komoraba tomo ni   We'll be there together, love—
   Na omoi wagase   Husband, do not be afraid.

Concerning the above, the story has come down that once there was a maiden who unbeknownst to her father and mother secretly became intimate with a young man. The youth trembled when he thought how her parents would take him to task, and he gradually began to have second thoughts. And so it was that the young woman fashioned this poem and sent it to her husband.

❋ The following love poem was a famous one in post-Man'yō times, and is referred to in the early anonymous annotation of the *Kana Preface* to *Kokinshū* as one of two poems used regularly for calligraphy practice. Mount Asaka is thought to have been near present Kōriyama City in Fukushima Prefecture. The provincial headquarters of Michinoku was farther north, near Sendai, and so the palace woman (uneme) in the attached anecdote is to be thought of not as composing the poem, but as quoting one appropriate to the northland. Asaka Mountain is echoed in *asaki* ("shallow") in line 4, which also serves as a syntactic double (kakekotoba), being the predicate of *yama no i* ("mountain spring") and the modifier of *kokoro* ("heart"). This jo is interesting because it is at once a positive and negative analogy. Unlike the mountain spring, the woman's heart is not shallow; but like the spring, it is so clear and pure that a mountain (or a man) could be reflected in it. The Prince Kazuraki of this no doubt apocryphal account was probably understood to be Tachibana no Moroe as a young man before he adopted non-royal status.

1543   [MYS XVI: 3829 / 3807]

   Asakayama   Asaka Mountain—
Kage sae miyuru   In a shallow mountain spring
   Yama no i no   A clear reflection:
Asaki kokoro o   Not so shallow is the heart
Wa ga omowanaku ni   Where my thoughts have mirrored you.

Concerning the above, the story has come down that when Prince Kazuraki was dispatched to Michinoku Province, the provincial officials were shockingly lax in their courtesies. The Prince was displeased at this, and his annoyance showed in his face. They set food and drink before him, but he was in no mood for a party. Now, there was a former palace woman there, a young lady of courtly sophistication. She offered the winecup with her left hand and held water in her right. She slapped the Prince's knee and recited this poem. At this the Prince relaxed and began to enjoy himself, drinking all day to his heart's content.

❉ The deserted wife in the following poem has brewed "waiting *sake*" (*machizake*), a beverage with which a woman traditionally welcomed her husband.

1544   [MYS XVI: 3832/3810]

Umaii o	It did me no good
Mizu ni kaminashi	To ferment the tasty rice,
Wa ga machishi	Brewing with water,
Kai wa sane nashi	Waiting for you—none at all,
Tada ni shi araneba	For you're not here to have it.

Concerning the above, it is related that there was once a young woman who was separated from her husband. Years went by while she longed for him and hoped for his return. But then he took another wife. Instead of coming himself, he just sent gifts. Thus the young woman fashioned this resentful poem and sent it back in response.

❉ Perhaps the most powerful of the poems in the genre of the abandoned wife is the following chōka. Spoken by a woman at the point of death, its use of bitter sarcasm and irony is particularly effective. In her insistence on the truth and integrity of her suffering, she turns angrily against attempts to look to supernatural sources for reasons or to shift the blame onto the gods. Lines 19–20 show her to be losing touch with her surroundings. Burning tortoise shell (line 10) to read the resultant cracks was a method of divination similar to scapulamancy (no. 1497); it is said to have been introduced from the continent. On the "evening augury" (line 26), see no. 1513. Both envoys seem slightly beside the main point of the poem—that the wife is dying in anger—and were probably put together with the chōka because of the diviners in the first and the ruddy-cheeked lord in the second.

1545–47   [MYS XVI: 3833–35/3811–13]

A poem of longing for her husband; with *tanka*

Sanitsurafu	My ruddy-cheeked lord,
Kimi ga mikoto to	Because no message-bearer
Tamazusa no	Comes with catalpa staff

Tsukai mo koneba	To bring me your precious words,
5 Omoiyamu	Sick with my yearning,
Wa ga mi hitori so	I only am forsaken.
Chihayaburu	Do not put it on
Kami ni mo na ōse	The thousand-rock-smashing gods,
Urahe sue	Nor call diviners,
10 Kame mo na yaki so	Having them burn tortoise shell.
Koishiku ni	It is love of you
Itaki wa ga mi so	That torments me with this pain.
Ichishiroku	Sharp through my body
Mi ni shimitōri	Penetrates the agony;
15 Murakimo no	And where my entrails
Kokoro kudakete	Cluster in my breast, my heart
Shinamu inochi	Is crushed, and my life
Niwaka ni narinu	Is urgent with coming death.
Imasara ni	Do you even now,
20 Kimi ka wa o yobu	My lord, call me by my name?
Tarachine no	Or does my mother,
Haha no mikoto ka	She who fed me from her breasts,
Momotarazu	Go to the crossroads
Yaso no chimata ni	Where the eighty ways branch out,
25 Yūke ni mo	Seeking of strangers
Ura ni mo so tou	Through the evening augury
Shinubeki wa ga yue	Why it is that I must die?

Envoy

Urabe o mo	Ask the diviners,
Yaso no chimata mo	Or strangers at the crossroads
Ura toedo	Of the eighty ways—
Kimi o aimimu	To meet you, see you, my lord,
Tadoki shirazu mo	No stratagem do they know.

In a certain text the envoy reads:

Wa ga inochi wa	It is not that life
Oshiku mo arazu	Is a thing that I begrudge,
Sanitsurafu	But, my ruddy-cheeked lord,
Kimi ni yorite so	Because of you, you only,
Nagaku hori suru	Do I desire length of days.

Concerning the above, it is related that there was once a young woman whose family name was that of the Kurumamochi clan. Her husband let many years go by without inquiring after her. Sick at heart with her endless yearning, the young woman fell ill and took to her bed, wasting away day by day. Now all at once she faced the road to the [Yellow] Springs. At this she sent a messenger to call her husband. According to the story, she murmured this poem in a voice choked with tears and then passed away.

❋ Book XVI contains among its miscellaneous poems the following nugget of pedantry. The "old poem" (no. 1548) speaks openly of licentiousness in a Buddhist temple, or perhaps merely of a lucky escapade that escaped the attention of temple authorities. The poem provides the kind of fondly amorous memory also found in no. 1384. Its impropriety shocked one Shii no Nagatoshi, otherwise unknown, into an act of bowdlerization (no. 1549). Nagatoshi was probably of kikajin origin, and perhaps a doctor. In any case his analysis is cast in medical terms, with an "examination" that is literally a "[taking of] the pulse," and a "diagnosis." The references to the "belly line" (line 4) and the "tail line" (line 5) show that he is referring to the theory of "poetic ills," or *uta no yamai*, expounded in *Kakyō Hyōshiki*, Japan's earliest work on poetics, by Fujiwara no Hamanari (724-90). (*Kakyō Hyōshiki* dates from 772, and Tachibanadera, the "Orange Tree Temple" of the poem, burned in 739. There is evidence here of the currency of the theory of "poetic ills" before Hamanari.) The poem, in short, is treated as a patient to be cured of its disease. This is done by changing *tera no nagaya* ("temple longhouse") to *tereru nagaya* ("shining longhouse"), and making *tachibana* an actual orange tree rather than the temple's name. The other matter that concerns Nagatoshi is the definition of *unaihanari*. *Unai* means "nape of the neck," and *hanari* means "loose." The term *should* refer to loose shoulder-length hair, the way girls in their early teens wore it before they adopted the adult woman's hairdo, which in the Nara period consisted of tying the hair in twin loops on top of the head. Yet Nagatoshi insists that *unaihanari* means "loose hair done up," that is, the "youthful coif" of the woman who has come of age at about sixteen. Nagatoshi may well have known what he was talking about—*obanari* in no. 574 seems to mean something of the sort he had in mind—but etymology is against him. In his revision *unai* is separated from *hanari* as a term meaning "loose-haired girl," and *hanari* is taken to refer to bound-up hair.

1548-49   [MYS XVI: 3844-45 / 3822-23]

(1548)   [3844 / 3822]

An old poem reads:

Tachibana no	She whose hair hung loose
Tera no nagaya ni	When I led her to the longhouse
Wa ga ineshi	And slept with her there
Unaihanari wa	At the Temple of the Orange Tree—
Kami agetsuramu ka	Has she now bound up her locks?

Concerning the above poem, Shii no Muraji Nagatoshi examined it and said, "Now, in the first place, temple buildings have no sleeping quarters for the laity. Furthermore, a woman who has received the youthful coif is what is called *unaihanari* ['loose hair done up']. Therefore, since the belly line already says 'loose hair done up,' is it not inappropriate for the tail line to speak again of wearing the coif?" His diagnosis reads:

(1549)   [3845/3823]

Tachibana no	She whose hair hung loose
Tereru nagaya ni	When I led her to the longhouse
Wa ga ineshi	And slept with her there
Unai hanari ni	Where the orange tree shone with light—
Kami agetsuramu ka	Has she parted and bound up her locks?

❋ Another love poem from Book XVI is of the hiyuka type. The speaker, no doubt an ama lad, is pleased that his sweetheart pleases only him. *Wakame* ("maiden-weed") and *nikime* ("tender-weed") refer to the same kind of seaweed, of a higher quality than *arame* ("rough-weed"). Tsunoshima is an island off the western extremity of Honshū.

1550   [MYS XVI: 3893/3871]

Tsunoshima no	The maiden-weed that grows
Seto no wakame wa	In the narrows off Tsuno Isle
Hito no muta	Is rough and harsh
Arakarishikado	To the touch of other men,
Wa ga muta wa nikime	But tender-weed to me.

❋ Two poems of a strongly folk quality follow. The first is in the contrastive pattern between nature and man exemplified by nos. 115, 920, and 1280. The song is by a woman, and no doubt intends a comparison between the "fruit" so avidly sought by the birds and her own neglected charms. In the second poem *oki yo oki yo* ("Get up! Get up!") is the cry of the birds as well as of the woman. *Hitoyozuma* ("husband of a single night") implies a casual one-night amour rather than the beginning of a marriage.

1551–52   [MYS XVI: 3894–95/3872–73]

(1551)   [3894/3872]

Wa ga kado no	To strip my nettle tree
E no mi morihamu	And gobble down its fruit they come,

Momochitori	Birds in their hundreds,
Chitori wa kuredo	Birds in their thousands come:
Kimi so kimasanu	But my love comes not to me.

(1552)   [3895 / 3873]

Wa ga kado ni	At my gate they cry,
Chitori shibanaku	Thousands of birds, incessantly,
Oki yo oki yo	Get up! Get up!
Wa ga hitoyozuma	My husband of a single night,
Hito ni shirayu na	Don't let people know you're here!

❊ The jo of the following poem appears also in no. 188, a lament. In both instances the "soft grass" (*nikogusa*) serves to introduce the idea of youth. The relevance of the elaborate image of the wounded deer to a love poem is not so immediately obvious. If there is one, it could be through the sexual implications of arrows, wounds, etc., or simply the double image of disappearance, of loss through death and time.

1553   [MYS XVI: 3896 / 3874]

Iyu shishi o	A wounded deer
Tsunagu kawahe no	Leaves a trail by the river
Nikogusa no	Into the soft grass:
Mi no wakakae ni	But where is the girl I slept with
Saneshi kora wa mo	In my green and tender years?

❊ Among the folk songs in Book XVI is the following derisive ballad. The Noto Peninsula on the Japan Sea coast of Honshū was a separate province from 718 to 741; from 741 to 757 it became part of Etchū, the province Ōtomo no Yakamochi governed from 746 to 751. Yakamochi could well have collected the song while he was Governor, and written the headnote later. He was interested in obtaining pearls from the divers of Noto (see no. 821-25), and very likely songs as well. Kumaki was on Nanao Bay, halfway up the peninsula. A Shiraki axe would be one imported from the Korean state of Silla or modeled on it. The song is an old, irregular chōka, no doubt the oldest form of Japanese prosody. *Washi* (rendered "heave-ho!" in lines 5 and 10) is a refrain-like exclamation of the sort also found in English ballads. The voice of the community can be heard ridiculing the carelessness and stupidity of its local fool, alternately narrating his actions and addressing him. The footnote is a learned collector's commentary. The obscure term *yara* (rendered "fen water") is replaced by *umi* ("sea") in the note.

1554 [MYS XVI: 3900/3878]

[One of] three songs from Noto Province

	Hashitate no	In the fen water
	Kumaki no yara ni	At ladder-steep Kumaki,
	Shiraki ono	Well, he dropped it,
	Otoshiire	That Shiraki axe.
5	Washi	Heave-ho!
	Agete agete	And he wailed, and he railed—
	Na nakashi so ne	Oh, please don't cry so!
	Ukiizuru ya to	It'll come floating up someday,
	Mimu	Let's say—
10	Washi	Heave-ho!

Concerning the above poem, tradition has it that there was a certain fool who when his axe dropped down to the bottom of the sea did not understand that iron sinks and does not have the property of floating in water. And so they made up this song and sang it to teach him.

❋ Among the most interesting poems in Book XVI are two examples of the songs of a class of wandering beggar-minstrels called *hokai* who provided entertainment and a blessing on a house in exchange for something to eat. Both songs concern food, probably the dishes consumed at the feast for which the hokai provided entertainment, and are highly reminiscent of the opening passage of no. 42. The first song (no. 1555) is about a deer and has an ingenious double introduction in which (lines 1–11) the hokai first flatteringly addresses his host as a great hunter who catches tigers in Korea, skins them, and sits on layers of their skins. This jo is joined to the next by the mock epithet *yaedatami* ("piled up eightfold"), applying to Heguri Mountain (line 12) through *he* ("layer"). The speaker then relates how he himself went hunting in the Heguri Mountains, on a *kusurigari*, or "medicine hunt" for herbs and the new antlers of deer. A deer approaches in lines 27–28 and speaks the rest of the poem. The speech of the deer is a long catalogue of its body parts, all of which it willingly sacrifices to the "great lord" who will feast upon or use them. This felicitous song provides rich opportunities for mime and, presumably, dance. The use of the eyes, and perhaps the ears, is metaphorical, but by and large the catalogue reflects actual material culture and diet. The diet is obviously pre- and highly un-Buddhist. Writing brushes (line 42) indicate literacy, however. So perhaps do the "inkwells" (*misumi no tsubo*) of line 36, though it has been suggested that they were a device for inking the *suminawa* ("inkstring") used in carpentry (see nos. 150 and 636). The repeated mention of the ancient lucky number eight contributes to the auspicious effect of the song rather than providing a literal enumeration. The body parts turn out to be nine in number—a baker's dozen?

The second song (no. 1556) is about a crab. The introduction is less elaborate—six lines by the narrator bring the crab onstage to speak its part. The four rhetorical questions (lines 7–16) make it clear the crab has been summoned to be eaten and give glimpses of the musicians who accompany the song (and, no doubt, dance). Lines 19–28 are particularly close to lines 3–12 of no. 42 and suggest the existence of a group of mimetic crab songs. Lines 19–20 are based on a pun in which *asu* ("tomorrow") in "Asuka" relates to *kyō* ("today"). The wordplay in lines 21–22 links *tatedo mo* ("though I stand up") to *oki* ("lie flat") in "Okina," and in lines 23–24 *tsuku* ("poke") in "Tsukuno" is brought to life by the pun *tsukanedo mo* ("though I do not poke"). The whole six-line passage is meant to blend verbal and mimetic jollity in a depiction of a hurrying, scurrying crab. Lines 29–32 imply that crabs as well as horses and oxen may be tied—here the crab has been hung up to dry. The "belly cinch" (*fumodashi*) was a rope passed around a horse's middle and tied to an overhead beam to keep it from leaving its stall. Bark from the hazel tree (*momunire*) was ground and used as a flavoring (lines 35–42 explain its preparation). Mixed with brine brought from Naniwa in a pot of high-fired *sue* ware, it makes a tasty glaze for the dried crab (lines 47–52). Both the deer song and the crab song conclude with felicitous exclamations congratulating the host on the menu he has provided his guests.

1555–56   [MYS XVI: 3907–8 / 3885–86]

Two songs of the beggar folk

(1555)   [3907 / 3885]

	Itoko	Sweet sir,
	Nase no kimi	Dear lord my brother,
	Oriorite	Here, here do you dwell;
	Mono ni iyuku to wa	And when you travel somewhere, why,
5	Karakuni no	It's off to Kara
	Tora tou kami o	To catch the gods called tigers:
	Ikedori ni	Taking them alive,
	Yatsu torimochiki	Eight of them, you bring them back.
	Sono kawa o	Their skins
10	Tatami ni sashi	You spread out for mats,
	Yaedatami	Piled up eightfold:
	Heguri no yama ni	Ranges of Heguri Mountain,
	Uzuki to	Whither in the months
	Satsuki to no ma ni	Of May and June I go to serve
15	Kusurigari	In the medicine hunt.
	Tsukauru toki ni	Once on such duty I was there

	Ashihiki no	On this foot-dragging
	Kono katayama ni	Solitary mountain peak,
	Futatsu tatsu	Waiting underneath
20	Ichihi ga moto ni	Where two oaks stood side by side—
	Azusayumi	Catalpa bows,
	Yatsu tabasami	Eight of them, clutched in my hand,
	Himekabura	Wood-splitting bulb-shafts,
	Yatsu tabasami	Eight of them, clutched in my hand—
25	Shishi matsu to	For the game to come,
	Wa ga oru toki ni	When, right up to where I was
	Saoshika no	There came a stag,
	Kitachinagekaku	And stood there, thus lamenting:
	Tachimachi ni	I stand, I wait,
30	Ware wa shinubeshi	In a moment I must die.
	Ōkimi ni	To the great lord
	Ware wa tsukaemu	I shall render service:
	Wa ga tsuno wa	My antlers
	Mikasa no hayashi	An adornment for his hat,
35	Wa ga mimi wa	My ears
	Misumi no tsubo	Wells for his ink,
	Wa ga mera wa	My eyes
	Masumi no kagami	Cloudless mirrors,
	Wa ga tsume wa	My hooves
40	Miyumi no yuhazu	Bowtips for his bow,
	Wa ga kera wa	My hair
	Mifumite hayashi	Splendid makings for his brush,
	Wa ga kawa wa	My hide
	Mihako no kawa ni	Skin to make a box for him,
45	Wa ga shishi wa	My flesh
	Minamasu hayashi	Splendid venison sliced raw,
	Wa ga kimo mo	My liver too
	Minamasu hayashi	Splendid sliced up raw,
	Wa ga mige wa	My stomach
50	Mishio no hayashi	Splendid makings for salt tripe.
	Oitaru yatsuko	That in my single body,
	Wa ga mi hitotsu ni	The body of this aged slave,
	Nanae hana saku	Sevenfold the flowers bloom,
	Yae hana saku to	Eightfold the flowers bloom,
55	Mōshihayasane	Report and make me glorious,
	Mōshihayasane	Report and make me glorious.

The above poem was composed on behalf of the deer, to relate its pains.

(1556)   [3908 / 3886]

Oshiteru ya	In far-shining
Naniwa no oe ni	Naniwa there built a hut
Io tsukuri	In a little creek
Namarite oru	Where it lived all out of sight
5 Ashigani o	A reed-crab,
Ōkimi mesu to	And the great lord summoned him:
Nani semu ni	Now why can it be
Wa mesurame ya	That you summon me, my lord?
Akirakeku	I know the reason—
10 Wa ga shiru koto o	It's as clear as it can be.
Utabito to	Is it as a singer
Wa o mesurame ya	That you summon me, my lord?
Fuefuki to	Is it as a piper
Wa o mesurame ya	That you summon me, my lord?
15 Kotohiki to	Is it as a strummer
Wa o mesurame ya	That you summon me, my lord?
Ka mo kaku mo	Be it as it may,
Mikoto ukemu to	To receive your high command
Kyō kyō to	Today, today,
20 Asuka ni itari	Tomorrow I reach Asuka;
Tatedo mo	Though I stand up
Okina ni itari	I fall flat on Okina;
Tsukanedo mo	Though I have no cane
Tsukuno ni itari	I poke on to Tsukuno.
25 Himukashi no	Through the eastern gate
Naka no mikado yu	Of the inner palace close
Mairikite	Humbly I approach
Mikoto ukureba	To receive the dictates of my lord:
Uma ni koso	Everybody knows
30 Fumodashi kaku mono	Horses have a belly cinch;
Ushi ni koso	Everybody knows
Hananawa hakure	Oxen wear ropes in their noses.
Ashihiki no	On this foot-dragging
Kono katayama no	Solitary mountain peak
35 Momunire o	From the hazel tree
Ioe hagitari	Stripping fifty branches' bark,
Ama teru ya	In the heaven-shining
Hi no ke ni hoshi	Sun-bright air they dry it
Saizuru ya	And in squeaky-voiced
40 Karausu ni tsuki	Foot-pedaled mortars they pound it,

	Niwa ni tatsu	Pound it in mortars
	Usu ni tsuki	That stand in the yard.
	Oshiteru ya	From far-shining
	Naniwa no oe no	Naniwa the first drippings
45	Hatsutari o	From the little creek
	Karaku tarikite	They come dripping all briny.
	Suehito no	My lord goes today
	Tsukureru kame o	And tomorrow he brings back
	Kyō yuki	A jar fashioned
50	Asu tori mochiki	By the *sue* potters,
	Wa ga mera ni	And in my eyes
	Shio nuritamai	He smears a glaze of salt:
	Kitai hayasu mo	Look, a splendid crab dried whole!
	Kitai hayasu mo	Look, a splendid crab dried whole!

The above poem was composed on behalf of the crab, to relate its pains.

❋ Book XVI ends with three mysterious tanka "on frightening things." The first poem (no. 1557) seems to refer merely to the experience of being startled by a quail suddenly flying up from underfoot, but it has been suggested that this poem like the other two relates to death. The field of Sasara, said to be in heaven, appears also in a lament in Book III (MYS 423/420), where it is a location for cutting sedge to use in a purification ceremony. *Sasara* may refer to fine-leaved plants such as bamboo grass (*sasa*). *Karibaka* ("grasspatch") is the patch assigned to one cutter. The quail may or may not refer to the spirit of the dead (see nos. 35–37 and 348). In the second poem (no. 1558) the Inner Country (*okitsukuni*) is the land of the dead, here regarded as being beyond or under the sea, and the yellow-lacquered houseboat (yellow like the Yellow Springs?) is to transport the dead thither. This poem has been linked to NS 123 (no. 191), the *kami ga to* ("gate of the gods") being equated with the *minato* ("harbor" or "water gate") in that song. This suggestion points toward a haunting ambiguity between Tokoyo as an undersea realm of eternal youth and Tokoyo as another version of Yomi, the land of the dead (compare nos. 579–80 with no. 574). The final poem (no. 1559) is about seeing a *hitodama*, a fox fire or phosphorescent apparition taken to be the soul of the newly dead.

1557–59   [MYS XVI: 3909–11/3887–89]

Three poems on frightening things

(1557)   [3909/3887]

Ame naru ya	Way up in the heavens
Sasara no ono ni	In the field of Sasara

Chigaya kari
Kaya karibaka ni
Uzura o tatsu mo

Cutting bladygrass,
Cutting grass in the grasspatch—
Whew, I start a quail!

(1558)   [3910/3888]

Okitsukuni
Ushihaku kimi ga
Nuriyakata
Kinuri no yakata
Kami ga to wataru

The lord who has power
Over the Inner Country—
His lacquered houseboat,
His yellow-lacquered houseboat
Passes the Gate of the Gods.

(1559)   [3911/3889]

Hitodama no
Sao naru kimi ga
Tada hitori
Aerishi amayo no
Haburi o so omou

Pale blue phantom
In the rainy night, you came,
And all alone
You met me; the memory
Lingers of that burial.

The Buddha's Footstone Poems

Twenty-one poems carved on a stone at Yakushiji in Nara constitute the most important Japanese poetic text from the eighth century outside those preserved in the chronicles, fudoki, and *Man'yōshū*. They are Buddhist devotional verses, and as such provide evidence of a new use for native prosody, one essentially excluded from *Man'yōshū* and other early sources, despite Okura's kambun allusions and Yakamochi's confessions of his desire to "seek the Way" (nos. 849–50). One may well wonder how many collections of sacred Buddhist hymns have not weathered the vicissitudes of time even as well as the battered engravings at Yakushiji. Pious anecdotes abound, and the Nara period was one of a perfervid faith at the center that sponsored literally towering achievements in Buddhist art and architecture. But little poetry remains to give an inner dimension to the monumental expressions of that faith. The Yakushiji poems thus afford an invaluable glimpse of the flame of worship burning within the mighty fanes of the time.

The twenty-one poems are engraved on a slab of slate now housed in the newly rebuilt Main Hall at Yakushiji, a temple devoted to the Buddha of Healing, Bhaiṣajya-guru, or Yakushi, "the Medicine Master." The date and authorship of the poems are unknown, but the stele on which they are carved accompanies another stone, the "Footprint Stone," or Bussokuseki, on which are incised outlines of the soles of the feet of the historical Buddha, Śākyamuni. These representatives of the footprints of the Enlightened One are among the primary icons of early Buddhism and were worshiped in ceremonies of circumambulation. It seems clear that the poems were intended to accompany—perhaps as a liturgical text—such a ritual. The Footprint Stone at Yakushiji is known to have been donated by Prince Chinu (Fumiya no Chinu; see note to nos. 1169–73) and has an inscription dated in correspondence with the year 753.

The poems are in the syllabic form 5-7-5-7-7-7, of which they are the chief surviving corpus, and which is named after them *bussokuseki no uta tai* ("Buddha's footprint stone poem form"). The poems are of two structural types. In poems BSS 1, 3–4, 6–7, 9–10, 13–15, and 17–19, the last line is an altered repetition of line 5; in poems 2, 5, 8, 12, 16, and 20 this is not the case, the last line usually being an exclamation. These two types will be referred to as A and B. Poems 11 and 21 are unfortunately too damaged to describe with certainty. In both type A and type B the tanka + 1 structure is suitable for antiphonal or responsive recitation. The content of the poems is doctrinal, and their expression is intense: we are clearly in the presence of a work of great religious power.

Roy Andrew Miller has studied the poems in depth in his monograph *Footprints of the Buddha*, tracing content and arrangement to particular Buddhist scriptures, most notably to the "Twelve Great Vows of Bhaiṣajya-guru" as set forth in *(Bussetsu) Yakushi Nyorai Hongangyō, Yakushi Rurikō Nyorai Hongan Kudokukyō*, and *Yakushi Rurikō Shichibutsu Hongan Kudokukyō*, a closely related group of sutras translated from the Sanskrit by Dharmagupta (d. 619), Hsüan-tsang (602–64), and I-ching (635–713), respectively. While my understanding of the poems is greatly indebted to Miller, in what follows I make no attempt to retrace all his analytical directions or reproduce all his conclusions. It is, however, of particular importance that he has pointed out the presence in the third of the Yakushi sutras mentioned above of Śākyamuni and the worship of his feet, since the poem-sequence itself is largely devoted to Śākyamuni, even though its institutional context is a Bhaiṣajya-guru temple. It has also seemed appropriate, if inconsistent, to follow Miller, a noted authority, in presenting this final group of poems in reconstructed Old Japanese, especially inasmuch as they are engraved in purely phonogram orthography on the original stone.

The Buddha's Footstone Poems

No. 1560 opens the sequence with a bold announcement of the icon's fashioning, at once awesome and compassionate. The ringing of hammer on chisel, chisel on stone, echoes between heaven and earth, informing all the universe of a new thing: the sacred, salvific emblem raised to the surface of an obdurate matrix by the power of faith. This faith, the poem tells us, is not merely gentle, but muscular, a sure guard and guide for all humanity. The cosmic frame, the kinetic rage of controlled force, the dedication to family and world, make this poem a resonant reply to Okura's destitute Everyman (no. 634), who also crouches between heaven and earth, striking the resistant soil for his living, himself struck by the village chief, and surrounded by his starving and moaning brood.

1560   [BSS 1]

Miatö tukuru	May the ringing
Isi nö Fibiki Fa	Of the stone whereon we fashion
Amë ni itari	The holy footprints
Tuti saFë yusure	Reach heaven, and earth itself resound—
Titi FaFa ga tamë ni	For the sake of father and mother,
MoröFitö nö tamë ni	For the sake of all people.

✳ No. 1561 constitutes a polar opposite to no. 1560 in two respects. For the resolute proclamation of the human act of devotion is substituted a vision of godly power; the artisan's proud assertion fades into humility before the miracle of the trodden footprints. The two versions are complementary, not contradictory: they express an outer and an inner truth. The other polarity is in the form of the refrain, changing from type A to type B, from altered echo to exclamation. The tension set up by these two oppositional sets, of form and of concept, intertwines and runs through the sequence. The hero of the thirty-two marks and eighty signs is a Buddha or a Cakravartī ("Wheel King"). Some of these marks and signs have in fact to do with the form and symbolic character of his feet, which leave prints though he walks four finger-breadths off the ground. The first of the "Great Vows" of Bhaiṣajya-guru is that when in a future world he attains enlightenment all creatures will come to share these physical characteristics.

1561   [BSS 2]

    Misoti amari   He who is complete
  Futatu nö katati   With the two-and-thirty marks
    Yasokusa tö   And the eighty signs
 Södareru Fitö nö   Has trodden his footprints:
Fumisi atötökörö   Here in this very place,
Mare ni mo aru kamo Wonderfully, they are!

✻ No. 1562 picks up the burden of no. 1560 and reverts to its antiphonal formula of altered repetition. But the *Fitö*, the Person, of no. 1561 is kept in view as the ultimate author of the footprints, whose originals have never been seen by the carver or carvers (*ware* can be either singular or plural). The Buddha lived long ago in another country, and the *Fitö* (which also can be singular or plural) of no. 1562 are his original disciples, followers, or simply those who heard and saw him. By this association they become *yöki*, "good," a term implying "wellborn" in the Japanese social context. No. 1562 occupies an intermediate position between the devotional act of BSS 1 and the miracle of BSS 2.

1562   [BSS 3]

    Yöki Fitö nö   The good men of old
 Masamë ni mikemu   Must have seen with their own eyes
   Miatö sura wo   Him whose holy prints,
 Ware Fa emisute   Themselves beyond our seeing,
 IFa ni werituku   We now carve upon the rock,
 Tama ni werituku   We now carve upon fine stone.

✻ The beneficent effect of the footprint icon is the subject of no. 1563, which reverts in this regard to no. 1560. There the sound, here the light, is the vehicle of salvation. The second of the "Great Vows" promises a vast flood of light, greater than the sun and moon, from Yakushi's immaculate lapis lazuli body. Salvation is a crossing over ("lead kindly light") to a further shore, as in Amida belief. But shining footprints suggest a pilgrimage overland. This is the only poem in the sequence that is openly and fully a prayer, though no. 1560, of which it is the visual counterpart, is a hortatory appeal.

1563   [BSS 4]

  Könö miatö ya   These holy footprints—
 Yörödu Figari wo   Let them shine forth with the shining

Fanatiidasi	Of a myriad lights,
Morömorö sukuFi	Saving all the multitude:
WatasitamaFana	Bring us across, we beseech thee,
SukuFitamaFana	Save us, we beseech thee.

✳ No. 1564, like no. 1561, belongs to type B, having an exclamatory instead of a repetitive last line, and like no. 1561 it uses *Fitö* to refer to the Buddha, similarly expressing wonder at his magically impressed footprints. The two clearly form a pair, conceptually and structurally. *Yakushi Nyorai Hongangyö* speaks of Yakushi the Lapis Lazuli Shining One as making lapis lazuli the ground of his dwelling. The image of leaving a footprint on rock as if it were earth also calls up the battle scene in high heaven in *Kojiki*, where Amaterasu the sun goddess confronts her brother Susanoo, "treading the hard ground till she sank in to her opposing thighs, kicking the earth aside like light snow." The Shining One of the Yakushi cult is no less the hero here.

1564   [BSS 5]

Ika naru ya	What manner of man
Fitö ni imase ka	Could He have been who on rock
IFa nö uFë wo	Pressed down His foot
Tuti tö Fuminasi	As in earth to leave a print
Atö nökeruramu	Trodden for the after-time?
TaFutoku mo aru ka	He is reverend indeed!

✳ Nos. 1565–66 form a pair, answering the question in no. 1564. He who left the footprints is indeed a hero, a masurao (O. J. *masurawo*), the valiant or stalwart man that haunted the Man'yö poets from Hitomaro to Yakamochi, usually because they felt they did not measure up to the standard. Here translated "that Greater Man," *masurawo* is itself a translation of the Chinese *chang-fu* ("great man," "heroic man"), a term used for the Buddha in sacred scripture. This spiritual hero has gone on ahead, leaving his footprints to remind and inspire his followers.

1565   [BSS 6]

Masurawo nö	That Greater Man
Susumisakitati	Has gone on ahead, first leaving
Fumeru atö wo	These trodden footprints:
Mitutu sinöFamu	Let us gaze and be mindful
Tada ni aFu mate ni	Till we meet Him face to face,
Masa ni aFu mate ni	Till we meet Him in good truth.

1566   [BSS 7]

Masurawo nö	That Greater Man
Fumiokeru atö Fa	Trod and left His footprints here
IFa nö uFë ni	Upon the rock;
Ima mo nököreri	They remain here even now:
Mitutu sinöFe tö	"Gaze and be mindful!"
Nagaku sinöFe tö	"Forever be mindful!"

❋ Although no. 1567 belongs structurally to type B, it is the unique example among the still legible poems in which the final line is neither an altered repetition of line 5 nor an exclamation. Instead, it is a reversed-syntax expansion of the declaration that constitutes this poem. The speaker—and the sequence pauses here in a statement, rather than an incantation—reacts to the devotional intensity of nos. 1565–66 by announcing that he indeed intends to set off to meet the Great Man "face to face." Here that Man is *yöki Fitö,* "the Good Man." The "country" where he dwells is at once India, where the "good men" of no. 1562 saw him, and the paradise to which, in Mahāyāna belief, he has "gone on ahead." The speaker will be a pilgrim and a leader of pilgrims.

1567   [BSS 8]

Könö miatö wo	These holy footprints
Tadunemotömëte	Shall I follow, questing:
Yöki Fitö nö	To the country
Imasu kuni ni Fa	Where the Good Man is, I too
Ware mo mawitemu	Shall go as a pilgrim,
Morömorö wo wite	Leading all the multitude.

❋ On the other side of no. 1567 comes another pair of type A matched poems. Nos. 1565–66 concern the miracle of the *masurawo* and the footprints he has left; the concept of nos. 1568–69 reverts to the carving of the prints by the worshipers. But the future orientation of "Forever be mindful!" is picked up and adapted to a new formulation. The footprints are to be offered to Maitreya, the Buddha yet to come, as a link to Śākyamuni, the historical Buddha who left his prints on the soil of India. Nos. 1568 and 1572 are the only poems in the series to mention any Buddha by name.

One cannot but be impressed that the archaic footprint icon should have inspired this outpouring of intense religious poetry in an ecclesiastical context like that of Nara, where complete sculpted and painted representations of canonical figures of the Buddhist pantheon, from the exquisite Maitreya of Chūgūji to the colossal Vairocana of Tōdaiji and the superb frescoes of

Hōryūji, shone in their pristine splendor from newly erected temples all over the capital area, like the magnificent bronzes of Yakushiji itself, unsung.

It has been well remarked that the use of the respect form *imase*, applied to living beings, in no. 1569 is a form of personification of the symbolic icon. The last word of the poem has flaked away from the surface of the stele.

1568 [BSS 9]

Saka nö miatö	These footprints of Śākya
IFa ni utusioki	We now copy onto rock
UyamaFite	And give reverence:
Nöti nö Fotökë ni	To the Buddha yet to come
Yudurimaturamu	Let us humbly bequeath them,
Sasagëmausamu	Let us offer them held high!

1569 [BSS 10]

Köre nö yö Fa	Though this present world
Uturisaru tö mo	Will alter and pass away,
TökötöFa ni	In eternal stone
Sanököriimase	Let these remain in being
Nöti nö yö nö tamë	For the sake of worlds to come,
Mata nö yö nö [tamë]	For the sake of other worlds.

❋ BSS 11 comes at the left edge of the upper part of the stele, where severe flaking has occurred, and too little remains to say much about. The poem appears to have begun *Masurawo nö / Miatö*, "The footprints of that Greater Man," but doubt has been cast on the genuineness of even this fragment. With BSS 12 (no. 1570) the sequence moves back to the exclamatory mode, with double references to the *yöki Fitö* ("good men") of no. 1562 and the theme of pilgrimage to the unique *yöki Fitö* of no. 1567. The "good men" are now a "band of comrades" (*tömokara*) who were able to make pilgrimage in the past, a piece of good fortune that the speaker both envies and rejoices in. There is also damage to the text of this poem, situated at the lower right of the stele, and some editors prefer to read *atö* for *Fitö* in line 5. The present translation follows Miller rather than Tsuchihashi Yutaka in this regard. Miller points out that the fifth Great Vow has to do with the rewards of correct monasticism, the life of the *tömokara* who are the *saṅgha*, or Buddhist Community.

1570 [BSS 12]

SakiFaFi nö	That band of comrades
Atuki tömokara	Rich in blessings, arriving

771

Mawitarite	After pilgrimage,
Masamë ni mikemu	Must have seen with their own eyes:
Fitö nö tömosisa	Oh, how enviable, they!
Uresiku mo aru ka	What joy we feel for them!

✸ Once again paired poems emerge in nos. 1571–72. Here the concept is the one with which the series began, that the footprints are fashioned by human agency, but here a new humility is enunciated in the auxiliary verb *maturu*, and in the image of human frailty. As in no. 1565, the Buddha is a savior who will rescue humanity in no. 1571, which has specific reference to the sixth of the Great Vows, the promise of succor, healing, and wholeness for the physically and mentally impaired and diseased. No. 1572 echoes and partially repeats no. 1568, carrying the icon forward from offering to use. Here again there is textual reference to the worship of Śākyamuni's feet in the set of Yakushi sutras lying behind these poems. The worship is in the form of circumambulation, a rehearsing in small of the pilgrimage treated elsewhere in the series. The intense religiosity of a poem like no. 1572 epitomizes the faith of the Nara period in its new Master, as did the declaration of Emperor Shōmu that he was the "slave of the Three Treasures" (see commentaries to nos. 525–30 and 814–17).

1571   [BSS 13]

Wodinaki ya	Old and decrepit
Ware ni otöreru	Though I am, there are many
Fitö wo oFomi	In worse plight than I—
Watasamu tamë tö	To bring all of us across
Utusimatureri	I have humbly copied these,
TukaFëmatureri	I have humbly served.

1572   [BSS 14]

Saka nö miatö	Śākya's holy prints
IFa ni utusioki	I now copy onto rock,
Yukimëguri	Circumambulate,
UyamaFimaturi	And give humble reverence:
Wa ga yö Fa woFëmu	So shall I end my span,
Könö yö Fa woFëmu	So shall I end this age.

✸ The "New Medicine Master" of no. 1573 is Bhaiṣajya-guru, Yakushi Nyorai himself, come from abroad—a parallel on the theological level to the influx of medical specialists from the continent in the seventh and eighth centuries. "The wonted ones" (*tune nö*) may refer to the Shintō deities of medicine Ōnamuchi and Sukuna Hikona, as well as to native shamanistic

772

healers. The familiar many-one device from secular poetry is put to use as
the mechanism for expressing this contrast. This poem, the most specific
reference to the *honzon*, or main object of worship, at Yakushiji, stands in
counterpoint to the stated worship of Śākyamuni in no. 1572. Throughout
the series the footprints are those of Śākyamuni, footprints that, as symbol
and icon, themselves have the power to save, to "bring across" through pilgrimage and its reenactment in circumambulation. The cults of Śākyamuni
and Bhaiṣajya-guru are thus aspects of the same quest for healing. No. 1571
combines them in its reference to the sixth Great Vow and to the copying
of the footprints. Nos. 1572 and 1573 separate out the two cultic strands,
naming Śākyamuni and making clear reference to the Buddha as healer
respectively.

1573   [BSS 15]

Kusurisi Fa	Medicine masters:
Tune nö mo aretö	There are also the wonted ones,
MaraFitö nö	But this visitant,
Ima nö kusurisi	The New Medicine Master,
TaFutokarikeri	Behold, how reverend!
Mëdasikarikeri	Behold, how laudable!

✱ No. 1574 reverts to the ritual of circumambulation mentioned in no.
1572 and is the last reference to this devotional act in the surviving portions
of the series. The poem is of type B, in which line 6 is not an echo of line 5.
Looking back, one can see that verses of this type form a series defining and
questing after the "Lord of the Footprints." No. 1561 presents him with all
his cultic verifying marks and signs; no. 1564 asks a deeper question about
his miraculous nature; in no. 1567 the speaker sets off on a pilgrimage to
find him; no. 1570 has the pilgrims arrive at their destination; and in no.
1574 a new image arises in the minds of the worshipers. This image super-
imposes the Bodhisattva, the future Buddha, now still adorned in princely
finery, on the more austere Buddha figure. The *atönusi* thus is not only the
"Lord of the Footprints" (Śākyamuni), but the "Lord of Time to Come,"
the future Buddha Maitreya, referred to previously in conjunction with
Śākyamuni in no. 1568.

1574   [BSS 16]

Könö miatö wo	How as we circle
MaFarimatureFa	Humbly these holy footprints
Atönusi nö	There rises to mind
Tama nö yösöFoFi	The apparel all of jewels
OmoFoyuru kamo	Of the Lord of the Footprints:
Miru götö mo aru ka	It is as if we could see Him!

✳ In no. 1575 attention shifts again to the benefits to be derived from worshiping—or merely coming to see, as here—the holy footprints, the theme enunciated at the beginning. No. 1569 proclaimed the eternal potency of the prints for good; no. 1575 extends their effect back over sins accumulated in previous lives. This is the final statement of the theme of salvation through dependence on "the strength of another" (*tariki*), a basic article of Mahāyāna faith. "Thus have I heard" (*tö zö kiku*) in the final refrain line translates a common opening formula in sutra texts.

1575   [BSS 17]

OFomiatö wo	For whoso comes
Mi ni kuru Fitö nö	To see the great holy footprints,
Inisi kata	Even the sins
Tiyö nö tumi saFë	Of a thousand lifetimes past
Foröbu tö sö iFu	Crumble, so it is said;
Nösöku tö zö kiku	He clears them away, thus have I heard.

✳ Nos. 1576–77 are a contrastive pair introducing a final section concerned with mortality and what it is to be human, rather than with the footprint cult per se. No. 1576 presents the positive aspect of human incarnation, enunciating the Buddhist truism that compared with lower forms of existence the human body is "hard to obtain"—is in fact a reward for merit accumulated in past lives. A human being is fortunate because he can devote himself to the Law (dharma), becoming, as it were, a living stronghold for the doctrine of the faith. Having done so, he must redouble his efforts to attain salvation. The image of *tutömë* and *susume* ("Strive onward . . . press forward!") is no doubt that of the circumambulatory ritual of which these poems are putatively the liturgy.

Another and equally compelling vision of the human condition is provided by no. 1577. The Four Serpents (the four elements of earth, water, fire, and wind making up matter) and the Five Demons (the Five Skandhas; see note to nos. 632–33) wriggle and swarm, and their gathering is the filth of our flesh and being. Human incarnation is only a stage—to accept it as final is to fall into its horrific trap. The passage seems plausibly related to the ninth of the Great Vows of Bhaiṣajya-guru, which promises release from "the nets of demons," as well as to other scriptural passages providing canonical sources for the serpents / demons metaphor.

1576   [BSS 18]

Fitö nö mï Fa	The human body
Egataku areFa	Is a hard thing to attain:
Nöri nö ta nö	It has become

Yösuka tö nareri   For the Law a refuge;
Tutömë morömorö   Strive onward, all!
Susume morömorö   Press forward, all!

1577   [BSS 19]

   Yötu nö Fëmi   Where the Four Serpents
Itutu nö monö nö   And the Five Demonic Things
   Atumareru   All in-gathered are:
Kitanaki mï wo Fa   These our filthy bodies—them
ItöFisutuFësi   We must loathe and cast away;
Fanaresutubësi   Must get free and cast them off.

※ No. 1578, the last legible poem, reverts to type B, with the exclamatory last line. It picks up the dread generated by no. 1577 and concentrates it in the figure of the Lord of Death (*sini nö oFokimi*), the opposite and counterpart of the savior figure who is the Lord of the Footprints (no. 1574, the last previous item in the B series). The human condition is not only filthy and agonizing (no. 1577) but ephemeral. "The fearsome hammer" is an etymological translation of *ikaduti* ("thunder"), and the "flash of light" (*Fikari*) is of course the lightning. The entire phrase is inspired by *tien-kuang* ("lightning flash"), a scriptural metaphor for human life. The Lord of Death as Yama (Emma), the King of Hell, is blended with the earthly King as oppressor, who appears in the tenth of the Great Vows. There also lurks on the border of this field of reference the Japanese snake/thunder deity Ōmononushi (see no. 122 and note). As the sequence now stands, this penultimate poem resonates darkly with no. 1560, in which the artisan's hammer echoed with salvific force. The legible portion of BSS 21 speaks of seeking the Medicine Master, the Good Man, for the end of awakening (from the evil dream of life?), but its authenticity has been brought into question. At all odds, one may feel that the last poem would have provided some such avenue of escape.

1578   [BSS 20]

   Ikaduti nö   The fearsome hammer,
Fikari nö götöki   And the flash of light: even so,
   Köre nö mï Fa   This our body;
Sini nö oFokimi   The Great Lord of Death
Tune ni taguFeri   Is always beside us—
OduFëkarazu ya   Should we not be afraid?

Reference Matter

Glossary

Items in small capitals appear elsewhere in the list.

Ageuta. A notation after some *Kojiki* songs, thought to indicate a high-pitched manner of delivery.

Ama. "Seafolk," dwellers along the shore who made their living from the sea, by fishing, seaweed-gathering, diving, and providing boat services.

Amadaburi. A notation after some *Kojiki* songs, thought to refer to their opening epithets.

Amahasezukai. "The seafolk couriers," the singers designated for some of the songs in the chronicles. Apparently a "corporation" (BE) of the AMA or seafolk of Ise that rendered service to the court in song as well as produce.

Amakataribe. A "corporation" or BE of AMA, the "seafolk reciters," thought to be identical to the AMAHASEZUKAI.

Apsaras. Buddhist goddesses, depicted as soaring through the air in 7th- and 8th-century Japanese art.

Asomi. A "new" KABANE, established as 2d in Emperor Temmu's list of eight. Given to 52 former OMI clans, more distantly related to the imperial clan than the KIMI.

Atae (also **Atai**). A KABANE of the occupational type, held by local magnates loyal to the court (KUNI NO MIYATSUKO). Eliminated from Emperor Temmu's list of eight. Some former holders were given IMIKI.

Aware. As an exclamation, an expression of strong emotion, whether happy or sad. As an esthetic term it is associated with HEIAN belles lettres, where its focus is on the pathos inherent in an awareness of human and natural perishability.

Ayui. A cord used to tie up trousers below the knee.

Azuma. A general term for the part of Honshū east of the YAMATO region.

Azumaasobiuta. "Songs for the Eastern Dances," a special group of folk songs of the FŪZOKUUTA type with provenance in eastern Japan. Performed as a special repertory at the HEIAN court. Not included in this volume.

Banka. A major category of Man'yō poetry. *Banka* are laments or elegies, lit., "[coffin]-pulling songs," a term adopted from *Wen-hsüan.*

Be (also called **Tomo** and **Tomo no o**). Groups of workers and specialists, ranging from low-ranking officials to peasants, who provided services to the court and clans and were under their control. *Be* was presumably a Sino-Korean word applied by PAEKCHE scholars to the Japanese institution.

Bussokuseki. The Buddha's Footprint Stone at YAKUSHIJI in Nara, an icon with incised representations of the feet of Śākyamuni, dated in correspondence with 753. It accompanies another stone, on which are engraved 21 poems in the BUSSOKUSEKIKA form.

Bussokusekika. An ancient poetic form in the syllabic pattern 5-7-5-7-7-7. The major corpus is carved on a stone at YAKUSHIJI and constitutes a liturgy of worship of the footprints of the Buddha, whence its name ("Buddha's footprint stone poem").

Ch'ing T'an. The "pure talk" of a bibulous group of Taoist recluses during the Western Chin Dynasty (A.D. 265–317); *carpe diem* escapist philosophy.

Chōka. "Long poem," a major poetic form in *Man'yōshū*, with alternating lines of five and seven syllables to any length, characteristically ending with a 7-7 couplet, and often followed by one or more envoys (HANKA) in TANKA form. It evolved from less firmly structured long songs preserved in the chronicles.

Chüeh, *see* **Chüeh-chü**

Chüeh-chü. A four-line form of Chinese poetry. There are two types, one with five characters per line and one with seven.

Chwap'yong. "Minister," the highest category in the administrative structure of the Korean state of PAEKCHE.

Cithern. A term used to translate KOTO in this book. Not to be confused with the Western cittern or zither.

Clan title, *see* **Kabane**

Dainin, *see* **Great Benevolence**

Dasoku. "The leg of a snake"; something superfluous.

Day of the Rat. A day in the cycle of the Twelve Beasts. The first Day of the Rat of the new year was considered auspicious and was celebrated in various ways, e.g., by picking spring herbs for medicinal purposes, pulling up seedling pines as symbols of longevity, and displaying the "jewel brooms" used for the ceremonial sweeping of the silkworm platforms.

Eibutsu. "Poems on Things," a Chinese genre adapted to WAKA. In *Man'yōshū* these are usually nature poems, often with images such as flowering trees showing emulation of Chinese tastes. The "things" were drawn from Chinese encyclopedias of poetic topics.

Engo. "Related words," a WAKA technique whereby a given word relates conceptually to a secondary meaning of a second word, thereby creating a sense of cohesion in the poem. The second word becomes a sort of KAKEKOTOBA, but one that does not function as a syntactic double, its homophone ghost being allowed to float free and "relate" to the first word. As a major technique *engo* is a post-Man'yō development, but see #965 and #1401 for early examples.

Expressing Thoughts by Reference to Things, *see* **Kibutsu chinshi**

Expressing Thoughts Directly, *see* **Seijutsu shinsho**

Five-agent system. A pseudo-scientific Chinese system adopted in Japan in which the five elements or agents of Wood, Fire, Earth, Metal, and Water corresponded to various directions, times, etc. Divided into Senior and Junior, they formed ten categories that interlocked with the Twelve Beasts of the zodiac to constitute the basic 60-part calendrical cycle.

Fu. A Chinese poetic form sometimes referred to as rhyme-prose or as rhapsodies. The *fu* were compositions of considerable length, combining narration and description, characterized by florid vocabulary used in an attempt to impress the reader with the sensuosity or majesty of the topic. They became popular in the Han Dynasty and remained so through the Six Dynasties. Influence from *fu* on CHŌKA has been alleged, and it is notable that Ōtomo no Yakamochi and his cousin Ikenushi referred to their CHŌKA as *fu* when in their Sinitic mode.

Fubito, *see* **Fuhito**

Fudoki. Provincial gazetteers listing local geographical data, products, and lore compiled in response to an imperial command issued in 713.

Fuhito. A court occupational title used in the manner of a KABANE. Those to whom it was assigned were scribes, recorders, and readers of texts.

Fujiwara Teika. Poet, critic, scholar, anthologist, redactor of manuscripts, Teika (1162–1241) was the central figure in medieval poetics and an authority for later poets.

Fumi no Tsukasa. Department of Letters, a unit of the administrative structure established by Emperor Tenji in 671 under the Ōmi Administrative Code (*Ōmi Ryō*).

Fūzokuuta. Folk songs collected and sung at the HEIAN court. Made up of two types, those based on the TANKA form, with repetitions and HAYASHIKOTOBA, and those employing looser structures. The older examples are considered to date from the 8th century. Not included in this volume.

Genji. The hero of *The Tale of Genji*, an 11th-century novel by Murasaki Shikibu.

Gigaku. A form of elaborately costumed and masked dance introduced from China in the 7th century and briefly popular in the NARA period. Now defunct, but the masks have been preserved.

Gosechi dances. Dating from the reign of Emperor Temmu (672–86), they were performed at court by young girls as part of the imperial harvest ceremony in the 11th month.

Goshichi-chō. The five-seven rhythm of TANKA, leading to a scansion of 5-7/5-7/7, a characteristic of much Man'yō verse. *See also* SHICHIGO-CHŌ.

Great Benevolence. Third rank in a Japanese court rank system instituted in 603.

Greater Brocade Lower. The 9th level from the top in a court rank system instituted by Emperor Tenji in 663.

Greater Mountain Lower. The 15th level from the top in a court rank system instituted by Emperor Tenji in 663.

Hada (also **Hata**). A clan of Korean origin that claimed descent from China's First Emperor. Specialists in textile manufacture, its members were very rich and influential in 7th-century Japan.

Haiku. A poetic form in 5-7-5 syllables, derived from the *hokku* or opening verse of a RENGA sequence.

Hakuhō. An art-historical period named after the YEAR PERIOD of the same name, 672–86. *Hakuhō* refers to late-7th-century, pre-NARA art in general, when Buddhist sculpture in particular was characterized by a serene, classic repose and youthful beauty expressed through fully sophisticated technical control.

Half poem, *see* **Katauta**

Hanka. An envoy, usually in TANKA form, after a CHŌKA.

Hareflower. A translation of *unohana* (*Deutzia thunbergii*), used in this book, suggested by the character *u* ("hare") in its orthography. *Unohana* has white blossoms.

Hata, *see* **Hada**

Hayashikotoba. Meaningless words and phrases in KAYŌ, sung as refrains or for their rhythm.

Heian. The period from 794 to 1192 during which the imperial court in theory ruled Japan without let or hindrance from its capital in Heian-kyō (modern Kyōto). Its culture marks the apogee of courtly civilization in Japan.

Hinaburi. "Rustic measure," a label for certain songs in *Kojiki*, thought to derive from the fact that one of them contains the word *hinatsume*, "rustic maid."

Hiyuka. A poem in the allegorical mode. A major category in *Man'yōshū*. Properly the term refers to poems in which the tenor of the metaphor is kept dark, but not all poems listed under the rubric are of this type.

Hon'i. The "basic concept" of a poem, a term in medieval poetics governing the prescribed treatment of a topic.

Imiki. A "new" KABANE, the 4th in Emperor Temmu's revised list of eight. It was given to KUNI NO MIYATSUKO clans that previously had been ATAI. Over half of these clans were of foreign origin.

Imo. A very common endearment for women in WAKA of our period. The word refers to women who are objects of desire and affection on the part of either men or women, most frequently wives and sweethearts. It is sometimes written with the character for "younger sister," and the modern word *imōto* ("younger sister") is derived from it. Some authorities believe that the meaning of "sister" is a later limitation on the term, others that it is the basic denotation. Half-sibling marriages were in fact common among the aristocracy during the 8th century and earlier.

Inaki (also **Inagi**). The lowest-ranking KABANE in Emperor Temmu's list of eight. It is an old term referring to local officials inferior to the KUNI NO MIYATSUKO, managers of imperial granaries (MIYAKE). There is no record of its having been bestowed under the reformed system.

Iwaki. "Stone fort," perhaps a hilltop stonghold or the stone crypt of a mound burial.

Izanagi. The progenitor god in Japanese myth. With IZANAMI he created the islands of Japan and many deities, mostly by sexual means.

Izanami. The progenitor goddess in Japanese myth. With IZANAGI she created the islands of Japan and many deities, mostly by sexual means.

Ji. Maitreya, from the Sino-Japanese reading of the character for "compassion."

Jinshin War. A conflict in 672 (the year Jinshin or Water-Senior/Monkey) in which Prince Ōama, the brother of the recently deceased Emperor Tenji, overthrew Tenji's son and heir, Prince Ōtomo (Emperor Kōbun), and seized power for himself as Emperor Temmu.

Jo. "Preface." With MAKURAKOTOBA, one of the two types of preposited rhetorical structures in WAKA. Longer than the MAKURAKOTOBA, the *jo* may occupy two or more lines. It leads up to a word that it introduces either by juxtaposition or some form of doubling or echoing. The relation between the *jo* and the MAIN STATEMENT may be purely phonetic, in which case the *jo* is *mushin* ("meaningless"). If the two parts of the poem are related by sense, the *jo* is *ushin* ("meaningful").

Jukkai. A Chinese-derived genre of poetry "stating one's feelings," often in the manner of a melancholy complaint.

Kabane. Clan titles, a complex system of which existed in the period dealt with in this book. The older phase of the system assigned the titles according to two criteria, genealogical and occupational. OMI and MURAJI are examples of the former, ATAI (or *Atae*) and OBITO of the latter. The system was reformed in 684 by Emperor Temmu, then constituting a hierarchy of eight titles: MAHITO, ASOMI, SUKUNE, IMIKI, MICHINOSHI, OMI, MURAJI, and INAGI (or *Inaki*).

Kagai, *see* **Utagaki**

Kagura. Shintō dances intended to please the gods. Song texts accompanying such dances performed at court have been preserved from the HEIAN period.

Kagurauta. Songs used in the Shintō ceremony known as KAGURA. They include both TANKA and folk song types. A small corpus has been preserved from HEIAN times. Not included in this anthology.

Kakekotoba. "Pivot word," a form of zeugma in which a set of syllables functions in two senses through an exploitation of homophony, or in which the same word serves double syntactical functions. Often found as a form of juncture between JO and MAIN STATEMENT in Man'yō poetry.

Kami-ichidan. The "upper one-step" conjugation of Japanese verbs.

Kamunabi. A place where a god descends into the wood (= MIMORO). MIMORO refers to the grove (*mori*) itself, while *kamunabi* means "place of the god." It is used to refer to specific hills in the Asuka area and has somewhat the quality of a place-name.

Kamunagi. Shamans, mediums.

Kan'ami. A famous Nō playwright and actor (1333–84), together with his son Zeami (1364?–1443) the founder of the classic Nō.

Kanshi. A poem in Chinese.

Kara. A unit of KAYA (also called Mimana); used also of Korea generally, and, with different orthography, of China.

Katami. A "keepsake," something by which to remember a person who has died or is away. An important concept in the laments of Hitomaro.

Kataoroshi. A notation ("lowered part") after some *Kojiki* songs, thought to indicate rendition at a lowered pitch.

Katauta. "Half poem," an ancient poetic structure in the syllabic pattern 5-7-7, often used as one-half of a poetic exchange.

Kaya (also called **Mimana**). A Japanese-dominated confederation of petty states on the south coast of Korea. It was overrun by SILLA in 562.

Kayō. Song, sung poetry. *See also* KODAI KAYŌ

Kazuraki. A mountain range between the Yamato basin and the sea. Also a clan of OMI status that intermarried with the imperial clan.

Kibutsu. "Referring to Things." A Japanese genre on the model of EIBUTSU, but characterized by the use of the traditional oblique metaphorical technique of the JO. Characteristically love poems. *See also* KIBUTSU CHINSHI

Kibutsu chinshi (also **Mono ni yosete omoi o noburu**). "Expressing Thoughts by Reference to Things," a metaphorical mode usually employing the technique of the JO. Characteristically love TANKA of a traditional type.

Kibutsu hasshi. "Arousing Thoughts by Reference to Things," a Man'yō category essentially the same as KIBUTSU CHINSHI.

Kikajin. A term referring to immigrants from the continent who remained in Japan and became Japanese subjects in our period.

Kikō. Travel literature, typically diaries, a genre developed from the 10th century on.

Kimi. A term translatable as "lord," but also used as a polite second person. Also a KABANE, among the ancient clans carried by chieftains claiming blood relation to the imperial clan, but enjoying a half-independent status in remote areas. Eliminated from Emperor Temmu's revised list of eight. These clans were reclassified as MAHITO.

Kishi. A KABANE-type title adopted directly from Korea, where it was 14th in the 17-rank court system of SILLA. Used by clans of Korean extraction.

Kō-rui, *see under* **Otsu-rui**

Kodai Kayō. "Ancient Song," a term referring to poetic texts in the chronicles and FUDOKI, as well as other early songs preserved in folk-song collections compiled at court, but not usually to the content of *Man'yōshū*.

Koguryŏ. A state in northern Korea and southern Manchuria conquered by SILLA in 668.

Koto. Any of various stringed instruments played horizontally by plucking. The ancient *wagon* or Japanese koto had six strings and could be held in the lap. Koto playing had magical as well as entertainment value, the plucked string of a musical instrument or a bow being thought to have power over gods and spirits of the dead. Sometimes translated as CITHERN in this book.

Kotoage. "Lifting up words," a form of Shintō spell in which the words, by being "lifted up," achieved their content through the force of the KOTODAMA.

Kotodama. The "word soul," the word regarded as having magical force, the focus of an ancient belief in the power of the Japanese language to work weal or woe.

Kotodate. An oath.

Ku. A prosodic unit referred to herein as a "line," though not visually represented as such in most Japanese texts. Characteristically either five or seven syllables in length.

Kumaso. Inhabitants of Kyūshū who were unsubmissive to the Yamato court during the times covered in this volume. Perhaps ethnically distinct.

Kumebe. A warrior group organized into a BE. The Kume are mentioned as fierce warriors in the service of the founding hero of Yamato in *Kojiki* and *Nihonshoki*.

Kuni no Miyatsuko. Hereditary heads of *kuni* ("lands," later the term for "province") in pre-TAIKA Japan.

Kunimi. The rite of imperial inspection of the land from a mountaintop.

Kurabito. A court occupational title used in the manner of a KABANE, one of a large class ending with *hito* ("person"). The KURABITO were storers.

Kuzu. Inhabitants of the Yoshino mountains, an autochthonous people who came to court with their songs, dances, and products in early Japan. They were regarded as simple and primitive.

Lesser Brocade Lower. The 12th level from the top in a court rank system instituted by Emperor Tenji in 663.

Lesser Mountain Lower. The 18th level from the top in a court rank system instituted by Emperor Tenji in 663.

Lesser Mountain Upper. The 16th level from the top in a court rank system instituted by Emperor Tenji in 663.

Lesser Virtue. Second rank in a Japanese court rank system instituted in 603.

Magatama. A curved, comma-shaped gem of jade or some other polished stone. A sacred emblem in ancient Japan, often strung on strings.

Mahito. The first class of KABANE as revised by Emperor Temmu in 684. Given to 13 former KIMI clans.

Main statement. The part of the poem introduced by the JO.

Makurakotoba. "Pillow word," a characteristically five-syllable modifying structure of two types, adjectival and adverbial. The adjectival type is epithetical, while the adverbial tends to function as a kind of metaphor.

Man'yōgana. An orthographic system employed in *Man'yōshū* and elsewhere in which Chinese characters are used phonetically (*see* PHONOGRAM) to represent the sounds of Japanese. It includes not only Sino-Japanese (ON-YOMI) readings, but "borrowed *kun*," assigned Japanese readings, as well as highly playful extrapolations, to represent the syllables of Japanese words. *Man'yōshū* is not written in *man'yōgana* alone, however, but combines it with SEMANTOGRAM uses of Chinese characters.

Masurao. A valiant, stalwart, or heroic man. A Man'yō ideal largely treated in the negative—as one the poet cannot live up to.

Michi no shiri. The after part of a province, more distant from the capital than *michi no kuchi*, the entrance of a province.

Michiyuki. A travel scene in Nō, Bunraku, and Kabuki drama.

Miki. An honorific term for SAKE.

Mimana, *see* **Kaya**

Mimoro. A sacred grove or tree into which a god would descend.

Minashiro. A "namesake group," a BE of farmers who presented their produce to the person for whom their *be* was named, usually a member of the imperial clan. To have a *minashiro* was regarded as a way to perpetuate one's name.

Miwa. A mountain in the YAMATO area, the seat of the ŌMONONUSHI cult. Also a word meaning "offertory wine."

Miyabio. An elegant man, one of refined tastes and savoir faire; a courtly play-boy. A Man'yō ideal treated with humorous irony.

Miyahitoburi. "Courtly measure," a notation after a *Kojiki* song, thought to re-fer to its opening word.

Miyake. Direct imperial domains; also the granaries on such domains. Also a colony such as Mimana (KAYA) belonging directly to the YAMATO state.

Miyatsuko. An occupational KABANE given to masters of workers' corporations (BE) from the late 5th century. *See also* KUNI NO MIYATSUKO

Mock epithet. A term used in this book for a MAKURAKOTOBA that modifies a word embedded in a longer word, as when *tsuno sahau* ("vine-swarming") serves as an epithet for the place-name Iwami through the word *iwa* ("rock").

Mono ni yosete omoi o noburu, *see* **Kibutsu chinshi**

Mononobe. An ancient MURAJI clan, specialists in warfare.

Mononofu. A general term for the court officials. Also used to refer specifically to military officials.

Mononofu no Yasotomo no o. A phrase combining MONONOFU as a MAKURA-KOTOBA or epithet with YASOTOMO NO O. Technically, *mononofu no* relates to *yaso* ("eighty") because of the large numbers of officials implied by *mononofu*. (An alternate explanation is that *mononofu* means "warriors" and relates as a MOCK EPITHET to *ya* ["arrow"].) The real point of the collocation, however, is in the orotund sound of the joined phrases, combined with an awesome vision of court officials high and low.

Mori. A sacred grove or tree (= MIMORO in this sense).

Muraji. A KABANE held by clans claiming descent from deities other than the an-cestress of the imperial family, the sun goddess Amaterasu. They did not marry into the imperial family, but served it in various capacities, as for in-stance the Ōtomo with their warrior tradition. With OMI one of the two politi-cally most prominent ancient KABANE, but demoted to 7th in Emperor Temmu's list of eight. Former Muraji were granted the new SUKUNE status after 684. *See also* ŌMURAJI

Mushin, *see under* **Jo**

Nara. The capital of Japan from 710 to 784; also the period of the Nara capital.

Nori no Tsukasa. Department of Laws, a unit of the administrative structure established by Emperor Tenji in 671 under the Ōmi Administrative Code (*Ōmi Ryō*).

Norito. Ancient Shintō prayers, an important early Japanese language source with stylistic similarities to CHŌKA style. They are preserved in *Engishiki*, a 10th-century compilation of the then-current law code, but such ritual incantations go back to the period represented in this volume, as may be seen in #153.

Nunawa. Water shield, an edible plant that grows in fresh water, now known in Japan as *junsai*.

Ō-Omi. ("Great OMI"), the leading civil court official in the pre-TAIKA system. This official was chosen from leading OMI clans such as Kazuraki, Heguri, Kose, and Soga.

Obito. A KABANE. *Obito* were village and district chiefs and supervisors of MIYAKE. They controlled corporations (BE) of workers.

Oborozukiyo. A character in the 11th-century novel *The Tale of Genji*. GENJI's indiscreet affair with this woman gives his enemies a handle against him.

Ochimizu. Water restorative of youth, according to myth to be found on the moon.

Ōkuninushi. "Great Land Master," a descendant of the unruly deity Susanoo no Mikoto. Worshiped at the Grand Shrine of Izumo, he rather than IZANAGI and IZANAMI is the creator deity in Izumo myth. Also known as Yachihoko no Kami, he is the hero of amorous adventures, and as the reconciled husband of Suserihime no Mikoto is worshiped as the god of marriage.

Omi. A KABANE held by clans claiming descent from the imperial clan, as for instance the Soga and the Kazuraki, which had the privilege of providing consorts for the Emperor. In the reformed system of Emperor Temmu, Omi was demoted to 6th in the list of eight KABANE, the former Omi clans being assigned the new ASOMI status. The term also had the general sense of "court noble" and may originally have meant "human being." *See also* Ō-OMI

Ōmononushi. The deity of Ōmiwa Shrine at Mount MIWA, one of whose forms is a snake. He appears as an amorous deity in SHINKON SETSUWA. According to the Izumo version of the creation myth, Ōmononushi helped ŌKUNINUSHI in the creation of the land; he is also described as a manifestation of Ōkuninushi.

Ōmuraji. ("Great MURAJI"), the two leading military officials in the pre-TAIKA system. They were chosen from the Mononobe and Ōtomo clans.

On-yomi. The Sino-Japanese reading of a character, as distinguished from the native Japanese reading assigned to it.

Otsu-rui. Old Japanese, the language of the poems in this volume, had eight vowels rather than the modern five. Two varieties of *i*, *e*, and *o* are distinguished as kō-rui (type A) and otsu-rui (type B). Otsu-rui vowels are marked in romanization by an umlaut diacritical (see the Buddha's Footstone Poems in this anthology).

Paekche. A kingdom in the southwestern quarter of the Korean peninsula, traditionally an ally of Japan against the rival kingdom of SILLA in the southeast. Destroyed by Silla in 663. There was heavy immigration from Paekche into Japan during the last century of its existence.

Phonogram. A Chinese character used for phonetic representation as opposed to a semantogram, a Chinese character used for its meaning. The terms are from the works of Roy Andrew Miller.

P'ien-wen. A Chinese prose style employing echoic phraseology, antithesis, and balanced "lines" of four and six characters.

Pillow word, *see* **Makurakotoba**

Pivot word, *see* **Kakekotoba**

Pon Kaya. One of the petty states of the KAYA confederation.

Quiet songs, *see* **Shizuuta**

Renga. Linked verse, a poetic form of alternating 5-7-5 and 7-7 syllabic units composed in alternation by two or more poets. It evolved from splitting the TANKA between two poets, and developed into a major kind of poetry in the 13th century and later, with elaborate rules and a characteristic length of 100 verses.

Rustic measure, *see* **Hinaburi**

Saibara. A form of KODAI KAYŌ. Folk songs collected at court and sung to musical accompaniment by the courtiers of the HEIAN period. Some have been preserved in TANKA form, but most do not follow classical syllabic schemes and are characterized by repetitions and ballad-like exclamations called HAYA-SHIKOTOBA. Such songs are thought to date back to the 8th century. Not included in this anthology.

Saikakuesque. Typical of characters or situations found in the work of Ihara Saikaku (1642–93), a poet and picaresque novelist whose heroes and heroines seize time by the forelock when it comes to making love and money.

Sake. A beverage made from fermented rice, usually translated herein as "wine."

Sakikusa. ("Split-grass"), a trifurcated plant whose identity is uncertain. Cypress, *Lilium auratum*, sweet-smelling daphne, and *Edgeworthia papyrifera* are among the possibilities.

Sami, *see* **Śrāmaṇera**

Sedōka. An ancient poetic form in the syllabic pattern 5-7-7-5-7-7.

Seijutsu shinsho (also **Tada ni omoi o noburu**). "Expressing Thoughts Directly." A mode of WAKA distinguished in *Man'yōshū*. These are poems of direct expression eschewing metaphor and allegory. Typically love poems.

Sekigahara, Battle of. A crucial battle in 1600 by which Tokugawa Ieyasu (1542–1616) won dominance over his feudal rivals.

Semantogram, *see under* **Phonogram**

Semmyō. Imperial edicts, a source for an early form of Japanese prose, to be found in *Shoku Nihongi*.

Shaku. Śākyamuni, from the first character used to write his name in Chinese.

Shichigo-chō. The seven-five rhythm of TANKA, leading to scansions of 5/7-5/7-7 or 5-7-5/7-7; increasingly characteristic of post-Man'yō poetry. *See also* GOSHICHI-CHŌ

Shih. A general term for the dominant form, or forms, of Chinese poetry, a rhyming verse characteristically in lines of equal length, either four, five, or seven characters. It includes the CHÜEH-CHÜ and the *Lü Shih* or regulated verse.

Shinkon setsuwa. Stories of marriage between gods and mortals, a feature of Japanese myth referred to several times in this volume.

Shirageuta. A notation after some *Kojiki* songs, thought to indicate a method of singing with the voice rising in the last line.

Shiritori. A prosodic pattern ("tail-catching") in which a line repeats or closely echoes part of the immediately preceding line.

Shizuuta. "Quiet songs" in *Kojiki*, thought to have been those intoned in a stately manner.

Shōsōin. A generic term for storehouses. Specifically, the building and institution housing the personal collection of art objects, manuscripts, and objects of material culture from all over Asia belonging to Emperor Shōmu and his consort Empress Kōmyō. Kōmyō donated the collection to the state on Shōmu's death in 756. Both the building and the collection have remained intact since the 8th century. The Shōsōin is located at TŌDAIJI.

Silla. A kingdom in the southeast quadrant of the Korean peninsula. It conquered the other Korean kingdoms of PAEKCHE in 663 and KOGURYŎ in 668, thus unifying the peninsula under its rule. It was an ally of T'ang China, and traditionally unfriendly to Japan.

Sōmon. A major category of Man'yō poetry, essentially love poetry, though the word means "mutual inquiry" and suggests an exchange.

Śrāmaṇera. A male Buddhist novice, defined as one who has taken vows not to kill, steal, lie or speak evil, have sexual intercourse, use perfumes or decorate himself with flowers, occupy high beds, sing or dance, possess wealth, eat out of regulation hours, or drink wine. There is evidence in *Man'yōshū* that the Japanese novice, or sami, represented by Mikata no Sami and Manzei Sami in this anthology, did not necessarily abstain from sex.

Sukuna Mikami. A tiny deity associated with the art of brewing; in Izumo mythology a helper of ŌKUNINUSHI in creating the land. Said to have left his task unfinished and returned to TOKOYO by being flipped off a stalk of millet. His task was completed by ŌMONONUSHI.

Sukune. A term of respect for loyal servants of the crown such as Takeshi Uchi no Sukune; supposedly derived from *sukuna* ("lesser") + *e* ("elder brother"). Later a KABANE, the 3d in Emperor Temmu's list of 684. It was assigned to former MURAJI clans.

Symbolic Equation. A term from Stephen Reckert, *Lyra Minima*, in which a metaphor is implied by the juxtaposition of a natural image with a statement about a human being in syntactically independent halves of a poem.

Tachibana. The ancient Japanese orange, according to Japanese legend imported from TOKOYO no Kuni by Tajimamori, a person of Korean descent, in the 3d century. The tree was admired for its fragrance, and both the fruit and the flowers were strung in garlands, but it is not clear whether the fruit was eaten in *Man'yō* times.

Taika. The reforms associated with the government dominated by Prince Naka no Ōe, and the period after they were introduced, named after the Taika YEAR PERIOD (645–50).

Talsol. The 2d rank in the administrative structure of the Korean state of PAEKCHE.

Tanka. "Short poem," the oldest form of Japanese literature still in use. A syllabic structure of five KU in the pattern 5-7-5-7-7.

Tōdaiji. The enormous temple of the Kegon Sect erected in Nara at the order of Emperor Shōmu to house the Great Buddha, a bronze icon of Vairocana. Both the icon and the building were the largest of their kind in the world. The dedication took place in 752. The site of the SHŌSŌIN.

Tōka. A Chinese dance introduced to the Japanese court in the 7th century. Performed by young men and women in the 1st month.

Tokoyo. "Everworld" (also Tokoyo no Kuni; the Land of Everworld), the mythic realm of immortality and the TACHIBANA or mandarin orange. It was conceived of as being across, in the midst of, or at the bottom of the sea.

Tomo. A native Japanese word meaning the same thing as BE.

Tomo no o. Synonymous with TOMO and BE. O originally probably meant "controller," but came also to be written with the character for "man" (both O.J. *wo*).

Toneri. Personal attendants on members of the imperial clan.

Tsuchigumo. An ancient people in Japan, perhaps ethnically distinct, who are recorded to have fought against the early heroes of Yamato.

Ukehi. An oath in which one's veracity or the will of the gods is tested by the occurrence, or not, of a specified alternative between two possible outcomes of an event.

Uneme. Translated "palace woman" in this anthology, the term refers to women sent from the provinces to serve at court. They were selected for their beauty by KUNI NO MIYATSUKO and were expected to remain unmarried and serve the Emperor.

Ushin, *see* **Jo**

Utagaki (also **Kagai**). Originally a fertility rite; as seen in sources in this volume, an opportunity for young men and women to pursue sexual liaisons, typically in the mountains, in a picnic-like atmosphere. Songs were exchanged between the sexes, and between male rivals, as means of conquest and rebuff. It is thought that these challenges were influential on the wit and pointedness of the poetic exchange.

Utaikaeshi. "Responses," a notation after some *Kojiki* songs, thought to refer to short CHŌKA sung in a lively manner.

Utamakura. "Song-pillow," a term for places rich in poetic associations.

Utamonogatari. A 10th-century literary genre with antecedents in the chronicles and *Man'yōshū*. Poems accompanied by a prose setting; short stories culminating in expression through poems.

Uzumasa (also **Utsumasa**). A location in present Kyōto, anciently the seat of the HATA (Hada) clan, whose clan title it became.

Waka. The forms of poetry represented in this book: essentially, TANKA, CHŌKA, SEDŌKA, and BUSSOKUSEKIKA.

Wani. A creature mentioned in the chronicles and FUDOKI, thought to have been either a crocodile or a shark.

Wazauta. A premonitory song of apparently innocent content, interpreted as referring to political matters and said to have been sung by children, the common people, or animals. Found principally in *Nihonshoki*, though it appears in other sources as well.

Yakushiji. A temple in NARA that is the site of the BUSSOKUSEKI and accompanying BUSSOKUSEKIKA stele, as well as other major icons of 8th-century Buddhism.

Yamato. The inland region extending from north of NARA south to the Yoshino mountains, where the Japanese court was usually located during the centuries before the move to Heian-kyō (modern Kyōto) in 794. Also the state that emerged in the Yamato area and the adjacent littoral in the 4th century. Also Japan as a whole as contrasted with the Korean states and China, especially in the period prior to the 7th century.

Yasotomo no o. "The Eighty Crafts," a term for a type of BE or "corporation" composed of two types. One was the TOMO NO O proper, made up of low-ranking officials who performed specialty functions in the palace, such as serving as scribes and taking care of the storehouses. The other, the Shinabe, were spread widely throughout the capital area. They were artisans—metalworkers, saddle-makers, brocade-makers, etc.—and were largely of continental origin, especially Korean, reflecting the large immigration from PAEKCHE in the 6th and 7th centuries.

Year period. Named eras, a Chinese invention adopted by the Japanese in the 7th century.

Yodan. The "four-step" conjugation of Japanese verbs.

Yōen. A medieval poetic term referring to a style of seductive and mysterious beauty, associated especially with FUJIWARA TEIKA.

Yomiuta. A notation after some *Kojiki* songs, thought to indicate they are songs of praise.

Zō. "Miscellaneous," a major category of Japanese poetry beginning with *Man'yōshū*, where it is one member of a tripartite grouping into ZŌKA, SŌMON ("Love Poetry"), and BANKA ("Laments"). In *Man'yōshū* it includes a great deal of formal public poetry.

Zōka. "Miscellaneous Poem," *see* ZŌ

Notes

For complete authors' names, titles, and places of publication on works cited in short form in the Notes, see the Bibliography, pp. 863–71. The following abbreviations are used:

Jōdai   Kojima Noriyuki, *Jōdai Nihon Bungaku to Chūgoku Bungaku*
NKBT   *Man'yōshū*, ed. Takagi Ichinosuke et al.
NKBZ   *Man'yōshū*, ed. Kojima Noriyuki et al.

INTRODUCTION

1. See Miller, pp. 66–69, for a discussion of the rules of synaloepha.

2. Trenchant critiques of the concept of the tanka as a five-line poem and defenses of its unilinearity are found in Morris and in Sato. The earliest detailed statements on Japanese prosody are in *Kakyō Hyōshiki* by Fujiwara no Hamanari (724–90). (See notes to #278 and #1548–49.) This work, dating from 772, proposes stringent phonetic rules for the five ku of a tanka.

3. My first encounters with waka in translation were in Donald Keene's *Japanese Literature* (1955) and *Anthology of Japanese Literature* (1956).

4. On the phonology of Old Japanese, see Miller, pp. 56–66. Miller acknowledges that Old Japanese cannot actually be pronounced with any assurance of correctness.

5. For Getsi's bilingual book, see Trakl. German and English are on facing pages.

6. Other than *Japanese Court Poetry* itself, the most highly recommended book on the period covered in this volume is McCullough, *Brocade by Night*. The first two chapters of that work are particularly valuable background reading and contain many excellent translations of Man'yō poetry and *kodai kayō*. Donald L. Philippi's translations of early song are also excellent. His *This Wine of Peace, This Wine of Laughter* (1968) collects them all. Brooks, "A Yakamochi Sampler," contains some of the finest tanka translations I have seen. The major project in the field at present is Ian Levy's complete translation of *Man'yōshū* under the title *The Ten Thousand Leaves*, the first volume of which was published by Princeton University Press in 1981.

7. The resolution of a syntactic doubling into the comparative pattern "no more . . . than . . . ," illustrated in MYS XI: 2680/2672, is a technique learned from Brooks, "A Yakamochi Sampler."

SONGS FROM THE CHRONICLES AND 'FUDOKI'

The *Six National Histories* (*Rikkokushi*), and the period covered by each, are *Nihonshoki* (also *Nihongi*), earliest times to 697; *Shoku Nihongi*, 697–791; *Nihon Kōki*, 792–833; *Shoku Nihon Kōki*, 833–50; *Montoku Jitsuroku*, 850–58; and *Sandai Jitsuroku*, 858–87. All are in Chinese, and the series halted with the decline of Chinese studies at the end of the 9th century. The first two contain waka and are of interest in the history of Japanese poetry (but see also #886–88 and note).

Evidence of 7th-century determination to compile a national history focuses on the reigns of Empress Suiko (r. 593–628) and Emperor Temmu (r. 672–86). *Nihonshoki* records that in 620 Suiko's nephew the scholar-statesman Prince Shōtoku (574–621) and the chief minister Soga no Umako (d. 626) together set down a *Record of the Emperors* (*Tennōki* or *Sumera Mikoto no Fumi*), a *National Record* (*Kokki* or *Kuni tsu Fumi*), and *Basic Records* (*Hongi* or *Moto tsu Fumi*) of the several classes of society (Sakamoto et al., II, 203 [Aston, II, 148]). These documents were burned by Umako's son Emishi during a coup d'état in 645; part of the *National Record*, however, was rescued from the flames (Sakamoto et al., II, 264, 265 [Aston, II, 193]). Later, in 681, Emperor Temmu ordered the "correction and recording" of the *Chronicle of the Sovereigns* (*Teiki* or *Sumera Mikoto no Fumi*) and what are referred to as "matters of high antiquity" (*jōko shoji* or *inishie no moromoro no koto*). It is thought that this commission eventually resulted in *Nihonshoki*. In addition to Princes Kawashima and Osakabe, Emperor Temmu's committee of historians included Prince Hirose (d. 722), Prince Takeda (d. 715), Prince Kuwata, Prince Mino, Kamitsukeno no Michiji (d. 681), Imube no Obito (d. 719), Azumi no Inashiki, Naniwa no Ōkata, Nakatomi no Ōshima (d. ca. 693), and Heguri no Koobito. *Nihonshoki* states that the last two, Ōshima and Koobito, "personally took their brushes and did the recording" (Sakamoto et al., II, 445–47 [Aston, II, 350]).

Another historiographical project started in Emperor Temmu's reign led to *Kojiki*. At an unspecified date, as recorded in Ō no Yasumaro's preface to *Kojiki*, the Emperor commissioned Hieda no Are, a *toneri*, or court attendant, credited with unusual powers of memory, to "learn" (i.e., memorize) the *Teiki* and *Honji* or *Basic Narrative*. All three projects, that of 620 and the two recorded for Temmu's reign, apparently dealt with two kinds of documents, genealogical and anecdotal, which were to be combined into a general history. In 711 (again according to the *Kojiki* preface), Empress Gemmei commanded Ō no Yasumaro to "record and present" what Hieda no Are had memorized. Yasumaro fulfilled this commission the following year, 712 (Kurano, pp. 45–49 [Philippi, *Kojiki*, pp. 41–44]). It has never been quite clear what the point of having documents memorized and then re-recorded was, but it has been suggested that Are was an expert in deciphering the stylistic and orthographical peculiarities of ancient documentary writing (Philippi, *Kojiki*, p. 8). Yasumaro may have been working with documents already re-recorded from Are's memorization or directly with Are himself (or herself: Are may have been a woman). Both *Kojiki* and *Nihonshoki* materialized three to four decades after the initiatives of Temmu's reign, and little is known about the inter-mediate stages. The date of Prince Toneri's appointment as final compiler of *Nihonshoki* is not recorded, nor is it known how large a staff he had working under him, though the names of two members, Ki no Kiyohito and Miyahe no Fujimaro, are known (*Shoku Nihongi*, pp. 55, 81). For an account of the formation of both *Kojiki* and *Nihonshoki*, Philippi, *Kojiki*, pp. 4–18, is useful.

The term fudoki stems from the Chinese work of that name (*Feng-t'u-chi*) by Chou Ch'u of the Chin dynasty (A.D. 265–420). The Japanese fudoki of the Nara period were a kind of *gebun*, or document submitted on imperial command. It is thought that the original manuscripts did not include the title fudoki. The first dated use of the term is in *Iken Fūji*, a work of 914 by Miyoshi Kiyoyuki (847–918; Akimoto, p. 8). The order for the compilation of the Nara documents now known as fudoki appears in *Shoku Nihongi*, Wadō 6 (713).5; see KT, II, 32. Sources of fudoki fragments (*itsubun*) begin with the *Iken Fūji* mentioned above and include *Man'yōshū Chūshaku* (1269) by Sengaku (b. 1203); *Shaku Nihongi* (dating from the Bun'ei-Kōan periods, 1264–88) by Urabe Kanekata; and *Chiribukuro* (dating from the period 1274–81), attributed to the monk Ryōin. Edo-period researches brought together these and other sources. Akimoto particularly cites *Man'yōi* (1717 or earlier) by Imai Jikan (1657–1723) and *Shokoku Fudoki Itsubunkō* by Ban No-butomo (1773–1846).

The compilation of *Shoku Nihongi* may have begun in the reign of Junnin (758–64) or earlier, and proceeded in a series of additions and revisions. The final stages of the project were under the direction of Fujiwara no Tsuginawa (727–96) and Sugano no Mamichi (ca. 738–ca. 811). (Yanagi [2], pp. 20–21; *Nihon Kōki*, pp. 10–11.)

The distinction between *dokuritsu kayō* ("independent songs") and *monogatari-uta* (songs composed for the story) is drawn by Tsuchihashi Yutaka in *Kodai Ka-yōshū*, pp. 10–18. He adds wazauta and other "popular songs" as a third category and divides the independent songs into *min'yō* ("folk songs"), *geiyō* ("art songs"; i.e., those by professional entertainers), and *kyūtei kayō* ("court songs"). The cate-gories sometimes overlap.

2–5 [K 2–5]. The translation "Eight Thousand Spears" for the name of the god Yachihoko no Kami is adopted, with gratitude, from Brower and Miner, pp. 62–64. The *amakataribe* were a corporation of reciters drawn from the seafolk (*ama*) of Ise, according to *Kodai Kayōshū*, p. 13. Their recitations were part of their annual service at court at the harvest ceremony of "first tasting" (*niinamesai*). They were also apparently used as couriers, whence the name *amahasezukai* ("seafolk couriers"). As seen in #167, the identity of the hero who was "unable to bed a wife" is interchangeable. #4–5 indicate rather that Eight Thousand Spears was famed for his amorous prowess.

6 [K 6]. If the *ototanabata* ("young maiden of the loom") is to be identified with the heroine of the Tanabata myth (see #398), the song cannot be earlier than the

late 7th century. The term *tanabata*, however, simply means "loom," and by extension "weaver," and need not refer to the Chinese myth. Another heavenly weaving woman is mentioned earlier in *Kojiki*, in the passage describing Susanoo's outrageous behavior after besting his sister the sun goddess in a progeny-producing contest. She is referred to as the "clothing-weaving woman" (*hataorime*) and is said to have mortally wounded herself by colliding with the shuttle of her loom after Susanoo flung a heavenly piebald colt flayed with a backward flaying through the roof of the heavenly weaving chamber (Kurano, p. 80-81 [Philippi, *Kojiki*, p. 80]).

7 [K 7]. Jewels are mentioned twice previously in the tale of Ho-ori no Mikoto. When he was sitting in the cassia tree before the sea god's palace prior to meeting Toyotamahime, he removed a red jewel from around his neck, put it in his mouth, and spat it into the water vessel offered him by Toyotamahime's handmaid. The jewel adhered to the vessel and aroused Toyotamahime's interest when shown to her. Later, before Ho-ori's return to land, the sea god gave him two magic jewels, the tide-flowing jewel and the tide-ebbing jewel, with which to control the waters and gain mastery over his elder brother. Ho-ori is the mythical ancestor of the Japanese imperial house.

9 [K 9]. The *ichisakaki* has been identified as the *Eurya japonica*, a bush producing numerous reddish-black berries.

10 [K 10]. See Philippi, *Kojiki*, p. 175, for the comment on the envoy-like ending of this song. The Tsuchigumo, like other early peoples in Japan, seem to have lived in pit-dwellings, but the no doubt derogatory description of them as having tails is puzzling. As a group unsubmissive to Yamato power, they may have brought upon themselves the opprobrium of an animalistic caricaturization. Their name appears to mean "earth-spiders," and in *Hitachi Fudoki* (Akimoto, pp. 46-47) they are described as having the nature of wolves and the feelings of owls. Opinion is divided on whether they were ethnically distinct from the people who conquered them (Kurano, p. 344; *Kodai Kayōshū*, p. 45). Sakamoto et al., I, 580, summarizes relevant theories. The "son of the heavenly deity" is Emperor Jimmu, according to *Kojiki* genealogy a descendant of the sun goddess in the fifth generation. The knob-mallet (*kubutsutsu*) and stone-mallet (*ishitsutsu*) swords had hilts in the shape of clubs.

11-14 [K 11-14]. Tomibiko was a Yamato chief who killed Jimmu's brother Itsuse no Mikoto in battle. The elder and younger Shiki were the chiefs of the Shiki District in Yamato. All these songs, though placed in the mouth of the Emperor in the *Kojiki* narrative, were traditionally sung by the Kume warriors, in ancient times an imperial guard. *Kamukaze no* ("of the divine wind") as an epithet for Ise (#13) may stem from the violent winds that strike the Ise-Shima peninsula. Another explanation has it as a mock epithet through *i*, the first syllable of *ibuki* ("breath"). For a poetic instance of the effect of the divine wind or breath of the sun goddess Amaterasu, enshrined at Ise, see #341. In #14 *tata namete* ("shields aligned") is a mock epithet for Inasa through the *i* in *iru* ("to shoot").

15–19 [K 15–19]. Isukeyorihime, the consort of Emperor Jimmu, was the daughter of Ōmononushi, the god of Mount Miwa, who came to Yamato from Izumo. A dynastic marriage of Yamato and Izumo seems hinted here. See Philippi, *Kojiki*, pp. 178–79, for the story of Isukeyorihime's birth, and pp. 415–16 for similar tales. *Sakeru tome* ("split, sharp eyes") is interpreted as tattooing around the eyes and is translated that way in the introductory sentence to #17, but literally in the two katauta. In connection with Isukeyorihime's avian riddle, see #1237.

20–22 [K 20–22]. On wazauta, see Nishimura, "Retrospective Comprehension." #20–21 and other premonitory songs in *Kojiki* are not usually discussed as wazauta, the earliest of which is technically considered to be #178. A less restrictive use of the term would include #176 (q.v. for further discussion), which, however, is not predictive. #20–21 qualify in this regard but are not credited to children or other anonymous sources, as are wazauta in the strict sense. #22 is premonitory, but not in the allegorical mode normal to the genre. #66–68, #137–38, and #157 are also in one respect or another similar to wazauta. The girl who sings #22 is seemingly a manifestation of a god, rather than a mortal mouthpiece, from the way she mysteriously vanishes.

23 [K 23]. This song is attached to a different anecdote in *Nihonshoki*, where it appears as NS 20. The text is almost identical and so has been omitted from the present anthology. In the *Kojiki* context it is a song of ridicule, and the matching sea and land images of seaweed and vines are perhaps intended as a mockery of the rich outward show of an impotent and defeated Izumo. The Brave of Izumo and the Brave of Yamato stand for their respective cultic and political powers.

24 [K 24]. The place of Oto-Tachibanahime's self-immolation is supposed to have been Uraga Strait, the entrance to Tōkyō Bay. It is likely that Oto-Tachibanahime is being offered as a bride to the sea god. When Ho-ori no Mikoto wedded Toyotamahime he was seated similarly on eight thicknesses of skin mats and eight thicknesses of silk mats (Kurano, pp. 138–39 [Philippi, *Kojiki*, pp. 151–52]). Oto-Tachibanahime's song implies that she is the daughter of the ruler of Sagamu. There is a parallel here with an earlier story in which Ōkuninushi (= Yachihoko no Kami) woos Suserihime, the daughter of Susanoo no Mikoto. Susanoo tries in various ways to kill his daughter's suitor, in one instance by trapping him on a burning plain. The same motif is employed in the story of Yamato Takeru in Sagamu, except that the daughter is not mentioned until the next episode (Kurano, pp. 96–97 [Philippi, *Kojiki*, pp. 99–100]). The stories of Ōkuninushi and Suserihime, Yamato Takeru and Oto-Tachibanahime, Ho-ori no Mikoto and Toyotamahime, and Urashima and the sea god's daughter (see #216–20 and #579–80) are all versions of a descent-to-the-underworld myth. The underworld or otherworld exists in two versions, one horrible (Yomi) and the other paradisal (Tokoyo), and the father of the hero's bride-to-be may be menacing or welcoming. In the story of Oto-Tachibanahime's sacrifice, the roles of god and hero are reversed—it is the human hero who has to surrender his bride to the capricious deity of the sea. For more on early beliefs concerning the sea and the netherworld, see Akima, "Songs of the Dead." For another reference to the burial of a comb, see #837–38.

25–26 [K 25–26]. From this exchange of katauta the later art of linked verse took its name of Tsukuba no Michi ("the Way of Tsukuba"). The allusion is unhistorical; linked verse evolved from split tanka, not from paired katauta.

27 [K 27]. The word used for "swan," *kubi*, is phonetically identical to *kubi*, "neck."

28 [K 28]. *Aratama* ("rough gem") as an epithet for *toshi* ("year") and *tsuki* ("month") may be a shortened form of *aratamaru* ("to renew"). *Kodai Kayōshū*, p. 113, analyzes the normally hortatory desiderative *tatanamu* in the last line as a speculative derived from *tachi-ari*.

30–32 [K 30–32]. These three songs are attributed to Yamato Takeru's father, Emperor Keikō, in *Nihonshoki*, where they appear in the order c-a-b as NS 21–23.

34–37 [K 34–37]. *Kodai Kayōshū*, p. 58, apparently takes #34 as an amorous folk song. See Kurano, pp. 60–61 (Philippi, *Kojiki*, p. 58), for the description of how the creator god Izanagi crawled around the corpse of his wife Izanami. #341, lines 107–18, is also instructive on the behavior of the bereaved. The repetition of *inagara* in lines 2 and 3 of #34, the so-called *shiritori* or tail-catching pattern, is exemplary of one of the basic structures of early verse. Another image of the soul as a bird is provided by #348. See Akima, "Songs of the Dead," pp. 492–95, for a discussion of the possible significance of this song sequence and of the relation of birds to beliefs about the dead. The "today" of the note following #34–37 may not be the early 8th century, when *Kojiki* was submitted, but the 6th century, when, presumably, record-keeping began (Philippi, *Kojiki*, p. 5).

39–40 [K 39–40]. On "waiting *sake*," see #1544. The puzzling myth of the tiny god Sukuna Hikona is recounted in variant versions in *Kojiki* and *Nihonshoki*. See Kurano, pp. 106–9 (Philippi, *Kojiki*, pp. 115–17); and Sakamoto et al., I, 128–29 (Aston, I, 59–60). According to Izumo mythology, Sukuna and Ōkuninushi (here called Ōnamuji) were the deities who created the land, rather than Izanagi and Izanami. Sukuna (his name means "little") was small enough to fit in a wagtail's skin and came from across the sea, whither he returned before finishing the land. Here he figures as the god of brewing. His connection with grains other than rice is suggested by the version of the myth in which he goes to the island of Awa ("Millet") and returns to Tokoyo by being flicked off a millet stalk (Sakamoto et al., I, 128–29 [Aston, I, 60]). There is some disagreement on whether the drum in #40 is stood up "like a mortar" (*Kodai Kayōshū*, p. 61; Sakamoto et al., I, 351) or "beside the mortar" (Kurano, p. 237). These two songs were sung to koto accompaniment at the early Heian court. Very close versions appear in the 10th-century *Kinkafu* (*Scores for Koto Songs*), with directions for vocalization (*Kodai Kayōshū*, pp. 472–73 [Brannen, pp. 253–54, 293–94]).

43 [K 43]. Takeshi Uchi no Sukune, who figures in several episodes from the reign of Chūai to that of Nintoku (mid-4th–early 5th c. A.D.?), was the first bearer of the title Ō-Omi, the "Great Omi." The Ō-Omi came from the Omi class of clans claiming imperial descent and served as chief officer at court. Philippi's note on Takeshi Uchi no Sukune summarizes the essential information (Philippi, *Kojiki*, pp. 602–3). The reference to an oak-leaf winecup alludes to the ancient custom of drinking wine from oak (*kashiwa*) leaves on ceremonial occasions.

44 [K 44]. In *Nihonshoki* this song is attributed, less appropriately, to Prince Ōsazaki.

47–48 [K 47–48]. On the Kuzu, see Kurano, pp. 154–55 (Philippi, *Kojiki*, p. 170). NS 39, which corresponds to K 48, is followed by this description:

> After they finished singing, they beat upon their mouths, threw back their heads, and laughed. Thus when nowadays on the day the Kuzu present their local products, they finish singing, beat upon their mouths, throw back their heads, and laugh, it would seem they are following an ancient custom. Now, the Kuzu are very simple people by nature. Year in and year out they gather and eat the fruits of the mountains; they also boil frogs, which they call *momi* and consider a delicacy. Their country is southeast of the capital, across the mountains along the Yoshino River. The peaks are precipitous, the valleys deep; the road is narrow and steep. And so although they were not far from the capital, they would rarely come to court. But after this they came frequently to present their local products. These included chestnuts, mushrooms, and trout. (Sakamoto et al., I, 372–73; *Kodai Kayōshū*, p. 149.)

There is a reference to the attendance of the Kuzu at court as late as the 12th century (*Heike Monogatari*, II, 164). It is not clear what connection there was between the Kuzu of Yoshino and Hitachi beyond the name (a contraction of *kunisu*, "earthlings"). *Hitachi Fudoki* lumps the Kuzu of Hitachi with the Tsuchigumo (see note to #10). The reference in Kurano, pp. 154–55, states that the ancestor of the Kuzu of Yoshino, though submissive, had a tail.

As *Kodai Kayōshū*, pp. 67, 115–16, points out, Homuta in #47, while the name of Prince Ōsazaki's father (Homuta-wake), is basically a place-name in Kawachi Province and serves here to refer to Prince Ōsazaki, who was raised there.

49 [K 49]. *Kushi*, translated "potion" here and in #39, is a word for liquor related to *kusushi* ("wondrous") and *kusuri* ("medicine"). The Ōsaka ("Great Slope") road led over the northern end of the Kazuraki Mountains, a range that separates inland Yamato from the sea and the site of the modern city of Ōsaka.

51 [K 51]. *Chihayahito* ("raging men") is a mock epithet for the place Uji through *uji* ("clan"). *Mayumi* ("true-bow"; line 5) is the name of a tree; *azusayumi* ("catalpa bow") serves as a decorative prelude to create a prosodically pleasing pattern of altered repetition (compare #168, line 5). The mention of bows undoubtedly serves to relate this song to the story context and could be one reason why it is attached to the narrative. Speculations about the identity of the *kimi* ("lord") and *imo* ("sister"—or "sweetheart"?) assume that the song was composed to go with the story (see *Kodai Kayōshū*, p. 69).

52 [K 52]. The translation follows ibid., pp. 116–17, in adopting Motoori Norinaga's reading *kurozaya* instead of *morozaya*.

53 [K 53]. Naniwa was perhaps called "far-shining" (*oshiteru ya*) from the sunlight reflected off the surface of the sea that surrounded it in the then much more watery environment of Ōsaka Bay (see the foldout map in NKBZ, 1). Viewed from the mountains separating Naniwa from Yamato, the panorama may well have been blinding in the late afternoon. The islands of Awa and Onogoro are mentioned in the creation sequence of *Kojiki*. Awa was the second-born of the children of the primordial pair Izanami and Izanagi, but like its elder sibling the "leech-child," it was excluded from the count of their progeny because of the incorrect marriage ceremony they had performed, with the woman speaking first. Onogoro, the "self-coagulating" island, which was formed from the brine dripping off the spear Izanagi thrust into the chaos of primeval waters, became the first solid land and base of operations for the procreative activities leading to the birth of the other islands of Japan. (Kurano, pp. 52–53, 54–55 [Philippi, *Kojiki*, pp. 49–51].

55 [K 55]. The *Tango Fudoki* song (#217) is from a version of the Urashima legend, for which see also #579–80. Both the *Kojiki* and fudoki versions of the song are structured on a jo, with semantic doubling in line 4. In the *Kojiki* context the reference to Yamato in the jo is particularly effective, for Kurohime's lover must return there "when the west wind blows."

56 [K 56]. Tsuchihashi Yutaka refers to the pattern of repetition in this song and such other examples as #80 as *kyakuinshiki kurikaeshi* ("end-rhyme-type repetition"), distinguished from the *shiritorishiki kurikaeshi* ("tail-catching repetition") exemplified in #34 and #43, lines 2–3, and notably in #5, lines 27–31. He refers to *komorizu no* in the analogical pattern of *komorizu no shita* ("underneath [like] hidden water") as a *makurakotobateki joshi* or "pillow-word-type jo" because it is limited to five syllables like a makurakotoba but is not an adjectival fixed epithet (*Kodai Kayōshū*, pp. 19, 24). This distinction is useful, but it is equally possible to divide makurakotoba into two types, adjectival and adverbial, a nomenclature that will cover the usual breadth of the term. This latter way of conceiving the matter guides the thinking behind the present anthology.

57 [K 57]. The Naniwa Canal was dug in the reign of Nintoku to control flooding on the Yodo River (Kurano, pp. 266–67 [Philippi, *Kojiki*, p. 302]). Iwanohime's route takes her up the Yodo, then east into its tributary, the Yamashiro (now called the Kizu), and finally south toward her home in the Kazuraki Mountains. *Kodai Kayōshū*, p. 117, lists instances of the camellia's use in ceremonies, its planting in open-air markets, shrines dedicated to it, etc. According to

Nihonshoki, Emperor Keikō (father of Yamato Takeru) used mallets made of camellia trees in his attack on the Tsuchigumo of Tsukushi (Sakamoto et al., I, 288–89 [Aston, I, 194]).

58 [K 58]. From the *Kojiki* account it is not clear whether the Empress ever reached home, or why she lodged with Nurinomi in Tsutsuki. Iwanohime was the granddaughter of the elder statesman Takeshi Uchi no Sukune; her clan, the Kazuraki, supplied consorts to the imperial house. Nurinomi was one of the many Korean immigrants who came to Japan during the reign of Nintoku's father Ōjin. No doubt a man of importance in fostering silk culture in Japan, he may have had a dependent relationship with the Kazuraki.

61 [K 61]. Johnson, "Juxta- and Other Positions," has proved very helpful in appreciating the sexual implications of ancient song.

63 [K 63]. For a discussion of "quiet songs" and their "responses," see *Kodai Kayōshū*, p. 117. There are seven songs, not six, in the series, but one is sung by Kuchihime. Hers is presumably not a *shizuuta no utaikaeshi*.

66–68 [K 66–68]. The similarity of these menacing allegories to the wazauta genre has been remarked above (note to #20–22).

69 [K 69]. The *Hizen Fudoki* version of this song is part of a description of what goes on at an utagaki; see #215. For the *Man'yōshū* version, see #886.

71–73 [K 71–73]. For other references to Takeshi Uchi no Sukune, consult #40, #43, and #124–26. This is his farewell appearance in *Kojiki*. Hime Island was one of the archipelago of islands formerly lying at the mouth of the Yodo River and now part of the city of Ōsaka (see the foldout map in NKBZ, I). *Tamakiwaru* is also interpreted as "soul-climaxing" when it modifies *inochi* ("life"), and as serving in that sense as a mock epithet for Uchi through *uchi* ("inner," "heart"). For the myth of Nigihayahi, see Sakamoto et al., I, 189, 209, 215–17 (Aston, I, 110–11, 127–28, 135). This deity, who came to earth in his heavenly rock boat, was the brother of Hikoho no Ninigi no Mikoto, the grandson of the sun goddess, who descended from heaven as the progenitor of the imperial line. *Kojiki* states that Nigihayahi descended after Ninigi no Mikoto (Kurano, pp. 160–61 [Philippi, *Kojiki*, p. 177]); *Nihonshoki* is unclear on this point. Unlike Ninigi no Mikoto, who landed on Mount Takachiho in Kyūshū, Nigihayahi came directly to Yamato in his rock boat, presumably seeing the land from the sky, and thus giving rise to the epithet *sora mitsu*. (Nigihayahi was submissive to Emperor Jimmu when the Emperor reached Yamato, and is accounted the ancestor of the Mononobe clan.)

74 [K 74]. The legend of the giant tree turned into a cithern also appears in *Ch'in Fu* ("Rhyme-Prose on the Cithern") by Chi Shu-yeh (A.D. 223–62), one of the "Seven Sages of the Bamboo Grove" (see #592–604). Just as in the *Kojiki* passage, this poem conveys the tree's immensity by a morning-evening contrast (*Monzen*, ed. Obi, II, 399). *Man'yōshū* contains an exchange of waka and kambun passages inspired by *Ch'in Fu* (MYS V: 814–16/810–12, not included in the present anthology). The exchange is between Ōtomo no Tabito and Fujiwara no Fusasaki (681–737). A maiden speaks to Fusasaki in a dream, telling him how she was once a paulownia tree and was chopped down and fashioned into a koto. Now she hopes to find a cultivated master to play upon her strings. Fusasaki sends this dream communication to Tabito, who replies in like manner. The *Kojiki* version of the story appears to be the only one that has the tree made into a ship first, and then into a koto. The song and the anecdote also appear as NS 41, but without any reference to the giant tree legend. In this version the incident occurs in the reign of Emperor Ōjin, who is credited with the song (Sakamoto et al., I, 376–79 [Aston, I, 268–69]). See #123 for the *Nihonshoki* adaptation of the giant tree legend.

There is no consensus on how to read the name of the river, which is written with Morohashi graphs 1358 and 7411; Philippi, *Kojiki*, p. 322, suggests "Uki," "Tönöki," or "Tuki." The river, whatever its name, was apparently in the province of Kawachi. Takayasu Mountain is on the border between that province and Yamato. It is not clear whether "burned it for salt" means that salt was to be leached from the burned timbers of the ship or that the timbers were to be firewood for boiling down brine. "Over seven leagues" can also be read as "through seven villages." For "response to a quiet song," see #63.

75–77 [K 75–77]. The "great rice-tasting" was the annual ritual banquet in which the Emperor formally partook of the rice harvest. Richū makes his escape over the Kazuraki Mountains separating the seacoast from inland Yamato. At Hanifu Slope the road forks, and the Emperor is warned to take the southern fork through Tagima (now Taima) rather than the Ōsaka road (note to #49). Isonokami is an ancient shrine near the present city of Tenri, between Nara and Asuka.

78 [K 78]. This song was sung to koto music at the early Heian court. It appears in *Kinkafu* to illustrate the category shirageuta (*Kodai Kayōshū*, p. 474 [Brannen, pp. 259–60, 295–96]). *Nihonshoki*, where some of the same songs appear, has this to say about the affair of Prince and Princess Karu:

> In the twenty-third year [of his father's reign] . . . Prince Kinashi no Karu was made Crown Prince. In face and form he was fair and lovely, so that those who saw him were spontaneously moved. His younger sister by the same mother, Princess Karu no Ōiratsume, was also alluring and exquisite. The Prince was constantly preoccupied with his desire to tryst with Princess Ōiratsume but kept silent, dreading the guilt he would incur. Thus his emotions built up to a peak of intensity, and he was ready to die. And so he thought, "Now I am going to die for nothing—even if I am held guilty, how can I endure this?" Finally he began a secret liaison, and his fretful brooding was somewhat alleviated. . . . In the twenty-fourth year, summer, in the sixth month, the Emperor's broth congealed and turned to ice. The Emperor was baffled and had the cause sought by divination. The diviner said, "There is disorder in the house. Perhaps close kin have committed folly." At that time there was someone who said, "Crown Prince Kinashi no Karu has committed folly with his

full sister Princess Ōiratsume." The Emperor had inquiries made and found this was indeed true. (Sakamoto et al., I, 446–49.)

"Folly," in the old sense of lewd behavior, translates *tawake*, which covers a similar range from foolery to immorality. Incest is the specific intent of the term in this passage. Prince and Princess Karu were guilty of this crime only because they were full brother and sister.

81 [K 81]. Prince Anaho (the future Emperor Ankō) was Prince Karu's younger full brother. The name Ōmae-Omae no Sukune may represent a conflation of two brothers named Ōmae and Omae ("Great Presence" and "Small Presence") or may simply be a decorative usage, as *Kodai Kayōshū*, p. 86, suggests. *Nihonshoki* refers to him as Mononobe no Ōmae no Sukune, though it includes the same song as #81 (Sakamoto et al., I, 451). The reference to two kinds of arrowheads, bronze and iron, provides evidence of a shift in weapon technology in the 5th century. The "light" (*karu*) arrows pun on Prince Karu's name. The sentences in parentheses are interlinear notes, probably added by Ō no Yasumaro (Philippi, *Kojiki*, p. 48).

83 [K 83]. In the *Nihonshoki* version Prince Karu is not handed over to Prince Anaho, but commits suicide in Ōmae no Sukune's house. This version separates the incest story from the death of Prince Karu, which is made to occur eighteen years later, but again because of sexual misbehavior on the part of the Prince. *Nihonshoki* asserts that it was Princess Karu, not the Prince, who was sent into exile for the incest (Sakamoto et al., I, 448–49, 450–51 [Aston, I, 324–25, 328–29].

85 [K 85]. Iyo was the northwestern province of Shikoku. For another reference to the hot springs there, see #255. Earlier in *Kojiki* the pheasant Nakime ("Weeping Woman") was sent as a messenger from heaven to the traitorous emissary Ame no Wakahiko (see #6), and later the *yatagarasu*, or "eight-span crow," was sent down to guide Emperor Jimmu on his campaign of conquest (Kurano, pp. 152–53 [Philippi, *Kojiki*, p. 169]). One of the poetic conventions about the cuckoo (*hototogisu*) in Heian times was that it flew back and forth between the lands of the living and the dead. For another treatment of the cuckoo as messenger, see #966. The story of Su Wu (ca. 140 B.C.–60 B.C.), the Han official who sent a message tied to the leg of a wild goose from his captivity with the Hsiung-nu, was well known in Japan by the 8th century, and no doubt earlier (*Han Shu*, VI, 2459–69, especially p. 2466). Kojima sees #85 as alluding directly to this anecdote (*Jōdai*, I, 574). *Man'yōshū* also contains several references, e.g., MYS VIII: 1618/1614, IX: 1712/1708 (#389), XV: 3698/3676. For more on birds and ancient Japanese beliefs, see Philippi, *Kojiki*, p. 321; and Akima, "Songs of the Dead," pp. 491–96.

89–90 [K 89–90]. On yomiuta, see *Kodai Kayōshū*, p. 119, n. 90. In handling his poem-tale in such a way that it builds up to a double suicide, Yasumaro or whoever was responsible for the structuring of the narrative showed a superior literary sense to the compilers of *Nihonshoki*, who let Princess Karu go off into exile alone, and Prince Karu die years later for another reason. For examples where the reverse is true, see #137–38.

91 [K 91]. The "Great Consort" refers to Yūryaku's consort Princess Wakakusakabe, a daughter of Emperor Nintoku. Her home was at Kusaka, then on the shore of Kusaka Inlet, an area now in East Ōsaka City (consult the foldout map in NKBZ, I). For a discussion of taboos concerning facing or turning one's back to the sun, see Philippi, *Kojiki*, p. 413.

92–95 [K 92–95]. This story should be compared with #236, attributed to Emperor Yūryaku, and with #1511; all are amorous encounters on one level or another in which a man accosts a young woman he has discovered crouched over her work. It is striking that in the present instance the encounter takes place along the Miwa River, the name given to the Hatsuse River as it flows past Mount Miwa. Mount Miwa is sacred to the god Ōmononushi, whose amorous proclivities are attested in several legends (see, e.g., #260). In one particular anecdote he turns himself into a red-painted arrow and floats down a ditch where a young woman crouches defecating. The arrow strikes her genitals and after she has taken it home, turns into a handsome young man who becomes her husband (Kurano, pp. 160–61 [Philippi, *Kojiki*, p. 178]). *Kodai Kayōshū*, p. 93, traces connections among the Hikitabe, Hikita shrines, and the Ōmiwa clan that provided the priests of the Ōmiwa Shrine on Mount Miwa; these make an intended connection between the story of Akaiko and the Ōmononushi group of legends even more plausible. In #92 Yūryaku treats Akaiko as a shaman of the Ōmiwa Shrine, and she replies as such in #94. In one sense Yūryaku is superimposed on Ōmononushi as the lustful deity; in another, he is the rival who has been unable to win the maiden from the embraces of the god. In *Kodai Kayōshū*, pp. 94–95, Tsuchihashi Yutaka remarks that #93 and #94 are probably from utagaki. In that context they are the balancing laments over lost youth of an old man and an old woman. Thus, though the emphasis in the prose anecdote is on Akaiko's aging, and #93 is translated with that in mind, it is quite possible to reinterpret the story as an old man's regret that he did not sleep with the woman while he was young, translating, "Young I would have been," and "But now I have grown old." The "great array of offerings," literally, "a hundred tables' worth of offerings," Akaiko brings to Yūryaku refers to the wedding gifts of a bride. #94 appears in *Kinkafu* and thus is known to have been sung in the Heian period (*Kodai Kayōshū*, p. 460 [Brannen, pp. 235, 277–78]).

97 [K 97]. This song and its commentary provide folk etymologies both for Akizushima, a name for Japan as a whole, and for the "fields of Akizu" by the Yoshino River (see #293). Akizushima also applies in a more limited sense to the Yamato homeland, for which usage *Nihonshoki* provides another folk etymology, likening the mountain-enclosed basin to mating dragonflies flying in a ring formation (Sakamoto et al., I, 225 [Aston, I, 134–35]). (Aston, it may be noted, does not understand *toname*, "licking the hinder parts," to refer to mating.) Actually, Akizushima was probably a specific place in Yamato whose name gradually became extended to refer to larger areas (*Jidaibetsu*, p. 8). *Akizu* can be read as "autumn cove" (Philippi, *Kojiki*, p. 452), from which etymology Aston may have derived his "region of harvests" (Aston, I, 134).

98 [K 98]. With its encomiastic opening and contrasting first-person flight, the song is clearly intended to be sung by someone other than the Emperor.

100 [K 100]. "Palace woman" renders *uneme*, a class of women of good family sent from the provinces on a compulsory basis to wait on the Emperor at court. The setting for #100 is one of a number of instances in which Emperor Yūryaku is dissuaded from violence, usually by a song. The others are in *Nihonshoki* (see #146, #148, #150–51). The palace of Hishiro at Makimuku was that of Emperor Keikō, the father of Yamato Takeru no Mikoto (Kurano, pp. 202–3 [Philippi, *Kojiki*, p. 228]). The tree from which the leaf falls is a *Zelkova serrata* var. *tsuki*, a tall tree with spreading branches resembling an American elm.

101 [K 101]. *Kodai Kayōshū*, pp. 101, 119–20, discusses the "high gathering place" (*takechi*) and "assembly grounds" (*ichi*) as a sacred place set aside for ceremonial purposes and planted with trees. *Ichi* usually denotes a marketplace. This takechi may have been the origin of the place-name Takechi in Yamato.

102 [K 102]. Philippi sees a similarity between the analogies of this lively scene and the funeral ceremonies of Ame no Wakahiko, in which the officiants are birds (Kurano, p. 117 [Philippi, *Kojiki*, pp. 126–27]). He is of the opinion that the "courtiers" are court women (Philippi, *Kojiki*, p. 366).

103 [K 103]. *Omi* here denotes a person (male or female) in service to an overlord, and not the clan title (*kabane*) of the same name. A "winecup song" (*ukiuta*) is one sung on offering the wine. This song appears in *Kinkafu* (*Kodai Kayōshū*, p. 468 [Brannen, pp. 256–57, 288–89]). Konishi Jin'ichi questions the phonetic relevance of *mina sosoku* to *omi* as a mock epithet, since the initial vowel of *omi* is different from that for the word denoting "fish," in Old Japanese *uwo*, *iwo*, or *wo*. He suggests a paradigm in which "lord" is to "courtier" as "sea" is to "fish" (*Kodai Kayōshū*, p. 468).

104 [K 104]. Tsuchihashi Yutaka considers this a courtly song of blessing (*hokiuta*) rather than a love song, pointing out its similarity to a kagura song in which the speaker wishes to be a sacred offering (*mitegura*) given into the hands of a god (*Kodai Kayōshū*, p. 104).

105 [K 105]. Tsuchihashi Yutaka specifies several instances of the ancient use of red to ward off evil. How a banner would be "raised" on a cord is problematical. Tsuchihashi discusses and rejects proposals by Motoori Norinaga that the character to which he (Tsuchihashi) gives the reading *tate* ("raise"; Morohashi 38309) is a mistake for *tate* ("cut"; Morohashi 34258), and that *hata* ("banner"; Morohashi 9086) is a phonetic substitute for *hata* ("cloth"; Morohashi 14345). (*Kodai Kayōshū*, p. 120; *Motoori Norinaga Zenshū*, pp. 337–38.) Kurano, pp. 324–25, reads Morohashi 38309 as *kazari* ("adorn"), and Tsuchihashi admits the term may mean *tsuke* ("attach"). Philippi translates "is attached" (Philippi, *Kojiki*, p. 371). Line 9 contains an unambiguous radical 117, however. If a jo-type structure is to be proposed between a small banner attached to a cord and a large banner that floats on the air, the reading of *tate* given by Tsuchihashi is preferable. But the exegesis of the passage remains uncertain. The matching names Oke and Woke are thought to carry the sense of elder and younger (Philippi, *Kojiki*, p. 535). *Harima Fudoki* contains another set of songs attributed to Prince Woke (see #211-12).

106–11 [K 106-11]. *Omi* is used in this sequence both as a clan title (Heguri no Omi) and as a status title (Shibi no Omi, Omi no ko), underlining the fact that Shibi is the subject and Woke the Prince. There seems to be some connection between *hatade* in #106 and #109, though one refers to a house and the other to a fish. The projecting "eaves" and "fins" are played off against each other. As Tsuchihashi Yutaka points out, #108 could be reinterpreted as the utterance of the Prince, with *kokoro o yurumi* ("your heart is slack, my lord") coming out as "I am generous of heart, [and so won't smash your flimsy fence]" (*Kodai Kayōshū*, p. 106). #110 is the only example of a 5-7-5-7-7-7 poem in the chronicles. The bussokusekika, or "Buddha's footstone poem," so-called from the 21 examples engraved on a stele accompanying a Buddha's footprint icon at Yakushiji in Nara, is essentially a tanka with an extra final line that functions in a refrain-like pattern of altered repetition.

114–15 [NS 3–4]. #114 employs both types of repetition analyzed by Tsuchihashi Yutaka as basic to early song—"tail-catching" (*shiritorishiki*) in lines 4-5 and 7-8, and "end-rhyme type" (*kyakuinshiki*) in lines 4 and 9. The ellipses in the narrative introducing NS 4 indicate that the original document incorporated into *Nihonshoki* left out the speech of the Imperial Grandchild, understood to be the same as in the first of the series of accounts of this incident.

116 [NS 10]. In the annals of Kao Ti (r. 206 B.C.–195 B.C.), the ruthlessness of his rival Hsiang Yü (232 B.C.–202 B.C.) is criticized in the following terms: "Once he attacked [the city] Hsiang Ch'eng, and in Hsiang Ch'eng there was not left a creature that eats; nothing that moved did he fail to annihilate" (*Han Shu*, I, 16).

118–20 [NS 15–17]. For references to Ōmononushi, see Kurano, pp. 108–9, 160–63, 178–83 (Philippi, *Kojiki*, pp. 117, 178–79, 201–4); Sakamoto et al., I, 128–31, 151–53, 238–43, 246–49 (Aston, I, 59, 61, 81, 151–55, 158–59); and NS 19. See Sakamoto et al., I, 563–65, for a discussion of the complex of deities amalgamated in Izumo mythology. Tsuchihashi Yutaka suggests that #119–20 would normally appear in the opposite order, but his reading of the song ascribed to the Emperor as an attempt to detain his guests is not convincing (*Kodai Kayōshū*, pp. 135, 209).

122 [NS 19]. The manner of Todohime's death brings to mind that of the *hataorime* referred to in the note to #6. She too, alarmed by the outrageous male, struck her genitals on a sharp object and died. Susanoo, the embodiment of the untamed male principle in this myth, was the ancestor of Ōkuninushi, of whom Ōmononushi was supposed to be a manifestation. The red-painted arrow story is given in Kurano, pp. 161–63 (Philippi, *Kojiki*, pp. 178–79; see note to #92–95). The other anecdote in which Ōmononushi appears as a snake is found in Kurano, pp. 180–83 (Philippi, *Kojiki*, pp. 203–4). *Yamashiro Fudoki* relates another story of impregnation by a red-painted arrow in its account of the origin of the Kamo shrines, ancient cultic sites antedating the city of Kyōto, in which they are now located. According to this account, Tamayorihime, a daughter of the god Kamotaketsunomi no Mikoto, was playing in the Kamo River when a red-painted arrow came floating downstream. She took it home and placed it by her bed, whereupon she became pregnant. The resulting child, a boy, later correctly identified his father as Honoikazuchi no Mikoto and leaped up into the sky through the roof of a ceremonial drinking hall to offer him the sacred liquor. Thus the child was named Kamowakeikazuchi no Mikoto, "Kamo" for his grandfather, "Ikazuchi" for his father, and "Wake" for the way he split the roof tiles. "Honoikazuchi" means "Fire-Thunder," and "Wakeikazuchi" may be understood as "Split-Thunder." The progenitor Kamotaketsunomi no Mikoto and his daughter Tamayorihime are the joint deities of the Shimogamo Shrine. Kamowakeikazuchi no Mikoto is worshiped at the Kamigamo Shrine, and Honoikazuchi no Mikoto at the Otokuni Shrine at Nagaoka in Otokuni District, Kyōto Prefecture. (Akimoto, pp. 414–15.)

123 [NS 24]. The "back province" of Tsukushi was Chikugo (as contrasted to Chikuzen, the "front province"), both parts of modern Fukuoka Prefecture in northern Kyūshū. Kishima was northwest in Hizen Province, and Aso southeast in Higo Province. The giant tree legend appears also in the fudoki of Chikugo (Akimoto, pp. 510–11), Hizen (Akimoto, pp. 390–93), and Harima (#213). This last resembles the story attached to #74 in that the tree is cut down and the lumber used to make a swift ship.

124 [NS 28]. "Bulb arrows" (*mariya*) had a hollow bulb-shaped whistle fitted behind the arrowhead.

127 [NS 40]. *Tasarearachishi* may be analyzable as *ta* (meaningless prefix) + *sare* (equivalent of *sari*, "depart") + *arachi* ("separate") + *shi* (past suffix). This solution, proposed in *Kodai Kayōshū*, p. 150, and *Iwanami Kogo Jiten*, p. 778, assumes the existence of an otherwise unattested transitive verb *aratsu* and of a form *sare*, best interpreted as a transitive equivalent of the intransitive *sari*.

129 [NS 45]. The Kuni no Miyatsuko were hereditary Governors of provinces (*kuni*) under the system prevailing before the Taika Reforms of 645.

130–34 [NS 46–50]. Nintoku's reputation for benevolence rests chiefly on an anecdote recounted in both *Kojiki* and *Nihonshoki* to the effect that he remitted taxes and forced labor for three years when he noticed no smoke rising from cooking fires among his people (Kurano, pp. 266–67 [Philippi, *Kojiki*, pp. 303–4]; Sakamoto et al., 1, 390–93 [Aston, 1, 278–80]). "Nintoku," the posthumous name by which the monarch Ōsazaki is known, means "Benevolent Virtue" and no doubt derives from these passages. The whole image of a benevolent monarch is Chinese in inspiration and detail, and contrasts sharply with the sexually oriented thrust of the native narrative tradition. For the passage from *Izumi Shikibu Nikki*, see Endō, p. 443 (Cranston, *Izumi Shikibu Diary*, p. 188). *Kodai Kayōshū*, p. 210, gives the two-generation theory on silkworms, and Sakamoto et al., I, 399, proposes the alternate interpretation of #134.

136 [NS 56]. The interpretation of this song for the most part follows Sakamoto et al., I, 402. *Kodai Kayōshū*, p. 159, sees the movements of the branch as a metaphor for Empress Iwanohime's journey. *Uraguwa* ("tip mulberry") is translated "leafy mulberry" based on the suggestion in *Iwanami Kogo Jiten* that the term refers to branches lushly leaved at the tip.

137 [NS 59]. Sakamoto et al., I, 405, suggest that the metal loom was a recent import from Korea. *Ame* ("heaven") is taken to be simply an encomium.

138 [NS 60]. The omission in the narrative is Tsuchihashi's.

140 [NS 65]. The *hsiao-shao* spider, or "long-legs," is said to be called "happy mother," and its lighting on a person's clothing to be an omen of the arrival of an intimate guest, in the Lu Chi commentary to *Shih Ching* song 156 (Chang, p. 293 [Waley, *Book of Songs*, p. 116]).

144 [NS 74]. *Analects*, IX:25: "The Master said, 'The commander of the three-army [state] can be taken by force; the will of a common man cannot be taken by force'" (Yoshikawa, I, 295–96).

146 [NS 76]. Yūryaku's speech to his attendant makes a significant adaptation of its original. Instead of *feng* ("meets"), *Han Shu* has *te* ("gets"). The source is an anecdote about Lady Feng, the heroic concubine who saved Emperor Yüan (r. 49 B.C.–33 B.C.) from an escaping bear by confronting it while all the other ladies and officials fled. When questioned by the Emperor, she replied, "A wild animal always stops when it gets someone. I was afraid it would reach Your Majesty's seat and so put myself in front of it" (*Han Shu*, VIII, 4005). Thus the point of the passage has been reversed. Yūryaku's attendant would hardly have been reassured by the original version. The immediate source for Yūryaku's dialogue with his Empress seems to be the early T'ang encyclopedia of poetic topics *I-wen Lei-chü*, compiled by Ou-yang Hsün (557–641). Under the topic "Field Hunting," *I-wen Lei-chü* quotes the relevant sentences from *Chuang-tzu* and *An-tzu Ch'un Ch'iu* (An Ying; d. 500 B.C.) containing the remonstrances of statesmen. Sentences from these two sources are integrated in *Nihonshoki*, but only minimally adapted to the new context (Wang, II, 1171–72). The passage attributed to *Chuang-tzu* does not appear in that work as it has come down to us. The passage from *An-tzu Ch'un Ch'iu* as excerpted in *I-wen Lei-chü* reads somewhat differently from the transmitted text of *An-tzu Ch'un Ch'iu* itself, which can be rendered, "All your subjects are of the opinion that Your Lordship takes his ease in the fields and not his country, takes his pleasure in the beasts, but hates his people. This is hardly proper" (Wu, I, 83). It is clear that the line attributed to the Empress in *Nihonshoki* draws from the *I-wen Lei-chü* excerpt, which can be rendered, "Your subjects are all saying that Your Lordship takes his ease in the fields and his pleasure in the beasts. This is hardly proper." The passages attributed to *Chuang-tzu* in *I-wen Lei-chü* also appear in the Han work *Hsin Hsü* by Liang Hsiang (79 B.C.–8 B.C.), from which Tsuchihashi Yutaka seems to assume they were drawn (*Kodai Kayōshū*, p. 173). But a comparison of the three texts shows that *Nihonshoki* is closer to the somewhat abbreviated *I-wen Lei-chü* version (Sakamoto et al., I, 471; *Hsin Hsü*, pp. 471–72; Wang, II, 1172).

147 [NS 77]. *Washiride* (line 5) is given an interpretation ("running forth"; i.e., the view of the mountain as a person would see it on stepping out of the door of his house) in conformity with that suggested in *Kodai Kayōshū*, p. 174. *Hashiride* in #348 is presumably the same word but is rendered according to an alternate interpretation, which sees in it a reference to a trailing line of foothills.

148 [NS 78]. *Chuang-tzu* is particularly rich in tales of skill, all used to illustrate a philosophical point. In Japan, the setsuwa collections include stories of unusual skill. See Watson, *Complete Works of Chuang Tzu*, especially pp. 50–51, 104, 152–53, 206. Several of the tales of strength and skill collected in *Konjaku Monogatari Shū* are translated in Jones, pp. 62–67, and Ury, pp. 142–45. *Kodai Kayōshū*, p. 210, discusses the magico-medicinal uses of vegetation in ancient Japan.

149 [NS 79]. For more on Sahohiko and his rebellion against Emperor Suinin, see Kurano, pp. 188–97 (Philippi, *Kojiki*, pp. 213–18); and Sakamoto et al., I, 261–65 (Aston, I, 170–72). Tsuchihashi Yutaka's reading *terau* in line 3 of the song has been rejected in favor of the *nerau* given in Sakamoto et al., I, 488. The phonogram for the first syllable is Morohashi 17521. Tsuchihashi's version could be translated "Such as are a man's pride."

152 [NS 82]. Events on the Korean peninsula during the 5th century, dominated by the expansion of Koguryŏ, are outlined in Lee, pp. 38–41. *Jidaibetsu*, p. 49, suggests that *amo* ("mother") is an eastern dialect word, but it bears an intriguing resemblance to Korean *ŏmŏni*, meaning the same thing. One textual lineage of *Nihonshoki* has *ame*, "heaven," interpreted to mean "the court" (Sakamoto et al., I, 501).

153 [NS 83]. For another translation of this ritual chant, see Philippi, *Norito*, p. 80.

154 [NS 84]. The *Eiga Monogatari* version, referred to as an "old song," goes as follows: Kawazoiyanagi / Kaze fukeba / Ugoku to suredo / Ne wa shizuka nari ("River-lining willow fronds / When the wind does blow / Move and make to follow it— / But the roots are always still"). (Matsumura and Yamanaka, I, 375; see also McCullough and McCullough, II, 441.) Concerning the pillow word *inamushiro*, one might hazard an imagistic link to *kawa* through the rippling effect of

wind over a rice field (a "rice mat," or *inamushiro*), likened to the ripples on a river.

160 [NS 92]. *Sue* ("end"/"tip") is both temporal and the tip of the sword.

161 [NS 93]. There is some question about the meaning of *amashijimi*. The translation follows Sakamoto et al., II, 10, in relating it to the verb *amu* ("to weave"). *Kodai Kayōshū*, p. 185, prefers *ama* ("sweet," "bland") + *shijimi* ("scowl") and sees it as a sneer, properly directed by the Prince toward his opponent: "I could erect a fine fence, but I despise you so much that I won't bother."

167 [NS 99]. *Fei jan chih tsao* ("a pattern of flowing lines") allegedly adapts *fei jan ch'eng chang* ("compose gracefully"; *Lun Yü*, V, 21 [Legge, I, 181]). *Tsao* ("waterweed") is used in the sense of literary embellishment, a usage derived from the sinuous patterns formed by grasses in the water, as pointed out in the Li Shan commentary to *Wen Fu* (*Wen-hsüan*, XVII, fasc. 6, 17.1b).

169 [NS 101]. Most of the *Nihonshoki* account of Keitai's reign is taken up with Korean relations. For the affair of Kena no Omi, see Sakamoto et al., II, 38–47 (Aston, II, 18–25). Lee, pp. 40–44, gives an overview of the Korean situation at this time. Kara was one of the units of Mimana, but the name came to be used for Korea generally.

171–72 [NS 103–4]. The annals of Emperor Kimmei (r. 539–71) are largely taken up with Korean affairs. For the account of the fall of Mimana, see Sakamoto et al., II, 119–27 (Aston, II, 80–85).

175 [NS 107]. For the *Nihon Ryōiki* version, see Endō and Kasuga, pp. 77–81; and Nakamura, pp. 108–10. The sense in which the pillow word *shinateru* ("slope-shining") applies to *kata* is obscure. See also Nishimura, "Prince and Pauper," for a study of the legend of Shōtoku and the wayfarer, including other versions of the song, such as SIS XX: 1350.

177 [NS 109]. On the eight-column dance, see *Lun Yü*, III, 1 (Legge, I, 154). The King was permitted eight rows of eight dancers, and the nobility, in order of rank, correspondingly fewer rows.

178 [NS 110]. The significance of "Upper Palace" (*jōgū* or *kami tsu miya*) as explained in the annals of Empress Suiko is that Prince Shōtoku's father Yōmei so loved his son that he had him live in a hall so designated, to the south of his own palace (Sakamoto et al., II, 174–75 [Aston, II, 122–23]). The Prince's sons are here referred to in the same way. Nishimura, "Retrospective Comprehension," pp. 45–48, translates and provides references to several Chinese examples of song interpretation. In *Kodai Kayōshū*, pp. 213–14, Tsuchihashi argues that *tōrase* is a teasingly honorific version of the *tōre* in #84 and #87, utagaki songs in which the sex partner "goes off" after the love-making is over. "One man against a thousand" (*i jen tang ch'ien*) derives from a passage from the annals of Hsiang Yü in *Shih Chi* (Yoshida, II, 442), in which, however, "A thousand" is usually replaced by "ten": "None of the troops of Ch'u but could cope with ten." (The characters for "ten" and "thousand" differ by only one stroke.)

180–82 [NS 112–14]. The *Wen-hsüan* quotation is from *Ch'i Ch'i Pa Shou* by Ts'ao Chih (A.D. 192–232): "Popular music [*san yüeh*] changes customs, makes the country rich, and the people healthy" (*Wen-hsüan*, fasc. 11, 34.24a). Its expression *i feng* ("cause a shift in customs") stems from *Li Chi* in a passage referring to the effect of music (Takeuchi, II, 573–74). The reference to adjacent palaces in the interpretation of #180 may be to those built at the top and foot of Amagashi Hill by Emishi and Iruka (Sakamoto et al., II, 259–61). For an account of Iruka's assassination, see Sakamoto et al., II, 261–65 (Aston, II, 190–93).

183 [NS 115]. On the tachibana and Tokoyo, see the commentary to #826–27.

184–85 [NS 116–17]. Soga no Kurayamada Ishikawa no Maro was the founder of the famous temple Yamadadera at Asuka, where he died. The temple has recently been excavated (see Parent, "Excavations" and "Tragedy and Triumph"). Maro's elder daughter, Ochi no Iratsume, was offered to Prince Naka no Ōe to shore up the latter's political alliances just before the coup d'état of 645. Nakatomi no Kamako served as the go-between. But Maro's half brother Himuka (also known as Musashi) abducted her on the eve of the wedding. Maro's second daughter, Mei no Iratsume, saved the situation by volunteering to marry Naka no Ōe in her sister's stead. Naka no Ōe later retrieved Ochi no Iratsume and had children by both consorts. Ochi no Iratsume had two daughters and one son. The daughters were Princess Uno (later Empress Jitō) and Princess Ōta, mother of Prince Ōtsu and Princess Ōku. The son was a deaf-mute, Prince Takeru. Mei no Iratsume was the mother of Princess Ahe (later Empress Gemmei). It is thought that Miyatsuko-hime was another name for Ochi no Iratsume, but the possibility exists that she was Mei no Iratsume. See Sakamoto et al., II, 255, n. 23; 310, n. 10; 331, n. 39; 367, n. 38; also 368–69 (Aston, II, 185–86, 252–53, 287–88). Musashi, who abducted Ochi no Iratsume, was the same half brother who slandered Ishikawa no Maro in 649. For an account of the slander and its outcome, see Sakamoto et al., II, 306–11 (Aston, II, 232–35). The first song in *Shih Ching* (Waley, *Book of Songs*, #87) provides parallels to the bride and the ospreys in the river, but lacks the image of paired birds. For positive analogy followed by a sad twist, see Mao #150 (Waley #62). Negative analogy is much less common, but is found in Mao #26 and #32 (Waley #75, #78). The term "symbolic equation" is from Reckert. The symbolic equation is a basic technique of *Shih Ching* poetry. Mao #63 (Waley #41) is an excellent example, as is Mao #1 (Waley #87).

186 [NS 118]. Yamazaki, where Emperor Kōtoku went during the last year of his life, is southwest of modern Kyōto, on what was then the border of Settsu and Yamashiro provinces.

187–92 [NS 119–24]. Akima argues that #190 expresses the pleasure of the dead in the "new tomb" (*imaki*) when properly appeased and comforted by dance and song. He takes #191 as a reference to ancient boat-burials. The boat carries the soul of the dead down the *unasaka*, or "slope of the sea," to the undersea realm of Tokoyo. This is where the sea flows down, *ushio no kudari, unakudari*. The dead person leaves the survivors behind (Akima, "Songs of the Dead," pp. 486–90). See #579–80 and #1558. Akima also discusses #187–89, though those three songs are not central to his argument. For other poems by Empress Saimei and further information about her, see #242–44.

193 [NS 125]. For an account of the fall of Paekche, see Sakamoto et al., II, 344–60 (Aston, II, 266–80). Lee, pp. 66–67, covers the same ground without mentioning the Japanese intervention. On Tsu no Omi Kutsuma, who apparently is mentioned nowhere else, see Sakamoto et al., II, 330, 331 (Aston, II, 252), where it is noted that Kutsuma and his fellow envoy Azumi no Tsuratari presented a camel and two asses on their return from Paekche. Tsuratari's report of Paekche's successful military operations against Silla in 657 is given in Sakamoto et al., II, 336, 337 (Aston, I, 259). "Cutworm bandits" translates *mao tse* (Sakamoto et al., II, 346, 347). Aston, II, 268, has "maggot-pests." The swarm of flies over Shinano prior to Empress Suiko's death was observed heading east rather than west (Sakamoto et al., II, 212–13 [Aston, II, 155]). Tsuchihashi Yutaka describes #193 as the most difficult to decipher of any song in the chronicles. His version is achieved by an ingenious rearrangement of the phonogram orthography, which he speculates was deliberately scrambled because the sense was highly uncomplimentary to the imperial house (*Kodai Kayōshū*, pp. 205–6).

196 [NS 128]. The Korean rank systems are tabulated in Lee, p. 52, and Sakamoto et al., II, 617–23. The Japanese systems under the Ōmi and Kiyomihara codes of the late 7th century are given in the latter, pp. 624–27.

Hitachi Fudoki. Akimoto, pp. 27, 73, 89, speculates that the text of *Hitachi Fudoki* may have been worked over for literary effect by Umakai and Mushimaro after their arrival in the province in 719. The basic document seems to date from before the establishment of Iwaki District in Michinoku Province as the separate province of Iwaki in Yōrō 2 (718).5 (*Shoku Nihongi*, p. 74).

200 [F 1]. *Nihonshoki* mentions a female tsuchigumo leader in the province of Chikugo in northern Kyūshū in the reign of Empress Jingū (4th c. A.D.?; Sakamoto et al., I, 332, 333 [Aston, I, 226–27]).

201 [F 2]. The translation "thousand autumns" in line 11 follows the kambun text in Akimoto, p. 40, as well as the Japanese rendering in both Akimoto and *Kodai Kayōshū*. The kambun text in *Kodai Kayōshū* has "hundred autumns."

204 [F 5]. "Village youths" follows Akimoto, p. 49; *Kodai Kayōshū*, p. 227, reads *miyaotoko* ("youths from the shrines"). The term is *sharō* (Morohashi 24631/39431). Shrines in the area include the major one at Kashima. But the Chinese term *she* (Sino-Japanese *sha*) referred to a village population unit as well as to the altar of its earth god. The case is argued by Kojima, *Jōdai*, I, 612. The "ninefold luminary" comes from the myth of the nine suns in the lower branches of the Fu-sang tree, a giant double-trunked mulberry growing by the eastern sea. The probably early Han poem "Yüan Yu" ("Distant Wandering"), traditionally attributed to Ch'ü Yüan (4th–3d c. B.C.), author of the chief poems in the *Ch'u Tz'u* anthology, contains a line translatable as "In the evening I dried my body in the ninefold luminary" (Hoshikawa, p. 260). The fudoki passage also associates the multiple-sun image with evening, suggesting the *Ch'u Tz'u* poem as a source. The association seems anomalous, since the tree was supposed to stand at the point of sunrise. The last two lines can also be read to mean that even if (like the waves) other young women make advances, the speaker will respond only to his girl (Akimoto, p. 49).

207–8 [F 8–9]. The reading and interpretation of the songs is based on Akimoto, pp. 73–74. Tsuchihashi Yutaka reads the last line of #207 as *Azeko shi mawamo,* "Oh, how the Aze girl dances!" Similarly, he gives a different reading for the last line of #208: *Wa o misaba shirishi,* "I knew him because he looked at me," assuming that it is the man who is "hidden" in a line of competing youths (*Kodai Kayōshū,* pp. 228–29). Akimoto has also been preferred for the name of the pine grove. Tsuchihashi has *Otome* ("Maiden"). The characters are Morohashi 25775/6930/6036, *dō/shi/jo* (Ch. *t'ung/tzu/nü*). The presence of the second graph makes Akimoto's reading preferable. *Unai* (O.J. *unawi*), a child of either sex with hair hanging loose around its neck (*una*), is to be distinguished from the place-name Unai (O.J. *unaFi*) in #574–76. Akimoto asserts that the former in this instance is a corruption of the latter, whose basic meaning is "seaside." It seems likely, however, that the recorders of the legend intended by their choice of characters to convey the meaning "the pine grove of the youth and maiden." The ancient phonetic interlinear note, translated in parentheses ("They are commonly referred to. . . ."), suggests that the young man and woman were a shaman and a shrine maiden. Akimoto points out that members of these occupations wore their hair loose regardless of age and gives the reading *unawi* to the characters *dōji* (Ch. *t'ung-tzu;* Morohashi 1132/6930). Tsuchihashi follows a manuscript tradition with the character *jo* (Ch. *nü;* Morohashi 6036) as the final element in a three-character series, thus making the name of the pine grove identical with the designation of the dramatis personae. The translation follows the kambun text in this version.

209 [F 10]. Akimoto, p. 77, arrives at his reading of the problematic fourth line by assuming scribal error and altering its fifth graph from Morohashi 23105, phonetic for *mo* in *Kodai Kayōshū,* p. 229, to Morohashi 30095, read by Akimoto as phonetic for *shi.* Both Akimoto and Tsuchihashi allege that the song text is fragmentary.

Harima Fudoki. Sazanami no Kafuchi appears in *Man'yōshū* with the clan name and title Takaoka no Muraji, granted in 724. He was a colleague of Yamanoue no Okura in 721 as Tutor to the future Emperor Shōmu. He left two poems in *Man'yōshū.*

213 [F 14]. The story of "Swift Bird" is a fragment not included in the surviving *Harima Fudoki*. The earliest source for this fragment is *Shaku Nihongi* (13th c.), p. 114.

214 [F 15]. For the *Nihonshoki* accounts of Sadehiko's expeditions to Korea, see Sakamoto et al., II, 59, 126–27 (Aston, II, 35, 86). Kurano, pp. 180–83, gives the story of how Ikutamayorihime traced her lover by sewing a thread to his garment. The passage is translated in Philippi, *Kojiki*, pp. 203–4 (see also Philippi, *Kojiki*, pp. 415–16). For the story of the lost mirror, see Akimoto, pp. 394–97.

215 [F 16]. #215 is a fragment. The earliest source is Sengaku's *Man'yōshū Chūshaku* (1269; Muromatsu, p. 77).

216–20 [F 17–21]. The earliest source for this fragment is *Shaku Nihongi*, pp. 165–66. "The small man yearns for his native earth" in the prose introduction is based on *Lun Yü* IV.11, translated by Waley, "Where gentlemen set their hearts upon moral force (*tê*), the commoners set theirs upon the soil" (Waley, *Analects*, p. 104). *Huai t'u* ("cherish the earth") is the same phrase appearing earlier in the sentence "Suddenly there arose within him a yearning for his native earth." "The dying fox rests its head upon its own hill" appears to derive from analogues in *Li Chi* and *Ch'u Tz'u*. The *Ch'u Tz'u* quotation is a line from "A Lament for Ying" (*Ai Ying*), one of the "Nine Declarations" (*Chiu Chang*) on the fall of the Ch'u capital in 278 B.C. (Hoshikawa, p. 201). Hawkes, p. 67, translates, "And the fox when he dies turns his head toward his earth." See also *Li Chi*, III, "The ancients had the saying, 'The fox when it dies rests its head right on [its own] hill. This is *jen* [the essence of humanity]'" (Takeuchi I, 93). The text of #220 is corrupt. The translation follows *Kodai Kayōshū*, #16. Akimoto, p. 475, reads lines 3–4 as *tayumaku mo / hatsuka madoishi* ("faltering, I went slightly astray").

221 [F 22]. The earliest sources for this fragment are *Chiribukuro*, an encyclopedia dating from the period 1274–81 attributed to the monk Ryōin; *Kojiki Uragaki*, a medieval commentary on *Kojiki* of obscure date and authorship attributed to Urabe Kanefumi (13th c.); and *Gengenshū* (ca. 1337), a work on the Ise Shintō cult by Kitabatake Chikafusa (1292–1354; Ōmiya and Nakajima, II, 6; Masamune, pp. 224–25). Toyoukanome is probably Toyouke no Kami, who descended from the high plain of heaven with the Imperial Grandchild and is worshiped at the Outer Shrine at Ise (see Kurano, pp. 128, 129 [Philippi, *Kojiki*, pp. 140, 616–17]). The debate between divine simplicity and mundane duplicity has become a part of the *Hagoromo* version of the myth (Akimoto, p. 467). *Kojiki Uragaki* lacks the passage, which Akimoto supplies from *Gengenshū* (Masamune, p. 224).

222 [F 23]. The earliest source for this fragment is Sengaku's *Man'yōshū Chūshaku* (Muromatsu, p. 36). A derivative relationship with MYS 1:61 (#476) is argued by Omodaka, I, 388.

223 [SN 1]. For the *Tso Chuan* passage, from Duke Chao, year 1, see Kamada, III, 1225, 1227, 1228. The legend about Emperor Temmu is recounted in *Seiji*

Yōryaku, p. 145. For reference to the performance of *tamai* ("field dances") in the 10th year of Emperor Tenji (671), see Sakamoto et al., II, 376, 377 (Aston, II, 296). The first reference to the *tōka* is in the 7th year of Empress Jitō (693; Sakamoto et al., II, 518, 519 [Aston, II, 411]). On the saibara identical to #223 (except for repetitions and *hayashikotoba* [i.e. meaningless refrains]), see *Kodai Kayōshū*, p. 395.

224 [SN 2]. For the longer version of this song, see *Kodai Kayōshū*, pp. 467–68 (Brannen, pp. 252–53, 287–88). The *Kinkafu* version makes no reference to a dance.

227 [SN 5]. For the complete text of this semmyō, with commentary, see Mikanagi, pp. 125–45.

229 [SN 7]. The Hakata River was a local stream near the detached palace in Kawachi. Its function in #229 is that of the Yoshino River in the many Yoshino poems in *Man'yōshū*. The *tan* as a measure of trade cloth was defined as two *jō*, six *shaku* in 714 (*Shoku Nihongi*, p. 54). Depending on whether the *komajaku* (35.4 cm) or the *tōshaku* (29.6 cm) was used as the standard, this would yield a length of 920.4 cm or 769.2 cm for a *tan*. A *ton* as a measure of silk floss was equal to six *ryō*, or about 22.2 kg.

230 [SN 8]. For songs similar to #230, see particularly Fūzokuuta 20 and Saibara 37, in *Kodai Kayōshū*, pp. 440–41 and 402–3, respectively.

SELECTIONS FROM 'MAN'YŌSHŪ'

Kojima et al. provide abundant documentation for the interpretation of the second syllable of *Man'yōshū* in the sense of "age" or "generation" (NKBZ I, 11–13). It will suffice to cite two items here. One is from the annals of Emperor Kenzō in *Nihonshoki* (Sakamoto et al., I, 516–17), a passage in which Prince Oke exhorts his brother Prince Woke to assume the imperial dignity, saying that if he does so, the world will flourish for 10,000 generations (*man'yō*). The other is from *Nihon Kōki* (p. 11), in a memorial to the throne on the completion of *Shoku Nihongi* in 797, expressing the wish that that work be passed down as a model for 10,000 generations (*man'yō*). Morohashi (no. 31387) cites a Chinese usage of the character for "leaf" in the sense of "age" from *Shih Ching*.

236 [MYS I:1]. The last three lines have also been read (NKBT, I, 9): Ware ni koso wa / Norame / Ie o mo na o mo ("Then to me, surely, You'll tell them, Your home and your name").

237 [MYS III:418/415]. The Well of Takahara was the site of a detached palace on the road from Yamato to Naniwa; Mount Tatsuta rises between Takahara and the Prince's home at Ikaruga. Both NKBZ and NKBT give the old reading Shōtoko for the Prince's name. *Nihonshoki* states in the annals of Emperor Yōmei that Prince Shōtoku "first lived in the Upper Palace and later moved to Ikaruga" (Sakamoto et al., II, 155 [Aston, II, 107]). See Nishimura, "Prince and Pauper," for a comparative study of this poem and its analogues.

238 [MYS 1:2]. *Toriyorou* is a *hapax legomenon* whose meaning is in doubt.
"Lush" (Omodaka), "particularly fine" (NKBZ), and "close at hand" (NKBT) are
among the tentative interpretations. *Iwanami Kogo Jiten* suggests "point of reliance
for the feelings and livelihood." Here it is freely rendered "our rampart." Mount
Kagu defines the northeastern boundary of the Asuka area. *Iyo Fudoki* recounts a
tale of how Mount Kagu split in two when it descended from heaven, one part
becoming Amayama in Iyo Province (northwestern Shikoku), and the other Ama
no Kaguyama in Yamato (Akimoto, p. 496).

240–41 [MYS 1:5–6]. The reading "Ikusa" is based on the character *gun* ("military"; Morohashi 38179) used to write the name. *Kishi* seems to be a Korean title
of honor attached to *kon*, which is represented by the same graph. On the reference to the *Chronicles*, see Sakamoto et al., II, 234–35 (Aston, II, 169). ("*Chronicles*" in the *Man'yōshū* editorial notes translates *ki*, short for *Nihonshoki, Chronicles
of Japan*.) *Iyo Fudoki* recounts Emperor Jomei's feeding of the birds in the two trees
(Akimoto, p. 495).

242 [MYS IV:488/485]. Omodaka, IV, 22–23, traces similarities between this
poem and an anonymous *chōka*, #1455, and suggests both were derived from a no
longer extant folk song.

249 [MYS 1:12]. Noshima is on the west coast of the Kii Peninsula; the location
of Agone is unknown.

251 [MYS 1:14]. The relevant story in *Harima Fudoki* (Akimoto, pp. 286–87)
takes place in Iibo District rather than Inami District. The god Abo comes from
Izumo to stop the fighting among Unebi, Kagu, and Miminashi, but stops at
Kamioka Village when he hears the quarrel has ceased. He turns over his boat
and takes shelter beneath it, an image of entombment (see Akima, "Songs of the
Dead"; and #190–92).

255 [MYS 1:8]. *Nihonshoki* fails to note an imperial excursion to Iyo in 637.
The reference could be to the excursion of 639 mentioned in the editorial note to
#240–41. The cyclical date given for the first of the twelfth month matches that for 639.

256 [MYS 1:16]. Kojima cites *Ch'iu Hsing Fu* by P'an An-jen (3d. c. A.D.) as a
Wen-hsüan parallel to Princess Nukata's debate on spring vs. fall. A line that can be
translated "Sighing over summer lushness that falls in autumn" is particularly suggestive (Kojima, *Jōdai*, II, 895; *Wen-hsüan*, XIII, 5a).

257–58 [MYS 1:17–18]. The cyclical date for 667, incorrectly given in *Man'yōshū* as Fire-Senior/Tiger, was Fire-Junior/Hare (Sakamoto et al., II, 366–67 [Aston,
II, 285]).

259 [MYS IV:491/488]. The following are examples of Six Dynasties analogues
cited by Kojima, *Jōdai*, II, 896:

The autumn breeze comes in my window;
The gauze curtain lifts and flutters:

Raising my head, I look at the bright moon,
Letting my feelings sweep across a thousand leagues of light.
—"Nine Modern Songs of Wu," *Yü-t'ai Hsin-yung*, X

Thinking of him at night—
The breeze blows through the window, the blind stirs,
Saying, "He is coming, he in whom you joy."
—*Yüeh-fu Shih-chi*, XLVI

260 [MYS I:19]. NKBZ suggests that this poem was intended to express Princess Nukata's admiration for Emperor Tenji. The story of Ōmononushi and the thread is given in Kurano, pp. 180–83 (Philippi, *Kojiki*, pp. 203–4). For more on Ōmononushi, see #118–20 and #122. *Hesokata* is an engo for *hari* meaning "spool thread."

264 [MYS I:27]. The cyclical date for 680, the 8th year of Temmu's reign according to modern chronologies, is Metal-Senior/Dragon instead of Earth-Junior/Hare, which corresponds to 679. It is evident that *Man'yōshū*, like *Nihonshoki*, dates Temmu's reign from his seizure of power in 672 rather than from his enthronement in 673. It was at Yoshino, on the 6th day of the 5th month of 679, that Temmu exacted an oath from his Empress-consort (later Empress Jitō) and six of his sons that after his death there would be no contention among them. Yoshino no doubt had a special significance to Temmu as the base from which he started his successful campaign in the Jinshin War of 672. The oath was broken almost immediately after Temmu's death by the forced suicide of Prince Ōtsu in 686 (#269). Prince Kusakabe, who pronounced the oath, which carried the penalty of death for dissension, died in 689 without succeeding to the throne. The further penalty Kusakabe stipulated, extinction of the abrogator's line, did not fall upon him, however. His son, Prince Karu, succeeded as Emperor Mommu in 697 (see #331–35). For the oath, see Sakamoto et al., II, 434–35 (Aston, II, 341–42).

266 [MYS I:22]. Princess Ahe was the future Empress Gemmei (r. 707–15), daughter of Emperor Tenji, consort of Prince Kusakabe, and mother of Emperor Mommu and Empress Genshō.

269–70 [MYS II:109; MYS III:419/16]. On Prince Ōtsu, see Sakamoto et al., II, 486–87 (Aston, II, 383–84); and Kojima, *Kaifūsō*, pp. 73–75. *Kaifūsō* states that the Prince was urged on to revolt by the Silla monk Haeng Sim and specifies that he died by suicide. The Prince's Chinese farewell poem is KFS 7: "The golden crow descends on the western lodge; / The voice of the drum hastens brief life. / On the road to the Springs there is neither host nor guest— / At evening tonight I leave home and set out." For analogues by Chinese poets, see Kojima, *Kaifūsō*, p. 451.

278 [MYS I:34]. This poem recurs in a slightly variant version as MYS IX: 1720/1716, attributed to Yamanoue no Okura, the author of another poem on the tragic fate of Prince Arima, #858, and another variant appears in *Kakyō Hyōshiki*, the earliest Japanese work on poetics (772), where it is attributed to one Tsuno no Sami Kihama (Sasaki, p. 5; Rabinovitch, pp. 507–8, 545–46).

286 [MYS II:160]. NKBZ provides no reading for the final line. The translation is a free rendering of NKBT (I, 94), which parses the line to include *omo* (Morohashi 42618). *Omo shiru* is taken to mean, "to know thoroughly and control." The editors of NKBZ object to this reading on the grounds that *nan* (Morohashi 21730) cannot represent the syllable *na* (NKBZ, I, 148).

301 [MYS III:240/239]. *Wakakomo* ("young rush," line 7) is a mock epithet for Kariji, a place-name, through *kari* ("cut"), whose object it is marked to be by *o*. This syntactic arrangement is a variant on the more common adjectival *no*.

311–13 [MYS I:40–42]. From its placement it seems likely that this series refers to Empress Jitō's excursion to Ise from the 6th to the 20th of the 3d month of 692 (see #473). At this time the new capital at Fujiwara-kyō was still under construction. Therefore the "capital" at which Hitomaro remained was the Kiyomihara Palace at Asuka. For more on Kiyomihara and Fujiwara, see #998–99 and #1245–47; also see #467.

315 [MYS IV:500/497]. When Genji has arrived with Yūgao at the deserted mansion where she is to meet her weird end, he looks up at the crumbling gate through the dawn mist and murmurs: Inishie no / Kaku ya wa hito no / Madoikemu / Wa ga mada shiranu / Shinonome no michi ("Did men thus wander, / Then too in the long ago, / Lost on errant ways, / Paths that I have yet to learn / Through the white light of dawn?"). For this passage, see Yamagishi, I, 142.

318 [MYS IV:504/501]. #419, a poem from the "Hitomaro Collection," provides an extremely close variant. NKBZ argues that it is a less personal expression than #318.

320 [MYS IV:506/503]. This poem has a close variant in MYS 3500/3481, one of the Azumauta in Book XIV. The interpretation of *saisai shizumi* is along the lines suggested by NKBZ. NKBT considers it a jo.

328–30 [MYS II:167–69]. For the text of "Minazuki no Tsugomori no Ōharae," see Takeda, pp. 422–27; for a translation, Philippi, *Norito*, pp. 45–49. *Fusō Ryakki*, a work of Heian historiography, is the source of the entry about the red pheasant (*Fusō Ryakki*, p. 66). *Nihonshoki* merely notes that the year (686) was changed to Shuchō ("Red Bird") 1, and that the Kiyomihara Palace was called Asuka no Kiyomihara no Miya, "Asuka" being written with the characters "flying bird." (Apparently this passage marks the origin of one of the traditional orthographies of the place.) Emperor Temmu was ill (he died two months later), and the assignment of a new year period was no doubt intended as an auspicious curative measure. It is thought that Temmu prized the color red (see the banners in #341), emulating the founder of the Han dynasty, who described himself as the son of the God of Red. Temmu was presented a red crow, a solar symbol, in 677, and a red sparrow, symbol of the south, perched on his southern gate in 680. (Sakamoto et al., II, 430–31, 442–43, 480–81, 589 [Aston, II, 337–38, 347, 379].)

336–37 [MYS II:194–95]. Under the Kiyomihara Code instituted by Emperor Temmu in 685, Jōdaisan was the fifth in a category of "pure" (*jō*) ranks; it corresponded to Senior Fifth Upper under the Taihō Code of 701. Akamitori ("Red Bird") is the Japanese reading of the year period Shuchō.

338 [MYS II:196]. "Well-ordered" freely renders *mike mukau* ("set out on a tray"; line 44), a mock epithet for Kinoe through *ki* ("leek," or its homophone meaning "liquor"). *Aji sahau* (line 47) is obscure, perhaps meaning "ducks flock," a mock epithet for *megoto* ("eyes and words") through *me*, putatively related to *mure* ("flock").

341 [MYS II:199]. Offended by her brother Susanoo's obstreperous behavior, the sun goddess Amaterasu hides in the rock cave of heaven, depriving the world of light (Kurano, pp. 80–83 [Philippi, *Kojiki*, pp. 81–85]). This early myth seems to provide the model for one aspect of the divine intervention in the climactic battle of the Jinshin War as recreated by Hitomaro. The other aspect—the wind— may have been suggested by the ancient epithet for Ise. Watarai is the name of the district in which the Ise shrines are located. The *Nihonshoki* account of the Jinshin War mentions Temmu's worship of Amaterasu at the outset of the campaign. The next day he entrusts the conduct of the war to his son Takechi, who makes a heroic speech but does not figure largely in the subsequent battle reports. That night there is a thunderstorm, which serves as the occasion for an *ukehi*, a test of divine intentions. The thunder and rain stop after Temmu declares that their cessation will be taken as a sign of the gods' favor. The climactic battle takes place a month later at Seta Bridge, the eastern approach to the Ōmi capital, and there is mention of banners, drums, and arrows that fall like rain, but no divine intervention. There are, however, accounts of oracles by the gods Kotoshironushi and Ikumitama (or Ikazuchi) and the goddess of Muraya. (Sakamoto et al., II, 390–91, 394–95, 400– 401, 404–5 [Aston, II, 307, 310, 314–15, 317–18].)

348–50 [MYS II:210–12]. The variant of this poem is MYS II:213–16, where the *chōka* ends *hai nite maseba* ("since she is ash"). For other poems dealing with cremation, see #355–56, #1313–16, and #1319.

351–53 [MYS II:217–19]. Omodaka, II, 478–79, agrees with Tsuchiya Bummei in regarding this poem as analogous to the rehearsals of the legendary deaths of Unai and Mama no Tegona by Mushimaro and others (see #553–55, #572–73, #574–76, and #837–38). *Sora kazou* ("counting vacantly") in the second envoy is a mock epithet for Ōtsu through *ō* ("vague"). It is freely rendered "vacantly musing."

357 [MYS III:429/426]. The edict on the treatment of fallen stragglers among the corvée laborers returning home was issued in the 1st month of 712. The living were to be fed and cared for, and the dead buried and their names reported to local authorities (*Shoku Nihongi*, p. 47).

358–60 [MYS II:220–22]. The island of Shikoku (called Iyo, the same as one of its constituent provinces) is the second-born of the offspring of Izanami and Izanagi after their second wedding ceremony. Each province has two names, the second being that of a god. Sanuki is named Iiyorihiko, probably a rice (*ii*) god (Kurano, pp. 54–57 [Philippi, *Kojiki*, p. 53]).

361 [MYS II:223]. It has also been suggested that Kamo Mountain was in Yamato or elsewhere (NKBZ, I, 181).

362–63 [MYS II:224–25]. NKBZ, I, 447, points out that there was a place named Yosami in Kawachi Province.

The "Hitomaro Collection." The other collections of the works of individual poets named in *Man'yōshū* are those of Tanabe no Sakimaro, Takahashi no Mushimaro, and Kasa no Kanamura. Akima Toshio concludes on the basis of an exhaustive study of the orthography and vocabulary of the "Hitomaro Collection" poems in Book XI that all are by Hitomaro except those directly attributed to someone else. He compares four categories of poems: (1) Hitomaro's accepted oeuvre; (2) the "Hitomaro Collection" poems in Book XI in regular Man'yō orthography; (3) the "Hitomaro Collection" poems in Book XI written in an abbreviated orthographic style—the so-called *shih*-type (*shitaika*), sometimes supposed to have been folk songs collected by Hitomaro; and (4) the anonymous poems of Book XI not taken from the "Hitomaro Collection." He finds greater correspondences among (1), (2), and (3) than between those categories and (4). (Akima, "Hitomaro Kashū"; findings summarized in Part 2, pp. 40–41.) Akima's research is impressive, but his conclusions are perhaps too sweeping; also, he does not seem to have considered the possibility of a distinction between poet and scribe when thinking about orthography. A cogent statement of the skeptical view is given by Morimoto Jikichi in *Waka Bungaku Daijiten*, pp. 151–53. One factor of possible significance is the inclusion of 38 poems on the Tanabata myth (see, e.g., #398) in the "Hitomaro Collection" portion of Book X. The last of these, MYS X: 2037/2033, has the cyclical date Metal-Senior/Dragon, corresponding either to 680 or to 740. Tanabata poems were common by 740, but none has been identified as early as 680. Morimoto and others argue that the dating places the poem, and presumably the whole collection, outside Hitomaro's lifetime. But Kojima points out that MYS IX:1686, by one Hashihito no Sukune, a poem on the Tanabata theme, must date from the reign of Emperor Mommu (697–707), during at least part of which Hitomaro is known to have been active (*Jōdai*, II, 1153). It is also worth noting that there is a Tanabata poem—MYS XV:3633/3611—in the collection from the embassy to Silla of 736 that is ascribed directly to Hitomaro in a footnote. It is included among a number of "old poems" recited on the journey. Naitō, p. 17, concludes on the basis of thematic and chronological analysis that Hitomaro was the pioneer of the Tanabata theme, beginning with the poem of 680. His analysis throws light on the naturalization of the Chinese myth, links the development of the Tanabata poem conventions to general love poetry in Japan, and proposes a setting for Hitomaro's putative composition of them at the parties held in the Yoshino detached palace during the reigns of Temmu and Jitō. Much in his article is suggestive, but the case for authorship of "Hitomaro Collection" poems by Hitomaro is assumed rather than proved.

365 [MYS VII: 1072/1068]. For the full text of Emperor Mommu's kanshi, see KFS 15, in Kojima, *Kaifūsō*, pp. 86–87. Kojima remarks that he has not been able to discover other uses of the moon-boat metaphor (in either Chinese or Japanese?) beyond #365 and KFS 15. The image is familiar in English through Alfred Noyes's "The Highwayman": "The moon was a ghostly galleon tossed upon cloudy seas" (Noyes, p. 192). "Cassia oar" refers to the cassia tree believed to grow on the moon (see #895).

370 [MYS VII: 1287/1283]. NKBZ has the reading *watashiteshi* in line 5: "[the bridge] I placed across." The translation follows NKBT.

375–81 [MYS IX: 1698–1704/1694–1700]. Sagisaka was south of Ogura Pond, which was fed by the Izumi and Naki rivers. NKBZ, II, 395, presents a map of the area as it might have been in Man'yō times.

389 [MYS IX: 1712/1708]. Kuiyama was a hill in the area south of Ogura Pond (see preceding note). On Su Wu, see the note to #85.

405 [MYS XI: 2359/2355]. The juxtaposition of the tender and the grim for effect is recurrent in such lines of Housman's as "Dear to friends and food for powder" and "Lovely lads and dead and rotten" (*A Shropshire Lad*, XXXV; Housman, p. 52).

408 [MYS XI: 2366/2362]. "Yamashiro" is Saibara 31 (*Kodai Kayōshū*, pp. 398–99).

411 [MYS XI: 2374/2370]. The poem appears as SIS XV: 937.

417 [MYS XI: 2394/2390]. The poem appears as SIS XV: 935, with the 4th line reading *chitabi zo ware wa*.

418 [MYS XI: 2405/2401]. The poem appears in a variant version as SIS XV: 936, as Koite shine / Koite shine to ya / Wagimoko ga / Wagaya no kado o / Sugite yukuramu ("'Love and die of it, / Love and die of it!' Is that / What she would tell me, / My girl who passes by my gate / And never stops to see me?").

420 [MYS XI: 2420/2416]. A variant of this poem appears as SIS X: 596, attributed to Hitomaro, with *tamoteru* for *motaseru*, *tare ga tame ni ka* for *ta ga tame ni ka mo*, and *nagaku to omowan* for *nagaku hori semu*.

Poems Attributed to Hitomaro in Later Collections. Kokinrokujō (full title *Kokinwakarokujō*) is an anthology of about 4,500 poems arranged by the topics of Chinese poetic encyclopedias. It is thought to have been compiled as a reference work for poets some time in the period 976–82, perhaps by Emperor Daigo's son Prince Kaneakira (914–87) or Minamoto no Shitagau (911–83). The count of 123 poems by Hitomaro includes only those immediately preceded by his name. *Kokinrokujō* does not appear to follow the practice of the imperial anthologies, in which a poet's name applies to all the poems following until the occurrence of the next name. It draws partially on *Man'yōshū*, including the "Hitomaro Collection," for poems it attributes to Hitomaro. *Kokinrokujō* is included in *Shimpen Kokka Taikan*, II, *Shisenshūhen*. *Shūishū* (full title *Shūiwakashū*) is thought to have been completed about 1005 or 1006 by ex-Emperor Kazan, based on the earlier *Shūishō* (997) in ten books, compiled perhaps by Fujiwara no Kintō (966–1041). Three versions of *Kakinomoto no Hitomaro Shū* (not to be confused with the "Hitomaro Collection" in *Man'yōshū*) are included in the first volume of *Shikashū Taisei*. Of these only one appears in *Shimpen Kokka Taikan*, III, *Shikashūhen* (I). The cross-references in the present anthology refer to the *Shikashū Taisei* texts.

431 [KKS VI:334]. Also SIS I:12 (Hitomaro); KHS I:170, II:4, III:29. Compare MYS X:2348/2344 (Anon.) and MYS VIII:1430/1426 (Yamabe no Akahito).

432 [KKS IX:409]. Also KHS I:210, II:213, III:613; KKRJ 1818 (Hitomaro). For the tone and concept of this poem, see #445 and #449 by Takechi no Kurohito and #611 and its variant SIS XX:1327 (see note to #611), attributed to Manzei.

433 [KKS XIII:621]. Also KHS II:313, III:466; KKRJ 693 (Hitomaro).

435 [SIS XII:700]. Also KHS I:193, II:569, III:429.

436 [SIS XIII:778]. Also KHS I:207, II:333; MYS XI:2813/2802a (Anon.); KKRJ 924.

437 [SKKS IV:346]. Also KHS I:218, II:351; MYS X:2281/2277 (Anon.); KKRJ 3691.

438 [SKKS V:459]. Also KHS II:168; MYS X:2224/2220 (Anon.).

439 [SKKS VI:582]. Also KHS I:131, 222, II:161; MYS X:2200/2196 (Anon.).

440 [SKKS VI:657]. Also KHS I:163, II:171, III:205; *Yakamochi Shū* II:143; MYS X:2335/2331 (Anon.); KKRJ 851. It is worth noting that this poem is attributed to both Hitomaro and Ōtomo no Yakamochi. Like Hitomaro, Yakamochi and Yamabe no Akahito drew the attention of Heian anthologizers. Their purported personal collections are printed in *Shikashū Taisei*, I.

441 [SKKS XI:992]. Also KHS I:15, II:297; MYS XI:2657/2649 (Anon.); KKRJ 783.

442 [SKKS XI:993]. Also KHS II:382, III:286; MYS IX:1772/1768 (variant, Nukike no Obito); KKRJ 2678.

443–44 [MYS II:228–29]. "Year-station" translates *saishi*, a term referring to the position of the "year star" (Jupiter) in its duodecimal progression along the zodiac. Here it refers to the position of the year in the 60-year cycle of the ten stems and twelve branches. The most famous use of the moss metaphor occurs in KKS VII:343, an anonymous poem adapted as the Japanese national anthem: Wa ga kimi wa / Chiyo ni yachiyo ni / Sazareishi no / Iwao to narite / Koke no musu made ("May our lord live / A thousand and eight thousand ages, / Until pebbles / Become boulders / And are overgrown with moss").

445 [MYS I:58]. Mikawa Province was just east of the modern city of Nagoya. The location of the headland of Are is not known.

448–55 [MYS III: 273–80/271–77]. The footnote to #450 points to the assembly of the set from various sources. Sakurada (#448) was at the location of the modern city of Nagoya; Shihatsu Mountain and Kasanui Island (#449) may have been either in the Ōsaka area or south of Nagoya; Futami ("Twin Views") in Mikawa Province (#453) is thought to have been where the Tōkaidō, the main east–west route, forks at modern Toyokawa City, one branch going north, and one south, of Lake Hamana; and Taka in Yamashiro Province (#455) was near Ide, between Uji and Nara. For a poem very similar to #451, see #1294.

456 [MYS III: 308/305]. Modern scholarship has fared no better than the compilers in identifying Shōben, perhaps an official title—"Minor Controller."

459 [MYS I: 43]. Nabari is on the border between Nara and Mie prefectures (or, anciently, Yamato and Ise provinces).

464 [MYS IV: 512/509]. The places named on this journey down the Inland Sea toward Tsukushi (Kyūshū) stretch from Mitsu ("the Royal Port," i.e., Naniwa) to Ie no Shima, off the present city of Himeji, only a small fraction of the total distance.

469 [MYS I: 66]. Ōtomo is the coast from Naniwa south to present-day Sakai. Takashi Beach included the area now known as Hamadera, the site of a famous poetry party in 1900, hosted by the young poets of the Sakai-Ōsaka area in honor of their guest, Yosano Tekkan (1873–1935). Then, too, some of the poets reclined on the beach to compose their verses. The occasion is supposed to have been that on which Tekkan and Hō (Yosano) Akiko (1878–1942) fell in love (see Cranston, "Young Akiko," p. 28).

471–72 [MYS III: 285, 287/282, 284]. Iware, in the hills east of Mount Kagu, was nearly ten kilometers southwest of Hatsuse. The action of #472 takes place around the present city of Shizuoka.

478 [MYS III: 293/290]. Speculations on the location of Mount Kurahashi center on the Tōnomine range east of Asuka.

479–80 [MYS IX: 1689–90/1685–86]. The Izumi, the present Kizu River, flowed north into Ogura Pond at the confluence of the Uji and Yodo rivers.

482 [MYS II: 115]. According to NKBZ, Sūfukuji was founded in Ōtsu in 668, the year after the capital was transferred there.

490 [MYS III: 267/265]. This Miwa is not the mountain mentioned in #119, #120, #257–58, and elsewhere, but a cape along the coast of the Kii Peninsula at present-day Shingū City. Teika's allusive variation is SKKS VI: 671: Koma tomete / Sode uchiharau / Kage mo nashi / Sano no watari no / Yuki no yūgure ("Here to stop my horse / And to brush my laden sleeves / There is no shelter; / Over the Sano crossing / Twilight amid the snow").

494 [MYS XVI: 3849/3827]. Text and translation follow the readings in NKBT. The point seems to be that *suguroku* dice have more "eyes" (*me*), i.e., markings, than human beings. The apparent play on *sae* ("even") and *sae* ("dice"), suggesting the "even . . . oddly" of the translation, may or may not be vitiated by restoring the 8th-century phonetic distinction between these two words, *saFë* and *saye*. A more searching exegesis would depend on a knowledge of how backgammon was played in Man'yō times. NKBZ provides the reading *Ichi ni no me / Nomi ni wa arazu / Go roku samu / Shi sae arikeri / Suguroku no sae*.

495 [MYS XVI:3850/3828]. The graffito, supposedly the work of a temple artisan, was discovered at Tōshōdaiji. For illustrations, see Tanaka, p. 126, fig. 101; and Noma, p. 180, fig. 74. It is one of hundreds of freehand ink sketches found at Tōshōdaiji and Hōryūji.

497–98 [MYS XVI:3852–53/3830–31]. A gem-whisk in the Shōsōin collection is illustrated in the prefatory pages of NKBZ, IV. The rikishimai is described in *Kyōkunshō*, a 1233 work devoted to ancient continental music by Koma Chikazane (Hayashi, pp. 88–89). For illustrations of Gigaku masks, see Kameda et al.; and Noma, color plate 10, black-and-white plates 44–47.

Prince Nagaya. Shoku Nihongi, p. 115 (Tempyō 1 [729].2.10–15), gives a terse account of the fall of the Prince, who was Minister of the Left at the time. He was accused of studying unorthodox doctrines, as well as of treason. His wife and sons followed him in his obligatory suicide.

509 [MYS IV:646/643]. Anase (or Anashi) River is thought to be the stretch of Makimuku River between Mount Miwa and Mount Anashi northeast of Asuka.

516–20 [MYS II:230–34]. Takamato and Mikasa are mountains east of Nara in the Kasuga area. *Shoku Nihongi*, p. 66, enters Prince Shiki's death as having occurred on Reiki 2 [716].8.11.

Yamabe no Akahito. For the award of the clan name Yamabe to Kumebe no Odate, see Sakamoto et al., I, 520–21 (Aston, I, 388). This clan was in charge of the Yamamoribe, or "guardians of the mountains." Tsurayuki's assessment of the relative merit of Hitomaro and Akahito is expressed in what may be a formula of faulty logic; unless, that is, Tsurayuki meant what his words say, that Akahito is not to be considered inferior to Hitomaro: "It would be hard to place Hitomaro above Akahito, or to set Akahito below Hitomaro" (Kubota, *Kokinwakashū*, I, 82).

538 [MYS III:321/318]. A variant of this envoy, attributed to Akahito, appears as an independent poem as SKKS VI:675: Tago no ura ni / Uchiidete mireba / Shirotae no / Fuji no takane ni / Yuki wa furitsutsu ("When on Tago Bay / We rowed far out and turned to look, / On the towering cone / Of Fuji white as barken cloth / A steady snow was falling"). The poem does not appear in either the Heian *Akahito Shū* or *Kokinrokujō*.

561 [MYS VI:930/925]. A nearly identical version of this envoy, attributed to Akahito, appears as SKKS VI:641. The last line reads *chidori naku nari*. The poem does not appear in either the Heian *Akahito Shū* or *Kokinrokujō*.

568 [MYS VIII:1431/1427]. This poem appears as SKKS I:11, with *asu kara* rather than *asu yori*. It does not appear in either the Heian *Akahito Shū* or *Kokinrokujō*.

569–71 [MYS III:322–24/319–21]. Kojima et al. list this set under Mushimaro in NKBZ, though they point out that the *Man'yōshū Mokuroku* (Table of Contents) attributes it to Kasa no Kanamura. NKBZ also states that *se* (line 21), written "stone flower" and meaning "barnacle," is a "borrowed *kun*," a phonetic substitute, but does not suggest the actual meaning of the name. The lake was located northwest of the mountain; it was split into Lakes Sai and Shōjin (NKBT, I, 170). The Fuji River flows past the mountain to the west, not down its slopes, as Mushimaro implies.

574–76 [MYS IX:1813–15/1809–11]. Kojima, *Jōdai*, II, 1116–17, points out a few similarities between Mushimaro's chōka-hanka set and the long anonymous narrative poem "For the Wife of Chiao Chung-ch'ing." The families of the suicides confer at the end and decide to bury them together, planting trees on the graves. And the young woman in each case speaks of waiting or meeting in the underworld ("Yellow Springs" in both poems). The situations in the two poems are fundamentally different, however. The Chinese case is a classic example of an abused daughter-in-law and a husband who can defy his mother only through suicide. The tale of the marriage-refusing maiden, so haunting to the Japanese imagination, does not stem from this source. The Chinese poem is set at the end of the Han dynasty in the early 3d century A.D. and is thought to be the product of several unknown poets in the succeeding decades (Uchida, I, 106–26).

The Nō play *Motomezuka* is based directly on a version of the Unai legend in tale 147 of *Yamato Monogatari*, a collection of poem-tales of the mid-10th century. In this grimmer, more detailed version, the suitors compete by shooting at a waterbird on the Ikuta River. Their arrows strike simultaneously, and Unai in despair throws herself into the river. The suitors leap in after her, and all drown. They are buried in adjoining graves, as in Mushimaro's poem, but one youth's parents bury weapons with him, and the other is buried without such protection. Later, a traveler hears sounds of conflict within the grave mounds, and a bloodied figure comes to him in a dream, asking to borrow his sword. The traveler lends it, and the hitherto defenseless suitor kills his rival. Kan'ami drew from this tale the theme of bitter passion lasting beyond the grave and intensified it, turning the grave mound into a flaming furnace, and the slain bird into an iron monster feeding on Unai's brain with its piercing beak. Unai is doomed to repeat forever the drama of hate and desire, with the suitors reappearing to seize and pull her in opposite directions. Even the prayers of a traveling priest to whom she confesses cannot save her soul. (Abe and Imai, pp. 311–16; Yokomichi and Omote, pp. 67–74.)

578 [MYS IX:1743/1739]. *Kanato* ("metal gate") is thought to mean a wooden gate with metal fittings.

579–80 [MYS IX:1744–45/1740–41]. In the *Tango Fudoki* and *Nihonshoki* versions of the Urashima story, the woman first appears in the form of a tortoise. The

Nihonshoki account is brief, noting that the pair married and went to Hōrai, where they saw the immortals (Sakamoto et al., I, 497 [Aston, I, 368]). For the story of Ho-ori and Toyotamahime, see Kurano, pp. 134–47 (Philippi, *Kojiki*, pp. 148–58). In *Nihonshoki* the hero is called Hikohohodemi no Mikoto (Sakamoto et al., I, 163–87 [Aston, I, 92–108]; see also the commentary to #1528–39). On Tokoyo and the "sea slope" (*unasaka*) of line 15, see Akima, "Songs of the Dead," pp. 486–90. The story attached to #122 is also a version of "the mysterious box," though there what is forbidden is not opening the box but overreacting to its contents. The Kyōgen play *Busu* is a comic variant, in which the "forbidden" content is sugar. *Tsurugitachi* ("sword") in line 3 of the envoy is a mock epithet for *na* ("you") through its homophone meaning "blade." The wordplay is rendered freely in the translation.

581–82 [MYS VI:976–77/971–72]. The appointment of the setsudoshi is given in *Shoku Nihongi*, p. 129. For Umakai's reaction to his appointment, see KFS 93 (Kojima, *Kaifūsō*, p. 156). And for a Man'yō poem by him, see #885. "Mountain sprite" renders *yamabiko*, the echo conceived as a deity answering far off in the mountains. *Yama* ("mountain") is meant to balance *tani* ("valley") in *taniguku*. The expression about the wandering toad is found in *Toshigoi no Matsuri*, a norito for rich harvest (see Takeda, pp. 390–91; [Philippi, *Norito*, p. 19]). For another instance of kotoage, see #1457. Tatsuta was one of the mountains separating inland Yamato from Naniwa and the sea.

584 [MYS IX:1752/1748]. Tatsutahiko and Tatsutahime, worshiped at Tatsuta Shrine, were male and female wind deities.

585 [MYS IX:1761/1757]. Lake Toba, west of Mount Tsukuha, has disappeared.

588 [MYS IX:1764/1760]. The clouds-and-rain metaphor finds its source in *Kao T'ang Fu*, attributed to Sung Yü, who lived in the state of Ch'u during the Warring States period (403 B.C.–221 B.C.). There a King of Ch'u has a dream in which a woman from Mount Wu comes and shares his couch in Kao-T'ang tower. As she departs she tells him that in the morning she takes the form of a cloud, and in the evening of a passing shower (*Wen-hsüan*, XIX, fasc. 7, 2a). For a discussion identifying this woman as "an ancient fertility goddess whose ritual mating with a shaman-king was necessary to the well-being of the land," see Schafer, *Divine Woman*, pp. 34–38.

592–604 [MYS III:341–53/338–50]. Tabito's wife died in the summer of 728, according to an interpretation of several poems and prose passages at the beginning of Book V. These include one chōka-hanka set, MYS V:798–803/794–99 by Yamanoue no Okura, entitled *Nihon Banka* ("Japanese Lament") and dated Jinki 5 [728].7.21. There are two schools of thought on this poem, one claiming that Okura is lamenting his own wife's demise, and the other holding that the poem is a *daisaku*, or "substitute composition," expressing Tabito's grief.

The passage on the origins of the terms "Sage" and "Worthy" for clear and cloudy wine is quoted in Wang, II, 1247, from a lost historical work on the Wei dynasty titled *Wei Lüeh*. Anecdotes about the Seven Sages of the Bamboo Grove are recounted in *Shih-shuo Hsin-yü*, a 5th-century collection by Liu I-ch'ing (A.D. 402–44). According to one, Liu Ling, one of the company of seven, was reproached by his wife for his drunkenness. Refusing to serve him any more wine, she begged him to give up his evil habit. "Very well," he replied. "Since I cannot do so unassisted, I shall make a vow to the gods. Prepare wine and meat for the sacrifice!" To this she readily agreed, but when she urged him to make his vow, Ling announced, "Heaven produced this Liu Ling and made him a name because of wine. He drinks a barrel at a time and five quarts for the hangover. Beware of listening to his wife!" And reaching for the wine and meat, he was soon roaring drunk again. (Mekada, III, 911). In another anecdote Liu Ling was censured by visitors for being drunk and naked in his own house. Ling replied, "Heaven and earth are my dwelling; my house is merely my loincloth. What are you doing in my loincloth?" (Mekada, III, 914.)

Cheng Hsüan asked his son to bury him beside the kiln, where he would turn to earth after several hundred years and hope to be dug up and fashioned into a wine vessel. The anecdote is in a fragmentary Six Dynasties collection, *T'ao-yü-chi*. A Japanese copy of this work was made as early as 759. Chüan XII and XIV were collected by Li Shu-ch'ang in Japan during the Meiji period and included with other Chinese works surviving in Japan in a collection called *Ku-i Ts'ung-shu* (*T'ao-yü-chi*, XIV). The "priceless jewel" that is the source of Tabito's *atai naki takara* is mentioned in the *Lotus Sutra*, chap. 8, in the parable of the man who lived in poverty, unaware that his friend (the Buddha) had sewn such a jewel (i.e., knowledge of the prophecy of supreme perfect enlightenment) into the lining of his garment (Takakusu, IX, 29 [Hurvitz, pp. 164–66]). *Shu-i-chi*, a Liang dynasty work attributed to Jen Fang (460–508), includes in its account of the marvels of the Southern Seas the following information: "In the Southern Seas there are gems that are the pupils of the eyes of whale-fish. When the whale dies the eyes lose their aqueous humor and can be used as mirrors. They call them 'night-shiners'" (*Shu-i-chi*, 19a, in Ch'eng, XXXII).

608 [MYS III: 339/336]. The orthography for *shiranuhi* ("white-sewn") fits the content of the poem and may have been chosen for that reason. It also rules out the old interpretation, "unknown fires," since "fire" is *Fï* (*otsu-rui*), and the *ren'yōkei* of a *yodan* verb is *kō-rui* (*siranuFi*).

611 [MYS III: 354/351]. A better-known version of this poem appears as SIS XX: 1327, attributed to Manzei: Yo no naka o / Nani ni tatoemu / Asaborake / Kogi-yuku fune no / Ato no shiranami ("To what / Shall we compare the world? / To the white wave / Behind a boat that rows away, / No one knows where, at dawn"). *Asabiraki*, a verb meaning "to leave port in the morning," has been altered to the noun (used adverbially) *asaborake* ("morning murk"), and the last line has been changed to include the pivot word *shiranami* ("not knowing" / "white wave"). The result makes a superior poem to the original—imagistically richer, phonetically sweeter, technically more intricate, and endowed with overtones by the strong noun ending. Here is proof that a poem can improve with age if it remains alive in a world of reciters instead of being set down once and for all in written form.

612 [MYS III: 395/392]. The *nuba*-bead (*nubatama*) is the fruit of the *hiōgi*, the blackberry lily or leopard flower, an emblem for blackness in the epithet *nubatama no*, translated elsewhere as "jet black," "berry black," "black as leopard-flower fruit," etc.

616 [MYS IV: 565/562]. A similar superstition concerning the eyes appears in *Yu-hsien-k'u*, where the involuntary fluttering or twitching of the hero's eyelids predicts his meeting lovely women (Yagisawa, pp. 566–67).

Yamanoue no Okura. The conclusion that Okura was a Korean by birth is that of Nakanishi. For his evidence, see his *Yamanoue no Okura*, pp. 23–45. Nakanishi, pp. 37–39, places the Yamanoue property at Yamanao, a location in Ōmi Province.

619 [MYS I: 63]. The place-name Ōtomo supposedly has a connection with Ōtomo clan holdings in the area (NKBZ, I, 452).

624 [MYS V: 804/800]. The cast-off shoe (or sandal) appears in the "Inscription at T'ou-t'o Temple" (*T'ou-t'o-ssu Pei-wen*) by Wang Chien-ch'i (d. 505). It is part of a metaphor for the casting aside of the world by Śākyamuni. Li Shan traces the image to *Shih Chi*, annals of Wu Ti, in a passage that specifically likens abandoning wife and children to the casting aside of a shoe (*Monzen*, ed. Obi, VII, 457–58, 461). Burton Watson translates the *Shih Chi* passage, "Ah! If I could only become like the Yellow Emperor, I would think no more of my wife and children than of a castoff slipper!" (Watson, *Records*, II, 52.) Emperor Wu (r. 141 B.C. – 87 B.C.) utters this exclamation on hearing how the mythical Yellow Emperor ascended to heaven on the back of a dragon. Watson points out that the "Basic Annals of Emperor Wu" do not exist as such but are identical to the "Treatise on the Feng and Shan Sacrifices" (*Records*, I, 375). The Chinese text is given in Yoshida, II, 717. The term *bōmei santaku* ("absconding into the hills and marshes") is mentioned as a crime in the chapter on banditry in the Yōrō Code (KT, XXII, 57).

626 [MYS III: 340/337]. The *ra* suffix on Okura's name is understood to be a humilific.

627–28 [MYS V: 806–7/802–3]. For a list and sources of the 32 marks of a Buddha, one of which is golden color, see Soothill and Hodous, p. 60. On Rāhula, see *Konkōmyō Saishōōkyō* (Takakusu, XVI, 406), "If the Tathagata . . . regards the multitudinous living things universally, and loves them without partiality, as he does Rāhula"; also *Gōbu Konkōmyōkyō* (Takakusu, XVI, 361), "If Buddha, the World-Honored, regards the multitudinous living things equally with Rāhula, I pray Buddha to grant me one favor." On "There is no love surpassing that for a child," compare *Zōagongyō* (Takakusu, II, 263), "There is nothing which is loved more than a child."

In *Man'yōshū* and *Nihonshoki*, *aohitokusa* is a reading supplied by tradition to the Chinese compound *ts'ang-sheng* ("green growth"; Morohashi 31627.82). In *Kojiki*, however, the term *hitokusa* appears in unambiguous semantogram orthography. Both the Chinese and the Japanese term are metaphors for the lusty growth and numerousness of the common people. It seems plausible that *aohitokusa* is a translation of *ts'ang-sheng*. The locus classicus of the latter is in *Shu Ching*, part II, book IV, chap. 1.7 (Legge, III, 83). For the Japanese references, see Sakamoto et al., I, 102–3 (Aston, I, 33); and Kurano, pp. 66–67 (Philippi, *Kojiki*, p. 65).

The T'ao Ch'ien reference is to a couplet in his poem *Tsê Tzu* ("Finding Fault with My Sons"): "T'ung-tzu is getting on toward nine / And all he wants are pears and chestnuts" (Hightower, p. 163). See also Nakanishi, p. 264.

629–31 [MYS V:909–11/904–6]. Nakanishi, pp. 480–81, argues that the note following #631 is meant to apply only to that poem, and that #629–30, like the preceding set left without an author's name, #640–46, are to be understood as definitely of Okura's composition. He points out the contrasting conceptions of the afterlife between #630 and #631, but seems inclined to accept #631 also as Okura's. NKBZ, II, 505, lists the entire set as by Okura. The research on the name "Furuhi" is also by Nakanishi, pp. 498–504. Even within the *Lotus* there are various lists of the Seven Treasures. The list given in the commentary (and in NKBZ, II, 116) appears in the sixth chapter, "Bestowal of Prophecy" (Takakusu, IX, 21 [Hurvitz, p. 125]). The identity of the plant *sakikusa* ("split-grass"?) is uncertain. NKBZ suggests *mitsumata* ("three-fork"; *Edgeworthia papyrifera*), daphne, or gold-banded lily (*Lilium auratum*). The phrase *sakikusa no* serves as an epithet for *naka* ("middle"). The role of the mirror in the prayer of the father (lines 41–42) no doubt has to do with its solar symbolism.

632–33 [MYS V:808–9/804–5]. For the Eight Great Pains, see Takakusu, I, 195. The Five Skandhas, or components of an intelligent being, are form, sensation, discernment, discrimination, and cognition (Soothill and Hodous, p. 126). The two [colors of] hair were lamented by P'an Yüeh (A.D. 247–300) in his *Ch'iu Hsing Fu*. P'an experienced their onset at the age of thirty-two (*Monzen*, ed. Obi, II, 166). The district seat of Kama District in Chikuzen Province was about 40 km east of Dazaifu. Okura is thought to have stopped there on a tour of his province.

634–35 [MYS V:896–97/892–93]. The title of Okura's poem can be interpreted as "debate between *bin* (poverty) and *gū* (destitution)" or as "debate on poverty (*bingū*)." The characters for *bingū* can also be read *hinkyū*. On T'ao Ch'ien, retirement, and poverty, see Hightower, pp. 1–6; and Owen, pp. 168–76. Owen's essay on a poem by Su Shih (1037–1101) in the same book is an instructive companion piece for reading "Dialogue on Poverty." Here the pitiless ironies of natural splendor as an indifferent backdrop for human suffering are explored by the persona of the magistrate rather than the peasant. And the poem ends with a somber bird flying up and away (Owen, pp. 176–79). Okura should also be read in conjunction with the kanshi of the great 9th-century poet-statesman Sugawara no Michizane (845–903), especially the set of ten on suffering from the cold, *Kanke Bunsō* 200–209. Okura's work, though in Japanese, belongs to this Chinese tradition. For translations, see Watson, *Japanese Literature in Chinese*, I, 93–94; and Borgen, pp. 187–88.

The lines about the spiderweb in the pot may have been suggested by a passage in *Tu-chia Li-ch'eng*, an early T'ang correspondence manual by Tu Cheng-tsung, a copy of which, in the hand of Empress Kōmyō, the consort of Emperor Shōmu, is preserved in the Shōsōin. This work, which was lost in China, contains phraseology translatable as "Dust gathers and fills the pot; the poor woman forgets how to cook" (NKBZ, II, 97). A photograph of a section of the Shōsōin manuscript is presented in Doi, p. 22.

Concerning Tajihi no Agatamori, Nakanishi points out that Okura would have become acquainted with him during his years in Kyūshū, where Agatamori was second in command (*daini*) at Dazaifu. Agatamori was appointed "Pacification Officer" (*chimbushi*) for the San'yōdō, the provinces north of the Inland Sea, in 731, and Regional Commander (*setsudoshi*) for the San'indō, the western provinces along the Japan Sea, in 732 (Nakanishi, pp. 371–72; *Shoku Nihongi*, pp. 127, 129).

639 [MYS V:901/896a]. *Ji* (Ch. *tz'u*), "compassion," is a quality associated with the future Buddha Maitreya, known as Jishi or Tz'u-chih, "the Compassionate One." The metaphor for the brevity of life is that of a horse glimpsed through a crack in a wall as it gallops past. The color is optional. See, for example, *Chuang-tzu*, XXII and XXIV (Ichikawa and Endō, II, 584, 749 [Watson, *Complete Works*, pp. 240, 330]). The story of Chi Cha and the "sword of faith" is in *Shih Chi*, XXXI, "The Hereditary House of Wu T'ai-po" (Yoshida, V, 23). The line about the white poplar is from no. 14 of "Nineteen Old Poems" of the Han (Saku, I, 53). The term *ch'ang yeh t'ai* ("platform of long night") appears in the first of three funeral poems by Lu Shih-heng (A.D. 261–303) in *Wen-hsüan* (*Monzen*, ed. Uchida, II, 541). *Mahāsattva*, an honorific for a great man, bodhisattva, or Buddha, is the Sanskrit equivalent of the title *daiji* in the text. "Jade body" is an encomium to balance the iconographic "golden countenance" of the Buddha. For the reference relating to Kālarātri and Lakṣmī, see, among others, *Daihatsu Nehangyō*, XII (Takakusu, XII, 435). The drifting cloud metaphor in the third line of the quatrain may have been suggested by a passage in *Yuimakyō* or *Vimalakīrti Sūtra* (Takakusu, XVI, 539). In the original lines 2 and 4 employ end rhyme.

640–46 [MYS V:902–8/897–903]. In the second envoy, *köra*, "these," differs in vowel from *kora*, "children" (*otsu* vs. *kō-rui*), but the phonetics may have been such that one could suggest the other, in the way of half-rhyme.

647 [MYS VI:983/978]. Okura did not advance in rank after 714, when he achieved Junior Fifth Lower. As a holder of this rank, he served as Governor of Hōki, Tutor to the Crown Prince, and Governor of Chikuzen. His friend Tabito died in Junior Second Rank, and Tabito's son Yakamochi in Junior Third. Holders of the Third and Second ranks were high court nobles (kugyō) and eligible for the positions of power. Four and Fifth Rank holders were *tenjōbito*, i.e., could be admitted to the audience room (*tenjō no ma*), and were the middle-level officials. Ordinary bureaucrats held Sixth Rank and below. Thus Okura was on the lower fringes of the middle group during his last two decades. But in any case real power was concentrated in the hands of particular members of the imperial clan or the

Fujiwara clan, or, from 737 to 756, of Tachibana no Moroe. People of Okura's rank could expect to spend much of their lives in provincial administration, and though he rose higher, this was true of Yakamochi as well. Tabito's provincial duty was at a higher level, as Governor-General of Dazaifu, a post calling for Junior Third Rank (Tabito actually was Senior Third at the time).

648–57 [MYS XVI: 3882–91/3860–69]. Shika is the peninsula enclosing the north side of Hakata Bay. This was the location of Kasuya District. Munakata was the neighboring district to the northeast. Matsura District occupied the northwestern quarter of Hizen Province, southwest of Chikuzen. The location of Cape Mineraku is uncertain. Cape Yara is the northern point on Noko Island in Hakata Bay (see #920).

658–59 [MYS VI: 981–82/976–77]. The clan title Imiki is discussed in the commentary to #488.

663 [MYS III: 378/375]. This poem appears, with the same attribution, as SKKS VI: 654.

666 [MYS III: 990/985]. The birth of the moon deity from the right eye of Izanagi during his ablutions after his visit to Yomi is narrated in Kurano, pp. 70–71 (Philippi, *Kojiki*, p. 70). See also Sakamoto et al., I, 87–89, 96–97 (Aston, I, 18–20, 28), for various versions of his birth. *Tsukuyomi* is properly "mooncount," a reference to the lunar calendar. The translation is based on the alternate name *tsukuyumi* ("moon-bow") found in some of the *Nihonshoki* accounts.

674 [MYS VI: 1051/1047]. The *kaho* bird (line 23) is thought by some to be the cuckoo (*kakkō*), but is to be distinguished from the smaller variety known as *hototogisu*, translated "cuckoo" herein. The signal-fire (*tobuhi*, line 28) station on Mount Ikoma between Nara and the coast at Naniwa was part of a warning system set up by Emperor Tenji during the 660's, at a time of alarm over the possibility of foreign invasion; see #193–94. (Sakamoto et al., II, 362–63 [Aston, II, 283]; see also Batten, pp. 215ff.)

677–85 [MYS VI: 1054–62/1050–58]. The reference in #677, lines 11–12, may be to the confluence of the Wazuka and Izumi (now Kizu) rivers near Kuni. Koma Mountain (#685) was west of Kuni, across the Izumi from Mount Kase.

693 [MYS III: 484/481]. The Sagaraka Mountains are thought to be those in southern Yamashiro around Kuni, where no doubt Takahashi no Asomi was in service at court.

698–99 [MYS VI: 978–79/973–74]. Rule by virtue, allowing the ruler to fold his hands in inactivity, is described in *Shu Ching*, V, III.10 (Legge, III, 316).

Princess Yashiro. On her reduction in rank, see *Shoku Nihongi*, Tempyō-Hōji 2 [758], p. 257.

Lady Ōtomo of Sakanoue. Much of the information on Lady Ōtomo in this section has been drawn from Aoki.

716–17 [MYS III:382–83/379–80]. The role of Ame no Oshihi no Mikoto in the divine descent is mentioned in Kurano, pp. 128–29 (Philippi, *Kojiki*, p. 141); and Sakamoto et al., I, 156–57 (Aston, I, 86–87). The translation interprets the somewhat obscure term *shiraka* ("white-tresses") in line 7 as finely split strands of *yū* (whitened mulberry-bark fiber cloth). *Shiraka tsuku* is a possible reading for the line, in which case it becomes an epithet for *yū*.

718 [MYS VI:984/979]. The Saho River flows south and west through Nara. The Sakanoue estate is thought to have been northeast of the imperial palace, probably across the river from the Saho estate.

719 [MYS VI:986/981]. Karitaka ("Hunting Heights") and Takamato ("High Target") are places southeast of Nara, associated here in an epithetical fashion. They suggest the third *taka*, providing the main device of the poem.

723–24 [MYS III:463–64/460–61]. Silla drove its erstwhile T'ang ally out of the Han River basin in 676 (Lee, p. 69). Rigan's age at death is not stated, nor the number of "dozens of years" (*sūki*) she lived in Japan. If she came as an infant and later became a nun in Japan, she could have been part of the wave of refugees that supposedly brought Yamanoue no Okura and his father in 663. But both chōka and footnote imply she came as an adult. Lady Ōtomo's mother was Lady Ishikawa (d. ca. 737). She held the court office of *naimyōbu*, a position in the women's quarters of the imperial palace. *Ōtoji*, or "Grand Mistress," refers to her position within the family. Arima, near Kōbe, is still famous for its hot springs. *Takuzuno no* ("of the *taku* ropes"; line 1) is a mock epithet for Shiraki through *shira* ("white"), a reference to the white fibers of *taku* (also *tae*) made from paper-mulberry bark. The related epithets *shikitae no* and *shirotae no* are also among the formulas used in the poem.

734 [MYS IV:688/685]. A triple sheath from the Shōsōin collection is illustrated in NKBZ, I, 363.

740 [MYS IV:724/721]. For more on *miyabi*, see #1000–1001; and Aoki, pp. 363–79.

Ōtomo no Yakamochi. The arguments on Yakamochi's year of birth are summarized in Doe, *Warbler's Song*, pp. 13, 14. For Prince Nagaya, see #505. The Prince and his family were forced by Fujiwara no Muchimaro to commit suicide on Jinki 6 (729).2.12 (*Shoku Nihongi*, p. 115). Tabito's membership in Prince Nagaya's clique, and the significance of his appointment to Dazaifu just at this time, are discussed in Takazaki, pp. 178, 201. *Shoku Nihongi* is the main source for Yakamochi's career after 759, and of course for the other historical events. See *Shoku Nihongi*, pp. 145, 146, 223, 229–40, 247, 285, 300, 303–10, 324, 336, 361, 368–69, 379, 380–81, 382, 402, 415, 418, 424, 427, 430, 436, 439, 456–57, 467, 469, 470, 476, 477, 481, 482, 484, 494, 497, 512–13. See also *Nihon Kōki*, p. 53.

On Tachibana no Moroe's relation to Yakamochi and *Man'yōshū*, Doe writes (p. 33): "Moroe is thought . . . to have edited or at least seen to the editing of the first two books of the *Man'yōshū*, and to have entrusted his protégé Yakamochi with the rest." The theory that both Moroe and Yakamochi were involved in the compilation of *Man'yōshū* is an old one, dating back at least to Sengaku (1203–ca. 1272). See Muromatsu, pp. 4–5. A detailed if speculative scenario is provided in Hisamatsu, "Ōtomo no Yakamochi," pp. 438–41.

761 [MYS XVII:3922/3900]. On *kai* (Ch. *huai*), the second element of *jukkai*, see Owen, pp. 12–13. The term means "what is on one's mind" and may refer to a scene, as well as to what is felt about it.

765–67 [MYS IV:683–85/680–82]. The Chinese term for the "companion" Yakamochi uses is *chiao-yu* (Morohashi 291.9).

768 [MYS IV:694/691]. The other two poems with the phrase *kokoro ni norite* are anonymous, MYS XIII:3292/3278 and MYS XIV:3538/3517.

778 [MYS IV:730/727]. The proximate source for "forgetting grass" is *Yang-sheng Lun*, a work on medicinal lore by Chi Shu-ye, one of the "Seven Sages of the Bamboo Grove" (*Monzen*, ed. Obi, VII, 16–17).

780 [MYS IV:744/741]. The *Yu-hsien-k'u* source for this poem is a scene early in the story, in which the hero dreams of the heroine before he has met her: "For a brief time I sat and dozed, and in a dream I saw the Tenth Maiden. I awoke with a start and grasped her, but suddenly my hands were empty. How could I describe the disappointment I felt in my heart?" (Yagisawa, p. 44; see Levy, p. 78, for a list of *Yu-hsien-k'u* sources for Man'yō poems.) Other translations include this by Kenneth Rexroth (*One Hundred Poems from the Japanese*, p. 99):

> Now to meet only in dreams,
> Bitterly seeking,
> Starting from sleep,
> Groping in the dark
> With hands that touch nothing.

Also this by E. Bruce Brooks ("A Yakamochi Sampler," p. 87):

> Our meeting in dream
> brought me at last only pain
> for, when I wakened,
> grope as I would to find you
> I felt no touch of your hand

781 [MYS IV:745/742]. The *Yu-hsien-k'u* reference here comes at the end of the story, after the lovers part: "My clothes hung looser day by day; my sash was slacker each morning" (Yagisawa, p. 190).

782 [MYS IV:746/743]. On the "thousand-puller stone," see Kurano, pp. 66–67 (Philippi, *Kojiki*, p. 65); and Sakamoto et al., I, 93 (Aston, I, 25).

783 [MYS IV:747/744]. The conceit of the open door derives from a poem in

Yu-hsien-k'u, where the hero tells the heroine before parting, "Do not bar your door tonight / I shall come to your side in a dream" (Yagisawa, p. 166).

793 [MYS IV:757/754]. Compare the following by Teika, *Shūi Gusō* 866: Omokage mo / Wakare ni kawaru / Kane no oto ni / Narai kanashiki / Shinonome no sora ("Shadow of a face / Changing into parting / At the sound of the bell / The accustomed sadness / Of the white dawn sky").

794 [MYS IV:758/755]. This poem draws its ultimate images from a passage in *Yu-hsien-k'u* describing the agonies of unfulfilled passion: "I have never devoured [burning] charcoal, but my entrails are as hot as if they were on fire; I have no recollection of swallowing a blade, but my belly is pierced and seems split in two" (Yagisawa, p. 33).

795-96 [MYS VIII:1631-32/1627-28]. "Went back and forth" (*ōrai*) seems to imply that the poems are an exchange. Since the headnote contradicts this assumption, perhaps the intent is that they were part of an exchange.

807-11 [MYS XVII:4035-39/4011-15]. According to NKBZ, IV, 225, n. 5, the proper season for hawking is winter, especially on clear days after snow. Windy or drizzly days are unsuitable. Yakamochi composed the poem on a date corresponding to November 4 by the Julian calendar, and he states in one of the envoys that a month has gone by since he last hunted. The date on which he had the dream is not clear. If it was immediately prior to the composition of the poem, he may indeed have still hoped for a happy outcome. The description of cormorant fishing in lines 15-18 shows the fishermen wading in the stream, holding their torches in one hand and guiding the cormorants with the other, instead of fishing from boats, as is the custom nowadays. A *haniwa* in the Yamato Bunkakan collection, serving as frontispiece for NKBZ, III, shows a hawk with a tinkle bell perched on a hunter's gauntlet. The bell is on the bird's lower back, attached to a strap that appears to be confining its wings. The places mentioned in the poem and note are all at the base of the Noto Peninsula, on the eastern side, facing Toyama Bay. See the map in NKBZ, IV, 130. The term "rotten mouse" in the note may have been drawn from *Chuang-tzu* (Ichikawa, II, 485 [Watson, *Complete Works*, p. 188]). The phrase translated "expending your vital force in vain" is adapted from *Yu-hsien-k'u* (Yagisawa, p. 31 [Levy, p. 13]).

812 [MYS XVII:4045/4021]. The Okami River is thought to be the present Shō River, flowing north into Toyama Bay past the town of Tonami.

813 [MYS XVIII:4078/4054]. Hisamatsu, p. 439, cites favorably a hypothesis of Oyama Tokujirō that Sakimaro brought a commission from Moroe for the compilation of *Man'yōshū*. The date of the banquet, the 26th of the 3d month, or April 28 by the Western calendar, was opportune for hearing the hototogisu on its northward migration. NKBZ, IV, 240, n. 3, gives the particulars of time and place.

814-17 [MYS XVIII:4118-21/4094-97]. On the discovery of gold in Michinoku, see *Shoku Nihongi*, Tempyō-Shōhō 1 [749].2.22, p. 197. Texts of the two semmyō (nos. 12 and 13) are in Mikanagi, pp. 121–45. The following passage from *Semmyō* 13 is relevant for lines 20–58.

> Now that thus the mission of the Heavenly Sun-Succession to govern and to bless has come down to this Our Sovereign reign, We take care, weigh heavily, are ashamed, and are in fear before the mind of heaven and earth as We sustain rule over these lands of Our sustenance: in whose eastern quarter, in the province of Michinoku and the district of Oda, report reaches Us that gold has been discovered. When We consider this, We hear that among the various and sundry doctrines the great dicta of the Buddha are the best for protecting the nation; We deposit the *Uttamarāja Sūtra* and fashion figures of Vairocana Buddha in the lands of Our sustenance, the several provinces of the Subcelestial Realm; We humbly pray to the gods of heaven and the deities of earth, and render worship to the souls of the successive Sovereigns, beginning with the remote Sovereign Ancestors dreadful even to bring to mind; and We lead the people with high exhortation in this act of service, believing that misfortune will cease and turn to good, peril alter to complete tranquility. But the people have doubted that the work could be completed, and We have afflicted Our mind lest gold be in short supply. Now We are given a sign—the divine and superlative efficacy of the great dicta of the Three Treasures. The gods of heaven and the deities of earth rejoice, bringing good fortune. And when We consider how the souls of the Sovereign Ancestors have blessed Us, stroked Us, thus, surely, revealing and pointing to this discovery, We receive it humbly, We receive it with joy. In Our reverence We know not whether to go forward or back; night and day We are in awe and fear. We feel unworthy and ashamed when We reflect that what would have been proper to the reign of a lord seated in the righteousness whereby he strokes and blesses the Subcelestial Realm has been made manifest in Our unseasoned and incompetent day. Hence how can We alone receive this great and worshipful Sign? In righteousness We must accept it humbly together with the Subcelestial Realm, bringing joy to the people: so We in all Our godhead do believe, blessing and governing the people. (Mikanagi, pp. 126–29).

The passage in Semmyō 13 concerning the Ōtomo can be translated:

> Further, as you Ōtomo and Saeki no Sukune have always said, you are the men who guard the Emperor's court without a backward glance, men, We hear, whose forefathers handed down these words:

Umi yukaba	If we go on the sea,
Mizuku kabane	Our dead are sodden in water;
Yama yukaba	If we go on the mountains,
Kusamusu kabane	Our dead are grown over with grass.
Ōkimi no	We shall die

| He ni koso shiname | By the side of our lord, |
| Nodo ni wa shinaji | We shall not die in peace. |

And because of this, from the age of the distant Sovereigns down to Our own reign, the Emperors have considered you to be inner palace troops and employed you as such. Therefore, let the children fulfill the faith of their fathers. Let them not lose their spirit, but serve with bright, pure hearts. We shall select one or two men, and likewise women, for special honor. (Ibid., pp. 138–41.)

For complete translations of Semmyō 12 and 13, see Sansom.

As a result of the discovery of gold in Tsushima, the era name was changed to Taihō (or Daihō; "Great Treasure") in 701. An old textual note in *Shoku Nihongi* states that Miyuki was the victim of some sort of deception by Mita no Itsuse, the man he dispatched to Tsushima to take charge of refining the gold (NKBZ, IV, 262; *Shoku Nihongi*, pp. 10, 12). On the descent of the ancestors of the Ōtomo and the Kume, see Kurano, pp. 128–29 (Philippi, *Kojiki*, p. 141).

821–25 [MYS XVIII:4125–29/4101–5]. For photographs and a description of the lives of the ama women of Hekura (which now has a permanent population) and the Seven Islands, see Maraini.

826–27 [MYS XVIII:4135–36/4111–12]. For descriptions of the varied citrus fruits of East Asia in their South Chinese and Vietnamese lands of origin, see Schafer, *Vermilion Bird*, pp. 183–85. The association of some of them with Taoist magic (p. 185) is worth noting. Whatever historicity may lie behind the Tajimamori legend seems to link Tokoyo with these southern regions. The celebration of the orange in poetry, both European and Oriental, is mentioned in Reckert, pp. 21–50, as well as Schafer. The account of Tajimamori and the "Seasonless Fragrant Tree" is given in Kurano, pp. 202–3 (Philippi, *Kojiki*, p. 226); and Sakamoto et al., I, 279–81 (Aston, I, 186–87). The term "eight spears" (*yahoko*) is found also in the *Kojiki* account, where it is thought to mean "eight saplings" and is paired with the expression "eight garlands" (*yakage*), perhaps referring to branches with leaves and fruit attached. For the story of the red jewel, see Kurano, pp. 254–57 (Philippi, *Kojiki*, pp. 291–93). *Nihonshoki* has a version featuring a white stone instead of a red jewel (Sakamoto et al., I, 258–61 [Aston, I, 166–68]). Both jewel and stone magically transform into a woman.

828 [MYS XIX:4163/4139]. The syntactic ambiguity of *niou* ("radiates"), which is both predicative and attributive, contributes to the mysterious double image of blossoms and young woman. The peach blossoms glow, and so does the garden as a whole, and if the poem is read with a break in the second line, it becomes the maiden who is the implied source of the suffused light. If a break is supplied after line 3, a "symbolic equation" is set up, in which the blossoms are the maiden.

830 [MYS XIX:4167/4143]. The *katakago* is the adder's-tongue lily, or dogtooth violet, *Erythronium japonicum*. "Pink sweet-lily" is my invention.

831–32 [MYS XIX:4170–71/4146–47]. The "irritable reaching after fact & reason" that Keats condemned as the contrary of the "Negative Capability" is certainly far from Yakamochi's passive resonance to the quiet sounds of nature, but could, mutatis mutandis, serve as a label for one of the alleged excesses of the "reasoning technique" in Six Dynasties poetry and its Japanese imitations. For "irritable" in this latter context, one might substitute "compulsive." See Konishi, "Genesis"; and McCullough, *Brocade*, pp. 68–71 passim. The Keats dictum is in Letter 45 in Rollins, I, 193. Yakamochi himself was an early practitioner of "reasoning," as in #829, as well as of other aspects of Six Dynasties style.

837–38 [MYS XIX:4235–36/4211–12]. A third poem-set on the legend of Unai, MYS IX:1805–7/1801–3 by Tanabe no Sakimaro, is not included in the present anthology.

839–41 [MYS XIX:4238–40/4214–16]. Fujiwara no Tsuginawa (727–96) was married to Meishin [K. Myŏnsin], apparently a woman of Paekche extraction. His mother was a daughter of Michi no Mahito Mushimaro. Kuzumaro, the eldest son of Nakamaro, had as wife a Princess Samman; his mother was the daughter of his great-uncle Fujiwara no Fusasaki (681–737). Nakamaro's second son was Mamitsu (Masaki, according to NKBZ, IV, 329, n. 1), whose mother is unknown (*Sompi Bummyaku*, II, 415, 417). The Southern House of the Fujiwara is one of four principal lineages descended from Kamatari's son Fuhito (659–720).

843–45 [MYS XIX:4314–16/4290–92]. The *ts'ang-keng* mentioned in Yakamochi's prose note is the Chinese oriole and corresponds to the Japanese *uguisu* ("warbler") in #843. The passage is derived from *Shih Ching* 168, lines 41–44: "The spring days are lengthening, / Grass and trees grow thick; / Cry, cry the orioles, / Troop, troop to pluck the flossweed." The sources of Chinese poetic theory are set forth concisely in McCullough, *Brocade*, pp. 303–11. Of particular relevance to Yakamochi's remark on poetry dispelling his cares is the "[idea], repeatedly expressed in Chinese writings of all kinds and all periods, . . . that poetry is peculiarly suited to the expression of such emotions as indignation, bitterness, grief, and melancholy, and that in such expression the author is able to relieve his feelings" (p. 310).

846–48 [MYS XX:4384–86/4360–62]. The digging of a drainage canal at Naniwa in the 11th year of Nintoku's reign is described in *Nihonshoki* (Sakamoto et al., I, 392–95 [Aston, I, 280–82]).

849–50 [MYS XX:4492–93/4468–69]. According to a note that Yakamochi appended to MYS XX:4489–91/4465–67, his cousin Koshibi (also Kojihi; 695–777) was dismissed from his post as Governor of Izumo because of a slander by Ōmi no Mifune. *Shoku Nihongi* gives a different account, stating that both Koshibi and Mifune were imprisoned on the 10th of the 5th month (eight days after former Emperor Shōmu's death) on a charge of reviling the government but were released three days later. The accusation was due to a slander by Fujiwara no Nakamaro

(*Shoku Nihongi*, pp. 225, 436). Kojima et al. suggest that Yakamochi's version may be closer to the truth, and that the *Shoku Nihongi* editors shifted the blame away from Mifune, who became a hero for his action in burning Seta Bridge, thus preventing the escape of Nakamaro in his abortive coup of 764 (*Shoku Nihongi*, p. 510). In 756 Mifune may have betrayed Koshibi, who belonged to the Naramaro faction, to Nakamaro (NKBZ, IV, 433). Yakamochi's reaction to the involvement of Koshibi was a chōka-hanka set (MYS XX : 4489–91/4465–67) admonishing his clan to be true to its tradition of loyalty to the throne. For an account of Nakamaro's end, see *Shoku Nihongi*, pp. 305–6.

854–59 [MYS II : 141–46]. For the *Nihonshoki* account of the Arima affair, see Sakamoto et al., II, 330–331, 334–37 (Aston, II, 251, 255–57). According to this account, Prince Arima feigned madness, no doubt to divert suspicion. Unlike Hamlet, however, he did not escape from captivity and return to court. It was he who induced the Empress and Prince Naka no Ōe to visit the Muro hot springs, presumably intending to strike during their absence. Tying branches together meant that one's soul was firmly fastened to them, and therefore safe (Kubota, *Man'yōshū*, I, 222).

860–61 [MYS I : 20–21]. The cyclical signs quoted for the year of this event are one year behind the date derived from *Nihonshoki* chronology; they should read "Earth-Senior/Dragon," corresponding to 668 (Sakamoto et al., II, 368–69 [Aston, II, 288]). However, the 7th year from Empress Saimei's death in 661 would in fact be 667, for which the stated cyclical date is correct. It is customary to consider 662 the 1st year of Tenji's reign, but the *Man'yōshū* compiler clearly counts from 661. The formal enthronement took place in 668, according to the main *Nihonshoki* account, or in 667 in a source it cites as a variant (Sakamoto et al., II, 367 [Aston, II, 287]).

869 [MYS II : 104]. The *okami* is thought to have been a snake or dragon deity that controlled rainfall. *Kojiki* identifies it with the deity Kura-okami, born from the blood that dripped between Izanagi's fingers after he cut off the head of the fire god (Kurano, pp. 62–63 [Philippi, *Kojiki*, p. 59]; see also Philippi, *Kojiki*, pp. 507, 508). The *Nihonshoki* version of this myth uses Morohashi 48844, a dragon character with the rain radical, in the name of this deity (Sakamoto et al., I, 93). The concept of rain-controlling dragons would seem Chinese in origin, but *Kojiki* hints at a perhaps independent association of Okami with water in naming his daughter Hikawahime, "Princess Sun-River," and his granddaughter Fukabuchi no Mizuya-rehana no Kami, "Deity Deep-Pool-Water-Pour[?]-Flower" (Kurano, pp. 88–91 [Philippi, *Kojiki*, p. 92]). Philippi, pp. 573–74, tentatively translates the granddaughter's name as "Deity Sprinkle-Water-on-the-Flowers of Pukabuti."

870–71 [MYS I : 23–24]. Modern chronologies make the 4th year of Temmu's reign correspond to 676, but *Nihonshoki* and *Man'yōshū*, not counting Tenji's son Kōbun (Prince Ōtomo) as having reigned at all, start Temmu's reign in the year of Jinshin (Water-Senior/Monkey, 672) instead of 673 (Water-Junior/Cock). The extant text of *Nihonshoki* differs from that quoted in *Man'yōshū* in starting the 4th month of 675 on Wood-Senior/Dog instead of Earth-Senior/Dog. The date of Prince Omi's exile according to *Nihonshoki* is thus Metal-Junior/Hare rather than Wood-Junior/Hare (Sakamoto et al., II, 419 [Aston, II, 329]). In either case it works out to the 18th of the 4th month, or May 17, 675, by the Julian calendar. (May 20, given in NKBZ, I, 77, n. 4, is in error if Paul Tsuchihashi's *Tables* are correct.)

886–88 [MYS III:388–90/385–87]. The *Kaifūsō* poems referring to the mulberry-branch legend are KFS 31, 45, 72, 98–100, and 102. They merely glance at the story, with references to Umashine, the branch, the nymph, and Yoshino. The chōka in *Shoku Nihon Kōki*, pp. 223–24, contains the following passage (lines 176–87):

Miyoshino ni	And Kumashine,
Arishi Kumashine	Who lived in fair Yoshino—
Amatsume no	A maid from heaven
Kitarikayoite	Came to him, frequented him;
Sono nochi wa	But afterward,
Seme kagafurite	Having borne his reproach,
Hiregoromo	Put on her garment
Kite tobiniki to iu	Of the trailing scarves, and flew away,
Kore mo mata	They say: She too
Kore no shimane no	Was a person of this island,
Hito ni koso	So it is said,
Ariki to iu nare	So have we heard for sure.

The poem was presented to Emperor Nimmyō (810–50; r. 833–50) in 849 by the Kōfukuji monks in honor of his 40th year. Among the several other gifts from the temple on this occasion were images of Urashima and "the maid of Yoshino," both of whom are referred to in the poem as visitors or denizens of Tokoyoshima, the "Isle of Everworld." (In this version Urashima attains eternal life; for other versions, see #216–20 and #579–80.) The gifts and references were clearly significant for their auspicious associations with longevity; nevertheless, Emperor Nimmyō died the following year. At 310 lines, the Kōfukuji chōka is over twice the length of #341, the longest poem in *Man'yōshū*. Exegetical difficulties hamper accurate description of this poem, but it is clearly unusual (from the standpoint of earlier chōka) in its copious Buddhist content. Prosodically, like other post-Man'yō chōka, it is prolix and lax. Nevertheless, it is of great interest as a late survival of the form in Nara and as a specimen of the uses to which extended versification was put in the poetically obscure 9th century. The translated section is based on readings supplied in Kojima, *Jōdai*, II, 1088. In his discussion of the mulberry-branch legend (pp. 1084–93), Kojima rejects a Chinese origin for the story, while allowing for accretions and embellishments that may have resulted in various versions. However, the story type to which the legend belongs, as far as can be judged from its extant fragments, is of wide distribution—that of metamorphosis and trans-human marriage.

889-91 [MYS III:407-9/404-6]. The four deities of Kasuga Shrine are the thunder god Takemikazuchi no Mikoto ("Brave Lord of the Awesome Hammer"), Iwainushi no Mikoto ("Lord Master of Abstinence"), Ame no Koyane no Mikoto ("Lord of the Heavenly Small Roof"), and Himegami ("Princess [or 'Sun Female'] Deity").

895 [MYS IV:635/632]. The "cassia" tree, or Chinese cinnamon, *kuei* (Sino-Japanese *kei*; Morohashi 14755), is here represented by the character *feng* (S.J. *fū*; Morohashi 15126), commonly meaning "maple," but also used for the male *katsura*. *Katsura*, the reading given *feng* in this poem, is a native Japanese tree, but the name was also from early times used to refer to the Chinese *kuei*. NBKZ, I, 348, cites *An-t'ien Lun* by Yü Hsi (4th c.) as a source for the myth of the *kuei* on the moon.

918-23 [MYS XV:3690-95/3668-73]. On "this blossom," see *Yung Yüeh* ("On the Moon") by Shen Yüeh (441-513), *Yü-t'ai Hsin-yung*, V, whose first line may be rendered: "The moon-blossom overlooks the still night" (Uchida, I, 312). A complete translation is in Birrell, p. 140.

The *Kokinshū* poem analogous to #920 is KKS XI:489: Suruga naru / Tago no uranami / Tatanu hi wa / Aredo mo kimi o / Koinu hi wa nashi ("Though there are days / Waves do not rise on Tago Bay / Along Suruga shore, / There's not a day I do not yearn / With all my heart for you").

Sano no Otogami and Nakatomi no Yakamori. NKBZ IV, 495, raises the possibility that Yakamori's exile was not due to his marriage. The *Man'yōshū Mokuroku* (Table of Contents) for Book XV uses the character read *metoru* (Morohashi 6365) rather than that read *okasu* (Morohashi 6045) to describe it, indicating that the nuptials were regarded as normal and not a violation. (The date of the *Mokuroku* is unknown; see NKBZ, IV, 13.) Otogami's name is sometimes given as Chigami, based on the text in *Ruijū Koshū*, a late Heian rearrangement of *Man'yōshū*, which has Morohashi 30836 instead of Morohashi 9737.

953 [MYS XV:3763/3741]. "Long as the silk of the silkworm" attempts to render the pillow-word construction *arikinu no arite* with its juncture through phonetic repetition. *Arite nochi* is "after we have lived"—"after persevering." *Arikinu*, whose apparent meaning is "ant garments," presumably means "moth garments" because of the interchangeability of the characters for "ant" (*ari*; Morohashi 33672) and "moth" (Morohashi 33082). The "moth" would be that of the silkworm, and thus the denotation of *arikinu*, apparently attested only in its epithetical form *arikinu no*, is "silk garments" (see *Jidaibetsu*, pp. 57, 58). The translation attempts to explore an associational level through the image of long skeins of silk, as well as relying on linkage through phonetic duplication.

960 [MYS XV:3770/3748]. For translations and discussions of *Chao Hun*, see Hawkes, pp. 101-9; and Owen, pp. 259-66.

966 [MYS XV: 3776/3754]. The 4th line is left undeciphered in NKBZ. The reading adopted is that in NKBT.

973 [MYS XV: 3783/3761]. NKBZ IV, 93, suggests that *tsune no kotowari*, which is written in phonogram orthography, may be a rendering of some such expression as *jōten* (Morohashi 8955.265), a Chinese lexical item appearing in *Nihonshoki*, translated "general principle" by Aston (Sakamoto et al., I, 383 [Aston, I, 273]). For illustrations of the *E-ingakyō* (*Illustrated Sutra of Cause and Effect*), see Noma, color plate 13, black and white 50; and Tanaka, color plate 5.

984 [MYS XV: 3794/3772]. On the release from exile of several people in 740, see *Shoku Nihongi*, p. 158.

1000–1002 [MYS II: 126–28]. On the identities of the several Ishikawa ladies referred to in *Man'yōshū*, see NKBZ, I, 429. Kojima et al. trace an evolution in the meaning of the word *feng-liu* (J. *fūryū*), used as a semantogram orthography for *miyabi*, from denoting a person's moral character in the Chin dynasty to denoting a person's decadent and sensual charm in the T'ang period. They suggest that the lady has the second meaning in mind, the gentleman the first (NKBZ, I, 131). The expression *tung-lin* ("neighbor to the east") occurs in *Mei-jen Fu*, attributed to Ssu-ma Hsiang-ju (179 B.C.–117 B.C.). In this fu the neighbor is also a young woman with amorous designs on the poet, who like Tanushi prides himself on not obliging her (see Lin, p. 249; for a French translation, see Margouliès, pp. 324–26). *Yu-hsien-k'u* and the *Teng-t'u-tzu Hao-ssu Fu* of Sung Yü (3d century B.C.) are also thought to lie behind the prose passage (NKBZ, I, 131–32).

1003–10 [MYS IV: 525–32/522–29]. Kojima et al. feel that the exchange took place about 717, but that it was placed, for some reason about which they do not speculate, in a sequence in Book IV that would suggest it belongs to 721, by which time Maro was the chief municipal officer of the capital (*kyōshiki no daibu*; NKBZ, I, 313). The issues surrounding the period to which the affair of Maro and Lady Ōtomo should be assigned are summarized in Aoki. The only firm dates are 715, when Prince Hozumi died, and 721, when Maro became Kyōshiki no Daibu. Since Lady Ōtomo subsequently married her half brother Sukunamaro and gave birth to a daughter ("the Elder Maiden of Sakanoue") who was being wooed by Yaka-mochi in the late 730's, scholars tend to believe that the affair with Maro did not continue very long.

Tabito's Plum-Blossom Party. Tsurayuki's poem "On Snow Having Fallen" (KKS I: 9), the example cited in the commentary, blends elegant confusion (an imported mode) with the native preparation-conclusion technique in a seamless miniature masterpiece. The preparation (i.e., the jo) is harmoniously consonant with the main statement, to which it is joined by the pivot word *haru* ("swell"/"spring"): Kasumi tachi / Ko no me mo haru no / Yuki fureba / Hana naki sato mo / Hana zo chirikeru ("The soft mist rises, / Buds swell on the trees in spring / Snow still will fall, / And even in blossomless villages / Blossoms scatter from the sky"). It is an oversimplification to assert that earlier poetry avoids jo except for analogical purposes. Sheer delight in language brings the jo into play in such examples as #1257, #1287, and #1295. The jo is an amplifier much like a pillow word in such cases.

Chinese example and Japanese adaptation in the period of *Man'yōshū* are discussed in detail in the first two chapters of McCullough, *Brocade*. According to NKBZ, II, 67–68, the following phrases in the preface are adapted from *Lan-t'ing-chi Hsü*: "The weather is fine, the wind is soft"; "words are forgotten in the chamber"; and "in pleasure contentment." The gathering at the Orchid Pavilion at Hui-chi in Chekiang Province that Wang Hsi-chih's preface commemorates took place in the 3d month of 353. It was attended by 41 luminaries who composed poems at a winding-water banquet. "Silken veils" and "heaven as a parasol and earth as a mat" are based on metaphors common to a number of Chinese texts. For a complete inventory of references, see Omodaka, V, 99–108. Omodaka gives the complete text of *Lan-t'ing-chi Hsü*, pp. 106–7, and an analysis by Kojima Noriyuki of the structure of poetic prefaces, pp. 107–8. NKBZ, II, 68, takes "sets on the fallen plum blossoms" to be a general rather than a specific reference.

1011 [MYS V:819/815]. The author is thought to have been Ki no Ohito (682–738). He became Assistant Governor-General (*daini*) in 728; this position carried the rank of Junior Fourth Lower. Ohito went on to higher offices and ranks, but was once again serving as Daini at his death, probably in a temporary appointment to fill in for Ono no Oyu, who died in the epidemic of 737. Three of his Chinese verses are preserved in *Kaifūsō*.

1012 [MYS V:820/816]. The author is Ono no Oyu (d. 737). Oyu became Junior Assistant Governor-General (*shōni*) in about 729 and was promoted to Daini probably about 735. His death two years later came in the midst of the great smallpox epidemic of 737. There were two Shōni at a time, and the position entitled its incumbents to Senior Fifth Rank Upper. Oyu, however, held only Junior Fifth Upper at this time. The appellation "Officer" (*daibu*) went with the Fourth and Fifth ranks.

1013 [MYS V:821/817]. Opinion divides on the identity of this author—either Awata no Hitokami or Awata no Hito. Hito is considered more likely because Hitokami held Senior Fifth Rank Upper in 730, whereas Hito apparently never advanced beyond Junior Fifth Upper. Although Hitokami was of the proper rank for a Shōni, it would seem anomalous to list him after Ono no Oyu, who held only Junior Fifth Upper.

1015 [MYS V:823/819]. It is not clear which member of the Ōtomo clan was the author of this poem. One candidate is Tabito's cousin Miyori (d. 774), but Miyori's rank in 730 was too low to be Governor of Bungo, a position entailing Junior Fifth Lower. Bungo corresponds to modern Ōita Prefecture, including Beppu and the Kunisaki Peninsula.

1016 [MYS V:824/820]. The author is Fujii no Ōnari, thought to be of immigrant lineage. Chikugo Province was south of Chikuzen, i.e., the southern half of present Fukuoka Prefecture. Its Governor was entitled to Junior Fifth Rank Lower.

1017 [MYS V: 825/821]. For this author, see commentary to #608 (Manzei's lay name was Kasa no Maro). The Novice (*sami*) Kasa was at this time Intendant for the Construction of Kanzeonji near Dazaifu and as such held Junior Fourth Rank Upper. NKBZ speculates that he is listed after men he outranked because of his clerical status.

1018 [MYS V: 826/822]. Tabito's kanshi "Attending a Banquet at the Beginning of Spring," KFS 44, can be rendered:

> Lenient rule—compassion come from afar,
> Following the old—a path still new.
> Pomp and circumstance—guests at the four gates,
> Far and wide the array—men of the three virtues.
> Plum-snow swirls on the shelving bank,
> Smoky haze envelops early spring.
> Together we wander by the sagely monarch's lake,
> As one we celebrate his gong-striking benevolence.

1020 [MYS V: 828/824]. From MYS V: 827/823 on, the clan names of these low-ranking poets are abbreviated to one character. Thus, Ōtomo is "Mr. Ban," from the Sino-Japanese reading of the second character, and the present instance is "Mr. A," from the first character of (presumably) Ahe. NKBZ suggests that this person was Ahe no Okishima. The two Junior Secretaries (*shōgen*) in the Dazaifu administration ranked Junior Sixth Upper.

1021 [MYS V: 829/825]. Hanishi no Momomura, the conjectural "Mr. To," had served along with Yamanoue no Okura as a lecturer to the Crown Prince (future Emperor Shōmu) in 721.

1022 [MYS V: 830/826]. The Senior Clerk (there were two) ranked Senior Seventh Upper. "Mr. Shi" is thought to refer to a member of the Fubito clan, but Fubito no Ōhara is obscure.

1023 [MYS V: 831/827]. For another poem by Yamaguchi no Wakamaro, see #1072. Junior Clerk (*shōten*) carried Senior Eighth Rank Upper.

1024 [MYS V: 832/828]. The author, "Mr. Tan," may have been either a Tajihi or a Taniwa clan member. Nothing is known of him other than that he attended Tabito's garden party and composed this poem. Senior Judge (*daihanji*) ranked above Senior and Junior Clerk, carrying Junior Sixth Lower.

1025 [MYS V: 833/829]. That the author of this poem was of continental origin is obvious from his un-Japanized name. It will be recalled that Okura was also the offspring of a Korean medical specialist. A Master of Medicine (*kusurishi*) held Senior Eighth Rank Upper.

1026 [MYS V:834/830]. Saeki no Koobito, tentatively identified in NKBZ, II, 498, as the author of this poem, was entitled to Junior Sixth Rank Upper as Assistant Governor (*suke*) of Chikuzen, which makes anomalous the notation "Senior Third Rank Upper, Fifth Order of Merit" in a provincial document.

1027 [MYS V:835/831]. The offshore islands of Iki were an Inferior Province (*gekoku*), and thus the Governor (*kami*) rated only Junior Sixth Rank Lower. (Chikuzen was a Superior Province [*jōkoku*].)

1028 [MYS V:836/832]. Nothing is known of the sacerdotal functionary who composed this poem. Even his name is obscure. "Mr. Kō" (Kōji) may have been an Arai, an Araki, or an Aratai. The Head Shintō Priest (*kamutsukasa*) ranked Senior Seventh Lower.

1029 [MYS V:837/833]. The Senior Legal Secretary (*dairyōshi*) ranked Greater Initial Rank Upper. The Initial ranks, Greater and Lesser, were below Junior Eighth Lower. It is known from Shōsōin documents that Sukunamaro later served in Izumo Province.

1030 [MYS V:838/834]. The Junior Legal Secretary (*shōryōshi*) ranked Greater Initial Lower. "Mr. Den" may have been a Taguchi, a Tanaka, a Tanabe, or some other kind of Ta ("Field"). He is unknown except for this poem.

1031 [MYS V:839/835]. It is speculated that this Master of Medicine (see note to #1025) may have been from the Korean kingdom of Koguryŏ, from his name "Mr. Kō," or else a Takada, Takahashi, etc.

1032 [MYS V:840/836]. The Master of Divination, or Yin-Yang Master (*on'yōshi*), held Senior Eighth Rank Upper. Norimaro is otherwise unknown. He is referred to as "Mr. Ki," and "Ki" (Morohashi 24465) may be an abbreviation for Isobe.

1033 [MYS V:841/837]. The Master of Computation (*sanshi*), a kind of accountant, held Senior Eighth Rank Upper. Shiki no Ōmichi was a specialist in calendrical science.

1034 [MYS V:842/838]. The Clerk (*sakan*) of Ōsumi Province, an Intermediate Province (*chūgoku*), was entitled to Greater Initial Rank Lower. Hachimaro ("Mr. Ka") may have been an Enoi. He is otherwise unknown.

1035 [MYS V:843/839]. Since Chikuzen was a Superior Province, its clerk ranked Junior Eighth Lower. A Tanabe no Makami is mentioned in Shōsōin documents.

1036 [MYS V:844/840]. Iki being an Inferior Province, its Clerk rated Lesser Initial Rank Upper. "Mr. Son" (probably Murakuni or Murakami) no Ochikata is otherwise unknown.

1037 [MYS V:845/841]. Like Iki, the islands of Tsushima constituted an Inferior Province. Takamuko no Oyu is a tentative identification of the "Mr. Kō" of the text. He appears in references in Shōsōin documents and *Shoku Nihongi*.

1038 [MYS V:846/842]. This "Mr. Kō" is unknown. As Clerk of an Intermediate Province he rated Greater Initial Rank Lower.

1039 [MYS V:847/843]. Hanishi no Mimichi was the author of four poems preserved in *Man'yōshū*. His official position is not given.

1040 [MYS V:848/844]. Ono no Kunikata probably had yet to achieve court rank. Later he was active in the scriptorium of Tōdaiji, and several examples of his calligraphy have survived.

1041 [MYS V:849/845]. Kadobe no Isotari was on the gubernatorial staff of Yamanoue no Okura. As Secretary (*jō*) of Chikuzen he had Junior Seventh Rank Upper.

1042 [MYS V:850/846]. Ono no Tamori (no position given) may be the man of that name (but with Tamori written with Morohashi 21723:7071 rather than 1766:21014) who became Junior Assistant Governor-General of Dazaifu in 749 and twice served as an Ambassador—to Silla in 753 and to Parhae (Pohai) in 758.

1043–44 [MYS V:851–52/847–48]. *Pao-p'u-tzu*, by Ko Hung (A.D. 283–ca. 343), discusses the alleged benefits of ingesting all manner of exotic substances, including "gold and cinnabar" and mica. Immortality and the ability to fly are mentioned as results (see, e.g., chüan 4 and 11; see also Schafer, *Golden Peaches*, p. 178). *I-wen Lei-chü* quotes from *Ling-hsien*, by Chang Heng (A.D. 78–139), the story of Heng O, wife of the famous archer Yi, who stole an elixir of immortality from the Queen Mother of the West, fled to the moon, and became an immortal (Wang, 1, 7).

1046 [MYS V:854/850]. Kojima, *Jōdai*, II, 937, lists analogues in Six Dynasties and later poetry for the notion of a flower "stealing" its color from something else. NKBZ, II, 76, specifically cites *Mei-hua Fu* ("*Fu* on Plum Blossoms") by Emperor Chien Wen of the Liang (r. 549–51). (That fu is not in *Wen-hsüan*, however, as stated in NKBZ.) For a translation, see Frankel, pp. 1–3. The Chinese text is provided in this work, reconstituted from quotations in *I-wen Lei-chü* and *Ch'u-hsüeh Chi*, another T'ang encyclopedia, compiled by Hsü Chien (659–729).

1048 [MYS V:856/852]. The flower-garden scene in *Yu-hsien-k'u* (Levy, pp. 41–45) is most relevant to this poem, but provides no personification in a dream.

An Excursion to Matsura River: Preface. For a translation of *Lo-shen Fu*, see Watson, *Chinese Rhyme-Prose*, pp. 55–60. The reference to "sit[ting] on the banks of the Lo" is to this fu, in which the traveler-narrator meets the goddess of the Lo River and exchanges amorous talk with her. The "gorges of Wu" reference comes from *Kao-t'ang Fu* by Sung Yü, another account of a sexual encounter between man and immortal. These works were familiar from *Wen-hsüan* (see *Monzen*, ed. Obi, II, 440–52, 467–75). The salutation of the traveler and modest reply of the maidens echo a similar passage at the beginning of *Yu-hsien-k'u*, and the phrases translated "Willow leaves opened in their brows; peach blossoms bloomed upon their cheeks" have been traced to a number of models in that work (Yagisawa, pp. 26, 63, 121, 169; Levy, pp. 11, 22, 38, 51). "We are merely those whose nature it is to take pleasure in the water, and whose hearts delight in the mountains" derives from *Lun Yü* VI.21 (Legge, I, 192), though there these characteristics apply to the wise and the virtuous rather than to seductive females. The author of the preface has made interesting use of this passage, integrating its water and mountain motifs into the pleasant Shangri-la, that is, ultimately, the Peach-Blossom Spring, of his (Chinese) imagination.

1049–59 [MYS V:857–67/853–63]. For a sifting of the evidence on authorship of these poems, see Kinoshita. The tripartite division is one proposed by Doi Kōchi, whose arguments Kinoshita summarizes (p. 467) but does not endorse. The evidence concerning #1050 has to do with the *man'yōgana* phonogram used to write the syllable *Fe* in the line *iFe Fa aredö* (*ie wa aredo*). This character is Morohashi 38758. Since it is grouped in the *Kuang Yün* table of rhymes with other characters having the reconstructed T'ang medial and final pronunciation *iⁿɐn*, its use to represent the Old Japanese *kō-rui* syllable *Fe* is anomalous, i.e., in terms of the predictable derivation of *man'yōgana* it should be pronounced *Fa* instead of *Fe*. To drastically foreshorten Kinoshita's detailed phonological reasoning, the speculative conclusion that he reaches is that the *on-yomi Fen*, and thus the *man'yōgana Fe*, are derived from the local dialect of Ch'ang-an in the 8th century. Since Okura, but not Tabito, had visited China and lived in Ch'ang-an, he is likely to have been responsible for at least the orthography of #1050. (Morohashi 38758 is used twice as a phonogram in *Man'yōshū*, and the other instance, MYS V:875/871, is also in a poem plausibly associated with Okura; a third instance, in MYS III:262/260, occurs only in the Kan'ei block-printed edition.) It should be noted, however, that the modern Japanese *on-yomi* of the character at issue is *hen*, as in *henji*, "reply."

A Letter from Yoshida no Yoroshi. Kinoshita dismisses Tsuchiya Bummei's argument that the letter was intended for Okura (NKBZ, II, 467, 473). For T'ai Ch'u, see Mekada, III, 763; and Mather, p. 309; for Yüeh Kuang, see *Chin Shu*, p. 598). Tabito's sorrows no doubt included the loss of his wife, who died in the summer of 728, shortly after his assignment to Dazaifu. For the *Chuang-tzu* passage on the perfected man, see Ichikawa, I, 272–73 (Watson, *Complete Works*, p. 78). The princely man as "submerged dragon" who does not agonize though living in neglect and poverty, is described in *I Ching* (Suzuki, I, 68–69 [Wilhelm/Baynes, p. 379]).

The anecdote about Lu Kung and the pheasant is cited in the Li Shan commentary to "Inscription for the Late Prince An Lu-chao of Ch'i" by Shen Yüeh as given in the Han court compilation *Tung-kuan Han-chi* (*Monzen*, ed. Obi, VII, 509). *I-wen Lei-chü* also gives it as from *Hsü Han Shu* by Ssu-ma Piao (d. 306: Wang, I, 908–9). K'ung Yü and the turtle also appear in *I-wen Lei-chü* (Wang, II, 1668–69). For Chang and Chao, see "Pei-shan-i Wen" by K'ung Te-chang (448–502), in *Monzen*, ed. Obi, VI, 96. Ch'ih Sung Tzu was a legendary immortal who controlled rain and fire, and rode on a swan; Wang Tzu Ch'iao was a son of King Ling (r. 571 B.C.–545 B.C.) of the Chou dynasty who attained immortality and flew off on a crane. They are mentioned in *Wen-hsüan* in poems on wandering immortals by Kuo Ching-ch'un (276–324) and Ho Ching-tsu (d. 301), respectively (*Monzen*, ed. Obi III, 248, 242).

The "Apricot Altar" passage is *Chuang-tzu* XXXI (Ichikawa, II, 771–82 [Watson, *Complete Works*, pp. 344–52]). *Lun Yü* XI.25 makes an attractive companion piece (Waley, *Analects*, pp. 159–61). These two complementary (Taoist and Confucian) versions of wisdom literature bear little resemblance to the goings-on at Tabito's poetry party, to which Yoroshi compares them. The point of the comparison must be that both the party and the gathering at the Apricot Altar were assemblages of gentlemen engaged in refined talk, whereas Matsura River and Spikenard Marshes, the other half of the double equation, brought together men and women in amorous badinage. The Ts'ao Chih fu is translated in Watson, *Rhyme-Prose*, pp. 55–60.

Likening fidelity to the faithfulness of a dog or horse draws on such sources as the "Memorial Seeking to Establish Intimacy" (*Ch'iu T'ung Ch'in Piao*) by Ts'ao Chih (A.D. 192–232), which is also the source of the sunflower metaphor (*Monzen*, ed. Obi, V, 203).

1070 [MYS III:338/335]. Tabito's poem is reminiscent of an anonymous tanka in *Kokinshū*, KKS XVIII:933: Yo no naka wa / Nani ka tsune naru / Asukagawa / Kinō no fuchi zo / Kyō wa se ni naru ("What in this our world / Is a thing that will remain? / Tomorrow River / Yesterday was lined with pools / Where today there are shallows").

1073–76 [MYS VI:970–73/965–68]. On the building of the Mizuki, see Sakamoto et al., II, 362, 363 (Aston, II, 283). NKBZ, II, 519, reports skepticism about this fortification actually having been used to back up water, but Sakamoto et al., II, 581, states that a culvert has been excavated from the remaining dike, indicating that in peacetime the stored water would be drained off. The river that was dammed up was the Mikasa. *Furitaki* in #1073 may be an early example of the *-tashi* desiderative, which otherwise is not attested before late Heian. NKBZ, II, 154, rejects the interpretation "intense" (*itashi*) suggested by the orthography as inappropriate for a transitive verb. "Grieving over how easy it was to part, and sighing over how hard it was to meet" in the footnote derives from *Yu-hsien-k'u* (Yagisawa, p. 166; Levy, p. 50). The epithet *mizukuki no* ("of the juicy stems") usually went with *oka* ("hill") in Man'yō times (later it referred to a writing brush). In #1076 Tabito adds sound-play to the sense.

1106 [MYS IV:609/606]. *Ōnawa ni*, here translated "ceaselessly," is apparently a *hapax legomenon* of obscure meaning.

Ōtomo no Surugamaro and Lady Ōtomo of Sakanoue. A reading of Lady Ōtomo's amorous exchanges as playful banquet poems is offered in Aoki, p. 352. Aoki also implies that Lady Ōtomo was stimulated to "creativity" by the presence of Tabito, Okura, and other male poets during her time at Dazaifu.

1122 [MYS IV:662/659]. The last line of this poem contains an interesting bit of orthographic play, the verb *arame* ("there will be") being represented by the "borrowed" phonetic reading *arame* ("rough seaweed"), which works well with a sec-ondary meaning of *oki* (here rendered "ahead") as "the offing," as well as reinforcing the vegetal implications of *shigeshi* ("rife," here rendered "a swamp") in line 2.

Ahe no Mushimaro and Lady Ōtomo of Sakanoue. Aoki, p. 361, presents Lady Ōtomo's poetic activity as a way of binding the clan together in affection, and as a species of instruction in how to write love poems, but admits that the lady may also have had a love life of her own. The *myōbu* ("palace ladies") were functionaries in the women's quarters of the imperial palace. The *naimyōbu*, or "Inner Palace Lady," had Fifth or higher court rank in her own right, whereas the *gemyōbu* ("Outer Palace Lady") was married to a husband of such rank (NKBZ, I, 358).

1133-34 [MYS IV:708-9/705-6]. Various suggestions for interpreting *hane-kazura* ("feather chaplet") are discussed at length in Omodaka, IV, 498-99. Two other Man'yō poems, VII:1116/1112 and XI:2634/2627, contain the lines *hane-kazura / ima suru imo*, and both emphasize the girl's youth (*urawakami* in both in-stances). Under the circumstances the connection of *hanekazura* with a coming-of-age ceremony seems plausible.

1138 [MYS III:468/465]. NKBZ, I, 279, discusses the orthography of the verb given here as *shinobitsuru* and translated "remember." The *yodan* verb *shinofu* (*si-noFu*) ("to remember," "to yearn for") later acquired a voiced consonant and un-derwent literarily productive mutual contamination with the *kami-nidan* verb *shinobu* (*sinöbu*) ("to keep secret," "to endure"). The two verbs were quite distinct in pre-Heian Japanese, and so the spelling in the present instance with a phonogram for *bi* (Morohashi 6103) constitutes an anomaly. Kojima et al. accept it as the earliest recorded instance of the phonetic shift, an opinion supported by *Jidaibetsu*, p. 363. NKBT, I, 218-19, prefers a textual variant (the *Kyōdaibon*) yielding the unvoiced *hi* (*Fi*). The same verb in the preceding poem (*shinohe*) is written in semantogram orthography with Morohashi 10462.

1156 [MYS IV:767/764]. Thomas Moore, "Believe Me, If All Those Endearing Young Charms," from *Irish Melodies*, in *Poetical Works*, p. 235.

1160 [MYS VIII:1638/1634]. The "clapper" (*hikita*) was apparently a device for frightening birds and animals that involved a board (*ita*) attached to a cord that could be pulled (*hiki*) from a distance.

1161 [MYS VIII:1639/1635]. The terms *tōku* ("head *ku*") and *matsuku* ("end *ku*") here clearly indicate the 5-7-5/7-7 structure of tanka that was the seed of linked verse. But "head" is used elsewhere in *Man'yōshū* variously to refer to the first line (XVIII:4067/4043), the first two lines (XII:2970/2958), and the first six lines (of a chōka: XIII:3313/3299). NKBZ, II, 366, suggests that *hitori* in the last line means that the "planter" will stay single, i.e., be disappointed, and reads *kareru hatsuii* rather than *karu wasaii* for Yakamochi's first line. It is interesting that the metaphors for sexual possession (if that is indeed what these poems are about) are "seeing" and "eating," along with "hearing" fundamental components in old honorifics mean-ing "to rule."

1169–73 [MYS XVII:3944–48/3922–26]. The first four participants listed below have their *kabane* entered after their names, presumably as a courtesy:

Fujiwara no Toyonari (704–65). Eldest son of Muchimaro (680–737) and older brother of Nakamaro (706–64). At this time Toyonari was a Middle Counselor, rather than a Major Counselor as stated in Yakamochi's prefatory account. NKBZ, IV, 172, suggests that Yakamochi, writing the account after the promotion, which occurred two years later, applies the later title. Toyonari became Minister of the Right in 749. He fell afoul of his brother Nakamaro's ambitions, however, and was demoted and exiled in 657 because of his imputed involvement in the attempted coup of Tachibana no Naramaro. He was restored to favor and promoted to Junior First Rank on the fall of Nakamaro in 764, only to die the following year. His chance for poetic immortality was foiled by the impromptu nature of the snow party; *Man'yōshū* records no other poem by him.

Kose no Natemaro (670–753). Also a Middle Counselor in 746, he was then 76. He was promoted to Major Counselor three years later.

Ōtomo no Ushikai (d. 749). A first cousin of Yakamochi's grandfather Yasumaro, Ushikai rose to Middle Counselor but was Imperial Adviser in 746.

Fujiwara no Nakamaro (706–64). The stormy petrel of mid-Nara, Nakamaro was 40 at the time of the snow party and had yet to rise to power. He held concurrently the offices of Minister of Popular Affairs, Imperial Adviser, Master of the Left Capital, and Governor of Ōmi. *Man'yōshū* preserves no poem by him.

Prince Mihara (d. 752). Son of Prince Toneri (676–735), the chief compiler of *Nihonshoki*. His brother Prince Ōi later was enthroned by Nakamaro as Junnin Tennō (733–65; r. 758–64). Prince Mihara was Minister of Civil Affairs in 746 and later became Minister of Central Affairs.

Prince Chinu (693–770). Son of Prince Naga (d. 715), for whose poems see #460–62. Prince Chinu was rewarded for his services in planning the temporary capitals at Kuni and Shigaraki as Head of the Bureau of Carpentry. In 752 he left the imperial family and took a clan name and kabane as Fumiya (or Fun'ya) no Mahito Chinu. He eventually rose to Junior Second Rank and held an office corresponding to Major Counselor. He was the donor of the Buddha's footprint icon at Yakushiji and was formerly thought to have written the 21 *Bussokuseki no uta* inscribed on the companion stone (#1560–78; see Miller, pp. 20, 46).

Prince Funa. Another son of Prince Toneri and elder brother of Emperor Junnin. After Junnin was deposed by former Empress Kōken and Dōkyō in 764, Prince Funa took part in Nakamaro's revolt and was exiled to the Oki Islands.

Prince Ōchi (704–80). Another son of Prince Naga, who like his brother Prince Chinu took the name Fumiya no Mahito in 752. In 746 he was Minister of Justice. He eventually rose to Major Counselor.

Prince Oda. Genealogy unknown. In 746 he was Head of the Bureau of Carpentry.

Prince Hayashi. An obscure Prince who was Head of the Bureau of Books and Drawings at the time of the snow party.

Hozumi no Oyu (d. 749). A minor official who had been exiled to Sado Island in 722 for criticizing Empress Genshō. He was pardoned in 740 and was Senior Assistant Minister of the Treasury in 746. He and Prince Hayashi were the only snow-sweepers not promoted shortly after the party.

Oda no Morohito. Obscure. Possibly Oharida no Morohito, who was promoted from Outer to regular Junior Fifth Rank Lower in the 5th month of 746.

Ono no Tsunate. Chief of the Imperial Storehouse in 746.

Takahashi no Kunitari. Director of the Rice Wine Office and Chief Server of the Imperial Table Office.

Ō no Tokotari. Obscure. Held Outer Junior Fifth Rank Lower in 746.

Takaoka no Kafuchi. Original name Sasanami no Kafuchi. Of Paekche origin, his father emigrated in 663. Kafuchi was appointed Tutor to the Crown Prince in 721. He received the clan name and kabane Takaoka no Muraji in 724. Eventually he became President of the Court University. Two of his poems are preserved in *Man'yōshū*.

Narahara no Azumato. Served as Senior Secretary of Dazaifu starting in 738.

1185–86 [MYS XVII: 3987–88/3965–66]. NKBZ, IV, 189, suggests that by his use of the ardent term *keiren* (Ch. *hsi-lien*; Morohashi 663.29), Yakamochi is deliberately giving a touch of the love letter to his correspondence. The term is used for a wife's yearning in the appended anecdote to #1547. "Unable to face the effort of hobbling along with a cane" has an analogue in *Tu-chia Li-ch'eng* (for which see the note to #634). *I-wen Lei-chü* quotes *Han Shu* to the effect that K'uang Hang (1st c. B.C.), an expert at explaining poetry, "loosened people's jaws" by his explanations, though it is not clear whether with amusement or amazement (Wang, I, 1003). The large discrepancy between the Japanese and Julian calendars in 747 was due to the insertion of an intercalary 9th month in the Japanese calendar the previous year.

1187–88 [MYS XVII: 3989–90/3967–68]. "Spring is a time for enjoyment" (*Ch'un k'e le*) is the title and opening phrase in a fu by Hsia-hou Chan of the Chin dynasty (late 3d–4th c.; Wang, I, 45). The red peach / green willow pairing occurs in *Yu-hsien-k'u* (Yagisawa, p. 169 [Levy, p. 51]). "The merry butterfly" and "the charming oriole" are also images found in *Yu-hsien-k'u* (Yagisawa, pp. 96, 97, 132 [Levy, pp. 31, 41]). The *lan* ("orchid") and *huei* ("melilotus") are mentioned in adjacent lines in *Li Sao* among the flowers and plants cultivated by the poet-statesman Ch'ü Yüan (ca. 343 B.C.–ca. 277 B.C.; Hoshikawa, p. 27 [Hawkes, p. 23]). The orchid image for friendship goes back to *I Ching*: "Speech that comes from minds that are the same is as fragrant as an orchid" (Suzuki, II, 332). The term translated "nature" is *busshoku* (Ch. *wu-ssu*), the "coloration [or 'nature'] of things." There is a source in the poem "Drinking Alone in a Landscape Garden" by Wang Po (ca. 650–76; *Ch'üan T'ang Shih*, II, 681).

1189–92 [MYS XVII: 3991–94/3969–72]. NKBZ, IV, 193, nn. 7–8, traces the phraseology translated "I am overwhelmed by your attentions" to the correspondence manual *Tu-chia Li-ch'eng*. The "products" of Yakamochi's brush are "water-grasses," and for "niceties of style" he uses the metaphor "carving insects." The metaphor does not refer, as might be imagined, to a master carver's fashioning of an insect, but to insects "carving" leaves by eating holes in them (Morohashi 9995.55). Several textual variations and additions to Yakamochi's letter, apparently reflecting different drafts, are given in NKBZ, IV, 193–94.

1193 [MYS XVII:3995/3972a]. *I-wen Lei-chü* devotes over ten pages to quotations of sources on the festivities of the 3d of the 3d month (Wang, I, 62–74). NKBZ, IV, 196, n. 4, mentions an opinion that "eyelids" (Morohashi 23744) is an error for "cheeks" (Morohashi 22254). For "mellowing its light," see Abe and Yamamoto, p. 17. (Lau, p. 60, has "soften the glare.") Morohashi 10243.208 traces the "gathering of stars of virtue" to an incident in Later Han when a fortunate conjunction of stars was interpreted as a sign of a gathering of worthies.

For a Chinese text and English translation of *Wen Fu*, see Fang, who renders the passage adapted by Ikenushi as "We [poets] struggle with Non-being to force it to yield Being; we knock upon Silence for an answering Music" (p. 534). The *Shu-tu Fu* passage is in Obi, I, 257 (Knechtges, I, 371). "Mouth phrases" is a literal rendering of *ganshō* (Ch. *han chang*; Morohashi 3350/25761) that attempts to match the physical quality of "strike silence." Knechtges translates "cherished elegance."

The poem by Ch'en Tzu-ang is "On the Third Day of the Third Month, Banqueting at a Small Pavilion of County Magistrate Wang," in *Ch'üan T'ang Shih*, II, 917. For "Peach Blossom Spring," see Saku, I, 448–49 (Hightower, pp. 254–56).

"Clear wine" in line 5 of Ikenushi's Chinese poem is a rendering of *sansei* (Ch. *san-ch'ing*), "thrice clear," which goes with "nine bends" in the next line. Kojima discusses the origin of the term in NKBZ, IV, 467–68. Ikenushi's proximate source may have been a poem by Chiang Tsung (6th c.) quoted in *I-wen Lei-chü* (Wang, I, 716). For the "nine bends," see Yagisawa, p. 71 (Levy, p. 24).

1194–96 [MYS XVII:3996–98/3973–75]. For the Wang Po references, see "Preface on Seeing Off Po Seven" and "Preface: At a Party with All the Officials of Chin-chou, Parting from Hsüeh-Sheng-Hua on an Autumn Night," in *Ch'u-T'ang Ssu Chieh Wen-chi*, chüan 6.1a, 2b. The reference to waters and mountains is to *Lun Yü* VI.21 (Legge, I, 192). For the *Shih P'in* quotation on Lu Chi and P'an Yüeh, see Ch'en Yen-chieh, *Shih P'in Chü*, in Yang, *Li-tai*, III, 15.

The anecdote concerning Ts'ao Chih is *Shih-shuo Hsin-yü* 66, in Mekada, I, 307. It is translated in Mather, p. 126, as follows:

Emperor Wen of Wei (Ts'ao P'ei, r. 220–226) once ordered [his younger brother] the Prince of Tung-o (Ts'ao Chih) to compose a poem in the time it would take to walk seven paces. If it was not completed, the maximum penalty was to be inflicted. On the spur of the moment Chih then composed the following poem:

Boiled beans are taken to make soup,
Strained lentils utilized for stock.
While stalks beneath the pot are blazing up,

The beans within the pot are shedding tears.
Originally from the same root grown,
For one to cook the other, why such haste?

The Emperor looked profoundly ashamed.

The passage on carving dragons by Liu Hsiang can be found in his *Ch'i-lüeh Pieh-lu*. Ikenushi was no doubt familiar with the version quoted in the Li Shan commentary to Chiang Wen-tung's (444–505) *Pieh Fu*, at the end of chüan 16 of *Wen-hsüan*. The expression "dragon-carver" originally referred to the skill of the builder Tsou Yen. NKBZ, IV, 199, tentatively identifies the *kaho* bird in line 27 of Ikenushi's chōka with the cuckoo (*kakkō*, a larger species than the hototogisu, regularly translated "cuckoo" herein).

1197 [MYS XVII:3999/3975a]. Concerning the convalescent Yakamochi's admission to "a nature difficult to carve," it is interesting to note that *Lun Yü* v.9 has Confucius say of a disciple asleep during the day, "Rotten wood cannot be carved" (Legge, I, 176). Serious tonal errors in Yakamochi's kanshi occur in line 1, position 6 (deflected instead of level); line 4, positions 4 (level instead of deflected) and 6 (deflected instead of level); and line 6, positions 4 (deflected instead of level) and 6 (level instead of deflected). In Ikenushi's poem one occurs at line 8, position 2 (deflected instead of level). The whole question of the "seriousness" of such errors in terms of the models available to Yakamochi and Ikenushi deserves further investigation.

Yakamochi has echoed Ikenushi's *ming-ting* ("soused") with his own *ling-ting* ("tottery") in the last line. For the *Shih Ching* reference, see Karlgren, pp. 218–19: "there are no words that are not answered." The bracketed passage appears to be a variant draft of the immediately preceding lines, beginning, "By searching for characters." It occurs in the Nishi Honganji texts used as basic by both NKBZ and NKBT, but not in the Genryaku Collated Text (*Genryaku Kōhon*) of 1184.

The Old Poem with the swallows bringing mud to build their nest is no. 12 of the series (Uchida, II, 565 [Waley, *Translations*, p. 44]). For the *Huai-nan-tzu* passage, see Yang, *Ssu-hsiang Ming-chu*, pp. 295, 338.

1200 [MYS XVII:4015/3991]. *Uchikuchiburi* in line 6 is obscure. I have followed suggestions in NKBZ and NKBT to take it as meaning *ochikochiburi*, "far and near."

1210 [MYS XVII:4030/4006]. NKBZ, IV, 217, and NKBT, IV, 233, both suggest that Yakamochi and Ikenushi are root and branch.

1212–14 [MYS XVII:4032–34/4008–10]. The hero of *Yu-hsien-k'u* expresses his desire for the heroine with the entrails hyperbole, translated by Levy "My heart [is] about to break," perhaps to avoid repeating the image, appearing a few lines before as "my entrails feel hot as fire" (Yagisawa, p. 33 [Levy, pp. 14, 15]). The *ayui* in line 14 of the chōka are bands to tie up the *hakama*, or bifurcated skirt, for travel. The sense in which *wakakusa no* modifies them is obscure. NKBT, IV, 234, suggests that the *ayui* are fashioned from strands of grass, NKBZ, IV, 219, that *waka-kusa no* is a pillow-word construction alluding to the fact that Yakamochi is going to visit his wife, *wakakusa no tsuma* ("wife [tender as] the young grass") being a traditional formula. Lines 25–27 are a jo introducing the word *ne* ("cry"), but they are also part of the "narrative" of the poem, in addition to echoing Yakamochi's reference to the hototogisu and his more developed panorama of the harbor.

1215–17 [MYS XVIII: 4097–99/4073–75]. The expression translated "I face the paper and am overcome by grief" is apparently modeled on similar expressions in the calligraphic manuals of Wang Hsi-chih (ca. A.D. 307–ca. 365) and his son Wang Hsien-chih (NKBT, IV, 270, n. 5).

1220 [MYS XVIII: 4102/4078]. The "poem left by a man of old" to which Yakamochi refers appears to have escaped his attention as compiler.

Songs of the Sakimori. Little is known of Sakamoto no Hitokami, the recruitment officer of the Tōtōmi sakimori, other than that he served at one point as a minor functionary in the office for the construction of Tōdaiji. The officer for Sagami, on the other hand, was a Fujiwara of some consequence. The second son of Umakai, Sukunamaro (later known as Yoshitsugu; 716–77), Governor of Sagami in 755, eventually rose to be Palace Minister (*naidaijin*), with Junior Second Rank (Junior First was awarded posthumously). Sukunamaro was much involved in the political troubles of the Nara period, as a supporter of his rebel brother Hirotsugu in 740, and later as the enemy of his cousin Nakamaro. He was exiled for two years for his role in the Hirotsugu rebellion and later was stripped of his rank for a plot against Nakamaro in 762 (in which Ōtomo no Yakamochi also took part). However, he emerged as one of the heroes of 764, when Nakamaro became an enemy of the state, leading several hundred troops against Nakamaro when he fled to Ōmi. (*Shoku Nihongi*, II, 436.) The recruitment officer of the Suruga sakimori, Fuse no Hitonushi, visited China as a low-ranking member of the official embassy of 750, returning to Japan in 751. He became Governor of Suruga shortly after his return and spent the rest of his career in provincial offices. Of the sakimori themselves, practically nothing is known other than that they composed the poems attributed to them in *Man'yōshū*, which has rescued their names from oblivion.

1245 [MYS I: 50]. The K'ung An-kuo commentary to *Shu Ching* states that Heaven gave the ancient ruler Yü a writing from the Lo River in the form of markings on the back of a divine tortoise (*Shang Shu*, chüan 7.2a).

MYS Book VII. NKBZ, II, 30, suggests that the scheme of this book is modeled on the original "Hitomaro Collection." On *yung wu* (J. *eibutsu*) poems as a Chinese category, see McCullough, *Brocade*, chap. 1 passim. *Kibutsu* and *hiyu* are not commonly recognized as categories in Chinese poetics.

1265 [MYS VII: 1106/1102]. The river-sash conceit appears a number of times in *Man'yōshū*, as well as in an anonymous *Kokinshū* poem, KKS XX: 1082: Magane fuku / Kibi no Nakayama / Obi ni seru / Hosotanigawa no / Oto no sayakesa

("How pure the sound / The narrow valley rivulet / Makes that winds about, / A sash on the Middlemount / In iron-smelting Kibi!").

1310 [MYS VII: 1399/1395]. For the *Yu-hsien-k'u* passage, see Yagisawa, p. 41 (Levy, p. 15). NKBZ, II, 278, prefers the reading *tsutsumi* ("taboo"), rather than *yamai* ("illness").

1328 [MYS X: 1893/1889]. NKBT, III, 68, takes the speaker of the poem to be the girl's mother; NKBZ, III, 62, the girl herself. The translation follows NKBZ, as also in the interpretation of *utate* ("so strange").

"On Yellow Leaves." NKBZ, III, 127, n. 1, suggests Chinese influence for the Man'yō orthographic preference, "yellow" being the common color designation for fall leaves through High T'ang. And *Jidaibetsu*, p. 748, suggests that yellow was the dominant fall color in the Yamato region.

1362 [MYS X: 2200/2196]. The post-Man'yō collections of poems attributed to Hitomaro are items 2–4 in *Shikashū Taisei*, I.

1363 [MYS X: 2206/2202]. On the Chinese moon-man, who is always hewing away at the cassia, only for it to reconstitute itself (the waxing and waning of the moon), see Morohashi 14330.94.

1365 [MYS X: 2255/2251]. The suggestion about watchmen for orange trees is Kojima et al.'s (NKBZ, III, 143).

1395 [MYS XI: 2763/2753]. The poem appears again as SIS XIV: 856, with *namima yori* in place of *nami no ma yu*.

1402 [MYS XI: 2813/2802a]. The poem of which this is a variant is MYS XI: 2812/2802: Omoedo mo / Omoi mo kanetsu / Ashihiki no / Yamadori no o no / Nagaki kono yo o ("For all my longing, / All my longing is in vain: / A pheasant's tail / From the leg-cramping mountains / Is no longer than this night"). The more famous variant version is Hitomaro I: 207 and II: 333 in *Shikashū Taisei*, I.

1420 [MYS XI: 2831/2820]. The suggestion that *kimi* was changed to *imo* in the process of oral transmission is made in NKBZ, III, 275.

1423 [MYS XI: 2834/2823]. The poem has an irregular *kakari-musubi* construction in which *koso* takes a *rentai* (*naki*) instead of an *izen* (*nakere*) form of the adjective.

1428 [MYS XI: 2841/2830]. Tsurayuki's KKS XII: 605: Te mo furede / Tsukihi henikeru / Shiramayumi / Okifushi yoru wa / I koso nerarene ("Hands have not touched, / Months and days gone by, white / Spindletree bow: / Drawn taut, I quiver in the night, / Rising, sinking, far from sleep"). More closely analogous to #1428 is the old and anonymous KKS XX: 1078: Michinoku no / Adachi no mayumi / Wa ga hikaba / Sue sae yoriko / Shinobi shinobi ni ("From famed Adachi / In far Michinoku come / Bows of spindlewood: / When I draw you, bend to me, / Softly, softly, always bend!").

1430 [MYS XI:2843/2832]. NKBT regularizes the scansion of line 2 by supplying the particle *shi*; NKBZ has *ue o fusete*.

1448 [MYS XIII:3236/3222]. The suggestion that this poem is a lullaby is Kojima et al.'s (NKBZ, III, 373).

1453 [MYS XIII:3259/3245]. On Tsukuyomi, see Kurano, pp. 70–73 (Philippi, *Kojiki*, pp. 70, 71, 618); and Sakamoto et al., I, 87, 554 (Aston, I, 18, 19). The name may have originally meant "moon-count" (*tukuyŏmi*), from which *tukuyomi* ("moon-night-see"), *tukuyo* ("moon-night" = "moon"), and *tukuyumi* ("moon-bow") derived.

"*Love Poems.*" This is a functional translation for the term sōmon, which literally means something like "mutual inquiry."

1488 [MYS XIV:3366/3352]. The designation zōka ("Miscellaneous Poem") is lacking, but the first five poems (of which one is included in the present anthology) of Book XIV are considered to be of that type by Kojima et al. (NKBZ, III, 445, n. 1). The rubric for *azumauta* ("Songs of the Eastland") is placed in such a way that it misleadingly seems to apply only to the first five verses instead of to the whole book.

1495 [MYS XIV:3388/3371]. For the *Kojiki* passage, see Kurano, pp. 214–15 (Philippi, *Kojiki*, p. 242).

1501 [MYS XIV:3417/3399]. On the opening of the Kiso Road through Shinano, see *Shoku Nihongi*, II, 54.

1512 [MYS XIV:3478/3459]. NKBZ, III, 477, suggests the poem is a work song. Whether tanka were used as work songs is problematical.

1528–30 [MYS XVI:3813–15/3791–93]. The *Genji* passage referring to *Taketori Monogatari* is in "Eawase," the "Picture Competition" chapter, in which the work turns up in illustrated form (Tamagami, IV, 39 [Seidensticker, I, 311]). For "Their hundred charms were beyond compare, their flowerlike faces without peer," see Yagisawa, p. 27 (Levy, p. 12). Also note the similarity to the description of the nymphs in the Matsura River sequence (#1049–59). The phrase translated "started to . . . nudge each other," more literally, "pushed and gave way to each other," is perhaps based on another passage from *Yu-hsien-k'u* (Yagisawa, p. 68; Levy, p. 23). Levy translates, "Everyone yielded to the others, and no one was willing to sit down first." The phraseology behind the first sentence in the Old Bamboo-Cutter's speech is modeled on Yagisawa, pp. 33, 46 (Levy, pp. 14, 17). These last are translated by Levy, "Suddenly encountering an immortal, I was unable to suppress my enchantment. . . . [S]eeing you intensifies my spiritual delusion." Kojima et al. point out other uses of *Yu-hsien-k'u* vocabulary as well (NKBZ, IV; 109, 110). The passages in the chōka relating how women wooed the Bamboo-Cutter with gifts could also have been suggested by *Yu-hsien-k'u* (Yagisawa, p. 32 [Levy, p. 13]).

NKBZ renders line 2 of the chōka as *wakugogami*, "youngster's hair," but as a babe in arms the hero probably as yet had little. Lines 6 and 10 are read in this way, too. The translation follows NKBT, as it does for lines 34, 44–46, 98–99, and 106–7, on which NKBZ gives no reading.

Lines 36 and 38 function as pillow-word constructions, adding a rhetorical adornment to the sartorial complexity of the passage. The flax-spinning girls (*omi no kora*) and the treasure-fashioning girls (*takara no kora*) are meant to be a balanced low-high culture pair. The "treasure" intended is that of luxury fabrics.

"Grainkeeper's girl" renders *inaki omina* in line 47. *Inaki* was the lowest of the reorganized list of kabane promulgated by Emperor Temmu, but the term here probably refers to the more ancient functional sense of the word. I am indebted to Dr. Judith N. Rabinovitch for the translation. The "stockings" (*shitakutsu*; "undershoes") of line 51 were a kind of tabi, or bifurcated sock. The black lacquer shoes (line 55) would have been court wear.

Two versions of the exemplary tale of Yüan Ku are preserved in the 10th-century Japanese legal commentary *Ryō no Shūge* by Koremune no Naomoto, in KT, XXIII, 410, 411. They are based on a fragmentarily preserved Chinese genre, the *Hsiao-tzu Chuan* (*Traditions of Filial Children*).

1540–41 [MYS XVI: 3826–27/3804–5]. On "His duties kept him bound," compare *Yu-hsien-k'u*, "my royal duties are fixed" (Yagisawa, p. 166 [Levy, p. 50]). "Words stuck in their throats": Yagisawa, p. 168 (Levy, p. 51), "Both of us wept and choked with inner grief." NKBZ, IV, 118, n. 8, assigns the woman as subject; I have preferred to follow the model in *Yu-hsien-k'u* by applying the sentence to both husband and wife. "In reply to his voice": NKBZ, IV, 118, n. 10, points out that this is a narrative formula used frequently in *Yu-hsien-k'u*.

1543 [MYS XVI: 3829/3807]. The other poem cited in the *Kana Preface* as basic to calligraphy practice is the famous *Naniwazu*: Naniwazu ni / Saku ya kono hana / Fuyugomori / Ima wa harube to / Saku ya kono hana ("At Port Naniwa / How it blossoms, this flower— / Closed up all winter, / Now because the spring has come, / How it blossoms, this flower!"). According to the *Kana Preface*, the poem was composed by Wani (see commentary to #124) to urge Prince Ōsazaki (Emperor Nintoku) to accept the throne. The two poems are called "the father and mother of poetry." See Kubota, *Kokinwakashū*, I, 62 (McCullough, *Kokin Wakashū*, pp. 3, 4, 9).

1548–49 [MYS XVI: 3844–45/3822–23]. On *Kakyō Hyōshiki*, see Rabinovitch. NKBZ has "waist line" (*koshi no ku*) in place of "belly line" (*hara no ku*). I have followed NKBT.

1555 [MYS XVI: 3907/3885]. Continental tiger hunts and men seated on tiger or other wild animal skins are depicted on the plectrum guards of musical instruments preserved in the Shōsōin (see Doi, plates 19 and 20). Tiger skins were also imported to Japan (NKBZ, IV, 151). Fierce beasts like tigers and wolves (*ōkami*; "great gods") were *kami*. The suggestion about inkwells is made in NKBZ, IV, 152. Lines 13 and 14 mention *uzuki* and *satsuki*, the 4th and 5th months, more nearly equivalent to May and June in the current calendar.

1557-59 [MYS XVI: 3909-11/3887-89]. These poems are discussed in Akima, "Songs of the Dead," pp. 495-97. Akima sees them as expressions of an ancient funeral cult. Kojima et al. speculate that the topic "Frightening Things" was drawn from an encyclopedic reference work of the type exemplified by *I-wen Lei-chü* (NKBZ, IV, 155, n. 1). NKBZ reads *ninuri* ("cinnabar-painted") for *kinuri* ("yellow-painted") in #1558, and leaves the final line of #1559 partially undeciphered. The translation follows NKBT.

THE BUDDHA'S FOOTSTONE POEMS

A few other Buddhist waka do remain from the Nara period. The following, for instance, was presented by the monks of Gangōji (also known as Asukadera), the oldest temple in Japan, to Tōdaiji on the occasion of the dedication of the Great Buddha in 752: Minamoto no / Nori no okorishi / Tobu ya tori / Asuka no tera no / Uta tatematsuru ("From the very Source / Whence the Doctrine first arose, / Flying-bird / Asuka Temple, now / We make offering of song"). (*Tōdaiji Yōroku*, p. 46.) There is also the following anecdote about how Gyōki (668-749), an itinerant monk and culture hero who is popularly remembered as Gyōki Bosatsu, "the Bodhisattva Gyōki," welcomed the Indian monk Bodhisena (704-60, later in charge of the "eye-opening ceremony" for the Great Buddha) on the latter's arrival in Japan in 736:

The little boat reached shore, and an Indian monk alighted on the beach. Bodhisattva took his hand, looked at him, and smiled. Bodhisattva sang a *waka*:

Washiyama no	On the Holy Mount,
Shaka no yamabe ni	In the mountains of Śākya,
Chigiriteshi	The self-consistent
Shinnyo kuchi sezu	Truth we swore has not decayed:
Aimitsuru kamo	I have met with you again!

The foreign holy man replied:

Kapirae ni	The vow we swore
Tomo ni chigirishi	Together in Kapilavastu
Kai arite	Has borne fruit:
Monju no mikao	For the face of Mañjuśri
Aimitsuru kana	I have seen again today!

Gyōki Bosatsu spoke to the monks and laity, saying, "This foreign holy man is a Brahman from South India; his name is Bodhi." The assembled people then knew that Gyōki was an incarnation of Mañjuśri. (*Tōdaiji Yōroku*, p. 46)

For translations of the Chinese inscriptions on the Footprint Stone, see Mills. The poems themselves are studied and translated in both Mills and Miller. Types A and B as used herein are to be distinguished from Miller's series A and B, which refer to a different analytical grouping. The three Yakushi sutras cited by Miller are nos. 449–51 in Takakusu, XIV. For the passage on the worship of Śākyamuni's feet, see p. 416.

1561 [BSS 2]. For lists of the 32 marks (*sanjūni sō*) and 80 signs (or "80 virtues"; *hachijū shukō*), see Mochizuki, II, 1554–60, and V, 4212–13. Soothill and Hodous list only the former. For the first Great Vow, see Takakusu, XIV, 401. A tanka version of this poem appears as SIS XX:1345, attributed to Empress Kōmyō, the consort of Emperor Shōmu. Its headnote claims it was affixed to a footprint stone at a temple known as Yamashinadera (probably Kōfukuji; or a temple in Yamashina?). For a discussion, see Miller, pp. 14–19, 84–90. See also Miller, p. 94, for the source of the notion that the Buddha walked four finger-breadths off the ground (this is the 68th of the 80 signs).

1563–64 [BSS 4–5]. On the second Great Vow, see Takakusu, XIV, 401; for the reference to *Yakushi Nyorai Hongangyō*, see ibid., p. 402; and on the battle in heaven, see Kurano, pp. 74, 75 (Philippi, *Kojiki*, pp. 74–80).

1565–66 [BSS 6–7]. *T'iao-yü chang-fu*, "the strong-man tamer [of man's passions]," is given as one of the appellations of Yakushi the Lapis Lazuli Shining Buddha immediately preceding the list of Great Vows in Takakusu, XIV, 401. See also Miller, p. 109; and Soothill and Hodous, p. 444. The translation of *masurawo* as "that Greater Man" calls for an apprehensive appeasement of the shade of John Milton, but may be justified in Japanese terms by the etymology *masu* ("increase") + *ra* (suffix) + *wo* ("man"). See *Jidaibetsu*, p. 677.

1567 [BSS 8]. Miller, p. 29, assigns the poem to Vows 4 and 5 (Takakusu, XIV, 401), which have to do with guiding the misguided, but since the guide (rather than the goal) is Yakushi himself, the reference seems dubious.

1569 [BSS 10]. Miller, p. 118, brings forward several Man'yō poems contrasting enduring stone and transient world (e.g., #633), but the point seems a trifle obvious. #266 would make a refreshing comparison, but has no more (or less) to do with the case.

BSS 11. Miller, p. 123, appears to subscribe to the view of Kariya Ekisai (1775–1835) that the surviving text of BSS 11 has been recut (i.e., is not necessarily the original). Kariya, p. 50, marks six of the eight surviving characters as dubious.

1570 [BSS 12]. Miller, p. 29; Takakusu, XIV, 401. *Kodai Kayōshū*, p. 243, has *atö*. Miller, apparently unintentionally, argues for both *atö* and *Fitö* (pp. 50–51, 125); *Fitö* is the reading he adopts in his translation, p. 124.

1571 [BSS 13]. See Takakusu, XIV, 401, for Vow 6. *Wodinasi* (*wodinaki*; line 1) is defined in *Jidaibetsu*, p. 835, as *otote iru* ("inferior"), *shikkari shite inai* ("not firm"—i.e., "infirm"?). I have added the idea of "old" under the influence of Miller's interesting attempt (pp. 131–33) to relate the *wodi* of *wodinasi* to the *woti* of *wotimidu* ("water to restore youth"), *wotikaFeru* ("become young again"), etc. (see #713, #1043, and #1453).

1572 [BSS 14]. *Yakushi Rurikō Shichibutsu Hongan Kudokukyō* mentions the circumambulation and worship of Śākyamuni's feet by Mañjuśri (Takakusu, XIV, 416).

1573 [BSS 15]. Ōnamuchi is another name for Ōkuninushi (also Yachihoko no Kami, the deity Eight Thousand Spears, see #2–5). For Sukuna Hikona as the "potion-master," see #39. For Ōnamuchi and Sukuna Hikona as the deities of medicine, see Sakamoto et al., I, 128, 129 (Aston, I, 59). These two are co-creators of the world in Izumo myth; see note to #39–40. This poem is related to Vows 6 and 7, promising healing to the sick and succor to the afflicted (Takakusu, XIV, 401).

1576–78 [BSS 18–20]. A four-character Chinese inscription is carved in the blank space immediately above these poems, the first three characters above #1576 and the last above #1578. Miller, pp. 152–55, dismisses this inscription as an interpolation, essentially a pious graffito irrelevant to the original text. Nevertheless, it may be of some significance as indicating an awareness of a sudden shift in the sequence from the footprints to the more general question of life and death. The four characters are Morohashi 3459, 4204, 21670, and 16365, and the inscription can be read to mean "Rebuking Birth and Death," i.e., rejecting *saṃsāra*, the everrecurring cycle of transmigration. (For Okura's meditation on the subject, see #639.) As Miller points out, #1576 does not qualify as a "rebuke"; but #1577–78 surely do. On the top part of the stele a similar "caption" has been engraved, one that can be translated "Reverencing Buddha's Footprints . . . seventeen poems," with the first part over #1560, and the second over #1568. Whoever wrote these inscriptions clearly read the sequence as falling into two parts, BSS 1–17 and BSS 18–21.

1576 [BSS 18]. A canonical source for "the human body is hard to obtain" is provided in *Yakushi Nyorai Hongangyō* (Takakusu, XIV, 403). A reference to Vow 8 (ibid., p. 401), a promise that women will be able to change into men, seems dubious, despite Miller, p. 30.

1577 [BSS 19]. For Vow 9, see Takakusu, XIV, 401–2. The same sutra promises release from the fear of poisonous snakes, also from the fear of evil elephants, lions, tigers, wolves, and various kinds of crawling things (ibid., p. 403). *Konkōmyō Saishōōkyō* has a passage explaining the "Four Poisonous Serpents" in detail (ibid., XVI, 424). The same passage mentions the five Skandhas, but does not call them "demons." The word translated "Demonic Things" in #1577 is *monö*, which in addition to the ordinary sense of "thing" has an ancient special use to denote mysterious supernatural powers, demons, etc. (*Jidaibetsu*, pp. 743–44). *Daihatsu Nehangyō* (Takakusu no. 374) likens the five Skandhas to five Caṇḍālas, "outcasts," or "untouchables." The same passage also deals with the Four Poisonous Serpents (Takakusu, XII, 499–500).

1578 [BSS 20]. For Vow 10, which offers release to those bound, beaten, and thrown into prison by the King's law, see Takakusu, XIV, 402. Yama, the judge of the dead, appears in a subsequent passage, p. 403. For the lightning metaphor, see ibid., XII, 606. This version of *Daihatsu Nehangyō*, Takakusu no. 375, unlike no. 374, cited in the note to #1577, contains additions by the Sung monk Hui Yen and others from another version of *Nehangyō*. Of "the ordinary, ignorant person," the passage says, "His body is not hard, it is like a reed, a passion tree (*airāvana*), a fleck of spume, a plaintain tree. His body is ephemeral, his thoughts inconstant. They are like a lightning flash, rushing water, or a fantasmal flame."

BSS 21. The poem stele reads as follows:

> — tu — — —
> — — — — Fitaru
> — — nö ta ni
> Kusurisi motömu
> Yöki Fitö motömu
> Samasamu ga tamë ni

Miller, pp. 171–72, strongly rejects this inscription as an example of later "vandalism." The text has been (re?)engraved on a portion of the stone (lower left edge) already damaged by flaking.

Bibliography

Unless otherwise specified, the place of publication of Japanese-language works is Tōkyō. The following abbreviations are used in this list.

KT   *Shintei Zōho Kokushi Taikei*, ed. Kuroita Katsumi. 66 vols. Yoshikawa Kōbunkan, 1929–66

MN   *Monumenta Nipponica*

SKT   *Shinshaku Kambun Taikei*. 96 vols. Meiji Shoin, 1960–81

Takakusu   Takakusu Junjirō, ed., Taishō Shinshū Daizōkyō. 85 vols. Taishō Issaikyō Kankōkai, 1924–32

Abe Toshiko and Imai Gen'e, eds. *Yamato Monogatari*. In *Nihon Koten Bungaku Taikei*, IX. Iwanami Shoten, 1957.

Abe Yoshio and Yamamoto Toshio, eds. *Rōshi*. In *SKT*, VII. 1966.

Akima Toshio. "Kakinomoto no Hitomaro Kashū Sakkakō—Shitaika o Chūshin ni," *Bungaku*, LI, 9, 10 (1983).

———. "The Songs of the Dead: Poetry, Drama, and Ancient Death Rituals in Japan," *Journal of Asian Studies*, XLI, 3 (May 1982).

Akimoto Kichirō, ed. *Fudoki*. *Nihon Koten Bungaku Taikei*, II. Iwanami Shoten, 1958.

Aoki Ikuko. "Ōtomo no Sakanoue no Iratsume." In Hisamatsu Sen'ichi and Sanekata Kiyoshi, eds., *Jōkō no Kajin*.

Aston, W. G., tr. *Nihongi: Chronicles of Japan from the Earliest Times to A.D. 697*. 2 vols. printed as one. London: Allen & Unwin, 1956. Originally published in 1896.

Batten, Bruce L. "Foreign Threat and Domestic Reform: The Emergence of the *Ritsuryō* State," *MN*, 41, 2 (Summer 1986).

Birrell, Anne, tr. *New Songs from a Jade Terrace: An Anthology of Early Chinese Love Poetry*. London: Allen & Unwin, 1982.

Borgen, Robert. *Sugawara no Michizane and the Early Heian Court*. Harvard East Asian Monographs, 120. Cambridge, Mass.: Harvard University Press, 1986.

Brannen, Noah S. "The *Kinkafu* Collection of Ancient Japanese Songs," *MN*, XXIII, 3–4 (1968).

Brooks, E. Bruce. "A Yakamochi Sampler," *The East-West Review*, III, 1 (Winter 1966–67).

Brower, Robert H., and Earl Miner. *Japanese Court Poetry*, Stanford, Calif.: Stanford University Press, 1961.

(*Bussetsu*) *Yakushi Nyorai Hongangyō* (tr. Dharmagupta). In Takakusu, XIV. 1925.

Chang Hai-p'eng, ed. *Mao Shih Lu Shu Kuang-yao*. In *Hsüeh Chin Tao Yüan*, VI. Taipei: Hsin Ta-feng Ch'u-pan Kung-ssu, 1980.

Ch'en Yen-chieh. *Shih-p'in Chü*. In Yang Chia-lo, ed., *Li-tai Shih-shih Ch'ang-pien*, III. Taipei: Wen-shu-chü, 1971.

Ch'eng Jung, comp. *Han-Wei Ts'ung-shu*.

Chin Shu, I. I-Wen Yin-shu-kuan, n.d.

Chung-hua Shu-chü Pien-chi-pu, ed. *Wen-hsüan*. 1974.

Ch'u T'ang Ssu Chieh Wen-chi. In *Ssu-pu Pi-yao*. Shanghai: Chung-hua Shu-chü.

Ch'üan T'ang Shih. 12 vols. Taipei: Ming-ling Ch'u-pan-she, 1971.

Cranston, Edwin A., tr. *The Izumi Shikibu Diary: A Romance of the Heian Court*. *Harvard-Yenching Institute Monograph Series*, 19. Cambridge, Mass.: Harvard University Press, 1969.

———. "Young Akiko: The Literary Debut of Yosano Akiko (1878–1942)," *Literature East & West*, XVIII, 1 (March 1974).

Daihatsu Nehangyō (tr. Fa Hsien). In Takakusu, I. 1924.

Daihatsu Nehangyō (tr. Tao-lang). In Takakusu, XII. 1925.

Doe, Paula Nold. "Ōtomo Yakamochi and the Man'yō Tradition of Elegy." Ph.D. dissertation, University of Wisconsin–Madison, 1978.

———. *A Warbler's Song in the Dusk: The Life and Work of Ōtomo no Yakamochi (718–785)*. Berkeley: University of California Press, 1982.

Doi Hiromu. *Shōshōin*. *Genshoku Nihon no Bijutsu*, IV. Shōgakukan, 1968.

Endō Yoshimoto, ed. *Izumi Shikibu Nikki*. In *Nihon Koten Bungaku Taikei*, XX. Iwanami Shoten, 1957.

Endō Yoshimoto and Kasuga Kazuo, eds. *Nihon Ryōiki*. *Nihon Koten Bungaku Taikei*, LXX. Iwanami Shoten, 1967.

Fang, Achilles, tr. and ed. "Rhyme-prose on Literature: The *Wen-fu* of Lu Chi (A.D. 261–303)." In John L. Bishop, ed., *Studies in Chinese Literature*. *Harvard-Yenching Institute Studies*, XXI. Cambridge, Mass.: Harvard University Press, 1966.

Frankel, Hans H. *The Flowering Plum and the Palace Lady: Interpretations of Chinese Poetry*. New Haven, Conn.: Yale University Press, 1976.

Fusō Ryakki. *KT*, XII.

Gengenshū (Kitabatake Chikafusa), *see* Masamune Atsuo, ed.

Gōbu Konkyōmyōkyō. In Takakusu, XVI. 1925.

Gyokudai Shin'ei, *see* Uchida Sennosuke, ed.

Han Shu. Peking: Chung-hua Shu-chü, 1962.

Hawkes, David, tr. *Ch'u Tz'u, the Songs of the South: An Ancient Chinese Anthology*. London: Oxford University Press, 1959.

Hayashi Tatsusaburō, ed. *Kodai Chūsei Geijutsuron*. *Nihon Shisō Taikei*, XXIII. Iwanami Shoten, 1973.

Heike Monogatari. Ed. Takagi Ichinosuke, Ozawa Masao, Atsumi Kaoru, and

Kindaichi Haruhiko. 2 vols. *Nihon Koten Bungaku Taikei*, XXXII–XXXIII. Iwanami Shoten, 1959–60.

Hightower, James Robert, tr. *The Poetry of T'ao Ch'ien*. London: Oxford University Press, 1970.

Hisamatsu Sen'ichi. "Ōtomo no Yakamochi." In Hisamatsu Sen'ichi and Sanekata Kiyoshi, eds., *Jōkō no Kajin. Nihon Kajin Kōza*, I. Kōbundō, 1968–69.

Hisamatsu Sen'ichi and Sanekata Kiyoshi, eds. *Jōkō no Kajin. Nihon Kajin Kōza*, I. Kōbundō, 1968–69.

Hoshikawa Kiyotaka, ed. *Soji. SKT*, XXXIV. 1970.

Housman, A.E. *The Collected Poems of A.E. Housman*. New York: Holt, 1950.

Hsin Hsü. In *Chung-kuo Tzu-hsüeh Ming-chu Chi-ch'eng*, 027. Taipei: Chung-kuo Tzu-hsüeh Ming-chu Chi-ch'eng Yin-chi Ch'üan-hui, 1978.

Hurvitz, Leon, tr. *Scripture of the Lotus Blossom of the Fine Dharma (The Lotus Sutra), translated from the Chinese of Kumarajiva*. New York: Columbia University Press, 1976.

Ichijima Kenkichi, ed. *Zokuzoku Gunsho Ruijū*, XI. Naigai Insatsu Kabushiki Kaisha, 1907.

Ichikawa Yasushi and Endō Tetsuo, ed. *Sōshi*. 2 vols. *SKT*, VII–VIII. Meiji Shoin, 1967.

Itō Yoshio et al., eds. *Waka Bungaku Daijiten*. Meiji Shoin, 1962.

Iwanami Kogo Jiten. Ed. Ōno Susumu, Satake Akihiro, and Maeda Kingorō. Iwanami Shoten, 1974.

I-wen Lei-chü. Ed. Wang Shao-ying. 2 vols. Shanghai: Ku-chi Ch'u-pen-she, 1965–83.

Jen Fang. *Shu-i-chi*. In Ch'eng Jung, comp., *Han-Wei Ts'ung-shu*.

Jidaibetsu Kokugo Daijiten: Jōdaihen. Ed. Jōdaigo Jiten Henshū Iinkai. Sanseidō, 1967.

Johnson, Regine. "Juxta- and Other Positions: Sexual Figuration in the Songs of the *Kojiki*." Unpublished seminar paper. Harvard University.

Jones, S.W., tr. *Ages Ago: Thirty-seven Tales from the Konjaku Monogatari Collection*. Cambridge, Mass.: Harvard University Press, 1959.

Kamada Tadashi, ed. *Shunjū Sashiden*. 3 vols. *SKT*, XXX–XXXII. 1971–77.

Kameda Tsutomu et al. *Men to Shōzō. Genshoku Nihon no Bijutsu*, XXIII. Shōgakukan, 1972.

Kariya Ekisai. *Kokyō Ibun*. Ed. Yamada Yoshio. Hōbunkan, 1912.

Karlgren, Bernhard, tr. *The Book of Odes*. Stockholm: Museum of Far Eastern Antiquities, 1950.

Kinoshita Masatoshi. "Hōkyaku to Matsura Sayohime—'Fe' no Kana kara," Supplementary Article I, *Man'yōshū*, ed. Kojima Noriyuki et al., II, 465–74.

Knechtges, David R., tr. *Wen Xuan, or Selections of Refined Literature*, I: *Rhapsodies on Metropolises and Capitals* (Xiao Tong; 501–31). Princeton, N.J.: Princeton University Press, 1982.

Kodai Kayōshū. Ed. Tsuchihashi Yutaka and Konishi Jin'ichi. *Nihon Koten Bungaku Taikei*, III. Iwanami Shoten, 1957.

Ko Hung. *Pao-p'u-tzu*. Shanghai: Sao-yeh Shan-fang, 1920.

Kojiki, see Kurano Kenji, ed; and Donald Philippi, tr.

Kojiki Uragaki, see Ōmiya Heima and Nakajima Hakkō, eds., II.

Kojima Noriyuki. *Jōdai Nihon Bungaku to Chūgoku Bungaku: Shuttenron o Chūshin to Suru Hikakubungakuteki Kōsatsu*. 3 vols. Hanawa Shobō, 1962–65.

Kojima Noriyuki, ed. *Kaifūsō*. In *Nihon Koten Bungaku Taikei*, LXIX. Iwanami Shoten, 1964.

Kokka Taikan. Ed. Matsushita Daisaburō and Watanabe Fumio. 2 vols. Kadokawa Shoten, 1951–63.

Koma Chikazane, *Kyōkunshō, see* Hayashi Tatsusaburō, ed.

Konishi Jin'ichi. "The Genesis of the *Kokinshū* Style," tr. Helen C. McCullough, *Harvard Journal of Asiatic Studies*, 38, 1 (1978).

———. *A History of Japanese Literature. Volume One: The Archaic and Ancient Ages*. Tr. Aileen Gatten and Nicholas Teele. Ed. Earl Miner. Princeton, N.J.: Princeton University Press, 1984.

Konkōmyō Saishōōkyō. Tr. I-ching. In Takakusu, XVI. 1925.

Koremune no Naomoto. *Ryō no Shūge*. In *KT*, XIII.

Kubota Utsubo. *Man'yōshū Hyōshaku*. 7 vols. Kadokawa Shoten, 1966–67.

———, ed. *Kokinwakashū Hyōshaku*. 3 vols. Tōkyōdō, 1960.

Kurano Kenji, ed. *Kojiki*. In *Nihon Koten Bungaku Taikei*, I. Iwanami Shoten, 1958.

Kyōkunshō, see Hayashi Tatsusaburō, ed.

Lau, D.C., tr. *Tao Te Ching*. Harmondsworth, Eng.: Penguin Books, 1963.

Lee, Ki-baik. *A New History of Korea*. Tr. Edward W. Wagner, with Edward J. Shultz. Cambridge, Mass.: Harvard University Press, 1984.

Legge, James, tr. *The Chinese Classics, with a Translation, Critical and Exegetical Notes, and Copious Indexes*. 5 vols. Taipei: Wen-shih-che Ch'u-pan-she, 1971.

Levy, Howard S., tr. *China's First Novelette: The Dwelling of Playful Goddesses* (Chang Wen-ch'eng; ca. 657–730). Dai Nippon Insatsu, 1965.

Li Shu-ch'ang. *Ku-i Ts'ung-shu*. Nippon Tōkyō Shisho Kambon, 1884. 50 vols.

Lin Yin, ed. *Liang-Han San-kuo Wen-hui*. Taipei: Ch'i-ch'eng Tu-shu Kung-ssu, 1960.

Man'yōshū. 4 vols. Kojima Noriyuki, Kinoshita Masatoshi, and Satake Akihiro, eds., *Nihon Koten Bungaku Zenshū*, II–V. Shōgakukan, 1971–75.

Man'yōshū. 4 vols. Takagi Ichinosuke, Gomi Tomohide, and Ōno Susumu, eds., *Nihon Koten Bungaku Taikei*, IV–VII. Iwanami Shoten, 1957–69.

Mao Shih Lu Shu Kuang-yao, see Chang Hai-p'eng, ed.

Maraini, Fosco. *Hekura: The Diving Girls' Island*. Tr. Eric Mosbacher. London: Hamish Hamilton, 1962.

Margouliès, Georges. *Anthologie raisonnée de la littérature chinoise*. Paris: Payot, 1948.

Masamune Atsuo, ed. *Nihon Koten Zenshū*, XI. Nihon Koten Zenshū Kankōkai, 1934.

Mather, Richard B., tr. *Shih-shuo Hsin-yü: A New Account of Tales of the World* (Liu I-ch'ing). Minneapolis: University of Minnesota Press, 1976.

Matsumura Hiroshi and Yamanaka Yutaka, eds. *Eiga Monogatari*. 2 vols. *Nihon Koten Bungaku Taikei*, LXXV–LXXVI. Iwanami Shoten, 1964–65.

Matsushita Daisaburō and Watanabe Fumio, eds. *Kokka Taikan*. 2 vols. Kadokawa Shoten, 1951–63.

McCullough, Helen Craig. *Brocade by Night: 'Kokin Wakashū' and the Court Style in Japanese Classical Poetry*. Stanford, Calif.: Stanford University Press, 1985.

———. *Kokin Wakashū: The First Imperial Anthology of Japanese Poetry; with 'Tosa Nikki' and 'Shinsen Waka'*. Stanford, Calif.: Stanford University Press, 1985.

McCullough, William H., and Helen Craig McCullough, trs. *A Tale of Flowering Fortunes: Annals of Japanese Aristocratic Life in the Heian Period*. 2 vols. Stanford, Calif.: Stanford University Press, 1980.

Mekada Makoto, ed. *Sesetsu Shingo*. 3 vols. *SKT*, LXXVI–LXXVIII. 1975–81.

Mikanagi Kiyotake. *Semmyō Shōkai*. Yūbun Shoin, 1936.

Miller, Roy Andrew. *'The Footprints of the Buddha': An Eighth-Century Old Japanese Poetic Sequence*. New Haven, Conn.: American Oriental Society, 1975.

Mills, Douglas E. "The Buddha's Footprint Stone Poems," *Journal of the American Oriental Society*, LXXX (1960).

Mochizuki Shinkyō, ed. *Bukkyō Daijiten*. 5 vols. Bukkyō Daijiten Hakkōsho, 1931–36. Plus 5 supplemental vols. Kyōto: Sekai Seiten Kankō Kyōkai, 1955–63.

Monzen. Ed. Obi Kōichi. 7 vols. *Zenshaku Kambun Taikei*, XXVI–XXXII, Shūeisha, 1974–76.

Monzen (Shihen I, II). Ed. Uchida Sennosuke and Ami Yūji. *SKT*, XIV–XV. 1963–72.

Moore, Thomas. *The Poetical Works of Thomas Moore*. New York: Sheldon, 1861.

Morohashi Tetsuji, ed. *Daikanwa Jiten*. 13 vols. Daishūkan Shoten, 1955–78.

Morris, Mark. "Waka and Form, Waka and History," *Harvard Journal of Asiatic Studies*, 46, 2 (Dec. 1986).

Motoori Norinaga Zenshū, XII. Ed. Ōno Susumu. Chikuma Shobō, 1974.

Murasaki Shikibu. *The Tale of Genji*. Tr. Edward G. Seidensticker. 2 vols. New York: Knopf, 1976.

Muromatsu Iwao, ed. *Kokubun Chūshaku Zensho*, XVII. Kokugakuin Daigaku Shuppambu, 1910.

Naitō Akira. "Hitomaro Kashū Tanabata-uta no Seiritsu to Sono Wakashiteki Ichi," *Kodai Kenkyū*, XVII (Nov. 1984).

Nakamura, Kyoko Motomochi, tr. *Miraculous Stories from the Japanese Buddhist Tradition: The Nihon ryōiki of the Monk Kyōkai*. Harvard-Yenching Institute

Monograph Series, 20. Cambridge, Mass.: Harvard University Press, 1973.

Nakanishi Susumu. *Yamanoue no Okura*. Kawade Shobō, 1973.

Nihon Kōki. In *KT*, III. 1934.

Nihonshoki, see Sakamoto Tarō et al., eds.

Nishimura, Sey. "The Prince and the Pauper: The Dynamics of a Shōtoku Legend," *MN*, 40, 3 (Autumn 1985).

———. "Retrospective Comprehension: Japanese Foretelling Songs," *Asian Folklore Studies*, XLV, 1 (1986).

Noma Seiroku, ed. *Nihon (3): Nara. Sekai Bijutsu Zenshū*, III. Kadokawa Shoten, 1968.

Noyes, Alfred. *Collected Poems*, I. New York: Stokes, 1913.

Ōmiya Heima and Nakajima Hakkō, eds. *Shintō Sōsho*. 4 vols. Yoshikawa Hanshichi, 1896.

Omodaka Hisataka. *Man'yōshū Chūshaku*. 20 vols. Chūō Kōronsha, 1957–69.

Owen, Stephen. *Traditional Chinese Poetry and Poetics: Omen of the World*. Madison: University of Wisconsin Press, 1985.

Parent, Mary Neighbour. "Yamadadera: Excavations 1984," *MN*, 40, 2 (Summer 1985).

———. "Yamadadera: Tragedy and Triumph," *MN*, 39, 3 (Autumn 1984).

Philippi, Donald L., tr. *Kojiki*. Princeton, N.J.: Princeton University Press, 1969.

———. *Norito: A New Translation of the Ancient Japanese Ritual Prayers*. Tōkyō: Institute for Japanese Culture and Classics, Kokugakuin University, 1959.

Rabinovitch, Judith. "Wasp Waists and Monkey Tails: A Study and Translation of Hamanari's *Uta no shiki* (*The Code of Poetry*, 772), Also Known as *Kakyō Hyōshiki* (*A Formulary for Verse Based on the Canons of Poetry*)," *Harvard Journal of Asiatic Studies*, 51, 2 (Dec. 1991).

Reckert, Stephen. *Lyra Minima: Structure and Symbol in Iberian Traditional Verse*. London: University of London, 1970.

Rexroth, Kenneth, tr. *One Hundred Poems from the Japanese*. New York: New Directions, 1964.

Rollins, Hyder Edward, ed. *The Letters of John Keats, 1814–1821*. 2 vols. Cambridge, Mass.: Harvard University Press, 1958.

Rōshi, see Abe Yoshio and Yamamoto Toshio, eds.

Ryō no Shūge. KT, XIII.

Sakamoto Tarō, Ienaga Saburō, Inoue Mitsusada, and Ōno Susumu, eds. *Nihonshoki*. 2 vols. *Nihon Koten Bungaku Taikei*, LXVII–LXVIII. 1967.

Saku Setsu, ed. *Kanshi Taikan*. 5 vols. Hō Shuppan, 1974.

Sansom, G. B. "The Imperial Edicts in the *Shoku Nihongi* (700–790)," *Transactions of the Asiatic Society of Japan*, 2d ser., 1 (1924).

Sasaki Nobutsuna, ed. *Nihon Kagaku Taikei*, I. Kazama Shobō, 1969.

Sato, Hiroaki. "Lineation of Tanka in English Translation," *MN*, 42, 3 (Autumn 1987).

Schafer, Edward H. *The Divine Woman: Dragon Ladies and Rain Maidens in T'ang Literature*. Berkeley: University of California Press, 1973.

———. *The Golden Peaches of Samarkand: A Study of T'ang Exotics*. Berkeley: University of California Press, 1963.

———. *The Vermilion Bird: T'ang Images of the South*. Berkeley: University of California Press, 1967.

Seidensticker, Edward G., tr. *The Tale of Genji* (Murasaki Shikibu). 2 vols. New York: Knopf, 1976.

Seiji Yōryaku. *KT*, XXVIII. 1935.

Sengaku. *Man'yōshū Chūshaku*, *see* Muromatsu Iwao, ed.

Shaku Nihongi (Urabe Kanekata). In *KT*, VIII. 1932.

Shang Shu. In *Ssu-pu Pi-yao*. Shanghai: Chung-hua Shu-chü.

Shikashū Taisei. Ed. Wakashi Kenkyūkai. 7 vols. and supplement. Meiji Shoin, 1973–76.

Shimpen Kokka Taikan Henshū Iinkai, ed. *Shimpen Kokka Taikan*. 9 sections (each composed of a text and an index volume) to date. Kadokawa Shoten, 1983–.

Shoku Nihongi. *KT*, II. 1937.

Shoku Nihonkōki. In *KT*, III. 1934.

Shunjū Sashiden. Ed. Kamada Tadashi. 3 vols. *SKT*, XXX–XXXII. 1971–77.

Sompi Bummyaku. 5 vols. *KT*, LVIII–LX and 2 supplemental vols. 1966–67.

Soothill, William Edward, and Lewis Hodous, comps. *A Dictionary of Chinese Buddhist Terms, with Sanskrit and English Equivalents and a Sanskrit-Pali Index*. Taipei: Ch'eng-wen Publishing Co., 1968. Originally published in London in 1937.

Ssu-ma Hsiang-ju. "Mei-jen Fu." In Lin Yin, ed., *Liang-Han San-kuo Wen-hui*. Taipei: Ch'i-ch'eng Tu-shu Kung-ssu, 1960.

Suzuki Yūjirō, ed. *Ekikyō*. 2 vols. *Zenshaku Kambun Taikei*, IX–X. Shūeisha, 1974.

Takakusu Junjirō, ed. *Taishō Daizōkyō*. 85 vols. Taishō Issaikyō Kankōkai. 1924–32.

Takazaki Masahide. "Ōtomo no Tabito." In Hisamatsu Sen'ichi and Sanekata Kiyoshi, eds., *Jōkō no Kajin*. *Nihon Kajin Kōza*, I. Kōbundō, 1968–69.

Takeda Yūkichi, ed. *Norito*. In *Nihon Koten Bungaku Taikei*, I. 1958.

Takeuchi Teruo, ed. *Raiki*. 3 vols. *SKT*, XXVII–XXIX. 1971–79.

Tamagami Takuya. *Genji Monogatari Hyōshaku*. 14 vols. Kadokawa Shoten, 1964–69.

Tanaka Ichimatsu. *Kodai Kaiga*. *Nihon Bijutsu Taikei*, III. Kōdansha, 1960.

T'ao-yü-chi. In Li Shu-ch'ang, *Ku-i Ts'ung-shu*, XXXII. Nippon Tōkyō Shisho Kambon, 1884.

Tōdaiji Yōroku. In Ichijima Kenkichi, ed., *Zokuzoku Gunsho Ruijū*, XI. Naigai Insatsu Kabushiki Kaisha, 1967.

Trakl, Georg. *Poems*. Tr. Lucia Getsi. Athens, Ohio: Mundus Artium Press, 1973.

Tsuchihashi, Paul Yachita, S.J. *Japanese Chronological Tables from 601 to 1872 A.D.* Tōkyō: Sophia University Press, 1952.

Tsuchihashi Yutaka and Konishi Jin'ichi, eds. *Kodai Kayōshū*. *Nihon Koten Bungaku Taikei*, III. Iwanami Shoten, 1957.

Uchida Sennosuke, ed. *Gyokudai Shin'ei*. 2 vols. *SKT*, LX–LXI. 1974–85.

Urabe Kanefumi. *Kojiki Uragaki*. In Ōmiya Heima and Nakajima Hakkō, eds., *Shintō Sōshō*, II. Yoshikawa Hanshichi, 1896.

Urabe Kanekata. *Shaku Nihongi*. In *KT*, VIII. 1932.

Ury, Marian, tr. *Tales of Times Now Past: Sixty-Two Stories from a Medieval Japanese Collection*. Berkeley: University of California Press, 1979.

Waka Bungaku Daijiten. Ed. Itō Yoshio et al. Meiji Shoin, 1962.

Wakashi Kenkyūkai, ed. *Shikashū Taisei*. 7 vols. and supplement. Meiji Shoin, 1973–76.

Waley, Arthur, tr. *The Analects of Confucius*. London: Allen & Unwin, 1938. Reprint, Vintage Books, n.d.

————. *The Book of Songs*. New York: Grove Press, 1960. Originally published in 1937.

————. *Translations from the Chinese*. New York: Knopf, 1964.

Wang Shao-ying, ed. *I-wen Lei-chü* (Ou-yang Hsün). 2 vols. Shanghai: Ku-chi Ch'u-pen-she, 1965–83.

Watson, Burton. *Chinese Rhyme-Prose*. New York: Columbia University Press, 1971.

————. *The Complete Works of Chuang Tzu*. New York: Columbia University Press, 1968.

————. *Japanese Literature in Chinese*. 2 vols. New York: Columbia University Press, 1975.

————. *Records of the Grand Historian, translated from the Shih chi of Ssu-ma Ch'ien*. 2 vols. New York: Columbia University Press, 1961.

Wen-hsüan. Ed. Chung-hua Shu-chü Pien-chi-pu. 1974.

Wilhelm, Richard, tr. *The I Ching or Book of Changes*. Rendered into English by Cary F. Baynes. *Bollingen Series*, XIX. Princeton, N.J.: Princeton University Press, 1977.

Wu Tse-yü, ed. *An-tzu Ch'un Ch'iu Shih Chi*. 2 vols. in 1. Beijing: Chung-hua Shu-chü, 1962.

Xiao Tong. *Wen Xuan, or Selections of Refined Literature*, I: *Rhapsodies on Metropolises and Capitals*. Tr. David R. Knechtges. Princeton, N.J.: Princeton University Press, 1982.

Yagisawa Hajime, ed. *Yūsenkutsu Zenkō*. Meiji Shoin, 1967.

Yakushi Rurikō Nyorai Hongan Kudokukyō (tr. Hsüan-tsang). In Takakusu, XIV. 1925.

Yakushi Rurikō Shichibutsu Hongan Kudokukyō (tr. I-ching). In Takakusu, XIV. 1925.

Yamagishi Tokuhei, ed. *Genji Monogatari*, 5 vols. *Nihon Koten Bungaku Taikei*, XIV–XVIII. 1958–63.

Yanagi Kōkichi. "*Shoku Nihongi* no Seiritsu," 1–3, *Shoku Nihongi Kenkyū*, 10, 1–5 (1963).

Yang Chia-lo, ed. *Chung-kuo Ssu-hsiang Ming-chu*, x. Taipei: Shih-chieh Shu-chü Yin-hang, 1959.

———. *Li-tai Shih-shih Ch'ang-pien*. 24 vols. Taipei: Wen-shu-chü, 1971.

Yokomichi Mario and Omote Akira, eds. *Yōkyokushū*, I. *Nihon Koten Bungaku Taikei*, XL. 1960.

Yōrō Ritsuryō. In *KT*, XXII. 1939.

Yoshida Kenkō, ed. *Shiki*, II, v. *SKT*, XXXIX, LXXXV. 1973–82.

Yoshikawa Kōjirō, ed. *Rongo*, I. *Shintei Chūgoku Kotensen*, II. Asahi Shimbunsha, 1968.

Yuimakitsu Shosekkyō (tr. Kumārajīva). In Takakusu, XIV. 1925.

Zōagangyō (tr. Guṇabhadra). In Takakusu, II. 1924.

Conversion Table 1:
Anthology Number to Source Number

The *Kojiki* numbers run in parallel with the anthology numbers: 1–113 = K 1–K 113

114	NS 3	144	NS 74	174	NS 106
115	NS 4	145	NS 75	175	NS 107
116	NS 10	146	NS 76	176	NS 108
117	NS 11	147	NS 77	177	NS 109
118	NS 15	148	NS 78	178	NS 110
119	NS 16	149	NS 79	179	NS 111
120	NS 17	150	NS 80	180	NS 112
121	NS 18	151	NS 81	181	NS 113
122	NS 19	152	NS 82	182	NS 114
123	NS 24	153	NS 83	183	NS 115
124	NS 28	154	NS 84	184	NS 116
125	NS 30	155	NS 85	185	NS 117
126	NS 31	156	NS 86	186	NS 118
127	NS 40	157	NS 87	187	NS 119
128	NS 44	158	NS 90	188	NS 120
129	NS 45	159	NS 91	189	NS 121
130	NS 46	160	NS 92	190	NS 122
131	NS 47	161	NS 93	191	NS 123
132	NS 48	162	NS 94	192	NS 124
133	NS 49	163	NS 95	193	NS 125
134	NS 50	164	NS 96	194	NS 126
135	NS 51	165	NS 97	195	NS 127
136	NS 56	166	NS 98	196	NS 128
137	NS 59	167	NS 99	197	NS 129
138	NS 60	168	NS 100	198	NS 130
139	NS 61	169	NS 101	199	NS 131
140	NS 65	170	NS 102	200	F 1
141	NS 66	171	NS 103	201	F 2
142	NS 67	172	NS 104	202	F 3
143	NS 68	173	NS 105	203	F 4

204	F 5	245	MYS I:3	286	MYS II:160
205	F 6	246	MYS I:4	287	MYS II:161
206	F 7	247	MYS I:10	288	MYS I:29
207	F 8	248	MYS I:11	289	MYS I:30
208	F 9	249	MYS I:12	290	MYS I:31
209	F 10	250	MYS I:13	291	MYS III:268/266
210	F 11	251	MYS I:14	292	MYS III:266/264
211	F 12	252	MYS I:15	293	MYS I:36
212	F 13	253	GSS VI:302	294	MYS I:37
213	F 14	254	MYS I:7	295	MYS I:38
214	F 15	255	MYS I:8	296	MYS I:39
215	F 16	256	MYS I:16	297	MYS III:235
216	F 17	257	MYS I:17	298	MYS III:236/235a
217	F 18	258	MYS I:18	299	MYS III:263/261
218	F 19	259	MYS IV:491/488	300	MYS III:264/262
219	F 20	260	MYS I:19	301	MYS III:240/239
220	F 21	261	MYS II:148	302	MYS III:241/240
221	F 22	262	MYS II:149	303	MYS III:242/241
222	F 23	263	MYS I:25	304	MYS III:251/250
223	SN 1	264	MYS I:27	305	MYS III:252/251
224	SN 2	265	MYS III:393/390	306	MYS III:253/252
225	SN 3	266	MYS I:22	307	MYS III:254/253
226	SN 4	267	MYS IV:493/490	308	MYS III:255/254
227	SN 5	268	MYS IV:494/491	309	MYS III:256/255
228	SN 6	269	MYS II:109	310	MYS III:257/256
229	SN 7	270	MYS III:419/416	311	MYS I:40
230	SN 8	271	MYS II:110	312	MYS I:41
231	MYS II:85	272	MYS II:105	313	MYS I:42
232	MYS II:86	273	MYS II:106	314	MYS IV:499/496
233	MYS II:87	274	MYS II:163	315	MYS IV:500/497
234	MYS II:88	275	MYS II:164	316	MYS IV:501/498
235	MYS IV:487/484	276	MYS II:165	317	MYS IV:502/499
236	MYS I:1	277	MYS II:166	318	MYS IV:504/501
237	MYS III:418/415	278	MYS I:34	319	MYS IV:505/502
238	MYS I:2	279	MYS II:119	320	MYS IV:506/503
239	MYS VIII:1515/1511	280	MYS II:120	321	MYS II:131
240	MYS I:5	281	MYS II:121	322	MYS II:132
241	MYS I:6	282	MYS II:122	323	MYS II:133
242	MYS IV:488/485	283	MYS VIII:1471/1467	324	MYS II:134
243	MYS IV:489/486	284	MYS VIII:1612/1608	325	MYS II:135
244	MYS IV:490/487	285	MYS I:28	326	MYS II:136

327	MYS II:137	368	MYS VII:1273/1269	409	MYS XI:2372/2368
328	MYS II:167	369	MYS VII:1286/1282	410	MYS XI:2373/2369
329	MYS II:168	370	MYS VII:1287/1283	411	MYS XI:2374/2370
330	MYS II:169	371	MYS VII:1288/1284	412	MYS XI:2375/2371
331	MYS I:45	372	MYS VII:1298/1294	413	MYS XI:2376/2372
332	MYS I:46	373	MYS VII:1303/1299	414	MYS XI:2377/2373
333	MYS I:47	374	MYS IX:1697/1693	415	MYS XI:2378/2374
334	MYS I:48	375	MYS IX:1698/1694	416	MYS XI:2381/2377
335	MYS I:49	376	MYS IX:1699/1695	417	MYS XI:2394/2390
336	MYS II:194	377	MYS IX:1700/1696	418	MYS XI:2405/2401
337	MYS II:195	378	MYS IX:1701/1697	419	MYS XI:2419/2415
338	MYS II:196	379	MYS IX:1702/1698	420	MYS XI:2420/2416
339	MYS II:197	380	MYS IX:1703/1699	421	MYS XI:2421/2417
340	MYS II:198	381	MYS IX:1704/1700	422	MYS XI:2422/2418
341	MYS II:199	382	MYS IX:1705/1701	423	MYS XI:2423/2419
342	MYS II:200	383	MYS IX:1706/1702	424	MYS XI:2424/2420
343	MYS II:201	384	MYS IX:1707/1703	425	MYS XI:2425/2421
344	MYS II:202	385	MYS IX:1708/1704	426	MYS XI:2426/2422
345	MYS II:207	386	MYS IX:1709/1705	427	MYS XI:2441/2437
346	MYS II:208	387	MYS IX:1710/1706	428	MYS XI:2444/2440
347	MYS II:209	388	MYS IX:1711/1707	429	MYS XI:2487/2483
348	MYS II:210	389	MYS IX:1712/1708	430	MYS XIII:3323/3309
349	MYS II:211	390	MYS IX:1713/1709	431	KKS VI:334
350	MYS II:212	391	MYS IX:1724/1720	432	KKS IX:409
351	MYS II:217	392	MYS IX:1725/1721	433	KKS XIII:621
352	MYS II:218	393	MYS IX:1726/1722	434	SIS X:597
353	MYS II:219	394	MYS IX:1727/1723	435	SIS XII:700
354	MYS III:431/428	395	MYS IX:1728/1724	436	SIS XIII:778
355	MYS III:432/429	396	MYS IX:1729/1725	437	SKKS IV:346
356	MYS III:433/430	397	MYS X:1816/1812	438	SKKS V:459
357	MYS III:429/426	398	MYS X:2004/2000	439	SKKS VI:582
358	MYS II:220	399	MYS X:2182/2178	440	SKKS VI:657
359	MYS II:221	400	MYS X:2183/2179	441	SKKS XI:992
360	MYS II:222	401	MYS XI:2355/2351	442	SKKS XI:993
361	MYS II:223	402	MYS XI:2356/2352	443	MYS II:228
362	MYS II:224	403	MYS XI:2357/2353	444	MYS II:229
363	MYS II:225	404	MYS XI:2358/2354	445	MYS I:58
364	MYS II:226	405	MYS XI:2359/2355	446	MYS I:70
365	MYS VII:1072/1068	406	MYS XI:2360/2356	447	MYS III:272/270
366	MYS VII:1105/1101	407	MYS XI:2361/2357	448	MYS III:273/271
367	MYS VII:1191/1187	408	MYS XI:2366/2362	449	MYS III:274/272

450	MYS III:275/273	491	MYS XVI:3846/3824	532	MYS VI:926/921
451	MYS III:276/274	492	MYS XVI:3847/3825	533	MYS VI:927/922
452	MYS III:277/275	493	MYS XVI:3848/3826	534	MYS VI:940/935
453	MYS III:278/276	494	MYS XVI:3849/3827	535	MYS VI:941/936
454	MYS III:279/276a	495	MYS XVI:3850/3828	536	MYS VI:942/937
455	MYS III:280/277	496	MYS XVI:3851/3829	537	MYS III:320/317
456	MYS III:308/305	497	MYS XVI:3852/3830	538	MYS III:321/318
457	MYS I:32	498	MYS XVI:3853/3831	539	MYS III:325/322
458	MYS I:33	499	MYS IV:511/508	540	MYS III:326/323
459	MYS I:43	500	MYS XIX:4251/4227	541	MYS III:327/324
460	MYS I:60	501	MYS XIX:4252/4228	542	MYS III:328/325
461	MYS I:65	502	MYS III:316/313	543	MYS III:360/357
462	MYS I:73	503	MYS VIII:1474/1470	544	MYS III:361/358
463	MYS I:69	504	MYS I:68	545	MYS III:362/359
464	MYS IV:512/509	505	MYS I:75	546	MYS III:363/360
465	MYS IV:513/510	506	MYS VIII:1559/1555	547	MYS III:364/361
466	MYS I:59	507	MYS IV:537/534	548	MYS III:365/362
467	MYS I:51	508	MYS IV:538/535	549	MYS III:375/372
468	MYS I:64	509	MYS IV:646/643	550	MYS III:376/373
469	MYS I:66	510	MYS IV:647/644	551	MYS III:381/378
470	MYS I:62	511	MYS IV:648/645	552	MYS III:387/384
471	MYS III:285/282	512	MYS VI:918/913	553	MYS III:434/431
472	MYS III:287/284	513	MYS VI:919/914	554	MYS III:435/432
473	MYS I:44	514	MYS VI:920/915	555	MYS III:436/433
474	MYS I:35	515	MYS VI:921/916	556	MYS VI:922/917
475	MYS I:76	516	MYS II:230	557	MYS VI:923/918
476	MYS I:61	517	MYS II:231	558	MYS VI:924/919
477	MYS III:292/289	518	MYS II:232	559	MYS VI:928/923
478	MYS III:293/290	519	MYS II:233	560	MYS VI:929/924
479	MYS IX:1689/1685	520	MYS II:234	561	MYS VI:930/925
480	MYS IX:1690/1686	521	MYS III:367/364	562	MYS VI:931/926
481	MYS II:114	522	MYS III:368/365	563	MYS VI:932/927
482	MYS II:115	523	MYS III:369/366	564	MYS VI:1006/1001
483	MYS II:116	524	MYS III:370/367	565	MYS VIII:1428/1424
484	MYS II:203	525	MYS VI:912/907	566	MYS VIII:1429/1425
485	MYS VIII:1517/1513	526	MYS VI:913/908	567	MYS VIII:1430/1426
486	MYS VIII:1518/1514	527	MYS VI:914/909	568	MYS VIII:1431/1427
487	MYS XVI:3838/3816	528	MYS VI:915/910	569	MYS III:322/319
488	MYS I:57	529	MYS VI:916/911	570	MYS III:323/320
489	MYS III:239/238	530	MYS VI:917/912	571	MYS III:324/321
490	MYS III:267/265	531	MYS VI:925/920	572	MYS IX:1811/1807

573	MYS IX:1812/1808	614	MYS IV:563/560	655	MYS XVI:3889/3867
574	MYS IX:1813/1809	615	MYS IV:564/561	656	MYS XVI:3890/3868
575	MYS IX:1814/1810	616	MYS IV:565/562	657	MYS XVI:3891/3869
576	MYS IX:1815/1811	617	MYS III:397/394	658	MYS VI:981/976
577	MYS IX:1742/1738	618	MYS VI:980/975	659	MYS VI:982/977
578	MYS IX:1743/1739	619	MYS I:63	660	MYS III:331/328
579	MYS IX:1744/1740	620	MYS VIII:1522/1518	661	MYS VI:1001/996
580	MYS IX:1745/1741	621	MYS VIII:1531/1527	662	MYS III:416/413
581	MYS VI:976/971	622	MYS VIII:1532/1528	663	MYS III:378/375
582	MYS VI:977/972	623	MYS VIII:1533/1529	664	MYS III:379/376
583	MYS IX:1751/1747	624	MYS V:804/800	665	MYS III:380/377
584	MYS IX:1752/1748	625	MYS V:805/801	666	MYS VI:990/985
585	MYS IX:1761/1757	626	MYS III:340/337	667	MYS VI:991/986
586	MYS IX:1762/1758	627	MYS V:806/802	668	MYS VI:989/984
587	MYS IX:1763/1759	628	MYS V:807/803	669	MYS IV:713/710
588	MYS IX:1764/1760	629	MYS V:909/904	670	MYS III:313/310
589	MYS III:318/315	630	MYS V:910/905	671	MYS III:329/326
590	MYS III:319/316	631	MYS V:911/906	672	MYS III:374/371
591	MYS VI:965/960	632	MYS V:808/804	673	MYS IV:539/536
592	MYS III:341/338	633	MYS V:809/805	674	MYS VI:1051/1047
593	MYS III:342/339	634	MYS V:896/892	675	MYS VI:1052/1048
594	MYS III:343/340	635	MYS V:897/893	676	MYS VI:1053/1049
595	MYS III:344/341	636	MYS V:898/894	677	MYS VI:1054/1050
596	MYS III:345/342	637	MYS V:899/895	678	MYS VI:1055/1051
597	MYS III:346/343	638	MYS V:900/896	679	MYS VI:1056/1052
598	MYS III:347/344	639	MYS V:901/896a	680	MYS VI:1057/1053
599	MYS III:348/345	640	MYS V:902/897	681	MYS VI:1058/1054
600	MYS III:349/346	641	MYS V:903/898	682	MYS VI:1059/1055
601	MYS III:350/347	642	MYS V:904/899	683	MYS VI:1060/1056
602	MYS III:351/348	643	MYS V:905/900	684	MYS VI:1061/1057
603	MYS III:352/349	644	MYS V:906/901	685	MYS VI:1062/1058
604	MYS III:353/350	645	MYS V:907/902	686	MYS VI:1063/1059
605	MYS IV:574/571	646	MYS V:908/903	687	MYS VI:1064/1060
606	MYS IV:632/629	647	MYS VI:983/978	688	MYS VI:1065/1061
607	MYS III:384/381	648	MYS XVI:3882/3860	689	MYS VI:1069/1065
608	MYS III:339/336	649	MYS XVI:3883/3861	690	MYS VI:1070/1066
609	MYS III:394/391	650	MYS XVI:3884/3862	691	MYS VI:1071/1067
610	MYS III:396/393	651	MYS XVI:3885/3863	692	MYS IX:1804/1800
611	MYS III:354/351	652	MYS XVI:3886/3864	693	MYS III:484/481
612	MYS III:395/392	653	MYS XVI:3887/3865	694	MYS III:485/482
613	MYS IV:562/559	654	MYS XVI:3888/3866	695	MYS III:486/483

696	MYS VI:985/980	737	MYS IV:691/688	778	MYS IV:730/727
697	KKS IX:406	738	MYS IV:692/689	779	MYS IV:731/728
698	MYS VI:978/973	739	MYS VIII:1454/1450	780	MYS IV:744/741
699	MYS VI:979/974	740	MYS IV:724/721	781	MYS IV:745/742
700	MYS IV:629/626	741	MYS IV:728/725	782	MYS IV:746/743
701	SKKS XV:1376/1375	742	MYS IV:729/726	783	MYS IV:747/744
702	MYS XIX:4294/4270	743	MYS IV:759/756	784	MYS IV:748/745
703	MYS VIII:1594/1590	744	MYS IV:760/757	785	MYS IV:749/746
704	MYS III:385/382	745	MYS IV:761/758	786	MYS IV:750/747
705	MYS III:386/383	746	MYS IV:762/759	787	MYS IV:751/748
706	MYS VIII:1560/1556	747	MYS VIII:1626/1622	788	MYS IV:752/749
707	MYS XVI:3870/3848	748	MYS VIII:1627/1623	789	MYS IV:753/750
708	MYS III:401/398	749	MYS IV:584/581	790	MYS IV:754/751
709	MYS III:402/399	750	MYS IV:585/582	791	MYS IV:755/752
710	MYS VIII:1444/1440	751	MYS IV:586/583	792	MYS IV:756/753
711	MYS IV:700/697	752	MYS IV:587/584	793	MYS IV:757/754
712	MYS IV:555/552	753	MYS III:398/395	794	MYS IV:758/755
713	MYS IV:653/650	754	MYS III:399/396	795	MYS VIII:1631/1627
714	MYS IV:559/556	755	MYS III:400/397	796	MYS VIII:1632/1628
715	MYS IV:568/565	756	MYS VI:999/994	797	MYS VIII:1633/1629
716	MYS III:382/379	757	MYS VIII:1570/1566	798	MYS VIII:1634/1630
717	MYS III:383/380	758	MYS VIII:1571/1567	799	MYS VI:1033/1029
718	MYS VI:984/979	759	MYS VIII:1572/1568	800	MYS VI:1036/1032
719	MYS VI:986/981	760	MYS VIII:1573/1569	801	MYS VI:1037/1033
720	MYS VI:987/982	761	MYS XVII:3922/3900	802	MYS VI:1039/1035
721	MYS VI:988/983	762	MYS III:406/403	803	MYS VI:1040/1036
722	MYS VI:998/993	763	MYS III:411/408	804	MYS VIII:1468/1464
723	MYS III:463/460	764	MYS III:417/414	805	MYS IV:770/767
724	MYS III:464/461	765	MYS IV:683/680	806	MYS IV:771/768
725	MYS IV:654/651	766	MYS IV:684/681	807	MYS XVII:4035/4011
726	MYS IV:655/652	767	MYS IV:685/682	808	MYS XVII:4036/4012
727	MYS IV:726/723	768	MYS IV:694/691	809	MYS XVII:4037/4013
728	MYS IV:727/724	769	MYS IV:695/692	810	MYS XVII:4038/4014
729	MYS IV:763/760	770	MYS IV:703/700	811	MYS XVII:4039/4015
730	MYS VIII:1564/1560	771	MYS IV:717/714	812	MYS XVII:4045/4021
731	MYS VIII:1565/1561	772	MYS IV:718/715	813	MYS XVIII:4078/4054
732	MYS IV:686/683	773	MYS IV:719/716	814	MYS XVIII:4118/4094
733	MYS IV:687/684	774	MYS IV:720/717	815	MYS XVIII:4119/4095
734	MYS IV:688/685	775	MYS IV:721/718	816	MYS XVIII:4120/4096
735	MYS IV:689/686	776	MYS IV:722/719	817	MYS XVIII:4121/4097
736	MYS IV:690/687	777	MYS IV:723/720	818	MYS XVIII:4122/4098

819	MYS XVIII:4123/4099	860	MYS I:20	901	MYS IV:641/638
820	MYS XVIII:4124/4100	861	MYS I:21	902	MYS IV:642/639
821	MYS XVIII:4125/4101	862	MYS II:151	903	MYS IV:643/640
822	MYS XVIII:4126/4102	863	MYS II:152	904	MYS IV:644/641
823	MYS XVIII:4127/4103	864	MYS IV:495/492	905	MYS IV:645/642
824	MYS XVIII:4128/4104	865	MYS IV:496/493	906	MYS VIII:1561/1557
825	MYS XVIII:4129/4105	866	MYS IV:497/494	907	MYS VIII:1562/1558
826	MYS XVIII:4135/4111	867	MYS IV:498/495	908	MYS VIII:1563/1559
827	MYS XVIII:4136/4112	868	MYS II:103	909	MYS XV:3600/3578
828	MYS XIX:4163/4139	869	MYS II:104	910	MYS XV:3601/3579
829	MYS XIX:4164/4140	870	MYS I:23	911	MYS XV:3602/3580
830	MYS XIX:4167/4143	871	MYS I:24	912	MYS XV:3603/3581
831	MYS XIX:4170/4146	872	MYS II:107	913	MYS XV:3660/3638
832	MYS XIX:4171/4147	873	MYS II:108	914	MYS XV:3669/3647
833	MYS XIX:4174/4150	874	MYS II:111	915	MYS XV:3670/3648
834	MYS XIX:4180/4156	875	MYS II:112	916	MYS XV:3673/3651
835	MYS XIX:4181/4157	876	MYS II:113	917	MYS XV:3685/3663
836	MYS XIX:4182/4158	877	MYS III:243/242	918	MYS XV:3690/3668
837	MYS XIX:4235/4211	878	MYS III:244/243	919	MYS XV:3691/3669
838	MYS XIX:4236/4212	879	MYS II:117	920	MYS XV:3692/3670
839	MYS XIX:4238/4214	880	MYS II:118	921	MYS XV:3693/3671
840	MYS XIX:4239/4215	881	MYS II:123	922	MYS XV:3694/3672
841	MYS XIX:4240/4216	882	MYS II:124	923	MYS XV:3695/3673
842	MYS XIX:4242/4218	883	MYS II:125	924	MYS XV:3710/3688
843	MYS XIX:4314/4290	884	MYS I:71	925	MYS XV:3711/3689
844	MYS XIX:4315/4291	885	MYS I:72	926	MYS XV:3712/3690
845	MYS XIX:4316/4292	886	MYS III:388/385	927	MYS XV:3726/3704
846	MYS XX:4384/4360	887	MYS III:389/386	928	MYS XV:3727/3705
847	MYS XX:4385/4361	888	MYS III:390/387	929	MYS XV:3738/3716
848	MYS XX:4386/4362	889	MYS III:407/404	930	MYS XV:3739/3717
849	MYS XX:4492/4468	890	MYS III:408/405	931	MYS VI:1018/1013
850	MYS XX:4493/4469	891	MYS III:409/406	932	MYS VI:1019/1014
851	MYS XX:4517/4493	892	MYS IV:630/627	933	MYS VI:1028/1024
852	MYS XX:4536/4512	893	MYS IV:631/628	934	MYS VI:1029/1025
853	MYS XX:4540/4516	894	MYS IV:634/631	935	MYS XV:3745/3723
854	MYS II:141	895	MYS IV:635/632	936	MYS XV:3746/3724
855	MYS II:142	896	MYS IV:636/633	937	MYS XV:3747/3725
856	MYS II:143	897	MYS IV:637/634	938	MYS XV:3748/3726
857	MYS II:144	898	MYS IV:638/635	939	MYS XV:3749/3727
858	MYS II:145	899	MYS IV:639/636	940	MYS XV:3750/3728
859	MYS II:146	900	MYS IV:640/637	941	MYS XV:3751/3729

942	MYS XV:3752/3730	983	MYS XV:3793/3771	1024	MYS V:832/828
943	MYS XV:3753/3731	984	MYS XV:3794/3772	1025	MYS V:833/829
944	MYS XV:3754/3732	985	MYS XV:3795/3773	1026	MYS V:834/830
945	MYS XV:3755/3733	986	MYS XV:3796/3774	1027	MYS V:835/831
946	MYS XV:3756/3734	987	MYS XV:3797/3775	1028	MYS V:836/832
947	MYS XV:3757/3735	988	MYS XV:3798/3776	1029	MYS V:837/833
948	MYS XV:3758/3736	989	MYS XV:3799/3777	1030	MYS V:838/834
949	MYS XV:3759/3737	990	MYS XV:3800/3778	1031	MYS V:839/835
950	MYS XV:3760/3738	991	MYS XV:3801/3779	1032	MYS V:840/836
951	MYS XV:3761/3739	992	MYS XV:3802/3780	1033	MYS V:841/837
952	MYS XV:3762/3740	993	MYS XV:3803/3781	1034	MYS V:842/838
953	MYS XV:3763/3741	994	MYS XV:3804/3782	1035	MYS V:843/839
954	MYS XV:3764/3742	995	MYS XV:3805/3783	1036	MYS V:844/840
955	MYS XV:3765/3743	996	MYS XV:3806/3784	1037	MYS V:845/841
956	MYS XV:3766/3744	997	MYS XV:3807/3785	1038	MYS V:846/842
957	MYS XV:3767/3745	998	MYS XIX:4284/4260	1039	MYS V:847/843
958	MYS XV:3768/3746	999	MYS XIX:4285/4261	1040	MYS V:848/844
959	MYS XV:3769/3747	1000	MYS II:126	1041	MYS V:849/845
960	MYS XV:3770/3748	1001	MYS II:127	1042	MYS V:850/846
961	MYS XV:3771/3749	1002	MYS II:128	1043	MYS V:851/847
962	MYS XV:3772/3750	1003	MYS IV:525/522	1044	MYS V:852/848
963	MYS XV:3773/3751	1004	MYS IV:526/523	1045	MYS V:853/849
964	MYS XV:3774/3752	1005	MYS IV:527/524	1046	MYS V:854/850
965	MYS XV:3775/3753	1006	MYS IV:528/525	1047	MYS V:855/851
966	MYS XV:3776/3754	1007	MYS IV:529/526	1048	MYS V:856/852
967	MYS XV:3777/3755	1008	MYS IV:530/527	1049	MYS V:857/853
968	MYS XV:3778/3756	1009	MYS IV:531/528	1050	MYS V:858/854
969	MYS XV:3779/3757	1010	MYS IV:532/529	1051	MYS V:859/855
970	MYS XV:3780/3758	1011	MYS V:819/815	1052	MYS V:860/856
971	MYS XV:3781/3759	1012	MYS V:820/816	1053	MYS V:861/857
972	MYS XV:3782/3760	1013	MYS V:821/817	1054	MYS V:862/858
973	MYS XV:3783/3761	1014	MYS V:822/818	1055	MYS V:863/859
974	MYS XV:3784/3762	1015	MYS V:823/819	1056	MYS V:864/860
975	MYS XV:3785/3763	1016	MYS V:824/820	1057	MYS V:865/861
976	MYS XV:3786/3764	1017	MYS V:825/821	1058	MYS V:866/862
977	MYS XV:3787/3765	1018	MYS V:826/822	1059	MYS V:867/863
978	MYS XV:3788/3766	1019	MYS V:827/823	1060	MYS V:868/864
979	MYS XV:3789/3767	1020	MYS V:828/824	1061	MYS V:869/865
980	MYS XV:3790/3768	1021	MYS V:829/825	1062	MYS V:870/866
981	MYS XV:3791/3769	1022	MYS V:830/826	1063	MYS V:871/867
982	MYS XV:3792/3770	1023	MYS V:831/827	1064	MYS III:332/329

1065 MYS III:333/330	1106 MYS IV:609/606	1147 MYS VIII:1630/1626
1066 MYS III:334/331	1107 MYS IV:610/607	1148 MYS IV:732/729
1067 MYS III:335/332	1108 MYS IV:611/608	1149 MYS IV:733/730
1068 MYS III:336/333	1109 MYS IV:612/609	1150 MYS IV:734/731
1069 MYS III:337/334	1110 MYS IV:613/610	1151 MYS IV:735/732
1070 MYS III:338/335	1111 MYS IV:614/611	1152 MYS IV:736/733
1071 MYS IV:569/566	1112 MYS IV:615/612	1153 MYS IV:737/734
1072 MYS IV:570/567	1113 MYS IV:649/646	1154 MYS IV:765/762
1073 MYS VI:970/965	1114 MYS IV:650/647	1155 MYS IV:766/763
1074 MYS VI:971/966	1115 MYS IV:651/648	1156 MYS IV:767/764
1075 MYS VI:972/967	1116 MYS IV:652/649	1157 MYS IV:768/765
1076 MYS VI:973/968	1117 MYS IV:656/653	1158 MYS IV:769/766
1077 MYS IV:575/572	1118 MYS IV:657/654	1159 MYS VIII:1637/1633
1078 MYS IV:576/573	1119 MYS IV:659/656	1160 MYS VIII:1638/1634
1079 MYS IV:577/574	1120 MYS IV:660/657	1161 MYS VIII:1639/1635
1080 MYS IV:578/575	1121 MYS IV:661/658	1162 MYS IV:789/786
1081 MYS VIII:1557/1553	1122 MYS IV:662/659	1163 MYS IV:790/787
1082 MYS VIII:1558/1554	1123 MYS IV:663/660	1164 MYS IV:791/788
1083 MYS VIII:1566/1562	1124 MYS IV:664/661	1165 MYS IV:792/789
1084 MYS VIII:1567/1563	1125 MYS III:403/400	1166 MYS IV:793/790
1085 MYS VIII:1568/1564	1126 MYS III:404/401	1167 MYS IV:794/791
1086 MYS VIII:1569/1565	1127 MYS III:405/402	1168 MYS IV:795/792
1087 MYS IV:590/587	1128 MYS III:413/410	1169 MYS XVII:3944/3922
1088 MYS IV:591/588	1129 MYS III:414/411	1170 MYS XVII:3945/3923
1089 MYS IV:592/589	1130 MYS IV:668/665	1171 MYS XVII:3946/3924
1090 MYS IV:593/590	1131 MYS IV:669/666	1172 MYS XVII:3947/3925
1091 MYS IV:594/591	1132 MYS IV:670/667	1173 MYS XVII:3948/3926
1092 MYS IV:595/592	1133 MYS IV:708/705	1174 MYS XVII:3965/3943
1093 MYS IV:596/593	1134 MYS IV:709/706	1175 MYS XVII:3966/3944
1094 MYS IV:597/594	1135 MYS III:465/462	1176 MYS XVII:3967/3945
1095 MYS IV:598/595	1136 MYS III:466/463	1177 MYS XVII:3968/3946
1096 MYS IV:599/596	1137 MYS III:467/464	1178 MYS XVII:3969/3947
1097 MYS IV:600/597	1138 MYS III:468/465	1179 MYS XVII:3970/3948
1098 MYS IV:601/598	1139 MYS III:469/466	1180 MYS XVII:3971/3949
1099 MYS IV:602/599	1140 MYS III:470/467	1181 MYS XVII:3972/3950
1100 MYS IV:603/600	1141 MYS III:471/468	1182 MYS XVII:3984/3962
1101 MYS IV:604/601	1142 MYS III:472/469	1183 MYS XVII:3985/3963
1102 MYS IV:605/602	1143 MYS VIII:1623/1619	1184 MYS XVII:3986/3964
1103 MYS IV:606/603	1144 MYS VIII:1624/1620	1185 MYS XVII:3987/3965
1104 MYS IV:607/604	1145 MYS VIII:1628/1624	1186 MYS XVII:3988/3966
1105 MYS IV:608/605	1146 MYS VIII:1629/1625	1187 MYS XVII:3989/3967

1188	MYS XVII: 3990/3968	1229	MYS XX: 4352/4328	1270	MYS VII: 1111/1107
1189	MYS XVII: 3991/3969	1230	MYS XX: 4353/4329	1271	MYS VII: 1112/1108
1190	MYS XVII: 3992/3970	1231	MYS XX: 4354/4330	1272	MYS VII: 1113/1109
1191	MYS XVII: 3993/3971	1232	MYS XX: 4358/4334	1273	MYS VII: 1115/1111
1192	MYS XVII: 3994/3972	1233	MYS XX: 4359/4335	1274	MYS VII: 1124/1120
1193	MYS XVII: 3995/3972a	1234	MYS XX: 4360/4336	1275	MYS VII: 1133/1129
1194	MYS XVII: 3996/3973	1235	MYS XX: 4361/4337	1276	MYS VII: 1135/1131
1195	MYS XVII: 3997/3974	1236	MYS XX: 4362/4338	1277	MYS VII: 1138/1134
1196	MYS XVII: 3998/3975	1237	MYS XX: 4363/4339	1278	MYS VII: 1171/1167
1197	MYS XVII: 3999/3975a	1238	MYS XX: 4364/4340	1279	MYS VII: 1172/1168
1198	MYS XVII: 4000/3976	1239	MYS XX: 4365/4341	1280	MYS VII: 1179/1176
1199	MYS XVII: 4001/3977	1240	MYS XX: 4366/4342	1281	MYS VII: 1181/1177
1200	MYS XVII: 4015/3991	1241	MYS XX: 4367/4343	1282	MYS VII: 1182/1178
1201	MYS XVII: 4016/3992	1242	MYS XX: 4368/4344	1283	MYS VII: 1183/1179
1202	MYS XVII: 4017/3993	1243	MYS XX: 4369/4345	1284	MYS VII: 1184/1180
1203	MYS XVII: 4018/3994	1244	MYS XX: 4370/4346	1285	MYS VII: 1185/1181
1204	MYS XVII: 4024/4000	1245	MYS I: 50	1286	MYS VII: 1186/1182
1205	MYS XVII: 4025/4001	1246	MYS I: 52	1287	MYS VII: 1187/1183
1206	MYS XVII: 4026/4002	1247	MYS I: 53	1288	MYS VII: 1188/1184
1207	MYS XVII: 4027/4003	1248	MYS I: 74	1289	MYS VII: 1189/1185
1208	MYS XVII: 4028/4004	1249	MYS II: 89	1290	MYS VII: 1190/1186
1209	MYS XVII: 4029/4005	1250	MYS II: 227	1291	MYS VII: 1192/1188
1210	MYS XVII: 4030/4006	1251	MYS III: 391/388	1292	MYS VII: 1193/1189
1211	MYS XVII: 4031/4007	1252	MYS III: 392/389	1293	MYS VII: 1194/1190
1212	MYS XVII: 4032/4008	1253	MYS VI: 1048/1044	1294	MYS VII: 1233/1229
1213	MYS XVII: 4033/4009	1254	MYS VI: 1049/1045	1295	MYS VII: 1248/1244
1214	MYS XVII: 4034/4010	1255	MYS VI: 1050/1046	1296	MYS VII: 1250/1246
1215	MYS XVIII: 4097/4073	1256	MYS VII: 1073/1069	1297	MYS VII: 1260/1256
1216	MYS XVIII: 4098/4074	1257	MYS VII: 1074/1070	1298	MYS VII: 1274/1270
1217	MYS XVIII: 4099/4075	1258	MYS VII: 1075/1071	1299	MYS VII: 1320/1316
1218	MYS XVIII: 4100/4076	1259	MYS VII: 1076/1072	1300	MYS VII: 1321/1317
1219	MYS XVIII: 4101/4077	1260	MYS VII: 1077/1073	1301	MYS VII: 1322/1318
1220	MYS XVIII: 4102/4078	1261	MYS VII: 1080/1076	1302	MYS VII: 1340/1336
1221	MYS XVIII: 4103/4079	1262	MYS VII: 1081/1077	1303	MYS VII: 1356/1352
1222	MYS XX: 4345/4321	1263	MYS VII: 1094/1090	1304	MYS VII: 1357/1353
1223	MYS XX: 4346/4322	1264	MYS VII: 1100/1096	1305	MYS VII: 1373/1369
1224	MYS XX: 4347/4323	1265	MYS VII: 1106/1102	1306	MYS VII: 1378/1374
1225	MYS XX: 4348/4324	1266	MYS VII: 1107/1103	1307	MYS VII: 1379/1375
1226	MYS XX: 4349/4325	1267	MYS VII: 1108/1104	1308	MYS VII: 1384/1380
1227	MYS XX: 4350/4326	1268	MYS VII: 1109/1105	1309	MYS VII: 1398/1394
1228	MYS XX: 4351/4327	1269	MYS VII: 1110/1106	1310	MYS VII: 1399/1395

1311	MYS VII: 1400/1396	1352	MYS X: 2186/2182	1393	MYS XI: 2680/2672
1312	MYS VII: 1401/1397	1353	MYS X: 2187/2183	1394	MYS XI: 2743/2734
1313	MYS VII: 1408/1404	1354	MYS X: 2188/2184	1395	MYS XI: 2763/2753
1314	MYS VII: 1409/1405	1355	MYS X: 2189/2185	1396	MYS XI: 2772/2762
1315	MYS VII: 1410/1406	1356	MYS X: 2190/2186	1397	MYS XI: 2788/2778
1316	MYS VII: 1411/1407	1357	MYS X: 2191/2187	1398	MYS XI: 2789/2779
1317	MYS VII: 1412/1408	1358	MYS X: 2192/2188	1399	MYS XI: 2790/2780
1318	MYS VII: 1413/1409	1359	MYS X: 2193/2189	1400	MYS XI: 2792/2782
1319	MYS VII: 1420/1416	1360	MYS X: 2194/2190	1401	MYS XI: 2798/2788
1320	MYS IX: 1669/1665	1361	MYS X: 2195/2191	1402	MYS XI: 2813/2802a
1321	MYS IX: 1670/1666	1362	MYS X: 2200/2196	1403	MYS XI: 2814/2803
1322	MYS IX: 1717/1713	1363	MYS X: 2206/2202	1404	MYS XI: 2815/2804
1323	MYS IX: 1718/1714	1364	MYS X: 2227/2223	1405	MYS XI: 2816/2805
1324	MYS X: 1833/1829	1365	MYS X: 2255/2251	1406	MYS XI: 2817/2806
1325	MYS X: 1834/1830	1366	MYS X: 2274/2270	1407	MYS XI: 2818/2807
1326	MYS X: 1843/1839	1367	MYS X: 2281/2277	1408	MYS XI: 2819/2808
1327	MYS X: 1882/1878	1368	MYS X: 2297/2293	1409	MYS XI: 2820/2809
1328	MYS X: 1893/1889	1369	MYS X: 2305/2301	1410	MYS XI: 2821/2810
1329	MYS X: 1901/1897	1370	MYS X: 2306/2302	1411	MYS XI: 2822/2811
1330	MYS X: 1903/1899	1371	MYS X: 2307/2303	1412	MYS XI: 2823/2812
1331	MYS X: 1912/1908	1372	MYS X: 2327/2323	1413	MYS XI: 2824/2813
1332	MYS X: 1913/1909	1373	MYS X: 2329/2325	1414	MYS XI: 2825/2814
1333	MYS X: 1919/1915	1374	MYS X: 2334/2330	1415	MYS XI: 2826/2815
1334	MYS X: 1978/1974	1375	MYS X: 2335/2331	1416	MYS XI: 2827/2816
1335	MYS X: 1979/1975	1376	MYS X: 2340/2336	1417	MYS XI: 2828/2817
1336	MYS X: 1980/1976	1377	MYS X: 2341/2337	1418	MYS XI: 2829/2818
1337	MYS X: 1981/1977	1378	MYS X: 2353/2349	1419	MYS XI: 2830/2819
1338	MYS X: 1982/1978	1379	MYS X: 2354/2350	1420	MYS XI: 2831/2820
1339	MYS X: 1983/1979	1380	MYS XI: 2369/2365	1421	MYS XI: 2832/2821
1340	MYS X: 1986/1982	1381	MYS XI: 2529/2524	1422	MYS XI: 2833/2822
1341	MYS X: 1987/1983	1382	MYS XI: 2534/2529	1423	MYS XI: 2834/2823
1342	MYS X: 1991/1987	1383	MYS XI: 2543/2538	1424	MYS XI: 2835/2824
1343	MYS X: 1998/1994	1384	MYS XI: 2545/2540	1425	MYS XI: 2836/2825
1344	MYS X: 2163/2159	1385	MYS XI: 2583/2578	1426	MYS XI: 2839/2828
1345	MYS X: 2165/2161	1386	MYS XI: 2610/2605	1427	MYS XI: 2840/2829
1346	MYS X: 2178/2174	1387	MYS XI: 2613/2608	1428	MYS XI: 2841/2830
1347	MYS X: 2179/2175	1388	MYS XI: 2641/2633	1429	MYS XI: 2842/2831
1348	MYS X: 2180/2176	1389	MYS XI: 2650/2642	1430	MYS XI: 2843/2832
1349	MYS X: 2181/2177	1390	MYS XI: 2657/2649	1431	MYS XI: 2844/2833
1350	MYS X: 2184/2180	1391	MYS XI: 2659/2651	1432	MYS XII: 2879/2867
1351	MYS X: 2185/2181	1392	MYS XI: 2660/2652	1433	MYS XII: 2929/2917

1434	MYS XII: 2949/2937	1475	MYS XIII: 3324/3310	1516	MYS XIV: 3561/3539
1435	MYS XII: 3093/3079	1476	MYS XIII: 3325/3311	1517	MYS XIV: 3570/3548
1436	MYS XII: 3094/3080	1477	MYS XIII: 3326/3312	1518	MYS XIV: 3572/3550
1437	MYS XII: 3095/3081	1478	MYS XIII: 3327/3313	1519	MYS XIV: 3585/3563
1438	MYS XII: 3191/3177	1479	MYS XIII: 3328/3314	1520	MYS XIV: 3589/3567
1439	MYS XII: 3196/3182	1480	MYS XIII: 3329/3315	1521	MYS XIV: 3590/3568
1440	MYS XII: 3197/3183	1481	MYS XIII: 3330/3316	1522	MYS XIV: 3591/3569
1441	MYS XII: 3198/3184	1482	MYS XIII: 3331/3317	1523	MYS XIV: 3592/3570
1442	MYS XII: 3199/3185	1483	MYS XIII: 3338/3324	1524	MYS XIV: 3593/3571
1443	MYS XII: 3200/3186	1484	MYS XIII: 3339/3325	1525	MYS XIV: 3595/3573
1444	MYS XII: 3201/3187	1485	MYS XIII: 3344/3330	1526	MYS XIV: 3598/3576
1445	MYS XII: 3202/3188	1486	MYS XIII: 3345/3331	1527	MYS XIV: 3599/3577
1446	MYS XII: 3217/3203	1487	MYS XIII: 3346/3332	1528	MYS XVI: 3813/3791
1447	MYS XII: 3220/3206	1488	MYS XIV: 3366/3352	1529	MYS XVI: 3814/3792
1448	MYS XIII: 3236/3222	1489	MYS XIV: 3368/3354	1530	MYS XVI: 3815/3793
1449	MYS XIII: 3246/3232	1490	MYS XIV: 3375/3359	1531	MYS XVI: 3816/3794
1450	MYS XIII: 3247/3233	1491	MYS XIV: 3377/3361	1532	MYS XVI: 3817/3795
1451	MYS XIII: 3257/3243	1492	MYS XIV: 3383/3366	1533	MYS XVI: 3818/3796
1452	MYS XIII: 3258/3244	1493	MYS XIV: 3386/3369	1534	MYS XVI: 3819/3797
1453	MYS XIII: 3259/3245	1494	MYS XIV: 3387/3370	1535	MYS XVI: 3820/3798
1454	MYS XIII: 3260/3246	1495	MYS XIV: 3388/3371	1536	MYS XVI: 3821/3799
1455	MYS XIII: 3262/3248	1496	MYS XIV: 3390/3373	1537	MYS XVI: 3822/3800
1456	MYS XIII: 3263/3249	1497	MYS XIV: 3391/3374	1538	MYS XVI: 3823/3801
1457	MYS XIII: 3264/3250	1498	MYS XIV: 3401/3383	1539	MYS XVI: 3824/3802
1458	MYS XIII: 3265/3251	1499	MYS XIV: 3404/3386	1540	MYS XVI: 3826/3804
1459	MYS XIII: 3266/3252	1500	MYS XIV: 3406/3388	1541	MYS XVI: 3827/3805
1460	MYS XIII: 3274/3260	1501	MYS XIV: 3417/3399	1542	MYS XVI: 3828/3806
1461	MYS XIII: 3275/3261	1502	MYS XIV: 3422/3404	1543	MYS XVI: 3829/3807
1462	MYS XIII: 3276/3262	1503	MYS XIV: 3443/3424	1544	MYS XVI: 3832/3810
1463	MYS XIII: 3277/3263	1504	MYS XIV: 3446/3427	1545	MYS XVI: 3833/3811
1464	MYS XIII: 3278/3264	1505	MYS XIV: 3448/3429	1546	MYS XVI: 3834/3812
1465	MYS XIII: 3279/3265	1506	MYS XIV: 3449/3430	1547	MYS XVI: 3835/3813
1466	MYS XIII: 3282/3268	1507	MYS XIV: 3450/3431	1548	MYS XVI: 3844/3822
1467	MYS XIII: 3283/3269	1508	MYS XIV: 3454/3435	1549	MYS XVI: 3845/3823
1468	MYS XIII: 3307/3293	1509	MYS XIV: 3456/3437	1550	MYS XVI: 3893/3871
1469	MYS XIII: 3308/3294	1510	MYS XIV: 3458/3439	1551	MYS XVI: 3894/3872
1470	MYS XIII: 3316/3302	1511	MYS XIV: 3459/3440	1552	MYS XVI: 3895/3873
1471	MYS XIII: 3319/3305	1512	MYS XIV: 3478/3459	1553	MYS XVI: 3896/3874
1472	MYS XIII: 3320/3306	1513	MYS XIV: 3488/3469	1554	MYS XVI: 3900/3878
1473	MYS XIII: 3321/3307	1514	MYS XIV: 3491/3472	1555	MYS XVI: 3907/3885
1474	MYS XIII: 3322/3308	1515	MYS XIV: 3550/3529	1556	MYS XVI: 3908/3886

884

1557	MYS XVI:3909/3887	1565	BSS 6	1573	BSS 15
1558	MYS XVI:3910/3888	1566	BSS 7	1574	BSS 16
1559	MYS XVI:3911/3889	1567	BSS 8	1575	BSS 17
1560	BSS 1	1568	BSS 9	1576	BSS 18
1561	BSS 2	1569	BSS 10	1577	BSS 19
1562	BSS 3	1570	BSS 12	1578	BSS 20
1563	BSS 4	1571	BSS 13		
1564	BSS 5	1572	BSS 14		

Conversion Table 2:
Source Number to Anthology Number

NIHONSHOKI			NS 75	145		NS 109	177
			NS 76	146		NS 110	178
NS 3	114		NS 77	147		NS 111	179
NS 4	115		NS 78	148		NS 112	180
NS 10	116		NS 79	149		NS 113	181
NS 11	117		NS 80	150		NS 114	182
NS 15	118		NS 81	151		NS 115	183
NS 16	119		NS 82	152		NS 116	184
NS 17	120		NS 83	153		NS 117	185
NS 18	121		NS 84	154		NS 118	186
NS 19	122		NS 85	155		NS 119	187
NS 24	123		NS 86	156		NS 120	188
NS 28	124		NS 87	157		NS 121	189
NS 30	125		NS 90	158		NS 122	190
NS 31	126		NS 91	159		NS 123	191
NS 40	127		NS 92	160		NS 124	192
NS 44	128		NS 93	161		NS 125	193
NS 45	129		NS 94	162		NS 126	194
NS 46	130		NS 95	163		NS 127	195
NS 47	131		NS 96	164		NS 128	196
NS 48	132		NS 97	165		NS 129	197
NS 49	133		NS 98	166		NS 130	198
NS 50	134		NS 99	167		NS 131	199
NS 51	135		NS 100	168			
NS 56	136		NS 101	169		FUDOKI	
NS 59	137		NS 102	170			
NS 60	138		NS 103	171		F 1	200
NS 61	139		NS 104	172		F 2	201
NS 65	140		NS 105	173		F 3	202
NS 66	141		NS 106	174		F 4	203
NS 67	142		NS 107	175		F 5	204
NS 68	143		NS 108	176		F 6	205
NS 74	144					F 7	206

F 8	207		MYS I:14	251		MYS I:59	466
F 9	208		MYS I:15	252		MYS I:60	460
F 10	209		MYS I:16	256		MYS I:61	476
F 11	210		MYS I:17	257		MYS I:62	470
F 12	211		MYS I:18	258		MYS I:63	619
F 13	212		MYS I:19	260		MYS I:64	468
F 14	213		MYS I:20	860		MYS I:65	461
F 15	214		MYS I:21	861		MYS I:66	469
F 16	215		MYS I:22	266		MYS I:68	504
F 17	216		MYS I:23	870		MYS I:69	463
F 18	217		MYS I:24	871		MYS I:70	446
F 19	218		MYS I:25	263		MYS I:71	884
F 20	219		MYS I:27	264		MYS I:72	885
F 21	220		MYS I:28	285		MYS I:73	462
F 22	221		MYS I:29	288		MYS I:74	1248
F 23	222		MYS I:30	289		MYS I:75	505
			MYS I:31	290		MYS I:76	475
SHOKU NIHONGI			MYS I:32	457			
			MYS I:33	458		MYS II:85	231
SN 1	223		MYS I:34	278		MYS II:86	232
SN 2	224		MYS I:35	474		MYS II:87	233
SN 3	225		MYS I:36	293		MYS II:88	234
SN 4	226		MYS I:37	294		MYS II:89	1249
SN 5	227		MYS I:38	295		MYS II:103	868
SN 6	228		MYS I:39	296		MYS II:104	869
SN 7	229		MYS I:40	311		MYS II:105	272
SN 8	230		MYS I:41	312		MYS II:106	273
			MYS I:42	313		MYS II:107	872
MAN'YŌSHŪ			MYS I:43	459		MYS II:108	873
			MYS I:44	473		MYS II:109	269
MYS I:1	236		MYS I:45	331		MYS II:110	271
MYS I:2	238		MYS I:46	332		MYS II:111	874
MYS I:3	245		MYS I:47	333		MYS II:112	875
MYS I:4	246		MYS I:48	334		MYS II:113	876
MYS I:5	240		MYS I:49	335		MYS II:114	481
MYS I:6	241		MYS I:50	1245		MYS II:115	482
MYS I:7	254		MYS I:51	467		MYS II:116	483
MYS I:8	255		MYS I:52	1246		MYS II:117	879
MYS I:10	247		MYS I:53	1247		MYS II:118	880
MYS I:11	248		MYS I:57	488		MYS II:119	279
MYS I:12	249		MYS I:58	445		MYS II:120	280
MYS I:13	250						

MYS II:121	281		MYS II:201	343		MYS III:256/255	309
MYS II:122	282		MYS II:202	344		MYS III:257/256	310
MYS II:123	881		MYS II:203	484		MYS III:263/261	299
MYS II:124	882		MYS II:207	345		MYS III:264/262	300
MYS II:125	883		MYS II:208	346		MYS III:266/264	292
MYS II:126	1000		MYS II:209	347		MYS III:267/265	490
MYS II:127	1001		MYS II:210	348		MYS III:268/266	291
MYS II:128	1002		MYS II:211	349		MYS III:272/270	447
MYS II:131	321		MYS II:212	350		MYS III:273/271	448
MYS II:132	322		MYS II:217	351		MYS III:274/272	449
MYS II:133	323		MYS II:218	352		MYS III:275/273	450
MYS II:134	324		MYS II:219	353		MYS III:276/274	451
MYS II:135	325		MYS II:220	358		MYS III:277/275	452
MYS II:136	326		MYS II:221	359		MYS III:278/276	453
MYS II:137	327		MYS II:222	360		MYS III:279/276a	454
MYS II:141	854		MYS II:223	361		MYS III:280/277	455
MYS II:142	855		MYS II:224	362		MYS III:285/282	471
MYS II:143	856		MYS II:225	363		MYS III:287/284	472
MYS II:144	857		MYS II:226	364		MYS III:292/289	477
MYS II:145	858		MYS II:227	1250		MYS III:293/290	478
MYS II:146	859		MYS II:228	443		MYS III:308/305	456
MYS II:148	261		MYS II:229	444		MYS III:313/310	670
MYS II:149	262		MYS II:230	516		MYS III:316/313	502
MYS II:151	862		MYS II:231	517		MYS III:318/315	589
MYS II:152	863		MYS II:232	518		MYS III:319/316	590
MYS II:160	286		MYS II:233	519		MYS III:320/317	537
MYS II:161	287		MYS II:234	520		MYS III:321/318	538
MYS II:163	274					MYS III:322/319	569
MYS II:164	275		MYS III:235	297		MYS III:323/320	570
MYS II:165	276		MYS III:236/235a	298		MYS III:324/321	571
MYS II:166	277		MYS III:239/238	489		MYS III:325/322	539
MYS II:167	328		MYS III:240/239	301		MYS III:326/323	540
MYS II:168	329		MYS III:241/240	302		MYS III:327/324	541
MYS II:169	330		MYS III:242/241	303		MYS III:328/325	542
MYS II:194	336		MYS III:243/242	877		MYS III:329/326	671
MYS II:195	337		MYS III:244/243	878		MYS III:331/328	660
MYS II:196	338		MYS III:251/250	304		MYS III:332/329	1064
MYS II:197	339		MYS III:252/251	305		MYS III:333/330	1065
MYS II:198	340		MYS III:253/252	306		MYS III:334/331	1066
MYS II:199	341		MYS III:254/253	307		MYS III:335/332	1067
MYS II:200	342		MYS III:255/254	308		MYS III:336/333	1068

MYS III: 337/334	1069	MYS III: 388/385	886	MYS III: 468/465	1138
MYS III: 338/335	1070	MYS III: 389/386	887	MYS III: 469/466	1139
MYS III: 339/336	608	MYS III: 390/387	888	MYS III: 470/467	1140
MYS III: 340/337	626	MYS III: 391/388	1251	MYS III: 471/468	1141
MYS III: 341/338	592	MYS III: 392/389	1252	MYS III: 472/469	1142
MYS III: 342/339	593	MYS III: 393/390	265	MYS III: 484/481	693
MYS III: 343/340	594	MYS III: 394/391	609	MYS III: 485/482	694
MYS III: 344/341	595	MYS III: 395/392	612	MYS III: 486/483	695
MYS III: 345/342	596	MYS III: 396/393	610		
MYS III: 346/343	597	MYS III: 397/394	617	MYS IV: 487/484	235
MYS III: 347/344	598	MYS III: 398/395	753	MYS IV: 488/485	242
MYS III: 348/345	599	MYS III: 399/396	754	MYS IV: 489/486	243
MYS III: 349/346	600	MYS III: 400/397	755	MYS IV: 490/487	244
MYS III: 350/347	601	MYS III: 401/398	708	MYS IV: 491/488	259
MYS III: 351/348	602	MYS III: 402/399	709	MYS IV: 493/490	267
MYS III: 352/349	603	MYS III: 403/400	1125	MYS IV: 494/491	268
MYS III: 353/350	604	MYS III: 404/401	1126	MYS IV: 495/492	864
MYS III: 354/351	611	MYS III: 405/402	1127	MYS IV: 496/493	865
MYS III: 360/357	543	MYS III: 406/403	762	MYS IV: 497/494	866
MYS III: 361/358	544	MYS III: 407/404	889	MYS IV: 498/495	867
MYS III: 362/359	545	MYS III: 408/405	890	MYS IV: 499/496	314
MYS III: 363/360	546	MYS III: 409/406	891	MYS IV: 500/497	315
MYS III: 364/361	547	MYS III: 411/408	763	MYS IV: 501/498	316
MYS III: 365/362	548	MYS III: 413/410	1128	MYS IV: 502/499	317
MYS III: 367/364	521	MYS III: 414/411	1129	MYS IV: 504/501	318
MYS III: 368/365	522	MYS III: 416/413	662	MYS IV: 505/502	319
MYS III: 369/366	523	MYS III: 417/414	764	MYS IV: 506/503	320
MYS III: 370/367	524	MYS III: 418/415	237	MYS IV: 511/508	499
MYS III: 374/371	672	MYS III: 419/416	270	MYS IV: 512/509	464
MYS III: 375/372	549	MYS III: 429/426	357	MYS IV: 513/510	465
MYS III: 376/373	550	MYS III: 431/428	354	MYS IV: 525/522	1003
MYS III: 378/375	663	MYS III: 432/429	355	MYS IV: 526/523	1004
MYS III: 379/376	664	MYS III: 433/430	356	MYS IV: 527/524	1005
MYS III: 380/377	665	MYS III: 434/431	553	MYS IV: 528/525	1006
MYS III: 381/378	551	MYS III: 435/432	554	MYS IV: 529/526	1007
MYS III: 382/379	716	MYS III: 436/433	555	MYS IV: 530/527	1008
MYS III: 383/380	717	MYS III: 463/460	723	MYS IV: 531/528	1009
MYS III: 384/381	607	MYS III: 464/461	724	MYS IV: 532/529	1010
MYS III: 385/382	704	MYS III: 465/462	1135	MYS IV: 537/534	507
MYS III: 386/383	705	MYS III: 466/463	1136	MYS IV: 538/535	508
MYS III: 387/384	552	MYS III: 467/464	1137	MYS IV: 539/536	673

MYS IV:555/552	712	MYS IV:613/610	1110	MYS IV:684/681	766
MYS IV:559/556	714	MYS IV:614/611	1111	MYS IV:685/682	767
MYS IV:562/559	613	MYS IV:615/612	1112	MYS IV:686/683	732
MYS IV:563/560	614	MYS IV:629/626	700	MYS IV:687/684	733
MYS IV:564/561	615	MYS IV:630/627	892	MYS IV:688/685	734
MYS IV:565/562	616	MYS IV:631/628	893	MYS IV:689/686	735
MYS IV:568/565	715	MYS IV:632/629	606	MYS IV:690/687	736
MYS IV:569/566	1071	MYS IV:634/631	894	MYS IV:691/688	737
MYS IV:570/567	1072	MYS IV:635/632	895	MYS IV:692/689	738
MYS IV:574/571	605	MYS IV:636/633	896	MYS IV:694/691	768
MYS IV:575/572	1077	MYS IV:637/634	897	MYS IV:695/692	769
MYS IV:576/573	1078	MYS IV:638/635	898	MYS IV:700/697	711
MYS IV:577/574	1079	MYS IV:639/636	899	MYS IV:703/700	770
MYS IV:578/575	1080	MYS IV:640/637	900	MYS IV:708/705	1133
MYS IV:584/581	749	MYS IV:641/638	901	MYS IV:709/706	1134
MYS IV:585/582	750	MYS IV:642/639	902	MYS IV:713/710	669
MYS IV:586/583	751	MYS IV:643/640	903	MYS IV:717/714	771
MYS IV:587/584	752	MYS IV:644/641	904	MYS IV:718/715	772
MYS IV:590/587	1087	MYS IV:645/642	905	MYS IV:719/716	773
MYS IV:591/588	1088	MYS IV:646/643	509	MYS IV:720/717	774
MYS IV:592/589	1089	MYS IV:647/644	510	MYS IV:721/718	775
MYS IV:593/590	1090	MYS IV:648/645	511	MYS IV:722/719	776
MYS IV:594/591	1091	MYS IV:649/646	1113	MYS IV:723/720	777
MYS IV:595/592	1092	MYS IV:650/647	1114	MYS IV:724/721	740
MYS IV:596/593	1093	MYS IV:651/648	1115	MYS IV:726/723	727
MYS IV:597/594	1094	MYS IV:652/649	1116	MYS IV:727/724	728
MYS IV:598/595	1095	MYS IV:653/650	713	MYS IV:728/725	741
MYS IV:599/596	1096	MYS IV:654/651	725	MYS IV:729/726	742
MYS IV:600/597	1097	MYS IV:655/652	726	MYS IV:730/727	778
MYS IV:601/598	1098	MYS IV:656/653	1117	MYS IV:731/728	779
MYS IV:602/599	1099	MYS IV:657/654	1118	MYS IV:732/729	1148
MYS IV:603/600	1100	MYS IV:659/656	1119	MYS IV:733/730	1149
MYS IV:604/601	1101	MYS IV:660/657	1120	MYS IV:734/731	1150
MYS IV:605/602	1102	MYS IV:661/658	1121	MYS IV:735/732	1151
MYS IV:606/603	1103	MYS IV:662/659	1122	MYS IV:736/733	1152
MYS IV:607/604	1104	MYS IV:663/660	1123	MYS IV:737/734	1153
MYS IV:608/605	1105	MYS IV:664/661	1124	MYS IV:744/741	780
MYS IV:609/606	1106	MYS IV:668/665	1130	MYS IV:745/742	781
MYS IV:610/607	1107	MYS IV:669/666	1131	MYS IV:746/743	782
MYS IV:611/608	1108	MYS IV:670/667	1132	MYS IV:747/744	783
MYS IV:612/609	1109	MYS IV:683/680	765	MYS IV:748/745	784

MYS IV:749/746	785	MYS V:824/820	1016	MYS V:865/861	1057
MYS IV:750/747	786	MYS V:825/821	1017	MYS V:866/862	1058
MYS IV:751/748	787	MYS V:826/822	1018	MYS V:867/863	1059
MYS IV:752/749	788	MYS V:827/823	1019	MYS V:868/864	1060
MYS IV:753/750	789	MYS V:828/824	1020	MYS V:869/865	1061
MYS IV:754/751	790	MYS V:829/825	1021	MYS V:870/866	1062
MYS IV:755/752	791	MYS V:830/826	1022	MYS V:871/867	1063
MYS IV:756/753	792	MYS V:831/827	1023	MYS V:896/892	634
MYS IV:757/754	793	MYS V:832/828	1024	MYS V:897/893	635
MYS IV:758/755	794	MYS V:833/829	1025	MYS V:898/894	636
MYS IV:759/756	743	MYS V:834/830	1026	MYS V:899/895	637
MYS IV:760/757	744	MYS V:835/831	1027	MYS V:900/896	638
MYS IV:761/758	745	MYS V:836/832	1028	MYS V:901/896a	639
MYS IV:762/759	746	MYS V:837/833	1029	MYS V:902/897	640
MYS IV:763/760	729	MYS V:838/834	1030	MYS V:903/898	641
MYS IV:765/762	1154	MYS V:839/835	1031	MYS V:904/899	642
MYS IV:766/763	1155	MYS V:840/836	1032	MYS V:905/900	643
MYS IV:767/764	1156	MYS V:841/837	1033	MYS V:906/901	644
MYS IV:768/765	1157	MYS V:842/838	1034	MYS V:907/902	645
MYS IV:769/766	1158	MYS V:843/839	1035	MYS V:908/903	646
MYS IV:770/767	805	MYS V:844/840	1036	MYS V:909/904	629
MYS IV:771/768	806	MYS V:845/841	1037	MYS V:910/905	630
MYS IV:789/786	1162	MYS V:846/842	1038	MYS V:911/906	631
MYS IV:790/787	1163	MYS V:847/843	1039		
MYS IV:791/788	1164	MYS V:848/844	1040	MYS VI:912/907	525
MYS IV:792/789	1165	MYS V:849/845	1041	MYS VI:913/908	526
MYS IV:793/790	1166	MYS V:850/846	1042	MYS VI:914/909	527
MYS IV:794/791	1167	MYS V:851/847	1043	MYS VI:915/910	528
MYS IV:795/792	1168	MYS V:852/848	1044	MYS VI:916/911	529
		MYS V:853/849	1045	MYS VI:917/912	530
MYS V:804/800	624	MYS V:854/850	1046	MYS VI:918/913	512
MYS V:805/801	625	MYS V:855/851	1047	MYS VI:919/914	513
MYS V:806/802	627	MYS V:856/852	1048	MYS VI:920/915	514
MYS V:807/803	628	MYS V:857/853	1049	MYS VI:921/916	515
MYS V:808/804	632	MYS V:858/854	1050	MYS VI:922/917	556
MYS V:809/805	633	MYS V:859/855	1051	MYS VI:923/918	557
MYS V:819/815	1011	MYS V:860/856	1052	MYS VI:924/919	558
MYS V:820/816	1012	MYS V:861/857	1053	MYS VI:925/920	531
MYS V:821/817	1013	MYS V:862/858	1054	MYS VI:926/921	532
MYS V:822/818	1014	MYS V:863/859	1055	MYS VI:927/922	533
MYS V:823/819	1015	MYS V:864/860	1056	MYS VI:928/923	559

MYS VI:929/924	560	MYS VI:1048/1044	1253	MYS VII:1115/1111	1273
MYS VI:930/925	561	MYS VI:1049/1045	1254	MYS VII:1124/1120	1274
MYS VI:931/926	562	MYS VI:1050/1046	1255	MYS VII:1133/1129	1275
MYS VI:932/927	563	MYS VI:1051/1047	674	MYS VII:1135/1131	1276
MYS VI:940/935	534	MYS VI:1052/1048	675	MYS VII:1138/1134	1277
MYS VI:941/936	535	MYS VI:1053/1049	676	MYS VII:1171/1167	1278
MYS VI:942/937	536	MYS VI:1054/1050	677	MYS VII:1172/1168	1279
MYS VI:965/960	591	MYS VI:1055/1051	678	MYS VII:1179/1176	1280
MYS VI:970/965	1073	MYS VI:1056/1052	679	MYS VII:1181/1177	1281
MYS VI:971/966	1074	MYS VI:1057/1053	680	MYS VII:1182/1178	1282
MYS VI:972/967	1075	MYS VI:1058/1054	681	MYS VII:1183/1179	1283
MYS VI:973/968	1076	MYS VI:1059/1055	682	MYS VII:1184/1180	1284
MYS VI:976/971	581	MYS VI:1060/1056	683	MYS VII:1185/1181	1285
MYS VI:977/972	582	MYS VI:1061/1057	684	MYS VII:1186/1182	1286
MYS VI:978/973	698	MYS VI:1062/1058	685	MYS VII:1187/1183	1287
MYS VI:979/974	699	MYS VI:1063/1059	686	MYS VII:1188/1184	1288
MYS VI:980/975	618	MYS VI:1064/1060	687	MYS VII:1189/1185	1289
MYS VI:981/976	658	MYS VI:1065/1061	688	MYS VII:1190/1186	1290
MYS VI:982/977	659	MYS VI:1069/1065	689	MYS VII:1191/1187	367
MYS VI:983/978	647	MYS VI:1070/1066	690	MYS VII:1192/1188	1291
MYS VI:984/979	718	MYS VI:1071/1067	691	MYS VII:1193/1189	1292
MYS VI:985/980	696			MYS VII:1194/1190	1293
MYS VI:986/981	719	MYS VII:1072/1068	365	MYS VII:1233/1229	1294
MYS VI:987/982	720	MYS VII:1073/1069	1256	MYS VII:1248/1244	1295
MYS VI:988/983	721	MYS VII:1074/1070	1257	MYS VII:1250/1246	1296
MYS VI:989/984	668	MYS VII:1075/1071	1258	MYS VII:1260/1256	1297
MYS VI:990/985	666	MYS VII:1076/1072	1259	MYS VII:1273/1269	368
MYS VI:991/986	667	MYS VII:1077/1073	1260	MYS VII:1274/1270	1298
MYS VI:998/993	722	MYS VII:1080/1076	1261	MYS VII:1286/1282	369
MYS VI:999/994	756	MYS VII:1081/1077	1262	MYS VII:1287/1283	370
MYS VI:1001/996	661	MYS VII:1094/1090	1263	MYS VII:1288/1284	371
MYS VI:1006/1001	564	MYS VII:1100/1096	1264	MYS VII:1298/1294	372
MYS VI:1018/1013	931	MYS VII:1105/1101	366	MYS VII:1303/1299	373
MYS VI:1019/1014	932	MYS VII:1106/1102	1265	MYS VII:1320/1316	1299
MYS VI:1028/1024	933	MYS VII:1107/1103	1266	MYS VII:1321/1317	1300
MYS VI:1029/1025	934	MYS VII:1108/1104	1267	MYS VII:1322/1318	1301
MYS VI:1033/1029	799	MYS VII:1109/1105	1268	MYS VII:1340/1336	1302
MYS VI:1036/1032	800	MYS VII:1110/1106	1269	MYS VII:1356/1352	1303
MYS VI:1037/1033	801	MYS VII:1111/1107	1270	MYS VII:1357/1353	1304
MYS VI:1039/1035	802	MYS VII:1112/1108	1271	MYS VII:1373/1369	1305
MYS VI:1040/1036	803	MYS VII:1113/1109	1272	MYS VII:1378/1374	1306

MYS VII: 1379/1375	1307	MYS VIII: 1568/1564	1085	MYS IX: 1711/1707	388
MYS VII: 1384/1380	1308	MYS VIII: 1569/1565	1086	MYS IX: 1712/1708	389
MYS VII: 1398/1394	1309	MYS VIII: 1570/1566	757	MYS IX: 1713/1709	390
MYS VII: 1399/1395	1310	MYS VIII: 1571/1567	758	MYS IX: 1717/1713	1322
MYS VII: 1400/1396	1311	MYS VIII: 1572/1568	759	MYS IX: 1718/1714	1323
MYS VII: 1401/1397	1312	MYS VIII: 1573/1569	760	MYS IX: 1724/1720	391
MYS VII: 1408/1404	1313	MYS VIII: 1594/1590	703	MYS IX: 1725/1721	392
MYS VII: 1409/1405	1314	MYS VIII: 1612/1608	284	MYS IX: 1726/1722	393
MYS VII: 1410/1406	1315	MYS VIII: 1623/1619	1143	MYS IX: 1727/1723	394
MYS VII: 1411/1407	1316	MYS VIII: 1624/1620	1144	MYS IX: 1728/1724	395
MYS VII: 1412/1408	1317	MYS VIII: 1626/1622	747	MYS IX: 1729/1725	396
MYS VII: 1413/1409	1318	MYS VIII: 1627/1623	748	MYS IX: 1742/1738	577
MYS VII: 1420/1416	1319	MYS VIII: 1628/1624	1145	MYS IX: 1743/1739	578
		MYS VIII: 1629/1625	1146	MYS IX: 1744/1740	579
MYS VIII: 1428/1424	565	MYS VIII: 1630/1626	1147	MYS IX: 1745/1741	580
MYS VIII: 1429/1425	566	MYS VIII: 1631/1627	795	MYS IX: 1751/1747	583
MYS VIII: 1430/1426	567	MYS VIII: 1632/1628	796	MYS IX: 1752/1748	584
MYS VIII: 1431/1427	568	MYS VIII: 1633/1629	797	MYS IX: 1761/1757	585
MYS VIII: 1444/1440	710	MYS VIII: 1634/1630	798	MYS IX: 1762/1758	586
MYS VIII: 1454/1450	739	MYS VIII: 1637/1633	1159	MYS IX: 1763/1759	587
MYS VIII: 1468/1464	804	MYS VIII: 1638/1634	1160	MYS IX: 1764/1760	588
MYS VIII: 1471/1467	283	MYS VIII: 1639/1635	1161	MYS IX: 1804/1800	692
MYS VIII: 1474/1470	503			MYS IX: 1811/1807	572
MYS VIII: 1515/1511	239	MYS IX: 1669/1665	1320	MYS IX: 1812/1808	573
MYS VIII: 1517/1513	485	MYS IX: 1670/1666	1321	MYS IX: 1813/1809	574
MYS VIII: 1518/1514	486	MYS IX: 1689/1685	479	MYS IX: 1814/1810	575
MYS VIII: 1522/1518	620	MYS IX: 1690/1686	480	MYS IX: 1815/1811	576
MYS VIII: 1531/1527	621	MYS IX: 1697/1693	374		
MYS VIII: 1532/1528	622	MYS IX: 1698/1694	375	MYS X: 1816/1812	397
MYS VIII: 1533/1529	623	MYS IX: 1699/1695	376	MYS X: 1833/1829	1324
MYS VIII: 1557/1553	1081	MYS IX: 1700/1696	377	MYS X: 1834/1830	1325
MYS VIII: 1558/1554	1082	MYS IX: 1701/1697	378	MYS X: 1843/1839	1326
MYS VIII: 1559/1555	506	MYS IX: 1702/1698	379	MYS X: 1882/1878	1327
MYS VIII: 1560/1556	706	MYS IX: 1703/1699	380	MYS X: 1893/1889	1328
MYS VIII: 1561/1557	906	MYS IX: 1704/1700	381	MYS X: 1901/1897	1329
MYS VIII: 1562/1558	907	MYS IX: 1705/1701	382	MYS X: 1903/1899	1330
MYS VIII: 1563/1559	908	MYS IX: 1706/1702	383	MYS X: 1912/1908	1331
MYS VIII: 1564/1560	730	MYS IX: 1707/1703	384	MYS X: 1913/1909	1332
MYS VIII: 1565/1561	731	MYS IX: 1708/1704	385	MYS X: 1919/1915	1333
MYS VIII: 1566/1562	1083	MYS IX: 1709/1705	386	MYS X: 1978/1974	1334
MYS VIII: 1567/1563	1084	MYS IX: 1710/1706	387	MYS X: 1979/1975	1335

MYS X:1980/1976	1336	MYS X:2334/2330	1374	MYS XI:2583/2578	1385
MYS X:1981/1977	1337	MYS X:2335/2331	1375	MYS XI:2610/2605	1386
MYS X:1982/1978	1338	MYS X:2340/2336	1376	MYS XI:2613/2608	1387
MYS X:1983/1979	1339	MYS X:2341/2337	1377	MYS XI:2641/2633	1388
MYS X:1986/1982	1340	MYS X:2353/2349	1378	MYS XI:2650/2642	1389
MYS X:1987/1983	1341	MYS X:2354/2350	1379	MYS XI:2657/2649	1390
MYS X:1991/1987	1342			MYS XI:2659/2651	1391
MYS X:1998/1994	1343	MYS XI:2355/2351	401	MYS XI:2660/2652	1392
MYS X:2004/2000	398	MYS XI:2356/2352	402	MYS XI:2680/2672	1393
MYS X:2163/2159	1344	MYS XI:2357/2353	403	MYS XI:2743/2734	1394
MYS X:2165/2161	1345	MYS XI:2358/2354	404	MYS XI:2763/2753	1395
MYS X:2178/2174	1346	MYS XI:2359/2355	405	MYS XI:2772/2762	1396
MYS X:2179/2175	1347	MYS XI:2360/2356	406	MYS XI:2788/2778	1397
MYS X:2180/2176	1348	MYS XI:2361/2357	407	MYS XI:2789/2779	1398
MYS X:2181/2177	1349	MYS XI:2366/2362	408	MYS XI:2790/2780	1399
MYS X:2182/2178	399	MYS XI:2369/2365	1380	MYS XI:2792/2782	1400
MYS X:2183/2179	400	MYS XI:2372/2368	409	MYS XI:2798/2788	1401
MYS X:2184/2180	1350	MYS XI:2373/2369	410	MYS XI:2813/2802a	1402
MYS X:2185/2181	1351	MYS XI:2374/2370	411	MYS XI:2814/2803	1403
MYS X:2186/2182	1352	MYS XI:2375/2371	412	MYS XI:2815/2804	1404
MYS X:2187/2183	1353	MYS XI:2376/2372	413	MYS XI:2816/2805	1405
MYS X:2188/2184	1354	MYS XI:2377/2373	414	MYS XI:2817/2806	1406
MYS X:2189/2185	1355	MYS XI:2378/2374	415	MYS XI:2818/2807	1407
MYS X:2190/2186	1356	MYS XI:2381/2377	416	MYS XI:2819/2808	1408
MYS X:2191/2187	1357	MYS XI:2394/2390	417	MYS XI:2820/2809	1409
MYS X:2192/2188	1358	MYS XI:2405/2401	418	MYS XI:2821/2810	1410
MYS X:2193/2189	1359	MYS XI:2419/2415	419	MYS XI:2822/2811	1411
MYS X:2194/2190	1360	MYS XI:2420/2416	420	MYS XI:2823/2812	1412
MYS X:2195/2191	1361	MYS XI:2421/2417	421	MYS XI:2824/2813	1413
MYS X:2200/2196	1362	MYS XI:2422/2418	422	MYS XI:2825/2814	1414
MYS X:2206/2202	1363	MYS XI:2423/2419	423	MYS XI:2826/2815	1415
MYS X:2227/2223	1364	MYS XI:2424/2420	424	MYS XI:2827/2816	1416
MYS X:2255/2251	1365	MYS XI:2425/2421	425	MYS XI:2828/2817	1417
MYS X:2274/2270	1366	MYS XI:2426/2422	426	MYS XI:2829/2818	1418
MYS X:2281/2277	1367	MYS XI:2441/2437	427	MYS XI:2830/2819	1419
MYS X:2297/2293	1368	MYS XI:2444/2440	428	MYS XI:2831/2820	1420
MYS X:2305/2301	1369	MYS XI:2487/2483	429	MYS XI:2832/2821	1421
MYS X:2306/2302	1370	MYS XI:2529/2524	1381	MYS XI:2833/2822	1422
MYS X:2307/2303	1371	MYS XI:2534/2529	1382	MYS XI:2834/2823	1423
MYS X:2327/2323	1372	MYS XI:2543/2538	1383	MYS XI:2835/2824	1424
MYS X:2329/2325	1373	MYS XI:2545/2540	1384	MYS XI:2836/2825	1425

MYS XI: 2839/2828	1426	MYS XIII: 3279/3265	1465	MYS XIV: 3446/3427	1504
MYS XI: 2840/2829	1427	MYS XIII: 3282/3268	1466	MYS XIV: 3448/3429	1505
MYS XI: 2841/2830	1428	MYS XIII: 3283/3269	1467	MYS XIV: 3449/3430	1506
MYS XI: 2842/2831	1429	MYS XIII: 3307/3293	1468	MYS XIV: 3450/3431	1507
MYS XI: 2843/2832	1430	MYS XIII: 3308/3294	1469	MYS XIV: 3454/3435	1508
MYS XI: 2844/2833	1431	MYS XIII: 3316/3302	1470	MYS XIV: 3456/3437	1509
		MYS XIII: 3319/3305	1471	MYS XIV: 3458/3439	1510
MYS XII: 2879/2867	1432	MYS XIII: 3320/3306	1472	MYS XIV: 3459/3440	1511
MYS XII: 2929/2917	1433	MYS XIII: 3321/3307	1473	MYS XIV: 3478/3459	1512
MYS XII: 2949/2937	1434	MYS XIII: 3322/3308	1474	MYS XIV: 3488/3469	1513
MYS XII: 3093/3079	1435	MYS XIII: 3323/3309	430	MYS XIV: 3491/3472	1514
MYS XII: 3094/3080	1436	MYS XIII: 3324/3310	1475	MYS XIV: 3550/3529	1515
MYS XII: 3095/3081	1437	MYS XIII: 3325/3311	1476	MYS XIV: 3561/3539	1516
MYS XII: 3191/3177	1438	MYS XIII: 3326/3312	1477	MYS XIV: 3570/3548	1517
MYS XII: 3196/3182	1439	MYS XIII: 3327/3313	1478	MYS XIV: 3572/3550	1518
MYS XII: 3197/3183	1440	MYS XIII: 3328/3314	1479	MYS XIV: 3585/3563	1519
MYS XII: 3198/3184	1441	MYS XIII: 3329/3315	1480	MYS XIV: 3589/3567	1520
MYS XII: 3199/3185	1442	MYS XIII: 3330/3316	1481	MYS XIV: 3590/3568	1521
MYS XII: 3200/3186	1443	MYS XIII: 3331/3317	1482	MYS XIV: 3591/3569	1522
MYS XII: 3201/3187	1444	MYS XIII: 3338/3324	1483	MYS XIV: 3592/3570	1523
MYS XII: 3202/3188	1445	MYS XIII: 3339/3325	1484	MYS XIV: 3593/3571	1524
MYS XII: 3217/3203	1446	MYS XIII: 3344/3330	1485	MYS XIV: 3595/3573	1525
MYS XII: 3220/3206	1447	MYS XIII: 3345/3331	1486	MYS XIV: 3598/3576	1526
		MYS XIII: 3346/3332	1487	MYS XIV: 3599/3577	1527
MYS XIII: 3236/3222	1448				
MYS XIII: 3246/3232	1449	MYS XIV: 3366/3352	1488	MYS XV: 3600/3578	909
MYS XIII: 3247/3233	1450	MYS XIV: 3368/3354	1489	MYS XV: 3601/3579	910
MYS XIII: 3257/3243	1451	MYS XIV: 3375/3359	1490	MYS XV: 3602/3580	911
MYS XIII: 3258/3244	1452	MYS XIV: 3377/3361	1491	MYS XV: 3603/3581	912
MYS XIII: 3259/3245	1453	MYS XIV: 3383/3366	1492	MYS XV: 3660/3638	913
MYS XIII: 3260/3246	1454	MYS XIV: 3386/3369	1493	MYS XV: 3669/3647	914
MYS XIII: 3262/3248	1455	MYS XIV: 3387/3370	1494	MYS XV: 3670/3648	915
MYS XIII: 3263/3249	1456	MYS XIV: 3388/3371	1495	MYS XV: 3673/3651	916
MYS XIII: 3264/3250	1457	MYS XIV: 3390/3373	1496	MYS XV: 3685/3663	917
MYS XIII: 3265/3251	1458	MYS XIV: 3391/3374	1497	MYS XV: 3690/3668	918
MYS XIII: 3266/3252	1459	MYS XIV: 3401/3383	1498	MYS XV: 3691/3669	919
MYS XIII: 3274/3260	1460	MYS XIV: 3404/3386	1499	MYS XV: 3692/3670	920
MYS XIII: 3275/3261	1461	MYS XIV: 3406/3388	1500	MYS XV: 3693/3671	921
MYS XIII: 3276/3262	1462	MYS XIV: 3417/3399	1501	MYS XV: 3694/3672	922
MYS XIII: 3277/3263	1463	MYS XIV: 3422/3404	1502	MYS XV: 3695/3673	923
MYS XIII: 3278/3264	1464	MYS XIV: 3443/3424	1503	MYS XV: 3710/3688	924

MYS XV:3711/3689	925	MYS XV:3780/3758	970	MYS XVI:3826/3804	1540
MYS XV:3712/3690	926	MYS XV:3781/3759	971	MYS XVI:3827/3805	1541
MYS XV:3726/3704	927	MYS XV:3782/3760	972	MYS XVI:3828/3806	1542
MYS XV:3727/3705	928	MYS XV:3783/3761	973	MYS XVI:3829/3807	1543
MYS XV:3738/3716	929	MYS XV:3784/3762	974	MYS XVI:3832/3810	1544
MYS XV:3739/3717	930	MYS XV:3785/3763	975	MYS XVI:3833/3811	1545
MYS XV:3745/3723	935	MYS XV:3786/3764	976	MYS XVI:3834/3812	1546
MYS XV:3746/3724	936	MYS XV:3787/3765	977	MYS XVI:3835/3813	1547
MYS XV:3747/3725	937	MYS XV:3788/3766	978	MYS XVI:3838/3816	487
MYS XV:3748/3726	938	MYS XV:3789/3767	979	MYS XVI:3844/3822	1548
MYS XV:3749/3727	939	MYS XV:3790/3768	980	MYS XVI:3845/3823	1549
MYS XV:3750/3728	940	MYS XV:3791/3769	981	MYS XVI:3846/3824	491
MYS XV:3751/3729	941	MYS XV:3792/3770	982	MYS XVI:3847/3825	492
MYS XV:3752/3730	942	MYS XV:3793/3771	983	MYS XVI:3848/3826	493
MYS XV:3753/3731	943	MYS XV:3794/3772	984	MYS XVI:3849/3827	494
MYS XV:3754/3732	944	MYS XV:3795/3773	985	MYS XVI:3850/3828	495
MYS XV:3755/3733	945	MYS XV:3796/3774	986	MYS XVI:3851/3829	496
MYS XV:3756/3734	946	MYS XV:3797/3775	987	MYS XVI:3852/3830	497
MYS XV:3757/3735	947	MYS XV:3798/3776	988	MYS XVI:3853/3831	498
MYS XV:3758/3736	948	MYS XV:3799/3777	989	MYS XVI:3870/3848	707
MYS XV:3759/3737	949	MYS XV:3800/3778	990	MYS XVI:3882/3860	648
MYS XV:3760/3738	950	MYS XV:3801/3779	991	MYS XVI:3883/3861	649
MYS XV:3761/3739	951	MYS XV:3802/3780	992	MYS XVI:3884/3862	650
MYS XV:3762/3740	952	MYS XV:3803/3781	993	MYS XVI:3885/3863	651
MYS XV:3763/3741	953	MYS XV:3804/3782	994	MYS XVI:3886/3864	652
MYS XV:3764/3742	954	MYS XV:3805/3783	995	MYS XVI:3887/3865	653
MYS XV:3765/3743	955	MYS XV:3806/3784	996	MYS XVI:3888/3866	654
MYS XV:3766/3744	956	MYS XV:3807/3785	997	MYS XVI:3889/3867	655
MYS XV:3767/3745	957			MYS XVI:3890/3868	656
MYS XV:3768/3746	958	MYS XVI:3813/3791	1528	MYS XVI:3891/3869	657
MYS XV:3769/3747	959	MYS XVI:3814/3792	1529	MYS XVI:3893/3871	1550
MYS XV:3770/3748	960	MYS XVI:3815/3793	1530	MYS XVI:3894/3872	1551
MYS XV:3771/3749	961	MYS XVI:3816/3794	1531	MYS XVI:3895/3873	1552
MYS XV:3772/3750	962	MYS XVI:3817/3795	1532	MYS XVI:3896/3874	1553
MYS XV:3773/3751	963	MYS XVI:3818/3796	1533	MYS XVI:3900/3878	1554
MYS XV:3774/3752	964	MYS XVI:3819/3797	1534	MYS XVI:3907/3885	1555
MYS XV:3775/3753	965	MYS XVI:3820/3798	1535	MYS XVI:3908/3886	1556
MYS XV:3776/3754	966	MYS XVI:3821/3799	1536	MYS XVI:3909/3887	1557
MYS XV:3777/3755	967	MYS XVI:3822/3800	1537	MYS XVI:3910/3888	1558
MYS XV:3778/3756	968	MYS XVI:3823/3801	1538	MYS XVI:3911/3889	1559
MYS XV:3779/3757	969	MYS XVI:3824/3802	1539		

MYS XVII: 3922/3900	761	MYS XVII: 4029/4005	1209	MYS XIX: 4174/4150	833
MYS XVII: 3944/3922	1169	MYS XVII: 4030/4006	1210	MYS XIX: 4180/4156	834
MYS XVII: 3945/3923	1170	MYS XVII: 4031/4007	1211	MYS XIX: 4181/4157	835
MYS XVII: 3946/3924	1171	MYS XVII: 4032/4008	1212	MYS XIX: 4182/4158	836
MYS XVII: 3947/3925	1172	MYS XVII: 4033/4009	1213	MYS XIX: 4235/4211	837
MYS XVII: 3948/3926	1173	MYS XVII: 4034/4010	1214	MYS XIX: 4236/4212	838
MYS XVII: 3965/3943	1174	MYS XVII: 4035/4011	807	MYS XIX: 4238/4214	839
MYS XVII: 3966/3944	1175	MYS XVII: 4036/4012	808	MYS XIX: 4239/4215	840
MYS XVII: 3967/3945	1176	MYS XVII: 4037/4013	809	MYS XIX: 4240/4216	841
MYS XVII: 3968/3946	1177	MYS XVII: 4038/4014	810	MYS XIX: 4242/4218	842
MYS XVII: 3969/3947	1178	MYS XVII: 4039/4015	811	MYS XIX: 4251/4227	500
MYS XVII: 3970/3948	1179	MYS XVII: 4045/4021	812	MYS XIX: 4252/4228	501
MYS XVII: 3971/3949	1180			MYS XIX: 4284/4260	998
MYS XVII: 3972/3950	1181	MYS XVIII: 4078/4054	813	MYS XIX: 4285/4261	999
MYS XVII: 3984/3962	1182	MYS XVIII: 4097/4073	1215	MYS XIX: 4294/4270	702
MYS XVII: 3985/3963	1183	MYS XVIII: 4098/4074	1216	MYS XIX: 4314/4290	843
MYS XVII: 3986/3964	1184	MYS XVIII: 4099/4075	1217	MYS XIX: 4315/4291	844
MYS XVII: 3987/3965	1185	MYS XVIII: 4100/4076	1218	MYS XIX: 4316/4292	845
MYS XVII: 3988/3966	1186	MYS XVIII: 4101/4077	1219		
MYS XVII: 3989/3967	1187	MYS XVIII: 4102/4078	1220	MYS XX: 4345/4321	1222
MYS XVII: 3990/3968	1188	MYS XVIII: 4103/4079	1221	MYS XX: 4346/4322	1223
MYS XVII: 3991/3969	1189	MYS XVIII: 4118/4094	814	MYS XX: 4347/4323	1224
MYS XVII: 3992/3970	1190	MYS XVIII: 4119/4095	815	MYS XX: 4348/4324	1225
MYS XVII: 3993/3971	1191	MYS XVIII: 4120/4096	816	MYS XX: 4349/4325	1226
MYS XVII: 3994/3972	1192	MYS XVIII: 4121/4097	817	MYS XX: 4350/4326	1227
MYS XVII: 3995/3972a	1193	MYS XVIII: 4122/4098	818	MYS XX: 4351/4327	1228
MYS XVII: 3996/3973	1194	MYS XVIII: 4123/4099	819	MYS XX: 4352/4328	1229
MYS XVII: 3997/3974	1195	MYS XVIII: 4124/4100	820	MYS XX: 4353/4329	1230
MYS XVII: 3998/3975	1196	MYS XVIII: 4125/4101	821	MYS XX: 4354/4330	1231
MYS XVII: 3999/3975a	1197	MYS XVIII: 4126/4102	822	MYS XX: 4358/4334	1232
MYS XVII: 4000/3976	1198	MYS XVIII: 4127/4103	823	MYS XX: 4359/4335	1233
MYS XVII: 4001/3977	1199	MYS XVIII: 4128/4104	824	MYS XX: 4360/4336	1234
MYS XVII: 4015/3991	1200	MYS XVIII: 4129/4105	825	MYS XX: 4361/4337	1235
MYS XVII: 4016/3992	1201	MYS XVIII: 4135/4111	826	MYS XX: 4362/4338	1236
MYS XVII: 4017/3993	1202	MYS XVIII: 4136/4112	827	MYS XX: 4363/4339	1237
MYS XVII: 4018/3994	1203			MYS XX: 4364/4340	1238
MYS XVII: 4024/4000	1204	MYS XIX: 4163/4139	828	MYS XX: 4365/4341	1239
MYS XVII: 4025/4001	1205	MYS XIX: 4164/4140	829	MYS XX: 4366/4342	1240
MYS XVII: 4026/4002	1206	MYS XIX: 4167/4143	830	MYS XX: 4367/4343	1241
MYS XVII: 4027/4003	1207	MYS XIX: 4170/4146	831	MYS XX: 4368/4344	1242
MYS XVII: 4028/4004	1208	MYS XIX: 4171/4147	832	MYS XX: 4369/4345	1243

MYS XX:4370/4346	1244	BSS 8	1567	**GOSENSHŪ**	
MYS XX:4384/4360	846	BSS 9	1568		
MYS XX:4385/4361	847	BSS 10	1569	GSS VI:302	253
MYS XX:4386/4362	848	BSS 12	1570		
MYS XX:4492/4468	849	BSS 13	1571	**SHŪISHŪ**	
MYS XX:4493/4469	850	BSS 14	1572	SIS X:597	434
MYS XX:4517/4493	851	BSS 15	1573	SIS XII:700	435
MYS XX:4536/4512	852	BSS 16	1574	SIS XIII:778	436
MYS XX:4540/4516	853	BSS 17	1575		
		BSS 18	1576	**SHINKOKINSHŪ**	
BUSSOKUSEKIKA		BSS 19	1577		
		BSS 20	1578	SKKS IV:346	437
BSS 1	1560			SKKS V:459	438
BSS 2	1561	**KOKINSHŪ**		SKKS VI:582	439
BSS 3	1562			SKKS VI:657	440
BSS 4	1563	KKS VI:334	431	SKKS XI:992	441
BSS 5	1564	KKS IX:406	697	SKKS XI:993	442
BSS 6	1565	KKS IX:409	432	SKKS XV:1376/1375	701
BSS 7	1566	KKS XIII:621	433		

Index of Poems by Author

Songs from the chronicles and *fudoki* are listed under the singer or author assigned to them in the narrative. Only attributed poems (including questionable attributions) are given. Anthology numbers are in boldface.

Ōtomo no Fumimochi: **1136**, MYS III:466/463

Ōtomo no Ikenushi: **703**, MYS VIII:1594/1590; **1175–77**, MYS XVII:
3966–68/3944–46; **1180**, MYS XVII:3971/3949; **1187–88**, MYS XVII:
3989–90/3967–68; **1193**, MYS XVII:3995/3972a; **1194–96**, MYS XVII:
3996–98/3973–75; **1202–3**, MYS XVII:4017–18/3993–94; **1207–9**,
MYS XVII:4027–29/4003–5; **1212–14**, MYS XVII:4032–34/4008–10;
1215–17, MYS XVIII:4097–99/4073–75

Ōtomo no Inagimi: **1081**, MYS VIII:1557/1553

Ōtomo no Katami: **711**, MYS IV:700/697

Ōtomo no Miyori: **712**, MYS IV:555/552; **713**, MYS IV:653/650

Ōtomo no Miyuki: **998**, MYS XIX:4284/4260

Ōtomo no Momoyo: **612**, MYS III:395/392; **613–16**, MYS IV:562–65/559–62;
1019, MYS V:827/823; **1071**, MYS IV:569/566

Ōtomo no Surugamaro: **1113**, MYS IV:649/646; **1115**, MYS IV:651/648;
1117–18, MYS IV:656–57/653–54; **1125**, MYS III:403/400; **1127**, MYS III:
405/402; **1129**, MYS III:414/411

Ōtomo no Tabito: **589–90**, MYS III:318–19/315–16; **591**, MYS VI:965/960;
592–604, MYS III:341–53/338–50; **1018**, MYS V:826/822; **1043–59**, MYS V:
851–67/847–63; **1066–70**, MYS III:334–38/331–35; **1075–76**, MYS VI:
972–73/967–68; **1079–80**, MYS IV:577–78/574–75

Ōtomo no Tanushi: **1001**, MYS II:127

Ōtomo no Yakamochi: **756**, MYS VI:999/994; **757–60**, MYS VIII:1570–73/
1566–69; **761**, MYS XVII:3922/3900; **762**, MYS III:406/403; **763**, MYS III:
411/408; **764**, MYS III:417/414; **765–67**, MYS IV:683–85/680–82;
768–69, MYS IV:694–95/691–92; **770**, MYS IV:703/700; **771–77**, MYS IV:
717–23/714–20; **778–79**, MYS IV:730–31/727–28; **780–94**, MYS IV:
744–58/741–55; **795–98**, MYS VIII:1631–34/1627–30; **799**, MYS VI:
1033/1029; **800–801**, MYS VI:1036–37/1032–33; **802–3**, MYS VI:1039–40/
1035–36; **804**, MYS VIII:1468/1464; **805–6**, MYS IV:770–71/767–68;
807–11, MYS XVII:4035–39/4011–15; **812**, MYS XVII:4045/4021; **813**,
MYS XVIII:4078/4054; **814–25**, MYS XVIII:4118–29/4094–4105; **826–27**,
MYS XVIII:4135–36/4111–12; **828–29**, MYS XIX:4163–64/4139–40; **830**,
MYS XIX:4167/4143; **831–32**, MYS XIX:4170–71/4146–47; **833**, MYS XIX:
4174/4150; **834–36**, MYS XIX:4180–82/4156–58; **837–38**, MYS XIX:
4235–36/4211–12; **839–41**, MYS XIX:4238–40/4214–16; **842**, MYS XIX:
4242/4218; **843–45**, MYS XIX:4314–16/4290–92; **846–48**, MYS XX:
4384–86/4360–62; **849–50**, MYS XX:4492–93/4468–69; **851**, MYS XX:
5417/4493; **852**, MYS XX:4536/4512; **853**, MYS XX:4540/4516; **1082**,
MYS VIII:1558/1554; **1084**, MYS VIII:1567/1563; **1086**, MYS VIII:1569/1565;
1111–12, MYS IV:614–15/611–12; **1133**, MYS IV:708/705; **1135**, MYS III:
465/462; **1137–42**, MYS III:467–72/464–69; **1143**, MYS VIII:1623/1619;
1146–47, MYS VIII:1629–30/1625–26; **1151–53**, MYS IV:735–37/732–34;

First-Line Index

Second, third, and fourth lines are supplied as needed, or indication is made that a poem is a variant. The last three items have only Chinese text.

General Index

In this index an "f" after a number indicates a separate reference on the next page, and an "ff" indicates separate references on the next two pages. A continuous discussion over two or more pages is indicated by a span of numbers, e.g., "pp. 57–58." *Passim* is used for a cluster of references in close but not consecutive sequence.

Achi no Atae, 45f
Adultery, 368, 486, 701, 737f
Agata Inukai Tachibana no Michiyo, 401
Ageuta, 48. *See also under Kojiki*
Ahe no Hironiwa, 343
Ahe no Miushi, 343
Ahe no Mushimaro, 396f, 410; and Lady Ōtomo of Sakanoue, 579–81
Ahe no Nakamaro, 345, 397f
Ahe no Okishima, 543, 845
Ahe no Tsugimaro, 507
Ahe, Princess, *see* Gemmei, Empress
Ajishiki Takahikone (also Ajisuki), 12f, 69
Akahito, *see* Yamabe no Akahito
Akahito Shū, 359, 826
Akaiko, 54–56, 806
Aki (place), 210–12, 398
Aki no Osa no Obito Maro, 637
Aki, Prince, 286f, 378, 588
Akizu (place), 56, 194, 295, 311, 664, 666, 806
Akizushima, 57, 89, 164, 712, 806
Allegory, 15, 84, 100, 114, 116, 122, 171, 211, 242, 306, 312, 339–40, 415, 421, 426, 443, 498, 590f, 648, 654, 657, 659, 669, 685, 699f, 727, 734f,

799, 803. *See also Hiyu; Hiyuka; Wazauta*
Ama (fisherfolk), xxv, 8f, 58, 61, 65, 70, 105, 166, 199f, 237, 279, 293f, 297f, 303, 372–75, 378, 447, 462f, 475, 478, 490f, 505–11 *passim*, 550–54, 556f, 618, 623, 654–63 *passim*, 704, 709, 716f, 729, 756, 797, 838
Ama no Inukai no Okamaro, 377, 383
Amadaburi (*Amada* measure), 50. *See also Kojiki*
Amagashi Hill, 503, 813
Amahasezukai, 7ff, 534, 797. *See also Ama*
Amakataribe, 58, 797. *See also Amahasezukai*
Amaterasu, *see* Sun goddess
Ame no Oshihi no Mikoto, 408, 456
Ame no Wakahiko, 12, 69, 805, 807
Anaho, Prince, *see* Ankō, Emperor
Analects (*Lun Yü*), 87, 105, 115, 145, 550, 556, 610, 612, 810, 812, 816, 848f, 853f
Analogy, xx, xxi, 12, 21, 24f, 29, 35, 40, 44, 51f, 70, 86, 120f, 187, 266, 340, 381, 417, 493, 551, 565f, 619, 661, 672f, 681, 688, 693, 698f, 703,

Library of Congress Cataloging-in-Publication Data

A Waka anthology / translated, with a commentary and notes by Edwin A. Cranston
  p.   cm.
Includes bibliographical references and index.
Contents: Vol. 1. Gem-glistening cup
ISBN 0-8047-1922-5 (cl.) : ISBN 0-8047-3157-8 (pbk.)
1. Japanese poetry—Translations into English. 2. Waka—
Translations into English. I. Cranston, Edwin A., 1932–
PL782.E3W27 1993
895.6'1008—dc20
91-48074 CIP

∞ This book is printed on acid-free, recycled paper. It has been typeset by G&S Typesetters, Inc. in 10/12 Bembo.

Original printing 1993
Last figure below indicates year of this printing:
07 06 05 04 03 02 01 00 99 98